DRAMATIC THEORY AND CRITICISM

DRAMATIC THEORY AND CRITICISM

Greeks to Grotowski

BERNARD F. DUKORE

University of Hawaii

HOLT, RINEHART AND WINSTON, INC.

New York   Chicago   San Francisco
Atlanta   Dallas   Montreal   Toronto

Library of Congress Cataloging in Publication Data

Dukore, Bernard F.
  Dramatic theory and criticism: Greeks to Grotowski.

  1. Drama.   2. Dramatic criticism.   I. Title.
PN1631.D83   808.2   73–9778
ISBN: 0–03–091152–4

Preface

The chief purpose of this book is to make available the major documents in dramatic theory. Some are important historically, some intrinsically; others have both historic and intrinsic value. Apart from presenting such writings by dramatic theorists and critics, *Dramatic Theory and Criticism: Greeks to Grotowski* also aims to offer works by philosophers, psychologists, and social theorists (though not always addressed directly to the drama, these writings —by Ortega y Gasset on modern art, for instance—are applicable or relevant to it), and by dramatic authors (this anthology begins with a selection by a playwright and ends with one by a director who is "author" of performance-texts).

The selections include theories and analyses of the major, traditional dramatic genres, from ancient to modern times, and of modern genres, forms of drama, and conceptions of theatre. In fact, dramatic genres constitute a thread that may be traced throughout the anthology. Another thread consists in the contrast of the more traditional drama with the newer drama ("avant-garde," it might be called in a figurative sense, though the phrase would, strictly speaking, be anachronistic in reference to periods preceding the modern). Other threads are the social contexts and resonances of the drama, dramatic action and playwriting, dramatic illusion, and Shakespearean criticism.

This book's subtitle, *Greeks to Grotowski*, suggests its scope and chief limitation. The scope is Ancient Greece to the present day; the limitation, the West. To include theorists of the Orient would have meant either to represent them inadequately or else, if justice were to be done, to double the size of this volume, which is large enough as is.

Despite its size, however, there are, inevitably, omissions. These derive from restrictions of copyright, space, the viewpoint of 1971–1972, and (admittedly) editorial tastes. The last limitation has no doubt resulted in inclusions as well as omissions. On this point, my plea must be *de gustibus non est disputandum:* there is no disputing concerning tastes.

v

Dramatic Theory and Criticism: Greeks to Grotowski is organized chronologically and by one or a group of countries. Initially, I had considered organization by subject matter, but fitting selections into subject-matter categories proved not only unwieldy, it also tended to become far more subjective than I felt was appropriate to a book like this. Apart from the validity of the chronological arrangement to a historical approach to dramatic theory and criticism, it is less subjective and it offers fewer problems than other methods I considered.

The introductions that precede all of the book's fourteen sections attempt to suggest the importance of various writers, connections among them, and some of the key issues they raise. Where helpful, the introductions try to provide a context, and cross-references direct the reader to writers in other sections. Briefly, though tautologically, each introduction attempts to introduce, rather than to offer long, overly tendentious explications of the selections that follow. To this end, I have tried to strike a Horatian balance between terseness and comprehensiblility.

Honolulu, Hawaii   B.F.D.
November 1973

Contents

RENAISSANCE ITALY 119

ELIZABETHAN AND JACOBEAN ENGLAND, AND SPAIN 157

SEVENTEENTH- AND EIGHTEENTH- CENTURY FRANCE 207

RESTORATION AND EIGHTEENTH-CENTURY ENGLAND 315

EIGHTEENTH- AND EARLY NINETEENTH-CENTURY GERMANY 427

NINETEENTH- AND TWENTIETH-CENTURY SCANDINAVIA 549

NINETEENTH- AND TWENTIETH-CENTURY ENGLAND AND IRELAND 577

NINETEENTH- AND TWENTIETH-CENTURY FRANCE, ITALY, AND SPAIN 673

NINETEENTH- AND TWENTIETH-CENTURY GERMANY, AUSTRIA, AND SWITZERLAND 773

NINETEENTH- AND TWENTIETH-CENTURY UNITED STATES AND CANADA 859

NINETEENTH- AND TWENTIETH-CENTURY RUSSIA AND HUNGARY 911

TWENTIETH-CENTURY POLAND 971

DRAMATIC THEORY
AND CRITICISM

Ancient Greece and Rome

The earliest critic whose work has survived is a playwright. In his satiric and farcical comedies, Aristophanes parodies tragedy in general and certain playwrights in particular (notably Euripides, his *bête noir*). Also, he explicitly discusses the value of specific tragedians, the nature of dramatic poetry, and the function of the poet—tragic as well as comic. In *The Frogs*, Aristophanes has two of Greece's major tragedians, Aeschylus and Euripides, debate their respective merits and failings, and in so doing he provides insights not only into the function and nature of tragedy and of dramatic poetry in general, but also into the question of realism and elevation in tragic drama.

Although the drama was not the main concern of any single work by Plato, dramatic poetry was a subject he touched on in several of his philosophical dialogues. Because poets tell lies (inventing stories that never happened), because dramatic and epic poets speak convincingly in the persons of wicked people, because tragedy makes spectators effeminate instead of manly, and because poetic imitation is several times removed from true reality, Plato would banish poets, particularly dramatic poets, from his ideal state. Medieval and Renaissance critics who opposed poetry, especially dramatic poetry, were to draw upon Plato's arguments to confound proponents of the drama.

Those who favored dramatic poetry, however, were to draw upon Aristotle's *Poetics*, the earliest surviving study of tragic theory and practice and probably the single most influential work on the subject. Distinguishing dramatic from epic and lyric poetry, Aristotle proposes a definition of tragedy that for centuries has been explicated by theorists, imitated by playwrights, and argued about by both. One reason for the many conflicting interpretations of the *Poetics* is that the work is sketchy and elliptical. It has even been suggested that the *Poetics* is but the outline of a book and perhaps notes for a lecture. Partly for this reason, I have included passages from Aristotle's *Rhetoric* on pity and fear (undefined in the *Poetics*) and from his *Nicomachean Ethics* on responsibility (related to a play offered as a model

1

in the *Poetics*, Sophocles' *Oedipus the King*). Another aspect of the problem of interpreting the *Poetics* is the matter of translation, and because of this I have included, in addition to a translation widely regarded as "standard," a more radical rendering of a few of the more important passages. Does Aristotle distinguish between tragic and epic poetry or between tragic and two types of epic poetry (Homeric and non-Homeric)? Does the important reference to time apply to the duration of the action or to the duration of the performance? Does the matter of purgation refer to the emotional effect on the audience or to the structure of the plot? Because a translation is itself an interpretation, these different renderings suggest different answers. Whereas Aristotle's *Poetics* focuses on tragedy to the neglect of comedy, the anonymous author of the *Tractatus Coislinianus* applies to the latter type of dramatic poetry the type of analysis Aristotle applies to tragedy.

More dogmatic than Aristotle, who describes the practice of tragic poets, Cicero and Horace in their writings on the subject often prescribe rules for tragic poets to follow. Horace's *Art of Poetry*, however, includes some loopholes that tend partly to mitigate his rigid dicta. Second in influence only to Aristotle's *Poetics*, Horace's *Art of Poetry*—the only complete treatise on dramatic theory to have survived from ancient Rome—was greatly admired by Renaissance critics and playwrights who shared his views on such subjects as didacticism in tragedy, decorum, and purity of genre. Unlike Cicero and Horace, Longinus was not prominent in the Renaissance. His importance was unrecognized until the late seventeenth century. A comparative critic, Longinus analyzes not only Greek and Roman poetry but also quotes from *Genesis*. As the title suggests, *On the Sublime* is concerned with what makes an extraordinary work extraordinary, and it goes far toward defining what is so often undefinable.

Aristophanes *c. 445–c. 385 B.C.*

The Frogs *405 B.C.*

AEACUS   Yes; there's a big business just astir,
   And hot dissension among all the dead.
XANTHIAS   About what?
AEACUS   There's a law established here
   Concerning all the large and liberal arts,
   Which grants the foremost master in each art
   Free entertainment at the Central Hearth,
   And also a special throne in Pluto's row . . .
XANTHIAS   Oh, now I understand!
AEACUS   To hold until
   There comes one greater; then he must make way.
XANTHIAS   But how has this affected Aeschylus?
AEACUS   Aeschylus held the throne of tragedy,
   As greatest . . .
XANTHIAS   Held it? Why, who holds it now?
AEACUS   Well, when Euripides came down, he gave
   Free exhibitions to our choicest sharpers,
   Footpads, cut-purses, burglars, father-beaters,
   —Of whom we have numbers here; and when they heard
   The neat retorts, the fencing, and the twists,
   They all went mad and thought him something splendid.
   And he, growing proud, laid hands upon the throne
   Where Aeschylus sat.
XANTHIAS   And wasn't pelted off?
AEACUS   Not he. The whole folk clamoured for a trial
   To see which most was master of his craft.
XANTHIAS   The sharper-folk?
AEACUS   Exactly;—loud as trumpets.
XANTHIAS   And were there none to fight for Aeschylus?
AEACUS   Goodness is scarce, you know. (*Indicating the audience*) The same
   as here!
XANTHIAS   And what does Pluto mean to do about it?
AEACUS   Why, hold a trial and contest on the spot
   To test their skill for certain.
XANTHIAS (*reflecting*)   But, I say,
   Sophocles surely must have claimed the throne?

Selections. From *The Frogs*, by Aristophanes, translated by Gilbert Murray. London: George Allen & Unwin, Ltd., 1965. Reprinted by permission of the publisher.

AEACUS Not he; as soon as ever he came down,
  He kissed old Aeschylus, and wrung his hand,
  And Aeschylus made room on half his seat.
  And now he means to wait—or so at least,
  Clidemides informs us—in reserve.
  If Aeschylus wins the day, he'll rest content;
  If not, why then, he says, for poor Art's sake,
  He must show fight against Euripides!

.   .   .   .

CHORUS
(the song is a parody of the meter and style of AESCHYLUS*).*
Eftsoons shall dire anger interne be the Thunderer's portion
  When his foe's glib tusk fresh whetted for blood he
    descries;
Then fell shall his heart be, and mad; and a pallid distortion
    Descend as a cloud on his eyes.
Yea, words with plume wild on the wind and with helmet
    that dances,
  With axle a-splinter and marble a-shiver, eftsoons
Shall bleed in the fray when our great Thought-builder
    advances
    His compounds in mounted platoons.
The deepcrest of his name shall uprise as he slowly un-
    limbers
  The long-drawn wrath of his brow, and lets loose with a
    roar
Epithets welded and screwed, like new torrent-swept
    timbers
    Blown loose by a giant at war.
Then rises the man of the Mouth; then battleward flashes
  A tester of verses, a smooth and serpentine tongue,
To dissect each phrase into mincemeat, and argue to ashes
    That high-towered labour of lung!

The door opens again. Enter EURIPIDES, DIONYSUS,
    and AESCHYLUS

EURIPIDES Pray, no advice to me! I won't give way.
  I claim that I'm more master of my art.
DIONYSUS You hear him, Aeschylus. Why don't you speak?
EURIPIDES He wants to open with an awful silence—
  The blood-curdling reserve of his first scenes.
DIONYSUS My dear sir, I must beg! Control your language.

EURIPIDES   I know him; I've seen through him years ago;
    Bard of the "noble savage," wooden-mouth,
    No door, no bolt, no bridle to his tongue,
    A torrent of pure bombast—tied in bundles!

AESCHYLUS (*breaking out*)   How say'st thou, Son o' the goddess of the
    Greens?—
    You dare speak thus of me, you phrase-collector,
    Blind-beggar-bard and scum of rifled rag-bags!
    Oh, you shall rue it!

DIONYSUS   Stop! Stop, Aeschylus;
    "Strike not thine heart to fire on rancour old."[1]

AESCHYLUS   No; I'll expose this crutch-and-cripple playwright,
    And what he's worth for all his insolence.

DIONYSUS (*to attendants*)   A lamb, a black lamb, quick, boys! Bring it out
    To sacrifice; a hurricane's let loose!

AESCHYLUS (*to* EURIPIDES)   You and your Cretan dancing-solos! You
    And the ugly amours that you set to verse!

DIONYSUS (*interposing*)   One moment, please, most noble Aeschylus!
    And you, poor wretch, if you have any prudence,
    Get out of the hailstones quick, or else, by Zeus,
    Some word as big as your head will catch you crash
    Behind the ear, and knock out all the . . . Telephus![2]
    Nay, Aeschylus, pray, pray control your anger;
    Examine and submit to be examined
    With a cool head. Two poets should not meet
    In fishwife style; but here are you, straight off,
    Ablaze and roaring like an oak on fire.

EURIPIDES   For my part I'm quite ready, with no shrinking,
    To bite first or be bitten, as he pleases.
    Here are my dialogue, music, and construction;
    Here's Peleus at your service, Meleâger,
    And Aeolus, and . . . yes, Telephus, by all means!

DIONYSUS   Do you consent to the trial, Aeschylus? Speak.

AESCHYLUS   I well might take objection to the place;
    It's no fair field for him and me.

DIONYSUS   Why not?

AESCHYLUS   Because my writings haven't died with me,
    As his have; so he'll have them all to hand. . . .
    However, I waive the point, if you think fit.

.   .   .   .

[1] The source of this quotation is unknown.
[2] Title character of a play by Euripides.

DIONYSUS   Now, quick to work. Be sure you both do justice to your cases,
    Clear sense, no loose analogies, and no long commonplaces.
EURIPIDES   A little later I will treat my own artistic mettle,
    This persons' claims I should prefer immediately to settle.
    I'll show you how he posed and prosed; with what audacious fooling
    He tricked an audience fresh and green from Phrynichus's[3] schooling.
    Those sole veiled figures on the stage were first among his graces,
    Achilles, say, or Niobe, who never showed their faces,
    But stood like so much scene-painting, and never a grunt they uttered!
DIONYSUS   Why, no, by Zeus, no more they did!
EURIPIDES   And on the Chorus spluttered
    Through long song-systems, four on end, the actors mute as fishes!
DIONYSUS   I somehow loved that silence, though; and felt it met my wishes
    As no one's talk does nowadays!
EURIPIDES   You hadn't yet seen through it!
    That's all.
DIONYSUS   I really think you're right! But still, what made him do it?
EURIPIDES   The instinct of a charlatan, to keep the audience guessing
    If Niobe ever meant to speak—the play meantime progressing!
DIONYSUS   Of course it was! The sly old dog, to think of how he tricked us!—
    Don't (*to* AESCHYLUS) ramp and fume!
EURIPIDES (*excusing* AESCHYLUS)   We're apt to do so when the facts con-
    vict us!
    —Then after this tomfoolery, the heroine, feeling calmer,
    Would utter some twelve wild-bull words, on mid-way in the drama,
    Long ones, with crests and beetling brows, and gorgons round the border,
    That no man ever heard on earth.
AESCHYLUS   The red plague . . . !
DIONYSUS   Order, order!
EURIPIDES   Intelligible—not one line!
DIONYSUS (*to* AESCHYLUS)   Please! Won't your teeth stop gnashing?
EURIPIDES   All fosses and Scamander-beds, and bloody targes flashing,
    With gryphon-eagles bronze-embossed, and crags, and riders reeling,
    Which somehow never quite joined on.
DIONYSUS   By Zeus, sir, quite my feeling!
    A question comes in Night's long hours, that haunts me like a spectre,[4]
    What kind of fish or fowl you'd call a "whirring hippalector."[5]
AESCHYLUS (*breaking in*)   It was a ship's sign, idiot, such as every joiner fixes!
DIONYSUS   Indeed! I thought perhaps it meant that music-man Eryxis![6]

---

[3] A tragic poet who preceded Aeschylus.
[4] From Euripides' *Hippolytus*.
[5] A flying horse with the tail of a bird.
[6] Unknown.

[EURIPIDES You like then, in a tragic play, a cock? You think it mixes?][7]

AESCHYLUS (*to* EURIPIDES) And what did you yourself produce, O fool with
    pride deluded?

EURIPIDES Not "hippalectors," thank the Lord, nor "tragelaphs,"[8] as you
    did—

  The sort of ornament they use to fill a Persian curtain!

  —I had the Drama straight from you, all bloated and uncertain,

  Weighed down with rich and heavy words, puffed out past comprehension.

  I took the case in hand; applied treatment for such distension—

  Beetroot, light phrases, little walks, hot book-juice, and cold reasoning;

  Then fed her up on solos. . . .

DIONYSUS (*aside*)   With Cephisophon[9] for seasoning!

EURIPEDES I didn't rave at random, or plunge in and make confusions.

  My first appearing character explained, with due allusions,

  The whole play's pedigree.

DIONYSUS (*aside*)   Your own you left in wise obscurity!

EURIPIDES Then no one from the start with me could idle with security.

  They had to work. The men, the slaves, the women, all made speeches,

  The kings, the little girls, the hags . . .

AESCHYLUS   Just see the things he teaches!

  And shouldn't you be hanged for that?

EURIPIDES   No, by the lord Apollo!

  It's democratic!

DIONYSUS (*to* EURIPIDES) That's no road for you, my friend, to follow;

  You'll find the "little walk" too steep; I recommend you quit it.

EURIPIDES Next, I taught all the town to talk with freedom.

AESCHYLUS   I admit it.

  'Twere better, ere you taught them, you had died amid their curses!

EURIPIDES I gave them canons to apply and squares for marking verses;

  Taught them to see, think, understand, to scheme for what they wanted,

  To fall in love, think evil, question all things. . . .

AESCHYLUS   Granted, granted!

EURIPIDES I put things on the stage that came from daily life and business.

  Where men could catch me if I tripped; could listen without dizziness

  To things they knew, and judge my art. I never crashed and lightened

  And bullied people's senses out; nor tried to keep them frightened

  With Magic Swans[10] and Aethiop knights,[11] loud barb and clanging vizor!

---

[7] Some critics consider this line to be spurious.

[8] Antelopes with huge horns.

[9] A friend of Euripides who, according to Euripides' detractors, helped him to write
his poetry.

[10] It is not known what play this refers to.

[11] In Aeschylus' *Memnon* and *The Soul Weighing*.

Then look at my disciples, too, and mark what creatures his are!
Phormisius[12] is his product and the looby lump Megainetus,[13]
All trumpet, lance, moustache, and glare, who twist their clubs of pine at us;
While Cleitophon is mine, sirs, and Theramenes the Matchless![14]

DIONYSUS   Theramenes! Ah, that's the man! All danger leaves him scratchless.
His friends may come to grief, and he be found in awkward fixes,
But always tumbles right end up, not aces—no: all sixes!

EURIPIDES
This was the kind of lore I brought
To school my town in ways of thought;
I mingled reasoning with my art
And shrewdness, till I fired their heart
To brood, to think through things and through;
And rule their houses better, too.

.   .   .   .

DIONYSUS   O thou who first of the Greeks did build great words to heaven-high towers,
And the essence of tragedy-padding distilled, give vent to thy pent-up showers.

AESCHYLUS   I freely admit that I take it amiss, and I think my anger is just,
At having to answer a man like this. Still, lest I should seem nonplussed,
Pray, tell me on what particular ground a poet should claim admiration?

EURIPIDES   If his art is true, and his council sound; and if he brings help to the nation,
By making men better in some respect.

AESCHYLUS   And suppose you have done the reverse,
And have had upon good strong men the effect of making them weaker and worse,
What, do you say, should your recompense be?

DIONYSUS   The gallows! You needn't ask him.

AESCHYLUS   Well, think what they were when he had them from me! Good six-footers, solid of limb,
Well-born, well-bred, not ready to fly from obeying their country's call,
Nor in latter-day fashion to loiter and lie, and keep their consciences small;
Their life was in shafts of ash and of elm, in bright plumes fluttering wide,

---

[12] A political figure who, it is said, died in a drinking bout.
[13] Obscure reference.
[14] Respected, moderate political figures.

In lance and greaves and corslet and helm, and hearts of seven-fold hide!

EURIPIDES (*aside*)   Oh, now he's begun and will probably run a whole arm-
ourer's shop on my head!

(*To* AESCHYLUS)   Stop! How was it due in especial to you, if they were so
very—well-bred?

DIONYSUS   Come, answer him, Aeschylus! Don't be so hot, or smoulder in
silent disdain.

AESCHYLUS (*crushingly*)   By a tragedy "brimming with Ares!"

DIONYSUS   A what?

AESCHYLUS   The *Seven against Thebes*.

DIONYSUS   Pray explain.

AESCHYLUS   There wasn't a man could see that play but he hungered for
havoc and gore.

DIONYSUS   I'm afraid that tells in the opposite way. For the Thebans profited
more,

It urged them to fight without flinching or fear, and they did so; and long
may you rue it!

AESCHYLUS   The same thing was open to all of you here, but it didn't amuse
you to do it!

Then next I taught you for glory to long, and against all odds stand fast;

That was *The Persians*, which bodied in song the noblest deed of the past.

DIONYSUS   Yes, yes! When Darius arose from the grave it gave me genuine joy,

And the Chorus stood with its arms a-wave, and observed, "Yow—oy, Yow
—oy!"

AESCHYLUS   Yes, that's the effect for a play to produce! For observe, from
the world's first start

Those poets have all been of practical use who have been supreme in their
art.

First, Orpheus withheld us from bloodshed impure, and vouchsafed us the
great revelation;

Musaeus was next, with wisdom to cure diseases and teach divination.

Then Hesiod showed us the season to plough, to sow, and to reap. And
the laurels

That shine upon Homer's celestial brow are equally due to his morals!

He taught men to stand, to march, and to arm. . . .

DIONYSUS   So that was old Homer's profession?

Then I wish he could keep his successors from harm, like Pantacles[15] in
the procession,

Who first got his helmet well strapped on his head, and then tried to put
in the plume!

---

[15] A lyric poet.

AESCHYLUS   There be many brave men that he fashioned and bred, like
Lamachus,[16] now in his tomb.

And in his great spirit my plays had a part, with their heroes many and
brave—

Teucers, Patrocluses, lions at heart; who made my citizens crave

To dash like them at the face of the foe, and leap at the call of a trumpet!—

But no Stheneboia I've given you, no; no Phaedra, no heroine-strumpet!

If I've once put a woman in love in one act of one play, may my teaching
be scouted!

EURIPIDES   No, you hadn't exactly the style to attract Aphrodite!

AESCHYLUS   I'm better without it.

A deal too much of that style she found in some of your friends and you,

And once, at the least, left you flat on the ground!

DIONYSUS   By Zeus, that's perfectly true.

If he dealt his neighbours such rattling blows, we must think how he suffered in person.

EURIPIDES   And what are the public defects you suppose my poor Stheneboia
to worsen?

AESCHYLUS (*evading the question with a jest*)   She makes good women, and
good men's wives, when their hearts are weary and want ease,

Drink jorums of hemlock and finish their lives, to gratify Bellerophontes![17]

EURIPIDES   But did I invent the story I told of—Phaedra, say? Wasn't it
history?

AESCHYLUS   It was true, right enough; but the poet should hold such a truth
enveloped in mystery,

And not represent it or make it a play. It's his duty to teach, and you
know it.

As a child learns from all who may come in his way, so the grown world
learns from the poet.

Oh, words of good counsel should flow from his voice—

EURIPIDES   And words like Mount Lycabettus

Or Parnes, such as you give us for choice, must needs be good counsel?—
Oh, let us,

Oh, let us at least use the language of men!

AESCHYLUS   Flat cavil, sir! cavil absurd!

When the subject is great and the sentiment, then, of necessity, great
grows the word;

When heroes give range to their hearts, is it strange if the speech of them
over us towers?

---

[16] A general.
[17] A hero who angrily wished that all women would poison themselves.

Nay, the garb of them too must be gorgeous to view, and majestical, nothing like ours.

All this I saw, and established as law, till you came and spoilt it.

EURIPIDES   How so?

AESCHYLUS   You wrapped them in rags from old beggarmen's bags, to express their heroical woe,

And reduce the spectator to tears of compassion!

EURIPIDES   Well, what was the harm if I did?

.   .   .   .

DIONYSUS   By Zeus the Saviour, still I can't decide!
The one so fine, and the other so convincing!
Well, I must ask you both for one more judgment;
What steps do you advise to save our country?

EURIPIDES   I know and am prepared to say!

DIONYSUS   Say on.

EURIPIDES   Where Mistrust now has sway, put Trust to dwell,
And where Trust is, Mistrust; and all is well.

DIONYSUS   I don't quite follow. Please say that again,
Not quite so cleverly and rather plainer.

EURIPIDES   If we count all the men whom now we trust,
Suspect; and call on those whom now we spurn
To serve us, we may find deliverance yet.

DIONYSUS   And what say you?

AESCHYLUS   First tell me about the City:
What servants does she choose? The good?

DIONYSUS   Great Heavens,
She loathes them!

AESCHYLUS   And takes pleasure in the vile?

DIONYSUS   Not she, but has perforce to let them serve her!

AESCHYLUS   What hope of comfort is there for a City
That quarrels with her silk and hates her hodden?

DIONYSUS   That's just what *you* must answer, if you want
To rise again!

AESCHYLUS   I'll answer there, not here.

DIONYSUS   No; better send up blessing from below.

AESCHYLUS   Her safety is to count her enemy's land
Her own, yea, and her own her enemy's;
Her ships her treasures, and her treasure dross!

DIONYSUS   Good;—though it all goes down the juror's throat!

PLUTO (*interrupting*)   Come, give your judgment!

DIONYSUS   Well, I'll judge like this;
    My choice shall fall on him my soul desires!
EURIPIDES   Remember all the gods by whom you swore
    To take me home with you, and choose your friend!
DIONYSUS   My tongue hath sworn;[18]—but I'll choose Aeschylus!

.   .   .   .

AESCHYLUS   I will do as you wish.—And as for my throne,
    I beg you let Sophocles sit there alone,
    On guard, till perchance I return some day;
    For he—all present may mark what I say—
            Is my Second in art and in wit.
    And see, above all, that this Devil-may-care
    Child of deceit with his mountebank air
    Shall never on that imperial chair
            By the wildest of accidents sit!

18 From Euripides' *Hippolytus*.

Plato   *c. 427–c. 347 B.C.*

The Republic   *c. 373 B.C.*

Book II[1]

Come then, and let us pass a leisure hour in story-telling, and our story
shall be the education of our heroes.

By all means.

And what shall be their education? Can we find a better than the traditional sort?—and this has two divisions, gymnastic for the body, and
music for the soul.

Selections from Books II, III, IV, and X. From *The Dialogues of Plato*, Third Edition,
Vol. III, translated by B. Jowet. New York: Oxford University Press, 1892.

1 The dialogue is between Socrates, who speaks first, and Adeimantus.

True.

Shall we begin education with music, and go on to gymnastic afterwards?

By all means.

And when you speak of music, do you include literature or not?

I do.

And literature may be either true or false?

Yes.

And the young should be trained in both kinds, and we begin with the false?

I do not understand your meaning, he said.

You know, I said, that we begin by telling children stories which, though not wholly destitute of truth, are in the main fictitious; and these stories are told them when they are not of an age to learn gymnastics.

Very true.

That was my meaning when I said that we must teach music before gymnastics.

Quite right, he said.

You know also that the beginning is the most important part of any work, especially in the case of a young and tender thing; for that is the time at which the character is being formed and the desired impression is more readily taken.

Quite true.

And shall we just carelessly allow children to hear any casual tales which may be devised by casual persons, and to receive into their minds ideas for the most part the very opposite of those which we should wish them to have when they grow up?

We cannot.

Then the first thing will be to establish a censorship of the writers of fiction, and let the censors receive any tale of fiction which is good, and reject the bad; and we will desire mothers and nurses to tell their children the authorized ones only. Let them fashion the mind with such tales, even more fondly than they mould the body with their hands; but most of those which are now in use must be discarded.

Of what tales are you speaking? he said.

You may find a model of the lesser in the greater, I said; for they are necessarily of the same type, and there is the same spirit in both of them.

Very likely, he replied; but I do not as yet know what you would term the greater.

Those, I said, which are narrated by Homer and Hesiod, and the rest of the poets, who have ever been the great story-tellers of mankind.

But which stories do you mean, he said; and what fault do you find with them?

A fault which is most serious, I said; the fault of telling a lie, and, what is more, a bad lie.

But when is this fault committed?

Whenever an erroneous representation is made of the nature of gods and heroes—as when a painter paints a portrait not having the shadow of a likeness to the original.

Book III[2]

. . . You may suppose . . . that the intermediate passages are omitted, and the dialogue only left.

That also, he said, I understand; you mean, for example, as in tragedy.

You have conceived my meaning perfectly; and if I mistake not, what you failed to apprehend before is now made clear to you, that poetry and mythology are, in some cases, wholly imitative—instances of this are supplied by tragedy and comedy; there is likewise the opposite style, in which the poet is the only speaker—of this dithyramb affords the best example; and the combination of both is found in epic, and in several other styles of poetry. Do I take you with me?

Yes, he said; I see now what you meant.

I will ask you to remember also what I began by saying, that we have done with the subject and might proceed to the style.

Yes, I remember.

In saying this, I intended to imply that we must come to an understanding about the mimetic art—whether the poets, in narrating their stories, are to be allowed by us to imitate, and if so, whether in whole or in part, and if the latter, in what parts; or should all imitation be prohibited?

You mean, I suspect, to ask whether tragedy and comedy shall be admitted into our State?

Yes, I said; but there may be more than this in question: I really do not know as yet, but whither the argument may blow, thither we go.

And go we will, he said.

Then, Adeimantus, let me ask you whether our guardians ought to be imitators; or rather, has not this question been decided by the rule already laid down that one man can only do one thing well, and not many; and that if he attempt many, he will altogether fail of gaining much reputation in any?

Certainly.

And this is equally true of imitation; no one man can imitate many things as well as he would imitate a single one?

---

[2] The dialogue is between Socrates, who speaks first, and Adeimantus.

He cannot.

Then the same person will hardly be able to play a serious part in life, and at the same time to be an imitator and imitate many other parts as well; for even when two species of imitation are nearly allied, the same persons cannot succeed in both, as, for example, the writers of tragedy and comedy—did you not just now call them imitations?

Yes, I did; and you are right in thinking that the same persons cannot succeed in both.

Any more than they can be rhapsodists and actors at once?

True.

Neither are comic and tragic actors the same; yet all these things are but imitations.

They are so.

And human nature, Adeimantus, appears to have been coined into yet smaller pieces, and to be as incapable of imitating many things well, as of performing well the actions of which the imitations are copies.

Quite true, he replied.

If then we adhere to our original notion and bear in mind that our guardians, setting aside every other business, are to dedicate themselves wholly to the maintenance of freedom in the State, making this their craft, and engaging in no work which does not bear on this end, they ought not to practice or imitate anything else; if they imitate at all, they should imitate from youth upward only those characters which are suitable to their profession—the courageous, temperate, holy, free, and the like; but they should not depict or be skilful at imitating any kind of illiberality or baseness, lest from imitation they should come to be what they imitate. Did you never observe how imitations, beginning in early youth and continued far into life, at length grow into habits and become a second nature, affecting body, voice, and mind?

Yes, certainly, he said.

Then, I said, we will not allow those for whom we profess a care and of whom we say that they ought to be good men, to imitate a woman, whether young or old, quarreling with her husband, or striving and vaunting against the gods in conceit of her happiness, or when she is in affliction, or sorrow, or weeping; and certainly not one who is in sickness, love, or labor.

Very right, he said.

Neither must they represent slaves, male or female, performing the offices of slaves?

They must not.

And surely not bad men, whether cowards or any others, who do the reverse of what we have just been prescribing, who scold or mock or revile one another in drink or out of drink, or who in any other manner sin against themselves and their neighbors in word or deed, as the manner of such is. Neither should they be trained to imitate the action or speech of men or women who are mad or bad; for madness, like vice, is to be known but not to be practiced or imitated.

Very true, he replied.

Neither may they imitate smiths or other artificers, or oarsmen, or boatswains, or the like?

How can they he said, when they are not allowed to apply their minds to the calling of any of these?

Nor may they imitate the neighing of horses, the bellowing of bulls, the murmur of rivers and roll of the ocean, thunder, and all that sort of thing?

Nay, he said, if madness be forbidden, neither may they copy the behavior of madmen.

You mean, I said, if I understand you aright, that there is one sort of narrative style which may be employed by a truly good man when he has anything to say, and that another sort will be used by a man of an opposite character and education.

And which are these two sorts? he asked.

Suppose, I answered, that a just and good man in the course of a narration comes on some saying or action of another good man, I should imagine that he will like to personate him, and will not be ashamed of this sort of imitation: He will be most ready to play the part of the good man when he is acting firmly and wisely; in a less degree when he is overtaken by illness or love or drink, or has met with any other disaster. But when he comes to a character which is unworthy of him, he will not make a study of that; he will disdain such a person, and will assume his likeness, if at all, for a moment only when he is performing some good action; at other times he will be ashamed to play a part which he has never practiced, nor will he like to fashion and frame himself after the baser models; he feels the employment of such an art, unless in jest, to be beneath him, and his mind revolts at it.

So I should expect, he replied.

Then he will adopt a mode of narration such as we have illustrated out of Homer, that is to say, his style will be both imitative and narrative; but there will be very little of the former, and a great deal of the latter. Do you agree?

Certainly, he said; that is the model which such a speaker must necessarily take.

But there is another sort of character who will narrate anything, and, the worse he is, the more unscrupulous he will be; nothing will be too bad for him; and he will be ready to imitate anything, not as a joke, but in right good earnest, and before a large company. As I was just now saying, he will attempt to represent the roll of thunder, the noise of wind and hail, or the creaking of wheels, and pulleys, and the various sounds of flutes, pipes, trumpets, and all sorts of instruments: He will bark like a dog, bleat like a sheep, or crow like a cock; his entire art will consist in imitation of voice and gesture, and there will be very little narration.

That, he said, will be his mode of speaking.

These, then, are the two kinds of style?

Yes.

And you would agree with me in saying that one of them is simple and has but slight changes; and if the harmony and rhythm are also chosen for their simplicity, the result is that the speaker, if he speaks correctly, is always pretty much the same in style, and he will keep within the limits of a single harmony (for the changes are not great), and in like manner he will make use of nearly the same rhythm?

That is quite true, he said.

Whereas the other requires all sorts of harmonies and all sorts of rhythms, if the music and the style are to correspond, because the style has all sorts of changes.

That is also perfectly true, he replied.

And do not the two styles, or the mixture of the two, comprehend all poetry, and every form of expression in words? No one can say anything except in one or other of them or in both together.

They include all, he said.

And shall we receive into our State all the three styles, or one only of the two unmixed styles? or would you include the mixed?

I should prefer only to admit the pure imitator of virtue.

Yes, I said, Adeimantus; but the mixed style is also very charming; and indeed the pantomimic, which is the opposite of the one chosen by you, is the most popular style with children and their attendants, and with the world in general.

I do not deny it.

But I suppose you would argue that such a style is unsuitable to our State, in which human nature is not twofold or manifold, for one man plays one part only?

Yes, quite unsuitable.

And this is the reason why in our State, and in our State only, we shall find a shoemaker to be a shoemaker and not a pilot also, and a husbandman to be a husbandman and not a dicast also, and a soldier a soldier and not a trader also, and the same throughout?

True, he said.

And therefore when any one of these pantomimic gentlemen, who are so clever that they can imitate anything, comes to us, and makes a proposal to exhibit himself and his poetry, we will fall down and worship him as a sweet and holy and wonderful being; but we must also inform him that in our State such as he are not permitted to exist; the law will not allow them. And so when we have anointed him with myrrh, and set a garland of wool upon his head, we shall send him away to another city. For we mean to employ for our souls' health the rougher and severer poet or story-teller, who will imitate the style of the virtuous only, and will follow those models which we prescribed at first when we began the education of our soldiers.

Book IV[3]

Then to sum up: This is the point to which, above all, the attention of our rulers should be directed, that music and gymnastic be preserved in their original form, and no innovation made. They must do their utmost to maintain them intact. And when anyone says that mankind most regard "The newest song which the singers have,"[4] they will be afraid that he may be praising, not new songs, but a new kind of song; and this ought not to be praised, or conceived to be the meaning of the poet; for any musical innovation is full of danger to the whole State, and ought to be prohibited. So Damon tells me, and I can quite believe him; he says that when modes of music change, the fundamental laws of the State always change with them.

Yes, said Adeimantus; and you may add my suffrage to Damon's and your own.

Then, I said, our guardians must lay the foundations of their fortress in music?

Yes, he said; the lawlessness of which you speak too easily steals in.

Yes, I replied, in the form of amusement; and at first sight it appears harmless.

Why, yes, he said, and there is no harm; were it not that little by little this spirit of license, finding a home, imperceptibly penetrates into manners and customs; whence, issuing with greater force, it invades contracts between man and man, and from contracts goes on to laws and constitutions, in utter recklessness, ending at last, Socrates, by an overthrow of all rights, private as well as public.

Is that true? I said.

That is my belief, he replied.

Then, as I was saying, our youth should be trained from the first in a stricter system, for if amusements become lawless, and the youths themselves become lawless, they can never grow up into well-conducted and virtuous citizens.

---

[3] The dialogue is between Socrates, who speaks first, and Adeimantus.
[4] *Odyssey*, i, 352 [translator's note].

Book X[5]

Of the many excellences which I perceive in the order of our State, there is none which upon reflection pleases me better than the rule about poetry.

To what do you refer?

To the rejection of imitative poetry, which certainly ought not to be received; as I see far more clearly now that the parts of the soul have been distinguished.

What do you mean?

Speaking in confidence, for I should not like to have my words repeated to the tragedians and the rest of the imitative tribe—but I do not mind saying to you, that all poetical imitations are ruinous to the understanding of the hearers, and that the knowledge of their true nature is the only antidote to them.

Explain the purport of your remark.

Well, I will tell you, although I have always from my earliest youth had an awe and love of Homer, which even now makes the words falter on my lips, for he is the great captain and teacher of the whole of that charming tragic company; but a man is not to be reverenced more than the truth, and therefore I will speak out.

Very good, he said.

Listen to me then, or rather, answer me.

Put your question.

Can you tell me what imitation is? for I really do not know.

A likely thing, then, that I should know.

Why not? for the duller eye may often see a thing sooner than the keener.

Very true, he said; but in your presence, even if I had any faint notion, I could not muster courage to utter it. Will you enquire yourself?

Well then, shall we begin the enquiry in our usual manner: Whenever a number of individuals have a common name, we assume them to have also a corresponding idea or form—do you understand me?

I do.

Let us take any common instance; there are beds and tables in the world—plenty of them, are there not?

Yes.

But there are only two ideas or forms of them—one of the idea of a bed, the other of a table.

True.

And the maker of either of them makes a bed or he makes a table for our use, in accordance with the idea—that is our way of speaking in this

---

[5] The dialogue is between Socrates, who speaks first, and Glaucon.

and similar instances—but no artificer makes the ideas themselves: how could he?

Impossible.

And there is another artist—I should like to know what you would say of him.

Who is he?

One who is the maker of all the works of all other workmen.

What an extraordinary man!

Wait a little, and there will be more reason for your saying so. For this is he who is able to make not only vessels of every kind, but plants and animals, himself and all other things—the earth and heaven, and the things which are in heaven or under the earth; he makes the gods also.

He must be a wizard and no mistake.

Oh! you are incredulous, are you? Do you mean that there is no such maker or creator, or that in one sense there might be a maker of all these things but in another not? Do you see that there is a way in which you could make them all yourself?

What way?

An easy way enough; or rather, there are many ways in which the feat might be quickly and easily accomplished, none quicker than that of turning a mirror round and round—you would soon enough make the sun and the heavens, and the earth and yourself, and other animals and plants, and all the other things of which we were just now speaking, in the mirror.

Yes, he said; but they would be appearances only.

Very good, I said, you are coming to the point now. And the painter too, is, as I conceive, just such another—a creator of appearances, is he not?

Of course.

But then I suppose you will say that what he creates is untrue. And yet there is a sense in which the painter also creates a bed?

Yes, he said, but not a real bed.

And what of the maker of the bed? were you not saying that he too makes, not the idea which, according to our view, is the essence of the bed, but only a particular bed?

Yes, I did.

Then if he does not make that which exists he cannot make true existence, but only some semblance of existence; and if anyone were to say that the work of the maker of the bed, or of any other workman, has real existence he could hardly be supposed to be speaking the truth.

At any rate, he replied, philosophers would say that he was not speaking the truth.

No wonder, then, that his work too is an indistinct expression of truth.

No wonder.

Suppose now that by the light of the examples just offered we enquire who this imitator is?

If you please.

Well then, here are three beds: one existing in nature, which is made by God, as I think that we may say—for no one else can be the maker?

No.

There is another which is the work of the carpenter?

Yes.

And the work of the painter is a third?

Yes.

Beds, then, are of three kinds, and there are three artists who superintend them: God, the maker of the bed, and the painter?

Yes, there are three of them.

God, whether from choice or from necessity, made one bed in nature and one only; two or more such ideal beds neither ever have nor ever will be made by God.

Why is that?

Because even if He had made but two, a third would still appear behind them which both of them would have for their idea, and that would be the ideal bed and not the two others.

Very true, he said.

God knew this, and He desired to be the real maker of a real bed, not a particular maker of a particular bed, and therefore He created a bed which is essentially and by nature one only.

So we believe.

Shall we, then, speak of Him as the natural author or maker of the bed?

Yes, he replied; inasmuch as by the natural process of creation He is the author of this and of all other things.

And what shall we say of the carpenter—is not he also the maker of the bed?

Yes.

But would you call the painter a creator and maker?

Certainly not.

Yet if he is not the maker, what is he in relation to the bed?

I think, he said, that we may fairly designate him as the imitator of that which the others make.

Good, I said; then you call him who is third in the descent from nature an imitator?

Certainly, he said.

And the tragic poet is an imitator, and therefore, like all other imitators, he is thrice removed from the king and from the truth?

That appears to be so.

Then about the imitator we are agreed. And what about the painter?— I would like to know whether he may be thought to imitate that which originally exists in nature, or only the creations of artists?

The latter.

As they are or as they appear? you have still to determine this.

What do you mean?

I mean, that you may look at a bed from different points of view, obliquely or indirectly or from any other point of view, and the bed will appear different, but there is no difference in reality. And the same of all things.

Yes, he said, the difference is only apparent.

Now let me ask you another question: Which is the art of painting designed to be—an imitation of things as they are, or as they appear—of appearance or of reality?

Of appearance.

Then the imitator, I said, is a long way off the truth, and can do all things because he lightly touches on a small part of them, and that part an image. For example: A painter will paint a cobbler, carpenter, or any other artist, though he knows nothing of their arts; and, if he is a good artist, he may deceive children or simple persons, when he shows them his picture of a carpenter from a distance, and they will fancy that they are looking at a real carpenter.

Certainly.

And whenever any one informs us that he has found a man who knows all the arts, and all things else that anybody knows, and every single thing with a higher degree of accuracy than any other man—whoever tells us this, I think that we can only imagine him to be a simple creature who is likely to have been deceived by some wizard or actor whom he met, and whom he thought all-knowing, because he himself was unable to analyze the nature of knowledge and ignorance and imitation.

Most true.

And so, when we hear persons saying that the tragedians, and Homer, who is at their head, know all the arts and all things human, virtue as well as vice, and divine things too, for that the good poet cannot compose well unless he knows his subject, and that he who has not this knowledge can never be a poet, we ought to consider whether here also there may not be a similar illusion. Perhaps they may have come across imitators and been deceived by them; they may not have remembered when they saw their works that these were but imitators and been deceived by them; they may not have remembered when they saw their works that these were but imitations thrice removed from the truth, and could easily be made without any knowledge of the truth, because they are appearances only and not realities? Or, after all, they may be in the right, and poets do really know the things about which they seem to the many to speak so well?

The question, he said, should by all means be considered.

Now do you suppose that if a person were able to make the original as well, as the image, he would seriously devote himself to the image-making branch? Would he allow imitation to be the ruling principle of his life, as if he had nothing higher in him?

I should say not.

The real artist, who knew what he was imitating, would be interested in realities and not in imitations; and would desire to leave as memorials of himself works many and fair; and, instead of being the author of encomiums, he would prefer to be the theme of them.

Yes, he said, that would be to him a source of much greater honor and profit.

Then, I said, we must put a question to Homer; not about medicine, or any of the arts to which his poems only incidentally refer: We are not going to ask him, or any other poet, whether he has cured patients like Asclepius, or left behind him a school of medicine such as the Asclepiads were, or whether he only talks about medicine and other arts at second-hand; but we have a right to know respecting military tactics, politics, education, which are the chiefest and noblest subjects of his poems, and we may fairly ask him about them. "Friend Homer," then we say to him, "if you are only in the second remove from truth in what you say of virtue, and not in the third—not an image maker or imitator—and if you are able to discern what pursuits make men better or worse in private or public life, tell us what State was ever better governed by your help? The good order of Lacedaemon is due to Lycurgus, and many other cities great and small have been similarly benefited by others; but who says that you have been a good legislator to them and have done them any good? Italy and Sicily boast of Charondas, and there is Solon who is renowned among us; but what city has anything to say about you?" Is there any city which he might name?

I think not, said Glaucon; not even the Homerids themselves pretend that he was a legislator.

Well, but is there any war on record which was carried on successfully by him, or aided by his counsels, when he was alive?

There is not.

Or is there any invention of his, applicable to the arts or to human life, such as Thales the Milesian or Anacharsis the Scythian, and other ingenious men have conceived, which is attributed to him?

There is absolutely nothing of the kind.

But, if Homer never did any public service, was he privately a guide or a teacher of any? Had he in his lifetime friends who loved to associate with him, and who handed down to posterity an Homeric way of life, such as was established by Pythagoras who was so greatly beloved for his wisdom, and whose followers are to this day quite celebrated for the order which was named after him?

Nothing of the kind is recorded of him. For surely, Socrates, Creophylus, the companion of Homer, that child of flesh, whose name always makes us laugh, might be more justly ridiculed for his stupidity, if as is said, Homer was greatly neglected by him and others in his own day when he was alive?

Yes, I replied, that is the tradition. But can you imagine, Glaucon, that if Homer had really been able to educate and improve mankind—if he had possessed knowledge and not been a mere imitator—can you imagine, I say, that he would not have had many followers, and been honored and loved by them? Protagoras of Abdera, and Prodicus of Ceos, and a host of others, have only to whisper to their contemporaries: "You will never be able to manage either your own house or your own State until you appoint us to be your ministers of education"—and this ingenious device of theirs has such an effect in making men love them that their companions all but carry them about on their shoulders. And is it conceivable that the contemporaries of Homer, or again of Hesiod, would have allowed either of them to go about as rhapsodists, if they had really been able to make mankind virtuous? Would they not have been as unwilling to part with them as with gold, and have compelled them to stay at home with them? Or, if the master would not stay, then the disciples would have followed him about everywhere, until they had got education enough?

Yes, Socrates, that, I think, is quite true.

Then must we not infer that all these poetical individuals, beginning with Homer, are only imitators; they copy images of virtue and the like, but the truth they never reach? The poet is like a painter who, as we have already observed, will make a likeness of a cobbler though he understands nothing of cobbling; and his picture is good enough for those who know no more than he does, and judge only by colors and figures.

Quite so.

In like manner the poet with his words and phrases may be said to lay on the colors of the several arts, himself understanding their nature only enough to imitate them; and other people, who are as ignorant as he is, and judge only from his words, imagine that if he speaks of cobbling, or of military tactics, or of anything else, in meter and harmony and rhythm, he speaks very well—such is the sweet influence which melody and rhythm by nature have. And I think that you must have observed again and again what a poor appearance the tales of poets make when stripped of the colors which music puts upon them, and recited in simple prose.

Yes, he said.

They are like faces which were never really beautiful, but only blooming; and now the bloom of youth has passed away from them?

Exactly.

Here is another point: The imitator or maker of the image knows nothing of true existence; he knows appearances only. Am I not right?

Yes.

Then let us have a clear understanding, and not be satisfied with half an explanation.

Proceed.

Of the painter we say that he will paint reins, and he will paint a bit? Yes.

And the worker in leather and brass will make them?

Certainly.

But does the painter know the right form of the bit and reins? Nay, hardly even the workers in brass and leather who make them; only the horseman who knows how to use them—he knows their right form.

Most true.

And may we not say the same of all things?

What?

That there are three arts which are concerned with all things: one which uses, another which makes, a third which imitates them?

Yes.

And the excellence or beauty or truth of every structure, animate or inanimate, and of every action of man, is relative to the use for which nature or the artist has intended them.

True.

Then the user of them must have the greatest experience of them, and he must indicate to the maker the good or bad qualities which develop themselves in use; for example, the flute-player will tell the flute-maker which of his flutes is satisfactory to the performer; he will tell him how he ought to make them, and the other will attend to his instructions?

Of course.

The one knows and therefore speaks with authority about the goodness and badness of flutes, while the other, confiding in him, will do what he is told by him?

True.

The instrument is the same, but about the excellence or badness of it the maker will only attain to a correct belief; and this he will gain from him who knows, by talking to him and being compelled to hear what he has to say, whereas the user will have knowledge?

True.

But will the imitator have either? Will he know from use whether or no his drawing is correct or beautiful? or will he have right opinion from being compelled to associate with another who knows and gives him instructions about what he should draw?

Neither.

Then he will no more have true opinion than he will have knowledge about the goodness or badness of his imitations?

I suppose not.

The imitative artist will be in a brilliant state of intelligence about his own creations?

Nay, very much the reverse.

And still he will go on imitating without knowing what makes a thing good or bad, and may be expected therefore to imitate only that which appears to be good to the ignorant multitude?

Just so.

Thus far then we are pretty well agreed that the imitator has no knowledge worth mentioning of what he imitates. Imitation is only a kind of play or sport, and the tragic poets, whether they write in Iambic or Heroic verse, are imitators in the highest degree?

Very true.

And now tell me, I conjure you, has not imitation been shown by us to be concerned with that which is thrice removed from the truth?

Certainly.

And what is the faculty in man to which imitation is addressed?

What do you mean?

I will explain: The body which is large when seen near, appears small when seen at a distance?

True.

And the same objects appear straight when looked at out of the water, and crooked when in the water; and the concave becomes convex, owing to the illusion about colors to which the sight is liable. Thus every sort of confusion is revealed within us; and this is that weakness of the human mind on which the art of conjuring and of deceiving by light and shadow and other ingenious devices imposes, having an effect upon us like magic.

True.

And the arts of measuring and numbering and weighing come to the rescue of the human understanding—there is the beauty of them—and the apparent greater or less, or more or heavier, no longer have the mastery over us, but give way before calculation and measure and weight?

Most true.

And this, surely, must be the work of the calculating and rational principle in the soul?

To be sure.

And when this principle measures and certifies that some things are equal, or that some are greater or less than others, there occurs an apparent contradiction?

True.

But were we not saying that such a contradiction is impossible—the same faculty cannot have contrary opinions at the same time about the same thing?

Very true.

Then that part of the soul which has an opinion contrary to measure is not the same with that which has an opinion in accordance with measure?

True.

And the better part of the soul is likely to be that which trusts to measure and calculation?

Certainly.

And that which is opposed to them is one of the inferior principles of the soul?

No doubt.

This was the conclusion at which I was seeking to arrive when I said that painting or drawing, and imitation in general, when doing their own proper work, are far removed from truth, and the companions and friends and associates of a principle within us which is equally removed from reason, and that they have no true or healthy aim.

Exactly.

The imitative art is an inferior who marries an inferior, and has inferior offspring.

Very true.

And is this confined to the sight only, or does it extend to the hearing also, relating in fact to what we term poetry?

Probably the same would be true of poetry.

Do not rely, I said, on a probability derived from the analogy of painting; but let us examine further and see whether the faculty with which poetical imitation is concerned is good or bad.

By all means.

We may state the question thus: Imitation imitates the actions of men, whether voluntary or involuntary, on which, as they imagine, a good or bad result has ensued, and they rejoice or sorrow accordingly. Is there anything more?

No, there is nothing else.

But in all this variety of circumstances is the man at unity with himself— or rather, as in the instance of sight there was confusion and opposition in his opinions about the same things, so here also is there not strife and inconsistency in his life? Though I need hardly raise the question again, for I remember that all this has been already admitted; and the soul has been acknowledged by us to be full of these and ten thousand similar oppositions occurring at the same moment?

And we were right, he said.

Yes, I said, thus far we were right; but there was an omission which must now be supplied.

What was the omission?

Were we not saying that a good man, who has the misfortune to lose his son or anything else which is most dear to him, will bear the loss with more equanimity than another?

Yes.

But will he have no sorrow, or shall we say that although he cannot help sorrowing, he will moderate his sorrow?

The latter, he said, is the truer statement.

Tell me: Will he be more likely to struggle and hold out against his sorrow when he is seen by his equals, or when he is alone?

It will make a great difference whether he is seen or not.

When he is by himself he will not mind saying or doing many things which he would be ashamed of anyone hearing or seeing him do?

True.

There is a principle of law and reason in him which bids him resist, as well as a feeling of his misfortune which is forcing him to indulge his sorrow?

True.

But when a man is drawn in two opposite directions, to and from the same object, this, as we affirm, necessarily implies two distinct principles in him?

Certainly.

One of them is ready to follow the guidance of the law?

How do you mean?

The law would say that to be patient under suffering is best, and that we should not give way to impatience, as there is no knowing whether such things are good or evil; and nothing is gained by impatience; also, because no human thing is of serious importance, and grief stands in the way of that which at the moment is most required.

What is most required? he asked.

That we should take counsel about what has happened, and when the dice have been thrown order our affairs in the way which reason deems best; not, like children who have had a fall, keeping hold of the part struck and wasting time in setting up a howl, but always accustoming the soul forthwith to apply a remedy, raising up that which is sickly and fallen, banishing the cry of sorrow by the healing art.

Yes, he said, that is the true way of meeting the attacks of fortune.

Yes, I said; and the higher principle is ready to follow this suggestion of reason?

Clearly.

And the other principle, which inclines us to recollection of our troubles and to lamentation, and can never have enough of them, we may call irrational, useless, and cowardly?

Indeed, we may.

And does not the latter—I mean the rebellious principle—furnish a great variety of materials for imitation? Whereas the wise and calm temperament, being always nearly equable, is not easy to imitate or to appreciate when imitated, especially at a public festival when a promiscuous crowd is assembled in a theatre. For the feeling represented is one to which they are strangers.

Certainly.

Then the imitative poet who aims at being popular is not by nature made, nor is his art intended, to please or to affect the rational principle in the soul; but he will prefer the passionate and fitful temper, which is easily imitated?

Clearly.

And now we may fairly take him and place him by the side of the painter, for he is like him in two ways: first, inasmuch as his creations have an inferior degree of truth—in this, I say, he is like him; and he is also like him in being concerned with an inferior part of the soul; and therefore we shall be right in refusing to admit him into a well-ordered State, because he awakens and nourishes and strengthens the feelings and impairs the reason. As in a city when the evil are permitted to have authority and the good are put out of the way, so in the soul of man, as we maintain, the imitative poet implants an evil constitution, for he indulges the irrational nature which has no discernment of greater and less, but thinks the same thing at one time great and at another small—he is a manufacturer of images and is very far removed from the truth.

Exactly.

But we have not yet brought forward the heaviest count in our accusation—the power which poetry has of harming even the good (and there are very few who are not harmed), is surely an awful thing?

Yes, certainly, if the effect is what you say.

Hear and judge: The best of us, as I conceive, when we listen to a passage of Homer, or one of the tragedians, in which he represents some pitiful hero who is drawling out his sorrows in a long oration, or weeping, and smiting his breast—the best of us, you know, delight in giving way to sympathy, and are in raptures at the excellence of the poet who stirs our feelings most.

Yes, of course I know.

But when any sorrow of our own happens to us, then you may observe that we pride ourselves on the opposite quality—we would fain be quiet and patient; this is the manly part, and the other which delighted us in the recitation is now deemed to be the part of a woman.

Very true, he said.

Now can we be right in praising and admiring another who is doing that which any one of us would abominate and be ashamed of in his own person?

No, he said, that is certainly not reasonable.

Nay, I said, quite reasonable from one point of view.

What point of view?

If you consider, I said, that when in misfortune we feel a natural hunger and desire to relieve our sorrows by weeping and lamentation, and this feeling which is kept under control in our own calamities is satisfied and delighted by the poets—the better nature in each of us, not having been sufficiently trained by reason or habit, allows the sympathetic element to break loose because the sorrow is another's; and the spectator fancies that there can be no disgrace to himself in praising and pitying anyone who comes telling him what a good man he is, and making a fuss about his troubles; he thinks that the pleasure is a gain, and why should he be supercilious and lose this and the poem too? Few persons ever reflect, as I should imagine, that from the evil of other men something of evil is communicated to themselves. And so the feeling of sorrow which has gathered strength at the sight of the misfortunes of others is with difficulty repressed in our own.

How very true!

And does not the same hold also of the ridiculous? There are jests which you would be ashamed to make yourself, and yet on the comic stage, or indeed in private, when you hear them, you are greatly amused by them, and are not at all disgusted at their unseemliness—the case of pity is repeated—there is a principle in human nature which is disposed to raise a laugh, and this which you once restrained by reason, because you were afraid of being thought a buffoon, is now let out again; and having stimulated the risible faculty at the theatre, you are betrayed unconsciously to yourself into playing the comic poet at home.

Quite true, he said.

And the same may be said of lust and anger and all the other affections, of desire and pain and pleasure, which are held to be inseparable from every action—in all of them poetry feeds and waters the passions instead of drying them up; she lets them rule, although they ought to be controlled, if mankind are ever to increase in happiness and virtue.

I cannot deny it.

Therefore, Glaucon, I said, whenever you meet with any of the eulogists of Homer declaring that he has been the educator of Hellas, and that he is profitable for education and for the ordering of human things, and that you should take him up again and again and get to know him and regulate your whole life according to him, we may love and honor those who say these things—they are excellent people, as far as their lights extend; and we are ready to acknowledge that Homer is the greatest of poets and first of tragedy writers; but we must remain firm in our convictions that hymns to the gods and praises of famous men are the only poetry which ought to be admitted into our State. For if you go beyond this and allow the honeyed muse to enter, either in epic or lyric verse, not law and the reason of mankind, which by common consent have ever been deemed best, but pleasure and pain will be the rulers in our State.

That is most true, he said.

Aristotle   *384–322 B.C.*

Poetics   c. 335 B.C.

I

I propose to treat of Poetry in itself and of its various kinds, noting the essential quality of each; to inquire into the structure of the plot as requisite to a good poem; into the number and nature of the parts of which a poem is composed; and similarly into whatever else falls within the same inquiry. Following, then, the order of nature, let us begin with the principles which come first.

Epic poetry and Tragedy, Comedy also and Dithyrambic poetry, and the music of the flute and of the lyre in most of their forms, are all in their general conception modes of imitation. They differ, however, from one another in three respects—the medium, the objects, the manner or mode of imitation, being in each case distinct.

For as there are persons who, by conscious art or mere habit, imitate and represent various objects through the medium of color and form, or again by the voice; so in the arts above mentioned, taken as a whole, the imitation is produced by rhythm, language, or "harmony," either singly or combined.

Thus in the music of the flute and of the lyre, "harmony" and rhythm alone are employed; also in other arts, such as that of the shepherd's pipe,

Translated by S. H. Butcher. From S. H. Butcher, *Aristotle's Theory of Poetry and Fine Art*, Third Edition. London: Macmillan and Co., 1902. The editor has made minor omissions (Chapters XX, XXI, and parts of Chapters XXII, XXIII, and XXV) as well as minor changes, which are indicated by double brackets[[ ]]. Other typographical devices are the tranlator's: [ ] = a possible interpolation, < > = a conjectural supplement to the text, ** = a lacuna.

which are essentially similar to these. In dancing, rhythm alone is used without "harmony"; for even dancing imitates character, emotion, and action, by rhythmical movement.

There is another art which imitates by means of language alone, and that either in prose or verse—which verse, again, may either combine different meters or consist of but one kind—but this has hitherto been without a name. For there is no common term we could apply to the mimes of Sophron and Xenarchus and the Socratic dialogues on the one hand; and, on the other, to poetic imitations in iambic, elegiac, or any similar meter. People do, indeed, add the word "maker" or "poet" to the name of the meter, and speak of elegiac poets, or epic (that is, hexameter) poets, as if it were not the imitation that makes the poet, but the verse that entitles them all indiscriminately to the name. Even when a treatise on medicine or natural science is brought out in verse, the name of poet is by custom given to the author; and yet Homer and Empedocles have nothing in common but the meter, so that it would be right to call the one poet, the other physicist rather than poet. On the same principle, even if a writer in his poetic imitation were to combine all meters, as Chaeremon did in his *Centaur*, which is a medley composed of meters of all kinds, we should bring him too under the general term poet. So much then for these distinctions.

There are, again, some arts which employ all the means above mentioned—namely, rhythm, tune and meter. Such are Dithyrambic and Nomic poetry, and also Tragedy and Comedy; but between them the difference is, that in the first two cases these means are all employed in combination, in the latter, now one means is employed, now another.

Such, then, are the differences of the arts with respect to the medium of imitation.

II

Since the objects of imitation are men in action, and these men must be either of a higher or a lower type (for moral character mainly answers to these divisions, goodness and badness being the distinguishing marks of moral differences), it follows that we must represent men either as better than in real life, or as worse, or as they are. It is the same in painting. Polygnotus depicted men as nobler than they are, Pauson as less noble, Dionysius drew them true to life.

Now it is evident that each of the modes of imitation above mentioned will exhibit these differences, and become a distinct kind in imitating objects that are thus distinct. Such diversities may be found even in dancing, flute-playing, and lyre-playing. So again in language, whether prose or verse un-accompanied by music. Homer, for example, makes men better than they are; Cleophon as they are; Hegemon the Thasian, the inventor of parodies, and Nicochares, the author of *Deiliad*, worse than they are. The same thing holds good of Dithyrambs and Nomes; here too one may portray different types, as Timotheus and Philoxenus differed in representing their Cyclopes. The same distinction marks off Tragedy from Comedy; for Comedy aims at representing men as worse, Tragedy as better than in actual life.

III

There is still a third difference—the manner in which each of these objects may be imitated. For the medium being the same, and the objects the same, the poet may imitate by narration—in which case he can either take another personality as Homer does, or speak in his own person, unchanged—or he may present all his characters as living and moving before us.

These, then, as we said at the beginning, are the three differences which distinguish artistic imitation—the medium, the objects, and the manner. So that from one point of view, Sophocles is an imitator of the same kind as Homer—for both imitate higher types of character; from another point of view, of the same kind as Aristophanes—for both imitate persons acting and doing. Hence, some say, the name of "drama" is given to such poems, as representing action. For the same reason the Dorians claim the invention both of Tragedy and Comedy. The claim to Comedy is put forward by the Megarians—not only by those of Greece proper, who allege that it originated under their democracy, but also by the Megarians of Sicily, for the poet Epicharmus, who is much earlier than Chionides and Magnes, belonged to that country. Tragedy too is claimed by certain Dorians of the Peloponnese. In each case they appeal to the evidence of language. Villages, they say, are by them called κῶμαι, by the Athenians δῆμοι: and they assume that Comedians were so named not from κωμάζειν, "to revel," but because they wandered from village to village (κατὰ κώμας), being excluded contemptuously from the city. They add also that the Dorian word for "doing" is δρᾶν, and the Athenian, πράττειν.

This may suffice as to the number and nature of the various modes of imitation.

IV

Poetry in general seems to have sprung from two causes, each of them lying deep in our nature. First, the instinct of imitation is implanted in man from childhood, one difference between him and other animals being that he is the most imitative of living creatures; and through imitation he learns his earliest lessons; and no less universal is the pleasure felt in things imitated. We have evidence of this in the facts of experience. Objects which in themselves we view with pain, we delight to contemplate when reproduced with minute fidelity: such as the forms of the most ignoble animals and of dead bodies. The cause of this again is, that to learn gives the liveliest pleasure, not only to philosophers but to men in general; whose capacity, however, of learning is more limited. Thus the reason why men enjoy seeing a likeness is, that in contemplating it they find themselves learning or inferring, and saying perhaps, "Ah, that is he." For if you happen not to have seen the original, the pleasure will be due not to the imitation as such, but to the execution, the coloring, or some such other cause.

Imitation, then, is one instinct of our nature. Next, there is the instinct for "harmony" and rhythm, meters being manifestly sections of rhythm. Persons, therefore, starting with this natural gift developed by degrees their special aptitudes, till their rude improvisations gave birth to Poetry.

Poetry now diverged in two directions, according to the individual character of the writers. The graver spirits imitated noble actions, and the actions of good men. The more trivial sort imitated the actions of meaner persons, at first composing satires, as the former did hymns to the gods and the praises of famous men. A poem of the satirical kind cannot indeed be put down to any author earlier than Homer; though many such writers probably there were. But from Homer onward, instances can be cited—his own *Margites*, for example, and other similar compositions. The appropriate meter was also here introduced; hence the measure is still called the iambic or lampooning measure, being that in which people lampooned one another. Thus the older poets were distinguished as writers of heroic or of lampooning verse.

As, in the serious style, Homer is preeminent among poets, for he alone combined dramatic form with excellence of imitation, so he too first laid down the main lines of Comedy, by dramatizing the ludicrous instead of writing personal satire. His *Margites* bears the same relation to Comedy that the *Iliad* and *Odyssey* do to Tragedy. But when Tragedy and Comedy came to light, the two classes of poets still followed their natural bent: the lampooners became writers of Comedy, and the Epic poets were succeeded by Tragedians, since the drama was a larger and higher form of art.

Whether Tragedy has as yet perfected its proper types or not; and whether it is to be judged in itself, or in relation also to the audience, this raises another question. Be that as it may, Tragedy—as also Comedy—was at first mere improvisation. The one originated with the leaders of the Dithyramb, the other with those of the phallic songs, which are still in use in many of our cities. Tragedy advanced by slow degrees; each new element that showed itself was in turn developed. Having passed through many changes, it found its natural form, and there it stopped.

Aeschylus first introduced a second actor; he diminished the importance of the Chorus, and assigned the leading part to the dialogue. Sophocles raised the number of actors to three, and added scene-painting. Moreover, it was not till late that the short plot was discarded for one of greater compass, and the grotesque diction of the earlier satyric form for the stately manner of Tragedy. The iambic measure then replaced the trochaic tetrameter, which was originally employed when the poetry was of the satyric order, and had greater affinities with dancing. Once dialogue had come in, Nature herself discovered the appropriate measure. For the iambic is, of all measures, the most colloquial: we see it in the fact that conversational speech runs into iambic form more frequently than into any other kind of verse; rarely into hexameters, and only when we drop the colloquial intonation. The additions to the number of "episodes" or acts, and the other improvements of which tradition tells, must be taken as already described; for to discuss them in detail would, doubtless, be a large undertaking.

V

Comedy is, as we have said, an imitation of characters of a lower type— not, however, in the full sense of the word bad, the Ludicrous being merely a subdivision of the ugly. It consists in some defect or ugliness which is not painful or destructive. To take an obvious example, the comic mask is ugly and distorted, but does not imply pain.

The successive changes through which Tragedy passed, and the authors of these changes, are well known, whereas Comedy has had no history, because it was not at first treated seriously. It was late before the Archon[1] granted a comic chorus to a poet; the performers were till then voluntary. Comedy had already taken definite shape when comic poets, distinctively so called, are heard of. Who introduced masks, or prologues, or increased the number of actors—these and other similar details remain unknown. As for the plot, it came originally from Sicily; but of Athenian writers Crates was the first who, abandoning the "iambic" or lampooning form, generalized his themes and plots.

Epic poetry agrees with Tragedy in so far as it is an imitation in verse of characters of a higher type. They differ, in that Epic poetry admits but one kind of meter, and is narrative in form. They differ, again, in their length: for Tragedy endeavors, as far as possible, to confine itself to a single revolution of the sun, or but slightly to exceed this limit; whereas the Epic action has no limits of time. This, then, is a second point of difference; though at first the same freedom was admitted in Tragedy as in Epic poetry.

Of their constituent parts some are common to both, some peculiar to Tragedy. Whoever, therefore, knows what is good or bad Tragedy, knows also about Epic poetry: for all the elements of an Epic poem are found in Tragedy, but the elements of a Tragedy are not all found in the Epic poem.

---

[1] Principal civil magistrate of Athens, he was general supervisor of the City of Dionysia, a festival at which plays were presented.

VI

Of the poetry which imitates in hexameter verse, and of Comedy, we will speak hereafter. Let us now discuss Tragedy, resuming its formal definition, as resulting from what has been already said.

Tragedy, then, is an imitation of an action that is serious, complete, and of a certain magnitude; in language embellished with each kind of artistic ornament, the several kinds being found in separate parts of the play; in the form of action, not of narrative; through pity and fear affecting the proper purgation of these emotions. By "language embellished," I mean language into which rhythm, "harmony," and song enter. By "the several kinds in separate parts," I mean, that some parts are rendered through the medium of verse alone, others again with the aid of song.

Now as tragic imitation implies persons acting, it necessarily follows, in the first place, that Spectacular equipment will be a part of Tragedy. Next, Song and Diction, for these are the medium of imitation. By "Diction" I mean the mere metrical arrangement of the words: as for "Song," it is a term whose sense every one understands.

Again, Tragedy is the imitation of an action; and an action implies personal agents, who necessarily possess certain distinctive qualities both of character and thought; for it is by these that we qualify actions themselves, and these—thought and character—are the two natural causes from which actions spring, and on actions again all success or failure depends. Hence, the Plot is the imitation of the action—for by plot I here mean the arrangement of the incidents. By Character I mean that in virtue of which we ascribe certain qualities to the agents. Thought is required wherever a statement is proved, or, it may be, a general truth enunciated. Every Tragedy, therefore, must have six parts, which parts determine its quality—namely, Plot, Character, Diction, Thought, Spectacle, Song. Two of the parts constitute the medium of imitation, one the manner, and three the objects of imitation. And these complete the list. These elements have been employed, we may say, by the poets to a man; in fact, every play contains Spectacular elements as well as Character, Plot, Diction, Song, and Thought.

But most important of all is the structure of the incidents. For Tragedy is an imitation, not of men, but of an action and of life, and life consists in action, and its end is a mode of action, not a quality. Now character determines men's qualities, but it is by their actions that they are happy or the reverse. Dramatic action, therefore, is not with a view to the representation of character: character comes in as subsidiary to the actions. Hence the incidents and the plot are the end of a tragedy; and the end is the chief thing of all. Again, without action there cannot be a tragedy; there may be without character. The tragedies of most of our modern poets fail in the rendering of character; and of poets in general this is often true. It is the same in painting; and here lies the difference between Zeuxis and Polygnotus. Polygnotus delineates character well: the style of Zeuxis is devoid of ethical quality. Again, if you string together a set of speeches expressive of character, and well finished in point of diction and thought, you will not produce the essential tragic effect nearly so well as with a play which, however deficient in these respects, yet has a plot and artistically constructed incidents. Besides which, the most powerful elements of emotional interest in Tragedy—[[Peripeteia or unexpected Reversal of circumstances or situation]], and Recognition scenes—are parts of the plot. A further proof is, that novices in the art attain to finish of diction and precision of portraiture before they can construct the plot. It is the same with almost all the early poets.

The Plot, then, is the first principle, and, as it were, the soul of a tragedy: Character holds the second place. A similar fact is seen in painting. The most beautful colors, laid on confusedly, will not give as much pleasure as the chalk outline of a portrait. Thus Tragedy is the imitation of an action, and of the agents, mainly with a view to the action.

Third in order is Thought—that is, the faculty of saying what is possible and pertinent in given circumstances. In the case of oratory, this is the function of the political art and of the art of rhetoric: and so indeed the older poets make their characters speak the language of civic life; the poets of our time, the language of the rhetoricians. Character is that which reveals moral purpose, showing what kind of things a man chooses or avoids. Speeches, therefore, which do not make this manifest, or in which the speaker does not choose or avoid anything whatever, are not expressive of character. Thought, on the other hand, is found where something is proved to be or not to be, or a general maxim is enunciated.

Fourth among the elements enumerated comes Diction; by which I mean, as has been already said, the expression of the meaning in words; and its essence is the same both in verse and prose.

Of the remaining elements Song holds the chief place among the embellishments.

The Spectacle has, indeed, an emotional attraction of its own, but, of all the parts, it is the least artistic, and connected least with the art of poetry. For the power of Tragedy, we may be sure, is felt even apart from representation and actors. Besides, the production of spectacular effects depends more on the art of the stage machinist than on that of the poet.

VII

These principles being established, let us now discuss the proper structure of the Plot, since this is the first and most important part of Tragedy.

Now, according to our definition, Tragedy is an imitation of an action that is complete, and whole, and of a certain magnitude; for there may be a whole that is wanting in magnitude. A whole is that which has a beginning, a middle, and an end. A beginning is that which does not itself follow anything by causal necessity, but after which something naturally is or comes to be. An end, on the contrary, is that which itself naturally follows some other thing, either by necessity, or as a rule, but has nothing following it. A middle is that which follows something as some other thing follows it. A well-constructed plot, therefore, must neither begin nor end at haphazard, but conform to these principles.

Again, a beautiful object, whether it be a picture of a living organism or any whole composed of parts, must not only have an orderly arrangement of parts, but must also be of a certain magnitude; for beauty depends on magnitude and order. Hence an exceedingly small picture cannot be beautiful; for the view of it is confused, the object being seen in an almost imperceptible moment of time. Nor, again, can one of vast size be beautiful; for as the eye cannot take it all in at once, the unity and sense of the whole is lost for the spectator; as for instance if there were a picture a thousand miles long. As, therefore, in the case of animate bodies and pictures a certain magnitude is necessary, and a magnitude which may be easily embraced in one view; so in the plot, a certain length is necessary, and a length which can be easily embraced by the memory. The limit of length in relation to dramatic competition and sensuous presentment, is no part of artistic theory. For had it been the rule for a hundred tragedies to compete together, the performance would have been regulated by the water-clock—as indeed we are told was formerly done. But the limit as fixed by the nature of the drama itself is this: the greater the length, the more beautiful will the piece be by reason of its size, provided that the whole be perspicuous. And to define the matter roughly, we may say that the proper magnitude is comprised within such limits, that the sequence of events, according to the law of probability or necessity, will admit of a change from bad fortune to good, or from good fortune to bad.

VIII

Unity of plot does not, as some persons think, consist in the unity of the hero. For infinitely various are the incidents in one man's life, which cannot be reduced to unity; and so, too, there are many actions of one man out of which we cannot make one action. Hence the error, as it appears, of all poets who have composed a *Heracleid*, a *Theseid*, or other poems of the kind. They imagine that as Heracles was one man, the story of Heracles must also be a unity. But Homer, as in all else he is of surpassing merit, here too—whether from art or natural genius—seems to have happily discerned the truth. In composing the *Odyssey* he did not include all the adventures of Odysseus—such as his wound on Parnassus, or his feigned madness at the mustering of the host—incidents between which there was no necessary or probable connection: but he made the *Odyssey*, and likewise the *Iliad*, to center round an action that in our sense of the word is one. As therefore, in the other imitative arts, the imitation is one when the object imitated is one, so the plot, being an imitation of an action, must imitate one action and that a whole, the structural union of the parts being such that, if any one of them is displaced or removed, the whole will be disjointed and disturbed. For a thing whose presence or absence makes no visible difference, is not an organic part of the whole.

IX

It is, moreover, evident from what has been said, that it is not the function of the poet to relate what has happened, but what may happen— what is possible according to the law of probability or necessity. The poet and the historian differ not by writing in verse or in prose. The work of Herodotus might be put into verse, and it would still be a species of history, with meter no less than without it. The true difference is that one relates what has happened, the other what may happen. Poetry, therefore, is a more philosophical and a higher thing than history: for poetry tends to express the universal, history the particular. By the universal I mean how a person of a certain type will on occasion speak or act, according to the law of probability or necessity; and it is this universality at which poetry aims in the names she attaches to the personages. The particular is— for example—what Alcibiades did or suffered. In Comedy this is already apparent: for here the poet first constructs the plot on the lines of prob-abilty, and then inserts characteristic names—unlike the lampooners who write about particular individuals. But tragedians still keep to real names, the reason being that what is possible is credible: what has not happened we do not at once feel sure to be possible: but what has happened is manifestly possible: otherwise it would not have happened. Still there are some tragedies in which there are only one or two well-known names, the rest being fictitious. In others, none are well known—as in Agathon's *Antheus*, where incidents and names alike are fictitious, and yet they give none the less pleasure. We must not, therefore, at all costs keep to the received legends, which are the usual subjects of Tragedy. Indeed, it would be absurd to attempt it; for even subjects that are known are known only to a few, and yet give pleasure to all. It clearly follows that the poet or "maker" should be the maker of plots rather than of verses; since he is a poet because he imitates, and what he imitates are actions. And even if he chances to take an historical subject, he is none the less a poet; for there is no reason why some events that have actually happened should not conform to the law of the probable and possible, and in virtue of that quality in them he is their poet or maker.

Of all plots and actions the episodic are the worst. I call a plot "episodic" in which the episodes or acts succeed one another without probable or necessary sequence. Bad poets compose such pieces by their own fault, good poets, to please the players; for, as they write show pieces for competition, they stretch the plot beyond its capacity, and are often forced to break the natural continuity.

But again, Tragedy is an imitation not only of a complete action, but of events terrible and pitiful. Such an effect is best produced when the events come on us by surprise; and the effect is heightened when, at the same time, they follow as cause and effect. The tragic wonder will then be greater than if they happened of themselves or by accident; for even coincidences are most striking when they have an air of design. We may instance the statue of Mitys at Argos, which fell upon his murderer while he was a spectator at a festival, and killed him. Such events seem not to be due to mere chance. Plots, therefore, constructed on these principles are necessarily the best.

X

Plots are either Simple or Complex, for the actions in real life, of which the plots are an imitation, obviously show a similar distinction. An action which is one and continuous in the sense above defined, I call Simple, when the change of fortune takes place without [[Peripeteia, that is, unexpected Reversal of circumstances or situation,]] and without Recognition.

A Complex action is one in which the change is accompanied by such [[Peripeteia,]] or by Recognition, or by both. These last should arise from the internal structure of the plot, so that what follows should be the necessary or probable result of the preceding action. It makes all the difference whether any given event is a case of *propter hoc* or *post hoc*.

XI

[[Peripeteia]] is a change by which the action veers round to its opposite, subject always to our rule of probability or necessity. Thus in the *Oedipus*, the messenger comes to cheer Oedipus and free him from his alarms about his mother, but by revealing who he is, he produces the opposite effect. Again in the *Lynceus*, Lynceus is being led away to his death, and Danaus goes with him, meaning to slay him; but the outcome of the action is, that Danaus is killed and Lynceus saved.

Recognition, as the name indicates, is a change from ignorance to knowledge, producing love or hate between the persons destined by the poet for good or bad fortune. The best form of recognition is coincident with a [[Peripeteia,]] as in the *Oedipus*. There are indeed other forms. Even inanimate things of the most trivial kind may sometimes be objects of recognition. Again, we may recognize or discover whether a person has done a thing or not. But the recognition which is most intimately connected with the plot and action is, as we have said, the recognition of persons. This recognotion, combined with [[Peripeteia,]] will produce either pity or fear; and actions producing these effects are those which, by our definition, Tragedy represents. Moreover, it is upon such situations that the issues of good or bad fortune will depend. Recognition, then, being between persons, it may happen that one person only is recognized by the other—when the latter is already known—or it may be necessary that the recognition should be on both sides. Thus Iphigenia is revealed to Orestes by the sending of the letter; but another act of recognition is required to make Orestes known to Iphigenia.

Two parts, then, of the Plot—[[Peripeteia]] and Recognition—turn upon surprises. A third part is the [[Scene of Passion, that is, of suffering. The Scene of Passion is a fatal]] or painful action, such as death on the stage, bodily agony, wounds, and the like.

XII

[The parts of Tragedy which must be treated as elements of the whole have been already mentioned. We now come to the quantitative parts—the separate parts into which Tragedy is divided—namely, Prologue, Episode, Exodos, Choric song; this last being divided into Parodos and Stasimon. These are common to all plays: peculiar to some are the songs of actors from the stage and the Commoi.

The Prologos is that entire part of a tragedy which precedes the Parodos of the Chorus. The Episode is that entire part of a tragedy which is between complete choric songs. The Exodos is that entire part of a tragedy which has no choric song after it. Of the Choric part the Parodos is the first undivided utterance of the Chorus: the Stasimon is a Choric ode without anapests or trochaic tetrameters: the Commos is a joint lamentation of Chorus and actors. The parts of Tragedy which must be treated as elements of the whole have been already mentioned. The quantitative parts—the separate parts into which it is divided—are here enumerated.]

XIII

As the sequel to what has already been said, we must proceed to consider what the poet should aim at, and what he should avoid, in constructing his plots; and by what means the specific effect of Tragedy will be produced.

A perfect tragedy should, as we have seen, be arranged not on the simple but on the complex plan. It should, moreover, imitate actions which excite pity and fear, this being the distinctive mark of tragic imitation. It follows plainly, in the first place, that the change of fortune presented must not be the spectacle of a virtuous man brought from prosperity to adversity: for this moves neither pity nor fear; it merely shocks us. Nor, again, that of a bad man passing from adversity to prosperity: for nothing can be more alien to the spirit of Tragedy; it possess no single tragic quality; it neither satisfies the moral sense, nor calls forth pity or fear. Nor, again, should the downfall of the utter villain be exhibited. A plot of this kind would, doubltless, satisfy the moral sense, but it would inspire neither pity nor fear; for pity is aroused by unmerited misfortune, fear by the misfortune of a man like ourselves. Such an event, therefore, will be neither pitiful nor terrible. There remains, then, the character between these two extremes, that of a man who is not eminently good and just, yet whose misfortune is brought about not by vice or depravity, but by some error or fraility. He must be one who is highly renowned and prosperous—a personage like Oedipus, Thyestes, or other illustrious men of such families.

A well-constructed plot should, therefore, be single in its issue, rather than double as some maintain. The change of fortune should be not from bad to good, but, reversely, from good to bad. It should come about as the result not of vice, but of some great error or fraility, in a character either such as we have described, or better rather than worse. The practice of the stage bears out our view. At first the poets recounted any legend that came in their way. Now, the best tragedies are founded on the story of a few houses—on the fortunes of Alcmaeon, Oedipus, Orestes, Meleager, Thyestes, Telephus, and those others who have done or suffered something terrible. A tragedy, then, to be perfect according to the rules of art should be of this construction. Hence they are in error who censure Euripides just because he follows this principle in his plays, many of which end unhappily. It is, as we have said, the right ending. The best proof is that on the stage and in dramatic competition, such plays, if well worked out, are the most tragic in effect; and Euripides, faulty though he may be in the general management of his subject, yet is felt to be the most tragic of the poets.

In the second rank comes the kind of tragedy which some place first. Like the *Odyssey*, it has a double thread of plot, and also an opposite catastrophe for the good and for the bad. It is accounted the best because of the weakness of the spectators; for the poet is guided in what he writes by the wishes of his audience. The pleasure, however, thence derived is not the true tragic pleasure. It is proper rather to Comedy, where those who, in the piece, are the deadliest enemies—like Orestes and Aegisthus— quit the stage as friends at the close, and no one slays or is slain.

XIV

Fear and pity may be aroused by spectacular means; but they may also result from the inner structure of the piece, which is the better way, and indicates a superior poet. For the plot ought to be so constructed that, even without the aid of the eye, he who hears the tale told will thrill with horror and melt to pity at what takes place. This is the impression we should receive from hearing the story of the *Oedipus*. But to produce this effect by the mere spectacle is a less artistic method, and dependent on extraneous aids. Those who employ spectacular means to create a sense not of the terrible but only of the monstrous, are strangers to the purpose of Tragedy; for we must not demand of Tragedy any and every kind of pleasure, but only that which is proper to it. And since the pleasure which the poet should afford is that which comes from pity and fear through imitation, it is evident that this quality must be impressed upon the incidents.

Let us then determine what are the circumstances which strike us as terrible or pitiful.

Actions capable of this effect must happen between persons who are either friends or enemies or indifferent to one another. If an enemy kills an enemy, there is nothing to excite pity either in the act or the intention —except so far as the suffering in itself is pitiful. So again with indifferent persons. But when the traigc incident occurs between those who are near or dear to one another—if, for example, a brother kills, or intends to kill, a brother, a son his father, a mother her son, a son his mother, or any other deed of the kind is done—these are the situations to be looked for by the poet. He may not indeed destroy the framework of the received legends—the fact, for instance, that Clytemnestra was slain by Orestes and Eriphyle by Alcmaeon—but he ought to show invention of his own, and skilfully handle the traditional material. Let us explain more clearly what is meant by skilful handling.

The action may be done consciously and with knowledge of the persons, in the manner of the older poets. It is thus too that Euripides makes Medea slay her children. Or, again, the deed of horror may be done, but done in ignorance, and the tie of kinship or friendship be discovered afterwards. The *Oedipus* of Sophocles is an example. Here, indeed, the incident is outside the drama proper; but cases occur where it falls within the action of the play: one may cite the *Alcmaeon* of Astydamas, or Telegonus in the *Wounded Odysseus*. Again, there is a third case, < to be about to act with knowledge of the persons and then not to act. The fourth case is > when someone is about to do an irreparable deed through ignorance, and makes the discovery before it is done. These are the only possible ways.

For the deed must either be done or not done, and that wittingly or unwittingly. But of all these ways, to be about to act knowing the persons,
and then not to act, is the worst. It is shocking without being tragic, for
no disaster follows. It is, therefore, never, or very rarely, found in poetry.
One instance, however, is in the *Antigone*, where Haemon threatens to
kill Creon. The next and better way is that the deed should be perpetrated.
Still better, that it should be perpetrated in ignorance, and the discovery
made afterwards. There is then nothing to shock us, while the discovery
produces a startling effect. The last case is the best, as when in the
Cresphontes Merope is about to slay her son, but, recognizing who he is,
spares his life. So in the *Iphigenia*, the sister recognizes the brother just
in time. Again in the *Helle*, the son recognizes the mother when on the
point of giving her up. This, then, is why a few families only, as has been
already observed, furnish the subjects of tragedy. It was not art, but happy
chance, that led poets to look for such situations and so impress the tragic
quality upon their plots. They are compelled, therefore, to have recourse
to those houses whose history contains moving incidents like these.

Enough has now been said concerning the structure of the incidents, and
the proper constitution of the plot.

XV

In respect of Character there are four things to be aimed at. First, and
most important, it must be good. Now any speech or action that manifests
moral purpose of any kind will be expressive of character: the character
will be good if the purpose is good. This rule is relative to each class. Even
a woman may be good, and also a slave; though the woman may be said
to be an inferior being, and the slave quite worthless. The second thing
to aim at is propriety. There is a type of manly valor; but valor in a woman,
or unscrupulous cleverness, is inappropriate. Thirdly, character must be
true to life: for this is a distinct thing from goodness and propriety, as here
described. The fourth point is consistency: for though the subject of the
imitation, who suggested the type, be inconsistent, still he must be consistently inconsistent. As an example of motiveless degradation of character,
we have Menelaus in the *Orestes*: of character indecorous and inappropriate,
the lament of Odysseus in the *Scylla*, and the speech of Melanippe: of
inconsistency, the *Iphigenia at Aulis*, for Iphigenia the suppliant in no
way resembles her later self.

As in the structure of the plot, so too in the portraiture of character,
the poet should always aim either at the necessary or the probable. Thus a
person of a given character should speak or act in a given way, by the rule
either of necessity or of probability; just as this event should follow that
by necessary or probable sequence. It is therefore evident that the unraveling

of the plot, no less than the complication, must arise out of the plot itself; it must not be brought about by the *Deus ex Machina*[2]—as in the *Medea*, or in the Return of the Greeks in the *Iliad*. The *Deus ex Machina* should be employed only for events external to the drama—for antecedent or subsequent events, which lie beyond the range of human knowledge, and which require to be reported or foretold; for to the gods we ascribe the power of seeing all things. Within the action there must be nothing irrational. If the irrational cannot be excluded, it should be outside the scope of the tragedy. Such is the irrational element in the *Oedipus* of Sophocles.

Again, since Tragedy is an imitation of persons who are above the common level, the example of good portrait-painters should be followed. They, while reproducing the distinctive form of the original, make a likeness which is true to life and yet more beautiful. So too the poet, in representing men who are irascible or indolent, or have other defects of character, should preserve the type and yet ennoble it. In this way Achilles is portrayed by Agathon and Homer.

These then are rules the poet should observe. Nor should he neglect those appeals to the senses, which, though not among the essentials, are the concomitants of poetry; for here too there is much room for error. But of this enough has been said in the published treatises.

XVI

What Recognition is has been already explained. We will now enumerate its kinds.

First, the least artistic form, which, from poverty of wit, is most commonly employed—recognition by signs. Of these some are congenital, such as "the spear which the earth-born race bear on their bodies," or the stars introduced by Carcinus in his *Thyestes*. Others are acquired after birth; and of these some are bodily marks, as scars; some external tokens, as necklaces, or the little ark in the *Tyro* by which the discovery is effected. Even these admit of more or less skilful treatment. Thus in the recognition of Odysseus by his scar, the discovery is made in one way by the nurse, in another by the herdsmen. The use of tokens for the express purpose of proof —and, indeed, any formal proof with or without tokens—is a less artistic mode of recognition. A better kind is that which comes about by a turn of incident, as in the Bath Scene in the *Odyssey*.

Next come the recognitions invented at will by the poet, and on that account wanting in art. For example, Orestes in the *Iphigenia* reveals the fact that he is Orestes. She, indeed, makes herself known by the letter;

[2] Literally, a "god from the machine," that is, a god who descends from a stage machine in order to unravel the play's plot or problems; figuratively, an improbable device or character introduced at the end of the play in order to resolve a difficult situation.

but he, by speaking himself, and saying what the poet, not what the plot requires. This, therefore, is nearly allied to the fault above mentioned—for Orestes might as well have brought tokens with him. Another similar instance is the "voice of the shuttle" in the *Tereus* of Sophocles.

The third kind depends on memory when the sight of some object awakens a feeling: as in the *Cyprians* of Dicaeogenes, where the hero breaks into tears on seeing the picture; or again in the "Lay of Alcinous," where Odysseus, hearing the minstrel play the lyre, recalls the past and weeps; and hence the recognition.

The fourth kind is by process of reasoning. Thus in the *Choëphori*— "Someone resembling me has come: no one resembles me but Orestes: therefore Orestes has come." Such too is the discovery made by Iphigenia in the play of Polyidus the Sophist. It was a natural reflection for Orestes to make, "So I too must die at the altar like my sister." So, again, in the *Tydeus* of Theodectes, the father says, "I came to find my son and I lose my own life." So too in the *Phineidae*: the women, on seeing the place, inferred their fate: "Here we are doomed to die, for here we were cast forth." Again, there is a composite kind of recognition involving false inference on the part of one of the characters, as in the *Odysseus Disguised as a Messenger*. A said < that no one else was able to bend the bow; . . . hence B (the disguised Odysseus) imagined that A would > recognize the bow which, in fact, he had not seen; and to bring about a recognition by this means—the expectation that A would recognize the bow—is false inference.

But, of all recognitions, the best is that which arises from the incidents themselves, where the startling discovery is made by natural means. Such is that in the *Oedipus* of Sophocles, and in the *Iphigenia*; for it was natural that Iphigenia would wish to dispatch a letter. These recognitions alone dispense with the artificial aid of tokens or amulets. Next come the recognitions by process of reasoning.

XVII

In constructing the plot and working it out with the proper diction, the poet should place the scene, as far as possible, before his eyes. In this way, seeing everything with the utmost vividness, as if he were a spectator of the action, he will discover what is in keeping with it, and be most unlikely to overlook inconsistencies. The need of such a rule is shown by the fault found in *Carcinus*. Amphiaraus was on his way from the temple. This fact escaped the observation of one who did not see the situation. On the stage, however, the piece failed, the audience being offended at the oversight.

Again, the poet should work out his play, to the best of his power, with appropriate gestures; for those who feel emotion are most convincing through natural sympathy with the characters they represent; and one who is agitated storms, one who is angry rages, with the most lifelike reality. Hence poetry implies either a happy gift of nature or a strain of madness. In the one case a man can take the mould of any character; in the other, he is lifted out of his proper self.

As for the story, whether the poet takes it ready made or constructs it for himself, he should first sketch its general outline, and then fill in the episodes and amplify in detail. The general plan may be illustrated by the *Iphigenia*. A young girl is sacrificed; she disappears mysteriously from the eyes of those who sacrificed her; she is transported to another country, where the custom is to offer up all strangers to the goddess. To this ministry she is appointed. Some time later her own brother chances to arrive. The fact that the oracle for some reason ordered him to go there, is outside the general plan of the play. The purpose, again, of his coming is outside the action proper. However, he comes, he is seized, and, when on the point of being sacrificed, reveals who he is. The mode of recognition may be either that of Euripides or of Polyidus, in whose play he exclaims very naturally: "So it was not my sister only, but I too, who was doomed to be sacrificed"; and by that remark he is saved.

After this, the names being once given, it remains to fill in the episodes. We must see that they are relevant to the action. In the case of Orestes, for example, there is the madness which led to his capture, and his deliverance by means of the purificatory rite. In the drama, the episodes are short, but it is these that give extension to Epic poetry. Thus the story of the *Odyssey* can be stated briefly. A certain man is absent from home for many years; he is jealously watched by Poseidon, and left desolate. Meanwhile his home is in a wretched plight—suitors are wasting his substance and plotting against his son. At length, tempest-tossed, he himself arrives; he makes certain persons acquainted with him; he attacks the suitors with his own hand, and is himself preserved while he destroys them. This is the essence of the plot; the rest is episode.

XVIII

Every tragedy falls into two parts, Complication and Unraveling or Dénouement. Incidents extraneous to the action are frequently combined with a portion of the action proper, to form the Complication; the rest is the Unraveling. By the Complication I mean all that extends from the beginning of the action and the part which marks the turning-point to good or bad fortune. The Unraveling is that which extends from the beginning of the change to the end. Thus, in the *Lynecus* of Theodectes, the Complication consists of the incidents presupposed in the drama, the seizure of the child, and then again * * < The Unraveling > extends from the accusation of murder to the end.

There are four kinds of Tragedy, the Complex, depending entirely on [[Peripeteia]] and Recognition; the Pathetic (where the motive is passion), such as the tragedies on Ajax and Ixion; the Ethical (where the motives are ethical), such as the *Phthiotides* and the *Peleus*. The fourth kind is the Simple. < We here exclude the purely spectacular element >, exemplified by the *Phorcides*, the *Prometheus*, and scenes laid in Hades. The poet should endeavor, if possible, to combine all poetic merits; or failing that, the greatest number and those the most important; the more so, in face of the caviling criticism of the day. For whereas there have hitherto been good poets, each in his own branch, the critics now expect one man to surpass all others in their several lines of excellence.

In speaking of a tragedy as the same or different, the best test to take is the plot. Identity exists where the Complication and Unraveling are the same. Many poets tie the knot well, but unravel it ill. Both arts, however, should always be mastered.

Again, the poet should remember what has been often said, and not make a tragedy into an Epic structure. By an Epic structure I mean one with a multiplicity of plots: as if, for instance, you were to make a tragedy out of the entire story of the *Iliad*. In the Epic poem, owing to its length, each part assumes its proper magnitude. In the drama the result is far from answering to the poet's expectation. The proof is that the poets who have dramatized the whole story of the Fall of Troy, instead of selecting portions, like Euripides; or who have taken the whole tale of Niobe, and not a part of her story, like Aeschylus, either fail utterly or meet with poor success on the stage. Even Agathon has been known to fail from this one defect. In his [[Peripeteia,]] however, he shows a marvelous skill in the effort to hit the popular taste, to produce a tragic effect that satisfies the moral sense. This effect is produced when the clever rogue, like Sisyphus, is outwitted, or the brave villain defeated. Such an event is probable in Agathon's sense of the word: "it is probable," he says, "that many things should happen contrary to probability."

The Chorus too should be regarded as one of the actors; it should be an integral part of the whole, and share in the action, in the manner not of Euripides but of Sophocles. As for the later poets, their choral songs pertain as little to the subject of the piece as to that of any other tragedy. They are, therefore, sung as mere interludes—a practice first begun by Agathon. Yet what difference is there between introducing such choral interludes, and transferring a speech, or even a whole act, from one play to another?

XIX

It remains to speak of Diction and Thought, the other parts of Tragedy having been already discussed. Concerning Thought, we may assume what is said in the Rhetoric, to which inquiry the subject more strictly belongs.

Under Thought is included every effect which has to be produced by speech, the subdivisions being, proof and refutation; the excitation of the feelings, such as pity, fear, anger, and the like; the suggestion of importance or its opposite. Now, it is evident that the dramatic incidents must be treated from the same points of view as the dramatic speeches, when the object is to evoke the sense of pity, fear, importance, or probability. The only difference is, that the incidents should speak for themselves without verbal exposition; while the effects aimed at in speech should be produced by the speaker, and as a result of the speech. For what were the business of a speaker, if the Thought were revealed quite apart from what he says?

Next, as regards Diction. One branch of the inquiry treats of the Modes of Expression. But this province of knowledge belongs to the art of Delivery, and to the masters of that science. It includes, for instance, what is a command, a prayer, a narrative, a threat, a question, an answer, and so forth. To know or not to know these things involves no serious censure upon the poet's art. For who can admit the fault imputed to Homer by Protagoras, that in the words, "Sing, goddess, of the wrath," he gives a command under the idea that he utters a prayer? For to tell someone to do a thing or not to do it is, he says, a command. We may, therefore, pass this over as an inquiry that belongs to another art, not to poetry. . . .

XXII

The perfection of style is to be clear without being mean. The clearest style is that which uses only current or proper words; at the same time it is mean: witness the poetry of Cleophon and of Sthenelus. That diction, on the other hand, is lofty and raised above the commonplace which employs unusual words. By unusual, I mean strange (or rare) words, metaphorical, lengthened—anything, in short, that differs from the normal idiom. Yet a style wholly composed of such words is either a riddle or a jargon; a riddle, if it consists of metaphors; a jargon, if it consists of strange (or rare) words. For the essence of a riddle is to express true facts under impossible combinations. Now this cannot be done by any arrangement of ordinary words, but by the use of metaphor it can. Such is the riddle: "A man I saw who on another man had glued the bronze by aid of fire," and others of the same kind. A diction that is made up of strange (or rare) terms is a jargon. A certain infusion, therefore, of these elements is necessary to style; for the strange (or rare) word, the metaphorical, the ornamental, and the other kinds above mentioned, will raise it above the commonplace and mean, while the use of proper words will make it perspicuous. But nothing contributes more to produce a clearness of diction that is remote from commonness than the lengthening, contraction, and alteration of words. For by deviating in exceptional cases from the normal idiom, the language will gain distinction; while, at the same time, the partial conformity with usage will give perspicuity. The critics, therefore, are in error who censure these licenses of speech, and hold the author up to ridicule. . . .

It is a great matter to observe propriety in these several modes of expression —compound words, strange or (rare) words, and so forth. But the greatest thing by far is to have a command of metaphor. This alone cannot be imparted by another; it is the mark of genius—for to make good metaphors implies an eye for resemblances. . . .

XXIII

As to that poetic imitation which is narrative in form and employs a single meter, the plot manifestly ought, as in a tragedy, to be constructed on dramatic principles. It should have for its subject a single action, whole and complete, with a beginning, a middle, and an end. It will thus resemble a single and coherent picture of a living being, and produce the pleasure proper to it. It will differ in structure from historical compositions, which of necessity present not a single action, but a single period, and all that happened within that period to one person or to many, little connected together as the events may be. For as the sea-fight at Salamis and the battle with the Carthaginians in Sicily took place at the same time, but did not tend to any one result, so in the sequence of events, one thing sometimes follows another, and yet no single result is thereby produced. Such is the practice, we may say, of most poets. Here again, then, as has been already observed, the transcendant excellence of Homer is manifest. He never attempts to make the whole war of Troy the subject of his poem, though that war had a beginning and an end. It would have been too vast a theme, and not easily embraced in a single view. If, again, he had kept it within moderate limits, it must have been over-complicated by the variety of the incidents. As it is, he detaches a single portion, and admits as episodes many events from the general story of the war—such as the Catalogue of the ships and others—thus diversifying the poem. All other poets take a single hero, a single period, or an action single indeed, but with a multiplicity of parts. . . .

XXIV

Again, Epic poetry must have as many kinds as Tragedy: it must be simple, or complex, or "ethical," or "pathetic." The parts also, with the exception of song and scenery, are the same; for it requires [[Peripeteias,]] Recognitions, and [[Scenes of Passion.]] Moreover, the thoughts and the diction must be artistic. In all these respects Homer is our earliest and sufficient model. Indeed each of his poems has a twofold character. The *Iliad* is at once simple and "pathetic," and the *Odyssey* complex (for Recognition scenes run through it), and at the same time "ethical." Moreover, in diction and thought he is supreme.

Epic poetry differs from Tragedy in the scale on which it is constructed, and in its meter. As regards scale or length, we have already laid down an adequate limit: the beginning and the end must be capable of being brought within a single view. This condition will be satisfied by poems on a smaller scale than the old epics, and answering in length to the group of tragedies presented at a single sitting.

Epic poetry has, however, a great—a special—capacity for enlarging its dimensions, and we can see the reason. In Tragedy we cannot imitate several lines of actions carried on at one and the same time; we must confine ourselves to the action on the stage and the part taken by the players. But in Epic poetry, owing to the narrative form, many events simultaneously transacted can be presented; and these, if relevant to the subject, add mass and dignity to the poem. The Epic has here an advantage, and one that conduces to grandeur of effect, to diverting the mind of the hearer, and relieving the story with varying episodes. For sameness of incident soon produces satiety, and makes tragedies fail on the stage.

As for the meter, the heroic measure has proved its fitness by the test of experience. If a narrative poem in any other meter or in many meters were now composed, it would be found incongruous. For of all measures the heroic is the stateliest and the most massive; and hence it most readily admits rare words and metaphors, which is another point in which the narrative form of imitation stands alone. On the other hand, the iambic and the trochaic tetrameter are stirring measures, the latter being akin to dancing, the former expressive of action. Still more absurd would it be to mix together different meters, as was done by Chaeremon. Hence no one has ever composed a poem on a great scale in any other than heroic verse. Nature herself, as we have said, teaches the choice of the proper measure.

Homer, admirable in all respects, has the special merit of being the only poet who rightly appreciates the part he should take himself. The poet should speak as little as possible in his own person, for it is not this that makes him an imitator. Other poets appear themselves upon the scene throughout, and imitate but little and rarely. Homer, after a few prefatory words, at once brings in a man, or woman, or other personage; none of them wanting in characteristic qualities, but each with a character of his own.

The element of the wonderful is admitted in Tragedy. The irrational, on which the wonderful depends for its chief effects, has wider scope in Epic poetry, because there the person acting is not seen. Thus, the pursuit of Hector would be ludicrous if placed upon the stage—the Greeks standing still and not joining in the pursuit, and Achilles waving them back. But in the Epic poem the absurdity passes unnoticed. Now the wonderful is pleasing: as may be inferred from the fact that, in telling a story, everyone adds something startling of his own, knowing that his hearers like it. It is Homer who has chiefly taught other poets the art of telling lies skilfully. The secret of it lies in a fallacy. For, assuming that if one thing is or becomes, a second is or becomes, men imagine that, if the second is, the first likewise is or becomes. But this is a false inference. Hence, where the first thing is untrue, it is quite unnecessary, provided the second be true, to add that the first is or has become. For the mind, knowing the second to be true, falsely infers the truth of the first. There is an example of this in the Bath Scene of the *Odyssey*.

Accordingly, the poet should prefer probable impossibilities to improbable possibilities. The tragic plot must not be composed of irrational parts. Everything irrational should, if possible, be excluded; or, at all events, it should lie outside the action of the play (as, in the *Oedipus*, the hero's ignorance as to the manner of Laius' death); not within the drama—as in the *Electra*, the messenger's account of the Pythian games; or, as in the *Mysians*, the man who comes from Tegea to Mysia without speaking. The plea that otherwise the plot would have been ruined, is ridiculous; such a plot should not in the first instance be constructed. But once the irrational has been introduced and an air of likelihood imparted to it, we must accept it in spite of the absurdity. Take even the irrational incidents in the *Odyssey*, where Odysseus is left upon the shore of Ithaca. How intolerable even these might have been would be apparent if an inferior poet were to treat the subject. As it is, the absurdity is veiled by the poetic charm with which the poet invests it.

The diction should be elaborated in the pauses of the action, where there is no expression of character or thought. For, conversely, character and thought are merely obscured by a diction that is over brilliant.

XXV

With respect to critical difficulties and their solutions, the number and nature of the sources from which they may be drawn may be thus exhibited.

The poet being an imitator, like a painter or any other artist, must of necessity imitate one of three objects—things as they were or are, things as they are said or thought to be, or things as they ought to be. The vehicle of expression is language—either current terms or, it may be, rare words or metaphors. There are also many modifications of language, which we concede to the poets. Add to this, that the standard of correctness is not the same in poetry and politics, any more than in poetry and any other art. Within the art of poetry itself there are two kinds of faults—those which touch its essence, and those which are accidental. If a poet has chosen to imitate something, < but has imitated it incorrectly > through want of capacity, the error is inherent in the poetry. But if the failure is due to a wrong choice—if he has represented a horse as throwing out both his off legs at once, or introduced technical inaccuracies in medicine, for example, or in any other art—the error is not essential to the poetry. These are the points of view from which we should consider and answer the objections raised by the critics.

First as to matters which concern the poet's own art. If he describes the impossible, he is guilty of an error; but the error may be justified, if the end of the art be thereby attained (the end being that already mentioned)—if, that is, the effect of this or any other part of the poem is thus rendered more striking. A case in point is the pursuit of Hector. If, however, the end might have been as well, or better, attained without violating the special rules of the poetic art, the error is not justified: for every kind of error should, if possible, be avoided.

Again, does the error touch the essentials of the poetic art, or some accident of it? For example, not to know that a hind has no horns is a less serious matter than to paint it inartistically.

Further, if it be objected that the description is not true to fact, the poet may perhaps reply, "But the objects are as they ought to be": just as Sophocles said that he drew men as they ought to be; Euripides, as they are. In this way the objection may be met. If, however, the representation be of neither kind, the poet may answer, "This is how men say the thing is." This applies to tales about the gods. . . .

Again, in examining whether what has been said or done by some one is poetically right or not, we must not look merely to the particular act of saying, and ask whether it is poetically good or bad. We must also consider by whom it is said or done, to whom, when, in whose interest, or for what end; whether, for instance, it be to secure a greater good, or avert a greater evil.

Other difficulties may be resolved by due regard to the usage of language. . . .

Sometimes an expression is metaphorical, as "Now all gods and men were sleeping through the night," while at the same time the poet says: "Often indeed as he turned his gaze to the Trojan plain, he marveled at the sound of flutes and pipes." "All" is here used metaphroically for "many," all being a species of many. . . .

In general, the impossible must be justified by reference to artistic requirements, or to the higher reality, or to received opinion. With respect to the requirements of art, a probable impossibility is to be preferred to a thing improbable and yet possible. Again, it may be impossible that there should be men such as Zeuxis painted. "Yes," we say, "but the impossible is the higher thing; for the ideal type must surpass the reality." To justify the irrational, we appeal to what is commonly said to be. In addition to which, we urge that the irrational sometimes does not violate reason; just as "it is probable that a thing may happen contrary to probability."

Things that sound contradictory should be examined by the same rules as in dialectical refutation—whether the same thing is meant, in the same relation, and in the same sense. We should therefore solve the question by reference to what the poet says himself, or to what is tacitly assumed by a person of intelligence.

The element of the irrational, and, similarly, depravity of character, are justly censured when there is no inner necessity for introducing them. Such is the irrational element in the *Aegeus* of Euripides, and the badness of Menelaus in the *Orestes*.

Thus, there are five sources from which critical objections are drawn. Things are censured either as impossible, or irrational, or morally hurtful, or contradictory, or contrary to artistic correctness. . . .

XXVI

The question may be raised whether the Epic or Tragic mode of imitation is the higher. If the more refined art is the higher, and the more refined in every case is that which appeals to the better sort of audience, the art which imitates anything and everything is manifestly most unrefined. The audience is supposed to be too dull to comprehend unless something of their own is thrown in by the performers, who therefore indulge in restless movements. Bad flute-players twist and twirl, if they have to represent "the quoit-throw," or hustle the coryphaeus[3] when they perform the "Scylla." Tragedy, it is said, has this same defect. We may compare the opinion that the older actors entertained of their successors. Mynniscus used to call Callippides "ape" on account of the extravagance of his action, and the same view was held of Pindarus. Tragic art, then, as a whole, stands to Epic in the same relation as the younger to the elder actors. So we are told that Epic poetry is addressed to a cultivated audience, who do not need gesture; Tragedy, to an inferior public. Being then unrefined, it is evidently the lower of the two.

Now, in the first place, this censure attaches not to the poetic but to the histrionic art; for gesticulation may be equally overdone in epic recitation, as by Sosistratus, or in lyrical competition, as by Mnasitheus the Opuntian. Next, all action is not to be condemned—any more than all dancing—but only that of bad performers. Such was the fault found in Callippides, as also in others of our own day, who are censured for representing degraded women. Again, Tragedy like Epic poetry produces its effect even without action; it reveals its power by mere reading. If, then, in all other respects it is superior, this fault, we say, is not inherent in it.

And superior it is, because it has all the epic elements—it may even use the epic meter—with the music and scenic effects as important accessories; and these produce the most vivid of pleasures. Further, it has vividness of impression in reading as well as in representation. Moreover, the art attains its end within narrower limits; for the concentrated effect is more pleasurable than one which is spread over a long time and so diluted. What, for example,

[3] Leader of the Chorus.

would be the effect of the *Oedipus* of Sophocles, if it were cast into a form as long as the *Iliad*? Once more, the Epic imitation has less unity; as is shown by this, that any Epic poem will furnish subjects for several tragedies. Thus if the story adopted by the poet has a strict unity, it must either be concisely told and appear truncated; or, if it conform to the Epic canon of length, it must seem weak and watery. < Such length implies some loss of unity, > if, I mean, the poem is constructed out of several actions, like the *Iliad* and the *Odyssey*, which have many such parts, each with a certain magnitude of its own. Yet these poems are as perfect as possible in structure; each is, in the highest degree attainable, an imitation of a single action.

If, then, Tragedy is superior to Epic poetry in all these respects, and, moreover, fulfils its specific function better as an art—for each art ought to produce, not any chance pleasure, but the pleasure proper to it, as already stated—it plainly follows that Tragedy is the higher art, as attaining its end more perfectly.

Thus much may suffice concerning Tragic and Epic poetry in general; their several kinds and parts, with the number of each and their differences; the causes that make a poem good or bad; the objections of the critics and the answers to these objections. * *

Another Translation of Four Passages of Aristotle's Poetics

III

Further, a third differentiation of these arts is the way one can imitate each class of these objects. In fact it is possible to imitate in the same media, and the same objects, (1) by narrating at times < and then again bringing

Translated by Gerald F. Else, who uses the following typographical devices: < > indicates a word or words not in the Greek manuscript but presumed by the translator to have been written by Aristotle; [ ] indicates an interpolation not by Aristotle; ( ) around one or two words is a parenthesis by Aristotle or the translator's amplification or explanation of a term; [[ ]] is an addition by Aristotle to his own text. From Gerald F. Else, *Aristotle's Poetics: The Argument*. Cambridge: Harvard University Press, 1957. Copyright 1957 by the Presidents and Fellows of Harvard College. Reprinted by permission of the publisher.

on some dramatic character > [or, becoming something different], the way Homer composes, or (2) with the same person doing the imitating throughout, with no change, or (3) with all the imitators doing their work in and through action.

V

Furthermore, so far as their bulk is concerned the one (tragedy) strives hard to exist in a single daylight period, or to vary but little (in length), while the epic has no fixed limit as to its time and differs with respect to this; though at first they used to do this in tragedies in the same way as in epics.

VI

Tragedy, then, is an imitation of an action which is serious, complete, and has bulk, in speech that has been made attractive, using each of its species separately in the parts of the play; with persons performing the action rather than through narrative [[carrying to completion, through a course of events involving pity and fear, the purification of those painful or fatal acts which have that quality]].

XI

. . . "recognition," as in fact the term itself indicates, is a shift from ignorance to awareness, pointing either to a state of close natural ties (blood relationships) or to one of enmity, on the part of those persons who have been in a clearly marked status with respect to prosperity or misfortune. The recognition is finest artistically when a peripety takes place at the same time [as is the case in the *Oedipus*]. Now there are indeed other varieties of recognition also; that is, it is possible for it to take place in the aforementioned manner with respect to inanimate objects or chance events, and it is possible to recognize whether someone has done a thing or not done it. But the one which is most integrally a part of the plot, i.e., the action, is the one we have mentioned. For that kind of recognition and peripety will carry with it either pity or fear, which are the kind of actions of which we have defined tragedy to be an imitation; and furthermore happiness or unhappiness will be the natural result of such occurrences.

Rhetoric *347–343 B.C.*

Chapter V
The Nature of Fear

The sort of things which men fear, and the persons whom, and under what affections as regards themselves, will thus become plain. Now, let fear be defined to be "A sort of pain or agitation, arising out of an idea that an evil, capable either of destroying or giving pain, is impending on us." People do not fear every evil; for example, a man does not fear lest he shall become unjust or stupid; but people fear all those evils whose effect is either a considerable degree of pain, or destruction, and these, provided they be not far removed, but give one the idea of being close at hand, so as to be on the eve of happening; for they do not fear that which is very far off: for all know that they shall die; but since the event is not near, they pay no attention to it.

If then fear be this, it must follow that all those things are to be feared which appear to possess great power either of destroying, or of hurting, in points whose tendency is toward considerable pain. On which account even the symptoms of such things are alarming, for the evil appears to be at hand; since this in fact is danger, viz. "the approach of what excites fear." Of this description, however, are both the hatred and the anger of those who have it in their power to do us any harm; for it is evident that they have both the will and the power, so that they are not far from doing it. Also injustice, possessed of power; for [it is evident that it does not want inclination to do harm] since it is from settled inclination that the unjust man is unjust. Also insulted virtue, invested with power; for it is evident that, invariably, when it is insulted, it determines on a requital, and now it has the power of exacting one. The fear also of those who have the power of doing us any harm, is itself an object to be dreaded; for anyone, in such circumstances, will of course be prepared against us.

But as men in general are depraved, and may be prevailed on by gain, and are timid amid dangers; it is, generally speaking, a fearful thing to be at the disposal of another. So that accomplices in any deed of guilt are to be feared, lest either they should denounce you, or abandon you to trial. Also those who have the power to act unjustly, are always objects of fear to such as may be attacked by injustice; for, in nine cases out of ten, a man when he has the power, perpetrates the injustice. Also those who have been wronged, or who conceive themselves to have been wronged; for they are ever on the watch for an opportunity [of retaliating]. Also those who have wronged others, if possessed of power, are to be feared, from their apprehension of being retali-

Selections from Book Two. From *Aristotle's Treatise on Rhetoric,* translated by Thomas Hobbes. London: H. G. Bohn, 1847.

ated on; for cases of this kind were laid down to be such as to excite alarm. Those, too, who are rivals for the same objects, and which it is not possible should accrue to both, for people are ever at variance with those towards whom they stand on this footing. Those who are objects of fear to our superiors, are also objects of fear to ourselves; for much more will they be able to injure us, than our superiors: and for the same reason [we needs must fear those] whom our superiors fear. Men dread those also who have already annihilated persons superior to themselves; and those who have attacked their inferiors; for, either they are *already* deserving fear, or they will become so by being aggrandized in power. And among those who have been wronged, or are enemies, or opponents, it is not the passionate, and those who speak their minds freely, who are to be dreaded; but the mild, the dissembling, and the insidious; for they give us to doubt, whether they be not close upon us, so that they are never clearly known to be too far off to reach us.

But all those circumstances which excite fear, have a still greater tendency to do so, in respect of which should a man have committed a mistake, it is not possible for him to recover himself, but which either are impracticable altogether, or which cannot be corrected by himself, but by his enemies only: as have those also which we have no means, or no easy means, of averting. So that, to speak generally, all those things are to be feared, which, happening or being likely to happen in the case of others, excite compassion. The circumstances then of fear, and which men are alarmed at, those at least of greatest importance, are, as I may say, nearly those which I have enumerated: and now let me state under what dispositions, as regards themselves, men are susceptible of fear.

Now, if fear be attended by an apprehension of suffering some *destructive* evil, it is plain that none of those who consider that they shall not suffer any thing, is subject to fear; and that no one is subject to it, in regard to those things which he does not consider that he shall suffer; nor in regard to those persons at whose hands he does not apprehend anything; nor at a time when he is without apprehensions. It must follow, therefore, that those are subject to fear, who apprehend they shall suffer something, and this in regard to the persons at whose hands, and the things which, and at the times when, they so apprehend. But neither are those who are, and who think themselves to be, in the midst of great good fortune, at all apprehensive of suffering anything (on which account they are contumelious, contemptuous and rash; but it is wealth, strength, number of friends, power, which renders men of this temper), nor those who think that already they have suffered the sum of all that is horrible, and whose feelings have been chilled with respect to what awaits them, just as those who have been already beaten on the rack; but [in order to the existence of fear] there must needs arise some hope of safety, about which men feel the painful anxiety; and this is a proof of it, that fear makes men deliberate; and yet no one deliberates about that which is utterly hopeless. So that, when it shall better serve our cause that the audience be affected by fear, we must set them off as persons liable to suffer, inasmuch as others of greater power have suffered, and also to show that their equals are or have been exposed to sufferings; and this, at the hands of persons from whom they would not have apprehended it, and such things, and at times when they would not have apprehended it.

But since on the subject of fear, it is plain what it is; and on the subject of things exciting fear, and also with what dispositions men experience it; from this it will be plain both what confidence is, and on what points men are confident, and with what dispositions; for both confidence itself is the opposite of fear, and what inspires it is the opposite of what excites fear; so that it is the hope of things conducive to safety, accompanied by an idea that they are near; and of things to be feared, that they either do not exist, or are at a distance.

But these are circumstances inspiring confidence; to have danger afar off, and in that which we may confide, near also means of recovering from, or of averting loss, whether these be numerous, or valuable, or both: again, should we never have been injured, nor have ourselves injured others; also, if we have no rival at all; or should those we have, be devoid of power; or, supposing they have power, should they be our friends; or should they have benefited us, or have been themselves benefited by us; or should those, to whom the same things are an object as to ourselves, be more numerous than those to whom they are not, or more powerful, or both at once.

But, as regards themselves, people feel confidence when thus affected: should they conceive themselves to have been often successful, and this without having suffered; or should they often have fallen into danger, and have escaped: for there are two ways in which men become dead to apprehension, either from never having experienced, or from being possessed of resources against calamity; just as, in the case of danger by sea, both those who never experienced a storm feel confidence as to the result, and those who from their experience possess resources against it. Men feel it also, when the case does not alarm their equals, nor their inferiors, nor those to whom they conceive themselves superior; but they conceive thus of those whom, either *absolutely* in their own persons, or *virtually* in the persons of their superiors or of their equals, they have overcome. And again, if they conceive there belong to themselves, in greater number and degree, those things in which, when they have the advantage, men are objects of fear; and these are, store of wealth, and strength in respect to retainers, and friends, and territory, and warlike preparation, either *all together*, or the *most important* of them. Also, if they have not wronged anyone, or not many, or not any of such a character as men are apprehensive of. And, in a word, if their account stands well with heaven, as well in other respects, as in what regards omens and oracles: because anger is a thing which inspires confidence; and the being free from the commission of injustice, while you are wronged yourself, is productive of anger; and the deity is supposed to aid such as have been wronged. [Once more, people feel confidence] when, being the first aggressors, they think they can suffer nothing, or shall not, or shall succeed at last. And of the subject of what inspires confidence and fear, we have spoken.

Chapter VIII
Of Pity

Let us explain the circumstances which excite pity; and the persons whom men pity; and, as regards themselves, with what dispositions. Now let pity be defined to be, "a sort of pain occasioned by an evil capable of hurting or destroying,[1] appearing to befall one who does not deserve it, which one may himself expect to endure, or that someone connected with him will; and this when it appears near": for it evidently is necessary that a person likely to feel pity should be actually such as to deem that, either in his own person, or of someone connected with him, he may suffer some evil, and that an evil of *such a description* as has been stated in the definition, or one similar to it, or nearly equivalent to it. On which account neither do those who are absolutely lost, feel pity; for these think they shall no longer be exposed to suffering, for their sufferings are past; nor those who esteem themselves excessively happy, but these wax insolent; for evidently, if they esteem every good to be realized to them, they also esteem their lot to be incapable of suffering any evil; since this also enters into the number of goods. But of this description, viz. such as think they may yet suffer evil, are both who already have suffered and escaped; and those advanced in years, as well by reason of their prudence, as of their experience: and the weak; and those who are rather timid; and men of education, for these calculate life's contingencies aright; and those to whom belong parents, or children, or wives, for these attach to one's self, and are liable to suffer the above-mentioned evils. Those do not feel pity who are under the excitements of courage, for instance, under anger or confidence; for these feelings little calculate the future: nor do those feel pity who are under insolent dispositions; for these persons also calculate little of suffering anything: but those who are of the mean temperament between these are susceptible of pity: and those again are not susceptible of it who are vehemently affected by fear; for such as are horror-struck do not feel pity, by reason of its being akin to an evil which comes home to themselves. Also people are susceptible of pity, should they esteem some persons to be good; for he who esteems no one to be such, will think every one deserving of evil. And in a word, everyone, when he is so affected as to call to his recollection the fact, that evils of such a character have befallen either him or his, or to

---

[1] The evil in the case of pity is of the same character as was stated to be the object of fear. In fact, whatever when befalling another excites *pity*, in one's own case excites *fear*. [This and the following note are by Hobbes.]

apprehend that they may befall either him or his. And now it has been stated with what dispositions men feel pity.

The circumstances which excite their pity will be evident from the definition: for whatever things, of the number of those which cause pain and anguish, have a tendency to destroy, are all such as to cause pity: again, everything whose tendency is utter abolition; also all those evils which involve the quality of greatness, and of which chance is the cause. But the evils whose characteristic is great anguish and destruction, are as follows: death, assaults, personal injuries, and age, and sickness, and want of food. And the evils of which chance is the cause, are, absolute want, or fewness of friends (on which account even the being torn from friends and familiars is a circumstance to be pitied), ugliness, infirmity, deformity, and the circumstance that some evil befalls one from a source whence it were becoming for some good to have arisen; and the frequent occurrence of a similar thing: and the accession of some good, when one has already passed his sufferings; as for example, the gifts of the king were sent down to Diopithes after he was dead; and the fact either that no good has accrued, or of there being no enjoyment of it when it has arrived. These, then, and the like, are the circumstances on account of which men feel pity.

But people are sensible of pity toward their acquaintances, if they be not of extremely close connection, but about such they feel just as they do about themselves when on the eve of suffering: and on this account Amasis,[2] as they say, did not shed a tear over his *son* when he was being led to execution, but he did over his *friend* who was asking an alms; for this was a circumstance to call for pity; the other, to excite horror. For horror is distinct from pity, and has a tendency to expel pity from the breast, and is frequently available to produce a contrary effect. Still men feel pity while the evil is yet approaching. And they feel it towards their equals, whether in age, in temper, in habits, in rank, or in family; for in all these relations, the evil is seen with greater clearness as possible to befall also one's self. For we must here also assume generally, that whatever people *fear* in their own case, that they *pity* as happening in the case of others. But as the disasters which excite pity always appear to be close at hand, while, as to those removed at the distance of ten thousand years, men neither in the expectation of them, if *future*, nor in the remembrance of them, if *past*, are sensible of pity at all, or at least not in an equal degree; this being the case, it must follow that those characters which are got up with the aid of gesture, and voice, and dress, and of acting, generally have the greater effect in producing pity. For thus, by setting the evil before our eyes, as either being on the eve of taking place, or as having happened, men make it appear to be close at hand. Likewise things which have just taken place, or quickly about to do so, have on this very account a greater

---

[2] Perhaps Aristotle quoted from memory; and it is not improbable that he may have been mistaken as to the person to whom he attributes this conduct, since Herodotus relates the story, not of Amasis, but of his son Psammenitus.

tendency to excite pity. Also the indications and actions of persons; for instance, the garments of those who have suffered, and other things of that sort. And the expressions of those under suffering, for instance, of those already in act of dying. And especially is it a circumstance to move pity, that while in these crises the persons have borne themselves virtuously. For all these circumstances produce pity in a higher degree from its appearing *near*; also, the fact of the person's being *unworthy*, and his disaster appearing in view before our eyes.

Nicomachean Ethics   335–325 B.C.

Now that we have ascertained what is just and what is unjust, we may say that a man acts unjustly or justly when he does these things voluntarily; but when he does them involuntarily, he does not, strictly speaking, act either unjustly or justly, but only "accidentally," i.e., he does a thing which happens to be just or unjust. For whether an act is or is not to be called an act of injustice (or of justice) depends upon whether it is voluntary or involuntary; for if it be voluntary the agent is blamed, and at the same time the act becomes an act of injustice: so something unjust may be done, and yet it may not be an act of injustice, i.e., if this condition of voluntariness be absent.

By a voluntary act I mean, as I explained before, anything which, being within the doer's control, is done knowingly (i.e., with knowledge of the person, the instrument, and the result; e.g., the person whom and the instrument with which he is striking, and the effect of the blow), without the intervention at any point of accident or constraint; e.g., if another take your hand and with it strike a third person, that is not a voluntary act of yours, for it was not within your control; again, the man you strike may be your father, and you may know that it is a man, or perhaps that it is one of the company, that you are striking but not know that it is your father; and it must be understood that the same distinction is to be made with regard to the result, and, in a word, to the whole act. That then which either is done in ignorance, or, though not done in ignorance, is not under our control, or is done under compulsion, is involuntary; besides which, there are many natural processes in which we knowingly take an active or a passive part,

Book V, Chapter 8. From *The Nicomachean Ethics of Aristotle,* translated by F. H. Peters. London: Kegan Paul, Trench & Co., 1886.

which cannot be called either voluntary or involuntary, such as growing old and dying.

An accidentally unjust act and an accidentally just act are equally possible; e.g., a man might restore a deposit against his will for fear of consequences, and then you could not say that he did what was just or acted justly except accidentally:[1] and, similarly, a man who against his will was forcibly prevented from restoring a deposit would be said only accidentally to act unjustly or to do that which is unjust.

Voluntary acts, again, are divided into (1) those that are done of set purpose, and (2) those that are done without set purpose; i.e., (1) those that are done after previous deliberation, and (2) those that are done without previous deliberation.

Now, there are three ways in which we may hurt our neighbor. Firstly, a hurt done in ignorance is generally called a mistake when there is a misconception as to the person affected, or the thing done, or the instrument, or the result; e.g., I may not think to hit, or not to hit with this instrument, or not to hit this person, or not to produce this effect, but an effect follows other than that which was present to my mind; I may mean to inflict a prick, not a wound, or not to wound the person whom I wound, or not to deal a wound of this kind.

But [if we draw the distinction more accurately] when the hurt comes about contrary to what might reasonably be expected, it may be called a mishap: but when, though it is not contrary to what might reasonably be expected, there is still no vicious intention, it is a mistake; for a man makes a mistake when he sets the train of events in motion,[2] but he is unfortunate when an external agency interferes.[3]

Secondly, when the agent acts with knowledge but without previous deliberation, it is an act of injustice; e.g., when he is impelled by anger or any of the other passions to which man is necessarily or naturally subject. In doing such hurt and committing such errors, the doer acts unjustly and the acts are acts of injustice, though they are not such as to stamp him as unjust or wicked; for the hurt is not done out of wickedness.

But, thirdly, when it is done of set purpose, the doer is unjust and wicked.

On this account acts done in anger are rightly held not to be done of malice aforethought; for he who gave the provocation began it, not he who did the deed in the heat of anger.

Again, in such cases as this last, what men dispute about is usually not

---

[1] I.e., he willed the act not as just, but as a means of avoiding the painful consequences; the justice of it, therefore, was not part of the essence of the act to him, was not among the qualities of the act which moved him to choose it, or, in Aristotle's language, was "accidental" [translator's note].

[2] Which leads by a natural, though by him unforeseen, sequence to his neighbor's hurt: negligence, or error of judgment [translator's note].

[3] And gives a fatal termination to an act that would ordinarily be harmless: accident [translator's note].

whether the deed was done or not, but what the justice of the case is; for it is an apparent injustice that stirs the assailant's wrath. There is a difference between cases of this kind and disputes about contracts: in the latter the question is a question of fact, and one or other of the parties must be a vicious character, unless his memory be at fault; but in these cases they agree about the facts, but differ as to which side is in the right, so that the assailant (differing herein from the deliberate aggressor, who knows very well the rights of the case) thinks that he is wronged, while the other thinks differently.

But if a man hurt another of set purpose, he acts unjustly, and acts of injustice (i.e., violations of what is proportionate and fair), when so done, stamp the doer as an unjust character.

In like manner a man is a just character when he of set purpose acts justly; but he is said to act justly if he merely do voluntarily that which is just.

Of involuntary injuries, on the other hand, some are pardonable, some unpardonable. Errors that are committed not merely in ignorance but by reason of ignorance are pardonable; but those that are committed not through ignorance but rather in ignorance, through some unnatural or inhuman passion, are not pardonable.

Anonymous

The Tractatus
Coislinianus[1] *c. 4th–2d centuries B.C.*

Poetry is either (I) nonmimetic or (II) mimetic.
(I) Nonmimetic poetry is divided into (A) historical, (B) instructive.
(B) Instructive poetry is divided into (1) didactic, (2) theoretical.
(II) Mimetic poetry is divided into (A) narrative, (B) dramatic and

Translated by Lane Cooper. From Lane Cooper, *An Aristotelian Theory of Comedy.* New York: Kraus Reprint Co., 1969.

[1] I have discarded the schematic arrangement of the original, supplying such words as "is divided into" in place of the oblique lines and horizontal braces which there indicate divisions and subdivisons under the various heads, and likewise adding appropriate numerals and letters in parentheses [translator's note].

[directly] presenting action. (B) Dramatic poetry, or that [directly] presenting action, is divided into (1) comedy, (2) tragedy, (3) mimes, (4) satyr-dramas.

Tragedy removes the fearful emotions of the soul through compassion and terror. And [he says] that it aims at having a due proportion of fear. It has grief for its mother.

Comedy is an imitation of an action that is ludicrous and imperfect, of sufficient length, [in embellished language,] the several kinds [of embellishment being] separately [found] in the [several] parts [of the play]; [directly presented] by persons acting, and not [given] through narrative; through pleasure and laughter effecting the purgation of the like emotions. It has laughter for its mother.

Laughter arises (I) from the diction [= expression] (II) from the things [= content].

(I) From the diction, through the use of—
    (A)   Homonyms
    (B)   Synonyms
    (C)   Garrulity
    (D)   Paronyms, formed by
        (?1) addition and
        (?2) clipping
    (E)   Diminutives
    (F)   Perversion
        (1) by the voice
        (2) by other means of the same sort
    (G) Grammar and syntax
(II) Laughter is caused by the things—
    (A)   From assimilation, employed
        (1) toward the worse
        (2) toward the better
    (B)   From deception
    (C)   From the impossible
    (D)   From the possible and inconsequent
    (E)   From the unexpected
    (F)   From debasing the personages
    (G) From the use of clownish (pantomimic) dancing
    (H) When one of those having power, neglecting the greatest things, takes the most worthless
    (I)   When the story is disjointed, and has no sequence

Comedy differs from abuse, since abuse openly censures the bad qualities attaching [to men], whereas comedy requires the so-called emphasis [? or "innuendo"].

The joker will make game of faults in the soul and in the body.

As in tragedies there should be a due proportion of fear, so in comedies there should be a due proportion of laughter.

The substance of comedy consists of (1) plot, (2) *ethos*, (3) *dianoia*, (4) diction, (5) melody, (6) spectacle.

The comic plot is the structure binding together the ludicrous incidents.

The characters [*ethe*] of comedy are (1) the buffoonish, (2) the ironical, and (3) those of the impostors.

The parts of *dianoia* are two: (A) opinion and (B) proof. [Proofs (or "persuasions") are of] five [sorts]: (1) oaths, (2) compacts, (3) testimonies, (4) tortures ["tests" or "ordeals"], (5) laws.

The diction of comedy is the common, popular language. The comic poet must endow his personages with his own native idiom, but must endow an alien with the alien idiom.

Melody is the province of the art of music, and hence one must take its fundamental rules from that art.

Spectacle is of great advantage to dramas in supplying what is in concord with them.

Plot, diction, and melody are found in all comedies, *dianoia*, *ethos*, and spectacle in few.

The [quantitative] parts of comedy are four: (1) prologue, (2) the choral part, (3) episode, (4) exode. The prologue is that portion of a comedy extending as far as the entrance of the chorus. The choral part [*choricon*] is a song by the chorus when it [the song] is of adequate length. An episode is what lies between two choral songs. The exode is the utterance of the chorus at the end.

The kinds of comedy are: (1) Old, with a superabundance of the laughable; (2) New, which disregards laughter, and tends toward the serious; (3) Middle, which is a mixture of the two.

Cicero *106–43 B.C.*

On the Best Style of Orators[*] 46 B.C.

. . . Of poets there are a great many divisions; for of tragic, comic, epic, lyric, and also of dithyrambic poetry, which has been more cultivated by the Latins, each kind is very different from the rest. Therefore in tragedy anything comic is a defect, and in comedy anything tragic is out of place. And in the other kinds of poetry each has its own appropriate note, and a tone well known to those who understand the subject. . . . He is the best orator who by speaking both teaches, and delights, and moves the minds of his hearers. To teach them is his duty, to delight them is creditable to him, to move them is indispensable.

Horace *65–8 B.C.*

The Art of Poetry[†] 24–20 B.C.

Suppose a painter wished to couple a horse's neck with a man's head, and to lay feathers of every hue on limbs gathered here and there, so that a woman, lovely above, foully ended in an ugly fish below; would you restrain your laughter, my friends, if admitted to a private view? Believe me, dear Pisos,[1] a book will apear uncommonly like that picture, if impossible figures are wrought into it—like a sick man's dreams—with the result that neither head nor foot is ascribed to a single shape, and unity is lost.

"But poets and painters have always had an equal right to indulge their

*Selection. From *The Orations of Marcus Tullius Cicero*, Vol. IV, translated by C. D. Yonge. London: Henry G. Bohn, 1852.

†Translated by Edward Henry Blakeney. Reprinted, with minor omissions, from *Horace on the Art of Poetry*, edited by Edward Henry Blakeney. London: Scholartis Press, limited edition published by Oxford University Press, 1928. Reprinted by permission of Oxford University Press.

[1] The work is also called "Epistle to the Pisos."

whims." Quite so: and this excuse we claim for ourselves and grant to others: but not so that harsh may mate with gentle, serpents be paired with birds, lambs with tigers.

Frequently grave openings, that promise much, have one or two purple patches tagged on, to catch the eye and enhance the color. Thus, for example, we get descriptions of "Diana's grove and altar," "the moving waters hurrying through fair fields," or get a picture of the Rhine, or of a rainbow; but all the time there is no place for these scenes. Perhaps you know how to limn a cypress; but what avails this if your sailor, who has paid to have his portrait painted, is represented as struggling hopelessly to shore from a wreck? A wine-jar was designed: why, when the wheel goes round, does it come out a pitcher? In short, be your subject what you will, only let it be simple and consistent.

Most of us poets—O father, and sons worthy of your father—are misled by our idea of what is correct. I try to be terse, and end by being obscure; another strives after smoothness, to the sacrifice of vigor and spirit; a third aims at grandeur, and drops into bombast; a fourth, through excess of caution and a fear of squalls, goes creeping along the ground. He who is bent on lending variety to a theme that is by nature uniform, so as to produce an unnatural effect, is like a man who paints a dolphin in a forest or a wild boar in the waves. If artistic feeling is not there, mere avoidance of a fault leads to some worse defect.

The humblest bronze-smith who lives near the Aemilian training school will depict you nails, and imitate waving hair in metal, yet fail in his work because he cannot represent the figure as a whole. Now, if I wanted to compose a work, I should no more wish to be like that smith than to live admired for my dark eyes and dark hair while I had a crooked nose.

You writers, choose a subject that is within your powers, and ponder long what your shoulders can and cannot bear. He who makes every effort to select his theme aright will be at no loss for choice words or lucid arrangement. Unless I am mistaken, the force and charm of arrangement will be found in this: to say at once what ought at once to be said, deferring many points, and waiving them for the moment.

Careful and nice, too, in his choice of words, the author of the promised poem must reject one word and welcome another; you will have expressed yourself admirably if a clever setting gives a spice of novelty to a familiar word.

If by chance some abstruse subject needs new terms to make the meaning clear, it will be right to frame words never heard of by old-fashioned folk like the Cethegi, and the licence will be allowed if not abused; new and lately-minted words will be accepted if drawn from a Greek source, provided this be done sparingly. Why should a Roman grant to Caecilius and Plautus a privilege denied to Virgil and Varius? Why am I myself, if I can capture a phrase or two, grudged this freedom, seeing that the works of Cato and Ennius have enriched the mother-tongue and broadcasted new names for things? It has always been and always will be permissible to circulate a word stamped with the hallmark of the day.

As forests suffer change of leaves with each declining year, so the earliest-invented words are the first to fall: an elder generation passes away and new-born words, like youth, flourish and grow. Death claims both us and our works. What matter if the sea, let into the heart of the land, shelters our ships from the north winds—a right royal work; or the marsh, long barren and fit for boats alone, feeds neighboring cities and groans under the plow-share; or the river, taught a better channel, has changed its course once ruinous to crops? The works of men's hands must perish, much less can the glory and charm of words endure undecaying. Many a word long disused will revive, and many now high in esteem will fade, if Custom wills it, in whose power lie the arbitrament, the rule, and the standard of language.

Homer has shown in what meter the deeds of kings and captains and the sorrows of war may be written. First came the voice of lament, in couplets unequally paired; then the joy of the successful lover: but who the author was that first published the dainty measures, critics dispute, and the matter is still unjudged.

It was fury that armed Archilochus with his own device, the iamb; this meter comedy and stately tragedy adopted, as fitted for dialogue, drowning the din of the audience, and born for action.

The Muse has assigned to the lyre the work of celebrating gods and heroes, the champion boxer, the victorious steed, the fond desire of lovers, and the cup that banishes care.

In works of genius are clearly marked differences of subject and shades of style. If, through ignorance, I fail to maintain these, why hail me Poet? Why, from a false shame, do I prefer ignorance to knowledge? A subject for comedy refuses to be handled in tragic verse; the banquet of Thyestes[2] disdains to be rehearsed in lines suited to daily life and right enough for comedy. At times, however, even Comedy exalts her voice, and an angry Chremes[3] rants and raves; often, too, in a tragedy Telephus[4] or Peleus[5] utters his sorrow in the language of prose, when, poor and in exile, he flings aside his paint-pots and his words a yard long, in eagerness to touch the spectator's heart with his lamentable tale.

---

[2] Thyestes seduced the wife of his brother Atreus, who to avenge himself killed Thyestes' children and served them to him at a banquet.

[3] A character in Aristophanes' *The Ecclesiazusae*.

[4] Telepheus, son-in-law of King Priam of Troy, was wounded by Achilles, who according to an oracle was the only man who could cure the wound. Achilles agreed to help Telepheus only if the latter helped him besiege the Trojans.

[5] Achilles' father, Peleus was exiled from his native country because of a murder he committed.

It is not enough for poems to be fine; they must charm, and draw the mind of the listener at will. As the human face answers a smile with a smile, so does it wait upon tears; if you would have me weep, you must first of all feel grief yourself; then and not till then will your misfortunes, Telephus or Peleus, touch me. If the part assigned you is not in character, I shall fall asleep or laugh.

Sad words suit a gloomy countenance, menacing words an angry; sportive words a merry look, stern words a grim one. For Nature shapes first our inner thoughts to take the bent of circumstance; she moves to gladness or drives to anger, bows the heart to earth and tortures it with bitter grief. After, with the tongue her aid, does she express emotion.

If a speaker's words are out of gear with his fortunes, all Rome, horse and foot, will guffaw. It will make a world of difference whether god or demigod be talking; an old man well on in years or a stripling in the first flush of youth; a wealthy dame or some bustling nurse; a roving trader or a son of the soil; a Colchian or an Assyrian; one reared in Argos or in Thebes.

Either stick to tradition or see that your inventions be consistent. If when writing a play you introduce yet again the "far-famed Achilles," make him impatient, hot-tempered, ruthless, fierce; he must disown all laws: they were not made for *him*; his appeal will be to the sword. In like manner let Medea be high-hearted and unconquerable, Ino tearful, Ixion a traitor, Io a wanderer, Orestes forlorn.

If you bring on to the stage a subject unattempted yet, and are bold enough to create a fresh character, let him remain to the end such as he was when he first appeared—consistent throughout. It is hard to treat a hackneyed theme with originality, and you act more wisely by dramatizing the *Iliad* than by introducing a subject unknown and hitherto unsung. I shall aim at a poem so deftly fashioned out of familiar matter that anybody might hope to emulate the feat, yet for all his efforts sweat and labor in vain. Such is the power of order and arrangement; such the charm that waits upon common things. The common quarry will become your own by right, if you do not dally in the cheap and easy round; if you do not, an all too faithful translator, essay to render your author word for word; if you do not—a mere copyist—take a plunge into some narrow pit from which diffidence or the conditions of the work itself forbid you to escape.

Nor should your exordium be like that of the cyclic poet of old: "I'll sing the fate of Priam, and the famous war of Troy." What will this writer produce worthy of such mouthing? it will be a case of "mountains in labor and —a mouse comes out!" Much better he who makes no ill-judged effort: "Sing me, O Muse, the tale of that hero who, after the capture of Troy, surveyed the manners and cities of mankind."[6] His aim is to fetch not smoke from a

---

[6] The beginning of Homer's *Odyssey*.

flash but light from smoke, that afterwards he may bring you marvels of the picturesque—Antiphates and Cyclops, Scylla and Charybdis. He does not date "the Return of Diomed" from Meleager's death,[7] nor the Trojan war from the twin eggs:[8] he ever hurries to the crisis and carries the listener into the midst of the story as though it were already known; what he despairs of illuminating with his touch he omits; and so employs fiction, so blends false with true, that beginning, middle, and end all strike the same note.

Now hear what I, and the world at large, expect. If you want an appreciative audience that will sit quiet till the curtain drops and the call for "cheers" begins, you must observe the characteristics of each age and assign a fitting grace to natures that shift with the years. The child who can just talk and feel his feet with confidence longs to play with his peers; is quick to anger, as quick to cool; his moods change hourly. The beardless boy, his tutor out of the way, finds delight in horses and dogs and the turf of the sunny plain. Pliant as wax to vice, he is gruff with his counsellors, slow to provide for his own best interests, lavish with his money; high-spirited, passionate, ready to discard his fancies. With manhood comes a change of tastes: his aim now is money and friendship; he will be the slave of ambition, and will shun doing what, later on, he might wish to undo.

Many are the discomforts of age, partly because the old man, ever amassing, shrinks from his gains and dares not enjoy them; partly because he handles everything in chill and listless fashion—irresolute, a laggard in hope, lazy, greedy of long life, cross-grained, querulous, one who extols the past as it was "when I was a boy"; a censor and critic of the rising generation. The years as they come bring many blessings: many do they take as they go. Lest an old man's part be given to a youth, or a man's part to a boy, we shall do wisely to dwell on the attributes proper to each period of life.

An action either takes place on the stage, or is announced as having taken place off it. What finds entrance through the ear strikes the mind less vividly than what is brought before the trusty eyes of the spectator himself. And yet you will not present incidents which ought to be enacted behind the scenes, and will remove from sight a good deal for the actor to relate on the stage by and by—so that, for example, Medea may not butcher her boys or savage Atreus cook human flesh in front of the audience, Procne turn into a bird or Cadmus into a snake. Anything you thrust under my nose in this fashion moves my disgust—and incredulity.

A play which is to be in demand and, after production, to be revived, should consist of five acts—no more, no less. A god must not be introduced

---

[7] The death of Meleager, uncle of the hero Diomed, is unrelated to the Greek hero's return from Troy.

[8] Two eggs resulted from Leda's union with Jupiter (who took the form of a swan). Helen, cause of the Trojan War, resulted from one, the twins Castor and Pollux from the other.

unless a difficulty occurs worthy of such a deliverer; nor should a fourth actor be forward to speak. The Chorus should discharge the part and duty of an actor with vigor, and chant nothing between the acts that does not forward the action and fit into the plot naturally. The Chorus must back the good and give sage counsel; must control the passionate and cherish those that fear to do evil; it must praise the thrifty meal, the blessings of justice, the laws, and Peace with her unbarred gates. It will respect confidences and implore heaven that prosperity may revisit the miserable and quit the proud.

In days gone by the pipe, not as now bound with brass and rival of the trumpet, but soft and simple with its few stops, was useful to accompany a Chorus and give it its note. It could fill with sound the not yet overcrowded benches, to which of course the people would gather, readily counted (for they were few)—a thrifty folk, chaste and honest. When victorious nations began to extend their boundaries, and an ever-widening wall to compass their cities, and people were free to enjoy themselves uncensored on feast-days with early revels, a greater licence was granted to rhythms and tunes. What taste could you expect in some unlettered rustic, out for a holiday, when in company with a townsman—clown and gentleman together? So the piper added movement and wanton gestures to his art of old, and would trail his robes as he strutted about the stage; so were new notes added to the sober lyre; bold eloquence brought with it a language unknown before; and wise saws, prophetic of the future, would match the oracles of Delphi.

The poet who competed in tragic verse for a paltry goat soon made the rustic satyrs doff their garments and ventured on coarse jests without loss of dignity, sure that a spectator, fresh from the sacrifice, drunk and subject to no law, must needs be held by the charms and enticements of novelty.

It will be well so to commend to your audience the quips and laughter of Satyrs, so to pass from grave to gay, that no god or hero who is to be staged —so conspicuous of late in royal gold and purple—should in his discourse sink to the level of tavern-talk; or again, while shunning the ground, catch at clouds and emptiness. It is beneath the dignity of Tragedy to blurt out trivial verse: like a matron bidden to dance on holy days, the Muse, if she has to move among saucy Satyrs, will show a due reserve.

If I write satyric plays, I shall not choose only bald and everyday terms; nor so try to vary from tragic diction that none can guess whether Davus is the speaker, or bold Pythias who won a talent by wiping her master's eye, or Silenus—guide, philosopher, and friend of a god.[9]

In my judgment, when woodland Fauns are brought on to the stage they should be careful not to languish in love-verses, like city exquisites, nor rap out filthy and shameful jests. For those who possess horse, father, or estate

---

[9] The name Davus is often given to slaves in Roman comedy; Pythias is a maid-servant; Silenus is a companion of Dionysos.

take offence; nor do they receive with favor or award a crown to everything the purchaser of fried peas and chestnuts may approve. . . .

It is not every critic that notices false rhythms; and it is true that needless indulgence is given to Roman poets. Am I, therefore, to run riot and break the rules? or shall I assume that the public will mark my slips? If so, then, wary and safe within the hope of forgiveness, I have indeed escaped censure, praise I have deserved not.

Do you, my friends, study the Greek masterpieces: thumb them day and night.

"But," someone answers, "your forebears praised the measures and pleasantries of Plautus." True: they admired both far too tolerantly, not to say foolishly, if only you and I know how to distinguish vulgarity from wit, and are quick with fingers and ears alike to catch the right cadences.

Thespis is said to have discovered Tragedy—a form of poetry hitherto unknown—and to have carried his plays about in tumbrils, to be chanted and performed by actors with faces smeared with lees. After him Aeschylus, inventor of the mask and comely robe, laid his stage on short planks, teaching his company how to talk grandiloquently and strut with buskined feet. Next came the Old Comedy, praised by all; but freedom degenerated into licence and violence, to be checked by law; to law it yielded, and the Chorus, robbed of its power to hurt, fell silent—to its shame.

Our own poets have left no style untried; not the least of their merits was when they boldly forsook the footsteps of Greece and celebrated, in comedy and tragedy alike, our national deeds. Latium would not be mightier in valor or feats of arms than in letters, if only her poets, one and all, did not scorn the long labor of the file. Do you, O Pisos, sprung from Numa, censure the poem that has not been pruned by time and many a cancellation—corrected ten times over and finished to the finger-nail.

Because Democritus believes that genius is happier than miserable art, and shuts the gates of Helicon on all sane poets, a good few will not cut their nails or beard, but court solitude and shun the baths. The fact is, a poet may win a poet's name and reward if only he has never entrusted to Licinus, the barber, a pate that not three Anticyras could cure!

What a fool I am to get rid of the bile when spring comes on! but for that, no poet would write better. But nothing is worth that! I'll serve as a whetstone which, though it cannot cut of itself, can sharpen iron. Though I write nothing, I'll teach the business and duty of a writer; show where his materials may be found; what it is that trains and molds a poet; what becomes him, what does not; whither knowledge tends, and whither error.

The secret of all good writing is sound judgment. The works of the Socratics will supply you with the facts: get these in clear perspective and the words will follow naturally. Once a man has learned his duty to friend and fatherland, the just claims of parent, brother, or guest on his love, the obligations of senator or judge, or the duty of a general sent on active service, he will infallibly know how to assign to each character its fitting part. I shall bid the clever imitator look to life and morals for his real model, and draw thence language true to life. Sometimes a play, tricked out with commonplaces and with characters well drawn, even though it be void of charm, force, or artistic skill, delights the populace and holds their interest far better than "lines without sense, and tuneful trifles."

It was the Greeks, aye, the Greeks covetous of praise alone, that the Muse endowed with quick wit and rounded utterance. Our Roman youths by long calculations learn how to divide the shilling into a hundred parts. "Come, young Albinus, tell me this: take a penny from sixpence, and what is over? You ought to know." "Fivepence." "Good! you'll hold your own some day. Now add a penny: what's the result?" "Sevenpence." Ah, once this canker of avarice, this money-grubbing, has tainted the soul, can we hope that poems will be written worthy of cedar oil and to be treasured in polished cases?

The poet's aim is either to profit or to please, or to blend in one the delightful and the useful. Whatever the lesson you would convey, be brief, that your hearers may catch quickly what is said and faithfully retain it. Every superfluous word is spilled from the too-full memory. Fictions made to please should keep close to the truth of things; your play should not demand an unlimited credence; it will not do to describe how a living boy is ripped from Lamia's belly after she has just eaten him. Elder folk rail at what contains no serviceable lesson; our young aristocrats cannot away with grave verses: the man who mingles the useful with the sweet carries the day by charming his reader and at the same time instructing him. That's the book to enrich the publisher, to be posted overseas, and to prolong its author's fame.

Yet some faults there are that we can gladly overlook. The string does not invariably give the note intended by mind and hand; we listen for a flat, and often get a sharp; nor does the arrow always hit the target. But whenever beauties in a poem form a majority, I shall not stumble at a few blemishes that are due to carelessness or that the weakness of human nature has failed to guard against.

How, then, do we stand? A copyist who continually makes the same blunder, spite of constant warning, gets no quarter; a harpist who is for ever fumbling with the same string is laughed at; so, too, I rank the slovenly poet with Choerilus, whose occasional fine lines, though surprising, move one to mirth. Am I, then, to be indignant whenever good Homer nods?

"Yes, but it is natural for slumber to steal over a long work. Poetry is like painting: one piece takes your fancy if you stand close to it, another if you keep at some distance. One courts a dim light, another, challenging keen criticism, will fain be seen in the glare; this charms but once, that will please if ten times repeated."

Hope of the Pisos! although you have your father to guide your judgment aright and are yourself wise to boot, cherish this lesson and take it home: that only in limited fields is mediocrity tolerable or pardonable. A counsel or second-rate pleader at the bar may not rival Messalla in eloquence, nor possess the knowledge of Casellius; yet he has his value; but mediocrity in poets has never been tolerated by gods, men, or—booksellers. Just as, at some pleasant banquet, ugly music, coarse perfume, and poppy seed mixed with Sardinian honey offend the taste, because the meal could have passed without such things: so a poem, created to give delight, if it fails but a little of the highest sinks to the lowest. One who is ignorant of games will abstain from the weapons of the Campus; and if he knows nothing of ball, or quoit, or hoop, will hold aloof, lest the thronging onlookers laugh with none to check them; yet he who is no poet, presumes to write verses! "And why not? Is he not free, of gentle birth, rated at a knight's income, with nothing against him?" *You*, I know, will say and do nothing "against the grain"—such is your resolve, such your good sense. If, however, you should one day produce something, pray submit it first to Maecius the critic, to your father, to me; and then put back the manuscript in your desk and let it stand over for a decade. The unpublished may be canceled; but a word once uttered can never be recalled. . . .

Whether a good poem be the work of nature or of art is a moot point. For my part I fail to see the use of study without wit, or of wit without training: so true is it that each requires the other's aid in helpful union.

The athlete who is eager to reach the longed-for goal has endured and done much in boyhood, has borne heat and cold, has abstained from women and wine; the flute-player who plays at the Pythian games has first learned his lesson and trembled before a teacher. Nowadays people think it enough to say: "I make wonderful poems; devil take the hindmost! it's a shame for me to be outdone and to own I really do not know what I have never learned."

As a crier collects a crowd to buy his wares, so a poet, rich in land and rich in investments, bids flatterers flock to him for their profit. If there is one who can provide a costly feast, who will go bail for a poor man and rescue him from the law's grim toils, I shall be surprised if, for all his wealth, he is clever enough to distinguish the false friend from the true. Whether you have given another a present, or mean to do so, never call him, when filled with joy, to listen to your verses; for he will be sure to cry, "Splendid! bravo!" He will change color over them, drop tears of pleasure, leap, beat upon the floor.

Hired mourners outstrip in word and action those whose sorrow is real: so is the sham admirer moved far more than the honest one. Wealthy folk, when keen to mark whether a man be worthy of friendship, are said to ply him with many a bumper and put him to the ordeal of wine; so, if you write poems, you will never fail to detect the spirit that lurks beneath the fox's skin.

In days gone by, whenever you read a piece to Quintilius he would exclaim, "Correct this, I pray, or that." If you replied that you could do no better, that you had tried twice or thrice in vain, he would bid you cut out the ill-turned lines and bring them to the anvil agin. If you chose rather to defend than to mend the faulty line, not a word more would he say, or waste his efforts. Henceforth you might hug yourself and your works, alone, without a rival.

A kind and sensible critic will censure verses when they are weak, condemn them when they are rough; ugly lines he will score in black, will lop off pretentious ornaments, force you to clear up your obscurities, criticize a doubtful phrase, and mark what needs a change—in fact prove another Aristarchus. He will not say, "Why should I take my friend to task for mere trifles?"— it is such trifles that will bring into sad scrapes the poet who has been fooled and flattered unfairly. . . .

Longinus   *1st or 3d century A.D.*

On the Sublime

I

. . . As I am writing to you, good friend, who are well versed in literary studies, I feel almost absolved from the necessity of premising at any length that sublimity is a certain distinction and excellence in expression, and that it is from no other source than this that the greatest poets and writers have derived their eminence and gained an immortality of renown. The effect of elevated language upon an audience is not persuasion but transport. At every time and in every way imposing speech, with the spell it throws over us, prevails over that which aims at persuasion and gratification. Our persuasions we can usually control, but the influences of the sublime bring power and irresistible might to bear, and reign supreme over every hearer. Similarly, we see skill in invention, and due order and arrangement of matter, emerging as the hard-won result not of one thing nor of two, but

Selections. From Longinus, *On the Sublime*, translated by W. Rhys Roberts. Cambridge: University Press, 1899.

of the whole texture of the composition, whereas Sublimity flashing forth at the right moment scatters everything before it like a thunderbolt, and at once displays the power of the orator in all its plenitude. . . .

II

First of all, we must raise the question whether there is such a thing as an art of the sublime or lofty. Some hold that those are entirely in error who would bring such matters under the precepts of art. A lofty tone, says one, is innate, and does not come by teaching; nature is the only art that can compass it. Works of nature are, they think, made worse and altogether feebler when wizened by the rules of art. But I maintain that this will be found to be otherwise if it be observed that, while nature as a rule is free and independent in matters of passion and elevation, yet is she wont not to act at random and utterly without system. Further, nature is the original and vital underlying principle in all cases, but system can define limits and fitting seasons, and can also contribute the safest rules for use and practice. Moreover, the expression of the sublime is more exposed to danger when it goes its own way without the guidance of knowledge, when it is suffered to be unstable and unballasted, when it is left at the mercy of mere momentum and ignorant audacity. It is true that it often needs the spur, but it is also true that it often needs the curb. Demosthenes expresses the view, with regard to human life in general, that good fortune is the greatest of blessings, while good counsel, which occupies the second place, is hardly inferior in importance, since its absence contributes inevitably to the ruin of the former. This we may apply to diction, nature occupying the position of good fortune, art that of good counsel. Most important of all, we must remember that the very fact that there are some elements of expression which are in the hands of nature alone, can be learnt from no other source than art. . . .

III

. . . Since even in tragedy, which is in its very nature stately and prone to bombast, tasteless tumidity is unpardonable, still less, I presume, will it harmonize with the narration of fact. . . . Altogether, tumidity seems particularly hard to avoid. The explanation is that all who aim at elevation are so anxious to escape the reproach of being weak and dry that they are carried, as by some strange law of nature, into the opposite extreme. They put their trust in the maxim that "failure in a great attempt is at least a noble error." But evil are the swellings, both in the body and in diction, which are inflated and unreal, and threaten us with the reverse of our aim; for nothing, say they, is drier than a man who has the dropsy. While tumidity desires to transcend the limits of the sublime, the defect which is termed puerility is the direct antithesis of elevation, for it is utterly low and mean and in real truth the most ignoble vice of style. What, then, is this puerility? Clearly, a pedant's thoughts, which begin in learned trifling and end in frigidity. Men slip into this kind of error because, while they aim at the uncommon and elaborate and most of all at the attractive, they drift unawares into the tawdry and affected. A third, and closely allied, kind of defect in matters of passion is . . . unseasonable and empty passion, where no passion is required, or immoderate, were moderation is needed. For men are often carried away, as if by intoxication, into displays of emotion which are not caused by the nature of the subject, but are purely personal and wearisome. In consequence they seem to hearers who are in no wise affected to act in an ungainly way. And no wonder; for they are beside themselves, while their hearers are not. But the question of the passions we reserve for separate treatment. . . .

V

. . . Our defects usually spring, for the most part, from the same sources as our good points. Hence, while beauties of expression and touches of sublimity, and charming elegancies withal, are favorable to effective composition, yet these very things are the elements and foundation, not only of success, but also of the contrary. Something of the kind is true also of variations and hyperboles and the use of the plural number, and we shall show subsequently the dangers to which these seem severally to be exposed. It is necessary now to seek and to suggest means by which we may avoid the defects which attend the steps of the sublime.

VI

The best means would be, friend, to gain, first of all, clear knowledge and appreciation of the true sublime. The enterprise is, however, an arduous one. For the judgment of style is the last and crowning fruit of long experience. Nonetheless, if I must speak in the way of precept, it is not impossible perhaps to acquire discrimination in these matters by attention to some such hints as those which follow.

VII

. . . In the case of sublimity in poems and prose writings, we must consider whether some supposed examples have not simply the appearance of elevation with many idle accretions, so that when analyzed they are found to be mere vanity—objects which a noble nature will rather despise than admire. . . . When, therefore, a thing is heard repeatedly by a man of intelligence, who is well versed in literature, and its effect is not to dispose the soul to high thoughts, and it does not leave in the mind more food for reflection than the words seem to convey, but falls, if examined carefully through and through, into disesteem, it cannot rank as true sublimity because it does not survive a first hearing. For that is really great which bears a repeated examination, and which it is difficult or rather impossible to withstand, and the memory of which is strong and hard to efface. In general, consider those examples of sublimity to be fine and genuine which pleases all and always. For when men of different pursuits, lives, ambitions, ages, languages, hold identical views on one and the same subject, then that verdict which results, so to speak, from a concert of discordant elements makes our faith in the object of admiration strong and unassailable.

VIII

There are, it may be said, five principal sources of elevated language. Beneath these five varieties there lies, as though it were a common foundation, the gift of discourse, which is indispensable. First and most important is the power of forming great conceptions. . . . Secondly, there is vehement and inspired passion. These two components of the sublime are for the most part innate. Those which remain are partly the product of art. The due formation of figures deals with two sorts of figures, first those of thought and secondly those of expression. Next there is noble diction, which in turn comprises choice of words, and use of metaphors, and elaboration of language. The fifth cause of elevation—one which is the fitting conclusion of all that have preceded it—is dignified and elevated composition. . . .

IX

Now the first of the conditions mentioned, namely elevation of mind, holds the foremost rank among them all. We must, therefore, in this case also, although we have to do rather with an endowment than with an acquirement, nurture our souls (as far as that is possible) to thoughts sublime, and make them always pregnant, so to say, with noble inspiration. In what way, you may ask, is this to be done? Elsewhere I have written as follows: "Sublimity is the echo of a great soul." Hence also a bare idea, by itself and without a spoken word, sometimes excites admiration just because of the greatness of soul implied. . . . First, then, it is absolutely necessary to indicate the source of this elevation, namely, that the truly eloquent must be free from low and ignoble thoughts. For it is not possible that men with mean and servile ideas and aims prevailing throughout their lives should produce anything that is admirable and worthy of immortality. Great accents we expect to fall from the lips of those whose thoughts are deep and grave. . . .

X

Let us next consider whether we can point to anything further that contributes to sublimity of style. Now, there inhere in all things by nature certain constituents which are part and parcel of their substance. It must needs be, therefore, that we shall find one source of the sublime in the systematic selection of the most important elements, and the power of forming, by their mutual combination, what may be called one body. The former process attracts the hearer by the choice of the ideas, the latter by the aggregation of those chosen. . . .

XIII

. . . Plato . . . shows us, if only we were willing to pay him heed, that another way (beyond anything we have mentioned) leads to the sublime. And what, and what manner of way, may that be? It is the imitation and emulation of previous great poets and writers. And let this, my dear friend, be an aim to which we steadfastly apply ourselves. For many men are carried away by the spirit of others as if inspired, just as it is related of the Pythian priestess when she approaches the tripod, where there is a rift in the ground which (they say) exhales divine vapor. By heavenly power thus communicated she is impregnated and straightway delivers oracles in virtue of the afflatus. Similarly from the great natures of the men of old there are borne in upon the souls of those who emulate them (as from sacred caves) what we may decribe as *effluences,* so that even those who seem little likely to be possessed are thereby inspired and succumb to the spell of the others' greatness. . . . This proceeding is not plagiarism; it is like taking an impression from beautiful forms or figures or other works of art. . . .

XIV

Accordingly it is well that we ourselves also, when elaborating anything which requires lofty expression and elevated conception, should shape some idea in our minds as to how perchance Homer would have said this very thing, or how it would have been raised to the sublime by Plato or

Demosthenes or by the historian Thucydides. For those personages, presenting themselves to us and inflaming our ardor and as it were illuminating our path, will carry our minds in a mysterious way to the high standards of sublimity which are imaged within us. Still more effectual will it be to suggest this question to our thoughts, "What sort of hearing would Homer, had he been present, or Demosthenes have given to this or that when said by me, or how would they have been affected by the other?" For the ordeal is indeed a severe one, if we presuppose such a tribunal and theatre for our own utterances, and imagine that we are undergoing a scrutiny of our writings before these great heroes, acting as judges and witnesses. A greater incentive still will be supplied if you add the question, "In what spirit will each succeeding age listen to me who have written thus?" But if one shrinks from the very thought of uttering aught that may transcend the term of his own life and time, the conceptions of his mind must necessarily be incomplete, blind, and as it were untimely born, since they are by no means brought to the perfection needed to ensure a futurity of fame. . . .

XXXIII

Come, now, let us take some writer who is really immaculate and beyond reproach. Is it not worth while, on this very point, to raise the general question whether we ought to give the preference, in poems and prose writings, to grandeur with some attendant faults, or to success which is moderate but altogether sound and free from error? Aye, and further, whether a greater number of excellences, or excellences higher in quality, would in literature rightly bear away the palm? For these are inquiries appropriate to a treatise on the sublime, and they imperatively demand a settlement. For my part, I am well aware that lofty genius is far removed from flawlessness; for invariable accuracy incurs the risk of pettiness, and in the sublime, as in great fortunes, there must be something which is over-looked. It may be necessarily the case that low and average natures remain as a rule free from failing and in greater safety because they never run a risk or seek to scale the heights, while great endowments prove insecure because of their very greatness. In the second place, I am not ignorant that it naturally happens that the worse side of human character is always the more easily recognized, and that the memory of errors remains indelible, while that of excellences quickly dies away. I have myself noted not a few errors on the part of Homer and other writers of the greatest distinction, and the slips they have made afford me anything but pleasure. Still I do not term them wilful errors, but rather oversights of a random and casual kind, due to neglect and introduced with all the heedlessness of genius. Conse-quently I do not waver in my view that excellences higher in quality, even if not sustained throughout, should always on a comparison be voted the first place, because of their sheer elevation of spirit if for no other reason. . . .

XXXVI

. . . Nevertheless—and the counsel about to be given reverts to the beginning of our memoir—since freedom from failings is for the most part the successful result of art, and excellence (though it may be unevenly sustained) the result of sublimity, the employment of art is in every way a fitting aid to nature; for it is the conjunction of the two which tends to ensure perfection.

Late Antiquity through the Middle Ages

Writing before the fall of the Roman Empire, on the eve of the Middle Ages, the harsh, intolerant, "fierce Tertullian" (as Matthew Arnold called him) reflected and also had a great influence on Church policy. The first Christian work in Latin to deal with the morality of the theatre for Christians, his *On the Spectacles* takes the position that theatrical spectacles of all types—tragedies, circuses, whatever—are among the sins of the world, offend God, and should be shunned by all good Christians. Charging the theatre with belonging to the Devil rather than to God, Tertullian condemns theatrical pleasures as a form of lust and at the same time offers the pleasures of Christ's church as greater than those of theatrical spectacles. Saint Augustine too opposes the theatre, for apart from its dedication to pagan gods it moves people to immoral behavior. In decrying the depravities perpetrated by theatrical and other poets, he applauds Plato for having excluded poets from his ideal state. Later works, which attack miracle plays when they are not performed in a church (for example, *Handling Sin*), or which attack "miracle playing" altogether, employ assumptions and arguments similar to and perhaps derived from those found in Tertullian and Saint Augustine.

While the fortunes of drama were low, Donatus kept alive classical ideas about it, including the analysis of drama in rhetorical terms. Traditional differences between tragedy and comedy—based on plot, style, characters, and subjects—are well summarized by Dante, who like other medieval writers does not restrict tragedy and comedy to dramatic works. For reasons his *Letter to the Lord Can Grande della Scala* makes clear, for instance, he calls his nondramatic work *The Divine Comedy*. In any case, with persistent attacks on dramatic and other poetry, the main job of medieval theorists was not to analyze poetry but to defend its very existence. Quintessentially medieval in his vivid defense of poetry against its theological and Platonic detractors is Boccaccio, whose defense suggests that, despite his references to Plato's *Republic*, he had either not read it, or had not read all of it. Also quintessentially medieval is his denigration of dramatic poetry while he upholds the nondramatic.

Tertullian *c. 155–c. 220*

On the Spectacles *197–202*

Ye servants of God, about to draw near to God, that you may make
solemn consecration of yourselves to Him, seek well to understand the condition of faith, the reasons of the truth, the laws of Chrisitan discipline,
which forbid, among other sins of the world, the pleasures of the public
shows; ye who have testified and confessed that you have already done so,
review the subject, that there may be no sinning, whether through real or
wilful ignorance. For such is the power of earthly pleasures, that, to retain
the opportunity of still partaking of them, it contrives to prolong a willing
ignorance, and bribes knowledge into playing a dishonest part. To both
things, perhaps, some among you are allured by the views of the heathens,
who in this matter are wont to press us with such arguments as these: That
the exquisite enjoyments of ear and eye we have in external things are not
in the least opposed to religion in the mind and conscience; and that surely
no offence is offered to God in any human enjoyment, at any of our
pleasures which, with all due reverence and honor secured to Him, it is
not sinful to partake of in its own time and place. But this is precisely
what we are ready to prove—that these things are not consistent with true
religion, and true obedience to the true God. . . .

. . . Everyone is ready with the argument that all things, as we teach,
were created by God, and given to man for his use, and that they must all
be good as coming all from so good a source, but that among them are
found the various constituent elements of the public shows, such as the
horse, the lion, bodily strength, and musical voice. It cannot, then, be
thought that what exists by God's own creative will is either foreign or
hostile to Him; and if it is not opposed to Him, it cannot be regarded as
injurious to His worshipers, as certainly it is not foreign to them. Beyond
all doubt, too, the very buildings connected with the places of public amusement, composed as they are of rocks, stones, marbles, pillars, are things
of God, who has given these various things for the earth's embellishment;
nay, the very scenes are enacted under God's own heaven. . . . We must
not, then, consider merely by whom all things were made, but by whom
they have been perverted. We shall find out for what use they were made
at first, when we find for what they were not. There is a vast difference
between the corrupted state and that of primal purity, just because there
is a vast difference between the Creator and the corrupter. Why, all sorts of

Selections, translated by Reverend S. Thelwall. From *The Writings of Septimus Florens
Tertullianus*, Vol. I. Edinburgh: T. & T. Clark, 1869.

evils, which as indubitably evils even the heathens prohibit, and against which they guard themselves, come from the works of God. Take, for instance, murder, whether committed by iron, by poison, or by magical enchantments. Iron and herbs and demons are all equally creatures of God. Has the Creator, withal, provided these things for man's destruction? Nay, He puts His interdict on every sort of man-killing by that one summary precept, "Thou shalt not kill." Moreover, who but God, the Maker of the world, put in it gold, brass, silver, ivory, wood, and all the other materials used in the manufacture of idols? Yet has He done this that men may set up a worship in opposition to Himself? On the contrary, idolatry in His eyes is the crowning sin. What is there offensive to God which is not God's? But in offending Him, it ceases to be His; and in ceasing to be His, it is in His eyes an offending thing. Man himself, guilty as he is of every iniquity, is not only a work of God—he is His image, and yet both in soul and body he has severed himself from his Maker. For we did not get eyes to minister to lust, and the tongue for speaking evil with, and ears to be the receptacle of evil speech, and the throat to serve the vice of gluttony, and the belly to be gluttony's ally, and the genitals for unchaste excesses, and hands for deeds of violence, and the feet for an erring life; or was the soul placed in the body that it might become a thought-manufactory of snares, and frauds, and injustices? I think not; for if God, as the righteous extractor of innocence, hates everything like malignity, if He hates utterly such plotting of evil, it is clear beyond a doubt, that, of all things that have come from His hand, He has made none to lead to works which He condemns, even though these same works may be carried on by things of His making; for, in fact, it is the one ground of condemnation that the creature misuses the creation. . . .

. . . The faith of some, either too simple or too scrupulous, demands direct authority from Scripture for giving up the shows, and holds out that the matter is a doubtful one, because such abstinence is not clearly and in words imposed upon God's servants. Well, we never find it expressed with the same precision, "Thou shalt not enter circus or theatre, thou shalt not look on combat or show," as it is plainly laid down, "Thou shalt not kill; thou shalt not worship an idol; thou shalt not commit adultery or fraud."[1] But we find that that first word of David bears on this very sort of thing: "Blessed," he says, "is the man who has not gone into the assembly of the impious, nor stood in the way of sinners, nor sat in the seat of scorners."[2] For though he seems to have predicted beforehand of that just man, that he took no part in the meetings and deliberations of the Jews, taking counsel about the slaying of our Lord, yet divine Scripture has ever far-reaching applications: after the immediate sense has been exhausted, in all directions

---

[1] Exod. 20:14.
[2] Ps. 1.1.

it fortifies the practice of the religious life, so that here also you have an utterance which is not far from a plain interdicting of the shows. For if he called those few Jews an assembly of the wicked, how much more will he so designate so vast a gathering of heathens! Are the heathens less impious, less sinners, less enemies of Christ, than the Jews were then? And see, too, how other things agree. For at the shows they also stand in the way. For they call the spaces between the seats going round the amphitheatre, and the passages which separate the people running down, ways. The place in the curve where matrons sit is called a chair. Therefore on the contrary it holds, unblessed is he who has entered any council of wicked men, and has stood in any way of sinners, and has sat in any chair of scorners. We may understand a thing as spoken generally, even when it requires a certain special interpretation to be given to it. For some things spoken with a special reference contain in them general truth. When God admonishes the Israelites of their duty, or sharply reproves them, He has surely a reference to all men; when He threatens destruction to Egypt and Ethiopia, He surely precondemns every sinning nation whatever. If, reasoning from *species* to *genus*, every nation that sins against them is an Egypt and Ethiopia; so also, reasoning from genus to species, with reference to the origin of shows, every show is an assembly of the wicked. . . .

. . . Though Varro derives the name of *Ludi* from *Ludus*, that is, from play, as they called the Luperci also *Ludii*, because they ran about making sport; still that sporting of young men belongs, in his view, to festal days and temples, and objects of religious veneration. However, it is of little consequence the origin of the name, when it is certain that the thing springs from idolatry. For the Liberalia, under the general designation of Ludi, clearly declared the glory of Father Bacchus; for to Bacchus these festivities were first consecrated by grateful peasants, in return for the boon he conferred on them, as they say, making known the pleasures of wine. Then the Consualia were called *Ludi*, and at first were in honor of Neptune, for Neptune has the name of Consus also. Thereafter Romulus dedicated the Equiria to Mars, though they claim the Consualia too for Romulus, on the ground that he consecrated them to Consus, the god, as they will have it, of counsel; of the counsel, forsooth, in which he planned the rape of the Sabine virgins for wives to his soldiers. An excellent counsel truly; and still I suppose reckoned just and righteous by the Romans themselves, I may not say by God. For this goes also to taint the origin: you cannot surely hold that to be good which has sprung from sin, from shamelessness, from violence, from hatred, from a fratricidal founder, from a son of Mars. . . .

. . . You have festivals bearing the name of the great Mother and Apollo, of Ceres too, and Neptune, and Jupiter Latiaris, and Flora, all celebrated for a common end; the others have their religious origin in the birthdays and solemnities of kings, in public successes, in municipal holidays. There are also testamentary exhibitions, in which funeral honors are rendered to the memories of private persons; and this according to an institution of ancient times. For from the first the "Ludi" were regarded as of two sorts, sacred and funereal, that is, in honor of the heathen deities and of the dead. But in the matter of idolatry, it makes no difference with us under what name or title it is practiced, while it has to do with the wicked spirits whom we abjure. If it is lawful to offer homage to the dead, it will be just as lawful to offer it to their gods: you have the same origin in both cases; there is the same idolatry; there is on our part the same solemn renunciation against all idolatry. . . .

. . . For the tiny streamlet from its very spring-head, the little twig from its very budding, contains in it the essential nature of its origin. It may be grand or mean, no matter, any circus procession whatever is offensive to God. Though there be few images to grace it, there is idolatory in one; though there be no more than a single sacred car, it is a chariot of Jupiter: anything of idolatry whatever, whether meanly arrayed or modestly rich and gorgeous, taints it in its origin. . . .

. . . Satan and his angels have filled the whole world. It is not by merely being in the world, however, that we lapse from God, but by touching and tainting ourselves with the world's sins. I shall break with my Maker, that is, by going to the Capitol or the temple of Serapis to sacrifice or adore, as I shall also do by going as a spectator to the circus and the theatre. The places in themselves do not contaminate, but what is done in them, from which even the places themselves, we maintain, become defiled. The polluted things pollute us. . . .

Let us pass on now to theatrical exhibitions, which we have already shown have a common origin with the circus, and bear like idolatrous designations—even as from the first they have borne the name of "Ludi," and equally minister to idols. They resemble each other also in their pomp, having the same procession to the scene of their display from temples and altars and that mournful profusion of incense and blood, with music of pipes and trumpets, all under the direction of the soothsayer and the undertaker, those two foul masters of funeral rites and sacrifices. So as we went on from the origin of the "Ludi" to the circus games, we shall now direct our course thence to those of the theatre, beginning with the place of exhibition. At first the theatre was properly a temple of Venus; and, to speak briefly, it was owing to this that stage performances were allowed to escape censure, and got a footing in the world. . . . Pompey the Great, less only than his theatre, when he had erected that citadel of all impurities, fearing some time or other censorian condemnation of his memory, superposed on it a temple of Venus; and summoning by public proclamation the people to its consecration, he called it not a theatre, but a temple, "under which," said he, "we have placed tiers of seats for viewing the shows." So he threw a veil over a structure on which condemnation had been often passed, and which is ever to be held in reprobation, by pretending that it was a sacred place; and by means of superstition he blinded the eyes of a virtuous discipline. But Venus and Bacchus are close allies. These two evil spirits are in sworn confederacy with each other, as the patrons of drunkenness and lust. So the theatre of Venus is as well the house of Bacchus: for they properly gave the name of Liberalia also to other theatrical amusements—which besides being consecrated to Bacchus (as were the Dionysia of the Greeks), were instituted by him; and, without doubt, the performances of the theatre have the common patronage of these two deities. That immodesty of gesture and attire which so specially and peculiarly characterizes the stage are consecrated to them—the one deity wanton by her sex, the other by his drapery; while its services of voice, and song, and lute, and pipe, belong to Apollos, and Muses, and Minervas, and Mercuries. You will hate, O Christian, the things whose authors must be the objects of your utter detestation. So we would now make a remark about the arts of the theatre, about the things also whose authors in the names we execrate. We know that the names of the dead are nothing, as are their images; but we know well enough, too, who, when images are set up, under these names carry on their wicked work, and exult in the homage rendered to them, and pretend to be divine—none other than spirits accursed, than devils. We see, therefore, that the arts also are consecrated to the service of the beings who dwell in the names of their founders; and that things cannot be held free from the taint of idolatry whose inventors have got a place among the gods for their discoveries. Nay, as regards the arts, we ought to have gone further back, and barred all further argument by the position that the demons, predetermining in their own interests from the first, among other evils of idolatry, the pollutions of the public shows, with the object of drawing man away from his Lord and binding him to their own service, carried out their purpose by bestowing on him the artistic gifts which the shows require. For none but themselves would have made provision and preparation for the objects they had in view; nor would they have given the arts to the world by any but those in whose names, and images, and histories they set up for their own ends the artifice of consecration. . . .

. . . Let us now . . . look at the subject in another way, for the sake of those especially who keep themselves comfortable in the thought that the abstinence we urge is not in so many words enjoined, as if in the condemnation of the lusts of the world there was not involved a sufficient declaration against all these amusements. For as there is a lust of money, or rank, or eating, or impure enjoyment, or glory, so there is also a lust of pleasure. But the show is just a sort of pleasure. I think, then, that under the general designation of lusts, pleasures are included; in like manner, under the general idea of pleasures, you have as a specific class the "shows." . . .

. . . God has enjoined us to deal calmly, and gently, and quietly, and peacefully with the Holy Spirit, because these things are alone in keeping with the goodness of His nature, with His tenderness and sensitiveness, not to vex Him with rage, or ill-nature, or anger, or grief. Well, how shall this be made to accord with the shows? For the show always leads to spiritual agitation. For where there is pleasure, there is keenness of feeling giving pleasure its zest; and where there is keenness of feeling, there is rivalry giving in turn its zest to that. Then, too, where you have rivalry, you have rage, and bitterness, and wrath, and grief, and all bad things which flow from them—the whole entirely out of keeping with the religion of Christ. For even suppose one should enjoy the shows in a moderate way, as befits his rank or age or nature, still he is not undisturbed in mind, without some unuttered movings of the inner man. No one partakes of pleasures such as these without their strong excitements; no one comes under their excitements without their natural lapses. These lapses, again, create passionate desire. . . . It is not enough that we do no such things ourselves, unless we break all connection also with those who do. "If thou sawest a thief," says the Scripture, "thou consentedst with him."[3] Would that we did not even inhabit the same world with these wicked men! But though that wish cannot be realized, yet even now we are separate from them in what is of the world; for the world is God's, but the worldly is the devil's. . . .

Are we not . . . enjoined to put away from us all immodesty? On this ground, again, we are excluded from the theatre, which is immodesty's own peculiar abode, where nothing is in repute but what elsewhere is disreputable. So the best path to the highest favor of its god is the vileness which the Atellan gesticulates, which the buffoon in woman's clothes exhibits, destroying all natural modesty, so that they blush more readily at home than at the play, which finally is done from his childhood on the person of the pantomime, that he may become an actor. The very harlots, too, victims of the public lust, are brought upon the stage, their misery increased as being there in the presence of their own sex, from whom alone they are wont to hide themselves: they are paraded publicly before every age and every rank—their abode, their gains, their praises, are set forth, and that even in the hearing of those who should not hear such things. . . . But if we ought to abominate all that is immodest, on what ground is it right to hear what we must not speak? For all licentiousness of speech, nay, every idle word, is condemned by God. Why, in the same way, is it right to look on what it is disgraceful to do? How is it that the things which defile a man in going out of his mouth, are not regarded as doing so when they go in at his eyes and ears?—when eyes and ears are the immediate attendants on

[3] Ps. 49:18.

the spirit; and that can never be pure whose servants-in-waiting are impure. You have the theatre forbidden, then, in the forbidding of immodesty. If, again, we despise the teaching of secular literature as being foolishness in God's eyes, our duty is plain enough in regard to those spectacles, which from this source derive the tragic or comic play. If tragedies and comedies are the bloody and wanton, the impious and licentious inventors of crimes and lusts, it is not good even that there should be any calling to remembrance the atrocious or the vile. What you reject in deed, you are not to bid welcome to in word. . . .

We shall now see how the Scriptures condemn the amphitheatre. If we can maintain that it is right to indulge in the cruel, and the impious, and the fierce, let us go there. If we are what we are said to be, let us regale ourselves there with human blood! It is good, no doubt, to have the guilty punished. Who but the criminal himself will deny that? And yet the innocent can find no pleasure in another's sufferings: he rather mourns that a brother has sinned so heinously as to need a punishment so dreadful. But who is my guarantee that it is always the guilty who are adjudged to the wild beasts, or to some other doom, and that the guiltless never suffer from the revenge of the judge, or the weakness of the defence, or the pressure of the rack? How much better, then, is it for me to remain ignorant of the punishment inflicted on the wicked, lest I am obliged to know also of the good coming to untimely ends—if I may speak of goodness in the case at all! At any rate, gladiators not chargeable with crime are offered in sale for the games, that they may become the victims of the public pleasure. Even in the case of those who are judicially condemned to the ampitheatre, what a monstrous thing it is, that, in undergoing their punishment, they, from some less serious delinquency, advance to the criminality of man-slayers! . . .

How vain, then—nay, how desperate—is the reasoning of persons, who, just because they decline to lose a pleasure, hold out that we cannot point to the specific words or the very place where this abstinence is mentioned, and where the servants of God are directly forbidden to have anything to do with such assemblies! I heard lately a novel defence of himself by a certain play-lover. "The sun," said he, "nay, God Himself, looks down from heaven on the show, and no pollution is contracted." Yes, and the sun, too, pours down his rays into the common sewer without being defiled. As for God, would that all crimes were hid from His eye, that we might all escape judgment! But He looks on robberies too; He looks on falsehoods, and adulteries, and frauds, and idolatries, and these same shows; and precisely on that account *we* will not look on them, lest the All-seeing see us. You are putting on the same level, O man, the criminal and the judge; the criminal who is a criminal because he is seen, and the Judge who is a Judge because He sees. Are we set, then, on playing the madman outside the circus boundaries? Outside the gates of the theatre are we bent on lewdness, and outside the course on arrogance, and outside the amphitheatre on cruelty, because outside the porticoes and the tiers and the curtains, too, God has eyes? Never and nowhere is that free from blame which God ever condemns; never and nowhere is it right to do what you may not do at all times and in all places. . . .

. . . Will God have any pleasure in the charioteer who disquiets so many souls, who rouses up so many furious passions, and creates so many various moods, either crowned like a priest or wearing the colors of a pimp, decked out by the devil that he may be whirled away in his chariot, as though with the object of taking off Elijah? Will He be pleased with him who applies the razor to himself, and completely changes his features; who, with no respect for his face, is not content with making it as like as possible to Saturn and Isis and Bacchus, but gives it quietly over to contumelious blows, as if in mockery of our Lord? The devil, forsooth, makes it part, too, of his teaching, that the cheek is to be meekly offered to the smiter! In the same way, with their high shoes, he has made the tragic actors taller, because "none can add a cubit to his stature."[4] His desire is to make Christ a liar. And in regard to the wearing of masks, I ask is that according to the mind of God, who forbids the making of every likeness, and especially then the likeness of man who is His own image? The Author of truth hates all the false; He regards as adultery all that is unreal. Condemning, therefore, as He does hypocrisy in every form, He never will approve any putting on of voice, or sex, or age; He never will approve pretended loves, and wraths, and groans, and tears. Then, too, as in His law it is declared that the man is cursed who attires himself in female garments, what must be His judgment of the pantomime, who is even brought up to play the woman! . . .

Seated where there is nothing of God, will one be thinking of his Maker? Will there be peace in his soul when there is eager strife there for a charioteer? Wrought up into a frenzied excitement, will he learn to be modest? Nay, in the whole thing he will meet with no greater temptation than that gay attiring of the men and women. The very intermingling of emotions, the very agreements and disagreements with each other in the bestowment of their favors, where you have such close communion, blow up the sparks of passion. And then there is scarce any other object in going to the show, but to see and to be seen. When a tragic actor is declaiming, will one be giving thought to prophetic appeals? Amid the measures of the effeminate player, will he call up to himself a psalm? And when the athletes are hard at struggle, will he be ready to proclaim that there must be no striking again? And with his eye fixed on the bites of bears, and the sponge-nets of the net-fighters, can he be moved by compassion? May God avert

4 Matt. 6:27.

from His people any such passionate eagerness after a cruel enjoyment! For how monstrous it is to go from God's church to the devil's—from the sky to the stye, as they say; to raise your hands to God, and then to weary them in the applause of an actor. . . .

We ought to detest these heathen meetings and assemblies, if no other account than that there God's name is blasphemed—that there the cry "To the lions!" is daily raised against us—that from thence persecuting decrees are wont to emanate, and temptations are sent forth. What will you do if you are caught in that heaving tide of impious judgments? Not that there any harm is likely to come to you from men: nobody knows that you are a Christian; but think how it fares with you in heaven. For at the very time the devil is working havoc in the church, do you doubt that the angels are looking down from above, and marking every man, who speaks and who listens to the blaspheming word, who lends his tongue and who lends his ears to the service of Satan against God? Shall you not then shun those tiers where the enemies of Christ assemble, that seat of all that is pestilential, and the very superincumbent atmosphere all impure with wicked cries? Grant that you have there things that are pleasant, things both agreeable and innocent in themselves; even some things that are excellent. Nobody dilutes poison with gall and hellebore: the accursed thing is put into condiments well seasoned and of sweetest taste. So, too, the devil puts into the deadly draught which he prepares, things of God most pleasant and most acceptable. . . .

Even as things are, if your thought is to spend this period of existence in enjoyments, how are you so ungrateful as to reckon insufficient, as not thankfully to recognize the many and exquisite pleasures God has bestowed upon you? . . . If the literature of the stage delight you, we have literature in abundance of our own—plenty of verses, sentences, songs, proverbs; and these not fabulous, but true; not tricks of art, but plain realities. Would you have also fightings and wrestlings? Well, of these there is no lacking, and they are not of slight account. Behold unchastity overcome by chastity, perfidy slain by faithfulness, cruelty stricken by compassion, impudence thrown into the shade by modesty: these are contests we have among us, and in these *we* win our crowns. But would you have something of blood too? You have Christ's.

Saint Augustine 354–430

The City of God 413–426

Chapter 7—. . . Man's Natural Bias to Evil
Induces Him Rather to Follow the Examples of the Gods
Than to Obey the Precepts of Men

The young profligate in Terence, when he sees on the wall a fresco representing the fabled descent of Jupiter into the lap of Danaë in the form of
a golden shower, accepts this as authoritative precedent for his own licentiousness, and boasts that he is an imitator of God. "And what God?" he says. "He
who with His thunder shakes the loftiest temples. And was I, a poor creature
compared to Him, to make bones of it? No; I did it, and with all my heart."[1]

Chapter 8—That the Theatrical Exhibitions,
Publishing the Shameful Actions of the Gods,
Propitiated Rather Than Offended Them

But, someone will interpose, these are the fables of poets, not the deliver-
ances of the gods themselves. Well, I have no mind to arbitrate between the
lewdness of theatrical entertainments and of mystic rites; only this I say, and
history bears me out in making the assertion, that those same entertainments,
in which the fictions of poets are the main attraction, were not introduced in
the festivals of the gods by the ignorant devotion of the Romans, but that the
gods themselves gave the most urgent commands to this effect, and indeed
extorted from the Romans these solemnities and celebrations in their honor.
I touched on this in the preceding book, and mentioned that dramatic entertainments were first inaugurated at Rome on occasion of a pestilence, and by
authority of the pontiff. And what man is there who is not more likely to
adopt, for the regulation of his own life, the examples that are represented
in plays which have a divine sanction, rather than the precepts written and
promulgated with no more than human authority? If the poets gave a false
representation of Jove in describing him as adulterous, then it were to be
expected that the chaste gods should in anger avenge so wicked a fiction, in
place of encouraging the games which circulated it. Of these plays, the most
inoffensive are comedies and tragedies, that is to say, the dramas which poets
write for the stage, and which, though they often handle impure subjects, yet

Selections from Book Two, translated by Reverend Marcus Dods. From A *Select Library
of the Nicene and Post-Nicene Fathers of the Christian Church*, Vol. II, edited by Philip
Schaff. Buffalo: The Christian Literature Co., 1887.

[1] *The Eunuch* (161 B.C.).

do so without the filthiness of language which characterizes many other performances; and it is these dramas which boys are obliged by their seniors to read and learn as a part of what is called a liberal and gentlemanly education.

Chapter 9—That the Poetical License Which the Greeks, in Obedience to Their Gods, Allowed, Was Restrained by the Ancient Romans

The opinion of the ancient Romans on this matter is attested by Cicero in his work *De Republica,* in which Scipio, one of the interlocutors, says, "The lewdness of comedy could never have been suffered by audiences, unless the customs of society had previously sanctioned the same lewdness." And in the earlier days the Greeks preserved a certain reasonableness in their license, and made it a law, that whatever comedy wished to say of any one, it must say it of him by name. And so in the same work of Cicero's, Scipio says, "Whom has it not aspersed? Nay, whom has it not worried? Whom has it spared? Allow that it may assail demagogues and factions, men injurious to the commonwealth—a Cleon, a Cleophon, a Hyperbolus. That is tolerable, though it had been more seemly for the public censor to brand such men, than for a poet to lampoon them; but to blacken the fame of Pericles with scurrilous verse, after he had with the utmost dignity presided over their state alike in war and in peace, was as unworthy of a poet, as if our own Plautus or Naevius were to bring Publius and Cneius Scipio on the comic stage, or as if Caecilius were to caricature Cato." And then a little after he goes on: "Though our Twelve Tables attached the penalty of death only to a very few offences, yet among these few this one: if any man should have sung a pasquinade, or have composed a satire calculated to bring infamy or disgrace on another person. Wisely decreed. For it is by the decisions of magistrates, and by a well-informed justice, that our lives ought to be judged, and not by the flighty fancies of poets; neither ought we to be exposed to hear calumnies, save where we have the liberty of replying, and defending ourselves before an adequate tribunal." . . . Cicero makes some further remarks, and concludes the passage by showing that the ancient Romans did not permit any living man to be either praised or blamed on the stage. But the Greeks, as I said, though not so moral, were more logical in allowing this license which the Romans forbade; for they saw that their gods approved and enjoyed the scurrilous language of low comedy when directed not only against men, but even against themselves; and this, whether the infamous actions imputed to them were the fictions of poets, or were their actual iniquities commemorated and acted in the theatres. And would that the spectators had judged them worthy only of laughter, and not of imitation! Manifestly it had been a stretch of pride to spare the good name of the leading men and the common citizens, when the very deities did not grudge that their own reputation should be blemished.

Chapter 10—That the Devils, in Suffering Either False or True Crimes to Be Laid to Their Charge, Meant to Do Men a Mischief

It is alleged, in excuse of this practice, that the stories told of the gods are not true, but false, and mere inventions, but this only makes matters worse, if we form our estimate by the morality our religion teaches; and if we consider the malice of the devils, what more wily and astute artifice could they practice upon men? When a slander is uttered against a leading statesman of upright and useful life, is it not reprehensible in proportion to its untruth and groundlessness? What punishment, then, shall be sufficient when the gods are the objects of so wicked and outrageous an injustice? But the devils, whom these men repute gods, are content that even iniquities they are guiltless of should be ascribed to them, so long as they may entangle men's minds in the meshes of these opinions, and draw them on along with themselves to their predestinated punishment: whether such things were actually committed by the men whom these devils, delighting in human infatuation, cause to be worshipped as gods, and in whose stead they, by a thousand malign and deceitful artifices, substitute themselves, and so receive worship; or whether, though they were really the crimes of men, these wicked spirits gladly allowed them to be attributed to higher beings, that there might seem to be conveyed from heaven itself a sufficient sanction for the perpetration of shameful wickedness. The Greeks, therefore, seeing the character of the gods they served, thought that the poets should certainly not refrain from showing up human vices on the stage, either because they desired to be like their gods in this, or because they were afraid that, if they required for themselves a more unblemished reputation than they asserted for the gods, they might provoke them to anger.

Chapter 11—That the Greeks Admitted Players to Offices of State, on the Ground That Men Who Pleased the Gods Should Not Be Contemptuously Treated by Their Fellows

It was a part of this same reasonableness of the Greeks which induced them to bestow upon the actors of these same plays no inconsiderable civic honors. In the above-mentioned book of the *De Republica*,[2] it is mentioned that Aeschines, a very eloquent Athenian, who had been a tragic actor in his youth, became a statesman, and that the Athenians again and again sent another tragedian, Aristodemus, as their plenipotentiary to Philip. For they

[2] Book IV.

judged it unbecoming to condemn and treat as infamous persons those who were the chief actors in the scenic entertainments which they saw to be so pleasing to the gods. No doubt this was immoral of the Greeks, but there can be as little doubt they acted in conformity with the character of their gods; for how could they have presumed to protect the conduct of the citizens from being cut to pieces by the tongues of poets and players, who were allowed, and even enjoined by the gods, to tear their divine reputation to tatters? And how could they hold in contempt the men who acted in the theatres those dramas which, as they had ascertained, gave pleasure to the gods whom they worshipped? Nay, how could they but grant to them the highest civic honors? On what plea could they honor the priests who offered for them acceptable sacrifices to the gods, if they branded with infamy the actors who in behalf of the people gave to the gods that pleasure or honor which they demanded, and which, according to the account of the priests, they were angry at not receiving. . . .

Chapter 12—That the Romans, by Refusing to the Poets the Same Licence in Respect of Men Which They Allowed Them in the Case of the Gods, Showed a More Delicate Sensitiveness Regarding Themselves Than Regarding the Gods

The Romans, however, as Scipio boasts in that same discussion, declined having their conduct and good name subjected to the assaults and slanders of the poets, and went so far as to make it a capital crime if anyone should dare to compose such verses. This was a very honorable course to pursue, so far as they themselves were concerned, but in respect of the gods it was proud and irreligious: for they knew that the gods not only tolerated, but relished, being lashed by the injurious expressions of the poets, and yet they themselves would not suffer this same handling; and what their ritual prescribed as acceptable to the gods, their law prohibited as injurious to themselves. How then, Scipio, do you praise the Romans for refusing this license to the poets, so that no citizen could be calumniated, while you know that the gods were not included under this protection? Do you count your senate-house worthy of so much higher a regard than the Capitol? Is the one city of Rome more valuable in your eyes than the whole heaven of gods, that you prohibit your poets from uttering any injurious words against a citizen, though they may with impunity cast what imputations they please upon the gods, without the interference of senator, censor, prince, or pontiff? It was, forsooth, intolerable that Plautus or Naevius should attack Publius and Cneius Scipio, insufferable that Caecilius should lampoon Cato; but quite proper that your Terence should encourage youthful lust by the wicked example of supreme Jove.

Chapter 13—That the Romans Should Have Understood That Gods Who Desired to Be Worshipped in Licentious Entertainments Were Unworthy of Divine Honor

But Scipio, were he alive, would possibly reply: "How could we attach a penalty to that which the gods themselves have consecrated? For the theatrical entertainments in which such things are said, and acted, and performed, were introduced into Roman society by the gods, who ordered that they should be dedicated and exhibited in their honor." But was not this, then, the plainest proof that they were no true gods, nor in any respect worthy of receiving divine honors from the republic? Suppose they had required that in their honor the citizens of Rome should be held up to ridicule, every Roman would have resented the hateful proposal. How then, I would ask, can they be esteemed worthy of worship, when they propose that their own crimes be used as material for celebrating their praises? Does not this artifice expose them, and prove that they are detestable devils? Thus the Romans, though they were superstitious enough to serve as gods those who made no secret of their desire to be worshipped in licentious plays, yet had sufficient regard to their hereditary dignity and virtue, to prompt them to refuse to players any such rewards as the Greeks accorded them. On this point we have this testimony of Scipio, recorded in Cicero: "They [the Romans] considered comedy and all theatrical performances as disgraceful, and therefore not only debarred players from offices and honors open to ordinary citizens, but also decreed that their names should be branded by the censor, and erased from the roll of their tribe." An excellent decree, and another testimony to the sagacity of Rome; but I could wish their prudence had been more thorough-going and consistent. For when I hear that if any Roman citizen chose the stage as his profession, he not only closed to himself every laudable career, but even became an outcast from his own tribe, I cannot but exclaim: This is the true Roman spirit, this is worthy of a state jealous of its reputation. But then someone interrupts my rapture, by inquiring with what consistency players are debarred from all honors, while plays are counted among the honors due to the gods? . . . And the whole of this discussion may be summed up in the following syllogism. The Greeks give us the major premise: If such gods are to be worshipped, then certainly such men may be honored. The Romans add the minor: But such men must by no means be honored. The Christians draw the conclusion: Therefore such gods must by no means be worshipped.

Chapter 14—That Plato, Who Excluded Poets from a Well-Ordered City, Was Better Than These Gods Who Desire to Be Honored by Theatrical Plays

We have still to inquire why the poets who write the plays, and who by the law of the twelve tables are prohibited from injuring the good name of the citizens, are reckoned more estimable than the actors, though they so shamefully asperse the character of the gods? Is it right that the actors of these poetical and God-dishonoring effusions be branded, while their authors are honored? Must we not here award the palm to a Greek, Plato, who, in framing his ideal republic, conceived that poets should be banished from the city as enemies of the state? He could not brook that the gods be brought into disrepute, nor that the minds of the citizens be depraved and besotted, by the fictions of the poets. Compare now human nature as you see it in Plato, expelling poets from the city that the citizens be uninjured, with the divine nature as you see it in these gods exacting plays in their own honor. . . . Plato will not suffer poets even to dwell in his city: the laws of Rome prohibit actors from being enrolled as citizens; and if they had not feared to offend the gods who had asked the services of the players, they would in all likelihood have banished them altogether. . . . The gods demand stage-plays in their own honor; the Romans exclude the players from all civic honors; the former commanded that they should be celebrated by the scenic representation of their own disgrace; the latter commanded that no poet should dare to blemish the reputation of any citizen. But that demigod [as he is sometimes regarded] Plato resisted the lust of such gods as these, and showed the Romans what their genius had left incomplete; for he absolutely excluded poets from his ideal state, whether they composed fictions with no regard to truth, or set the worst possible examples before wretched men under the guise of divine actions.

Aelius Donatus   *4th century A.D.*

Comedy and Tragedy   *c. 350*

Comedy employs a story involving the various peculiarities of public and private behavior, which teaches us what is practical in life and what on the contrary is to be avoided. The Greeks define it in this way: "Comedy deals with private and public affairs without entailing danger to life."

Selections. Translated by Charles Gattnig from the 1735 edition of the *Thesaurus Graecarum Antiquitatum*, edited by Jacobo Gronovius (Venice). Copyright 1974 by Charles Gattnig. Printed with permission of the translator.

"Comedy," says Cicero, "is an imitation of life, a mirror of custom, an image of reality. . . ."

There are three types of comedy: (1) *palliata*, in which Greek costume is worn; some call this *tabernaria*; (2) *togata*, so called because of the type of characters; the toga costume is desired; (3) *attellana* is composed of witticisms and jokes which have acquired an elegance through tradition. However, comedy is divided into four parts: prologue, protasis, epitasis, and catastrophe. . . . In the prologue, only the argument is presented. In the protasis the action of the drama is initiated; part of the argument is given as exposition and part held back to develop audience suspense. The epitasis is the continuing development of the conflict and, as I said, the complication of the plot. Catastrophe is the conversion of events into a happy dénouement—a conclusion made clear to the audience by an explanation of what has happened. . . .

Because it is remembered as the oldest style, gleaming white costumes are worn by old men in comedy. Costumes of varied colors are given to young men. Comic slaves wear skimpy outfits either to indicate their former indigence or to allow them to move quickly. Parasites wear convoluted chitons. White clothing is given to happy characters, rags to the unhappy. The rich man wears royal purple, the pauper wears reddish-purple; the soldier receives a purple cloak; and a girl wears a foreign tunic. The pimp is given a multi-colored tunic; saffron-yellow is given to the whore to designate greed. These are called *syrmata*, or costumes with a train, because they are dragged. This custom resulted from the extravagant excesses of the stage. The same costumes on mourning characters appear sloppy because of personal neglect.

Tapestries are also draped on the stage. Their decoration is painted in the style of the Attalic kingdom which was brought to Rome. In place of these, smaller curtains were used in a later period. There is also an act curtain which cuts off the audience and which is used between the acts of the play.

The actors speak the dialogue. The playwright does not arrange the songs. This task is performed by an individual skilled in the art of music. . . . Those who wrote that kind of music put their names at the beginning of the play above the names of the dramatist and the cast.

These songs were written for flutes so that when they were heard, many people could tell which play would be produced before the title was announced to the spectators. Also, the songs were played on "equal" or "unequal" flutes which were either right-handed or left-handed. Because of their solemn tones, the right-handed, Lydian, flutes announced a serious play. The left-handed, Serranian, flutes indicated the joking of comedy with crisp light notes. But when the play called for both right-handed and left-handed flutes, the mixing of jokes and seriousness was announced.

Robert Mannyng
of Brunne *fl. 1288–1338*

Handling Sin *1303*

It is forbid him in the decree,
Miracles for to make or see;
For miracles, if thou begin,
It is a gathering, a sight of sin.
He may in the church, through this reason,
Play the resurrection—
That is to say, how God rose,
God and man in might and loss—
To make men be in belief good
That He rose with flesh and blood;
And he may play, without plight,
How God was born one holy night,
To make men to believe steadfastly
That he alighted in the virgin Mary.
If thou do it in ways or groves,[1]
A sight of sin truly it seems.
Saint Isadore, I take to witness,
For he it said, that such it is;
Thus he said, in his book,
They forsake that they took—
God and their Christendom—
That make such plays to any man
As miracles and bourdes,[2]
Or tournaments of great prize.
These are the pomps that thou forsook
First when thou thy Christendom took.
At the font, said the lewd[3] man,
"I forsake thee here, Satan,
And all thy pomps and all thy works":
This is thy lore, after the clerks.

Selection. From *Robert of Brunne's "Handlyng Synne,"* ed. Frederick J. Furnivall. London: Kegan Paul, Trench, Trübner & Co., Ltd., 1901. Spelling and punctuation modernized by the editor and Edward A. Langhans.

[1] That is, instead of in the church.
[2] Jests.
[3] Wicked.

Hadst thou foreword—aye, certain aye—
When thou makest such a draw?
Against God thou breakest covenant,
And servest thy sire, Termagant.[4]
Saint Isadore said in his writing,
"All those that delight to see such thing,
Or horse or harness lend thereto,
Yet have they guilt of their peril."
    If priest or clerk lend vestment,
That hallowed is through sacrament,
More than other they are to blame;
Of sacrilege they have the fame:
Fame, for they fall in plight,
They should be chastised, therefore, with right.

---

[4] A legendary Moslem deity, represented in medieval plays as a boisterous character.

Dante Alighieri *1265–1321*

Letter to the Lord Can Grande della Scala[1] *c. 1318*

The title of the book[2] is: "Here beginneth the Comedy of Dante Alighieri, a Florentine by birth, but not by character." And for the comprehension of this it must be understood that the word "comedy" is derived from κώμη, village, and ᾠδή, which meaneth song; hence comedy is, as it were, a *village song*. Comedy is in truth a certain kind of poetical narrative that differeth from all others. It differeth from Tragedy in its subject matter—in this way,

Selection. From *A Translation of Dante's Eleven Letters*, by Charles Sterrett Latham. Boston: Houghton Mifflin Co., 1891.

[1] The full title of this letter (the eleventh) is "To the magnificent and victorious lord, the Lord Can Grande della Scala, Vicar General of the Most Holy Roman Empire in the city of Verona and the town of Vicenza."
[2] *The Divine Comedy.*

that Tragedy in its beginning is admirable and quiet, in its ending or catastrophe foul and horrible; and because of this the word "tragedy" is derived
from τράγος, which meaneth *goat*, and ᾠδή. Tragedy is, then, as it were, a
goatish song; that is, foul like a goat, as doth appear in the tragedies of Seneca.
Comedy, indeed, beginneth with some adverse circumstances, but its theme
hath a happy termination, as doth appear in the comedies of Terence. And
hence certain writers were accustomed to say in their salutations in place of
a greeting, "a tragic beginning and a comic ending." Likewise they differ in
their style of language, for Tragedy is lofty and sublime, Comedy, mild and
humble, as Horace says in his *Poetica*, where he concedeth that sometimes
comedians speak like tragedians and conversely:

> Interdum tamen et vocem comoedia tollit,
> Iratusque Chremes tumido delitigat ore;
> Et tragicus plerumque dolet sermone pedestri.[3]

From this it is evident why the present work is called a comedy. For if we
consider the theme, in its beginning it is horrible and foul, because it is Hell;
in its ending, fortunate, desirable, and joyful, because it is Paradise; and if
we consider the style of language, the style is careless and humble, because
it is the vulgar tongue, in which even housewives hold converse. . . .

[3] See p. 69.

Giovanni Boccaccio 1313–1375

The Genealogy
of the Gentile Gods c. 1365

There is further a class of men, recognizable by the golden buckles of their
togas and almost regal decorations, and yet not less remarkable for their
impressive gait and bearing and their fluency of speech. Clients swarm at
their heels, and they are conspicuous and influential men. In reality they are

Selections from Book XIV. From *Boccaccio on Poetry*, by Charles G. Osgood, copyright
© 1930 by Princeton University Press, 1956, by The Liberal Arts Press, Inc., reprinted
by permission of the Liberal Arts Press Division of The Bobbs-Merrill Company, Inc.

eminent teachers of the law, and judges, and, in their proper administration of the law, hold a tight rein on the evil forces that pervert society. Thus by their help innocence is exalted, each man gets just rights, and the State is not only maintained in its natural strength, but, through an increasing tradition of justice, grows stronger and better. These men therefore deserve special reverence and honor.

But wisely as they purge the stains of others, yet are they themselves marked, almost to a man, with one taint—the love of money; they think nothing and nobody deserves approval that is not aglitter with gold. These, I expect, will come along with the rest, to see whether there is not some offence in my work against which they may take the law; and I know perfectly, if they stick to their precedent, what objection they will make. It is their practice, especially during a lull in their duties, to leave bench and court, and join an informal gathering of friends; if, in the course of the conversation, anyone happens to mention poets, they always praise them highly of course, as men of great learning and eloquence. But at length with the honey they mingle poison—not deadly, to be sure. They say poets can hardly be called wise to have spent their whole time following a profession that, after years of labor, yields never a cent. This explains, they add, why poets are always stark poor; they never make brilliant showing with dress, money, nor servants; from this they argue that, because poets are not rich, their profession is good for nothing. Such reasoning along with its unexpressed conclusion, finds easy access to the ears and minds of others, since we are all somewhat given to love of money, and foolishly take wealth to be the greatest thing in the world. . . .

I readily grant therefore their contention, that poetry does not make money, and poets have always been poor—if they can be called poor who of their own accord have scorned wealth. But I do not concede that they were fools to follow the study of poetry, since I regard them as the wisest of men, provided they have, like good Catholics, recognized the true God. . . .

. . . I repeat, poetry certainly never does make one rich, yet I do not admit their claim that it thereby makes for meanness. For money-getting is *not* the function and end of the speculative sciences, but of the applied sciences and finance. Indeed these last aim at nothing else, and, to achieve it quickly, they never render any service absolutely gratis. Likewise the court lawyers, out of their acquaintance with the law and out of the failings of their fellow men, rear offices wherein they fairly coin money with the stamp of a venal tongue, and make gold out of the tears of the wretched by the transmuting power of their own verbosity. But poetry, mindful of its high origin, utterly abhors and rejects such a practice, and if it is to be condemned and despised for this, then Philosophy, mistress of things, who teaches us the causes of all that exists, must sink into low price, or to none at all. The same is true of Theology, by which we attain to a true knowledge of God. I never have heard that *these* sciences implied zeal for the acquisition of wealth. . . .

They say poetry is absolutely of no account, and the making of poetry a useless and absurd craft; that poets are tale-mongers, or, in lower terms, liars; that they live in the country among the woods and mountains because they lack manners and polish. They say, besides, that their poems are false, obscure, lewd, and replete with absurd and silly tales of pagan gods, and that they make Jove, who was, in point of fact, an obscene and adulterous man, now the father of gods, now king of heaven, now fire, or air, or man, or bull, or eagle, or similar irrelevant things; in like manner poets exalt to fame Juno and infinite others under various names. Again and again they cry out that poets are seducers of the mind, prompters of crime, and, to make their foul charge fouler, if possible, they say they are philosophers' apes, that it is a heinous crime to read or possess the books of poets; and then, without making any distinction, they prop themselves up, as they say, with Plato's authority to the effect that poets ought to be turned out-of-doors—nay, out of town, and that the Muses, their mumming mistresses, as Boethius says, being sweet with deadly sweetness, are detestable, and should be driven out with them and utterly rejected. . . . Thus for a long time there have been "poets," if such deserve the name, who, either to get money or popularity, study contemporary fashions, pander to a licentious taste, and at the cost of all self-respect, the loss of all honor, abandon themselves to these literary fooleries. Their works certainly should be condemned, hated, and spurned, as I shall show later. Yet if a few writers of fiction erred thus, poetry does not therefore deserve universal condemnation, since it offers us so many inducements to virtue, in the monitions and teaching of poets whose care it has been to set forth with lofty intelligence, and utmost candor, in exquisite style and diction, men's thoughts on things of heaven. . . .

This poetry, which ignorant triflers cast aside, is a sort of fervid and exquisite invention, with fervid expression, in speech or writing, of that which the mind has invented. It proceeds from the bosom of God, and few, I find, are the souls in whom this gift is born; indeed so wonderful a gift it is that true poets have always been the rarest of men. This fervor of poesy is sublime in its effects: it impels the soul to a longing for utterance; it brings forth strange and unheard-of creations of the mind; it arranges these meditations in a fixed order, adorns the whole composition with unusual interweaving of words and thoughts; and thus it veils truth in a fair and fitting garment of fiction. Further, if in any case the invention so requires, it can arm kings, marshal them for war, launch whole fleets from their docks, nay, counterfeit sky, land, sea, adorn young maidens with flowery garlands, portray human character in its various phases, awake the idle, stimulate the dull, restrain the rash, subdue the criminal, and distinguish excellent men with their proper meed of praise: these, and many other such, are the effects of poetry. . . .

These fine cattle bellow still further to the effect that poets are tale-mongers, or, to use the lower and more hateful term which they sometimes employ in their resentment—liars. No doubt the ignorant will regard such an imputation as particularly objectionable. But I scorn it. The foul language of some men cannot infect the glorious name of the illustrious. Yet I grieve to see these revilers in a purple rage let themselves loose upon the innocent. If I conceded that poets deal in stories, in that they are composers of fiction, I think I hereby incur no further disgrace than a philosopher would in draw-ing up a syllogism. . . .

But, they may object, nature meant this gift for a useful purpose, not for idle nonsense; and fiction is just that—idle nonsense. True enough, if the poet had intended to compose a mere tale. But I have time and time again proved that the meaning of fiction is far from superficial. Wherefore, some writers have framed this definition of fiction (*fabula*): Fiction is a form of discourse, which, under guise of invention, illustrates or proves an idea; and, as its super-ficial aspect is removed, the meaning of the author is clear. If, then, sense is revealed from under the veil of fiction, the composition of fiction is not idle nonsense. Of fiction I distinguish four kinds: The first superficially lacks all appearance of truth; for example, when brutes or inanimate things converse. Aesop, an ancient Greek, grave and venerable, was past master in this form; and though it is a common and popular form both in city and country, yet Aristotle, chief of the Peripatetics, and a man of divine intellect, did not scorn to use it in his books. The sceond kind at times superficially mingles fiction with truth, as when we tell of the daughters of Minyas at their spin-ning, who, when they spurned the orgies of Bacchus, were turned to bats; or the mates of the sailor Acestes, who for contriving the rape of the boy Bac-chus, were turned to fish. This form has been employed from the beginning by the most ancient poets, whose object it has been to clothe in fiction divine and human matters alike; they who have followed the sublimer inventions of the poets have improved upon them; while some of the comic writers have perverted them, caring more for the approval of a licentious public than for honesty. The third kind is more like history than fiction, and famous poets have employed it in a variety of ways. For however much the heroic poets seem to be writing history—as Vergil in his description of Aeneas tossed by the storm, or Homer in his account of Ulysses bound to the mast to escape the lure of the Sirens' song—yet their hidden meaning is far other than ap-pears on the surface. The better of the comic poets, Terence and Plautus, for example, have also employed this form, but they intend naught other than the literal meaning of their lines. Yet by their art they portray varieties of human nature and conversation, incidentally teaching the reader and putting him on his guard. If the events they describe have not actually taken place, yet since they are common, they could have occurred, or might at some time. My opponents need not be so squeamish—Christ, who is God, used this sort of fiction again and again in his parables!

The fourth kind contains no truth at all, either superficial or hidden, since it consists only of old wives' tales.

Now, if my eminent opponents condemn the first kind of fiction, then they must include the account in Holy Writ describing the conference of the trees of the forest on choosing a king. If the second, then nearly the whole sacred body of the Old Testament will be rejected. God forbid, since the writings of the Old Testament and the writings of the poets seem as it were to keep step with each other, and that too in respect to the method of their composition. For where history is lacking, neither one concerns itself with the superficial possibility, but what the poet calls fable or fiction our theologians have named figure. The truth of this may be seen by fairer judges than my opponents, if they will but weigh in a true scale the outward literary semblance of the visions of Isaiah, Ezekiel, Daniel, and other sacred writers on the one hand, with the outward literary semblance of the fiction of poets on the other. If they find any real discrepancy in their methods, either of implication or exposition, I will accept their condemnation. If they condemn the third form of fiction, it is the same as condemning the form which our Savior Jesus Christ, the Son of God, often used when He was in the flesh, though Holy Writ does not call it "poetry," but "parable"; some call it "exemplum," because it is used as such.

I count as naught their condemnation of the fourth form of fiction, since it proceeds from no consistent principle, nor is fortified by the reinforcement of any of the arts, nor carried logically to a conclusion. Fiction of this kind has nothing in common with the works of the poets, though I imagine these objectors think poetry differs from it in no respect.

I now ask whether they are going to call the Holy Spirit, or Christ, the very God, liars, who both in the same Godhead have uttered fictions. I hardly think so, if they are wise. . . .

Such then is the power of fiction that it pleases the unlearned by its external appearance, and exercises the minds of the learned with its hidden truth and thus both are edified and delighted with one and the same perusal. . . .

These cavillers further object that poetry is often obscure, and that poets are to blame for it, since their end is to make an incomprehensible statement appear to be wrought with exquisite artistry; regardless of the old rule of the orators, that a speech must be simple and clear. Perverse notion! Who but a deceiver himself would have sunk low enough not merely to hate what he could not understand, but incriminate it, if he could? I admit that poets are at times obscure. At the same time will these accusers please answer me? Take those philosophers among whom they shamelessly intrude; do they always find their close reasoning as simple and clear as they say an oration should be? If they say yes, they lie; for the works of Plato and Aristotle, to go no further, abound in difficulties so tangled and involved that from their day to the present, though searched and pondered by many a man of keen insight, they have yielded no clear nor consistent meaning. But why do I talk of philosophers? There is the utterance of Holy Writ, of which they especially like to be thought expounders; though proceeding from the Holy Ghost, is it not full to overflowing with obscurities and ambiguities? It is indeed, and for all their denial, the truth will openly assert itself. . . . It seems that obscurities are not confined to poetry. Why then do they not criticise philosophers as well as poets? Why do they not say that the Holy Spirit wove obscure sayings into his works, just to give them an appearance of clever artistry? As if He were not the sublime Artificer of the Universe! . . . They should have realized that when things perfectly clear seem obscure, it is the beholder's fault. To a half-blind man, even when the sun is shining its brightest, the sky looks cloudy. Some things are naturally so profound that not without difficulty can the most exceptional keenness in intellect sound their depths; like the sun's globe, by which, before they can clearly discern it, strong eyes are sometimes repelled. On the other hand, some things, though naturally clear perhaps, are so veiled by the artist's skill that scarcely anyone could by mental effort derive sense from them; as the immense body of the sun when hidden in clouds cannot be exactly located by the eye of the most learned astronomer. That some of the prophetic poems are in this class, I do not deny.

Yet not by this token is it fair to condemn them; for surely it is not one of the poet's various functions to rip up and lay bare the meaning which lies hidden in his inventions. . . .

But I repeat my advice to those who would appreciate poetry, and unwind its difficult involutions. You must read, you must persevere, you must sit up nights, you must inquire, and exert the utmost power of your mind. If one way does not lead to the desired meaning, take another; if obstacles arise, then still another; until, if your strength holds out, you will find that clear which at first looked dark. For we are forbidden by divine command to give that which is holy to dogs, or to cast pearls before swine. . . .

Yet if they will insist that whatever is not literally true is, however uttered, a lie, I accept it for purposes of argument; if not, I will spend no more energy in demolishing this objection of theirs. Rather I will ask them to tell me what name should be applied to those parts of the Revelation of John the Evangelist—expressed with amazing majesty of inner sense, though often at first glance quite contrary to the truth—in which he has veiled the great mysteries of God. And what will they call John himself? . . .

But I do not expect these disturbers to hold their peace here. They will cry out the louder that poets have written many lies about this one true God —whom, as I have just said, they recognize—and on that count deserve to be called liars. Of course I do not doubt that pagan poets had an imperfect sense of the true God, and so sometimes wrote of him what was not altogether true—a lie, as their accusers call it. But for all that I think they should hardly be called liars. There are two kinds of liars: first, those who knowingly and wilfully lie, whether to injure another person or not, or even to help him. These should not be called merely liars, but, more appropriate, "wilful deceivers." The second class are those who have told a falsehood without knowing it. . . . Such are the pagan poets who, with all their knowledge of the Liberal Arts, poetry, and philosophy, could not know the truth of Christianity; for that light of the eternal truth which lighteth every man that cometh into the world had not yet shone forth upon the nations. . . . And if pagan poets wrote not the whole truth concerning the true God, though they thought they did, such ignorance is an acceptable excuse and they ought not to be called liars. . . .

Furthermore my opponents curse the poet and clamor for the extinction of poetry as replete with pranks and adulteries of pagan gods. . . .

But those seductive performances of the gods presented chiefly by comic poets, in whatever way, I neither praise nor commend, but detest, and I hold such writers to be as execrable as the scenes themselves. . . .

But to come now to my main point. The prattle of these reverend judges notwithstanding, poets are not corruptors of morals. Rather, if the reader is prompted by a healthy mind, not a diseased one, they will prove actual stimulators to virtue, either subtle or poignant, as occasion requires. . . .

A few of the enemies of poetry who would outdo the rest in their attack say that poets are but apes of the philosophers. . . . But the ignorant deceive themselves. If they but understood the works of the poets, they would see that, far from being apes, they should be reckoned of the very number of the philosophers, since they never veil with their inventions anything which is not wholly consonant with philosophy as judged by the opinions of the Ancients. And then, too, the pure imitator never sets foot outside his model's track—a fact not observed in poets. For though their destination is the same as that of the philosophers, they do not arrive by the same road. The philosopher, everyone knows, by a process of syllogizing, disproves what he considers false, and in like manner proves his theory, and does all this as obviously as he can. The poet conceives his thought by contemplation, and, wholly without the help of syllogism, veils it as subtly and skilfully as he can under the outward semblance of his invention. The philosopher as a rule employs an unadorned prose style, with something of scorn for literary embellishment. The poet writes in meter, with an artist's most scrupulous care, and in a style distinguished by exquisite charm. It is, furthermore, a philosopher's business to dispute in the lecture-room, but a poet's to sing in solitude. . . .

A mere trifle it seems to these barkers—the exposure of their vain attempt to drive the poets out of the homes and hands of men. For see! they rally and rush to the attack, and flourishing like a weapon the authority of Plato they belch out with hideous roar, that Plato ordered the poets banished from the cities. . . .

I wish my opponents would say whether they think that Plato, in his *Republic*, passed the stricture they mention upon Homer, so that Homer would have been an exile from his ideal city. Whatever they say, I cannot think so, having read so much in praise of Homer. . . . Nay Plato himself calls Homer to witness in the very book of the *Republic* in which he condemns poets, and elsewhere. If then the laws call him the father of virtues, and glory of the law, and if he is claimed as citizen of so many states, and if Plato, our very monitor, cites him to prove a point, isn't it utter folly to think so wise a man as he would have ordered such a poet to be excluded from his commonwealth? . . .

. . . Shall we suppose then, that Plato would have men of such virtue expelled from the state? Blockheads! I could say as much of Horace, and Persius of Volterra, and Juvenal of Aquinum, all to prove that it never entered Plato's mind to expel such men. . . . But let us never suppose the learned man meant what these "interpreters" say he did; for I can only believe that great poets and their kind are to be rightly regarded not as merely citizens of his state and all others, but as the princes and rulers thereof.

But they will spleen and say: "If not these, then what poets would Plato expel?" There is only one answer to such nonsense. Find out for yourselves, you incompetents! To be sure, allowance must be made for ignorance of all sorts. Every art, like every liquor, hath its lees; the lees may be but so much foul draff; yet an art, like a liquor, without lees is cheapened. What, for example, is truer than Philosophy, mistress of all sciences and arts? Yet she hath had as her dregs, so to speak, the Cynics and Epicureans—not to mention any more—who having got themselves tangled up in unspeakable errors, proceeded in various ways to defame her more like enemies than supporters. But shall we say that for the sake of these we must abandon also Socrates, Xenocrates, Anaxagoras, Panetius, and others adorned with the fair title of Philosopher? Such is the way of the knave and the fool! What is holier than the Christian religion? Yet she hath her Donatists, her Macedons, her Fotini, and far worse dregs of heresy than they; and we do not therefore regard Basil, and St. John Chrysostom, and Ambrose, and Pope Leo, and many another holy and reverend man as profane. Thus also poetry, like the other arts, contains likewise its dregs. There have been certain so-called comic poets, who, to be sure, included a few upright men such as Terence and Plautus, but who for the most part defiled the bright glory of poetry with their filthy creations. Even Ovid at times makes one of these. Whether from innate foulness of mind, or greed for money, or desire of popularity, they wrote dirty stories and presented them on the stage, and thus prompted lascivious men to crime, unsettled those who were established in virtue, and weakened the moral order of the whole state. What was worst of all, though the pagan religion was already in other respects reprehensible, yet they seduced various peoples into the practice of such licentious rites that its own disciples had to blush for it. It is such poets, I repeat, that paganism no less than Christianity abhors, and such it is that Plato would banish. Indeed I think they ought to be not expelled, but exterminated. . . .

. . . Amid clamor and discord they flourish the words of the most holy and learned Boethius, particularly those found near the beginning of his book on *Consolation.* It is the point where Philosophy speaks saying: "Who hath let these drabs of the stage approach unto this sick man; for they apply no manner of remedy to his sufferings, but only nurse them with sweet poisons," etc. Thus they shriek in triumph, and fill the place with hubbub, and try with cowardly insult to frighten them who take innocent sport therein. Little do they understand Boethius' words: they consider them only superficially; wherefore they bawl at the gentle and modest Muses, as if they were women in the flesh, simply because their names are feminine. They call them disreputable, obscene, witches, harlots, and, forcing the meaning of Boethius' diminutive, they would push them to the bottom of society, nay in the lowest brothel make them supine to the pleasure of the very dregs of the crowd. From this slander they deduce their contention that poets are dishonorable; for if, according to Boethius, the Muses are lewd, and disreputable, so also must be their familiars, the poets; since friendship and familiarity rest only upon affinity of character, and hence the Muses obviously are close familiars of the poets, as their songs aver, and therefore share their shame. . . . I think it safe to infer from previous demonstration that there are two kinds of poets —one worthy of praise and reverence, always acceptable to good men, the other obscene and detestable, who, I said, should be both expelled and exterminated. Now the same distinction holds of the Muses, of which there is one genus but two species. For though they all enjoy the same power, and are governed by the same laws, yet the fruits of their labors are unlike, since one beareth sweet, the other bitter. Accordingly one may be held in honor, the other in dishonor. The one deserves every title and epithet of praise; she dwells in laurel groves, near the Castalian spring, or in whatsoever places we hold sacred; she is the companion of Phoebus; she goeth forth adorned with garlands of flowers, and graced with the sweet sound of voices in song. The other is she who is seduced by disreptable comic poets to mount the stage, preempt theatres and street-corners: and there for a fee she calmly exhibits herself to loungers in low compositions, destitute of a single commendable grace. It is not hers to relieve or heal the sufferings of those who languish, with the consolations of goodness, and with holy remedies of salvation; she only enhances their suffering even unto death amid groans and complaints, and strangles them in the toils of sensual delight. Hence these poet-haters may learn what they were too stupid to see, that when Boethius called the Muses drabs of the stage, he spoke only of theatrical Muses.

Anonymous

A Sermon against Miracle Plays *late 14th century*

Know thee, Christian men, that as Christ, God, and man is both way, truth, and life, as saith the Gospel of John—way to the erring, truth to the unknowing and doubting, life to the striving to heaven and wearying—so Christ did nothing to us but effectually in way of mercy, in truth of righteousness, and in life of yielding everlasting joy for our continually mourning and sorrowing in this vale of tears. In miracles, therefore, that Christ did here in earth—other[1] in Himself, other[1] in his saints—were so effectual and in earnest done, that to sinful men that erred, they brought forgiveness of sin, setting them in the way of right relief; to doubtful men not steadfast, they brought in cunning[2] to better please God, and very[3] hope in God to be steadfast in Him; and to them weary of the way of God, for the great penance and sufferance of the tribulation that men must have therein, these brought in love of burning charity, to which all things [are] light, and He to suffer death, the which men most dread, for the everlasting life and joy that men most love

Selections. From *Reliquiae Antiquae*, Vol. II, ed. Thomas Wright and James Orchard Halliwell. London: William Pickering, 1843. Spelling and punctuation modernized by the editor and Edward A. Langhans.

[1] Other . . . other = either . . . or.
[2] Knowledge.
[3] True.

and desire, of the which thing very hope putteth away all weariness here in the way of God. Then, since miracles of Christ and of his saints were thus effectual, as by our belief we are in certain, no man should use in bourde[4] and play the miracles and works that Christ so earnestly wrought to our help; for whoever so doth, he erreth in the belief, reverseth Christ, and scorneth God. He erreth in the belief, for in that he taketh the most precious works of God in play and bourde, and so taketh His name in idle,[5] and so misuseth our belief. Ah! Lord! since an earthly servant dare not take in play and in bourde that their earthly lord taketh in earnest, much more we should not make our play and bourde of those miracles and works that God so earnestly wrought to us; for soothly,[6] when we do so, dread to sin is taken away, as a servant when he bourdeth with his master loseth his dread to offend him, namely, when he bourdeth with his master in that that his master taketh in earnest. And right as a nail smitten in holdeth two things together, so dread smitten to Godward holdest and sustaineth our belief to Him. Therefore, right as playing and jesting of the most earnestful works of God taketh away the dread of God that men should have in the same, so it taketh away our belief and so our most help of our salvation. And since taking away of our belief is more vengeance-taking than sudden taking away of our bodily life, and when we take in bourde and play the most earnestful works of God, as be his miracles, God taketh away from us His grace of meekness, dread, reverence, and of our belief; then, when we play his miracles as men do nowadays, God taketh more vengeance on us than a lord that suddenly slayeth his servant for he played too homely[7] with him; and right as that lord then indeed sayeth to his servant, "play not with me, but play with thy peer," so when we take in play and in bourde the miracles of God, He from us taking His grace, sayeth more earnestfully to us than the foresaid lord, "play not with Me, but play with thy peer." Therefore, such miracle playing reverseth Christ: first, in taking to play that that He took into most earnest; the second, in taking to miracles of our flesh, of our lust, and of our five wits, that that God took to the bringing in of His bitter death, and to teaching of penance-doing, and to fleeing of feeding of our wits, and to mortifying of them. . . .

But here again is they saying that they play these miracles in the worship of God, and so did not these Jews that bobbed[8] Christ? Also, often since by such miracle playing be men converted to good living, as men and women, seeing in miracle playing that the devil, by their array, by the which they move each another to lechery and to pride, make them his servants [in order] to bring themselves and many others to hell, and to have far more villainy

---

[4] Jest.
[5] Vain.
[6] Truly.
[7] Familiarly.
[8] Struck. Perhaps a reference to John 10:31–42.

hereafter by their proud array here than they have worshiped here, and seeing, furthermore, that all this worldly being here is but vanity for a while, as is miracle playing, wherefore they leave their pride and take to them afterward the meek conversation of Christ and of his saints, and so miracle playing turneth men to the belief, and not perverteth. Also, often since by such miracle playing men and women, seeing the passion of Christ and of his saints, are moved to compassion and devotion, weeping bitter tears, then they be not scorning of God but worshiping. Also, profitable to men and to the worship of God it is to fulfill and seek all the means by the which men see sin and [be drawn] to virtues; and since as there be men that only by earnestful doing will be converted to God, so there be other men that will be converted to God by games and play; and nowadays, men be not converted by the earnestful doing of God nor of men, then now it is time and skillful to assay to convert the people by play and games, as by miracle playing and other manner [of] mirths. Also, some recreation men must have, and better it is, or less evil, that they have their recreation by playing of miracles than by playing of other japes. Also, since it is leaveful to have the miracles of God painted, why is [it] not as well leaveful to have the miracles of God played, since men must better read the will of God and his marvelous works in the playing of them than in the painting, and better they be held in men's minds and oftener rehearsed by the playing of them than by the painting, for this is a dead book, the other a quick.

To the first reason, we answer, saying that such miracle playing is not to the worship of God, for they be done more to be seen of the world and to please to the world than to be seen by God or to please to him; as Christ never exampled them, but only heathen men that evermore dishonored God, saying that to the worship of God, that is to the most villainous of them, therefore, as the wickedness of the misbelief of heathen men lieth to themselves when they say that the worshiping of their maumetry[9] is to the worship of God, so men's lechery nowadays to have their own lust lieth to themselves, when they say that such miracle playing is to the worship of God. For Christ saith that folk of adultery seek such sinnings, as a lecher seeketh signs of very love, but no deeds of very love; so, since these miracle playings be only signs of love without deeds, they be not only contrarious to the worship of God— that is, both in sign and in deed—but also they be beginnings of the devil to catch men to believe of Anti-Christ, as words of love without very deeds be beginnings of the lecher to catch fellowship to fulfilling of his lechery. Both for these miracle playings be very leasings,[10] as they be signs without deeds, and for they be very idleness, as they take the miracles of God in idle after their own lust, and certainly idleness and leasings be the most begin-

---

[9] Idolatary.
[10] Lies.

nings of the devil to draw men to the belief of Anti-Christ, and therefore to priests it is utterly forbidden not only to be a miracle player, but also to hear or to see miracle playing, lest he that should be the gin[11] of God to catch men and to hold men in the belief of Christ, they be made otherwise by hypocrisy the gin of the devil to catch men to the belief of Anti-Christ. . . .

And as anent the second reason, we say that just as a virtuous deed is otherwhile[12] occasion of evil, as was the passion of Christ to the Jews, but not occasion given but taken of Him, so evil deeds be occasion of good deeds otherwhile, as was the sin of Adam occasion of the coming of Christ, but not occasion given of the sin, but occasion taken of the great mercy of God, [in] the same wise miracle playing, albeit that it be sin, is otherwhile occasion of converting of men, but as it is sin, it is far more occasion of perverting of men, not only of one single person but a whole community, as it maketh all a people to be occupied in vain against this hest[13] of the Psalter Book, that saith to all men, and namely to priests that each day read it in their service, "Turn away my eyes that they see not vanities," and after, "Lord, Thou hatest all waiting vanities." How then may a priest play in interludes, or give himself to the sight of them? since it is forbidden him so expressly by the foresaid hest of God, namely, since he curseth each day in his service all those that bow[14] away from the hests of God; but alas! more harm is, priests nowadays must shrew[15] themselves and all day, as many that all day crieth, "what, shrew!" shrewing themselves. Therefore, miracle playing, since it is against the hest of God, that biddeth that thou shalt not take God's name in idle, it is against our belief, and so it may not give occasion of turning men to the belief but of perverting; and therefore, many men ween[16] that there is no hell of everlasting pain, but that God doth but threaten us and not to do it in deed, as be playing of miracles in sign and not in deed. . . . So then, these men that say, "play we a play of Anti-Christ and of the day of doom, that some man may be converted thereby," fall into the heresy of them that reverse the apostle and say, "do we evil things that there come good things," of whom, as saith the apostle, damning is rightful.[17]

By this we answer to the third reason, saying that such miracle playing giveth no one occasion of very weeping and needful, but the weeping that falleth to men and women by the sight of such miracle playing, as they do not principally for their own sins nor of their good faith within sorrow, but more of their sight without. Sorrow is not allowable before God, but more reprovable; for since Christ himself reproved the women that wept upon Him

[11] Device.
[12] Sometimes.
[13] Command.
[14] Bend.
[15] Curse.
[16] Believe.
[17] Paul, in Rom. 3:8.

in His passion, much more they be reprovable that weep for the play of Christ's passion, leaving to weep for the sins of themselves and of their children, as Christ bade the women that wept on him.

And by this we answer to the fourth reason, saying that no man may be converted to God but only by the earnestful doing of God, and by no vain playing; for that that the word of God worketh not, nor his sacraments, how should playing work, that is of no virtue but full of defaults? Therefore, just as the weeping that men weep often in such plays commonly is false, witnessing that they love more the liking of their body and of prosperity of the world than liking in God and prosperity of virtue in the soul, and therefore, having more compassion of pain than of sin, they falsely weep for lacking of bodily prosperity more than for lacking of ghostly, as do damned men in hell; just so often since the converting that men seem to be converted by such playing is but feigned holiness, worse than is other sin beforehand. For if he were verily converted, he should hate to see all such vanities, as biddeth the hest of God, albeit that of such play he take occasion by the grace of God to flee sin and to follow virtue. . . . The priests that say themselves holy, and busy themselves about such plays, be very hypocrites and liars; and hereby we answer to the fifth reason, saying, that very recreation is leaveful[18] occupying in false works [in order] to more ardently working greater works; and therefore such miracle playing nor the sight of them is no very recreation, but false and worldy, as proved [by] the deeds of the authors of such plays, that yet never tasted verily sweetness in God, travailing so much therein that their body would not suffice to bear such a travail of the spirit; but as man goeth from virtue [into] virtue, so they go from lust into lust, that they more steadfastly dwell in them, and therefore as this feigned recreation of playing of miracles is false conceit, so it is double shrewdness,[19] worse than [if] they played pure vanities. . . . And if men ask what recreation men should have on the holiday after their holy contemplation in the church, we say to them two things, one, that if he had verily occupied him in contemplation before, neither he would ask that question nor have wish to see vanity; another, we say that his recreation should be in works of mercy to his neighbor, and in delighting [himself] in all good communications with his neighbor, as before he delighted [himself] in God, and in all other needful works that reason and kind ask. And to the last reason, we say that painting, if it be verily without meaning of leasings, and not curious to much feeding [of] men's wits and not occasion of maumetry to the people, they be but as naked letters to a clerk to read the truth; but so be not miracle playing, that be made more to delight men bodily than to be books to lewd men, and therefore, if they be quick books, they be quick books to shrewdness more than to goodness. Good men,

---

[18] Permissibly.
[19] Harmfulness.

therefore, seeing their time short do occupy [themselves] in good, earnest works, and seeing the day of the reckoning nearing fast, and unknowing when they shall go hence, flee all such idleness, hying, that they were with their spouse Christ in the bliss of Heaven. . . .

But peradventure here thou sayest that if playing of miracles be sin, [nevertheless] it is but little sin. But herefore, dear friend, know thee that each sin, be it never so little, if it be maintained and preached as good and profitable, is deadly sin; and therefore saith the prophet, "Woe to them that see good, evil, and evil, good!"[20] and therefore the wise man damneth them that gladden when they do evil; and therefore all saints say that humanish it is to fall, but devilish it is to abide still therein. Therefore, since this miracle playing is sin, as thou acknowledgest, and is steadfastly maintained, and also men delight them therein, no doubt but that it is deadly sin, and damnable, devilish not humanish. . . .

. . . Such miracle playing nowadays witnesseth three things: first, is great sin before thee; second, it witnesseth great folly in the doing; and the third, great vengeance after; for just as the children of Israel, when Moses was in the hill busily praying for them, they—mistrusting him—honored a calf of gold, and afterward ate and drank and rose to play, and afterwards were slain of them three and twenty thousand of men; so then, as this playing witnessed the sin of their maumetry before, and their mistrust to Moses when they should have trusted to him, and after their folly in their playing, and the third the vengeance that came after, so this miracle playing is verily witness of men's avarice and covetousness before, that is maumetry, as saith the apostle,[21] for that that they should spend upon the needs of their neighbors, they spend upon the plays, and to pay their rent and their debts they will grouch, and to spend twice so much upon their play they will nothing grouch. . . . So, since nowadays much of the people worshipeth and praiseth only the likeness of the miracles of God as much as the word of God in the preacher's mouth by the which all miracles be done, no doubt that the people do more maumetry now in such miracle playing than did the people of Israel that time in herrying[22] of the calf, inasmuch as the leasings and lusts of miracle playing that men worship in them is more contrarious to God, and more according with the devil, than was that golden calf that the people worshiped. And therefore . . . in such miracle playing the devil is most pleased, as the devil is best paid to deceive men in the likeness of that thing in which by God man were converted beforehand, and in which the devil was denied beforehand.

[20] Isa. 5:20.
[21] Paul, in Col. 3:5.
[22] Worshiping.

Renaissance Italy

The influence of Aristotle's *Poetics* on Renaissance writers started in 1536. That year, Alessandro Pazzi published a good Latin translation and Bernardino Daniello published his own *Poetics*, strongly influenced by Aristotle (and Horace too). Also influenced by these Greek and Roman theorists is Giraldi Cinthio, an important tragic dramatist who, however, sometimes rejects classical precepts if they do not harmonize with his own ideas. Although he approves of the five-act structure, for instance, he rejects the Aristotelian disapproval of double plots. The question of what was later called Unity of Time—based on Aristotle's statement that the action of a tragedy should occur during a single circuit of the sun (as it revolves around the earth, of course) or slightly more—is first raised by Cinthio, who fails to take a clear stand.

Robortellus does, however, restrictively asserting moreover that this means the artificial day of twelve hours rather than the natural day of twenty-four. Thoroughly Aristotelian, Robortellus applies to comedy the terms of Aristotle's analysis of tragedy. His synthesis of traditional theories of comedy (he contributes nothing new) made Robortellus one of the leading authorities on the subject in the Renaissance. Like Robortellus, Trissino analyzes comedy and tragedy in Aristotelian terms. His critical writing—as well as his play *Sofonisba* (1515), the first play in the vernacular in Western Europe to be cast in the tragic mold of the ancients—also reflects the influence of Seneca, whose sententious sayings were greatly admired in the Renaissance.

One of the most influential scholars of the Renaissance, Julius Caesar Scaliger regards Aristotle as a virtual dictator of poetry. Although the beginning of Aristotle's influence in Europe is due in large part to him, Scaliger himself feels free to differ from the Stagirite (according to the Italian, the end of poetry, for example, should include the Horatian ideal of instruction). On the basis of verisimilitude, Scaliger argues that the dramatic time of a play should be as concise as possible. A restricted place, which he only implies, is a consequence of restricted time, since (according to him) it is unreasonable for an audience to believe one could travel far in a short space of time. Though sometimes incorrectly called "Scaligerian," the three unities (of action, time, and place) are not mentioned by Scaliger but are formulated for the first time by Castelvetro, who though he disagrees with Scaliger on some important matters (character, for one) agrees with him that the basis of stage illusion is verisimilitude. Indeed, Castelvetro's unities, which he insists are inviolable laws of the drama, derive from verisimilitude.

Despite Horatian and Ciceronian injunctions against mixing genres, classical precedents in playwriting (satyr plays, happy endings in some tragedies of Euripides, and serious elements in comedies of Terence) and loopholes in both Aristotle and Horace helped provide academic justification for the mixed genre, tragicomedy. The name itself was used facetiously by Plautus, who in his *Amphitrion* has Mercury so label that play because a slave mingles with kings and gods. Guarini—author of one of the most popular and influential pastoral tragicomedies of the Renaissance, *The Faithful Shepherd*—argues in his *Compendium of Tragicomic Poetry* that tragicomedy is not merely one of the two component genres spoiled by the other, and he attempts to justify it as a separate, distinct, and legitimate genre.

Giovambattista Giraldi Cinthio 1504–1573

Discourse on Comedies and Tragedies 1543

There are many [ancient] comedies in which the action occurs in more than one day; e.g., Terence's *The Self-Tormenter*. In tragedy . . . it is obvious (unless I am mistaken) in the treatment of Euripides' *Heracles* that the action of the plot can only be developed with the greatest difficulty in merely one day. . . . It seems to me that more than the space of one day is needed. But the more learned (and I don't want to argue with anyone) claim [from Aristotle] that the action should occur in the space of one day.

In one respect the two plots [comedy and tragedy] resemble each other: they have a common purpose in that both attempt to inculcate good morals. However, while they have the same goal, their methods are different. Comedy exists without terror and without commiseration (because there are no interruptions of deaths or other terrible accidents; on the contrary, comedy seeks to bring about its conclusion through pleasure and with some funny jokes). And whether it has a happy ending or an unhappy one, tragedy— through the representation of extreme suffering and terrifying events— purges the spectators of vices and inculcates good morals. . . .

Although both comedy and tragedy are alike in that both employ a plot, nevertheless some people insist that the plot of tragedy must be taken from history and that of comedy must be fabricated by the poet. It seems that an adequate explanation can be given for such a distinction: comedy is drawn from matters affecting citizens and ordinary people, whereas tragedy has its source in illustrious and royal events. The former is concerned with citizens; the latter presents kings and great personages. Tragedy, then, would seem to break the rule of verisimilitude, because such personages, being in the eyes of the world, cannot perform any singular act which, as soon as it is done, is not heard by everyone. Thus, since tragic plots expose renowned events in order to describe the persons who are responsible for them, it does not seem that such happenings can be produced on the stage without their having been known before. But it is easy to fabricate the actions of citizens because the news of them does not usually spread beyond

Selections. Translated by Charles Gattnig from the 1554 edition. Copyright 1974 by Charles Gattnig. Printed with permission of the translator.

their own homes, and they are soon forgotten. Therefore, the poet has a wide area for fabricating whatever he wishes in order to bring new comic plots to the stage. However sound this logic may seem, nevertheless I propose that the poet can fabricate the tragic plot in the same way as he does the comic plot. Aristotle, always judicious, concedes this argument in several passages of his *Poetics*. . . . Also, it seems to me that reason can direct us quite sufficiently in this matter. Since the power of evoking the tragic emotions depends only on imitation which does not depart from the verisimilar, and since cold facts by themselves do not excite the emotions without rhythmical and appropriate language, it appears to me that it is in the poet's power to rouse at his will the tragic emotions in tragedy. He invents an action which, consistent with natural behavior, is not far removed from what can and usually does occur. And perhaps, because of the fabrication, the emotions are persuaded all the more to the inculcation of good morals since the invented plot calls greater attention to itself for being new in the minds of the audience, for the spectator, knowing that he cannot understand the plot of a play without seeing it presented, as soon as he has had an inkling of a plot which seems cleverly constructed, finds his attention aroused and is anxious not to miss a word of the play. . . . That an invented plot has this power has been demonstrated by the experience of my *Orbecche* (such as it is) every time it has been produced (. . . I mention this not to pat myself on the back but to verify my argument with a very recent example). Not only new spectators, but even those who returned each time it was presented were not able to hold back gasps and tears.[1] . . .

At this point, it should be noted that although double tragedies are not held in high esteem by Aristotle (however much others may disagree), nevertheless, the double plot is often acclaimed in comedy: witness how this very aspect of Terence's plots has made his plays extremely successful. I call that plot "double" when its action describes characters who belong to the same social grouping but exhibit different personalities; e.g., two lovers of different intellects, two old men with opposing dispositions, two servants with contrasting moral proclivities, etc. Such characters can be found in the *Andria,* and in other plots by the same playwright, where it is clear that such combinations offer the best solution to unraveling difficult complications of the plot. And I propose that if this double structure is correctly imitated in tragedy by a skilled poet, i.e., if the conflict he selects does not cause confusion, he will succeed as surely as he would in comedy (with all due respect to Aristotle). If there have been those who have supported this argument and have disagreed with Aristotle, they should not (I believe)

---

[1] Cinthio seems to contradict himself by claiming (a) that a play is more interesting when the story is unknown and (b) that spectators who saw his play several times were captivated each time [translator's note].

be criticized, especially if the tragedy has a happy ending—which makes it consonant with the ending of comedy. In this instance, then, the imitation of the action of both tragedy and comedy can be similar. . . .

Returning to our proposition: I say that just as great and royal characters convene in tragedy so are commonfolk gathered in comedy, as we said above. And however varied the actions of one or the other may be (though both comic and tragic plots aim at the same end, i.e., to inculcate good morals), they produce this effect differently. For tragedy, with horror and compassion showing what must be avoided, purges us of the obsessions which have trapped the tragic characters. But comedy's function is to imitate with passions and moderate sentiments mixed with games, with laughter and facetious jokes, in order to show us the right way to live.

Of the two types [of tragedy] one ends in sorrow. The other kind—which has a happy ending—does not lack terror-filled events and compassionate responses, because tragedy, however cunningly devised, cannot be made without events which inspire terror and compassion. Plautus referred to this mode of tragedy (to which Aristotle assigns the name "mixed") in the prologue of his *Amphitrion* when he said in his play that common men were mixed with the great and royal. However, he took this concept from the *Poetics* in which Aristotle speaks of this type of tragedy. Because of its cheerful ending, its very nature is more enjoyable to the spectators. In this mode of tragedy, the cognizance, or the recognition, which is what I mean, of the characters is especially appropriate.[2] Through this recognition they escape the dangers and deaths which arouse our horror and compassion. And among all the recognitions about which Aristotle instructs us (for it does not seem pertinent to speak of all of them now), the one which is praised more than the others is the change of fortune from a state of suffering to a state of happiness, as we will explain later. But this famous type of recognition is as suitable to tragedy with a happy ending as it is to one with an unhappy ending; it produces the opposite effect in the latter, i.e., it makes the happy become miserable and changes friends to enemies.

Of the Romans, Seneca never tried his hand at writing tragedies with happy dénouements, but dedicated himself only to those with serious resolutions. He did so with such excellence that in almost all his tragedies (so it seems to me) he surpassed in prudence, seriousness, dignity, majesty, and sententious sayings all the Greeks who ever wrote. However, his style could have been more clean cut and refined than it was. In spite of this, and to be more in tune with the times, I have composed some plays in this likeness [tragedy with a happy dénouement], e.g., *Altile, Selene, Antivalomeni,* and others, because the spectators demand them and they are more suc-

[2] See the *Poetics*, chap. 11 [translator's note].

cessful in the theatre. Though Aristotle claims that this is to pander to the ignorance of the spectators, and though many support his position, I have held that it is better to satisfy with a non-Aristotelian concept the audience for whose pleasure the play is produced, than to antagonize them by offering a stuffy work. There is little satisfaction in writing a play which, while adhering to academic standards, ends up being a failure in production. Those terrible plays (which seem to insult the esthetic sensibilities of the spectators) may be more appropriate as closet dramas; those with happy endings belong on the stage. . . .

You should know that tragedies which end happily are much better suited to intricate plot complications and are more successful when double than those which end unhappily; the latter are much better simple rather than double. By "simple" I do not mean the opposite of complex; rather, I refer to those plots whose action does not depend on pairs of characters with contrasting personality traits. . . .

In comedy, the dialogue of the characters should be so like familiar conversation that it seems exactly like the speech of friends and relatives, if they were to talk about such things. . . . The metrical lines in comedy should imitate the language of the citizenry, and those in tragedy the speech of the great and royal.

However, in comedies the verses used should be entirely without rhymes, for rhymed verses are more foreign to ordinary speech than any others, carrying with them more profound thought than those without rhymes. On the contrary, rhymes belong in certain parts of tragedy, as in the dialogue of characters and especially in the choral sections. Here, regular and irregular rhymes can be mixed for more effective harmony. I refer, however, to the choral odes which divide one act from the other, and not the chorus which appears with the actors, because then only one member of the chorus speaks and not the ensemble. . . .

Rhymes are also appropriate in tragedy in the ethical and emotional parts which are introduced either to motivate compassion or to show unexpected cheerfulness, for pleasant emotions and persuasive maxims can sometimes be expressed with similar verses in order that they may be received more easily in the mind of the listener. But this is not so essential that it cannot be omitted without reproach. The other parts of tragedy should be composed of complete verses without rhymes. . . .

The Romans insisted that a play be divided into five acts. They demanded that the argument should be contained in the first act. In the second, the conflicts contained in the argument begin to move to their conclusion. In the third come the obstacles and the complications. The fourth act begins to offer a way of resolving the troubles. The fifth act brings the desired dénouement with a proper solution for the whole argument. This outline is useful only for comedy, but with the necessary changes it can also be functional for tragedy. And this division has been common to both comedy and tragedy, even though others have interpreted that passage differently.

Franciscus Robortellus 1516–1567

On Comedy 1548

Comedy has the same purpose that all other kinds of poems have, to imitate the characters and actions of men. And since all poetic imitation is accomplished by three means, speech, rhythm, and harmony, these three have come to be used in Comedy, but separately, one after the other, not all together as in some other forms. This practice, however, it has in common with Tragedy, as Aristotle explains in the *Poetics*. Comedy differs, moreover, from other forms in the subject matter which it treats; for it imitates the actions of the lower, meaner people, and therefore differs from Tragedy, which imitates the better sort of people, as Aristotle also shows. . . .

The parts of Comedy are those which belong to the essence and can be called the essentials and those which belong to the quantity and can be called the parts that determine the magnitude. And first let us speak of the essentials.

These essentials are five or, as some reason, six in number: Plot, Character, Thought, Diction, Spectacle, Music. Aristotle allows just so many in the *Poetics*. As practice has demonstrated, no comedy can be recited if the Music and Spectacle are not employed so that the play on the stage appears to be enacted in city or town. Therefore these parts, Music and Spectacle, are necessary. The other parts are much more necessary, because without them Comedy cannot even be written. In composing a comedy it is first necessary to invent the matter which is to be written; this comprises the Plot (*fabula*). But, on the other hand, the Plot, because

Selections, translated by Marvin T. Herrick. From Marvin T. Herrick, *Comic Theory in the Sixteenth Century*. Urbana: University of Illinois Press, 1964. Copyright 1950 by the Board of Trustees of the University of Illinois. Reprinted by permission of the publisher.

it imitates, must bring out Character (*mores*) and accurately express the manners of diverse people. Therefore another part, Character, is necessary. Not every speech expresses Character, as, for example, speeches in mathematics, medicine, physiology, dialectics. Since it is necessary to express thoughts by means of speech (*oratio*), it is therefore necessary to add another part, Thought (*sententia*). But since Thought consists of words, it is necessary to add yet another part, Diction (*dictio*). One who is going to write Comedy properly should pay heed to all these parts; but let us speak of each one by one.

The comic play ought to represent low, trifling matter; for this very reason it differs from Tragedy. Moreover, it should imitate not many but merely one simple action which can be completed within a single circuit of the sun, as Aristotle most learnedly advises in the *Poetics*, where he talks about the tragic play. I suppose I ought to repeat that a single circuit of the sun is not what the mathematicians generally call the natural day but rather the artificial day;[1] I have fully said this is my commentary on the *Poetics*.

The Plot ought to have magnitude and order. Magnitude distinguishes it from extemporaneous poems and from short ones. Order makes all the parts fit together; on the one hand, it should not be ended just anywhere, as though thoughtlessly, nor should it begin just anywhere. There is a very definite rule for fixing the limits of magnitude in any plot, namely, that in managing the single action it extend just so far as is meet, that is, so long as it seems to be more pleasing, and as I shall briefly describe. The right magnitude of a comic plot is whatever is necessary to make plain the change and interchange of disturbances and quarrels. All the parts of the plot, indeed, ought to be so joined together that no part can be taken away or transplanted without ruining or disjoining the whole plot.

Further, the names of all comic characters should be fictitious. This is not done in Tragedy because Tragedy uses stories of the more pitiful events that have befallen certain well-known people, whose names must be declared. Comedy, however, feigns in a verisimilar manner and therefore, as Aristotle very clearly informs us in the *Poetics*, invents its names.

The plot ought not to be episodic, for such a plot is faulty. I call that plot episodic in which many things are inserted over and above the one action that was set up in the beginning—what was done in the ancient contests by unskilled poets so that the play would appear longer and give more pleasure. Since the imitation in Comedy is not only of low and trifling affairs, such as take place in the private actions of people, but also of disturbances, there should also be present that which is taken from the nature and custom of human actions, which always have in them

---

[1] That is, not twenty-four hours (the natural day) but twelve hours (the artificial day).

something troublesome or distressing. It is necessary to intermingle those things which are beyond our hope and expectation, such accidental events as bring unexpected joy, or grief, or wonder.

We say, therefore, that there are two kinds of comic plots: some are simple, others complex; and such, moreover, are the actions which they imitate. Simple actions are those which have nothing unexpected and contain no Discovery. Complex actions contain either one or both of these devices. Discovery occurs when we are led from ignorance to knowledge of some matter, out of which springs either grief or joy—nearly always joy, for Discoveries are, with good reason, placed in the last part of a comedy, where the disturbance in affairs begins to subside. An example of this sort can be drawn from the *Andrian* of Terence, and from many others in which there is Discovery.

There are five kinds of Discovery. The first is by means of signs, of which some are inborn and others accidental. These may be again divided into two classes, for they are either on the body, such as scars and birthmarks, or outside, such as necklaces. Some of the signs are of the better sort, some of the worse; some are artifiical, others inartificial. Artificial signs are those which are invented by the poet himself. Inartificial signs are those in the material itself and already at hand in the plot. We call those signs inborn which have customarily been atrributed to the habits of the characters—such as the club and lion's skin of Hercules. The second kind of Discovery occurs through memory: when, upon beholding something, the remembrance of something similar comes to mind and we acknowledge a likeness by means of a likeness. The third kind of Discovery is by means of inevitable reasoning: e.g., since we know that a certain man is like only one other person in the city, when we see one like this other person we therefore infer that he is this certain man. Another rational Discovery, the fourth kind, is effected by a paralogism; this is a fallacy derived from a false foundation, as is a paralogism in dialectic. A fifth kind of Discovery is that which arises from conjectured likenesses more carefully considered and brought together.

Let these remarks, in short, suffice for Discovery; we have spoken more fully in our commentary on Aristotle's *Poetics*.

One ought not to proceed to write a comic play at random; rather, one ought to have a sure plan and method such as Aristotle describes. First, the poet should establish the plot, which should be set down in few words and put before his eyes so that he can readily see what is appropriate and what is not, just as the spectator does while the play is acted on stage. The language which he uses to unfold the plot should be clear and plain so that he may perceive contradictions if they have appeared; the greatest part of the mistakes committed by bad and unskilled poets proceeds from these contradictions. When the poet has set down the substance of the whole matter in this way, he should invent names for his matter which should be appropriate. Afterwards the poet should provide the episodes and set them in place. Episodes enrich the poem, embellish and enlarge the action. What these episodes are I might have explained with some examples from Terentian and Plautine plots, nor more clearly but at greater length. Therefore it has seemed enough if I explained everything in few words, omitting examples.

In the art of writing Comedy it is important to recognize that its duration is limited by two goals, namely dénouement and complication. All that extends from the beginning of the play to the point where the bustle of affairs turns and a change takes place is called the complication, as I have related above. That part which extends from the beginning of the change to the end of the play is called the dénouement. He who will keep these things before his eyes will both readily judge the writings of the ancient poets and will himself write Comedy in an easier fashion. But let this be enough about Plot; now we shall discuss Character.

Four things should be considered in Character. First, one should see to it that goodness and badness are presented in the several kinds of people. If somebody is good, then the character assigned him should be good. Character is expressed by speech and by action, for we know from his speech and action whether some one is good or bad. This should be observed for all kinds of people, for it often happens that a trait which is praiseworthy in one person is not appropriate in another; persons may admit of great differences. Grant me that a certain slave is not a thief, and this is supreme merit and goodness in a slave; in a man of honor it is no commendation. To weave nicely, to embroider, to spin are commendable in a woman; these things ought not to be esteemed in a man. There is an old tale that Philip of Macedon rebuked Alexander when he once surprised his son singing in the midst of professional singers; such behaivor, as it were, was not sufficiently becoming in a king. It was considered a blemish in Nero that he was a trained singer, in Commodus that he shot and wrestled well. Therefore praises becoming to men of low birth are not praises if ascribed to men of higher breeding. The character of a servant, if applied to a gallant gentleman, would not only lower the gentleman, but even make him bad. Whence it is evident that what was the highest goodness in a servant is a very great vice in the master.

Second, what is requisite in Character is "appropriateness" (τὸ ἁρμόττον). As strength of body is certainly a very great virtue; if it be attributed to a woman, however, and if some poet or other portrays a woman in the same way Homer portrays Achilles, he would be severely censured.

Third, Character ought to be what Aristotle, in the *Poetics*, calls "like the reality" (τὸ ὅμοιον); that is to say, the imitation of character in any role should be expressed according to his traditional reputation and the common opinion of mankind. For then this τὸ ὅμοιον is preserved when a poet introduces somebody acting and speaking as people know he is accustomed to act and speak. For example, we know that Achilles was fierce and ruthless, and everybody thinks of him as so. Therefore he ought to be portrayed as such. The ancients report that Ulysses was shrewd and crafty. Therefore he is to be portrayed in this way. For a full treatment of this matter see Horace's *Epistle to Augustus.*

Fourth, it is necessary to make Character "consistent" (τὸ ὁμαλόν); characters should be consistent throughout the poem. If you once show somebody as cowardly, greedy, proud, you should show him the same at all times; not cowardly sometimes and then brave, not greedy sometimes and then generous; for such practice is the greatest blemish in a poem. But we shall discuss this matter fully in our commentary on Aristotle's *Poetics.* Horace also described it carefully in his *Poetica.*

It should be understood that characters are portrayed in two ways, either "according to the probable" (κατὰ τὸ εἰκός), or "according to the necessary" (κατὰ τὸ ἀναγκαιον), as Aristotle says in the *Poetics.* If, therefore, known persons are introduced and we know that they actually existed, their characters should be represented according to necessity. If, however, the persons are new and have been created for the first time by the poet himself, their characters should be represented according to probability. As the poet understands and can execute this, he must note the characters of all ages and classes, just as Horace learnedly teaches in his *Poetica,* and Aristotle in the second book of his *Rhetoric.* Nor yet should the poet be ignorant, as indeed we have said above, that he creates all the personages in his comedies, gives them whatever names he pleases, and that poems of this kind admit only to the "probable." Albeit Old Comedy once took real persons, I speak of New Comedy, which is much more praiseworthy. It is different in Tragedy; for when real matters of real people are imitated the real names should be kept and the characters represented "according to the necessary," although all personages are not real and new ones were introduced even into Tragedy. It suffices if some real names of people to whom the misfortunes befall are kept; the rest can be arbitrarily created by the poet in accord with probability, just as we say is done in Comedy.

Let this be enough about Character, upon which almost the whole art of the comic poet depends. Now, in what follows, we shall discuss Thought.

The power of Thought lies in fitly expressing the disposition of the soul; it encourages, stirs up, restains, comforts, ridicules, disparages, and produces innumerable results of this sort, just as Aristotle learnedly describes in the *Poetics.* Since comic discourse is simple or, as the Greek rhetoricians say, ἀφελης, its thoughts ought to be humble and not at all lofty; otherwise it would not differ from political discourse, that is, the speech which orators use in public. For this reason Aristides the rhetorician has very rightly determined the whole matter in his book, "On Simple Discourse." Aristides says, indeed: "Political thoughts are harsher, more illustrious, taken from more honorable matters, more striking since they are made up of striking turns of phrase, and therefore at the same time both less common and more illustrious. But thoughts in simple address are plain, common, insignificant, and taken from insignificant things." There is a further difference between the thoughts of political and comic discourse and this rises "from the treatment"; for in political or oratorical discourse there are declarations of issues and careful proof in order that the hearer may attentively perceive and believe what is being discussed. In comic discourse, however, there are no issues, but everything is revealed as if it were already decided and proved. There is also another difference in the "figures of speech"; for the figures in a political discourse seem to be "harsh, critical, and forcible" (as, indeed, Aristides the rhetorician writes); in a comic or "simple" discourse, however, they are "loose, plain, by no means critical nor exemplifying searching inquiry, but more common and obvious." Just as the former figures produce a lofty discourse and one distinctly "political," just so the latter make the discourse simple and distinctly comic since they are "conversable" and "commonplace."

And this will be enough to say about Thought. Now we shall speak about Diction.

Diction in comic discourse ought to be simple, easy, open, clear, familiar, and finally, taken from common usage: for, as Aristides the rhetorician says, simple discourse, such as comic discourse is, does not admit lofty diction since, as has been said, it has thoughts that are simple and humble. Forensic and political oratory, however, since it is lofty, ought to be adapted to this lofty diction. Such, therefore, is the difference established so far as dictions go between comic and political discourse. In the one, that is, the "simple"— these are the words of Aristides—"the diction is delivered as if by chance, appearing careless and by no means studied." In the political, however, the diction ought to be splendid, ornate, and symmetrical. I add also another difference which I have noted in the same passage in Aristides. Whatever one wishes to express in a political discourse must be separately uttered in distinct terms; the Greek words are: "In a political discourse only one meaning ought to appear." In simple or comic discourse, however, one expression often indicates two or three things; the Greek words are as follows: "In the simple discourse one expression means one or two or three things . . . [for example] ἱπποφορβός (horse-keeper)." Much that is splendid and ornamental is added by means of the composition. Now let us leave off our pursuit of Diction so that we may take up Spectacle.

Spectacle consists of the scene and the dress or costume of the personages. . . .

I would say something about Melody, which was mainly produced by flutes, if I did not see that it was sufficiently known to every one. I shall make an investigation in some other places as to the place and manner in which these things were used in the recitation of poems, and there is a fuller account of the whole matter in my commentary on Aristotle's *Poetics*.

So much for my explantion of the parts of Comedy, that is, the essentials. The other parts, which appertain to quantity, are enumerated by Donatus as four, and what these are is explained: Prologue, Prothesis, Epitasis, Catastrophe. I think Aristotle wrote about these in the second book of the *Poetics*, which I suspect has been lost; for in the extant first book he carefully describes similar parts of Tragedy. Comedy ought to be divided into five acts, as Horace recommends in his *Poetica*. Donatus observes that a character should not be permitted more than five entrances on the scene; in Tragedy the number should be even less. Finally, the Chorus would have been discussed, for the Old Comedy retained it; but since the New Comedy rejects the Chorus, it is not necessary to say more about these matters, especially since we have fully explained everything regarding the Chorus, the comic chorus moreover, in our commentary on Aristotle's *Poetics*; we have given an account of its nature and of why it was removed from the New Comedy.

Giovan Giorgio Trissino *1478–1550*

The Poetics *c. 1549*

(V)

Since we have pointed out all the ways of rhyming and all the types of poems that are arranged with rhymes, it will be well to set them aside now, for nonrhyming verses, i.e., those whose lines do not end with similar sounding words, are more apt to serve almost all kinds of drama than those with rhymes. It is quite true that in the choruses of tragedies and comedies and in the soliloquies which sing of love and praises, where sweetness and beauty are especially called for, rhymes with their rules are not to be avoided.

Selections. Translated by Charles Gattnig from the 1729 edition. Copyright 1974 by Charles Gattnig. Printed with permission of the translator.

Rather, they should be accepted and embraced for being principally responsible for this beauty and sweetness. And although a heavenly influence may have been at work perhaps it was only for this desire to achieve sweetness and beauty that that period of antiquity reduced not merely belles-lettres but all the fine arts to their nadir. Rhyming was pursued with much enthusiasm, so much so that during the period of decay of the Latin language, men of uncouth talents produced rhymes with great determination, as ecclesiastic hymns clearly demonstrate. And it happened that although rhyming was discovered by the earliest Greeks, it was infrequently used by them—perhaps because of its defects. However, the men of the age of which I spoke, finding it in the Latin which was becoming corrupt and disappearing, embraced it so passionately that they established the practice not only in the Sicilian and Italian vernacular, but passed it on to France and Spain and even returned rhyming to Greece itself. . . .

The action of tragedy should last one day, i.e., one revolution of the sun, or a little more. . . .

Since tragedy is the imitation of the most prestigious and the highest people, the maker of tragedy must imitate the best painters, who in their portraits, while expressing the proper image of those they portray, nevertheless depict their subjects as more beautiful than they are. So the poet in imitating angry, timid, lazy, and similar characters, ought to make their behavior better, i.e., more polite and generous, and not more arrogant and spiteful. This was Homer's method. He represented Achilles as angry, but loving and good. And Terence in *Hecuba* made the mother-in-law loving to the daughter-in-law, and the whore to the wife. Thus, the poet ought to adhere to what we have said, and afterwards he must carefully consider those things in poetry that necessarily affect the senses, i.e., seeing and hearing. I claim that he must be aware that the tragedy he is writing is to be recited, and the gestures seen, and the speeches and melody heard. Therefore, he must treat the play with beautiful and appropriate words. And in constructing the plot, he must place everything before his eyes, and behave as though he himself were participating in that action. Following this method, he will clearly see all the traits of his characters and will easily discover which characteristics are suitable to each one. His characters will not be able to conceal incongruous and hateful traits. And by placing as far as possible before his eyes the gestures and forms of those who are suffering emotions, he will almost experience those emotions, because those that experience passion are persuaded through the same nature to know how the tormented man most genuinely torments himself and how the obsessed man is most genuinely obsessed.

Maxims, then, should be used abundantly not only in tragedy but also in heroic poetry, comedy, and the other poems. Maxims are speeches which are sententious, moralistic, conclusive, and quickly understood. The Greeks called them *gnomai*. Some maxims are exhortations either to do or not to do something; others are affirmative, others simple, others compound, others credible, others true, and others hyperbolic. The exhortations to do something are like this one from Dante:

> Always to that truth, which has the face of mendacity,
> Must man close his lips, as much as he can,
> For they often unintentionally bring indignity.

The exhortations not to do something are like this one from *Italy Liberated from the Goths*:[1]

> He must never sleep all night
> Who keeps the seat of government.

The affirmative maxims are like this one from Petrarch:

> It is less of a disgrace to make mistakes when one is young.

The simple are like this one from Petrarch:

> Constant sighing solves nothing.

The compound are like that one of the same Petrarch:

> Old age praises life and the evening the day.

The credible are like that one from Dante:

> Love, that does not excuse the one who is loved from loving.

The true are like that from *Sofonisba*:[2]

> This mortal life
> Cannot be traversed without sorrow.

The hyperbolic are like that one again from Petrarch:

> The ranks of fools are infinite.

And it should be noted that nothing prevents the same maxim from having two, three, or four of the qualities discussed, i.e., it can be at the same time an exhortation to action, and simple, and true, and affirmative. And so it is with the other qualities, as long as they are not opposites and contraries, for the same maxim cannot be at the same time an exhortation to do and not to do something, both simple and compound, and both hyperbolic and true. . . .

[1] An epic poem by Trissino (1547).
[2] A tragedy by Trissino (1514–1515).

(VI)

Comedy, then, imitates the worse actions with speech, rhythm, and harmony, as does tragedy; and it imitates them in a single action which has completeness and magnitude, and a beginning, a middle, and an end. But in this it is different from tragedy, because tragedy achieves its end through compassion and fear, while comedy achieves its end by ridiculing and criticizing ugly and bad behavior. . . . It is enough to know that comedy is a representation of the bad and the vicious, but not all extremes of vice, only those that are ugly and from which arise the ridiculous—which is an ugly defect without pain and without deaths. . . .

. . . The plot of comedy is made up of actions different from and almost contrary to those of tragedy, because just as tragedy produces its essential effect through compassion, tears, and fear, which are sad things, so comedy attains its essential effect through jokes and laughter, which are cheerful things. Therefore, while in tragedy the compassion-causing actions of great and renowned men are expected, in comedy the humorous actions of lowly and obscure persons are expected. And while in tragedy, in which anguish and deaths occur and which almost always ends in unhappiness, in comedy, although some anxious moments may interrupt the action, these are not instances of injuries or deaths, and so everything ends happily. That is, comedy ends with marriages, peace-making, and tranquility; the final exit of the characters occurs in a state of conciliation. . . .

Comedy will also differ from tragedy in this respect: While in tragedy the events and names given are all or almost all real, in comedy both the events and the names are invented by the playwright. However, Plautus in his *Amphitrion* did not follow this procedure, and for this reason he called it a tragicomedy. . . .

Here we will specifically deal with the ridiculous, which (Aristotle claims) properly belongs to comedy. Aristotle tells us in his *Rhetoric* that he has dealt with the ridiculous in the *Poetics*. Perhaps it was in that part which discussed comedy, which because of the destructive nature of time is lost, and so the treatment of the ridiculous apparently became lost. Since it is important to investigate it, we will do it in another way—the way it was done by Marcus Tullius and Fabius Quintilianus,[3] although their method was more that of the orator than the philosopher. The ridiculous, therefore, as Aristotle says, is pertinent to the ugly, and is a defect and an ugliness which is neither deadly nor painful. Tully and Quintilian, who may have borrowed the idea from Aristotle, say, not inaccurately, that the place and essence of the ridiculous reside in ugliness and deformity. But they did not explain why this ugliness causes laughter. And that part of Aristotle in

[3] Cicero (106–43 B.C.) and Quintilian (1st century A.D.).

which he may have explained it is lost. Therefore, we will investigate it in this way.

It is clear that laughter is the result of the delight and pleasure experienced by the individual who laughs. This pleasure cannot come to him except through the senses, i.e., from seeing, hearing, touching, tasting, and smelling, or from the memory of pleasures already experienced, or from the anticipation of future pleasures. And such pleasure does not come from every object that delights and pleases the senses, but only from those objects that are to some degree ugly. For if someone sees a beautiful woman, or a beautiful jewel, or some similar thing that he likes, he does not laugh. Also, he does not laugh on hearing compliments, nor on touching, tasting, and smelling things which to the touch, taste, and smell are joyous and pleasant. Actually, these things together with pleasure bring admiration, not laughter. But if the object which stimulates the senses is mixed with some ugliness, it evokes laughter. An ugly and distorted face, an awkward movement, a silly word, a mispronunciation, an obscene gesture, a bitter wine, and a rancid rose immediately cause laughter. And these things especially make us laugh when we expected something different or better, because then not only our senses but even our expectations are slightly offended. And this kind of pleasure exists because man is by nature envious and spiteful, as is quite obvious in little children, for all of them are envious and always take delight in doing harm, if they can. It can also be seen that man is never naturally cheered by the good fortune of others, unless indirectly, i.e., because he expects to gain something. As Plautus says, "There is no one who would not envy the obtaining of a favorable thing." And therefore, if someone sees that another finds money, he does not laugh or rejoice. Instead, he is jealous. But if he sees someone fall into mud and dirty himself, he laughs, because (as Lucretius says) it is always sweeter to stare at the misfortune of others which we do not possess ourselves. But if we suffer similar misfortunes, we are not moved to laughter when we see them in others, for no hunchback laughs at another hunchback, nor a cripple at another cripple, unless perhaps he believes that those afflictions are less ugly in him than in that other. Then, if the sufferings seen in others are fatal and painful, as are wounds, fevers, blows, etc., they do not cause laughter. Instead, the result is compassion due to the fear that similar misfortunes may come to us or to our family, for we consider those who belong to us as parts of ourselves. Therefore, the small misfortune—not painful and fatal—that we see or hear in others, as an ugly body, stupid mind, or some such thing, when it is not or when we believe it is not part of ourselves, causes pleasure and laughter, for just as man is composed of mind and body, so the ugliness in him is double, i.e., of the mind and the body. And the special forms of ugliness of the mind are ignorance, imprudence, credulity, and similar things which are frequently interdependent, and thus in jokes we always laugh at the ignorance, rashness, and gullibility of someone else. And this is especially so when we see them in persons who are regarded as solid and shrewd, for in such as these the chances are greater that judgment and trust will be betrayed. All the jokes and mockeries written by Boccaccio and the Courtier[4] may be reduced to such kinds of ugliness, and similarly all the ridiculous stories, jokes, and witticisms recounted by Tully, Quintilian, Boccaccio, Poggio, and the Courtier. It is noteworthy that if the afore-mentioned ugliness and deformity of the mind have magnitude, as have betrayals and perjuries, etc., they do not evoke laughter but disdain. They are condemned and repudiated, as are lies, displays of ignorance, and similar kinds of clumsiness of mind and body. But if they are minor uglinesses, they are the source of laughter and ridicule and delight. And all such kinds of ridiculous ugliness are either demonstrated or narrated or are commented on with some urbanity.

Those that are demonstrated are of the kind that Tully assigns to Crassus, who, when speaking against Helvius Mancia, said: "Now I will show you who you are." And Mancia demanded: "Whom will you show who I am?" Whereupon Crassus turned and pointed a finger at a Cimbrian shield . . . on which was carved the face of a Frank, ugly and distorted, which certainly resembled the face of Mancia, whereupon everyone began to laugh.[5]

Deformities become evident when narrated, as was that story by Strepsiades in Aristophanes[6] in which he recites the differences between himself and his wife. Since he was a peasant and miser and she was urbane and arrogant, they disagreed on many things, especially when it came to naming the little son who was born to them. Strepsiades wanted to name him Hold-Your-Money, and the proud wife wanted the name Famous-Horses. They ended up by agreeing that each would give him half his name, i.e., Hold-Your-Horses or Phidippides. And almost the entire story evokes laughter, because in almost every part the ignorance and avarice of the peasant and the arrogance and rashness of the woman is revealed. These qualities are all examples of ugliness of the mind.

The said forms of ugliness of either the body or the mind may be commented on with an urbane witticism. For example, someone noted the ugliness of body in Testio Pinario, who contorted his chin when speaking, as if he had a nut in his mouth. And his adversary said to him: "Say whatever you like, after you have cracked that nut which you have in your mouth." . . . . This urbanity is a brief, shrewd, and swift thing, and excellently suited to matters of wit and ridicule which involve a give-and-take dialogue. And there are many such instances which are ripe for

---

[4] That is, by Castiglione in *The Courtier* [translator's note].

[5] The story occurs in Cicero's *De Oratore*, II, 66 [translator's note].

[6] *The Clouds* [translator's note].

ridicule, e.g., ambiguity, the unexpected, deriding another's nature, stupidity. All these things have various aspects which are ripe for ridicule, either by denial or refutation or defense or diminution. And these all excite laughter because they comment on some ugliness either in oneself or in others.

An example of ambiguity would be that sonnet by Antonio Alemani about Alemano Salviati. This Alemano was with other citizens on a committee which did not want to comply with the said Antonio in something that he wanted. Whereupon Alemano to excuse himself said to Antonio: "It is not I, that is, I am not the one who does not want to please you." And Antonio, making believe that he understood him to say that he was not Alemano Salviati, wrote this:

> Alemano says to me, I am not I,
> And this is not true, because he is he.
> But when he denies that he is himself,
> He thinks he will tell the truth of my predicament.

Here the ridiculous arises from the ambiguity of *I am not I*, with which he feigns his own ignorance and Alemano's lie, both of which are uglinesses of the mind. . . .

Another similarly ridiculous instance was the one in a response of Pievano Arlotto, who, finding himself on a street in Florence and passing near a very beautiful and bold girl, said to his companion, who was embarrassed: "This is a beautiful woman." And the bold girl turned towards him and said "I am not able to say the same about you." And Pievano immediately replied: "Of course, since you wish to tell a lie about me, just as I have told about you." By feigning ugliness of mind in himself, i.e., by having lied, Pievano in this way revealed another ugliness in the ungrateful nature of the woman who criticized the man who complimented her. And at the the same time he jokingly pretended that her body was ugly. . . .

There are many types of this ambiguity, such as the changing of letters— which some call a pun. For eaxmple, Garifilo, *Garofolo*; Luca Michiele, *Licamelculo*,[7] etc. A pun is also made by adding letters, as "moral," "mortal." . . .

The most appropriate instance of the ridiculous is the unexpected, because it uncovers the imprudence of the one who waits, e.g., the way Giovanni Cannaccio ridiculed Prior Pandolfini. The Prior firmly believed that the monk Girolamo Savonarola was a saint and that although he was dead he would rise up. And so one day he said to Cannaccio, who was one of those who sentenced the monk to death: "What will you say, Giovanni, when you see Brother Girolamo raised from the dead?" And Cannaccio

---

[7] These puns are untranslatable [translator's note].

replied, contrary to every expectation of Pandolfini: "I will say that next time we ought to hang him. . . .[8]"

A laugh is also evoked with a shrewd reply to some proverb which is uttered, such as was made by Maestro Gerardo Bolderio, a Veronese physician, to that Signora of Malaspini who asked him for a remedy for her only son. The physician told her that there was nothing wrong with the boy and that she should not give him any medicine. But the woman still insisted that he should prepare some remedy. And attempting to excuse herself for such insistence, she used a proverb, saying: "Oh sir, he who has only one eye often wipes it." And the physician added: "And he wipes it so much that he digs it out." And in that instance the ridiculous arises from the revelation of the rashness of that Signora who believes that medicine would help one who was not sick. . . .

. . . Words in comedy should not be designed to be noble, resounding, and refined, as are those in tragedy; they should sound humble, clear, and urbane. The metaphors and other figures must contain frivolity and should seem like common speech, which comedy especially imitates. But the words in comedy must not be taken from different languages nor use references which give the impression of being foreign. Also, they must not demonstrate too much culture and too many embellishments, because (as we have said) very splendid and cultured words obfuscate maxims and dispositions. Also, things not in common usage produce an elevated atmosphere—a thing that is not appropriate to comedy.

[8] Savonarola was burned at the stake.

Julius Caesar Scaliger *1484–1558*

Poetics *1561*[1]

Imitation, however, is not the end of poetry, but is intermediate to the end. The end is the giving of instruction in pleasurable form, for poetry teaches, and does not simply amuse, as some used to think. Whenever

Selections. From *Select Translations from Scaliger's Poetics,* by Frederick Morgan Padelford. Yale Studies in English, No. 26. New York: Henry Holt and Co., 1905.

[1] Date of posthumous publication.

language is used, the purpose, of course, is to acquaint the hearer with a fact or with the thought of the speaker, but because the primitive poetry was sung, its design seemed merely to please; yet underlying the music was that for the sake of which music was provided only as a sauce. In time this rude and pristine invention was enriched by philosophy, which made poetry the medium of its teaching. Let it be further said that when poetry describes military counsels, at one time open and frank, at another crafty—the στρατήγημα of the Greeks—when it tells of tempests, of wars, of routs, of various artifices, all is for one purpose: it imitates that it may teach. So in *The Frogs* of Aristophanes, to the one who asked him, "What merit in a poet can arouse the greatest admiration for him?" Euripides made a good answer when he replied, "The ability to impress adroitly upon citizens the need of being better men." . . .

Now is there not one end, and one only, in philosophical exposition, in oratory, and in the drama? Assuredly such is the case. All have one and the same end—persuasion; for, you see, just as we were saying above, whenever language is used it either expresses a fact or the opinion of the speaker. The end of learning is knowledge, that is, knowledge, of course, interpreted in no narrow sense. An accurate and simple definition of knowledge is as follows: Belief based either upon conclusive evidence, or upon a loose notion. Thus we say, "I know that Dido committed suicide because Aeneas departed." Now we do not know any such thing, but this is popularly accepted as the truth. Persuasion, again, means that the hearer accepts the words of the speaker. The soul of persuasion is truth, truth either fixed and absolute, or susceptible of question. Its end is to convince, or to secure the doing of something. Truth, in turn, is agreement between that which is said about a thing and the thing itself. . . .

. . . Comedy is a dramatic poem, which is filled with intrigue, full of action, happy in its outcome, and written in a popular style.

An inaccurate definition of the Latin comedy described it as "a plot free from the suggestion of danger, dealing with the life and affairs of the private citizen." In the first place, this definition covers other, nondramatic stories, which can be presented in simple narration. In the second place, there is always the suggestion of danger in comedy, although the outcome is invariably tame. What else is danger than the approach or the visitation of imminent danger? Further, there is not only danger in comedy, but violence at the hands of panderers, rivals, lovers, servants, or masters. Thus in the *Asinaria* and *The Ghost*[2] even the masters themselves are ill-treated. Once more, this definition would not admit the official class, wearers of the toga, for they are not private citizens. Finally, the definition would embrace memes and dramatic satires. . . .

Tragedy, like comedy, is patterned after real life, but it differs from

[2] Both by Plautus.

comedy in the rank of the characters, in the nature of the action, and in the outcome. These differences demand, in turn, differences in style. Comedy employs characters from rustic, or low city life, such as Chremes, Davus, and Thais.[3] The beginning of a comedy presents a confused state of affairs, and this confusion is happily cleared up at the end. The language is that of everyday life. Tragedy, on the other hand, employs kings and princes, whose affairs are those of the city, the fortress, and the camp. A tragedy opens more tranquilly than a comedy, but the outcome is horrifying. The language is grave, polished, removed from the colloquial. All things wear a troubled look; there is a pervading sense of doom, there are exiles and deaths. Tradition has it that the Macedonian king, Archelaus, the intimate friend and patron of Euripides, asked the poet to make him the hero of a tragedy, but that Euripides replied: "Indeed I cannot do it; your life presents no adequate misfortune."

The name tragedy is derived from $\tau\rho\acute{a}\gamma o_5$, the he-goat, for the simple reason that tragedy was acted in the honor of that divinity to whom the goat was wont to be sacrificed. Then, in turn, the goat was given as a prize, that the victor might sacrifice it to the god. It is recorded as an assured fact that tragedies were first acted in the vintage season, and this gave the grammarians an opportunity to derive the name from $\tau\rho\acute{v}\gamma\eta\mu a$, the vintage, just as if it were $\tau\rho\nu\gamma\omega\delta\acute{\iota}a$, a word which you actually find in the *Acharnians* of Aristophanes. . . .

The definition of tragedy given by Aristotle is as follows: "Tragedy is an imitation of an action that is illustrious, complete, and of a certain magnitude, in embellished language, the different kinds of embellishments being variously employed in the different parts, and not in the form of narration, but through pity and fear effecting the purgation of such like passions." I do not wish to attack this definition other than by adding my own: A tragedy is the imitation of the adversity of a distinguished man; it employs the form of action, presents a disastrous dénouement, and is expressed in impressive metrical language. Though Aristotle adds harmony and song, they are not, as the philosophers say, of the essence of tragedy; its one and only essential is acting. Then the phrase "of a certain magnitude" is put in to differentiate the tragedy from the epic, which is sometimes prolix. . . . Further, the mention of "purgation" is too restrictive, for not every subject produces this effect. "A certain magnitude," to return to the phrase, means not too long and not too short, for a few verses would not satisfy the expectant public, who are prepared to atone for the disgusting prosiness of many a day by the enjoyment of a few hours. Prolixity, however, is just as bad, when you must say with Plautus: "My legs ache with sitting, and my eyes with looking." . . .

---

[3] In Roman comedy, Chremes is a young man or a father, Davus a slave, and Thais a courtesan.

Although tragedy resembles this epic poetry, it differs in rarely introducing persons of the lower classes, such as messengers, merchants, sailors, and the like. Comedies, on the other hand, never admit kings, save in such rare instances as the *Amphitrion* of Plautus. I would limit this generalization of course to those plays which employ Greek characters and the Greek dress, for the Romans have admitted at will the dignified toga and *trabea*. The wanton characters of the satyric plays are drinking, joking, jolly, sarcastic fellows. The mime employs cloth-fullers, shoemakers, butchers, poulterers, fish-dealers, and market-gardeners. Such characters, indeed, were admitted in the Old Comedy, as well, for the subject-matter of the Old Comedy was not very different from that of the mimes, and the difference between the two forms was largely in the division into acts, and the introduction of the chorus. Tragedy and comedy are alike in mode of representation, but differ in subject-matter and treatment (*ordo*). The matters of tragedy are great and terrible, as commands of kings, slaughters, despair, suicides, exiles, bereavements, parricides, incests, conflagrations, battles, the putting out of eyes, weeping, wailing, bewailing, funerals, eulogies, and dirges. In comedy we have jests, reveling, weddings with drunken carousals, tricks played by slaves, drunkenness, old men deceived and cheated of their money. To satyric plays belong dancing, banquets, potations, and biting raillery; to mimes, plebeian, ignoble trafficking, frauds, rustic pranks, drawling speeches, panderings, jokes, jests, deceits. The performances of the satyrs, at the close as at the beginning, are impudent, capricious, unexpected, varied, and incoherent. The action of the mimes is abrupt; thus if one character leave the stage, all the rest leave too, even though not much of a situation has been worked out. The characters run and skip about, they rail at one another, they are lazy and silly. Parodies imitate, but so imitate as to subvert that which is serious, and give a thought an unexpected turn. . . .

Now a tragedy, provided it is a genuine tragedy, is altogether serious, but there have been some satyrical plays which differed little from comedies save in the gravity of some of the characters. We have an illustration in the *Cyclops* of Euripides, where all is wine and jesting, and where the outcome is so happy that all the companions of Ulysses are released, and the Cyclops alone suffers in the loss of his eye. The conclusion of this play was not unlike that of a mime, for the stage was wholly deserted on the exit of Ulysses, the giant with the rock alone remaining.

There are, on the other hand, many comedies which end unhappily for some of the characters. Such are *The Braggart Captain*, *The Persian*, and the *Asinaria* of Plautus. So too, there are not a few tragedies which end happily. Thus in the *Electra* of Euripides, except for the slaughter of Aegisthus, joy came to many. In the *Ion* and the *Helen* the outcome was happy. Again, though *The Eumenides* of Aeschylus contains tragic events, for example slaughters and furies, its treatment is more like that of comedy.

The opening part is gratifying to the guard, and disturbing to Clytemnestra because of the arrival of her husband; then comes the murder, which makes Electra and Orestes happy; and then succeeds the dénouement, which brings happiness to all—Apollo, Orestes, the people, Pallas, and the Eumenides. Hence it is by no means true, as has hitherto been taught, that an unhappy issue is essential to tragedy. It is enough that the play contain horrible events.

When authors take their plots from history, they must be careful not to depart too widely from the records. In the early writers such care was by no means taken. Thus Aeschylus followed Greek history in binding Prometheus to the rock, but he invented the fiction of his undoing by the thunderbolt, for tragic effect. There should be no dire event at the end, but only at the beginning, where he is bound to Caucasus. . . . Euripides invented stories about Helen, which were utterly contrary to well-known history. The same author has been censured for bringing wicked and impure women into his plays. What is viler, the critic says, than Phaedra, Jocasta, Canace, and Pasiphae, by whose infamy society is corrupted? But we reply that these women were not creatures of his imagination, but were taken from life. Forsooth, if we are to hear of no wickedness, history must be done away with. So those comedies should be prized which make us condemn the vices which they bring to our ears, especially when the life of impure women ends in an unhappy death. . . .

The events themselves should be made to have such sequence and arrangement as to approach as near as possible to truth, for the play is not acted solely to strike the spectator with admiration or consternation—a fault of which, according to the critics, Aeschylus was often guilty—but should also teach, move, and please. We are pleased either with jests, as in comedy, or with things serious, if rightly ordered. Disregard of truth is hateful to almost every man. Therefore, neither those battles or sieges at Thebes which are fought through in two hours please me, nor do I take it to be the part of a discreet poet to pass from Delphi to Athens, or from Athens to Thebes, in a moment of time. Thus, Aeschylus has Agamemnon killed and buried so suddenly that the actor has scarcely time to breathe. Nor is the casting of Lichas into the sea by Hercules to be approved, for it cannot be represented without doing violence to truth.

The content of a play should be as concise as possible, yet also as varied and manifold as possible; for example, Hecuba in Thrace, Achilles forbidding her return, Polydorus already killed, the murder of Polyxena, and the blinding of Polymnestor. Since dead persons cannot be introduced, their apparitions, or ghosts, or spectres, are substituted. Thus, as noted above, Aeschylus introduces the apparitions of Polydorus and Darius, and in Ovid, Ceÿx appears to Alcyone. If a tragedy is to be composed from this last story, it should not begin with the departure of Ceÿx, for as the whole time for stage-representation is only six or eight hours, it is not true to life to have a storm arise, and the ship founder, in a part of the sea from which no land is visible. Let the first act be a passionate lamentation, the chorus to follow with execrations of sea life; the second act, a priest with votive offerings conversing with Alcyone and her nurse, altars, fire, pious sentiments, the chorus following with approbation of the vows; the third act, a messenger announcing the rising of a storm, together with rumors as to the ship, the chorus to follow with mention of shipwrecks, and much apostrophizing of Neptune; the fourth act tumultuous, the report found true, shipwrecks described by sailors and merchants, the chorus bewailing the event as though all were lost; the fifth act, Alcyone peering anxiously over the sea and sighting far off a corpse, followed by the resolution, when she was about to take her own life. This sample outline can be expanded by the introduction of other characters.

Lodovico Castelvetro *1505–1571*

On Aristotle's Poetics *1570*

Poetry is imitation and its general mode is imitation. . . .[1]

The qualified poet's duty . . . is to imitate through speculation the reality of people caught in the accidents of fortune. . . . He should leave the discovery of the reality hidden in the accidents of nature to the philosopher and the scientist.

Now, since drama was invented, as I say, to delight and provide recreation for the common people, it must have subject matter which the common people can understand and which when they understand it may make them happy. This subject matter should include such things as everyday occur-

Selections. Translated by Charles Gattnig from the 1576 revised and amended edition. Copyright 1974 by Charles Gattnig. Printed with permission of the translator.

[1] Whereas earlier Italian critics translated Aristotle's term μίμησις as *imitazione* (e.g., Cinthio and Trissino; even Donatus uses the Latin *imitationem*), Castelvetro uses the word *rassomiglianza* exclusively. I translate the latter as "representation" [translator's note].

rences and such things which people discuss, e.g., world news and history. And for this reason we assert that the subject matter of poetry is historical similitude or imitation. Because it is an imitation, poetry not only rewards its inventor with glory—and makes and constitutes him a poet—but it delights us much more than the history of actual past events. . . . Therefore, because the data of the sciences and arts are not comprehensible to the people, not only must they be avoided and discarded as the general subjects of poetry, but care must also be taken that no specific reference to the matters of arts and sciences is made in any part of the poem. . . .

Tragedy puts compassion and fright in the souls of the spectators or the audience. . . . Fright and compassion are the two objectives of tragedy. . . .

Murders, and other such difficult things, are not shown onstage because they are difficult to perform with dignity and verisimilitude. It is better to have them occur offstage and then be recounted by a messenger. [Dramatic and narrative poetry] are also different because the narrative can interpret in a few hours many things which happened in many hours and in many hours a few things which happened in a few hours. But drama, which represents the events as taking place, is incapable of creating this effect because the time spent in performance is the same as the time needed by the actions themselves. This is why tragedy and comedy, which are types of representational poetry, cannot last longer than that time which the comfort of the spectators tolerates. Nor can tragedy and comedy represent more events than those which occurred in the space of time required by these plays. As I say, the comfort of the public should be considered, for after some hours people have to leave the theatre because of human needs— eating, drinking, sleeping, and other functions. . . .

Because it only utilizes words, the epic can with no awkwardness recount an action which lasted many years and occurred in many different places. Words can make us imagine faraway places and remote times. Tragedy is incapable of doing the same thing, for it requires as its subject an action that happened in a limited place and a short space of time; i.e., in whatever place and time the actors actually use in the performance, and not anywhere else or in any other time. But just as the boundary of place is the stage, so is the boundary of time that period in which the spectators can comfortably remain sitting in the theatre. For this reason, I don't see how "the revolution of the sun," as Aristotle says, can elapse; that would be twelve hours. Because of the needs of the body, such as eating, drinking, dismissing superfluous burdens of the stomach and bladder, sleeping, and other necessities, the public cannot tolerate any kind of delay in the theatre beyond the aforesaid limitation. Nor is it possible to make the spectators believe that many days and nights have passed when they sensibly know that only a few hours have elapsed. The deception is not allowed to take place because it is still recognized by sense. Since Plautus and Terence were aware of that limitation, how could they excuse their error? For in some of their comedies they have represented actions which are longer than one day. . . .

The end of tragedy is action and not the ethical predilections of characters, for if teaching morals were the ultimate aim of tragedy, actions would determine morality; but it is the nature of the characters which determines the actions. Therefore, actions are the end of tragedy, not morals. Aristotle explained it with these words: οὐχουν πράκτουσι, i.e., playwrights do not make the plot, or the actions, to represent characters; rather, they employ characters to accompany the actions. . . . Thus, it doesn't much matter whether the characters are determined by the plot and are secondary, or whether the plot is determined by the characters and is secondary, because the plot is the end of tragedy, and consequently of every type of poem, since the plot has the same function in all poems as it has in tragedy. That is, plot is the ultimate goal, and is not secondary to the morality revealed by the characters. Therefore, if the morality revealed by the characters is not the ultimate goal, it follows that many highly touted men of letters, both ancient and modern, among whom we even find Julius Caesar dalla Scala or Scaliger, have seriously erred, for they claim that fine poets like Homer and Virgil intended in their most famous works—the *Iliad*, the *Odyssey*, and the *Aeneid*—to portray and to show the world, let us say, a captain despised in a most touching way, or a brave leader, or a wise man, and their natures, and similar nonsense. For if this were true, the moral nature of the characters would not have been selected by the poets to support the action, as Aristotle says, but the action would have been selected to comply with the moral nature of the characters. There is only one exception; if such material were principal and not accessory, it could not be the stuff of poetry, but would be by its nature philosophical. . . .

Here[2] and in other passages, Aristotle stubbornly demands that the action structuring the plot should be single and be concerned with one person only. And if there actually are multiple actions, one should grow out of the other. The only reason or proof he offers for this contention is the example of the tragic poets and Homer, who in making the plot restricted themselves to the representation of the action of one person. But he could easily perceive that in tragedy and comedy the plot contains one action only—or two which because of dependency can be thought of as one—and more often of one person than of one family or group, not because the plot cannot contain multiple actions but because the twelve-hour maximum time limit and the narrowness of place in which the action is presented do not permit a multitude of actions, or even the actions of one family or group. On the contrary, quite often these limitations do not

[2] See *Poetics*, chap. 8 [translator's note].

permit the presentation of the whole of a single complete action, if the action is quite long. And this is the principal and essential reason why the plot of tragedy and comedy must be single, i.e., it must contain only one action concerning one person, or two regarded as one because of their interdependency. . . .

The plot of [tragedy and the epic] must contain action which is not only human but also magnificent and royal. And if it is to contain action by a member of the royalty, it follows that the plot must contain action which definitely occurred and which involves a king who has lived and who is known to have lived. . . . Therefore, the plots of all tragedies and all epics are and must be made up of mishaps which can be called historical, although for some reason Aristotle had a different opinion. . . .[3] But these happenings must not be revealed by means of history or renown, except briefly and generally, so that the poet can exercise his function and show his talent in finding the ways and particular methods of dramatizing the above-mentioned situations. . . .

We are willing to admit the possibility that it is easier to make the plot of a tragedy and an epic than of a comedy, because in the plots of the first two, the poet does not invent everything, as he does comedy. . . . It is the poet's special talent to structure the plot of comedy by inventing the general and particular aspects of a situation. Because he invents everything, and because actual events or history have no part in it, the poet can even assign whatever names he wishes to his characters. He can do this without offense, and within reason he must do it. He can design a happening entirely invented by himself. Therefore, it must be a situation dealing with private persons of which no one remembers either the incident or the people involved, since they have not been preserved for posterity as history or renown. . . .

In order that the plot may be beautiful, the sixth essential requirement is that it be astonishing. Earlier we explained while defining tragedy that it is not only a representation of an action that is magnificent, complete, etc., but also a representation of terror-causing and compassion-making things. And since these terror-causing and compassion-making things are fundamentally terror causing and compassion making through the employment of the astonishing, one should not omit saying that the astonishing generates and increases terror and compassion. This will not give us a complete understanding of what scares us and what fills us with compassion. The essential elements of the action or of the plot of tragedy are terror and compassion.

The objective of tragedy, or of the plot of tragedy, is happiness or sadness, but not every kind of happiness or sadness. We must not con-

[3] See *Poetics*, chap. 9 [translator's note].

fuse the happy or sad conclusion of tragedy with the joy or sadness which are the objectives of comedy or of the plot of comedy. Therefore, the happy conclusion of tragedy consists in and restricts itself to the preservation of self, or of a loved one, from death or from a sorrowful life, or from the loss of kinship. Conversely, the sad conclusion of tragedy consists in and restricts itself to the occurrence to self, or to loved ones, of death or of a sorrowful life, or of the loss of the crown. And these two are its proper goals. . . .

The purpose of comedy, as I say, is similarly happiness or sadness, but neither that same happiness nor the same sadness which we claim suitable for tragedy. For the joy which is the aim of comedy consists in the concealment of some disgrace brought on oneself, or on some loved one, or in the preservation from some shame which others did not believe was possible, or in the recovery of a person, or a precious possession which was lost, or in the successful pursuit of love. But the sadness of comedy consists in and restricts itself to the reception by oneself, or by loved ones, of some disgrace or moderate shame, or in slight damage to property, or in unrequited love, etc. And these are the two proper purposes of comedy.

. . . The characters of tragedy are not the same as those of comedy. Those of tragedy are royal and are more dynamic and proud; they intensely want what they want. If offended, or if they think they have been offended, they do not appeal to the courts to take legal action concerning the injury. Nor do they endure injury patiently. Instead, they take justice in their own hands, following their instincts. And in revenge, they kill both strangers and relatives; in desperation, they kill not only members of their family but sometimes even themselves. When placed on the throne, which is considered to be the zenith of human happiness, such characters are powerful enough to revenge any outrages perpetrated on them. What they inflict upon others is never moderate. Nor are they affected by minor damages to their property. Their cheerfulness is not augmented either through marriage or through the successful pursuit of love. Actually, they exist in perpetual marriage and in continual amorous satisfaction, to such an extent that if they are to realize cheerfulness, they must first be separated from happiness, or at least they must be caught in an obvious danger, and derive happiness by escaping from it. And to cause sadness they must fall heavily into misery or disgrace with a spectacular plunge.

But the characters of comedy are meek and are accustomed to obey the courts. They live under the law and endure offense and damages. They appeal to officials to enforce by means of their statutes the restitution of their self-respect or the payment of damages. They do not take the law into their own hands and they do not resort to killing relatives or themselves or others for things which kings resolve by murder. And because their condition is poor and humble, it is not necessary first to remove their happiness in order for them to appreciate cheerfulness. Their happiness can grow by many degrees and by a little bit of luck, such as a desired wedding or something similar. And conversely, injury or medium disgrace can make them unhappy. And these are the reasons why the happy and sad endings of tragedy are different from the happy and sad endings of comedy. . . .

Therefore, tragedy has either a happy or a sad ending. And even when it has a happy ending, it generates terror and compassion to a lesser extent because the royal character falls into great danger.[4] Because the danger is mixed, the joy is not without sadness, as we will explain later. However, tragedy generates similar emotions to a greater extent when it has a sad ending. Thus, the purpose of the plot of tragedy is the joy and sadness produced in the way we have explained. . . .

If poetry was invented essentially for esthetic delight and not for practical usefulness, as Aristotle shows when he speaks of the origin of poetry in general, why does he contend that we should look primarily for usefulness in tragedy, which is one type of poetry? Why not concentrate primarily on delight and forget usefulness? Let's not waste too much effort on this subject. Otherwise, if one follows Aristotle too far, all the other types of tragedies which are devoid of usefulness would be rejected. Tragedies should be restricted to only one kind of usefulness, i.e., only to the achieving of the purification of terror and compassion. Nevertheless, if one insists on discussing usefulness, other kinds of tragedies should be examined, e.g., those that contain the transformation of good men from a condition of misery to happiness, or the change of evil men from happiness to misery. In this way, the public, being persuaded by the examples presented, may be strengthened in its holy faith that god [sic] is in charge of the world and that his special province over his own protects them and confuses their enemies. . . .

Thus, the delight which is appropriate to tragedy is that which is derived from the terror and compassion proceeding from the spectacle of a character neither wholly good nor wholly bad passing from happiness to misery because of a mistake. But others may question the kind of delight derived from seeing a good man who has unjustly lost happiness being drowned in misery. Reason dictates that such an occurrence would not cause delight but displeasure. Now there is no doubt that Aristotle took the word ἡδονὴν to mean the purification and the expulsion of terror and compassion from human souls by the action of these same emotions in the manner we have discussed at length above. Assuming that that purification and that expulsion would proceed, as he asserts, from these same emotions, it may become

[4] Elsewhere, Castelvetro again mentions this point—with a difference, however: "Tragedy without a sad conclusion cannot reasonably generate terror and compassion; experience shows that such a tragedy does not cause terror and compassion" [translator's note].

clear how they can correctly be called ἡδονή, i.e., pleasure or delight. And it must immediately be described as a utilitarian function, since the soul is made healthy by means of very bitter medicine. That pleasure arising from compassion and terror, which is really pleasure, is that which we have earlier referred to as "oblique pleasure." At the time, when we experience displeasure because others unjustly suffer misery, we acknowledge that we are good, because injustice bothers us. The natural love that we bring to ourselves is a very great pleasure for which we are grateful. To this pleasure is added still another that is not at all small. When we see others being unjustly oppressed and realize that the same could happen to us or to people like us, we learn quietly and unconsciously that we are subject to many misfortunes, and that it is not wise to place trust in the tranquil course of events. We are much more delighted by this self-taught lesson than if another, e.g., a teacher, were openly to lecture us on this same subject, for experience of things that have happened firmly impresses understanding in our souls more effectively than can be accomplished by the mere voice of a learned authority. And we rejoice more in the little we learn for ourselves than in the much we learn from others, for we are not able to learn from others unless we admit ignorance of that which we learn and an obligation to our teachers for what we learn from them. . . .

Those who maintain that poetry was invented essentially for utilitarian purposes, or for usefulness and delight together, should beware of setting themselves against Aristotle's authority. In this part of the *Poetics* and elsewhere, it does not seem that he allows any end other than delight.[5] And if he indeed grants some utilitarian function, he concedes it as incidental, as is the purification of terror and compassion by means of tragedy. . . .

In tragedy, the place of the action is restricted not only to one city or house or countryside, or similar site, but to that scene which alone can be absorbed by the vision of one person.

---

[5] See *Poetics*, chap. 23 [translator's note].

Giovanni Battista Guarini 1538–1612

Compendium of Tragicomic Poetry 1599

Some may say that there are two ways in which the precept of unity is not obeyed in the poem of *The Faithful Shepherd*: first, because it has two genres, tragic and comic; second, because it has more than one theme, like almost all the plays of Terence. So that our exact terminology may be swiftly and clearly understood, we will refer to the first [the combination of tragic and comic genres] by the usual name of "mixed" and the second [multiple themes] as "grafted." As to the first, it must be understood that tragicomedy is not made up of two complete plots—a perfect tragedy plus a perfect comedy—joined together in such a way that any separation would damage both. Nor should anyone imagine that tragicomedy is a tragic story spoiled by the triviality of comedy or that it is a comic plot contaminated by the deaths of tragedy, since that would not be the correct composition of tragicomedy, because anyone who makes tragicomedy does not intend to write either tragedy or comedy separately but a third perfect genre which contains those many elements of comedy and tragedy which can coexist with versimilitude. Thus, in judging it, it is not necessary to confuse the terms "mixed" and "double," as do those who know little and who do not realize that nothing can be mixed if it is not one and if the parts that comprise it do not give the impression that they can any longer be individually identified or separated from each other....

. . . And there is no doubt that anyone who imagines that he can make one of these genres slip in its entirety into the confines of the other, and that he can put into tragedy that which is only proper to comedy, or vice versa, would produce an improper and monstrous play. But it remains to be seen if these specific differences are so inconsistent that, in whatever way it is formed, a third genre—which would be a reasonable and legitimate drama —is not possible.

Regarding these specific differences, in tragedy there is the great or publicly responsible character, the serious action, terror, and commiseration; in comedy there is the private character, private business, laughter, and wit. About the first I confess, and also it is the doctrine of Aristotle, that great personages come together in tragedy, and that the humble gather in comedy.[1]

Selections. Translated by Charles Gattnig from the 1601 edition. Copyright 1974 by Charles Gattnig. Printed with permission of the translator.

[1] See Aristotle's *Poetics*, chap. 5 [translator's note].

150

But I firmly deny that it is inconsistent with nature, and poetic art in general, to introduce public and private characters in a single plot. Has there ever been a tragedy which has not had many more servants and other characters of this ilk than characters of great consequence? Who unties that very beautiful knot in Sophocles' *Oedipus*? Not the king, not the queen, not Creon, not Tiresias, but two servants who are shepherds. Therefore, the joining of the great and the nongreat is not contrary to the nature of the stage, regardless of whether the dramatic poem is called "mixed" drama— as is tragicomedy—or pure tragedy. And this is true even in comedy, if we point to Aristophanes who, for your pleasure, mixed men and gods, city people and peasants, and who went so far as to bring in beasts and clouds to speak in his plays.

I cannot see why it is unsuitable to have public and private affairs in one and the same plot, not entirely tragic, if they are judiciously inserted. Can't amusing occurrences intervene between serious events? Aren't they often the reasons for bringing dangerous situations to a happy resolution? Not at all? Is it possible for princes always to be majestic? Don't they ever deal in pivate matters? Certainly they do. Therefore, why can't great persons who deal in private matters be represented in a stage play? This is exactly what Euripides did in *The Cyclops*, where Ulysses [Odysseus], a tragic character with serious danger to his life, becomes entangled with the drunkenness of the Cyclops—which is a comic situation. And of the Romans, Plautus did the same thing in *Amphitrion*, which couples the laughter and practical jokes of Mercury with great characters—not only with Amphitrion, but even with the king of the gods. Therefore, it is not unreasonable to say that great characters and private affairs can coexist in a single stage play.

The same can be said of commiseration, a tragic quality, and of laughter, a comic quality. And still, they do not seem to me to be so mutually exclusive that the same plot cannot include them in diverse situations and characters. . . . I do not say that consequently there can be cheerfulness and sorrow in the same plot, but that there can be compassion with laughter. And so the sum total of this contradiction may seem to be reduced to only one difference, i.e., the terror-filled event which can only occur in a tragic plot but never in a comedy, because terror can only be induced by means of serious and deadly representations; where it is found, there is no room for laughter and jokes. . . .

Aren't the horse and the ass two distinct species? Certainly, and yet from both is produced a third, the mule, which is neither one nor the other. . . . Bronze is made of copper and tin, and the body of one enters that of the other, and vice versa. And they and their natures are so well mixed that that third which results is neither tin nor copper. . . .

Whoever puts together tragicomedies takes from tragedy its great characters but not its great actions, its versimilar plot but not its historically true one, its stirred emotions but not its furious ones, its delight but not its sadness, its danger but not its death. From comedy he takes laughter that is not immoderate, modest amusement, the fabricated complication, happy reversal, and above all the comic order—which we will discuss in its appropriate place. . . .

But a new question could be asked here: what actually is this mixture of tragicomedy? And I would reply that it is the compromise of tragic and comic delight which does not allow the audience to be carried away by excessive tragic melancholy and comic immoderation.

. . . If at this point we concede that tragicomedy is reasonably mixed, what does it attempt to do? What is its end, laughter or tears? For the two cannot be accomplished at the same time. Therefore, what does it do first? What to a greater extent? What to a lesser? What principally? What subordinately? We cannot respond to these questions until we can determine the objectives of tragedy and comedy. . . .

Beginning with comedy, its "instrumental" objective is to represent those actions of private characters whose faults make us laugh; this concept comes from Aristotle. But the "structural"[2] objective cannot be found in his extant works. For in that treatise of his poetics which we have, the analysis of comedy is missing. We must assume that there he would also have assigned a "structural" objective for comedy as effectively as he did for tragedy. But from the "instrumental" objective that he assigned in his work, we can well conjecture what he would have fixed as the "structural" objective, since this is the model which the author holds up for himself. . . .

. . . Comedy purges melancholy, an emotion so noxious that it often drives man to madness and suicide. . . . As the wind is able to dissipate condensed air, comedy, by provoking laughter, also shakes off that dark and misty mood generated in us by the excessive mental concentration which often makes us lazy and slow-witted in our activities. For this reason comedy only presents private characters with faults deemed worthy of laughter, jokes, games, and intrigues which are small in consequence, short in time, and end happily. In this way comedy achieves its "structural" objective.

But tragedy, on the other hand, recalls the loose and wandering soul; therefore, its objectives are very different [from those of comedy]. Aristotle, in his *Poetics*, has discussed both objectives in the passage where he defines tragedy (in this respect, much more satisfactorily than comedy). The "instrumental" objective is the imitation of some horrible and compassionate event; the "structural" objective is the purgation of terror and com-

[2] *Poetics*, chap. 5.

passion. . . . Tragedy is a story and its purpose is not to teach virtue but to purge—as much as one story can—those two disturbances of the soul which are obstacles to fortitude, which is so noble and necessary a virtue in all human activities. . . .

For quite a while now I have been saying that tragicomedy is like the others; it also has two objectives: the "instrumental," which is the form resulting from the imitation of tragic and comic situations mixed together; and the "structural," which purges souls of the ill effect of melancholy. Since it is entirely comic and simple, the "structural" objective [of tragicomedy] is not connected in any way with tragedy because the effects of the purging in the two genres are actually opposite: one cheers and the other saddens, one relaxes and the other restrains. These are inconsistent emotions, since one moves from the center to the circumference, while the other travels in the opposite direction. In drama, these objectives can be called contradictory. However, since tragedy has many parts, the "instrumental" objective can be "mixed," if the terror-causing event is removed, for there are enough other parts which have the power of producing comic delight. Therefore, since Aristotle concedes delight in tragedy, delight smoothly concurs with delight. And what is tragic delight? It is the imitation of serious actions by illustrous characters with new and unexpected accidents. Now, by eliminating the terror and reducing only the danger, by fabricating a new plot and new names, all tempered with laughter, the delight of the imitation which remains will be potentially but not actually tragic. And only the outward appearance of terror will remain, but not that essential aspect of it which induces purgation, for the purging of terror can only be induced when all the tragic elements are intact. Otherwise, the story itself would still be a tragedy. And there is a great difference between these two genres, because tragicomedy, with its simple narration, has no intention of purging [terror], and tragedy—with its seriousness, with decoration, harmony, rhythm, magnificent and luxurious language, and with other tragic spectacle—intends to induce a terrifying and pitiful ambience in order to purge those resulting reactions. And that is why where Aristotle says that the plots with unhappy endings are tragic in the truest sense, he quickly adds "when they are well managed," meaning that all representations do not produce a tragic effect, but only those which are accompanied by all the other elements which are appropriate to them. Tragic pleasure consists, therefore, in the imitation of horrifying and pitiful events which in itself, Aristotle says, is delightful. But this is insufficient. It is necessary that the other elements also be such that the objective of purgation can be properly achieved. Otherwise, a tragedy will only be an equivocal one, i.e., outside the definition given by the Philosopher. Therefore, in developing some subject which is not intended to purge terror, the poet modifies it with laughter and other comic qualities in such a way that, although the subject is by nature terrifying and pitiful, it is unable to produce terror and compassion. And it is still less able to purge them, but it retains the single virtue of delighting through representation. And just as every terrifying event is not suitable for the purpose of purging terror (which is proved in paintings, however horrifying and frightening, and in things of the same quality which are only narrated but not dramatized), so every representation of the terrible does not produce tragedy if it is not combined with the other elements which are essential to it. . . .

As for comedy, it has become so tedious and contemptible that unless it is accompanied by the wonders of the interludes no one today will tolerate it any longer. And this has happened because sordid and mercenary people have contaminated it and reduced it to its nadir, carrying here and there, for a notorious profit, that excellent type of play which once would have crowned its makers with glory. Consequently, in order to raise comedy from such meanness, in order for it to delight the alert ears of modern audiences, the makers of tragicomedy—following in the footsteps of Menander and Terence, who elevated it to more serious and respectful dignity—strive to blend in between pleasurable situations those aspects of tragedy which can accompany the comic to the point that they can achieve purgation. . . .

But to conclude once and for all that which was my primary intention to demonstrate, if I am asked what the objective of tragicomedy is, I will answer that it is to imitate through the mise en scène a fabricated action, mixed with all those tragic and comic elements which could with verisimilitude and decorum be joined together into a single dramatic form, whose purpose is to purge with delight the sadness of the audience. The mode of imitation, which is the "instrumental" objective, is "mixed" because it represents a mixture of tragic and comic events. But the purging, which is the "structural" objective, exists only as a single mode because it reduces the combination of two qualities to only one purpose: to free the audience from melancholy.

Although all four of the elements,[3] however blunted, are found in natural compounds, as has been said, there nevertheless remains in every one of them one particular quality which is dominated by either this or that element and which subordinates the others and favors the element most compatible with it. So also in the "mixed" drama of which we speak, although all the elements in it are tragic and comic, it is not impossible, however, for the plot to favor one genre more than the other. This depends on the playwright's preference, provided he remains within the limits discussed above. Plautus' *Amphitrion* leans more toward the comic, Euripides' *Cyclops* more toward the tragic. However, it is not true that neither one of them is a tragicomedy: neither has as its objective the purging of terror

[3] Earth, air, fire, and water [translator's note].

and compassion, because this purgation cannot occur when there is laughter, disposing souls to relax rather than restrain themselves. . . .

. . . The proper and principal linguistic style of tragicomedy is the magnificent. When the magnificent is accompanied by the serious, this mode of expression becomes the quintessence of tragedy. But when the magnificient is mixed with polished language, the resulting mood is suitable to tragicomedy. Because it deals with high-ranking characters and heroes, humble language is not appropriate. And because we do not want terror-causing events and atrocities in it—on the contrary, we run away from them—tragicomedy sets aside the serious and takes the sweet, which modifies the magnitude and sublimity which is proper to the purely tragic. . . .

Now, how does the tragicomic playwright temper his style? Obviously, he will not devise a maxim or figure of speech whose style is sublime, nor will he fabricate the language and rhythm of the humble. But by modifying the seriousness of the maxim with those devices which usually make it unpretentious, and with other devices that sustain the humble nature of some character or theme with which he deals, with a little of that nobility of speech which is proper to the wonderful, he will arrive at a concept appropriate to his subject matter. It should not be so elevated that it rises to the level of the tragic, nor so unpretentious that it approaches the comic. . . .

Laughter would not be suitable to the double form of tragedy because the tragic cannot take shape where there is laughter. So also, although malefactors are punished in the double form of tragedy, pain is not suitable to tragicomedy, in which according to comic tradition, the worst characters are not punished. . . . Ordinarily, comedy would also be inclined to give a prosperous end to its worst characters.

Elizabethan
and Jacobean England,
and Spain

Although actors and audiences of dramatic productions had on numerous occasions been condemned in England as sinful, the earliest systematic, separate attack, apart from sermons, occurred in 1577, in John Northbrooke's *Treatise*, whose full title links plays with gambling. Written after and possibly because of the opening of the Theatre, the Curtain, and the Blackfriars— all homes for "Satan's banquets"—Northbrooke's *Treatise* vividly reveals the hostile attitude many Elizabethans held toward the theatre. Paradoxically, this antidramatic tract is written in quasidramatic form: a dialogue between Youth and Age. No less violent an attack came two years later, when Stephen Gosson's more famous *School of Abuse* charged the theatre with responsibility for the deterioration of England's manners and morals. Because of the theatre—"a whore's fair for whores" in Elizabethan England as in ancient Rome—Englishmen, charges Gosson, are more gluttonous than Greeks, more wanton than Italians, prouder than Spaniards, more deceitful than the French, and greater drinkers than the Dutch. Himself a former actor and an unsuccessful playwright, Gosson repents his sins, warns others who may fall into the pit, and maintains that moral instruction should be sought in the Church and not in the theatre. Although he claims to condemn only the abuses of poetry rather than all poetry, he leaves little uncondemned.

The first reply to Gosson, by Thomas Lodge, later a playwright and translator of Seneca, came the same year, 1579. For the most part, Lodge's *Defense* rests on conventional Renaissance arguments, such as the citation of admired poets. Failing to come to grips with the issues, he leaves the field to Sir Philip Sidney, who head-on tackles Gosson's objections. Sidney's *Defense of Poesy* (that is, of imaginative literature in general) was written, it should be noted, *before* the great period of Elizabethan drama; Shakespeare and Marlowe had not then turned twenty, and all Sidney could find to admire in English drama was *Gorboduc*, which falls short of classical models but which he praised for its pithy Senecan *sententiae*. Stressing the usual neo-classical ideals of instruction, decorum, the three unities, and purity of genre, every essential principle of Sidney's *Defense* can be traced to Italy. Through

157

Sidney's rigidly classical *Apology*, which mentions the unities for the first time in English criticism, Aristotle—as filtered through neoclassical principles—began to be influential in England.

These principles did not, however, influence English or Spanish playwrights, who seem to have been aware of them. Shakespeare, for instance, remarks on "the abuse of distance" as the locale of *Henry* V is about to change from England to France, and in *The Winter's Tale* he suggests it is no crime for him to "slide o'er sixteen years." Like most Elizabethan and Jacobean playwrights of the popular theatre, John Webster admits that he willingly disregards neoclassical rules of playwriting in favor of the sort of play his audience prefers.

Likewise familiar with classical and neoclassical critics and poets, Lope de Vega nevertheless rejects their dicta on the general ground that he writes for a Spanish audience whose demands differ from those of academic critics. He also justifies his heretical mixture of "Terence with Seneca," in his words, on the basis that such variety exists in nature and is beautiful.

Atypically, Ben Jonson tried to establish "correct" literary standards in England. Although he did not succeed in his own time, he influenced later generations. A classicist, Jonson preferred adherence to the rules of the ancients, but not blind obedience to them. Insisting on the moral purposes of comedy, to act as a social monitor and to condemn vice by ridicule, Jonson also proposed (in the Induction to *Every Man out of his Humour*) the "humours" theory of comic characterization, which he based on an imbalance of one or more of four basic human characteristics that derive from the four elements. Finally, Jonson was the first important critic of Shakespeare, and he set the tone of much important Shakespearean criticism to come: reasoned admiration and an absence of what Bernard Shaw was to call "bardolatry."

The question of dramatic genres interested Elizabethan and Jacobean playwrights and critics (one recalls Polonius' famous speech about genres). In *The Art of English Poesy*, George Puttenham—confusing "satyr" with "satire"—links changes in genres with the development of drama and of civilization itself. The anonymous author of *A Warning for Fair Women* personifies three genres: Tragedy, Comedy, and History. In his Preface to *The Faithful Shepherdess*, John Fletcher—like Guarini, who influenced both preface and play—tries to justify tragicomedy as a separate, legitimate genre. Another question that interested Elizabethans and Jacobeans was that of rhyme. Campion attacked it as a vulgar and unseemly ornament that made the poet excessively strain and extend a metaphor at the expense of subject matter. Defending rhyme, Daniel cited such matters as custom, but he argued more substantively that, for example, rhyme helps people remember what is said.

John Northbrooke *16th century*

A Treatise against Dicing, Dancing, Plays, and Interludes *1577*

YOUTH   What say you to . . . players and plays? Are they good and godly, meet to be used, haunted, and looked upon, which now are practiced?

AGE   To speak my mind and conscience plainly (and in the fear of God) they are not tolerable nor sufferable in any commonweal, especially where the gospel is preached, for it is right prodigality, which is opposite to liberality, for as liberality is to help and succor with worldly goods the man which is poor and stands needful thereof, and also to give to the marriage of poor maidens, highways, or poor scholars, etc., so prodigality is to bestow money and goods in such sort as it [is] spent either in banqueting, feasting, rewards to players of interludes, dicing, and dancing, etc., for the which no great fame or memory can remain to the spenders or receivers thereof.

YOUTH   I have heard say that one Plautus, a comical poet, spent all his substance upon players' garments; also one Roscius, a Roman and a player in comedies (whom for his excellence in pronunciation and gesture, noble Cicero called his jewel), the Romans also gave him (as histories report) a stipend of one thousand groats for every day (which is in our money sixteen pounds, fourteen shillings, four pence). . . . Why may we not do the like?

AGE   Because these are no examples for Christians to follow, for Christ hath given us a far better rule and order: how to bestow our goods upon his needy members which lie in the streets, prisons, and other places, and also those that are afflicted and persecuted for the testimony of a good conscience for the gospel's cause, etc. . . . Saint Augustine saith, *Donare quippe res suas histrionibus, vitium est immane, non virtus*: whosoever give their goods to interlude and stage players is [*sic*] a great vice and sin, and not a virtue. . . .

YOUTH   Do you speak against those places also which are made up and built for such plays and interludes, as the Theatre and Curtain is, and other suchlike places besides?

AGE   Yea, truly, for I am persuaded that Satan hath not a more speedy way

Selections. From John Northbrooke, *A Treatise against Dicing, Dancing, Plays, and Interludes*. London: Reprinted for the Shakespeare Society, 1843. Spelling and punctuation modernized by the editor.

and fitter school to work and teach his desire to bring men and women into his snare of concupiscence and filthy lusts of wicked whoredom than those places and plays and theatres are, and [it is] therefore necessary that those places and players should be forbidden and dissolved and put down by authority, as the brothel houses and stews are. How did the Benjamites overcome and take away the daughters of Israel but in watching them in a special open place where they were accustomed upon the festival days to sport and dance most idly and wantonly? . . .[1] Saint Augustine saith that the women of Saba, being of curiosity desirous to be present at open spectacles, were raped and ravished by the Romans, whereof followed such wars that both nations were almost destroyed. . . .

YOUTH I have heard many, both men and women, say that they can resort to such plays and behold them without any hurt to themselves or to others, and that no lust nor concupiscence is inflamed or stirred up in them in the beholding of any person or of the plays themselves. How say you: may it be so?

AGE Saint Chrysostom shall answer them, who wrote only of such as you speak of, that resorted to such playing places. . . . David (saith he) was sore hurt in beholding Bathsheba, and thinkest thou to escape? He did not behold a harlot but on the top of his house, *tu autem in theatro, ubi condemnat animam sapientis*: thou beholdest them in an open theatre, a place where the soul of the wise is snared and condemned. In those places (saith he) thou seest not only *res infaustas*, unlawful things, but also hearest *spurciloquia*, filthy speeches, whereof is (saith he) *incessu meretricis*, the beginning of whoredom, and the habit of all evilness and mischief, where thou shalt, by hearing devilish and filthy songs, hurt thy chaste ears, and also shalt see that which shall be grievous unto thine eyes, for our eyes are as windows of the mind. . . . Art thou wiser, stronger, and holier than David? A little sparkle of fire cast into straw beginneth quickly to kindle and flame. Our flesh is straw and will burn quickly, and for that cause the Holy Ghost setteth David for an example to us, that we should beware of such contagiousness. . . .

YOUTH I perceive by your communication that none ought to haunt and frequent those theatres and places where interludes are, and especially women and maids.

AGE You have collected the meaning of my sayings—nay, rather of the fathers' sayings—truly. You may see daily what multitudes are gathered together at those plays, of all sorts, to the great displeasure of Almighty God and danger of their souls, etc., for they learn nothing thereby but that which is fleshy and carnal. . . . In the Synod of Laodicea, it was decreed that no Christians, and especially priests, should come into any

[1] Judg. 21:20–23.

place where interludes and plays are, for that Christians must abstain from such places where blasphemy is commonly used. Chrysostom calleth those places and playing of interludes, *festa Satanae*, Satan's banquets. . . .

YOUTH Notwithstanding all this that you have alleged out of the fathers and councils, I suppose a man or woman doth not sin to behold and lust one for another except they commit carnal copulation together.

AGE My son, how dost thou read or hear the word of Christ in the gospel, that saith he that looketh on a woman and desireth to have her, he hath committed adultery already in his heart, etc. . . .[2] I dare boldly say that few men or women come from plays and resorts of men with safe and chaste minds. . . .

YOUTH I marvel why you do speak against such interludes and places for plays, seeing that many times they play histories out of the Scriptures.

AGE Assuredly, that is very evil so to do, to mingle scurrility with divinity; that is to eat meat with unwashed hands. Theopompus intermingled a portion of Moses' law with his writings, for the which God struck him mad. Theodectes began the same practice and was stricken stark blind. And will God suffer them unpunished that with impure and wicked manners and doings do use and handle upon God's divine mysteries with such unreverentness and irreligiousness? What fellowship hath righteousness with unrighteousness? What communion hath light with darkness? . . . Saint Augustine saith it is better that spiritual things be utterly omitted than unworthily and unreverently handled and touched. . . . By the long suffering and permitting of these vain plays, it hath stricken such a blind zeal into the hearts of people that they shame not to say, and affirm openly, that plays are as good as sermons and that they learn as much or more at a play than they do at God's word preached. . . . Saint Ambrose saith that all such plays, though they seem pleasant and full of sport, must utterly be abolished, because no such plays are mentioned or expressed in Holy Scripture. Saint Augustine saith that such interludes and plays are filthy spectacles, for when the heathen did appoint and ordain (says he) plays and interludes to their gods for the avoiding of the pestilence of their bodies, your bishops for the avoiding of the pestilence of your souls have forbidden and prohibited those kind of scenical and interlude plays. . . . In the decrees, it is so decreed that all interlude players and comedy players, heretics, Jews, and pagans are infamous persons and ought to be taken as no accusers of any, nor yet to be produced as witnesses in any matter or cause before any judge. If they be, the law is that the party may lawfully except against them and say they are infamous persons, for that they are players of interludes. . . . Also, there is a notable statute made against vagabonds, rogues, etc., wherein is expressed what

[2] Matt. 5:28.

they are that shall be taken and accounted for rogues. Amongst all the whole rabblement, common players in interludes are to be taken for rogues and punishment is appointed for them to be burnt through the ear with a hot iron of an inch [in] compass, and for the second fault to be hanged as felon, etc. The reason is for that their trade is such an idle, loitering life, a practice to all mischief, as you have heard before.

YOUTH   If they leave this life and become good, true laborers of the commonwealth, to get their own livings with their own hands, in the sweat of their face, shall they not be admitted and taken again to the Lord's table and afterward to be reputed and taken for honest men?

AGE   Yes, truly, and therefore in the Third Council of Carthage, it is put down in these words: *Scenicis, atque histrionibus, caeterisque personis hujusmodi, vel Apostatis, conversis ad Dominum, gratia vel reconciliatio non negetur,* to players of interludes and comedies and other suchlike infamous persons and apostates converting and returning to the Lord, by repentance, grace and reconciliation is not to be denied.

Stephen Gosson   *1554–1623*

The School of Abuse[1]   *1579*

. . . Ovid says that Romulus built his theatre as a whores' fair for whores, made triumphs and set out plays to gather the fair women together, [so] that every one of his soldiers might take where he liked a snatch for his share. . . . Dion so straightly forbids the ancient families of Rome, and gentlewomen that tender their name and honor, to come to theatres, and rebukes them so sharply when he takes them napping, that if they be but once seen there he judges it sufficient cause to speak ill of them and think worse. The shadow

Selections. From Stephen Gosson, *The School of Abuse*. London: Reprinted for The Shakespeare Society, 1841. Spelling and punctuation modernized by the editor.

[1] The full title is *The School of Abuse: Containing a Pleasant Invective against Poets, Pipers, Players, Jesters, and such like caterpillars of a commonwealth, setting up the flag of defiance to their mischievous exercise and overthrowing their bulwarks by profane writers, natural reason, and common experience, a discourse as pleasant for gentlemen that favor learning as profitable for all that will follow virtue.*

of a knave hurts an honest man, the scent of the stews a sober matron, and the show of the theatres a simple gazer. . . .

Consider with thyself, gentle reader, the old discipline of England: mark what we were before and what we are now. Leave Rome awhile and cast thine eyes back to thy predecessors, and tell me how wonderfully we have been changed since we were schooled with these abuses. Dion says that Englishmen could suffer watching and labor, hunger and thirst, and bear all storms with head and shoulders; they fed upon roots and barks of trees; they would stand up to the chin many days in marshes without victuals, and they had a kind of sustenance in time of need, of which if they had taken but the quantity of a bean or the weight of a pea they did neither gape after meat nor long for the cup a great while after. The men in valor not yielding to Scythia, the women in courage passing the Amazons, the exercise of both was shooting and darting, running and wrestling, and trying such mastery as either consisted in swiftness of feet, agility of body, strength of arms, or martial discipline.

But the exercise that is now among us is banqueting, playing, piping, and dancing, and all such delights as may win us to pleasure or rock us in sleep. *Quantum mutatus ab illo!*[2] Oh, what a wonderful change is this! Our wrestling at arms is turned to wallowing in ladies' laps, our courage to cowardice, our cunning to riot, our bows into bowls, and our darts to dishes. We have robbed Greece of gluttony, Italy of wantonness, Spain of pride, France of deceit, and Dutchland of quaffing. Compare London to Rome and England to Italy: you shall find the theatres of the one, the abuses of the other, to be rife among us. . . . In our assemblies at plays in London, you shall see such heaving and shoving, such itching and shouldering to sit by women, such care for their garments that they be not trod on, such eyes to their laps that no chips light in them, such pillows to their backs that they take no hurt, such masking in their ears, I know not what; such giving them pippins to pass the time, such playing at foot-saunt[3] without cards, such ticking, such toying, such smiling, such winking, and such manning them home when the sports are ended that it is a right comedy to mark their behavior, to watch their conceits, as the cat for the mouse, and as good as a course[4] at the game itself to dog them a little or follow aloof by the print of their feet, and so discover by slot where the deer takes soil.

If this were as well noted as ill seen, or as openly punished as secretly practiced, I have no doubt but the cause would be sered to dry up the effect, and these pretty rabbits very cunningly ferreted from their burrows. For they that lack customers all the week, either because their haunt is unknown, or the constables and officers of their parish watch them so narrowly that they dear

[2] Vergil, *Aeneid*, ii, 274. Gosson's English version follows.
[3] A game of cards.
[4] A hunt.

not queach,[5] to celebrate the Sabbath [they] flock to theatres and there keep a general market of bawdry. Not that any filthiness in deed is committed within the compass of that ground, as was once done in Rome, but that every John and his Joan, every knave and his queen are there first acquainted and cheapen the merchandise in that place, which they pay for elsewhere, as they can agree. These worms, when they dare not nestle in the peascod at home, find refuge abroad and are hid in the ears of other men's corn. . . .

Solon made no law for parricides because he feared that he should rather put men in mind to commit such offences than by any strange punishment give them a bit to keep them under, and I intend not to show you all that I see, nor half that I hear of these abuses, lest you judge me more willful to teach them than willing to forbid them. . . . The carpenter raises not his frame without tools, nor the Devil his work without instruments: were not players the means to make these assemblies, such multitudes would hardly be drawn in so narrow a room. They seek not to hurt, but desire to please: they have purged their comedies of wanton speeches, yet the corn which they sell is full of cockle and the drink that they draw overcharged with dregs. There is more in them than we perceive: the Devil stands at our elbow when we see not, speaks when we hear him not, strikes when we feel not, and wounds sore when he raises no skin nor rends the flesh. In those things that we least mistrust the greatest danger does often lurk: the countryman is more afraid of the serpent that is hid in the grass than the wild beast that openly feeds upon the mountains, the mariner is more endangered by private shelves than known rocks, the soldier is sooner killed with a little bullet than a long sword. There is more peril in close fistulas than outward sores, in secret ambush than main battles, in undermining than plain assaulting, in friends than foes, in civil discord than foreign wars. Small are the abuses and slight are the faults that now in theatres escape the poet's pen, but tall cedars from little grains shoot high, great oaks from slender roots spread wide, large streams from narrow springs run far, one spark fires a whole city. . . . The abuses of plays cannot be shown because they pass the degrees of the instrument, reach of the plummet, sight of the mind, and for trial are never brought to the touchstone. Therefore, he that will avoid the open shame of private sin, the common plague of private offences, the great wracks of little rocks, the sure disease of uncertain causes, must set hand to the stern and eye to his steps to shun the occasion as near as he can, neither running to bushes for rending his clothes, nor rend his clothes for impairing his thrift, nor walk upon ice for taking of a fall, nor take a fall for bruising himself, nor go to theatres for being allured, nor once be allured for fear of abuse.

. . . It is well known that some [players] are sober, discreet, properly learned, honest householders, and citizens well thought on among their neigh-

---

[5] Stir.

bors at home, though the pride of their shadows (I mean those hangbyes whom they succor with stipend) cause them to be somewhat ill talked of abroad.

And as some of the players are far from abuse, so some of their plays are without rebuke, which are easily remembered, as quickly reckoned: the two prose books played at the Belsavage, where you shall find never a word without wit, never a line without pith, never a letter placed in vain; *The Jew* and *Ptolemy*, shown at the Bull,[6] the one representing the greediness of worldly choosers and bloody minds of userers, the other very lively describing how seditious estates with their own devices, false friends with their own swords, and rebellious commons in their own snares are overthrown, neither with amorous gesture wounding the eye nor with slovenly talk hurting the ears of the chaste hearers; *The Blacksmith's Daughter*[7] and *Catiline's Conspiracies*,[8] usually brought in at the Theatre, the first containing the treachery of Turks, the honorable bounty of a noble mind, the shining of virtue in distress. The last, because it is known to be a pig of mine own sow, I will speak the less of it, only giving you to understand that the whole mark which I shot at in that work was to show the reward of traitors in Catiline and the necessary government of learned men in the person of Cicero, which foresees every danger that is likely to happen and forestalls it continually ere it take effect. Therefore, I give these plays the commendation that Maximus Tyrius gave to Homer's works:[9] καλὰ μὲν γὰρ τὰ Ὁμήρου ἔπη, καὶ ἔπων τὰ κάλλιστα, καὶ φανότατα, καὶ ἄδεσθαι μουσαῖς πρέποντα ἀλλα οὐ πᾶσι καλὰ, οὐδὲ ἀεὶ καλά.

These plays are good plays and sweet plays, and of all plays the best plays, and most to be liked, worthy to be sung of the Muses, or set out with the cunning of Roscius himself; yet are they not fit for every man's diet; neither ought they commonly to be shown. Now, if any man ask me why myself have penned comedies[10] in time past and inveigh so eagerly against them here, let him know that *Semel insanavimus omnes.*[11] I have sinned and am sorry for my fault. He runs far that never turns. Better late than never. I gave myself to that exercise in hope to thrive, but I burnt one candle to seek another and lost both my time and my travel when I had done. . . .

This have I set down of the abuses of poets, pipers, and players, which bring us to pleasure, sloth, sleep, sin, and without repentance to death and

[6] *The Jew*, or *The Practice of Parasites* and *Ptolemy*, both anon., performed 1576–1579 at the Bull Inn.

[7] Anon., performed 1576–1579.

[8] A didactic history play by Gosson, written and performed 1578.

[9] "The poetry of Homer is beautiful, the most beautiful, the most brilliant poetry of its genre, the most harmonious, and worthy to be sung by the Muses themselves." —*Dissertations*, iii.

[10] His other plays (see n. 8) are *Captain Mario*, a comedy, and *Praise at Parting*, a morality, both written 1577.

[11] "We have all been mad at one time."—Mantuan, *Eclogues*, i, 118.

the Devil. . . . The patient that will be cured of his own accord must seek the means. . . . Let us but shut up our ears to poets, pipers, and players, pull our feet back from resort to theatres, and turn away our eyes from beholding of vanity, the greatest storm of abuse will be overblown and a fair path trod to amendment of life. Were not we so foolish to taste every drug and buy every trifle, players would shut in their shops and carry their trash to some other country.

Themistocles, in setting a piece of his ground to sale, among all the commodities which were reckoned up, straightly charged the crier to proclaim this, that he which bought it should have a good neighbor. If players can promise in words and perform it in deeds, proclaim it in their bills and make it good in their theatres, that there is nothing there noisome to the body nor hurtful to the soul, and that everyone which comes to buy their jests shall have an honest neighbor, tag and rag, cut and long tail, go thither and spare not. Otherwise, I advise you to keep you thence; myself will begin to lead the dance.

Thomas Lodge *c. 1558–1625*

A Defence of Poetry, Music, and Stage Plays *1579–1580*

And first let me familiarly consider . . . what the learned have always esteemed of poetry. Seneca, though a stoic, would have a poetical son, and amongst the ancientest, Homer was no less accounted than *Humanus deus*.[1] What made Alexander, I pray you, esteem of him so much? Why allotted he for his works so curious a closet? Was there no fitter underprop for his pillow than a simple pamphlet? In all Darius' coffers was there no jewel so costly?[2]

Selections. From Thomas Lodge, A *Defence of Poetry, Music, and Stage Plays*. London: The Shakespeare Society, 1853. Spelling and punctuation modernized by the editor.

[1] A god in human form.
[2] When Alexander the Great (356–323 B.C.) set out to conquer Persia, he took with him the works of Homer, compiled for him by Aristotle, his former teacher. According to tradition, the conquest of Darius III (King of Persia, 336–330 B.C.) meant less to Alexander than this "pamphlet" of Homer.

Forsooth, methinks these two (the one the father of philosophers, the other the chieftain of chivalry) were both deceived if all were as a Gosson[3] would wish them; if poets paint naught but paltry toys in verse, their studies tended to foolishness. . . .

Poets, you say, use colors to cover their inconveniences and witty sentences to burnish their bawdry, and you divinity to cover your knavery. But tell me truth, Gosson, speakest thou as thou thinkest? What colors findest thou in a poet not to be admitted? . . . Are their gods displeasant unto thee? . . . Thou knowest them not, for wot thou that in the person of Saturn our decaying years are signified; in the person of Juno our affections are deciphered; in the person of Minerva is our understanding signified, both in respect of war as [of] policy. When they say that Pallas was begotten of the brain of Jupiter, their meaning is none other but that all wisdom (as the learned say) is from above, and cometh from the Father of Lights. . . . What so they wrote was to this purpose: in the way of pleasure to draw men to wisdom. . . .

Though Plato could wish the expulsion of poets from his well publics [commonwealth], which he might do with reason, yet the wisest had not all that same opinion. . . . Seneca saith that the study of poets is to make children ready to the understanding of wisdom. . . . What made Erasmus labor in Euripides' tragedies? Did he endeavor by painting them out of Greek into Latin to manifest sin with us? or to confirm us in goodness? . . . Who then doth not wonder at poetry? Who thinketh not that it proceedeth from above? . . . Horace reporteth, in his *de Arte Poetica*, all the answers of the oracles were in verse. Among the precise Jews you shall find poets. . . . David was a poet. . . . Solomon vouchsafed poetical practices. . . .

Men that have knowledge what comedies and tragedies be will commend them, but it is sufferable in the foolish to reprove what they know not. . . . If it not be tedious to Gosson to hearken to the learned, the reader shall perceive the antiquity of playmaking, the inventors of comedies, and therewithal the use and commodity of them. . . . Tragedy and comedy, Donatus the grammarian saith, they were invented by learned fathers of the old time to no other purpose but to yield praise unto God for a happy harvest or plentiful year. . . . The first matter of tragedies was to give thanks and praise to God and a grateful prayer of the countrymen for a happy harvest. . . . [Later] they presented the lives of satyrs, so that they might wisely, under abuse of that name, discover the follies of many [of] their fellow citizens. As for comedies . . . Horace himself . . . saith there was no abuse but these men reprehended it: a thief was loth to be seen [at] one [of] their spectacles, a coward was never present at their assemblies, a backbiter abhorred their company, and I myself could not have blamed you, Gosson, for exempting yourself from the theatre. . . .

I must confess with Aristotle that men are greatly delighted with imitation

---

[3] Stephen Gosson, to whose *School of Abuse* (see pp. 162–166) this is a reply.

and that it were good to bring those things on stage that were altogether attending to virtue. . . . I wish as zealously as the best that all abuses of playing were abolished, but for the thing, the antiquity causeth me to allow it, so it be used as it should be. . . . Sure it were pity to abolish that which hath so great virtue in it because it is abused.

Sir Philip Sidney 1554–1586

The Defense of Poesy 1583

And first, truly, to all them that, professing learning, inveigh against poetry, may justly be objected that they go very near to ungratefulness, to seek to deface that which, in the noblest nations and languages that are known, hath been the first light-giver to ignorance, and first nurse, whose milk by little and little enabled them to feed afterwards of tougher knowledges. And will they now play the hedgehog, that, being received into the den, drave out his host? Or rather the vipers, that with their birth kill their parents? Let learned Greece in any of her manifold sciences be able to show me one book before Musaeus, Homer, and Hesiod, all three nothing else but poets. Nay, let any history be brought that can say any writers were there before them, if they were not men of the same skill, as Orpheus, Linus, and some other are named, who, having been the first of that country that made pens deliverers of their knowledge to their posterity, may justly challenge to be called their fathers in learning. For not only in time they had this priority—although in itself antiquity be venerable—but went before them as causes, to draw with their charming sweetness the wild untamed wits to an admiration of knowledge. So as Amphion was said to move stones with his poetry to build Thebes, and Orpheus to be listened to by beasts—indeed stony and beastly people. So among the Romans were Livius Andronicus and Ennius; so in the Italian language the first that made it aspire to be a treasure-house of science were the poets Dante, Boccace, and Petrarch; so in our English were Gower and Chaucer, after whom, encouraged and delighted with their excellent fore-

Selections. From Sir Philip Sidney, *The Defense of Poesy, Otherwise Known as An Apology for Poetry*, edited by Albert S. Cook. Boston: Ginn & Co., 1890.

going, others have followed to beautify our mother-tongue, as well in the same kind as in other arts.

This did so notably show itself, that the philosophers of Greece durst not a long time appear to the world but under the masks of poets. . . . And truly even Plato whosoever well considereth, shall find that in the body of his work though the inside and strength were philosophy, the skin as it were and beauty depended most of poetry. . . .

So that truly neither philosopher nor historiographer could at the first have entered into the gates of popular judgments, if they had not taken a great passport of poetry, which in all nations at this day, where learning flourisheth not, is plain to be seen; in all which they have some feeling of poetry. In Turkey, besides their lawgiving divines they have no other writers but poets. In our neighbor country Ireland, where truly learning goeth very bare, yet are their poets held in a devout reverence. Even among the most barbarous and simple Indians, where no writing is, yet have they their poets, who make and sing songs (which they call *areytos*), both of their ancestors' deeds and praises of their gods—a sufficient probability that, if ever learning come among them, it must be by having their hard dull wits softened and sharpened with the sweet delights of poetry; for until they find a pleasure in the exercise of the mind, great promises of much knowledge will little persuade them that know not the fruits of knowledge. In Wales, the true remnant of the ancient Britons, as there are good authorities to show the long time they had poets which they called bards, so through all the conquests of Romans, Saxons, Danes, and Normans, some of whom did seek to ruin all memory of learning from among them, yet do their poets even to this day last; so as it is not more notable in soon beginning, than in long continuing.

But since the authors of most of our sciences were the Romans, and before them the Greeks, let us a little stand upon their authorities. . . .

Poesy, therefore, is an art of imitation, for so Aristotle termeth it in his word μίμησις, that is to say, a representing, counterfeiting, or figuring forth; to speak metaphorically, a speaking picture, with this end—to teach and delight.

Of this have been three general kinds. The chief, both in antiquity and excellency, were they that did imitate the inconceivable excellencies of God. Such were David in his Psalms; Solomon in his Song of Songs, in his Ecclesiastes and Proverbs; Moses and Deborah in their Hymns; and the writer of Job; which, beside other, the learned Emanuel Tremellius and Franciscus Junius do entitle the poetical part of the Scripture.[1] Against these none will speak that hath the Holy Ghost in due holy reverence. . . .

The second kind is of them that deal with matters philosophical: either

---

[1] Emanuel Tremellius (1510–1580) and Franciscus Junius or Dujon or DuJon (1545–1602), scholars who edited the Bible.

moral, as Tyrtaeus, Phocylides, and Cato; or natural, as Lucretius and Virgil's *Georgics*; or astronomical, as Manilius and Pontanus; or historical, as Lucan; which who mislike, the fault is in their judgment quite out of taste, and not in the sweet food of sweetly uttered knowledge.

But because this second sort is wrapped within the fold of the proposed subject, and takes not the free course of his own invention, whether they properly be poets or no let grammarians dispute, and go to the third, indeed right poets, of whom chiefly this question ariseth. Betwixt whom and these second is such a kind of difference as betwixt the meaner sort of painters, who counterfeit only such faces as are set before them, and the more excellent, who having no law but wit, bestow that in colors upon you which is fittest for the eye to see—as the constant though lamenting look of Lucretia, when she punished in herself another's fault; wherein he painteth not Lucretia, whom he never saw, but painteth the outward beauty of such a virtue. For these third be they which most properly do imitate to teach and delight; and to imitate borrow nothing of what is, hath been, or shall be; but range, only reined with learned discretion, into the divine consideration of what may be and should be. These be they that, as the first and most noble sort may justly be termed *vates*, so these are waited on in the excellentest languages and best understandings with the foredescribed name of poets. For these, indeed, do merely make to imitate, and imitate both to delight and teach, and delight to move men to take that goodness in hand, which without delight they would fly as from a stranger; and teach to make them know that goodness whereunto they are moved—which being the noblest scope to which ever any learning was directed, yet want there not idle tongues to bark at them. . . .

For conclusion, I say the philosopher teacheth, but he teacheth obscurely, so as the learned only can understand him; that is to say, he teacheth them that are already taught. But the poet is the food for the tenderest stomachs; the poet is indeed the right popular philosopher. Whereof Aesop's tales give good proof; whose pretty allegories, stealing under the formal tales of beasts, make many, more beastly than beasts, begin to hear the sound of virtue from those dumb speakers. . . .

So, then, the best of the historian is subject to the poet; for whatsoever action or faction, whatsoever counsel, policy, or war-stratagem the historian is bound to recite, that may the poet, if he list, with his imitation make his own, beautifying it both for further teaching and more delighting, as it pleaseth him; having all, from Dante's Heaven to his Hell, under the authority of his pen. Which if I be asked what poets have done? so as I might well name some, yet say I, and say again, I speak of the art, and not of the artificer.

Now, to that which commonly is attributed to the praise of history, in respect of the notable learning is gotten by marking the success, as though therein a man should see virtue exalted and vice punished—truly that commendation is peculiar to poetry and far off from history. For, indeed, poetry ever setteth virtue so out in her best colors, making Fortune her well-waiting handmaid, that one must needs be enamored of her. . . .

. . . It is the comic whom naughty play-makers and stage-keepers have justly made odious. To the argument of abuse I will answer after. Only thus much now is to be said, that the comedy is an imitation of the common errors of our life, which he representeth in the most ridiculous and scornful sort that may be, so as it is impossible that any beholder can be content to be such a one. Now, as in geometry the oblique must be known as well as the right, and in arithmetic the odd as well as the even; so in the actions of our life who seeth not the filthiness of evil, wanteth a great foil to perceive the beauty of virtue. This doth the comedy handle so, in our private and domestical matters, as with hearing it we get, as it were, an experience what is to be looked for of a niggardly Demea, of a crafty Davus, of a flattering Gnatho, of a vainglorious Thraso;[2] and not only to know what effects are to be expected, but to know who be such, by the signifying badge given them by the comedian. And little reason hath any man to say that men learn evil by seeing it so set out; since, as I said before, there is no man living, but by the force truth hath in nature, no sooner seeth these men play their parts, but wisheth them *in pistrinum*,[3] although perchance the sack of his own faults lie so behind his back, that he seeth not himself to dance the same measure— whereto yet nothing can more open his eyes than to find his own actions contemptibly set forth.

So that the right use of comedy will, I think, by nobody be blamed, and much less of the high and excellent tragedy, that openeth the greatest wounds, and showeth forth the ulcers that are covered with tissue; that maketh kings fear to be tyrants, and tyrants manifest their tyrannical humors; that with stirring the effects of admiration and commiseration teacheth the uncertainty of this world, and upon how weak foundations gilden roofs are builded; that maketh us know:

Qui sceptra saevus duro imperio regit,
Timet timentes, metus in auctorem redit.[4]

But how much it can move, Plutarch yieldeth a notable testimony of the abominable tyrant Alexander Pheraeus; from whose eyes a tragedy, well made and represented, drew abundance of tears, who without all pity had murdered infinite numbers, and some of his own blood; so as he that was not

---

[2] Characters in the plays of Terence: a stingy old man (Demea), a wily slave (Davus), a parasite (Gnatho), a braggart (Thraso).

[3] In the mill. For punishment, Roman masters sent their slaves to labor there.

[4] From Seneca, *Oedipus*, 705–706: "The savage tyrant, bearing sternest rule, / Dreads those who dread him, and his fear recoils / To plague the inventor." —translation by Albert S. Cook.

ashamed to make matters for tragedies, yet could not resist the sweet violence of a tragedy. And if it wrought no further good in him, it was that he, in despite of himself, withdrew himself from hearkening to that which might mollify his hardened heart. But it is not the tragedy they do mislike, for it were too absurd to cast out so excellent a representation of whatsoever is most worthy to be learned. . . .

Now then go we to the most important imputations laid to the poor poets; for aught I can yet learn they are these.

First, that there being many other more fruitful knowledges, a man might better spend his time in them than in this.

Secondly, that it is the mother of lies.

Thirdly, that it is the nurse of abuse, infecting us with many pestilent desires, with a siren's sweetness drawing the mind to the serpent's tail of sinful fancies—and herein especially comedies give the largest field to ear, as Chaucer saith; how, both in other nations and in ours, before poets did soften us, we were full of courage, given to martial exercises, the pillars of manlike liberty, and not lulled asleep in shady idleness with poets' pastimes.

And, lastly and chiefly, they cry out with an open mouth, as if they had overshot Robin Hood, that Plato banished them out of his Commonwealth. Truly this is much, if there be much truth in it.

First, to the first, that a man might better spend his time is a reason indeed; but it doth, as they say, but *petere principium.*[5] For if it be, as I affirm, that no learning is so good as that which teacheth and moveth to virtue, and that none can both teach and move thereto so much as poesy, then is the conclusion manifest that ink and paper cannot be to a more profitable purpose employed. And certainly, though a man should grant their first assumption, it should follow, me thinks, very unwillingly, that good is not good because better is better. But I still and utterly deny that there is sprung out of earth a more fruitful knowledge.

To the second, therefore, that they should be the principal liars, I answer paradoxically, but truly, I think truly, that of all writers under the sun the poet is the least liar; and though he would, as a poet can scarcely be a liar. The astronomer, with his cousin the geometrician, can hardly escape when they take upon them to measure the height of the stars. How often, think you, do the physicians lie, when they aver things good for sicknesses, which afterwards send Charon a great number of souls drowned in a potion before they come to his ferry? And no less of the rest which take upon them to affirm. Now for the poet, he nothing affirmeth, and therefore never lieth. For, as I take it, to lie is to affirm that to be true which is false; so as the other artists, and especially the historian, affirming many things, can, in the cloudy knowledge of mankind, hardly escape from many lies. But the poet, as I said

[5] Beg the question.

before, never affirmeth. The poet never maketh any circles about your imagination, to conjure you to believe for true what he writeth. He citeth not authorities of other histories, but even for his entry calleth the sweet Muses to inspire into him a good invention; in troth, not laboring to tell you what is or is not, but what should or should not be. And therefore though he recount things not true, yet because he telleth them not for true he lieth not; without we will say that Nathan lied in his speech, before alleged, to David; which, as a wicked man durst scarce say, so think I none so simple would say that Aesop lied in the tales of his beasts; for who thinketh that Aesop wrote it for actually true, were well worthy to have his name chronicled among the beasts he writeth of. What child is there that, coming to a play, and seeing Thebes written in great letters upon an old door, doth believe that it is Thebes? If then a man can arrive at that child's age, to know that the poet's persons and doings are but pictures what should be, and not stories what have been, they will never give the lie to things not affirmatively but allegorically and figuratively written. And therefore, as in history looking for truth, they may go away full-fraught with falsehood, so in poesy looking but for fiction, they shall use the narration but as an imaginative ground-plot of a profitable invention. . . .

Their third is, how much it abuseth men's wit, training it to wanton sinfulness and lustful love. For indeed that is the principal, if not the only, abuse I can hear alleged. They say the comedies rather teach than reprehend amorous conceits. They say the lyric is larded with passionate sonnets, the elegiac weeps the want of his mistress, and that even to the heroical Cupid hath ambitiously climbed. Alas! Love, I would thou couldst as well defend thyself as thou canst offend others! I would those on whom thou dost attend could either put thee away, or yield good reason why they keep thee! But grant love of beauty to be a beastly fault, although it be very hard, since only man, and no beast, hath that gift to discern beauty; grant that lovely name of Love to deserve all hateful reproaches, although even some of my masters the philosophers spent a good deal of their lamp-oil in setting forth the excellency of it; grant, I say, whatsoever they will have granted, that not only love, but lust, but vanity, but, if they list, scurrility, possesseth many leaves of the poets' books; yet think I when this is granted, they will find their sentence may with good manners put the last words foremost, and not say that poetry abuseth man's wit, but that man's wit abuseth poetry. . . . But what! shall the abuse of a thing make the right use odious? . . . Do we not see the skill of physic, the best rampire to our often-assaulted bodies, being abused, teach poison, the most violent destroyer? Doth not knowledge of law, whose end is to even and right all things, being abused, grow the crooked fosterer of horrible injuries? Doth not, to go in the highest, God's word abused breed heresy, and his name abused become blasphemy? Truly a needle cannot do much hurt, and as truly—with leave of ladies be it spoken—it cannot do much good. With a sword thou mayst kill thy father, and with a sword thou mayst defend thy prince and country. . . .

But now, indeed, my burden is great, that Plato's name is laid upon me, whom, I must confess, of all philosophers I have ever esteemed most worthy of reverence; and with great reason, since of all philosophers he is the most poetical; yet if he will defile the fountain out of which his flowing streams have proceeded, let us boldly examine with what reasons he did it. . . .

Again, a man might ask out of what commonwealth Plato doth banish them. In sooth, thence where he himself alloweth community of women. So as belike this banishment grew not for effeminate wantonness, since little should poetical sonnets be hurtful when a man might have what woman he listed. But I honor philosophical instructions, and bless the wits which bred them, so as they be not abused, which is likewise stretched to poetry. Saint Paul himself, who yet, for the credit of poets, allegeth twice two poets,[6] and one of them by the name of a prophet, setteth a watchword upon philosophy —indeed upon the abuse. So doth Plato upon the abuse, not upon poetry. Plato found fault that the poets of his time filled the world with wrong opinions of the gods, making light tales of that unspotted essence, and there-fore would not have the youth depraved with such opinions. . . .

. . . And a man need go no further than to Plato himself to know his meaning; who, in his dialogue called *Ion*, giveth high and rightly divine com-mendation unto poetry. So as Plato, banishing the abuse, not the thing, not banishing it, but giving due honor unto it, shall be our patron and not our adversary. . . .

Our tragedies and comedies not without cause cried out against, observing rules neither of honest civility nor of skilful poetry, excepting *Gorboduc*— again I say of those that I have seen. Which notwithstanding as it is full of stately speeches and well-sounding phrases, climbing to the height of Seneca's style, and as full of notable morality, which it doth most delightfully teach, and so obtain the very end of poesy; yet in truth it is very defectious in the circumstances, which grieveth me, because it might not remain as an exact model of all tragedies. For it is faulty both in place and time, the two neces-sary companions of all corporal actions. For where the stage should always represent but one place, and the uttermost time presupposed in it should be, both by Aristotle's precept and common reason, but one day; there is both many days and many places inartificially imagined.

But if it be so in *Gorboduc*, how much more in all the rest? where you shall have Asia of the one side, and Afric of the other, and so many other under-kingdoms, that the player, when he cometh in, must ever begin with

----

[6] Aratus and Cleanthes (Acts 17:28), Epimenides (Titus 1:12), and Menander (1 Cor. 15:33).

telling where he is, or else the tale will not be conceived. Now ye shall have three ladies walk to gather flowers, and then we must believe the stage to be a garden. By and by we hear news of shipwreck in the same place, and then we are to blame if we accept it not for a rock. Upon the back of that comes out a hideous monster with fire and smoke, and then the miserable beholders are bound to take it for a cave. While in the mean time two armies fly in, represented with four swords and bucklers, and then what hard heart will not receive it for a pitched field?

Now of time they are much more liberal. For ordinary it is that two young princes fall in love; after many traverses she is got with child, delivered of a fair boy, he is lost, groweth a man, falleth in love, and is ready to get another child—and all this in two hours' space; which how absurd it is in sense even sense may imagine, and art hath taught, and all ancient examples justified, and at this day the ordinary players in Italy will not err in. Yet will some bring in an example of *Eunuchus* in Terence, that containeth matter of two days, yet far short of twenty years. True it is, and so was it to be played in two days, and so fitted to the time it set forth. And though Plautus have in one place done amiss, let us hit with him, and not miss with him. But they will say, How then shall we set forth a story which containeth both many places and many times? And do they not know that a tragedy is tied to the laws of poesy, and not of history; not bound to follow the story, but having liberty either to feign a quite new matter, or to frame the history to the most tragical conveniency? Again, many things may be told which cannot be showed—if they know the difference betwixt reporting and representing. As for example I may speak, though I am here, of Peru, and in speech digress from that to the description of Calicut; but in action I cannot represent it without Pacolet's horse. And so was the manner the ancients took, by some *Nuntius*[7] to recount things done in former time or other place.

Lastly, if they will represent a history, they must not, as Horace saith, begin *ab ovo*,[8] but they must come to the principal point of that one action which they will represent. By example this will be best expressed.[9] I have a story of young Polydorus, delivered for safety's sake, with great riches, by his father Priamus to Polymnestor, King of Thrace, in the Trojan war time. He, after some years, hearing the overthrow of Priamus, for to make the treasure his own murdereth the child; the body of the child is taken up by Hecuba; she, the same day, findeth a sleight to be revenged most cruelly of the tyrant. Where now would one of our tragedy-writers begin, but with the delivery of the child? Then should he sail over into Thrace, and so spend I know not how many years, and travel numbers of places. But where doth Euripides?

---

[7] Messenger.
[8] Literally, from the egg; that is, from its origin or from the beginning.
[9] His example is the *Hecuba* of Euripides.

Even with the finding of the body, leaving the rest to be told by the spirit of Polydorus. This needs no further to be enlarged; the dullest wit may conceive it.

But, besides these gross absurdities, how all their plays be neither right tragedies nor right comedies, mingling kings and clowns, not because the matter so carrieth it, but thrust in the clown by head and shoulders to play a part in majestical matters, with neither decency nor discretion; so as neither the admiration and commiseration, nor the right sportfulness, is by their mongrel tragicomedy obtained. I know Apuleius[10] did somewhat so, but that is a thing recounted with space of time, not represented in one moment; and I know the ancients have one or two examples of tragicomedies, as Plautus hath *Amphitrion*. But, if we mark them well, we shall find that they never, or very daintily, match hornpipes and funerals. So falleth it out that, having indeed no right comedy in that comical part of our tragedy, we have nothing but scurrility, unworthy of any chaste ears, or some extreme show of doltishness, indeed fit to lift up a loud laughter, and nothing else; where the whole tract of a comedy should be full of delight, as the tragedy should be still maintained in a well-raised admiration.

But our comedians think there is no delight without laughter, which is very wrong; for though laughter may come with delight, yet cometh it not of delight, as though delight should be the cause of laughter; but well may one thing breed both together. Nay, rather in themselves they have, as it were, a kind of contrariety. For delight we scarcely do, but in things that have a conveniency to ourselves, or to the general nature; laughter almost ever cometh of things most disproportioned to ourselves and nature. Delight hath a joy in it either permanent or present; laughter hath only a scornful tickling. For example, we are ravished with delight to see a fair woman, and yet are far from being moved to laughter. We laugh at deformed creatures, wherein certainly we cannot delight. We delight in good chances, we laugh at mischances. We delight to hear the happiness of our friends and country, at which he were worthy to be laughed at that would laugh. We shall, contrarily, laugh sometimes to find a matter quite mistaken and go down the hill against the bias, in the mouth of some such men, as for the respect of them one shall be heartily sorry he cannot choose but laugh, and so is rather pained that delighted with laughter. Yet deny I not but that they may go well together. For as in Alexander's picture well set out we delight without laughter, and in twenty mad antics we laught without delight; so in Hercules, painted, with his great beard and furious countenance, in woman's attire, spinning at Omphale's commandment, it breedeth both delight and laughter; for the representing of so strange a power in love, procureth delight, and the scornfulness of the action stirreth laughter.

[10] In *The Golden Ass.*

But I speak to this purpose, that all the end of the comical part be not upon such scornful matters as stir laughter only, but mixed with it that delightful teaching which is the end of poesy. And the great fault, even in that point of laughter, and forbidden plainly by Aristotle, is that they stir laughter in sinful things, which are rather execrable than ridiculous; or in miserable, which are rather to be pitied than scorned. For what is it to make folks gape at a wretched beggar or a beggarly clown, or, against law of hospitality, to jest at strangers because they speak not English so well as we do? what do we learn? since it is certain:

> Nil habet infelix paupertas durius in se,
> Quam quod ridiculos homines facit.[11]

[11] From Juvenal, *Satires*, III, 152–153: "Poverty, bitter though it be, has no sharper pang than this, that it makes men ridiculous." —translation by Albert S. Cook.

George Puttenham   *c. 1529–1590*

The Art of English Poesy   *1589*

Then, as there was no art in the world till by experience found out, so if poesy be now an art, and of all antiquity has been among the Greeks and Latins, and yet were none until by studious persons fashioned and reduced into a method of rules and precepts, then no doubt may there be the like with us. And if the art of poesy be but a skill appertaining to utterance, why may not the same be with us as well as with them, our language being no less copious, pithy, and significative than theirs, our concepts the same, and our wits no less apt to devise and imitate than theirs were? If again art be but a certain order of rules prescribed by reason and gathered by experience, why should not poesy be a vulgar art with us as well as with the Greeks and Latins, our language admitting no fewer rules and nice diversities than theirs but peradventure more by a peculiar, which our speech has in many things differing from theirs? . . .

Selections from Book One. From Joseph Haslewood, ed., *Ancient Critical Essays upon English Poets and Poesy*, Vol. I. London: Robert Triphook, 1811. Spelling and punctuation modernized by the editor.

The profession and use of poesy is most ancient from the beginning, and not as many erroneously suppose after but before any civil society was among men. For it is written that poesy was the original cause and occasion of their first assemblies, when before the people remained in the woods and mountains, vagrant and dispersed like the wild beasts, lawless and naked, or very ill clad, and of all good and necessary provision for harbor or sustenance utterly unfurnished, so as they little differed for their manner of life from the very brute beasts of the field. Whereupon it is said that Amphion and Orpheus, two poets of the first ages, one of them, to wit Amphion, built up cities and reared walls with the stones that came in heaps to the sound of his harp, figuring thereby the mollifying of hard and stony hearts by his sweet and eloquent persuasion. And Orpheus assembled the wild beasts to come in herds to harken to his music, and by that means made them tame, implying thereby how by his discreet and wholesome lessons uttered in harmony and with melodious instruments he brought the rude and savage people to a more civil and orderly life. . . . Poets therefore are of great antiquity. Then, forasmuch as they were the first that attended to the observation of nature and her works, and especially of the celestial courses, by reason of the continual motion of the heavens, searching after the first mover, and from thence by degrees coming to know and consider of the substances separate and abstract which we call the divine intelligences or good angels (*Demones*), they were the first that instituted sacrifices of placation, with invocations and worship to them, as to gods, and invented and established all the rest of the observances and ceremonies of religion and so were the first priests and ministers of the holy mysteries. And because for the better execution of that high charge and function, it behooved them to live chaste and in all holiness of life and in continual study and contemplation, they came by instinct divine and by deep mediation and much abstinence (the same subtling and refining their spirits) to be made apt to receive visions, both waking and sleeping, which made them utter prophecies and foretell things to come. So also were they the first prophets or seers, *Videntes*, for so the Scripture terms them in Latin after the Hebrew word, and all the oracles and answers of the gods were given in meter or verse and published to the people by their direction. And for that they were aged and grave men and of much wisdom and experience in the affairs of the world, they were the first lawmakers to the people, and the first politicians, devising all expedient means for the establishment of commonwealth, to hold and contain the people in order and duty by force and virtue of good and wholesome laws made for the preservation of the public peace and tranquility. . . .

. . . Speech itself is artificial and made by man, and the more pleasing it is, the more it prevails to such purpose as it is intended for, but speech by meter is a kind of utterance more cleanly couched and more delicate to the ear than prose is. . . . It is briefer and more compendious, and easier to bear away and be retained in memory than that which is contained in multitude of words and full of tedious ambage and long periods. It is besides a manner of utterance more eloquent and rhetorical than the ordinary prose which we use in our daily talk because it is decked and set out with all manner of fresh colors and figures, which makes that it sooner inveigles the judgment of man and carries his opinion this way and that, whithersoever the heart by impression of the ear shall be most affectionately bent and directed. . . . So as the poets were also from the beginning the best persuaders and their eloquence the first rhetoric of the world, even so it became that the high mysteries of the gods should be revealed and taught by a manner of utterance and language of extraordinary phrase and brief and compendious and above all others sweet and civil as the metrical is. The same also was meetest to register the lives and noble gests of princes and of the great monarchs of the world and all other the memorable accidents of time, so as the poet was also the first historiographer. Then, forasmuch as they were the first observers of all natural causes and effects in the things generable and corruptible, and from thence mounted up to search after the celestial courses and influences, and yet penetrated further to know the divine essences and substances separate, as is said before, they were the first astronomers and philosophists and metaphysics. Finally, because they did altogether endeavor themselves to reduce the life of man to a certain method of good manners and made the first differences between virtue and vice . . . therefore were they the first philosophers ethic . . . of the world. . . .

But it came to pass, when fortune fled far from the Greeks and Latins, and that their towns flourished no more in traffic nor their universities in learning as they had done continuing those monarchies, the barbarous conquerors invading them with innumerable swarms of strange nations, the poesy metrical of the Grecians and Latins came to be much corrupted and altered. . . . The very Greeks and Latins themselves took pleasure in rhyming verses and used it as a rare and gallant thing. . . . From the time of the Emperors Gracian and Valentinian downwards . . . began the declination of the Roman Empire by the notable inundations of the Huns and Vandals. . . . This brought the rhyming poesy in grace and made it prevail in Italy and Greece (their own long time cast aside and almost neglected). . . .

For the respects aforesaid in all former ages and in the most civil countries and commonwealths, good poets and poesy were highly esteemed and much favored of the greatest princes, for proof whereof we read how much Amyntas, King of Macedonia, made of the tragical poet Euripides, and the Athenians of Sophocles. . . . And King Henry VIII, Her Majesty's father, for a few Psalms of David turned into English meter by Sternhold made him Groom of His Privy Chamber and gave him many other good gifts. . . . We find that Julius Caesar, the first Emperor and a most noble captain, was not only the most eloquent orator of his time but also a very good poet, though none of his doings therein be now extant. . . . But in these days, although some learned princes may take delight in them, yet universally it is not so, for as well poets as poesy are despised and the name become . . . subject to scorn and derision. . . .

Some perchance would think that next after the praise and honoring of their gods should commence the worshiping and praise of good men, and especially of great princes and governors of the earth in sovereignty and function next unto the gods, but it is not so, for before that came to pass, the poets, or holy priests, chiefly studied the rebuke of vice and to carp at the common abuses such as were most offensive to the public and private, for as yet for lack of good civility and wholesome doctrines there was greater store of lewd lurdanes than of wise and learned lords, or of noble and virtuous princes and governors. So as next after the honors exhibited to their gods, the poets, finding in man generally much to reprove and little to praise, made certain poems in plain meters, more like to sermons or preachings than otherwise, and when the people were assembled together in those hallowed places dedicated to their gods, because they had yet no large halls or places of conventicle, nor had any other correction of their faults, but such as rested only in rebukes of wise and grave men, such as at these days make the people ashamed rather than afraid, the said ancient poets used for that purpose three kinds of poems reprehensive, to wit, the Satire, the Comedy, and the Tragedy, and the first and most bitter invective against vice and vicious men was the Satire, which to the intent their bitterness should breed no one ill will, either to the poets or to the reciters (which could not have been chosen if they had been openly known), and besides, to make their admonitions and reproofs seem graver and of more efficacy, they made wise as if the gods of the woods, whom they called *Satyrs* or *Silenuses*, should appear and recite those verses of rebuke, whereas indeed they were but disguised persons under the shape of satyrs, as who would say, these terrene and base gods, being conversant with man's affairs and spiers-out of all their secret faults, had some great care over man and desired by good admonitions to reform the evil of their life and to bring the bad to amendment by those kind of preachings, whereupon the poets [who were] inventors of the device were called satirists.

But when this manner of solitary speeches and recitals of rebuke, uttered by the rural gods out of bushes and briars, seemed not to the finer heads sufficiently persuasive, nor so popular as if it were reduced into action of many persons or by many voices lively represented to the ear and eye, so as a man might think it were even now adoing, the poets devised to have many parts played at once by two or three or four persons that debated the matters of the world, sometimes of their own private affairs, sometimes of their neighbors, but never meddling with any princes' matters nor such high personages, but commonly of merchants, soldiers, artificers, good honest householders, and also of unthrifty youths, young damsels, old nurses, bawds, brokers, ruffians, and parasites, with such like, in whose behavior lie in effect the whole course and trade of man's life, and therefore tended altogether to the good amendment of man by discipline and example. It was also much for the solace and recreation of the common people by reason of the pageants and shows. And this kind of poem was called Comedy and followed next after the Satire, and by that occasion was somewhat sharp and bitter after the nature of the Satire, openly and by express names taxing men more maliciously and impudently than became [it], so as they were enforced for fear of quarrel and blame to disguise their players with strange apparel, and by coloring their faces and carrying hats and caps of diverse fashions to make themselves less known. But as time and experience do reform everything that is amiss, so this bitter poem called the Old Comedy, being disused and taken away, the New Comedy came in place, more civil and pleasant a great deal and not touching any man by name, but in a certain generality glancing at every abuse. So as from thenceforth fearing no ill will or enmity at anybody's hands, they left aside their disguisings and played bareface till one Roscius Gallus, the most excellent player among the Romans, brought up these vizards, which we see at this day used, partly to supply the want of players, when there were more parts than there were persons, or that it was not thought meet to trouble and pester princes' chambers with too many folks. Now, by the change of a vizard, one man might play the king and the carter, the old nurse and the young damsel, the merchant and the soldier or any other part he listed very conveniently. There be [those] that say Roscius did it for another purpose, for being himself the best *histrion* or buffoon that was in his day to be found . . . yet because he was squint-eyed and had a very unpleasant countenance, and looks which made him ridiculous or rather odious to the presence, he devised these vizards to hide his own ill-favored face. . . .

But because in those days, when the poets first taxed [people] by Satire and Comedy, there was no great store of kings or emperors or such high estates, all men being yet for the most part rude and in a manner popularly equal, they could not say of them or of their behavior anything to the purpose, which cases of princes are since taken for the highest and greatest matters of all. But after that, some men among the more became mighty and famous in the world, sovereignty and dominion having learned them all manner of lusts and licentiousness of life, by which occasions also their high estates and felicities fell many times into most low and lamentable fortune. Whereas before, in their great prosperity, they were both feared and reverenced in the highest degree, after their deaths, when the posterity stood no more in dread of them, their infamous life and tyrannies were laid open to all the world, their wickedness reproached, their follies and extreme insolences derided, and their miserable ends painted out in plays and pageants to show the mutability of fortune and the just punishment of God in revenge of a vicious and evil life. These matters were also handled by the poets and represented by action, as that of the Comedies, but because the matter was higher than that of the Comedies, the poets' style was also higher and more lofty, the provision greater, the place more magnificent, for which purpose also the players' garments were made more rich and costly and solemn, and every other thing appertaining, according to that rate, so as where the Satire was pronounced by rustical and naked sylvans speaking out of a bush, and the common players of Interludes, called *Planipes*, played barefoot upon the floor, the later Comedies upon scaffolds and by men well and cleanly hosed and shod. These matters of great princes were played upon lofty stages and the actors thereof wore upon their legs buskins of leather called *Cothorni*, and other solemn habits, and for a special preeminence did walk upon those high, corked shoes, or pantofles, which now they call in Spain and Italy *Chopines*. And because those buskins and high shoes were commonly made of goatskins very finely tanned and died into colors, or for that as some say the best player's reward was a goat to be given him, or for that as others think a goat was the peculiar sacrifice to the god Pan, king of all the gods of the woods, forasmuch as a goat in Greek is called *Tragos*, therefore these stately plays were called Tragedies. . . .

But as the bad and illaudable parts of all estates and degrees were taxed by the poets in one sort or another, and those of great princes by Tragedy in especial, and not till after their deaths, as has been before remembered, to the intent that such exemplifying, as it were, of their blames and adversities, being now dead, might work for a secret reprehension to others that were alive, living in the same or like abuses, so was it great reason that all good and virtuous persons should for their well doings be rewarded with commendation, and the great princes above all others with honors and praises, being for many respects of greater moment, to have them good and virtuous than any inferior sort of men. . . .

As it has been declared, the Satires were first uttered in their hallowed places within the woods where they honored their gods under the open heaven, because they had no other housing fit for great assemblies. The Old Comedies were played in the broad streets upon wagons or carts uncovered, which carts were floored with boards and made for removable stages, to pass from one street of their town to another, where all the people might stand at their ease to gaze upon the sights. Their New Comedies, or civil interludes, were played in open pavilions or tents of linen cloth or leather, half displayed, that the people might see. Afterward, when Tragedies came up, they devised to present them upon scaffolds, or stages of timber, shadowed with linen or leather as the other, and these stages were made in the form of a semicircle, whereof the bow served for the beholders to sit in, and the string, or forepart, was appointed for the floor, or place where the players uttered, and had in it sundry little divisions by curtains, as traverses, to serve for several rooms where they might repair unto and change their garments and come in again, as their speeches and parts were to be renewed. Also, there was place appointed for the musicians to sing or to play upon their instruments at the end of every scene, to the intent the people might be refreshed and kept occupied. This manner of stage in half circle, the Greeks called *theatrum,* as much to say as a beholding place, which was also in such sort contrived by benches and greces to stand or sit upon, as no man should impeach another's sight.

Anonymous

Induction to
A Warning for Fair Women *1599*

COMEDY   But History! what, all three met at once?
What wonder's towards, that we are got together?
HISTORY   My meaning was to have been here to-day,
But meeting with my lady Tragedy
She scolds me off:
And, Comedy, except thou canst prevail
I think she means to banish us the stage.
COMEDY   Tut, tut, she cannot; she may for a day
Or two, perhaps, be had in some request
But once a week if we do not appear,
She shall find few that will attend her here.
TRAGEDY   I must confess you have some sparks of wit
Some odd ends of old jests scrap'd up together,
To tickle shallow unjudicial ears:
Perhaps some puling passion of a lover,
But slight and childish. What is this to me?
I must have passions that must move the soul;
Make the heart heavy and throb within the bosom,
Extorting tears out of the strictest eyes—

Selection. From *The School of Shakspere,* Vol. II, edited by Richard Simpson. London: Chatto and Windus, 1878.

To rack a thought, and strain it to his form,
Until I rap the senses from their course.
This is my office.

COMEDY   How some damn'd tyrant to obtain a crown
Stabs, hangs, impoisons, smothers, cutteth throats:
And then a Chorus, too, comes howling in
And tells us of the worrying of a cat:
Then, too, a filthy whining ghost,
Lapt in some foul sheet, or a leather pilch,
Comes screaming like a pig half stick'd,
And cries, V*indicta!*—Revenge, Revenge!
With that a little rosin flasheth forth,
Like smoke out of a tobacco pipe, or a boy's squib.
Then comes in two or three [more] like to drovers,
With tailors' bodkins, stabbing one another—
Is not this trim? Is not here goodly things,
That you should be so much accounted of?
I would not else—

HISTORY   Now, before God, thou'lt make her mad anon;
Thy jests are like a whisp unto a scold.

COMEDY   Why, say I could, what care I, History?
Then shall we have a Tragedy indeed;
Pure purple buskin, blood and murther right.

TRAGEDY   Thus, with your loose and idle similies,
You have abused me; but I'll whip you hence:
                    [*She whips them.*]
I'll scourge and lash you both from off the stage.
Tis you have kept the Theatres so long,
Painted in play-bills upon every post,
That I am scorned of the multitude,
My name profan'd. But now I'll reign as Queen.
In great Appollo's name, and all the Muses,
By virtue of whose Godhead I am sent,
I charge you to begone and leave this place!

HISTORY   Look, Comedy, I mark'd it not till now,
The stage is hung with black, and I perceive
The auditors prepar'd for Tragedy.

COMEDY   Nay, then, I see she shall be entertain'd.
These ornaments beseem not thee and me.
Then Tragedy kill them to-day with sorrow,
We'll make them laugh with mirthful jests tomorrow.

HISTORY   And, Tragedy, although to-day thou reign,
Tomorrow here I'll domineer again.   [*Exeunt.*]

Ben Jonson 1573–1637

Induction to
Every Man out of His Humour 1600

ASPER   ... Gracious, and kind spectators, you are welcome,
Apollo and the Muses feast your eyes
With graceful objects, and may our Minerva
Answer your hopes, unto their largest strain!
Yet here mistake me not, judicious friends.
I do not this, to beg your patience,
Or servilely to fawn on your applause,
Like some dry brain, despairing in his merit.
Let me be censured by the austerest brow,
Where I want art, or judgment; tax me freely:
Let envious censors, with their broadest eyes,
Look through, and through me, I pursue no favor.
Only vouchsafe me your attentions,
And I will give you music worth your ears,
O, how I hate the monstrousness of time,
Where every servile imitating spirit,
Plagued with an itching leprosy of wit,
In a mere halting fury, strives to fling
His ulcerous body in the Thespian spring,
And straight leaps forth a poet! but as lame
As Vulcan, or the founder of Cripplegate.
MITIS   In faith, this humour will come ill to some,
You will be thought to be too peremptory.
ASPER   "This humour"? good! and why "this humour," Mitis?
Nay, do not turn, but answer.
MITIS   Answer, what?
ASPER   I will not stir your patience, pardon me,
I urged it for some reasons, and the rather
To give these ignorant, well-spoken days
Some taste of their abuse of this word "humour."
CORDATUS   O, do not let your purpose fall, good Asper,
It cannot but arrive most acceptable,
Chiefly to such, as have the happiness

Selections. From *Ben Jonson*, Vol. I, edited by Brinsley Nicholson. London: T. Fisher Unwin, 1894.

Daily to see how the poor innocent word
Is racked and tortured.
MITIS   Ay, I pray you proceed.
ASPER   Ha! what? what is't?
CORDATUS   For the abuse of humour.
ASPER   O, I crave pardon, I had lost my thoughts.
Why, humour, as 'tis *ens*,[1] we thus define it.
To be a quality of air, or water,
And in itself holds these two properties,
Moisture, and fluxure: as, for demonstration,
Pour water on this floor, 'twill wet, and run:
Likewise the air, forced through a horn, or trumpet,
Flows instantly away, and leaves behind
A kind of dew; and hence we do conclude,
That whatsoe'er hath fluxure, and humidity,
As wanting power to contain itself,
Is humour. So in every human body,
The choler, melancholy, phlegm, and blood,
By reason that they flow continually
In some one part, and are not continent,[2]
Receive the name of Humours. Now thus far
It may, by metaphor, apply itself
Unto the general disposition:
As when some one peculiar quality
Doth so possess a man, that it doth draw
All his affects,[3] his spirits, and his powers,
In their confluctions, all to run one way,
This may be truly said to be a humour.
But that a rook,[4] by wearing a pied feather,
The cable hat-band, or the three-piled[5] ruff,
A yard of shoe-tie, or the Switzer's knot
On his French garters, should affect a "humour"!
O, it is more than most ridiculous.
CORDATUS   He speaks pure truth, now, if an idiot
Have but an apish, or fantastic strain,
It is "his humour."
ASPER   Well, I will scourge those apes.
And to these courteous eyes oppose a mirror,

---

[1] A thing existing [all notes are Nicholson's].
[2] Staying together in one place.
[3] Affections.
[4] Simpleton-prater.
[5] Three-tiered.

As large as is the stage whereon we act,
Where they shall see the time's deformity
Anatomized in every nerve, and sinew,
With constant courage, and contempt of fear. . . .
ASPER   . . . Attentive auditors,
Such as will join their profits with their pleasure,
And come to feed their understanding parts:
For these, I'll prodigally spend myself,
And speak away my spirit into air;
For these, I'll melt my brain into invention,
Coin new conceits, and hang my richest words
As polished jewels in their bounteous ears?
But stay, I lose myself, and wrong their patience;
If I dwell here, they'll not begin, I see.
Friends, sit you still, and entertain this troop
With some familiar, and by-conference,
I'll haste them sound. [*To audience.*] Now, gentlemen, I go
To turn an actor, and a humourist,
Where, ere I do resume my present person,
We hope to make the circles of your eyes
Flow with distillèd laughter: if we fail,
We must impute it to this only chance,
Art hath an enemy called Ignorance.   [*Exit*]
CORDATUS   How do you like his spirit, Mitis?
MITIS   I should like it much better, if he were less confident.
CORDATUS   Why, do you suspect his merit?
MITIS   No, but I fear this will procure him much envy.[6]
CORDATUS   O, that sets the stronger seal on his desert; if he had no enemies,
   I should esteem his fortunes most wretched at this instant.
MITIS   You have seen his play, Cordatus? pray you, how is't?
CORDATUS   Faith sir, I must refrain to judge; only this I can say of it, 'tis
   strange, and of a particular kind by itself, somewhat like *Vetus Comoedia;*[7]
   a work that hath bounteously pleased me; how it will answer the general
   expectation, I know not.
MITIS   Does he observe all the laws of comedy in it?
CORDATUS   What laws mean you?
MITIS   Why, the equal division of it into acts, and scenes, according to
   the Terentian manner; his true number of actors; the furnishing of the
   scene with Grex, or Chorus, and that the whole argument fall within
   compass of a day's business.

---

[6] Dislike.
[7] The ancient comedy.

CORDATUS   O no, these are too nice observations.

MITIS   They are such as must be received, by your favor, or it cannot be authentic.

CORDATUS   Troth, I can discern no such necessity.

MITIS   No?

CORDATUS   No, I assure you signior. If those laws, you speak of, had been delivered us, *ab initio*,[8] and in their present virtue and perfection, there had been some reason of obeying their powers: but 'tis extant, that that which we called *Comoedia*, was at first nothing but a simple and continued song, sung by one only person, till Susario invented a second; after him, Epicharmus a third; Phormus and Chionides devised to have four actors, with a prologue and chorus; to which Cratinus, long after, added a fifth, and sixth; Eupolis, more; Aristophanes, more than they; every man in the dignity of his spirit and judgment supplied something. And, though that in him this kind of poem appeared absolute, and fully perfected, yet how is the face of it changed since, in Menander, Philemon, Cecilius, Plautus, and the rest; who have utterly excluded the chorus, altered the property of the persons, their names, and natures, and augmented it with all liberty, according to the elegancy and disposition of those times, wherein they wrote. I see not then, but we should enjoy the same licence of free power to illustrate and heighten our invention, as they did; and not be tied to those strict and regular forms, which the niceness of a few—who are nothing but form—would thrust upon us.

MITIS   Well, we will not dispute of this now; but what's his scene?

CORDATUS   Marry, *Insula Fortunata*, sir.

MITIS   O, "the Fortunate Island!"[9] mass, he has bound himself to a strict law there.

CORDATUS   Why so?

MITIS   He cannot lightly alter the scene, without crossing the seas.

CORDATUS   He needs not, having a whole island to run through, I think.

MITIS   No? how comes it then, that in some one play we see so many seas, countries, and kingdoms, passed over with such admirable dexterity?

CORDATUS   O, that but shows how well the authors can travel[10] in their vocation, and outrun the apprehension of their auditory. But, leaving this, I would they begin once: this protraction is able to sour the best settled patience in the theatre.

[8] From the beginning.
[9] England.
[10] He puns on this and "travail."

Preface to
Sejanus, His Fall[*] 1605

First, if it be objected, that what I publish is no true poem, in the strict laws of time, I confess it: as also in the want of a proper chorus; whose habit and moods are such and so difficult, as not any, whom I have seen, since the ancients, no, not they who have most presently affected laws, have yet come in the way of. Nor is it needful, or almost possible in these our times, and to such auditors as commonly things are presented, to observe the old state and splendor of dramatic poems, with preservation of any popular delight. But this I shall take more seasonable cause to speak, in my observations upon Horace his *Art of Poetry*, which, with the text translated, I intend shortly to publish. In the meantime, if in truth of argument, dignity of persons, gravity and height of elocution, fulness and frequency of sentence, I have discharged the other offices of a tragic writer, let not the absence of these forms be imputed to me, wherein I shall give you occasion hereafter, and without my boast, to think I could better prescribe, than omit the due use for want of a convenient knowledge.

Dedication to
Volpone^{†1} 1607

. . . If men will impartially, and not asquint, look toward the offices and function of a poet, they will easily conclude to themselves the impossibility of any man's being the good poet without first being a good man.

* Selection. From *Ben Jonson*, Vol. II, edited by Brinsley Nicholson. London: T. Fisher Unwin, 1894.

† Selections. Spelling and punctuation modernized by the editor.

¹ The Dedication is "To the most noble and most equal sisters, the two famous universities, for their love and acceptance shown to his poem in the presentation, Ben Jonson, the grateful acknowledger, dedicates both it and himself."

He that is said to be able to inform young men to all good disciplines, inflame grown men to all great virtues, keep old men in their best and supreme state, or, as they decline to childhood, recover them to their first strength; that comes forth the interpreter and arbiter of nature, a teacher of things divine no less than human, a master in manners, and can alone (or with a few) effect the business of mankind; this, I take him, is no subject for pride and ignorance to exercise their railing rhetoric upon. But it will here be hastily answered that the writers of these days are other things; that not only their manners but their natures are inverted, and nothing remaining with them of the dignity of poet but the abused name, which every scribe usurps; that now, especially in dramatic or (as they term it) stage poetry, nothing but ribaldry, profanation, blasphemy, all license of offence to God and man is practiced. I dare not deny a great part of this (and am sorry I dare not) because in some men's abortive features (and would they had never boasted the light) it is over-true. But that all are embarked in this bold adventure for Hell is a most uncharitable thought and, uttered, a more malicious slander. For my own particular, I can (and from a most clear conscience) affirm that I have ever trembled to think toward the least profaneness, have loathed the use of such foul and unwashed bawdry as is now made the food of the scene. . . .[2] In this my latest work . . . I have labored for their instruction and amendment to reduce not only the ancient forms but manners of the scene, the easiness, the propriety, the innocence, and, last, the doctrine, which is the principal end of poesy, to inform men in the best reason of living. And though my catastrophe may in the strict rigor of comic law meet with censure . . . my special aim being to put the snaffle in their mouths that cry out, "We never punish vice in our interludes," etc., I took the more liberty, though not without some lines of example, drawn even in the ancients themselves, the goings-out[3] of whose comedies are not always joyful, but ofttimes the bawds, the servants, the rivals, yea, and the masters are mulcted, and fitly, it being the office of a comic poet to imitate justice and instruct to life, as well as purity of language, or stir up gentle affections.[4]

[2] The stage.
[3] Conclusions.
[4] Emotions.

Timber,
or Discoveries Made
upon Men and Matter 1620–1625

I remember the players have often mentioned it as an honor to Shakespeare, that in his writing, whatsoever he penned, he never blotted out a line. My answer hath been, "Would he had blotted a thousand," which they thought a malevolent speech. I had not told posterity this but for their ignorance, who chose that circumstance to commend their friend by wherein he most faulted; and to justify mine own candor, for I loved the man, and do honor his memory on this side idolatry as much as any. He was, indeed, honest, and of open and free nature; had an excellent fancy, brave notions, and gentle expressions, wherein he flowed with that facility that sometime it was necessary he should be stopped. "*Sufflaminandust erat*,"[1] as Augustus said of Haterius. His wit was in his own power; would the rule of it had been so too. Many times he fell into those things, could not escape laughter, as when he said in the person of Caesar, one speaking to him: "Caesar, thou dost me wrong." He replied: "Caesar did never wrong but with just cause";[2] and such like, which were ridiculous. But he redeemed his vices with his virtues. There was ever more in him to be praised than to be pardoned. . . .

Poetry and picture are arts of a like nature, and both are busy about imitation. It was excellently said of Plutarch, poetry was a speaking picture, and picture a mute poesy.[3] For they both invent, feign, and devise many things, and accommodate all they invent to the use and service of Nature. Yet of the two the pen is more noble than the pencil; for that can speak to the understanding, the other but to the sense. They both behold pleasure and profit as their common object; but should abstain from all base pleasures, lest they should err from their end, and, while they seek to better men's minds, destroy their manners. They both are born artificers, not made. Nature is more powerful in them than study.

Whosoever loves not picture is injurious to truth and all the wisdom of poetry. Picture is the invention of heaven, the most ancient and most akin to Nature. It is itself a silent work, and always of one and the same

Selections. From Ben Jonson, *Timber, or Discoveries Made upon Men and Matter*, edited by Felix E. Schelling. Boston: Ginn & Co., 1892.

[1] He should have been stopped.
[2] Cf. *Julius Caesar*, III, i, 47–48.
[3] Plutarch, *De Audiendis Poetis*, 3.

habit; yet it doth so enter and penetrate the inmost affection (being done by an excellent artificer) as sometimes it o'ercomes the power of speech and oratory. There are divers graces in it, so are there in the artificers. One excels in care, another in reason, a third in easiness, a fourth in nature and grace. Some have diligence and comeliness, but they want majesty. They can express a human form in all the graces, sweetness, and elegancy, but they miss the authority. They can hit nothing but smooth cheeks; they cannot express roughness or gravity. Others aspire to truth so much as they are rather lovers of likeness and beauty. . . .

I take this labor in teaching others, that they should not be always to be taught, and I would bring my precepts into practice, for rules are ever of less force and value than experiments; yet with this purpose, rather to show the right way to those that come after, than to detect any that have slipped before by error. And I hope it will be more profitable; for men do more willingly listen, and with more favor, to precept, than reprehension. Among divers opinions of an art, and most of them contrary in themselves, it is hard to make election; and, therefore, though a man cannot invent new things after so many, he may do a welcome work yet to help posterity to judge rightly of the old. But arts and precepts avail nothing, except Nature be beneficial and aiding. And therefore these things are no more written to a dull disposition, than rules of husbandry to a barren soil. No precepts will profit a fool, no more than beauty will the blind, or music the deaf. As we should take care that our style in writing be neither dry nor empty, we should look again it be not winding, or wanton with farfetched descriptions: either is a vice. But that is worse which proceeds out of want, than that which riots out of plenty. The remedy of fruitfulness is easy, but no labor will help the contrary. I will like and praise some things in a young writer which yet, if he continues in, I cannot but justly hate him for the same. There is a time to be given all things for maturity, and that even your country husbandman can teach, who to a young plant will not put the pruning-knife, because it seems to fear the iron, as not able to admit the scar. No more would I tell a green writer all his faults, lest I should make him grieve and faint, and at last despair. For nothing doth more hurt than to make him so afraid of all things as he can endeavor nothing. Therefore youth ought to be instructed betimes, and in the best things; for we hold those longest we take soonest, as the first scent of a vessel lasts, and the tinct the wool first receives. Therefore a master should temper his own powers, and descend to the other's infirmity. If you pour a glut of water upon a bottle, it receives little of it; but with a funnel, and by degrees, you shall fill many of them, and spill little of your own; to their capacity they will all receive and be full. . . .

A poet, *poeta*, is that which by the Greeks is called κατ' ἐξοχήν, ὁ ποιητής, a maker, or a feigner: his art, an art of imitation or feigning; expressing the life of man in fit measure, numbers, and harmony; according to Aristotle from the word ποιεῖν, which signifies to make or feign. Hence he is called a poet, not he which writeth in measure only, but that feigneth and formeth a fable, and writes things like the truth. For the fable and fiction is, as it were, the form and soul of any poetical work or poem. . . .

The parts of a comedy are the same with a tragedy, and the end is partly the same, for they both delight and teach; the comics are called διδάσκαλοι[4] of the Greeks no less than the tragics. Nor is the moving of laughter always the end of comedy; that is rather a fowling for the people's delight, or their fooling. For, as Aristotle says rightly, the moving of laughter is a fault in comedy, a kind of turpitude that depraves some part of a man's nature without a disease. As a wry face without pain moves laughter, or a deformed vizard, or a rude clown dressed in a lady's habit and using her actions; we dislike and scorn such representations which made the ancient philosophers ever think laughter unfitting in a wise man. And this induced Plato to esteem of Homer as a sacrilegious person, because he presented the gods sometimes laughing. As also it is divinely said of Aristotle, that to seem ridiculous is a part of dishonesty, and foolish. So that what either in the words or sense of an author, or in the language or actions of men, is awry or depraved doth strangely stir mean affections, and provoke for the most part to laughter. And therefore it was clear that all insolent and obscene speeches, jests upon the best men, injuries to particular persons, perverse and sinister sayings and the rather unexpected in the old comedy did move laughter, especially where it did imitate any dishonesty; and scurrility came forth in the place of wit, which, who understands the nature and genius of laughter cannot but perfectly know.

Of which Aristophanes affords an ample harvest, having not only out-gone Plautus or any other in that kind, but expressed all the moods and figures of what is ridiculous oddly. In short, as vinegar is not accounted good until the wine be corrupted, so jests that are true and natural seldom raise laughter with the beast, the multitude. They love nothing that is right and proper. The farther it runs from reason or possibility with them the better it is. What could have made them laugh, like to see Socrates presented, that example of all good life, honesty, and virtue, to have him hoisted up with a pulley, and there play the philosopher in a basket; measure how many foot a flea could skip geometrically, by a just scale, and edify the people from the engine. This was theatrical wit, right stage jesting, and relishing a playhouse, invented for scorn and laughter; whereas, if it had savored of equity, truth, perspicuity, and candor, to have tasten a wise or learned palate—spit it out presently! this is bitter and profitable: this instructs and would inform us! what need we know anything, that are nobly

4 Teachers.

born, more than a horse-race, or a hunting-match, our day to break with citizens, and such innate mysteries? This is truly leaping from the stage to the tumbril again, reducing all wit to the original dung-cart. . . .

. . . The fable is called the imitation of one entire and perfect action, whose parts are so joined and knit together, as nothing in the structure can be changed, or taken away, without impairing or troubling the whole, of which there is a proportionable magnitude in the members. . . .

Whole we call that, and perfect, which hath a beginning, a midst, and an end. So the place of any building may be whole and entire for that work, though too little for a palace. As to a tragedy or a comedy, the action may be convenient and perfect that would not fit an epic poem in magnitude. So a lion is a perfect creature in himself, though it be less than that of a buffalo or a rhinocerote. They differ but in specie: either in the kind is absolute; both have their parts, and either the whole. Therefore, as in every body so in every action, which is the subject of a just work, there is required a certain proportionable greatness, neither too vast nor too minute. For that which happens to the eyes when we behold a body, the same happens to the memory when we contemplate an action. . . .

Now in every action it behoves the poet to know which is his utmost bound, how far with fitness and a necessary proportion he may produce and determine it; that is, till either good fortune change into the worse, or the worse into the better. For as a body without proportion cannot be goodly, no more can the action, either in comedy or tragedy, without his fit bounds. And every bound, for the nature of the subject, is esteemed the best that is largest, till it can increase no more; so it behoves the action in tragedy or comedy to be let grow till the necessity ask a conclusion; wherein two things are to be considered: first, that it exceed not the compass of one day; next, that there be place left for digression and art. For the episodes and digressions in a fable are the same that household stuff and other furniture are in a house. And so far form the measure and extent of a fable dramatic.

Thomas Campion *1567–1620*

Observations on the Art of English Poesy *1602*

Learning first flourished in Greece, from thence it was derived unto the Romans, both diligent observers of the number and quantity of syllables, not in their verses only but likewise in their prose. Learning after the declining of the Roman Empire and the pollution of their language through the conquest of the Barbarians lay most pitifully deformed. . . . In those lack-learning times, and in barbarized Italy, began that vulgar and easy kind of poesy which is now in use throughout most parts of Christendom, which we abusively call rhyme and meter. . . .

I am not ignorant that whosoever shall by way of reprehension examine the imperfections of rhyme must encounter with many glorious enemies, and those very expert and ready at their weapon that can if need be extempore (as they say) rhyme a man to death. . . . All this and more cannot yet deter me from a lawful defence of perfection or make me any whit the sooner adhere to that which is lame and unbeseeming. [As] for custom, I allege that ill uses are to be abolished and that things naturally imperfect cannot be perfected by use. . . . By rhyme is understood that which ends in the like sound, so that verses in such manner composed yield but a continual repetition of that rhetorical figure which we term *similiter desinentia*,[1] and that being but *figura verbi*[2] ought, as Tully and all other rhetoricians have judicially observed, sparingly to be used, lest it should offend the ear with tedious affection. . . . But there is yet another fault in rhyme altogether intolerable, which is that it enforces a man oftentimes to abjure his matter and extend a short conceit beyond all bounds of art.

Selections. From Joseph Haslewood, ed., *Ancient Critical Essays upon English Poets and Poesy*, Vol. II. London: Robert Triphook, 1815. Spelling and punctuation modernized by the editor.

[1] Similar endings.
[2] A figure of speech.

Samuel Daniel c. 1562–1619

A Defense of Rhyme 1603

Against a Pamphlet Entitled
Observations in the Art of English Poesy

The general custom and use of rhyme in this kingdom . . . having been so long (as from a grant of nature) held unquestionable, made me to imagine that it lay altogether out of the way of contradiction and was become so natural as we should never have had a thought to cast it off into reproach or be made to think that it ill became our language. But now . . . we are told how that our measures go wrong, all rhyming is gross, vulgar, barbarous. . . .

. . . Both custom and nature do most powerfully defend [rhyme]: custom that is before all law, nature that is above all art. Every language has her proper number or measure fitted to use and delight, which custom, entertaining by the allowance of the ear, does endenizen and make natural. All verse is but a frame of words confined within certain measure, differing from the ordinary speech and introduced the better to express men's conceits both for delight and memory, which frame of words, consisting of *rhythmus* or *metrum*, number or measure . . . fall as naturally already in our langue as ever art can make them. . . . Rhyme, which is an excellence added to this work of measure and a harmony far happier than any proportion antiquity could ever show us, does add more grace and has more of delight than ever bare numbers, howsoever they can be forced to run in our slow language, can possibly yield; which . . . consisting of an agreeing sound in the last syllables of several verses, [gives] both to the ear an echo of a delightful report and to the memory a deeper impression of what is delivered therein. . . . And so natural a melody is it, and so universal as it seems to be generally borne with all the nations of the world, as an hereditary eloquence proper to all mankind. The universality argues the general power of it, for if the Barbarian use it then it shows that it sways the affection of the Barbarian. . . . The Slavonian and Arabian tongues acquaint a great part of Asia and Africa with it, the Muscovite, Polack, Hungarian, German, Italian, French, and Spaniard use no other harmony of words. The Irish, Briton, Scot, Dane, Saxon, English, and all the inhabiters of this island either have hither brought it or here found the same in use. And such a force has it in nature, or so made by nature, as the Latin numbers, notwithstanding their excellence, seemed not sufficient to satisfy the ear of the world thereunto accustomed without this harmonical cadence. . . .

Selections. From Joseph Haslewood, ed., *Ancient Critical Essays upon English Poets and Poesy*, Vol. II. London: Robert Triphook, 1815. Spelling and punctuation modernized by the editor.

"Ill customs are to be left." I grant it, but I see not how that can be taken for an ill custom which nature has thus ratified, all nations received, time so long confirmed. . . . Be the verse never so good, never so full, it seems not to satisfy nor breed that delight as when it is met and combined with a like sounding accent, which seems as the jointure without which it hangs loose, and cannot subsist, but runs wildly on like a tedious fancy without a close. Suffer then the world to enjoy that which it knows and what it likes. . . .

. . . In an eminent spirit whom nature has fitted for that mastery, rhyme is no impediment to his conceit but rather gives him wings to mount and carries him not out of his course but, as it were, beyond his power to a far happier flight. All excellences being sold us at the hard price of labor, it follows, where we bestow most thereof, we buy the best success; and rhyme, being far more laborious than loose measures (whatsoever is objected), must needs, meeting with wit and industry, breed greater and worthier effects in our language, so that if our labors have wrought out a manumission from bondage, and that we go at liberty, nothwithstanding these ties, we are no longer the slaves of rhyme but we make it a most excellent instrument to serve us. . . . Besides, is it not most delightful to see much excellently ordered in a small room, or little gallantly disposed and made to fill up a space of like capacity, in such sort that the one would not appear so beautiful in a larger circuit nor the other do well in a less? . . . The apt planting the sentence where it may best stand to hit the certain close of delight with the full body of a just period well carried is such as neither the Greeks nor Latins ever attained unto, for their boundless running on often so confounds the reader that, having once lost himself, must either give off unsatisfied or uncertainly cast back to retrieve the escaped sense and to find way again into this matter.

Methinks we should not so soon yield our consents captive to the authority of antiquity unless we saw more reason. All our understandings are not to be built by the square of Greece and Italy. We are the children of nature as well as they; we are not so placed out of the way of judgment but that the same sun of discretion shines upon us; we have our portion of the same virtues as well as the same vices.

Lope de Vega 1562–1635

The New Art of Writing Plays 1609

1. You command me, noble spirits, flower of Spain[1]—who in this congress and renowned academy will in short space of time surpass not only the assemblies of Italy which Cicero, envious of Greece, made famous with his own name, hard by the Lake of Avernus, but also Athens where in the Lyceum of Plato was seen high conclave of philosophers—to write you an art of the play which is today acceptable to the taste of the crowd.

2. Easy seems this subject, and easy it would be for anyone of you who had written very few comedies, and who knows more about the art of writing them and of all these things; for what condemns me in this task is that I have written them without art.

3. Not because I was ignorant of the precepts; thank God, even while I was a tyro in grammar, I went through the books which treated the subject, before I had seen the sun run its course ten times from the Ram to the Fishes;

4. But because, in fine, I found that comedies were not at that time, in Spain, as their first devisers in the world thought that they should be written; but rather as many rude fellows managed them, who confirmed the crowd in its own crudeness; and so they were introduced in such wise that he who now writes them artistically dies without fame and guerdon; for customs can do more among those who lack light of art than reason and force.

5. True it is that I have sometimes written in accordance with the art which few know; but, no sooner do I see coming from some other source the monstrosities full of painted scenes where the crowd congregates and the women who canonize this sad business, than I return to that same barbarous habit, and when I have to write a comedy I lock in the precepts with six keys, I banish Terence and Plautus from my study that they may not cry out at me; for truth, even in dumb books, is wont to call aloud; and I write in accordance with that art which they devised who aspired to the applause of the crowd; for, since the crowd pays for the comedies, it is fitting to talk foolishly to it to satisfy its taste.

6. Yet true comedy has its end established like every kind of poem or

Complete. Translated by William T. Brewster. From *Papers on Playmaking*, edited by Brander Matthews. New York: Hill and Wang Dramabook, 1957. Reprinted by permission of the Brander Matthews Dramatic Museum of Columbia University.

[1] An address to the Academy at Madrid.

poetic art, and that has always been to imitate the actions of men and to paint the customs of their age. Furthermore, all poetic imitation whatsoever is composed of three things, which are discourse, agreeable verse, harmony, that is to say music, which so far was common also to tragedy; comedy being different from tragedy in that it treats of lowly and plebeian actions, and tragedy of royal and great ones. Look whether there be in our comedies few failings.

7. *Auto* was the name given to them, for they imitate the actions and the doings of the crowd. Lope de Reuda was an example in Spain of these principles, and today are to be seen in print prose comedies of his so lowly that he introduces into them the doings of mechanics and the love of the daughter of a smith; whence there has remained the custom of calling the old comedies *entremeses*, where the art persists in all its force, there being one action and that between plebeian people; for an *entremés* with a king has never been seen. And thus it is shown how the art, for very lowness of style, came to be held in great disrepute, and the king in the comedy to be introduced for the ignorant.

8. Aristotle depicts in his *Poetics*—although obscurely—the beginning of comedy; the strife between Athens and Megara as to which of them was the first inventor; they of Megara say that it was Epicarmus, while Athens would have it that Magnetes was the man. Elias Donatus says it had its origin in ancient sacrifices. He names Thespis as the author of tragedy—following Horace, who affirms the same—as of comedies, Aristophanes. Homer composed the *Odyssey* in imitation of comedy, but the *Iliad* was a famous example of tragedy, in imitation of which I called my *Jerusalem* an epic, and added the term *tragic*; and in the same manner all people commonly term the *Inferno*, the *Purgatorio*, and the *Paradiso* of the celebrated poet Dante Alighieri a comedy, and this Manetti recognizes in his prologue.

9. Now everybody knows that comedy, as if under suspicion, was silenced for a certain time, and that hence also satire was born, which, being more cruel, more quickly came to an end, and gave place to the New Comedy. The choruses were the first things; then the fixed number of the characters was introduced; but Menander, whom Terence followed, held the choruses in despite, as offensive. Terence was more circumspect as to the principles; since he never elevated the style of comedy to the greatness of tragedy, which many have condemned as vicious in Plautus; for in this respect Terence was more wary.

10. Tragedy has as its argument history, and comedy fiction; for this reason it was called flat-footed, of humble argument, since the actor performed without buskin or stage. There were comedies with the *pallium*, mimes, comedies with the toga, *fabulae atellanae*, and comedies of the tavern, which were also, as now, of various sorts.

11. With Attic elegance the men of Athens chided vice and evil custom

in their comedies, and they gave their prizes both to the writers of verse and to the devisers of action. For this Tully called comedies "the mirror of custom and a living image of the truth"—a very high tribute, in that comedy ran even with history. Look whether it be worthy of this crown and glory!

12. But now I perceive that you are saying that this is merely translating books and wearying you with painting this mixed-up affair. Believe me, there has been a reason why you should be reminded of some of these things; for you see that you ask me to describe the art of writing plays in Spain, where whatever is written is in defiance of art; and to tell how they are now written contrary to the ancient rule and to what is founded on reason, is to ask me to draw on my experience, not on art, for art speaks truth which the ignorant crowd gainsays.

13. If, then, you desire art, I beseech you, men of genius, to read the very learned Robortello[2] of Udine and you will see in what he says concerning Aristotle, and especially in what he writes about comedy, as much as is scattered among many books; for everything of today is in a state of confusion.

14. If you wish to have my opinion of the comedies which now have the upper hand and to know why it is necessary that the crowd with its laws should maintain the vile chimera of this comic monster, I will tell you what I hold, and do you pardon me, since I must obey whoever has power to command me—that, gilding the error of the crowd, I desire to tell you of what sort I would have them; for there is no recourse but to follow art observing a mean between the two extremes.

15. Let the subject be chosen and do not be amused—may you excuse these precepts!—if it happens to deal with kings; though, for that matter, I understand that Philip the Prudent, King of Spain and our lord, was offended at seeing a king in them; either because the matter was hostile to art or because the royal authority ought not to be represented among the lowly and the vulgar.

16. This is merely turning back to the Old Comedy, where we see that Plautus introduced gods, as in his *Amphitrion* he represents Jupiter. God knows that I have difficulty in giving this my approbation, since Plutarch, speaking of Menander, does not highly esteem Old Comedy. But since we are so far away from art and in Spain do it a thousand wrongs, let the learned this once close their lips.

17. Tragedy mixed with comedy and Terence with Seneca, though it be like another minotaur of Pasiphaë, will render one part grave, the other ridiculous; for this variety causes much delight. Nature gives us good example, for through such variety it is beautiful.

[2] Or Robortellus. See above, pp. 125–131.

18. Bear in mind that this subject should contain one action only, seeing to it that the story in no manner be episodic; I mean the introduction of other things which are beside the main purpose; nor that any member be omitted which might ruin the whole of the context. There is no use in advising that it should take place in the period of one sun, though this is the view of Aristotle; but we lose our respect for him when we mingle tragic style with the humbleness of mean comedy. Let it take place in as little time as possible, except when the poet is writing history in which some years have to pass; these he can relegate to the space between the acts, wherein, if necessary, he can have a character go on some journey; a thing that greatly offends whoever perceives it. But let not him who is offended go to see them.

19. Oh! how lost in admiration are many at this very time at seeing that years are passed in an affair to which an artificial day sets a limit; though for this they would not allow the mathematical day! But, considering that the wrath of a seated Spaniard is immoderate, when in two hours there is not presented to him everything from Genesis to the Last Judgment, I deem it most fitting, if it be for us here to please him, for us to adjust everything so that it succeeds.

20. The subject once chosen, write in prose, and divide the matter into three acts of time, seeing to it, if possible, that in each one the space of the day be not broken. Captain Verués, a worthy wit, divided comedy into three acts, which before had gone on all fours, as on baby's feet, for comedies were then infants. I wrote them myself, when eleven or twelve years of age, of four acts and of four sheets of paper, for a sheet contained each act; and then it was the fashion that for the three intermissions were made three little *entremeses*, but today scarce one, and then a dance, for the dancing is so important in comedy that Aristotle approves of it, and Athenaeus, Plato, and Xenophon treat of it, though this last disapproves of indecorous dancing; and for this reason he is vexed at Callipides, wherein he pretends to ape the ancient chorus. The matter divided into two parts, see to the connection from the beginning until the action runs down; but do not permit the untying of the plot until reaching the last scene; for the crowd, knowing what the end is, will turn its face to the door and its shoulder to what it has awaited three hours face to face; for in what appears nothing more is to be known.

21. Very seldom should the stage remain without someone speaking, because the crowd becomes restless in these intervals and the story spins itself out at great length; for, besides its being a great defect, the avoidance of it increases grace and artifice.

22. Begin then, and, with simple language, do not spend sententious thoughts and witty sayings on family trifles, which is all that the familiar

talk of two or three people is representing. But when the character who is introduced persuades, counsels, or dissuades, then there should be gravity and wit; for then doubtless is truth observed, since a man speaks in a different style from what is common when he gives counsel, or persuades, or argues against anything. Aristides, the rhetorician, gave us warrant for this; for he wishes the language of comedy to be pure, clear, and flexible, and he adds also that it should be taken from the usage of the people, this being different from that of polite society; for in the latter case the diction will be elegant, sonorous, and adorned. Do not drag in quotations, nor let your language offend because of exquisite words; for, if one is to imitate those who speak, it should not be by the language of Panchaia, of the Metaurus, of hippogriffs, demigods, and centaurs.

23. If the king should speak, imitate as much as possible the gravity of a king; if the sage speak, observe a sententious modesty; describe lovers with those passions which greatly move whoever listens to them; manage soliloquies in such a manner that the recitant is quite transformed, and in changing himself, changes the listener. Let him ask questions and reply to himself, and if he shall make plaints, let him observe the respect due to women. Let not ladies disregard their character, and if they change costumes, let it be in such wise that it may be excused; for male disguise usually is very pleasing. Let him be on his guard against impossible things, for it is of the chiefest importance that only the likeness of truth should be represented. The lackey should not discourse of lofty affairs, nor express the conceits which we have seen in certain foreign plays; and in no wise let the character contradict himself in what he has said; I mean to say, forget—as in Sophocles one blames Oedipus for not remembering that he has killed Laius with his own hand. Let the scenes end with epigram, with wit, and with elegant verse, in such wise that, at his exit, he who spouts leave not the audience disgusted. In the first act set forth the case. In the second weave together the events, in such wise that until the middle of the third act one may hardly guess the outcome. Always trick expectancy; and hence it may come to pass that something quite far from what is promised may be left to the understanding. Tactfully suit your verse to the subjects being treated. *Décimas* are good for complainings; the sonnet is good for those who are waiting in expectation; recitals of events ask for *romances*, though they shine brilliantly in *octavas*. *Tercets* are for grave affairs and *redondillas* for affairs of love. Let rhetorical figures be brought in, as repetition or anadiplosis, and in the beginning of these same verses the various forms of anaphora; and also irony, questions, apostrophes, and exclamations.

24. To deceive the audience with the truth is a thing that has seemed well,

as Miguel Sánchez, worthy of this memorial for the invention, was wont to do in all his comedies. Equivoque and the uncertainty arising from ambiguity have always held a large place among the crowd, for it thinks that it alone understands what the other one is saying. Better still are the subjects in which honor has a part, since they deeply stir everybody; along with them go virtuous deeds, for virtue is everywhere loved; hence we see, if an actor chance to represent a traitor, he is so hateful to everyone that what he wishes to buy is not sold him, and the crowd flees when it meets him; but if he is loyal, they lend to him and invite him, and even the chief men honor him, love him, seek him out, entertain him, and acclaim him.

25. Let each act have but four sheets, for twelve are well suited to the time and the patience of him who is listening. In satirical parts, be not clear or open, since it is known that for this very reason comedies were forbidden by law in Greece and Italy; wound without hate, for if, perchance, slander be done, expect not applause, nor aspire to fame.

26. These things you may regard as aphorisms which you get not from the ancient art, which the present occasion allows no further space for treating; since whatever has to do with the three kinds of stage properties which Vitruvius speaks of concerns the impresario; just as Valerius Maximus, Petrus Crinitus, Horace in his epistles, and others describe these properties, with their drops, trees, cabins, houses, and simulated marbles.

27. Of costume Julius Pollux would tell us if it were necessary, for in Spain it is the case that the comedy of today is replete with barbarous things: a Turk wearing the neck-gear of a Christian and a Roman in tight breeches.

28. But of all, nobody can I call more barbarous than myself, since in defiance of art I dare to lay down precepts, and I allow myself to be borne along in the vulgar current, wherefore Italy and France call me ignorant. But what can I do if I have written four hundred and eighty-three comedies, along with one which I finished this week? For all of these, except six, gravely sin against art. Yet, in fine, I defend what I have written, and I know that, though they might have been better in another manner, they would not have had the vogue which they have had; for sometimes that which is contrary to what is just, for that very reason, pleases the taste.

> How Comedy reflects this life of man,
>   How true her portraiture of young and old;
> How subtle wit, polished in narrow span,
>   And purest speech, and more too you behold;
> What grave consideration mixed with smiles,

What seriousness, along with pleasant jest;
Deceit of slaves; how woman oft beguiles
   How full of slyness is her treacherous breast;
How silly, awkward swains to sadness run,
   How rare success, though all seems well begun,

Let one hear with attention, and dispute not of the art; for in comedy everything will be found of such a sort that in listening to it everything becomes evident.

John Fletcher   *1579–1625*

Preface to
The Faithful Shepherdess   *1609*

If you be not reasonably assured of your knowledge in this kind of poem, lay down the book, or read this, which I would wish had been the Prologue. It is a pastoral tragicomedy, which the people seeing when it was played, having ever a singular gift in defining, concluded to be a play of country-hired shepherds, in grey cloaks, with cur-tailed dogs in strings, sometimes laughing together, and sometimes killing one another; and missing Whitsun-ales, cream, wassel, and morris-dances, began to be angry. In their error I would not have you fall, lest you incur their censure. Understand, therefore, a pastoral to be a representation of shepherds and shepherdesses with their actions and passions, which must be such as may agree with their natures, at least not exceeding former fictions and vulgar traditions; they are not to be adorned with any art, but such improper ones as nature is said to bestow, as singing and poetry; or such as experience may teach them, as the virtues of herbs and fountains, the ordinary course of the sun, moon and stars, and such like. But you are ever to remember shepherds to be such as all the ancient poets, and modern, of understanding, have received them: that is, the owners of flocks, and not hirelings. A tragicomedy is not so called in

"To the Reader," from *The Works of Beaumont and Fletcher*, Vol. I. London: George Routledge & Sons, 1872.

respect of mirth and killing, but in respect it wants deaths, which is enough to make it no tragedy, yet brings some near it, which is enough to make it no comedy, which must be a representation of familiar people, with such kind of trouble as no life be questioned; so that a god is as lawful in this as in a tragedy, and mean people as in a comedy. Thus much I hope will serve to justify my poem, and make you understand it; to teach you more for nothing, I do not know that I am in conscience bound.

John Webster *1580?–1634?*

Preface to
The White Devil *1612*

If it be objected this is no true dramatic poem, I shall easily confess it; *nonpotes in nugas dicere plura meas ipse ego quam dixi.*[1] Willingly, and not ignorantly, in this kind have I faulted: for, should a man present to such an auditory the most sententious tragedy that ever was written, observing all the critical laws, as height of style, and gravity of person, enrich it with the sententious Chorus, and, as it were, liven death in the passionate and weighty Nuntius[2]; yet, after all this divine rapture, *O dura messorum ilia,*[3] the breath that comes from the uncapable multitude is able to poison it. . . .

Selection from "To the Reader." From *Webster and Tourneur*, ed. John Addington Symonds. The Mermaid Series. London: Vizetelly & Co., 1888.

[1] "You can say no more against these trifles of mine than what I myself have said." —Martial, XIII, 2.

[2] Messenger.

[3] "O strong stomachs of harvesters!" —Horace, *Epodes*, III, 4.

Seventeenth- and Eighteenth-Century France

Whereas popular taste in early seventeenth-century France favored the more expansive, panoramic drama derived from medieval tradition and unfettered by rules of playwriting, the academic critics sensitive to Italiante theatrical innovations promoted classical regularity and order, as set forth by Italian scholars, and they therefore sought to promote a classically correct French theatre that would rival if not surpass the glories of Greece and Rome. In 1635 the French Academy was established by Cardinal Richelieu, who favored order and a central authority (his own) in the drama as well as in politics (in fact, much neoclassical tragedy reflects such political goals as a strong monarch and total subservience to him). Crucial to the establishment of classically inspired, innovative rules as the norm and standard for France, and to the power of the Academy, was the controversy engendered by the production in 1636 of Corneille's *The Cid.* An immense success, Corneille's incident-packed story of love, duty, and bravery nevertheless claimed correctness: adherence to all of the neoclassical precepts, including the three unities. Rival authors, such as Scudéry, attacked the play—perhaps because of jealousy at the play's popularity, but also because *The Cid,* though superficially conforming to the rules, violated (according to its hostile critics) the bases of such rules, verisimilitude and decorum. Although Corneille first tried to stand above the battle, he was soon drawn into it. Then, Scudéry appealed to Richelieu's new Academy. The Academy's *Opinions,* written mainly by Jean Chapelain (1595–1674), was submitted for approval to Richelieu, who returned it with injunctions to make it harsher. "It is necessary to set an example," said the Cardinal in one of his marginal exclamations. The example was set, Corneille chastened, and both Richelieu's Academy and the neoclassical rules that were its guidelines made triumphant.

In one sense, the neoclassical rules were bound to triumph no matter how harsh or lenient the judgment against *The Cid,* for both Corneille and his attackers proceeded from the same set of values. The issue was not whether the neoclassical rules and assumptions were correct but

whether the play lived up to them. In Corneille's three *Discourses,*
written more than twenty years after the contention surrounding *The Cid,*
he occasionally refers to his controversial play, which he relates to
general precepts, such as the instructive aspect of tragedy, the questions of
probability and necessity, the unities (unity of action, says he, consists
of unity of danger), and so forth. Like Corneille, though to a far lesser
extent, Racine, France's other major seventeenth-century tragedian,
also explored theoretical questions that were the common concern of
seventeenth-century neoclassicists: for instance, the nature of the tragic
hero, condensation and simplicity of design, and the purpose of tragedy.

References to the emotional aim of tragedy notwithstanding,
neoclassicists usually preferred that it—and comedy too—fulfill an
instructive aim as well. The social and political bases of such instruction is
explicit in Hédelin's influential *Whole Art of the Stage.* A dogmatist,
Hédelin begins with the premise that in order to be good a play must be
written to conform to the rules, and he predictably concludes, for
instance, that if an "irregular" play pleases then only those parts please
that conform to the rules.

Even more influential was Boileau, called "the lawgiver of the French
Parnassus." His *Art of Poetry* expressed systematically, in aphoristic rhyming
couplets, and with clarity, polish, and elegance, the neoclassical ideals of
poetry. "Half of his verses became maxims or proverbs at their birth,"
said Brunetière in 1889. Also influential is Rapin, who dogmatizes on
instruction as inherently the basic goal of both tragedy and comedy
and who regards the other rules as means to that end. Erroneously, he
claims Aristotle's *Poetics* as authority; and though he cites Horace as
well, with more accuracy, he erroneously calls him Aristotle's interpreter.

Veneration of the rules, though variously interpreted as to details, was
widespread, but it was by no means universal. Molière (Jean-Baptiste
Poquelin), regarding them as shackles, insisted that the only rule was to
please the audience. Nevertheless, he shared some of the premises of
the rule-mongering critics. Like them, he maintained that the end of comedy
was moral instruction and that comedy should depict universal types
rather than individuals. Saint-Évremond too was far from rigid. Although
his criticism of the theatre was based on such concepts as verisimilitude,
still, he questions Aristotle, repudiates dogmatism, and scrutinizes the
theatre with common sense, which is revealed in his anecdote of the
Prince of Condé's expression of gratitude that Hédelin followed Aristotle's
rules and of regret that these rules caused Hédelin to write so bad a
tragedy. Saint-Évremond's perception that tragedy should excite admiration
accurately assesses what many French tragedians, consciously or not, were
aiming to do.

Verisimilitude and nature, decorum and the unities, noble heroes who
speak in rhymed verse—such fundamentals of seventeenth-century

tragic theory were eroding in the eighteenth. A theatrical reactionary, though a political liberal, Voltaire (François Marie Arouet) insisted on the inviolability of the neoclassical formulas and considered Addison's *Cato* to be England's best tragedy. Times were changing, however. In 1751 —two decades after Voltaire's *Discourse on Tragedy*, seventeen years before his *Letter to Walpole*—came the first volume of Diderot's *Encyclopedia*, which was to advocate (sometimes between the lines, sometimes explicitly) civil rights and to help pave the way for the Revolution of 1789. Turmoil in the arts reflects social turmoil. Like conceptions of society, conceptions of theatre were being redefined according to the value and viewpoint not of the aristocracy but of the rising middle class, which wanted a theatre and a world based on their values. Such dramatic critics as Diderot (the major French theorist of this movement), his disciple Beaumarchais (Pierre-Augustin Caron), and Mercier tried to change and extend the range of theatre. Neoclassical rules, artistocratically inspired, were, they charged, as inapplicable to the theatre as to eighteenth-century life. Mercier went so far as to urge the abandonment of the concept of a single character as hero in favor of the portrayal of groups. Whereas the two pure genres, tragedy and comedy, may have been appropriate for aristocratic audiences a century earlier, a new genre fit for bourgeois, eighteenth-century audiences was wanted, said these critics: the Serious Drama, a middle ground between tragedy and comedy, for middle-class people. Stories of royalty, as Beaumarchais said, appeal merely to the spectator's voyeuristic vanity; these critics rejected them. They wanted plays that would truthfully depict men as they are, not as they should be according to aristocratic ideals; show people who work for a living at various occupations; reveal the concerns of such people (family and money); be composed in prose rather than verse. They advocated tear-jerking plays that would impel audiences toward virtue—not aristocratic virtue but bourgeois virtue—and they claimed that the Serious Drama performed this task better than other genres. Rousseau, meanwhile, vigorously denied that any kind of drama achieves such a goal. In any case, plays were written to fit the formula: Diderot's *Father of the Family*, for instance, Michel-Jean Sedaine's *The Philosopher in Spite of Himself* (the most original and successful French realization of the theory in the eighteenth century), Beaumarchais' *Eugenie*. Although Beauchmarchais' more famous *Marriage of Figaro* is not a Serious Drama, it satirizes the corruption of the nobility and hails the servants. With realism in playwriting goes realism in production, as Diderot shows, for the play focuses on contemporaries as they actually live. In his concept of production, then, in calling for a prose play reflective of bourgeois values, and in aiming to give audiences something to recognize from their own lives, we see what may be regarded as the starting point of modern drama.

The Cid Controversy

Georges de Scudéry 1601–1667

Observations on The Cid[1] 1637

There are certain plays, as there are certain natural creatures, that from a distance appear to be stars but that close up are nothing but worms. Everything that shines is not necessarily precious; beauty may be illusory as well as actual, and we often misread the appearance of substance as substance itself. Therefore it does not astound me that the groundlings, whose discernment is largely visual, fall into error from trusting that one of the senses most easily deceived. But that the vulgar effluvia of the pit should invade the boxes and that a mirage should delude both ignorance and knowledge and the courtiers as well as the bourgeoisie, is a wonder at which I marvel. It is in this sense only that I find *The Cid* marvelous. But just as in olden times a Macedonian appealed the judgment of a prejudiced Philip to a Philip seeing the light, so I urge all gentlemen to reserve their decisions and not to condemn without a hearing the *Sofonisbas*, the *Caesars*, the *Cleopatras*, the *Herculeses*, the *Mariamnes*, the *Cleomedons*, and the countless other illustrious heroes who have delighted them in the theatre. As for myself, however dazzling the success of *The Cid* may have been, I look on it as I do the beautiful rainbows that disappear almost as soon as the sun has stamped their sumptuous but illusive forms on the clouds. Though I did not, advisedly, envy something merely pitiful, I neglected to point out the flaws that I saw in this work. Instead, since without boasting I can call myself generous and kind, I gave voice to sentiments that I did not actually feel, I led others to believe what I did not believe myself, and I contented myself with recognizing error without exposing it and truth without becoming an evangelist. But when I saw that that sage who observed that prosperity is harder for most of us to bear than misfortune, and that restraint in the face of the former is rarer than

[1] Selection.

patience in the face of the latter, seemed to have painted a portrait of the author of *The Cid*; when I saw, moreover, that he was deifying himself by his own hand, that he was speaking of himself as we normally speak of others, that he was even committing his self-praise to print, that he seems to believe that he is conferring too great an honor on the greatest minds of the age to offer them his left hand, I realized that it would be unjust and cowardly of me not to act on the public behalf, and that it would be proper to impel him to read that serviceable inscription that the ancients could find carved above the door of one of the Greek temples:

KNOW THOU THYSELF

Not that I wish to counter his scorn with insults. Only those with no other weapons should stoop to using these, and, whatever one's need to defend one's self, I deem them unfit for my use. I am attacking *The Cid* and not its author. My complaint is against the work rather than the man. And since disagreements need not be disagreeable, I would raise the foil to my lips before I have at him. I shall deal in neither satire nor libel, but in simple observations, and no acrimony, aside from that which my subject matter implies, will taint my words. I conjure him to employ the same restraint if he replies, for I can neither offer nor endure insults. As regards the play *The Cid*, I intend to prove

That the plot is worthless;
That it abuses the basic rules of dramatic poetry;
That it pursues an erratic course;
That much of its verse is poor;
That virtually all its beauties are stolen.

Therefore, it does not deserve the plaudits it has won. But having stated this premise and being obliged to justify it, I am now required to acquit myself with honor.

Those who wish to topple one of those proud structures that human vanity raises so high do not waste their time smashing columns or breaking balustrades; they begin by undermining the foundation so that the whole mass will crumble and fall at the same moment. Wishful to achieve their end, I shall imitate their actions, and to insure my success I shall state that the opinion of Aristotle, and of all later theorists, has established as an incontrovertible rule that invention is the primary test of both the poet and the poem. The etymology of the words themselves supports this truth, for they derive from the Greek verb for "to make." To the extent that *The Cid* shows good invention, the credit belongs to its Spanish author, Guillen de Castro, rather than to its French translator, but I contend that the plot is worthless. For a tragedy to conform to the rules of art, it must have only one principal action, to which all the others converge as the radii of a circle converge at its center. And, the argument being drawn from history or from familiar myths (according to the precepts handed down to us), the object is not to surprise the spectator, since he already knows the outcome. But such is not the case with tragicomedy, for, although it was almost unknown to antiquity, nevertheless, since it is a mixture of tragedy and of comedy, and since its ending would seem to incline it more toward the latter, the first act of this kind of play must spin an intrigue that keeps us constantly in suspense without disentangling until the end. In *The Cid*, this Gordian knot has no need of an Alexander to cut it. There, Chimène's father dies almost at the beginning. Throughout the play, neither she nor Rodrigue engage or can engage in but a single action. There is no variety, no plot, no complication. The least visionary spectator guesses, or, rather, foresees the end of this story as soon as it begins. The preceding evidence, I believe, clearly demonstrates that the plot is worthless since I have shown that it lacks all that could make it good, but has in abundance all that makes it bad. I shall find it just as easy to prove that it abuses the basic rules of drama, and I am fully confident that, once I have reminded him, everyone will agree that the most important of the rules of which I speak, that on which a work will stand or fall, is plausibility. If that is missing, no amount of hocus-pocus, however fascinating, can truly interest us in the success or failure of these fictional protagonists. The poet who aims at stirring the audience's passions by means of those of his characters, must be wise enough to see that, no matter how vivid, forceful, and well expressed they are, he will fail to achieve the desired effect unless he attains to plausibility. The great masters who have preceded us, and from whom I have learned all that I here set down for those who may not have heard it, have always insisted that the poet and the historian ought not to travel the same route and that it is better for the former to treat a subject that is plausible but not true than one that is true but not plausible. It is scarcely necessary for me to add that in the mind of the reader, though it is true that Chimène married the Cid, it is not plausible that an honorable daughter would marry her father's murderer. Such an occurrence would serve for an historian, but it is worthless for a poet, and it makes it no better to depict Chimène's revulsion or her struggles between duty and love, or to hear a thousand contradictions from her lips, or for the King to interpose his authority, since, in the end, none of these measures saves her from being a parricide when, at last, she agrees to marry her father's murderer. And, although she will not do so right away, her consent (without which there can be no marriage) seems already to be given, and Chimène is a parricide. Such a plot is not plausible. Consequently, it abuses one of the basic rules of drama. But, to ground my reasons in ancient authority, I recall that the name "myth," which Aristotle gave to the plot of tragedy, although Homer uses it to mean only a simple discourse, everywhere else refers to an account of something unreal which, nevertheless, contains a kind of truth. It is such myths that the tragic poets, in Aristotle's day, and even earlier, used for the plots of their plays, indifferent as to whether they were true as long as they were plausible. That is why, as the Philosopher observes, the first tragedians, though they began by taking their plots from any source, ended by restricting themselves to those which are or can be made plausible, and which, for no other reason, many authors have dramatized, for example, Medea, Alcmeon, Oedipus, Orestes, Meleager, Thyestes, and Telephus. As one can see, these are myths that they could change if they saw fit to bring them in line with plausibility. Thus, Sophocles, Aeschylus, and Euripides have treated the myth of Philoctetes quite differently, and, equally, that of Medea is not identical in Seneca, Ovid, and Euripides. But they were dealing, as it were, with religion; they could not have allowed themselves to change history in their treatments or to belie the facts. Finally, not finding all history to be plausible, though true, and being able neither to make it so nor to alter it, they came, because of this difficulty, to use it less and less, and to choose instead, for the most part, mythological material as easier to handle plausibly. Continuing, our Philosopher shows that the art of the poet is more demanding than that of the historian because the latter simply reports what has happened whereas the former represents not what is but what should be. In this respect, the author of *The Cid* has failed, for, finding in Spanish history that this daughter had married her father's murderer, he should have considered that, being historic and consequently true, but not plausible, to the extent that it goes against reason and custom, it was not and could not become suitable material for dramatic poetry. But one error leads to another, and to preserve the unity of time (an excellent rule when properly understood), the French author falters more clumsily than the Spaniard, and does ill by straining to do well. Castro at least compensates for his fault with some color because since his poem is irregular, the extended time period, though it always diminishes intensity of pain, somehow results in making the whole more plausible. But to enclose within the space of twenty-four hours both the father's murder and the daughter's pledge to marry the man who murdered him, and murdered him not without knowing who he was, or accidentally, but in a duel to which he had challenged him, is to present what (as one of my friends has cleverly remarked), far from being acceptable in twenty-four hours, would not be endurable after twenty-four years. And therefore (I repeat) he does not observe the rule of plausibility though that rule is indispensable. Indeed, all the noble deeds that it took the Cid many years to accomplish, are in this play so tightly compressed into twenty-four hours that the characters seem to be *dei ex machina* fallen to Earth from Heaven, for in the short period of one day, the King chooses a tutor for the Prince of Castile, Don Diègue and the Count quarrel and come to blows, Rodrigue and the Count fight a duel, Rodrigue defeats the Moors and returns to duel with Don Sanche, and Rodrigue and Chimène contract their betrothal. I leave you to judge whether this has been a very busy day and whether one would not be gravely in error to accuse these characters of laziness. The plot of a dramatic poem, like all corporeal forms, in order to be perfect requires the proper magnitude, neither too vast nor too narrowly constricted. Thus, when we observe such a work, what normally happens is what takes place when the eye sees an object. One who views a form of excessive magnitude, in working at encompassing all the parts, cannot take in the whole that they make up; similarly, if the action of a play is too extensive, one who contemplates it will not find a way for his memory to retain all the parts. On the other hand, if a form is too small, the eyes, skimming over it too quickly, for in almost the same instant the image appears and is gone, find nothing pleasurable. Thus, with the poem, which is to the memory as the object is to the eye, the mind takes delight neither in what it overlooks nor in what it cannot scan. And, certainly, as forms in order to be beautiful need two things, namely, order and magnitude, for which reason Aristotle denies that one can attribute beauty to small men, however pleasing their appearance, since, although harmoniously ordered, nevertheless they lack that advantageous stature necessary to beauty—likewise, it is not enough for a poem to have all its parts artfully arranged if it fails of the exact magnitude for the mind to apprehend it with ease. Now what should this magnitude be? Aristotle, on whose judgment we rely to the extent that we scorn those who do not, has determined that this period must be the time elapsed between two suns. The represented action then must neither exceed nor fall short of the length that he prescribes. That is why Aristophanes, the Greek comic poet, once ridiculed the tragic poet Aeschylus who, in his *Niobe*, to depict the sustained grief of his heroine, introduced her sitting at the tomb of her children, where, without saying a word, she remained for three days. And that is why the learned Heinsius found Buchanan to have erred in his tragedy *Jephtha*, where, within a twenty-four-hour period, he encloses an action that, history tells us, lasted two months, the time the daughter spent in lamenting her virginity. But the author of *The Cid* carries error much farther since he squeezes several years into one day and since the the marriage to Chimène and the capture of the Moorish kings, which according to Spanish history did not take place until two or three years after the death of the Count, here take place on the same day. For although the ceremony does not take place at once, Chimène and Rodrigue give their consent, and are, from that point on, married, since according to jurisconsults, consent is the only requirement even without considering that Chimène is his by virtue of his victory over Don Sanche and by the King's decree. But this is not the only law transgressed in this part of the play; the author breaks one more crucial in that he violates good form as well as the rules of drama. To see this truth, one must know that that drama was invented to instruct while delighting and that under this pleasant garb Philosophy is in disguise for fear lest she reveal herself as too austere for the eyes of the world, and, through the author's art, she sugarcoats the pills (so to speak) so that we will swallow them without distaste and find ourselves cured almost without being aware of the remedy. Therefore, she never fails to show us in the theatre virtue rewarded and vice always punished. If we sometimes see the wicked prosper, the good persecuted, with apparently no hope of change, by the end of the performance she unfailingly shows the triumph of the innocents, the punishment of the guilty. In this way, imperceptibly, the theatre impresses on our minds a horror of vice and a love for virtue. But the play *The Cid* falls so far short of this desideratum as to serve as an atrocious example. We see therein an unnatural daughter speaking of only distraction when she should be speaking of her bereavement, and lamenting the loss of her lover when she should be thinking only of her father, still loving where she should abhor, regretting at the same time and on the same premises the loss of both the murderer and the wretched corpse, and, for a crowning impiety, joining her hand to a hand defiled with the blood of her father. After this horrible crime, does not the spectator have the right to expect a thunderbolt from the playwright's fictive heaven to strike this danaid down? Or, should he be familiar with the rule against onstage violence, has he not reason to believe, at the very least, that directly after her exit, a Messenger will arrive to proclaim her punishment? Nevertheless, neither event takes place. On the contrary, this immodest creature basks in the royal favor; her vice appears to be rewarded, and virtue seems to be banished from the conclusion of the play. It is therefore a guide to evil, a goad to urge us toward it, and, because of these egregious and dangerous flaws, diametrically opposed to the basic rules of drama. It was because of such works as these that Plato would not admit poetry into his Republic—all poetry, but chiefly he proscribed the poetry of the theatre that imitates through action, the more so that it offers up to our consideration all sorts of behavior, vices and virtues, crimes and noble deeds, and that it indiscriminately presents Atreus or Nestor. Now, deriving no more pleasure from the expression of good actions than from bad, since in poetry, as in painting, one confronts only the image, and a well-executed portrait of Thersites is as satisfying as one of Narcissus—to proceed from there, this satisfaction corrupted the spectator's spirits, and he came to find as much pleasure in imitating the bad actions that he saw presented with artistry, and to which human nature is prone, as in imitating the good, which require effort. Thus, the theatre was as much a school for vice as for virtue. This realization obliged Plato to exile poets from his Republic, and, although he crowned Homer with flowers, he did not hesitate to banish him. But, with a view toward softening Plato's hard line, Aristotle, who recognized the uses of poetry, and of dramatic poetry especially, which inclines us more successfully than epic or lyric poetry toward goodness rather than toward evil, and, since that which we see affects more deeply than that which we merely hear (as Horace has observed), Aristotle (I say) states in his *Poetics* that the behavior represented on the stage should be for the most part good and that, if we must include persons full of vice, the virtuous should outnumber them. The result was that critics of later times have blamed certain classical tragedies for depicting fewer good than evil actions. An example is the *Orestes* of Euripides, in which, with the exception of Pylades, all the characters have evil inclinations. If the author under discussion had known these precepts as well as the others I have cited, he would not have allowed himself to let wickedness triumph on the stage, and his characters would have had higher ideals than those of the personages that he has created. Fernand would have been a greater statesman, Urraque less basely tempted, Don Gomes less ambitious and less insolent, Don Sanche nobler, and Elvire would have provided a better example for ladies-in-waiting to follow, and the author would not have preached vengeance through the words of the daughter of the very one whose actions another must avenge. Chimène would not have said:

Forgo all hope of reconciliation;
Affronted honor knows no reparation.
Resolve and prudence counsel us in vain.
Beneath appearances, the wounds remain.

Pierre Corneille *1606–1684*

Apologetic Letter[1] *1637*

Sir,

It was not enough for you that your libels wound me publicly; your letters hound me in the privacy of my chamber, and you send me unjust accusations when the least that you owe me is apologies. I did not write the document that you find so disturbing; I received it with a letter from Paris that informed me of its author's name. He addresses it to one of our friends who will be able to give you further information. I myself pass no judgment on the matter but leave that up to you. I am all the more noncommittal for not wishing to offend a man of so exalted a station, with whom I do not have the honor of being acquainted, as well as for fearing his resentment less than yours. All

[1] Complete.

that I can say to you is that I question neither your rank nor your qualifications, and, in matters of this kind, in which I have no interest, I take the world on faith; let us not confuse our argument with such problems. It is not a question of knowing how noble or how much more qualified you are when it comes to judging how much better *The Cid* is than *The Generous Lover.* The intelligentsia consider your *Observations* to be a great masterpiece of erudition and theory. The modesty and generosity that you display seem to them to be rare qualities. And throughout your wonderfully sincere and cordial behavior toward a friend, you deny insulting me, and immediately afterward you accuse me of ignorance of my craft and of a want of judgment in the execution of my best creation. Do you call that professional courtesy? I should need no more than the text of your slanderous pamphlet and the contradictions therein to convict you of both the crimes with which you charge me and to tie to your coattail the insulting quatrain that you wish to attach to mine—even if the text itself did not make me see that you do not deserve the praise due to an author of good reputation, for it drew my attention to yet another of your deficiencies along these lines when it exclaimed, "O reason of the audience, could you have been at work?" When you delivered this infamous quip had you forgotten that *The Cid* had had five performances at the Louvre and two at Richelieu's palace? When you called poor Chimène immodest, a prostitute, a parricide, a monster, had you forgotten that the Queen, the Princesses, and the most virtuous ladies of Paris and of the Court had received her and cherished her as a woman of honor? When you reproached me with vanity and dismissed the Count de Gormas as a *commedia dell'arte* Captain,[2] had you forgotten your own preface to *Ligdamon* and the poetic and military excesses that cause the reader to deride almost all your books? To convince others of my ignorance, you have imposed upon the credulous and have entirely on your own authority put forth theatrical dicta from which, even if they were true, you could not draw the fanciful conclusions that you do. You have blithely passed yourself off as an Aristotle; and on other authors whom you have not read and may never have understood and who do not strengthen your position, you play the Royal Censor in order to attribute bad examples to me. In your fastidiousness, you have gone so far as to accuse me of omitting a caesura. If you knew the technical language of the craft in which you meddle, you would have called it the hemistichal pause. You have attempted to classify me as a simple translator on the strength of seventy verses (out of a total of two thousand) though no expert would ever call them simple translations. You have attacked me for suppressing the name of the Spanish author although you would not have known it except for me and although you know full well that I have not concealed it from anyone, but instead have actually shown a copy of the Spanish original to His Eminence,

[2] Il Capitano, the braggart soldier.

the Cardinal,[3] your master and mine. Finally, you wish to snatch from me in one day what it has taken me years of application to acquire. It is no thanks to you that I have not descended from the position of leadership in which many honest gentlemen have placed me to one below that of Claveret.[4] And, to make amends for these signal offenses, you find it sufficient to urge me to answer you civilly lest we both have cause to repent of our follies later, and you imperiously command me, despite the foregoing exchange of jibes, to be your friend so that you may still be mine as if, after your petulant insults, your friendship could still be of value to me and as if I were obliged to take note of only the harm that you have successfully inflicted rather than of all that you intended. You complain of a letter that I wrote . . . in which I did not speak of you as an equal—and justly so, since in revealing your envy of me you admit to being my inferior, although you call the professional vices to which you have succumbed sheer madness, and the remorse that you show signalizes your shame. It is not enough to say "Be my friend once more" to regain a friendship so outrageously violated. I am not one of your enlightened beings, you may be certain of that. Treat me henceforward as one as much unknown as I wish to let you remain now that I know you. But you have no right to complain when I assume the same authority over your works as you have assumed over mine. Should one volume of *Observations* not be enough for you, write fifty more; until the basis of your attack is much firmer, I shall not have cause to defend myself, and, for my part, I, along with my friends, shall do nothing until we have seen whether it be worth ruining whatever you have left me of my reputation. When you request my friendship in politer language, I shall be gracious enough not to refuse you and to hold my peace about the lack of wit that you display in your books. Until then, I am vain enough to tell you in a neighborly fashion that I neither fear you nor love you. After all, to speak seriously, and to show you that I am not so much annoyed as you may imagine, it will not be my fault if we fail to resume our former good relationship, in which you have expressed an interest. But after so public an attack, I rightfully stand on ceremony. Not that I intend to make things difficult. I shall submit my case to whichever of your friends you may choose, for I am certain that a man who might overlook doing himself harm, would condemn you for doing that harm to yourself, rather than me, who wish you none at all and in whom reading your *Observations* aroused nothing but pity. And, certainly, I should deserve society's censure if I held a grudge against you for augmenting my reputation with a

---

[3] Richelieu.

[4] Jean Claveret (*c.* 1600–1666). After some success as a poet, he turned to writing for the theatre, despite Corneille's attempts to dissuade him. He later angered Corneille by writing *The Author of the True Spanish Cid to His French Translator*, which maintained that Corneille had stolen the form and the best parts of *The Cid* from the Spanish source. Claveret's tragicomedy *The Rape of Proserpine* (1637–1638) violated the unity of place by enacting scenes in Heaven, Sicily, and Hell [translator's note].

tract that has proved to be beneficial to *The Cid*, which, of all the fine poems
that have appeared to date, has been the only one whose dazzling success
has prompted Envy to take up her pen. I seek no better apologia than that
which you admit it has received, the approbation of the scholars and of the
Court. That truthful praise with which you began your denigrations negates
everything you can find to say afterward. It is enough that you were insane
enough to attack me without my being equally insane and answering you as
you would wish me to. And, since in such things brevity is always best, I shall
not resuscitate your insanity by prolonging my own. And you must resist the
temptation of those sallies that make the public laugh at your expense. Continue wishing to be my friend so that I may still be yours.

—Corneille

The Opinions
of the French Academy[1] 1638

We cannot deny that at first we were astounded that the Observer, having
undertaken to convict this play of irregularity, decided on a method differing
from the one that Aristotle employs to guide us in creating epic and dramatic
poems. It seems to us that instead of adopting his own procedure for examining the matter, he might better have exemplified regularity and considered
in sequence plot, which comprises the invention and arrangement of the
subject matter; character, which covers the predispositions of the soul and
its various passions; dianoia, the expression of the ideas inherent in the story;
and language, which is nothing else than poetic diction—for we find that the
result of his having used a different method is that his reasoning appears to
be less sound, with even the strongest of his objections weakened. We should
not, however, have cited this new method at this time if we had not understood that in some way our silence condoned it. But in whatever way he may
or may not have erred in selecting this method, we do not err in following it,
since we are examining his work, and whatever path he may have taken, we
may not deviated from it without giving him cause for the complaint that we
have chosen another route in order to make him look bad.

---

[1] Selections. The *Opinions* are mainly the work of Jean Chapelain (1595–1674).

He first submits that the plot of *The Cid is* worthless, but by our lights, when he states that we find there neither nodus nor intrigue and that we guess the outcome as soon as we see the beginning, he aims at rather than succeeds in proving its worthlessness—for since the nodus of theatrical works is an unlooked-for incident that stays the course of the represented action, and the dénouement another that brings that action to completion, we find that both these elements are present in the structure of *The Cid*, and that its plot would not be bad, this objection notwithstanding, if there were not stronger objections that could be made.

One has only to remember that since the Count had approved the marriage of Chimène and Rodrigue in his own mind, his quarrel immediately afterward with Don Diègue throws the affair into question, and with his subsequent death at Rodrigue's hands, the possibility is even more remote. And in this succession of difficulties we easily recognize the nodus or intrigue. The dénouement also will be no less apparent if we consider that when, after Rodrigue has suffered many ordeals, Chimène offers her hand to whoever will bring her his head, Don Sanche steps forward, and the King not only does not exact further punishment of Rodrigue for the death of the Count than to fight one duel, but also, against everyone's expectations, requires Chimène to marry whichever of the two is the victor. Now, whether or not the dénouement be artistic is another question, to be settled elsewhere. Such as it is, it does not lack surprise, and therefore a plot and its unraveling are not absent from this play. This much the Observer himself cannot avoid recognizing a little farther on when, faulting the play for its plethora of detached episodes, he states that the author had all the fewer justifications for including so many in *The Cid* in that, the plot being tragicomic, there was no need for them—referring to what he had just said about tragicomic plots, which being sufficiently involved by their nature scarcely require additional embellishment. Therefore, if the plot of *The Cid* is bad, we do not see that it is because it lacks a nodus, but rather because it is not plausible. The Observer is aiming in the proper direction, but when he attempts to prove that it abuses the basic rules of dramatic poetry, he has not hit the mark.

As far as we can judge from the opinions of Aristotle on the subject of the probable, he recognizes only two species, the usual and the extraordinary. The usual embraces what normally happens to human beings according to their station, age, habits, and temperament; for example, it is probable that a businessman will seek profits, that a child will act thoughtlessly, that a wastrel will sink into poverty, that an angry man will pursue vengeance, and all such events that regularly occur. The extraordinary embraces what rarely happens, what is outside the realm of the predictable, as when a clever scoundrel is tricked, when a strong man is beaten. Included are those incidents that we usually attribute to luck provided they result from a sequence of ordinary events. A case in point is when Hecuba by a strange coincidence comes to the shore to bathe her daughter's corpse at the moment that the waves cast her son's to the shore. Now, for a mother to come to the shore to bathe her daughter's corpse and for the sea to cast up another are two events that, considered separately, are in no wise out of the ordinary; but at the same time, and in the same place that she is bathing her daughter's corpse, for the corpse of her son, whom she thought to be alive and well, to appear before her is a thoroughly strange event, and by the result of their combination is something extreme, something wondrous. There is nothing outside these two categories that one can classify as probable. And we must describe any event that fits under neither heading as merely possible, as for example it is possible for one who all his life has been an honest man to commit a crime of his own volition. But such an action is not serviceable for the plot of a narrative or of a dramatic poem since, to be thus serviceable, what is possible must also be both probable and necessary. But the probable, both the usual and the extraordinary, must have the special quality—whether upon first examination or later, after reflection—of inspiring the audience or the reader to believe with no other proof that what the poet sets before them is entirely true because they find nothing there to resist. As for the reasons for assigning to the probable rather than to the possible a role in epic and dramatic poetry, the purpose of these art forms is useful delight, to which they more easily lead men through the readily accepted probable than through the possible, which may be so strange and incredible that they would refuse to be convinced or to trust it as a model and guide. But as several things are required for an action to be probable, and as it must retain its appropriateness to the period, the place, the circumstances, the character, the emotions, of which the most essential to the poem is the consistency of the *dramatis personae* with the character alloted them—that, for example, an evil man should not perform good deeds—what argues for so scrupulous an obedience of these laws is that there is no other way to achieve the wondrous and its delightful effects of surprise and delectation in the soul; it is therefore the perfect means for making good poetry useful as well.

It is on this basis that we charge the plot of *The Cid* with being essentially defective, since it displays neither the kind of probability that we have termed "usual" nor that which we have termed "extraordinary," for not only does the playwright violate consistency of character by introducing a virtuous daughter who later consents to marry her father's murderer, but also no unforeseen twist of fate that is nevertheless the culmination of a sequence of probable events brings about the ending. On the contrary, nothing constrains the daughter to agree to this marriage but the depth of her passion, and the unraveling of the plot results from the injustice that Ferdinand unexpectedly perpetrates by decreeing a union that, rightly, he ought only to suggest. We freely admit that the historicity of this event works in the playwright's favor and makes us readier to excuse him than if the plot were of his own invention. But we maintain that not all actual occurrences are suitable for the theatre and that some of them are like those crimes whose trial records the judges burn with the criminals. There are some truths that are monstrous or that we must suppress for the good of society, or, if we cannot keep them hidden, we must settle for singling them out as abnormal. It is chiefly in such instances that the poet should prefer probability to possibility and work with material that though fictitious is probable, rather than with that which is actual but excessive. If he must use historical material, then he ought to make it, even at the expense of the truth, compatible with decorum, and he should rather change it completely than leave a trace of anything unconformable to the rules of art, which, addressing itself to universal concepts, purifies reality of the defects and of the individual irregularities with which the rigid laws of history compel the latter to bear. The upshot is that there would unquestionably have been fewer embarrassments in the working out of *The Cid* if the author, despite history, had imagined either that the Count in the end would turn out not to be Chimène's real father; or that, contrary to the general belief, he had not died of his wounds; or that the well-being of the King and of his kingdom absolutely depended on this marriage, so that the benefits to the sovereign and to his state might compensate for the violence that these proceedings inflict upon natural feelings. The whole affair, we submit, would then be more pardonable than the stage presentation of the event intact and wholly as scandalous as history reports it. But most suitable of all would have been not to dramatize it, since it was too well known to be changed in so essential a point and too bad an example to set before the public without having first refined it. Besides, the Observer, who rightly complains of the slight probability of Chimène's marriage, does not strengthen his sound case, as he believes, by the alleged meaning of the word "myth," which Aristotle uses to designate the plot of the dramatic poem. And this error is one that he shares with certain of this philosopher's commentators, who have inferred from this word "myth" that truth has no place whatsoever in the theatre, and that a playwright is forbidden to touch upon history and use it for his subject matter because he may not change it to reduce it to probability. On this score, we judge them not to have sufficiently pondered Aristotle's meaning; he undoubtedly used the word to suggest not that the plot had to be mythical, but only that it had to be plausible. As proof, there is that passage in his *Poetics* in which he expressly states that the poet should be deemed no less a poet for treating actual events because such data are not *ipso facto* improbable, and in several other passages where he would have it that the tragic or epic plot be, or be accepted as, substantially true but in which he seemingly means no more than that if not all the details are known, the poet is free to supply them from his imagination and, to that extent at least, deserves the title of poet. And, certainly, it would be a strange doctrine indeed if in order to remain within the literal meaning of the word "myth," it required us to view as "mythical" those adventures of the Medeas, the Oedipuses, the Oresteses, etc., which all Antiquity has handed down to us as true accounts of at least the overall substance of the stories, although there may be differing opinions about the details. Of those considered to be pure myths, there is not one, however bizarre and extravagant it may be, that the sages of olden times have not rearranged to make it teach a better lesson. This is why we must say, contrary to the Observer's opinion, that the poet need not fear lest he commit a sacrilege in deviating from the truth of history. The most religious of poets confirms us in this belief by corrupting history to portray Dido as unchaste for no other reasons than to embellish his narrative with an admirable incident and to flatter the Romans at the expense of the Carthaginians; thus, following his overall plan, he has created an Aeneas ardently patriotic and victorious over the heroes of Latium, although there are historians who report that he was one of the traitors who sold out Troy to the Greeks and others who assert that Mezentius killed him and bore away the spoils. Therefore, as we see it, the Observer is ill advised in saying that *The Cid* is a poor subject for a dramatic poem because, since it is historic and consequently factual, it cannot be changed or made suitable to the stage. Just as Vergil, for example, triumphed by turning an honest woman into a licentious one, so another poet, in the public interest, might by making the proper adjustments and by taking the proper care to correct its faults be allowed to refashion an unthinkable marriage into one that we could accept. We are well aware that there are those who have blamed Vergil for using such methods, but, aside from our doubting whether the opinion of those critics be viable, and whether they know as much as he of the purviews of poetry, we believe that if they blamed him it was not simply for having changed history, but for having changed good into evil, so that their complaint is not that he sinned against art by deviating from the truth, but against good form by slandering a human being who would rather have died than live without her good name. It was just the opposite with Chimène; the changes to be made in the plot of *The Cid* were of bad examples in the historical account that, in the public interest, poetry might have reformed.

The objection that the Observer next raises strikes us as a most serious one, for a primary precept of poetic mimesis is not to make use of more material than one can properly develop but to allow the necessary space to the action that one is imitating. Most certainly, the author cannot deny that it is an artistic failure to have compressed so many unusual incidents into a twenty-four-hour period and to have found no other way of filling out his five acts than piling event on event in a short space of time. But if we find him justly taken to task for the multitude of actions in his play, we feel that there is even greater reason to reproach him for having Chimène consent to marry Rodrigue on the very day that he has killed the Count. Such behavior is beyond all belief: No human being, not even one most devoid of honor and humanity, let alone a proper daughter, would be.capable of it. The question here is not simply one of assembling so many great and varied adventures within so small a space of time, but of implanting in the same mind, and in fewer than twenty-four hours, two ideas as much opposed to each other as retribution for a father's death and betrothal to his murder, and reconciling within the same day two acts that could not be suffered in a whole lifetime. The Spanish author sinned less against propriety in allowing several days to elapse between her prosecution of Rodrigue and her consenting to marry him, but the French author, wishing to conform to the rule of the unity of time, has to avoid one error fallen into another, and for fear of violating the rules of art has preferred to sin against human nature.

All that the Observer says concerning the proper magnitude for a poem that is to delight the spirit without causing it to strain, derives from a sound and solid doctrine based on Aristotle's authority, or, better, on that of reason. But its application does not seem to us to be correct when he explicates this magnitude in terms of time rather than of material so that he would have it that the magnitude of *The Cid* is excessive because it includes within one day actions that would take several years when he should be demonstrating that there are too many actions for the mind to encompass at one time. Therefore, for all his demonstration that the plot of *The Cid* is so diffuse as to overtax the memory, we do not consider its excessive magnitude to lie in its having crowded the action of several years into a single day, for it might not be implausible that they could happen in one day, but that it is the abundance of the material rather than the extent of time that overtaxes the mind and that makes the play oversized. It is easy to deduce from the epic, which may extend over the period of an entire year, a succession of the four seasons, and, notwithstanding, make a distinct impression on the mind, which might nevertheless seem to be too vast if the number of events resulted in a confusion that prevented our taking them in at a glance. Indeed, Aristotle has prescribed the amount of time that plays should comprise and has ascribed to the actions that make up their plots a period no longer than sunrise to sunset. In setting forth so judicious a rule, however, he did so for reasons far removed from those that the Observer here alleges. But this is one of the thorniest questions in the field of poetry, and as it is not necessary to settle it at this time, we shall treat it later in an *Art of Poetry* that we are planning to write. As for the question that some others have raised as to whether a poet should be blamed for making events that happened at different times happen at the same time, in our opinion, he should not be—providing he does it judiciously, and restricts himself to unfamiliar or unimportant matters. Without making himself the slave of the circumstances that surround their basic truth, the poet considers only the plausibility of events, so much so that if it be plausible for several actions to take place either at once or separately, he is free to conjoin them if in so doing he can create a more admirable poem. . . .

As regards the unity of place, there is no one to whom it is not plain that here is a concept that the author of this play poorly understand, for the stage represents more than one locale. It is true that it shares this fault with most of our dramatic poems, the negligence of our playwrights having, it would seem, inured our audiences to it, but since the author of this one has set himself the narrow limits that conform with the unity of time, he should also have striven to comply with the unity of place, which is no less essential than the other, and which, for want of being carefully observed, leaves the audience no less confused and benighted.

Pierre Corneille *1606–1684*

Discourses *1660*

First Discourse

*On the Uses and the Parts
of the Dramatic Poem*

Although, according to Aristotle, the sole end of dramatic poetry should be to please the spectator, and although most of these plays have pleased, I always contend that many among them have not attained the goal of art. "It must not be pretended," says the philospher, "that this genre of poetry gives us all kinds of pleasure, but only that which is proper to it"; and in order to find this pleasure that is proper and give it to the audience, one must follow the rules of the art and please the audience according to these rules. It is an established fact that there are rules since there is an art, but what they are is not established. We agree to the name without agreeing to the thing and we agree upon the words only to argue about their meaning. Unity of action, of place, of time must be observed, no one has any doubt, but it is not a little difficult to know what this unity of action is, and how far unity of time and place extend. . . .

We should know, then, what these rules are; but it is our misfortune that Aristotle, and Horace after him, wrote so obscurely as to need inter-

Selections. Translated by Arlin Hiken Armstrong. Copyright 1974 by Arlin Hiken Armstrong. Printed with permission of the translator.

preters, and that until now those who have volunteered to act as such have often interpreted these writers only for the benefit of grammarians and philosophers. As they were more scholarly and theoretical than experienced in the theatre, their scholarship was able to make us more erudite, but not to give us much real insight into how to succeed in the theatre.

I will venture something on fifty years of work for the stage, and will speak my thoughts about it quite simply, without the spirit of contest which compels me to affirm them, and without intending that anybody renounce in my favor those that he will have conceived.

Thus, what I asserted at the beginning of this discourse—that dramatic poetry has for its end solely to please the spectators—is not for the purpose of stubbornly getting the better of those who think to ennoble the art by giving it for its object usefulness as well as pleasure. Such a dispute would be quite useless since it is impossible to please according to the rules without at the same time providing a great deal of usefulness. It is true that Aristotle, in the whole of his *Poetics*, never used this word once; that he attributed the origin of the drama to the pleasure that we take in seeing the actions of men imitated; that he preferred that part of the play which dealt with the plot to that which dealt with the characterizations, because the former contained what was most pleasing, like recognitions and reversals; that he included in the definition of tragedy the pleasing quality of the language of which it is composed; and that, finally, he esteemed it more highly than the epic poem because it has more spectacle and music (which are powerful pleasures), and because, since it is shorter and less diffuse, the pleasure that one takes in it is more perfect. But it is not less true that Horace teaches us we will not be able to please everyone if we do not blend in some useful things and that grave and serious men, old men, lovers of virtue will be bored if they find nothing from which to profit: *"Centuriae seniorum agitant expertia frugis."*[1] Thus, although the usefulness enters only in the guise of the delightful, it is no less necessary (and it is more profitable) to examine what place we should assign to it than to dispute, as I said before, a useless question regarding use in this sort of poetry. I think, then, that it is possible to meet with four kinds of use.

The first consists in maxims and moral instructions that are strewn almost everywhere; but they must be used moderately and rarely put into general conversation or even more than uttered, especially when one makes a passionate man speak or be in sympathy with another who speaks to him; for he should have neither the patience to listen nor the easy mind to conceive and to say them. . . .

The second use in the dramatic poem lies in the simple painting of

---

[1] "Elder folk rail at what contains no serviceable lesson. . . ." (see above, *Art of Poetry*, p. 74).

vices and virtues, which never fails to make its effect when it is well achieved and when the traits are so recognizable that one cannot confuse them with each other, nor take vice for virtue. Virtue is always to be loved, though unhappy; and vice is always to be hated, though triumphant. The ancients are often quite happy with this depiction without taking the trouble to have good deeds recompensed and bad ones punished. Clytemnestra and her lover kill Agamemnon with impunity. Medea does away with her children and Atreus with those of his brother, Thyestes, and makes Thyestes eat them. It is true that close consideration of the actions which they chose for the catastrophes of their tragedies shows that those they had punished were criminals, but they were punished by crimes greater than their own. Thyestes had abused his brother's wife but the vengeance that Atreus takes for it is somewhat more horrible than the first crime. Jason was perfidious to abandon Medea, to whom he owed all; but to murder his children under his very eyes is something else again. Clytemnestra complained of the concubines that Agamemnon brought home from Troy; but he had not made a criminal attempt on her life as she did on his, and these masters of the art found the crime of his son, Orestes, who killed to avenge his father, still greater than hers since they gave Orestes the avenging Furies to torment him and did not give them to his mother, who is allowed to enjoy peaceably, with her Aegisthus, the kingdom of a husband she has murdered.

Our theatre tolerates such subjects with difficulty: the *Thyestes* of Seneca was not very successful; his *Medea* found more favor; but also, to be perfectly clear, the perfidy of Jason and the violence of the king of Corinth make her seem so unjustly oppressed that the spectator easily sides with her and regards her vengeance as justice, which she performs herself on those who oppress her.

It is this interest that we love to take in the virtuous that has constrained us to arrive at this other manner of finishing the dramatic poem—by the punishment of evil acts and the rewarding of good ones—which is not a rule of the art, but a usage which we have embraced, from which every man can deviate at his own peril. . . .

It is in this that the third use in the theatre consists, as the fourth lies in the purging of emotions by means of pity and terror. But as this use is peculiar to tragedy I will expound on this subject in the second volume. . . . [Aristotle says] that the difference between these two kinds of plays [comedy and tragedy] consists only in the nobility of the characters and of the actions that they imitate and not in the manner of imitating them, nor in the means which serve for this imitation. . . .

The requirements of the subject are different for tragedy and for comedy. I will touch at present only on the latter, which Aristotle simply defines as an imitation of low and knavish persons. I cannot forbear to say that this definition does not satisfy me; and since many wise men hold that Aristotle's *Poetics* has not come down to us in its entirety, I wish to believe that in the version of which time has robbed us, there would be a more complete definition.

Dramatic poetry, according to Aristotle, is an imitation of actions and he stops short at the condition of the persons, without saying what these actions should be. However that may be, this definition is in accord with the usage of his times where only persons in a moderate condition of life were made to speak in comedy; but it is not entirely precise for ours, where kings themselves can come on in comedy when their actions are not above it. When one puts on the stage a simple intrigue of love between kings, and when they imperil neither their lives nor their states, I do not believe that, although the characters are illustrious, the action should be elevated to the level of tragedy. Its dignity demands some great interest of state or some passion more noble and virile than love, such as ambition or vengeance, and it should lead us to fear greater misfortune than the loss of a mistress. It is proper to intermingle love with tragedy, because it is always so pleasurable and can serve as the foundation for these concerns and these other passions of which I speak; but it must always be content with the second level of the play and leave the first to the others.

This maxim will seem new at first; but it is always the practice of the ancients, in whom we see no tragedy where there is simply a love interest to clear up. On the contrary, they often did away with it completely; and those who wish to consider my plays will admit that, at their example, I have never allowed it to assume the most important place, and that in *The Cid* itself, which is undoubtedly more full of love than my other plays, obligation of birth and pride of honor carry it above all the endearments that love inspires in the play's lovers. . . .

Second Discourse

*On Tragedy and the Means of Treating It
according to the Probable or the Necessary*

Aside from the three uses in the dramatic poem of which I have spoken in the discourse which serves as the preface to the first part of this collection, tragedy has this special one, that "through pity and terror it purges us of these same emotions." These are the terms which Aristotle uses in his definition and they inform us of two things: one, that tragedy excites pity and terror; two, that by means of pity and terror, it purges these same emotions. Aristotle explains the first at some length, but he does not say one word about the second, and, of all the terms that he uses in this definition, purgation is the only one that he does not clarify. . . .

"We pity," says he, "those whom we see suffer a misfortune that they do not deserve, and we fear that a like fate will come to us when we see men like ourselves suffer." Thus, pity embraces concern for the person we see suffering; terror, which follows upon it, concerns our own; and this "following upon," alone, gives us enough means to find the manner in which the emotions are purged in tragedy. Pity for a misfortune into which we see men like ourselves fall takes us to terror of a like one for ourselves; this terror to the desire to avoid it; this desire to the wish to purge, to moderate, to rectify, even to eradicate in ourselves the emotion which, before our eyes, plunges persons that we pity into misfortune; for this ordinary but natural and indubitable reason: that to avoid the effect one must cut out the cause. . . . It is true that, ordinarily, only kings are presented as the principal characters in a tragedy and that the spectators hold no sceptres as they do to give them good reason to fear the misfortune which befalls these kings; but these kings are men like the spectators and fall into misfortune because of transports of passion of which the spectators are capable. They themselves present easily comprehensible evidence of a fall from the greatest to the least; the audience can easily comprehend that if a king, by abandoning himself so completely to ambition, to love, to hate, to vengeance, falls into misfortune so great that the audience pities him, there is much more necessity for one who is only a common man to bridle such emotions for fear that they will hurl him into equal misfortune. Outside of that it is not necessary that the theatre only show the misfortunes of kings. The misfortune of other men could take place there if it befell any who were illustrous and extraordinary enough to merit it and if history cared enough about them to teach us. . . .

To facilitate for us the means of engendering this pity and terror to which Aristotle seems to compel us, he helps us to choose people and events which can excite one or the other. Concerning which I grant what is very true, that our audience is composed neither of wicked men nor of saints, but of people of ordinary integrity, who are not so severely entrenched in absolute virtue that they would not be susceptible to emotions and capable of falling into dangers which engage those who submit to them too much. That being granted, let us examine those whom the philosopher excludes from tragedy in order to arrive, with him, at those in whom he believes perfection to consist.

In the first place he does not want a "completely virtuous man to pass from prosperity into adversity," and he maintains that "that produces neither pity nor terror because it is a completely unjust occurrence." Some interpreters emphasize the Greek word, μιαρόν, which he uses as an epithet for this occurrence, even to translating it "abominable." To which I add that such a passage excites more indignation and hatred against him who causes the suffering than pity for the one who suffers, and that this feeling, which is not proper to tragedy, at least to well-contrived tragedy, can thus stifle the emotion that it ought to produce and leave the spectator dissatisfied with the anger he feels, anger that is mingled with pity, which would please him if he felt only pity.

Aristotle does not want a "bad man to pass from adversity to prosperity, because such a passage not only cannot engender pity or terror, but it cannot even move us to the natural feeling of joy for a principal character on whom we have bestowed our favor." The downfall of a wicked man in some way pleases us because of the aversion we feel for him, but, as it is only a just punishment, it does not make us feel pity, nor does it instil any terror in us, inasmuch as we are not so wicked, like him, as to be capable of his crimes, and to fear from them an equally fatal result.

There remains, then, the finding of a middle ground between these two extremes, with the choice of a man who is neither completely good nor completely bad, and who, through an error, or a human frailty, falls into misfortune that he does not deserve. Aristotle gives as examples Oedipus and Thyestes, wherein truthfully, I do not understand his thinking. The former seems to me not to make any error, although he kills his father, because he does not know him and only disputes the right of way, like a man of mettle, with an unknown man who attacks him with the odds on his side. Nevertheless, as the meaning of the Greek word ἁμάρτημα can be extended to a simple error of recognition, such as his was, let us concede the point to the philosopher, although I cannot see what passion it gives us to purge nor what we can correct in ourselves from his example. But, for Thyestes, I cannot discover in him this ordinary integrity, nor this error without crime which plunges him into adversity. If we regard him before the tragedy that bears his name, he is an incestuous man who abuses the wife of his brother; if we consider him in the tragedy, he is a man of good faith who has confidence in the word of his brother, with whom he is reconciled. In the first instance, he is very criminal; in the second, he is a right-thinking man. If we attribute his adversity to his incest, it is a crime of which the audience is not capable, and the pity which it will feel for him will by no means lead to that terror which purges because he in no way resembles the audience. If we impute his disaster to his good faith, some terror may follow the pity that we will have, but it will purge only a readiness of confidence in the word of a reconciled enemy, which is rather a trait of an honest man than a vicious habit, and this purgation will not only banish sincerity from any reconciliations. I therefore frankly confess that I do not at all understand the application of this example.

I will confess more. If the purgation of the emotions is achieved in tragedy, I hold that it ought to be done in the manner that I have explained; but I doubt if it is ever achieved, even in those same tragedies that have the conditions Aristotle demanded. One finds such conditions in *The Cid* and they caused its great success. Rodrigue and Chimène have this virtue; it is exposed to passions; and their passions cause their misfortune, although they are unfortunate only insofar as they are in agony over each other. They fall into adversity through human frailty, of which we like they are capable; their adversity invariably causes pity, and it has cost the spectators enough tears not to argue the point at all. This pity ought to give us the fear of falling into like adversity and purge in us this excess of love which causes their adversity and makes us pity them. But I do not know if it gives us terror or if it purges it, and I greatly fear that the reasoning of Aristotle on this point is only a beautiful idea which in reality never has this result. I leave it to those who saw productions of *The Cid*: they may look into their secret hearts and think over again what moved them in the theatre to find out if they came thus to this reflexive terror, and if it rectified in them the passion which caused the disgrace that they feared. . . . If the conditions that Aristotle demands are necessary to produce tragedy, they are encountered so rarely that Robortellus finds them only in the *Oedipus* and maintains that the philosopher does not prescribe them to us as so necessary that their absence renders a work defective except as ideas regarding the perfection of tragedy. Our century saw them in *The Cid*, but I do not know if it saw them in many others; and if we wish to cast another glance at this rule we will confess that their success justified many plays where it was not observed.

The exclusion of perfectly virtuous persons who fall into adversity banishes martyrs from our theatre. *Polyeucte* succeeded contrary to this maxim and *Heraclius* and *Nicomède*[2] pleased (although they imprinted only pity on us and did not give us anything to fear nor any passion to purge), even though we see them[3] oppressed and on the point of perishing without any fault on their part which we ourselves might be able to correct on the basis of their examples.

The adversity of a completely bad man excites neither pity nor terror, because it is not worthy of the former and because the audience, who unlike him is not wicked, cannot conceive terror at the sight of his punishment. But it would be fitting to make some distinction among crimes. There are some, of which honest people are capable through an excess of passion, the evil success of which can have an effect on the soul of the spectator. An honest man will not steal in a dark corner of the woods, nor commit a murder in cold blood; but if he is deeply in love he can hoodwink his rival, he can fly into a fit of anger and kill in a single movement, and ambition can entangle him in a crime or a blameworthy action. . . .

[2] All are by Corneille.
[3] The title characters.

Nevertheless, whatever difficulty there might be in finding this effective and palpable purgation of the emotions by means of pity and terror, it is easy to reconcile ourselves with Aristotle. We have only to say that by this way of wording it, he did not mean that these two methods always attended together, and that it suffices, according to him, for one of the two to effect the catharsis, with this difference however, that pity cannot occur without terror and terror cannot happen without pity. The death of the Count does not cause either in *The Cid* and it can still better purge us of the sort of arrogance that is envious of the glory of others, than all the compassion that we feel for Rodrigue and Chimène purges the sentiments of that violent love which makes them both objects of pity. . . .

To sum up this discourse before moving to another matter, let us establish as a maxim that the perfection of tragedy best consists in exciting pity and terror by means of a principal character, as Rodrigue is able to function in *The Cid* and Placide in *Théodore*, but that that is not so absolutely necessary that one cannot make use of different persons to engender these emotions, as in *Rodogune*,[4] and even to move the listener to one of the two, as in *Polyeucte*, whose performance is marked only by pity without any terror. That being set down, let us find some mitigation to the rigidity of the philosopher's rules, or at least some favorable interpretation, so as not to be obliged to condemn some plays that we have seen succeed in our theatres.

Aristotle does not want a completely good man to fall into adversity because, that being abominable, it excites more indignation against the one who persecutes him than pity for his misfortune. Neither does he want a completely bad man to fall, because one cannot feel pity for a misfortune that he deserves or engender terror of a like misfortune among spectators he does not resemble; but when these two reasons are not present, so that a good man who suffers excites more pity for himself than indignation against the one who made him suffer, or the punishment of a great crime can correct in us some imperfection which has something in common with it, I believe that it is not necessary to raise obstacles to showing on the stage very good or very bad men in adversity. . . .

The end of the poet is to please according to the rules of his art. In order to please, he sometimes needs to heighten the brilliance of beautiful actions and to extenuate the horror of fatal ones. These are some necessities of embellishment with which he may greatly shock particular probability by some alteration of history but not so as to exempt himself from general probability except rarely, and for things that may be of utmost beauty and so brilliant that they dazzle. Above all, it should never be necessary to

[4] All plays cited are by Corneille.

push them beyond extraordinary probability because these ornaments that the poet adds out of his own invention are not absolutely necessary, and it is better to dispense with them completely than to adorn his play contrary to all manner of probability. In order to please according to the rules of his art he must confine his action to unity of time and of place, and as that is an absolute and indispensable necessity, much more leeway is permitted to him in these two items than in that of embellishment.

It is so difficult to encounter, in history or in the imagination of men, a great number of these illustrious events worthy of tragedy, whose resolutions and their execution can happen in the same place and on the same day without doing a little violence to the usual order of things that I cannot believe this sort of violence completely condemnable provided it does not skirt the impossible. There are beautiful plots where one cannot avoid it, and a scrupulous playwright will deprive himself of an opportunity for glory and the public of a great deal of satisfaction if he does not make bold to put them on the stage, for fear of seeing himself forced to make them move more quickly than probability permits him to. I will, in this case, give him some advice that he will find salutary: It is that he should not specify any appointed time in his play nor any fixed place where he puts his characters. The imagination of the spectator will have more liberty to let itself flow with the action if it is not fixed by these boundaries, and he will be more likely not to notice this haste if the boundaries do not make him remember and apply his mind to it in spite of himself. I have always regretted having made the king say, in *The Cid,* that he wished Rodrigue might wait an hour or two after the defeat of the Moors before contending against Don Sanche. I had done it to show that the play was within the twenty-four hours, and that served only to alert the audience to the constraint to which I subjugated it. If I had ended the combat without designating the hour perhaps no one would have taken notice of it.

I do not think that in comedy the poet should have this liberty of condensing his action because of the necessity of condensing it into the unity of time. Aristotle wishes all actions that are shown to be probable, and he does not add the phrase "or necessary," as he does for tragedy. Also, the difference is rather great between the actions of the one and of the other. Those of comedy proceed from common persons and consist only of intrigues of love and of knavery, which are developed so easily in a day that, often enough, in Plautus and in Terence, the time of their duration scarcely exceeds that of their performance. But in tragedy public affairs are ordinarily mingled with the private interests of the illustrious people who are made to appear in it. There are battles, captured cities, great dangers, revolutions of state, and all of these are arduously reconciled with the speed that the rule obliges us to give to what happens on the stage.

Third Discourse

*On the Three Unities
of Action, of Time, and of Place*

I maintain, then, and I have already said so, that in comedy unity of action consists in unity of intrigue or of obstacle to the designs of the principal characters; and in tragedy, it consists in unity of danger, whether the hero perishes in it or escapes from it. I do not mean that one cannot allow several dangers in the latter and several intrigues or obstacles in the former, provided that one necessarily flows into the other; because then the end of the first danger does not render the action complete, since it brings with it a second one; and the clearing up of one intrigue does not bring the actors to a complete rest, since it entangles them in a new one. My memory does not provide me any examples in former times of this multiplicity of dangers linked to each other, so as not to destroy unity of action; but I have branded as a defect the unsubordinated double action in *Horace* and in *Théodore*, where there is no need for the former to kill his sister as he sallies forth from his victory, nor for the latter[5] to offer herself as a martyr after having escaped prostitution; and I am greatly deceived if the deaths of Polyxena and of Astyanax, in *The Trojan Women* of Seneca, do not create the same irregularity.

In the second place, this phrase "unity of action" does not mean that the tragedy should show only one action on the stage. What the poet chooses for his subject must have a beginning, a middle, and an end; and these three parts are not only so many actions coming to a head in the main action, but, further, each of these actions can consist of several actions similarly subordinated. There must be only one complete action . . . but it can evolve only through several other incomplete actions, which serve as progressions and keep the spectator in a pleasant state of suspense. The playwright must contrive this suspense at the end of each act in order to render the action continuous. There is no need to know precisely all that the actors do during the intermissions, nor what they are doing when they do not appear on the stage, but each act must leave an expectation of something that will be shown in the one that follows it. . . .

The rule of unity of time has its foundation in the statement of Aristotle that "tragedy must confine the duration of its action to one revolution of the sun or not exceed it by very much." These words give rise to that famous argument over whether Aristotle means a natural day of twenty-four hours or an artificial day of twelve. There are two views, of which each has several partisans; and, as for me, I find that there are some subjects so difficult

---

[5] The title characters of the former and latter plays (both by Corneille).

to confine in so little time that not only do I accord them the entire twenty-four hours, but I will even avail myself of the liberty that the philosopher gives of exceeding them a little, and will, without scruple, extend them to thirty hours. . . . I find that a writer is ill at ease under this constraint which forced several of our ancients to skirt the impossible. . . .

Many speak out against this rule which they call tyrannical, and they would be right if it were based only on the authority of Aristotle; but what ought to give it general acceptance is the natural reason that supports him. A dramatic poem is an imitation, or to express it better, a portrait of the actions of men; and, without doubt, portraits are in the same proportion more excellent as they more closely resemble the original. The performance lasts two hours and would perfectly resemble the original if the action that it performs took no longer for its realization. Thus, let us by no means stop either at twelve hours or at twenty-four; but let us tighten up the action of the play into the smallest duration of time that we can, in order that the performance may resemble more closely and be more perfect. . . .

I repeat what I said, moreover, that when we take a longer time, like ten hours, I would want the eight that must be lost to be spent during the intermissions between the acts, and each of them to spend in privacy only what the performance wastes—primarily when there is continuous liaison of the scenes, because this liaison does not permit any empty space between two scenes. I always consider that the fifth act, by special privilege, has some right to squeeze the time a little, so that the part of the action that it shows may take longer than it needs for its performance. The reason for this is that the spectator is then impatient to see the end and, when it depends on actors who have left the stage, all the dialogue that one gives to those who remain there waiting for their news only makes it flag and seem to stand still without action. . . .

As for unity of place, I do not find any such rule either in Aristotle or in Horace. This is what leads some to believe that the rule was established only because of the unity of time and to persuade themselves, accordingly, that one can extend it as far as a man can go and return in twenty-four hours. This opinion is a little free, and if one made an actor go by coach, the two sides of the stage could represent Paris and Rouen. I wish, in order not to put the spectator out at all, that what is performed for him in two hours might be able to happen in fact in two hours and that what one has him see on a stage that does not change at all might be confined to one bedroom or one drawing room, according to the choice that is made for it; but often that is so difficult, not to say impossible, that one must find some freedom for the place as one does for the time. . . .

I maintain, then, that one must search for this exact unity as far as possible; but, as it does not adapt itself to all sorts of subjects, I should very willingly concede that what happens in a single city conforms to unity of place. I would not want the stage to show the entire city—that would be a little too comprehensive—but only two or three special places included within the enclosure of its walls. Thus the action of *Cinna* does not leave Rome, and is sometimes in the apartment of Auguste in his place and sometimes in Emilie's house. *The Liar* has the Tuileries and the Place Royale in Paris, and *The Sequel* [to *The Liar*][6] shows the prison and the lodgings of Mélisse in Lyons. *The Cid* multiplies the number of places still more without leaving Séville; and, as the liaison of the scenes is not preserved in it, the stage, as early as the first act, is in the house of Chimène, in the apartments of the Infanta in the king's palace, and in the public square. The second act adds the king's chamber, and doubtless this liberty is somewhat excessive. To rectify this duplication of places when it is unavoidable, I would like two things to be done: one, the set should never be changed in the same act, but only between one act and another, as is done in the first three acts of *Cinna*; the other, these two places should by no means need different sets and neither of the two should ever be named, but only the general place where both are contained, like Paris, Rome, Lyon, Constantinople, etc. That will help to beguile the spectator, who, seeing nothing that marks for him a difference in places, will not remark any, at least in a malicious and critical way (of which there are a few who are capable), the majority hanging eagerly on the action that they see being shown. The pleasure that they take in it is grounds for their not wanting to search out a lack of precision in order to take a dislike to it and they recognize it only perforce, when it is too visible, as in *The Liar* and *The Sequel* where the different sets make them recognize the duplication of place, notwithstanding what one may have done. . . .

Many of my plays will fail if one does not permit this mitigation with which I shall always be content henceforth when I cannot satisfy the extreme rigor of the rule. I have been able to condense only three plays: *Horace, Polyeucte,* and *Pompée.* If I indulge myself too much in the others, I will have still more indulgence for those whose works I shall see succeed on the stage with some appearance of regularity. It is easy for men of speculative mind to be severe. But if they wished to show ten or twelve plays of this nature to the public, perhaps they would widen the rules even more than I have done, as soon as they recognized from experience what constraint their exactitude causes and what beautful things they banish from our theatre. However that may be, there are my opinions, or, if you like, my heresies concerning the principle points of the art; and I simply do not know how to reconcile ancient rules with modern pleasures any better. I do not in the least doubt that it would be easy to find better ways to do it and I will always be ready to follow them when they have been put into practice as happily as mine have been seen to be.

[6] Both by Corneille.

François Hédelin, Abbot of Aubignac 1604–1676

The Whole Art of the Stage 1657

Book One

Chapter I

As for those spectacles which consist as much in discourse as action, such as formerly were the disputes upon the stage between the epic and dramatic poets, they are not only useful but absolutely necessary to instruct the people and give them some tincture of moral virtues.

The minds of those who are of the meanest rank and condition in a state are generally so little acquainted with any notions of morality that the most general maxims of it are hardly known to them. 'Tis in vain, therefore, to make fine discourses, full of convincing reasons and strengthened with examples, to them: they can neither understand the first nor have any deference for the latter. All the elevated truths of philosophy are lights too strong for their weak eyes. Tell them of these maxims—that happiness consists less in the possession of worldly things than in the despising of them, that virtue ought to seek its recompence in itself, that there is no interest in the world considerable enough to oblige a man of honor to do a base thing—all these, I say, are paradoxes to them, which makes them suspect philosophy itself and turn it into ridicule. They must therefore be instructed by a more sensible way, which may fall more under their senses, and such are the representations of the stage, which may therefore properly be called the People's School.

One of the chiefest and indeed the most indispensable rule of dramatic poems is that in them virtues always ought to be rewarded, or at least commended, in spite of all the injuries of fortune, and that likewise vices be always punished, or at least detested with horror, though they triumph upon the stage for that time. The stage being thus regulated, what can philosophy teach that won't become much more sensibly touching by representation? 'Tis there that the meanest capacities may visibly see that favors of fortune are not real enjoyments, when they see the ruin of the royal family of Priam; all that they hear from the mouth of Hecuba seems very probable, having before their eyes the sad example of her calamities. 'Tis there that they are convinced that Heaven punishes the horrid crimes of the guilty

Selections. From François Hédelin, Abbot of Aubignac, *The Whole Art of the Stage*, trans. anonymous. London: William Cadman, 1684. Spelling and punctuation modernized by the editor.

238

with the remorse of them, when they see Orestes tormented by his own conscience and driven about by furies within his own breast. 'Tis there that ambition seems to them a very dangerous passion, when they see a man engaged in crimes to attain his ends, and after having violated the laws of heaven and earth, fall into misfortunes as great as those he had overwhelmed others in and [be] more tormented by himself than by his enemies. 'Tis there again that covetousness appears a disease of the soul, when they see a covetous man persecuted with continual restlessness and fears of want in the midst of all his riches. And lastly, 'tis there that a man, by representation, makes them penetrate into the most hidden secrets of human nature, while they seem to touch and feel in this living picture those truths which else they would scarce be capable of. But that which is most remarkable is that they never go from the theatre without carrying along with them the idea of the persons represented, the knowledge of those virtues and vices of which they have seen the examples, their memory repeating continually to them those lessons which have been derived to them from sensible and present objects.

Besides, in all governments there is a number of idle people, either because they hate taking pains or because they need not do it to live. This idleness carries them generally to many debaucheries, where they consume in a very little time what might suffice for the keeping of their families many months and are then forced upon ill actions for a supply to their present wants. Now, I think nothing worthier the care of a great prince than to prevent, if possible, his subjects from taking these extravagant courses, and as it would be too severe to enjoin them perpetual labor, so I think that public spectacles and entertainments would most innocently amuse those who have no other employment. Their own pleasure would carry them thither without constraint, their hours would slide away without regret, and their very idleness being busy, they would there lose all the thoughts of doing ill. . . .

Chapter IV

. . . Here are five objections which have been ordinarily made to me against the rules of the ancients.

First, that we are not to make laws to ourselves from custom and example but from reason, which ought to prevail over any authority.

Secondly, that the ancients themselves have often violated their own rules.

Thirdly, that diverse poems of the ancients have been translated and acted upon our stage with very ill success.

Fourthly, that divers of our modern plays, though quite contrary to these rules, had been acted with great applause.

And last of all, that if these rigorous maxims should be followed we should very often lose the greatest beauty of all true stories, their incidents having most commonly happened at different times and in different places.

As to the first objection, I answer that the rules of the stage are not founded upon authority but upon reason. They are not so much settled by example as by the natural judgment of mankind, and if we call them the rules and the art of the ancients, 'tis only because they have practiced them with great regularity, and much to their glory, having first made many observations upon the nature of moral actions and upon the probability of human accidents in this life and thereby drawing the pictures after the truth of the original; and observing all due circumstances, they reduced to an art this kind of poem, whose progress was very slow, though it were much in use among them and much admired all the world over. But, however, I am very sparing of citing their poems, and when I do it, it is only to show with what agreeable artifice they kept to these rules and not to buoy up my opinion by their authority.

As for the second objection, it seems not considerable, for reason, being alike all the world over, does equally require everybody's submission to it, and if our modern authors cannot without offense be dispensed from the rules of the stage, no more could the ancients; and where they have failed, I do not pretend to excuse them. . . . I do propose the ancients for models only in such things as they shall appear to have followed reason in, and their example will always be an ill pretext for faults, for which there is no excuse against reason. In things which are founded only in custom, as in grammar or in the art of making a verse with long or short syllables, the learned may often use a license against the received practice and be imitated in it by others, because custom may often have countenanced a thing not well of itself. But in all that depends upon common sense and reason, such as the rules of the stage, there to take license is a crime, because it offends not custom but natural light, which ought never to suffer an eclipse.

I must not omit, for the glory of the ancients, that if they have sometimes violated the art of dramatic poems, they have done it for some more powerful and inducing reason than all the interest of the play could amount to, as for example, Euripides in *The Suppliants* has preferred the glory of his country to that of his art. . . .

The third objection has no force but in the ignorance of those that allege it, for if some poems of the ancients, and even those which were most in esteem with them, have not succeeded upon our stage, the subject and not the want of art has been the cause of it, and sometimes likewise the changes made by the translators, which destroyed all the graces of the original: they have added improbable scenes between princes and have showed out of time that which the ancients had carefully concealed with art, and very often changed a fine relation into an impertinent, ridiculous spectacle. But that which is more worthy our consideration is that there were certain stories fitted for the stage of Athens with great ornaments which would be in abomination upon ours, for example, the story of Thyestes, so that we may say that either the moderns have corrupted the ancients by changing their whole economy or the imperfection of the matter stifled the excellence of the art.

To destroy the fourth objection, we need only to remember that those plays of ours which took with the people and with the court were not liked in all their parts but only in those things which were reasonable and in which they were comformable to the rules. When there were any passionate scenes they were praised, and when there was any great appearance or noble spectacle it was esteemed, and if some notable event was well managed there was great satisfaction shown; but if in the rest of the play, or even in these beauties of it, any irregularities were discovered, or any fault against probability and decency, either in the persons, time, or place, or as to the state of the things represented, they were condemned as faults. And all the favor that was showed the poet was that out of the desire of preserving what was fine, the spectators were somewhat more indulgent to what was amiss. Therefore, that success so much bragged on is so far from contradicting the rules of the stage that, quite [the] contrary, it establishes their authority. . . .

The fifth objection is absolutely ridiculous, for the rules of the stage do not at all reject the most notable incidents of any story, but they furnish us with inventions how so to adjust the circumstances of the action, time, and place as not to go against all probable appearance and yet not to represent them always as they are in story but such as they ought to be, to have nothing but what's agreeable in them. . . .

Book Two

Chapter III

'Tis one of Aristotle's rules, and without doubt a very rational one, that a dramatic poem ought to comprehend but one action, and he does very pertinently condemn those who make a play of the whole story or life of a hero, for though we speak but of one principal part on which all the other events, bad and good, do depend, yet there are diverse, subordinate actions. . . .

'Tis certain that the stage is but a picture or image of human life, and as a picture cannot show us at the same time two originals and be an accomplished picture, it is likewise impossible that two actions (I mean principal ones) should be represented reasonably by one play. Let us consider what the painter does who is to make a picture of some story. He has no other design but to give the image of some action, and that action so limited that it cannot represent two parts of a story together, and less all the story upon which he has fixed, because it would be necessary that the same person should be painted and appear in different places, which would make a strange confusion in the whole picture, and it would be hard to distinguish any order among so many different actions; and, by consequence, the story would be very obscure and confused. Therefore, instead of that, the painter would choose, among all the actions which made up the story, the most important one and the fittest for the excellence of his art, and [the one] which in some measure should contain all the others, so that with one look one might have a sufficient knowledge of all that he designed to express; and if he desired to express two parts of the same story, he would make in some corner of the picture a *lontananza*, where he would paint that other action which he had a mind to represent, that he might make it be understood that he designed the painting of two different actions, and that it was two pictures and not one.

As for example, suppose he designed to draw the story of Iphigenia, it would be hard for him to comprehend in one picture all the adventures of that princess. Therefore, he would choose that of the sacrifice which the Greeks were going to make of her to Diana to appease her anger and the storms of the sea, for in this action her whole story would in some measure be comprehended. . . . Then, if he had a mind to express that Diana carried her to Tauris, where she was upon the point of sacrificing her brother Orestes, he would put her in one of the corners of his picture in the particular dress of Diana's priestess, with some other marks of this second adventure, and so make two pictures of two different actions of the same story.

The dramatic poet must imitate the painter, and when he undertakes the composition of a play, he must reckon that he undertakes to make a living, speaking picture and that therefore he cannot comprehend in it a whole history or the life of a hero, because he would be necessitated to represent an infinite number of events and employ a vast number of actors and mingle so many things that he would make up a work of perfect confusion and would be forced in most places to offend against probability and decency, and to go beyond the time and extent ordinarily allowed to dramatic poems, or if he would keep within the limits of the rules of his art, he would be forced to hasten all the incidents and as it were heap them one upon another, without either graces or distinction, and so be obliged to stifle and suppress all the passionate strokes and, in a word, show such a monstrous, extravagant image as they have done who have represented in the first act of a tragedy the marriage of a princess, in the second the birth of her son, in the third the amours of that young prince, in the fourth his victories, and in the fifth his death, in all [of] which there was matter enough for above twenty plays. Our poet, therefore, amid this vast extent, shall pitch upon some one remarkable action, and, as one may say, a point of story notable by the happiness or misfortune of some illustrious person, in which point he may comprehend, as circumstances, all the rest of the story, and by representing one chief part make the whole known by some slight to the spectators without multiplying the principal action and without retrenching any of the necessary beauties to the perfection of his work; and if by chance he should meet in the same story with two or more actions, so considerable that they each of them deserved a play, and so independent or opposite to each other as not to be reconciled, he ought to make two or more plays of them or choose the most important, and particularly the most pathetic, for his subject.

Thus, *The Suppliants* of Euripides does not contain the whole war of Thebes but only the burial of the two princes of Argos. *Hecuba* contains not the taking of Troy but the last misfortunes of that queen in her captivity. The *Ajax* of Sophocles shows not all the exploits of war of that hero, nor his disputes with Ulysses for the arms of Achilles, but only represents his madness, which was the cause of his death. And so we may say of most of the ancient plays. But in all these, the poets have showed so much art as to instruct the spectators either by narrations, discourses, complaints, or other slights of the art, in all the circumstances of those stories which they treated. . . .

Chapter VI

. . . To make his actors appear in different places would render his play ridiculous by the want of probability, which is to be the foundation of it. This rule of Unity of Place begins now to be looked upon as certain, but yet the ignorant and some others of weak judgment do still imagine that it cannot but be repugnant to the beauty of the incidents of a play. . . . As for the truly learned, they are thoroughly convinced of the necessity of this rule because they see clearly that probability can no ways be preserved without it. . . .

Aristotle has said nothing of it, and I believe he omitted it because this rule was in his time too well known, the Choruses, which ordinarily remained upon the stage from one end of the play to the other, marking the unity of the scene too visibly to need a rule for it. . . . The three famous tragedians of the Greeks whose works we have are so punctual in the observation of this rule and so often make their actors say where they are and whence they come that Aristotle must have supposed too much ignorance in his age and in those who should read these poets if he had gone about to explain so settled a rule. . . .

. . . One and the same image remaining in the same state cannot represent two different things. Now, it is highly improbable that the same space and the same floor, which receives no change at all, should represent two different places, as, for example, France and Denmark, or, within Paris itself, the Tuileries and the Exchange. . . .

Let it then be allowed for a certain truth that the place where the first actor, who opens the play, is supposed to be ought to be the same place to the end of the play, and that, it not being in the ordinary course of nature that the place can receive any change, there can be none likewise in the representation, and, by consequence, that all your other actors cannot rationally appear in any other place.

But we must remember that this place which cannot be supposed to change is the area or floor of the stage, upon which the actors walk. . . . 'Tis not the same with the sides and end of the theatre, for as they do but represent those things which did actually environ the persons acting and which might receive some change, they may likewise receive some in the representation, and 'tis in that that consists the changing of scenes and other ornaments of decoration, which always ravish the people and please the best judges when they are well done. So we have seen upon our stage a temple adorned with a noble front of architecture which, coming to be set open, showed the inside of it, where in perspective were descried pillars and an altar and all the other ornaments of a church extremely well done, so that the place did not change and yet had a fine decoration. . . . So, for example, [the poet] might feign a palace upon the seaside, forsaken and left to be inhabited by poor fishermen; a prince landing or being cast away there might adorn it with all the rich furniture fit for it; after this, by some accident, it might be set on fire; and then, behind it, the sea might appear, upon which one might represent a sea fight, so that in all the five changes of the stage the Unity of Place would still be ingeniously preserved. . . .

As for the extent which the poet may allow to the scene he chooses, when it is not in a house but open, I believe it may be as far as a man can see another walk and yet not know perfectly that 'tis he, for to take a smaller space would be ridiculous, it being improbable that two people being each of them at one end of the stage without any object between should look at one another and yet not see one another, whereas this distance, which we allow often, contributes to the working of the play by the mistakes and doubts which a man may make by seeing another at a distance. . . .

Chapter VII

. . . One must consider that a dramatic poem has two sorts of time, each of which has a different and proper lasting. The first is the true time of the representation . . . that is, from the opening of the stage to the end of the play. . . . Of this time, the measure can be no other but so much time as will reasonably spend the patience of the audience, for this sort of poem being made for pleasure, it ought not to weary and fatigue the mind, and it must not likewise be so short as that the spectators go away with an opinion of not having been well nor enough diverted. In all this, experience is the faithfulest guide and tells us most commonly that a play cannot last above three hours without wearying of us nor less without coming short of pleasing us. . . .

The other time of the dramatic poem is that of the action represented . . . containing all that space which is necessary to the performing of those things which are to be exposed to the knowledge of the spectators from the first to the last act of the play. . . . The three Greek tragics, Aeschylus, Euripides, and Sophocles, allow but a few hours to the lasting of the theatrical action in their poems, but their example was not followed by the poets who succeeded them, for Aristotle blames those of his time for giving too long an extent to the lasting of their plays, which makes him set down the rule, or rather renew it from the model of the ancients, saying that tragedy ought to be comprehended in the revolution of one sun. . . . As the day is considered two ways, the one with regard to the *primum mobile*,[1] which is called the natural day, and is of twenty-four hours, and the other by the sun's presence upon the horizon, between his rising and setting, which is called the artificial day, it is necessary to observe that Aristotle means only the artificial day, in the extent of which he makes the theatrical action to be comprehended. Castelvetro and Piccolomini,[2] upon Aristotle's *Poetics*, are of this opinion, against Segni,[3] who extends the rule to the natural day of twenty-four hours.

The reason of this is certain, and founded upon the nature of dramatic poems, for this sort of poem ought to carry a sensible image of the actions of human life. Now, we do not see that regularly men are busy before day, nor much after night, and accordingly, in all well-governed places, there are magistrates to watch those who employ the night, naturally designed for rest, in the actions of the day.

Besides, we have said, and it cannot be called in question, that the theatrical action ought to be one and not comprehend any other actions which are not necessary to the intrigue of the stage. Now, how can that be observed in a play of twenty-four hours? Would it not be a necessity that

---

[1] Literally, the first moving thing, the sun was supposed to revolve around the earth in twenty-four hours, moving from east to west.

[2] Alessandro Piccolomini (1508–1578) translated Aristotle's *Poetics* and appended notes interpreting that work.

[3] Bernardo Segni (1504–1558) translated Aristotle's *Poetics* into Italian (the first vernacular translation) in 1549.

the persons acting should sleep and eat and busy themselves in many things which would not be of the subject of the play, and though the poet should say nothing of it, yet the spectators must needs conceive it so?

But besides, the action of the stage is to be continued and not interrupted or broken. Now, that could not be in a play of twenty-four hours. Nature could not without some rest endure so long an action. . . .

Moreover, we cannot omit a reason of the ancients, which is essential to tragedy, which is that the Choruses, which they used, did not regularly use to stir off the stage for the whole play, or at least from the time they first came on, and I do not know with what appearance of probability the spectators could have been persuaded that people who were never out of their sight should have stayed twenty-four hours in that place, nor how in the truth of the action they could imagine that those whom they represented had passed all that time without satisfying some necessities of nature.

After all, we can never better understand Aristotle than by those three excellent tragic poets whom he always proposes for examples, who have regularly observed not to give above twelve hours to their plays. And I do not think that there are any of their works which do comprehend the whole space between the rising and setting of the sun.

It being most certain that their stage generally opens after sunrise and is shut up before sunset, as one may observe in the comedies of Plautus and Terence, 'tis therefore that Rossi, an Italian, allows but eight or ten hours. And Scaliger, more rigorously but more reasonably, would have the action performed in six hours. It were even to be wished that the action of the poem did not take up more time than that of the representation, but that being hard, and almost impossible, in certain occasions the poet has the liberty to suppose a longer time by some hours, in which the music that marks the intervals of the acts, and the relations of the actors upon the stage while the others are busy off of it, with the natural desire of the spectators to see the event, do all contribute very much and help to deceive the audience so as to make them think there has passed time enough for the performance of the things represented. . . .

Book Four

Chapter V

The stage . . . became a sensible and moving image of all human life. Now, there being three sorts of conditions or ways of living—that of great persons in the courts of kings, that of citizens and gentry in towns, and that of the country people in the country—the stage has likewise received three kinds of dramatic poems, to wit, Tragedy, Comedy, and Pastoral.

Tragedy represented the life of princes and great people full of disquiets, suspicions, troubles, rebellions, wars, murders, and all sorts of violent passions and mighty adventures. . . . Now, to distinguish Tragedies by their catastrophe, they were of two sorts. The one were calamitous and bloody in their events, ending generally by the death or some great misfortune of the hero. The others were more happy and concluded by the felicity of the chief persons upon the stage. And yet, because the poets, out of complaisance to the Athenians, who loved spectacles of horror, ended often their tragedies by unfortunate catastrophes, many people have thought that the word Tragical never signifies anything but some sad, bloody event, and that a dramatic poem could not be called a Tragedy if the catastrophe did not contain the death of the chief persons in the play. But they are mistaken, that word in its true signification meaning nothing else but a magnificent, serious, grave poem, conformable to the agitations and sudden turns of the fortune of great people. And accordingly, in the nineteen tragedies of Euripides, many of them have a happy conclusion. . . .

Comedy was the picture of the actions of the people, in which were generally represented the debaucheries of young people, with the tricks and jests of slaves and courtesans, full of raileries and jests, and ending in marriages or some other pleasant adventure of common life; and this poem was so confined to represent a popular life that the style of it was to be low and mean, the expressions taken out of the mouths of ordinary people, the passions were to be short and without violence. In a word, all the intrigues were to be upheld by slight and cunning and not by the sublime and marvelous part of human life. . . .

Pastoral or Satyr had a mixture of serious and pleasant; heroes and satyrs were its actors; and this sort of poem ought to be considered two ways. At first, it was nothing but a little poem called Idyllium or Eclogue, sung or recited by one man alone and seldom by two or more, and they were generally shepherds, gardeners, husbandmen, satyrs, nymphs, and all sorts of country people. There was nothing but complaints of lovers, cruelties of shepherdesses, disputes for singing, ambuscados of satyrs, and ravishing of nymphs, with such like diverting, easy adventures. But the poems were all loose pieces without any story or necessity of action. . . . The other sort was a dramatic poem, carried on according to the rules of the stage, where heroes and satyrs were mingled together, representing both grave and pleasant, ridiculous things, and for that reason this poem had the name of Satyrical Tragedy. This sort of poem had not any course among the Romans, at least that ever I could observe either in their historians or poets, that which they called Satire being only a copy of verses made to slander or reprove and never used for the stage but with the mimes and by way of interlude. . . .

These three sorts of poems are not now upon the stage in the same manner as they were anciently, for, to begin with Pastorals, they are now a dramatic poem according to the rules of all other dramas, composed of five acts and many agreeable events and intrigues, but all regarding a country life, so that we have borrowed the matter of the Eclogues from the ancients and applied it to the rules of Satyrical Tragedy.

Comedy among us has remained long not only in meanness and obscurity but looked upon as infamous, being changed into that sort of Farce which we still retain at the end of some of our tragedies, though they are certainly things without art or grace and only recommendable to the rascally sort of mankind. . . .

As for Tragedy, it has been preserved a little better among us because, the manners of our nobility being serious and heroic, they have with more pleasure seen upon the stage the adventures of such persons and have showed no disposition at all to that mixture of serious and burlesque which we blame in the Italians. But besides the niceties of the art, which as well as the Italians we have long been ignorant of, we have done two things, one of which is very reasonable and the other without any good grounds. The first is that we have rejected all those stories full of horror and cruelty which made the pleasure of the Roman and Athenian stages. . . . But the second thing, which we do without any ground at all, is that we have taken away the name of Tragedy from all those plays where the catastrophe is happy and without blood, though both the subject and persons are heroic, and have given them the name of Tragicomedy. . . .

I shall not absolutely fall out with this name but I shall show that it is at least superfluous, since the word Tragedy signifies as well those plays that end in joy as those that end in blood, provided still the adventures be of illustrious persons. And besides, the signification of the word Tragicomedy is not true in the sense we use it, for in those plays that we apply it to there is nothing at all comical; all is grave and heroic, nothing popular and burlesque.

But moreover, this title alone may destroy all the beauty of a play, which, consisting particularly in the Peripeteia, or return of affairs, it may discover that too soon, since the most agreeable thing in a drama is that out of many sad and tragic appearances the event should at last be happy against the expectation of the whole audience. But when once the word Tragicomedy is prefixed, the catastrophe is presently known and the audience is less concerned with all the incidents that trouble the designs of the chief actors, so that all their pathetic complaints do but weakly move the spectator, who is prepossessed with an opinion that all will end well, whereas if we were ignorant of the event we should tremble for them and be likewise more delighted with the return of good fortune that should deliver them.

One thing which surprises me the most in this occasion is that there are men of learning and parts who out of complaisance to popular errors do maintain that this was a word used by the Romans, for, for my part, I cannot imagine where they can find that a drama containing the adventures of heroic persons and ending in a happy catastrophe had the name of Tragicomedy. We see nothing of this in what remains of the works of the ancients, nor in those who have compiled fragments or written their own sense about the art and maxims of the stage. 'Tis true that Plautus in the Prologue to his *Amphitrion* uses the word Tragicomedy, but as he is the only Roman that has used it, so has he done it in a sense very remote from the use we make of it.

Molière (Jean-Baptiste Poquelin) 1622–1673

Critique of School for Wives 1663

THE MARQUIS   It is necessary merely to take note of the continual bursts of laughter coming from the pit. That's all the evidence I need to prove that the play is worthless.

DORANTE   Are you then, Marquis, one of those fashionable gentlemen who will not have it that the pit may possess common sense, and who would be annoyed if you were to laugh with them, even at the funniest joke in the world? The other day at the theatre I saw one of our friends making himself ridiculous in this manner. He listened to the entire play with the most somber seriousness in the world, and everything that made other people smile made him frown. At every burst of laughter he would shrug his shoulders and look at the pit with pity; and sometimes too, looking at them with annoyance, he would loudly tell them, "Laugh away, pit, laugh away." It was a second comedy, our friend's irritation; like a true gentleman, he played it for everyone without charging an admission price, and they all agreed that no one else could have played it better. Learn, Marquis, I beg of you, and others as well, that in the theatre good sense is not restricted to any particular part of the house, that differences in the price of admission have nothing whatever to do with good taste, that those who stand and those who sit can both render poor judgments, and that, finally, if I may generalize, I would rather obtain the approval of the pit, because a few of its members can judge a play according to the rules, but the others judge it by the right method of judging it, which is to let themselves be caught up by it, with neither blind prejudice, affected complaisance, nor ridiculous fastidiousness. . . .

URANIE   . . . No doubt tragedy is a thing of beauty when it is well done, but comedy has its charms, and I maintain that one is no less difficult than the other.

DORANTE   Assuredly, madam, and you might not be wrong if you were to put the difficulty more on the side of comedy. After all, I find it considerably easier to force great sentiments, to defy fortune in verse, to accuse destiny, and to challenge the gods, than to essay properly the ridicule of men and to dramatize the faults of mankind in a pleasant manner. When you portray heroes you do as you like. These portraits are gratuitous. No one looks for fidelity to life in them, and all you have to do is give free play to your imagination, which often leaves truth behind in order to go after the marvelous. But when you portray men as they are, you must use nature as your model. People want these portraits to look lifelike, and if you do not make people recognize your contemporaries, you have accomplished nothing. In a word, all that is necessary to escape criticism in serious plays is to say sensible things in a well-written manner. But in comedy this is not enough. You must amuse, and to make decent people laugh is an odd sort of business. . . .

LYSIDAS   Those who know Aristotle and Horace see at once, madam, that *School for Wives* sins against all the rules of art.

URANIE   I'm not familiar with those gentlemen, I confess, and I know nothing about rules of art.

DORANTE   You people are laughable with your rules that embarrass the ignorant and that perpetually deafen us. To hear you talk, it would seem that these rules of art are the most mysterious things in the world. Yet they are only a few simple observations which good sense has made on what can take away the pleasure one receives from these types of poems; and the same good sense that made these observations in days gone by easily makes them every day without any help from Horace and Aristotle. I would very much like to know: isn't the great rule of all the rules simply to please, and hasn't a play that has achieved this goal done what is appropriate for it to do? Do you consider that an entire audience can be mistaken about such things and that each person in the theatre is not a proper judge of the pleasure he gets there?

URANIE   I have noticed one thing about those gentlemen who talk the most about rules and who know them better than anyone else: they write comedies that no one likes.

DORANTE   And this shows, madam, how little attention one should pay to their complicated explanations. After all, if those plays written according to the rules do not please, and those not written according to the rules do please, one must necessarily conclude that the rules have been badly formulated. Let us therefore laugh at this chicanery to which they would subject public taste, and let us consider only the effect a play has on us. Let us honestly go to whatever grips us and not search out any reasons that might prevent us from having pleasure.

URANIE   As for me, when I see a play, I am interested only in whether it affects me. When it entertains me I am certainly not going to ask whether I was wrong or whether the rules of Aristotle forbade me to laugh.

DORANTE   It's just as if a man were to taste an excellent sauce and then want to know whether it were good according to the rules of a cook book.

The Improvisation at Versailles 1663

MOLIÈRE [*playing a ridiculous marquis*]   We're arguing about who the marquis in Molière's *Critique* is based on. He bets it's me and I bet it's him.

BRECOURT [*playing a gentleman of quality*]   And I consider that it's neither of you. You're both mad if you want to apply this sort of thing to yourselves, and that's the very thing I heard Molière complaining about the other day when he was talking to some people who made the same accusations against him that you're making. He said that nothing displeased him as much as being accused of basing his characters on particular persons; that his object is to portray manners in general rather than to try to draw individuals; and that the characters he depicts are invented—phantoms, actually, imaginatively delineated for the spectators' delight. He would be most pained, he said, if he had ever drawn a portrait of any-

Selection. Translated by Richard Kerr. All rights reserved. Printed with permission of the translator.

one who really existed, and he insisted that if any one thing could make him sick of writing plays it would be these resemblances that people always wanted to find, which his enemies maliciously tried to prove in order to make things bad for him with certain people he had never thought of. In point of fact, I believe he is right, for—let me ask you—why would one want to apply every one of those words, and to try to make trouble for him by saying loudly, "He's mocking so-and-so," when all the words and all the gestures typify a hundred people? Since the business of comedy is to represent in a general way the faults of all men, and chiefly men of our own time, it is impossible for Molière to dramatize a character someone will not come across somewhere in this world; and if Molière has to be accused of having in mind every person in whom one can find the faults he depicts, he will undoubtedly have to stop writing comedies.

Preface to Tartuffe *1669*

If the purpose of comedy is to correct men's vices, I do not see why any group of men should have special privileges. If this were so, it would have a far more dangerous social consequence than all the other vices, and we have seen that the theatre's great virtue is its ability to correct vices. The most beautiful expression of a serious moral is most often less powerful than that of satire; and nothing reforms the majority of men better than the portrayal of their faults. To expose vices to everyone's laughter is to deal them a mighty blow. People easily endure reproofs, but they cannot at all endure being made fun of. People have no objection to being considered wicked, but they are not willing to be considered ridiculous.

Jean Racine *1639–1699*

First Preface to Andromache* *1668*

However that may be, the public has been too indulgent to me for me to concern myself with the personal annoyance of two or three people who would like all the heroes of antiquity to be reformed and made into perfect heroes. I find very praiseworthy their desire that only flawless characters be shown on the stage. But I beg them to remember that it is not up to me to change the rules of the theatre. Horace charges us to depict Achilles as fierce, inexorable, violent, just as he was and just as his son is depicted. And Aristotle, far from demanding perfect heroes of us, on the contrary wants tragic characters (that is, those whose misfortune causes the catastrophe of the tragedy) to be neither completely good nor completely evil. He does not want them to be wholly good because the punishment of a good man excites in the spectator more indignation than pity; nor to be wholly evil because one has no pity for a villain. Therefore, they must be moderately good—that is, good but capable of weakness—and they should fall into misfortune through some error that makes us pity rather than hate them.

First Preface to Britannicus† *1670*

What should one do to satisfy such trying judges? It would be an easy thing if only one were willing to throw away his good sense One need only stray from the natural to plunge into the extraordinary. Instead of a simple action, laden with few incidents—such as an action ought to be that takes place in a single day and that, proceeding gradually to its end, is held together only by the concerns, the feelings, the passions of the characters—one would have to cram into this same action a multitude of incidents that could not take place in less than a month, a great number of theatrical tricks, the more amazing as they are less probable, and an infinite number of high-flown speeches in which one would have to make the actors say exactly the opposite of what they ought to say. For example one would have to show some drunken hero who would attempt to make his mistress hate him out of sheer wantonness, a Spartan who would be all talk, a conqueror who would spout nothing but maxims of love, a woman who would give conquerors lessons in arrogance. Doubtless this would be the stuff to make all these gentlemen exclaim in admiration. But, in the meantime, what would the limited number of sensible people whom I strive to please be saying? What face would I dare to put on, so to speak, to appear before the great men of antiquity whom I have chosen as models? Because, to avail myself of the opinion of one man of antiquity, those are the true audiences we ought to have in view; and we ought ceaselessly to ask ourselves: "What would Homer and Vergil say if they read these lines? What would Sophocles say if he saw this scene played?"

Preface to Bérénice   *1674*

. . . For a long time I had wanted to try my hand at a tragedy with that simplicity of action which was so central to the taste of men of antiquity, because it is one of the prime precepts that they have left us. Whatever your work," said Horace, "let it be simple and let it be unified. . . ."

And it must not be thought that this rule is based only in the whim of those who made it. It is only the probable that moves us in tragedy. And what probability is there when in one day a multitude of things happens that could scarcely happen in several weeks? There are those who think that this simplicity is a sign of lack of inventiveness. They do not dream that, on the contrary, the whole of inventiveness consists in making something out of nothing and that this huge number of incidents has always been the refuge of poets who do not perceive in their talent either enough richness or enough authority to engage their audiences for five acts through a simple action

Selections. Translated by Arlin Hiken Armstrong. Copyright 1974 by Arlin Hiken Armstrong. Printed with permission of the translator.

sustained by violence of passion, beauty of thought and elegance of expression. . . .

. . . The prime rule is to please and to move. All the others are set forth only to attain this principal one.

Preface to Phaedra 1677

Moreover, I do not yet venture to say that this play is, in fact, the best of my tragedies. I let readers and time determine its true value. What I can say is that I have written none where virtue looked better than in this one. The smallest errors are here harshly punished; the thought of a crime alone is here regarded with as much abhorrence as the crime itself; the weaknesses of love are here considered as real weaknesses; the passions are here displayed only to show all the confusion they cause; and vice is here painted on all sides in colors that render its ugliness recognizable and despised. This is properly the goal that any man who works for the public ought to set for himself. And this is the one that the first tragic poets kept above all in sight. Their theatre was a school where virtue was taught no less well than in the schools of the philosophers. So Aristotle had no objection to giving rules for dramatic poetry; and Socrates, the wisest of all philosophers, was not above putting his hand to the tragedies of Euripides. It is desirable that our works should be as solid and as full of useful instruction as those of these poets. This would be, perhaps, a way of reconciling tragedy to a number of people, famous for their piety and for their dogma, who have condemned it in recent times and who would doubtless judge it more favorably if playwrights envisioned teaching their audiences as much as amusing them, and thus observed the true purpose of tragedy.

Nicholas Boileau-Despréaux 1636–1711

The Art of Poetry 1674

Canto I

Rash author, 'tis a vain presumptuous crime
To undertake the sacred art of rime;
If at thy birth the stars that ruled thy sense
Shone not with a poetic influence,
In thy strait genius thou wilt still be bound,
Find Phoebus deaf, and Pegasus unsound.
You, then, that burn with a desire to try
The dangerous course of charming poetry,
Forbear in fruitless verse to lose your time,
Or take for genius the desire of rime;
Fear the allurements of a specious bait,
And well consider your own force and weight. . . .

Whate'er you write of pleasant or sublime,
Always let sense accompany your rime;
Falsely they seem each other to oppose—
Rime must be made with reason's law to close;
And when to conquer her you bend your force,
The mind will triumph in the noble course;
To reason's yoke she quickly will incline,
Which, far from hurting, renders her divine;
But if neglected, will as easily stray,
And master reason, which she should obey.
Love reason then; and let whate'er you write
Borrow from her its beauty, force, and light.
Most writers mounted on a resty muse,
Extravagant and senseless objects choose;
They think they err, if in their verse they fall
On any thought that's plain or natural.
Fly this excess; and let Italians be
Vain authors of false glittering poetry. . . .

Sometimes an author, fond of his own thought,
Pursues its object till it's overwrought:

Selections. Translated by Sir William Soame and John Dryden. From *The Art of Poetry: the Poetical Treatises of Horace, Vida, and Boileau,* edited by Albert S. Cook. Boston: Ginn, 1892. The translators anglicize Boileau's examples as well as his words.

If he describes a house, he shows the face,
And after walks you round from place to place;
Here is a vista, there the doors unfold,
Balconies here are balustered with gold;
Then counts the rounds and ovals in the halls,
"The festoons, friezes, and the astragals";
Tired with his tedious pomp, away I run,
And skip o'er twenty pages, to be gone.
Of such descriptions the vain folly see,
And shun their barren superfluity.
All that is needless carefully avoid;
The mind once satisfied is quickly cloyed.
He cannot write who knows not to give o'er,
To mend one fault he makes a hundred more:
A verse was weak, you turn it much too strong,
And grow obscure for fear you should be long;
Some are not gaudy, but are flat and dry;
Not to be low, another soars too high.

    Would you of every one deserve the praise?
In writing vary your discourse and phrase;
A frozen style, that neither ebbs nor flows,
Instead of pleasing, makes us gape and doze.
Those tedious authors are esteemed by none,
Who tire us, humming the same heavy tone.

    Happy who in his verse can gently steer
From grave to light, from pleasant to severe!
His works will be admired wherever found,
And oft with buyers will be compassed round.

    In all you write be neither low nor vile;
The meanest theme may have a proper style.
The dull burlesque appeared with impudence,
And pleased by novelty in spite of sense;
All, except trivial points, grew out of date;
Parnassus spoke the cant of Billingsgate;
Boundless and mad, disordered rime was seen;
Disguised Apollo changed to Harlequin. . . .
Choose a just style. Be grave without constraint,
Great without pride, and lovely without paint.

    Write what your reader may be pleased to hear,
And for the measure have a careful ear;
On easy numbers fix your happy choice;
Of jarring sounds avoid the odious noise;
The fullest verse, and the most labored sense,
Displease us if the ear once take offense. . . .

There is a kind of writer pleased with sound,
Whose fustian head with clouds is compassed round—
No reason can disperse them with its light;
Learn then to think ere you pretend to write.
As your idea's clear, or else obscure,
The expression follows, perfect or impure;
What we conceive with ease we can express;
Words to the notions flow with readiness.
　　Observe the language well in all you write,
And swerve not from it in your loftiest flight.
The smoothest verse and the exactest sense
Displease us, if ill English give offense;
A barbarous phrase no reader can approve,
Nor bombast, noise, or affectation love.
In short, without pure language, what you write
Can never yield us profit or delight.
　　Take time for thinking; never work in haste;
And value not yourself for writing fast;
A rapid poem, with such fury writ,
Shows want of judgment, not abounding wit.
More pleased we are to see a river lead
His gentle streams along a flowery mead,
Than from high banks to hear loud torrents roar,
With foamy waters, on a muddy shore.
Gently make haste, of labor not afraid;
A hundred times consider what you've said;
Polish, repolish, every color lay,
And sometimes add, but oftener take away.
　　'Tis not enough, when swarming faults are writ,
That here and there are scattered sparks of wit;
Each object must be fixed in the due place,
And differing parts have corresponding grace;
Till, by a curious art disposed, we find
One perfect whole of all the pieces joined.
Keep to your subject close in all you say,
Nor for a sounding sentence ever stray.
　　The public censure for your writings fear,
And to yourself be critic most severe.
Fantastic wits their darling follies love;
But find you faithful friends that will reprove,
That on your works may look with careful eyes,
And of your faults be zealous enemies.
Lay by an author's pride and vanity,

And from a friend a flatterer descry,
Who seems to like, but means not what he says;
Embrace true counsel, but suspect false praise.
   A sycophant will everything admire;
Each verse, each sentence, sets his soul on fire;
All is divine! there's not a word amiss!
He shakes with joy, and weeps with tenderness;
He overpowers you with his mighty praise.
Truth never moves in those impetuous ways.
   A faithful friend is careful of your fame,
And freely will your heedless errors blame. . . .

Canto III

There's not a monster bred beneath the sky,
But, well-disposed by art, may please the eye;
A curious workman, by his skill divine,
From an ill object makes a good design.
Thus to delight us, Tragedy, in tears
For Oedipus, provokes our hopes and fears;
For parricide Orestes asks relief,
And to increase our pleasure, causes grief. . . .

In all you write observe with care and art
To move the passions and incline the heart.
If in a labored act, the pleasing rage
Cannot our hopes and fears by turns engage,
Nor in our mind a feeling pity raise,
In vain with learned scenes you fill your plays;
Your cold discourse can never move the mind
Of a stern critic, naturally unkind,
Who, justly tired with your pedantic flight,
Or falls asleep or censures all you write.
The secret is, attention first to gain,
To move our minds and then to entertain,
That, from the very opening of the scenes,
The first may show us what the author means.
   I'm tired to see an actor on the stage
That knows not whether he's to laugh or rage;
Who, an intrigue unraveling in vain,
Instead of pleasing keeps my mind in pain.
I'd rather much the nauseous dunce should say
Downright, "My name is Hector in the play,"

Than with a mass of miracles, ill-joined,
Confound my ears, and not instruct my mind.
The subject's never soon enough expressed.
  Your place of action must be fixed, and rest.
A Spanish poet may with good event
In one day's space whole ages represent;
There oft the hero of the wandering stage
Begins a child, and ends the play of age.
But we, that are by reason's rule confined,
Will that with art the poem be designed,
That unity of action, time, and place,
Keep the stage full, and all our labors grace.
  Write not what cannot be with ease conceived;
Some truths may be too strong to be believed.
A foolish wonder cannot entertain;
My mind's not moved if your discourse be vain.
You may relate what would offend the eye;
Seeing indeed would better satisfy,
But there are objects which a curious art
Hides from the eyes, yet offers to the heart. . . .

  Of romance heroes shun the low design,
Yet to great hearts some human frailties join.
Achilles must with Homer's heart engage—
For an affront I'm pleased to see him rage;
Those little failings in your hero's heart
Show that of man and nature he has part.
To leave known rules you cannot be allowed;
Make Agamemnon covetous and proud,
Aeneas in religious rites austere;
Keep to each man his proper character.
Of countries and of times the humors know,
From different climates different customs grow;
And strive to shun their fault, who vainly dress
An antique hero like a modern ass,
Who make old Romans like our English move,
Show Cato sparkish, or make Brutus love.
In a romance those errors are excused;
There 'tis enough that, reading, we're amused,
Rules too severe would there be useless found;
But the strict scene must have a juster bound,
Exact decorum we must always find.

If then you form some hero in your mind,
Be sure your image with itself agree,
For what he first appears he still must be. . . .

Wise nature by variety does please;
Clothe differing passions in a differing dress:
Bold anger in rough haughty words appears;
Sorrow is humble and dissolves in tears.
Make not your Hecuba with fury rage,
And show a ranting grief upon the stage,
Or tell in vain how "the rough Tanais bore
His sevenfold waters to the Euxine shore."
These swollen expressions, this affected noise,
Shows like some pedant that declaims to boys.
In sorrow you must softer methods keep,
And, to excite our tears, yourself must weep.
Those noisy words with which ill plays abound
Come not from hearts that are in sadness drowned. . . .

The great success which tragic writers found
In Athens first the comedy renowned.
The abusive Grecian[1] there, by pleasing ways,
Dispersed his natural malice in his plays;
Wisdom and virtue, honor, wit, and sense,
Were subject to buffooning insolence;
Poets were publicly approved and sought,
That vice extolled and virtue set at naught;
A Socrates himself, in that loose age,
Was made the pastime of a scoffing stage.
At last the public took in hand the cause,
And cured this madness by the power of laws,
Forbade, at any time or any place,
To name the persons or describe the face.
The stage its ancient fury thus let fall,
And comedy diverted without gall,
By mild reproofs recovered minds diseased,
And, sparing persons, innocently pleased.
Each one was nicely shown in this new glass,
And smiled to think he was not meant the ass.
A miser oft would laugh at first, to find
A faithful draught of his own sordid mind;

[1] Aristophanes.

And fops were with such care and cunning writ,
They liked the piece for which themselves did sit.
   You, then, that would the comic laurels wear,
To study nature be your only care.
Whoe'er knows man, and by a curious art
Discerns the hidden secrets of the heart;
He who observes, and naturally can paint
The jealous fool, the fawning sycophant,
A sober wit, an enterprising ass,
A humorous Otter,[2] or a Hudibras—
May safely in those noble lists engage,
And make them act and speak upon the stage.
Strive to be natural in all you write,
And paint with colors that may please the sight.
Nature in various figures does abound,
And in each mind are different humors found. . . .

   In this example we may have our part;
Rather be mason ('tis a useful art)
Than a dull poet; for that trade accursed
Admits no mean betwixt the best and worst.
In other sciences, without disgrace,
A candidate may fill a second place,
But poetry no medium can admit,
No reader suffers an indifferent wit. . . .

   Be not affected with that empty praise
Which your vain flatterers will sometimes raise,
And, when you read, with ecstasy will say,
"The finished piece! the admirable play!"—
Which, when exposed to censure and to light,
Cannot endure a critic's piercing sight. . . .

   Choose a sure judge to censure what you write,
Whose reason leads, and knowledge gives you light,
Whose steady hand will prove your faithful guide,
And touch the darling follies you would hide;
He, in your doubts, will carefully advise,
And clear the mist before your feeble eyes. . . .

   Would you in this great art acquire renown?
Authors, observe the rules I here lay down.

[2] Mrs. Otter is a character in Ben Jonson's *Epicoene, or The Silent Woman* (1609).

In prudent lessons everywhere abound,
With pleasant join the useful and the sound;
A sober reader a vain tale will slight,
He seeks as well instruction as delight.

    Let all your thoughts to virtue be confined,
Still offering nobler figures to our mind.
I like not those loose writers, who employ
Their guilty muse good manners to destroy,
Who with false colors still deceive our eyes,
And show us vice dressed in a fair disguise.

    Yet do I not their sullen muse approve,
Who from all modest writings banish love. . . .

    Write for immortal fame, nor ever choose
Gold for the object of a generous muse.
I know a noble wit may, without crime,
Receive a lawful tribute for his time,
Yet I abhor those writers who despise
Their honor, and alone their profits prize,
Who their Apollo basely will degrade,
And of a noble science make a trade.

    The comic wit, born with a smiling air,
Must tragic grief and pompous verse forbear;
Yet may he not, as on a market-place,
With bawdy jests amuse the populace.
With well-bred conversation you must please,
And your intrigue unravelled be with ease;
Your action still should reason's rules obey,
Nor in an empty scene may lose its way.
Your humble style must sometimes gently rise,
And your discourse sententious be and wise,
The passions must to nature be confined,
And scenes to scenes with artful weaving joined. . . .

    I like an author that reforms the age,
And keeps the right decorum of the stage,
That always pleases by just reason's rule;
But for a tedious droll, a quibbling fool,
Who with low nauseous bawdry fills his plays,
Let him be gone, and on two trestles raise
Some Smithfield stage, where he may act his pranks,
And make Jack-Puddings speak to mountebanks.

Canto IV

In Florence dwelt a doctor of renown,
The scourge of God, and terror of the town,
Who all the cant of physic had by heart,
And never murdered but by rules of art.
The public mischief was his private gain:
Children their slaughtered parents sought in vain;
A brother here his poisoned brother wept;
Some bloodless died, and some by opium slept;
Colds, at his presence, would to frenzies turn,
And agues like malignant fevers burn. . . .

René Rapin   *1621–1687*

Reflections on Aristotle's Treatise of Poesy   *1674*

In General

It is not easily decided what [is] the nature and what precisely is the end of this art. The interpreters of Aristotle differ in their opinions. Some will have the end to be delight, and that 'tis on this account it labors to move the passions. . . . 'Tis true, delight is the end poetry aims at, but not the principal end, as others pretend. In effect, poetry, being an art, ought to be profitable by the quality of its own nature and by the essential subordination that all arts should have to polity, whose end in general is the public good. This is the judgment of Aristotle and of Horace, his chief interpreter. . . .

. . . Morality, which undertakes to regulate the motions of the heart by its precepts, ought to make itself delightful that it may be listened to, which can by no means be so happily effected as by poetry. 'Tis by this that morality,

Selections. From René Rapin, *Reflections on Aristotle's Treatise of Poesy*, trans. Thomas Rymer. London: H. Herringman, 1674. Spelling and punctuation modernized by the editor.

in curing the maladies of men, makes use of the same artifice that physicians have recourse to in the sickness of children: they mingle honey with the medicine to take off the bitterness. The principal design, therefore, of this art is to render pleasant that which is wholesome. . . .

For no other end is poetry delightful than that it may be profitable. Pleasure is only the means by which the profit is conveyed, and all poetry when 'tis perfect ought of necessity to be a public lesson of good manners for the instruction of the world. Heroic poetry proposes the example of great virtues and great vices to excite men to abhor these and to be in love with the other: it gives us an esteem for Achilles in Homer, and contempt for Thersites; it begets in us a veneration for the piety of Aeneas in Vergil, and horror for the profaneness of Mezentius.[1] Tragedy rectifies the use of passions by moderating our fear and our pity, which are obstacles of virtue; it lets men see that vice never escapes unpunished when it represents Aegisthus, in the *Electra* of Sophocles, punished after the ten years enjoyment of his crime. It teaches us that the favors of fortune and the grandeurs of the world are not always true goods when it shows on the theatre a queen so unhappy as Hecuba deploring with that pathetic air her misfortunes in Euripides.[2] Comedy, which is an image of common conversation, corrects the public vices by letting us see how ridiculous they are in particulars. Aristophanes does not mock at the foolish vanity of Praxagora in his *Parliament of Women* but to cure the vanity of the other Athenian women, and 'twas only to teach the Roman soldiers in what consisted true valor that Plautus exposed in public the extravagance of false bravery in his Braggadocio Captain in that comedy of the *Glorious Soldier*.

But because poetry is only profitable so far as it is delightful, 'tis of greatest importance in this art to please; the only certain way to please is by rules . . . for unless a man adhere to principles, he . . . falls into errors as often as he sets out. . . . I pretend not by a long discourse to justify the necessity, the justness, and the truth of these rules, nor to make an history of Aristotle's *Treatise of Poesy* or examine whether it is complete, which many others have done. All these things I suppose. Only I affirm that these rules well considered, one shall find them made only to reduce nature into method, to trace it step by step and not suffer the least mark of it to escape us. 'Tis only by these rules that the verisimility in fictions is maintained, which is the soul of poesy, for unless there be the unity of place, of time, and of the action in the great poems, there can be no verisimility. In fine, 'tis by these rules that all becomes just, proportionate, and natural, for they are founded upon good sense and sound reason rather than on authority and example. Horace's *Book of Poesy*, which is but an interpretation of that of Aristotle, discovers suffi-

---

[1] *The Iliad* of Homer and *The Aeneid* of Vergil.
[2] *Hecuba* (425–424 B.C.) by Euripides.

ciently the necessity of being subject to rules by the ridiculous absurdities one is apt to fall into, who follows only his fancy, for though poesy be the effect of fancy, yet if this fancy be not regulated, 'tis a mere caprice, not capable of producing anything reasonable. . . .

. . . A poet that designs to wrote nothing but what is just and accurate above all things ought to apply himself with great attention to the precepts of Aristotle as the best master that ever writ of this art. . . .

Besides all the rules taken from Aristotle, there remains one mentioned by Horace, to which all the other rules must be subject, as to the most essential, which is the decorum, without which the other rules of poetry are false, it being the most solid foundation of that probability so essential to this art, because it is only by the decorum that this probability gains its effect; all becomes probable where the decorum is strictly preserved in all circumstances. One ordinarily transgresses this rule either by confounding the serious with the pleasant, as Pulci has done in his poem of *Morgante*; or by giving manners disproportionate to the condition of the persons, as Guarini has done to his shepherds, which are too polite[3] . . . or because no regard is had to make the wonderful adventures probable, whereof Ariosto is guilty in his *Orlando*; or that a due preparation is not made for the great events by a natural conduct, in which Bernardo Tasso transgressed in his poem of *Amadis* and in his *Floridante*; or by want of care to sustain the characters of persons, as Theophile in his tragedy of *Pyramus and Thisbe*; or by following rather a capricious genius than nature, as Lope de Vega, who gives his wit too much swing and is ever foisting in his own fancies on all occasions. . . . Finally, whatever is against the rules of time, of manners, of thought, of expression is contrary to the decorum, which is the most universal of all the rules. . . .

In Particular

. . . [Aristotle] alleges that tragedy is a public lecture, without comparison more instructive than philosophy because it teaches the mind by the sense and rectifies the passions themselves, calming by their emotion the troubles they excite in the heart. The philosopher had observed two important faults in man to be regulated, pride and hardness of heart, and he found for both vices a cure in tragedy, for it makes man modest by representing the great masters of the earth humbled and it makes him tender and merciful by showing him on the theatre the strange accidents of life and the unforeseen disgraces to which the most important persons are subject. . . . But as the end of tragedy is to teach men not to fear too weakly the commonly misfortunes and manage their fear, it makes account also to teach them to spare their compassion for objects that deserve it, for there is an injustice in being moved at the afflictions of those who deserve to be miserable. One may see without

---

[3] In *Pastor fido* (*The Faithful Shepherd*, 1590).

pity Clytemnestra slain by her son Orestes in Aeschylus[4] because she had cut the throat of Agamemnon, her husband. . . .

Modern tragedy turns on other principles. The genius of our [the French] nation is not strong enough to sustain an action on the theatre by moving only terror and pity. These are machines that will not play as they ought but by great thoughts and noble expressions, of which we are not indeed altogether so capable as the Greeks. Perhaps our nation, which is naturally gallant, has been obliged by the necessity of our character to frame for ourselves a new system of tragedy to suit with our humor. The Greeks, who were popular estates and who hated monarchy, took delight in their spectacles to see kings humbled and high fortunes cast down, because the exaltation grieved them. The English, our neighbors, love blood in their sports, by the quality of their temperament. These are insularies, separated from the rest of men. We are more humane. Gallantry, moreover, agrees with our manners, and our poets believed that they could not succeed well on the theatre but by sweet and tender sentiments, in which perhaps they had some reason, for, in effect, the passions represented become deformed and insipid unless they are founded on sentiments conformable to those of the spectator. 'Tis this that obliges our poets to stand up so strongly for the privilege of gallantry on the theatre and to bend all their subjects to love and tenderness, the rather to please the women, who have made themselves judges of these divertissements and usurped the right to pass sentence. . . . However it be, for I am not hardy enough to declare myself against the public, 'tis to degrade tragedy from that majesty which is proper to it, to mingle in it love, which is of a character always light and little suitable to that gravity of which tragedy makes profession. Hence it proceeds that these tragedies mixed with gallantries never make such admirable impressions on the spirit as did those of Sophocles and Euripides, for all the bowels were moved by the great objects of terror and pity which they proposed. 'Tis likewise for this that the reputation of our modern tragedies so soon decays and yields but small delight at two years' end, whereas the Greek please yet to those that have a good taste after two thousand years, because what is not grave and serious in the theatre, though it give delight at present, after a short time grows distasteful and unpleasant, and because what is not proper for great thoughts and great figures in tragedy cannot support itself. The ancients, who perceived this, did not interweave their gallantry and love save in comedy, for love is of a character that always degenerates from that heroic air of which tragedy must never divest itself, and nothing to me shows so mean and senseless as for one to amuse himself with whining about frivolous kindnesses when he may be admirable by great and noble thoughts and sublime expressions. But I dare not presume so far on my own capacity and credit to oppose myself of my own head against a usage so established. I must be content modestly to propose my doubts. . . .

---

[4] *The Libation Bearers*, the second play in the *Oresteia* trilogy (458 B.C.).

Comedy is an image of common life. Its end is to show on the stage the faults of particulars in order to amend the faults of the public and to correct the people through a fear of being rendered ridiculous, so that which is most proper to excite laughter is that which is most essential to comedy. One may be ridiculous in words or ridiculous in things: there is an honest laughter and a buffoon laughter. 'Tis merely a gift of nature to make everything ridiculous, for all the actions of human life have their fair and their wrong side, their serious and their ridiculous. But Aristotle, who gives precepts to make men weep, leaves none to make them laugh. This proceeds purely from the genius; art and method have little to do with it; 'tis the work of nature alone. . . . Fine raillery, which is the flower of wit, is the talent which comedy demands, but it must always be observed that the true ridiculous of art, for the entertainment on the theatre, ought to be no other but the copy of the ridiculous that is found in nature. Comedy is as it should be when the spectator believes himself really in the company of such persons as he has represented and takes himself to be in a family while he is at the theatre, and that he there sees nothing but what he sees in the world, for comedy is worth nothing at all unless he know and can compare the manners that are exhibited on the stage with those of such persons as he has conversation withall. . . . 'Tis the great art of comedy to keep close to nature and never leave it, to have common thoughts and expressions fitted to the capacity of all the world, for it is most certainly true that the most gross strokes of nature, whatever they be, please always more than the most delicate that are not natural. Nevertheless, base and vulgar terms are not to be permitted on the theatre unless supported by some kind of wit. The proverbs and wise sayings of the people ought not to be suffered unless they have some pleasant meaning and unless they are natural. This is the most general principle of comedy, by which whatever is represented cannot fail to please; but without it, nothing. 'Tis only by adhering to nature that the probability can be maintained, which is the sole infallible guide that may be followed on the theatre. Without probability, all is lame and faulty; with it, all goes well. None can run astray who follow it, and the most ordinary faults of comedy happen from thence, that the decencies are not well observed nor the incidents enough prepared. 'Tis likewise necessary to take heed that the colors employed to prepare the incidents be not too gross, to leave the spectator the pleasure of finding out himself what they signify. But the most ordinary weakness of our comedies is the unraveling. Scarce ever any succeed well in that, by the difficulty there is in untying happily that knot which had been tied. It is easy to wind up an intrigue—'tis only the work of fancy—but the unraveling is the pure and perfect work of the judgment. 'Tis this that makes the success difficult, and if one would thereon make a little reflection, he might find that the most universal fault of comedies is that the catastrophe of it is not natural. It rests to examine whether in comedy the images may be drawn greater than the natural, the more to move the minds of the spectators by more shining portraits and by stronger impressions: that is to say, whether a poet may make a miser more covetous, a morose man more morose and troublesome than the original. To which I answer that Plautus, who studied to please the common people, made them so but Terence, who would please the better sort, confined himself within the bounds of nature, and he represented vices without making them either better or worse. . . .

. . . But among the French, never any carried comedy so high as Molière, for the ancient comic poets had only the folk of the family to make mirth with on the theatre but . . . Molière has made bold with all Paris and the court. He is the only man among them who has discovered those lines of nature that distinguish and make her known. The beauties of the portraits he draws are so natural that they make themselves perceived by the grossest apprehensions, and his talent of being pleasant is improved one half the more by that he has of counterfeiting to the life. His *Misanthrope*, in my opinion, is the most complete character, and withal the most singular, that ever appeared on the theatre. But the contrivance of his comedies is always defective in something, and his plots are never handsomely unraveled.

Charles de Marguetel de Saint-Denis, Seigneur de Saint-Évremond *1610–1703*

On the Characters of Tragedies *1671–1675*

. . . Every time that I go to hear our most moving tragedies, the tears of the actors draw forth mine with a secret pleasure which I find in being moved, but if the affliction continues, I am uneasy and impatiently expect some turn

Selections. From *The Works of Monsieur de Saint-Évremond*, Vol. II, trans. anonymous. London: J. Churchill, 1714. Spelling and punctuation modernized by the editor.

of the scene to deliver me from these melancholy impressions. I have frequently seen it happen in those long discourses of tenderness that toward the end the author gives us another idea than that of a lover whom he designs to represent. This lover sometimes commences a philosopher and reasons gravely in his passion, or by way of lecture explains to us after what manner it is formed. Sometimes, the spectator who at first suffered his imagination to range with the person represented comes home to himself and finds that 'tis not the hero but the poet that speaks, who in doleful strain of elegy would needs have us weep at some feigned misfortune.

An author mistakes when he thinks to get my good opinion at this rate. He provokes my laughter when he pretends to possess me with pity. But what is more ridiculous even than this is to hear a man declaim eloquently on his misfortunes. He that takes a great deal of pains in describing them saves me the trouble of condoling with him. 'Tis nature that suffers and 'tis she that ought to complain. She sometimes loves to speak her private thoughts in order to gain relief by it, but not to expatiate eloquently, to show her fine parts.

Neither have I any mighty opinion of the violence of that passion which is ingenious to express itself with great pomp and magnificence. The soul, when it is sensibly touched, does not afford the mind an opportunity to think intensely, much less to ramble and divert itself in the variety of its conceptions. . . .

. . . As for those long conversations of tenderness, those sighs we hear incessantly and those tears that are shed every moment . . . in my opinion, they are not so much the effects of love as the folly of the lover. I have a greater respect for that passion than to load it with any scandal which does not belong to it. A few tears are sufficient for a lover to express his love by. When they are immoderate or unseasonable, they rather show his infirmity than his passion. I dare venture to say that a lady who might have some compassion for her lover when she sees him discreetly and respectfully expressing the inquietudes she gives him, would laugh at him for a chickenhearted milksop if he whined and fobbed eternally before her.

Of Ancient and Modern Tragedy 1672

There never were so many rules to write a good tragedy by, and yet so few good ones are now made that the players are obliged to revive and act all the old ones. I remember that the Abbé d'Aubignac wrote one according to the laws he had imperiously prescribed for the stage. This piece had no success, notwithstanding which he boasted in all companies that he was the only French writer that had exactly followed the precepts of Aristotle, whereupon the Prince of Condé said wittily, "I am obliged to M. d'Aubignac for having so exactly followed Aristotle's rules, but I will never forgive the rules of Aristotle for having put M. d'Aubignac upon writing so bad a tragedy."

It must be acknowledged that Aristotle's *Art of Poetry* is an excellent piece of work. But, however, there's nothing so perfect in it as to be the standing rule of all nations and all ages. Descartes and Gassendi have found out truths that were unknown to Aristotle; Corneille has discovered beauties for the stage of which Aristotle was ignorant; and as our philosophers have observed errors in his *Physics*, our poets have spied out faults in his *Poetics*, at least with respect to us, considering what great change all things have undergone since his time. The gods and goddesses among the ancients brought about everything that was great and extraordinary upon the theatre, either by their hatred or their friendship, by their revenge or by their protection; and among so many supernatural things, nothing appeared fabulous to the people, who believed there passed a familiar correspondence between gods and men. Their gods, generally speaking, acted by human passions. Their men undertook nothing without the counsel of their gods and executed nothing without their assistance. Thus, in this mixture of the divinity and humanity, there was nothing which was not credible.

But all this profusion of miracles is downright romance to us at this time of day. The gods are wanting to us and we are wanting to the gods, and if in imitation of the ancients an author would introduce his angels and saints upon our stage, the bigots and puritans would be offended at it and look on him as a profane person, and the libertines would certainly think him weak. Our preachers would by no means suffer a confusion of the pulpit and the theatre, or that the people should go and learn those matters from the mouth of comedians which themselves deliver with such authority to the whole people.

Besides this, it would give too great an advantage to the libertines, who might ridicule in a comedy those very things which they receive at church with a seeming submission, either out of respect to the place where they are delivered or to the character of the person that utters them.

From *The Works of Monsieur de Saint-Évremond*, Vol. II, trans. anonymous. London: J. Churchill, 1714. Spelling and punctuation modernized by the editor.

But let us put the case that our doctors should freely leave all holy matters to the liberty of the stage. Let us likewise take it for granted that men of the least devotion would hear them with as great an inclination to be edified as persons of the profoundest resignation. Yet certain it is that the soundest doctrines, the most Christian actions, and the most useful truths would produce a kind of tragedy that would please us the least of anything in the world.

The spirit of our religion is directly opposite to that of tragedy. The humility and patience of our saints carry too direct an opposition to those heroical virtues that are so necessary for the theatre. What zeal, what force is there which Heaven does not bestow upon Nearchus and Polyeucte?[1] And what is there wanting on the part of these new Christians to answer fully the end of these happy gifts? The passion and charms of a young, lovely bride make not the least impression upon the mind of Polyeucte. The politic considerations of Felix, as they less affect us, so they make a less impression. Insensible both of prayers and menaces, Polyeucte has a greater desire to die for God than other men have to live for themselves. Nevertheless, this very subject, which would make one of the finest sermons in the world, would have made a wretched tragedy if the conversation of Pauline and Sévère, heightened with other sentiments and other passions, had not preserved that reputation to the author which the Christian virtues of our martyrs had made him lose.

The theatre loses all its agreeableness when it pretends to represent sacred things, and sacred things lose a great deal of the religious opinion that is due to them by being represented upon the theater.

To say the truth, the histories of the Old Testament are infinitely better suited to our stage. Moses, Samson, and Joshua would meet with much better success than Polyeucte and Nearchus, for the wonders they would work there would be a fitter subject for the theatre. But I am apt to believe that the priests would not fail to exclaim against the profanation of these sacred histories with which they fill their ordinary conversations, their books, and their sermons; and to speak soberly upon the point, the miraculous passage through the Red Sea, the sun stopped in his career by the prayer of Joshua, and whole armies defeated by Samson with the jawbone of an ass, all these miracles, I say, would not be credited in a play because we believe them in the Bible, but we should be rather apt to question them in the Bible because we should believe nothing of them in a play.

If what I have delivered is founded on good and solid reasons, we ought to content ourselves with things purely natural but at the same time such as are extraordinary, and in our heroes to choose the principal actions which we may believe possible as humane and which may cause admiration in us as being rare and of an elevated character. In a word, we should have nothing

---

[1] Characters in *Polyeucte* (1640) by Pierre Corneille.

but what is great; yet still let it be human. In the human we must carefully avoid mediocrity and [in the] fable [have] that which is great.

I am by no means willing to compare the *Pharsalia* to the *Aeneid*. I know the just difference of their value. But as for what purely regards elevation, Pompey, Caesar, Cato, Curio, and Labienus have done more for Lucan than Jupiter, Mercury, Juno, Venus, and all the train of the other gods and goddesses have done for Vergil.

The ideas which Lucan gives us of these great men are truly greater and affect us more sensibly than those which Vergil gives us of his deities. The latter has clothed his gods with human infirmities to adapt them to the capacity of men. The other has raised his heroes so as to bring them into competition with the gods themselves.

Victrix causa deis placuit, sed victa Catoni.[2]

In Vergil, the gods are not so valuable as the heroes; in Lucan, the heroes equal the gods.

To give you my opinion freely, I believe that the tragedies of the ancients might have suffered a happy loss in the banishment of their gods, their oracles, and [their] soothsayers, for it proceeded from these gods, these oracles, and these diviners that the stage was swayed by a spirit of superstition and terror capable of infecting mankind with a thousand errors and overwhelming them with more numerous mischiefs. And if we consider the usual impressions which tragedy made at Athens in the minds of the spectators, we may safely affirm that Plato was more in the right who prohibited the use of them than Aristotle who recommended them, for as their tragedies wholly consisted in excessive motions of fear and pity, was not this the direct way to make the theatre a school of terror and compassion, where people only learned to be affrighted at all dangers and to abandon themselves to despair upon every misfortune?

It will be a hard matter to persuade me that a soul accustomed to be terrified for what regards another, has strength enough to support the misfortunes that concern itself. This perhaps was the reason why the Athenians became so susceptible of the impressions of fear, and that this spirit of terror, which the theatre inspired into them with so much art, became at last but too natural to their armies.

At Sparta and Rome, where only examples of valor and constancy were publicly shown, the people were no less brave and resolute in battle than they were unshaken and constant in the calamities of the republic. Ever since this art of fearing and lamenting was set up at Athens, all those disorderly passions, which they had as it were imbibed at their public representations, got footing in their camps and attended them in their wars.

---

[2] "The victorious found favor with the gods, the defeated with Cato." —Lucan, *Pharsalia*, Book I, l. 128.

Thus, a spirit of superstition occasioned the defeat of their armies as a spirit of lamentation made them sit down contented with bewailing their great misfortunes when they ought to have found out proper remedies for them, for how was it possible for them not to learn despair in this pitiful school of commiseration? The persons they usually represented upon it were examples of the greatest misery and subjects but of ordinary virtues.

So great was their desire to lament that they represented fewer virtues than misfortunes, lest a soul raised to the admiration of heroes should be less inclined to pity the distressed. And in order to imprint these sentiments of affliction the deeper in their spectators, they had always upon their theatre a chorus of virgins or of old men who furnished them upon every event either with their terrors or their tears.

Aristotle was sensible enough what prejudice this might do the Athenians, but he thought he sufficiently prevented it by establishing a certain purgation, which no one hitherto has understood and which in my opinion he himself never fully comprehended, for can anything be so ridiculous as to form a science which will infallibly discompose our minds only to set up another which does not certainly pretend to cure us, or to raise a perturbation in our souls for no other end than to endeavor afterwards to calm it by obliging it to reflect upon the dejected condition it has been in?

Among a thousand persons that are present at the theatre, perhaps there may be six philosophers that are capable of recovering their former tranquility by the assistance of these prudent and useful meditations, but the multitude will scarce make any such judicious reflections and we may be almost assured that what we see constantly represented on the theatre will not fail at long run to produce in us a habit of these unhappy motions.

Our theatrical representations are not subject to the same inconveniences as those of the ancients were, since our fear never goes so far as to raise this superstitious terror which produced such ill effects upon valor. Our fear, generally speaking, is nothing else but an agreeable uneasiness which consists in the suspension of our minds. 'Tis a dear concern which our soul has for those subjects that draw its affection to them.

We may almost say the same of pity as 'tis used on our stage. We divest it of all its weaknesses and leave it all that we call charitable and human. I love to see the misfortune of some great, unhappy person lamented. I am content with all my heart that he should attract our compassion—nay, sometimes command our tears—but then I would have these tender and generous tears paid to his misfortunes and virtues together, and that this melancholy sentiment of pity be accompanied with vigorous admiration, which shall stir up in our souls a sort of amorous desire to imitate him.

We were obliged to mingle somewhat of love in the new tragedy, the better to remove those black ideas which the ancient tragedy caused in us by superstition and terror. And in truth, there is no passion that more excites us to everything that is noble and generous than a virtuous love. A man who may cowardly suffer himself to be insulted by a contemptible enemy will yet defend what he loves, though to the apparent hazard of his life, against the attacks of the most valiant. The weakest and most fearful creatures, those creatures that are naturally inclined to fear and to run away, will fiercely encounter what they dread most to preserve the object of their love. Love has a certain heat which supplies the defect of courage in those that want it most. But, to confess the truth, our authors have made as ill a use of this noble passion as the ancients did of their fear and pity, for if we except eight or ten plays where its impulses have been managed to great advantage, we have no tragedies in which both lovers and love are not equally injured.

We have an affected tenderness where we ought to place the noblest sentiments. We bestow a softness on what ought to be most moving; and sometimes, when we mean plainly to express the graces of nature, we fall into a vicious and mean simplicity.

We imagine we make kings and emperors perfect lovers, but in truth we make ridiculous princes of them; and by the complaints and sighs which we bestow upon them, where they ought neither to complain nor sigh, we represent them weak, both as lovers and as princes.

Our great heroes upon the theatre generally make love like shepherds, and thus the innocence of a sort of rural passion supplies with them the place of glory and valor.

If an actress has the art to weep and bemoan herself after a moving, lively manner, we give her our tears at certain places which demand gravity, and because she pleases best when she seems to be affected, she shall put on grief all along, indifferently.

Sometimes, we must have a plain, unartificial, sometimes a tender, and sometimes a melancholy, whining love, without regarding where that simplicity, tenderness, or grief is requisite. And the reason of it is plain, for as we must needs have love everywhere, we look for diversity in the manners and seldom or never place it in the passions.

I am in good hopes we shall one day find out the true use of this passion, which is now become too common. That which ought to sweeten cruel or calamitous accidents, that which ought to affect our very souls, to animate our courage and raise our spirits, will not certainly be always made the subject of a little affected tenderness or of a weak simplicity. Whenever this happens, we need not envy the ancients, and without paying too great a respect to antiquity or being too much prejudiced against the present age, we shall not set up the tragedies of Sophocles and Euripides as the only models for the dramatic compositions of our times.

However, I don't say that these tragedies wanted anything that was necessary to recommend them to the palate of the Athenians. But should a man translate even the *Oedipus*, the best performance of all antiquity, into French, with the same spirit and force as we see it in the original, I dare be bold to affirm that nothing in the world would appear to us more cruel, more opposite to the true sentiments which mankind ought to have.

Our age has at least this advantage over theirs, that we are allowed the liberty to hate vice and love virtue. As the gods occasioned the greatest crimes on the theatre of the ancients, these crimes captivated the respect of the spectators and the people durst not find fault with those things which were really abominable. When they saw Agamemnon sacrifice his own daughter, and a daughter too that was so tenderly beloved by him, to appease the indignation of the gods, they only considered this barbarous sacrifice as a pious obedience and the highest proof of a religious submission.

Now, in that superstitious age, if a man still preserved the common sentiments of humanity, he could not avoid murmuring at the cruelty of the gods, he must needs be cruel and barbarous to his own fellow creatures, he must like Agamemnon offer the greatest violence both to nature and to his own affection.

Tantum religio potuit suadere malorum,[3]

says Lucretius upon the account of this barbarous sacrifice.

Nowadays, we see men represented upon the theatre without the interposition of the gods, and this conduct is infinitely more useful both to the public and to private persons, for in our tragedies we neither introduce any villain who is not detested nor any hero who does not cause himself to be admired. With us, few crimes escape unpunished and few virtues go off unrewarded. In short, by the good examples we publicly represent on the theatre, by the agreeable sentiments of love and admiration that are discreetly interwoven with a rectified fear and pity, we are in a capacity of arriving to that perfection which Horace desires—

Omne tulit punctum qui miscuit utile dulci[4]

—which can never be effected by the rules of the ancient tragedy.

I shall conclude with a new and daring thought of my own, and that is this: we ought in tragedy, before all things whatever, to look after a greatness of soul well expressed, which excites in us a tender admiration. By this sort of admiration, our minds are sensibly ravished, our courages elevated, and our souls deeply affected.

---

[3] "To such evil deeds could religion impel people." —Lucretius, *De rerum natura* (*On the Nature of Things*), Book I, l. 101.

[4] Horace, *The Art of Poetry*: ". . . the man who mingles the useful with the sweet carries the day by charming his reader and at the same time instructing him." See above, p. 74.

To an Author Who Asked My Opinion of a Play Where the Heroine Does Nothing but Lament Herself 1675

The princess you make the heroine of your play would have pleased me well enough had you managed her tears with more frugality, but you make her shed them so prodigally that when the audience come to themselves, this profusion of tears cannot but make the person you represent less affecting and those that behold the representation less sensible. . . .

I own that nothing is so moving as the lively representation of a beautiful person in distress. 'Tis a new sort of a charm that unites everything that is tender within us by impressions of love and pity mingled together. But if the fair lady continues to bewail her misfortunes too long, that which at first affected us makes us sad, and as we are soon weary of comforting one that takes a pleasure in whining and complaining, we leave her as a troublesome creature in the hands of old women and relations who know how to manage one in this sad condition by the received rules of condoling. . . .

I cannot endure to see a dying person upon the stage who is more lamented by him that dies than by the spectators that see him die. I love great griefs attended with few complaints but deep concern. I love a despair which does not waste itself in words but where nature is overcome, and sinks under the violence of the passion. Long, tedious discourses rather show our desire of life than our resolutions to die.

Selections. From *The Works of Monsieur de Saint-Évremond*, Vol. II, trans. anonymous. London: J. Churchill, 1714. Spelling and punctuation modernized by the editor.

Voltaire
(François Marie Arouet) 1694–1778

Preface to Oedipus 1729

... The principles of all the arts that depend on the imagination are easy and simple, all drawn from nature and from reason. . . . But since Monsieur de la Motte[1] seems desirous of establishing rules directly opposite to those which our great masters submitted to, it is but just to defend the ancient laws —not because they are ancient but because they are good and necessary, and because those laws might find a very powerful adversary in a man of his distinguished merit.

M. de la Motte would abolish the unities of action, time, and place. The French were the first of the moderns who revived the wise rules of the ancient theatre. Other nations refused for a long time submission to a yoke which they thought too severe, but as the laws were just, and reason must triumph at last, in process of time they yielded also. Even in England, at this day, authors give us notice at the beginning of their pieces that the time employed in the action is equal to that of the representation and thus go further than ourselves, who taught them. All nations now begin to look upon those ages as barbarous when this practice was entirely unknown to the greatest geniuses, such as Lope de Vega and Shakespeare; they acknowledge their obligation to us for awakening them from this Gothicism. And shall a Frenchman, after this, exercise all his wit and abilities to reduce us once more to the same standard? . . .

What is a theatrical performance? The representation of an action. Why of a single action, and not of two or three? Doubtless, because the human mind is incapable of embracing more than one object at a time; because the interest which is divided is soon destroyed; because we are disgusted at seeing two different events even in a picture; it is, in short, because nature alone points out to us this precept, which is as invariable as herself.

For the same reason unity of place is essential, for a single action cannot possibly happen in several places at a time. If the persons of the drama are at Athens in the first act, how can they be at Persia in the second? . . .

Selections. From *The Dramatic Works of Mr. de Voltaire*, Vol. I, translated by the Reverend Mr. Francklin. London: J. Newbery, R. Baldwin, S. Crowder, & Co., 1761. Spelling and punctuation modernized by the editor.

[1] Monsieur de la Motte presented the world with two *Oedipuses*, one verse, the other in prose, in the year 1726; that in verse was played four times, the prose was never represented at all [Voltaire's note].

The unity of time naturally follows the other two, of which this is, I think, an incontestable proof: I come to a tragedy, that is to say, to the representation of an action; the subject is the accomplishment of this single action. A conspiracy is formed against Augustus at Rome; I want to know what happens to Augustus and to the conspirators. If the poet makes the action last fifteen days, he ought to give me an account of what passes during that time; I come there to be informed of every circumstance, and nothing should pass that is useless. If he represents the events of fifteen days, there must be at least fifteen different actions, however inconsiderable they may all be. It is no longer the accomplishment of that single action of the conspiracy, toward which we are to proceed as speedily as possible, but a long, tedious history, which cannot be interesting because it is not lively; because the whole will be at too great a distance from the decisive moment, from the catastrophe, which is the principal thing I am in expectation of. I don't go to the play to hear the history of a hero, but to see one single event of his life, and there perhaps I meet with many. But further, the spectator is but three hours at the theatre, the action therefore should last no longer than that time. *Cinna*,[2] *Andromache*,[3] *Oedipus* (Corneille's,[4] la Motte's, and my own,[5] if I may be permitted to mention it) are all within this rule. If some other pieces require more time, it is a license which can only be pardoned in favor of great beauties in the work, and the more of this license is indulged, the more faulty it becomes.

We often extend the unity of time to twenty-four hours and the unity of place to the whole circumference of a palace. More severity would prevent the handling [of] some very fine subjects, and more indulgence would open the way to intolerable abuses, for if it was once made an established rule that a theatric action might continue for two days, one author would soon extend it to two weeks and another to two years, and in the same manner, if the place of the scene was not confined to certain limits, we should soon see tragedies, like the old *Julius Caesar* of the English, where Brutus and Cassius are at Rome in the first act and in Thessaly in the fifth.

The observation of these rules serves not only to prevent faults, but it is likewise productive of true beauties, in the same manner as the rules of fine architecture well followed necessarily compose a building agreeable to the eye. We easily perceive that by adhering to the unities of time, place, and action, the piece must be simple. It is this which constitutes the merit of all Racine's performances and is that very perfection which Aristotle required. . . . Let us, then, with the great Corneille, adhere to the three unities, in which we shall find all the other rules, that is to say, all other beauties, comprehended.

[2] By Pierre Corneille (1639).
[3] By Jean Racine (1668).
[4] 1659.
[5] First performed in 1718.

A Discourse on Tragedy [1] *1731*

. . . I must own, my lord, on my return from England, where I had passed almost two years in the continual study of your language, I found myself at a loss when I set about a French tragedy. I was accustomed almost to think in English, and perceived that the French idioms did not present themselves to my imagination with that facility that they did formerly; it was like a rivulet, whose current had been turned another way; some time and pains were requisite to make it flow again in its proper channel. I began then to be convinced that to succeed in any art, we must cultivate it all our lives.

What deterred me more than anything from works of this kind were the severe rules of our poetry, and the slavery of rhyme. I regretted that happy liberty which you enjoy of writing tragedy in blank verse; of lengthening out, of shortening almost all our words; of running one verse into another; and, upon occasion, coining new expressions; which are generally adopted, if they sound well, and are useful, and intelligible. "An English poet," said I, "is a freeman, who can subject his language to his genius; while the Frenchman is a slave to rhyme, obliged sometimes to make four verses to express a sentiment that an Englishman can give you in one." An Englishman says what he will; a Frenchman only what he can. One runs along a large and open field, while the other walks in shackles, through a narrow and slippery road; but, in spite of all these reflections and complaints, we can never shake off the yoke of rhyme; it is absolutely essential to French poetry. Our language will not admit of inversions; nor our verses bear to be run one into another: our syllables can never produce a sensible harmony, by their long or short measures; our caesuras, and a certain number of feet, would not be sufficient to distinguish prose from verse; rhyme is therefore indispensably necessary; besides, so many of our great masters, who have written in rhyme, such as Corneille, Racine, and Despréaux, have so accustomed our ears to this kind of harmony, that we could never bear any other; and I once more therefore insist upon it, that whoever can be absurd enough to shake off a burden which the great Corneille was obliged to carry, would be looked upon, and with great reason, not as a bold and enterprising genius, striking out into a new road, but as a weak and impotent writer, who had not strength to support himself in the old path.

Some have attempted to give us tragedies in prose; but it is a thing which, I believe, can never succeed. Those who already have much, are seldom contented with a little; and he who says, "I come to lessen your pleasure," will

Selections. Translated by William F. Fleming, slightly revised by the editor. From *The Works of Voltaire*, Vol. XXXIX. Paris: E. R. DuMont, 1901.

[1] In a letter to Lord Bolingbroke, prefixed to Voltaire's play *Brutus*.

always be a very unwelcome guest to the public. If, in the midst of Paul Veronese's or Rubens' pictures, any one should come and place his sketches with a pencil, would he have any right to compare himself with those great artists? We are used at feasts to dancing and singing; would it be enough on these occasions merely for us to walk and speak, only under the pretence that we walked and spoke well, and that it was more easy, and more natural?

It is probable that verse will always be made use of in tragedy, rhymed verse in ours. It is even to this constraint of rhyme, and the extreme severity of our versification, that we are indebted for the most excellent performances in our language. We require in our rhymes that they should never prejudice the sentiment; that they should never be trivial, nor labored; and are so rigorous as to expect the same purity, and the same exactness in verse, as in prose. We do not permit the least licence; we force our authors to carry all the chains without breaking one link, and at the same time to appear entirely free, and never acknowledge any as poets who have not fulfilled all these conditions.

Such are the reasons why it is more easy to make a hundred verses in any other language than four in French. . . .

. . . Depend on it, my lord, the more a stranger knows of our language, the sooner will he reconcile himself to that rhyme which is a first so formidable to him. It is not only necessary to our tragedies, but is even an ornament to our comedies themselves. A good thing in verse is more easily retained: the various pictures of human life will be always more striking in verse—when a Frenchman says verse, he always means rhyme—and we have comedies in prose, by the celebrated Molière, which we have been obliged to put into verse after his death, and which are never played but in their new dress.

Not daring, therefore, my lord, to hazard on the French theatre that kind of verse which is used in Italy and in England, I have endeavored at least to transplant into our scene some of the beauties of yours; at the same time I am sufficently satisfied that the English theatre is extremely defective. I have heard you say you have not one good tragedy; but to make you amends, in those wild pieces which you have, there are some admirable scenes. Hitherto there has been wanting, in all the tragic authors of your nation, that purity, that regular conduct, that decorum in the action and style, and all those strokes of art which have established the reputation of the French theatre since the time of the great Corneille: though, at the same time, it must be acknowledged, that your most irregular pieces have very great merit with regard to the action.

We have in France some tragedies in high repute, which are rather conversations than the representation of an event. . . . Our excessive delicacy obliges us frequently to put into narration what we would gladly have brought before the eyes of the spectator; but we are afraid to hazard on the scene new spectacles, before a people accustomed to turn into ridicule everything which they are not used to.

The place where our comedies are acted, and the abuses which have crept into it, are another cause of that dryness which appears in some of our pieces. The benches on the stage, appropriated to the spectators, confine the scene, and make all action almost impracticable; and this is the reason why the decorations, so highly recommended by the ancients, are with us seldom well adapted to the piece: and above all, it prevents the actors from passing out of one apartment into the other in sight of the spectators; as was the sensible practice of the Greeks and Romans, to preserve at once unity of place and probability.

How, for instance, could we dare, on our theatre, to bring on the ghost of Pompey, or the genius of Brutus, among a crowd of young fellows who seldom look upon the most serious things but with the view of showing their wit by a *bon mot* on the occasion? . . .

With what pleasure have I seen at London your tragedy of Julius Caesar, which for these hundred and fifty years past has been the delight of your nation! not that I approve the barbarous irregularities which it abounds with; it only astonishes me, that there are not many more in a work written in an age of ignorance, by a man who did not even understand Latin, and had no instructor but his own genius: and yet, among so many gross faults, with what rapture did I behold Brutus, holding in his hand a dagger, still wet with the blood of Caesar, assemble the Roman people, and . . . harangue them from the tribunal. . . .

After this scene Antony comes to excite the compassion of those very Romans whom Brutus had just before inspired with his own rigor and barbarity. Antony, by an artful discourse, leads back as it were insensibly these haughty spirits, and when he sees them softened a little, shows them the body of Caesar; and making use of the most pathetic figures of rhetoric, excites them to sedition and revenge. The French, perhaps, would never suffer on their stage a chorus composed of Roman artisans and plebians; would never permit the bleeding body of Caesar to be exposed in public; or the people to be excited to rebellion by a harangue from the tribunal; custom alone, who is the queen of this world, can change the taste of nations, and make the objects of our aversion pleasing and agreeable.

The Greeks produced spectacles on the stage that appear not less shocking and absurd to us. Hippolytus, bruised with his fall, comes on to count his wounds, and make hideous lamentations. Philoctetes falls into a trance, occasioned by the violence of his pains, and the black blood flows from his wound. Oedipus, covered with blood that drops from the remaining part of his eyes, which he had been just tearing out, complains both of gods and men. We hear the shrieks of Clytemnestra, murdered by her own son; and Electra cries out from the stage: "Strike, spare her not, she did not spare our father." Prometheus is fastened to a rock, by nails driven into his arms and stomach. The furies answer the bloody ghost of Clytemnestra by horrid and inarticulate noises. In short, many of the Greek tragedies are filled with terror of this kind, that is to the last degree extravant. The Greek tragedians, in other respects superior to the English, were certainly wrong in often mistaking horror for terror; and the disgusting and incredible for the tragic and the marvelous. . . . But if the Greeks and you have both passed the bounds of decorum, and the English more particularly abound in the frightful instead of the terrible, we, on the other hand, as overscrupulous as you have been rash, for fear of going too far, stop too short, and very often fail of reaching the tragic, for fear of going beyond it.

I am far from proposing that the stage should be a scene of bloodshed, as it is in Shakespeare, and many of his successors, who, without his genius, have imitated his faults; but I dare believe that there are some certain circumstances and situations, which at present appear shocking and disgusting to a French audience, that, if well conducted, represented with art, and above all softened by the charms of good verse, might give us a species of pleasure we are as yet unacquainted with, which notwithstanding may certainly be attained. . . .

At least I should wish to be informed why our heroes and heroines should be permitted to kill themselves and nobody else. . . .

All these laws of banishing murder from the stage, of not suffering more than three persons to speak, are such as, in my opinion, might admit of some exceptions among us, as they did among the Greeks. It is not with the rules of decorum, that are always a little arbitrary, as it is with the fundamental laws of the theatre, which are the three unities; it would be a mark of weakness and sterility to extend an action beyond that degree of space and time suitable to it. Ask any man, who has crowded too many events into his piece, what is the reason of this fault, and, if he has sincerity enough, he will fairly confess, that he had not sufficient genius to fill up his performance with a single action: and if he takes up two days, and places his scene in two different places, you may take it for granted, it is because he has not skill enough to confine his plan within the limits of three hours, or bring it into the walls of a palace, as probability requires he should. But it is quite another thing with regard to hazarding a horrible spectacle cn the stage; this would not in the least shock probability: a boldness like this, far from implying any weakness in the author, would, on the contrary, demand a great genius to give his verses true grandeur in an action, which, without sublimity of style, would appear savage and disgusting.

This was what our great Corneille once attempted in his *Rodogune*. He brings upon the stage a mother, who, in the presence of an ambassador and the whole court, wants to poison her son and her daughter-in-law, after having killed her other son with her own hand. She presents them the poisoned cup, and on their refusing to taste it, occasioned by their suspicions of her, drinks it herself, and dies by the poison which she had designed for them.

Strokes so terrible as these should be very rare; it is not every one who should dare to strike them. Such novelties require great circumspection, and a masterly hand in the execution. The English themselves allow that Shakespeare, for example, was the only poet who could call up ghosts, and make them speak with success.

Within that circle none durst move but he.

The more majestic and full of terror a theatrical action is, the more insipid would it become if it were often repeated; in the same manner as details of battles, which, being in their own nature everything that is terrible, become dry and tedious, by appearing often in history. The only piece of Racine, where there is any spectacle, is his masterpiece, *Athalie*; there we see a child on the throne, his nurse and the priests attending him, a queen who commands her soldiers to massacre him, and the Levites running to take up arms in his defence: the whole of this action is pathetic; and yet, if the style was not so too, it would appear childish and ridiculous.

The more we strike the eye with splendid appearances, the stronger obligation do we lay ourselves under of supporting them by sublimity of diction; otherwise the writer will only be considered as a decorator, and not as a tragic poet. It is nearly thirty years since the tragedy of *Montezuma* was represented at Paris; the scene opened with a spectacle entirely new: a palace in a magnificent but barbarous taste; Montezuma in a dress very singular and uncommon; at the end of the stage a number of his slaves, armed with bows and arrows according to the custom of their country; round the king were eight grandees of his court prostrate on the earth, with their faces to the ground; Montezuma begins the piece with these words:

Arise; your king permits you on this day
To look on, and to speak to him.

The spectacle charmed the spectators, but nothing else gave the least pleasure throughout the whole tragedy.

With regard to myself I must own, it was not without fear that I introduced on our stage the Roman senate in scarlet robes delivering their opinions. I recollected, that when I brought into my *Oedipe* a chorus of Thebans, saying:

Strike, strike ye gods, O death deliver us,
And we will thank you for the boon.

The paterre, instead of being struck with the pathetic in this passage, only felt the absurdity, if any such there were, of putting these verses into the mouths of raw actors, not much used to choruses, and immediately set up a loud laugh. This prevented me from making the senators in *Brutus* speak, when Titus is accused before them, of heightening the terror of the incident by expressing the astonishment and grief of these reverend fathers of their country, who, no doubt, should have signified their surprise in another manner than by dumb show: but they did not do even so much as this.

The English are more fond of action than we are, and speak more to the eye; the French give more attention to elegance, harmony, and the charms of verse. It is certainly more difficult to write well than to bring upon the stage assassinations, wheels of torture, mechanical powers, ghosts, and sorcerers. The tragedy of *Cato*, which reflects so much honor on Mr. Addison, your successor in the ministry, and which is the only tragedy your country has produced that is well written from start to finish, I have heard you say, owes its great reputation to its fine poetry; that is to say, to just and noble sentiments expressed in harmonious verses. It is these detached beauties that support poetical performances, and hand them down to posterity. It is only a peculiar manner of saying common things; it is the art of embellishing by diction what all men think and feel that constitutes the true poet. . . . M. Racine is superior to all those who have said the same things as himself only because he has said them better: and Corneille is never truly great, except when he expresses himself as well as he thinks. . . .

To exact love in every tragedy shows an effeminate taste; and entirely to proscribe and banish it from the theatre is equally unreasonable and ridiculous. The stage, either in tragedy or comedy, is a lively picture of the human passions: one perhaps represents the ambition of a prince, the other ridicules the vanity of a citizen. Here you laugh at the coquetry and intrigues of a citizen's lady; there you weep at the unhappy passion of Phaedra: love amuses you in a romance, or charms you in the Dido of Virgil. Love in a tragedy is not more essentially a fault than it is in the *Aeneid*. In short, it is never blamable but when it is brought in unseasonably or treated inartistically. . . .

To render love worthy of the tragic scene, it ought to arise naturally from the business of the piece, and not be brought in by mere force, only to fill up a vacancy, as it generally does in your tragedies, and in ours, which are both of them too long: it should be a passion entirely tragical, considered as a weakness, and opposed by remorse; it should either lead to misfortunes or to crimes, to convince us how dangerous it is; or it should be subdued by virtue, to show us that it is not invincible. In all other cases, it is no more than the love of an eclogue, or a comedy.

Letter to Horace Walpole *July 15, 1768*

Quite some time ago I said that if Shakespeare had been born in the age of Addison he would have joined to his genius the elegance and purity which make Addison so commendable. I said, "his genius was his very own and his faults were those of his time." In my opinion, he is precisely like the Spaniard Lope de Vega, and like Calderon. His nature is beautiful but uncivilized; he has neither regularity, decorum, nor art; mixing meanness with grandeur, buffoonery with terror; in his chaotic tragedies are a hundred flashes of light. . . .

You free Britons do not observe the unity of place, or of time, or of action. In truth, by failing to do so you do not improve things; verisimilitude should count for something. Art is the more difficult because of it, and difficulties which are overcome provide pleasure and glory in every genre.

Permit me, sir, even though you are thoroughly English, to take up a little the cause of my country. Since I lecture her with wholesome truths so often, it is only just for me to congratulate her when she is in the right. Yes, sir, I have believed, I do believe, and I will believe that in the composition of tragedy and comedy, Paris is quite superior to Athens. Molière and even Regnard seem to me to surpass Aristophanes as much as Demosthenes surpasses our lawyers. I'll be so bold as to say frankly that in comparison to the sublime scenes of Corneille and the perfect tragedies of Racine all the Greek tragedies seem to me the work of schoolboys. Even Boileau, who admired the ancients as much as he did, felt the same way. He did not think twice of writing at the bottom of a portrait of Racine that this great man had surpassed Euripides and equalled Corneille. . . .

Selections. Translated by Richard Kerr. All rights reserved. Printed by permission of the translator.

Denis Diderot *1713–1784*

Encyclopedia[1] *1755–1780*

Comedy

[2] Comedy is the imitation of manners and morals in terms of action. . . .
The starting point of comedy is the malice natural to all men. When the
shortcomings of our fellow men are not pathetic enough to arouse passion,
revolting enough to create hatred, or dangerous enough to inspire fear, we
regard these shortcomings with a self-satisfaction mixed with contempt. These
images make us smile if they are depicted with delicacy. If the strokes of this
malicious joy, as striking as they are unexpected, are sharpened by surprise,
these images make us laugh. From this propensity to seize hold of the ridiculous, comedy derives its power and its resources. It would undoubtedly be
more beneficial if we could transform this vicious self-satisfaction into a philosophical pity; but it has proved easier and more certain to make human malice
serve to correct the other vices of mankind—much as the sharp edges of the
diamond are used to polish the diamond itself.

This is the goal which comedy sets for itself; and the theatre is for vice
and the ridiculous what the courts of justice and the scaffolds are for crime
—the place where it is judged and the place where it is punished.

[3] Why should we forbid the painter of manners every subject that isn't
laughable? Why would we regard man's likable and reasonable side with less
pleasure than his shortcomings and his ridiculous traits?

It is undoubtedly very useful to expose the follies of man in their true light,
but would it be less useful to offer examples of honest dealings, of noble sentiments, of decent behavior, of all the virtues of social life, so that these examples could touch us, move us, and make a lasting impression on us? And
there is no need to fear that what is beautiful and virtuous is less suited to
giving pleasure than what is ridiculous; on the contrary, we see that Plautus
and Molière are nowhere more successful than when they are serious. Thus,
without taking away anything of value from satiric and mirthful comedy, let
us not close our theatres to comedy which entertains us by more noble pictures, and which instead of making us laugh at the failings of mankind delights
us by the sight of its perfections. . . .

[1] Diderot edited the *Encyclopedia* but did not write all the articles in it. Where the
authors of these selections are known, they will be identified in footnotes.

[2] By Jean-François Marmontel (1723–1799).

[3] By Johann Georg Sulzer (1720–1779).

The comic poet will then undertake a very special study of the divers temperaments of men. He will observe how these temperaments are nonetheless modified by the kind of life, the external relationships, the social obligations, the duties, and the other circumstances. In order to arouse our attention, he will create contrasts among the temperaments, duties, passions, and situations; he will often present to us the conflict between reason and inclination; he will unmask before our eyes the rogue and the hypocrite, and he will show them to us in their true colors; he will put the decent, honest man in the various crucial situations of life, and he will take care to place him in a light which will give us high regard and affection for him. . . .

Comedy is much more suited than tragedy to present instructive scenes. Tragic events are outside the ordinary course of nature, whereas every day instances occur where the successful outcome depends on good sense, on prudence, on moderation, on knowledge of the world, on decent behavior, or on some particular virtue, and where the opposite of these qualities produces disorder and confusion.

Who would want to be the man so bereft of reason—one could say so brutish—as not to want to have before his eyes—in a thousand occasions on which depend his peace of mind, his honor, often the entire happiness of his life—exact and clearly defined models which would indicate to him in a striking fashion what is appropriate for him to do and what he should avoid? It would be in vain for him to want to consult treatises on morality; these works, no matter how excellent they may be, are presented in too general a manner, and the application of their precepts to the particular case which occurs is neither certain nor easy. For all the scenes of human life, only the comic theatre can provide true models of good and evil, of a reasonable way of behaving and a foolish one; besides, the instances are determined there by circumstances so precise that the spectator does not simply learn what he should do, he also learns how he should do it. Comedy does not limit itself to speculative wisdom, it adds practical wisdom, which is the only useful kind in life. . . .

Since according to this notion comedy is nothing but practical philosophy put into action, it is clear that in order to work successfully in this field, the talents of the poet must be accompanied by the range of knowledge of the true moral philosopher. . . .

[4] The misuse of comedy is to make the most serious professions appear ridiculous and to strip important people of that mask of solemnity which protects them from the insolence and malignity of envy. . . . Fops, pretentious bluestockings, and similar useless beings who are nuisances to so-

---

[4] This paragraph appeared in the *Encyclopedia* under the heading "Gravité" (Gravity, Seriousness). Author anonymous.

ciety are comic subjects. But doctors, lawyers, and all those who perform a useful service must be respected. There is nothing objectionable about presenting *Turcaret* on the stage, but there perhaps is about performing *Tartuffe*. . . . True piety loses a great deal because of the ridicule that is cast on hypocritical bigots.[5]

Illusion

[6] In the arts of imitation the truth is nothing, verisimilitude everything, and not only does one not ask them to be real, one does not even want the pretence to be the exact resemblance.

In tragedy it has been very justly observed that the illusion is not complete: (1) it cannot be; (2) it ought not to be.

It cannot be because it is impossible to disregard totally the actual place of the theatrical performance and its attendant inconsistencies. No matter how our imagination may be engaged, our eyes inform us that we are in Paris while the represented scene is in Rome; and the proof that we never lose sight of the actor in the character whom he portrays is that at the moment when we are the most moved, we exclaim: "Oh! How well it's acted!" Thus, we know that it is only acting. . . .

But even if by a perfect likeness it would be possible to create a total illusion, art would avoid it, just as sculpture does by not coloring the marble for fear of making it frightening. There are similar theatrical representations of which moderate illusion is pleasing, but of which total illusion would be revolting or painfully distressing. . . .

But even if in comedy the illusion were complete, the spectator, imagining what he was seeing was nature, would forget the art and would be deprived by the illusion itself of one of the pleasures of theatrical representation. This is common to all the genres.

The pleasure of being moved to pity and fear by the misfortunes of one's fellow men, and the pleasure of laughing at the expense of the failings and ridiculous traits of others are not the only ones which the stage offers us: the pleasure of seeing to what degree of power and truth genius and art can go, the pleasure of admiring in the scene presented the superiority of the depiction over the thing depicted—these would be lost if the illusion were complete. . . . It is the same with all kinds of imitation: at the same time we wish to enjoy both nature and art; we thus wish to be aware that art goes hand in hand with nature.

[5] The refererences are to Alain René Le Sage's comedy *Turcaret* (1709) and to Molière's famous attack on religious hypocrisy [translator's note].

[6] By Marmontel.

Tragedy

[7] Man falls into danger and into misfortune through a cause which is *outside him* or *within him*. *Outside him*, it is his destiny, his situation, his duties, his bonds, all the accidents of life, and the action which the gods, nature, and other men exercise on him. . . . *Within him*, it is his weakness, his imprudence, his inclinations, his passions, his vices, sometimes his virtues; of these causes the most fruitful, the most pathetic, and the most moral is passion combined with natural goodness. . . .

This distinction of the causes of misfortune, either *outside us*, or *within us*, brings about the division into two systems of tragedy, the ancient and the modern. . . . In addition to having the advantage of creating, in a republican commonwealth exposed to the greatest disasters, a body of men ready for anything and determined to do anything, the ancient system of tragedy also had the advantage of making its audiences see that all men were equal in the hands of destiny; that the most highly placed were subject to rashness and error; that the gods made sport of kings; that everything that flattered human pride was fragile and perishable; and that since the greatest calamities and the greatest crimes were reserved for royalty, it was equally insane to aspire to the state of royalty as to endure its existence. This is what it was important to inculcate in a free people. . . .

This mass of chance happenings, from which nothing could be deduced, succeeded in arresting the attention of our ancestors at the renaissance of letters when neither understanding, nor taste, nor even judgment were properly developed. . . .

Finally, once Corneille had discovered, in the middle of this chaos, a new source of tragic actions, as interesting in their causes as dreadful in their effects, it was universally acclaimed; and modern Europe found the form of tragedy which was appropriate to it.

Man with free will under a just God who permits evil without being the cause of it, man at the mercy of his passions, exposed to those of his fellow men, and made miserable by himself or by them, became the object of tragedy and the new spectacle, both pathetic and dreadful, by which it powerfully affected the mind and heart.

The advantages of this new system are that it is more fruitful, more universal, more moral, more adapted to the form and dimensions of our theatres, more suited to all the attractions of performance. . . .

In a commonwealth exposed to great dangers, subject to great revolutions, where each man had to be resolute to risk everything, to endure everything, perhaps this abandonment of oneself to the decrees of destiny was the virtue of the first order, and it was needed to mold the national character; but in

[7] By Marmontel.

a vast and peaceful monarchy where a part of the forces of the nation suffices for its defense, the public good basically requires a moderate set of manners and morals. A form of tragedy which keeps in check the agitations of the heart is thus a political lesson at the same time as a lesson in manners and morals. Hatred, anger, vengeance, ambition, black envy, and above all love spread their devastation in all stations of life, in all the ranks of society. These are the true domestic enemies, and it is most essential that we be made to fear them by the depiction of those misfortunes to which they can lead us, since they have brought to similar misfortunes men often less weak, more prudent, and more virtuous than we; and this is what the Greeks never even thought of. If in ancient tragedy passion is sometimes the cause or instrument of misfortune, this misfortune does not fall on the person carried away by passion, but on some innocent victim. But to keep passion in check within us, it is not a matter of making us see that it is fatal to others, but of making us see that it is fatal to ourselves. . . . Of all the active passions love is the most theatrical, the most interesting, the most fruitful in producing touching scenes, the most useful in showing its dreadful excesses. . . . This pathetic genre is equally adapted to both systems of tragedy; but here a new difference between them lies in the freedom which we have, and which the ancients did not, to place the tragic action in the humble realms of private life. . . .

According to our theory, the aim of tragedy is to correct manners and morals by imitating them, by an action which serves as an example: then, whether or not the victim of passion is famous, whether or not his ruin is dazzling, the lesson is no less general in import. The same cause which spreads desolation in a state can spread it in a family. Love, hate, ambition, jealousy, and vengeance poison the sources of domestic happiness just as they poison those of the public good. . . .

But it is to wrong the human heart and to misjudge nature to believe that nature needs titles to move us. The sacred names of friend, father, lover, spouse, son, mother, brother, sister, in a word man, with interesting manners and morals—these are the touching qualities. What matters the station, name, birth of the unfortunate person who has been drawn into the snares of gambling by his complaisance toward unworthy friends and by the enticement of their example, and who now groans in prison devoured by remorse and by shame? If you ask what he is, I answer you: he was a virtuous man, and to make his sufferings worse, he is a husband and father: his wife whom he loves and by whom he is loved pines away, reduced to extreme indigence, and she can offer only tears when her children ask for bread. In the accounts of heroes, one could hardly find a situation more touching, more moral, in brief more tragic. . . .[8]

---

[8] Marmontel is referring to Edward Moore's domestic tragedy *The Gamester* (1753), which under its French title *Beverley* was much admired by Diderot and his associates as an example of what the new serious genre could accomplish [translator's note].

On Dramatic Poetry 1758

In *The Illegitimate Son* I tried to give the idea of a drama that would occupy a place between Comedy and Tragedy.

The Father of the Family, which I then promised to complete but which was delayed by constant interruptions, occupies a place between the Serious Drama of *The Illegitmate Son* and Comedy.

And if ever I have spare time and the courage to do so, I do not despair of writing a drama which would occupy a place between the Serious Drama and Tragedy.

Whether one recognizes some worth in these works, or whether one regards them as worthless, they will nonetheless demonstrate that the gap which I have noticed between the two established genres is not imaginary.

Here then is the entire range of the dramatic scale: Happy Comedy, whose subject is ridicule and vice, Serious Comedy, whose subject is virtue and the duties of man; that Tragedy whose subject may be our domestic misfortunes, and that Tragedy whose subject is public catastrophes and the misfortunes of the great. . . .

. . . All of the obligations and disadvantages of a particular social class are not equally important. It seems to me that one can dwell on the main ones, make them the basis of one's work, and discard the rest of them. That is what I proposed doing in *The Father of the Family*, whose two major pivots are the terms of the marriage settlement concerning the son and those concerning the daughter. Fortune, birth, education, the duties of fathers toward their children and of children toward their parents, marriage, celebacy, everything that is a consideration of the position of a father of the family has been brought up in my dialogue. May another join the playwriting profession, may he have the talent I lack, and then you will see what a play like this will become!

People's objections to this genre prove only that it is difficult to handle, that a child cannot write it, and that it requires more art, more understanding, more gravity, and more mental power than one who writes for the theatre generally has. . . .

The duties of man are as rich a fund for the dramatic poet as man's follies and vices; and honest and serious plays will succeed everywhere, but more surely will their success be repeated in a more corrupt society. It is by going to the theatre that one runs away from the company of the evil people who surround one; it is on stage that one finds those among whom one would like to live; it is on stage that one sees mankind as it is and there that one is reconciled to it. Good people are rare; but they exist. Whoever thinks otherwise accuses himself and shows how unhappy he is with his wife, with his relatives, with his friends, with his acquaintances. . . .

It is always necessary to have virtue and virtuous people in mind when one writes. . . .

One must accuse the miserable conventions that pervert man and not man's basic nature. Really, what affects us as much as the account of a generous act? Where is the unhappy person who can listen indifferently to the plea of a good man?

The theatre is the only place where the tears of the virtuous man and the evil man are mingled. There, the evil man grows angry at the injustices he might have committed; feels compassion for the bad things he might have caused; and grows indignant toward a man like himself. But the impression is absorbed; it lives within us, in spite of ourselves; and the evil person leaves the theatre less apt to do evil than he would had he been scolded by a severe and tough orator. . . .

Whether you write plays or whether you play them, do not think any more about the spectator than you would if he didn't exist. Imagine on the edge of the stage a large wall that separates you from the audience; write or act the play as if the curtain had not risen. . . .

Let an intelligent author bring into his work characteristics that the spectator may apply to himself—I'll agree to that; let him call attention to current follies, prevailing vices, public events; let him instruct and let him please—but let him do all this without thinking about it. If anyone notices what his purpose is, he will fail to achieve it; he will stop writing dialogue and instead will preach.

Jean-Jacques Rousseau *1712–1778*

Politics and the Arts *1758*

Hence, there is a combination of general and particular causes which keeps the theatre from being given that perfection of which it is thought to be susceptible and from producing the advantageous effects that seem

Selections. From *Politics and the Arts: Letter to M. d'Alembert on the Theatre*, by Jean-Jacques Rousseau, translated by Allan Bloom. Reprinted with permission of The Macmillan Company from *Politics and the Arts* by Rousseau. © The Free Press, A Corporation, 1960.

to be expected from it. Even if this perfection is supposed to be as great as it can be, and the people as well disposed as could be wished, nevertheless these effects would be reduced to nothing for want of means to make them felt. I know of only three instruments with which the morals [manners] of a people can be acted upon: the force of the laws, the empire of opinion, and the appeal of pleasure. Now the laws have no access to the theatre where the least constraint would make it a pain and not an amusement.[1] Opinion does not depend on the theatre, since rather than giving the law to the public, the theatre receives the law from it. And, as to the pleasure that can be had in the theatre, its whole effect is to bring us back more often.

Let us see if there can be other means. The theatre, I am told, directed as it can and ought to be, makes virtue lovable and vice odious. What? Before there were dramas, were not virtuous men loved, were not the vicious hated, and are these sentiments feebler in the places that lack a theatre? The theatre makes virtue lovable . . . It accomplishes a great miracle in doing what nature and reason do before it! The vicious are hated on the stage. . . . Are they loved in society when they are known to be such? Is it quite certain that this hate is the work of the author rather than of the crimes that he makes the vicious commit? Is it quite certain that the simple account of these crimes would produce less horror in us than all the colors with which he has painted them? If his whole art consists in producing malefactors for us in order to render them hateful, I am unable to see what is so admirable in this art, and we get, in this regard, only too many lessons without need of this one. Dare I add a suspicion which comes to me? I suspect that any man, to whom the crimes of Phaedra or Medea were told beforehand, would hate them more at the beginning of the play than at the end. And if this suspicion is well founded, then what are we to think of this much-vaunted effect of the theatre?

I should like to be clearly shown, without wasting words, how it could produce sentiments in us that we did not have and could cause us to judge moral beings otherwise than we judge them by ourselves? How puerile and senseless are these vain pretensions when examined closely! If the beauty of virtue were the product of art, virtue would have long since been disfigured! As for me, even if I am again to be regarded as wicked for daring to assert that man is born good, I think it and believe that I have proved it. The source of the concern which attaches us to what is decent and which inspires us with

---

[1] The laws can detemine the subjects of the plays, and their form, and the way to play them; but the laws cannot force the public to enjoy them. The emperor Nero sang at the theatre and had all those who fell asleep put to death; still he could not keep everybody awake. And the pleasure of a short nap came close to causing Vespasian his life. Noble Actors of the Paris Opera, if you had enjoyed the imperial power, I should not now complain about having lived too long [Rousseau's note].

aversion for evil is in us and not in the plays. There is no art for producing this concern, but only for taking advantage of it. The love of the beautiful[2] is a sentiment as natural to the human heart as the love of self; it is not born out of an arrangement of scenes; the author does not bring it; he finds it there; and out of this pure sentiment, to which he appeals, are born the sweet tears that he causes to flow.

Imagine a play as perfect as you like. Where is the man who, going for the first time, does not go already convinced of what is to be proved in it and already predisposed toward those whom he is meant to like? But this is not the question; what is important is to act consistently with one's principles and to imitate the people whom one esteems. The heart of man is always right concerning that which has no personal relation to himself. In the quarrels at which we are purely spectators, we immediately take the side of justice, and there is no act of viciousness which does not give us a lively sentiment of indignation so long as we receive no profit from it. But when our interest is involved, our sentiments are soon corrupted. And it is only then that we prefer the evil which is useful to us to the good that nature makes us love. Is it not a necessary effect of the constitution of things that the vicious man profits doubly, from his injustice and the probity of others? What more advantageous treaty could he conclude than one obliging the whole world, excepting himself, to be just, so that everyone will faithfully render unto him what is due him, while he renders to no one what he owes? He loves virtue, unquestionably; but he loves it in others because he hopes to profit from it. He wants none of it for himself because it would be costly to him. What then does he go to see at the theatre? Precisely what he wants to find everywhere: lessons of virtue for the public, from which he excepts himself, and people sacrificing everything to their duty while nothing is exacted from him.

I hear it said that tragedy leads to pity through fear. So it does; but what is this pity? A fleeting and vain emotion which lasts no longer than the illusion which produced it; a vestige of natural sentiment soon stifled by the passions; a sterile pity which feeds on a few tears and which has never produced the slightest act of humanity. . . .

In the final accounting, when a man has gone to admire fine actions in stories and to cry for imaginary miseries, what more can be asked of him? Is he not satisfied with himself? Does he not applaud his fine soul? Has he not acquitted himself of all that he owes to virtue by the homage which he

---

[2] We have to do with the morally beautiful here. Whatever the philosophers may say of it, this love is innate to man and serves as principle to his conscience. (I can cite as an example of this the little play *Nanine*, which has caused the audience to grumble and is only protected by the great reputation of its author. All this is only because honor, virtue, and the pure sentiments of nature are preferred in it to the impertinent prejudice of social station.) [Rousseau's note; the play is by Voltaire].

has just rendered it? What more could one want of him? That he practice it himself? He has no role to play; he is no actor. . . .

. . . The theatre has rules, principles, and a morality apart, just as it has a language and a style of dress that is its own. We say to ourselves that none of this is suitable for us, and that we should think ourselves as ridiculous to adopt the virtues of its heroes as it would be to speak in verse or to put on Roman clothing. This is pretty nearly the use of all these great sentiments and of all these brilliant maxims that are vaunted with so much emphasis—to relegate them forever to the stage, and to present virtue to us as a theatrical game, good for amusing the public but which it would be folly seriously to attempt introducing into society. Thus the most advantageous impression of the best tragedies is to reduce all the duties of man to some passing and sterile emotions that have no consequences, to make us applaud our courage in praising that of others, our humanity in pitying the ills that we could have cured, our charity in saying to the poor, God will help you!

To be sure, a simpler style can be adopted on the stage, and the tone of the theatre can be reconciled in the drama with that of the world. But in this way, morals [manners] are not corrected; they are depicted, and an ugly face does not appear ugly to him who wears it. If we wish to correct them by caricaturing them, we leave the realm of probability and nature, and the picture no longer produces an effect. Caricature does not render objects hateful; it only renders them ridiculous. And out of this arises a very great difficulty; afraid of being ridiculous, men are no longer afraid of being vicious. The former cannot be remedied without promoting the latter. Why, you will ask, must I suppose this to be a necessary opposition? Why, Sir? Because the good do not make evil men objects of derision, but crush them with their contempt, and nothing is less funny or laughable than virtue's indignation. Ridicule, on the other hand, is the favorite arm of vice. With it, the respect that the heart owes to virtue is attacked at its root, and the love that is felt for it is finally extinguished.

Thus everything compels us to abandon this vain idea that some wish to give us of the perfection of a form of theatre directed toward public utility. . . .

I will be told that in these plays crime is always punished and virtue always rewarded. I answer that, even if this were so, most tragic actions are only pure fables, events known to be inventions of the poet, and so do not make a strong impression on the audience; as a result of showing them that we want to instruct them, we no longer instruct them. I answer, moreover, that these punishments and rewards are always effected by such extraordinary means that nothing similar is expected in the natural course of human things. Finally, I answer by denying the fact. It is not, nor can it be, generally true. For, since this end is not the one toward which authors direct their plays, they are likely to attain it rarely; and often it would be an obstacle to success. Vice or virtue?—what is the difference, provided that the public is overawed by an impression of greatness?

Beaumarchais (Pierre Augustin Caron) *1732–1799*

An Essay on Serious Drama *1767*

I do not merit the name of author. I have lacked both the time and talent to become one; but about eight years ago I amused myself by jotting down on paper some ideas about Serious Drama, that intermediate form between heroic Tragedy and pleasant Comedy. I might have tried my hand at any of the several genres of literature but I gave this one preference, perhaps because it was the least important one. I have always been too busy with serious occupations to look to literature for anything more than honest relaxation. *Neque semper arcum tendit Apollo.*[1] I liked the subject; it engaged me; but I soon learned I was wrong to wish to use reasonable persuasions in a genre where only sentiment prevails. I soon wished passionately to be able to substitute examples for precepts. When it is successful, an example is an infallible way to proselytize but the unfortunate man who fails is exposed to the double sorrow of missing his aim and being burdened with the shame of having presumed on his skills.

I was too excited to be capable of the latter thought, and so I composed [*Eugenie,*] the drama I present today. . . .

Shortly thereafter, Diderot presented his *The Father of the Family.* This poet's genius, the strength of his style, the virile and vigorous tone of his work made me drop the pencil from my hand. But the path he had just created held so many charms for me that I reflected less on my inadequacies than on my taste. I returned to my play with a renewed eagerness. I polished it one final time and then delivered it to the actors. Thus, the

Selections. Translated by Thomas B. Markus. Copyright 1974 by Thomas B. Markus.

[1] And Apollo does not always stretch the bow.

child who is made stubborn by a man's success sometimes reaches the fruits he has desired. He is happy while tasting them, so long as he does not find them filled with bitterness! Here is the history of my play. . . .

I have seen people grow truly angry when they found that Serious Drama attracted supporters. "An equivocal genre," they said, "we don't know what it is. What kind of a play is it in which nothing makes us laugh? in which for five deadly acts of dawdling prose—without comic relief, maxims, or characters—we are kept suspended by the thread of an imaginary incident which has no more probability than reality? Does not the toleration of such work open the door to licentiousness and encourage laziness? The easiness of writing prose will discourage our young authors from the difficult work of writing verse, and our theatre will quickly fall back into the state of barbarity from which our poets took such pains to raise it. Some of these plays have touched us (we don't know how) but it would be frightful if such a genre became popular; additionally, it would do a disservice to our nation, as it is widely known what the authoritative voices of our famous authors think of it. They have proscribed it as a genre equally disclaimed by Melpomene and Thalia.[2] Shall we have to create a new muse to preside over this vulgar cothurnus, this graceless comedy? Tragicomedy, Bourgeois Tragedy, Lachrymose Comedy—what are we to name these monstrosities? And let not some vain author take pride in the momentary applause of the public's justified reward for the actors' work and talent! The Public! What is the Public? When this collective identity begins to dissolve, when its dismembered parts are scattered, what remains as a foundation for general opinion except that of the individual? And among these individuals the most enlightened have a natural influence upon the others and will eventually bring them back to share their private opinions. Thus, it is clear that we must rely on the judgment of the few and not on that of the Public."

Enough! Let us dare to answer this stream of objections which I have quoted, taking care neither to weaken or disguise them. Let us start by defending our judge's rights, and disposing him to be favorable to us. In spite of what critics say, the Public is the only judge of works designed to entertain it; and all come before this judge as equals. To want to stop the efforts of genius from creating a new kind of theatre (to add to those kinds that are already known) is a criminal assault against his rights, an outrage against his pleasures. I agree that a difficult truth will be more swiftly recognized, better understood, and more sanely judged by a small number of enlightened people than by the roaring multitude, since otherwise this truth would not be called difficult; but the matters of taste, of feelings, of pure effect, in one word of theatre, would never be acknowl-

[2] Muses of Tragedy and Comedy, respectively.

edged but for the powerful and sudden feelings which they produced in all spectators. Must all be judged by the same rules? Since this theatre aims less at questions of discussion and philosophy than of feeling, of being amused or touched, is it not hazardous to assert that the judgment of the responsive Public is wrong or unsuitable as to pretend that the kind of play by which an entire nation could be very deeply moved, and which is generally pleasing, would not be of a suitable stature for this nation? What weight will certain authors' satires on Serious Drama have against the opinion of the Public, especially when their remarks slander quite charming plays of this very kind which they themselves have written? In addition to the fact that one ought to be consistent, this light and playful weapon called sarcasm has never decided any dispute; it is barely able to begin one. That is why it is the weapon most sanctioned by those cowardly antagonists who, hiding behind shields of Authority, refuse to confront the champions of Reason on an open field. Their position is still preferred by society's "Gifted Spirits," who only glance over what they are to judge and who are like light advance troops or literature's lost children. But now, as the result of an odd reversal, stern people are making jokes while worldly people dispute. I hear wordy arguments everywhere, and set against Serious Drama are Aristotle, the ancients, the poets, the purpose of theatre, the Rules (especially the Rules, those eternal clichés of critics, that scarecrow for the simple minded). In what genre have masterpieces ever been produced according to Rules? On the contrary, have not the examples of great plays always been the basis and the foundation for these same Rules, which now are placed in opposition to genius by those who reverse the order of things? Would advancements in the Arts and Sciences ever have been made if men had servilely respected the boundaries prescribed by their predecessors? The new world would still be unknown to us if the bold Genoese sailor—as arrogant as he was proud—had not trod upon the *ne plus ultra* of the Alcides columns.[3] The genius is always curious and impatient, always cramped for room in the circle of acquired knowledge. He suspects there is more to be known than everyone accepts; he is excited by the feeling which presses within him; and so he worries, strives, expands, and at last, breaking the constraints of prejudice, he darts forth beyond known boundaries. Sometimes he only wanders, but he is the only one who carries, far ahead into the night of the possible, the signal-light all hasten to follow. He takes a giant stride and Art is extended—Let us stop. This is not a question to be discussed heatedly, but one to be considered calmly. Let us reduce to simple terms a question which has never been well posed. In taking it before the Tribunal of Reason, here is how I should express it:

[3] The pillars of Hercules (now Gibralter and Ceuta), a memorial of his journey. Treading upon the notion that there was "nothing more than these" or nothing beyond them, Columbus went farther and discovered America.

Is it permissible in the theatre to try to interest an audience and to cause it to shed tears over an event which would never fail to produce those same tears if it were a real-life event and took place before their very eyes? For such is the honest aim of Serious Drama. . . .

The essence of Serious Drama is to offer (all things being equal) a more immediate interest and a more direct moral lesson than heroic Tragedy and a deeper meaning than pleasant Comedy.

I already hear a thousand voices rise and shout against this impious idea, but before it is pronounced an anathema, I ask in all grace to be heard through. These ideas are too new not to be developed.

While watching a tragedy of the ancients, I am seized by an involuntary indignation against their cruel gods when I witness the torments which they permit an innocent victim to suffer. Oedipus, Jocasta, Phaedra, Ariadne, Philoctetes, Orestes, and so many others inspire more terror in me than interest. I am terrified more than moved by the fate of these devoted and passive characters, these blind instruments of the angry and whimsical gods. Everything in these plays is enormous. The passions are always frenzied; the crimes are atrocities, as far removed from nature as they are alien to today's mores. In these plays, one walks only among debris, through streams of blood, past heaps of corpses, and finally reaches the catastrophe only by way of poisoning, murder, incest, and parricide. Tears produced by these plays are painful, rare, and burning; they well up behind the eyes a long time before they fall. Incredible efforts are required to tear them from us, and the genius of a sublime author is barely sufficient for the task.

Moreover, the inevitable blows of fate do not offer the mind any moral lesson. When one can only shudder and be silent, is not the act of reflection the worst thing one might do? If a morality were extracted from this genre of play, it would be a dreadful one which might lead many souls toward crime, since its fatalistic vision would provide them with a justification; it would discourage many from following the ways of virtue, and all such efforts, according to this system, would be for naught. If there is no virtue without sacrifice, so too there is no sacrifice without hope of reward. Any belief in fatalism degrades man by depriving him of the freedom without which his actions reveal no sense of morality to him.

On the other hand, let us examine the type of interest which is exciting to us in the actions of the heroes and kings of heroic Tragedy, and we shall perhaps admit that these important events, these fatuous characters, are only traps set for our vanity which makes us wish to be initiated into the secrets of an elegant court, to be a party to consultations which might change the face of a state, to enter the forbidden throne room of a queen. We like to imagine ourselves as the confidants of an unhappy prince, because his sorrows, his tears, his weaknesses seem to reconcile his condition with ours, to console us for his apparent superiority. Without noticing it, each of us tries to enlarge his sphere, and our pride nourishes itself on the pleasures we get at the theatre by judging these Masters of the World who elsewhere would spurn us. Men are more dupes of themselves than they think; the wisest is often motivated by incentives which would make him blush if he knew them. But if our heart gains something from the identification we find with the characters of a tragedy, it is less because they are heroes and kings than because they are men and unfortunate. Is it the Queen of Messina who moves me in *Merope*?[4] It is the mother of Aegisthus. Only nature has rights upon our hearts.

If the theatre is a faithful reflection of the world's happenings, the interest it excites in us must necessarily have some relation to our way of seeing real objects. Now, I see that often a great prince—at the peak of his fortunes, covered with glory, and shining with success—stirs us only to that sterile sentiment Admiration—a foreigner to our heart. We probably never sense how much we like him until he falls into disgrace; this stirring enthusiasm of the people, the eulogy and reward of good kings, does not touch him until he sees them unhappy and about to lose him. Then his compassion for the suffering man is a sentiment so true and so profound that it can be said he should be acquitted from responsibility for all the good deeds of the happy monarch. The true interest of the heart, the true relation, is therefore always between Man and Man and not between Man and King. And thus, exalted rank, far from increasing my interest in tragic characters, diminishes it. The closer the suffering man is to my station in life, the more I take his misfortune to my heart. "Should we not wish," asks Rousseau, "that our sublime authors might deign to come down occassionally from their incessant elevation and move us with the sufferings of humanity, for fear that—having had pity for unhappy heroes only—we might never feel pity for a common man?"

What do the revolutions of Athens and Rome mean to me, the quiet subject of an eighteenth-century monarchy? What interest can I possibly take in the death of a Peloponnesian tyrant? in the sacrifice of a young princess in Aulis? In all this, there is nothing for me to learn, no moral lesson which applies to me. For what is morality? It is the fruitful result of the personal application of thoughts which are torn out of us by a specific experience. What is interest? It is the involuntary feeling by which we adapt the experience to ourselves, the sympathy which puts us in the place of the sufferer, in the very midst of his situation. . . . Thus, heroic Tragedy touches us only to the degree that it approaches Serious Drama in portraying men and not kings. When the subject set in action is far from our life and the characters foreign to our civil state, then our interest becomes less intense than it does for Serious Drama, and is usually lost upon us—unless it

[4] Voltaire (1736).

serves to console us for our mediocrity by showing us that great crimes and great misfortunes are the standard lot for those who are involved with governing the world.

After rereading this last argument, I do not believe I need to prove that there is more interest in Serious Drama than in Comedy. Everyone accepts that, in plays of equal merit, stirring subjects affect us more than pleasing ones. It should be sufficient for me to explain the causes of this effect, which is as constant as it is natural, and to examine the moral object by comparing the two genres.

Gaiety entertains us; in a unique way it draws our souls out of us and spreads them before us: we only laugh well when we're in the company of others. But if the bright display of ridicule entertains the spirit for a moment during a play, experience teaches us that a gibe which never touches our hearts may excite us to laughter, but will certainly fail to amuse its victim. Pride makes us careful to remove ourselves from vulnerability, and as we are reprieved by the outbursts of the crowd, we take advantage of the general tumult to separate ourselves from everything that could tie us to the epigram. Up till now the harm has not been too great since the public has only laughed at pedants, fops, coquettes, eccentrics, imbeciles, grotesques, in a word the butts of society's ridicule. But is the mockery which punishes them the weapon with which to attack vice? Does the playwright believe he can conquer through jokes? Not only would he miss his target, he would accomplish the exact opposite of what he proposed! We see this happen in most comedies. To morality's shame, the audience too often finds itself interested in the rascal rather than the honest man, since the latter is less engaging. But even if the mirth of a scene can sweep me up for a moment, I soon become humiliated at having let myself fall for the jokes and theatrical tricks, and I draw back, unhappy with the author, with the play, and with myself. The morality of Comedy is therefore shallow, or worthless, or even the inverse of what the theatre must present.

Such is not the effect of a touching drama, drawn from life. If noisy laughter is the enemy of thought, sympathy is silent. It collects our thoughts; it isolates us from everything. Whoever cries at a performance is alone; the more he feels alone, the more he delights in his tears, especially in the honest plays of Serious Drama which isolate the heart through such true and natural means. Often, in the midst of a pleasant scene, a charming emotion leads us to copious and easy tears, which then blend with the traces of a smile to paint the face with sympathy and joy. Is such a touching conflict not the most beautiful triumph of art and the sweetest state for the sensitive soul which feels it?

Furthermore, sympathy has a moral advantage over laughter: it is not dependent on any other object, which might concurrently produce a powerful counteremotion.

The painting of an honest man's unhappiness knocks at the door to our heart, opens it gently, takes possession of it, and soon obliges it to examine itself. When I see virtue persecuted—a victim of wickedness, but still beautiful, glorious, and admirable above all else even at the depth of misfortune —the effect of drama is not ambiguous. It is virtue alone which interests me; and if I am not happy, if vile envy strives to sully me, if it attacks my own person, my honor or my wealth, how much I enjoy this kind of play! And what a nice moral lesson I draw from it! Naturally, I am interested in the subject only as I am interested in the unfortunate person who suffers unjustly; I consider that if by frivolity of character, error of behavior, excessive ambition, or dishonest connivance, I have attracted the hatred of those who persecute me, then my conclusion is surely to try to correct myself. I leave the play better than I entered it, only because I have been touched by it.

If the offense I have suffered is glaring and arises more from another's action than from my own, the morality of a sympathetic drama will be even sweeter for me; I shall reach down into my heart with pleasure, and there, if I have fulfilled all my duties toward society (if I am a good father, a fair master, a concerned friend, an equitable man, and a useful citizen)— the internal feeling consoling me from the unwarranted offense—I shall cherish the play which will have reminded me of the reward I get from the practice of virtue, that greatest gentleness to which a wise man can pretend, the one to make a man satisfied with himself. I shall delight once again in crying before the portrait of innocence or of the persecution of virtue. . . .

Serious Drama admits only a simple style, without flourishes or ornamentation; it must draw its beauty from the essence, texture, interest, and development of its subject. The embellishments and plumage of Tragedy and the cap and bells of Comedy are as absolutely forbidden to it as they are to nature itself: no maxims unless they are essential to the action. Its characters must always have an appearance which makes them so interesting that they hardly need to speak. Its real eloquence is that of situation and the only coloration which is allowed is the bright, fast, vital, and real language of passions—removed from that compass of caesura and the affectation of rhyme, which can never be obscured if the poet's drama is in verse. In order that Serious Drama might have all the truth that we have the right to require of it, the first aim of the author must be to carry me far from the backstage world and to make it impossible for me to remember the banter of actors and the machinery of the theatre even once during the performance. Now, is not the first effect of rhymed conversation, which has convention as its only virtue, to bring me back into the theatre and consequently to destroy any illusion which might have been established? It is in the salon of Vanderk that I completely lose sight of Préville and

Brizard and see only the good Antoine and his excellent master,[5] and in which I am truly moved by them. Do you believe this would happen to me in the same way if they spoke verse? Not only would I find the actors in the characters but, and this is worse, I would find, through each rhyme, the poet in the actors. So, all the truth which is so precious to this play would disappear. And this Antoine—whom I find to be so true, so sympathetic—would seem to me as sulky and clumsy with his borrowed language as a naïve peasant badly disguised in a wealthy livery. Therefore I hold, along with Diderot, that Serious Drama must be written in prose. I hold that it must not be burdened with trimmings and that elegance must always be sacrificed to energy—whenever we must choose between them.

My work will be quite successful if I succeed in convincing my readers that Serious Drama exists, that it is good, that it offers a very keen interest, a direct and profound morality, that this genre can use only the one language found in nature, and that in addition to the merits common to other genres, Serious Drama has a great beauty of its own. Serious Drama is a new path where genius can take an extended flight because it encompasses every station of life and all the situations of each station. Once again the great comic characters who have been almost exhausted through overuse can be introduced. Through the creation of Serious Drama, society has been provided with an abundant source of pleasures and moral lessons.

Preface to
The Marriage of Figaro 1784

... When I staged *Eugenie* ... all our self-righteous spokesmen for decency flamed up in the foyer, for I had dared to show a libertine lord disguising his valets as priests and pretending to marry a young woman who appeared pregnant on the stage, although she had not been married previously.

In spite of their shouts, the play was judged if not the finest then at least

Selections. Translated by Thomas B. Markus. Copyright 1974 by Thomas B. Markus.

[5] In *The Philosopher in Spite of Himself* (1765) by Michel Jean Sedaine (1719–1797).

the most moral of dramas, and it has been played repeatedly on every stage and has been translated into every language. Intelligent audiences saw that the morality of the play, its interest, arose entirely from a powerful and vicious man's misuse of his name and influence in order to torment a weak, helpless, abused, virtuous, and forsaken girl. And thus everything in the play that is good or useful was born of the author's courage, for he dared to carry social inequity to the highest degree of freedom.

Later I wrote *The Two Comrades,* a play in which a father confesses to his supposed niece that she is his illegitimate daughter. This too is a very moral play. The author takes pains to show, by presenting the sacrifices made of a perfect friendship, that the duties demanded by nature of the offspring of such an affair frequently cause these children to be abandoned—the result of the rigors of social conventions, or more accurately of their abuse.

Among other criticisms of the play, I heard a young "gallant" of the Court delight the ladies in the box next to mine by saying "the author, doubtless, is a rag picker who has seen nothing more elevated than farmhands and dry-goods merchants; and it is in the rear of such merchants' shops that he finds these noble friends he brings to the French stage." "Alas, sir," I said, presenting myself, "they must at least have been drawn from some place one might imagine finding them. The author would make you laugh even harder if he had drawn these two friends from the antechambers of Versailles or the coaches of elite society. There must remain a little verisimilitude, even for virtuous stories."

Giving myself up to my happier temper, I next attempted, with *The Barber of Seville,* to restore to the theatre an old-fashioned but vital gaiety, combining it with the frivolous tone of our present humor; but as even this was a kind of innovation, the play was sharply attacked. It seemed I had shaken the State; the excessive cautions which were taken and the loud protests which were made against me revealed the fear that certain vicious persons had when they saw themselves unmasked. The play was censored four times, canceled at the moment of performance three times, and even denounced in Parliament. Shocked by this tumult, I persisted in demanding that the public be the judge of what I had destined for the public's entertainment.

Three years later I got satisfaction. After the riots, the eulogies. Everyone whispered to me: write more plays like this one, because you're the only one who dares to laugh freely.

An author who is grieved by the shouting and the cabal, but who sees his play succeed at last, regains heart; and so did I. The late Prince of Conti, of patriotic memory (even now, when his name rings in the air that antique word *Fatherland* vibrates in echo), gave me the public's challenge—to put the family of Figaro from my Preface to *The Barber of Seville* into theatrical form and to present in a play what had in the Preface been only a description.

"My lord," I answered him, "if I presented this character on the stage a second time, since I would need to show him older and wiser, there would surely be another commotion, and who knows if the play would ever be presented?" However, I dutifully accepted the challenge and respectfully composed *The Marriage of Figaro*, which causes such uproar today. The Prince deigned to be the first to see it. He was a man of great spirit, an august Prince, a noble and proud thinker: shall I say it? He enjoyed it. . . .

Nevertheless, *The Marriage of Figaro* stayed in my portfolio for five years. The actors knew I had it and finally they wrenched it from me. Whether they acted rightly or wrongly for themselves has been seen since; whether they felt they needed new works of comedy to please the public, no matter. Never before had so difficult a play been performed with such ensemble effort; and if the author (as has been claimed) did not achieve his highest standards, there is no actor whose reputation has not been established, increased, or confirmed by this work. But let us return to its reading and adoption by the actors.

Because of the extreme praise they gave it, every producing Society wanted to see it. From that time on I had either to engage in endless disputes or to give it up to all requests. From that time, also, the author's great enemies began to rumor at Court that the play—"no more than a foolish trifle"—attacked Religion, Government, all classes of society, good manners, and above all it was rumored that virtue was debased in it and vice made triumphant. "What else would you expect?" they added. If these earnest gentlemen who repeated these thoughts so often will honor me by reading this preface, they will discover that I have quoted them accurately, at least, and that the bourgeois integrity my quotations reflect merely points up the noble infidelity of theirs.

Therefore, if *The Barber of Seville* shook the State, this far more infamous and seditious new work turned it upside down. If this work were allowed, nothing would remain sacred! The author was abused by the most insidious reports; powerful groups plotted; timorous ladies grew alarmed; I made enemies on the very prayer-stools of chapels. But I offset these base intrigues, whenever men and circumstances permitted, with my extreme patience, my firmness of respect, my docile obstinacy, and, when anyone would hear it, by Reason.

This fight continued for four years. Add these to the five years before the play was first given and what remains of the allusions one strives to see in the work? Alas! When it was written the circumstances of today's world had not yet been imagined. It was another world then.

During the four years of debate I asked for only one censor; I was awarded five or six. And what did they see in this work which had become the object of such invective? The most playful of plots. An important Spanish lord is in love with a girl he wants to seduce—and the efforts of this maiden, the man she loves, and the lord's wife combine to thwart the intention of this absolute tyrant whose class, wealth, and prodigality make him all-powerful. That's all; nothing more. The play is before you.

Then why all these shrill complaints? Because instead of exposing only one vicious character (as the Gambler, the Opportunist, the Miser, or the Hypocrite), which would have brought only one group of enemies down upon me, I took advantage of a frivolous composition, or rather arranged my plot so as to include in it the criticism of many abuses which society suffers. But since this does not debase a work in the eyes of any enlightened censor, all approved it, and returned it to the theatre. The theatre was then obliged to endure it and finally the Greats of this World were scandalized to behold

This play where an insolent valet is portrayed
Shamelessly protecting his wife from his master.
                    M. Gudin

Oh how I regret not having written a truly gory tragedy on this moral subject! I should have placed a dagger in the hand of the outraged husband (who should never have been named Figaro) and in his jealous passion I would have had him stab his mighty but corrupt antagonist; and he would have defended his honor with perfectly rounded verses and pompous phrases. My jealous hero, himself at least a General of the Armies, would have as a distinguished rival some fearful and villainous tyrant who reigned cruelly over a downtrodden people. All of this—since it is totally removed from our habits and our morals—would, I suppose, have hurt no one. "Bravo!" they would have cried, "a truly moral work!" We escaped, me and my *savage* Figaro.

But wanting only to entertain the public and not to make our French wives' eyes stream with tears, I made my guilty lover a young nobleman: prodigal, courteous enough, but a bit of a libertine—looking like most of the other lords of his time. But what could one dare to say about one nobleman in the theatre which would not offend them all, unless it were to reproach him for his excessive gallantry? Is not that their least denied fault? I see many, even now, blushing modestly (and it is a noble effort) as they admit I am right.

As I wanted to make my nobleman guilty, I had, out of generous respect, to give him no vice common to the people. You would have said that this was impossible? That to do so would be to destroy verisimilitude? Then judge in support of my play, because that, at least, I did not do.

Thus my play—which might have been a harsh struggle opposing the abuse of power, the forgetfulness of principles, prodigality, opportunity (and everything that makes seduction attractive) to the fire and resourcefulness which the socially inferior can use to oppose the attack when they become excited by the challenge—is a pleasant game of intrigues in which a crafty husband is vexed, wearied, harassed, and always stopped from achieving his goals, and is obliged three times in the same day to kneel before his wife, who is kind, indulgent, and sensitive, and who concludes always by forgiving him. Isn't that what such women always do? What is exceptional about such morality, I ask you Gentlemen?

Do you find this morality a little frivolous for the serious treatment I have given it? Your eyes might be even more offended by an even more severe moral which is in the work, though you have not seen it. Here it is: a nobleman who is vicious enough to make all his vassals contribute to his capricious wish to seduce every young maiden in his land finally becomes the laughing stock of his valets. . . .

When Figaro takes liberties with his master, why does he delight me instead of shocking me? It is because he is clearly different from other valets. He is not, and you know it well, the villain of the play. We see that his situation obliges him to repulse the insults with wit, and we forgive him everything because we know he only outwits his master in order to protect his love and to defend his proper rights.

Therefore, except for the Count and his agents, everyone in the play behaves as he should. . . .

Guilty of a moral lapse years before—of which Figaro is the issue—some would say that she (Marceline) ought to suffer at least the embarrassment of her shame when she recognizes her son. The author ought to have drawn an important moral from the situation. That is, as a corrective lesson, a seduced girl's sin should be shown to be the responsibility of the man's action and not only her own. Why didn't he do that?

He did, reasonable censor! Study the following scene, which is the core of the third act, but which the actors asked me to shorten for fear that such a somber moment might dim the merriment of the action.

When Molière finally humiliates the coquette, the tease, in *The Misanthrope*, through the public reading of her letters to her several lovers, he leaves her flayed under the lashes he has given her. He is right; what else should he do with her? She is vicious by taste and by choice, a hardened widow, a courtesan without any excuse for her behavior, and the plague of a fully honest man. He abandons her to our contempt. That is the moral of the play. As for me, using Marceline's credulous confession at the moment of recognition, I have shown this humiliated woman, Bartholo who has rejected her, and Figaro, their common son, so as to guide the public's attention to the true creators of that sin to which all common girls who have nice faces are mercilessly drawn.

Sebastien Mercier *1740–1814*

On the Theatre *1773*

Introduction

The Theatre is a lie; the thing to do is to bring it as close as possible to the greatest truthfulness. The Theatre is a painting; the thing to do is to make this painting useful, that is to say, to make it accessible to the greatest possible number of people, so that the picture which it presents will serve to link men together through the triumphant feeling of compassion and pity. It is therefore not enough that the soul be engrossed, or even moved; it is essential that it be incited to righteousness; it is essential that the moral purpose, without being either hidden or too explicit, gain possession of the heart and hold on to it with complete authority. . . .

(I)

On the Goal Which
the Art of the Drama
Ought to Set Itself

The effect of the Theatre resides in impressions, not in lessons. Step aside, cold moralist, take away your thick book. What is the sense of stringing together your dry maxims when an eloquent painting could deck out the picture in all its colors! . . .

It would be possible to judge the soul of each man by the degree of emotion which he shows in the theatre; if his face remains indifferent, if his eye is not moist, when the Father of the Family[1] says to his son, "Where are you going, wretched boy?" and if the flames of indignation don't sear his heart, when Narcisse brings about the final stage in Nero's corruption,[2] he is a wicked person, without any doubt; he can escape such an appellation only by confessing to his complete idiocy.

(V)

On Comedy

Now there are certain people who say: "Entertain us, we want to laugh; it is absolutely essential that you be amusing. Can a Comedy be composed in

Translated by Daniel C. Gerould. Copyright 1974 by Daniel C. Gerould. Printed by permission of the translator.

[1] Diderot's play *The Father of the Family* (1758).
[2] Racine's tragedy *Britannicus* (1669).

any other way? Come now, Mr. Author, be gay and lively: we want to laugh; do you hear, imitate Molière." Gladly, gentleman, I like to laugh as much as you: but the wise laugh is seen, and not heard, as Solomon says. Only extravagant characters and temperaments produce laughter. There is a delicate smile which is not loud, and which is worth more than the laughs that you want me to give you. . . . Immoderate laughter indicates only extravagance of the soul, pushed beyond the limits of reason. . . . Mechanical laughter does not speak to the soul, as is the case with this sweet smile which acclaims what is respectable, noble, and touching. . . .

In Molière the actor is often the only one who laughs. . . . Those people who want to laugh ask you—with a sad look and in a sepulchral tone—for comedies like those Molière wrote; but if Molière himself were to come back, he wouldn't make them laugh. Their Molière is played every Friday, enriched by the best actors, and no one goes to the theatre to see him. If Molière returned to the world in 1773, he certainly wouldn't have the same gaiety; he wouldn't be able to laugh in the midst of a country which no longer has any occasion for laughing. The two muscles in the mouth, which are called the zygomatic muscles, still flexible in his time, have now become paralyzed in all Frenchmen; they have become serious, and we know why Molière if he came back today would unquestionably be a better Misanthrope. . . .[3]

Mixed feelings are the most agreeable of all; they bring the soul a new feeling which is more delightful. Therefore, we must turn over to farce the tumultuous laughs which are appropriate to the populace. . . .

Only a buffoon can't see that *laughter and tears*, those two emotions of the soul, have in reality the same origin, that they are not separated from one another, that they blend together, that one is not an absolute sign of joy, nor the other an absolute sign of sorrow; that twenty people are differently affected by the same thing, and that there is a bitter laugh that is painful, as there are tears that are delightful. Therefore, let's no longer say: "I want to make the audience laugh in this play, I want to make them cry in that one"; let's give an exact, lively, faithful portrayal and leave to the audience the responsibility of how they respond to it. . . .

I notice that in those plays that are called plays of *character*, the dominating figure is always distorted so as to bring out this principal character or temperament; I notice that all the others are subordinated to him, that they are cut down to make him bigger, that everything that surrounds him is sacrificed to him. . . .

In Comedy the point is to give not individual portraits but pictures emphasizing a group. It is not so much the individual that we must attempt to depict but the species. We must draw various figures, group them, set them in motion, give all of them equal voice and life. A figure too set off from the

---

[3] A reference to Molière's play *The Misanthrope* (1666).

others will quickly appear isolated; I'm not asking for a statue on a pedestal, but a picture of various, different people. I want to see large groupings, contradictory preferences, miscellaneous eccentricities and shortcomings, and above all the consequences of our current way of life. Let the dramatic poet disclose to me the stage of the world, and not the sanctuary of a single man. Whoever has thought over the manner, mentality, behavior, and temperament of the different men whom he has seen will not depict them in an isolated way, but in action: it is action, the simultaneous and reciprocal action of all the characters, which alone animates the drama and gives weight to its moral message. In all the plays which are called plays of character, the chief character always is of a colossal stature and dominates to such a degree that the others serve as nothing more than shadows in the background to highlight him. . . .

The chief character doesn't have any counterbalance, he seems to move all by himself, he acts without having any clearly defined reason for doing so, he is seen carried along by an irresistible power: it is the hand of the dramatic poet which, similar to that of fate, makes him move the way he does. . . .

Truth of experience, in short, is not observed; the proportions are above and beyond nature. The common people laugh as they laugh at any caricature, but in society they never come across the model that they have been presented in the theatre.

(VIII)

On the Serious Drama

I am going to prove that the new genre, called the Serious Drama (*Drame*), which arises from Tragedy and from Comedy, having the pathos of the first, and the simple portrayals of life of the second, is infinitely more useful, more truthful, more interesting, since it is more accessible to the great mass of citizens. . . .

"I am a man," I can cry out to the dramatic poet! "Show me what I am, unfold before my very eyes my own abilities and possibilities; it's up to you to interest me, to instruct me, to stir me deeply. Up until now have you done that? Where are the fruits of your labors? Why have you been working? Have your accomplishments been corroborated by the applause of the common people? Perhaps they aren't aware of either your labors or of your existence. What then is the influence of your art on your age and on your compatriots?"

There has been an attempt here in France to do away with the word Serious Drama (*Drame*), which is the collective word, the original word, the proper word. But I'd venture to say that the distinction between tragedy and comedy has surely been extremely pernicious to art. The dramatic poet, who has written a tragedy, has felt himself obliged to be always strained, serious, impressive; he has disdained those details which could well be noble, even though ordinary, and those simple graces and the naturalness which animate a work and give it its true colors. The idea that tragedy necessarily had to produce tears has filled the stage with unforeseen deaths which make the author's pen like the bloody scythe of death; and following a false idea, always wishing to call forth tears, the tragic poet has dried up their source. The writer of comedy, on the other hand, has attempted to make people laugh and has had virtually nothing but this single goal in view; for this effect he has exaggerated his portraits; he has felt obliged to be the exact opposite of the tragic writer; he has virtually disdained the art of his counterpart and everything that was in the province of the pathetic; he hasn't been able to take a step unless it supported his false conception, forgetting that to want to make the audience always laugh is a more ridiculous aim than that of making us always cry.

The Greek tragedies were appropriate for the Greeks; and what about us, won't we venture to have our own theatre, to portray our contemporaries, be moved by them and interested in them? Will we always have to have men dressed in purple, surrounded by guards and wearing diadems on their heads? The misfortunes which affect us directly, which concern us, which are all around us, won't they have any right to our tears? In short, why shouldn't we have the courage to declare to the country the virtues of a man of humble station? Even though such a man were born in the lowest stratum of society, rest assured (as soon as he has a man of genius to present him to us), that he will become greater in our eyes than those kings whose haughty language has been grating on our ears for a long time now. . . .

(IX)

The Differences between the Serious Drama and Comedy

It is therefore time to portray the details and above all the duties of the individual in society, to break new ground in this richly fruitful field, whereas other areas have been worked over, used up by laborious hands. New productions are going to arise out of this soil which has recently been discovered. . . . Let us look at our neighbors; let us live with our compatriots, form a republic where the torch of morality will illumine the virtues which it is still permitted us to practice. . . . These plays . . . will teach us to know ourselves.

The Serious Drama can therefore be at the same time an interesting picture, because all the human classes will come and take their places in it; a moral picture because moral uprightness can and must lay down its laws in it; a picture of absurdities all the more effectively portrayed because vice alone will convey the characteristic features of what is absurd; a cheerful picture because virtue after several reverses will enjoy a complete triumph; finally, a picture of the age, because the characters, the virtues, and the vices will be essentially those of the day and of the country.

Fall, fall, walls which separate the genres! Let the poet gaze freely over the broad countryside and no longer feel his genius confined by those partitions where art is circumscribed and reduced in scope.

It will be said: "But is it Comedy?" I'll answer: "No, it's not comedy. Comedy has never presented such touching, pathetic, noble scenes, such an atmosphere of decent, respectable people, such fine developments of theme and action, such lessons of animated morality, such characters and temperaments which contrast without being opposed, which without overshadowing each other are joined and blended together."

In Comedy the chief character determines the action. Here, in the Serious Drama, the action flows from the interplay among the characters. One character is no longer the despot to whom all the other characters are subordinated or sacrificed; he is not a kind of pivot around which all the events and discussions of the play turn. In a word, the Serious Drama is not an action that is far-fetched, rapid, extreme: it is a typical moment of human life which reveals the private existence of a family where—without neglecting the broad strokes—one carefully garners up the details. It does not present an artificial character, to whom all the faults or virtues of mankind are rigorously attributed; it presents a truer, more reasonable, less colossal character, who produces a greater effect than he would have if he had been much heralded. To interweave and link the facts in accordance with the truth, in the choice of events to follow the ordinary course of things, to avoid all that has any trace of being fiction, to shape the progress of the play, so that the outline of the action seems to be a story where the most exact verisimilitude prevails, to arouse interest and sustain it without overelaboration, never to allow the eye to cease being moist without assaulting the heart in too violent a fashion, and finally to call forth at different moments the smile which is felt in the soul, and to make joy as delicate as compassion—all that is what the Serious Drama sets out to do and what Comedy has not attempted.

In Comedy, I repeat, an absolute character and temperament almost always dominates. By trying to make him energetic, one makes him far-fetched, and then he grimaces: the same fault as in tragedy. The perfection of a play would consist in its being impossible to tell who the chief character is, and in all the characters being so interconnected that you couldn't take out a single one without destroying the totality. We haven't given enough attention to mixed characters which comprise the whole human race. Men, whether they are good or bad, are not entirely given over to goodness or evil; they have moments of inaction, just as they have moments of action, and the nuances of the virtues and the vices are infinitely varied. What new possibilities for those who know the mixture of colors, who understand what unites in the same person baseness of soul and grandeur, savagery and compassion! Who knows on the basis of what hidden motives an old man behaves like a young man, or a young man like an old man? Now the coward summons up all his strength; the arrogant, haughty man becomes a low flatterer; the just man succumbs to gold; and the tyrant, out of ambition, performs an act of justice.

Man does not stay in the same state. . . .

And if we condescend to look at the various occupations, how many interesting things there are to learn! To what a great extent the shuttle, the hammer, the scales, the square, the quadrant, the chisel, give diversity to these subjects of interest, though at first sight they seem monotonous. What! You'll read with great delight technical descriptions of the different trades, and the man who invents these ingenious machines, who operates them, who understands their theory, wouldn't be interesting? This prodigious diversity of skills, of notions, of lines of reasoning will appear to me a hundred times more lively than the nonsense of these marquises who are presented to us as the only men who exist, and who despite their endless chatter don't have one hundredth the intelligence that a decent craftsman possesses. . . .

(X)

Continuation

But the Serious Drama, interesting and purified, does not banish gaiety; it only refines it and makes it more lively, more sweet, more lasting. It does not aim to provoke that mechanical convulsion of the body which is expressed by prolonged outbursts; rather, it attempts to create that subtle, delicate, peaceful smile which is as far removed from tumultuous joy as true pleasure is from debauchery.

Restoration and Eighteenth-Century England

Restoration England was a period of strong contrasts: extreme wealth and extreme poverty; courtly love and libertinage; Puritans and Pepys; the values of *Pilgrim's Progress* and those of *The Man of Mode*; the stagey, rhetorical, heroic tragedy and the Comedy of Manners, which was more realistic (since it featured painted scenes of locales audiences knew and characters in recognizable situations); the expansive, native tradition of dramaturgy and the contractive, neoclassical tradition—the latter reinforced during the court's enforced sojourn in France during the Interregnum. Although Dryden's professed aim in his *Essay of Dramatic Poesy* is "chiefly to vindicate the honor of our English writers from the censure of those who unjustly prefer the French before them," the dialogue form in which he casts his essay enables him to give effective expression to different sides. Often if not always, Neander may speak for Dryden, but—unlike Northbrooke in his antitheatrical *Treatise* almost a century earlier—Dryden the playwright plays fair: his characters argue from their own points of view. A practicing playwright, Dryden sometimes appears to engage in dialogue with himself—weighing pros and cons, changing his mind as a result of his own practice. Whereas his Preface to *All for Love* patriotically declares that French laws of the theatre should not rule in England, the play itself follows such laws (more precisely, he admits in the same preface, than is necessary for the English stage).

Unlike Dryden, Milton did not write for the stage, as he admits in his classically inspired essay on tragedy, prefixed to *Samson Agonistes*, which obeys foreign laws—Grecian and Roman, as interpreted by Italian jurists. Obedience to these laws is also fundamental to the dramatic theory of Thomas Rymer, whose basic premises center on their absolute authority and inviolability. Logically, then, the inflexible Rymer can demonstrate that because Shakespeare did not follow neoclassical precepts, his tragedies are bad. The reductive methods of such pedants as Rymer prompted rejoinders like Samuel Butler's satire included here. Also employing satire, and anticipating Samuel Johnson's arguments, the comic playwright Farquhar attacks verisimilitude and the unities of time and place—the cornerstones of neoclassicism. But they were not so easily laughed or reasoned away.

It was in the name of reason itself that neoclassicism held sway. To the neoclassicists, restrictive rules on dramatic and other poetry are compatible with nature, and in fact—to use Alexander Pope's famous phrase—"Are Nature still, but Nature methodiz'd."

The philosopher David Hume, another major figure of the age, discusses not rules of tragedy but a more substantive question, the source of our pleasure in things that in real life would make us terribly uneasy. Samuel Johnson's ground-breaking *Dictionary* aimed to provide comprehensive definitions; and his definitions of different dramatic genres, of drama and criticism themselves, and his illustrative examples, summarize much eighteenth-century English thought. In his essays on criticism, and in his criticism of Shakespeare, Johnson combines eclectically many of the best features of neoclassical doctrine without its rigidity. Distinguishing, for example, what is right because it is established from what is established because it is right, he employs common sense in his Shakespeare criticism. And yet his disapprobation of Shakespeare's obscenity and his general preference for moral purpose (in Nahum Tate's *Lear*, for example) serve as reminders that even he is very much of his age.

Morality is the chief preoccupation of Jeremy Collier's diatribe against Restoration comedy. His title spells out his two basic charges: immorality and profaneness. Solidly grounded, since Restoration comedy does offend against conventional morality, Collier's *Short View* set the tone of much criticism of this type of comedy—Sir Richard Steele's, for instance, whose condemnation of it generally and Etherege's *The Man of Mode* in particular derives from Collier. Among those who answered such charges was John Dennis, who in 1722 defended Etherege's play against Steele, just as two dozen years earlier he had defended the stage against Collier in a systematic brief that endeavored to demonstrate the theatre's usefulness first to man's happiness, then to government, and finally to religion itself. Just as systematically, playwright William Congreve, attacked by Collier, defended his own comedies and counterattacked.

But times had changed. Comedy was turning sentimental and such unrepentant rakes as Etherege's unvirtuous hero could no longer win the heroine's person and property unless they sincerely repented, perhaps not even then. Poetic justice was debated—Addison, for instance, against; Dennis for. Tearful or sentimental comedy was also argued—this time, Dennis was against; Steele, author of one of the genre's exemplars, *The Conscious Lovers*, defined and defended that genre in his preface to the play. In the late eighteenth century, Goldsmith regrets the decline of laughing comedy and the popularity of the sentimental type. As comedy loses its lightness, tragedy loses its heaviness. In his Dedication to his exemplary bourgeois tragedy *The London Merchant*, Lillo—in phrases resembling those Arthur Miller would use two centuries later—justifies people of humbler stations in life as tragic heroes.

John Dryden *1631–1700*

An Essay of Dramatic Poesy *1668*

. . . There are so few who write well in this age, said Crites, that methinks any praises should be welcome; they neither rise to the dignity of the last age, nor to any of the ancients: and we may cry out of the writers of this time, with more reason than Petronius of his, *Pace vestra liceat dixisse, primi omnium eloquentiam perdidistis*: you have debauched the true old poetry so far, that nature, which is the soul of it, is not in any of your writings.

If your quarrel (said Eugenius) to those who now write, be grounded only on your reverence to antiquity, there is no man more ready to adore those great Greeks and Romans than I am: but, on the other side, I cannot think so contemptibly of the age in which I live, or so dishonourably of my own country, as not to judge we equal the ancients in most kinds of poesy, and in some surpass them; neither know I any reason why I may not be as zealous for the reputation of our age, as we find the ancients themselves were in reverence to those who lived before them. . . .

But I see I am engaging in a wide dispute, where the arguments are not like to reach close on either side; for poesy is of so large an extent, and so many, both of the ancients and moderns, have done well in all kinds of it, that in citing one against the other, we shall take up more time this evening, than each man's occasions will allow him: therefore I would ask Crites to what part of poesy he would confine his arguments, and whether he would defend the general cause of the ancients against the moderns, or oppose any age of the moderns against this of ours.

Crites, a little while considering upon this demand, told Eugenius, that if he pleased he would limit their dispute to Dramatic Poesy; in which he thought it not difficult to prove, either that the ancients were superior to the moderns, or the last age to this of ours. . . .

Eugenius was going to continue this discourse, when Lisideius told him, that it was necessary, before they proceeded further, to take a standing measure of their controversy; for how was it possible to be decided, who wrote the best plays, before we know what a play should be? but, this once agreed on by both parties, each might have recourse to it, either to prove his own advantages, or to discover the failings of his adversary.

He had no sooner said this, but all desired the favour of him to give the definition of a play; and they were the more importunate, because neither Aristotle, nor Horace, nor any other, who had writ of that subject, had ever done it.

Lisideius, after some modest denials, at last confessed he had a rude notion

Selections. From *The Works of John Dryden*, Vol. XV, edited by Sir Walter Scott, revised by George Saintsbury. Edinburgh: William Patterson, 1883.

of it; indeed rather a description than a definition; but which served to guide him in his private thoughts, when he was to make a judgment of what others writ: that he conceived a play ought to be, "Any just and lively image of human nature, representing its passions and humours, and the changes of fortune to which it is subject, for the delight and instruction of mankind."

This definition (though Crites raised a logic objection against it—that it was only *a genere et fine*,[1] and so not altogether perfect) was yet well received by the rest: and after they had given order to the watermen to turn their barge, and row softly, that they might take the cool of the evening in their return, Crites, being desired by the company to begin, spoke on behalf of the ancients, in this manner:

If confidence presage a victory, Eugenius, in his own opinion, has already triumphed over the ancients: nothing seems more easy to him, than to over-come those whom it is our greatest praise to have imitated well; for we do not only build upon their foundations, but by their models. Dramatic Poesy had time enough, reckoning from Thespis (who first invented it) to Aristophanes, to be born, to grow up, and to flourish in maturity....

... Those ancients have been faithful imitators, and wise observers of that nature which is so torn and ill represented in our plays; they have handed down to us a perfect resemblance of her; which we, like ill copiers, neglecting to look on, have rendered monstrous, and disfigured. But, that you may know how much you are indebted to those your masters, and be ashamed to have so ill requited them, I must remember you, that all the rules by which we practice the drama at this day (either such as relate to the justness and sym-metry of the plot; or the episodical ornaments, such as descriptions, narra-tions, and other beauties, which are not essential to the play), were delivered to us from the observations which Aristotle made of those poets, who either lived before him, or were his contemporaries. We have added nothing of our own, except we have the confidence to say, our wit is better; of which none boast in this our age, but such as understand not theirs. Of that book which Aristotle has left us, περὶ τῆς Ποιητικῆς, Horace his *Art of Poetry* is an excel-lent comment, and, I believe, restores to us that Second Book of his con-cerning comedy, which is wanting in him.

Out of these two have been extracted the famous rules which the French call *Des Trois Unités*, or the Three Unities, which ought to be observed in every regular play; namely, of time, place, and action.

The unity of time they comprehend in twenty-four hours, the compass of a natural day, or as near as it can be contrived; and the reason of it is obvious to every one, that the time of the feigned action, or fable of the play, should be proportioned as near as can be to the duration of that time in which it is represented: since, therefore, all plays are acted on the theatre in a space

---

[1] By general classification and aim.

of time much within the compass of twenty-four hours, that play is to be thought the nearest imitation of nature, whose plot or action is confined within that time. And, by the same rule which concludes this general proportion of time, it follows, that all the parts of it are (as near as may be) to be equally subdivided; namely, that one act take not up the supposed time of half a day, which is out of proportion to the rest; since the other four are then to be straitened within the compass of the remaining half: for it is unnatural, that one act, which being spoke or written, is not longer than the rest, should be supposed longer by the audience; it is therefore the poet's duty, to take care that no act should be imagined to exceed the time in which it is represented on the stage; and that the intervals and inequalities of time be supposed to fall out between the acts.

This rule of time, how well it has been observed by the ancients, most of their plays will witness. You see them in their tragedies (wherein to follow this rule is certainly most difficult), from the very beginning of their plays, falling close into that part of the story which they intend for the action, or principal object of it, leaving the former part to be delivered by narration: so that they set the audience, as it were, at the post where the race is to be concluded; and saving them the tedious expectation of seeing the poet set out and ride the beginning of the course, they suffer you not to behold him till he is in sight of the goal, and just upon you.

For the second unity, which is that of place, the ancients meant by it, that the scene ought to be continued through the play, in the same place where it was laid in the beginning: for the stage, on which it is represented, being but one and the same place, it is unnatural to conceive it many; and those far distant from one another. I will not deny, but by the variation of painted scenes, the fancy (which in these cases will contribute to its own deceit) may sometimes imagine it several places, with some appearance of probability; yet it still carries the greater likelihood of truth, if those places be supposed so near each other, as in the same town or city, which may all be comprehended under the larger denomination of one place: for a greater distance will bear no proportion to the shortness of time which is allotted, in the acting, to pass from one of them to another. For the observation of this, next to the ancients, the French are to be most commended. They tie themselves so strictly to the unity of place, that you never see in any of their plays a scene changed in the middle of an act: if the act begins in a garden, a street, or chamber, 'tis ended in the same place; and that you may know it to be the same, the stage is so supplied with persons, that it is never empty all the time: he who enters second has business with him who was on before: and before the second quits the stage, a third appears who has business with him. This Corneille calls *la liaison des Scènes*, the continuity or joining of the scenes; and 'tis a good mark of a well-contrived play, when all the persons are known to each other, and every one of them has some affairs with all the rest.

As for the third unity, which is that of action, the ancients meant no other by it than what the logicians do by their *finis*, the end or scope of any action; that which is the first in intention, and last in execution. Now the poet is to aim at one great and complete action, to the carrying on of which all things in his play, even the very obstacles, are to be subservient; and the reason of this is as evident as any of the former.

For two actions equally laboured and driven on by the writer, would destroy the unity of the poem; it would be no longer one play, but two: not but that there may be many actions in a play, as Ben Johnson has observed in his *Discoveries*; but they must be all subservient to the great one, which our language happily expresses in the name of underplots: such as in Terence's *Eunuch* is the difference and reconcilement of Thais and Phaedria, which is not the chief business of the play, but promotes the marriage of Chaerea and Chremes's sister, principally intended by the poet. There ought to be but one action, says Corneille, that is, one complete action, which leaves the mind of the audience in a full repose; but this cannot be brought to pass, but by many other imperfect actions, which conduce to it, and hold the audience in a delightful suspense of what will be.

If by these rules (to omit many other drawn from the precepts and practice of the ancients) we should judge our modern plays, 'tis probable that few of them would endure the trial: that which should be the business of a day, takes up in some of them an age; instead of one action, they are the epitomes of a man's life; and for one spot of ground (which the stage should represent) we are sometimes in more countries than the map can show us. . . .

Crites had no sooner left speaking, but Eugenius, who had waited with some impatience for it, thus began:

I have observed in your speech, that the former part of it is convincing, as to what the moderns have profited by the rules of the ancients; but in the latter you are careful to conceal how much they have excelled them. We own all the helps we have from them, and want neither veneration nor gratitude, while we acknowledge, that to overcome them we must make use of the advantages we have received from them: but to these assistances we have joined our own industry; for, had we sat down with a dull imitation of them, we might then have lost somewhat of the old perfection, but never acquired any that was new. We draw not therefore after their lines, but those of nature; and having the life before us, besides the experience of all they knew, it is no wonder if we hit some airs and features which they have missed. . . .

Be pleased then, in the first place, to take notice, that the Greek poesy, which Crites has affirmed to have arrived to perfection in the reign of the old comedy, was so far from it, that the distinction of it into acts was not known to them; or if it were, it is yet so darkly delivered to us, that we cannot make it out.

All we know of it is, from the singing of their chorus; and that, too, is so uncertain, that in some of their plays we have reason to conjecture they sung more than five times. Aristotle indeed divides the integral parts of a play into four. First, the *Protasis*, or entrance, which gives light only to the characters of the persons, and proceeds very little into any part of the action. Secondly, the *Epitasis*, or working up of the plot; where the play grows warmer, the design or action of it is drawing on, and you see something promising that it will come to pass. Thirdly, the *Catastasis*, called by the Romans, *Status*, the height and full growth of the play: we may call it properly the counterturn which destroys that expectation, embroils the action in new difficulties, and leaves you far distant from that hope in which it found you; as you may have observed in a violent stream, resisted by a narrow passage, it runs round to an eddy, and carries back the waters with more swiftness than it brought them on. Lastly, the *Catastrophe*, which the Grecians called λυσις, the French *le dénouement*, and we the discovery, or unraveling of the plot: there you see all things settling again upon their first foundations, and, the obstacles which hindered the design or action of the play once removed, it ends with that resemblance of truth and nature, that the audience are satisfied with the conduct of it. Thus this great man delivered to us the image of a play; and I must confess it so lively, that from thence much light has been derived to the forming it more perfectly into acts and scenes: but what poet first limited to five the number of the acts, I know not; only we see it so firmly established in the time of Horace, that he gives it for a rule in comedy, *Neu brevior quinto, neu sit productior actu.*[2] So that you see the Grecians cannot be said to have consummated this art; writing rather by entrances than by acts, and having rather a general indigested notion of a play, than knowing how and where to bestow the particular graces of it.

But since the Spaniards at this day allow but three acts, which they call *Jornadas*, to a play, and the Italians in many of theirs follow them, when I condemn the ancients, I declare it is not altogether because they have not five acts to every play, but because they have not confined themselves to one certain number: it is building an house without a model; and when they succeeded in such undertakings, they ought to have sacrificed to Fortune, not to the Muses.

Next, for the plot, which Aristotle called τὸ μυθός, and often τῶν πραγμάτων σύνθεσις, and from him the Romans *Fabula*, it has already been judiciously observed by a late writer, that in their tragedies it was only some tale derived from Thebes or Troy, or at least something that happened in those two ages; which was worn so threadbare by the pens of all the epic poets, and even by tradition itself of the talkative Greeklings (as Ben Jonson calls them), that before it came upon the stage, it was already known to all the audience;

[2] See *The Art of Poetry*, above, p. 71.

and the people, so soon as ever they heard the name of Oedipus, knew as well as the poet, that he had killed his father by a mistake, and committed incest with his mother, before the play; that they were now to hear of a great plague, an oracle, and the ghost of Laius; so that they sate with a yawning kind of expectation, till he was to come with his eyes pulled out, and speak a hundred or more verses in a tragic tone, in complaint of his misfortunes. But one Oedipus, Hercules, or Medea had been tolerable; poor people, they escaped not so good cheap; they had still the *chapon bouillé*[3] set before them, till their appetites were cloyed with the same dish, and, the novelty being gone, the pleasure vanished; so that one main end of Dramatic Poesy in its definition, which was to cause delight, was of consequence destroyed.

In their comedies, the Romans generally borrowed their plots from the Greek poets; and theirs was commonly a little girl stolen or wandered from her parents, brought back unknown to the city, there got with child by some lewd young fellow, who, by the help of his servant, cheats his father; and when her time comes to cry, *Juno Lucina, fer opem,*[4] one or other sees a little box or cabinet which was carried away with her, and so discovers her to her friends, if some god do not prevent it, by coming down in a machine, and taking the thanks of it to himself.

By the plot you may guess much of the characters of the persons. An old father, who would willingly, before he dies, see his son well married; his debauched son, kind in his nature to his mistress, but miserably in want of money; a servant or slave, who has so much wit to strike in with him, and help to dupe his father; a braggadocio captain, a parasite, and a lady of pleasure.

As for the poor honest maid, on whom the story is built, and who ought to be one of the principal actors in the play, she is commonly a mute in it; she has the breeding of the old Elizabeth way, which was for maids to be seen, and not to be heard; and it is enough you know she is willing to be married, when the fifth act requires it.

These are plots built after the Italian mode of houses—you see through them all at once: the characters are indeed the imitations of nature, but so narrow, as if they had imitated only an eye or an hand, and did not dare to venture on the lines of a face, or the proportion of a body.

But in how straight a compass soever they have bounded their plots and characters, we will pass it by, if they have regularly pursued them, and perfectly observed those three unities of time, place, and action; the knowledge of which you say is derived to us from them. But, in the first place, give me leave to tell you that the unity of place, however it might be practiced by them, was never any of their rules: we neither find it in Aristotle, Horace,

---

[3] Boiled capon.
[4] "Juno, goddess of childbirth, help me!"

or any who have written of it, till in our age the French poets first made it a precept of the stage. The unity of time, even Terence himself, who was the best and most regular of them, has neglected: his *Heautontimorumenos*, or *Self-punisher*, takes up visibly two days, says Scaliger; the two first acts concluding the first day, the three last the day ensuing; and Euripides, in tying himself to one day, has committed an absurdity never to be forgiven him; for in one of his tragedies[5] he has made Theseus go from Athens to Thebes, which was about forty English miles, under the walls of it to give battle, and appear victorious in the next act; and yet, from the time of his departure to the return of the Nuntius, who gives the relation of his victory, Aethra and the chorus have but thirty-six verses; which is not for every mile a verse. . . .

It is true, they [the French] have kept the continuity, or, as you call it, *liaison des Scènes*, somewhat better: two do not perpetually come in together, talk, and go out together; and other two succeed them, and do the same throughout the act, which the English call by the name of single scenes; but the reason is, because they have seldom above two or three scenes, properly so called, in every act; for it is to be accounted a new scene, not only every time the stage is empty, but every person who enters, though to others, makes it so; because he introduces a new business. Now the plots of their plays being narrow, and the persons few, one of their acts was written in a less compass than one of our well-wrought scenes; and yet they are often deficient even in this. . . .

But as they have failed both in laying of their plots and in the management, swerving from the rules of their own art, by misrepresenting nature to us, in which they have ill satisfied one intention of a play, which was delight; so in the instructive part they have erred worse: instead of punishing vice, and rewarding virtue, they have often shown a prosperous wickedness, and an unhappy piety: they have set before us a bloody image of revenge in Medea, and given her dragons to convey her safe from punishment, a Priam and Astyanax murdered, and Cassandra ravished, and the lust and murder ending in the victory of him who acted them. In short, there is no indecorum in any of our modern plays, which, if I would excuse, I could not shadow with some authority from the ancients. . . .

But, to return from whence I have digressed, to the consideration of the ancients' writing, and their wit; of which, by this time, you will grant us in some measure to be fit judges. Though I see many excellent thoughts in Seneca, yet he, of them who had a genius most proper for the stage, was Ovid; he had a way of writing so fit to stir up a pleasing admiration and concernment, which are the objects of a tragedy, and to show the various movements of a soul combating betwixt two different passions, that had he

[5] *The Suppliant Women.*

lived in our age, or in his own could have writ with our advantages, no man but must have yielded to him. . . . For love-scenes you will find few among them; their tragic poets dealt not with that soft passion, but with lust, cruelty, revenge, ambition, and those bloody actions they produced; which were more capable of raising horror than compassion in an audience: leaving love untouched, whose gentleness would have tempered them, which is the most frequent of all the passions, and which, being the private concernment of every person, is soothed by viewing its own image in a public entertainment. . . .

Eugenius was proceeding in that part of his discourse, when Crites interrupted him. I see, said he, Eugenius and I are never like to have this question decided betwixt us; for he maintains, the moderns have acquired a new perfection in writing, I can only grant they have altered the mode of it. . . .

This moderation of Crites, as it was pleasing to all the company, so it put an end to that dispute; which Eugenius, who seemed to have the better of the argument, would urge no farther. But Lisideius, after he had acknowledged himself of Eugenius his opinion concerning the ancients, yet told him, he had forborne, till his discourse were ended, to ask him, why he preferred the English plays above those of other nations? and whether we ought not to submit our stage to the exactness of our next neighbours?

Though, said Eugenius, I am at all times ready to defend the honour of my country against the French, and to maintain, we are as well able to vanquish them with our pens as our ancestors have been with their swords; yet, if you please, added he, looking upon Neander, I will commit this cause to to my friend's management; his opinion of our plays is the same with mine: and besides, there is no reason that Crites and I, who have now left the stage, should reenter so suddenly upon it; which is against the laws of comedy.

If the question had been stated, replied Lisideius, who had writ best, the French or English, forty years ago, I should have been of your opinion, and adjudged the honour to our own nation; but since that time (said he, turning towards Neander) we have been so long together bad Englishmen, that we had not leisure to be good poets. Beaumont, Fletcher, and Jonson (who were only capable of bringing us to that degree of perfection which we have) were just then leaving the world; as if in an age of so much horror, wit, and those milder studies of humanity, had no further business among us. But the Muses, who ever follow peace, went to plant in another country: it was then that the great Cardinal of Richelieu began to take them into his protection; and that, by his encouragement, Corneille, and some other Frenchmen, reformed their theatre, which before was as much below ours as it now surpasses it and the rest of Europe. But because Crites, in his discourse for the ancients, has prevented me, by observing many rules of the stage, which the moderns have borrowed from them, I shall only, in short demand of you, whether you are not convinced that of all nations the French have best observed them? In the unity of time you find them so scrupulous, that it yet remains a dispute among their poets, whether the artificial day of twelve hours, more or less, be not meant by Aristotle, rather than the natural one of twenty-four; and consequently, whether all plays ought not to be reduced into that compass. This I can testify, that in all dramas writ within these last twenty years and upwards, I have not observed any that have extended the time to thirty hours. In the unity of place they are full as scrupulous; for many of their critics limit it to that very spot of ground where the play is supposed to begin; none of them exceed the compass of the same town or city.

The unity of action in all their plays is yet more conspicuous; for they do not burden them with underplots, as the English do: which is the reason why many scenes of our tragicomedies carry on a design that is nothing of kin to the main plot; and that we see two distinct webs in a play, like those in ill-wrought stuffs; and two actions, that is, two plays, carried on together, to the confounding of the audience; who, before they are warm in their concernments for one part, are diverted to another; and by that means espouse the interest of neither. From hence likewise it arises, that the one-half of our actors are not known to the other. They keep their distances, as if they were Montagues and Capulets, and seldom begin an acquaintance till the last scene of the fifth act, when they are all to meet upon the stage. There is no theatre in the world has anything so absurd as the English tragicomedy; it is a drama of our own invention, and the fashion of it is enough to proclaim it so; here a course of mirth, there another of sadness and passion, and a third of honour and a duel: thus, in two hours and a half we run through all the fits of Bedlam. The French affords you as much variety on the same day, but they do it not so unseasonably, or *mal à propos*, as we: our poets present you the play and the farce together....

The end of tragedies or serious plays, says Aristotle, is to beget admiration, compassion, or concernment; but are not mirth and compassion things incompatible? and is it not evident, that the poet must of necessity destroy the former by intermingling of the latter? that is, he must ruin the sole end and object of his tragedy, to introduce somewhat what is forced into it, and is not of the body of it. Would you not think that physician mad, who, having prescribed a purge, should immediately order you to take restringents?

But to leave our plays, and return to theirs. I have noted one great advantage they have had in the plotting of their tragedies; that is, they are always grounded upon some known history: according to that of Horace, *Ex noto fictum carmen sequar;*[6] and in that they have so imitated the ancients, that they have surpassed them. For the ancients, as was observed before,

---

[6] Horace, *The Art of Poetry*: "I shall aim at a poem so deftly fashioned out of familiar matter. . . ."

took for the foundation of their plays some poetical fiction, such as under that consideration could move but little concernment in the audience, because they already knew the event of it. But the French goes farther—.

> *Atque ita mentitur, sic veris falsa remiscet,*
> *Primo ne medium, medio ne discrept imum.*[7]

He so interweaves truth with probable fiction, that he puts a pleasing fallacy upon us, mends the intrigues of fate, and dispenses with the severity of history, to reward that virtue which has been rendered to us there unfortunate. . . . On the other side, if you consider the historical plays of Shakespeare, they are rather so many chronicles of kings, or the business many times of thirty or forty years, cramped into a representation of two hours and a half; which is not to imitate or paint Nature, but rather to draw her in minature, to take her in little; to look upon her through the wrong end of a perspective, and receive her images not only much less, but infinitely more imperfect than the life: this, instead of making a play delightful, renders it ridiculous. . . .

Another thing in which the French differ from us and from the Spaniards, is, that they do not embarrass, or cumber themselves with too much plot; they only represent so much of a story as will constitute one whole and great action sufficient for a play: we, who undertake more, do but multiply adventures; which, not being produced from one another, as effects from causes, but barely following, constitute many actions in the drama, and consequently make it many plays.

But by pursuing closely one argument, which is not cloyed with many turns, the French have gained more liberty for verse, in which they write: they have leisure to dwell on a subject which deserves it; and to represent the passions (which we have acknowledged to be the poet's work) without being hurried from one thing to another, as we are in the plays of Calderon, which we have seen lately upon our theatres, under the name of Spanish plots. . . .

But there is another sort of relations, that is, of things happening in the action of the play, and supposed to be done behind the scenes; and this is many times both convenient and beautiful: for by it the French avoid the tumult to which we are subject in England, by representing duels, battles, and the like; which renders our stage too like the theatres where they fight prizes. For what is more ridiculous than to represent an army with a drum and five men behind it; all which, the hero of the other side is to drive in before him? or to see a duel fought, and one slain with two or three thrusts of the foils, which we know are so blunted, that we might give a man an hour to kill another in good earnest with them?

---

[7] Horace, *The Art of Poetry*: ". . . and so employs fiction, so blends false with true, that beginning, middle, and end all strike the same note."

I have observed, that in all our tragedies the audience cannot forbear laughing when the actors are to die; it is the most comic part of the whole play. All passions may be lively represented on the stage, if to the well-writing of them the actor supplies a good commanded voice, and limbs that move easily, and without stiffness; but there are many actions which can never be imitated to a just height: dying especially is a thing which none but a Roman gladiator could naturally perform on the stage, when he did not imitate, or represent, but do it; and therefore it is better to omit the representation of it.

The words of a good writer, which describe it lively, will make a deeper impression of belief in us, than all the actor can insinuate into us, when he seems to fall dead before us; as a poet in the description of a beautiful garden, or a meadow, will please our imagination more than the place itself can please our sight. When we see death represented, we are convinced it is but fiction; but when we hear it related, our eyes (the strongest witnesses) are wanting, which might have undeceived us; and we are all willing to favour the slight when the poet does not too grossly impose on us. . . .

But I find I have been too long in this discourse, since the French have many other excellences not common to us; as that you never see any of their plays end with a conversion, or simple change of will, which is the ordinary way which our poets use to end theirs. It shows little art in the conclusion of a dramatic poem, when they who have hindered the felicity during the four acts, desist from it in the fifth, without some powerful cause to take them off their design; and though I deny not but such reasons may be found, yet it is a path that is cautiously to be trod, and the poet is to be sure he convinces the audience that the motive is strong enough. . . .

Lisideius concluded in this manner; and Neander, after a little pause, thus answered him:

I shall grant Lisideius, without much dispute, a great part of what he has urged against us; for I acknowledge, that the French contrive their plots more regularly, and observe the laws of comedy, and decorum of the stage (to speak generally), with more exactness than the English. Further, I deny not but he has taxed us justly in some irregularities of ours, which he has mentioned; yet, after all, I am of opinion, that neither our faults nor their virtues are considerable enough to place them above us.

For the lively imitation of nature being in the definition of a play, those which best fulfill that law ought to be esteemed superior to the others. 'Tis true, those beauties of the French poesy are such as will raise perfection higher where it is, but are not sufficient to give it where it is not: they are indeed the beauties of a statue, but not of a man, because not animated with the soul of poesy, which is imitation of humour and passions: and this Lisideius himself, or any other, however biased to their party, cannot but acknowledge, if he will either compare the humours of our comedies, or the characters of our serious plays, with theirs. He who will look upon theirs which have been written till these last ten years, or thereabouts, will find it an hard matter to pick out two or three passable humours amongst them. Corneille himself, their arch-poet, what has he produced except *The Liar*, and you know how it was cried up in France; but when it came upon the English stage, though well translated, and that part of Dorant acted to so much advantage as I am confident it never received in its own country, the most favourable to it would not put it in competition with many of Fletcher's or Ben Jonson's. In the rest of Corneille's comedies you have little humour; he tells you himself, his way is, first to show two lovers in good intelligence with each other; in the working up of the play, to embroil them by some mistake, and in the latter end to clear it, and reconcile them.

But of late years Molière, the younger Corneille,[8] Quinault, and some others, have been imitating afar off the quick turns and graces of the English stage. They have mixed their serious plays with mirth, like our tragicomedies, since the death of Cardinal Richelieu, which Lisideius and many others, not observing, have commended that in them a virtue, which they themselves no longer practise. Most of their new plays are, like some of ours, derived from the Spanish novels. There is scarce one of them without a veil, and a trusty Diego, who drolls much after the rate of the *Adventures.*[9] But their humours, if I may grace them with that name, are so thin sown, that never above one of them comes up in any play. I dare take upon me to find more variety of them in some one play of Ben Jonson's than in all theirs together: as he who has seen the *Alchemist, The Silent Woman*, or *Bartholomew Fair*, cannot but acknowledge with me.

I grant the French have performed what was possible on the groundwork of the Spanish plays; what was pleasant before, they have made regular: but there is not above one good play to be writ on all those plots; they are too much alike to please often, which we need not the experience of our own stage to justify. As for their new way of mingling mirth with serious plot, I do not, with Lisideius, condemn the thing, though I cannot approve their manner of doing it. He tells us, we cannot so speedily recollect ourselves after a scene of great passion and concernment, as to pass to another of mirth and humour, and to enjoy it with any relish: but why should he imagine the soul of man more heavy than his senses? Does not the eye pass from an unpleasant object to a pleasant, in a much shorter time than is required to this? and does not the unpleasantness of the first commend the beauty of the latter? The old rule of logic might have convinced him, that contraries, when placed near, set off each other. A continued gravity keeps the spirit too much bent; we must refresh it sometimes, as we bait in

[8] Thomas Corneille (1625–1709), brother of Pierre.
[9] *The Adventures of Five Hours* (1663) by Sir Samuel Tuke and the Earl of Bristol, based on the Spanish of Calderon.

a journey, that we may go on with greater ease. A scene of mirth, mixed with tragedy, has the same effect upon us which our music has betwixt the acts; which we find a relief to us from the best plots and language of the stage, if the discourses have been long. I must therefore have stronger arguments, ere I am convinced that compassion and mirth in the same subject destroy each other; and in the meantime, cannot but conclude, to the honour of our nation, that we have invented, increased, and perfected a more pleasant way of writing for the stage, than was ever known to the ancients or moderns of any nation, which is tragicomedy.

And this leads me to wonder why Lisideius and many others should cry up the barrenness of the French plots, above the variety and copiousness of the English. Their plots are single, they carry on one design, which is pushed forward by all the actors, every scene in the play contributing and moving towards it. Our plays, besides the main design, have underplots, or by-concernments, of less considerable persons and intrigues, which are carried on with the motion of the main plot: as they say the orb of the fixed stars, and those of the planets, though they have motions of their own, are whirled about by the motion of the *primum mobile*, in which they are contained. That similitude expresses much of the English stage; for if contrary motions may be found in nature to agree, if a planet can go east and west at the same time—one way by virtue of his own motion, the other by the force of the first mover—it will not be difficult to imagine how the under-plot, which is only different, not contrary to the great design, may naturally be conducted along with it.

Eugenius has already shown us, from the confession of the French poets, that the unity of action is sufficiently preserved, if all the imperfect actions of the play are conducing to the main design; but when those petty intrigues of a play are so ill ordered, that they have no coherence with the other, I must grant that Lisideius has reason to tax that want of due connection—for coordination in a play is as dangerous and unnatural as in a state. In the meantime, he must acknowledge, our variety, if well ordered, will afford, a greater pleasure to the audience.

As for his other argument, that by pursuing one single theme they gain an advantage to express and work up the passions, I wish any example he could bring from them would make it good; for I confess their verses are to me the coldest I have ever read. Neither, indeed, is it possible for them, in the way they take, so to express passion, as that the effects of it should appear in the concernment of an audience, their speeches being so many declamations, which tire us with the length; so that instead of persuading us to grieve for their imaginary heroes, we are concerned for our own trouble, as we are in tedious visits of bad company; we are in pain till they are gone. . . . But to speak generally: it cannot be denied, that short speeches and replies are more apt to move the passions, and beget concernment in us, than the other; for it is unnatural for any one, in a gust of passion, to speak long together; or for another, in the same condition, to suffer him without interruption. Grief and passion are like floods raised in little brooks by a sudden rain, they are quickly up, and if the concernment be poured unexpectedly in upon us, it overflows us: but a long sober shower gives them leisure to run out as they came in, without troubling the ordinary current. . . .

But to leave this, and pass to the latter part of Lisideius's discourse, which concerns relations, I must acknowledge with him, that the French have reason to hide that part of the action which would occasion too much tumult on the stage, and to choose rather to have it made known by narration to the audience. Further, I think it very convenient, for the reasons he has given, that all incredible actions were removed; but, whether custom has so insinuated itself into our countrymen, or nature has so formed them to fierceness, I know not; but they will scarcely suffer combats and other objects of horror to be taken from them. And indeed, the indecency of tumults is all which can be objected against fighting: for why may not our imagination as well suffer itself to be deluded with the probability of it, as with any other thing in the play? For my part, I can with as great ease persuade myself, that the blows are given in good earnest, as I can, that they who strike them are kings or princes, or those persons which they represent. . . . To conclude on this subject of relations, if we are to be blamed for showing too much of the action, the French are as faulty for discovering too little of it; a mean betwixt both should be observed by every judicious writer, so as the audience may neither be left unsatisfied by not seeing what is beautiful, or shocked by beholding what is either incredible or undecent.

I hope I have already proved in this discourse, that though we are not altogether so punctual as the French, in observing the laws of comedy, yet our errors are so few, and little, and those things wherein we excel them so considerable, that we ought of right to be preferred before them. . . . By their servile observations of the unities of time and place, and integrity of scenes, they have brought on themselves that dearth of plot, and narrowness of imagination, which may be observed in all their plays. How many beautiful accidents might naturally happen in two or three days, which cannot arrive with any probability in the compass of twenty-four hours? There is time to be allowed also for maturity of design, which amongst great and prudent persons, such as are often represented in tragedy, cannot, with any likelihood of truth, be brought to pass at so short a warning. Further, by tying themselves strictly to the unity of place, and unbroken scenes, they are forced many times to omit some beauties which cannot be shown where the act began; but might, if the scene were interrupted, and the stage cleared for the persons to enter in another place; and therefore the French poets are often forced upon absurdities: for if the act begins in a chamber, all the persons in the play must have some business or other to come thither, or else they are not to be shown that act; and sometimes their characters are very unfitting to appear there: as suppose it were the king's bed-chamber, yet the meanest man in the tragedy must come and dispatch his business there, rather than in the lobby, or courtyard (which is fitter for him), for fear the stage should be cleared, and the scenes broken. . . .

If they content themselves, as Corneille did, with some flat design, which, like an ill riddle, is found ere it be half proposed, such plots we can make every way regular as easily as they; but whenever they endeavour to rise to any quick turns and counterturns of plot, as some of them have attempted since Corneille's plays have been less in vogue, you see they write as irregularly as we, though they cover it more speciously. Hence the reason is perspicuous, why no French plays, when translated, have, or ever can succeed on the English stage. For, if you consider the plots, our own are fuller of variety; if the writing, ours are more quick and fuller of spirit; and therefore 'tis a strange mistake in those who decry the way of writing plays in verse, as if the English therein imitated the French. We have borrowed nothing from them; our plots are weaved in English looms; we endeavour therein to follow the variety and greatness of characters, which are derived to us from Shakespeare and Fletcher; the copiousness and well-knitting of the intrigues we have from Jonson; and for the verse itself we have English precedents of elder date than any of Corneille's plays. . . .

But to return whence I have digressed: I dare boldly affirm these two things of the English drama: First, that we have many plays of ours as regular as any of theirs, and which besides, have more variety of plot and characters; and, secondly, that in most of the irregular plays of Shakespeare or Fletcher (for Ben Jonson's are for the most part regular), there is a more masculine fancy, and greater spirit in the writing, than there is in any of the French. I could produce even in Shakespeare's and Fletcher's works, some plays which are almost exactly formed; as the *Merry Wives of Windsor* and *The Scornful Lady*. . . .

To begin then with Shakespeare. He was the man who of all modern, and perhaps ancient poets, had the largest and most comprehensive soul. All the images of nature were still present to him, and he drew them not laboriously, but luckily: when he describes anything, you more than see it, you feel it too. Those who accuse him to have wanted learning, give him the greater commendation: he was naturally learned; he needed not the spectacles of books to read nature; he looked inwards, and found her there. I cannot say he is everywhere alike; were he so, I should do him injury to compare him with the greatest of mankind. He is many times flat, insipid; his comic wit degenerating into clenches, his serious swelling into bombast.

But he is always great, when some great occasion is presented to him: no man can say, he ever had a fit subject for his wit, and did not then raise himself as high above the rest of poets—

Quantum lenta solent inter viburna cupressi.[10]

The consideration of this made Mr. Hales of Eton[11] say, that there was no subject of which any poet ever writ, but he would produce it much better done in Shakespeare. . . .

[10] Virgil, *Eclogues*, I: "as cypresses often do among bending willows."
[11] John Hales (1585–1656).

A Defence of an Essay
of Dramatic Poesy *1668*

. . . As for the question as he states it,[1] whether rhyme be nearest the nature of what it represents, I wonder he should think me so ridiculous as to dispute whether prose or verse be nearest to ordinary conversation.

It still remains for him to prove his inference; that, since verse is granted to be more remote than prose from ordinary conversation, therefore no serious plays ought to be writ in verse: and when he clearly makes that good, I will acknowledge his victory as absolutely as he can desire it. . . .

But to return to verse, whether it be natural or not in plays, is a problem which is not demonstrable of either side: It is enough for me, that he acknowledges he had rather read good verse than prose: for if all the enemies of verse will confess as much, I shall not need to prove that it is natural. I am satisfied if it cause delight; for delight is the chief, if not the only, end of poesy: Instruction can be admitted but in the second place, for poesy only instructs as it delights. It is true, that to imitate well is a poet's work; but to affect the soul, and excite the passions, and, above all to move admira-

Selections. From *The Works of John Dryden*, Vol. II, edited by Sir Walter Scott, revised by George Saintsbury. Edinburgh: William Patterson, 1883.

[1] Sir Robert Howard (1626–1698), the model for Crites in *An Essay of Dramatic Poesy*, defended blank verse in the Preface to his tragedy *The Great Favourite* (1668). Dryden published this response as Preface to the second edition of *The Indian Emperor*.

tion (which is the delight of serious plays), a bare imitation will not serve. The converse, therefore, which a poet is to imitate, must be heightened with all the arts and ornaments of poesy; and must be such as, strictly considered, could never be supposed spoken by any without premeditation.

As for what he urges, that "a play will still be supposed to be a composition of several persons speaking *extempore,* and that good verses are the hardest things which can be imagined to be so spoken"; I must crave leave to dissent from his opinion, as to the former part of it: For, if I am not deceived, a play is supposed to be the work of the poet, imitating, or representing, the conversation of several persons: and this I think to be as clear, as he thinks the contrary.

But I will be bolder, and do not doubt to make it good, though a paradox, that one great reason why prose is not to be used in serious plays, is, because it is too near the nature of converse: There may be too great a likeness; as the most skilful painters affirm, that there may be too near a resemblance in a picture: To take every lineament and feature is not to make an excellent piece, but to take so much only as will make a beautiful resemblance of the whole: and, with an ingenious flattery of nature, to heighten the beauties of some parts, and hide the deformities of the rest. . . .

Thus Prose, though the rightful prince, yet is by common consent deposed, as too weak for the government of serious plays: and he failing, there now start up two competitors; one, the nearer in blood, which is Blank Verse; the other, more fit for the ends of government, which is Rhyme. Blank Verse is, indeed, the nearer Prose, but he is blemished with the weakness of his predecessor. Rhyme (for I will deal clearly) has somewhat of the usurper in him; but he is brave, and generous, and his dominion pleasing. For this reason of delight, the ancients (whom I will still believe as wise as those who so confidently correct them) wrote all their tragedies in verse, though they knew it most remote from conversation.

But I perceive I am falling into the danger of another rebuke from my opponent; for when I plead that the ancients used verse, I prove not that they would have admitted rhyme, had it then been written. All I can say is only this, that it seems to have succeeded verse by the general consent of poets in all modern languages; for almost all their serious plays are written in it; which, though it be no demonstration that therefore they ought to be so, yet at least the practice first, and then the continuation of it, shows that it attained the end, which was to please; and if that cannot be compassed here, I will be the first who shall lay it down: for I confess my chief endeavours are to delight the age in which I live. If the humour of this be for low comedy, small accidents, and raillery, I will force my genius to obey it, though with more reputation I could write in verse. I know I am not so fitted by nature to write comedy: I want that gaiety of humour which is required to it.

Preface to
An Evening's Love 1671

But I have descended, before I was aware, from comedy to farce; which consists principally of grimaces. That I admire not any comedy equally with tragedy, is, perhaps, from the sullenness of my humour; but that I detest those farces, which are now the most frequent entertainments of the stage, I am sure I have reason on my side. Comedy consists, though of low persons, yet of natural actions and characters; I mean such humours, adventures, and designs, as are to be found and met with in the world. Farce, on the other side, consists of forced humours, and unnatural events. Comedy presents us with the imperfections of human nature: Farce entertains us with what is monstrous and chimerical. The one causes laughter in those who can judge of men and manners, by the lively representation of their folly or corruption: The other produces the same effect in those who can judge of neither, and that only by its extravagances. The first works on the judgment and fancy; the latter on the fancy only: There is more of satisfaction in the former kind of laughter, and in the latter more of scorn. But, how it happens, that an impossible adventure should cause our mirth, I cannot so easily imagine. Something there may be in the oddness of it, because on the stage it is the common effect of things unexpected, to surprise us into a delight: and that is to be ascribed to the strange appetite, as I may call it, of fancy; which, like that of a longing woman, often runs out into the most extravagant desires; and is better satisfied sometimes with loam, or with the rinds of trees, than with the wholesome nourishments of life. In short, there is the same difference betwixt farce and comedy, as betwixt an empiric and a true physician: Both of them may attain their ends; but what the one performs by hazard, the other does by skill. And as the artist is often unsuccessful, while the montebank succeeds; so farces more commonly take the people than comedies. For, to write unnatural things, is the most probable way of pleasing them, who understand not nature. And a true poet often misses of applause, because he cannot debase himself to write so ill as to please his audience. . . .

. . . In tragedy, where the actions and persons are great, and the crimes horrid, the laws of justice are more strictly observed; and examples of punishment to be made, to deter mankind from the pursuit of vice. Faults of this kind have been rare amongst the ancient poets: for they have punished in *Oedipus*, and in his posterity, the sin which he knew not he had committed. *Medea* is the only example I remember at present, who escapes from punishment after murder. Thus tragedy fulfils one great part of its

Selections. From *The Works of John Dryden*, Vol. III, edited by Sir Walter Scott, revised by George Saintsbury. Edinburgh: William Patterson, 1883.

institution; which is, by example, to instruct. But in comedy it is not so; for the chief end of it is divertissement and delight. . . . The business of the poet is to make you laugh: when he writes humour, he makes folly ridiculous; when wit, he moves you, if not always to laughter, yet to a pleasure that is more noble. And if he works a cure on folly, and the small imperfections in mankind, by exposing them to public view, that cure is not performed by an immediate operation: For it works first on the ill-nature of the audience; they are moved to laugh by the representation of deformity; and the shame of that laughter teaches us to amend what is ridiculous in our manners. This being then established, that the first end of comedy is delight, and instruction only the second; it may reasonably be inferred, that comedy is not so much obliged to the punishment of faults which it represents, as tragedy. For the persons in comedy are of a lower quality, the action is little, and the faults and vices are but the sallies of youth, and the frailties of human nature, and not premeditated crimes: such to which all men are obnoxious; not such as are attempted only by few, and those abandoned to all sense of virtue: such as move pity and commiseration; not detestation and horror: such, in short, as may be forgiven; not such as must of necessity be punished. But, lest any man should think that I write this to make libertinism amiable, or that I cared not to debase the end and institution of comedy, so I might thereby maintain my own errors, and those of better poets, I must further declare, both for them and for myself, that we make not vicious persons happy, but only as Heaven makes sinners so; that is, by reclaiming them first from vice. For so it is to be supposed they are, when they resolve to marry; for then, enjoying what they desire in one, they cease to pursue the love of many.

Preface to
All for Love 1678

The death of Antony and Cleopatra is a subject which has been treated by the greatest wits of our nation, after Shakespeare; and by all so variously, that their example has given me the confidence to try myself in this bow

Selections. From *The Works of John Dryden*, Vol. V, edited by Sir Walter Scott, revised by George Saintsbury. Edinburgh: William Patterson, 1883.

of Ulysses amongst the crowd of suitors; and, withal, to take my own measures, in aiming at the mark. I doubt not but the same motive has prevailed with all of us in this attempt; I mean the excellency of the moral: For the chief persons represented were famous patterns of unlawful love; and their end accordingly was unfortunate. All reasonable men have long since concluded, that the hero of the poem ought not to be a character of perfect virtue, for then he could not, without injustice, be made unhappy; nor yet altogether wicked, because he could not then be pitied. I have therefore steered the middle course; and have drawn the character of Antony as favourably as Plutarch, Appian, and Dion Cassius would give me leave; the like I have observed in Cleopatra. That which is wanting to work up the pity to a greater height, was not afforded me by the story; for the crimes of love, which they both committed, were not occasioned by any necessity, or fatal ignorance, but were wholly voluntary; since our passions are, or ought to be, within our power. The fabric of the play is regular enough, as to the inferior parts of it; and the unities of time, place, and action, more exactly observed, than perhaps the English theatre requires. Particularly, the action is so much one, that it is the only of the kind without episode, or underplot; every scene in the tragedy conducing to the main design, and every act concluding with a turn of it. The greatest error in the contrivance seems to be in the person of Octavia; for, though I might use the privilege of a poet, to introduce her into Alexandria, yet I had not enough considered, that the compassion she moves to herself and children was destructive to that which I reserved for Antony and Cleopatra; whose mutual love being founded upon vice, must lessen the favour of the audience to them, when virtue and innocence were oppressed by it. And, though I justified Antony in some measure, by making Octavia's departure to proceed wholly from herself; yet the force of the first machine still remained; and the dividing of pity, like the cutting of a river into many channels, abated the strength of the natural stream. But this is an objection which none of my critics have urged against me; and therefore I might have let it pass, if I could have resolved to have been partial of myself. . . .

Yet, in this nicety of manners does the excellency of French poetry consist. Their heroes are the most civil people breathing; but their good breeding seldom extends to a word of sense; all their wit is in their ceremony; they want the genius which animates our stage and therefore it is but necessary, when they cannot please, that they should take care not to offend. But as the civilest man in the company is commonly the dullest, so these authors, while they are afraid to make you laugh or cry, out of pure good manners make you sleep. They are so careful not to exasperate a critic, that they never leave him any work; so busy with the broom, and make so clean a riddance, that there is little left either for censure or for praise: For no part of a poem is worth our discommending, where the whole is

insipid; as when we have once tasted of palled wine, we stay not to examine it glass by glass. But while they affect to shine in trifles, they are often
careless in essentials. Thus, their Hippolytus is so scrupulous in point of
decency, that he will rather expose himself to death, than accuse his step-
mother to his father; and my critics I am sure will commend him for it.
But we of grosser apprehensions are apt to think that this excess of generosity is not practicable, but with fools and madmen. This was good manners
with a vengeance; and the audience is like to be much concerned at the
misfortunes of this admirable hero. But take Hippolytus out of his poetic
fit, and I suppose he would think it a wiser part to set the saddle on the
right horse, and choose rather to live with the reputation of a plain-spoken,
honest man, than to die with the infamy of an incestuous villain. . . . But
for my part, I desire to be tried by the laws of my own country; for it seems
unjust to me, that the French should prescribe here, till they have conquered. Our litle sonneteers, who follow them, have too narrow souls to
judge of poetry. Poets themselves are the most proper, though I conclude
not the only critics. But till some genius, as universal as Aristotle, shall arise,
one who can penetrate into all arts and sciences, without the practice of
them, I shall think it reasonable, that the judgment of an artificer in his
own art should be preferable to the opinion of another man; at least where
he is not bribed by interest, or prejudiced by malice.

John Milton *1608–1674*

Of That Sort of Dramatic Poem Called Tragedy *1671*

Tragedy, as it was anciently composed, hath been ever held the gravest,
moralest, and most profitable of all other poems; therefore said by Aristotle
to be of power, by raising pity and fear, or terror, to purge the mind of those

From *The Poetical Works of John Milton*, Vol. II, edited by David Masson. London:
Macmillan & Co., 1874.

and such-like passions—that is, to temper and reduce them to just measure with a kind of delight, stirred up by reading or seeing those passions well imitated. Nor is Nature wanting in her own effects to make good his assertion; for so, in physic, things of melancholic hue and quality are used against melancholy, sour against sour, salt to remove salt humours. Hence philosophers and other gravest writers, as Cicero, Plutarch, and others, frequently cite out of tragic poets, both to adorn and illustrate their discourse. The Apostle Paul himself thought it not unworthy to insert a verse of Euripides into the text of Holy Scripture, 1 Cor. 15:33; and Paraeus, commenting on the *Revelation*, divides the whole book, as a tragedy, into acts, distinguished each by a Chorus of heavenly harpings and song between. Heretofore men in highest dignity have laboured not a little to be thought able to compose a tragedy. Of that honour Dionysius the elder was no less ambitious than before of his attaining to the tyranny. Augustus Caesar also had begun his *Ajax*, but, unable to please his own judgment with what he had begun, left it unfinished. Seneca, the philosopher, is by some thought the author of those tragedies (at least the best of them) that go under that name. Gregory Nazianzen, a Father of the Church, thought it not unbeseeming the sanctity of his person to write a tragedy, which he entitled *Christ Suffering*. This is mentioned to vindicate Tragedy from the small esteem, or rather infamy, which in the account of many it undergoes at this day, with other common interludes; happening through the poet's error of intermixing comic stuff with tragic sadness and gravity, or introducing trivial and vulgar persons: which by all judicious hath been counted absurd, and brought in without discretion, corruptly to gratify the people. And, though ancient Tragedy use no Prologue, yet using sometimes, in case of self-defence or explanation, that which Martial calls an Epistle, in behalf of this tragedy, coming forth after the ancient manner, much different from what among us passes for best, thus much beforehand may be *epistled*— that Chorus is here introduced after the Greek manner, not ancient only, but modern, and still in use among the Italians. In the modeling therefore of this poem, with good reason, the Ancients and Italians are rather followed, as of much more authority and fame. The measure of verse used in the Chorus is of all sorts, called by the Greeks *Monostrophic*, or rather *Apolelymenon*, without regard had to Strophe, Antistrophe, or Epode, which were a kind of stanzas framed only for the music, then used with the Chorus that sung; not essential to the poem, and therefore not material; or, being divided into stanzas or pauses, they may be called *Allaeostropha*. Division into act and scene, referring chiefly to the stage (to which this work[1] never was intended), is here omitted.

It suffices if the whole drama be found not produced beyond the fifth

---

[1] *Samson Agonistes*, a tragedy to which this essay is prefixed.

act. Of the style and uniformity, and that commonly called the plot, whether intricate or explicit—which is nothing indeed but such economy, or disposition of the fable, as may stand best with verisimilitude and decorum—they only will best judge who are not unacquainted with Aeschylus, Sophocles, and Euripides, the three tragic poets unequaled yet by any, and the best rule to all who endeavour to write Tragedy. The circumscription of time, wherein the whole drama begins and ends, is, according to ancient rule and best example, within the space of twenty-four hours.

Samuel Butler *1612–1680*

Upon Critics Who Judge of Modern Plays Precisely by the Rules of the Ancients *1678*

Who ever will regard poetic fury,
When it is once found idiot by a jury;
And ev'ry pert and arbitrary fool
Can all poetic licence over-rule;
Assume a barbarous tyranny to handle
The Muses worse than Ostrogoth and Vandal;
Make 'em submit to verdict and report,
And stand or fall to th' orders of a court?
Much less be sentenced by the arbitrary
Proceedings of a witless plagiary,
That forges old records and ordinances
Against the right and property of fancies,
More false and nice than weighing of the weather

Selections. From *The Poetical Works of Samuel Butler*, Vol. II, edited by the Reverend George Gilfillan. Edinburgh: James Nichol, 1854.

To th' hundredth atom of the lightest feather;
Or measuring of air upon Parnassus
With cylinders of Torricellian glasses;
Reduce all Tragedy, by rules of art,
Back to its antique theatre, a cart;
And make them henceforth keep the beaten roads
Of reverend choruses and episodes;
Reform and regulate a puppet-play,
According to the true and ancient way;
That not an actor shall presume to squeak,
Unless he have a licence for 't in Greek;
Nor Whittington henceforward sell his cat in
Plain vulgar English, without mewing Latin:
No pudding shall be suffer'd to be witty,
Unless it be in order to raise pity;
Nor Devil in the puppet-play b' allow'd
To roar and spit fire, but to fright the crowd,
Unless some god or demon chance t' have piques
Against on ancient family of Greeks;
That other men may tremble, and take warning,
How such a fatal progeny they're born in.
For none but such for Tragedy are fitted,
That have been ruin'd only to be pity'd;
And only those held proper to deter,
Who've had th' ill luck against their wills to err.
Whence only such as are of middling sizes,
Between morality and venial vices,
Are qualify'd to be destroy'd by Fate,
For other mortals to take warning at. . . .

These are the reformations of the Stage,
Like other reformations of the age,
On purpose to destroy all wit and sense,
As th' other did all law and conscience. . . .

An English poet should be try'd b' his peers,
And not by pedants and philosophers,
Incompetent to judge poetic fury,
As butchers are forbid to be of a jury;
Besides the most intolerable wrong
To try their matters in a foreign tongue. . . .
Enough to furnish all the lewd impeachers
Of witty Beaumont's poetry and Fletcher's;

Who, for a few misprisions of wit,
Are charged by those who ten times worse commit;
And, for misjudging some unhappy scenes,
Are censured for 't with more unlucky sense;
When all their worst miscarriages delight,
And please more, than the best that pedants write.

Thomas Rymer *1641–1713*

A Short View of Tragedy *1693*

Chapter I

What reformation may not we expect now that in France they see the necessity of a chorus to their tragedies? Boyer and Racine, both of the Royal Academy, have led the dance; they have tried the success in the last plays that were presented by them.

The chorus was the root and original and is certainly always the most necessary part of tragedy.

The spectators thereby are secured that their poet shall not juggle or put upon them in the matter of place and time other than is just and reasonable for the representation.

And the poet has this benefit: The chorus is a goodly show, so that he need not ramble from his subject out of his wits for some foreign toy or hobbyhorse to humor the multitude.

Aristotle[1] tells us of two senses that must be pleased, our sight and our ears, and it is vain for a poet (with Bayes in *The Rehearsal*)[2] to complain of injustice and the wrong judgment in his audience unless these two senses be gratified.

Selections. From Thomas Rymer, *A Short View of Tragedy*. London: Richard Baldwin, 1693. Spelling and punctuation modernized by the editor.

[1] *Poetica* [Rymer's note].
[2] (1671). A parody of heroic tragedy by George Villiers, Second Duke of Buckingham, and others.

The worst of it is that most people are wholly led by these two senses and follow them upon content without ever troubling their noodle farther.

How many plays owe all their success to a rare show? Even in the days of Horace, enter on the stage a person in a costly, strange habit: Lord! What clapping, what noise and thunder as [if] Heaven and earth were coming together! Yet not one word spoken.

> *Dixit adhuc aliquid? nil, sane, quid placit ergo?*
> *Lana Tarentino violas imitata veneno.*[3]

Was there ought said? troth, no. What then did touch you?
Some Prince of Bantam, or a Mamamouche.

It matters not whether there be any plot, any characters, any sense, or a wise word from one end to the other provided in our play we have the Senate of Rome, the Venetian Senate in their Pontificalibus, or a Blackamoor ruffian, or Tom Dove or other four-legged hero of the Bear Garden.

The eye is a quick sense, will be in with our fancy, and prepossesses the head strangely. Another means whereby the eye misleads our judgment is the action. We go to see a play acted. In tragedy is represented a memorable action. So the spectators are always pleased to see action and are not often so ill natured to pry into and examine whether it be proper, just, natural, in season, or out of season. Bayes in *The Rehearsal* well knew this secret: the two Kings are at their Coranto; nay, the Moon and the Earth dance the Hey; anything in nature or against nature rather than allow the serious council or other dull business to interrupt or obstruct action.

This thing of action finds the blind side of humankind a hundred ways. We laugh and weep with those that laugh or weep. We gape, stretch, and are very dotterels by example.

Action is speaking to the eyes, and all Europe over plays have been represented with great applause in a tongue unknown and sometimes without any language at all.

Many, peradventure, of the tragical scenes in Shakespeare, cried up for the action, might do yet better without words. Words are a sort of heavy baggage that were better out of the way at the push of action, especially in his bombast circumstance, where the words and action are seldom akin, generally are inconsistent, at cross-purposes, embarrass or destroy each other; yet to those who take not the words distinctly there may be something in the buzz and sound that like a drone to a bagpipe may serve to set off the action. For an instance of the former, would not a rap at the door better express Iago's meaning than:

---

[3] Horace, *Epistles*, II, 1, ll. 206–207.

> . . . Call aloud.
> IAGO   Do, with like timorous accent and dire yell,
>   As when by night and negligence the fire
>   Is spied in populous cities.

For "What ship? Who is arrived?" the answer is:

> [GENTLEMAN]   'Tis one Iago, Ancient to the General.
> [CASSIO]   He 'as had most fav'rable and happy speed;
>   Tempests themselves, high seas, and howling winds,
>   The guttered rocks and congregated sands,
>   Traitors ensteeped, t' enclog the guiltless keel,
>   As having sense of beauty, do omit
>   Their [mortal] natures, letting go safely by
>   The divine Desdemona.

Is this the language of the Exchange or the Insuring Office? Once in a man's life he might be content at Bedlam to hear such a rapture. In a play one should speak like a man of business; his speech must be Πολιτινος, which the French render *agissante*, the Italians *negotiosa* and *operativa*.[4] But by this gentleman's talk one may well guess he has nothing to do. And he has many companions that are

> . . . Hey day!
> I know not what to do nor what to say.[5]

It was then a strange imagination in Ben Jonson to go stuff out a play[6] with Tully's orations, and in Seneca to think his dry morals and a tedious train of sentences might do feats or have any wonderful operation in the drama.

Some go to see, others to hear a play. The poet should please both, but be sure that the spectators be satisfied, whatever entertainment he give his audience.

But if neither the show nor the action cheats us, there remains still a notable vehicle to carry off nonsense, which is the pronunciation.

> By the loud trumpet, which our courage aids,
> We learn that sound as well as our sense persuades.[7]

Demosthenes[8] had a good stock of sense, was a great master of words, could turn a period and draw up his tropes in a line of battle, and fain would he have seen some effect of his orations; nobody was moved, nobody

---

[4] Busy, bustling; businesslike; effective.
[5] *The Rehearsal* [Rymer's note].
[6] *Cataline* (1611).
[7] Edmund Waller, "Upon the Earl of Roscommon's Translation of Horace" (1680).
[8] Plutarch, *Demosthenes* [Rymer's note].

minded him. He goes to the playhouse, bargains with an actor, and learned of him to speak roundly and gracefully. From that time, who but Demosthenes? Never such a leading man! Whenever he spoke, no division, not a vote to the contrary, the whole house were with him, *nemine contradicente.*[9] This change observed, a friend went to him for the secret. "Tell me," says he, "your nostrum. Tell me your receipt. What is the main ingredient that makes an orator?" Demosthenes answered, "Pronunciation." "What then the next thing?" "Pronunciation." "Pray then, what the third?" Still the answer was, "Pronunciation."

Now, this was at Athens, where want of wit was never an objection against them. So that it is not in song only that a good voice diverts us from the wit and sense. From the stage, the bar, or the pulpit, a good voice will prepossess our ears and, having seized that pass, is in a fair way to surprise our judgment.

Considering then what power the show, the action, and the pronunciation have over us, it is no wonder that wise men often mistake and give a hasty judgment, which upon a review is justly set aside. . . .

But among the moderns, never was a cause canvassed with so much heat between the play judges as that in France about Corneille's tragedy of *The Cid.* The majority were so fond of it that with them it became a proverb "*Cela est plus beau que Le Cid.*"[10] On the other side, Cardinal Richelieu damned it and said, "All the pudder about it was only between the ignorant people and the men of judgment."

Yet this Cardinal, with so nice a taste, had not many years before been several times to see acted the tragedy of *Sir Thomas More* and as often wept at the representation. Never were known so many people crowded to death as at that play,[11] yet was it the manufacture of Jean de [la] Serre, one about the form of our Flecknoe[12] or Thomas Jordan,[13] the same de [la] Serre that dedicated a *Book of Meditations* to K[ing] Charles I and went home with pockets full of medals and reward.

By this instance we see a man the most sharp and of the greatest penetration was imposed upon by these cheating senses, the eyes and the ears, which greedily took in the impression from the show, the action, and from the emphasis and pronunciation, though there was no great matter of fable, no manners, no fine thoughts, no language, that is, nothing of a tragedy, nothing of a poet all the while.

Horace was very angry with these empty shows and vanity, which the

---

[9] No one contradicting.

[10] Pelisson, *Hist. Acad.* [Rymer's note]. "That is more beautiful than *The Cid.*"

[11] *Parnasse Reform* [Rymer's note].

[12] Richard Flecknoe (d.c. 1678), an Irish Catholic priest whose name became synonymous with bad poetry.

[13] (c. 1620–c. 1685), actor-playwright.

gentlemen of his time ran like mad after. . . . What would he have said to the French opera, of late so much in vogue? There it is, for you to bewitch your eyes and to charm your ears. . . . 'Tis a debauch the most insinuating and the most pernicious. . . . Away with your opera from the theatre! Better had they become the heathen temples. . . .

Chapter VIII

From all the tragedies acted on our English stage, *Othello* is said to bear the bell away. The subject is more of a piece and there is indeed something like, there is, as it were, some phantom of a fable. The fable is always accounted the soul of tragedy, and it is the fable which is properly the poet's part, because the other three parts of tragedy, to wit, the characters are taken from the moral philosopher, the thoughts or sense from them that teach rhetoric, and the last part, which is the expression, we learn from the grammarians.

This fable is drawn from a novel, composed in Italian by Geraldi Cinthio, who also was a writer of tragedies and to that use employed such of his tales as he judged proper for the stage. But with this of the Moor, he meddled no farther.

Shakespeare alters it from the original in several particulars, but always, unfortunately, for the worse. He bestows a name on his Moor and styles him the Moor of Venice, a note of preeminence which neither history nor heraldry can allow him. Cinthio, who knew him best and whose creature he was, calls him simply a Moor. We say the Piper of Strasbourg, the Jew of Florence, and, if you please, the Pinder of Wakefield—all upon record and memorable in their places. But we see no such cause for the Moor's preferment to that dignity. And it is an affront to all chroniclers and antiquaries to top upon 'em a Moor, with that mark of renown, who yet had never fallen within the sphere of their cognizance.

Then is the Moor's life from a simple citizen in Cinthio dressed up with her topknots and raised to be Desdemona, a Senator's daughter. All this is very strange and therefore pleases such as reflect not on the improbability. This match might well be without the parents' consent. . . .

. . . The moral . . . of this fable is very instructive.

First, this may be a caution to all maidens of quality how without their parents' consent they run away with Blackamoors. . . .

Secondly, this may be a warning to all good wives that they look well to their linen.

Thirdly, this may be a lesson to husbands that before their jealously be tragical, the proofs may be mathematical.

Cinthio affirms that she was not overcome by a womanish appetite but by the virtue of the Moor. It must be a good-natured reader that takes

Cinthio's word in this case, though in a novel. Shakespeare, who is accountable both to the eyes and to the ears, and to convince the very heart of an audience, shows that Desdemona was won by hearing Othello talk:

> OTHELLO   ... I spoke of most disastrous chances,
>   Of moving accidents by flood and field,
>   Of hairbreadth 'scapes i' th' imm'nent deadly breach,
>   Of being taken by th' insolent foe
>   And sold to slavery, of my redemption thence
>   And [portance] in my [trav'lers'] history,
>   Wherein of antres vast and deserts idle,
>   Rough quarries, rocks, and hills whose heads touch Heaven,
>   It was my hint to speak—such was my process—
>   And of the cann'bals that each other eat,
>   The Anthropophagi, and men whose heads
>   Do grow beneath their shoulders. ...

This was the charm, this was the philtre, the love powder that took the daughter of this noble Venetian. This was sufficient to make the Blackamoor white and reconcile all, though there had been a cloven foot into the bargain.

A meaner woman might be as soon taken by *aqua tetrachymagogon*.[14]

... The Doge himself tells us: "I think this tale would win my daughter too. . . ." Shakespeare in this play calls 'em the supersubtle Venetians. Yet examine throughout the tragedy: there is nothing in the noble Desdemona that is not below any country chambermaid with us. ...

The character of that state is to employ strangers in their wars, but shall a poet thence fancy that they will set a Negro to be their general, or trust a Moor to defend them against the Turk? With us, a Blackamoor might rise to be a trumpeter, but Shakespeare would not have him less than a lieutenant-general. With us, a Moor might marry some little drab or small-coal wench; Shakespeare would provide him the daughter and heir of some great lord or Privy Councillor. And all the town should reckon it a very suitable match! Yet the English are not bred up with that hatred and aversion to the Moors as are the Venetians, who suffer by a perpetual hostility from them. ...

Nothing is more odious in nature than an improbable lie, and certainly never was any play fraught, like this *Othello*, with improbabilities.

The character or manners, which are the second part in a tragedy, are not less unnatural and improper than the fable was improbable and absurd.

Othello is made a Venetian general. We see nothing done by him nor related concerning him that comports with the condition of a general, or indeed of a man, unless the killing himself to avoid a death the law was

---

[14] A meaningless name, used by quacks.

about to inflict upon him. When his jealousy had wrought him up to a resolution of [his] taking revenge for the supposed injury, he sets Iago to the fighting part, to kill Cassio, and chooses himself to murder the silly woman, his wife, that was like to make no resistance.

His love and his jealousy are no part of a soldier's character, unless for comedy.

But what is most intolerable is Iago. . . . Shakespeare knew his character of Iago was inconsistent. . . . But to entertain the audience with something new and surprising, against common sense and nature, he would pass upon us a close, dissembling, false, insinuating rascal instead of an openhearted, frank, plain-dealing soldier, a character constantly worn by them for some thousands of years in the world. . . . Our ensigns and subalterns, when disgusted by the captain, throw up their commissions, bluster, and are bare faced. Iago, I hope, is not brought on the stage in a red coat. . . .

Nor is our poet more discreet in his Desdemona. He had chosen a soldier for his knave, and a Venetian lady is to be the fool.

This Senator's daughter runs away to a carrier's inn, the Sagittary, with a Blackmoor, is no sooner wedded to him but the very night she beds him is importuning and teasing him for a young, smock-faced lieutenant, Cassio. And though she perceives the Moor jealous of Cassio, yet will she not forbear but still rings Cassio, Cassio in both his ears.

. . . There can be nothing in the characters either for the profit or to delight an audience.

The third thing to be considered is the thoughts. But from such characters we need not expect many that are either true or fine or noble.

And without these, that is, without sense or meaning, the fourth part of tragedy, which is the expression, can hardly deserve to be treated on distinctly. The verses rumbling in our ears are of good use to help off the action.

In the neighing of a horse or in the growling of a mastiff there is a meaning, there is as lively expression, and may I say more humanity than many times in the tragical flights of Shakespeare.

Step then among the scenes to observe the conduct in this tragedy.

The first we see are Iago and Roderigo by night in the streets of Venice. After growling a long time together, they resolve to tell Brabantio that his daughter is run away with the Blackamoor. Iago and Roderigo were not of quality to be familiar with Brabantio, nor had any provocation from him to deserve a rude thing at their hands. Brabantio was a noble Venetian, one of the sovereign lords and principal persons in the government, peer to the most serene Doge, one attended with more state, ceremony, and punctilio than any English duke or nobleman in the government will pretend to. This misfortune in his daughter is so prodigious, so tender a point as might puzzle the finest wit of the most supersubtle Venetian to touch upon it, or break the discovery to her father. See then how delicately Shakespeare minces the matter:

> RODERIGO   What ho, Brabantio, Signior Brabantio, ho!
> IAGO   Awake! What ho, Brabantio! Thieves, thieves!
>   Look to your house, your daughter, and your bags!
>   Thieves, thieves!
>   [*Brabantio at a window.*]
> BRABANTIO   What is the reason for this terrible summons?
>   What is the matter there?
> RODERIGO   Signior, is all your family within?
> IAGO   Are your doors locked?
> BRABANTIO   Why, wherefore ask you this?
> IAGO   ['Zounds,] sir, you're robbed. For shame, put on your gown;
>   Your heart is burst, you have lost half your soul;
>   E'en now, [now,] very now, an old black ram
>   Is tupping your white ewe. Arise, arise!
>   Awake the snorting cit'zens with the bell,
>   Or else the Dev'l will make a grandsire of you.
>   Arise, I say!

Nor have they yet done. Amongst other ribaldry, they tell him:

> IAGO   Sir, you are one of those that will not serve God if the Devil bid you. Because we come to do you service [and] you think [we are] ruffians, you'll have your daughter covered with a Barbary [horse], you'll have your nephews neigh to you, you'll have coursers for cousins and gennets for germans.
> BRABANTIO   What prophane wretch art thou?
> IAGO   I am one sir, that comes to tell you your daughter and the Moor are now making the beast with two backs.

In former days, there wont to be kept at the courts of princes somebody in a fool's coat that in pure simplicity might let slip something which made way for the ill news and blunted the shock which otherwise might have come too violent upon the party. . . . But besides the manners to a magnifico, humanity cannot bear that an old gentleman in his misfortune should be insulted over with such a rabble of scoundrel language when no cause or provocation. Yet thus it is on our stage. This is our school of good manners and the *Speculum Vitae*. . . .[15]

For the second act, our poet having dispatched his affairs at Venice shows the action next (I know not how many leagues off) in the island of Cyprus. The audience must be there too, and yet our Bayes had it never in his head to make any provision of transport ships for them.

In the days that the Old Testament was acted in Clerkenwell by the parish clerks of London, the Israelites might pass through the Red Sea.

[15] Mirror of life.

But alas, at this time we have no Moses to bid the waters make way and to usher us along. Well, the absurdities of this kind break no bones. They may make fools of us, but [they] do not hurt our morals. . . .

I thought it enough that Cassio should be acquainted with a virgin of that rank and consideration in Venice as Desdemona. I wondered that in the Senate house everyone should know her so familiarly. Yet here also at Cyprus everybody is in a rapture at the name of Desdemona, except only Montano, who must be ignorant that Cassio, who has an excellent cut in shaping an answer, may give him the satisfaction. . . .

Now follows a long rabble of Jack-pudding farce betwixt Iago and Desdemona that runs on with all the little plays, jingles, and trash below the patience of any country kitchenmaid with her sweetheart. . . . And this is all when they are newly got on shore from a dismal tempest and when every moment she might expect to hear her lord (as she calls him), that she runs so mad after, is arrived or lost. . . . The company for acting Christ's passion or the Old Testament were carpenters, cobblers, and illiterate fellows who found that the drolls and fooleries interlarded by them brought in the rabble and lengthened their time, so they got money by the bargain. . . . These carpenters and cobblers were the guides [Shakespeare] followed. And it is then no wonder that we find so much farce and apocryphal matter in his tragedies, thereby unhallowing the theatre, profaning the name of tragedy, and instead of representing men and manners, turning all morality, good sense, and humanity into mockery and derision. . . .

The last act begins with Iago and Roderigo. . . . Our gallant grows angry and would have satisfaction from Iago, who sets all right by telling him Cassio is to be Governor, Othello is going with Desdemona into Mauritania. To prevent this, you are to murder Cassio and then all may be well. . . . Why Roderigo should take this for payment and risk his person where the prospect of advantage is so very uncertain and remote, nobody can imagine. It had need be a supersubtle Venetian that this plot will pass upon. . . .

So much ado, so much stress, so much passion and repetition about a handkerchief! Why was not this called the *Tragedy of the Handkerchief*? . . . Had it been Desdemona's garter, the sagacious Moor might have smelled a rat, but the handkerchief is so remote a trifle, no booby on this side Mauritania could make any consequence from it.

We may learn here that a woman never loses her tongue even though after she is stifled.

DESDEMONA   Oh, falsely, falsely murdered! [. . .]
EMILIA   Sweet Desdemona, oh, sweet mistress, speak!
DESDEMONA   A guiltless death I die.
EMILIA   Oh, who [hath] done [this] deed?
DESDEMONA   Nobody! I, myself! Farewell.
    Commend me to my kind lord. Oh, farewell!

... But hark what follows:[16]

> OTHELLO   ... Oh, heavy hour!
>   Methinks it should be now a huge eclipse
>   Of sun and moon, and that th' affrighted globe
>   [Did] yawn at alteration.

This is wonderful. Here is poetry to elevate and amuse. Here is found all-sufficient. It would be uncivil to ask Flamsteed[17] if the sun and moon can both together be so hugely eclipsed in any heavy hour whatsoever. . . . These are physical circumstances a poet may be ignorant in without any harm to the public. These slips have no influence on our manners and good life, which are the poet's province.

Rather may we ask here what unnatural crime Desdemona or her parents had committed to bring this judgment down upon her, to wed a Blackamoor and, innocent, to be thus cruelly murdered by him. What instruction can we make out of this catastrophe? O whither must our reflection lead us? Is not this to envenom and sour our spirits, to make us repine and grumble at Providence and the government of the world? If this be our end, what boots it to be virtuous?

Desdemona dropped the handkerchief and missed it that very day after her marriage. It might have been rumpled up with her wedding sheets. And this night that she lay in her wedding sheets the Fairy Napkin, while Othello was stifling her, might have started up to disarm his fury and stop his ungracious mouth. Then might she, in a trance for fear, have lain as dead. Then might he, believing her dead, touched with remorse, have honestly cut his own throat by the good leave and with the applause of all the spectators, who might thereupon have gone home with a quiet mind, admiring the beauty of Providence, fairly and truly represented on the theatre. . . .

But from this scene to the end of the play we meet with nothing but blood and butchery, described much what to the style of the last speeches and confessions of the persons executed at Tyburn, with this difference, that there we have the fact and the due course of justice, whereas our poet, against all justice and reason, against all law, humanity, and nature, in a barbarous, arbitrary way executes and makes havoc of his subjects, hab-nab, as they come to hand. Desdemona dropped her handkerchief; therefore she must be stifled. Othello, by law to be broken on the wheel, by the poet's cunning escapes with cutting his own throat. Cassio, for I know not what, comes off with a broken shin. Iago murders his benefactor, Roderigo, as [if] this were poetical gratitude. Iago is not yet killed because there yet never was such a villain alive. . . .

---

[16] Actually, it precedes.
[17] John Flamsteed, the Astronomer Royal (1646–1719).

What can remain with the audience to carry home with them from this sort of poetry for their use and edification? How can it work, unless (instead of settling the mind and purging our passions) to delude our senses, disorder our thoughts, addle our brain, pervert our affections, hare our imaginations, corrupt our appetite, and fill our head with vanity, confusion, Tintamarre, and jingle-jangle, beyond what all the parish clerks of London, with their Old Testament farces and interludes in Richard the Second's time, could ever pretend to? Our only hopes, for the good of their souls, can be that these people go to the playhouse as they do to church: to sit still, look on one another, make no reflection, nor mind the play more than they would a sermon.

There is in this play some burlesque, some humor and ramble of comical wit, some show, and some mimicry to divert the spectators, but the tragical part is plainly none other than a bloody farce without salt or savor.

Jeremy Collier *1650–1726*

A Short View of the Immorality and Profaneness of the English Stage *1698*

Introduction

The business of plays is to recommend virtue and discountenance vice; to show the uncertainty of human greatness, the sudden turns of fate, and the unhappy conclusions of violence and injustice; 'tis to expose the singularities of pride and fancy, to make folly and falsehood contemptible, and to bring everything that is ill under infamy and neglect. This design has been oddly pursued by the English stage. Our poets write with a different view

Selections. From Jeremy Collier, *A Short View of the Immorality and Profaneness of the English Stage*. London: S. Keble, 1698. Spelling and punctuation modernized by the editor.

and are gone into another interest. 'Tis true, were their intentions fair they might be serviceable to this purpose. They have in great measure the springs of thought and inclination in their power. Show, music, action, and rhetoric are moving entertainments, and rightly employed would be very significant. But force and motion are things indifferent and the use lies chiefly in the application. These advantages are now in the enemies' hands and under a very dangerous management. Like cannon seized, they are pointed the wrong way, and by the strength of the defence the mischief is made the greater. That this complaint is not unreasonable I shall endeavor to prove by showing the misbehavior of the stage with respect to morality and religion. Their liberties in the following particulars are intolerable, viz., their smuttiness of expression; their swearing, profaneness, and lewd application of Scripture; their abuse of the clergy; their making their top characters libertines and giving them success in their debauchery. . . .

Chapter I

The Immodesty of the Stage

In treating this head, I hope the reader does not expect that I should set down chapter and page and give him the citations at length. To do this would be a very unacceptable and foreign employment. Indeed, the passages, many of them, are in no condition to be handled. He that is desirous to see these flowers, let him do it in their own soil. 'Tis my business rather to kill the root than transplant it. But that the poets may not complain of injustice, I shall point to the infection at a distance and refer in general to play and person.

Now, among the curiosities of this kind we may reckon Mrs. Pinchwife, Horner, and Lady Fidget in *The Country Wife*; Widow Blackacre and Olivia in *The Plain Dealer*. . . .[1] Some people appear coarse and slovenly out of poverty. They can't well go to the charge of sense. They are offensive, like beggars, for want of necessaries. But this is none of *The Plain Dealer's* case. He can afford his muse a better dress when he pleases. But then the rule is: where the motive is the less, the fault is the greater. To proceed. Jacinta, Elvira, Dalinda, and Lady Pliant in the *Mock Astrologer*, *Spanish Friar*, *Love Triumphant*, and *Double Dealer* forget themselves extremely; and almost all the characters in *The Old Bachelor* are foul and nauseous. *Love for Love* and *The Relapse* strike sometimes upon this sand and so likewise does *Don Sebastian*. . . .[2]

[1] *The Country Wife* (1675) and *The Plain Dealer* (1676) by William Wycherley.

[2] *The Mock Astrologer* (1668), *The Spanish Friar* (1680), and *Love Triumphant* (1694) by John Dryden; *The Double Dealer* (1693), *The Old Bachelor* (1693), and *Love for Love* (1695) by William Congreve; *The Relapse* (1696) by Sir John Vanbrugh; *Don Sebastian* (1690) by John Dryden.

. . . Here is a large collection of debauchery. . . . Sometimes you have it in image and description, sometimes by way of allusion, sometimes in disguise, and sometimes without it. And what can be the meaning of such a representation unless it be to tincture the audience, to extinguish shame, and make lewdness a diversion? This is the natural consequence and therefore one would think 'twas the intention too. Such licentious discourse tends to no point but to stain the imagination, to awaken folly, and to weaken the defences of virtue. It was upon the account of these disorders that Plato banished poets [from] his Commonwealth. And one of the fathers calls poetry *Vinum Daemonum*, an intoxicating draught made up of the Devil's dispensatory.

I grant the abuse of a thing is no argument against the use of it. However, young people particularly should not entertain themselves with a lewd picture, especially when 'tis drawn by a masterly hand, for such a liberty may probably raise those passions which can neither be discharged without trouble nor satisfied without a crime. 'Tis not safe for a man to trust his virtue too far, for fear it should give him the slip. But the danger of such an entertainment is but part of the objection. 'Tis all scandal and meanness into the bargain. It does in effect degrade human nature, sinks reason into appetite, and breaks down the distinctions between man and beast. . . .

Smuttiness is a fault in behavior as well as in religion. 'Tis a very coarse diversion, the entertainment of those who are generally least both in sense and station. The looser part of the mob have no true relish of decency and honor, and want education and thought to furnish out a genteel conversation. Barrenness of fancy makes them often take up with those scandalous liberties. . . . The modern poets seem to use smut as the old ones did machines, to relieve a fainting invention. . . .

Obscenity in any company is a rustic, uncreditable talent, but among women 'tis particularly rude. Such talk would be very affrontive in conversation and not endured by any lady of reputation. Whence then comes it to pass that those liberties which disoblige so much in conversation should entertain upon the stage? Do the women leave all the regards to decency and conscience behind them when they come to the playhouse? Or does the place transform their inclinations and turn their former aversions into pleasure? Or were their pretences to sobriety elsewhere nothing but hypocrisy and grimace? Such suppositions as these are all satire and invective. They are rude imputations upon the whole sex. To treat the ladies with such stuff is no better than taking their money to abuse them. It supposes their imaginations vicious and their memories ill furnished, that they are practiced in the language of the stews and pleased with the scenes of brutishness when at the same time the customs of education and the laws of decency are so very cautious and reserved in regard to women—I say so very reserved—that 'tis almost a fault for them to understand they are ill used. . . .

. . . The stage is faulty to a scandalous degree of nauseousness and aggravation, for:

First, the poets make women speak smuttily. Of this, the places before mentioned are sufficient evidence, and if there was occasion they might be multiplied to a much greater number. Indeed, the comedies are seldom clear of these blemishes, and sometimes you have them in tragedy. For instance, *The Orphan*'s Monimia[3] makes a very improper description, and the royal Leonora, in *The Spanish Friar*, runs a strange length in the history of love. . . . Now, to bring women under such misbehavior is violence to their native modesty and misrepresentation of their sex, for modesty, as Mr. Rapin observes,[4] is the character of women. To represent them without this quality is to make monsters of them and throw them out of their kind. Euripides, who was no negligent observer of human nature, is always careful of this decorum. Thus, Phaedra,[5] when possessed with an infamous passion, takes all imaginable pains to conceal it. She is as regular and reserved in her language as the most virtuous matron. 'Tis true, the force of shame and desire, the scandal of satisfying and the difficulty of parting with her inclinations disorder her to distraction. However, her frenzy is not lewd. She keeps her modesty even after she has lost her wits. Had Shakespeare secured this point for his young virgin Ophelia, the play[6] had been better contrived. Since he was resolved to drown the lady like a kitten, he should have set her aswimming a little sooner. To keep her alive only to sully her reputation and discover the rankness of her breath was very cruel. . . .

Secondly, they represent their single ladies and persons of condition under these disorders of liberty. This makes the irregularity still more monstrous and a greater contradiction to nature and probability. . . . *The Double Dealer* is particularly remarkable. There are but four ladies in this play and three of the biggest of them are whores. A great compliment to quality, to tell them there is not above a quarter of them honest! . . .

Thirdly, they have oftentimes not so much as the poor refuge of a double meaning to fly to, so that you are under a necessity either of taking ribaldry or nonsense. And when the sentence has two handles, the worst is generally turned to the audience. . . .

Fourthly, and which is still more extraordinary, the Prologues and Epilogues are sometimes scandalous to the last degree. I shall discover them for once and let them stand like rocks in the margin. . . .[7] These preliminary and

---

[3] By Thomas Otway (1680).
[4] *Reflections on Aristole* [Collier's note].
[5] Euripides, *Hippolytus* [Collier's note].
[6] *Hamlet* [Collier's note].
[7] *Mock Astrologer, Country Wife, Cleomenes* [(1692) by John Dryden], *Old Bachelor* [Collier's note; these notes were in the margin rather than at the foot of the page].

concluding parts are designed to justify the conduct of the play and bespeak the favor of the company. Upon such occasions one would imagine, if ever, the ladies should be used with respect and the measures of decency observed. But here we have lewdness without shame or example. Here the poet exceeds himself. Here are such strains as would turn the stomach of an ordinary debauchee and be almost nauseous in the stews. And to make it the more agreeable, women are commonly picked out for this service. . . .

Chapter II

The Profaneness of the Stage

Another instance of the disorders of the stage is their profaneness. This charge may come under these two particulars: first, their cursing and swearing; secondly, their abuse of religion and Holy Scripture.

First, their cursing and swearing.

What is more frequent than their wishes of Hell and confusion, Devils and diseases, all the plagues of this world and the next to each other? And as for swearing, 'tis used by all persons and upon all occasions: by heroes and poltroons, by gentlemen and clowns; love and quarrels, success and disappointment, temper and passion must be varnished and set off with oaths. At some times and with some poets, swearing is no ordinary relief. . . . 'Tis almost all the rhetoric and reason some people are masters of. The manner of performance is different. Sometimes they mince the matter—change the letter and keep the sense[8]—as if they had a mind to steal a swearing and break the Commandment without sin. . . . When the fit comes on them, they make no difficulty of swearing at length. Instances of all these kinds may be met with in the *Old Bachelor, Double Dealer,* and *Love for Love.* . . .

. . . What sin [is] more contemptuous than common swearing? What can be more insolent and irreligious than to bring in God to attest our trifles, to give security for our follies, and to make part of our diversion? . . . And if religion signifies nothing, as I am afraid it does with some people, there is law as well as Gospel against swearing. . . .

For the preventing and avoiding of the great abuse of the holy Name of God in stage plays, interludes, etc., be it enacted by our Sovereign Lord, etc. that if at any time or times after the end of this present session of Parliament, any person or persons do or shall in any stage play, interlude, show, etc. jestingly or profanely speak or use the holy Name of God, or of Christ Jesus, or of the Holy Ghost, or of the Trinity, which are not to be spoken but with fear and reverence, shall forfeit for every such offence by him

[8] Gad for God [Collier's note].

or them committed ten pounds: the one moiety thereof to the King's Majesty, his Heirs, and Successors; the other moiety thereof to him or them that will sue for the same in any Court of Record at Westminster, wherein no essoin, protection, or wager of law shall be allowed.

By this Act not only direct swearing but all vain invocation of the name of God is forbidden. This Statute well executed would mend the poets or sweep the box, and the stage must either reform or not thrive upon profaneness. . . .

A second branch of the profaneness of the stage is their abuse of religion and Holy Scripture. And here sometimes they don't stop short of blasphemy. To cite all that might be collected of this kind would be tedious. I shall give the reader enough to justify the charge and, I hope, to abhor the practice.

To begin with *The Mock Astrologer* . . . Wildwood swears by Mahomet, rallies smuttily upon the other world, and gives the preference to the Turkish Paradise. This gentleman, to encourage Jacinta to a compliance in debauchery, tells her, "Heaven is all eyes and no tongue." That is, it sees wickedness but conceals it. . . . In the close of the play, they make sport with apparitions and fiends. One of the devils sneezes; upon this, they give him the blessing of the occasion and conclude he has got cold by being too long out of the fire. . . .

In *The Old Bachelor*, Vainlove asks Bellmour, "Could you not be content to go to Heaven?" Bellmore: "Hum, not immediately in my conscience, not heartily—" . . . To go to Heaven in jest is the way to go to Hell in earnest. . . .

Chapter III

The Clergy Abused by the Stage

The satire of the stage upon the clergy is extremely particular. In other cases they level at a single mark and confine themselves to persons. But here their buffoonery takes an unusual compass. They shoot chain shot and strike at universals. They play upon the character and endeavor to expose not only the men but the business. 'Tis true, the clergy are no small rub in the poet's way. 'Tis by their ministrations that religion is perpetuated, the other world refreshed, and the interest of virtue kept up. . . . As long as these men are looked on as the messengers of Heaven and the supports of government and enjoy their old pretensions in credit and authority . . . the stage must decline, of course, and atheism give ground and lewdness lie under censure and discouragement. Therefore, that liberty may not be embarrassed nor principles make head against pleasure, the clergy must be attacked and rendered ridiculous.

To represent a person fairly and without disserve to his reputation, two things are to be observed. First, he must not be ill used by others, nor, secondly, be made to play the fool himself. . . . The contradiction of both these methods is practiced by the stage. . . .

To give some instances of their civility: in *The Spanish Friar*, Dominick is made a pimp for Lorenzo, he is called a parcel of holy guts and garbage and said to have room in his belly for his church steeple. . . . And to make the railing more effectual, you have a general stroke or two upon the profession. Would you know what are the infallible church remedies? Why, 'tis to lie impudently and swear devoutly. . . .

. . . In *The Provoked Wife*,[9] Sir John Brute puts on the habit of a clergyman, counterfeits himself drunk, quarrels with the constable, and is knocked down and seized. He rails, swears, curses, is lewd and profane to all the heights of madness and debauchery. The officers and justice break jests upon him and make him a sort of representative of this order.

. . . *The Relapse* is, if possible, more singularly abusive. Bull, the chaplain, wishes the married couple joy in language horribly smutty and profane. To transcribe it would blot the paper too much. . . .[10] At the end of this act, Bull speaks to the case of bigamy and determines it thus: "I do confess, to take two husbands for the satisfaction of . . . is to commit the sin of exorbitancy, but to do it for the peace of the spirit is no more than to be drunk by way of physic. Besides, to prevent a parent's wrath is to avoid the sin of disobedience, for when the parent is angry the child is froward. . . ."[11] Coupler instructs Young Fashion which way Bull was to be managed. He tells him as chaplains go now he must be bribed high: "He wants money, preferment, wine, and a whore. . . ."

I could cite more plays to this purpose, but these are sufficient to show the temper of the stage. . . .

Chapter IV

The Stage Poets Make Their Principal Persons Vicious and Reward Them at the End of the Play

. . . When vice is varnished over with pleasure and comes in the shape of convenience . . . then the fancy may be gained and the guards corrupted and reason suborned against itself. . . . Innocence is often owing to fear, and appetite is kept under by shame, but when these restraints are once taken off, when profit and liberty lie on the same side and a man can debauch

---

[9] By Sir John Vanbrough (1697).

[10] The offending speech: "I hope, since it has been my lot to join you in the holy bands of wedlock, you will so well cultivate the soil, which I have craved a blessing on, that your children may swarm about you like bees about a honeycomb."

[11] The elipsis in this quotation from Act IV is Collier's, the missing words: "the flesh."

himself into credit, what can be expected in such a case but that pleasure should grow absolute and madness carry all before it? The stage seems eager to bring matters to this issue. They have made a considerable progress and are still pushing their point with all the vigor imaginable. If this be not their aim, why is lewdness so much considered in character and success? Why are their favorites atheistical and their fine gentlemen debauched? To what purpose is vice thus preferred, thus ornamented and caressed, unless for imitation? . . . Wildblood[12] sets up for debauchery, ridicules marriage, and swears by Mahomet. . . . Horner is horribly smutty and Harcourt false to his friend who used him kindly.[13] In *The Plain Dealer*, Freeman talks coarsely, cheats the widow, debauches her son, and makes him undutiful. . . . These sparks generally marry the top ladies and those that do not are brought to no penance but go off with the character of fine gentlemen. . . . Valentine[14] is altogether compounded of vice. He is a prodigal debauchee, unnatural and profane, obscene, saucy, and undutiful. And yet this libertine is crowned for the man of merit, has his wishes thrown into his lap, and makes the happy exit. . . .

To sum up the evidence, a fine gentleman is a fine whoring, swearing, smutty, atheistical man. These qualifications, it seems, complete the idea of honor. They are the top improvements of fortune and the distinguishing glories of birth and breeding! This is the stage test for quality, and those that can't stand it ought to be disclaimed. The restraints of conscience and the pedantry of virtue are unbecoming a cavalier; future securities and reaching beyond life are vulgar provisions. . . . A fine gentleman . . . has neither honesty nor honor, conscience nor manners, good nature nor civil hypocrisy: fine only in the insignificancy of life, the abuse of religion, and the scandals of conversation. These wonderful things are the poet's favorites. . . . And what can be the meaning of this wretched distribution of honor? Is it not to give credit and countenance to vice and to shame young people out of all pretence to conscience and regularity?

---

[12] *Mock Astrologer* [Collier's note].
[13] *Country Wife* [Collier's note].
[14] *Love for Love* [Collier's note].

William Congreve 1670–1729

Amendments of Mr. Collier's False and Imperfect Citations, etc. 1698

I have no intention to examine all the absurdities and falsehoods in Mr. Collier's book.[1] To use the gentleman's own metaphor in his preface, an inventory of such a warehouse would be a large work. My detection of his malice and ignorance, of his sophistry and vast assurance, will lie within a narrow compass and only bear a proportion to so much of his book as concerns myself.

Least of all would I undertake to defend the corruptions of the stage. Indeed, if I were so inclined, Mr. Collier has given me no occasion, for the greater part of those examples which he has produced are only demonstrations of his own impurity. They only savor of his utterance and were sweet enough till tainted by his breath.

I will not justify any of my own errors. I am sensible of many, and if Mr. Collier has by any accident stumbled on one or two, I will freely give them up to him. . . .

My intention, therefore, is to do little else but to restore those passages to their primitive station which have suffered so much in being transplanted by him. I will remove 'em from his dunghill and replant 'em in the field of nature; and when I have washed 'em of that filth which they have contracted in passing through his very dirty hands, let their own innocence protect them.

Mr. Collier, in the high vigor of his obscenity, first commits a rape upon my words and then arraigns 'em of immodesty; he has barbarity enough to accuse the very virgins that he has deflowered. . . . Where the expression is unblameable in its own clear and genuine signification, he enters into it himself like the evil spirit; he possesses the innocent phrase and makes it bellow forth his own blasphemies. . . .

To reprimand him a little in his own words, if these passages produced by Mr. Collier are obscene and profane, why were they raked in and disturbed unless it were to conjure up vice and revive impurities? Indeed, Mr. Collier has a very untoward way with him. His pen has such a libertine stroke that 'tis a question whether the practice or the reproof be the more licentious.

Selections. From William Congreve, *Amendments of Mr. Collier's False and Imperfect Citations, etc.* London: F. Tonson, 1698. Spelling and punctuation modernized by the editor.

[1] *A Short View of the Immorality and Profaneness of the English Stage* (see above, pp. 351–358).

He teaches those vices he would correct and writes more like a pimp than a p - - - -. Since the business must be undertaken, why was not the thought blanched, the expression made remote, and the ill features cast into shadows? . . . He has blackened the thoughts with his own smut. The expression that was remote, he has brought nearer. . . .

Before I proceed, for method's sake I must premise some few things to the reader, which if he thinks in his conscience are too much to be granted me I desire he would proceed no further in his perusal of these animadversions but return to Mr. Collier's *Short View, etc.*

First, I desire that I may lay down Aristotle's definition of comedy, which has been the compass by which all the comic poets since his time have steered their course. . . . Comedy, says Aristotle, is an imitation of the worse sort of people. . . . He does not mean the worse sort of people in respect to their quality but in respect to their manners. . . . There are crimes too daring and too horrid for comedy, but the vices most frequent and which are the common practice of the looser sort of livers are the subject matter of comedy. He tells us farther that they must be exposed after a ridiculous manner, for men are to be laughed out of their vices in comedy. The business of comedy is to delight as well as to instruct, and as vicious people are made ashamed of their follies or faults by seeing them exposed in a ridiculous manner, so are good people at once both warned and diverted at their expense.

Thus much I thought necessary to premise, that by showing the nature and end of comedy, we may be prepared to expect characters agreeable to it.

Secondly, since comic poets are obliged by the laws of comedy and to the intent that comedy may answer its true end and purpose, abovementioned, to represent vicious and foolish characters, in consideration of this, I desire that it may not be imputed to the persuasion or private sentiments of the author if at any time one of these vicious characters in any of his plays shall behave himself foolishly or immorally in word or deed. I hope I am not yet unreasonable; it were very hard that a painter should be believed to resemble all the ugly faces that he draws.

Thirdly, I must desire the impartial reader not to consider any expression or passage cited from any play as it appears in Mr. Collier's book, nor to pass any sentence or censure upon it out of its proper scene or alienated from the character by which it is spoken, for in that place alone and in his mouth alone can it have its proper and true signification. . . .

Fourthly, because Mr. Collier, in his chapter of the profaneness of the stage, has founded great part of his accusation upon the liberty which poets take of using some words in their plays which have been sometimes employed by the translators of the Holy Scriptures, I desire that the following distinction may be admitted, viz., that when words are applied to sacred things, and with a purpose to treat of sacred things, they ought to be understood accordingly, but when they are otherwise applied, the diversity of the subject gives a diversity of signification. And, in truth, he might as well except against the common use of the alphabet in poetry because the same letters are necessary to the spelling of words which are mentioned in sacred writ. . . .

It may not be impertinent in this place to remind the reader of a very common expedient which is made use of to recommend the instruction of our plays, which is this. After the action of the play is over and the delight of the representation at an end, there is generally care taken that the moral of the whole shall be summed up and delivered to the audience in the very last and concluding lines of the poem. The intention of this is that the delight of the representation may not so strongly possess the minds of the audience as to make them forget or oversee the instruction. It is the last thing said, that it may make the last impression, and it is always comprehended in a few lines and put into rhyme, that it may be easy and engaging to the memory. . . .

In his chapter of the immodesty of the stage, he has not made any quotation from my comedies but in general finds fault with the lightness of some characters. . . . "*The Double Dealer* is particularly remarkable. There are but four ladies in this play and three of the biggest of them are whores." These are very *big* words, very much too *big* for the sense, for to say "three of the biggest" when there are but four in number is stark nonsense. Whatever the matter may be in this gentleman's book, I perceive his style at least is admirable. . . . But mark: he gives us an instance of his *big* good breeding. "A great complement to quality, to tell them there is not above a quarter of them honest!" This computation, I suppose, he makes by the help of political arithmetic, as thus: The stage is the image of the world; by the men and women represented there are signified all the men and women in the world; so that if four women are shown upon the stage and three of them are vicious, it is as much as to say that three parts in four of the whole sex are stark naught. He who dares be so hardy as to gainsay this argument, let him do it; for my part, I love to meddle with my match. It was a mercy that all the four women were not naught, for that had been maintaining that there was not one woman of quality honest. What has Vergil to answer for at this rate in his *Aeneid*, where for two of the fair sex that do good, viz., Venus and the Sibyl (for Cybele and Andromache are but well-wishers), he has the following catalogue who are always engaged in mischief, viz., Juno, Juturna, Dido, her sister, her nurse, an old witch, Allecto the Fury, all the Harpies? To these you are reminded of Helen, the first incendiary; Sylvia is produced as a second; next Camilla; then Amata, who despised the decrees of the gods; nay, poor Creusa and Lavinia are made subservient to unfortunate events. . . .

Mr. Collier, in his second chapter, charges the stage with profaneness. Almost all the quotations which he has made from my plays in this chapter are represented falsely or by halves, so that I have very little to do in their vindication but to represent 'em as they are in the original fairly and at length and to fill up the blanks which this worthy, honest gentleman has left.

"In *The Old Bachelor*," says he, "Vainlove asks Bellmour, 'Could you be content to go to Heaven?' Bellmour: 'Hum, not immediately, in my conscience, not heartily—.' " Here, Mr. Collier concludes this quotation with a dash, as if both the sense and the words of the whole sentence were at an end. But the remainder of it in the play—Act III, Scene 2— is in these words: "I would do a little more good in my generation first in order to deserve it."

I think the meaning of the whole is very different from the meaning of the first half of this expression. 'Tis one thing for a man to say positively he will not go to Heaven and another to say that he does not think himself worthy till he is better prepared. . . .

In his next chapter, he charges the stage with the abuse of the clergy. . . . He seems to be apprehensive of being brought upon the stage and in some places endeavors to prove that as he is a priest he should be exempted from the correction of the drama. . . . I would ask Mr. Collier whether a man, after he has received holy orders, is become incapable of either playing the knave or the fool. . . . Such a character neither does nor can asperse the sacred order of priesthood; neither does it at all reflect upon the persons of the pious and good clergy. . . .

I come now to his chapter of the immorality of the stage. His objections here are rather objections against comedy in general than against mine or anybody's comedies in particular. He says the sparks that marry up the top ladies and are rewarded with wives and fortunes in the last acts are generally debauched characters. In answer to this, I refer to my first and second proposition. He is a little particular in his remarks upon Valentine in *Love for Love*. . . . Valentine is in debt and in love; he has honesty enough to close with a hard bargain rather than not pay his debts, in the first act; and he has generosity and sincerity enough in the last act to sacrifice everything to his love, and when he is in danger of losing his mistress thinks everything else of little worth. This, I hope, may be allowed a reason for the lady to say, "He has virtues." They are such in respect to her, and her once saying so in the last act is all the notice that is taken of his virtue quite through the play.

Mr. Collier says he is prodigal. He was prodigal and is shown in the first act under hard circumstances, which are the effects of his prodigality. That he is unnatural and undutiful, I don't understand: he has indeed a very unnatural father, and if he does not very passively submit to his tyranny and barbarous usage, I conceive there is a moral to be applied from thence to such fathers. That he is profane and obscene is a false accusation and without any evidence. In short, the character is a mixed character; his faults are fewer than his good qualities and as the world goes he may pass well enough for the best character in a comedy, where even the best must be shown to have faults, that the best spectators may be warned not to think too well of themselves. . . .

To give him his due, he seems everywhere to write more from prejudice than opinion; he rails when he should reason and for gentle reproofs uses scurrilous reproaches. . . . If there is any spirit in his arguments, it evaporates and flies off unseen through the heat of his passion. . . . That which shows the face of wit in his writing has indeed no more than the face, for the head is wanting.

John Dennis *1657–1734*

The Usefulness of the Stage to the Happiness of Mankind, to Government, and to Religion *1698*

Since . . . the stage is acknowledged by its greatest adversaries to be in itself good, and instrumental to the instruction of mankind, nothing can be more unreasonable than to exhort people to ruin it instead of reforming it, since at that rate we must think of abolishing much more important establishments. Yet that is apparently the design of Mr. Collier's book,[1] though his malice infinitely surpassing his ability, as it certainly does, whatever some people may think of him, his performance is somewhat awkward, for in the Introduction to his book he gives you reasons why the stage in general ought to be commended, in the first chapters of his book he pretends to show cause why the English stage ought to be reformed, and in the sixth and last chapter he pretends to prove by authority that no stage ought to be allowed. . . . If

Selections. From John Dennis, *The Usefulness of the Stage to the Happiness of Mankind, to Government, and to Religion. Occasioned by a late book, written by Jeremy Collier,* M. A. London: Richard Parker, 1698. Spelling and punctuation modernized by the editor.

[1] *A Short View of the Immortality and Profaneness of the English Stage* (see above, pp. 351–358).

Mr. Collier had only attacked the corruptions of the stage, for my part I should have been so far from blaming him that I should have publicly returned him my thinks, for the abuses are so great that there is a necessity for the reforming them. Not that I think that with all its corruptions the stage has debauched the people—I am fully convinced it has not, and I believe I have said enough in the following treatise to convince the reader of it—but this is certain, that the corruptions of the stage hinder its efficacy in the reformation of manners. . . . My business therefore is a vindication of the stage and not of the corruptions or the abuses of it. . . .

. . . The chief end and design of man is to make himself happy. . . . And 'tis by this universal principle that God maintains the harmony and order and quiet of the reasonable world. . . . The stage is instrumental to the happiness of mankind in general. . . .

. . . They who have made the most reflections on it . . . and above all philosophers . . . have declared themselves sensible that to be happy is a very difficult thing. And the reason why they of all men have always found it so difficult is because they always propounded to owe their happiness to reason, though one would think that experience might have convinced them of the folly of such a design because they had seen that the most thinking and the most reasonable had always most complained. . . . Nothing but passion in effect can please us, which everyone may know by experience, for when any man is pleased he may find by reflection that at the same time he is moved. The pleasure that any man meets with oftenest is the pleasure of sense. Let anyone examine himself in that and he will find that the pleasure is owing to passion, for the pleasure vanishes with the desire and is succeeded by loathing, which is a sort of grief. . . . But though we can never be happy by the force of reason, yet while we are in this life we cannot possibly be happy without it or against it, for since man is by his nature a reasonable creature, to suppose man happy against reason is to suppose him happy against nature, which is absurd and monstrous. . . . If reason resists, a man's breast becomes the seat of civil war, and the combat makes him miserable. . . . Now, in the world it is so very rare to have our passions thus raised and so improved that that is the reason why we are so seldom thoroughly and sincerely pleased. But in the drama the passions are false and abominable unless they are moved by their true springs and raised by their just degrees. Thus are they moved, thus are they raised in every well-writ tragedy till they come to as great a height as reason can very well bear. Besides, the very motion has a tendency to the subjecting them to reason and the very raising purges and moderates them so that the passions are seldom anywhere so pleasing and nowhere so safe as they are in tragedy. . . .

But now we come to the . . . pretended reason why the drama tends to the making of men unhappy, and that is, say the adversaries of the stage, because it encourages and indulges their vices. To which we answer that the drama, and particularly tragedy in its purity is so far from having that effect that it must of necessity make men virtuous: first, because it moderates the passions whose excesses cause their vices; secondly, because it instructs them in their duties, both by its fable and by its sentences. But here they start an objection which some imagine a strong one, that is, that the nation has been more corrupted since the establishment of the drama upon the Restoration than ever it was before. To which I answer . . . first . . . if the corruption of manners proceeded from the abuses of the stage, how comes it to pass that we never heard any complaint of the like corruption of manners before the restoration of Charles the Second, since it is plain from Mr. Collier's book that the drama flourished in the reign of King James I and flourished with the like licentiousness? But secondly, if this general corruption of manners is to be attributed to the abuses of the stage, from hence it will follow that there should be the greatest corruption of manners where the theatres are most frequented or most licentious, which is not true, for in France the theatres are less licentious than ours and yet the corruption of manners is there as great, if you only except our drinking, which . . . can never proceed from any encouragement of the stage. . . . But thirdly, the corruption of manners upon the Restoration appeared with all the fury of libertinism even before the playhouse was reestablished and long before it could have any influence on manners, so that another cause of that corruption is to be inquired after than the reestablishment of the drama, and that can be nothing but that beastly Reformation, which in the time of the late civil wars . . . oppressed and persecuted men's inclinations instead of correcting and converting them, which afterwards broke out with the same violence that a raging fire does upon its first getting vent. And that which gave it so licentious a vent was not only the permission but the example of the Court, which for the most part was just arrived from abroad with the King, where it had endeavored by foreign corruption to sweeten or at least to soften adversity, and having sojourned for a considerable time both at Paris and in the Low Countries united the spirit of the French whoring to the fury of the Dutch drinking, so that the poets who writ immediately after the Restoration were obliged to humor the depraved tastes of their audience. . . . The spirit of libertinism which came in with the Court and for which the people were so well prepared by the sham restoration of manners caused the lewdness of their plays and not the lewdness of plays the spirit of libertinism. . . . Fourthly, that the corruption of manners is not to be attributed to the licentiousness of the drama may appear from the consideration of the reigning vices. . . . For drinking and gaming, their excesses cannot be reasonably charged upon the stage . . . because these two vices have been made odious and ridiculous by our plays, instead of being shown agreeable . . . [and] because those two vices flourish in places that are too remote and in persons that are too abject to be encouraged or influenced by the stage. There is drinking and gaming in the furthest north and the furthest west, among peasants as well as among dukes and peers. . . . As for . . . unnatural sin, which is another growing vice of the age, it would be monstrous to urge that it is in the least encouraged by the stage, for it is either never mentioned there or mentioned with the last detestation. And now lastly, for the love of women fomented by the corruption and not by the genuine art of the stage: though the augmenting and nourishing it cannot be defended, yet it may be in some measure excused: (1) because it has more of nature, and consequently more temptation, and consequently less malice, than the preceding three, which the drama does not encourage; (2) because it has a check upon the other vices, and peculiarly upon that unnatural sin, in the restraining of which the happiness of mankind is in so evident a manner concerned. . . .

The stage is instrumental to the welfare of the government in general. . . . Maladministration has always its source from the passions or vices of those who govern. The passions which cause it are for the most part ambition or the immoderate love of pleasure. Now, as tragedy checks the first by showing the great ones of the earth humbled, so it corrects the last by firing the mind and raising it to something nobler. The vices which cause the maladministration of governors are either vices of weakness or of malice, the first of which cause governors to neglect and the last to oppress their people. The vices of weakness are inconsiderateness and effeminacy, inconstancy and irresolution. Now, nothing can be a better remedy than tragedy for inconsiderateness, which reminds men of their duty and perpetually instructs them, either by its fable or by its sentences, and shows them the ill and the fatal consequences of irregular administration; and nothing is more capable of raising the soul and giving it that greatness, that courage, that force, and that constancy which are the qualifications that make men deserve to command others. . . . That vice of malice which for the most part causes the maladministration of governers is cruelty, which nothing is more capable of correcting than tragedy. . . .

. . . The stage is useful to government with respect to those who are governed. . . . Tragedy is very proper to check the emotions that they may at any time feel to rebellion or disobedience by stopping the very sources of them, for tragedy naturally checks their ambition by showing them the great ones of the earth humbled, by setting before their eyes—to make use of Mr. Collier's words—the uncertainty of human greatness, the sudden turns of state, and the unhappy conclusion of violence and injustice. Tragedy too diverts their apprehension of grievances by the delight which it gives them, discovers the designs of their factious guides by opening their eyes and instructing them in their duty by the like examples; and lastly, it dispels their unreasonable jealousies, for people who are melted or terrified with the sufferings of the great, which are set before their eyes, are rather apt to feel a secret pleasure from the sense that they have that they are free from the like calamities than to torment themselves with the vain and uncertain apprehensions of futurity. . . . Tragedy diverts them from their unjust designs by the pleasure which it gives them, since no man as long as he is easy himself is in a humor to disturb others, and by purging those passions whose excesses cause their injustice, by instructing them in their duty by its fable and by its sentences, by raising their minds and setting them above injustice, by touching them with compassion and making them good upon a principle of self-love, and lastly, by terrifying them with setting before their eyes the unhappy conclusion—to use Mr. Collier's words—of violence and injustice.

Thirdly, the stage is useful to government by having an influence over those who are governed in relation to the common enemy, for nothing more raises and exalts their minds and fires them with a noble emulation, who shall best perform their duty. . . .

We have shown . . . that the drama, and particularly tragedy, is among other reasons useful to government because it is proper to restrain a people from rebellion and disobedience and to keep them in good correspondence among themselves. For this reason, the drama may be said to be instrumental in a peculiar manner to the welfare of the English government, because there is no people on the face of the earth so prone to rebellion as the English or so apt to quarrel among themselves. And this seems very remarkable: that since the drama began first to flourish among us, we have been longer at quiet than ever we were before since the Conquest, and the only civil war which has been among us since that time is notoriously known to have been begun and carried on by those who had an utter aversion to the stage, as on the other side he who now discovers so great an aversion to the stage has notoriously done all that lay in his little power to plunge us in another civil war. . . . But farther, the stage is beneficial to the present government if you consider a third sort of people who daily frequent it, and they are such who are always indifferent what government they live under so they can live but agreeably. Now, these are of all others the most addicted to their pleasures and would take it most heinously to be deprived of them. . . .

We now come to answer what is objected from religion, which is that there is no need of the stage to make people good subjects, for that the pulpit teaches men their duty to their prince better than all the philosophy and all the poetry in the world. 'Tis indeed undeniable. But the validity of this objection depends upon two suppositions, which are that all the subjects of the state go to church and that all attend when they are there, whereas it is manifest that our atheists and deists seldom go thither and that our doubting, cold, and lukewarm Christians seldom attend when they are there. . . .

. . . Let any man show me where terror is moved to a height and I will show him that that place requires the belief of a God and particular providence. . . . Poetic justice would be a jest if it were not an image of divine and if it did not consequently suppose the being of a God and providence. It supposes too the immortality of the soul and future rewards and punishments. . . .

. . . It was the business of tragedy to exhort men to piety and the worship of the gods, to persuade them to justice, to humility, and to fidelity, and to incline them to moderation and temperance. And 'tis for the omission of one of these duties that the persons of the modern tragedy are shown unfortunate in their catastrophes. Thus, Don John is destroyed for his libertinism and his impiety, Timon for his profusion and his intemperance, Macbeth for his lawless ambition and cruelty, Castalio for his falsehood to his brother and friend, Jaffeir for his clandestine marriage with the daughter of his benefactor, and Belvidera for her disobedience.[2]

. . . The stage is useful for the advancing the Christian and particularly the reformed religion. . . . The human virtues are a part of natural religion, which since the stage advances, as we have shown above, it follows that it partly advances Christianity. The stage too in some measure may be made to recommend humility, patience, and meekness to us, which are true Christian virtues, and though a dramatic poet neither can nor ought to teach the mysteries of the Christian religion, yet by recommending the human and the Christian virtues to the practice of our audience, he admirably prepares men for the belief of the mysteries. For this is undeniable, that it is not reason but passion and vice that keeps any man from being a Christian. That therefore that moderates our passions and instructs us in our duty must consequently advance our faith, so that the stage is not only absolutely necessary for the instructing and humanizing those who are not Christians but the best of all human things to prepare them for the sublimer doctrines of the church. Now, that which inclines us to the Christian religion will incline us to the purer sort of it and that which has the least affinity with idolatry, which is the reformed religion. That which opens men's eyes, as the stage does, by purging our passions and instructing us in our duty and that which raises their minds will make them naturally averse from superstitious foppery and from being slaves to priestcraft. And that which exposes hypocrisy, as the stage does, must naturally make men averse from fanaticism and the affected austerity of bigots. And therefore the Jesuits on the one hand and the fanatics on the other have always been inveterate enemies to plays. . . .

The objections from reason are chiefly three: that the stage makes its characters sometimes talk profanely, that it encourages pride, that it exposes religion in the priesthood. . . . To [the first] I answer that if the character which speaks is well marked and the profaneness be necessary for the fable and for the action, then the profaneness is not unjustifiable, for to assert the contrary would be to affirm that it is unlawful for a dramatic poet to write against profaneness, which is ridiculous. A poet has no other way in the

---

[2] Don John in *The Libertine* (1676), based on the Don Juan legend, by Thomas Shadwell; Timon in Shakespeare's *Timon of Athens* (1605–1609); Shakespeare's *Macbeth* (1606); Castalio in *The Orphan* (1680) by Thomas Otway; Jaffeir and Belvidera in *Venice Preserved* (1682) by Otway.

drama of giving an audience an aversion for any vice than by exposing or punishing it in the persons of the drama. . . . But secondly, the stage encourages pride. . . . For the generality of mankind, greatness of mind may be very serviceable for the assisting them to command their passions and the restraining them from committing enormous crimes. But thirdly, the stage exposes religion by exposing the priesthood. To which I answer that . . . I cannot for my life conceive why the bringing a foolish or a vicious priest upon the stage should be such an abominable thing, for since persons of all degrees, from monarch to peasant, are daily brought upon the stage, why should the clergy be exempted? . . . None of the superior clergy have been ever exposed in our comedies, which is one sign of the good intention of the poets and that they only show the follies and vices of some while they reverence the piety and learning of others and the order in general. . . . And whereas Mr. Collier says that to affront a priest is to affront the Deity, so it is to affront a peasant who is a good Christian. . . . The exposing upon the stage a priest who is an ill or a ridiculous person can never make the order contemptible, for nothing can make the priesthood contemptible but priests. . . . It appears to be full as necessary to expose a priest who is an ill man as one of the laity, because his example is more contagious and the salvation of so many souls depend on it, whereas a layman influences fewer.

To The Spectator upon His Paper of the 16th of April *1712*

I cannot wonder that criticism should degenerate so vilely at a time when poetry and acting are sunk so low. . . .

To set a few of his errors in their proper light, he[1] tells us in the begin-

Selections. From John Dennis, *Original Letters: Familiar, Moral, and Critical*. London: W. Mears, 1721. Spelling and punctuation modernized by the editor.

[1] Joseph Addison, to whose article in *The Spectator*, No. 40, this is a reply. See pp. 388–390.

ning that "The English writers of tragedy are possessed with a notion that when they represent a virtuous or innocent person in distress, they ought not to leave him till they have delivered him out of his troubles and made him triumph over his enemies."

But, Mr. Spectator, is this peculiar to the *English* writers of tragedy? Have not the French writers of tragedy the same notion? Does not Racine tell us, in the Preface to his *Iphigenia,* that it would have been horrible to have defiled the stage with the murder of a princess so virtuous and so lovely as was Iphigenia?

But your correspondent goes on. "This error," says he, with an insolent and dogmatic air, "they have been led into by a ridiculous doctrine in modern criticism, that they are obliged to an equal distribution of rewards and punishments, and an impartial execution of poetical justice."

But who were the first who established this rule he is not able to tell. I take it for granted that a man who is ingenuous enough to own his ignorance is willing to be instructed. Let me tell him, then, that the first who established this ridiculous doctrine of modern criticism was a certain modern critic who lived above two thousand years ago and who tells us expressly in the thirteenth chapter of his critical *Spectator,* which pedants call his *Poetic,* that since a tragedy, to have all the beauty of which it is capable, ought to be complex and not simple (by the way, Mr. Spectator, you must bear with this critical cant as we do with your speculations and lucubrations) and ought to move compassion and terror, for we have already shown that the exciting these passions is the proper effect of a tragical imitation; it follows necessarily that we must not choose a very good man to plunge him from a prosperous condition into adversity, for instead of moving compassion and terror, that on the contrary would create horror and be detested by all the world.

And does not the same deluded philosopher tell us in the very same chapter that the fable to which he gives the second preference is that which has a double constitution and which ends by a double catastrophe, a catastrophe favorable to the good and fatal to the wicked? Is not here, Mr. Spectator, a very formal recommendation of the impartial and exact execution of poetical justice? Thus, Aristotle was the first who established this ridiculous doctrine of modern criticism. . . . This contemptible doctrine of poetical justice is not only founded in reason and nature but is itself the foundation of all the rules and even of tragedy itself, for what tragedy can there be without a fable, or what fable without a moral, or what moral without poetical justice? What moral, where the good and the bad are confounded by destiny and perish alike promiscuously? . . . Well! But the practice of the ancients is against this poetical justice! What, always, Mr. Spectator! Will your correspondent have the assurance to affirm that? No, but sometimes. Why, then, sometimes the ancients offended against reason and nature. And who ever believed that the ancients were without fault or brought tragedy to its perfection? . . .

Poetical justice, says your correspondent, has no foundation in nature and reason because "We find that good and evil happen alike to all men on this side [of] the grave." In answer to which he must give me leave to tell him that this is not only a very false but a dangerous assertion, that we neither know what men really are nor what they really suffer.

'Tis not always that we know men's crimes, but how seldom do we know their passions, and especially their darling passions? And as passion is the occasion of infinitely more disorder in the world than malice—for where one man falls a sacrifice to inveterate malice, a thousand become victims to revenge and ambition; and whereas malice has something that shocks human nature, passion is pleasingly catching and contagious—can anything be more just than that that providence which governs the world should punish men for indulging their passions as much as for obeying the dictates of their most envenomed hatred and malice?

Thus, you see, for ought we know, good and evil does not happen alike to all men on this side [of] the grave, because 'tis for the most part by their passions that men offend and 'tis by their passions for the most part that they are punished. But this is certain, that the more virtue a man has, the more he commands his passions, but the virtuous alone command them. The wicked take the utmost care to dissemble and conceal them, for which reason we neither know what our neighbors are nor what they really suffer. Man is too finite, too shallow, and too empty a creature to know another man thoroughly, to know the creature of an infinite Creator, but dramatical persons are creatures of which a poet is himself the creator, and though a mortal is not able to know the Almighty's creatures, he may be allowed to know his own, to know the utmost extent of their guilt and what they ought to suffer; nay, he must be allowed not only to know this himself but to make it manifest and unquestionable to all his readers and hearers. The creatures of a poetical creator have no dissimulation and no reserve. We see their passions in all their height and in all their deformity; and when they are unfortunate, we are never to seek for the cause.

But suppose I should grant that there is not always an equal distribution of affliction and happiness here below. Man is a creature who was created immortal, and a creature consequently that will find a compensation in futurity for any seeming inequality in his destiny here. But the creatures of a poetical creator are imaginary and transitory. They have no longer duration than the representation of their respective fables; and, consequently, if they offend they must be punished during that representation. And therefore we are very far from pretending that poetical justice is an equal representation of the justice of the Almighty. We freely confess that 'tis but a very narrow and a very imperfect type of it—so very narrow and so very imperfect that 'tis forced by temporal to represent eternal punishments—and therefore, when we show a man unfortunate in tragedy for not restraining his passions, we mean that everyone will for such neglect, unless he timely repents, be infallibly punished by infinite justice either here or hereafter.

A Defence of
Sir Fopling Flutter   *1722*

. . . As tragedy instructs chiefly by its design, comedy instructs by its characters, which not only ought to be drawn truly in nature but to be the resembling pictures of our contemporaries, both in court and town. Tragedy answers to history painting, but comedy to drawing of portraits.

How little do they know of the nature of true comedy who believe that its proper business is to set us patterns for imitation, for all such patterns are serious things and laughter is the life and the very soul of comedy. 'Tis its proper business to expose persons to our view whose views we may shun and whose follies we may despise, and by showing us what is done upon the comic stage to show us what ought never to be done upon the stage of the world.

All the characters in *Sir Fopling Flutter*,[1] and especially the principal characters, are admirably drawn both to please and to instruct. First, they are drawn to please because they are drawn in the truth of nature. . . . But secondly, the characters in *Sir Fopling Flutter* are admirably contrived to please, and more particularly the principal ones, because we find in those characters a true resemblance of the persons both in court and town who lived at the time when that comedy was writ. For Rapin tells us with a great deal of judgment "That comedy is as it ought to be when an audience is apt to

Selections. From John Dennis, *A Defence of Sir Fopling Flutter*. London: T. Warner, 1722. Spelling and punctuation modernized by the editor.

[1] The subtitle of Sir George Etherege's play *The Man of Mode* (1676), by which it is often refered to Dennis's defence is a reply to the attack of Sir Richard Steele (whom he calls "the knight") in *The Spectator*, No. 65 (see pp. 393–395).

imagine that instead of being in the pit and boxes they are in some assembly of the neighborhood or in some family meeting and that we see nothing done in it but what is done in the world. For it is," says he, "not worth one farthing if we do not discover ourselves in it and do not find in it both our own manners and those of the persons with whom we live and converse."[2] The reason of this rule is manifest, for as 'tis the business of a comic poet to cure his spectators of vice and folly by the apprehension of being laughed at, 'tis plain that his business must be with the reigning follies and vices. The violent passions which are the subjects of tragedy are the same in every age and appear with the same face, but those vices and follies which are the subjects of comedy are seen to vary continually. Some of those that belonged to our ancestors have no relation to us and can no more come under the cognizance of our present comic poets than the sweating and sneezing sickness can come under the practice of our contemporary physicians. What vices and follies may infect those who are to come after us, we know not. 'Tis the present, the reigning vices and follies that must be the subjects of our present comedy. The comic poet must therefore take characters from such persons as are his contemporaries and are infected with the aforesaid follies and vices. . . .

Now, I remember very well that upon the first acting this comedy it was generally believed to be an agreeable representation of the persons of condition of both sexes, both in court and town, and that all the world was charmed with Dorimant, and that it was unanimously agreed that he had in him several of the qualities of Wilmot, Earl of Rochester, as his wit, his spirit, his amorous temper, the charms that he had for the fair sex, his falsehood and his inconstancy, the agreeable manner of his chiding his servants . . . and lastly, his repeating on every occasion the verses of Waller, for whom that noble lord had a very particular esteem. . . . They who were acquainted with the late Sir Fleetwood Shepherd know very well that not a little of that gentleman's character is to be found in Medley.

But the characters in this comedy are very well formed to instruct as well as to please, especially those of Dorimant and of Loveit, and they instruct by the same qualities to which the knight has taken so much whimsical exception, as Dorimant instructs by his insulting and his perfidiousness, and Loveit by the violence of her resentment and her anguish, for Loveit has youth, beauty, quality, wit, and spirit, and it was depending upon these that she reposed so dangerous a trust in Dorimant, which is a just caution to the fair sex never to be so conceited of the power of their charms or their other extraordinary qualities as to believe they can engage a man to be true to them to whom they grant the best favor without the only sure engagement,

---

[2] René Rapin, *Reflections on Aristotle's Treatise of Poesy.* See p. 268 (in different translation).

without which they can never be certain that they shall not be hated and despised by that very person whom they have done everything to oblige.

To conclude with one general observation: that comedy may be qualified in a powerful manner both to instruct and to please, the very constitution of its subject ought always to be ridiculous. "Comedy," says Rapin, "is an image of common life, and its end is to expose upon the stage the defects of particular persons in order to cure the defects of the public and to correct and amend the people by the fear of being laughed at. That therefore," says he, "which is most essential to comedy is certainly the ridicule."[3] Every poem is qualified to instruct and to please most powerfully by that very quality which makes the forte and the characteristic of it and which distinguishes it from all other kinds of poems. As tragedy is qualified to instruct and to please by terror and compassion, which two passions ought always to be predominant in it, and to distinguish it from all other poems; epic poetry pleases and instructs chiefly by admiration, which reigns throughout it and distinguishes it from poems of every other kind; thus comedy instructs and pleases most powerfully by the ridicule, because that is the quality which distinguishes it from every other poem. The subject, therefore, of every comedy ought to be ridiculous by its constitution; the ridicule ought to be of the very nature and essence of it. Where there is none of that, there can be no comedy.

[3] Rapin, *Reflections*, p. 268.

Remarks on a Play Called The Conscious Lovers: A Comedy   *1723*

When Sir Richard[1] says that anything that has its foundation in happiness and success must be the subject of a comedy, he confounds comedy with that species of tragedy which has a happy catastrophe. When he says that 'tis an

Selections from the section subtitled "The Preface." From John Dennis, *Remarks on a Play Called* The Conscious Lovers: A Comedy. London: T. Warner, 1723. Spelling and punctuation modernized by the editor.

[1] Sir Richard Steele, to whose play *The Conscious Lovers*, and its preface, this is a reply. See pp. 396–397.

improvement of comedy to introduce a joy too exquisite for laughter, he takes all the care that he can to show that he knows nothing of the nature of comedy. . . . Let Sir Richard, or anyone, look into that little piece of Molière called *La Critique de l'ècole des femmes*[2] and he shall find there that in Molière's opinion 'tis the business of a comic poet to enter into the ridicule of men and to expose the blind sides of all sorts of people agreeably, that he does nothing at all if he does not draw the pictures of his contemporaries and does not raise the mirth of the sensible part of an audience, which, says he, 'tis no easy matter to do. This is the sense of Molière, though the words are not his exactly.

When Sir Richard talks of a joy too exquisite for laughter, he seems not to know that joy, generally taken, is common—like anger, indignation, love —to all sorts of poetry—to the epic, the dramatic, the lyric—but that that kind of joy which is attended with laughter is the characteristic of comedy, as terror and compassion, according as one or the other is predominant, makes the characteristic of tragedy, as admiration does of epic poetry.

When Sir Richard says that weeping upon the sight of a deplorable object is not a subject for laughter but that 'tis agreeable to good sense and to humanity, he says nothing but what all the sensible part of the world has already granted; but then all that sensible part of the world have always denied that a deplorable object is fit to be shown in comedy. When Sir George Etherege in his comedy of *Sir Fopling Flutter*[3] shows Loveit in all the height and violence of grief and rage, the judicious poet takes care to give those passions a ridiculous turn by the mouth of Dorimant. Besides that, the subject is at the bottom ridiculous, for Loveit is a mistress who has abandoned herself to Dorimant, and by falling into these violent passions only because she fancies that something of which she is very desirous has gone beside her, makes herself truly ridiculous. Thus is this famous scene in the second act of *Sir Fopling*, by the character of Loveit and the dexterous handling of the subject, kept within the bounds of comedy. But the scene of the discovery in *The Conscious Lovers* is truly tragical. Indiana was strictly virtuous. She had indeed conceived a violent passion for Bevil, but all young people in full health are liable to such a passion, and perhaps the most sensible and the most virtuous are more than others liable. But besides that, she had kept this passion within the bounds of honor; it was the natural effect of her esteem for her benefactor and of her gratitude, that is, of her virtue. These considerations rendered her case deplorable and the catastrophe downright tragical, which of a comedy ought to be the most comical part for the same reason that it ought to be the most tragical part of a tragedy.

[2] *Critique of School for Wives* (1663). See pp. 249–251.
[3] See John Dennis's *A Defence of Sir Fopling Flutter*, above, pp. 372–374.

George Farquhar 1677–1707

A Discourse upon Comedy in Reference to the English Stage 1702

But in the first place I must beg you, sir, to lay aside your superstitious veneration for antiquity and the usual expressions on that score: that the present age is illiterate or their taste is vitiated, that we live in the decay of time and the dotage of the world is fallen to our share. 'Tis a mistake, sir. The world was never more active or youthful, and true sense was never more universal than at this very day; 'tis neither confined to one nation in the world nor to one party of a city; 'tis remarkable in England as well as France, and good, genuine reason is nourished as well by the cold of Swedeland as by the warmth of Italy; 'tis neither abdicated the court with the late reigns nor expelled the city with the playhouse bills; you may find it in the Grand Jury at Hick's Hall and upon the bench sometimes among the justices. Then why should we be hampered so in our opinions as if all the ruins of antiquity lay so heartily on the bones of us that we could not stir hand and foot? No, no, sir, *ipse dixit*[1] is removed long ago, and all the rubbish of old philosophy that in a manner buried the judgment of mankind for many centuries is now carried off; the vast tomes of Aristotle and his commentators are all taken to pieces and their infallibility is lost with all persons of a free and unprejudiced reason.

Then above all men living, why should the poets be hoodwinked at this rate and by what authority should Aristotle's rules of poetry stand so fixed and immutable? Why, by the authority of two thousand years' standing, because through this long revolution of time the world has still continued the same, by the authority of their being received at Athens, a city the very same with London in every particular—their habits the same, their humours alike, their public transactions and private societies *à la mode de France*,[2] in short, so very much the same in every circumstance—that Aristotle's criticisms may give rules to Drury Lane, the Areopagus[3] give judgment upon a case in the King's Bench, and old Solon[4] shall give laws to the House of Commons!

Selections. From *The Works of the Late Ingenious Mr. George Farquhar*, Vol. I. London: John Rivington, 1772. Spelling and punctuation modernized by the editor.

[1] An assertion not proved but made on authority.
[2] Fashionably French.
[3] The supreme Athenian tribunal.
[4] (*c.* 638–*c.* 558 B.C.), Athenian statesman and lawmaker.

But to examine this matter a little further: All arts and professions are compounded of these two parts, a speculative knowledge and a practical use, and from an excellence in both [of] these any person is raised to eminence and authority in his calling. The lawyer has his years of student in the speculative part of his business, and when promoted to the bar he falls upon the practice, which is the trial of his ability. . . . The physician, to gain credit to his prescriptions, must labor for a reputation in the cure of such and such distempers, and before he sets up for a Galen[5] or Hippocrates[6] must make many experiments upon his patients. Philosophy itself, which is a science the most abstract from practice, has its public acts and disputations; it is raised gradually, and its professor commences doctor by degrees; he has the labor of maintaining theses, methodizing his arguments, and clearing objections; his memory and understanding is often puzzled by oppositions couched in fallacies and sophisms, in solving all [of] which he must make himself remarkable before he pretends to impose his own systems upon the world. Now, if the case be thus in philosophy—or in any branch thereof, as in ethics, physics, which are called sciences—what must be done in poetry, that is denominated an art, and consequently implies a practice in its perfection?

Is it reasonable that any person that has never writ a distich of verses in his life should set up for a dictator in poetry, and without the least practice in his own performance must give laws and rules to that of others? Upon what foundation is poetry made so very cheap and so easy a task by these gentlemen? An excellent poet is the single production of an age when we have crowds of philosophers, physicians, lawyers, divines every day and all of them competently famous in their callings. In the two learned commonwealths of Rome and Athens, there was but one Vergil and one Homer, yet have we above a hundred philosophers in each, and most part of 'em, forsooth, must have a touch of poetry. . . .

Of all these I shall mention only Aristotle, the first and great lawgiver in this respect, and upon whom all that followed him are only commentators. Among all the vast tracts of this voluminous author, we don't find any fragment of an epic poem or the least scene of a play to authorize his skill and excellence in that art. . . .

I have talked so long to lay a foundation for these following conclusions. Aristotle was no poet and consequently not capable of giving instructions in the art of poetry. His *Ars Poetica* are only some observations drawn from the works of Homer and Euripides, which may be mere accidents resulting casually from the compositions of the works and not any of the essential principles on which they are compiled, that without giving himself the trouble of searching into the nature of poetry he has only complimented the heroes

---

[5] (*c.* 130–*c.* 200), Greek physician and writer on medicine.
[6] (460?–357 B.C.), Greek physician, called the father of medicine.

of wit and valor of his age by joining with them in their approbation, with this difference, that their applause was plain and his more scholastic.

But to leave these only as suppositions to be relished by every man at his pleasure, I shall without complimenting any author, either ancient or modern, inquire into the first invention of comedy, what were the true designs and honest intentions of that art, and from a knowledge of the end seek out the means—without one quotation of Aristotle or authority of Euripides.

In all productions, either divine or human, the final cause is the first mover because the end or intention of any rational action must first be considered before the material or efficient causes are put in execution. Now, to determine the final cause of comedy we must run back beyond the material and formal agents and take it in its very infancy, or rather in the very first act of its generation, when its primary parent, by proposing such or such an end of his labor, laid down the first sketches or shadows of the piece. Now, as all arts and sciences have their first rise from a final cause, so 'tis certain that they have grown from very small beginnings and that the current of time has swelled them to such a bulk that nobody can find the fountain by any proportion between the head and the body; this, with the corruption of time, which has debauched things from their primitive innocence to selfish designs and purposes, render it difficult to find the origin of any offspring so very unlike its parent.

This is not only the case of comedy as it stands at present, but the condition also of the ancient theatres, when great men made shows of this nature a rising step to their ambition, mixing many lewd and lascivious representations to gain the favor of the populace, to whose taste and entertainment the plays were chiefly adapted. We must therefore go higher than either Aristophanes or Menander to discover comedy in its primitive institution if we would draw any moral design of its invention to warrant and authorize its continuance. . . .

Comedy is no more at present than a *well-framed tale handsomely told as an agreeable vehicle for counsel or reproof.* This is all we can say for the credit of its institution and is the stress of its charter for liberty and toleration. Then where should we seek for a foundation but in Aesop's symbolical way of moralizing upon tales and fables, with this difference, that his stories were shorter than ours? He had his tyrant lion, his statesman fox, his beau magpie, his coward hare, his bravo ass, and his buffoon ape, with all the characters that crowd our stages every day, with this distinction, that Aesop made his beast speak good Greek and our heroes sometimes can't talk English.

But whatever difference time has produced in the form we must in our own defence stick to the end and intention of his fables. *Utile dulce*[7] was

---

[7] The profitable mixed with the pleasant.

his motto and must be our business; we have no other defence against the presentment of the Grand Jury and for aught I know it might prove a good means to mollify the rigor of that persecution to inform the inquisitors that the great Aesop was the first inventor of these poor comedies that they are prosecuting with so much eagerness and fury, that the first laureat was as just, as prudent, as pious, as reforming, and as ugly as any of themselves, and that the beasts which are lugged upon the stage by the horn are not caught in the city as they suppose but brought out of Aesop's own forest. We should inform them, besides, that those very tales and fables which they apprehend as obstacles to reformation were the main instruments and machines used by the wise Aesop for its propagation, and as he would improve men by the policy of beasts, so we endeavor to reform brutes with the examples of men. . . . Here are precepts, admonitions, and salutary innuendoes for the ordering [of] our lives and conversations, couched in these allegories and allusions. . . . By ancient practice and modern example, by the authority of pagans, Jews, and Christians, the world is furnished with this so sure, so pleasant, and expedient an art of schooling mankind into better manners. Now here is the primary design of comedy illustrated from its first institution, and the same end is equally alleged for its daily practice and continuance. Then, without all dispute, whatever means are most proper and expedient for compassing this end and intention, they must be the just rules of comedy and the true art of the stage.

We must consider, then, in the first place, that our business lies not with a French or a Spanish audience, that our design is not to hold forth to ancient Greece, nor to moralize upon the vices and defaults of the Roman commonwealth. No, no: an English play is intended for the use and instruction of an English audience, a people not only separated from the rest of the world by situation but different also from other nations as well in the complexion and temperament of the natural body as in the constitution of our body politic. As we are a mixture of many nations, so we have the most unaccountable medley of humours among us of any people upon earth. These humours produce variety of follies, some of 'em unknown to former ages. These distempers must have new remedies, which are nothing but new counsels and instructions.

Now, sir, if our *utile*, which is the end, be different from the ancients, pray let our *dulce*, which is the means, be so too, for you know that to different towns there are different ways, or if you would have it more scholastically, *ad diversos fines non idem conducit medium*, or mathematically, one and the same line cannot terminate in two centers. But waiving this manner of concluding by induction, I shall gain my point a nearer way and draw it immediately from the first principle I set down, *that we have the most unaccountable medley of humours among us of any nation upon earth*, and this is demonstrable from common experience. We shall find a Wildair[8] in one corner and a Morose[9] in another; nay, the space of an hour or two shall create such vicissitudes of temper in the same person that he can hardly be taken for the same man. We shall have a fellow bestir his stumps from Chocolate to Coffee House with all the joy and gaiety imaginable, though he wants a shilling to pay for a hack; while another, drawn about in a coach and six, is eaten up with the spleen and shall loll in state with as much melancholy, vexation, and discontent as if he were making the Tour of Tyburn.[10] Then what sort of a *dulce* (which I take for the pleasantry of the tale or the plot of the play) must a man make use of to engage the attention of so many different humours and inclinations? Will a single plot satisfy everybody? Will the turns and surprises that may result naturally from the ancient limits of time be sufficient to rip open the spleen of some and physic the melancholy of others, screw up the attention of a rover and fix him to the stage, in spite of his volatile temper and the temptation of a mask?[11] To make the moral instructive, you must make the story diverting. The splenetic wit, the beau courtier, the heavy citizen, the fine lady, and her fine footman come all to be instructed and therefore must all be diverted, and he that can do this best and with most applause writes the best comedy, let him do it by what rules he pleases, so they be not offensive to religion and good manners.

But *hic labor, hic opus.*[12] How must this secret of pleasing so many different tastes be discovered? Not by tumbling over volumes of the ancients but by studying the humours of the moderns. The rules of English comedy don't lie in the compass of Aristotle or his followers, but in the pit, box, and galleries. And to examine into the humour of an English audience, let us see by what means our own English poets have succeeded in this point. To determine a suit at law, we don't look into the archives of Greece or Rome but inspect the reports of our own lawyers and the acts and statutes of our parliaments; and by the same rule we have nothing to do with the models of Menander or Plautus, but must consult Shakespeare, Jonson, Fletcher, and others who have supported the English stage and made themselves famous to posterity. We shall find that these gentlemen have fairly dispensed with the greatest part of critical formalities; the decorums of time and place, so much cried up of late, had no force of decorum with them; the economy of their plays was *ad libitum*[13] and the extent of their plots only limited by the convenience of action. I would willingly understand the irregularities of *Ham-*

[8] Sir Harry Wildair, a character in Farquhar's *The Constant Couple, or A Trip to the Jubilee* (1699) and its sequel, *Sir Harry Wildair* (1701).
[9] A character in Ben Jonson's *Epicoene, or The Silent Woman* (1609).
[10] The trip from Newgate Prison to the gallows.
[11] A woman wearing a mask.
[12] From this effort, this result.
[13] Unrestricted.

let, Macbeth, Harry the Fourth, and of Fletcher's plays, and yet these have long been the darlings of the English audience and are like to continue with the same applause in defiance of all the criticisms that ever were published in Greek and Latin.

But are there no rules, no decorums to be observed in comedy? Must we make the condition of the English stage a state of anarchy? No, sir, for there are extremes in irregularity as dangerous to an author as too scrupulous a deference to criticism, and as I have given you an instance of one, so I shall present you an example of the other.

There are a sort of gentlemen that have had the jaunty education of dancing, French, and a fiddle, who coming to age before they arrive at years of discretion make a shift to spend a handsome patrimony of two or three thousand pounds by soaking in the tavern all night, lolling abed all the morning, and sauntering away all the evening between the two playhouses with their hands in their pockets. You shall have a gentleman of this size, upon his knowledge of Covent Garden and a knack of witticizing in his cups, set up immediately for a playwright. But besides the gentleman's wit and experience, here is another motive. There are a parcel of fancy, impudent fellows about the playhouse called "doorkeepers" that can't let a gentleman see a play in peace without jogging and nudging him every minute: "Sir, will you please to pay?—Sir, the act's done. Will you please to pay, sir?" . . . "I'll be plagued with 'em no longer [says the gentleman]; I'll e'en write a play myself, by which means my character of wit shall be established, I shall enjoy the freedom of the house, and to pin up the basket, Miss —— shall have the profits of my Third Night[14] for her maidenhead. . . . But stay, what shall I call it first? Let me see: *The Rival Theatres*. Very good, by gad, because I reckon the two houses will have a contest about this very play." Thus having found a name for his play, in the next place he makes a play to his name, and thus he begins: "Act I. *Scene:* Covent Garden. *Enter* PORTICO, PIAZZA, *and* TURNSTILE."

Here you must note that Portico, being a compound of practical rake and speculative gentleman, is ten to one the author's own character, and the leading card in the pack, Piazza, is his mistress, who lives in the square and is daughter to old Pillariso, an odd, out o' the way gentleman, something between the character of Alexander the Great and Solon, which must please because 'tis new.

Turnstile is maid and confidante to Piazza, who for a bribe of ten pieces lets Portico in at the back door. So the first act concludes.

In the second, enter Spiggotoso, who was butler perhaps to the Czar of Muscovy, and Faucetana, his wife. After these characters are run dry, he

---

[14] The Third Night Benefit: proceeds from the third night's performance were traditionally the author's.

brings you in at the third act Whinewell and Charmarillis for a scene of love to please the ladies, and so he goes on without fear or wit till he comes to a marriage or two, and then he writes, *"Finis."* . . .

Now, such a play may be written with all the exactness imaginable in respect of unity in time and place, but if you inquire its character of any person, though of the meanest understanding of the whole audience, he will tell you 'tis intolerable stuff, and upon your demanding his reasons his answer is, "I don't like it." His humour is the only rule that he can judge a comedy by, but you find that mere nature is offended with some irregularities and though he be not so learned in the drama to give you an inventory of the faults, yet I can tell you that one part of the plot had no dependence upon another, which made this simple man drop his attention and concern for the event, and so disengaging his thoughts from the business of the action he sat there very uneasy, thought the time very tedious because he had nothing to do. The characters were so incoherent in themselves and composed of such variety of absurdities that in his knowledge of nature he could find no original for such a copy, and being therefore unacquainted with any folly they reproved or any virtue that they recommended, their business was as flat and tiresome to him as if the actors had talked Arabic.

Now, these are the material irregularities of a play, and these are the faults which downright mother sense can censure and be offended at as much as the most learned critic in the pit. And although the one cannot give me the reasons of his approbation or dislike, yet I will take his word for the credit or disrepute of a comedy sooner perhaps than the opinion of some virtuosos, for there are some gentlemen that have fortified their spleen so impregnably with criticism and hold out so stiffly against all attacks of pleasantry that the most powerful efforts of wit and humor cannot make the least impression. What a misfortune is it to these gentlemen to be natives of such an ignorant, self-willed, impertinent island, where let a critic and a scholar find never so many irregularities in a play, yet five hundred saucy people will give him the lie to his face and come to see this wicked play forty or fifty times in a year! But this *vox populi*[15] is the Devil, though in a place of more authority than Aristotle it is called *vox Dei.*[16] "Here is a play with a vengeance," says a critic, "to bring the transactions of a year's time into the compass of three hours, to carry the whole audience with him from one kingdom to another by the changing of a scene. Where's the probability—nay, the possibility, of all this? The Devil's in the poet, sure, he don't think to put contradictions upon us!"

Look 'e, sir, don't be in a passion. The poet does not impose contradictions upon you because he has told you no lie, for that only is a lie which is related

---

[15] Voice of the people.
[16] Voice of God.

with some fallacious intention that you should believe it for a truth. Now, the poet expects no more that you should believe the plot of his play than old Aesop designed the world should think his eagle and lion talked like you and I, which I think was every jot as improbable as what you quarrel with; and yet the fables took and I'll be hanged if you yourself don't like 'em. But besides, sir, if you are so inveterate against improbabilities you must never come near the playhouse at all, for there are several improbabilities—nay, impossibilities—that all the criticism in nature cannot correct. As for instance: in the part of Alexander the Great, to be affected with the transactions of the play, we must suppose that we see that great conqueror after all his triumphs shunned by the woman he loves and importuned by her he hates, crossed in his cups and jollity by his own subjects, and at last miserably ending his life in a raging madness. We must suppose that we see the very Alexander, the son of Philip, in all these unhappy circumstances, else we are not touched by the moral, which represents to us the uneasiness of human life in the greatest state and the instability of fortune in respect of worldly pomp. Yet the whole audience at the same time knows that this is Mr. Betterton who is strutting upon the stage and tearing his lungs for a livelihood, and that the same person should be Mr. Betterton and Alexander the Great at the same time is somewhat like an impossibility in my mind. Yet you must grant this impossibility in spite of your teeth if you haven't power to raise the old hero from the grave to act his own part.

Now for another impossibility. The less rigid critics allow·to a comedy the space of an artificial day, or twenty-four hours; but those of the thorough reformation will confine it to the natural or solar day, which is but half the time. Now, admitting this for a decorum absolutely requisite, this play begins when it is exactly six by your watch and ends precisely at nine, which is the usual time of the representation. Now, is it feasible *in rerum natura*[17] that the same space or extent of time can be three hours by your watch and twelve hours upon the stage, admitting the same number of minutes or the same measure of sand to both? I am afraid, sir, you must allow this for an impossibility too, and you may with as much reason allow the play the extent of a whole year, and if you grant me a year you may give me seven, and so to a thousand, for that a thousand years should come within the compass of three hours is no more an impossibility than that two minutes should be contained in one. *Nullum minus continet in se majus*[18] is equally applicable to both.

So much for the decorum of time, now for the regularity of place. I might make the one a consequence of t'other and allege that by allowing me any extent of time you must grant me any change of place, for the one depends

---

[17] In the nature of things.
[18] There is nothing smaller that does not contain in itself something greater.

upon t'other, and having five or six years for the action of a play I may travel from Constantinople to Denmark, so to France, and home to England, and rest long enough in each country besides. But you'll say, "How can you carry us with you?" Very easily, sir, if you will be willing to go, as for example, here is a new play, the house is thronged, the Prologue spoken, and the curtain drawn represents you the scene of Grand Cairo. Whereabouts are you now, sir? Were you not the very minute before in the pit in the English playhouse talking to a wench, and now, *praesto pass*,[19] you are spirited away to the banks of the River Nile. Surely, sir, this is a most intolerable improbability, yet this you must allow me or else you destroy the very constitution of representation. Then in the second act, with a flourish of the fiddles, I change the scene to Astrachan. "O, this is intolerable!" Look 'e, sir, 'tis not a jot more intolerable than the other, for you'll find that 'tis much about the same distance between Egypt and Astrachan as it is between Drury Lane and Grand Cairo, and if you please to let your fancy take post, it will perform the journey in the same moment of time without any disturbance in the world to your person. . . .

I am as little a friend to those rambling plays as anybody, nor have I ever espoused their party by my own practice; yet I could not forbear saying something in vindication of the great Shakespeare, whom every little fellow that can form an *aoristus primus*[20] will presume to condemn for indecorums and absurdities, sparks that are so spruce upon their Greek and Latin that, like our fops in travels, they can relish nothing but what is foreign to let the world know they have been abroad, forsooth. "But it must be so, because Aristotle said it!" Now, I say it must be otherwise, because Shakespeare said it, and I'm sure that Shakespeare was the greater poet of the two. But you'll say that Aristotle was the greater critic. That's a mistake, sir, for criticism in poetry is no more than judgment in poetry, which you will find in your Lexicon. Now, if Shakespeare was the better poet he must have the most judgment in his art, for everybody knows that judgment is an essential part of poetry and without it no writer is worth a farthing. But to stoop to the authority of either, without consulting the reason of the consequence, is an abuse to a man's understanding, and neither the precept of the philosopher nor example of the poet should go down with me without examining the weight of their assertions. We can expect no more decorum or regularity in any business than the nature of the thing will bear. Now, if the stage cannot subsist without the strength of supposition and force of fancy in the audience, why should a poet fetter the business of his plot and starve his action for the nicety of an hour or the change of a scene, since the thought of man can fly over a thousand years with the same ease and in the same instant of

[19] Step quickly.
[20] A verb declension in Greek.

time that your eye glances from the figure of six [to] seven on the dial plate and can glide from the Cape of Good Hope to the Bay of St. Nicholas, which is quite 'cross the world, with the same quickness and activity as between Covent Garden Church and Will's Coffee House. Then I must beg of these gentlemen to let our old English authors alone. If they have left vice unpunished, virtue unrewarded, folly unexposed, or prudence unsuccessful, the contrary of which is the *utile* of comedy, let them be lashed to some purpose; if any part of their plots have been independent of the rest or any of their characters forced or unnatural, which destroys the *dulce* of plays, let them be hissed off the stage. But if by a true decorum in these material points they have writ successfully and answered the end of dramatic poetry in every respect, let them rest in peace and their memories enjoy the encomiums due to their merit. . . .

Joseph Addison   *1672–1718*

The Spectator, No. 39   *April 14, 1711*

As a perfect tragedy is the noblest production of human nature, so it is capable of giving the mind one of the most delightful and most improving entertainments. A virtuous man, says Seneca,[1] struggling with misfortunes, is such a spectacle as gods might look upon with pleasure; and such a pleasure it is which one meets with in the representation of a well-written tragedy. Diversions of this kind wear out of our thoughts everything that is mean and little. They cherish and cultivate that humanity which is the ornament of our nature. They soften insolence, soothe affliction, and subdue the mind to the dispensations of Providence.

It is no wonder, therefore, that in all the polite nations of the world, this part of the drama has met with public encouragement.

The modern tragedy excels that of Greece and Rome in the intricacy and disposition of the fable; but, what a Christian writer would be ashamed to own, falls infinitely short of it in the moral part of the performance.

Selections. From *The Spectator*, Vol. I. Philadelphia: Crissy & Markley, 1853.

[1] *De Providentia*, II, 8–9.

This I may show more at large hereafter; and, in the meantime, that I may contribute something towards the improvement of the English tragedy, I shall take notice in this and in other following papers of some particular parts in it that seem liable to exception.

Aristotle observes that the iambic verse in the Greek tongue was the most proper for tragedy; because, at the same time that it lifted up the discourse from prose, it was that which approached nearer to it than any other kind of verse. For, says he, we may observe that men in ordinary discourse very often speak iambics, without taking notice of it. We may make the same observation of our English blank verse, which often enters into our common discourse, though we do not attend to it; and is such a due medium between rhyme and prose, that it seems wonderfully adapted to tragedy. I am, therefore, very much offended when I see a play in rhyme; which is as absurd in English as a tragedy of hexameters would have been in Greek or Latin. The solecism is, I think, still greater in those plays that have some scenes in rhyme and some in blank verse, which are to be looked upon as two several languages; or where we see some particular similies dignified in rhyme, at the same time that everything about them lies in blank verse. I would not, however, debar the poet from concluding his tragedy, or, if he pleases, every act of it, with two or three couplets, which may have the same effect as an air in the Italian opera after a long recitativo, and give the actor a graceful exit. Besides that, we see a diversity of numbers in some parts of the old tragedy, in order to hinder the ear from being tired with the same continued modulation of voice. For the same reason I do not dislike the speeches in our English tragedy that close with a hemistich, or half verse, notwithstanding the person who speaks after it begins a new verse, without filling up the preceding one; nor with abrupt pauses and breakings-off in the middle of a verse, when they humour any passion that is expressed by it.

Since I am upon this subject, I must observe that our English poets have succeeded much better in the style than in the sentiments of their tragedies. Their language is very often noble and sonorous, but the sense either very trifling or very common. On the contrary, in the ancient tragedies, and indeed in those of Corneille and Racine, though the expressions are very great, it is the thought that bears them up and swells them. For my own part I prefer a noble sentiment that is depressed with homely language, infinitely before a vulgar one that is blown up with all the sound and energy of expression. Whether this defect in our tragedies may arise from want of genius, knowledge, or experience in the writers, or from their compliance with the vicious taste of their readers, who are better judges of the language than of the sentiments, and consequently relish the one more than the other, I cannot determine. But I believe it might rectify the conduct both of the one and of the other, if the writer laid down the whole contexture of his dialogue in plain English before he turned it into blank verse; and if the reader, after the perusal of a scene, would consider the naked thought of every speech in it, when divested of all its tragic ornaments: by this means, without being imposed upon by words, we may judge impartially of the thought, and consider whether it be natural or great enough for the person that utters it, whether it deserves to shine in such a blaze of eloquence, or show itself in such a variety of lights, as are generally made use of by the writers of our English tragedy.

I must in the next place observe, that when our thoughts are great and just, they are often obscured by the sounding phrases, hard metaphors, and forced expressions, in which they are clothed. Shakespeare is often very faulty in this particular. . . .

Otway[2] has followed nature in the language of his tragedy, and therefore shines in the passionate parts more than any of our English poets. As there is something familiar and domestic in the fable of his tragedy, more than in those of any other poet, he has little pomp, but great force in his expressions. For which reason, though he has admirably succeeded in the tender and melting part of his tragedies, he sometimes falls into too great a familiarity of phrase in those parts, which by Aristotle's rule, ought to have been raised and supported by the dignity of expression.

It has been observed by others, that this poet has founded his tragedy of *Venice Preserved* on so wrong a plot, that the greatest characters in it are those of rebels and traitors. Had the hero of his play discovered the same good qualities in the defence of his country that he showed for its ruin and subversion, the audience could not enough pity and admire him; but as he is now represented, we can only say of him, what the Roman historian[3] says of Catiline, that his fall would have been glorious (*si pro patriâ sic concidisset*) had he so fallen in the service of his country.

[2] Thomas Otway (1652–1685).
[3] Lucius Annaeus Florus, *Epitome*, II, 12.

The Spectator, No. 40[1] *April 16, 1711*

The English writers of tragedy are possessed with a notion, that when they represent a virtuous or innocent person in distress, they ought not to leave him, till they have delivered him out of his troubles, or made him triumph over his enemies. This error they have been led into by a ridiculous doctrine in modern criticism, that they are obliged to an equal distribution of rewards and punishments, and an impartial execution of poetical justice. Who were the first that established this rule, I know not; but I am sure it has no foundation in nature, in reason, or in the practice of the ancients. We find that good and evil happen alike to all men on this side the grave; and as the principal design of tragedy is to raise commiseration and terror in the minds of the audience, we shall defeat this great end, if we always make virtue and innocence happy and successful. Whatever crosses and disappointments a good man suffers in the body of the tragedy, they will make but a small impression on our minds, when we know that in the last act he is to arrive at the end of his wishes and desires. When we see him engaged in the depth of his afflictions, we are apt to comfort ourselves, because we are sure he will find his way out of them; and that his grief, how great soever it may be at present, will soon terminate in gladness. For this reason the ancient writers of tragedy treated men in their plays, as they are dealt with in the world, by making virtue sometimes happy and sometimes miserable, as they found it in the fable which they made choice of, or as it might affect their audience in the most agreeable manner. Aristotle considers the tragedies that were written in either of these kinds, and observes, that those which ended unhappily had always pleased the people and carried away the prize, in the public disputes of the stage, from those that ended happily. Terror and commiseration leave a pleasing anguish in the mind; and fix the audience in such a serious composure of thought, as is much more lasting and delightful than any little transient starts of joy and satisfaction. Accordingly, we find, that more of our English tragedies have succeeded, in which the favourites of the audience sink under their calamities, than those in which they recover themselves out of them. . . . *King Lear* is an admirable tragedy . . . as Shakespeare wrote it; but as it is reformed according to the chimerical notion of poetical justice,[2] in my humble opinion it has lost half its beauty. At the same time I must allow that there are very noble tragedies which have been framed upon the other plan, and have ended happily. . . . I must also allow, that many of

Selections. From *The Spectator*, Vol. I. Philadelphia: Crissy & Markley, 1853.

[1] See John Dennis's reply to this essay, above, pp. 369–372.
[2] In the adaptation by Nahum Tate (1652–1715), first performed in 1681, Cordelia lives and marries Edgar.

Shakespeare's, and several of the celebrated tragedies of antiquity, are cast in the same form. I do not therefore dispute against this way of writing tragedies, but against the criticism that would establish this as the only method; and by that means would very much cramp the English tragedy, and perhaps give a wrong bent to the genius of our writers.

The tragicomedy, which is the product of the English theatre, is one of the most monstrous inventions that ever entered into a poet's thoughts. An author might as well think of weaving the adventures of Aeneas and Hudibras into one poem, as of writing such a motley piece of mirth and sorrow. But the absurdity of these performances is so very visible, that I shall not insist upon it.

The same objections which are made to tragicomedy, may, in some measure, be applied to all tragedies that have a double plot in them, which are likewise more frequent upon the English stage than upon any other; for though the grief of the audience, in such performances, be not changed into another passion, as in tragicomedies, it is diverted upon another object, which weakens their concern for the principal action, and breaks the tide of sorrow, by throwing it into different channels. This inconvenience, however, may in a great measure be cured, if not wholly removed, by the skilful choice of an underplot, which may bear such a near relation to the principal design, as to contribute towards the completion of it, and be concluded by the same catastrophe.

There is also another particular, which may be reckoned among the blemishes, or rather the false beauties, of our English tragedy: I mean those particular speeches which are commonly known by the name of *rants*. The warm and passionate parts of a tragedy are always the most taking with the audience; for which reason we often see the players pronouncing in all the violence of action, several parts of the tragedy which the author writ with great temper, and designed that they should have been so acted. I have seen Powell[3] very often raise himself a loud clap by this artifice. The poets that were acquainted with this secret, have given frequent occasion for such emotions in the actor, by adding vehemence to words where there was no passion, or inflaming a real passion into fustian. This hath filled the mouths of our heroes with bombast; and given them such sentiments as proceed rather from a swelling than a greatness of mind. Unnatural exclamations, curses, vows, blasphemies, a defiance of mankind, and an outraging of the gods, frequently pass upon the audience for towering thoughts, and have accordingly met with infinite applause.

I shall here add a remark, which I am afraid our tragic writers may make an ill use of. As our heroes are generally lovers, their swelling and blustering upon the stage very much recommends them to the fair part of their audi-

---

[3] George Powell (1668–1714).

ence. The ladies are wonderfully pleased to see a man insulting kings, or affronting the gods in one scene, and throwing himself at the feet of his mistress in another. Let him behave himself insolently towards the men, and abjectly towards the fair one, and it is ten to one but he proves a favourite of the boxes.

Sir Richard Steele   *1672–1729*

The Spectator, No. 51   *April 28, 1711*

"Mr. Spectator,

"My fortune, quality, and person are such, as render me as conspicuous as any young woman in town. It is in my power to enjoy it in all its vanities; but I have from a very careful education contracted a great aversion to the forward air and fashion which is practiced in all public places and assemblies. I attribute this very much to the style and manner of our plays. I was last night at the *Funeral*,[1] where a confident lover in the play, speaking of his mistress, cries out—'Oh that Harriot! to fold these arms about the waist of that beauteous, struggling, and at last yielding fair!' Such an image as this ought by no means to be presented to a chaste and regular audience. I expect your opinion of this sentence, and recommend to your consideration, as a *Spectator*, the conduct of the stage at present with relation to chastity and modesty. I am, sir, your constant reader and well wisher."

The complaint of this young lady is so just, that the offence is gross enough to have displeased persons who cannot pretend to that delicacy and modesty of which she is mistress. But there is a great deal to be said in behalf of an author: If the audience would but consider the difficulty of keeping up a sprightly dialogue for five acts together, they would allow a writer, when he wants wit, and cannot please any otherwise, to help it out with a little smut-

Selections. From *The Spectator*, Vol. I. Philadelphia: Crissy & Markley, 1853.

[1] Steele's first comedy (1701). Because it was performed at Drury Lane on April 26, 1711 (two nights before the publications of this paper), it may be that Steele himself wrote the letter.

tiness. I will answer for the poets, that no one ever writ bawdry for any other reason but dearth of invention. When the author cannot strike out of himself any more of that which he has superior to those who make up the bulk of his audience, his natural recourse is to that which he has in common with them: and a description which gratifies a sensual appetite will please, when the author has nothing about him to delight a refined imagination. It is to such a poverty we must impute this and all other sentences in plays, which are of this kind, and which are commonly termed luscious expressions.

This expedient to supply the deficiencies of wit has been used, more or less, by most of the authors who have succeeded on the stage; though I know but one who has professedly writ a play upon the basis of the desire of multiplying our species, and that is the polite Sir George Etherege; if I understand what the lady would be at in the play called *She Would If She Could*.[2] Other poets have, here and there, given an intimation that there is this design under all the disguises and affectations which a lady may put on; but no author, except this, has made sure work of it, and put the imaginations of the audience upon this one purpose, from the beginning to the end of the comedy. It has always fared accordingly; for whether it be, that all who go to this piece, would if they could, or that the innocents go to it, to guess only what *She Would If She Could*, the play has always been well received.

It lifts a heavy empty sentence, when there is added to it a lascivious gesture of body; and when it is too low to be raised even by that, a flat meaning is enlivened by making it a double one. Writers who want genius never fail of keeping this secret in reserve to create a laugh, or raise a clap. I, who know nothing of women but from seeing plays, can give great guesses at the whole structure of the fair sex, by being innocently placed in the pit, and insulted by the petticoats of their dancers; the advantages of whose pretty persons are a great help to a dull play. When a poet flags in writing lusciously, a pretty girl can move lasciviously, and have the same good consequences for the author. Dull poets in this case use their audiences, as dull parasites do their patrons; when they can not longer divert them with their wit or humour, they bait their ears with something which is agreeable to their temper, though below their understanding. . . . But, as I have before observed, it is easier to talk to the man than to the man of sense.

It is remarkable, that the writers of least learning are best skilled in the luscious way. The poetesses of the age have done wonders in this kind; and we are obliged to the lady who writ *Ibrahim*,[3] for introducing a preparatory scene to the very action, when the emperor throws his handkerchief as a signal for his mistress to follow him into the most retired part of the seraglio. . . . This ingenious gentlewoman, in this piece of bawdry, refined upon an

[2] (1668).
[3] (1696) by Mrs. Mary Pix.

author of the same sex, who, in *The Rover*,[4] makes a country squire strip to his Holland drawers. . . .

If men of wit, who think fit to write for the stage, instead of this pitiful way of giving delight, would turn their thoughts upon raising it from such good natural impulses as are in the audience, but are choked up by vice and luxury, they would not only please, but befriend us at the same time. If a man had a mind to be new in his way of writing, might not he who is now represented as a fine gentleman, though he betrays the honour and bed of his neighbour and friend, and lies with half the women in the play, and is at last rewarded with her of the best character in it; I say upon giving the comedy another cast, might not such a one divert the audience quite as well, if at the catastrophe he were found out for a traitor, and met with contempt accordingly? There is seldom a person devoted to above one darling vice at a time, so that there is room enough to catch at men's hearts to their good and advantage, if the poets will attempt it with the honesty which becomes their characters.

There is no man who loves his bottle or his mistress in a manner so very abandoned, as not to be capable of relishing an agreeable character, that is no way a slave to either of those pursuits. A man that is temperate, generous, valiant, chaste, faithful, and honest, may, at the same time, have wit, humour, mirth, good breeding, and gallantry. While he exerts these latter qualities, twenty occasions might be invented to show he is master of the other noble virtues. Such characters would smite and reprove the heart of a man of sense, when he is given up to his pleasures. He would see he has been mistaken all this while, and be convinced that a sound constitution and an innocent mind are the true ingredients for becoming and enjoying life. All men of true taste would call a man of wit, who should turn his ambition this way, a friend and benefactor to his country; but I am at a loss what name they would give him, who makes use of his capacity for contrary purposes.

[4] (1677) by Mrs. Aphra Behn.

The Spectator, No. 65[1] *May 15, 1711*

. . . The seat of wit, when one speaks as a man of the town and the world, is the playhouse; I shall therefore fill this paper with reflections upon the use of it in that place. The application of wit in the theatre has as strong an effect upon the manners of our gentlemen, as the taste of it has upon the writings of our authors. . . .

Without further preface, I am going to look into some of our most applauded plays, and see whether they deserve the figure they at present bear in the imaginations of men, or not.

In reflecting upon those works, I shall chiefly dwell upon that for which each respective play is most celebrated. The present paper shall be employed upon *Sir Fopling Flutter*. The received character of this play is, that it is the pattern of genteel comedy. Dorimant and Harriot are the characters of greatest consequence: and if these are low and mean, the reputation of the play is very unjust.

I will take for granted, that a fine gentleman should be honest in his actions, and refined in his language. Instead of this, our hero in this piece is a direct knave in his designs, and a clown in his language. Bellair is his admirer and friend; in return for which, because he is forsooth a greater wit than his said friend, he thinks it reasonable to persuade him to marry a young lady, whose virtue, he thinks, will last no longer than till she is a wife, and then she cannot but fall to his share, as he is an irresistible fine gentleman. The falsehood to Mrs. Loveit, and the barbarity of triumphing over her anguish for losing him, is another instance of his honesty, as well as his good nature. As to his fine language, he calls the orange-woman, who, it seems, is inclined to grow fat, "an overgrown jade with a flasket of guts before her"; and salutes her with a pretty phrase of, "How now, double tripe?" Upon the mention of a country gentlewoman, whom he knows nothing of (no one can imagine why), he "will lay his life she is some awkward, ill-fashioned country toad, who, not having above four dozen of hairs on her head, has adorned her baldness with a large white fruz, that she may look sparkishly in the fore-front of the king's box at an old play." Unnatural mixture of senseless commonplace!

As to the generosity of his temper, he tells his poor footman: "If he did not wait better," he would turn him away, in the insolent phrase of, "I'll uncase you."

Selections. From *The Spectator*, Vol. II. Philadelphia: Crissy & Markley, 1853.

[1] See John Dennis's reply, "A Defence of Sir Fopling Flutter," above, pp. 372–374. Sir Fopling Flutter gives his name to the subtitle of Sir George Etherege's *The Man of Mode* (1676), which is often referred to by its subtitle.

Now for Mrs Harriot: she laughs at obedience to an absent mother, whose tenderness Busy describes to be very exquisite; "for, that she is so pleased with finding Harriot again, that she cannot chide her for being out of the way." This witty daughter and fine lady, has so little respect for this good woman, that she ridicules her air in taking leave, and cries, "In what struggle is my poor mother yonder? See, see, her head tottering, her eyes staring, and her underlip trembling." But all this is atoned for, because "she has more wit than is usual in her sex, and as much malice, though she is as wild as you could wish her, and has a demureness in her looks that makes it so surprising!" Then to recommend her as a fit spouse for his hero, the poet makes her speak her sense of marriage very ingenuously; "I think," says she, "I might be brought to endure him, and that is all a reasonable woman should expect in a husband." It is, methinks, unnatural that we are not made to understand how she, that was bred up under a silly, pious old mother, that would never trust her out of her sight, came to be so polite.

It cannot be denied, but that the negligence of everything which engages the attention of the sober and valuable part of mankind, appears very well drawn in this piece; but it is denied, that it is necessary to the character of a fine gentleman, that he should in that manner trample upon all order and decency. As for the character of Dorimant, it is more of a coxcomb than that of Fopling. He says of one of his companions, that a good correspondence between them is their mutual interest. Speaking of that friend, he declares, their being much together, "makes the women think the better of his understanding, and judge more favourably of my reputation. It makes him pass upon some for a man of very good sense, and me upon others for a very civil person."

This whole celebrated piece is a perfect contradiction to good manners, good sense, and common honesty, and as there is nothing in it but what is built upon the ruin of virtue and innocence, according to the notion of merit in this comedy, I take the shoemaker to be, in reality, the fine gentleman of the play; for it seems he is an atheist, if we may depend upon his character as given by the orange woman, who is herself far from being the lowest in the play. She says of a fine man, who is Dorimant's companion, there "is not such another heathen in the town, except the shoemaker." His pretension to be the hero of the drama appears still more in his own description of his way of living with his lady. "There is," says he, "never a man in town lives more like a gentleman with his wife than I do; I never mind her emotions; she never inquires into mine. We speak to one another civilly, hate one another heartily; and because it is vulgar to lie and soak together, we have each of us our several settle-bed." That of *soaking together*, is as good as if Dorimant had spoken it himself; and, I think, since he puts human nature in as ugly a form as the circumstance will bear, and is a staunch unbeliever, he is very much wronged in having no part of the good fortune bestowed in the last act.

To speak plainly of this whole work, I think nothing but being lost to a sense of innocence and virtue can make anyone see this comedy without observing more frequent occasion to move sorrow and indignation than mirth and laughter. At the same time, I allow it to be nature, but it is nature in its utmost corruption and degeneracy.

The Spectator, No. 290 *February 1, 1712*

The players, who know I am very much their friend, take all opportunities to express a gratitude to me for being so. They could not have a better occasion of obliging me than one which they lately took hold of. They desired my friend, Will Honeycomb, to bring me to the reading of a new tragedy; it is called *The Distressed Mother*.[1] I must confess, though some days are passed since I enjoyed that entertainment, the passions of the several characters dwell strongly upon my imagination; and I congratulate the age, that they are at last to see truth and human life represented in the incidents which concern heroes and heroines. The style of the play is such as becomes those of the first education, and the sentiments worthy those of the highest figure. It was a most exquisite pleasure to me, to observe real tears drop from the eyes of those who had long made it their profession to dissemble affliction; and the player who read, frequently threw down the book, till he had given vent to the humanity which rose in him at some irresistible touches of the imagined sorrow. We have seldom had any female distress on the stage, which did not, upon cool examination, appear to flow from the weakness rather than the misfortune of the person represented: but in this tragedy you are not entertained with the ungoverned passions of such as are enamoured of each other merely as they are men and women, but their regards are founded upon high conceptions of each other's virtue and merit; and the

Selections. From *The Spectator*, Vol. VI. Philadelphia: Crissy & Markley, 1853.

[1] An adaptation by Ambrose Philips of Racine's *Andromaque*, first performed at Drury Lane on March 17, 1712.

character which gives name to the play, is one who has behaved herself with heroic virtue in the most important circumstances of a female life, those of a wife, a widow, and a mother. If there be those whose minds have been too attentive upon the affairs of life, to have any notion of the passion of love in such extremes as are known only to particular tempers, yet in the above-mentioned considerations, the sorrow of the heroine will move even the generality of mankind. Domestic virtues concern all the world, and there is no one living who is not interested that Andromache should be an imitable character. The generous affection to the memory of her deceased husband, that tender care for her son, which is ever heightened with the consideration of his father, and these regards preserved in spite of being tempted with the possession of the highest greatness, are what can not but be venerable even to such an audience as at present frequents the English theatre. . . . As to the work itself, it is everywhere nature. The persons are of the highest quality in life, even that of princes; but their quality is not represented by the poet, with directions that guards and waiters should follow them in every scene, but their grandeur appears in greatness of sentiments, flowing from minds worthy their condition. To make a character truly great, this author understands that it should have its foundation in superior thought and maxims of conduct. . . . What is further very extraordinary in this work is, that the persons are all of them laudable, and their misfortunes arise rather from unguarded virtue than propensity to vice.

Preface to
The Conscious Lovers[1]   *1723*

This comedy has been received with universal acceptance, for it was in every part excellently performed, and there needs no other applause of the actors but that they excelled according to the dignity and difficulty of the

Selection. From Sir Richard Steele, *The Conscious Lovers*. London: J. Tonson, 1730. The play was first performed in 1722 and first published the following year. Spelling and punctuation modernized by the editor.

[1] See John Dennis's reply, *Remarks on a Play Called* The Conscious Lovers: A Comedy, pp. 374–375.

character they represented. But this great favor done to the work in acting renders the expectation still the greater from the author to keep up the spirit in the representation of the closet, or any other circumstance of the reader, whether alone or in company: to which I can only say that it must be remembered a play is to be seen, and is made to be represented with the advantage of action, nor can appear but with half the spirit without it, for the greatest effect of a play in reading is to excite the reader to go see it; and when he does so, it is then a play has the effect of example and precept.

The chief design of this was to be an innocent performance, and the audience have abundantly showed how ready they are to support what is visibly intended that way; nor do I make any difficulty to acknowledge that the whole was writ for the sake of the scene of the fourth act, wherein Mr. Bevil evades the quarrel with his friend, and hope it may have some effect upon the Goths and Vandals that frequent the theatres, or a more polite audience may supply their absence.

But this incident, and the case of the father and daughter, are esteemed by some people no subjects of comedy. But I cannot be of their mind, for anything that has its foundation in happiness and success must be allowed to be the object of comedy, and sure it must be an improvement of it to introduce a joy too exquisite for laughter, that can have no spring but in delight, which is the case of this young lady. I must therefore contend that the tears which were shed on that occasion flowed from reason and good sense, and that men ought not to be laughed at for weeping till we are come to a more clear notion of what is to be imputed to the hardness of the head and the softness of the heart; and I think it was very politely said of Mr. Wilks to one who told him there was a General weeping for Indiana, "I'll warrant he'll fight ne'er the worse for that." To be apt to give way to the impressions of humanity is the excellence of a right disposition and the natural working of a well-turned spirit.

George Lillo 1693?–1739

Dedication to
The London Merchant[1] 1731

If Tragic Poetry be, as Mr. Dryden has somewhere said, the most excellent and most useful kind of writing, the more extensively useful the moral of any tragedy is, the more excellent that piece must be of its kind.

I hope I shall not be thought to insinuate that this, to which I have presumed to prefix your name, is such; that depends on its fitness to answer the end of tragedy, the exciting of the passions, in order to the correcting such of them as are criminal, either in their nature, or through their excess. Whether the following scenes do this in any tolerable degree, is, with the deference that becomes one who would not be thought vain, submitted to your candid and impartial judgment.

What I would infer is this, I think, evident truth; that tragedy is so far from losing its dignity, by being accommodated to the circumstances of the generality of mankind, that it is more truly august in proportion to the extent of its influence, and the numbers that are properly affected by it. As it is more truly great to be the instrument of good to many, who stand in need of our assistance, than to a very small part of that number.

If Princes, etc. were alone liable to misfortunes, arising from vice, or weakness in themselves, or others, there would be good reason for confining the characters in tragedy to those of superior rank; but, since the contrary is evident, nothing can be more reasonable than to proportion the remedy to the disease.

I am far from denying that tragedies, founded on any instructive and extraordinary events in History, or well-invented Fable, where the persons introduced are of the highest rank, are without their use, even to the bulk of the audience. The strong contrast between a Tamerlane and a Bajazet, may have its weight with an unsteady people, and contribute to the fixing of them in the interest of a Prince of the character of the former, when, through their own levity, or the arts of designing men, they are rendered factious and uneasy, though they have the highest reason to be satisfied. The sentiments and example of a Cato, may inspire his spectators with a just sense of the value of liberty, when they see that honest patriot prefer death to an obligation from a tyrant, who would sacrifice the constitution of his country, and the liberties of mankind, to his ambition or revenge. I have

Selection. From *Lillo's Dramatic Works*, Vol. I. London: W. Lowndes, 1810.

[1] To Sir John Eyles, Baronet.

attempted, indeed, to enlarge the province of the graver kind of poetry, and should be glad to see it carried on by some abler hand. Plays, founded on moral tales in private life, may be of admirable use, by carrying conviction to the mind, with such irresistible force, as to engage all the faculties and powers of the soul in the cause of virtue, by stifling vice in its first principles. They who imagine this too much to be attributed to Tragedy, must be strangers to the energy of that noble species of poetry. Shakespeare, who has given such amazing proofs of his genius, in that as well as in Comedy, in his Hamlet, has the following lines:

> Had he the motive and the cue for passion
> That I have; he would drown the stage with tears
> And cleave the general ear with horrid speech;
> Make mad the guilty, and appal the free,
> Confound the ignorant; and amaze indeed
> The very faculties of eyes and ears.

And farther, in the same speech,

> . . . . .I have heard,
> . . . . . That guilty creatures sitting at a play,
> Have, by the very cunning of the scene,
> Been struck so to the soul, that presently
> They have proclaim'd their malefactions.

Prodigious! yet strictly just. But I shall not take up your valuable time with my remarks; only give me leave just to observe, that he seems so firmly persuaded of the power of a well wrote piece to produce the effect here ascribed to it, as to make Hamlet venture his soul on the event, and rather trust that, than a messenger from the other world, though it assumed, as he expresses it, his noble father's form, and assured him, that it was his spirit. I'll have, says Hamlet, grounds more relative,

> . . . . . The Play's the thing,
> Wherein I'll catch the conscience of the king.

Such Plays are the best answers to them who deny the lawfulness of the stage.

Considering the novelty of this attempt, I thought it would be expected from me to say something in its excuse; and I was unwilling to lose the opportunity of saying something of the usefulness of Tragedy in general, and what may be reasonably expected from the farther improvement of this excellent kind of poetry.

Samuel Johnson *1709–1784*

The Rambler, No. 92* *February 2, 1751*

It is . . . the task of criticism to establish principles; to improve opinion
into knowledge, and to distinguish those means of pleasing which depend
upon known causes and rational deduction, from the nameless and inexplicable elegances which appeal wholly to the fancy, from which we feel delight,
but know not how they produce it, and which may well be termed the en-
chantresses of the soul. Criticism reduces those regions of literature under
the dominion of science, which have hitherto known only the anarchy of
ignorance, the caprices of fancy, and the tyranny of prescription.

The Rambler, No. 156† *September 4, 1751*

Every government, say the politicians, is perpetually degenerating towards
corruption, from which it must be rescued at certain periods by the resusci-
tation of its first principles, and the re-establishment of its original constitution. Every animal body, according to the methodic physicians, is, by the
predominance of some exuberant quality, continually declining towards disease and death, which must be obviated by a seasonable reduction of the
pecant humour to the just equipoise which health requires.

In the same manner the studies of mankind, all at least which, not being
subject to rigorous demonstration, admit the influence of fancy and caprice,
are perpetually tending to error and confusion. Of the great principles of
truth which the first speculatists discovered, the simplicity is embarrassed by
ambitious additions, or the evidence obscured by inaccurate argumentation;
and as they descend from one succession of writers to another, like light
transmitted from room to room, they lose their strength and splendour, and
fade at last in total evanescence.

* Selection. From Samuel Johnson, *The Rambler*, Vol. II. Philadelphia: J. J. Woodward,
1827.

† From Samuel Johnson, *The Rambler*, Vol. IV. Philadelphia: J. J. Woodward, 1827.

The systems of learning therefore must be sometimes reviewed, complications analyzed into principles, and knowledge disentangled from opinion. It is not always possible, without a close inspection, to separate the genuine shoots of consequential reasoning, which grow out of some radical postulate, from the branches which art has engrafted on it. The accidental prescriptions of authority, when time has procured them veneration, are often confounded with the laws of nature, and those rules are supposed coeval with reason, of which the first rise cannot be discovered.

Criticism has sometimes permitted fancy to dictate the laws by which fancy ought to be restrained, and fallacy to perplex the principles by which fallacy is to be detected; her superintendance of others has betrayed her to negligence of herself; and like the ancient Scythians, by extending her conquests over distant regions, she has left her throne vacant to her slaves.

Among the laws of which the desire of extending authority, or ardour of promoting knowledge, has prompted the prescription, all which writers have received, had not the same original right to our regard. Some are to be considered as fundamental and indispensable, others only as useful and convenient; some as dedicated by reason and necessity, others as enacted by despotic antiquity; some as invincibly supported by their conformity to the order of nature and operations of the intellect; others as formed by accident, or instituted by example, and therefore always liable to dispute and alteration.

That many rules have been advanced without consulting nature or reason, we cannot but suspect, when we find it peremptorily decreed by the ancient masters, that *only three speaking personages should appear at once upon the stage*; a law which, as the variety and intricacy of modern plays has made it impossible to be observed, we now violate without scruple, and as experience proves, with inconvenience.

The original of this precept was merely accidental. Tragedy was a monody or solitary song in honour of Bacchus, improved afterwards into a dialogue by the addition of another speaker, but the ancients remembering that the tragedy was first pronounced only by one, durst not for some time venture beyond two; at last when custom and impunity had made them daring, they extended their liberty to the admission of three, but restrained themselves by a critical edict from further exorbitance.

By what accident the number of acts was limited to five, I know not that any author has informed us; but certainly it is not determined by any necessity arising either from the nature of action or propriety of exhibition. An act is only the representation of such a part of the business of the play as proceeds in an unbroken tenour, or without any intermediate pause. Nothing is more evident than that of every real, and by consequence of every dramatic action, the intervals may be more or fewer than five; and indeed the rule is upon the *English* stage every day broken in effect, without any other mischief than that which arises from an absurd endeavour to observe it in appearance.

Whenever the scene is shifted the act ceases, since some time is necessarily supposed to elapse while the personages of the drama change their place.

With no greater right to our obedience have the critics confined the dramatic action to a certain number of hours. Probability requires that the time of action should approach somewhat nearly to that of exhibition, and those plays will always be thought most happily conducted which crowd the greatest variety into the least space. But since it will frequently happen that some delusion must be admitted, I know not where the limits of imagination can be fixed. It is rarely observed that minds, not prepossessed by mechanical criticism, feel any offence from the extension of the intervals between the acts; nor can I perceive it absurd or impossible, that he who can multiply three hours into twelve or twenty-four, might image with equal ease a greater number.

I know not whether he that professes to regard no other laws than those of nature, will not be inclined to receive tragicomedy to his protection, whom, however generally condemned, her own laurels have hitherto shaded from the fulminations of criticism. For what is there in the mingled drama which impartial reason can condemn? The connexion of important with trivial incidents, since it is not only common but perpetual, in the world, may surely be allowed upon the stage, which pretends only to be the mirror of life. The impropriety of suppressing passions before we have raised them to the intended agitation, and of diverting the expectation from an event which we keep suspended only to raise it, may be speciously urged. But will not experience show this objection to be rather subtle than just? Is it not certain that the tragic and comic affections have been moved alternately with equal force, and that no plays have oftener filled the eye with tears, and the breast with palpitation, than those which are varigated with interludes of mirth?

I do not however think it safe to judge of works of genius merely by the event. The resistless vicissitudes of the heart, this alternate prevalance of merriment and solemnity, may sometimes be more properly ascribed to the vigour of the writer than the justness of the design; and instead of vindicating tragicomedy by the success of Shakespeare, we ought perhaps to pay new honours to that transcendent and unbounded genius that could preside over the passions in sport; who, to actuate the affections needed not the slow gradation of common means, but could fill the heart with instantaneous jollity or sorrow, and vary our disposition as he changed his scenes. Perhaps the effects even of Shakespeare's poetry might have been yet greater, had he not counteracted himself; and we might have been more interested in the distresses of his heroes, had we not been so frequently diverted by the jokes of his buffoons.

There are other rules more fixed and obligatory. It is necessary that of every play the chief action should be single; for since a play represents some transaction, through its regular maturation to its final event two actions equally important must evidently constitute two plays.

As the design of tragedy is to instruct by moving the passions, it must always have a hero, a personage apparently and incontestably superior to the rest, upon whom the attention may be fixed and the anxiety suspended. For though of two persons opposing each other with equal abilities and equal virtue, the auditor will inevitably in time choose his favourite, yet as that choice must be without any cogency of conviction, the hopes or fears which it raises will be faint and languid. Of two heroes acting in confederacy against a common enemy, the virtues or dangers will give little emotion, because each claims our concern with the same right, and the heart lies at rest between equal motives.

It ought to be the first endeavour of a writer to distinguish nature from custom; or that which is established because it is right, from that which is right only because it is established; that he may neither violate essential principles by a desire of novelty, nor debar himself from the attainments of beauties within his view, by a needless fear of breaking rules which no literary dictator had authority to enact.

A Dictionary of the English Language 1755

Comedy. A dramatic representation of the lighter faults of mankind.

> In every scene some moral let it teach,
> And, if it can, at once both please and preach. —Pope.[1]

Critic. A man skilled in the art of judging literature; a man able to distinguish the faults and beauties of writing.

Selections. From Samuel Johnson, A *Dictionary of the English Language*. London: W. Strahan, 1755. Spelling and punctuation modernized by the editor.

[1] Alexander Pope, *Epistle to Miss Blount, with the Works of Voiture* (1700–1710), verses 23–24.

Criticism (from **Critic**).

> Criticism, as it was first instituted by Aristotle, was meant a standard of judging well. —Dryden's *Innocence*, Preface.[2]

Drama. A poem accommodated to action; a poem in which the action is not related but represented and in which, therefore, such rules are to be observed as make the representation possible.

> Many rules of imitating nature Aristotle drew from Homer, which he fitted to the drama, furnishing himself also with observations from the theatre when it flourished under Aeschylus, Euripides, and Sophocles. —Dryden's *Aeneis*, Dedication.[3]

Farce. A dramatic representation written without regularity and stuffed with wild and ludicrous conceits.

> They object against it as a farce, because the irregularity of the plot should answer to the extravagance of the characters, which they say this piece wants, and therefore is no farce. —Gay.[4]

Tragedy. A dramatic representation of a serious action.

> All our tragedies are of kings and princes, but you never see a poor man have a part, unless it be as a chorus or to fill up the scenes, to dance, or to be derided. —Taylor's *Holy Living*.[5]

Tragicomedy. A drama compounded of merry and serious events.

> We have often had tragicomedies upon the English theatre with success, but in that sort of composition the tragedy and comedy are in distinct scenes. —Gay.

Tragicomical. Relating to **Tragicomedy**.

> The whole art of the tragicomical farce lies in interweaving the several kinds of the drama so that they cannot be distinguished. —Gay's *What D'Ye Call It*.[6]

---

[2] John Dryden, "The Author's Apology for Heroic Poetry and Poetic License," prefixed to *The State of Innocence* (1677).

[3] A minor misquotation from John Dryden, *Aeneis* (1697), II, 226.

[4] With a minor ellipsis, from John Gay, Preface to *The What D'Ye Call It: A Tragi-Comi-Pastoral Farce* (1715). The two John Gay quotations that follow are from the same Preface.

[5] Jeremy Taylor, *Holy Living* (1650).

[6] A misquotation from Gay's Preface to the play, which reads "But the whole art of the Tragi-Comi-Pastoral Farce," etc. Like the play itself, the Preface is parody. Still, Johnson's misquotation—perhaps deliberate, perhaps an inspired error—is an apt description of much late nineteenth- and twentieth-century tragicomedy.

Preface to The Plays of William Shakespeare 1765

Nothing can please many, and please long, but just representations of general nature. Particular manners can be known to few, and therefore few only can judge how nearly they are copied. The irregular combinations of fanciful invention may delight awhile, by that novelty of which the common satiety of life sends us all in quest; but the pleasures of sudden wonders are soon exhausted, and the mind can only repose on the stability of truth.

Shakespeare is, above all writers, at least above all modern writers, the poet of nature; the poet that holds up to his readers a faithful mirror of manners and of life. His characters are not modified by the customs of particular places, unpracticed by the rest of the world; by the peculiarities of studies or professions, which can operate but upon small numbers; or by the accidents of transient fashions or temporary opinions: they are the genuine progeny of common humanity, such as the world will always supply, and observation will always find. His persons act and speak by the influence of those general passions and principles by which all minds are agitated, and the whole system of life is continued in motion. In the writings of other poets a character is too often an individual: in those of Shakespeare it is commonly a species.

It is from this wide extension of design that so much instruction is derived. It is this which fills the plays of Shakespeare with practical axioms and domestic wisdom. It was said of Euripides, that every verse was a precept; and it may be said of Shakespeare, that from his works may be collected a system of civil and economical prudence. Yet his real power is not shown in the splendour of particular passages, but by the progress of his fable, and the tenour of his dialogue; and he that tries to recommend him by select quotations, will succeed like the pedant in Hierocles, who when he offered his house to sale, carried a brick in his pocket as a specimen.

It will not easily be imagined how much Shakespeare excels in accommodating his sentiments to real life, but by comparing him with other authors. It was observed of the ancient schools of declamation, that the more diligently they were frequented, the more was the student disqualified for the world, because he found nothing there which he should ever meet in any other place. The same remark may be applied to every stage but that of

Selections. From *The Works of Samuel Johnson*, Vol. II. New York: Harper & Brothers, 1851.

Shakespeare. The theatre, when it is under any other direction, is peopled by such characters as were never seen, conversing in a language which was never heard, upon topics which will never arise in the commerce of mankind. But the dialogue of this author is often so evidently determined by the incident which produces it, and is pursued with so much ease and simplicity, that it seems scarcely to claim the merit of fiction, but to have been gleaned by diligent selection out of common conversation, and common occurrences.

Upon every other stage the universal agent is love, by whose power all good and evil is distributed, and every action quickened or retarded. To bring a lover, a lady, and a rival into the fable; to entangle them in contradictory obligations, perplex them with oppositions of interest, and harass them with violence of desires inconsistent with each other; to make them meet in rapture, and part in agony; to fill their mouths with hyperbolical joy and outrageous sorrow; to distress them as nothing human ever was distressed; to deliver them as nothing human ever was delivered; is the business of a modern dramatist. For this, probability is violated, life is misrepresented, and language is depraved. But love is only one of many passions; and as it has no great influence upon the sum of life, it has little operation· in the dramas of a poet, who caught his ideas from the living world, and exhibited only what he saw before him. He knew that any other passion, as it was regular or exorbitant, was a cause of happiness or calamity.

Characters thus ample and general were not easily discriminated and preserved, yet perhaps no poet ever kept his personages more distinct from each other. I will not say with Pope, that every speech may be assigned to the proper speaker, because many speeches there are which have nothing characteristical; but, perhaps, though some may be equally adapted to every person, it will be difficult to find that any can be properly transferred from the present possessor to another claimant. The choice is right, when there is reason for choice.

Other dramatists can only gain attention by hyperbolical or aggravated characters, by fabulous and unexampled excellence or depravity, as the writers of barbarous romances invigorated the reader by a giant and a dwarf; and he that should form his expectations of human affairs from the play or from the tale, would be equally deceived. Shakespeare has no heroes; his scenes are occupied only by men, who act and speak as the reader thinks that he should himself have spoken or acted on the same occasion; even where the agency is supernatural, the dialogue is level with life. Other writers disguise the most natural passions and most frequent incidents; so that he who contemplates them in the book, will not know them in the world; Shakespeare approximates the remote, and familiarizes the wonderful; the event which he represents will not happen, but, if it were possible, its effects would probably be such as he has assigned; and it may be said, that he has not only shown human nature as it acts in real exigencies, but as it would be found in trials to which it cannot be exposed.

This therefore is the praise of Shakespeare, that his drama is the mirror of life; that he who has mazed his imagination, in following the phantoms which other writers raise up before him, may here be cured of his delirious ecstasies, by reading human sentiments in human language, by scenes from which a hermit may estimate the transactions of the world, and a confessor predict the progress of the passions.

His adherence to general nature has exposed him to the censure of critics, who form their judgments upon narrower principles. Dennis and Rymer think his *Romans* not sufficiently *Roman*; and Voltaire censures his kings as not completely royal. Dennis is offended, that Menenius, a senator of Rome, should play the buffoon: and Voltaire perhaps thinks decency violated when the Danish usurper is represented as a drunkard. But Shakespeare always makes nature predominate over accident; and, if he preserves the essential character, is not very careful of distinctions superinduced and adventitious. His story requires Romans or kings, but he thinks only on men. He knew that Rome, like every other city, had men of all dispositions; and wanting a buffoon, he went into the Senate-house for that which the senate-house would certainly have afforded him. He was inclined to show an usurper and a murderer not only odious, but despicable; he therefore added drunkenness to his other qualities, knowing that kings love wine like other men, and that wine exerts its natural power upon kings. These are the petty cavils of petty minds; a poet overlooks the casual distinction of country and condition, as a painter, satisfied with the figure, neglects the drapery.

The censure which he has incurred by mixing comic and tragic scenes, as it extends to all his works, deserves more consideration. Let the fact be first stated, and then examined.

Shakespeare's plays are not in the rigorous and critical sense either tragedies or comedies, but compositions of a distinct kind; exhibiting the real state of sublunary nature, which partakes of good and evil, joy and sorrow, mingled with endless variety of proportion and innumerable modes of combination; and expressing the course of the world, in which the loss of one is the gain of another; in which, at the same time, the reveller is hasting to his wine, and the mourner burying his friend; in which the malignity of one is sometimes defeated by the frolic of another; and many mischiefs and many benefits are done and hindered without design.

Out of this chaos of mingled purposes and casualties the ancient poets, according to the laws which custom had prescribed, selected some the crimes of men, and some their absurdities; some the momentous vicissitudes of life, and some the lighter occurrences; some the terrors of distress, and some the gaieties of prosperity. Thus rose the two modes of imitation, known by the names of *tragedy* and *comedy*, compositions intended to promote different ends by contrary means, and considered as so little allied, that I do not recollect among the Greeks or Romans a single writer who attempted both.

Shakespeare has united the powers of exciting laughter and sorrow not only in one mind, but in one composition. Almost all his plays are divided between serious and ludicrous characters, and, in the successive evolutions of the design, sometimes produce seriousness and sorrow, and sometimes levity and laughter.

That this is a practice contrary to the rules of criticism will be readily allowed; but there is always an appeal open from criticism to nature. The end of writing is to instruct; the end of poetry is to instruct by pleasing. That the mingled drama may convey all the instruction of tragedy or comedy cannot be denied, because it includes both in its alterations of exhibition, and approaches nearer than either to the appearance of life, by showing how great machinations and slender designs may promote or obviate one another, and the high and the low co-operate in the general system by unavoidable concatenation.

It is objected, that by this change of scenes the passions are interrupted in their progression, and that the principal event, being not advanced by a due gradation of preparatory incidents, wants at last the power to move, which constitutes the perfection of dramatic poetry. This reasoning is so specious, that it is received as true even by those who in daily experience feel it to be false. The interchanges of mingled scenes seldom fail to produce the intended vicissitudes of passion. Fiction cannot move so much, but that the attention may be easily transferred; and though it must be allowed that pleasing melancholy be sometimes interrupted by unwelcome levity, yet let it be considered likewise, that melancholy is often not pleasing, and that the disturbance of one man may be the relief of another; that different auditors have different habitudes; and that, upon the whole, all pleasure consists in variety.

The players, who in their edition divided our author's works into comedies, histories, and tragedies, seem not to have distinguished the three kinds by any very exact or definite ideas.

An action which ended happily to the principal persons, however serious or distressful through its intermediate incidents, in their opinion, constituted a comedy. This idea of a comedy continued long among us; and plays were written, which, by changing the catastrophe, were tragedies today and comedies tomorrow.

Tragedy was not in those times a poem of more general dignity or elevation than comedy; it required only a calamitous conclusion, with which the common criticism of that age was satisfied, whatever light pleasure it afforded in its progress.

History was a series of actions, with no other than chronological succession, independent on each other, and without any tendency to introduce or regulate the conclusion. It is not always very nicely distinguished from tragedy. There is not much nearer approach to unity of action in the tragedy of *Antony and Cleopatra*, than in the history of *Richard the Second*. But a history might be continued through many plays; as it had no plan, it had no limits.

Through all these denominations of the drama Shakespeare's mode of composition is the same; an interchange of seriousness and merriment, by which the mind is softened at one time, and exhilarated at another. But whatever be his purpose, whether to gladden or depress, or to conduct the story, without vehemence or emotion, through tracts of easy and familiar dialogues, he never fails to attain his purpose; as he commands us, we laugh or mourn, or sit silent with quiet expectation, in tranquilty without indifference.

When Shakespeare's plan is understood, most of the criticisms of Rymer and Voltaire vanish away. The play of *Hamlet* is opened, without impropriety, by two sentinels; Iago bellows at Brabantio's window, without injury to the scheme of the play, though in terms which a modern audience would not easily endure; the character of Polonius is seasonable and useful; and the grave-diggers themselves may be heard with applause.

Shakespeare engaged in dramatic poetry with the world open before him; the rules of the ancients were yet known to few; the public judgment was unformed; he had no example of such fame as might force him upon imitation, nor critics of such authority as might restrain his extravagance; he therefore indulged his natural disposition; and his disposition, as Rymer has remarked, led him to comedy. In tragedy he often writes, with great appearance of toil and study, what is written at last with little felicity; but, in his comic scenes, he seems to produce, without labour, what no labour can improve. In tragedy he is always struggling after some occasion to be comic; but in comedy he seems to repose, or to luxuriate, as in a mode of thinking congenial to his nature. In his tragic scenes there is always something wanting, but his comedy often surpasses expectation or desire. His comedy pleases by the thoughts and the language, and his tragedy for the greater part by incident and action. His tragedy seems to be skill, his comedy to be instinct.

The force of his comic scenes has suffered little diminution from the changes made by a century and a half, in manners or in words. As his personages act upon principles arising from genuine passion, very little modified by particular forms, their pleasures and vexations are communicable to all times and to all places; they are natural, and therefore durable: the adventitious pecularities of personal habits are only superficial dyes, bright and pleasing for a little while, yet soon fading to a dim tinct, without any remains of former lustre, but the discriminations of true passion are the colours of nature: they pervade the whole mass, and can only perish with the body that exhibits them. The accidental compositions of heterogeneous modes are dissolved by the chance which combined them; but the uniform simplicity of primitive qualities neither admits increase, nor suffers decay. The sand heaped by one flood is scattered by another, but the rock always continues in its place. The stream of time, which is continually washing the dissoluble fabrics of other poets, passes without injury by the adamant of Shakespeare.

If there be, what I believe there is, in every nation, a style which never becomes obsolete, a certain mode of phraseology so consonant and congenial to the analogy and principles of its respective language, as to remain settled and unaltered; this style is probably to be sought in the common intercourse of life, among those who speak only to be understood, without ambition of elegance. The polite are always catching modish innovations, and the learned depart from established forms of speech, in hope of finding or making better; those who wish for distinction forsake the vulgar, when the vulgar is right; but there is a conversation above grossness, and below refinement, where propriety resides, and where this poet seems to have gathered his comic dialogue. He is therefore more agreeable to the ears of the present age than any other author equally remote, and among his other excellencies deserves to be studied as one of the original masters of our language.

These observations are to be considered not as unexceptionably constant, but as containing general and predominant truth. Shakespeare's familiar dialogue is affirmed to be smooth and clear, yet not wholly without ruggedness or difficulty; as a country may be eminently fruitful, though it has spots unfit for cultivation: his characters are praised as natural, though their sentiments are sometimes forced, and their actions improbable; as the earth upon the whole is spherical, though its surface is varied with protuberances and cavities.

Shakespeare with his excellencies has likewise faults, and faults sufficient to obscure and overwhelm any other merit. I shall show them in the proportion in which they appear to me, without envious malignity or superstitious veneration. No question can be more innocently discussed than a dead poet's pretensions to renown; and little regard is due to that bigotry which sets candour higher than truth.

His first defect is that to which may be imputed most of the evil in books or in men. He sacrifices virtue to convenience, and is so much more careful to please than instruct, that he seems to write without any moral purpose. From his writings indeed a system of social duty may be selected, for he that thinks reasonably must think morally; but his precepts and axioms drop casually from him; he makes no just distribution of good or evil, nor is always careful to show in the virtuous a disapprobation of the wicked; he carries his persons indifferently through right and wrong, and at the close dismisses them without further care, and leaves their examples to operate by chance. This fault the barbarity of his age cannot extenuate; for it is always a writer's duty to make the world better, and justice is a virtue independent on time or place.

The plots are often so loosely formed, that a very slight consideration may improve them, and so carelessly pursued, that he seems not always fully to comprehend his own design. He omits opportunities of instructing or delighting, which the train of his story seems to force upon him, and apparently rejects those exhibitions which would be more affecting, for the sake of those which are more easy.

It may be observed, that in many of his plays the latter part is evidently neglected. When he found himself near the end of his work, and in view of his reward, he shortened the labour to snatch the profit. He therefore remits his efforts where he should most vigorously exert them, and his catastrophe is improbably produced or imperfectly represented.

He had no regard to distinction of time or place, but gives to one age or nation, without scruple, the customs, institutions, and opinions of another, at the expense not only of likelihood, but of possibility. These faults Pope has endeavoured, with more zeal than judgment, to transfer to his imagined interpolators. We need not wonder to find Hector quoting Aristotle, when we see the loves of Theseus and Hippolyta combined with the gothic mythology of fairies. Shakespeare, indeed, was not the only violator of chronology, for in the same age Sidney, who wanted not the advantages of learning, has, in his *Arcadia*, confounded the pastoral with the feudal times, the days of innocence, quiet, and security, with those of turbulence, violence, and adventure.

In his comic scenes he is seldom very successful, when he engages his characters in reciprocations of smartness and contents of sarcasm; their jests are commonly gross, and their pleasantry licentious; neither his gentlemen nor his ladies have much delicacy, nor are sufficiently distinguished from his clowns by any appearance of refined manners. Whether he represented the real conversation of his time is not easy to determine: the reign of Elizabeth is commonly supposed to have been a time of stateliness, formality, and reserve; yet perhaps the relaxations of that severity were not very elegant. There must, however, have been always some modes of gaiety preferable to others, and a writer ought to choose the best.

In tragedy his performance seems constantly to be worse as his labour is more. The effusions of passion, which exigence forces out, are for the most part striking and energetic; but whenever he solicits his invention, or strains his faculties, the offspring of his throne is tumour, meanness, tediousness, and obscurity.

In narration he affects a disproportionate pomp of diction, and a wearisome train of circumlocution, and tells the incident imperfectly in many words, which might have been more plainly delivered in few. Narration in dramatic poetry is naturally tedious, as it is unanimated and inactive, and obstructs the progress of the action; it should therefore always be rapid, and enlivened by frequent interruption. Shakespeare found it an incumbrance, and instead of lightening it by brevity, endeavoured to recommend it by dignity and splendour.

His declamations or set speeches are commonly cold and weak, for his power was the power of nature; when he endeavoured, like other tragic writers, to catch opportunities of amplification, and instead of inquiring what the occasion demanded, to show how much his stores of knowledge could supply, he seldom escapes without the pity or resentment of his reader.

It is incident to him to be now and then entangled with an unwieldy sentiment, which he cannot well express, and will not reject; he struggles with it awhile, and, if it continues stubborn, comprises it in words such as occur, and leaves it to be disentangled and evolved by those who have more leisure to bestow upon it.

Not that always where the language is intricate the thought is subtle, or the image always great where the line was bulky; the equality of words to things is very often neglected, and trivial sentiments and vulgar ideas disappoint the attention, to which they are recommended by sonorous epithets and swelling figures.

But the admirers of this great poet have most reason to complain when he approaches nearest to his highest excellence, and seems fully resolved to sink them in dejection, and mollify them with tender emotions, by the fall of greatness, the danger of innocence, or the crosses of love. What he does best, he soon ceases to do. He is not soft and pathetic without some idle conceit, or contemptible equivocation. He no sooner begins to move, than he counteracts himself; and terror and pity, as they are rising up the mind, are checked and blasted by sudden frigidity.

A quibble is to Shakespeare, what luminous vapours are to the traveller; he follows it at all adventures: it is sure to lead him out of his way, and sure to engulf him in the mire. It has some malignant power over his mind, and its fascinations are irresistible. Whatever be the dignity or profundity of his disquisition, whether he be enlarging knowledge or exalting affection, whether he be amusing attention with incidents, or enchaining it in suspense, let but a quibble spring up before him, and he leaves his work unfinished. A quibble is the golden apple for which he will always turn aside from his career, or stoop from his elevation. A quibble, poor and barren as it is, gave him such delight, that he was content to purchase it, by the sacrifice of reason, propriety, and truth. A quibble was to him the fatal *Cleopatra* for which he lost the world, and was content to lose it.

It will be thought strange, that, in enumerating the defects of this writer, I have not yet mentioned his neglect of the unities; his violation of those laws which have been instituted and established by the joint authority of poets and critics.

For his other deviations from the art of writing, I resign him to critical justice, without making any other demand in his favour, than that which must be indulged to all human excellence: that his virtues be rated with his failings; but from the censure which this irregularity may bring upon him, I shall, with due reverence to that learning which I must oppose, adventure to try how I can defend him.

His histories, being neither tragedies nor comedies, are not subject to any of their laws; nothing more is necessary to all the praise which they expect, than that the changes of action be so prepared as to be understood; that the incidents be various and affecting, and the characters consistent, natural, and distinct. No other unity is intended, and therefore none is to be sought.

In his other works he has well enough preserved the unity of action. He has not, indeed, an intrigue regularly perplexed and regularly unraveled: he does not endeavour to hide his design only to discover it, for this is seldom the order of real events, and Shakespeare is the poet of nature; but his plan has commonly, what Aristotle requires, a beginning, a middle and an end; one event is concatenated with another, and the conclusion follows by easy consequence. There are perhaps some incidents that might be spared, as in other poets there is much talk that only fills up time upon the stage; but the general system makes gradual advances, and the end of the play is the end of expectation.

To the unities of time and place he has shown no regard; and perhaps a nearer view of the principles on which they stand will diminish their value, and withdraw from them the veneration which, from the time of Corneille, they have very generally received, by discovering, that they have given more trouble to the poet, than pleasure to the auditor.

The necessity of observing the unities of time and place arises from the supposed necessity of making the drama creditable. The critics hold it impossible that an action of months or years can be possibly believed to pass in three hours; or that the spectator can suppose himself to sit in the theatre, while ambassadors go and return between distant kings, while armies are levied and towns besieged, while an exile wanders and returns, or till he whom they saw courting his mistress, shall lament the untimely fall of his son. The mind revolts from evident falsehood, and fiction loses its force when it departs from the resemblance of reality.

From the narrow limitation of time, necessarily arises the contraction of place. The spectator, who knows that he saw the first act at Alexandria, cannot suppose that he sees the next at Rome, at a distance to which not the dragons of Medea could, in so short a time, have transported him; he knows with certainty that he has not changed his place; and he knows that place cannot change itself; that what was a house cannot become a plain; that what was Thebes can never be Persepolis.

Such is the triumphant language with which a critic exults over the misery of an irregular poet, and exults commonly without resistance or reply. It is time, therefore, to tell him by the authority of Shakespeare, that he assumes, as an unquestionable principle, a position, which, while his breath is forming it into words, his understanding pronounces to be false. It is false, that any representation is mistaken for reality; that any dramatic fable in its materiality was ever credible, or, for a single moment, was ever credited.

The objection arising from the impossibility of passing the first hour at Alexandria, and the next at Rome, supposes, that when the play opens, the spectator really imagines himself at Alexandria, and believes that his walk to the theatre has been a voyage to Egypt, and that he lives in the days of Antony and Cleopatra. Surely he that imagines this, may imagine more. He that can take the stage at one time for the palace of the Ptolemies, may take it in half an hour for the promontory of Actium. Delusion, if delusion be admitted, has no certain limitation; if the spectator can be once persuaded, that his old acquaintance are Alexander and Caesar, that a room illuminated with candles is the plain of Pharsalia, or the bank of Granicus, he is in a state of elevation above the reach of reason or of truth, and from the heights of empyrean poetry, may despise the circumscriptions of terrestrial nature. There is no reason why a mind thus wandering in ecstacy, should count the clock, or why an hour should not be a century in that calenture of the brain that can make the stage a field.

The truth is, that the spectators are always in their senses, and know, from the first act to the last, that the stage is only a stage, and that the players are only players. They came to hear a certain number of lines recited with just gesture and elegant modulation. The lines relate to some action, and an action must be in some place; but the different actions that complete the story may be in places very remote from each other; and where is the absurdity of allowing that space to represent first Athens, and then Sicily, which was always known to be neither Sicily nor Athens, but a modern theatre?

By supposition, as place is introduced, time may be extended; the time required by the fable elapses for the most part between the acts; for, of so much of the action as is represented, the real and poetical duration is the same. If, in the first act, preparations for war against Mithridates are represented to be made in Rome, the event of the war may, without absurdity, be represented, in the catastrophe, as happening in Pontus; we know that there is neither war, nor preparation for war; we know that we are neither in Rome nor Pontus; that neither Mithridates nor Lucullus are before us. The drama exhibits successive imitations of successive actions; and why may not the second imitation represent an action that happened years after the first, if it be so connected with it, that nothing but time can be supposed to intervene? Time is, of all modes of existence, most obsequious to the imagination; a lapse of years is as easily conceived as a passage of hours. In contemplation we easily contract the time of real actions, and therefore willingly permit it to be contracted when we only see their imitation.

It will be asked, how the drama moves, if it is not credited. It is credited with all the credit due to a drama. It is credited whenever it moves, as a just picture of a real original; as representing to the auditor what he would him-self feel, if he were to do or suffer what is there feigned to be suffered or to be done. The reflection that strikes the heart is not, that the evils before us are real evils, but that they are evils to which we ourselves may be exposed. If there be any fallacy, it is not that we fancy the players, but that we fancy ourselves unhappy for a moment; but we rather lament the possibility than suppose the presence of misery, as a mother weeps over her babe, when she remembers that death may take it from her. The delight of tragedy proceeds from our consciousness of fiction; if we thought murders and treasons real, they would please no more.

Imitations produce pain or pleasure, not because they are mistaken for realities, but because they bring realities to mind. When the imagination is re-created by a painted landscape, the trees are not supposed capable to give us shade, or the fountains coolness; but we consider how we should be pleased with such fountains playing beside us, and such woods waving over us. We are agitated in reading the history of Henry the Fifth, yet no man takes his book for the field of Agincourt. A dramatic exhibition is a book recited with concomitants that increase or diminish its effect. Familiar comedy is often more powerful on the theatre than in the page; imperial tragedy is always less. The humour of Petruchio may be heightened by grimace; but what voice or what gesture can hope to add dignity or force to the soliloquy of Cato?

A play read affects the mind like a play acted. It is therefore evident, that the action is not supposed to be real; and it follows, that between the acts a longer or shorter time may be allowed to pass, and that no more account of space or duration is to be taken by the auditor of a drama, than by the reader of a narrative before whom may pass in an hour the life of a hero, or the revolutions of an empire.

Whether Shakespeare knew the unities, and rejected them by design, or deviated from them by happy ignorance, it is, I think, impossible to decide, and useless to inquire. We may reasonably suppose, that, when he rose to notice, he did not want the counsels and admonitions of scholars and critics, and that he at last deliberately persisted in a practice, which he might have begun by chance. As nothing is essential to the fable but unity of action, and as the unities of time and place arise evidently from false assumptions, and, by circumscribing the extent of the drama, lessen its variety, I cannot think it much to be lamented, that they were not known by him, or not observed: nor if such another poet could arise, should I very vehemently reproach him, that his first act passed at Venice, and his next in Cyprus. Such viola-tions of rules merely positive, become the comprehensive genius of Shake-speare, and such censures are suitable to the minute and slender criticisms of Voltaire. . . .

. . . The result of my inquiries, in which it would be ludicrous to boast of impartiality, is, that the unities of time and place are not essential to a just drama; that though they may sometimes conduce to pleasure, they are always to be sacrificed to the nobler beauties of variety and instruction; and that a play written with nice observation of critical rules, is to be contemplated as an elaborate curiosity, as the product of superfluous and ostentatious art, by which is shown, rather what is possible, than what is necessary.

He that, without diminution of any other excellence, shall preserve all the unities unbroken, deserves the like applause with the architect, who shall display all the orders of architecture in a citadel, without any deduction from its strength: but the principal beauty of a citadel is to exclude the enemy; and the greatest graces of a play are to copy nature, and instruct life. . . .

Voltaire expressed his wonder, that our author's extravagances are endured by a nation which has seen the tragedy of *Cato*. Let him be answered that Addison speaks the language of poets; and Shakespeare of men. We find in *Cato* innumerable beauties which enamour us of its author, but we see nothing that acquaints us with human sentiments or human actions; we place it with the fairest and the noblest progeny which judgment propagates by conjunction with learning; but *Othello* is the vigorous and vivacious offspring of observation impregnated by genius. *Cato* affords a splendid exhibition of artificial and fictitious manners, and delivers just and noble sentiments, in diction easy, elevated, and harmonious, but its hopes and fears communicate no vibration to the heart; the composition refers us only to the writer; we pronounce the name of Cato, but we think on Addison.

The work of a correct and regular writer is a garden accurately formed and diligently planted, varied with shades, and scented with flowers; the composition of Shakespeare is a forest, in which oaks extend their branches, and pines tower in the air, interspersed sometimes with weeds and brambles, and sometimes giving shelter to myrtles and to roses; filling the eye with awful pomp, and gratifying the mind with endless diversity. Other poets display cabinets of precious rarities, minutely finished, wrought into shape, and polished into brightness. Shakespeare opens a mine which contains gold and diamonds in unexhaustible plenty, though clouded by incrustations, debased by impurities, and mingled with a mass of meaner minerals.

General Observations on King Lear   *1765*

The tragedy of *Lear* is deservedly celebrated among the dramas of Shakespeare. There is perhaps no play which keeps the attention so strongly fixed; which so much agitates our passions and interests our curiosity. The artful involutions of distinct interests, the striking opposition of contrary characters, the sudden changes of fortune, and the quick succession of events, fill the mind with a perpetual tumult of indignation, pity, and hope. There is no scene which does not contribute to the aggravation of the distress or conduct of the action, and scarce a line which does not conduce to the progress of the scene. So powerful is the current of the poet's imagination, that the mind which once ventures within it, is hurried irresistibly along.

On the seeming improbability of Lear's conduct, it may be observed, that he is represented according to histories at that time vulgarly received as true. And, perhaps, if we turn our thoughts upon the barbarity and ignorance of the age to which this story is referred, it will appear not so unlikely as while we estimate Lear's manners by our own. Such preference of one daughter to another, or resignation of dominion on such conditions, would be yet credible, if told of a petty prince of Guinea or Madagascar. Shakespeare, indeed, by the mention of his earls and dukes, has given us the idea of times more civilized, and of life regulated by softer manners; and the truth is, that though he so nicely discriminates, and so minutely describes, the characters of men, he commonly neglects and confounds the characters of ages, by mingling customs, ancient and modern, English and foreign.

My learned friend Mr. Warton, who has in *The Adventurer*[1] very minutely criticised this play, remarks, that the instances of cruelty are too savage and shocking, and the intervention of Edmund destroys the simplicity of the story. These objections may, I think, be answered, by repeating, that the cruelty of the daughters is an historical fact, to which the poet has added little, having only drawn it into a series by dialogue and action. But I am not able to apologize with equal plausibility for the extrusion of Gloucester's eyes, which seems an act too horrid to be endured in dramatic exhibition, and such as must always compel the mind to relieve its distress by incredulity. Yet let it be remembered, that our author well knew what would please the audience for which he wrote.

Selections. From *The Works of Samuel Johnson*, Vol. II. New York: Harper & Brothers, 1851.

[1] Joseph Warton (1722–1800), critic and poet, contributed twenty-four papers to *The Adventurer* between 1752 and 1754, including several on Shakespeare.

The injury done by Edmund to the simplicity of the action, is abundantly recompensed by the addition of variety, by the art with which he is made to co-operate with the chief design, and the opportunity which he gives the poet of combining perfidy with perfidy, and connecting the wicked son with the wicked daughters, to impress this important moral, that villainy is never at a stop, that crimes lead to crimes, and at last terminate in ruin.

But though this moral be incidentally enforced, Shakespeare has suffered the virtue of Cordelia to perish in a just cause, contrary to the natural ideas of justice, to the hope of the reader, and, what is yet more strange, to the faith of chronicles. . . . A play in which the wicked prosper, and the virtuous miscarry, may doubtless be good, because it is a just representation of the common events of human life; but since all reasonable beings naturally love justice, I cannot easily be persuaded, that the observation of justice makes a play worse; or that, if other excellencies are equal, the audience will not always rise better pleased from the final triumph of persecuted virtue.

In the present case the public has decided. Cordelia, from the time of Tate,[2] has always retired with victory and felicity. And, if my sensations could add anything to the general suffrage, I might relate, I was many years ago so shocked by Cordelia's death, that I know not whether I ever endured to read again the last scenes of the play till I undertook to revise them as an editor.

David Hume *1711–1776*

Of Tragedy *1757*

It seems an unaccountable pleasure, which the spectators of a well-written tragedy receive from sorrow, terror, anxiety, and other passions, that are in themselves disagreeable and uneasy. The more they are touched and affected,

Selections. From David Hume, *Essays Moral, Political, and Literary*, Vol. I, edited by T. H. Green and T. H. Grose. London: Longmans, Green, and Co., 1875.

[2] Nahum Tate (1652–1715) revised Shakespeare's *Lear.* In Tate's version—performed for the first time in 1681—Cordelia does not die at the end but instead lives and marries Edgar.

the more are they delighted with the spectacle; and as soon as the uneasy passions cease to operate, the piece is at an end. One scene of full joy and contentment and security is the utmost, that any composition of this kind can bear; and it is sure always to be the concluding one. If, in the texture of the piece, there be interwoven any scenes of satisfaction, they afford only faint gleams of pleasure, which are thrown in by way of variety, and in order to plunge the actors into deeper distress, by means of that contrast and disappointment. The whole heart of the poet is employed, in rousing and supporting the compassion and indignation, the anxiety and resentment of his audience. They are pleased in proportion as they are afflicted, and never are so happy as when they employ tears, sobs, and cries to give vent to their sorrow, and relieve their heart, swollen with the tenderest sympathy and compassion.

The few critics who have had some tincture of philosophy, have remarked this singular phenomenon, and have endeavoured to account for it.

L'Abbé Dubos, in his reflections on poetry and painting,[1] asserts that nothing is in general so disagreeable to the mind as the languid, listless state of indolence, into which it falls upon the removal of all passion and occupation. To get rid of this painful situation, it seeks every amusement and pursuit; business, gaming, shows, executions; whatever will rouse the passions, and take its attention from itself. No matter what the passion is: Let it be disagreeable, afflicting, melancholy, disordered; it is still better than that insipid languor, which arises from perfect tranquillity and repose.

It is impossible not to admit this account, as being, at least in part, satisfactory. You may observe, when there are several tables of gaming, that all the company run to those, where the deepest play is, even though they find not there the best players. The view, or at least, imagination of high passions, arising from great loss or gain, affects the spectator by sympathy, gives him some touches of the same passions, and serves him for a momentary entertainment. It makes the time pass the easier with him, and is some relief to that oppression, under which men commonly labour, when left entirely to their own thoughts and meditations.

We find that common liars always magnify, in their narrations, all kinds of danger, pain, distress, sickness, deaths, murders, and cruelties; as well as joy, beauty, mirth, and magnificence. It is an absurd secret, which they have for pleasing their company, fixing their attention, and attaching them to such marvellous relations, by the passions and emotions, which they excite.

There is, however, a difficulty in applying to the present subject, in its full extent, this solution, however ingenious and satisfactory it may appear. It is certain, that the same object of distress, which pleases in a tragedy, were

---

[1] Jean-Baptiste Dubos or DuBos (1670–1742), *Critical Reflections on Poetry and Painting* (1719).

it really set before us, would give the most unfeigned uneasiness; though it be then the most effectual cure to languor and indolence. Monsieur Fontenelle seems to have been sensible of this difficulty; and accordingly attempts another solution of the phenomenon; at least makes some addition to the theory above mentioned.[2]

"Pleasure and pain," says he, "which are two sentiments so different in themselves, differ not so much in their cause. From the instance of tickling, it appears, that the movement of pleasure, pushed a little too far, becomes pain; and that the movement of pain, a little moderated, becomes pleasure. Hence it proceeds, that there is such a thing as a sorrow, soft and agreeable: It is a pain weakened and diminished. The heart likes naturally to be moved and affected. Melancholy objects suit it, and even disastrous and sorrowful, provided they are softened by some circumstance. It is certain, that, on the theatre, the representation has almost the effect of reality; yet it has not altogether that effect. However we may be hurried away by the spectacle; whatever dominion the senses and imagination may usurp over the reason, there still lurks at the bottom a certain idea of falsehood in the whole of what we see. This idea, though weak and disguised, suffices to diminish the pain which we suffer from the misfortunes of those whom we love, and to reduce that affliction to such a pitch as converts it into a pleasure. We weep for the misfortune of a hero, to whom we are attached. In the same instant we comfort ourselves, by reflecting, that it is nothing but a fiction: And it is precisely that mixture of sentiments, which composes an agreeable sorrow, and tears that delight us. But as that affliction, which is caused by exterior and sensible objects, is stronger than the consolation which arises from an internal reflection, they are the effects and symptoms of sorrow, that ought to predominate in the composition."

This solution seems just and convincing; but perhaps it wants still some new addition, in order to make it answer fully the phenomenon, which we here examine. All the passions, excited by eloquence, are agreeable in the highest degree, as well as those which are moved by painting and the theatre. The epilogues of Cicero are, on this account chiefly, the delight of every reader of taste; and it is difficult to read some of them without the deepest sympathy and sorrow. His merit as an orator, no doubt, depends much on his success in this particular. When he had raised tears in his judges and all his audience, they were then the most highly delighted, and expressed the greatest satisfaction with the pleader. The pathetic description of the butchery, made by Verres of the Sicilian captains, is a masterpiece of this kind: But I believe none will affirm, that the being present at a melancholy scene of that nature would afford any entertainment. Neither is the sorrow here

---

[2] Bernard Le Bovier de Fontenelle (1657–1757), "Digression on the Ancients and the Modern," part of *Pastoral Poetry* (1688).

softened by fiction: For the audience were convinced of the reality of every circumstance. What is it then, which in this case raises a pleasure from the bosom of uneasiness, so to speak; and a pleasure, which still retains all the features and outward symptoms of distress and sorrow?

I answer: This extraordinary effect proceeds from that very eloquence, with which the melancholy scene is represented. The genius required to paint objects in a lively manner, the art employed in collecting all the pathetic circumstances, the judgment displayed in disposing them: the exercise, I say, of these noble talents, together with the force of expression, and beauty of oratorical numbers, diffuse the highest satisfaction on the audience, and excite the most delightful movements. By this means, the uneasiness of the melancholy passions is not only overpowered and effaced by something stronger of an opposite kind; but the whole impulse of those passions is converted into pleasure, and swells the delight which the eloquence raises in us. The same force of oratory, employed on an uninteresting subject, would not please half so much, or rather would appear altogether ridiculous; and the mind, being left in absolute calmness and indifference, would relish none of those beauties of imagination or expression, which, if joined to passion, give it such exquisite entertainment. The impulse or vehemence, arising from sorrow, compassion, indignation, receives a new direction from the sentiments of beauty. The latter, being the predominant emotion, seize the whole mind, and convert the former into themselves, at least tincture them so strongly as totally to alter their nature. And the soul, being, at the same time, roused by passion, and charmed by eloquence, feels on the whole a strong movement, which is altogether delightful.

The same principle takes place in tragedy; with this addition, that tragedy is an imitation; and imitation is always of itself agreeable. This circumstance serves still farther to smooth the motions of passion, and convert the whole feeling into one uniform and strong enjoyment. Objects of the greatest terror and distress please in painting, and please more than the most beautiful objects, that appear calm and indifferent. The affection, rousing the mind, excites a large stock of spirit and vehemence; which is all transformed into pleasure by the force of the prevailing movement. It is thus the fiction of tragedy softens the passion, by an infusion of a new feeling, not merely by weakening or diminishing the sorrow. You may by degrees weaken a real sorrow, till it totally disappears; yet in none of its graduations will it ever give pleasure; except, perhaps, by accident, to a man sunk under lethargic indolence, whom it rouses from that languid state.

To confirm this theory, it will be sufficient to produce other instances, where the subordinate movement is converted into the predominant, and gives force to it, though of a different, and even sometimes though of a contrary nature.

Novelty naturally rouses the mind, and attracts our attention; and the movements, which it causes, are always converted into any passion, belonging to the object, and join their force to it. Whether an event excite joy or sorrow, pride or shame, anger or good will, it is sure to produce a stronger affection, when new or unusual. And though novelty of itself be agreeable, it fortifies the painful, as well as agreeable passions.

Had you any intention to move a person extremely by the narration of any event, the best method of increasing its effect would be artfully to delay informing him of it, and first to excite his curiosity and impatience before you let him into the secret. This is the artifice practiced by Iago in the famous scene of Shakespeare; and every spectator is sensible, that Othello's jealousy acquires additional force from his preceding impatience, and that the subordinate passion is here readily transformed into the predominant one.

Difficulties increase passions of every kind; and by rousing our attention, and exciting our active powers, they produce an emotion, which nourishes the prevailing affection.

Parents commonly love that child most, whose sickly infirm frame of body has occasioned them the greatest pains, trouble, and anxiety in rearing him. The agreeable sentiment of affection here acquires force from sentiments of uneasiness.

Nothing endears so much a friend as sorrow for his death. The pleasure of his company has not so powerful an influence. . . .

These instances (and many more might be collected) are sufficient to afford us some insight into the analogy of nature, and to show us, that the pleasure, which poets, orators, and musicians give us, by exciting grief, sorrow, indignation, compassion, is not so extraordinary or paradoxical, as it may at first sight appear. The force of imagination, the energy of expression, the power of numbers, the charms of imitation; all these are naturally, of themselves, delightful to the mind: And when the object presented lays also hold of some affection, the pleasure still rises upon us, by the conversion of this subordinate movement into that which is predominant. The passion, though, perhaps, naturally, and when excited by the simple appearance of a real object, it may be painful; yet is so smoothed, and softened, and mollified, when raised by the finer arts, that it affords the highest entertainment.

To confirm this reasoning, we may observe, that if the movements of the imagination be not predominant above those of the passion, a contrary effect follows; and the former, being now subordinate, is converted into the latter, and still farther increases the pain and affliction of the sufferer.

Who could ever think of it as a good expedient for comforting an afflicted parent, to exaggerate, with all the force of elocution, the irreparable loss, which he has met with by the death of a favourite child? The more power of imagination and expression you here employ, the more you increase his despair and affliction.

The shame, confusion, and terror of Verres, no doubt, rose in proportion to the noble eloquence and vehemence of Cicero: So also did his pain and uneasiness. These former passions were too strong for the pleasure arising from the beauties of elocution; and operated, though from the same principle, yet in a contrary manner, to the sympathy, compassion, and indignation of the audience.

Lord Clarendon, when he approaches towards the catastrophe of the royal party,[3] supposes, that his narration must then become infinitely disagreeable; and he hurries over the king's death, without giving us one circumstance of it. He considers it as too horrid a scene to be contemplated with any satisfaction, or even without the utmost pain and aversion. He himself, as well as the readers of that age, were too deeply concerned in the events, and felt a pain from subjects, which an historian and a reader of another age would regard as the most pathetic and most interesting, and, by consequence, the most agreeable.

An action, represented in tragedy, may be too bloody and atrocious. It may excite such movements of horror as will not soften into pleasure; and the greatest energy of expression, bestowed on descriptions of that nature, serves only to augment our uneasiness. . . .

Even the common sentiments of compassion require to be softened by some agreeable affection, in order to give a thorough satisfaction to the audience. The mere suffering of plaintive virtue, under the triumphant tyranny and oppression of vice, forms a disagreeable spectacle, and is carefully avoided by all masters of the drama. In order to dismiss the audience with entire satisfaction and contentment, the virture must either convert itself into a noble courageous despair, or the vice receive its proper punishment.

---

[3] Edward Hyde, First Earl of Clarendon (1609–1674), wrote of the execution of Charles I in his *History of the Great Rebellion and Civil Wars in England* (published posthumously, 1702–1704, in three volumes).

Oliver Goldsmith   *1730?–1774*

A Comparison between Sentimental and Laughing Comedy   *1772*

The theatre, like all other amusements, has its fashions and its prejudices; and when satiated with its excellence, mankind begin to mistake change for improvement. For some years tragedy was the reigning entertainment; but of late it has entirely given way to comedy, and our best efforts are now exerted in these lighter kinds of composition. The pompous train, the swelling phrase, and the unnatural rant, are displaced for that natural portrait of human folly and frailty, of which all are judges, because all have sat for the picture.

But as in describing nature it is presented with a double face, either of mirth or sadness, our modern writers find themselves at a loss which chiefly to copy from; and it is now debated, whether the exhibition of human distress is likely to afford the mind more entertainment than that of human absurdity?

Comedy is defined by Aristotle to be a picture of the frailties of the lower part of mankind, to distinguish it from tragedy, which is an exhibition of the misfortunes of the great. When comedy therefore ascends to produce the characters of princes or generals upon the stage, it is out of its walk, since low life and middle life are entirely its object. The principal question therefore is, whether in describing low or middle life, an exhibition of its follies be not preferable to a detail of its calamities? Or, in other words, which deserves the preference—the weeping sentimental comedy, so much in fashion at present, or the laughing and even low comedy, which seems to have been last exhibited by Vanbrugh and Cibber?[1]

If we apply to authorities, all the great masters in the dramatic art have but one opinion. Their rule is, that as tragedy displays the calamities of the great, so comedy should excite our laughter, by ridiculously exhibiting the follies of the lower part of mankind. Boileau, one of the best modern critics, asserts, that comedy will not admit of tragic distress:

> Le comique, ennemi des soupirs et des pleurs,
> N'admet point dans ses vers de tragiques douleurs."[2]

From *The Miscellaneous Works of Oliver Goldsmith*, Vol. I, edited by James Prior. New York: G. P. Putnam & Co., 1854.

[1] Sir John Vanbrugh (1664–1726) and Colley Cibber (1671–1757).

[2] "The comic muse, averse to tears and sighs, / From tragic sorrows with abhorrence flies" [Goldsmith's note].

424

Nor is this rule without the strongest foundation in nature, as the distresses of the mean by no means affect us so strongly as the calamities of the great. When tragedy exhibits to us some great man fallen from his height, and struggling with want and adversity, we feel his situation in the same manner as we suppose he himself must feel, and our pity is increased in proportion to the height from which he fell. On the contrary, we do not so strongly sympathize with one born in humbler circumstances, and encountering accidental distress: so that while we melt for Belisarius,[3] we scarcely give halfpence to the beggar who accosts us in the street. The one has our pity; the other our contempt. Distress, therefore, is the proper object of tragedy, since the great excite our pity by their fall; but not equally so of comedy, since the actors employed in it are originally so mean, that they sink but little by their fall.

Since the first origin of the stage, tragedy and comedy have run in distinct channels, and never till of late encroached upon the provinces of each other. Terence, who seems to have made the nearest approaches, always judiciously stops short before he comes to the downright pathetic; and yet he is even reproached by Caesar for wanting the *vis comica*.[4] All other comic writers of antiquity aim only at rendering folly or vice ridiculous, but never exalt their characters into buskin pomp, or make what Voltaire humorously calls "a tradesman's tragedy."

Yet notwithstanding this weight of authority, and the universal practice of former ages, a new species of dramatic composition has been introduced under the name of *sentimental comedy*, in which the virtues of private life are exhibited, rather than the vices exposed; and the distresses rather than the faults of mankind make our interest in the piece. These comedies have had of late great success, perhaps from their novelty, and also from their flattering every man in his favourite foible. In these plays almost all the characters are good, and exceedingly generous; they are lavish enough of their tin money on the stage; and though they want humour, have abundance of sentiment and feeling. If they happen to have faults or foibles, the spectator is taught not only to pardon, but to applaud them, in consideration of the goodness of their hearts; so that folly, instead of being ridiculed, is commended, and the comedy aims at touching our passions, without the power of being truly pathetic. In this manner we are likely to lose one great source of entertainment on the stage; for while the comic poet is invading the province of the tragic muse, he leaves her lovely sister quite neglected. Of this, however, he is no way solicitous, as he measures his fame by his profits.

But it will be said, that the theatre is formed to amuse mankind, and that it matters little, if this end be answered, by what means it is obtained. If

---

[3] A general under Emperor Justinian of Constantinople, Belisarius had successes that aroused Justinian's jealousy. He was disgraced and became a beggar.

[4] Comic spirit.

mankind find delight in weeping at comedy, it would be cruel to abridge them in that or any other innocent pleasure. If those pieces are denied the name of comedies, yet call them by any other name, and if they are delightful, they are good. Their success, it will be said, is a mark of their merit, and it is only abridging our happiness to deny us an inlet to amusement.

These objections, however, are rather specious than solid. It is true, that amusement is a great object at a theatre; and it will be allowed, that these sentimental pieces do often amuse us; but the question is, whether the true comedy would not amuse us more? The question is, whether a character supported throughout a piece, with its ridicule still attending, would not give us more delight than this species of bastard tragedy, which only is applauded because it is new.

A friend of mine who was sitting unmoved at one of the sentimental pieces, was asked how he could be so indifferent? "Why truly," says he, "as the hero is but a tradesman, it is indifferent to me whether he be turned out of his counting-house on Fishstreet Hill, since he will still have enough left to open shop in St. Giles's."

The other objection is as ill-grounded; for though we should give these pieces another name, it will not mend their efficacy. It will continue a kind of mulish production, with all the defects of its opposite parents, and marked with sterility. If we are permitted to make comedy weep, we have an equal right to make tragedy laugh, and to set down in blank verse the jests and repartees of all the attendants in a funeral procession.

But there is one argument in favor of sentimental comedy which will keep it on the stage, in spite of all that can be said against it. It is of all others the most easily written. Those abilities that can hammer out a novel, are fully sufficient for the production of a sentimental comedy. It is only sufficient to raise the characters a little; to deck out the hero with a riband, or give the heroine a title; then to put an insipid dialogue, without character or humour, into their mouths, give them mighty good hearts, very fine clothes, furnish a new set of scenes, make a pathetic scene or two, with a sprinkling of tender melancholy conversation through the whole, and there is no doubt but all the ladies will cry, and all the gentlemen applaud.

Humour at present seems to be departing from the stage; and it will soon happen that our comic players will have nothing left for it but a fine coat and a song. It depends upon the audience, whether they will actually drive those poor merry creatures from the stage, or sit at a play as gloomy as at the tabernacle. It is not easy to recover an art when once lost; and it will be but a just punishment, that when, by our being too fastidious, we have banished humour from the stage, we should ourselves be deprived of the art of laughing.

Eighteenth- and Early Nineteenth-Century Germany

Lessing is not only the author of Germany's first bourgeois tragedy
(*Miss Sara Sampson*), he is in addition Germany's first major drama critic.
His *Hamburg Dramaturgy*, which started as a twice-weekly series of reviews of
productions by the Hamburg National Theatre, soon appeared less frequently
and became more theoretical. Examining the nature of such subjects as
tragedy, comedy, and dramatic action, Lessing inveighed against the rule-
mongering French for their distortions of Aristotle and their baleful
influence on German drama. Opposed to rhetorical neoclassical tragedies
about royalty, he favored domestic tragedies in simple language about
humbler people. In less than a century, however, bourgeois tragedy was to
fall into disrepute. The reasons for this, and the remedy, are suggested by
one of its ablest practitioners, Hebbel.

Like Lessing, the playwrights of the German romantic movement,
appropriately named *Sturm und Drang* (Storm and Stress), reacted—
stormily, of course—against neoclassical strictures. Among them were
young Goethe and Schiller, who urges not the single tones of neoclassicism,
but a harmonious unity of dualities, such as monstrously grotesque
crime and the good, the common and the noble, the corporeal and the
spiritual, the sensual and the rational. Although Schiller regards the
stage as a moral institution, he distinguishes between esthetic and moral
criteria for plays, and he explores such related principles as the different
pleasures that derive from the esthetic and the moral spheres, and
(corresponding to them, respectively) from the beautiful and the sublime,
which he analyzes in relationship to both moral freedom and moral necessity.

Goethe, whose *Götz von Berlichingen* (1773) was the first dramatic
manifestation of the *Sturm und Drang* movement, admired Shakespeare—
as other romantic playwrights and theorists did, and as neoclassicists
often did not. Not only does the play reveal Shakespeare's influence, but
two years earlier Goethe had read a *Sturm und Drang* manifesto on
Shakespeare's birthday and a dozen years later, in his novel *Wilhelm
Meister's Apprenticeship*, he included a discussion of tragic fate in

427

relation to *Hamlet*. As he grew older, however, Goethe moved from romantic to classical values, as revealed in the *Conversations*—held more than half a century after his youthful *Götz*. But Goethe cannot be neatly pigeonholed; his observations on such subjects as dramatic illusion, the playwright as philosopher, and the practical problem of cutting a text for production transcend these categories.

In his *Lectures on Dramatic Art*, Schlegel discusses basic differences between romanticism and classicism. He analyzes such subjects as drama's necessary combination of the poetic and the theatrical; the nature of tragedy and comedy; and the three unities as revealed in the plays of Greece and France, and in those of Shakespeare, Calderon, and the Romantics. Also, in terms that Collier had established over a century earlier, he denounces Restoration comedy.

A decade after Schlegel first delivered his lectures, two major German philosophers turned their attention to the theatre. To Schopenhauer, the significance of tragedy, representing as it does the terrible side of life, lies in its revelation of the nature of existence itself and its source of sublimity in the surrender of the will to live. Hegel devotes considerably more attention to the analysis of dramatic art. He delves into important matters concerning art generally (the question of instruction as a goal, differences between classic and romantic), dramatic art less generally, and tragedy particularly. Differentiating between two types of tragic situation in the classical theatre (one centering on deeds committed without conscious intent, the other on opposition between different ethical imperatives, each morally good), Hegel contrasts both with "modern tragedy," that is, Shakespearean and Romantic. The modern, he finds, is characterized not by the ethical but by the subjective and personal, from which derive such characteristics as complexity of characterization, the large number of incidents potentially relevant to the play's action, and the relationship between personal responsibility and moral guilt. According to the Shakespearean critic A. C. Bradley, Hegel is the only philosopher since Aristotle who has treated the subject of tragedy in original and searching ways.

Gotthold Ephraim Lessing 1729–1781

Hamburg Dramaturgy 1767–1769

1

. . . If heroic sentiments are to arouse admiration, the poet must not be too lavish of them, for what we see often, what we see in many persons, no longer excites astonishment. Every Christian in *Olindo and Sophronia*[1] holds being martyred and dying as easy as drinking a glass of water. We hear these pious bravadoes so often and out of so many mouths, that they lose all their force.

2

. . . The first tragedy that deserves the name of Christian has beyond doubt still to appear. I mean a play in which the Christian interests us solely as a Christian. But is such a piece even possible? Is not the character of a true Christian something quite untheatrical? Does not the gentle pensiveness, the unchangeable meekness that are his essential features, war with the whole business of tragedy that strives to purify passions by passions? Does not his expectation of rewarding happiness after this life contradict the disinterestedness with which we wish to see all great and good actions undertaken and carried out on the stage?

Until a work of genius arises that incontestably decides these objections—for we know by experience what difficulties genius can surmount—my advice is this, to leave all existent Christian tragedies unperformed. . . .

. . . In another still worse tragedy where one of the principal characters died quite casually, a spectator asked his neighbor, "But what did she die of?" —"Of what? Of the fifth act," was the reply. In very truth the fifth act is an ugly evil disease that carries off many a one to whom the first four acts promised a longer life.

9

It is right and well if in everyday life we start with no undue mistrust of the character of others, if we give all credence to the testimony of honest

Selections, translated by Helen Zimmern as "Dramatic Works." From G. E. Lessing, *Selected Prose Works*. London: George Bell & Sons, 1879.

[1] By Baron Johann Friedrich von Kronegk (1731–1758), unfinished at his death.

folk. But may the dramatic poet put us off with such rules of justice? Certainly not, although he could much ease his business thereby. On the stage we want to see who the people are, and we can only see it from their actions. The goodness with which we are to credit them, merely upon the word of another, cannot possibly interest us in them. It leaves us quite indifferent, and if we never have the smallest personal experience of their goodness it even has a bad reflex upon those on whose faith we solely and only accepted the opinion. Far therefore from being willing to believe Siegmund to be a most perfect and excellent young man, because Julia, her mother, Clarissa, and Edward declare him to be such, we rather begin to suspect the judgment of these persons, if we never see for ourselves anything to justify their favorable opinion. It is true, a private person cannot achieve many great actions in the space of four-and-twenty hours. But who demands great actions? Even in the smallest, character can be revealed, and those that throw the most light upon character are the greatest according to poetical valuation.

14

Domestic tragedies found a very thorough defender in the person of the French art critic who first made *Sara*[2] known to his nation. As a rule the French rarely approve anything of which they have not a model among themselves.

The names of princes and heroes can lend pomp and majesty to a play, but they contribute nothing to our emotion. The misfortunes of those whose circumstances most resemble our own must naturally penetrate most deeply into our hearts, and if we pity kings, we pity them as human beings, not as kings. Though their position often renders their misfortunes more important, it does not make them more interesting. Whole nations may be involved in them, but our sympathy requires an individual object and a state is far too much an abstract conception to touch our feelings.

"We wrong the human heart," says Marmontel, "we misread nature, if we believe that it requires titles to rouse and touch us. The sacred names of friend, father, lover, husband, son, mother, of mankind in general, these are far more pathetic than aught else and retain their claims forever. What matters the rank, the surname, the genealogy of the unfortunate man whose easy good nature toward unworthy friends has involved him in gambling and who loses over this his wealth and honor and now sighs in prison distracted by shame and remorse? If asked, who is he? I reply: He was an honest man and to add to his grief he is a husband and a father; his wife whom he loves

---

[2] *Miss Sara Sampson* (1755), by Lessing.

and who loves him is suffering extreme need and can only give tears to the children who clamor for bread. Show me in the history of heroes a more touching, a more moral, indeed a more tragic situation! And when at last this miserable man takes poison and then learns that Heaven had willed his release, what is absent, in this painful terrible moment, when to the horrors of death are added the tortures of imagination, telling him how happily he could have lived, what I say is absent to render the situation worthy of a tragedy? The wonderful, will be replied. What! is there not matter wonderful enough in this sudden change from honor to shame, from innocence to guilt, from sweet peace to despair; in brief, in the extreme misfortune into which mere weakness has plunged him!"

But no matter how much their Diderots and Marmontels preach this to the French, it does not seem as though domestic tragedies were coming into vogue among them. The nation is too vain, too much enamored of titles and other external favors; even the humblest man desires to consort with aristocrats and considers the society of his equals as bad society.

16

. . . The only unpardonable fault of a tragic poet is this, that he leaves us cold; if he interests us he may do as he likes with the little mechanical rules.

29

Comedy is to do us good through laughter; but not through derision; not just to counteract those faults at which it laughs, nor simply and solely in those persons who possess these laughable faults. Its true general use consists in laughter itself, in the practice of our powers to discern the ridiculous, to discern it easily and quickly under all cloaks of passion and fashion; in all admixture of good and bad qualities, even in the wrinkles of solemn earnestness. Granted that Molière's *Miser* never cured a miser; nor Regnard's *Gambler*, a gambler; conceded that laughter never could improve these fools; the worse for them, but not for comedy. It is enough for comedy that, if it cannot cure an incurable disease, it can confirm the healthy in their health. The *Miser* is instructive also to the extravagant man; and to him who never plays the *Gambler* may prove of use. The follies they have not got themselves, others may have with whom they have to live. It is well to know those with whom we may come into collision; it is well to be preserved from all impressions by example. A preservative is also a valuable medicine, and all morality has none more powerful and effective, than the ridiculous.

45

. . . What good does it do the poet that the particular actions that occur in every act would not require much more time for their real occurrence than is occupied by the representation of each act; and that this time, including what is absorbed between the acts, would not nearly require a complete revolution of the sun; has he therefore regarded the unity of time? He has fulfilled the words of the rule, but not their spirit. For what he lets happen in one day, can be done in one day it is true, but no sane mortal would do it in one day. Physical unity of time is not sufficent: the moral unity must also be considered, whose neglect is felt by every one, while the neglect of the other, though it generally involves an impossibility, is yet not so generally offensive because this impossibility can remain unknown to many. If, for instance, in a play a person must travel from one place to another and this journey alone would require more than a day, the fault is only observed by those who know the distance of the locality. Not everybody knows geographical distances, while everybody can feel in themselves for what actions they would allow themselves one day, for what several. The poet therefore who does not know how to preserve physical unity of time except at the expense of moral unity, who does not hesitate to sacrifice the one to the other, consults his own interests badly and sacrifices the essential to the accidental. . . .

. . . It is not enough that a person says why he comes on, we ought also to perceive by the connection that he must therefore come. It is not enough that he says why he goes off, we ought to see subsequently that he really went on that account. Else that which the poet places in his mouth is mere excuse and no cause.

46

It is one thing to circumvent the rules, another to observe them. The French do the former, the latter was only understood by the ancients.

Unity of action was the first dramatic law of the ancients; unity of time and place were mere consequences of the former which they would scarcely have observed more strictly than exigency required had not the combination with the chorus arisen. For since their actions required the presence of a large body of people and this concourse always remained the same, who could go no further from their dwellings nor remain absent longer than it is customary to do from mere curiosity, they were almost obliged to make the scene of action one and the same spot and confine the time to one and the same day. They submitted *bona fide* to this restriction; but with a suppleness of understanding such that in seven cases out of nine they gained more than they lost thereby. For they used this restriction as a reason for simplifying the action and to cut away all that was superfluous, and thus, reduced to essentials, it became only the ideal of an action which was developed most felicitously in this form which required the least addition from circumstances of time and place.

The French, on the contrary, who found no charms in true unity of action, who had been spoilt by the wild intrigues of the Spanish school, before they had learnt to know Greek simplicity, regarded the unity of time and place not as consequences of unity of action, but as circumstances absolutely needful to the representation of an action, to which they must therefore adapt their richer and more complicated actions with all the severity required in the use of a chorus, which however they had totally abolished. When they found however, how difficult, nay at times how impossible this was, they made a truce with the tyrannical rules against which they had not the courage to rebel. Instead of a single place, they introduced an uncertain place, under which we could imagine now this, now that spot; enough if the places combined were not too far apart and none required special scenery, so that the same scenery could fit the one about as well as the other. Instead of the unity of a day they substituted unity of duration, and a certain period during which no one spoke of sunrise or sunset, or went to bed, or at least did not go to bed more than once, however much might occur in this space, they allowed to pass as a day.

Now no one would have objected to this, for unquestionably even thus excellent plays can be made, and the proverb says, cut the wood where it is thinnest. But I must allow my neighbor the same privelege. I must not always show him the thickest part, and cry, "There you must cut! That is where I cut!" Thus the French critics all exclaim, especially when they speak of the dramatic works of the English. What a to-do they then make of regularity, that regularity which they have made so easy to themselves! But I am weary of dwelling on this point!

As far as I am concerned Voltaire's and Maffei's *Merope* may extend over eight days and the scene may be laid in seven places in Greece! if only they had the beauties to make me forget these pedantries!

59

Many hold pompous and tragic to be much the same thing. Not only many of the readers but many of the poets themselves. What! their heroes are to talk like ordinary mortals! What sort of heroes would those be? "Ampullae et sesquipedalia verba,"[3] sentences and bubbles and words a yard long, this constitutes for them the true tone of tragedy.

[3] ". . . paint-pots and . . . words a yard long . . ."—Horace, *The Art of Poetry*.

Diderot says,[4] "We have not omitted anything that could spoil the drama from its very foundations." (Observe that he speaks especially of his countrymen.) "We have retained the whole splendid versification of the ancients that is really only suited to a language of very measured quantities and very marked accents, for very large stages and for a declamation fitted to music and accompanied with instruments. But its simplicity in plot and conversation and the truth of its pictures we have abandoned."

Diderot might have added another reason why we cannot throughout take the old tragedies for our pattern. There all the personages speak and converse in a free public place, in presence of an inquisitive multitude. They must therefore nearly always speak with reserve and due regard to their dignity; they cannot give vent to their thoughts and feelings in the first words that come, they must weigh and choose them. But we moderns, who have abolished the chorus, who generally leave our personages between four walls, what reason have we to let them employ such choice stilted rhetorical speech notwithstanding? Nobody hears it except those whom they permit to hear it; nobody speaks to them but people who are involved in the action, who are therefore themselves affected and have neither desire nor leisure to control expressions. This was only to be feared from the chorus who never acted, however much they might be involved in the play, and always rather judged the acting personages than took a real part in their fate. It is as useless to invoke the high rank of the personages; aristocratic persons have learned how to express themselves better than the common man, but they do not affect incessantly to express themselves better than he. Least of all in moments of passion; since every passion has its own eloquence, is alone inspired by nature, is learnt in no school, and is understood by the most uneducated as well as by the most polished.

There never can be feeling with a stilted, chosen, pompous language. It is not born of feeling, it cannot evoke it. But feeling agrees with the simplest, commonest, plainest words and expressions.

75

For it is certainly not Aristotle who has made the division so justly censured of tragic passions into terror and compassion. He has been falsely interpreted, falsely translated. He speaks of pity and *fear*, not of pity and *terror*; and his fear is by no means the fear excited in us by misfortune threatening another person. It is the fear which arises for ourselves from the similarity of our position with that of the sufferer; it is the fear that the calamities pending over the sufferers might also befall ourselves; it is the fear that we ourselves might thus become objects of pity. In a word this fear is compassion referred back to ourselves.

[4] Second Conversation following *The Natural Son* [Lessing's note].

80

To what end the hard work of dramatic form? Why build a theatre, disguise men and women, torture their memories, invite the whole town to assemble at one place if I intend to produce nothing more with my work and its representation, than some of those emotions that would be produced as well by any good story that everyone could read by his chimney-corner at home?

The dramatic form is the only one by which pity and fear can be excited, at least in no other form can these passions be excited to such a degree. Nevertheless it is preferred to excite all others rather than these; nevertheless it is preferred to employ it for any purpose but this, for which it is so especially adapted.

The public will put up with it; this is well, and yet not well. One has no special longing for the board at which one always has to put up with something.

It is well known how intent the Greek and Roman people were upon their theatres; especially the former on their tragic spectacles. Compared with this, how indifferent, how cold is our people towards the theatre! Whence this difference if it does not arise from the fact that the Greeks felt themselves animated by their stage with such intense, such extraordinary emotions, that they could hardly await the moment to experience them again and again, whereas we are conscious of such weak impressions from our stage that we rarely deem it worth time and money to attain them. We most of us go to the theatre from idle curiosity, from fashion, from ennui, to see people, from desire to see and be seen, and only a few, and those few very seldom, go from any other motive.

I say we, our people, our stage, but I do not mean the Germans only. We Germans confess openly enough that we do not as yet possess a theatre. What many of our critics who join in this confession and are great admirers of the French theatre think when they make it I cannot say, but I know well what I think. I think that not alone we Germans, but also that those who boast of having had a theatre for a hundred years, ay, who boast of having the best theatre in all Europe, even the French have as yet no theatre, certainly no tragic one. The impressions produced by French tragedy are so shallow, so cold.

81

Of the two it is Corneille who has done the greatest harm and exercised the most pernicious influence on these tragedians. Racine only seduced by his example, Corneille by his examples and doctrines together, the latter especially, which were accepted as oracles by the whole nation (excepting one or two pedants, a Hédelin, a Dacier who however did not know themselves what they desired) and followed by all succeeding poets. I would venture to prove bit by bit that these doctrines could produce nothing but the most shallow, vapid, and untragical stuff. . . .

1. Aristotle says tragedy is to excite pity and fear, Corneille says oh, yes, but as it happens, both together are not always necessary, we can be contented with one of them, now pity without fear, another time fear without pity. Else where should I be, I the great Corneille with my Rodrigue and my Chimène? These good children awaken pity, very great pity, but scarcely fear. And again where should I be with my Cleopatra, my Prusias, and my Phocas? Who can have pity on these wretches? but they create fear. So Corneille believed and the French believed it after him.

2. Aristotle says tragedy should excite pity and fear, both, be it understood, by means of one and the same person. Corneille says: if it so happens very good. It is not however absolutely necessary and we may employ two different persons to produce these two sensations as I have done in my *Rodogune*. This is what Corneille did and the French do after him.

3. Aristotle says by means of the pity and fear excited in us by tragedy our pity and our fear and all that is connected with them are to be purified. Corneille knows nothing of all this and imagines that Aristotle wished to say tragedy excites our pity in order to awaken our fear, in order to purify by this fear the passions which had drawn down misfortunes upon the person we commiserate. I will say nothing of the value of this aim, enough that it is not Aristotle's and that since Corneille gave to his tragedies quite another aim they necessarily became works totally different from those whence Aristotle had abstracted his theories, they needs became tragedies which were no true tragedies. And such not only his but all French tragedies became because their authors did not think of the aim of Aristotle, but the aim of Corneille.

101–104

. . . No nation has more misapprehended the rules of ancient drama than the French. They have adopted as the essential some incidental remarks made by Aristotle about the most fitting external division of drama, and have so enfeebled the essential by all manner of limitations and interpretations, that nothing else could necessarily arise therefrom but works that remained far below the highest effect on which the philosopher had reckoned in his rules.

Friedrich Schiller *1759–1805*

Preface to
The Robbers *1781*

This play is to be regarded merely as a *dramatic* narrative, in which, for the purpose of tracing out the innermost workings of the soul, advantage has been taken of the *dramatic* method, without otherwise conforming to the stringent rules of theatrical composition, or seeking the dubious advantage of stage adaptation. It must be admitted as somewhat inconsistent that three very remarkable people, whose acts are dependent on perhaps a thousand contingencies, should be completely developed within three hours, considering that it would scarcely be possible, in the ordinary course of events, that three such remarkable people should, even in twenty-four hours, fully reveal their characters to the most penetrating inquirer. A greater amount of incident is here crowded together than it was possible for me to confine within the narrow limits prescribed by Aristotle and Batteux.[1]

It is, however, not so much the bulk of my play as its contents which banish it from the stage. Its scheme and economy require that several characters should appear, who would offend the finer feelings of virtue, and shock the delicacy of our manners. Every delineator of human character is placed in the same dilemma, if he proposes to give a faithful picture of the world as it really is, and not an ideal phantasy, a mere creation of his own. It is the course of mortal things that the good should be shadowed by the bad, and virtue shine the brightest when contrasted with vice. Whoever proposes to discourage vice, and to vindicate religion, morality, and social order, against their adversaries, must unveil crime in all its deformity, and place it before the eyes of men in its colossal magnitude. He must diligently explore its dark mazes, and make himself familiar with sentiments at the wickedness of which his soul revolts.

Vice is here exposed in its innermost workings. In Francis it resolves all the confused terrors of conscience into wild abstractions, destroys virtuous sentiments by dissecting them, and holds up the earnest voice of religion to mockery and scorn. He who has gone so far (a distinction by no means enviable) as to quicken his understanding at the expense of his soul— to him the holiest things are no longer holy—to him God and man are alike indifferent, and both worlds are as nothing. Of such a monster I have

From *The Works of Frederick Schiller: Early Dramas and Romances,* translated by Henry G. Bohn. London: Henry G. Bohn, 1849.

[1] Charles Batteux (1713–1780), who in 1771 published a French translation, with commentary, of Aristotle's *Poetics.*

endeavored to sketch a striking and lifelike portrait, to hold up to abhorrence all the machinery of his scheme of vice, and to test its strength by contrasting with truth. How far my narrative is successful in accomplishing these objects, the reader is left to judge. My conviction is, that I have painted nature to the life.

Next to this man (Francis) stands another, who would perhaps puzzle not a few of my readers. A mind for which the greatest crimes have only charms through the glory which attaches to them, the energy which their perpetration requires, and the dangers which attend them. A remarkable and important personage, abundantly endowed with the power of becoming either a Brutus or a Catiline, according as that power is directed. An unhappy conjunction of circumstances determines him to choose the latter for his example, and it is only after a fearful straying that he is recalled to emulate the former. Erroneous notions of activity and power, an exuberance of strength which bursts through all the barriers of law, must of necessity conflict with the rules of social life. To these enthusiast dreams of greatness and efficiency it needed but a sarcastic bitterness against the unpoetic spirit of the age to complete the strange Don Quixote, whom, in the Robber Moor, we at once detest and love, admire and pity. It is, I hope, unnecessary to remark, that I no more hold up this picture as a warning exclusively to robbers, than the greatest Spanish satire was levelled exclusively at knight-errants.

It is nowadays so much the fashion to be witty at the expense of religion, that a man will hardly pass for a genius if he does not allow his impious satire to run a-tilt at its most sacred truths. The noble simplicity of holy writ must needs be abused and turned into ridicule at the daily assemblies of the so-called wits; for what is there so holy and serious that will not raise a laugh if a false sense be attached to it? Let me hope that I shall have rendered no inconsiderable service to the cause of true religion and morality in holding up these wanton misbelievers to the detestation of society, under the form of the most despicable robbers.

But still more. I have made these said immoral characters to stand out favorably in particular points, and even in some measure to compensate by qualities of the head for what they are deficient in those of the heart. Herein I have done no more than literally copy nature. Every man, even the most depraved, bears in some degree the impress of the Almighty's image, and perhaps the greatest villain is not farther removed from the most upright man than the petty offender; for the moral forces keep pace with the powers of the mind, and the greater the capacity bestowed on man, the greater and more enormous become his misapplication of it, the more responsible is he for his errors.

The "Adramelech" of Klopstock (in his *Messiah*)[2] awakens in us a feeling

---

[2] Friedrich Gottlieb Klopstock (1724–1803), poet and playwright, whose *Messiah* was published, several cantos at a time, from 1748 to 1773.

in which admiration is blended with detestation. We follow Milton's Satan with shuddering wonder through the pathless realms of chaos. The Medea of the old dramatists is, in spite of all her crimes, a great and wondrous woman, and Shakespeare's Richard the Third is sure to excite the admiration of the reader, much as he would hate the reality. If it is to be my task to portray men as they are, I must at the same time include their good qualities, of which even the most vicious are never totally destitute. If I would warn mankind against the tiger, I must not omit to describe his glossy, beautifully marked skin, lest, owing to this omission, the ferocious animal should not be recognized till too late. Besides this, a man who is so utterly depraved as to be without a single redeeming point is no meet subject for art, and would disgust rather than excite the interest of the reader, who would turn over with impatience the pages which concern him. A noble soul can no more endure a succession of moral discords, than the musical ear the grating of knives upon glass.

And for this reason I should have been ill advised in attempting to bring my drama on the stage. A certain strength of mind is required both on the part of the poet and the reader; in the former that he may not disguise vice, in the latter that he may not suffer brilliant qualities to beguile him into admiration of what is essentially detestable. Whether the author has fulfilled his duty, he leaves others to judge, that his readers will perform theirs he by no means feels assured. The vulgar—among whom I would not be understood to mean merely the rabble—the vulgar, I say (between ourselves) extend their influence far around, and unfortunately—set the fashion. Too short-sighted to reach my full meaning, too narrow-minded to comprehend the largeness of my views, too disingenuous to admit my moral aim—they will, I fear, almost frustrate my good intentions, and pretend to discover in my work an apology for the very vice which it has been my object to condemn, and will perhaps make the poor poet, to whom anything rather than justice is usually accorded, responsible for his simplicity.

Thus we have a *Da capo* of the old story of Democritus and the Abderitans,[3] and our worthy Hippocrates would needs exhaust whole plantations of hellebore, were it proposed to remedy this mischief by a healing decoction.

---

[3] This alludes to the fable amusingly recorded by Wieland in his *Geschichte der Abderiten*. The Abderitans, who were a byword among the ancients for their extreme simplicity, are said to have sent express for Hippocrates to cure their great townsman, Democritus, whom they believed to be out of his senses, because his sayings were beyond their comprehension. Hippocrates, on conversing with Democritus, having at once discovered that the cause lay with themselves, assembled the senate and principal inhabitants in the marketplace, with the promise of instructing them in the cure of Democritus. He then banteringly advised them to import six ship-loads of hellebore, of the very best quality; and on its arrival to distribute it among the citizens, at least seven pounds per head, but to the senators double that quantity, as they were bound to have an extra supply of sense. By the time these worthies discovered that they had been laughed at, Hippocrates was out of their reach. The story in Wieland is infinitely more amusing than this short quotation from memory enables me to show [translator's note].

Let as many friends of truth as you will instruct their fellow-citizens in the pulpit and on the stage, the vulgar will never cease to be vulgar, though the sun and moon may change their course, and "heaven and earth wax old as a garment." Perhaps, in order to please tender-hearted people, I might have been less true to nature; but if a certain beetle, of whom we have all heard, could extract filth even from pearls, if we have examples that fire has destroyed and water deluged, shall therefore pearls, fire, and water be condemned? In consequence of the remarkable catastrophe which ends my play, I may justly claim for it a place among books of morality, for crime meets at last with the punishment it deserves; the lost one enters again within the pale of the law, and virtue is triumphant. Whoever will but be courteous enough towards me to read my work through with a desire to understand it, from him I may expect—not that he will admire the poet, but that he will esteem the honest man.

The Stage as a Moral Institution *1784*

Sulzer[1] has remarked that the stage has arisen from an irresistible longing for the new and extraordinary. Man, oppressed by divided cares, and satiated with sensual pleasure, felt an emptiness or want. Man, neither altogether satisfied with the senses, nor forever capable of thought, wanted a middle state, a bridge between the two states, bringing them into harmony. Beauty and esthetics supplied that for him. But a good lawgiver is not satisfied with discovering the bent of his people—he turns it to account as an instrument for higher use, and hence he chose the stage, as giving nourishment to the soul, without straining it, and uniting the noblest education of the head and heart.

The man who first pronounced religion to be the strongest pillar of the

From Friedrich Schiller, *Complete Works*, Vol. VIII. Translator anonymous. New York: P. F. Collier & Son, 1902.

[1] Johann Georg Sulzer (1720–1779), critic and esthetician.

state unconsciously defended the stage, when he said so, in its noblest aspect. The uncertain nature of political events, rendering religion a necessity, also demands the stage as a moral force. Laws only prevent disturbances of social life; religion prescribes positive orders sustaining social order. Law only governs actions; religion controls the heart and follows thought to the source.

Laws are flexible and capricious; religion binds forever. If religion has this great sway over man's heart, can it also complete his culture? Separating the political from the divine element in it, religion acts mostly on the senses; she loses her sway if the senses are gone. By what channel does the stage operate? To most men religion vanishes with the loss of her symbols, images, and problems; and yet they are only pictures of the imagination, and insolvable problems. Both laws and religion are strengthened by a union with the stage, where virtue and vice, joy and sorrow, are thoroughly displayed in a truthful and popular way; where a variety of providential problems are solved; where all secrets are unmasked, all artifice ends, and truth alone is the judge, as incorruptible as Rhadamanthus.[2]

Where the influence of civil laws ends that of the stage begins. Where venality and corruption blind and bias justice and judgment, and intimidation perverts its ends, the stage seizes the sword and scales and pronounces a terrible verdict on vice. The fields of fancy and of history are open to the stage; great criminals of the past live over again in the drama, and thus benefit an indignant posterity. They pass before us as empty shadows of their age, and we heap curses on their memory while we enjoy on the stage the very horror of their crimes. When morality is no more taught, religion no longer received, or laws exist, Medea would still terrify us with her infanticide. The sight of Lady Macbeth, while it makes us shudder, will also make us rejoice in a good conscience, when we see her, the sleep-walker, washing her hands and seeking to destroy the awful smell of murder. Sight is always more powerful to man than description; hence the stage acts more powerfully than morality or law.

But in this the stage only aids justice. A far wider field is really open to it. There are a thousand vices unnoticed by human justice, but condemned by the stage; so, also, a thousand virtues overlooked by man's laws are honored on the stage. It is thus the handmaid of religion and philosophy. From these pure sources it draws its high principles and the exalted teachings, and presents them in a lovely form. The soul swells with noblest emotions when a divine ideal is placed before it. When Augustus offers his forgiving hand to Cinna, the conspirator, and says to him: "Let us be friends, Cinna!"[3] what man at the moment does not feel that he could do the same? Again, when

---

[2] Son of Zeus and Europa, Rhadamanthus was a judge in Elysium.
[3] *Cinna* (1641) by Pierre Corneille.

Francis von Sickingen,[4] proceeding to punish a prince and redress a stranger, on turning sees the house, where his wife and children are, in flames, and yet goes on for the sake of his word—how great humanity appears, how small the stern power of fate!

Vice is portrayed on the stage in an equally telling manner. Thus, when old Lear, blind, helpless, childless, is seen knocking in vain at his daughters' doors, and in tempest and night he recounts by telling his woes to the elements, and ends by saying: "I have given you all"—how strongly impressed we feel at the value of filial piety, and how hateful ingratitude seems to us!

The stage does even more than this. It cultivates the ground where religion and law do not think it dignified to stop. Folly often troubles the world as much as crime; and it has been justly said that the heaviest loads often hang suspended by the slightest threads. Tracing actions to their sources, the list of criminals diminish, and we laugh at the long catalogue of fools. In our sex all forms of evil emanate almost entirely from one source, and all our excesses are only varied and higher forms of one quality, and that a quality which in the end we smile at and love; and why should not nature have followed this course in the opposite sex too? In man there is only one secret to guard against depravity; that is, to protect his heart against wickedness.

Much of all this is shown up on the stage. It is a mirror to reflect fools and their thousand forms of folly, which are there turned to ridicule. It curbs vice by terror, and folly still more effectually by satire and jest. If a comparison be made between tragedy and comedy, guided by experience, we should probably give the palm to the latter as to effects produced. Hatred does not wound the conscience so much as mockery does the pride of man. We are exposed specially to the sting of satire by the very cowardice that shuns terrors. From sins we are guarded by law and conscience, but the ludicrous is specially punished on the stage. Where we allow a friend to correct our morals, we rarely forgive a laugh. We may bear heavy judgment on our transgressions, but our weaknesses and vulgarities must not be criticized by a witness.

The stage alone can do this with impunity, chatising us as the anonymous fool. We can bear this rebuke without a blush, and even gratefully.

But the stage does even more than this. It is a great school of practical wisdom, a guide for civil life, and a key to the mind in all its sinuosities. It does not, of course, remove egoism and stubbornness in evil ways; for a thousand vices hold up their heads in spite of the stage, and a thousand virtues make no impression on cold-hearted spectators. Thus, probably,

---

[4] Franz von Sickingen (1481–1523), one of the "free knights" of the early Reformation, also figures in Goethe's *Götz von Berlichingen* (1773).

Molière's Harpagon[5] never altered a usurer's heart, nor did the suicide in *Beverley*[6] save anyone from the gaming-table. Nor, again, is it likely that the high roads will be safer through Karl Moor's untimely end.[7] But, admitting this, and more than this, still how great is the influence of the stage! It has shown us the vices and virtues of men with whom we have to live. We are not surprised at their weaknesses, we are prepared for them. The stage points them out to us, and their remedy. It drags off the mask from the hypocrite, and betrays the meshes of intrigue. Duplicity and cunning have been forced by it to show their hideous features in the light of day. Perhaps the dying Sarah[8] may not deter a single debauchee, nor all the pictures of avenged seduction stop the evil; yet unguarded innocence has been shown the snares of the corrupter, and taught to distrust his oaths.

The stage also teaches men to bear the strokes of fortune. Chance and design have equal sway over life. We have to bow to the former, but we control the latter. It is a great advantage if inexorable facts do not find us unprepared and unexercised, and if our breast has been steeled to bear adversity. Much human woe is placed before us on the stage. It gives us momentary pain in the tears we shed for strangers' troubles, but as a compensation it fills us with a grand new stock of courage and endurance. We are led by it, with the abandoned Ariadne, through the Isle of Naxos,[9] and we descend the Tower of Starvation in *Ugolino*;[10] we ascend the terrible scaffold, and we are present at the awful moment of execution. Things remotely present in thought become palpable realities now. We see the deceived favorite abandoned by the queen. When about to die, the perfidious Moor[11] is abandoned by his own sophistry. Eternity reveals the secrets of the unknown through the dead, and the hateful wretch loses all screen of guilt when the tomb opens to condemn him.

Then the stage teaches us to be more considerate to the unfortunate, and to judge gently. We can only pronounce on a man when we know his whole being and circumstances. Theft is a base crime, but tears mingle with our condemnation when we read what obliged Edward Ruhberg to do the horrid deed. Suicide is shocking; but the condemnation of an enraged father, her love, and the fear of a convent, lead Marianne to drink

---

[5] Title character of *The Miser* (1668).

[6] Title character of Edward Moore's *The Gamester* (1753).

[7] In Schiller's *The Robbers* (1781).

[8] Title character of Lessing's *Miss Sara Sampson* (1755).

[9] Daughter of Minos, Ariadne fell in love with Theseus, helped him escape from the Labyrinth, and fled with him to the island of Naxos.

[10] A conspirator in Pisa during the thirteenth century, he was betrayed, captured, and starved to death in a tower which became known as the Tower of Starvation. He is the title character of Heinrich Wilhelm von Gerstenberg's tragedy *Ugolino* (1767).

[11] Shakespeare's *Othello* (1604).

the cup, and few would dare to condemn the victim of a dreadful tyranny. Humanity and tolerance have begun to prevail in our time at courts of princes and in courts of law. A large share of this may be due to the influence of the stage in showing man and his secret motives.

The great of the world ought to be especially grateful to the stage, for it is here alone that they hear the truth.

Not only man's mind, but also his intellectual culture, has been promoted by the higher drama. The lofty mind and the ardent patriot have often used the stage to spread enlightenment.

Considering nations and ages, the thinker sees the masses enchanted by opinion and cut off by adversity from happiness; truth only lights up a few minds, who perhaps have to acquire it by the trials of a lifetime. How can the wise ruler put these within the reach of his nation.

The thoughtful and the worthier section of the people diffuse the light of wisdom over the masses through the stage. Purer and better principles and motives issue from the stage and circulate through society; the night of barbarism and superstition vanishes. I would mention two glorious fruits of the higher class of dramas. Religious toleration has latterly become universal. Before Nathan the Jew and Saladin the Saracen put us to shame,[12] and showed that resignation to God's will did not depend on a fancied belief of His nature—even before Joseph II[13] contended with the hatred of a narrow piety—the stage had sown seeds of humanity and gentleness: pictures of fanaticism had taught a hatred of intolerance, and Christianity, seeing itself in this awful mirror, washed off its stains. It is to be hoped that the stage will equally combat mistaken systems of education. This is a subject of the first political importance, and yet none is so left to private whims and caprice. The stage might give stirring examples of mistaken education, and lead parents to juster, better views of the subject. Many teachers are led astray by false views, and methods are often artificial and fatal.

Opinions about governments and classes might be reformed by the stage. Legislation could thus justify itself by foreign symbols, and silence doubtful aspersions without offence.

Now, if poets would be patriotic they could do much on the stage to forward invention and industry. A standing theatre would be a material advantage to a nation. It would have a great influence on the national temper and mind by helping the nation to agree in opinions and inclinations. The stage alone can do this, because it commands all human knowledge, exhausts all positions, illumines all hearts, unites all classes, and makes its way to the heart and understanding by the most popular channels.

---

[12] Lessing's *Nathan the Wise* (1779).
[13] Emperor Joseph II (1741–1790) supported religious tolerance.

If one feature characterized all dramas; if the poets were allied in aim—that is, if they selected well and from national topics—there would be a national stage, and we should become a nation. It was this that knit the Greeks so strongly together, and this gave to them the all-absorbing interest in the republic and the advancement of humanity.

Another advantage belongs to the stage; one which seems to have become acknowledged even by its censurers. Its influence on intellectual and moral culture, which we have till now been advocating, may be doubted; but its very enemies have admitted that it has gained the palm over all other means of amusement. It has been of much higher service here than people are often ready to allow.

Human nature cannot bear to be always on the rack of business, and the charms of sense die out with their gratification. Man, oppressed by appetites, weary of long exertion, thirsts for refined pleasure, or rushes into dissipations that hasten his fall and ruin, and disturb social order. Bacchanal joys, gambling, follies of all sorts to disturb ennui, are unavoidable if the lawgiver produces nothing better. A man of public business, who has made noble sacrifices to the state, is apt to pay for them with melancholy, the scholar to become a pedant, and the people brutish, without the stage. The stage is an institution combining amusement with instruction, rest with exertion, where no faculty of the mind is overstrained, no pleasure enjoyed at the cost of the whole. When melancholy gnaws the heart, when trouble poisons our solitude, when we are disgusted with the world, and a thousand worries oppress us, or when our energies are destroyed by over-exercise, the stage revives us, we dream of another sphere, we recover ourselves, our torpid nature is roused by noble passions, our blood circulates more healthily. The unhappy man forgets his tears in weeping for another. The happy man is calmed, the secure made provident. Effeminate natures are steeled, savages made man, and, as the supreme triumph of nature, men of all ranks, zones, and conditions, emancipated from the chains of conventionality and fashion, fraternize here in a universal sympathy, forget the world, and come nearer to their heavenly destination. The individual shares in the general ecstasy, and his breast has now only space for an emotion: he is a *man*.

On the Cause of the Pleasure We Derive from Tragic Objects *1791*

The praiseworthy object of pursuing everywhere moral good as the supreme aim, which has already brought forth in art so much mediocrity, has caused also in theory a similar prejudice. To assign to the fine arts a really elevated position, to conciliate for them the favor of the State, the veneration of all men, they are pushed beyond their true domain, and a vocation is imposed upon them contrary to their nature. It is supposed that a great service is awarded them by substituting for a frivolous aim—that of charming—a moral aim; and their influence upon morality, which is so apparent, necessarily militates in favor of this pretension. It is found illogical that the art which contributes in so great a measure to the development of all that is most elevated in man should produce but accessorily this effect, and make its chief object an aim so vulgar as we imagine pleasure to be. But this apparent contradiction it would be very easy to conciliate if we had a good theory of pleasure, and a complete system of esthetic philosophy.

It would result from this theory that a free pleasure, as that which the fine arts procure for us, rests wholly upon moral conditions, and all the moral faculties of man are exercised in it. It would further result that this pleasure is an aim which can never be attained but by moral means, and consequently that art, to tend and perfectly attain to pleasure, as to a real aim, must follow the road of healthy morals. Thus it is perfectly indifferent for the dignity of art whether its aim should be a moral aim, or whether it should reach only through moral means; for in both cases it has always to do with the morality, and must be rigorously in unison with the sentiment of duty; but for the perfection of art, it is by no means indifferent which of the two should be the aim and which the means. If it is the aim that is moral, art loses all that by which it is powerful, I mean its freedom, and that which gives it so much influence over us—the charm of pleasure. The play which recreates is changed into serious occupation, and yet it is precisely in recreating us that art can the better complete the great affair—the moral work. It cannot have a salutary influence upon the morals but in exercising its highest esthetic action, and it can only produce the esthetic effect in its highest degree in fully exercising its liberty.

Selections. From Friedrich Schiller, *Complete Works*, Vol. VIII. Translator anonymous. New York: P. F. Collier & Son, 1902.

It is certain, besides, that all pleasure, the moment it flows from a moral source, renders man morally better, and then the effect in its turn becomes cause. The pleasure we find in what is beautiful, or touching, or sublime strengthens our moral sentiments, as the pleasure we find in kindness, in love, etc., strengthens these inclinations. And just as contentment of mind is the sure lot of the morally excellent man, so moral excellence willingly accompanies satisfaction of heart. Thus the moral efficacy of art is not only because it employs moral means in order to charm us, but also because even the pleasure which it procures us is a means of morality. . . .

But the sufferings of a criminal are as charming to us tragically as those of a virtuous man; yet here is the idea of moral impropriety. The antagonism of his conduct to moral law, and the moral imperfection which such conduct presupposes, ought to fill us with pain. Here there is no satisfaction in the morality of his person, nothing to compensate for his misconduct. Yet both supply a valuable object for art; this phenomenon can easily be made to agree with what has been said.

We find pleasure not only in obedience to morality, but in the punishment given to its infraction. The pain resulting from moral imperfections agrees with its opposite, the satisfaction at conformity with the law. Repentance, even despair, have nobleness morally, and can only exist if an incorruptible sense of justice exists at the bottom of the criminal heart, and if conscience maintains its ground against self-love. Repentance comes by comparing our acts with the moral law, hence in the moment of repenting the moral law speaks loudly in man. Its power must be greater than the gain resulting from the crime as the infraction poisons the enjoyment. Now, a state of mind where duty is sovereign is morally proper, and therefore a source of moral pleasure. What, then, sublimer than the heroic despair that tramples even life underfoot, because it cannot bear the judgment within? A good man sacrificing his life to conform to the moral law, or a criminal taking his own life because of the morality he has violated: in both cases our respect for the moral law is raised to the highest power. If there be any advantage it is in the case of the latter; for the good man may have been encouraged in his sacrifice by an approving conscience, thus detracting from his merit. Repentance and regret at past crimes show us some of the sublimest pictures of morality in active condition. A man who violates morality comes back to the moral law by repentance.

On the Tragic Art 1792

The state of passion in itself, independently of the good or bad influence of its object on our morality, has something in it that charms us. We aspire to transport ourselves into that state, even if it costs us some sacrifices. You will find this instinct at the bottom of all our most habitual pleasures. As to the nature itself of the affection, whether it be one of aversion or desire, agreeable or painful, this is what we take little into consideration. Experience teaches us that painful affections are those which have the most attraction for us, and thus that the pleasure we take in an affection is precisely in an inverse ratio to its nature. It is a phenomenon common to all men that sad, frightful things, even the horrible, exercise over us an irresistible seduction, and that in presence of a scene of desolation and of terror we feel at once repelled and attracted by two equal forces. Suppose the case be an assassination. Then everyone crowds round the narrator and shows a marked attention. Any ghost story, however embellished by romantic circumstances, is greedily devoured by us, and the more readily in proportion as the story is calculated to make our hair stand on end.

This disposition is developed in a more lively manner when the objects themselves are placed before our eyes. A tempest that would swallow up an entire fleet would be, seen from shore, a spectacle as attractive to our imagination as it would be shocking to our heart. It would be difficult to believe with Lucretius that this natural pleasure results from a comparison between our own safety and the danger of which we are witnesses. See what a crowd accompanies a criminal to the scene of his punishment! This phenomenon cannot be explained either by the pleasure of satisfying our love of justice, nor the ignoble joy of vengeance. Perhaps the unhappy man may find excuses in the hearts of those present; perhaps the sincerest pity takes an interest in his reprieve: this does not prevent a lively curiosity in the spectators to watch his expressions of pain with eye and ear. If an exception seems to exist here in the case of a well-bred man, endowed with a delicate sense, this does not imply that he is a complete stranger to this instinct; but in his case the painful strength of compassion carries the day over this instinct, or it is kept under the laws of decency. The man of nature, who is not chained down by any feeling of human delicacy, abandons himself without any sense of shame to this powerful instinct. This attraction must, therefore, have its spring of action in an original disposition, and it must be explained by a psychological law common to the whole species.

But if it seems to us that these brutal instincts of nature are incompatible with the dignity of man, and if we hesitate, for this reason, to establish on

Selections. From Friedrich Schiller, *Complete Works*, Vol. VIII. Translator anonymous. New York: P. F. Collier & Son, 1902.

this fact a law common to the whole species, yet no experiences are required to prove, with the completest evidence, that the pleasure we take in painful emotions is real, and that it is general. The painful struggle of a heart drawn asunder between its inclinations or contrary duties, a struggle which is a cause of misery to him who experiences it, delights the person who is a mere spectator. We follow with always heightening pleasure the progress of a passion to the abyss into which it hurries its unhappy victim. The same delicate feeling that makes us turn our eyes aside from the sight of physical suffering, or even from the physical expression of a purely moral pain, makes us experience a pleasure heightened in sweetness, in the sympathy for a purely moral pain. The interest with which we stop to look at the painting of these kinds of objects is a general phenomenon.

Of course this can only be understood of sympathetic affections, or those felt as a secondary effect after their *first impression*; for commonly *direct* and *personal* affections immediately call into life in us the instinct of our own happiness, they take up all our thoughts, and seize hold of us too powerfully to allow any room for the feeling of pleasure that accompanies them, when the affection is freed from all personal relation. Thus, in the mind that is really a prey to painful passion, the feeling of pain commands all others notwithstanding all the charm that the painting of its moral state may offer to the bearers and the spectators. And yet the painful affection is not deprived of all pleasures, even for him who experiences it directly; only this pleasure differs in degree according to the nature of each person's mind. The sports of chance would not have half so much attraction for us were there not a kind of enjoyment in anxiety, in doubt, and in fear; danger would not be encountered from mere foolhardiness; and the very sympathy which interests us in the trouble of another would not be to us that pleasure which is never more lively than at the very moment when the illusion is strongest, and when we substitute ourselves most entirely in the place of the person who suffers. But this does not imply that disagreeable affections cause pleasure of themselves, nor do I think any one will uphold this view; it suffices that these states of the mind are the conditions that alone make possible for us certain kinds of pleasure. Thus the hearts particularly sensitive to this kind of pleasure, and most greedy of them, will be more easily led to share these disagreeable affections, which are the condition of the former; and even in the most violent storms of passion they will always preserve some remains of their freedom.

The displeasure we feel in disagreeable affections comes from the relation of our sensuous faculty or of our moral faculty with their object. In like manner, the pleasure we experience in agreeable affections proceeds from the very same source. The degree of liberty that may prevail in the affections depends on the proportion between the moral nature and the sensuous nature of a man. Now it is well known that in the moral order there is nothing arbitrary for us, that, on the contrary, the sensuous instinct is subject to the laws of reason and consequently that we can keep our liberty full and entire in all those affections that are concerned with the instinct of self-love, and that we are the masters to determine the degree which they ought to attain. This degree will be less in proportion as the moral sense in a man will prevail over the instinct of happiness, and as by obeying the universal laws of reason he will have freed himself from the selfish requirements of his individuality, his Ego. A man of this kind must therefore, in a state of passion, feel much less vividly the relation of an object with his own instinct of happiness, and consequently he will be much less sensible of the displeasure that arises from this relation. On the other hand, he will be perpetually more attentive to the relation of this same object with his moral nature, and for this very reason he will be more sensible to the pleasure which the relation of the object with morality often mingles with the most painful affections. A mind thus constituted is better fitted than all others to enjoy the pleasure attaching to compassion, and even to regard a personal affection as an object of simple compassion. Hence the inestimable value of a moral philosophy, which, by raising our eyes constantly towards general laws, weakens in us the feeling of our individuality, teaches us to plunge our paltry personality in something great, and enables us thus to act to ourselves as to strangers. This sublime state of mind is the lot of strong philosophic minds, which by working assiduously on themselves have learned to bridle the egotistical instinct. Even the most cruel loss does not drive them beyond a certain degree of sadness, with which an appreciable sum of pleasure can always be reconciled. These souls, which are alone capable of separating themselves from themselves, alone enjoy the privilege of sympathizing with themselves and of receiving of their own sufferings only a reflex, softened by sympathy.

The indications contained in what precedes will suffice to direct our attention to the sources of the pleasure that the affection in itself causes, more particularly the sad affection. We have seen that this pleasure is more energetic in moral souls, and it acts with greater freedom in proportion as the soul is more independent of the egotistical instinct. This pleasure is, moreover, more vivid and stronger in sad affections, when self-love is painfully disquieted, than in gay affections, which imply a satisfaction of self-love. Accordingly, this pleasure increases when the egotistical instinct is wounded, and diminishes when that instinct is flattered. Now we only know of two sources of pleasure—the satisfaction of the instinct of happiness, and the accomplishment of the moral laws. Therefore, when it is shown that a particular pleasure does not emanate from the former source, it must of necessity issue from the second. It is therefore from our moral nature that issues the charm of the painful affections shared by sympathy, and the pleasure that we sometimes feel even where the painful affection directly affects ourselves.

Many attempts have been made to account for the pleasure of pity, but most of these solutions had little chance of meeting the problem, because the principle of this phenomenon was sought for rather in the accompanying circumstances than in the nature of the affection itself. To many persons the pleasure of pity is simply the pleasure taken by the mind in exercising its own sensibility. To others it is the pleasure of occupying their forces energetically, of exercising the social faculty vividly—in short, of satisfying the instinct of restlessness. Others again make it derived from the discovery of morally fine features of character, placed in a clear light by the struggle against adversity or against the passions. But there is still the difficulty to explain why it should be exactly the very feeling of pain—*suffering*, properly so called—that in objects of pity attracts us with the greatest force, while, according to those elucidations, a less degree of suffering ought evidently to be more favorable to those causes to which the source of the emotion is traced. Various matters may, no doubt, increase the pleasure of the emotion without occasioning it. Of this nature are: the vividness and force of the ideas awakened in our imagination, the moral excellence of the suffering persons, the reference to himself of the person feeling pity. I admit that the suffering of a weak soul, and the pain of a wicked character, do not procure us this enjoyment. But this is because they do not excite our pity to the same degree as the hero who suffers, or the virtuous man who struggles. Thus we are constantly brought back to the first question: Why is it precisely the degree of suffering that determines the degree of sympathetic pleasure which we take in an emotion? and one answer only is possible; it is because the attack made on our sensibility is precisely the condition necessary to set in motion that quality of mind of which the activity produces the pleasure we feel in sympathetic affections.

Now this faculty is no other than the reason; and because the free exercise of reason, as an absolutely independent activity, deserves *par excellence* the name of activity; as, moreover, the heart of man only feels itself perfectly free and independent in its moral acts, it follows that the charm of tragic emotions is really dependent on the fact that this instinct of activity finds its gratification in them. But, even admitting this, it is neither the great number nor the vivacity of the ideas that are awakened then in our imagination, nor in general the exercise of the social faculty, but a certain kind of ideas and a certain activity of the social faculty brought into play by reason, which is the foundation of this pleasure.

Thus the same sympathetic affections in general are for us a source of pleasure because they give satisfaction to our instinct of activity, and the sad affections produce this effect with more vividness because they give more satisfaction to this instinct. The mind only reveals all its activity when it is in full possession of its liberty, when it has a perfect consciousness of its rational nature, because it is only then that it displays a force superior to all resistance. . . .

Art attains its end by the *imitation of nature*, by satisfying the conditions which make pleasure possible in reality, and by combining, according to a plan traced by the intelligence, the scattered elements furnished by nature, so as to attain as a principal end to that which, for nature, was only an accessory end. Thus tragic art ought to imitate nature in those kinds of actions that are specially adapted to awaken pity. . . .

If the cause that has produced a misfortune gives us too much displeasure, our compassion for the victim is diminished thereby. The heart cannot feel simultaneously, in a high degree, two absolutely contrary affections. Indignation against the person who is the primary cause of the suffering becomes the prevailing affection, and all other feeling has to yield to it. Thus our interest is always enfeebled when the unhappy man whom it would be desirable to pity had cast himself into ruin by a personal and an inexcusable fault; or if, being able to save himself, he did not do so, either through feebleness of mind or pusillanimity. The interest we take in unhappy King Lear, ill-treated by two ungrateful daughters, is sensibly lessened by the circumstances that this aged man, in his second childhood, so weakly gave up his crown, and divided his love among his daughters with so little discernment. In the tragedy of Kronegk, *Olinda and Sophronia*,[1] the most terrible suffering to which we see these martyrs to their faith exposed only excites our pity feebly, and all their heroism only stirs our admiration moderately, because madness alone can suggest the act by which Olinda has placed himself and all his people on the brink of the precipice.

Our pity is equally lessened when the primary cause of a misfortune, whose innocent victim ought to inspire us with compassion, fills our mind with horror. When the tragic poet cannot clear himself of his plot without introducing a wretch, and when he is reduced to derive the greatness of suffering from the greatness of wickedness, the supreme beauty of his work must always be seriously injured. Iago and Lady Macbeth in Shakespeare, Cleopatra in the tragedy of *Rodogune*,[2] or Franz Moor in *The Robbers*,[3] are so many proofs in support of this assertion. A poet who understands his real interest will not bring about the catastrophe through a malicious will which proposes misfortune as its end; nor, and still less, by want of understanding: but rather through the imperious force of circumstances. If this catastrophe does not come from moral sources, but from outward things, which have no volition and are not subject to any will, the pity we experience is more pure, or at all events it is not weakened by any idea of moral incongruity. But then the spectator cannot be spared the disagreeable feeling of an incongruity in the order of nature, which can alone save in such a case moral propriety. Pity is far more excited when it has for its object both

---

[1] Unfinished at the death of the author, Baron Friedich von Kronegk (1731–1758).

[2] (1644) by Pierre Corneille.

[3] (1781) by Schiller.

him who suffers and him who is the primary cause of the suffering. This can only happen when the latter has neither elicited our contempt nor our hatred, but when he has been brought against his inclination to become the cause of this misfortune. It is a singular beauty of the German play of *Iphigenia*[4] that the King of Tauris, the only obstacle who thwarts the wishes of Orestes and of his sister, never loses our esteem, and that we love him to the end.

There is something superior even to this kind of emotion; this is the case when the cause of the misfortune not only is in no way repugnant to morality, but only becomes possible through morality, and when the reciprocal suffering comes simply from the idea that a fellow-creature has been made to suffer. This is the situation of Chimène and Rodrigue in *The Cid*[5] of Pierre Corneille, which is undeniably in point of intrigue the masterpiece of the tragic stage. Honor and filial love arm the hand of Rodrigue against the father of her whom he loves, and his valor gives him the victory. Honor and filial love rouse up against him, in the person of Chimène, the daughter of his victim, an accuser and a formidable persecutor. Both act in opposition to their inclination, and they tremble with anguish at the thought of the misfortune of the object against which they arm themselves, in proportion as zeal inspires them for their duty to inflict this misfortune. Accordingly both conciliate our esteem in the highest sense, as they accomplish a moral duty at the cost of inclination; both inflame our pity in the highest degree, because they suffer spontaneously for a motive that renders them in the highest degree to be respected. It results from this that our pity is in this case so little modified by any opposite feeling that it burns rather with a double flame; only the impossibility of reconciling the idea of misfortune with the idea of a morality so deserving of happiness might still disturb our sympathetic pleasure, and spread a shade of sadness over it. It is besides a great point, no doubt, that the discontent given us by this contradiction does not bear upon our moral being, but is turned *aside* to a harmless place, to necessity only; but this blind subjection to destiny is always afflicting and humiliating for free beings, who determine themselves. . . .

In the same manner as the tragic emotion is weakened by the admixture of conflicting ideas and feelings, and the charm attaching to it is thus diminished, so this emotion can also, on the contrary, by approaching the excess of direct and personal affection, become exaggerated to the point where pain carries the day over pleasure. It has been remarked that displeasure, in the affections, comes from the relation of their object with our senses, in the same way as the pleasure felt in them comes from the relation of the

---

[4] *Iphigenia in Tauris* (1788) by Goethe.
[5] (1636).

affection itself to our moral faculty. This implies, then, between our senses and our moral faculty a determined relation, which decides as regards the relation between pleasure and displeasure in tragic emotions. Nor could this relation be modified or overthrown without overthrowing at the same time the feelings of pleasure and displeasure which we find in the emotions, or even without changing them into their opposites. In the same ratio that the senses are vividly roused in us, the influence of morality will be proportionately diminished; and reciprocally, as the sensuous loses, morality gains ground. Therefore that which in our hearts gives a preponderance to the sensuous faculty, must of necessity, by placing restrictions on the moral faculty, diminish the pleasure that we take in tragic emotions, a pleasure which emanates exclusively from this moral faculty. In like manner, all that in our heart impresses an impetus on this latter faculty must blunt the stimulus of pain even in direct and personal affections. Now our sensuous nature actually acquires this preponderance, when the ideas of suffering rise to a degree of vividness that no longer allows us to distinguish a sympathetic affection from a personal affection, or our own proper Ego from the subject that suffers—reality, in short, from poetry. The sensuous also gains the upper hand when it finds an alignment in the great number of its objects, and in that dazzling light which an over-excited imagination diffuses over it. On the contrary, nothing is more fit to reduce the sensuous to its proper bounds than to place alongside it supersensuous ideas, moral ideas, to which reason, oppressed just before, clings as to a kind of spiritual props, to right and raise itself above the fogs of the sensuous to a serener atmosphere. Hence the great charm which general truths or moral sentences, scattered opportunely over dramatic dialogue, have for all cultivated nations, and the almost excessive use that the Greeks made of them. . . .

Every feeling of pity implies the idea of suffering, and the degree of pity is regulated according to the degree more or less of vividness, of truth, of intensity, and of duration of this idea. . . .

If we now form the proper deductions from the previous investigation, the following will be the conditions that form bases of the tragic art. It is necessary, in the first place, that the object of our pity should belong to our own species—I mean belong in the full sense of the term—and that the action in which it is sought to interest us be a moral action; that is, an action comprehended in the field of free will. It is necessary, in the second place, that suffering, its sources, its degrees, should be completely communicated by a series of events chained together. It is necessary, in the third place, that the object of the passion be rendered present to our senses, not in a mediate way and by description, but immediately and in action. In tragedy art unites all these conditions and satisfies them.

According to these principles tragedy might be defined as the poetic imitation of a coherent series of particular events (forming a complete action): an imitation which shows us man in a state of suffering, and which has for its end to excite our pity.

I say first that it is the *imitation* of an action; and this idea of imitation already distinguishes tragedy from the other kinds of poetry, which only narrate or describe. In tragedy particular events are presented to our imagination or to our senses at the very time of their accomplishment; they are present, we see them immediately, without the intervention of a third person. The epos, the romance, simple narrative, even in their form, withdraw action to a distance, causing the narrator to come between the acting person and the reader. Now what is distant and past always weakens, as we know, the impressions and the sympathetic affection; what is present makes them stronger. All narrative forms make of the present something past; all dramatic form makes of the past a present.

Secondly, I say that tragedy is the imitation of a succession of *events*, of an action. Tragedy has not only to represent by imitation the feelings and the affections of tragic persons, but also the events that have produced these feelings, and the occasion on which these affections are manifested. This distinguishes it from lyric poetry, and from its different forms, which no doubt offer, like tragedy, the poetic imitation of certain states of the mind, but not the poetic imitation of certain actions. An elegy, a song, an ode, can place before our eyes, by imitation, the moral state in which the poet actually is—whether he speaks in his own name, or in that of an ideal person—a state determined by particular circumstances; and up to this point these lyric forms seem certainly to be incorporated in the idea of tragedy; but they do not complete that idea, because they are confined to representing our feelings. There are still more essential differences, if the end of these lyrical forms and that of tragedy are kept in view.

I say, in the third place, that tragedy is the imitation of a complete action. A separate event, though it be ever so tragic, does not in itself constitute a tragedy. To do this, several events are required, based one on the other, like cause and effect, and suitably connected so as to form a whole; without which the truth of the feeling represented, of the character, etc.—that is, their conformity with the nature of our mind, a conformity which alone determines our sympathy—will not be recognized. If we do not feel that we ourselves in similar circumstances should have experienced the same feelings and acted in the same way, our pity would not be awakened. It is, therefore, important that we should be able to follow in all its concatenation the action that is represented to us, that we should see it issue from the mind of the agent by a natural gradation, under the influence and with the concurrence of external circumstances. It is thus that we see spring up, grow, and come to maturity under our eyes, the curiosity of Oedipus and the jealousy of Iago. It is also the only way to fill up the great gap that exists between the joy of an innocent soul and the torments of a guilty conscience, between the proud serenity of the happy man and his terrible catastrophe; in short, between the state of calm, in which the reader is at the beginning, and the violent agitation he ought to experience at the end.

A series of several connected incidents is required to produce in our souls a succession of different movements which arrest the attention, which, appealing to all the faculties of our minds, enliven our instinct of activity when it is exhausted, and which, by delaying the satisfaction of this instinct, do not kindle it the less. Against the suffering of sensuous nature the human heart has only recourse to its moral nature as counterpoise. It is, therefore, necessary, in order to stimulate this in a more pressing manner, for the tragic poet to prolong the torments of sense, but he must also give a glimpse to the latter of the satisfaction of its wants, so as to render the victory of the moral sense so much the more difficult and glorious. This twofold end can only be attained by a succession of actions judiciously chosen and combined to this end.

In the fourth place, I say that tragedy is the poetic *imitation* of an action deserving of pity, and, therefore, tragic imitation is opposed to *historic* imitation. It would only be a historic imitation if it proposed a historic end, if its principal object were to *teach* us that a thing has taken place, and how it took place. On this hypothesis it ought to keep rigorously to historic accuracy, for it would only attain its end by representing faithfully that which really took place. But tragedy has a *poetic* end, that is to say it represents an action to *move* us, and to *charm* our souls by the medium of this emotion. If, therefore, a matter being given, tragedy treats it conformably with this poetic end, which is proper to it, it becomes, by that very thing, free in its imitation. It is a right—nay, more, it is an obligation—for tragedy to subject historic truth to the laws of poetry; and to treat its matter in conformity with requirements of this art. But as it cannot attain its end, which is emotion, except on the condition of a perfect conformity with the laws of nature, tragedy is, notwithstanding its freedom in regard to history, strictly subject to the laws of natural truth, which, in opposition to the truth of history, takes the name of poetic truth. It may thus be understood how much poetic truth may lose, in many cases by a strict observance of historic truth, and, reciprocally, how much it may gain by even a very serious alteration of truth according to history. As the tragic poet, like poets in general, is only subject to the laws of poetic truth, the most conscientious observance of historic truth could never dispense him from his duties as poet, and could never excuse in him any infraction of poetic truth or lack of interest. It is, therefore, betraying very narrow ideas on tragic art, or rather on poetry in general, to drag the tragic poet before the tribunal of history, and to require *instruction* of the man who by his very title is only bound to move and charm you. Even supposing the poet, by a scrupulous submission to historic truth, had stripped himself of his privilege of artist, and that he had tacitly acknowledged in history a jurisdiction over his work, art retains all her rights to summon him before its bar; and pieces such as *The Death of Hermann,*[6] *Minona,*[7] *Fust of Stromberg,* if they could not stand the test on this side, would only be tragedies of mediocre value, notwithstanding all the minuteness of costume—of national costume—and of the manners of the time.

Fifthly, tragedy is the imitation of an action that lets us see *man suffering.* The word *man* is essential to mark the limits of tragedy. Only the suffering of a being like ourselves can move our pity. Thus, evil genii, demons—or even men like them, without morals—and again pure spirits, without our weaknesses, are unfit for tragedy. The very idea of suffering implies a man in the full sense of the term. A pure spirit cannot suffer, and a man approaching one will never awaken a high degree of sympathy. A purely sensuous being can indeed have terrible suffering; but without moral sense it is a prey to it, and a suffering with reason inactive is a disgusting spectacle. The tragedian is right to prefer mixed characters, and to place the idea of his hero halfway between utter perversity and entire perfection.

Lastly, tragedy unites all these requisites to excite pity. Many means the tragic poet takes might serve another object; but he frees himself from all requirements not relating to this end, and is thereby obliged to direct himself with a view to this supreme object.

The final aim to which all the laws tend is called the *end* of any style of poetry. The means by which it attains this are its *form.* The end and form are, therefore, closely related. The form is determined by the end, and when the form is well observed the end is generally attained. Each kind of poetry having a special end must have a distinguishing form. What it exclusively produces it does in virtue of this special nature it possesses. The end of tragedy is *emotion;* its form is the imitation of an action that leads to suffering. Many kinds may have the same object as tragedy, of emotion, though it be not their principal end. Therefore, what distinguishes tragedy is the relation of its form to its end, the way in which it attains its end by means of its subject.

If the end of tragedy is to awaken sympathy, and its form is the means of attaining it, the imitation of an action fit to move must have all that favors sympathy. Such is the form of tragedy.

The production of a kind of poetry is perfect when the form peculiar to its kind has been used in the best way. Thus, a perfect tragedy is that where the form is best used to awaken sympathy. Thus, the best tragedy is that where the pity excited results more from the treatment of the poet than the theme. Such is the ideal of a tragedy.

[6] (1787), third part of a trilogy on Hermann by Friedrich Gottlieb Klopstock (1724–1803).
[7] (1785) by Wilhelm von Gerstenberg.

A good number of tragedies, though fine as poems, are bad as dramas, because they do not seek their end by the best use of tragic form. Others, because they use the form to attain an end different from tragedy. Some very popular ones only touch us on account of the subject, and we are blind enough to make this a merit in the poet. There are others in which we seem to have quite forgotten the object of the poet, and, contented with pretty plays of fancy and wit, we issue with our hearts cold from the theatre. Must art, so holy and venerable, defend its cause by such champions before such judges? The indulgence of the public only emboldens mediocrity: it causes genius to blush, and discourages it.

The Pathetic   *1793*

The depicting of suffering, in the shape of simple suffering, is never the end of art, but it is of the greatest importance as a means of attaining its end. The highest aim of art is to represent the supersensuous, and this is effected in particular by tragic art, because it represents by sensible marks the moral man, maintaining himself in a state of passion, independently of the laws of nature. The principle of freedom in man becomes conscious of itself only by the resistance it offers to the violence of the feelings. Now the resistance can only be measured by the strength of the attack. In order, therefore, that the intelligence may reveal itself in man as a force independent of nature, it is necessary that nature should have first displayed all her power before our eyes. The *sensuous* being must be profoundly and strongly *affected, passion* must be in play, that the *reasonable* being may be able to testify his independence and manifest himself in *action*.

It is impossible to know if the empire which man has over his affections is the effect of a moral force, till we have acquired the certainty that it is not an effect of insensibility. There is no merit in mastering the feelings which only lightly and transitorily skim over the surface of the soul. But to resist a tempest which stirs up the whole of sensuous nature, and to preserve in it

Selections. From Friedrich Schiller. *Complete Works,* Vol. VIII. Translator anonymous. New York: P. F. Collier & Son, 1902.

the freedom of the soul, a faculty of resistance is required infinitely superior to the act of natural force. Accordingly it will not be possible to represent moral freedom, except by expressing passion, or suffering nature, with the greatest vividness; and the hero of tragedy must first have justified his claim to be a sensuous being before aspiring to our homage as a reasonable being, and making us believe in his strength of mind.

Therefore the *pathetic* is the first condition required most strictly in a tragic author, and he is allowed to carry his description of suffering as far as possible, without prejudice to the *highest end of his art*, that is, without moral freedom being oppressed by it. He must give in some sort to his hero, as to his reader, their full *load* of suffering, without which the question will always be put whether the resistance opposed to suffering is an act of the soul, something *positive*, or whether it is not rather a purely *negative* thing, a simple deficiency.

The latter case is offered in the purer French tragedy, where it is very rare, or perhaps unexampled, for the author to place before the reader suffering nature, and where generally, on the contrary, it is only the poet who warms up and declaims, or the comedian who struts about on stilts. The icy tone of declamation extinguishes all nature here, and the French tragedians, with their superstitious worship of *decorum*, make it quite impossible for them to paint human nature truly. Decorum, whenever it is, even in its proper place, always falsifies the expression of nature, and yet this expression is rigorously required by art. In a French tragedy, it is difficult for us to believe that the hero ever suffers, for he explains the state of his soul, as the coolest man would do, and always thinking of the effect he is making on others, he never lets nature pour forth freely. The kings, the princesses, and the heroes of Corneille or Voltaire never forget their *rank* even in the most violent excess of passion; and they part with their *humanity* much sooner than with their *dignity*. They are like those kings and emperors of our old picture-books, who go to bed with their crowns on.

What a difference from the Greeks and those of the moderns who have been inspired with their spirit in poetry! Never does the Greek poet blush at nature; he leaves to the sensuous all its rights, and yet he is quite certain never to be subdued by it. He has too much depth and too much rectitude in his mind not to distinguish the accidental, which is the principal point with false taste, from the really necessary; but all that is not humanity itself is accidental in man. The Greek artist who has to represent a Laocoon, a Niobe, and a Philoctetes, does not care for the king, the princess, or the king's son; he keeps to the *man*. Accordingly the skilful statuary sets aside the drapery, and shows us nude figures, though he knows quite well it is not so in real life. This is because drapery is to him an accidental thing, and because the necessary ought never to be sacrificed to the accidental. It is also because, if decency and physical necessities have their laws, these laws are not those of art. The statuary ought to show us, and wishes to show us, the *man* himself; drapery conceals him, therefore he sets that aside, and with reason.

The Greek sculptor rejects drapery as a useless and embarrassing load, to make way for *human nature*; and in like manner the Greek poet emancipates the human personages he brings forward from the equally useless constraint of decorum, and all those icy laws of propriety, which put nothing but what is artificial in man, and conceal nature in it. Take Homer and the tragedians; suffering nature speaks the language of truth and ingenuousness in their pages, and in a way to penetrate to the depths of our hearts. All the passions play their part freely, nor do the rules of propriety compress any feeling with the Greeks. The heroes are just as much under the influence of suffering as other men, and what makes them heroes is the very fact that they feel suffering strongly and deeply, without suffering overcoming them. They love life as ardently as others; but they are not so ruled by this feeling as to be unable to give up life when the duties of honor or humanity call on them to do so. Philoctetes filled the Greek stage with his lamentations; Hercules himself, when in fury, does not keep under his grief. Iphigenia, on the point of being sacrificed, confesses with a touching ingenuousness that she grieves to part with the light of the sun. Never does the Greek place his glory in being insensible or indifferent to suffering, but rather in s*upporting* it, though feeling it in its fullness. The very gods of the Greeks must pay their tribute to nature, when the poet wishes to make them approximate to humanity. Mars, when wounded, roars like ten thousand men together, and Venus, scratched by an iron lance, mounts again to Olympus, weeping, and cursing all battles.

This lively susceptibility on the score of suffering, this warm, ingenuous nature, showing itself uncovered and in all truth in the monuments of Greek art, and filling us with such deep and lively emotions—this is a model presented for the imitation of all artists; it is a law which Greek genius has laid down for the fine arts. It is always and eternally nature which has the first rights over man; she ought never to be fettered, because man, before being anything else, is a sensuous creature. After the rights of nature come those of *reason*, because man is a rational, sensuous being, a moral person, and because it is a duty for this person not to let himself be ruled by nature, but to rule her. It is only after satisfaction has been given in the *first place* to *nature*, and after reason in the *second place* has made its rights acknowledged, that it is permitted for decorum in the third place to make good its claims, to impose on man, in the expression of his moral feelings and of his sensations, considerations towards society, and to show in it the social being, the civilized man. The first law of the tragic art was to represent suffering nature. The second law is to represent the resistance of morality opposed to suffering. . . .

. . . Art ought to charm the mind and give satisfaction to the feeling of moral freedom. This man who is a prey to his pain is to me simply a tortured animate being, and not a man tried by suffering. For a moral resistance to painful affections is already required of man—a resistance which can alone allow the principle of moral freedom, the intelligence, to make itself known in it.

If it is so, the poets and the artists are poor adepts in their art when they seek to reach the pathetic only by the sensuous force of affection and by representing suffering in the most vivid manner. They forget that suffering in itself can never be the last end of imitation, nor the immediate source of the pleasure we experience in tragedy. The pathetic only has esthetic value in as far as it is sublime. Now, effects that only allow us to infer a purely sensuous cause, and that are founded only on the affection experienced by the faculty of sense, are never sublime, whatever energy they may display, for everything sublime proceeds *exclusively* from the reason.

I imply by passion the affections of pleasure as well as the painful affections, and to represent passion only, without coupling with it the expression of the supersensuous faculty which resists it, is to fall into what is properly called *vulgarity*; and the opposite is called *nobility*. Vulgarity and nobility are two ideas which, wherever they are applied, have more or less relation with the supersensuous share a man takes in a work. There is nothing noble but what has its source in the reason; all that issues from sensuousness alone is *vulgar* or *common*. We say of a man that he acts in a *vulgar* manner when he is satisfied with obeying the suggestions of his sensuous instinct; that he acts suitably when he only obeys his instinct in conformity with the laws; that he acts *nobly* when he obeys reason only, without having regard to his instincts. We say of a physiognomy that it is *common* when it does not show any trace of the spiritual man, the intelligence; we say it has expression when it is the mind which has determined its features; and that it is noble when a pure spirit has determined them. If an architectural work is in question we qualify it as *common* if it aims at nothing but a physical end; we name it noble if, independently of all physical aim, we find in it at the same time the expression of a conception.

Accordingly, I repeat it, correct taste disallows all painting of the affections, however energetic, which rests satisfied with expressing physical suffering and the physical resistance opposed to it by the subject, without making visible at the same time the superior principle of the nature of man, the presence of a supersensuous faculty. It does this in virtue of the principle developed farther back, namely, that it is not suffering in itself, but only the resistance opposed to suffering, that is pathetic and deserving of being represented. It is for this reason that all the absolutely extreme degrees of the affections are forbidden to the artist as well as to the poet. All of these, in fact, oppress the force that resists from within; or rather, all betray of themselves, and without any necessity of other symptoms, the oppression of this force, because no affection can reach this last degree of intensity as long as the intelligence in man makes any resistance. . . .

We are now in a position to point out in what way the supersensuous element, the moral and independent force of man, his Ego in short, can be represented in the phenomena of the affections. I understand that this is possible if the parts which only obey physical nature, those where will either disposes nothing at all, or only under certain circumstances, betray the presence of suffering; and if those, on the contrary, that escape the blind sway of instinct, that only obey physical nature, show no trace, or only a very feeble trace, of suffering, and consequently appear to have a certain degree of freedom. Now this want of harmony between the features imprinted on animal nature in virtue of the laws of physical necessity, and those determined with the spiritual and independent faculty of man, is precisely the point by which that supersensuous principle is discovered in man capable of placing limits to the effects produced by physical nature, and therefore distinct from the latter. The purely animal part of man obeys the physical law, and consequently may show itself oppressed by the affection. It is, therefore, in this part that all the strength of passion shows itself, and it answers in some degree as a measure to estimate the resistance—that is to say, of the energy of the moral faculty in man—which can only be judged according to the force of the attack. Thus in proportion as the affection manifests itself with decision and violence in the field of *animal nature*, without being able to exercise the same power in the field of *human nature*, so in proportion the latter makes itself manifestly known—in the same proportion the moral independence of man shows itself gloriously: the portraiture becomes pathetic and the pathetic sublime. . . .

Thus there are two conditions in every kind of the pathetic: first, suffering, to interest our sensuous nature; second, moral liberty, to interest our spiritual nature. All portraiture in which the expression of suffering nature is wanting remains without esthetic action, and our heart is untouched. All portraiture in which the expression of moral aptitude is wanting, even did it possess all the sensuous force possible, could not attain to the pathetic, and would infallibly revolt our feelings. Throughout moral liberty we require the human being who suffers; throughout all the sufferings of human nature we always desire to perceive the independent spirit, or the capacity for independence.

But the independence of the spiritual being in the state of suffering can manifest itself in two ways. Either negatively, when the moral man does not receive the law from the physical man, and his state exercises no influence over his manner of feeling; or positively, when the moral man is a ruler over the physical being, and his manner of feeling exercises an influence upon his state. In the first case, it is the sublime of disposition; in the second, it is the sublime of action.

The sublime of disposition is seen in all character independent of the accidents of fate. "A noble heart struggling against adversity," says Seneca, "is a spectacle full of attraction even for the gods."[1] Such for example is that which the Roman Senate offered after the disaster of Cannae. Lucifer even, in Milton,[2] when for the first time he contemplates hell—which is to be his future abode—penetrates us with a sentiment of admiration by the force of soul he displays:

> Hail, horrors, hail.
> Infernal world, and thou, profoundest Hell;
> Receive thy new possessor!—one who brings
> A mind not to be changed by place or time;
> The mind is its own place, and in itself
> Can make a Heaven of Hell. . . .
>   Here at least
> We shall be free, etc.

The reply of Medea in the tragedy belongs also to this order of the sublime.

The sublime of disposition makes itself seen, it is visible to the spectator, because it rests upon coexistence, the simultaneous; the sublime action, on the contrary, is *conceived only by the thought*, because the impression and the act are successive, and the intervention of the mind is necessary to infer from a free determination the idea of previous suffering.

It follows that the first alone can be expressed by the plastic arts, because these arts give but that which is simultaneous; but the poet can extend his domain over one and the other. Even more; when the plastic art has to represent a sublime action, it must necessarily bring it back to sublimity.

In order that the sublimity of action should take place, not only must the suffering of man have no influence upon the moral constitution, but rather the opposite must be the case. The affection is the work of his moral character. This can happen in two ways: either mediately, or according to the law of liberty, when out of respect for such and such a duty it decides from free choice to suffer—in this case, the idea of duty determines as a motive, and its suffering is a voluntary act—or immediately, and according to the necessity of nature, when he expiates by a moral suffering the violation of duty; in this second case, the idea of duty determines him as a *force*, and his suffering is no longer an *effect*. Regulus offers us an example of the first kind, when, to keep his word, he gives himself up to the vengeance of the Carthaginians;[3]

---

[1] *De Providentia*, II, 9.

[2] *Paradise Lost.*

[3] Marcus Attilus Regulus, a Roman general and consul, was captured by the Carthaginians in 255 B.C. Released on his word, he was sent to Rome in 250 B.C. to negotiate peace. In Rome, he urged the Senate to refuse the Carthaginian demands and then, true to his word, he returned to Carthage, where he was tortured to death. Although the story may have been fabricated in order to justify Rome's harsh treatment of Carthaginian prisoners of war, it nevertheless made Regulus a model of heroic endurance.

and he would serve as an example of the second class, if, having betrayed his trust, the consciousness of this crime would have made him miserable. In both cases suffering has a moral course, but with this difference, that on the one part Regulus shows us its moral character, and that, on the other, he only shows us that he was made to have such a character. In the first case he is in our eyes a morally great person; in the second he is only esthetically great.

This last distinction is important for the tragic art; it consequently deserves to be examined more closely.

Man is already a sublime object, but only in the esthetic sense, when the *state* in which he is gives us an idea of his human destination, even though we might not find this destination realized in his *person*. He only becomes sublime to us in a moral point of view, when he acts, moreover, as a person, in a manner conformable with this destination; if our respect bears not only on his moral faculty, but on the use he makes of this faculty; if dignity, in his case, is due, not only to his moral aptitude, but to the real morality of his conduct. It is quite a different thing to direct our judgment and attention to the moral faculty generally, and to the possibility of a will absolutely free, and to be directing it to the use of this faculty, and to the reality of this absolute freedom of willing.

It is, I repeat, quite a different thing; and this difference is connected not only with the objects to which we may have to direct our judgment, but to the very criterion of our judgment. The same object can displease us if we appreciate it in a moral point of view, and be very attractive to us in the esthetic point of view. But even if the moral judgment and the esthetic judgment were both satisfied, this object would produce this effect on one and the other in quite a different way. It is not morally satisfactory because it has an esthetic value, nor has it an esthetic value because it satisfies us morally. . . .

. . . Now, underlying every moral judgment there is a requirement of reason which requires us to act conformably with the moral law, and it is an absolute necessity that we should wish what is good. But as the will is free, it is physically an accidental thing that we should do in fact what is good. If we actually do it, this agreement between the contingent in the use of free will and the imperative demand of reason gives rise to our assent or approbation, which will be greater in proportion as the resistance of the inclinations made this use that we make of our free will more accidental and more doubtful. Every esthetic judgment, on the contrary, refers the object to the necessity which cannot help willing imperatively, but only desires that there should be an agreement between the accidental and its own interest.

. . . Now what is the interest of imagination? It is to emancipate itself from all laws, and to play its part freely. The obligation imposed on the will by the moral law, which prescribes its object in the strictest manner, is by no means favorable to this need of independence. And as the moral obligation of the will is the object of the moral judgment, it is clear that in this mode of judging, the imagination could not find its interest. But a moral obligation imposed on the will cannot be conceived, except by supposing this same will absolutely independent of the moral instincts and from their constraint. Accordingly the *possibility* of the moral act requires liberty, and therefore agrees here in the most perfect manner with the interest of imagination. But as imagination, through the medium of its wants, cannot give orders to the will of the individual, as reason does by its imperative character, it follows that the faculty of freedom, in relation to imagination, is something accidental, and consequently that the agreement between the accidental and the necessary (conditionally necessary) must excite pleasure. . . . Thus an act of virtue judged by the moral sense—by reason—will give us as its only satisfaction the feeling of approbation, because reason can never find *more*, and seldom finds *as much* as it requires. This same act, judged, on the contrary, by the esthetic sense—by imagination—will give us a positive pleasure, because the imagination, never requiring the end to agree with the demand, must be surprised, enraptured, at the real satisfaction of this demand as at a happy chance. . . .

It results, therefore, from all that which precedes, that the moral judgment and the esthetic, far from mutually corroborating each other, impede and hinder each other, because they impress on the soul two directions entirely opposite. In fact, this observance of rule which reason requires of us as moral judge is incompatible with the independence which the imagination calls for as esthetic judge. It follows that an object will have so much the less esthetic value the more it has the character of a moral object, and if the poet were obliged notwithstanding that to choose it, he would do well in treating of it, not to call the attention of our reason to the rule of the will, but that of our imagination to the power of the will. In his own interest it is necessary for the poet to enter on this path, for with our liberty his empire finishes. We belong to him only inasmuch as we look beyond ourselves; we escape from him the moment we reenter into our innermost selves, and that is what infallibly takes place the moment an object ceases to be a phenomenon in our consideration, and takes the character of a law which judges us.

Even in the manifestation of the most sublime virtue, the poet can only employ for his own views that which in those acts belongs to force. As to the direction of the force, he has no reason to be anxious. The poet, even when he places before our eyes the most perfect models of morality, has not, and ought not to have, any other end than that of rejoicing our soul by the contemplation of this spectacle. Moreover, nothing can rejoice our soul except that which improves our personality, and nothing can give us a spiritual joy except that which elevates the spiritual faculty. But in what way can the morality of another improve our own personality, and raise our spiritual force? That this other one really accomplishes his duty results from an accidental use which he makes of his liberty, and which for that very reason can prove nothing to us. We only have in common with him the faculty to conform ourselves equally to duty; the moral power which he exhibits reminds us also of our own, and that is why we then feel something which upraises our spiritual force. Thus it is only the idea of the possibility of an absolutely free will which makes the real exercise of this will in us charming to the esthetic feeling. . . .

. . . It is no doubt a very honorable aim in a poet to moralize the man, and excite the patriotism of the citizen, and the Muses know better than anyone how well the arts of the sublime and of the beautiful are adapted to exercise this influence. But that which poetry obtains excellently by indirect means it would accomplish very badly as an immediate end. Poetry is not made to serve in man for the accomplishment of a particular matter, nor could any instrument be selected less fitted to cause a particular object to succeed, or to carry out special projects and details. Poetry acts on the whole of human nature, and it is only by its general influence on the character of a man that it can influence particular acts. Poetry can be for man what love is for the hero. It can neither counsel him, nor strike for him, nor do anything for him in short; but it can form a hero in him, call him to great deeds, and arm him with a strength to be all that he ought to be.

Thus the degree of esthetical energy with which sublime feelings and sublime acts take possession of our souls, does not rest at all on the interest of reason, which requires every action to be *really* conformable with the idea of good. But it rests on the interest of the imagination, which requires conformity with good should be possible, or, in other terms, that no feeling, however strong, should oppress the freedom of the soul. Now this possibility is found in every act that testifies with energy to liberty, and to the force of the will; and if the poet meets with an action of this kind, it matters little where, he has a subject suitable for his art. To *him*, and to the interest we have in him, it is quite the same, to take his hero in one class of characters or in another, among the good or the wicked, as it often requires as much strength of character to do evil conscientiously and persistently as to do good. If a proof be required that in our esthetic judgments we attend more to the force than to its direction, to its freedom than to its lawfulness, this is sufficient for our evidence. We prefer to see force and freedom manifest themselves at the cost of moral regularity, rather than regularity at the cost of freedom and strength. For directly one of those cases offers itself, in which the general law agrees with the instincts which by their strength threaten to carry away the will, the esthetic value of the character is increased, if he be capable of resisting these instincts. A vicious person begins to interest us as soon as he must risk his happiness and life to carry out his perverse designs; on the contrary, a virtuous person loses in proportion as he finds it useful to be virtuous. Vengeance, for instance, is certainly an ignoble and a vile affection, but this does not prevent it from becoming esthetic, if to satisfy it we must endure painful sacrifice. Medea slaying her children aims at the heart of Jason, but at the same time she strikes a heavy blow at her own heart, and her vengeance esthetically becomes sublime directly we see in her a tender mother.

In this sense the esthetic judgment has more of truth than is ordinarily believed. The vices which show a great force of will evidently announce a greater aptitude for real moral liberty than do virtues which borrow support from inclination; seeing that it only requires of the man who persistently does evil to gain a single victory over himself, one simple upset of his maxims, to gain ever after to the service of virtue his whole plan of life, and all the force of will which he lavished on evil. And why is it we receive with dislike medium characters, while we at times follow with trembling admiration one which is altogether wicked? It is evident, that with regard to the former, we renounce all hope, we cannot even conceive the possibility of finding absolute liberty of the will; while with the other, on the contrary, each time he displays his faculties, we feel that one single act of the will would suffice to raise him up to the fullest height of human dignity.

Thus, in the esthetic judgment, that which excites our interest is not morality itself, but liberty alone; and moral purity can only please our imagination when it places in relief the forces of the will. It is then manifestly to confound two very distinct orders of ideas, to require in esthetic things so exact a morality, and, in order to stretch the domain of reason, to exclude the imagination from its own legitimate sphere.

Either it would be necessary to subject it entirely, then there would be an end to all esthetic effect; or it would share the realm of reason, then morality would not gain much. For if we pretend to pursue at the same time two different ends, there would be risk of missing both one and the other. The liberty of the imagination would be fettered by too great respect for the moral law; and violence would be done to the character of *necessity* which is in the reason, in missing the *liberty* which belongs to the imagination.

Reflections on the Use
of the Vulgar and Low Elements
in Works of Art *1793*

I call *vulgar* (common) all that does not speak to the mind, of which all the interest is addressed only to the senses. There are, no doubt, an infinite number of things vulgar in themselves from their material and subject. But as the vulgarity of the material can always be ennobled by the treatment, in respect of art the only question is that relating to the *vulgarity* in form. A vulgar mind will dishonor the most noble matter by treating it in a common manner. A great and noble mind, on the contrary, will ennoble even a common matter, and it will do so by superadding to it something spiritual and discovering in it some aspect in which this matter has greatness. Thus, for example, a vulgar historian will relate to us the most insignificant actions of a hero with a scrupulousness as great as that bestowed on his sublimest exploit, and will dwell as lengthily on his pedigree, his costume, and his household as on his projects and his enterprises. He will relate those of his actions that have the most grandeur in such wise that no one will perceive that character in them. On the contrary, a historian of genius, himself endowed with nobleness of mind, will give even to the private life and the least considerable actions of his hero an interest and a value that will make them considerable. Thus, again, in the matter of the plastic arts, the Dutch and Flemish painters have given proof of a vulgar taste; the Italians, and still more the ancient Greeks, of a grand and noble taste. The Greeks always went to the ideal; they rejected every vulgar feature, and chose no common subject.

A portrait painter can represent his model in a *common* manner or with *grandeur*; in a *common manner* if he reproduce the merely *accidental* details with the same care as the essential features, if he neglect the great to carry out the minutiae curiously. He does it grandly if he know how to find out and place in relief what is most *interesting*, and distinguish the accidental from the necessary; if he be satisfied with indicating what is paltry, reserving all the finish of the execution for what is great. And the only thing that is great is the expression of the soul itself, manifesting itself by actions, gestures, or attitudes.

The poet treats his subject in a common manner when in the execution of his theme he dwells on valueless facts and only skims rapidly over those that are important. He treats his theme with grandeur when he associates with it what is great. For example, Homer treated the shield of Achilles

Selection. From Friedrich Schiller, *Complete Works*, Vol. VIII. Translator anonymous. New York: P. F. Collier & Son, 1902.

grandly, though the making of a shield, looking merely at the matter, is a very commonplace affair.

One degree below the common or the vulgar is the element of the base or gross, which differs from the common in being not only something *negative*, a simple lack of inspiration or nobleness, but something *positive*, marking coarse feelings, bad morals, and contemptible manners. Vulgarity only testifies that an advantage is wanting, whereof the absence is a matter of regret; baseness indicates the want of quality which we are authorized to require in all. Thus, for example, revenge, considered in itself, in *whatever place or way* it manifests itself, is something vulgar, because it is the proof of a lack of generosity. But there is, moreover, a *base* vengeance, when the man, to satisfy it, employs means exposed to contempt. The base always implies something gross, or reminds one of the mob, while the common can be found in a well-born and well-bred man, who may think and act in a common manner if he has only mediocre faculties. A man acts in a *common* manner when he is only taken up with his own interest, and it is in this that he is in opposition with the really *noble* man, who, when necessary, knows how to forget himself to procure some enjoyment for others. But the same man would act in a *base* manner if he consulted his interests at the cost of his honor, and if in such a case he did not even take upon himself to respect the laws of decency. Thus the common is only the contrary of the noble; the base is the contrary both of the noble and the seemly. To give yourself up, unresisting, to all your passions, to satisfy all your impulses, without being checked even by the rules of propriety, still less by those of morality, is to conduct yourself basely, and to betray baseness of the soul.

The artist also may fall into a low style, not only by choosing ignoble subjects, offensive to decency and good taste, but moreover by treating them in a *base manner*. It is to treat a subject in a *base manner* if those sides are made prominent which propriety directs us to conceal, or if it is expressed in a manner that incidentally awakens low ideas. The lives of the greater part of men can present particulars of a low kind, but it is only a low imagination that will pick out these for representation.

There are pictures describing sacred history in which the Apostles, the Virgin, and even the Christ, are depicted in such wise that they might be supposed to be taken from the dregs of the populace. This style of execution always betrays a low taste, and might justly lead to the inference that the artist himself thinks coarsely and like the mob.

No doubt there are cases where art itself may be allowed to produce base images: for example, when the aim is to provoke laughter. A man of polished manners may also sometimes, and without betraying a corrupt taste, be amused by certain features when nature expresses herself crudely but with truth, and he may enjoy the contrast between the manners of polished society and those of the lower orders. A man of position appearing intoxicated will

always make a disagreeable impression on us; but a drunken driver, sailor, or
carter will only be a risible object. Jests that would be insufferable in a man
of education amuse us in the mouth of the people. Of this kind are many of
the scenes of Aristophanes, who unhappily sometimes exceeds this limit, and
becomes absolutely condemnable. This is, moreover, the source of the pleasure.
we take in parodies, when the feelings, the language, and the mode of action
of the common people are fictitiously lent to the same personages whom the
poet has treated with all possible dignity and decency. As soon as the poet
means only to jest, and seeks only to amuse, we can overlook traits of a low
kind, provided he never stirs up indignation or disgust.

He stirs up indignation when he places baseness where it is quite unpardonable, that is in the case of men who are expected to show fine moral sense.
In attributing baseness to them he will either *outrage* truth, for we prefer to
think him a liar than to believe that well-trained men can act in a base manner; or his personages will offend our moral sense, and, what is worse, excite
our imagination. I do not mean by this to condemn *farces*; a farce implies
between the poet and the spectator a tacit consent that *no* truth is to be
expected in the piece. In a farce we exempt the poet from all *faithfulness* in
his pictures; he has a kind of privilege to tell us untruths. Here, in fact, all
the comic consists exactly in its contrast with the truth, and so it cannot
possibly be true.

This is not all: even in the serious and the tragic there are certain places
where the low element can be brought into play. But in this case the affair
must pass into the *terrible*, and the momentary violation of our good taste
must be masked by a strong impression, which brings our passion into play.
In other words, the low impression must be absorbed by a superior tragic
impression. *Theft*, for example, is a thing absolutely *base*, and whatever arguments our heart may suggest to excuse the thief, whatever the pressure of
circumstances that led him to the theft, it is always an indelible brand
stamped upon him, and, esthetically speaking, he will always remain a base
object. On this point taste is even less forgiving than morality, and its tribunal is more severe; because an esthetical object is responsible even for the
accessory ideas that are awakened in us by such an object, while moral judgment eliminates all that is merely accidental. According to this view a man
who robs would always be an object to be rejected by the poet who wishes
to present serious pictures. But suppose this man is at the same time a murderer, he is even more to be condemned than before by the *moral* law. But
in the esthetic judgment he is raised one degree higher and made better
adapted to figure in a work of art. Continuing to judge him from the esthetic
point of view, it may be added that he who abases himself by a *vile* action
can to a certain extent be raised by a *crime*, and can be thus reinstated in
our *esthetic* estimation. This contradiction between the moral judgment and
the esthetic judgment is a fact entitled to attention and consideration. It may

be explained in different ways. First, I have already said that, as the esthetic judgment depends on the imagination, all the accessory ideas awakened in us by an object and naturally associated with it must themselves influence this judgment. Now, if these accessory ideas are base, they infallibly stamp this character on the principal object.

In the second place, what we look for in the esthetic judgment is *strength*; while in a judgment pronounced in the name of the moral sense we consider *lawfulness*. The lack of strength is something contemptible, and every action from which it may be inferred that the agent lacks strength is, by that very fact, a contemptible action. Every cowardly and underhand action is repugnant to us, because it is a proof of impotence; and, on the contrary, a devilish wickedness can, esthetically speaking, flatter our taste, as soon as it marks strength. Now, a theft testifies to a vile and grovelling mind: a murder has at least on its side the appearance of strength; the interest we take in it esthetically is in proportion to the strength that is manifested in it.

A third reason is, because in presence of a deep and horrible crime we no longer think of the *quality* but the awful consequences of the action. The stronger emotion covers and stifles the weaker one. We do not look back into the mind of the agent; we look onward into his destiny, we think of the effects of his action. Now, directly we begin to *tremble* all the delicacies of taste are reduced to silence. The principal impression entirely fills our mind: the accessory and accidental ideas, in which chiefly dwell all impressions of baseness, are effaced from it.

On the Use of the Chorus in Tragedy *1803*

The assertion so commonly made, that the public degrades art, is not well founded. It is the artist that brings the public to the level of his own conceptions; and, in every age in which art has gone to decay, it has fallen through

Selections. From *Schiller's Works*, Vol. III, edited by J. G. Fischer. Philadelphia: George Barrie, 1883.

its professors. The people need feeling alone, and feeling they possess. They take their station before the curtain with an unvoiced longing, with a multifarious capacity. They bring with them an aptitude for what is highest—they derive the greatest pleasure from what is judicious and true; and if, with these powers of appreciation, they begin to be satisfied with inferior productions, still, if they have once tasted what is excellent, they will, in the end, insist on having it supplied to them.

It is sometimes objected that the poet may labor according to an ideal—that the critic may judge from ideas, but that mere executive art is subject to contingencies, and depends for effect on the occasion. Managers will be obstinate; actors are bent on display—the audience is inattentive and unruly. Their object is relaxation, and they are disappointed if mental exertion be required, when they expected only amusement. But if the theatre be made instrumental towards higher objects, the pleasure of the spectator will not be increased, but ennobled. It will be a diversion, but a poetical one. All art is dedicated to pleasure, and there can be no higher and worthier end than to make men happy. The true art is that which provides the highest degree of pleasure; and this consists in the abandonment of the spirit to the free play of all its faculties. . . .

Art has for its object not merely to afford a transient pleasure, to excite to a momentary dream of liberty; its aim is to make us absolutely free; and this it accomplishes by awakening, exercising, and perfecting in us a power to remove to an objective distance the sensible world (which otherwise only burdens us as rugged matter, and presses us down with a brute influence); to transform it into the free working of our spirit, and thus acquire a dominion over the material by means of ideas. For the very reason also that true art requires somewhat of the objective and real, it is not satisfied with a show of truth. It rears its ideal edifice on truth itself—on the solid and deep foundations of Nature.

But how art can be at once altogether ideal, yet in the strictest sense real, how it can entirely leave the actual, and yet harmonize with nature, is a problem to the multitude—and hence the distorted views which prevail in regard to poetical and plastic works; for to ordinary judgments these two requisites seem to counteract each other.

It is commonly supposed that one may be attained by the sacrifice of the other: the result is a failure to arrive at either. One to whom nature has given a true sensibility, but denied the plastic imaginative power, will be a faithful painter of the real; he will adapt casual appearances, but never catch the spirit of nature. He will only reproduce to us the matter of the world, which, not being our own work, the product of our creative spirit, can never have the beneficent operation of art, of which the essence is freedom. Serious, indeed, but unpleasing, is the cast of thought with which such an artist and poet dismisses us; we feel ourselves painfully thrust back into the narrow sphere of reality by means of the very art which ought to have emancipated us. On the other hand, a writer endowed with a lively fancy, but destitute of warmth and individuality of feeling, will not concern himself in the least about truth; he will sport with the stuff of the world, and endeavor to surprise by whimsical combinations; and as his whole performance is nothing but foam and glitter, he will, it is true, engage the attention for a time, but build up and confirm nothing in the understanding. His playfulness is, like the gravity of the other, thoroughly unpoetical. To string together at will fantastical images is not to travel into the realm of the ideal; and the imitative reproduction of the actual cannot be called the representation of nature. Both requisites stand so little in contradiction to each other that they are rather one and the same thing; that art is only true insomuch as it altogether forsakes the actual, and becomes purely ideal. Nature herself is an idea of the mind, and is never presented to the senses. She lies under the veil of appearances, but is herself never apparent. To the art of the ideal alone is lent, or rather, absolutely given, the privilege to grasp the spirit of the All, and bind it in a corporeal form.

Yet, in truth, even art cannot present it to the senses, but by means of her creative power to the imaginative faculty alone; and it is thus that she becomes more true than all reality, and more real than all experience. It follows from these premises that the artist can use no single element taken from reality as he finds it—that his work must be ideal in all its parts, if it be designed to have, as it were, an intrinsic reality, and to harmonize with nature.

What is true of art and poetry, in the abstract, holds good as to their various kinds; and we may apply what has been advanced to the subject of tragedy. In this department, it is still necessary to controvert the ordinary notion of the natural, with which poetry is altogether incompatible. A certain ideality has been allowed in painting, though I fear, rather for conventional reasons, than on grounds of conviction; but in dramatic works what is desired is illusion, which, if it could be accomplished by means of the actual, would be, at least, a paltry deception. All the externals of a theatrical representation are opposed to this notion; all is merely a symbol of the real. The day itself in a theatre is an artificial one; the metrical dialogue is itself ideal; yet the conduct of the play must forsooth be real, and the general effect sacrificed to a part. Thus the French, who have utterly misconceived the spirit of the ancients, adopted on their stage the unities of time and place in the most common and empirical sense; as though there were any place but the bare ideal one, or any other time than the mere sequence of the incidents. . . .

It is well known that the Greek tragedy had its origins in the Chorus; and though, in process of time, it became independent, still it may be said that poetically, and in spirit, the Chorus was the source of its existence, and that without these persevering supporters and witnesses of the incident a totally different order of poetry would have grown out of the drama. The abolition of the Chorus, and the debasement of this sensibly powerful organ into the characterless substitute of a confidant, is, by no means, such an improvement in tragedy as the French, and their imitators, would have it supposed to be.

The old tragedy, which at first only concerned itself with gods, heroes, and kings, introduced the Chorus as an essential accompaniment. The poets found it in nature, and for that reason employed it. It grew out of the poetical aspect of real life. In the new tragedy it becomes an organ of art which aids in making the poetry prominent. The modern poet no longer finds the Chorus in nature; he must needs create and introduce it poetically; that is, he must resolve on such an adaptation of his story as will admit of its retrocession to those primitive times, and to that simple form of life.

The Chorus thus renders more substantial service to the modern dramatist than to the old poet—and for this reason, that it transforms the commonplace actual world into the old poetical one; that it enables him to dispense with all that is repugnant to poetry, and conducts him back to the most simple, original, and genuine motives of action. . . .

This is what the Chorus effects in tragedy. It is, in itself, not an individual but a general conception, yet it is represented by a palpable body which appeals to the senses with an imposing grandeur. It forsakes the contracted sphere of the incidents to dilate itself over the past and the future, over distant times and nations, and general humanity, to deduce the grand results of life, and pronounces the lessons of wisdom. But all this it does with the full power of fancy—with a bold lyrical freedom which ascends, as with godlike step, to the topmost height of worldly things; and it effects it in conjunction with the whole sensible influence of melody and rhythm, in tones and movements.

The Chorus thus exercises a purifying influence on tragic poetry, insomuch as it keeps reflection apart from the incidents, and by this separation arms it with a poetical vigor; as the painter, by means of a rich drapery, changes the ordinary poverty of costume into a charm and an ornament.

But as the painter finds himself obliged to strengthen the tone of color of the living subject, in order to counterbalance the material influences—so the lyrical effusions of the Chorus impose upon the poet the necessity of a proportionate elevation of his general diction. It is the Chorus alone which entitles the poet to employ this fullness of tone, which at once charms the senses, pervades the spirit, and expands the mind. This one giant form on his canvas obliges him to mount all his figures on the cothurnus, and thus impart a tragical grandeur to his picture. If the Chorus be taken away, the diction of the tragedy must generally be lowered, or what is now great and majestic will appear forced and overstrained. The old Chorus introduced into the French tragedy would present it in all its poverty, and reduce it to nothing; yet, without doubt, the same accompaniment would impart to Shakespeare's tragedy its true significance.

As the Chorus gives life to the language—so also it gives repose to the action; but it is that beautiful and lofty repose which is the characteristic of a true work of art. For the mind of the spectator ought to maintain its freedom through the most impassioned scenes; it should not be the mere prey of impressions, but calmly and severely detach itself from the emotions which it suffers. The commonplace objection made to the Chorus, that it disturbs the illusion, and blunts the edge of the feelings, is what constitutes its highest recommendation; for it is this blind force of the affections which the true artist deprecates—this illusion is what he disdains to excite. If the strokes which tragedy inflicts on our bosoms followed without respite— the passion would overpower the action. We should mix ourselves up with the subject matter, and no longer stand above it. It is by holding asunder the different parts, and stepping between the passions with its composing views, that the Chorus restores to us our freedom, which would else be lost in the tempest. The characters of the drama need this intermission in order to collect themselves; for they are no real beings who obey the impulse of the moment, and merely represent individuals—but ideal persons and representatives of their species, who enunciate the deep things of humanity.

Thus much on my attempt to revive the old Chorus on the tragic stage. It is true that choruses are not unknown to modern tragedy; but the Chorus of the Greek drama, as I have employed it—the Chorus, as a single ideal person, furthering and accompanying the whole plot—is of an entirely distinct character; and when, in discussion on the Greek tragedy, I hear mention made of choruses, I generally suspect the speakers's ignorance of his subject. In my view the Chorus has never been reproduced since the decline of the old tragedy.

I have divided it into two parts, and represented it in contest with itself; but this occurs where it acts as a real person, and as an unthinking multitude. As Chorus and an ideal person it is always one and entire. I have also several times dispensed with its presence on the stage. For this liberty I have the example of Aeschylus, the creator of tragedy, and Sophocles, the greatest master of his art.

Johann Wolfgang von Goethe 1749–1832

Wilhelm Meister's Apprenticeship 1795

One evening a dispute arose among our friends about the novel and the drama, and which of them deserved the preference. Serlo said it was a fruitless and misunderstood debate; both might be superior in their kinds, only each must keep within the limits proper to it.

"About their limits and their kinds," said Wilhelm, "I confess myself not altogether clear."

"Who *is* so?" said the other; "and yet perhaps it were worth while to come a little closer to the business."

They conversed together long upon the matter; and in fine, the following was nearly the result of their discussion:

"In the novel as well as in the drama, it is human nature and human action that we see. The difference between these sorts of fiction lies not merely in the circumstance that the personages of the one are made to speak, while those of the other have commonly their history narrated. Unfortunately many dramas are but novels, which proceed by dialogue; and it would not be impossible to write a drama in the shape of letters.

"But in the novel it is chiefly *sentiments* and *events* that are exhibited; in the drama it is *characters* and *deeds*. The novel must go slowly forward; and the sentiments of the hero, by some means or another, must restrain the tendency of the whole to unfold itself and to conclude. The drama, on the other hand, must hasten, and the character of the hero must press forward to the end; it does not restrain, but is restrained. The novel hero must be suffering, at least he must not in a high degree be active; in the dramatic one we look for activity and deeds. Grandison, Clarissa, Pamela, the Vicar of Wakefield, Tom Jones himself, are, if not suffering, at least retarding personages; and the incidents are all in some sort modeled by their sentiments. In the drama the hero models nothing by himself; all things withstand him, and he clears and casts away the hindrances from off his path, or else sinks under them."

Our friends were also of opinion that in the novel some degree of scope may be allowed to Chance; but that it must always be led and guided by

Selection, translated by Thomas Carlyle, from Book V, Chapter 7. From Johann Wolfgang von Goethe, *Works*, Vol. IV. Philadelphia: G. Barrie, 1885.

the sentiments of the personages; on the other hand, that Fate, which, by means of outward unconnected circumstances, carries forward men, without their own concurrence, to an unforeseen catastrophe, can have place only in the drama; that Chance may produce pathetic situations, but never tragic ones; Fate, on the other hand, ought always to be terrible; and is in the highest sense tragic, when it brings into a ruinous concatenation the guilty man, and the guiltless that was unconcerned with him.

These considerations led them back to the play of Hamlet, and the pecularities of its composition. The hero in this case, it was observed, is endowed more properly with sentiments than with a character; it is events alone that push him on; and accordingly the piece has in some measure the expansion of a novel. But as it is Fate that draws the plan; as the story issues from a deed of terror, and the hero is continually driven forward to a deed of terror, the work is tragic in the highest sense, and admits of no other than a tragic end.

On Truth and Probability in Works of Art *1798*

In a certain German theatre, there was represented a sort of oval amphitheatrical structure, with boxes filled with painted spectators, seemingly occupied with what was transacting below. Many of the real spectators in the pit and boxes were dissatisfied with this, and took it amiss that anything so untrue and improbable was put upon them. Whereupon the conversation took place, of which we here give the general purport.

THE FRIEND OF THE ARTIST Let us see if we cannot by some means agree more nearly.

THE SPECTATOR I do not see how such a representation can be defended.

FRIEND Tell me, when you go into a theatre, do you not expect all you see to be true and real?

SPECTATOR By no means! I only ask that what I see shall appear true and real.

From Johann Wolfgang von Goethe, *Essays on Art*, translated by Simon Gray Ward. Boston: James Munroe & Co., 1845.

FRIEND Pardon me if I contradict even your inmost conviction, and maintain this is by no means the thing you demand.

SPECTATOR That is singular! If I did not make this requisition, why should' the scene painter take so much pains to draw each line in the most perfect manner, according to the rules of perspective, and represent every object in the most perfect keeping? Why waste so much study on the costume? Why spend so much to ensure its truth, so that I may be carried back into those times? Why is that player most highly praised, who most truly expresses the sentiment, who in speech, gesture, delivery, comes nearest the truth, who persuades me that I behold, not an imitation, but the thing itself?

FRIEND You express your feelings admirably well, but it is harder than you may think to have a right comprehension of our feelings. What should you say, if I reply, that theatrical representations by no means seem really true to you, but rather to have only an appearance of truth?

SPECTATOR I should say that you advanced a subtlety that was little more than a play upon words.

FRIEND And I uphold, that when we are speaking of the operations of the soul, no words can be delicate and subtle enough; and that this sort of play upon words indicates a need of the soul, which, not being able adequately to express what passes within us, seeks to work by way of antithesis, to give an answer to each side of the question, and thus, as it were, find the thing between them.

SPECTATOR Very good. Only explain yourself more fully, and, if you will oblige me, by examples.

FRIEND I shall be glad to avail myself of them. For instance, when you are at an opera, do you not experience a lively and complete satisfaction?

SPECTATOR Yes, when everything is in harmony, one of the most complete I know.

FRIEND But when the good people there meet and compliment each other with a song, sing off billets that they hold in their hands, sing you their love, their hatred, and all their passions, fight singing, and die singing, can you say that the whole representation, or even any part of it, is true? or, I may say, has even an appearance of truth?

SPECTATOR In fact, when I consider, I could not say it had. None of these things seem true.

FRIEND And yet you are completely pleased and satisfied with the exhibition?

SPECTATOR Beyond question. I still remember how the opera used to be ridiculed on account of this gross improbability, and how I always received the greatest satisfaction from it, in spite of this, and find more and more pleasure the richer and more complete it becomes.

FRIEND And you do not then at the opera experience a complete deception?

SPECTATOR   Deception, that is not the proper word—and yet, yes!—But no——

FRIEND   Here you are in a complete contradiction, which is far worse than a quibble.

SPECTATOR   Let us proceed quietly; we shall soon see light.

FRIEND   As soon as we come into the light, we shall agree. Having reached this point, will you allow me to ask you some questions?

SPECTATOR   It is your duty, having questioned me into this dilemma, to question me out again.

FRIEND   The feeling you have at the exhibition of an opera, cannot be called deception?

SPECTATOR   I agree. Still it is a sort of deception; something nearly allied to it.

FRIEND   Tell me, do you not almost forget yourself?

SPECTATOR   Not almost, but quite, when the whole or some part is excellent.

FRIEND   You are enchanted?

SPECTATOR   It has happened more than once.

FRIEND   Can you explain under what circumstances?

SPECTATOR   Under so many, it would be hard to tell.

FRIEND   Yet you have already told when it is most apt to happen, viz., when all is in harmony.

SPECTATOR   Undoubtedly.

FRIEND   Did this complete representation harmonize with itself, or some other natural product?

SPECTATOR   With itself, certainly.

FRIEND   And this harmony was a work of art?

SPECTATOR   It must have been.

FRIEND   We have denied to the opera the possession of a certain sort of truth. We have maintained that it is by no means faithful to what it professes to represent. But can we deny to it a certain interior truth, which arises from its completeness as a work of art?

SPECTATOR   When the opera is good, it creates a little world of its own, in which all proceeds according to fixed laws, which must be judged by its own laws, felt according to its own spirit.

FRIEND   Does it not follow from this that truth of nature and truth of art are two distinct things, and that the artist neither should nor may endeavor to give his work the air of a work of nature?

SPECTATOR   But yet it has so often the air of a work of nature.

FRIEND   That I cannot deny. But may I on the other hand be equally frank?

SPECTATOR   Why not? Our business is not now with compliments.

FRIEND   I will then venture to affirm that a work of art can seem to be a work of nature only to a wholly uncultivated spectator; such a one the artist appreciates and values indeed, though he stands on the lowest step. But, unfortunately, he can only be satisfied when the artist descends to his level; he will never rise with him, when, prompted by his genius, the true artist must take wing, in order to complete the whole circle of his work.

SPECTATOR   Your remark is curious; but proceed.

FRIEND   You would not let it pass unless you had yourself attained a higher step.

SPECTATOR   Let me now make trial, and take the place of questioner, in order to arrange and advance our subject.

FRIEND   I shall like that better still.

SPECTATOR   You say that a work of art could appear as a work of nature only to an uncultivated person?

FRIEND   Certainly. You remember the birds that tried to eat the painted cherries of the great master?

SPECTATOR   Now, does not that show that the cherries were admirably painted?

FRIEND   By no means. It rather convinces me that these connoisseurs were true sparrows.

SPECTATOR   I cannot, however, for this reason, concede that this work could have been other than excellent.

FRIEND   Shall I tell you a more modern story.

SPECTATOR   I would rather listen to stories than arguments.

FRIEND   A certain great naturalist, among other animals, possessed an ape, which, missing one day he found after a long search in the library. There sat the beast on the ground, with the plates of an unbound work of Natural History scattered about him. Astonished at this zealous fit of study on the part of his familiar, the gentleman approached, and found, to his wonder and vexation, that the dainty ape had been making his dinner of the beetles that were pictured in various places.

SPECTATOR   It is a droll story.

FRIEND   And seasonable, I hope. You would not compare these colored copperplates with the work of so great an artist?

SPECTATOR   No, indeed.

FRIEND   But you would reckon the ape among the uncultivated amateurs?

SPECTATOR   Yes, and among the greedy ones! You awaken in me a singular idea. Does not the uncultivated amateur, just in the same way, desire a work to be natural, that he may be able to enjoy it in a natural, which is often a vulgar and common way?

FRIEND   I am entirely of that opinion.

SPECTATOR   And you maintain, therefore, that an artist lowers himself when he tries to produce this effect?

FRIEND   Such is my firm conviction.

SPECTATOR   But here again I feel a contradiction. You did me just now the honor to number me, at lowest, among the half-instructed spectators.

FRIEND   Among those who are on the way to become true connoisseurs.

SPECTATOR   Then explain to me, Why does a perfect work of art appear like a work of nature to me also?

FRIEND   Because it harmonizes with your better nature. Because it is above natural, yet not unnatural. A perfect work of art is a work of the human soul, and in this sense, also, a work of nature. But because it collects together the scattered objects, of which it displays even the most minute in all their significance and value, it is above nature. It will be comprehensible by a mind that is harmoniously formed and developed, and such a one, in proportion to its depth, discovers that which is perfect and completes in itself. The common spectator, on the contrary, has no idea of it; he treats a work of art as he would any object he meets with in the market. But the true connoisseur sees not only the truth of the imitation, but also the excellence of the selection, the refinement of the composition, the superiority of the little world of art; he feels that he must rise to the level of the artist, in order to enjoy his work; he feels that he must collect himself out of his scattered life, must live with the work of art, see it again and again, and through it receive a higher existence.

SPECTATOR   Well said, my friend. I have often made similar reflections upon pictures, the drama, and other species of poetry, and had an instinct of those things you require. I will in future give more heed, both to myself and to works of art. But if I am not mistaken, we have left the subject of our dispute quite behind. You would have persuaded me that I was to find these painted spectators at our opera admissible, and I do not yet see, though we have come to an agreement, by what arguments you mean to support this license, and under what rubric I am to admit these painted lookers-on.

FRIEND   Fortunately, the opera is repeated tonight; I trust you will not miss it.

SPECTATOR   On no account.

FRIEND   And the painted men?

SPECTATOR   Shall not alarm me, for I think myself something more than a sparrow.

FRIEND   I hope that a mutual interest may bring us together again.

Conversations of Goethe
with Eckermann and Soret[1] *1823–1830*

November 14, 1823 "I cannot but think that Schiller's turn for philosophy injured his poetry, because this led him to consider the idea far higher than all nature; indeed, thus to annihilate nature. What he could conceive must happen, whether it were in conformity with nature or not.

"It was sad," said Goethe, "to see how so highly gifted a man tormented himself with philosophical disquisitions which could in no way profit him. . . .

"It was not Schiller's plan," continued Goethe, "to go to work with a certain unconsciousness, and as it were instinctively; he was forced, on the contrary, to reflect on all he did. Hence it was that he never could leave off talking about his poetical projects, and thus he discussed with me all his late pieces, scene after scene.

"On the other hand, it was contrary to my nature to talk over my poetic plans with anybody—even with Schiller. I carried everything about with me in silence, and usually nothing was known to any one till the whole was completed."

March 30, 1824 This evening I was with Goethe. I was alone with him; we talked on various subjects, and drank a bottle of wine. We spoke of the French drama, as contrasted with the German.

"It will be very difficult," said Goethe, "for the German public to come to a kind of right judgment, as they do in Italy and France. We have a special obstacle in the circumstance, that on our stage a medley of all sorts of things is represented. On the same boards where we saw Hamlet yesterday, we see Staberle[2] today; and if tomorrow we are delighted with *Zauberflöte*,[3] the day after we shall be charmed with the oddities of the next lucky wight. Hence the public becomes confused in its judgment, mingling together various species, which it never learns rightly to appreciate and to understand. Furthermore, every one has his own individual demands and personal wishes, and returns to the spot where he finds them realized. On the tree where he has plucked figs today, he would pluck them again tomorrow,

Selections. From *Conversations of Goethe with Eckermann and Soret*, translated by John Oxenford. London: George Bell & Co., 1883.

[1] Johann Peter Eckermann (1791–1854) and Frédéric Jacob Soret (1795–1865). Unless otherwise indicated, the conversations are with Eckermann.

[2] A Viennese buffoon [translator's note].

[3] *The Magic Flute* (1791) by Mozart.

and would make a long face if sloes had grown in their stead during the night. If anyone is a friend to sloes, he goes to the thorns.

"Schiller had the happy thought of building a house for tragedy alone, and of giving a piece every week for the male sex exclusively. But this notion presupposed a very large city, and could not be realized with our humble means."

We talked about the plays of Iffland[4] and Kotzebue,[5] which, in their way, Goethe highly commended. "From this very fault," said he, "that people do not perfectly distinguish between *kinds* in art, the pieces of these men are often unjustly censured. We may wait a long time before a couple of such popular talents come again."

I praised Iffland's *Hagestolz* (*Old Bachelor*),[6] with which I had been highly pleased on the stage. "It is unquestionably Iffland's best piece," said Goethe; "it is the only one in which he goes from prose into the ideal."

He then told me of a piece, which he and Schiller had made as a continuation to the *Hagestolz*; that is to say, in conversation, without writing it down. Goethe told me the progress of the action, scene by scene; it was very pleasant and cheerful, and gave me great delight.

Goethe then spoke of some new plays by Platen.[7] "In these pieces," said he, "we may see the influence of Calderon.[8] They are very clever, and, in a certain sense, complete; but they want specific gravity, a certain weight of import. They are not of a kind to excite in the mind of the reader a deep and abiding interest; on the contrary, the strings of the soul are touched but lightly and transiently. They are like cork, which, when it swims on the water, makes no impression, but is easily sustained by the surface.

"The German requires a certain earnestness, a certain grandeur of thought, and a certain fulness of sentiment. It is on this account that Schiller is so highly esteemed by them all. I do not in the least doubt the abilities of Platen; but those, probably from mistaken views of art, are not manifested here. He shows distinguished culture, intellect, pungent wit, and artistical completness; but these, especially in Germany, are not enough."

February 24, 1825 "If I were still superintendent of the theatre," said Goethe, this evening, "I would bring out Byron's *Doge of Venice*.[9] The piece is indeed long, and would require shortening. Nothing, however, should be cut out, but the import of each scene should be taken, and expressed more

---

[4] August Wilhelm Iffland (1759–1814).
[5] August von Kotzebue (1761–1819).
[6] (1793).
[7] August Grav von Platen (1796–1835).
[8] Calderon de la Barca (1600–1681).
[9] *Marino Faliero, Doge of Venice* (1821), by George Gordon, Lord Byron (1788–1824).

concisely. The piece would thus be brought closer together, without being damaged by alterations, and it would gain a powerful effect, without any essential loss of beauty."

This opinion of Goethe's gave me a new view as to how we might proceed on the stage, in a hundred similar cases, and I was highly pleased with such a maxim, which, however, presupposes a fine intellect—nay, a poet, who understands his vocation.

We talked more about Lord Byron, and I mentioned how, in his conversations with Medwin, he had said there was something extremely difficult and unthankful in writing for the theatre. "The great point is," said Goethe, "for the poet to strike into the path which the taste and interest of the public have taken. If the direction of his talent accords with that of the public, everything is gained. . . . [Lord Byron's] tendency varied from that of the public. The greatness of the poet is by no means the important matter. On the contrary, one who is little elevated above the general public may often gain the most general favor precisely on that account."

We continued to converse about Byron, and Goethe admired his extraordinary talent. "That which I call invention," said he, "I never saw in anyone in the world to a greater degree than in him. His manner of loosing a dramatic knot is always better than one would anticipate."

"That," said I, "is what I feel about Shakespeare, especially when Falstaff has entangled himself in such a net of falsehoods, and I ask myself what I should do to help him out; for I find that Shakespeare surpasses all my notions. That you say the same of Lord Byron is the highest praise that can be bestowed on him. Nevertheless," I added, "the poet who takes a clear survey of beginning and end, has, by far, the advantage with the biased reader."

Goethe agreed with me, and laughed to think that Lord Byron, who, in practical life, could never adapt himself, and never even asked about a law, finally subjected himself to the stupidest of laws—that of the *three unities*.

"He understood the purpose of this law," said he, "no better than the rest of the world. *Comprehensibility* is the purpose, and the three unities are only so far good as they conduce to this end. If the observance of them hinders the comprehension of a work, it is foolish to treat them as laws, and to try to observe them. Even the Greeks, from whom the rule was taken, did not always follow it. In the *Phaeton* of Euripides, and in other pieces, there is a change of place, and it is obvious that good representation of their subject was with them more important than blind obedience to law, which, in itself, is of no great consequence. The pieces of Shakespeare deviate, as far as possible, from the unities of time and place; but they are comprehensible—nothing more so—and on this account, the Greeks would have found no fault in them. The French poets have endeavored to follow most rigidly the laws of the three unities, but they sin against comprehensibility, inasmuch as they solve a dramatic law, not dramatically, but by narration."

"I call to mind the *Feinde* (*Enemies*) of Houwald.[10] The author of this drama stood much in his own light, when, to preserve the unity of place, he sinned against comprehensibility in the first act, and altogether sacrificed what might have given greater effect to his piece to a whim, for which no one thanks him. I thought, too, on the other hand, of *Götz von Berlichingen*,[11] which deviates as far as possible from the unity of time and place; but which, as everything is visibly developed to us, and brought before our eyes, is as truly dramatic and comprehensible as any piece in the world. I thought, too, that the unities of time and place were natural, and in accordance with the intention of the Greeks, only when a subject is so limited in its range that it can develop itself before our eyes with all its details in the given time; but that with a large action, which occurs in several places, there is no reason to be confined to one place, especially as our present stage arrangements offer no obstacle to a change of scene."

July 26, 1826 I told him that one of my friends intended to arrange Lord Byron's *Two Foscari*[12] for the stage. Goethe doubted his success.

"It is indeed a temptation," he said. "When a piece makes a deep impression on us in reading, we think it will do the same on the stage, and that we could obtain such a result with little trouble. But this is by no means the case. A piece that is not originally, by the intent and skill of the poet, written for the boards, will not succeed; but whatever is done to it, will always remain something unmanageable. What trouble have I taken with my *Götz von Berlichingen*! yet it will not go right as an acting play, but is too long; and I have been forced to divide it into two parts, of which the last is indeed theatrically effective, while the first is to be looked upon as a mere introduction. If the first part were given only once as an introduction, and then the second repeatedly, it might succeed. It is the same with *Wallenstein*:[13] *The Piccolomini* does not bear repetition, but *Wallenstein's Death* is always seen with delight."

I asked how a piece must be constructed so as to be fit for the theatre.

"It must be symbolical," replied Goethe; "that is to say, each incident must be significant in itself, and lead to another still more important. The *Tartuffe*[14] of Molière is, in this respect, a great example. Only think what an introduction is the first scene! From the very beginning everything is

---

[10] *Enemies* (1825) by Christoph Ernst Freiherr von Houwald (1778–1845).
[11] (1773) by Goethe.
[12] (1821).
[13] Trilogy by Schiller: *Wallenstein's Camp* (1798), *The Piccolomini* (1799), and *Wallenstein's Death* (1799).
[14] (1669).

highly significant, and leads us to expect something still more important which is to come. The beginning of Lessing's *Minna von Barnhelm*[15] is also admirable; but that of the *Tartuffe* comes only once into the world: it is the greatest and best thing that exists of the kind."

January 31, 1827 ". . . No poet has ever known the historical characters which he has painted; if he had, he could scarcely have made use of them. The poet must know what effects he wishes to produce, and regulate the nature of his characters accordingly. If I had tried to make Egmont as history represents him, the father of a dozen children, his light-minded proceedings would have appeared very absurd. I needed an Egmont more in harmony with his own actions and my poetic views; and this is, as Clara says, *my* Egmont.[16]

"What would be the use of poets, if they only repeated the record of the historian? The poet must go further, and give us, if possible, something higher and better. All the characters of Sophocles bear something of that great poet's lofty soul; and it is the same with the characters of Shakespeare. This is as it ought to be. Nay, Shakespeare goes farther, and makes his Romans Englishmen; and there, too, he is right; for otherwise his nation would not have understood him.

"Here, again," continued Goethe, "the Greeks were so great, that they regarded fidelity to historic facts less than the treatment of them by the poet."

March 28, 1827 [Soret] ". . . But, to speak frankly, I am sorry that a man of undoubted innate power from the northern coast of Germany, like Hinrichs,[17] should be so spoilt by the philosophy of Hegel as to lose all unbiased and natural observation and thought, and gradually to get into an artificial and heavy style, both of thought and expression; so that we find passages in his book where our understanding comes to a standstill, and we no longer know what we are reading. . . .

"I think we have had enough of this. What must the English and French think of the language of our philosophers, when we Germans do not understand them ourselves." "And in spite of all this," said I, "we both agree that a noble purpose lies at the foundation of the book, and that it possesses the quality of awakening thoughts."

"His idea of the relation between family and state," said Goethe, "and the tragical conflicts that may arise from them, is certainly good and suggestive; still I cannot allow that it is the only right one, or even the best for tragic art. We are indeed all members both of a family and of a state, and

---

[15] (1767).
[16] Clara and Egmont are characters in Goethe's play *Egmont* (1787).
[17] Hermann Friedrich Wilhelm Hinrichs (1794–1861).

a tragical fate does not often befall us which does not wound us in both capacities. Still we might be very good tragical characters, if we were merely members of a family or merely members of a state; for, after all, the only point is to get a conflict which admits of no solution, and this may arise from an antagonistical position in any relation whatever, provided a person has a really natural foundation, and is himself really tragic. Thus Ajax falls a victim to the demon of wounded honor, and Hercules to the demon of jealousy. In neither of these cases is there the least conflict between family piety and political virtue; though this, according to Hinrichs, should be the element of Greek tragedy."

"One sees clearly," says I, "that in this theory he merely had *Antigone*[18] in his mind. He also appears to have had before his eyes merely the character and mode of action of this heroine, as he makes the assertion that family piety appears most pure in woman, and especially in a sister; and that a sister can love only a brother with perfect purity, and without sexual feeling."

"I should think," returned Goethe, "that the love of sister for sister was still more pure and unsexual. As if we did not know that numerous cases have occurred in which the most sensual inclinations have existed between brother and sister, both knowingly and unknowingly!

"You must have remarked generally," continued Goethe, that Hinrichs, in considering Greek tragedy, sets out from the *idea*; and that he looks upon Sophocles as one who, in the invention and arrangement of his pieces, likewise set out from an idea, and regulated the sex and rank of his characters accordingly. But Sophocles, when he wrote his pieces, by no means started from an *idea*; on the contrary, he seized upon some ancient ready-made popular tradition in which a good idea existed, and then only thought of adapting it in the best and most effective manner for the theatre. The Atreides will not allow Ajax to be buried; but as in *Antigone* the sister struggles for the brother, so in the *Ajax*[19] the brother struggles for the brother. That the sister takes charge of the unburied Polynices, and the brother takes charge of the fallen Ajax, is a contingent circumstance, and does not belong to the invention of the poet, but to the tradition, which the poet followed and was obliged to follow."

"What he says about Creon's conduct," replied I, "appears to be equally untenable. He tries to prove that, in prohibiting the burial of Polynices, Creon acts from pure political virtue; and since Creon is not merely a man, but also a prince, he lays down the proposition, that, as a man represents the tragic power of the state, this man can be no other than he who is himself the personification of the state itself—namely, the prince; and that

[18] (*c.* 442 B.C.).
[19] (*c.* 442 B.C.).

of all persons the man as prince must be just that person who displays the greatest political virtue."

"These are assertions which no one will believe," returned Goethe with a smile. "Besides, Creon by no means acts out of political virtue, but from hatred towards the dead. When Polynices endeavored to reconquer his paternal inheritance, from which he had been forcibly expelled, he did not commit such a monstrous crime against the state that his death was insufficient, and that the further punishment of the innocent corpse was required.

"An action should never be placed in the category of political virtue which is opposed to virtue in general. When Creon forbids the burial of Polynices, and not only taints the air with the decaying corpse, but also affords an opportunity for the dogs and birds of prey to drag about pieces torn from the dead body, and thus to defile the altars—an action so offensive both to gods and men is by no means politically virtuous, but on the contrary a political crime. Besides, he has everybody in the play against him. He has the elders of the state, who form the chorus, against him; he has the people at large against him; he has Teiresias against him; he has his own family against him; but he hears not, and obstinately persists in his impiety, until he has brought to ruin all who belong to him, and is himself at last nothing but a shadow."

"And still," said I, "when one hears him speak, one cannot help believing that he is somewhat in the right."

"That is the very thing," said Goethe, "in which Sophocles is a master; and in which consists the very life of the dramatic in general. His characters all possess this gift of eloquence, and know how to explain the motives for their action so convincingly that the hearer is almost always on the side of the last speaker.

"One can see that, in his youth, he enjoyed an excellent rhetorical education, by which he became trained to look for all the reasons and seeming reasons of things. Still, his great talent in this respect betrayed him into faults, as he sometimes went too far.

"There is a passage in Antigone which I always look upon as a blemish, and I would give a great deal for an apt philologist to prove that it is interpolated and spurious.

"After the heroine has, in the course of the piece, explained the noble motives for her action, and displayed the elevated purity of her soul, she at last, when she is led to death, brings forward a motive which is quite unworthy, and almost borders upon the comic.

"She says that, if she had been a mother, she would not have done, either for her dead children or for her dead husband, what she has done for her brother. 'For,' says she, 'if my husband died I could have had another, and if my children died I could have had others by my new husband. But with my brother the case is different. I cannot have another brother; for since my mother and father are dead, there is no one to beget one.'

"This is, at least, the bare sense of this passage, which in my opinion, when placed in the mouth of a heroine going to her death, disturbs the tragic tone, and appears to me very far-fetched—to savor too much of dialectical calculation. As I said, I should like a philologist to show us that the passage is spurious."

We then conversed further upon Sophocles, remarking that in his pieces he always less considered a moral tendency than an apt treatment of the subject in hand, particularly with regard to theatrical effect.

"I do not object," said Goethe, "to a dramatic poet having a moral influence in view; but when the point is to bring his subject clearly and effectively before his audience, his moral purpose proves of little use, and he needs much more a faculty for delineation and a familiarity with the stage to know what to do and what to leave undone. If there be a moral in the subject, it will appear, and the poet has nothing to consider but the effective and artistic treatment of his subject. If a poet has as high a soul as Sophocles, his influence will always be moral, let him do what he will. Besides, he knew the stage, and understood his craft thoroughly."

"How well he knew the theatre," answered I, "and how much he had in view a theatrical effect, we see in his *Philoctetes*,[20] and the great resemblance which this piece bears to *Oedipus in Colonos*,[21] both in the arrangement and the course of action.

"In both pieces we see the hero in a helpless condition; both are old and suffering from bodily infirmities. Oedipus has, at his side, his daughter as a guide and a prop; Philoctetes has his bow. The resemblance is carried still further. Both have been thrust aside in their afflictions; but when the oracle declares with respect to both of them that the victory can be obtained with their aid alone, an endeavor is made to get them back again; Ulysses comes to Philoctetes, Creon to Oedipus. Both begin their discourse with cunning and honeyed words; but when these are of no avail they use violence, and we see Philoctetes deprived of his bow, and Oedipus of his daughter."

"Such acts of violence," said Goethe, "give an opportunity for excellent altercations, and such situations of helplessness excited the emotions of the audience, on which account the poet, whose object it was to produce an effect upon the public, liked to introduce them. In order to strengthen this effect in the Oedipus, Sophocles brings him in as a weak old man, when he still, according to all circumstances, must have been a man in the prime

[20] (409 B.C.).
[21] (402 B.C.).

of life. But at this vigorous age, the poet could not have used him for his play; he would have produced no effect, and he therefore made him a weak, helpless old man."

"The resemblance to Philoctetes," continued I, "goes still further. The hero, in both pieces, does not act, but suffers. On the other hand, each of these passive heroes has two active characters against him. Oedipus has Creon and Polynices, Philoctetes has Neoptolemus and Ulysses; two such opposing characters were necessary to discuss the subject on all sides, and to gain the necessary body and fulness for the piece."

"You might add," interposed Goethe, "that both pieces bear this further resemblance, that we see in both the extremely effective situation of a happy change, since one hero, in his disconsolate situation, has his beloved daughter restored to him, and the other, his no less beloved bow.

"The happy conclusions of these two pieces are also similar; for both heroes are delivered from their sorrows: Oedipus is blissfully snatched away, and as for Philoctetes, we are forewarned by the oracle of his cure, before Troy, by Aesculapius.

"When we," continued Goethe, "for our modern purposes, wish to learn how to conduct ourselves upon the theatre, Molière is the man to whom we should apply.

"Do you know his *Malade Imaginaire*?[22] There is a scene in it which, as often as I read the piece, appears to me the symbol of a perfect knowledge of the boards. I mean the scene where the Malade Imaginaire asks his little daughter Louison, if there has not been a young man in the chamber of her eldest sister.

"Now, any other who did not understand his craft so well would have let the little Louison plainly tell the fact at once, and there would have been the end of the matter.

"But what various motives for delay are introduced by Molière into this examination, for the sake of life and effect. He first makes the little Louison act as if she did not understand her father; then she denies that she knows anything; then, threatened with the rod, she falls down as if dead; then, when her father bursts out in despair, she springs up from her feigned swoon with roguish hilarity, and at last, little by little, she confesses all.

"My explanation can only give you a very meager notion of the animation of the scene; but read this scene yourself till you become thoroughly impressed with its theatrical worth, and you will confess that there is more practical instruction contained in it than in all the theories in the world.

"I have known and loved Molière," continued Goethe, "from my youth, and have learned from him during my whole life. I never fail to read some of his plays every year, that I may keep up a constant intercourse with what

[22] *The Imaginary Invalid* (1673).

is excellent. It is not merely the perfect artistic treatment which delights me; but particularly the amiable nature, the highly formed mind, of the poet. There is in him a grace and a feeling for the decorous, and a tone of good society, which his innate beautiful nature could only attain by daily intercourse with the most eminent men of his age. . . .

"To a man like Schlegel," returned Goethe, "a genuine nature like Molière's is a veritable eyesore; he feels that he has nothing in common with him, he cannot endure him. . . . Schlegel cannot forgive Molière for ridiculing the affection of learned ladies;[23] he feels, probably as one of my friends has remarked, that he himself would have been ridiculed if he had lived with Molière.

"It is not to be denied," continued Goethe, "that Schlegel knows a great deal, and one is almost terrified at his extraordinary attainments and his extensive reading. But this is not enough. All the learning in the world is still no judgment. His criticism is completely one-sided, because in all theatrical pieces he merely regards the skeleton of the plot and arrangement, and only points out small points of resemblance to great predecessors, without troubling himself in the least as to what the author brings forward of graceful life and the culture of a high soul. But of what use are all the arts of a talent, if we do not find in a theatrical piece an amiable or great personality of the author. This alone influences the cultivation of the people."

April 2, 1829 We then came to the newest French poets, and the meaning of the terms "classic" and "romantic."

"A new expression occurs to me," said Goethe, "which does not ill define the state of the case. I call the classic *healthy*, the romantic *sickly*. . . . Most modern productions are romantic, not because they are new, but because they are weak, morbid, and sickly; and the antique is classic, not because it is old, but because it is strong, fresh, joyous, and healthy. If we distinguish 'classic' and 'romantic' by these qualities, it will be easy to see our way clearly."

March 14, 1830 [Soret] The conversation then returned to the French literature, and the modern ultraromantic tendency of some not unimportant talents. Goethe was of opinion that this poetic revolution, which was still in its infancy, would be very favorable to literature, but very prejudicial to the individual authors who effect it.

"Extremes are never to be avoided in any revolution," said he. "In a political one, nothing is generally desired in the beginning but the abolition of abuses; but before people are aware, they are deep in bloodshed and horror. Thus the French, in their present literary revolution, desired nothing

23 *Les Femmes savantes* (1672).

at first but a freer form; however, they will not stop there, but will reject the traditional contents together with the form. They begin to declare the representation of noble sentiments and deeds as tedious, and attempt to treat of all sorts of abominations. Instead of the beautiful subjects from Grecian mythology, there are devils, witches, and vampires, and the lofty heroes of antiquity must give place to jugglers and galley slaves. This is piquant! This is effective! But after the public has once tasted this highly seasoned food, and has become accustomed to it, it will always long for more, and that stronger. A young man of talent, who would produce an effect and be acknowledged, and who is great enough to go his own way, must accommodate himself to the taste of the day—nay, must seek to outdo his predecessors in the horrible and frightful. But in this chase after outward means of effect, all profound study, and all gradual and thorough development of the talent and the man from within, is entirely neglected. And this is the greatest injury which can befall a talent, although literature in general will gain by this tendency of the moment."

"But," added I, "how can an attempt which destroys individual talents be favorable to literature in general?"

"The extremes and excrescences which I have described," returned Goethe, "will gradually disappear; but at last this great advantage will remain—besides a freer form, richer and more diversified subjects will have been attained, and no object of the broadest world and the most manifold life will be any longer excluded as unpoetical. I compare the present literary epoch to a state of violent fever, which is not in itself good and desirable, but of which improved health is the happy consequence. That abomination which now often constitutes the whole subject of a poetical work, will in future only appear as an useful expedient; aye, the pure and the noble, which is now abandoned for the moment, will soon be resought with additional ardor."

August Wilhelm von Schlegel *1767–1845*

Lectures on Dramatic Art and Literature *1801–1811*[1]

I

Ordinarily, indeed, men entertain a very erroneous notion of criticism, and understanding by it nothing more than a certain shrewness in detecting and exposing the faults of a work of art. As I have devoted the greater part of my life to this pursuit, I may be excused if, by way of preface, I seek to lay before my auditors my own ideas of the true genius of criticism.

We see numbers of men, and even whole nations, so fettered by the conventions of education and habits of life, that, even in the appreciation of the fine arts, they cannot shake them off. Nothing to them appears natural, appropriate, or beautiful, which is alien to their own language, manners, and social relations. With this exclusive mode of seeing and feeling, it is no doubt possible to attain, by means of cultivation, to great nicety of discrimination within the narrow circle to which it limits and circumscribes them. But no man can be a true critic or connoisseur without universality of mind, without that flexibility which enables him, by renouncing all personal predilections and blind habits, to adapt himself to the pecularities of other ages and nations—to feel them, as it were, from their proper central point, and, what ennobles human nature, to recognize and duly appreciate whatever is beautiful and grand under the external accessories which were necessary to its embodying, even though occasionally they may seem to disguise and distort it. There is no monopoly of poetry for particular ages and nations; and consequently that despotism in taste, which would seek to invest with universal authority the rules which at first, perhaps, were but arbitrarily advanced, is but a vain and empty pretension. Poetry, taken in its widest acceptation, as the power of creating what is beautiful, and representing it to the eye or the ear, is a universal gift of Heaven, being shared to a certain extent even by those whom we call bar-

Selections. From Augustus William Schlegel, *A Course of Lectures on Dramatic Art and Literature,* translated by John Black, revised by the Reverend A. J. W. Morrison. London: Bell & Daldy, 1871.

[1] These lectures were delivered in 1808, then revised for publication in 1809 and again in 1811.

493

barians and savages. Internal excellence is alone decisive, and where this exists, we must not allow ourselves to be repelled by the external appearance. Everything must be traced up to the root of human nature: if it has sprung from thence, it has an undoubted worth of its own; but if, without possessing a living germ, it is merely externally attached thereto, it will never thrive nor acquire a proper growth. . . .

. . . It is well known that, three centuries and a half ago, the study of ancient literature received a new life, by the diffusion of the Grecian language (for the Latin never became extinct); the classical authors were brought to light, and rendered universally accessible by means of the press; and the monuments of ancient art were diligently disinterred and preserved. All this powerfully excited the human mind, and formed a decided epoch in the history of human civilization; its manifold effects have extended to our times, and will yet extend to an incalculable series of ages. But the study of the ancients was forthwith most fatally perverted. The learned, who were chiefly in the possession of this knowledge, and who were incapable of distinguishing themselves by works of their own, claimed for the ancients an unlimited authority, and with great appearance of reason, since they are models in their kind. Maintaining that nothing could be hoped for the human mind but from an imitation of antiquity, in the works of the moderns they only valued what resembled, or seemed to bear a resemblance to, those of the ancients. Everything else they rejected as barbarous and unnatural. With the great poets and artists it was quite otherwise. However strong their enthusiasm for the ancients, and however determined their purpose of entering into competition with them, they were compelled by their independence and originality of mind to strike out a path of their own, and to impress upon their productions the stamp of their own genius. . . . As the poets for the most part had their share of scholarship, it gave rise to a curious struggle between their natural inclination and their imaginary duty. When they sacrificed to the latter, they were praised by the learned; but by yielding to the former, they became the favorites of the people. . . .

Those very ages, nations, and ranks who felt least the want of a poetry of their own were the most assiduous in their imitation of the ancients; accordingly, its results are but dull school exercises, which at best excite a frigid admiration. But in the fine arts, mere imitation is always fruitless; even what we borrow from others, to assume a true poetical shape, must, as it were, be born again within us. Of what avail is all foreign imitation? Art cannot exist without nature, and man can give nothing to his fellow-men but himself.

Genuine successors and true rivals of the ancients, who, by virtue of congenial talents and cultivation have walked in their path and worked in their spirit, have ever been as rare as their mechanical spiritless copyists are common. Seduced by the form, the great body of critics have been but too indulgent to these servile imitators. These were held up as correct modern classics, while the great truly living and popular poets, whose reputation was a part of their nations' glory, and to whose sublimity it was impossible to be altogether blind, were at best but tolerated as rude and wild natural geniuses. But the unqualified separation of genius and taste on which such a judgment proceeds is altogether untenable. Genius is the almost unconscious choice of the highest degree of excellence, and, consequently, it is taste in its highest activity.

In this state, nearly, matters continued till a period not far back, when several inquiring minds, chiefly Germans, endeavored to clear up the misconception, and to give the ancients their due, without being insensible to the merits of the moderns, although of a totally different kind. The apparent contradiction did not intimidate them. The groundwork of human nature is no doubt everywhere the same; but in all our investigations, we may observe that, throughout the whole range of nature, there is no elementary power so simple, but that it is capable of dividing and diverging into opposite directions. The whole play of vital motion hinges on harmony and contrast. Why, then, should not this phenomenon recur on a grander scale in the history of man? In this idea we have perhaps discovered the true key to the ancient and modern history of poetry and the fine arts. Those who adopted it gave to the peculiar spirit of *modern* art, as contrasted with the *antique* or *classical*, the name of *romantic*. The term is certainly not inappropriate; the word is derived from *romance*—the name originally given to the languages which were formed from the mixture of the Latin and the old Teutonic dialects, in the same manner as modern civilization is the fruit of the heterogeneous union of the peculiarities of the northern nations and the fragments of antiquity; whereas the civilization of the ancients was much more of a piece. . . .

To the application! The Pantheon is not more different from Westminster Abbey or the church of St. Stephen at Vienna, than the structure of a tragedy of Sophocles from a drama of Shakespeare. The comparison between these wonderful productions of poetry and architecture might be carried still farther. But does our admiration of the one compel us to depreciate the other? May we not admit that each is great and admirable in its kind, although the one is, and is meant to be, different from the other? The experiment is worth attempting. We will quarrel with no man for his predilection either for the Grecian or the Gothic. The world is wide, and affords room for a great diversity of objects. Narrow and blindly adopted prepossessions will never constitute a genuine critic or connoisseur, who ought, on the contrary, to possess the power of dwelling with liberal impartiality on the most discrepant views, renouncing the while all personal inclinations.

II

. . . It will be necessary to examine what is meant by *dramatic, theatrical, tragic,* and *comic*.

What is dramatic? To many the answer will seem very easy: where various persons are introduced conversing together, and the poet does not speak in his own person. This is, however, merely the first external foundation of the form; and that is dialogue. But the characters may express thoughts and sentiments without operating any change on each other, and so leave the minds of both in exactly the same state in which they were at the commencement; in such a case, however interesting the conversation may be, it cannot be said to possess a dramatic interest. I shall make this clear by alluding to a more tranquil species of dialogue, not adapted for the stage, the philosophic. When, in Plato, Socrates asks the conceited sophist Hippias what is the meaning of the beautiful, the latter is at once ready with a superficial answer, but is afterwards compelled by the ironical objections of Socrates to give up his former definition, and to grope about him for other ideas, till, ashamed at last and irritated at the superiority of the sage who has convicted him of his ignorance, he is forced to quit the field: this dialogue is not merely philosophically instructive, but arrests the attention like a drama in miniature. And justly, therefore, has this lively movement in the thoughts, this stretch of expectation for the issue, in a word, the dramatic cast of the dialogues of Plato, been always celebrated.

From this we may conceive wherein consists the great charm of dramatic poetry. Action is the true enjoyment of life, nay, life itself. Mere passive enjoyments may lull us into a state of listless complacency, but even then, if possessed of the least internal activity, we cannot avoid being soon wearied. The great bulk of mankind merely from their situation in life, or from their incapacity for extraordinary exertions, are confined within a narrow circle of insignificant operations. Their days flow on in succession under the sleepy rule of custom, their life advances by an insensible progress, and the bursting torrent of the first passions of youth soon settles into a stagnant marsh. From the discontent which this occasions they are compelled to have recourse to all sorts of diversions, which uniformly consist in a species of occupation that may be renounced at pleasure, and though a struggle with difficulties, yet with difficulties that are easily surmounted. But of all diversions the theatre is undoubtedly the most entertaining. Here we may see others act even when we cannot act to any great purpose ourselves. The highest object of human activity is man, and in the drama we see men, measuring their powers with each other, as intellectual and moral beings, either as friends or foes, influencing each other by their opinions, sentiments, and passions, and decisively determining their reciprocal relations and circumstances. The art of the poet accordingly consists in separating from the fable whatever does not essentially belong to it, whatever, in the daily necessities of real life, and the petty occupations to which they give rise, interrupts the progress of important actions, and concentrating within a narrow space a number of events calculated to attract the minds of the hearers and to fill them with attention and expectation. In this manner he gives us a renovated picture of life; a compendium of whatever is moving and progressive in human existence.

But this is not all. Even in a lively oral narration, it is not unusual to introduce persons in conversation with each other, and to give a corresponding variety to the tone and the expression. But the gaps, which these conversations leave in the story, the narrator fills up in his own name with a description of the accompanying circumstances, and other particulars. The dramatic poet must renounce all such expedients; but for this he is richly recompensed in the following invention. He requires each of the characters in his story to be personated by a living individual; that this individual should, in sex, age, and figure, meet as near as may be the prevalent conceptions of his fictitious original, nay, assume his entire personality; that every speech should be delivered in a suitable tone of voice, and accompanied by appropriate action and gesture; and that those external circumstances should be added which are necessary to give the hearers a clear idea of what is going forward. Moreover, these representatives of the creatures of his imagination must appear in the costume belonging to their assumed rank, and to their age and country; partly for the sake of greater resemblance, and partly because, even in dress, there is something characteristic. Lastly, he must see them placed in a locality, which, in some degree, resembles that where, according to his fable, the action took place, because this also contributes to the resemblance: he places them, i.e., on a scene. All this brings us to the idea of the *theatre*. It is evident that the very form of dramatic poetry, that is, the exhibition of an action by dialogue without the aid of narrative, implies the theatre as its necessary complement. We allow that there are dramatic works which were not originally designed for the stage, and not calculated to produce any great effect there, which nevertheless afford great pleasure in the perusal. I am, however, very much inclined to doubt whether they would produce the same strong impression with which they affect us upon a person who had never seen or heard a description of a theatre. In reading dramatic works, we are accustomed ourselves to supply the representation. . . .

After this rapid sketch of what may be called the map of dramatic literature, we return to the examination of its fundamental ideas. Since, as we have already shown, visible representation is essential to the very form of the drama, a dramatic work may always be regarded from a double point of view—how far it is *poetical*, and how far it is *theatrical*. The two are by no means inseparable. Let not, however, the expression *poetical* be misunderstood: I am not now speaking of the versification and the ornaments of language; these, when not animated by some higher excellence, are the least effective on the stage; but I speak of the poetry in the spirit and design of a piece; and this may exist in as high a degree when the drama is written in prose as in verse. What is it, then, that makes a drama poetical? The very same, assuredly, that makes other works so. It must in the first place be a connected whole, complete and satisfactory within itself. But this is merely the negative definition of a work of art, by which it is distinguished from the phenomena of nature, which run into each other, and do not possess in themselves a complete and independent existence. To be poetical it is necessary that a composition should be a mirror of ideas, that is, thoughts and feelings which in their character are necessary and eternally true, and soar above this earthly life, and also that it should exhibit them embodied before us. What the ideas are, which in this view are essential to the different departments of the drama, will hereafter be the subject of our investigation. We shall also, on the other hand, show that without them a drama becomes altogether prosaic and empirical, that is to say, patched together by the understanding out of the observations it has gathered from literal reality.

But how does a dramatic work become theatrical, or fitted to appear with advantage on the stage? In single instances it is often difficult to determine whether a work possesses such a property or not. It is indeed frequently the subject of great controversy, especially when the self-love of authors and actors comes into collision; each shifts the blame of failure on the other, and those who advocate the cause of the author appeal to an imaginary perfection of the histrionc art, and complain of the insufficiency of the existing means for its realization. But in general the answer to this question is by no means so difficult. The object proposed is to produce an impression on an assembled multitude, to rivet their attention, and to excite their interest and sympathy. In this respect the poet's occupation coincides with that of the orator. How then does the latter attain his end? By perspicuity, rapidity, and energy. Whatever exceeds the ordinary measure of patience or comprehension he must diligently avoid. Moreover, when a number of men are assembled together, they mutually distract each other's attention whenever their eyes and ears are not drawn to a common object without and beyond themselves. Hence the dramatic poet, as well as the orator, must from the very commencement, by strong impressions, transport his hearers out of themselves, and, as it were, take bodily possession of their attention. There is a species of poetry which gently stirs a mind attuned to solitary contemplation, as soft breezes elicit melody from the Aeolian harp. However excellent this poetry may be in itself, without some other accompaniments its tones would be lost on the stage. The melting harmonica is not calculated to regulate the march of an army, and kindle its military enthusiasm. For this we must have piercing instruments, but above all a strongly marked rhythm, to quicken the pulsation and give a more rapid movement to the animal spirits. The grand repuisite in a drama is to make this rhythm perceptible in the onward progress of the action. When this has once been effected, the poet may all the sooner halt in his rapid career, and indulge the bent of his own genius. There are points when the most elaborate and polished style, the most enthusiastic lyrics, the most profound thoughts and remote allusions, the smartest coruscations of wit, and the most dazzling flights of a sportive or ethereal fancy, are all in their place, and when the willing audience, even those who cannot entirely comprehend them, follow the whole with a greedy ear, like music in unison with their feelings. Here the poet's great art lies in availing himself of the effect of contrasts, which enable him at one time to produce calm repose, profound contemplation, and even the self-abandoned indifference of exhaustion, or at another, the most tumultuous emotions, the most violent storm of the passions. With respect to theatrical fitness, however, it must not be forgotten that much must always depend on the capacities and humors of the audience, and, consequently, on the national character in general, and the particular degree of mental culture. Of all kinds of poetry the dramatic is, in a certain sense, the most secular; for, issuing from the stillness of an inspired mind, it yet fears not to exhibit itself in the midst of the noise and tumult of social life. The dramatic poet is, more than any other, obliged to court external favor and loud applause. But of course it is only in appearance that he thus lowers himself to his hearers; while, in reality, he is elevating them to himself.

III

The dramatic poet, as well as the epic, represents external events, but he represents them as real and present. In common with the lyric poet he also claims our mental participation, but not in the same calm composedness; the feeling of joy and sorrow which the dramatist excites is more immediate and vehement. He calls forth all the emotions which the sight of similar deeds and fortunes of living men would elicit, and it is only by the total sum of the impression which he produces that he ultimately resolves these conflicting emotions into a harmonious tone of feeling. As he stands in such close proximity to real life, and endeavors to endue his own imaginary creations with vitality, the equanimity of the epic poet would in him be indifference; he must decidedly take part with one or other of the leading views of human life, and constrain his audience also to participate in the same feeling.

To employ simpler and more intelligible language: the *tragic* and *comic* bear the same relation to one another as *earnest* and *sport*. Every man, from his own experience, is acquainted with both these states of mind; but to determine their essence and their source would demand deep philosophical investigation. Both, indeed, bear the stamp of our common nature; but earnestness belongs more to its moral, and mirth to its animal part. The creatures destitute of reason are incapable either of earnest or of sport. Animals seem indeed at times to labor as if they were earnestly intent upon some aim, and as if they made the present moment subordinate to the future; at other times they seem to sport, that is, they give themselves up without object or purpose to the pleasure of existence: but they do not possess consciousness, which alone can entitle these two conditions to the names of earnest and sport. Man alone, of all the animals with which we are acquainted, is capable of looking back toward the past, and forward into futurity; and he has to purchase the enjoyment of this noble privilege at a dear rate. Earnestness, in the most extensive signification, is the direction of our mental powers to some aim. But as soon as we begin to call ourselves to account for our actions, reason compels us to fix this aim higher and higher, till we come at last to the highest end of our existence: and here that longing for the infinite which is inherent in our being is baffled by the limits of our finite existence. All that we do, all that we effect, is vain and perishable; death stands everywhere in the background, and to it every well or ill-spent moment brings us nearer and closer; and even when a man has been so singularly fortunate as to reach the utmost term of life without any grievous calamity, the inevitable doom still awaits him to leave or to be left by all that is most dear to him on earth. There is no bond of love without a separation, no enjoyment without the grief of losing it. When, however, we contemplate the relations of our existence to the extreme limit of possibilities: when we reflect on its entire dependence on a chain of causes and effects, stretching beyond our ken: when we consider how weak and helpless, and doomed to struggle against the enormous powers of nature, and conflicting appetites, we are cast on the shores of an unknown world, as it were, shipwrecked at our very birth; how we are subject to all kinds of errors and deceptions, any one of which may be our ruin; that in our passions we cherish an enemy in our bosoms; how every moment demands from us, in the name of the most sacred duties, the sacrifice of of our dearest inclinations, and how at one blow we may be robbed of all that we have acquired with much toil and difficulty; that with every accession to our stores, the risk of loss is proportionately increased, and we are only the more exposed to the malice of hostile fortune: when we think upon all this, every heart which is not dead to feeling must be overpowered by an inexpressible melancholy, for which there is no other counterpoise than the consciousness of a vocation transcending the limits of this earthly life. This is the tragic tone of mind; and when the thought of the possible issues out of the mind as a living reality, when this tone pervades and animates a visible representation of the most striking instances of violent revolutions in a man's fortunes, either prostrating his mental energies or calling forth the most heroic endurance—then the result is *Tragic Poetry*. We thus see how this kind of poetry has its foundation in our nature, while to a certain extent we have also answered the question why we are fond of such mournful representations, and even find something consoling and elevating in them. This tone of mind we have described is inseparable from strong feeling; and although poetry cannot remove these internal dissonances, she must at least endeavor to effect an ideal reconciliation of them.

As earnestness, in the highest degree, is the essence of tragic representation; so is sport of the comic. The disposition to mirth is a forgetfulness of all gloomy considerations in the pleasant feeling of present happiness. We are then inclined to view everything in a sportive light, and to allow nothing to disturb or ruffle our minds. The imperfections and the irregularities of men are no longer an object of dislike and compassion, but serve, by their strange inconsistencies, to entertain the understanding and to amuse the fancy. The comic poet must therefore carefully abstain from whatever is calculated to excite moral indignation at the conduct, or sympathy with the situations of his personages, because this would inevitably bring us back again into earnestness. He must paint their irregularities as springing out of the predominance of the animal part of their nature, and the incidents which befall them as merely ludicrous distresses, which will be attended with no fatal consequences. This is uniformly what takes place in what we call Comedy, in which, however, there is still a mixture of seriousness. . . . The oldest comedy of the Greeks was, however, entirely sportive, and in that respect formed the most complete contrast to their tragedy. Not only were the characters and situations of individuals worked up into a comic picture of real life, but the whole frame of society, the constitution, nature, and the gods, were all fantastically painted in the most ridiculous and laughable colors.

IV

The tragical imitation of the ancients was altogether ideal and rhythmical; and in forming a judgment of it, we must always keep this in view. It was ideal, insofar as it aimed at the highest grace and dignity; and rhythmical, insomuch as the gestures and inflections of voice were more solemnly measured than in real life. As the statuary of the Greeks, setting out, with almost scientific strictness, with the most general conception, sought to embody it again in various general characters which were gradually invested with the charms of life, so that the individual was the last thing to which they descended; in like manner in the mimetic art, they began with the idea (the delineation of persons with heroical grandeur, more than human dignity, and ideal beauty), then passed to character, and made passion the last of all; which, in the collision with the requisitions of either of the others, was forced to give way. Fidelity of representation was less their object than beauty; with us it is exactly the reverse. On this principle, the use of masks, which appears astonishing to us, was not only justifiable, but absolutely essential; far from considering them as a makeshift, the Greeks would certainly, and with justice too, have looked upon it as a makeshift to be obliged to allow a player with vulgar, ignoble, or strongly marked features, to represent an Apollo or a Hercules; nay, rather they would have deemed it downright profanation.

V

We come now to the essence of Greek tragedy. That in conception it was ideal is universally allowed; this, however, must not be understood as implying that all its characters were depicted as morally perfect. In such a case what room could there be for that contrast and collision which the very plot of a drama requires?—They have their weaknesses, errors, and even crimes, but the manners are always elevated above reality, and every person is invested with as high a portion of dignity as was compatible with his part in the action. But this is not all. The ideality of the representation chiefly consisted in the elevation of everything in it to a higher sphere. Tragic poetry wished to separate the image of humanity which it presented to us from the level of nature to which man is in reality chained down, like a slave of the soil. How was this to be accomplished? By exhibiting to us an image hovering in the air? But this would have been incompatible with the law of gravitation and with the earthly materials of which our bodies are framed. Frequently, what is praised in art as *ideal* is really nothing more. But this would give us nothing more than airy evanescent shadows incapable of making any durable impression on the mind. The Greeks, however, in their artistic creations, succeeded most perfectly in combining the ideal with the real, or, to drop school terms, an elevation more than human with all the truth of life, and in investing the manifestation of an idea with energetic corporeity. They did not allow their figures to flit about without consistency in empty space, but they fixed the statue of humanity on the eternal and immovable basis of moral liberty; and that it might stand there unshaken, formed it of stone or brass, or some more massive substance than the bodies of living men, making an impression by its very weight, and from its very elevation and magnificence only the more completely subject to the laws of gravity.

Inward liberty and external necessity are the two poles or the tragic world. It is only by contrast with its opposite that each of these ideas is brought into full manifestation. As the feeling of an internal power of self-determination elevates the man above the unlimited dominion of impulse and the instincts of nature; in a word, absolves him from nature's guardianship, so the necessity, which alongside of her he must recognize, is no mere natural necessity, but one lying beyond the world of sense in the abyss of infinitude; consequently it exhibits itself as the unfathomable power of Destiny. Hence this power extends also to the world of gods: for the Grecian gods are mere powers of nature; and although immeasurably higher than mortal man, yet, compared with infinitude, they are on an equal footing with himself. In Homer and in the tragedians, the gods are introduced in a manner altogether different. In the former their appearance is arbitrary and accidental, and communicate to the epic poem no higher interest than the charm of the wonderful. But in Tragedy the gods either come forward as the servants of destiny, and mediate executors of its decrees; or else approve themselves godlike only by asserting their liberty of action, and entering upon the same struggles with fate which man himself has to encounter.

This is the essence of the tragical in the sense of the ancients. We are accustomed to give to all terrible or sorrowful events the appellation of tragic, and it is certain that such events are selected in preference by Tragedy, though a melancholy conclusion is by no means indispensably necessary; and several ancient tragedies, viz., the *Eumenides, Philoctetes,* and in some degree also the *Oedipus Coloneus,* without mentioning many of the pieces of Euripides, have a happy and cheerful termination.

But why does Tragedy select subjects so awfully repugnant to the wishes and the wants of our sensuous nature? This question has often been asked, and seldom satisfactorily answered. Some have said that the pleasure of such representations arises from the comparison we make between the calmness and tranquillity of our own situation, and the storms and perplexities to which the victims of passion are exposed. But when we take a warm interest in the persons of a tragedy, we cease to think of ourselves; and when this is not the case, it is the best of all proofs that we take but a feeble interest in the exhibited story, and that the tragedy has failed in its effect. Others again have had recourse to a supposed feeling for moral improvement, which is gratified by the view of poetical justice in the reward of the good and the punishment of the wicked. But he for whom the aspect of such dreadful examples could really be wholesome must be conscious of a base feeling of depression, very far removed from genuine morality, and would experience humiliation rather than elevation of mind. Besides, poetical justice is by no means indispensable to a good tragedy; it may end with the suffering of the just and the triumph of the wicked, if only the balance be preserved in the spectator's own consciousness by the prospect of futurity. Little does it mend the matter to say with Aristotle, that the object of tragedy is to purify the passions by pity and terror. In the first place commentators have never been able to agree as to the meaning of this proposition, and have had recourse to the most forced explanations of it. Look, for instance, into the *Dramaturgie* of Lessing. Lessing gives a new explanation of his own, and fancies he has found in Aristotle a poetical Euclid. But mathematical demonstrations are liable to no misconception, and geometrical evidence may well be supposed inapplicable to the theory of the fine arts. Supposing, however, that tragedy does operate this moral cure in us, still she does so by the painful feelings of terror and compassion: and it remains to be proved how it is that we take a pleasure in subjecting ourselves to such an operation.

Others have been pleased to say that we are attracted to theatrical representations from the want of some violent agitation to rouse us out of the torpor of our everyday life. Such a craving does exist; I have already acknowledged the existence of this want, when speaking of the attractions of the drama; but to it we must equally attribute the fights of wild beasts among the Romans, nay, even the combats of the gladiators. But must we, less indurated, and more inclined to tender feelings, require demigods and heroes to descend, like so many desperate gladiators, into the bloody arena of the tragic stage, in order to agitate our nerves by the spectacle of their sufferings? No: it is not the sight of suffering which constitutes the charm of a tragedy, or even of the games of the circus, or of the fight of wild beasts. In the latter we see a display of activity, strength, and courage; splendid qualities these, and related to the mental and moral powers of man. The satisfaction, therefore, which we derive from the representation, in a good tragedy, of powerful situations and overwhelming sorrows must be ascribed either to the feeling of the dignity of human nature, excited in us by such grand instances of it as are therein displayed, or to the trace of a higher order of things, impressed on the apparently irregular course of events, and mysteriously revealed in them; or perhaps to both these causes conjointly.

The true reason, therefore, why tragedy need not shun even the harshest subject is that a spiritual and invisible power can only be measured by the opposition which it encounters from some external force capable of being appreciated by the senses. The moral freedom of man, therefore, can only be displayed in a conflict with his sensuous impulses: so long as no higher call summons it to action, it is either actually dormant within him, or appears to slumber, since otherwise it does but mechanically fulfill its part as a mere power of nature. It is only amidst difficulties and struggles that the moral part of man's nature avouches itself. If, therefore, we must explain the distinctive aim of tragedy by way of theory, we would give it thus: that to establish the claims of the mind to a divine origin, its earthly existence must be disregarded as vain and insignificant, all sorrows endured and all difficulties overcome. . . .

I come now to another peculiarity which distinguishes the tragedy of the ancients from ours, I mean the Chorus. We must consider it as a personified reflection on the action which is going on; the incorporation into the representation itself of the sentiments of the poet, as the spokesman of the whole human race. This is its general poetical character; and that is all that here concerns us, and that character is by no means affected by the circumstance that the Chorus had a local origin in the feasts of Bacchus. . . .

. . . Whatever it might be and do in each particular piece, it represented in general, first the common mind of the nation, and then the general sympathy of all mankind. In a word, the Chorus is the ideal spectator. It mitigates the impression of a heart-rendering or moving story, while it conveys to the actual spectator a lyrical and musical expression of his own emotions, and elevates him to the region of contemplation.

XVII

The far-famed Three Unities, which have given rise to a whole Iliad of critical wars, are the Unities of Action, Time, and Place.

The validity of the first is universally allowed, but the difficulty is to agree about its true meaning; and, I may add, that it is no easy matter to come to an understanding on the subject.

The Unities of Time and Place are considered by some quite a subordinate matter, while others lay the greatest stress upon them, and affirm that out of the pale of them there is no safety for the dramatic poet. In France this zeal is not confined merely to the learned world, but seems to be shared by the whole nation in common. Every Frenchman who has sucked in his Boileau with his mother's milk considers himself a born champion of the Dramatic Unities, much in the same way that the kings of England since Henry VIII are hereditary Defenders of the Faith.

It amusing enough to see Aristotle driven perforce to lend his name to these three Unities, whereas the only one of which he speaks with any degree of fullness is the first, the Unity of Action. With respect to the Unity of Time he merely throws out a vague hint; while of the Unity of Place he says not a syllable.

I do not, therefore, find myself in a polemical relation to Aristotle, for I by no means contest the Unity of Action properly understood: I only claim a greater latitude with respect to place and time for many species of the drama, nay, hold it essential to them. . . .

Unity of Action is required. What is action? Most critics pass over this point, as if it were self-evident. In the higher, proper signification, action is an activity dependent on the will of man. Its unity will consist in the direction towards a single end; and to its completeness belongs all that lies between the first determination and the execution of the deed.

This idea of action is applicable to many tragedies of the ancients (for instance, Orestes' murder of his mother, Oedipus' determination to discover and punish the murderer of Laius), but by no means to all; still less does it apply to the greater part of modern tragedies, at least if the action is to be sought in the principal characters. What comes to pass through them, and proceeds with them, has frequently no more connection with a voluntary determination, than a ship's striking on a rock in a storm. But further, in the term action, as understood by the ancients, we must include the resolution to bear the consequences of the deed with heroic magnanimity, and the execution of this determination will belong to its completion. The pious resolve of Antigone to perform the last duties to her unburied brother is soon executed and without difficulty; but genuineness, on which alone rests its claim to be a fit subject for a tragedy, is only subsequently proved when, without repentance, and without any symptoms of weakness, she suffers death as its penalty. And to take an example from quite a different sphere, is not Shakespeare's *Julius Caesar*, as respects the action, constructed on the same principle? Brutus is the hero of the piece; the completion of his great resolve does not consist in the mere assassination of Caesar (an action ambiguous in itself, and of which the motives might have been ambition and jealousy), but in this, that he proves himself the pure champion of Roman liberty by the calm sacrifice of his amiable life.

Farther, there could be no complication of the plot without opposition, and this arises mostly out of the contradictory motives and views of the acting personages. If, therefore, we limit the notion of an action to the determination and the deed, then we shall, in most cases, have two or three actions in a single tragedy. Which now is the principal action? Every person thinks his own the most important, for every man is his own central point. Creon's determination to maintain his kingly authority, by punishing the burial of Polynices with death, is equally fixed with Antigone's determination, equally important, and, as we see at the end, not less dangerous, as it draws after it the ruin of his whole house. It may be perhaps urged that the merely negative determination is to be considered simply as the complement of the affirmative. But what if each determines on something not exactly opposite, but altogether different? In the *Andromache* of Racine, Orestes wishes to move Hermione to return his love; Hermione is resolved to compel Pyrrhus to marry her, or she will be revenged on him; Pyrrhus wishes to be rid of Hermione, and to be united to Andromache; Andromache is desirous of saving her son, and at the same time remaining true to the memory of her husband. Yet nobody ever questioned the unity of this piece, as the whole has a common connection, and ends with one common catastrophe. But which of the actions of the four persons is the main action? In strength of passion their endeavors are pretty nearly equal—in all the whole happiness of life is at stake; the action of Andromache has, however, the advantage in moral dignity, and Racine was therefore perfectly right in naming the piece after her.

We see here a new condition in the notion of action, namely, the reference to the idea of moral liberty, by which alone man is considered as the original author of his own resolutions. For, considered within the province of experience, the resolution, as the beginning of action, is not a cause merely, but is also an effect of antecedent motives. It was in this reference to a higher idea, that we previously found the *unity* and *wholeness* of Tragedy in the sense of the ancients; namely, its absolute beginning is the assertion of Free Will, and the acknowledgment of Necessity its absolute end. But we consider ourselves justified in affirming that Aristotle was altogether a stranger to this view; he nowhere speaks of the idea of Destiny as essential to Tragedy. In fact, we must not expect from him a strict idea of action as a resolution and deed. He says somewhere—"The extent of a tragedy is always sufficiently great, if, by a series of probable or necessary consequences, a reverse from adversity to prosperity, or from happiness to misery, is brought about." It is evident, therefore, that he, like all the moderns, understood by *action* something merely that takes place. This action, according to him, must have beginning, middle, and end, and consequently consist of a plurality of connected events. But where are the limits of this plurality? Is not the concatenation of causes and effects, backwards and forwards, without end? and may we then, with equal propriety, begin and break off wherever we please? In this province, can there be either beginning or end, corresponding to Aristotle's very accurate definition of these notions? Completeness would therefore be altogether impossible. If, however, for the unity of a plurality of events nothing more is requisite than causal connection, then this rule is indefinite in the extreme, and the unity admits of being narrowed or enlarged at pleasure. For every series of incidents or actions, which are occasioned by each other, however much it be prolonged, may always be comprehended under a single point of view, and denoted by a single name. When Calderon in a single drama describes the conversion of Peru to Christianity, from its very beginning (that is, from the discovery of the country) down to its completion, and when nothing actually occurs in the piece which had not some influence on that event, does he not give us as much Unity in the above sense as the simplest Greek tragedy, which, however, the champions of Aristotle's rules will by no means allow?

Corneille was well aware of the difficulty of a proper definition of unity, as applicable to an inevitable plurality of subordinate actions; and in this way did he endeavor to get rid of it. "I assume," says he, "that in Comedy, Unity of Action consists in Unity of the Intrigue; that is, of the obstacles raised to the designs of the principal persons; and in Tragedy, in the unity of the danger, whether the hero sinks under, or extricates himself from it. By this, however, I do not mean to assert that several dangers in Tragedy, and several intrigues or obstacles in Comedy, may not be allowable, provided only that the personage falls necessarily from one into the other; for then the escape from the first danger does not make the action complete, for it draws a second after it, as also the clearing up of one intrigue does not place the acting persons at their ease, because it involves them in another."

In the first place the difference here assumed between tragic and comic Unity is altogether unessential. For the manner of putting the play together is not influenced by the circumstance that the incidents in Tragedy are more serious, as affecting person and life; the embarrassment of the characters in Comedy when they cannot accomplish their design and intrigues, may equally be termed a danger. Corneille, like most others, refers all to the idea of connection between cause and effect. No doubt when the principal persons, either by marriage or death, are set at rest, the drama comes to a close; but if nothing more is necessary to its Unity than the uninterrupted progress of an opposition, which serves to keep up the dramatic movement, simplicity will then come but poorly off: for, without violating this rule of Unity, we may go on to an almost endless accumulation of events, as in the *Thousand and One Nights*, where the thread of the story is never once broken. . . .

. . . The idea of *One* and *Whole* is in no way whatever derived from experience, but arises out of the primary and spontaneous activity of the human mind. . . .

The external sense perceives in objects only an indefinite plurality of distinguishable parts; the judgment, by which we comprehend these into an entire and perfect unity, is in all cases founded on a reference to a higher sphere of ideas. Thus, for example, the mechanical unity of a watch consists in its aim of measuring time; this aim, however, exists only for the understanding, and is neither visible to the eye, nor palpable to the touch: the organic unity of a plant or an animal consists in the idea of life; but the inward intuition of life, which, in itself uncorporeal, nevertheless manifests itself through the medium of the corporeal world, is brought by us to the observation of the individual living object, otherwise we could not obtain it from that object.

The separate parts of a work of art, and (to return to the question before us) the separate parts, consequently, of a tragedy, must not be taken in by the eye and ear alone, but also comprehended by the understanding. Collectively, however, they are all subservient to one common aim, namely, to produce a joint impression on the mind. Here, therefore, as in the above examples, the Unity lies in a higher sphere, in the feeling or in the reference to ideas. This is all one; for the feeling, so far as it is not merely sensual and passive, is our sense, our organ for the Infinite, which forms itself into ideas for us.

Far, therefore, from rejecting the law of a perfect Unity in Tragedy as unnecessary, I require a deeper, more intrinsic, and more mysterious unity than that with which most critics are satisfied. This Unity I find in the tragical compositions of Shakespeare, in as great perfection as in those of Aeschylus and Sophocles; while, on the contrary, I do not find it in many of those tragedies which nevertheless are lauded as correct by the critics of the dissecting school.

Logical coherence, the causal connection, I hold to be equally essential to Tragedy and every serious drama, because all the mental powers act and react upon each other, and if the Understanding be compelled to take a leap, Imagination and Feeling do not follow the composition with equal alacrity. But unfortunately the champions of what is called regularity have applied this rule with a degree of petty subtlety, which can have no other effect than that of cramping the poet, and rendering true excellence impossible. . . .

So much for the Unity of Action. With respect to the Unity of Time. . . . Corneille with great reason finds the rule extremely inconvenient; he therefore prefers the more lenient interpretation, and says, "he would not scruple to extend the duration of the action even to thirty hours." Others, however, most rigorously insist on the principle that the action should not occupy a longer period than that of its representation, that is to say, from two to three hours. The dramatic poet must, according to them, be punctual to his hour. In the main, the latter plead a sounder cause than the more lenient critics. For the only ground of the rule is the observation of a probability which they suppose to be necessary for illusion, namely, that the actual time and that of the representation should be the same. If once a discrepancy be allowed, such as the difference between two hours and thirty, we may upon the same principle go much farther. This idea of illusion has occasioned great errors in the theory of art. By this term there has often been understood the unwittingly erroneous belief that the represented action is reality. In that case the terrors of Tragedy would be a true torture to us, they would be like an Alpine load on the fancy. No, the theatrical, as well as every other poetical illusion, is a waking dream, to which we voluntarily surrender ourselves. To produce it, the poet and actors must powerfully agitate the mind, and the probabilities of calculation do not in the least contribute towards it. This demand of literal deception, pushed to the extreme, would make all poetic form impossible; for we know well that the mythological and historical persons did not speak our language, that impassioned grief does not express itself in verse, etc. . . .

But, it will be objected, the ancient tragedians at least observed the Unity of Time. This expression is by no means precise. . . . What they observe is nothing but the *seeming* continuity of time. It is of importance to attend to this distinction—the seeming; for they unquestionably allow much more to take place during the choral songs than could really happen within their actual duration. . . .

The moderns have, in the division of their plays into acts, which, properly speaking, were unknown to Greek Tragedy, a convenient means of extending the period of representation without any ill effect. For the poet may fairly reckon so far on the spectator's imagination as to presume that during the entire suspension of the representation, he will readily conceive a much longer interval to have elapsed than that which is measured by the rhythmical time of the music between the acts; otherwise to make it appear the more natural to him, it might be as well to invite him to come and see the next act tomorrow. . . .

The romantic poets take the liberty even of changing the scene during the course of an act. As the stage is always previously left empty, these also are such interruptions of the continuity, as would warrant them in the assumption of as many intervals. . . .

The objection to the change of scene is founded on the same erroneous idea of illusion which we have already discussed. To transfer the action to another place would, it is urged, dispel the illusion. But now if we are in reality to consider the imaginary for the actual place, then must stage decoration and scenery be altogether different from what it now is. Johnson, a critic who, in general, is an advocate for the strict rules, very justly observes[2] that if our imagination once goes the length of transporting us eighteen hundred years back to Alexandria, in order to figure to ourselves the story of Antony and Cleopatra as actually taking place before us, the next step, of transporting ourselves from Alexandria to Rome, is easier.

XXII

. . . The poetic spirit requires to be limited, that it may move with a becoming liberty, within its proper precincts, as has been felt by all nations on the first invention of meter; it must act according to laws derivable from its own essence, otherwise its strength will evaporate in boundless vacuity.

The works of genius cannot therefore be permitted to be without form; but of this there is no danger. However, that we may answer this objection of want of form, we must understand the exact meaning of the term form, since most critics, and more especially those who insist on a stiff regularity, interpret it merely in a mechanical, and not in an organical sense. Form is mechanical when, through external force, it is imparted to any material merely as an accidental addition without reference to its quality; as, for example, when we give a particular shape to a soft mass that it may retain the same after its induration. Organical form, again, is innate; it unfolds itself from within, and acquires its determination contemporaneously with the perfect development of the germ. We everywhere discover such forms in nature throughout the whole range of living powers, from the crystallization

[2] See pp. 413–414.

of salts and minerals to plants and flowers, and from these again to the human body. In the fine arts, as well as in the domain of nature—the supreme artist—all genuine forms are organical, that is, determined by the quality of the work. In a word, the form is nothing but a significant exterior, the speaking physiognomy of each thing, which, as long as it is not disfigured by any destructive accident, gives a true evidence of its hidden essence.

Hence it is evident that the spirit of poetry, which, though imperishable, migrates, as it were, through different bodies, must, so often as it is newly born in the human race, mold to itself, out of the nutrimental substance of an altered age, a body of a different conformation. The forms vary with the direction taken by the poetical sense; and when we give to the new kinds of poetry the old names, and judge of them according to the ideas conveyed by these names, the application which we make of the authority of classical antiquity is altogether unjustifiable. No one should be tried before a tribunal to which he is not amenable. We may safely admit that the most of the English and Spanish dramatic works are neither tragedies nor comedies in the sense of the ancients: they are romantic dramas. That the stage of a people who, in its foundation and formation, neither knew nor wished to know anything of foreign models will possess many peculiarities, and not only deviate from, but even exhibit a striking contrast to, the theatres of other nations who had a common model for imitation before their eyes, is easily supposable, and we should only be astonished were it otherwise. But when in two nations, differing so widely as the English and Spanish, in physical, moral, political, and religious respects, the theatres (which, without being known to each other, arose about the same time) possess, along with external and internal diversities, the most striking features of affinity, the attention even of the most thoughtless cannot but be turned to this phenomenon; and the conjecture will naturally occur that the same, or, at least, a kindred principle must have prevailed in the development of both. . . .

The similarity of the English and Spanish theatres does not consist merely in the bold neglect of the Unities of Place and Time, and in the commixture of comic and tragic elements: that they were unwilling or unable to comply with the rules and with right reason (in the meaning of certain critics these terms are equivalent) may be considered as an evidence of merely negative properties. The ground of the resemblance lies far deeper, in the inmost substance of the fictions, and in the essential relations, through which every deviation of form becomes a true requisite, which, together with its validity, has also its significance. What they have in common with each other is the spirit of the romantic poetry, giving utterance to itself in a dramatic shape. . . .

Of the origin and essence of the romantic I treated in my first Lecture, and I shall here, therefore, merely briefly mention the subject. The ancient art and poetry rigorously separate things which are dissimilar; the romantic delights in indissoluble mixtures; all contrarieties: nature and art, poetry and prose, seriousness and mirth, recollection and anticipation, spirituality and sensuality, terrestrial and celestial, life and death, are by it blended together in the most intimate combination. As the oldest lawgivers delivered their mandatory instructions and prescriptions in measured melodies; as this is fabulously ascribed to Orpheus, the first softener of the yet untamed race of mortals; in like manner the whole of the ancient poetry and art is, as it were, a *rhythmical nomos* (law), an harmonious promulgation of the permanently established of a world submited to a beautiful order, and reflecting in itself the eternal images of things. Romantic poetry, on the other hand, is the expression of the secret attraction to a chaos which lies concealed in the very bosom of the ordered universe, and is perpetually striving after new and marvelous births; the life-giving spirit of primal love broods here anew on the face of the waters. The former is more simple, clear, and like to nature in the self-existent perfection of her separate works; the latter, notwithstanding its fragmentary appearance, approaches more to the secret of the universe. For Conception can only comprise each object separately, but nothing in truth can ever exist separately and by itself; Feeling perceives all in all at one and the same time.

Respecting the two species of poetry with which we are here principally occupied, we compared the ancient Tragedy to a group in sculpture: the figures corresponding to the characters, and their grouping to the action; and to these two in both productions of art is the consideration exclusively directed, as being all that is properly exhibited. But the romantic drama must be viewed as a large picture, where not merely figure and motion are exhibited in larger, richer groups, but where even all that surrounds the figures must also be portrayed; where we see not merely the nearest objects, but are indulged with the prospect of a considerable distance; and all this under a magical light, which assists in giving to the impression the particular character desired.

Such a picture must be bounded less perfectly and less distinctly, than the group; for it is like a fragment cut out of the optic scene of the world. However the painter, by the setting of his foreground, by throwing the whole of his light into the center, and by other mean of fixing the point of view, will learn that he must neither wander beyond the composition, nor omit anything within it. . . .

The very same description of beauties [is] peculiar to the Romantic drama. It does not (like the Old Tragedy) separate seriousness and the action, in a rigid manner, from among the whole ingredients of life; it embraces at once the whole of the chequered drama of life with all its circumstances; and while it seems only to represent subjects brought accidentally together, it satisfies the unconscious requisitions of fancy, buries us in reflections on the inexpressible signification of the objects which we view blended by order, nearness and distance, light and color, into one harmonious whole; and thus lends, as it were, a soul to the prospect before us.

The change of time and of place (supposing its influence on the mind to be included in the picture; and that it comes to the aid of the theatrical perspective, with reference to what is indicated in the distance, or half-concealed by intervening objects, the contrast of sport and earnest (supposing that in degree and kind they bear a proportion to each other), finally, the mixture of the dialogical and the lyrical elements, (by which the poet is enabled, more or less perfectly, to transform his personages into poetical beings)—these, in my opinion, are not mere licenses, but true beauties in the romantic drama. In all these points, and in many others also, the English and Spanish works, which are preeminently worthy of this title of Romantic, fully resemble each other, however different they may be in other respects.

XXIII

Our poet's want of scholarship has been the subject of endless controversy, and yet it is surely a very easy matter to decide. Shakespeare was poor in dead school-cram, but he possessed a rich treasury of living and intuitive knowledge. He knew a little Latin, and even something of Greek, though it may be not enough to read with ease the writers in the original. With modern languages also, the French and Italian, he had, perhaps, but a superficial acquaintance. The general direction of his mind was not to the collection of words but of facts. With English books, whether original or translated, he was extensively acquainted: we may safely affirm that he had read all that his native language and literature then contained that could be of any use to him in his poetical avocations. He was sufficiently intimate with mythology to employ it, in the only manner he could wish, in the way of symbolical ornament. He had formed a correct notion of the spirit of Ancient History, and more particularly of that of the Romans; and the history of his own country was familiar to him even in detail. Fortunately for him it had not as yet been treated in a diplomatic and pragmatic spirit, but merely in the chronicle style; in other words, it had not yet assumed the appearance of dry investigations respecting the development of political relations, diplomatic negotiations, finances, etc., but exhibited a visible image of the life and movement of an age prolific of great deeds. Shakespeare, moreover, was a nice observer of nature; he knew the technical language of mechanics and artisans; he seems to have been well traveled in the interior of his own country, while of others he inquired diligently of traveled navigators respecting their peculiarity of climate and customs. He thus became accurately acquainted with all the popular usages, opinions, and traditions which could be of use in poetry.

The proofs of his ignorance, on which the greatest stress is laid, are a few geographical blunders and anachronisms. Because in a comedy founded on an earlier tale, he makes ships visit Bohemia, he has been the subject of much laughter. But I conceive that we should be very unjust towards him were we to conclude that he did not, as well as ourselves, possess the useful but by no means difficult knowledge that Bohemia is nowhere bounded by the sea. He could never, in that case, have looked into a map of Germany who yet describes elsewhere, with great accuracy, the maps of both Indies, together with the discoveries of the latest navigators.[3] In such matters Shakespeare is only faithful to the details of the domestic stories. In the novels on which he worked, he avoided disturbing the associations of his audience, to whom they were known, by novelties—the correction of errors in secondary and unimportant particulars. The more wonderful the story, the more it ranged in a purely poetical region, which he transfers at will to an indefinite distance. These plays, whatever names they bear, take place in the true land of romance, and in the very century of wonderful love stories. He knew well that in the forest of Ardennes there were neither the lions and serpents of the Torrid Zone, nor the shepherdesses of Arcadia: but he transferred both to it,[4] because the design and import of his picture required them. Here he considered himself entitled to take the greatest liberties. He had not to do with a hair-splitting, hypercritical age like ours, which is always seeking in poetry for something else than poetry; his audience entered the theatre not to learn true chronology, geography, and natural history, but to witness a vivid exhibition. I will undertake to prove that Shakespeare's anachronisms are, for the most part, committed of set purpose and deliberately. It was frequently of importance to him to move the exhibited subject out of the background of time, and bring it quite near us. Hence in *Hamlet*, though avowedly an old Northern story, there runs a tone of modish society, and in every respect the costume of the most recent period. Without those circumstantialities it would not have been allowable to make a philosophical inquirer of Hamlet, on which trait, however, the meeting of the whole is made to rest. On that account he mentions his education at a university, though, in the age of the true Hamlet of history, universities were not in existence. He makes him study at Wittenberg, and no selection of a place could have been more suitable. The name was very popular: the story of *Dr. Faustus of Wittenberg* had made it well known; it was of particular celebrity in protestant England, as Luther had taught and written there

---

[3] *Twelfth Night, or What You Will*, III, ii [Schlegel's note].
[4] *As You Like It* [Schlegel's note].

shortly before, and the very name must have immediately suggested the idea of freedom in thinking. I cannot even consider it an anachronism that Richard the Third should speak of Macchiavelli. The word is here used altogether proverbially: the contents, at least, of the book entitled. *Of the Prince* (*Del Principe*) have been in existence ever since the existence of tyrants; Macchiavelli was merely the first to commit them to writing.

XXVIII

. . . The comic muse, instead of becoming familiar with life in the middle and lower ranks (her proper sphere), assumed an air of distinction: she squeezed herself into courts, and endeavored to snatch a resemblance of the *beau monde*. It was now[5] no longer an English national, but a London comedy. The whole turns almost exclusively on fashionable love-suits and fashionable raillery; the love-affairs are either disgusting or insipid, and the raillery is always puerile and destitute of wit. These comic writers may have accurately hit the tone of their time; in this they did their duty; but they have reared a lamentable memorial of their age. In few periods has taste in the fine arts been at such a low ebb as about the close of the seventeenth and during the first half of the eighteenth century. . . .

The last, and not the least defect of the English comedies is their offensiveness. I may sum up the whole in one word by saying that after all we know of the licentiousness of manners under Charles II, we are still lost in astonishment at the audacious ribaldry of Wycherley and Congreve. Decency is not merely violated in the grossest manner in single speeches, and frequently in the whole plot; but in the character of the rake, the fashionable debauchee, a moral scepticism is directly preached up, and marriage is the constant subject of their ridicule.

[5] During the Restoration.

Arthur Schopenhauer 1788–1860

The World as Will and Idea 1818

I

Tragedy is to be regarded, and is recognized, as the summit of poetical art, both on account of the greatness of its effect and the difficulty of its achievement. It is very significant for our whole system, and well worthy of observation, that the end of this highest poetical achievement is the representation of the terrible side of life. The unspeakable pain, the wail of humanity, the triumph of evil, the scornful mastery of chance, and the irretrievable fall of the just and innocent, is here presented to us; and in this lies a significant hint of the nature of the world and of existence. It is the strife of will with itself, which here, completely unfolded at the highest grade of its objectivity, comes into fearful prominence. It becomes visible in the suffering of men, which is now introduced, party through chance and error, which appear as the rulers of the world, personified as fate, on account of their insidiousness, which even reaches the appearance of design; partly it proceeds from man himself, through the self-mortifying efforts of a few, through the wickedness and perversity of most. It is one and the same will that lives and appears in them all, but whose phenomena fight against each other and destroy each other. In one individual it appears powerfully, in another more weakly; in one more subject to reason, and softened by the light of knowledge, in another less so, till at last, in some single case, this knowledge, purified and heightened by suffering itself, reaches the point at which the phenomenon, the veil of Maya,[1] no longer deceives it. It sees through the form of the phenomenon, the *principum individuationis*.[2] The egoism which rests on this perishes with it, so that now the *motives* that were so powerful before have lost their might, and instead of them the complete knowledge of the nature of the world, which has a *quieting* effect on the will, produces resignation, the surrender not merely of life, but of the very will to live. Thus we see in tragedies the noblest men, after long conflict and suffering, at last renounce the ends they have so keenly followed, and all the pleasures of life forever, or else freely and joyfully surrender life itself. So is it with the steadfast prince of Calderon; with Gretchen in *Faust*;[3] with

Selections. From Arthur Schopenhauer, *The World as Will and Idea*, translated by R. B. Haldane and J. Kemp. London: Trübner & Co., 1883.

[1] *Maya* means appearance or illusion; the veil of Maya separates appearance from truth or from the true reality.

[2] According to Thomas Aquinas, the principle of individuation.

[3] *The Constant Prince* (1629) by Calderon; *Faust*, Part I (1806), by Goethe.

Hamlet, whom his friend Horatio would willingly follow, but is bade remain a while, and in this harsh world draw his breath in pain, to tell the story of Hamlet, and clear his memory; so also is it with the Maid of Orleans, the Bride of Messina;[4] they all die purified by suffering, i.e., after the will to live which was formerly in them is dead. In the *Mohammed* of Voltaire this is actually expressed in the concluding words which the dying Palmira addresses to Mohammed: "The world is for tyrants: live!" On the other hand, the demand for so-called poetical justice rests on entire misconception of the nature of tragedy, and, indeed, of the nature of the world itself. It boldly appears in all its dullness in the criticisms which Dr. Samuel Johnson made on particular plays of Shakespeare, for he very naïvely laments its entire absence. And its absence is certainly obvious, for in what has Ophelia, Desdemona, or Cordelia offended? But only the dull, optimistic, Protestant-rationalistic, or peculiarly Jewish view of life will make the demand for poetical justice, and find satisfaction in it. The true sense of tragedy is the deeper insight, that it is not his own individual sins that the hero atones for, but original sin, i.e., the crime of existence itself:

> Pues el delito mayor
> Del hombre es haber nacido
>
> (For the greatest crime of man
> Is that he was born)

as Calderon exactly expresses it.[5]

I shall allow myself only one remark more closely concerning the treatment of tragedy. The representation of a great misfortune is alone essential to tragedy. But the many different ways in which this is introduced by the poet may be brought under three specific conceptions. It may happen by means of a character of extraordinary wickedness, touching the utmost limits of possibility, who becomes the author of the misfortune; examples of this kind are Richard III, Iago in *Othello*, Shylock in *The Merchant of Venice*, Franz Moor,[6] Phaedra of Euripides, Creon in the *Antigone*, etc., etc. Secondly, it may happen through blind fate, i.e., chance and error; a true pattern of this kind is the *Oedipus Rex* of Sophocles, the *Trachiniae* also; and in general most of the tragedies of the ancients belong to this class. Among modern tragedies, *Romeo and Juliet*, *Tancred* by Voltaire, and *The Bride of Messina* are examples. Lastly, the misfortune may be brought about by the mere position of the dramatis personae with regard to each other, through their relations; so that there is no need either for a tremendous error or an unheard-of accident, nor yet for a character whose wickedness reaches the limits of human

---

[4] The title characters of plays by Schiller.
[5] *Life Is a Dream* (1631–1632), Act I.
[6] *The Robbers* (1781) by Schiller.

possibility; but characters of ordinary morality, under circumstances such as often occur, are so situated with regard to each other that their position compels them, knowingly and with their eyes open, to do each other the greatest injury, without any one of them being entirely in the wrong. This last kind of tragedy seems to me far to surpass the other two, for it shows us the greatest misfortune not as an exception, not as something occasioned by rare circumstances or monstrous characters, but as arising easily and of itself out of the actions and characters of men, indeed almost as essential to them, and thus brings it terribly near to us. In the other two kinds we may look on the prodigious fate and the horrible wickedness as terrible powers which certainly threaten us, but only from afar, which we may very well escape without taking refuge in renunciation. But in the last kind of tragedy we see that those powers which destroy happiness and life are such that their path to us also is open at every moment; we see the greatest sufferings brought about by entanglements that our fate might also partake of, and through actions that perhaps we also are capable of performing, and so could not complain of injustice; then shuddering we feel ourselves already in the midst of hell. This last kind of tragedy is also the most difficult of achievement; for the greatest effect has to be produced in it with the least use of means and causes of movement, merely through the position and distribution of the characters; therefore even in many of the best tragedies this difficulty is evaded. Yet one tragedy may be referred to as a perfect model of this kind, a tragedy which in other respects is far surpassed by more than one work of the same great master; it is *Clavigo*.[7] Hamlet belongs to a certain extent to this class, as far as the relation of Hamlet to Laertes and Ophelia is concerned. *Wallenstien*[8] has also this excellence. *Faust* belongs entirely to this class, if we regard the events connected with Gretchen and her brother as the principal action; also *The Cid* of Corneille, only that it lacks the tragic conclusion, while on the contrary the analogous relation of Max to Thecla[9] has it. . . .

III

The end of the drama in general is to show us in an example what is the nature and existence of man. The sad or the bright side of these can be turned to us in it, or their transitions into each other. But the expression, "nature and existence of man," already contains the germ of the controversy whether the nature, i.e., the character, or the existence, i.e., the fate, the adventures, the action, is the principal thing. Moreover, the two have grown so firmly together that although they can certainly be separated in

[7] By Goethe.
[8] By Schiller.
[9] In the *Wallenstein* trilogy.

conception, they cannot be separated in the representation of them. For only the circumstances, the fate, the events, make the character manifest its nature, and only from the character does the action arise from which the events proceed. Certainly, in the representation, the one or the other may be made more prominent; and in this respect the piece which centers in the characters and the piece which centers in the plot are the two extremes.

The common end of the drama and the epic, to exhibit, in significant characters placed in significant situations, the extraordinary actions brought about by both, will be most completely attained by the poet if he first introduces the characters to us in a state of peace, in which merely their general color becomes visible, and allows a motive to enter which produces an action, out of which a new and stronger motive arises, which again calls forth a more significant action, which, in its turn, begets new and even stronger motives, whereby, then, in the time suitable to the form of the poem, the most passionate excitement takes the place of the original peace, and in this now the important actions occur in which the qualities of the characters which have hitherto slumbered are brought clearly to light, together with the course of the world.

Great poets transform themselves into each of the persons to be represented, and speak out of each of them like ventriloquists; now out of the hero, and immediately afterwards out of the young and innocent maiden, with equal truth and naturalness: so Shakespeare and Goethe. Poets of the second rank transform the principal person to be represented into themselves. This is what Byron does; and then the other persons often remain lifeless, as is the case even with the principal persons in the works of mediocre poets.

Our pleasure in tragedy belongs, not to the sense of the beautiful, but to that of the sublime; nay, it is the highest grade of this feeling. For, as at the sight of the sublime in nature we turn away from the interests of the will in order to be purely perceptive, so in the tragic catastrophe we turn away even from the will to live. In tragedy the terrible side of life is presented to us, the wail of humanity, the reign of chance and error, the fall of the just, the triumph of the wicked; thus the aspect of the world which directly strives against our will is brought before our eyes. At this sight we feel ourselves challenged to turn away our will from life, no longer to will it or love it. But just in this way become conscious that then there still remains something over to us, which we absolutely cannot know positively, but only negatively, as that which does not will life. As the chord of the seventh demands the fundamental chord; as the color red demands green, and even produces it in the eye; so every tragedy demands an entirely different kind of existence, another world, the knowledge of which can only be given us indirectly just as here by such a demand. In the moment of the tragic catastrophe the conviction becomes more distinct to us than ever that life is a bad dream from which we have to awake. So far the effect of the tragedy is analogous to that of the dynamical sublime, for like this it lifts us above the will and its interests, and puts us in such a mood that we find pleasure in the sight of what tends directly against it. What gives to all tragedy, in whatever form it may appear, the peculiar tendency towards the sublime is the awakening of the knowledge that the world, life, can afford us no true pleasure, and consequently is not worthy of our attachment. In this consists the tragic spirit: it therefore leads to resignation.

I admit that in ancient tragedy this spirit of resignation seldom appears and is expressed directly. Oedipus Colons certainly dies resigned and willing; yet he is comforted by the revenge on his country. Iphigenia at Aulis is very willing to die; yet it is the thought of the welfare of Greece that comforts her, and occasions the change of her mind, on account of which she willingly accepts the death which at first she sought to avoid by any means. Cassandra, in the *Agamemnon* of the great Aeschylus, dies willingly; but she also is comforted by the thought of revenge. Hercules, in the *Trachiniae*, submits to necessity, and dies composed, but not resigned. So also the Hippolytus of Euripides, in whose case it surprises us that Artemis, who appears to comfort him, promises him temples and fame, but never points him to an existence beyond life, and leaves him in death, as all gods forsake the dying: in Christianity they come to him; and so also in Brahmanism and Buddhism, although in the latter the gods are really exotic. Thus Hippolytus, like almost all the tragic heroes of the ancients, shows submission to inevitable fate and the inflexible will of the gods, but no surrender of the will to live itself. As the Stoic equanimity is fundamentally distinguished from Christian resignation by the fact that it teaches only patient endurance and composed expectation of unalterably necessary evil, while Christianity teaches renunciation, surrender of the will; so also the tragic heroes of the ancients show resolute subjection under the unavoidable blows of fate, while Christian tragedy, on the contrary, shows the surrender of the whole will to live, joyful forsaking of the world in the consciousness of its worthlessness and vanity. But I am also entirely of opinion that modern tragedy stands higher than that of the ancients. Shakespeare is much greater than Sophocles; in comparison with Goethe's *Iphigenia* one might find that of Euripides almost crude and vulgar. *The Bacchae* of Euripides is a revolting composition in favor of the heathen priests. Many ancient pieces have no tragic tendency at all, like the *Alcestis* and *Iphigenia in Tauris* of Euripides; some have disagreeable, or even disgusting motives, like the *Antigone* and *Philoctetes*. Almost all show the human race under the fearful rule of chance and error, but not the resignation which is occasioned by it, and delivers from it. All because the ancients had not yet attained to the summit and goal of tragedy, or indeed of the view of life itself.

Although, then, the ancients displayed little of the spirit of resignation, the turning away of the will from life, in their tragic heroes themselves, as their frame of mind, yet the peculiar tendency and effect of tragedy remains the awakening of that spirit in the beholder, the calling up of that frame of mind, even though only temporarily. The horrors upon the stage hold up to him the bitterness and worthlessness of life, thus the vanity of all its struggle. The effect of this impression must be that he becomes conscious, if only in obscure feeling, that it is better to tear his heart free from life, to turn his will from it, to love not the world nor life; whereby then in his deepest soul, the consciousness is aroused that for another kind of willing there must also be another existence. For if this were not so, then the tendency of tragedy would not be this rising above all the ends and good things of life, this turning away from it and its seductions, and the turning towards another kind of existence, which already lies in this, although an existence which is for us quite inconceivable. How would it, then, in general, be possible that the exhibition of the most terrible side of life, brought before our eyes in the most glaring light, could act upon us beneficently, and afford us a lofty satisfaction? Fear and sympathy, in the excitement of which Aristotle places the ultimate end of tragedy, certainly do not in themselves belong to the agreeable sensations: therefore they cannot be the end, but only the means. Thus the summons to turn away the will from life remains the true tendency of tragedy, the ultimate end of the intentional exhibition of the suffering of humanity, and is so accordingly even where this resigned exaltation of the mind is not shown in the hero himself, but is merely excited in the spectator by the sight of great, unmerited, nay, even merited suffering. Many of the moderns also are, like the ancients, satisfied with throwing the spectator into the mood which has been described, by the objective representation of human misfortune as a whole; while others exhibit this through the change of the frame of mind of the hero himself, effected by suffering. The former give, as it were, only the premises, and leave the conclusion to the spectator; while the latter give the conclusion, or the moral of the fable, also, as the change of the frame of mind of the hero, and even also as reflection, in the mouth of the chorus, as, for example, Schiller in *The Bride of Messina*: "Life is not the highest good. . . ."

If now we have found the tendency and ultimate intention of tragedy to be a turning to resignation, to the denial of the will to live, we shall easily recognize in its opposite, comedy, the incitement to the continued assertion of the will. It is true the comedy, like every representation of human life, without exception, must bring before our eyes suffering and adversity; but it presents it to us as passing, resolving itself into joy, in general mingled with success, victory, and hopes, which in the end preponderate; moreover, it brings out the inexhaustible material for laughter of which life, and even its adversities themselves are filled, and which under all circumstances ought to keep us in a good humor. Thus it declares, in the result, that life as a whole is thoroughly good, and especially is always amusing. Certainly it must hasten to drop the curtain at the moment of joy, so that we may not see what comes after; while the tragedy, as a rule, so ends that nothing can come after.

Georg Wilhelm Friedrich Hegel *1770–1831*

The End of Art *1818–1829*

. . . The end of art has been pronounced to be that it should *teach*. Thus, on the one side, the peculiar character of art would consist in the movement of the emotions and in the satisfaction which lies in this movement, even in fear, compassion, in painful pathos and shock—that is to say, in the satisfying engagement of the emotions and passions, and to that extent in a complacency, entertainment, and delight in the objects of art, in their representation and effect; but, on the other side, this purpose (of art) is held to find its higher standard only in its instructiveness, in the *fabula docet*,[1] and thus in the useful influence which the work of art succeeds in exerting on the subject.[2] In this respect the Horatian saw, "*Et prodesse volunt et delectare poetae*" ("Poets aim at utility and entertainment alike"), contains, concentrated in a few words, all that has subsequently been elaborated in infinite degrees, and diluted into the uttermost extreme of insipidity as a doctrine of art. As regards such instruction we have, then, to ask whether it is meant to be directly or indirectly, explicitly or implicitly contained in the work of art.

If, speaking generally, we are concerned about a purpose which is universal and not contingent, it follows that this purpose, considering the

Selections. From *Introduction to Hegel's Philosophy of Fine Art*, translated by Bernard Bosanquet. London: Kegan Paul, Trench & Co., 1886. The title is the present editor's.

[1] The moral [this note, and those that follow, are the translator's].
[2] Person, i.e., here, audience or spectator.

essentially spiritual nature of art, cannot but be itself spiritual, and indeed, moreover, one which is not contingent,[3] but actual in its nature and for its own sake. Such a purpose in relation to teaching could only consist in bringing before consciousness, by help of the work of art, a really and explicitly significant spiritual content. From this point of view it is to be asserted that the higher art ranks itself, the more it is bound to admit into itself such a content as this, and that only in the essence of such a content can it find the standard which determines whether what is expressed is appropriate or inappropriate. Art was, in fact, the first *instructress* of peoples.

But the purpose of instruction may be treated as *purpose*, to such a degree that the universal nature of the represented content is doomed to be exhibited and expounded directly and obviously as abstract proposition, prosaic reflection, or general theorem, and not merely in an indirect way in the concrete form of a work of art. By such a severance the sensuous plastic form, which is just what makes the work of art a work of *art*, becomes a mere otiose accessory, a husk which is expressly pronounced to be mere husk, a semblance expressly pronounced to be mere semblance. But thereby the very nature of the work of art is distorted. For the work of art ought to bring a content before the mind's eye, not in its generality as such, but with this generality made absolutely individual, and sensuously particularized. If the work of art does not proceed from this principle, but sets in relief its generalized aspect with the purpose of abstract instruction, then the imaginative and sensuous aspect is only an external and superfluous adornment, and the work of art is a thing divided against itself, in which form and content no longer appear as grown into one. In that case the sensuously individual and the spiritually general are become external to one another.

And further, if the purpose of art is limited to this *didactic* utility, then its other aspect, that of pleasure, entertainment, and delight, is pronounced to be in itself *unessential*, and ought to have its substance merely in the utility of the teaching on which it is attendant. But this amounts to pronouncing that art does not bear its vocation and purpose in itself, but that its conception is rooted in something else, to which it is a *means*. Art is, in this case, only one among the several means which prove useful and are applied for the purpose of instruction. This brings us to the boundary at which art is made no longer to be an end on its own merits, seeing that it is degraded into a mere toy of entertainment or a mere means of instruction.

This boundary becomes most sharply marked when a question is raised, in its turn, about a supreme end and aim for the sake of which the pas-

---

[3] "Contingent" means, not so much "what may or may not exist," as the trivial, which makes no difference whether it exists or not.

sions are to be purified and men are to be instructed. This aim has often, in modern times, been declared to be *moral* improvement, and the aim of art has been placed in the function of preparing the inclinations and impulses for moral perfection, and of leading them to this goal. This idea combines purification with instruction, inasmuch as art is, by communicating an insight into genuine moral goodness—that is, by instruction—at the same time to incite to purification, and in this way alone to bring about the improvement of mankind as its useful purpose and supreme goal.

Regarding art in reference to moral improvement, the same has *prima facie* to be said as about the didactic purpose. We may readily grant that art must not as a principle take for its aim the immoral and its furtherance. But it is one thing to take immorality for the express aim of representation, and another to abstain from taking morality. Every genuine work of art may have a good moral drawn from it, but, of course, in doing so much depends on interpretation and on him who draws the moral. Thus one may hear the most immoral representations defended by saying that we must know evil, or sin, in order to act morally; and, conversely, it has been said that the portrayal of Mary Magdalene, the beautful sinner who afterwards repented, has seduced many into sin, because art makes it look so beautiful to repent, and you must sin before you can repent. But the doctrine of moral improvement, if consistently carried out, goes in general yet further. It would not be satisfied with the possibility of extracting a moral from a work of art by interpretation, but it would, on the contrary, display the moral instruction as the substantive purpose of the work of art, and, indeed, would actually admit to portrayal none but moral subjects, moral characters, actions, and incidents. For art has the choice among its subjects, in contradistinction to history or the sciences which have their matter fixed for them....

. . . To be respectable and virtuous is not enough to make a man moral. Morality involves *reflection* and the definite consciousness of that which duty prescribes, and acting out of such a prior consciousness. Duty itself is the law of the will, which man nevertheless lays down freely out of his own self, and then is supposed to determine himself to this duty for duty's and its fulfilment's sake, by doing good solely from the conviction which he has attained that it is the good. Now this law, the duty which is chosen for duty's sake to be the guide of action, out of free conviction and the inner conscience, and is then acted upon, is, taken by itself, the abstract universal of the will, and is the direct antithesis of nature, the sensuous impulses, the self-seeking interests, the passions, and of all that is comprehensively entitled the feelings and the heart. In this antagonism the one side is regarded as *negativing* the other; and, seeing that both are present as antagonists within the subject (person), he has, as determining himself out of himself, the choice of following the one or the other. . . . For the modern moralistic view starts from the fixed antithesis of the will in its spiritual universality to its sensuous natural particularity,[4] and consists not in the completed reconciliation of these contrasted sides, but in their conflict with one another, which involves the requirement that the impulses which conflict with duty ought to yield to it.

This antithesis does not merely display itself for our consciousness in the limited region of moral action; but also emerges as a fundamental distinction and antagonism between that which is real essentially and in its own right, and that which is external reality and existence. Formulated in the abstract, it is the contrast of the universal and particular, when the former is explicitly fixed over against the latter, just as the latter is over against the former; more concretely, it appears in nature as the opposition of the abstract law against the abundance of individual phenomena, each having its own character; in the mind, as the sensuous and spiritual in man, as the battle of the spirit against the flesh, of duty for duty's sake, the cold command, with the individual interest, the warm feelings, the sensuous inclinations and impulses, the individual disposition as such; as the hard conflict of inward freedom and of natural necessity; further, as the contradiction of the dead conception—empty in itself—compared with full concrete vitality, or of theory and subjective thought contrasted with objective existence and experience. . . .

Now, as an ultimate aim implied a higher standpoint in the case of moral improvement, we shall have to vindicate this higher standpoint for art no less than for morals. Thereby we at once lay aside the false position, which has already been remarked upon, that art has to serve as a means for moral ends, and to conduce to the moral end of the world, as such, by instruction and moral improvement, and thereby has its substantive aim, not in itself, but in something else. If, therefore, we now continue to speak of an aim or purpose, we must, in the first instance, get rid of the perverse idea, which, in asking "What is the aim?" retains the accessory meaning of the question, "What is the *use*?" The perverseness of this lies in the point that the work of art would then be regarded as aspiring to something else which is set before consciousness as the essential and as what ought to be; so that then the work of art would only have value as a useful instrument in the realization of an end having substantive importance *outside* the sphere of art. Against this it is necessary to maintain that art has the vocation of revealing *the truth* in the form of sensuous artistic shape, of representing the reconciled antithesis just described, and, therefore, has its purpose in itself,

---

[4] As, e.g., if we suppose that an act done at the bidding of natural affection cannot also be a fulfilment of the command of duty. The "reconciliation" would be in supposing the natural affection, e.g., for parents, to operate as a moral motive, being transformed by a recognition of its sacred or spiritual character.

in this representation and revelation. For other objects, such as instruction, purification, improvement, pecuniary gain, endeavor after fame and honor, have nothing to do with the work of art as such, and do not determine its conception.

Symbolic, Classic, and Romantic *1818–1829*

. . . The idea of each epoch always finds its appropriate and adequate form; and these are what we designate as the special forms of art. The imperfection or the perfection can consist only in the degree of relative truth which belongs to the idea itself; for the matter must first be true, and developed in itself, before it can find a perfectly appropriate form.

We have, in this respect, *three principal forms* to consider:

1.   The first is the *Symbolic Form.* Here the idea seeks its true expression in art without finding it; because, being still abstract and indefinite, it cannot create an external manifestation which conforms to its real essence. It finds itself in presence of the phenomena of nature and of the events of human life, as if confronted by a foreign world. Thus it exhausts itself in useless efforts to produce a complete expression of conceptions vague and ill defined; it perverts and falsifies the forms of the real world which it seizes in arbitrary relations. Instead of combining and identifying, of blending totally the form and the idea, it arrives only at a superficial and abstract agreement between them. These two terms, thus brought into connection, manifest their disproportion and heterogeneity.

2.   But the idea, in virtue of its very nature, cannot remain thus, in abstraction and indetermination. As the principle of free activity, it seizes itself in its reality as spirit. The spirit, then, as free subject, is determined by and for itself, and in thus determining itself it finds in its own essence its appropriate outward form. This unity, this perfect harmony

Selections. From *The Philosophy of Art: Being the Second Part of Hegel's Aesthetik*, translated by William M. Bryant. New York: D. Appleton & Co., 1879.

between the idea and its external manifestation, constitutes the second form of art— the *Classic Form*.

Here art has attained its perfection, insofar as there is reached a perfect harmony between the idea as spiritual individuality, and the form as sensuous and corporeal reality. All hostility between the two elements has disappeared, in order to give place to a perfect harmony.

3.   Nevertheless, spirit cannot rest with this form, which is not its complete realization. To reach this perfect realization, spirit must pass beyond the classic form, must arrive at a pure spirituality, which, returning upon itself, descends into the depths of its own inmost nature. In the classic form, indeed, notwithstanding its generality, spirit reveals itself with a special determinate character; it does not escape from the finite. Its external form, as a form altogether visible, is limited. The matter, the idea itself, because there is perfect fusion, must present the same character. Only the finite spirit is able to unite itself with external manifestation so as to form an indissoluble unity.

When the idea of beauty seizes itself as absolute or infinite spirit, it also at the same time discovers itself to be no longer completely realized in the forms of the external world; it is only in the internal world of consciousness that it finds, as spirit, its true unity. It breaks up then this unity which forms the basis of Classic Art; it abandons the external world in order to take refuge within itself. This is what furnishes the type of the *Romantic Form*. Sensuous representation, with its images borrowed from the external world, no longer sufficing to express free spirituality, the form becomes foreign and indifferent to the idea. So that Romantic Art thus reproduces the separation of matter and form, but from the side opposite to that from which this separation takes place in Symbolic Art.

As a summary of the foregoing, we may say that Symbolic Art *seeks* this perfect unity of the idea with the external form; Classic Art *finds* it, for the senses and the imagination, in the representation of spiritual individuality; Romantic Art *transcends* it in its infinite spirituality, which rises above the visible world. . . .

The true content of Romantic thought, then, is absolute internality, the adequate and appropriate form of which is spiritual subjectivity, or conscious personality, as comprehension of its own independence and freedom. Now, that which is in itself infinite and wholly universal is the absolute negativity of all that is finite and particular. It is the simple unity with self which has destroyed all mutually exclusive objects, all processes of nature, with their circle of genesis, decay, and renewal—which, in short, has put an end to all limitation of spiritual existence, and dissolved all particular divinities into pure, infinite identity with itself. In this pantheon all the gods are dethroned. The flame of subjectivity has consumed them. In place of plastic polytheism, art now knows but *one* God, *one* Spirit, one absolute independence, which, as absolute knowing and determining, abides in free unity with itself, and no longer falls asunder into these special characters and functions whose sole bond of unity was the constraint of a mysterious necessity. Absolute subjectivity, or personality as such, however, would escape from art and be accessible only to abstract thought, if, in order to be an actual subjectivity commensurate with its idea, it did not pass into external existence, and again collect itself out of this reality into itself. . . .

But the external existence of God is not the natural and sensuous, as such, but the sensuous elevated to the supersensuous, to spiritual subjectivity, to personality, which, instead of losing the certainty of itself in its outer manifestation, truly for the first time attains to the present actual certainty of itself through its own reality. God in His truth is, therefore, no mere ideal created by the imagination. Rather, He places Himself in the midst of the finitude and outer accidentality of immediate existence, and yet knows Himself in all this as the divine principle which in itself remains infinite and creates for itself this infinitude. Since, therefore, actual subject or person is the manifestation of God, art now acquires the higher right of employing the human form, together with the modes and conditions of externality generally, for the expression of the Absolute. Nevertheless, the new problem for art can consist only in this: that in this form the inner shall not be submerged in outer corporeal existence, but shall, on the contrary, return into itself in order to bring into view the spiritual consciousness of God in the individual. The various moments or elements brought to light by the totality of this view of the world as totality of the truth itself, therefore, now find their manifestation in man. And this, in the sense that neither nature as such—as the sun, the sky, the stars, etc.—gives the content and the form, nor does the circle of the divinities of the Greek world of beauty, nor the heroes, nor external deeds in the province of the morality of the family and of political life, attain to infinite value. Rather it is the actual, individual subject or person who acquires this value, since it is in him alone that the eternal moments or elements of absolute truth, which exist actually only as spirit, are multifariously individualized and at the same time reduced to a consistent and abiding unity. . . .

If personal subjectivity—as it presents itself in its absolute independence —constitutes the essential characteristic in honor, so, and far more, the highest phase of love is the *devotion* of the subject or person to an individual of the opposite sex, the surrender of his independent consciousness, and of his individual isolated being, which feels itself to have become thoroughly penetrated with its own knowledge of itself, for the first time, in the consciousness of another. In this respect love and honor are contrasted the one with the other. On the other hand, however, we can also consider love as the realization of that which already lies in honor in so far as it is a necessity of honor, when this is itself recognized, to see the infinity of the one person accepted in another person. This recognition is for the first time true and complete when my personality is respected by another, not merely in the abstract, or in a concrete, individualized, and therefore limited instance, but when, in conformity with my entire subjectivity, with all that this is, and all that it contains in itself as this individual, past, present, and to be, I pervade the consciousness of another, and constitute his very will and thought, his endeavor and his possession. For this other lives only in me, as I, in turn, exist only in him. It is only in this completed unity that the two exist truly— each for himself—and in this identity place their whole souls and the entire world. In this respect it is the same internal infinity of the subject, or person, which gives to love its importance for Romantic Art, an importance which is still further enhanced through the greater wealth here contained in the conception of love.

But, again, love does not, as often happens with honor, rest upon the reflections and casuistry of the understanding. On the contrary, its origin is found to be in sentiment. It is thus that, where difference of sex assumes importance, love presents the characteristic of a spiritualized, natural-relationship. Here, however, it is essential only from the fact that in this relation the subject, or person, develops in accordance with its own inner nature; [i.e., in accordance] with its ideal infinitude. This absorption of consciousness in another; this appearance of disinterestedness and unselfishness, through which the individual, for the first time, again finds himself, and comes to himself; this forgetfulness of self, so that the lover does not exist for himself, does not live and care for himself, but finds the essence of his own existence in another, and yet completely enjoys himself in this other, constitutes the infinity of love. Again, the beauty to be found therein consists especially in this: that this feeling does not remain merely inclination and feeling, but that the fantasy extends its world in such measure that all else which, in interests, circumstances, and aims, previously belonged to actual being and life, it here elevates to [the rank of] an ornament of this feeling, draws all into this circle, and only in this respect assigns to it a value. It is especially in female characters that love rises to its highest beauty; for it is in woman that this devotion, this self-surrender, is the supreme point; for she concentrates and develops her whole spiritual and actual life in this sentiment, finds in it alone a context of existence, and disappears before the blast of misfortune, like a light extinguished at the first rude breath.

In Classic Art, love appears not in this subjective internality of sentiment, but rather for the most part only as a subordinate element of the representation, or again only on the side of sensual enjoyment. . . . The high tragedies of antiquity know nothing of the sorrows of love in the Romantic signification. Especially with Aeschylus and Sophocles, it makes no pretence to essential and independent interest. Thus, although Antigone is chosen to be the bride of Haemon,[1] and though Haemon himself espouses the cause of Antigone even in opposition to his own father, and proceeds to the extreme of destroying himself when he finds himself unable to save her, he nevertheless presents to Creon only objective relations, and not the subjective energy of his own passion, which, in truth, he does not at all experience in the sense of a modern sincere lover. Euripides, again (for example, in Phaedra),[2] treats love as a more essential passion. But here, also it appears as a reprehensible madness of the blood, as a sensual passion caused by Venus, who desires to destroy Hippolytus because he refuses to sacrifice to her. So, too, in the Venus de Medici, we have a plastic image of love against which nothing can be said respecting grace and the perfect execution of the form; but the expression of internality which Romantic art demands of it is wholly wanting. . . .

. . . With the Spanish it [love] abounds in images, is chivalrous, is sometimes subtle in seeking out and defending its rights and duties, as personal affairs of honor; and here, too, it is fanciful in its highest brillancy. With the modern French, again, it is more gallant, with a tendency toward vanity. It is an artificial sentiment which aims at poetic effect, and into the expression of which there often penetrates much spirit and a sophistic subtlety rich in significance. Sometimes it is a voluptuousness without passion, sometimes a passion without voluptuousness, a sublimated sentiment and susceptibility full of reflection. . . .

The most frequent collision which we have to mention, in this respect, is that between Love and Honor. On its side, honor possesses the same infinity as love, and may assume a content which will stand as an absolute hindrance in the way of love. The duty of honor may demand the sacrifice of love. From certain standpoints, for example, it would be contrary to honor for one in a higher station to love a woman of lower rank. The difference of rank is, from the nature of the case, something necessary and predetermined. If, now, secular life has not yet been regenerated, through the infinite comprehension of true freedom, in virtue of which the individual can himself choose his condition and determine his vocation, it is, on the one hand, and in greater or less degree, nature, birth, which assigns to man his permanent position; on the other hand, the distinctions which thus appear are also, through honor (in so far as this makes of its own position or rank an affair of honor), held fast as absolute and infinite.

But secondly, aside from honor, the eternal, substantial powers, the interests of the state, love of country, duty to one's family, etc., enter into conflict with love, and oppose its realization. It is in modern representations, in which the objective relations of life have already attained to importance,

---

[1] In the *Antigone* of Sophocles.
[2] In the character of Phaedra, that is; the play is the *Hippolytus* of Euripides.

that this collision is an especially favorite one. Here, love, as an independent and highly important right of the subjective soul, is placed in opposition to other rights and duties, as inferior, or that it may acknowledge them [as binding], in which case a struggle ensues between duty, on the one side, and the violence of passion on the other. *The Maid of Orleans*,[3] for example, is based upon this last collision.

Thirdly, however, there may be, in general, *external* relations and hindrances which oppose love—the ordinary course of things, the prose of life, unhappy accidents, passions, prejudices, narrownesses, egotism in others—incidents of the most manifold kinds. . . . This species of conflict, however, since it rests upon mere accidentality, is of an inferior order. . . .

. . . Romantic love has also its limits or imperfections. What is wanting in its content is independent and self-sufficing *universality*. It is only the *personal* sentiment of the special individual, who shows himself to be filled, not with the permanent interests and objective content of human existence —with family, political aims, fatherland, duties of a vocation, of position, of freedom, of religion—but only with himself. He seeks only to find himself reflected in another self—that is, to cause this other to reciprocate his passion. But this content of formal internality does not truly correspond to the totality, which must be a genuinely concrete individual. In the family, in marriage, in duty, in the state, the subjective sentiment, as such, and the consequent immediate union with this, and no other individual, is not the chief object for which effort is made. But, in Romantic love, everything is concentrated upon this, namely, that two individuals experience an affection each for the other. Why it is precisely this, and no other individual, has its explanation in subjective peculiarity, or personal preference, in the accident of caprice. To the man, his beloved appears the most beautiful, and to the maiden, the one whom she loves appears the most noble of all in the world; and this, notwithstanding the fact that others may find them both altogether ordinary individuals. . . . That the preference should be given always and absolutely to one, and only one, is, therefore, a mere private affair of the subjective heart, and of the individuality or particularity of the person; and the immeasurable obstinacy of necessarily finding precisely in this one alone his life, his highest consciousness, bears the appearance of a boundless caprice of necessity. . . .

. . . The personages in the high tragedies of the ancients—Agamemnon, Clytemnestra, Orestes, Oedipus, Antigone, Creon, etc.—have, it is true, an individual aim; but that which is substantial in them, the true pathos, that which impels them, and constitutes the read content of their deeds, is of absolute legitimacy, and hence also of essentially universal interest. The fate which befalls them in consequence of their acts, is, therefore, not touching

[3] By Schiller (1801).

because it is an unhappy destiny, but because it is an unhappiness such as commands absolute respect; for the pathos which rests only when it has attained satisfaction possesses an essential and necessary content. But those sorrows of love, those shattered hopes, that distressed existence in general, those infinite torments which a lover experiences, that immeasurable happiness and felicity which he pictures to himself, are by no means in themselves essential interests, but only something which concerns himself merely. Every man, it is true, has a heart for love, and has also the right to become happy through love. But should he, in precisely this case, under such or such circumstances, in respect to precisely this woman, fail to attain to happiness, he is not to be considered as thereby suffering injustice. For it is not in itself necessary that he should become enamored of this particular woman, or that we should interest ourselves in the merest accidentality, in the caprice of the individual, which possesses no extension or universality. This persists as the side of coldness which penetrates us throughout the representations of passion in spite of all their warmth.

Dramatic Poetry   *1818–1829*

The reason that dramatic poetry must be regarded as the highest phase of the art of poetry, and, indeed, of every kind of art, is due to the fact that it is elaborated, both in form and substance, in a whole that is the most complete. For in contrast to every other sort of sensuous *materia*, whether it be stone, wood, color, or tone, that of human speech is the only medium fully adequate to the presentation of spiritual life; and further, among the particular types of the art of articulate speech, dramatic poetry is the one in which we find the objective character of the Epos essentially united to the subjective principle of the Lyric. In other words it presents directly before our vision an essentially independent action as a definite fact, which does not merely originate from the personal life of character under the process of self-realization, but receives its determinate form as the result of the sub-

Selections. From *The Philosophy of Fine Art*, Vol. IV, by G. W. F. Hegel, translated by F. P. B. Osmaston. London: G. Bell & Sons, Ltd., 1920. Reprinted by permission of the publishers, G. Bell & Sons, Ltd.

stantive interaction in concrete life of ideal intention, many individuals, and collisions. This mediated form of epic art by means of the intimate personal life of an individual viewed in the very presence of his activity does not, however, permit the drama to describe the external aspects of local condition and environment, nor yet the action and event itself in the way that they are so described in the epic. Consequently, in order that the entire art product may receive the full animation of life, we require its complete scenic representation. . . .

. . . Dramatic action, however, is not confined to the simple and undisturbed execution of a definite purpose, but depends throughout on conditions of collision, human passion, and characters, and leads therefore to actions and reactions, which in their turn call for some further resolution of conflict and disruption. What we have consequently before us are definite ends individualized in living personalities and situations pregnant with conflict; we see these as they are asserted and maintained, as they work in cooperation or opposition—all in a momentary and kaleidoscopic interchange of expression—and along with this, too, the final result presupposed and issuing from the entirety of this interthreading and conflicting skein of human life, movement, and accomplishment, which has nonetheless to work out its tranquil resolution. . . .

The more obvious laws of dramatic composition may be summarized in the time-honored prescription of the so-called unities of place, time, and action.

The inalterability of one exclusive *locale* of the action proposed belongs to the type of those rigid rules which the French in particluar have deduced from classic tragedy and the critique of Aristotle thereupon. As a matter of fact, Aristotle merely says[1] that the duration of the tragic action should not exceed at the most the length of a day. He does not mention the unity of place at all; moreover, the ancient tragedians have not followed such a principle in the strict sense adopted by the French. As examples of such a deviation, we have a change of scene both in the *Eumenides* of Aeschylus and the *Ajax* of Sophocles. To a still less extent can our more modern dramatic writing, in its effort to portray a more extensive field of collision, dramatis personae of whatever kind and incidental event, and, in a word, an action the ideal explication of which requires, too, an external environment of greater breadth, subject itself to the yoke of a rigid identity of scene. Modern poetry, insofar, that is, as its creations are in harmony with the romantic type, which as a rule displays more variety and caprice in its attitude to external condition, has consequently freed itself from any such demand. If, however, the action is in truth concentrated in a few great

---

[1] *Poetics*, chap. 5 [translator's note].

motives, so that it can avoid complexity of external exposition, there will be no necessity for considerable alternation of scene. Indeed, the reverse will be a real advantage....

The unity of *time* is a precisely similar case. In the pure realm of imaginative idea we may no doubt, with no difficulty, combine vast periods of time; in the direct vision of perception we cannot so readily pass over a few years. If the action is, therefore, of a simple character, viewed in its entire content and conflict, we shall do best to concentrate the time of such a conflict, from its origin to its resolution, in a restricted period. If, on the contrary, it demands character richly diversified, whose development necessitates many situations which, in the matter of time, lie widely apart from one another, then the formal unity of a purely relative and entirely conventional duration of time will be essentially impossible. To attempt to remove such a representation from the domain of dramatic poetry, on the *prima facie* ground that it is inconsistent with the strict rule of time-unity would simply amount to making the prose of ordinary facts the final court of appeal, as against the truth of poetic creation. Least of all need we waste time in discussing the purely empirical probability that as audience we could, in the course of a few hours, witness also, directly through our sense, merely the passage of a short space of time. For it is precisely in the case where the poet is most at pains to illustrate this conclusion that, from other points of view, he well-nigh invariably perpetrates the most glaring improbabilities.

In contrast to the above examples of unity, that of *action* is the one truly inviolable rule. The true nature, however, of this unity may be a matter of considerable dispute. I will therefore develop my own views of its significance at greater length.

Every action must without exception have a *distinct object* which it seeks to achieve. It is through his action that man enters actively into the concrete actual world, in which also the most universal subject matter is in its turn accepted in the poetic work and defined under more specific manifestation. From this point of view, therefore, the unity will have to be sought for in the realization of an end itself essentially definite, and carried under the particular conditions and relations of concrete life to its consummation. The circumstances adapted to dramatic action are, however, as we have seen, of a kind that the individual end meets with obstructions at the hands of other personal agents, and this for the reason that a contradictory end stands in its path, which in its turn equally strives after fulfillment, so that it is invariably attached to the reciprocal relation of conflicts and their devolution. Dramatic action in consequence rests essentially upon an action that is involved with *resistance*; and the genuine unity can only find its *rationale* in the entire movement which consists in the assertion of this collision relatively to the definition of the particular circumstances, characters, and ends proposed, not merely under a mode consonant to such ends and characters, but in such a way as to resolve the opposition implied. Such a resolution has, precisely as the action itself has, an external and an inside point of view. In other words, on the one side, the conflict of the opposed *ends* is finally composed; and on the other the particular *characters*, to a greater or less extent, have committed their entire volitional energy and being to the undertaking they strive to accomplish. . . .

The genuine content of tragic action subject to the *aims* which arrest tragic characters is supplied by the world of those forces which carry in themselves their own justification, and are realized substantively in the volitional activity of mankind. Such are the love of husband and wife, of parents, children, and kinsfolk. Such are, further, the life of communities, the patriotism of citizens, the will of those in supreme power. Such are the life of churches, not, however, if regarded as a piety which submits to act with resignation, or as a divine judicial declaration in the heart of mankind over what is good or the reverse in action; but, on the contrary, conceived as the active engagement with and demand for veritable interests and relations. It is of a soundness and thoroughness consonant with these that the really tragical *characters* consist. They are throughout that which the essential notion of their character enables them and compels them to be. They are not merely a varied totality laid out in the series of views of it proper to the epic manner; they are, while no doubt remaining also essentially vital and individual, still only the one power of the particular character in question, the force in which such a character, in virtue of its essential personality, has made itself inseparably coalesce with some particular aspect of the capital and substantive life-content we have indicated above, and deliberately commits himself to that. It is at some such elevation, where the mere accidents of unmediated[2] individuality vanish altogether, that we find the tragic heroes of dramatic art, whether they be the living representatives of such spheres of concrete life or in any other way already so derive their greatness and stability from their own free self-reliance that they stand forth as works of sculpture, and as such interpret, too, under this aspect the essentially more abstract statues and figures of gods, as also the lofty tragic characters of the Greeks more completely than is possible for any other kind of elucidation or commentary. . . .

These ethical forces, as also the characters of the action, are *distinctively defined* in respect to their content and their individual personality, in virtue of the principle of differentiation to which everything is subject, which forms part of the objective world of things. If, then, these particular forces, in the way presupposed by dramatic poetry, are attached to the external expression of human activity, and are realized as the determinate aim of a human pathos which passes into action, their concordancy is cancelled, and they

---

[2] *Unmittelbaren Individualität.* Hegel means the individuality that is abstract, not soldered into the substance of concrete human life [translator's note].

are asserted *in contrast* to each other in interchangeable succession. Individual action will then, under given conditions, realize an object or character, which, under such a presupposed state, inevitably stimulates the presence of a pathos[3] opposed to itself, because it occupies a position of unique isolation in virtue of its independently fixed definition, and, by doing so, brings in its train unavoidable conflicts. Primitive tragedy, then, consists in this, that within a collision of this kind both sides of the contradiction, if taken by themselves, are *justified*; yet, from a further point of view, they tend to carry into effect the true and positive content of their end and specific characterization merely as the negation and *violation* of the other equally legitimate power, and consequently in their ethical purport and relatively to this so far fall under *condemnation.* . . .

As a result of this, however, an unmediated contradiction is posited, which no doubt may assert itself in the Real, but, for all that, is unable to maintain itself as that which is wholly substantive and verily real therein; which rather discovers, and only discovers, its essential justification in the fact that it is able to *annul* itself as such contradiction. In other words, whatever may be the claim of the tragic final purpose and personality, whatever may be the necessity of the tragic collision, it is, as a consequence of our present view, no less a claim that is asserted—this is our *third* and last point— by the tragic resolution of this division. It is through *this* latter result that Eternal Justice is operative in such aims and individuals under a mode whereby it restores the ethical substance and unity in and along with the downfall of the individuality which disturbs its repose. For, despite the fact that individual characters propose that which is itself essentially valid, yet they are only able to carry it out under the tragic demand in a manner that implies contradiction and with a onesidedness which is injurious. What, however, is substantive in truth, and the function of which is to secure realization, is not the battle of particular unities, however much such a conflict is essentially involved in the notion of a real world and human action; rather it is the reconciliation in which definite ends and individuals unite in harmonious action without mutual violation and contradiction. That which is abrogated in the tragic issue is merely the *one-sided* particularity which was unable to accommodate itself to this harmony, and consequently in the tragic course of its action, through inability to disengage itself from itself and its designs, either is committed in its entire totality to destruction or at least finds itself compelled to fall back upon a state of resignation in the execution of its aim in so far as it can carry this out. . . .

. . . That which preeminently is of valid force in ancient drama, therefore,

[3] Hegel appears to understand by pathos here little more than a psychological state [translator's note].

whether it be tragedy or comedy, is the universal and essential content of the end, which individuals seek to achieve. In tragedy this is the ethical claim of human consciousness in view of the particular action in question, the vindication of the act on its own account. And in the old comedy, too, it is in the same way at least the general public interests which are emphasized, whether it be in statesmen and the mode in which they direct the State, questions of peace or war, the general public and its moral conditions, or the condition of philosophy and its decline. . . .

In *modern* romantic poetry, on the contrary, it is the individual passion, the satisfaction of which can only be relative to a wholly personal end, generally speaking the destiny of some particular person or character placed under exceptional circumstances, which forms the subject-matter of all importance. . . .

. . . What we require therefore above all in such cases is at least the formal[4] greatness of character and power of the personal life which is able to ride out everything that negates it, and which, without denial of its acts or, indeed, without being materially discomposed by them, is capable of accepting their consequences. And on the other side we find that those substantive ends, such as patriotism, family devotion, loyalty, and the rest, are by no means to be excluded, although for the individual persons concerned the main question of importance is not so much the substantive force as their own individuality. But in such cases as a rule they rather form the particular ground upon which such persons, viewed in the light of their private character, take their stand and engage in conflict, rather than have supplied what we may regard as the real and ultimate content of their volition and action.

And further, in conjunction with a personal self-assertion of this type we may have presented the full extension of individual idiosyncrasy, not merely in respect to the soul-life simply, but also in relation to external circumstances and conditions, within which the action proceeds. And it is owing to this that in distinctive form the simple conflicts which characterize more classical dramatic composition, we now meet with the variety and exuberance of the characters dramatized, the unforeseen surprises of the ever new and complicated developments of plot, the maze of intrigue, the contingency of events, and, in a word, all those aspects of the modern drama which claim our attention, and the unfettered appearance of which, as opposed to the overwhelming emphasis attached to what is essentially most fundamental in the content, accentuates the type of romantic art in its distinction from the classic type. . . .

. . . In Greek tragedy it is not at all the bad will, crime, worthlessness, or mere misfortune, stupidity, and the like, which act as an incentive to such collisions, but rather, as I have frequently urged, the ethical right to a definite

---

[4] Formal as contrasted with really ethical content [translator's note].

course of action.[5] Abstract evil neither possesses truth in itself, nor does it arouse interest. At the same time, when we attribute ethical traits of characterization to the individual of the action, this ought not to appear merely as a matter of opinion. It is rather implied in their right or claim that they are actually there as essential on their own account. The hazards of crime, such as are present in modern drama—the useless, or quite as much the so-called noble criminal, with his empty talk about fate, we meet with in the tragedy of ancient literature, rarely, if at all, and for the good reason that the decision and deed depends on the wholly personal aspect of interest and character, upon lust for power, love, honor, or other similar passions, whose justification has its roots exclusively in the particular inclination and individuality. A resolve of this character, whose claim is based upon the content of its object, which it carries into execution in one restricted direction of particularization, violates, under certain circumstances, which are already essentially implied in the actual possibility of conflicts, a further and equally ethical sphere of human volition, which the character thus confronted adheres to, and, by his thus stimulated action, enforces, so that in this way the collision of powers and individuals equally entitled to the ethical claim is completely set up in its movement.

The sphere of this content,[6] although capable of great variety of detail, is not in its essential features very extensive. The principal source of opposition, which Sophocles in particular, in this respect following the lead of Aeschylus, has accepted and worked out in the finest way, is that of the *body politic*, the opposition, that is, between ethical life in its social universality and the family as the natural ground of moral relations. These are the purest forces of tragic representation. It is, in short, the harmony of these spheres and the concordant action within the bounds of their realized content, which constitute the perfected reality of the moral life. In this respect I need only recall to recollection the *Seven before Thebes* of Aeschylus and, as a yet stronger illustration, the *Antigone* of Sophocles. Antigone reverences the ties of blood-relationship, the gods of the nether world. Creon alone recognizes Zeus, the paramount Power of public life and the commonwealth. We come across a similar conflict in the *Iphigeneia in Aulis*, as also in the *Agamemnon*, the *Choephorae*, and *Eumenides* of Aeschylus, and in the *Electra* of Sophocles. Agamemnon, as king and leader of his army, sacrifices his daughter in the interest of the Greek folk and the Trojan expedition. He shatters thereby the bond of love as between himself and his daughter and wife, which Clytemnestra retains in the depths of a mother's heart, and in revenge pre-

---

[5] *Die sittliche Berechtigung zu einer bestimmten Tat.* The context shows that Hegel does not merely mean the justification in the individual conscience, which is demanded by and perfected in such activity, but the actual ethical claim which is vindicated in such action [translator's note].

[6] That is, the content of the dramatic action in Greek drama [translator's note].

pares an ignominious death for her husband on his return. Orestes, their son, respects his mother, but is bound to represent the right of his father, the king, and strikes dead the mother who bore him.

A content of this type retains its force through all times, and its presentation, despite all difference of nationality, vitally arrests our human and artistic sympathies.

Of a more formal type is that second kind of essential collision, an illustration of which in the tragic story of Oedipus the Greek tragedians especially favored. Of this Sophocles has left us the most complete example in his *Oedipus Rex*, and *Oedipus in Colonos*. The problem here is concerned with the claim of alertness in our intelligence, with the nature of the obligation[7] implied in that which a man carries out with a volition fully aware of its acts as contrasted with that which he has done in fact, but unconscious of and with no intention of doing what he has done under the directing providence of the gods. Oedipus slays his father, marries his mother, begets children in this incestuous alliance, and nevertheless is involved in these most terrible of crimes without active participation either in will or knowledge. The point of view of our profounder modern consciousness of right and wrong would be to recognize that crimes of this description, inasmuch as they were neither referable to a personal knowledge or volition, were not deeds for which the true personality of the perpetrator was responsible. The plastic nature of the Greek on the contrary adheres to the bare fact which an individual has achieved, and refuses to face the division implied by the purely ideal attitude of the soul in the self-conscious life on the one hand and the objective significance of the fact accomplished on the other.

For ourselves, to conclude this survey, other collisions, which either in general are related to the universally accepted association of personal action to the Greek conception of Destiny, or in some measure to more exceptional conditions, are comparatively speaking less important.

In all these tragic conflicts, however, we must above all place on one side the false notion of *guilt* or *innocence*. The heroes of tragedy are quite as much under one category as the other. If we accept the idea as valid that a man is guilty only in the case that a choice lay open to him, and he deliberately decided on the course of action which he carried out, then these plastic figures of ancient drama are guiltless. They act in accordance with a specific character, a specific pathos, for the simple reason that they are this character, this pathos. In such a case there is no lack of decision and no choice. The strength of great characters consists precisely in this that they do not choose, but are entirely and absolutely just that which they will and achieve. They are simply

---

[7] By *Rechtfertigung* Hegel here seems to mean not so much the vindicated right as the degree of responsibility which a certain attitude of mind involves. It is the nature of the subjection to the vindicated right, or its absence [translator's note].

themselves, and never anything else, and their greatness consists in that fact. Weakness in action, in other words, wholly consists in the division of the personal self as such from its content, so that character, volition, and final purpose do not appear as absolutely one unified growth; and inasmuch as no assured end lives in the soul as the very substance of the particular personality, as the pathos and might of the individual's entire will, he is still able to turn with indecision from this course to that, and his final decision is that of caprice. A wavering attitude of this description is alien to these plastic creations. The bond between the psychological state of mind and the content of the will is for them indissoluble. That which stirs them to action is just in this very pathos which implies an ethical justification and which, even in the pathetic aspects of the dialogue, is not enforced in and through the merely personal rhetoric of the heart and the sophistry of passion, but in the equally masculine and cultivated objective presence, in the profound possibilities, the harmony and vitally plastic beauty of which Sophocles was to a superlative degree master. At the same time, however, such a pathos, with its potential resources of collision, brings in its train deeds that are both injurious and wrongful. They have no desire to avoid the blame that results therefrom. On the contrary, it is their fame to have done what they have done. One can in fact urge nothing more intolerable against a hero of this type than by saying that he has acted innocently. It is a point of honor with such great characters that they are guilty. They have no desire to excite pity or our sensibilities. For it is not the substantive, but rather the wholly personal deepening[8] of the individual character which stirs our individual pain. These securely strong characters, however, coalesce entirely with their essential pathos, and this indivisible accord inspires wonder, but does not excite heart emotions. The drama of Euripides marks the transition to that.

The final result, then, of the development of tragedy conducts us to this issue and only this, namely, that the twofold vindication of the mutually conflicting aspects are no doubt retained, but the *one-sided* mode under which they were maintained is canceled, and the undisturbed ideal harmony brings back again that condition of the chorus, which attributes without reserve equal honor to all the gods. The true course of dramatic development consists in the annulment of *contradictions* viewed as such, in the reconciliation of the forces of human action, which alternately strive to negate each other in their conflict. Only so far is misfortune and suffering not the final issue, but rather the satisfaction of spirit, as for the first time, in virtue of such a conclusion, the necessity of all that particular individuals experience, is able to appear in complete accord with reason, and our emotional attitude is tranquillized on a true ethical basis, rudely shaken by the calamitous result

---

[8] By *die subjektive Vertiefung der Persönlichkeit* Hegel would seem to mean the psychological analysis of character on its own account [translator's note].

to the heroes, but reconciled in the substantial facts. And it is only in so far as we retain such a view securely that we shall be in a position to understand ancient tragedy. . . .

First, we have particularly to emphasize the fact, that if it is the one-sidedness of the pathos which constitutes the real basis of collisions this merely amounts to the statement that it is asserted in the action of life, and therewith has become the unique pathos of a particular individual. If this one-sideness is to be abrogated then it is this individual which, to the extent that his action is exclusively identified with this isolated pathos, must perforce be stripped and sacrificed. For the individual here is merely this single life, and, if this unity is not secured in its stability on its own account, the individual is shattered.

The most complete form of this development is possible when the individuals engaged in conflict relatively to their concrete or objective life appear in each case essentially involved in one whole, so that they stand fundamentally under the power of that against which they battle, and consequently infringe that, which, conformably to their own essential life, they ought to respect. Antigone, for example, lives under the political authority of Creon; she is herself the daughter of a king and the affianced of Haemon, so that her obedience to the royal prerogative is an obligation. But Creon also, who is on his part father and husband, is under obligation to respect the sacred ties of relationship, and only by breach of this can give an order that is in conflict with such a sense. In consequence of this we find immanent in the life of both that which each respectively combats, and they are seized and broken by that very bond which is rooted in the compass of their own social existence. Antigone is put to death before she can enjoy what she looks forward to as bride, and Creon too is punished in the fatal end of his son and wife, who commit suicide, the former on account of Antigone's death, and the latter owing to Haemon's. Among all the fine creations of the ancient and the modern world—and I am acquainted with pretty nearly everything in such a class, and one ought to know it, and it is quite possible—the *Antigone* of Sophocles is from this point of view in my judgment the most excellent and satisfying work of art.

The tragic issue does not, however, require in every case as a means of removing both overemphasized aspects and the equal honor which they respectively claim the downfall of the contestant parties. The *Eumenides* does not end, as we all know, with the death of Orestes, or the destruction of the Eumenides, these avenging spirits of matricide and filial affection, these opponents of Apollo, who seeks to protect unimpaired the worth of and reverence for the family chief and king, the god who had prompted Orestes to slay Clytemnestra, but will have Orestes released from the punishment and honor bestowed on both himself and the Furies. At the same time we cannot fail to see in this adjusted conclusion the nature of the authority which the Greeks attached to their gods when they presented them as mere individuals contending with each other. They appear, in short, to the Athenian of everyday life merely as definite aspects of ethical experience which the principles of morality viewed in their complete and harmonious coherence bind together. The votes of the Areopagus are equal on either side. It is Athena, the goddess, the life of Athens, that is, imagined in its essential unity, who adds the white pebble, who frees Orestes, and at the same time promises altars and a cult to the Eumenides no less than Apollo. . . .

But as a *further* and final class, and one more beautiful than the above rather external mode of resolution we have the reconciliation more properly of the soul itself, in which respect there is, in virtue of the personal significance, a real approach to our modern point of view. The most perfect example of this in ancient drama is to be found in the ever admirable *Oedipus in Colonos* of Sophocles. . . .

Modern tragedy accepts in its own province from the first the principle of subjectivity or self-assertion. It makes, therefore, the personal intimacy of character—the character, that is, which is no purely individual and vital embodiment of ethical forces in the classic sense—its peculiar object and content. It, moreover, makes, in a type of concurrence that is adapted to this end, human actions come into collision through the instrumentality of the external accident of circumstances in the way that a contingency of a similar character is also decisive in its effect on the consequence, or appears to be so decisive. . . .

To start with, we may observe that, however much in romantic tragedy the personal aspect of suffering and passions, in the true meaning of such an attitude, is the focal center, yet, for all that, it is impossible in human activity that the ground basis of definite ends borrowed from the concrete worlds of the family, the State, the Church, and others should be dispensed with. Insofar, however, as in the drama under discussion, it is not the substantive content as such in these spheres of life which constitutes the main interest of individuals. Such ends are from a certain point of view particularized in a breadth of extension and variety, as also in exceptional modes of presentment, in which it often happens that what is truly essential is only able to force itself on our attention with attenuated strength. . . .

And, from a further point of view in this drama, it is the right of subjectivity, as above defined, absolutely unqualified, which is retained as the dominating content; and for this reason personal love, honor, and the rest make such an exclusive appeal as ends of human action that, while in one direction other relations cannot fail to appear as the purely external background on which these interests of our modern life are set in motion, in another such relations on their own account actively conflict with the requirements of the more individual state of emotion. Of more profound significance still is wrong and crime, even assuming that a particular character does not deliberately and to start with place himself in either, yet does not avoid in order to attain his original purpose. . . .

Generally speaking, however, in modern tragedy it is not the substantive content of its object in the interest of which men act, and which is maintained as the stimulus of their passion; rather it is the inner experience of their heart and individual emotion, or the particular qualities of their personality, which insist on satisfaction. . . .

In order to emphasize still more distinctly the difference which in this respect obtains between ancient and modern tragedy, I will merely refer the reader to Shakespeare's *Hamlet*. Here we find fundamentally a collision similar to that which is introduced by Aeschylus into his *Choeporae* and that by Sophocles into his *Electra*. For Hamlet's father, too, and the King, as in these Greek plays, has been murdered, and his mother has wedded the murderer. That which, however, in the conception of the Greek dramatists possesses a certain ethical justification—I mean the death of Agamemnon—relatively to his sacrifice of Iphigenia in the contrasted case of Shakespeare's play, can only be viewed as an atrocious crime, of which Hamlet's mother is innocent; so that the son is merely concerned in his vengeance to direct his attention to the fratricidal king, and there is nothing in the latter's character that possesses any real claim to his respect. The real collision, therefore, does not turn on the fact that the son, in giving effect to a rightful sense of vengeance, is himself forced to violate morality, but rather on the particular personality, the inner life of Hamlet, whose noble soul is not steeled to this kind of energetic activity, but, while full of contempt for the world and life, what between making up his mind and attempting to carry into effect or. preparing to carry into effect its resolves, is bandied from pillar to post, and finally through his own procrastination and the external course of events meets his own doom.

If we now turn, in close connection with the above conclusions, to our *second* point of fundamental importance in modern tragedy—that is to say, the nature of the characters and their collisions—we may summarily take a point of departure from the following general observations.

The heroes of ancient classic tragedy discover circumstances under which they, so long as they irrefragably adhere to the *one* ethical state of pathos which alone corresponds to their own already formed personality, must infallibly come into conflict with an ethical Power which opposes them and possesses an equal ethical claim to recognition. Romantic characters, on the contrary, are from the first placed within a wide expanse of contingent relations and conditions, within which every sort of action is possible; so that the conflict, to which no doubt the external conditions presupposed supply the occasion, essentially abides within the *character* itself, to which the individuals concerned in their passion give effect, not, however, in the interests of the ethical vindication of the truly substantive claims, but for the simple reason that they are the kind of men they are. Greek heroes also no doubt act in accordance with their particular individuality; but this individuality, as before noted, if we take for our examples the supreme results of ancient tragedy, is itself necessarily identical with an ethical pathos which is substantive. In modern tragedy the peculiar character in its real significance, and to which it as a matter of accident remains constant, whether it happens to grasp after that which on its own account is on moral grounds justifiable, or is carried into wrong and crime, forms its resolves under the dictate of personal wishes and necessities, or among other things purely external considerations. In such a case, therefore, though we may have a coalescence between the moral aspect of the object and the character, yet, for all that, such a concurrence does not constitute, and cannot constitute—owing to the divided character of ends, passions, and the life wholly personal to the individual, the *essential* basis and objective condition of the depth and beauty of the tragic drama. . . .

. . . For even in the cases where a purely formal passion, as for instance ambition in Macbeth, or jealousy in Othello, claims as its field the entire pathos of his tragic hero, such an abstraction impairs by no fraction the full breadth of the personality. . . .

The last of the subjects which we have still to discuss as proposed is the nature of the *tragic issue* which characters in our present drama have to confront, as also the type of tragic *reconciliation* compatible with such a standpoint. In ancient tragedy it is the eternal justice which, as the absolute might of destiny, delivers and restores the harmony of substantive being in its ethical character by its opposition to the particular forces which, in their strain to assert an independent subsistence, come into collision, and which, in virtue of the rational ideality implied in its operations, satisfies us even where we see the downfall of particular men. Insofar as a justice of the same kind is present in modern tragedy, it is necessarily, in part, more abstract on account of the closer differentiation of ends and characters, and, in part, of a colder nature and one that is more akin to that of a criminal court, in virtue of the fact that the wrong and crime into which individuals are necessarily carried, insofar as they are intent upon executing their designs, are of a profounder significance. Macbeth, for instance, the elder daughters of Lear and their husbands, the president in *Kabale und Liebe*,[9] Richard III, and many similar examples, on account of their atrocious conduct, only deserve the fate they get. This type of dénouement usually is presented under the guise that individuals are crushed by an actual force which they have defied in order to carry out their personal aims. . . .

From another point of view, however, we may see the tragic issue also merely in the light of the effect of unhappy circumstances and external accidents, which might have brought about, quite as readily, a different re-

[9] *Love and Intrigue* (1783) by Schiller.

sult and a happy conclusion. From such a point of view we have merely left us the conception that the modern idea of individuality, with its searching definition of character, circumstances, and developments, is handed over essentially to the contingency of the earthly state, and must carry the fateful issues of such finitude. Pure commiseration of this sort is, however, destitute of meaning; and it is nothing less than a frightful kind of external necessity in the particular case where we see the downfall of essentially noble natures in their conflict thus assumed with the mischance of purely external accidents. Such a course of events can insistently arrest our attention; but in the result it can only be horrible, and the demand is direct and irresistible that the external accidents ought to accord with that which is identical with the spiritual nature of such noble characters. Only as thus regarded can we feel ourselves reconciled with the grievous end of Hamlet and Juliet. From a purely external point of view, the death of Hamlet appears as an accident occasioned by his duel with Laertes and the interchange of the daggers. But in the background of Hamlet's soul, death is already present from the first.

Friedrich Hebbel *1813–1863*

Preface to
Maria Magdalena *1844*

. . . Now a word more about the drama that I am offering to the public. It is a bourgeois tragedy. The bourgeois tragedy in Germany has fallen into into discredit, and chiefly because of two abuses. Principally because it has not been constructed of those inner elements which are inherent in it: the harsh determination with which the individuals, incapable of dialectic, stand face-to-face with one another in the most confined of spheres; and the terrible constraint of life in all its one-sidedness which results from this condition. Rather they have patched it together out of all kinds of externalities: lack of money, for example, surplus of hunger; but above all out of the

Selection. Translated by Carl R. Mueller. Acknowledgment is made to Carl R. Mueller for permission to reprint the excerpt from his translation of Hebbel's Preface to *Maria Magdalena*. Copyright © 1962 by Carl R. Mueller.

conflict between the third estate and the first and second estates in love-affairs. This undoubtedly gives rise to much that is pathetic, but not tragic, for the tragic must appear from the start as something necessary, as something postulated in life itself, such as death, as something which is utterly unavoidable. As soon as one can help himself with a "If only he had (thirty dollars)" which a touching sentimentality bolsters, with a "If only he had (come to me, I live in No. 32)," or with a "If only she had been (a lady, etc.)"—when one can help himself with the like of these, then the impression, which was meant to stir us deeply, becomes trivial, and the effect, if it is not utterly scattered to the winds, exists in the fact that the next day the spectator will pay his poorhouse taxes more readily than before or that he will treat his daughter with more consideration: facts for which the supervisor of the poorhouse and the daughter, respectively, may be grateful, but not dramatic art.

The second reason why bourgeois tragedy has fallen into discredit is that once our poets let themselves down to the people, because it occurred to them that perhaps one need only be human to have a fate and in certain circumstances a terrible fate, they assumed it necessary to ennoble the common people with whom they occupy themselves during such lost hours through beautiful speeches which they bestow upon them from their treasure chest; or else these poets thought it necessary to force them down below their actual station in life by imposing on them a wooden stupidity, so that their characters appear to us partly as bewitched princes and princesses—whom the magician out of sheer malice refused to turn into dragons and lions and other respectable worthies of the animal kingdom, but turned instead into base bakery maids and tailors' apprentices—but also partly as living blocks of wood, whose very ability to say Yes and No is cause for no little surprise. This, if possible, was even worse, because to the absurd and the ridiculous it added the trivial, and furthermore in a most obvious manner, for it is well known that the citizen and the farmer do not pluck their figures of speech, which they use just as well as the heroes of the salon and the promenade, from the starry firmament nor fish them from the sea; rather the artisan gathers them in his workshop, and the farmer from behind his plow, and many of us have learned that these simple people, though they may not be adept in the art of conversation, are nevertheless capable of lively speech, and know how to combine and illustrate their ideas.

These two abuses explain the prejudice against bourgeois tragedy, but they cannot justify it, because they are the fault not of the genre but of inferior tradesmen who have bungled so badly in it. It is in and of itself a matter of indifference whether the hands of a clock are made of gold or of brass, nor does it matter whether an action which is in itself significant, that is, symbolic, takes place in a lower or in a socially higher sphere. Whereas in the heroic tragedy the seriousness of the subject matter and the reflections directly bound up in it may compensate up to a point for the deficiency in the tragic form, in the bourgeois tragedy everything depends on whether the circle of the tragic form is completed, that is, whether the point has been reached where we no longer care about the fate of a single individual, arbitrarily chosen by the playwright, but are able in that individual fate to see a fate which is universally human. The tragic outcome, too, whatever the particular form it may assume, must be recognized as wholly inevitable and incontestable.

These are the only points to be concerned about in a play: the relationship of the story to the positive and negative aspects of the moral powers moving in its background—family, honor, the choice between good and evil. Never ask for the so-called flowery diction of the false poets, that lamentably colorful calico in which marionettes strut themselves about; nor for the many pretty figures, splendid aphorisms and descriptions and other spurious adornments, to be poor in which is the first result of richness. Those hereditary sins of the bourgeois tragedy, which I have mentioned above, are the very ones which I have avoided—of that I am certain. But I have undoubtedly committed others in their place.

Nineteenth- and Twentieth-Century Scandinavia

Just as crying is natural to all people, so according to the Danish philosopher Kierkegaard is there a common ground between ancient and modern tragedy. Nevertheless, he sees differences, including the modern syndrome of avoiding responsibility for one's deeds, a tendency that has comic significance. Like Hegel, Kierkegaard regards the crucial distinction between ancient and modern tragedy as stemming from the latter's emphasis on character. Whereas in ancient tragedy the destruction of the hero results not only from his own deeds but also from such strong external factors as state, family, and destiny, the hero of modern tragedy "stands and falls entirely on his own acts." Tending toward the psychological, modern tragedy emphasizes guilt and remorse—which diminishes the tragic element. Although tragedy requires guilt and remorse, which issue from character, it also requires action based outside of character. The distinctions between the tragic and the comic, says Kierkegaard, revolve around the different types of contradiction on which both are based: the tragic on the suffering contradiction, which despairs of a way out; the comic— despite the imaginary suffering of a comic character—on the painless contradiction, which sees a way out.

Regardless of Ibsen's claim that he read little Kierkegaard and understood less, critics have noted several resemblances between the Dane's philosophical writings and the Norwegian's plays—parallels that may (or may not) be coincidental. Champion of realistic playwriting in prose, Ibsen nevertheless considered himself even in his prose dramas to "have been more poet and less social philosopher than people generally seem inclined to believe." Although often associated with the social problem play, Ibsen is concerned with problems of humanity in general, of which social problems form a part. By drawing human beings, he admitted, he reached the same conclusions as political philosophers. Ibsen's plays and his scattered comments on the drama tend to confirm the statement of his first great critic, Shaw, that the "great dramatic poet"—such as Shakespeare, Goethe, and Ibsen—"is never a socialist, nor an individualist,

549

nor a positivist, nor a materialist, nor any other sort of 'ist,' though he comprehends all the 'isms,' and is generally quoted and claimed by all sections as an adherent."

Unlike Ibsen the Norwegian, Strindberg the Swede wrote at length on the drama. One of the major practitioners of naturalism, Strindberg is also one of its major theoreticians. In *An Effective Play*, he outlines the formula of the so-called well-made play, which he opposes. In his Preface to *Miss Julie*, he discusses such characteristics of naturalism as complexity of motive; lifelike, loosely structured dialogue; realistic acting; three-dimensional scenery; and the abolition of footlights, whose illumination looks artificial. In his comments on his expressionistic *Dream Play*, he outlines characteristics of this departure from surface realism that aims to penetrate more deeply beneath realism's surface.

Søren Kierkegaard 1813–1855

The Ancient Tragical Motive as Reflected in the Modern 1843

Should anyone feel called upon to say that the tragic always remains the tragic, I should in a sense have no objection to make, insofar as every historical evolution always remains within the sphere of the concept. Supposing, namely, that the word had a meaning, and that the twofold repetition of the word tragic should not be regarded as constituting a meaningless parenthesis about a contentless nothing, then the meaning must be this, that the content of a concept does not dethrone the concept, but enriches it. On the other hand, it can scarcely have escaped the attention of any observer, and it is something that the reading and theatre-going public already believes itself to be in lawful possession of, as its share dividend in the labors of the experts, that there is an essential difference between the ancient and modern tragedy. If one were again to emphasize this distinction absolutely, and by its aid, first stealthily, then perhaps forcibly, separate the conceptions of the ancient and modern tragical, his procedure would be no less absurd than that of the first, since he would forget that the foothold necessary for him was the tragic itself, and that this again was so far from being able to separate, that it really bound the ancient and modern together. And it must be regarded as a warning against every such prejudiced attempt to separate them, that estheticians still constantly turn back to established Aristotelian determinations and requirements in connection with the tragical; as being exhaustive of the concept; and the warning is needed so much the more, as no one can escape a feeling of sadness in observing that however much the world has changed, the conception of the tragic is still essentially unchanged, just as weeping is still natural to all men alike. . . .

. . . One characteristic our age certainly has to a greater degree than Greece, this, namely, that it is more melancholy, and hence it is more profoundly in despair. Thus, our age is melancholy enough to realize that there is something which is called responsibility, and this indicates something significant. While, therefore, everyone wishes to rule, no one wishes to accept responsibility. There is even yet a story fresh in our memories, that a French statesman, when a portfolio was offered to him for a second time,

Selections. From Søren Kierkegaard, *Either/Or*, Vol. I, translated by David F. Swenson and Lillian Marvin Swenson with revisions and a foreword by Howard A. Johnson (copyright 1949, © 1959 by Princeton University Press; Princeton Paperback, 1971), pp. 113, 115, 116, 117, 118, 120, 121, and 123. Reprinted by permission of Princeton University Press.

declared that he would accept it, but only on the condition that the secretary of the council should become responsible. It is well known that the king of France is not responsible, while his ministers are; the minister does not wish to be responsible, but will be minister on condition that the secretary of state becomes responsible; it finally results naturally in the watchmen or street commissioners becoming responsible. Would not this story of shifted responsibility really be a proper subject for Aristophanes! And on the other hand, why are the government and rulers so afraid of accepting responsibility, unless because they fear an attack from an opposition, which equally seeks to evade responsibility? When, then, one considers these two powers in opposition to one another, but not able to come to grips with each other, because the one constantly vanishes from the other, the one only a duplicate of the other, then such a lay-out is certainly not without its comic effect. This is sufficient to show that the bond which essentially holds the state together is disorganized, but that it should thereby result in isolation is naturally comic, and the comic lies in trying to stress the *subjective as mere form*. Every isolated individual always becomes comic by stressing his own accidental individuality over against necessary development. It would undoubtedly be most deeply comic for some accidental individual to get the universal idea of wishing to be the savior of the world. On the other hand, the appearance of Christ is in a certain sense (in another sense it is infinitely more) the deepest tragedy, because Christ came in the fullness of time, and, what I must later particularly emphasize, He bore the sins of the world.

It is well known that Aristotle mentions two things, thought and character, as the source of action in tragedy, but he notes also that the main thing is the plot, and the individuals do not act in order to present characters, but the characters are included for the sake of the action. Here one readily notices a divergence from modern tragedy. The peculiarity of ancient tragedy is that the action is not only the result of the character, that the action is not reflected sufficiently into the subject, but that the action itself has a relative addition of suffering. Hence the ancient tragedy has not developed the dialogue to the point of exhaustive reflection, so that everything is absorbed in it; it has in the monologue and the chorus exactly the factors supplemental to the dialogue. Whether the chorus approaches nearer the epic substantiality or the lyric exaltation, it thus still indicates, as it were, the more which will not be absorbed in the individuality; the monologue again is more the lyric concentration, and has the more which will not be absorbed in action and situation. In ancient tragedy the action itself has an epic moment in it, it is as much event as action. The reason for this naturally lies in the fact that the ancient world did not have the subjectivity reflected in it. Even if the individual moved freely, he still rested in the substantial categories of state, family, and destiny. This substantial category is exactly the fatalistic element in Greek tragedy, and its exact peculiarity. The hero's destruction is, therefore, not only a result of his own deeds, but is also a suffering, whereas in modern tragedy, the hero's destruction is really not suffering, but is action. In modern times, therefore, situation and character are really predominant. The tragic hero is subjectively reflected in himself, and this reflection has not only reflected him out of every immediate relation to state, race, and destiny, but has often even reflected him out of his own preceding life. We are interested in a certain definite moment of his life, considered as his own deed. Because of this the tragdy can be exhaustively represented in situation and dialogue, since nothing of the more immediate is left behind. Hence, modern tragedy has no epic foreground, no epic heritage. The hero stands and falls entirely on his own acts.

This brief but adequate analysis may be useful in illuminating the difference between ancient and modern tragedy, which I regard as having great significance, the difference, namely, in the nature of tragic guilt. It is well known that Aristotle requires the tragic hero to have guilt. But just as the action in Greek tragedy is intermediate between activity and passivity (action and suffering), so is also the hero's guilt, and therein lies the tragic collision. On the other hand, the more the subjectivity becomes reflected, the more one sees the individual left Pelagianally to himself, the more his guilt becomes ethical. The tragedy lies between these two extremes. If the individual is entirely without guilt, then is the tragic interest nullified, for the tragic collision is thereby enervated; if, on the other hand, he is absolutely guilty, then he can no longer interest us tragically. Hence, it is certainly a misunderstanding of the tragic, when our age strives to let the whole tragic destiny becomes transubstantiated in individuality and subjectivity. One would know nothing to say about the hero's past life, one would throw his whole life upon his own shoulders, as being the result of his own acts, would make him accountable for everything, but in so doing, one would also transform his esthetic guilt into an ethical one. The tragic hero thus becomes bad, the evil becomes precisely the tragic subject, but evil has no esthetic interest, and sin is not an esthetic element. This mistaken endeavor certainly has its cause in the whole tendency of our age toward the comic. The comic lies exactly in isolation; when one would maintain the tragic within this isolation, then one gets evil in all its baseness, not the truly tragic guilt in its ambiguous innocence. It is not difficult when one looks about in modern literature, to find examples. Thus, the very ingenious work of Grabbe, *Faust and Don Juan*, is precisely constructed around this evil. However, in order not to argue from a single work, I prefer to show it in the whole general consciousness of the age. If one wished to represent an individual whom an unhappy childhood had influenced so disturbingly that this impression occasioned his downfall, such a defense would simply not appeal to the present age, and this naturally not because it was wrongly handled, for I have a right to assume that it would be handled with distinction, but because our age employs another standard. It would know nothing about such coddling; without knowing, it holds every individual responsible for his own life. Hence, if he goes to the dogs, it is not tragic, but it is bad. One might now believe that this must be a kingdom of the gods, this generation in which I have the honor to live. On the contrary, this is by no means the case; the energy, the courage, which would thus be the creator of its own destiny, aye, its own creator, is an illusion, and when the age loses the tragic, it gains despair. There lies a sadness and a healing power in the tragic, which one truly should not despise, and when a man in the extraordinary manner our age affects, would gain himself, he loses himself and becomes comical. Every individual, however primitive he may be, is still a child of God, of his age, of his family and friends, herein lies its truth; if in this relativity he tries to be the absolute, then he becomes ridiculous. . . .

In ancient tragedy the sorrow is deeper, the pain less; in modern, the pain is greater, the sorrow less. Sorrow always contains something more substantial than pain. Pain always implies a reflection over suffering which sorrow does not know. From a psychological standpoint it is always interesting to watch a child when it sees an older person suffer. The child is not reflective enough to feel grief, and yet its sorrow is infinitely deep. It is not reflective enough to have any conception about sin and guilt; when it sees an older person suffer, it does not occur to it to reflect upon it, and yet when the cause of the suffering is concealed from it, there is a dim suspicion about it in its sorrow. Such, but in complete and profound harmony, is the Greek sorrow, and therefore it is at one and the same time so gentle and so deep. When an older person sees a child suffer, his pain is greater, his sorrow less. The more clearly the conception of guilt stands out, the greater is the pain, the less profound the sorrow. If one now applies this to the relation between ancient and modern tragedy, then must one say: in the ancient tragedy, the sorrow is deeper, and in the consciousness which corresponds to this, the sorrow is deeper. It must in fact be constantly remembered that the sorrow does not lie in myself, but it lies in the tragedy, and that I, in order to undersand the deep sorrow of the Greek tragedy, must myself live in the Greek consciousness. Hence, it is certainly often only an affectation when so many profess to admire the Greek tragedies; for it is very evident that our age, at least, has little sympathy for that which precisely constitutes Greek sorrow. The sorrow is deeper because the guilt has the esthetic ambiguity. In modern times, the pain is greater. It is a fearful thing to fall into the hands of the living God. One might say this about Greek tragedy. The wrath of the gods is terrible, but the pain is not so great as in modern tragedy where the hero bears the whole weight of his guilt, is himself transparent in his suffering of his guilt. Here it is relevant in conformity with the tragic guilt, to show which sorrow is the true esthetic sorrow, and which the true esthetic pain. The bitterest pain is manifestly remorse, but remorse has ethical not esthetic reality. It is the bitterest pain because it has the total transparency of the entire guilt, but just because of this transparency, it does not interest us esthetically. Remorse has a sacredness which obscures the esthetic, it may not be seen, least of all by the spectator, and it requires quite a different kind of self-activity. Modern comedy has sometimes presented remorse on the stage, but this only shows a lack of judgment on the part of the author. One may indeed be reminded of the psychological interest it can have to see remorse delineated on the stage, but again the psychological interest is not the esthetic. This is part of the confusion which in our age asserts itself in so many ways: we look for a thing where we ought not to look for it, and what is worse, we find it where we ought not to find it; we wish to be edified in the theater, esthetically impressd in church, we would be converted by novels, get enjoyment out of books of devotion, we want philosophy in the pulpit, and the preacher in the professorial chair. This pain of remorse is consequently not the esthetic pain, and yet it is apparently this which the modern age tends toward as the highest tragic interest. This is also true with regard to the tragic guilt. Our age has lost all the substantial categories of family, state, and race. It must leave the individual entirely to himself, so that in a stricter sense he becomes his own creator, his guilt is consequently sin, his pain remorse; but this nullifies the tragedy. Also, in a stricter sense, the tragedy of suffering has exactly lost its tragic interest, for the power from which the suffering comes has lost its significance, and the spectators cry: "Help yourself, and heaven will help you!" or, in other words, the spectator has lost his compassion, but compassion is in a subjective as well as an objective sense, the precise expression for the tragic. . . .

The true tragic sorrow consequently requires an element of guilt, the true tragic pain an element of innocence; the true tragic sorrow requires an element of transparency, the true tragic pain an element of obscurity. This I believe best indicates the dialectic wherein there is a synthesis of the categories of sorrow and pain, as well as also the dialectic which lies in the concept of tragic guilt.

The Comical 1846

The matter is quite simple. The comical is present in every stage of life (only that the relative positions are different), for wherever there is life, there is contradiction, and wherever there is contradiction, the comical is present. The tragic and the comic are the same, insofar as both are based on contradiction; but *the tragic is the suffering contradiction, the comical, the painless contradiction.* That something which the comic apprehension envisages as comical may entail imaginary suffering for the comical individual is quite irrelevant. In that case, for example, it would be incorrect to apprehend the hero of Holberg's *The Busy Man* as comical. Satire also entails pain, but this pain has a dialectic which gives it a teleology in the direction of a cure. The difference between the tragic and the comic lies in the relationship between the contradiction and the controlling idea. The comic apprehension evokes the contradiction or makes it manifest by having in mind the way out, which is why the contradiction is painless. The tragic apprehension sees the contradiction and despairs of a way out. It is at matter of course that this must be understood so that the various nuances of the comic are again kept subject to the qualitative dialectic of the different spheres, which passes judgment upon all subjective arbitrariness. Thus if one proposed to make everything comical by means of nothing, it is clear at once that his comedy is nowhere at home, since it lacks a foothold in any sphere. The discoverer of this type of comedy would himself be open to comic apprehensions from the standpoint of the ethical sphere, because as an existing individual he must himself in one way or another have a foothold in existence.

If one were to say: repentance is a contradiction, *ergo,*[1] it is comical, it would at once be apparent that this is nonsense. Repentance belongs in the ethico-religious sphere, and is hence so placed as to have only one higher sphere above it, namely, the religious in the strictest sense. But it was not the religious it was proposed to make use of in order to make repentance ridiculous; *ergo,* it must have been something lower, in which case the comic is illegitimate, or something only chimerically higher, as for example the sphere of abstraction; and then our friend of laughter is himself comical, as I have frequently in the preceding sought to show over against speculative philosophers, namely, that in consequence of having

Selections. From Søren Kierkegaard, *Concluding Unscientific Postscript*, translated by David F. Swenson and Walter Lowrie (copyright 1941, © 1969 by Princeton University Press; Princeton Paperback, 1968), pp. 459, 462, 463–465. Original footnotes have been omitted. Reprinted by permission of Princeton University Press. The title of these selections is the present editor's.

[1] Therefore.

made themselves fantastic, and in that manner having attained to the highest standpoint, they have made themselves comical. The lower can never make the higher comical, i.e., it cannot legitimately apprehend the higher as comical, and has not the power to make it comical. It is another thing that the lower, by being brought into conjunction with the higher, may make the relationship ridiculous. Thus it is possible for a horse to be the occasion for a man showing himself in a ridiculous light, but the horse has no power to make him ridiculous.

The different existential stages take rank in accordance with their relationship to the comical, depending on whether they have the comical within themselves or outside themselves; yet not in the sense that the comical is the highest stage. The immediate consciousness has the comical outside itself, for wherever there is life there is contradiction, but the contradiction is not represented in the immediate consciousness, which therefore has the contradiction coming from the outside. A finite worldly wisdom presumes to apprehend immediacy as comical, but thereby itself becomes comical; for the supposed justification of its comic apprehension is that it definitely knows the way out, but the way out which it knows is still more comical. This, then, is an illegitimate comic apprehension. Wherever there exists a contradiction and the way out is not known, where the contradiction is not canceled and corrected in something higher, there the contradiction is not painless; and where the correction is based on something only chimerically higher (from the frying-pan into the fire), it is itself still more comical, because the contradiction is greater. Thus in the relationship between immediacy and finite worldly wisdom. A comic apprehension on the basis of despair is also illegitimate, for despair is despair because it does not know the way out, does not know the contradiction canceled, and ought therefore to apprehend the contradiction tragically, which is precisely the way to its healing.

Humor has its justification precisely in its tragic side, in the fact that it reconciles itself to the pain, which despair seeks to abstract from, although it knows no way out. Irony is justified as over against immediacy, because its state of equilibrium, not as mere abstraction but as an existential art, is higher than the immediate consciousness. Only an existential ironist is therefore justified over against immediacy; total irony once for all, like a bargain-priced notion set down on paper, is, like all abstractions, illegitimate over against every sphere of existence. Irony is indeed an abstraction, and an abstract putting together of things, but the justification of the existential ironist is that he expresses this himself existentially, that he preserves his life in it, and does not toy with the grandeurs of irony while himself having his life in Philistinism; for then his comic apprehension is illegitimate.

The immediate consciousness has the comical outside itself; irony has it *within* itself. The ethicist who has irony as his incognito can again see the comic side of irony, but assures himself of justification only through constantly holding himself to the ethical, and therefore sees the comical only as constantly vanishing.

Humor has the comical *within* itself, and is justified in the existential humorist; for humor once for all *in abstracto*[2] is as illegitimate as everything else that is in this manner abstract; the humorist earns his justification by having his life in his humor. Against religiosity only it is not justified, but it is justified against everything that courts recognition as religiosity. The religiosity which has humor as its incognito can also see the humoristic as comical, but preserves its justification only by constantly keeping itself in religious passion with respect to the God-relationship, and hence it sees the comic aspect of humor only vanishingly.

Now we have reached the limit. The religiosity of hidden inwardness is *eo ipso*[3] inaccessible to comic apprehension. The comical cannot be outside it, precisely because it is hidden inwardness and therefore cannot come into contradiction with anything. The sphere of contradiction which humor dominates, including as it does the highest range of the comical, is something that such religiosity has itself brought to consciousness, and it has it within itself as something lower. Thus it is absolutely secured against the comical, or is by means of the comical secured against the comical.

[2] In the abstract.
[3] In itself.

Henrik Ibsen *1828–1906*

Letter to
Björnstjerne Björnson *December 9, 1867*

My book[1] *is* poetry; and if it is not, then it will be. The conception of poetry in our country, in Norway, shall be made to conform to the book. There is no stability in the world of ideas. The Scandinavians of this century are not Greeks. He says that the Strange Passenger is symbolic of terror. Supposing that I had been about to be executed, and that such an explanation would have saved my life, it would never have occurred to me. I never thought of such a thing. I stuck in the scene as a mere caprice. And tell me now, is Peer Gynt himself not a personality, complete and individual? *I* know that he is. And the mother, is she not? There are many things to be learned from Clemens Petersen, and I have learned much from him; but there is something that it might do him good to learn, and in which I, even though I cannot teach it to him, have the advantage of him—and that is what you in your letter call "loyalty." Yes, that is just the word! Not loyalty to a friend, a purpose, or the like, but to something infinitely higher.

However, I am glad of the injustice that has been done me. There has been something of the God-send, of the providential dispensation in it; for I feel that this anger is invigorating all my powers. If it is to be war, then let it be war! If I am no poet, then I have nothing to lose. I shall try my luck as a photographer. My contemporaries in the North I shall take in hand, one after the other, as I have already taken the nationalist language reformers.[2] I will not spare the child in the mother's womb, nor the thought or feeling that lies under the word of any living soul that deserves the honor of my notice.

Selection. From *Letters of Henrik Ibsen*. Translated by J. N. Laurvik and Mary Morison. New York: Fox, Duffield, and Co., 1905.

[1] The first edition of *Peer Gynt* was published in Copenhagen on the 14th of November 1867, and the second edition only a fortnight later. Björnson reviewed the book in a letter from Copenhagen to the *Norsk Folkeblad*. A week later it was reviewed in *Foederlandet* by Clemens Petersen. Petersen declared that the work is not "real poetry," because "in its transpositions from reality to art it neither completely fulfills the requirements of art nor those of reality." It is, in his opinion, "full of fallacious ideas" and of "riddles which are insoluble because there is nothing in them at all." He assigns it to the domain of polemical journalism. [This and the following note are the translators'.]

[2] In the figure "Huhu" in the Fourth Act of *Peer Gynt*, Ibsen aims at the "Maalstrae-vere," the would-be nationalizers of the Norwegian language.

Letter to Edmund Gosse[*] January 15, 1874

I am greatly obliged to you for your kind review of my new drama.[1]
There is only one remark in it about which I must say a word or two.
You are of the opinion that the drama ought to have been written in verse,
and that it would have gained by this. Here I must differ from you. The
play is, as you must have observed, conceived in the most realistic style;
the illusion I wished to produce was that of reality. I wished to produce
the impression on the reader that what he was reading was something that
had really happened. If I had employed verse, I should have counteracted
my own intention and prevented the accomplishment of the task I had
set myself. The many ordinary, insignificant characters whom I have intentionally introduced into the play would have become indistinct, and indistinguishable from one another, if I had allowed all of them to speak in one
and the same rhythmical measure. We are no longer living in the days of
Shakespeare. Among sculptors there is already talk of painting statues in the
natural colors. Much can be said both for and against this. I have no desire
to see the Venus of Milo painted, but I would rather see the head of a
Negro executed in black than in white marble. Speaking generally, the style
must conform to the degree of ideality which pervades the representation.
My new drama is no tragedy in the ancient acceptation; what I desired to
depict were human beings, and therefore I would not let them talk the
"language of the Gods."

Letter to Lucie Wolf[†] May 25, 1883

You wish me to write a prologue for the festival performance to be given
at the Christiania Theatre in June, on the thirtieth anniversary of your appearance on its stage.

* Selection. From *Letters of Henrik Ibsen*. Translated by J. N. Laurvik and Mary Morison.
New York: Fox, Duffield, and Co., 1905.

† Selection. From *Letters of Henrik Ibsen*. Translated by J. N. Laurvik and Mary Morison.
New York: Fox, Duffield, and Co., 1905.

[1] Gosse reviewed *Emperor and Galilean* in *The Spectator*, December 27, 1873.

I wish I could comply with your request. Nothing would please me more than to be able to do it. But I cannot; my convictions and my art-principles forbid me. Prologues, epilogues, and everything of the kind ought to be banished from the stage. The stage is for dramatic art alone; and declamation is not dramatic art.

The prologue would, of course, have to be in verse; for such is the established custom. But I will have no hand in perpetuating this custom. Verse has been most injurious to dramatic art. A scenic artist whose department is the drama of the present day should be unwilling to take a verse into his mouth. It is improbable that verse will be employed to any extent worth mentioning in the drama of the immediate future; the aims of the dramatists of the future are almost certain to be incompatible with it. It is therefore doomed. For art forms become extinct, just as the preposterous animal forms of prehistoric times became extinct when their day was over.

A tragedy in iambic pentameters is already as rare a phenomenon as that bird the dodo, of which only a few specimens are still in existence on some African island.

I myself have for the last seven or eight years hardly written a single verse; I have exclusively cultivated the very much more difficult art of writing the genuine, plain language spoken in real life. It is by no means of this language that you have become the excellent artist you now are. Smooth verse has never helped you to bribe any one's verdict.

But there is yet another argument, which appears to me to be the chief one. In a prologue all kinds of agreeable things are said to the public; it is thanked for its lenient and instructive criticism; the artist employs all the tricks of rhyme in making himself as insignificantly diminutive as possible. But is this an honest proceeding? You know, just as well as I, that it is not. The exact opposite is the truth. It is not you who are in debt to the public; it is the public that is deeply in debt to you for your thirty years' faithful work.

This, in my opinion, is the standpoint which it is the duty of an able artist to maintain, out of regard for himself and his profession. And I am certain that you yourself will admit that I cannot well, holding such opinions, undertake to compose a prologue for the occasion in question.

But though I am unable to serve you in this matter, I trust that you will, nevertheless, accept the tribute of thanks which I herewith offer you, thanks for all you have been and still are to our scenic art, and my special thanks for the important share you have taken in the rendering of so many of my own dramatic works.

Letter to
Hans Lien Braekstad *August 1890*

[I have had my attention called to a letter from Berlin relating to myself in the *Daily Chronicle* of August 13; and as several of the statements in this letter seem susceptible of misconstruction—have, in fact, been already misconstrued in the Scandinavian papers—I shall be very much obliged by your having some of the expressions attributed to me corrected. It appears to me that certain of them are not exact and complete reproductions of my utterances to the correspondent of the paper.][1]

I did not, for instance, say that I have never studied the question of Socialism—the fact being that I am much interested in the question, and have endeavored to the best of my ability to acquaint myself with its different sides. I only said that I have never had time to study the extensive literature dealing with the different socialistic systems.

Where the correspondent repeats my assertion that I do not belong to the Social-Democratic party, I wish that he had not omitted what I expressly added, namely, that I never have belonged, and probably never shall belong, to any party whatever.

I may add here that it has become an absolute necessity to me to work quite independently and to shape my own course.

What the correspondent writes about my surprise at seeing my name put forward by socialistic agitators as that of a supporter of their dogmas is particularly liable to be misunderstood.

What I really said was that I was surprised that I, who had made it my chief life-task to depict human characters and human destinies, should, without conscious or direct intention, have arrived in several matters at the same conclusions as the social-democratic moral philosophers had arrived at by scientific processes.

What led me to express this surprise (and, I may here add, satisfaction) was a statement made by the correspondent to the effect that one or more lectures had lately been given in London, dealing, according to him, chiefly with *A Doll's House*.[2]

Selection. From *Letters of Henrik Ibsen*. Translated by J. N. Laurvik and Mary Morison. New York: Fox, Duffield, and Co., 1905.

[1] [This letter] has been reconstructed from the extracts from the original letter (which is no longer in existence), inserted by Mr. Braekstad in the *Daily Chronicle* of the 28th of August 1890, and the *Münchener Post*, No. 200 [translators' note].

[2] Ibsen refers to Bernard Shaw's lecture to the Fabian Society. This lecture was the basis of Shaw's *The Quintessence of Ibsenism* [see below, pp. 638–647].

Speech at the Festival of the Norwegian Women's Rights League, Christiana May 26, 1898

I am not a member of the Women's Rights League. Whatever I have written has been without any conscious thought of making propaganda. I have been more poet and less social philosopher than people generally seem inclined to believe. I thank you for the toast, but must disclaim the honor of having consciously worked for the women's rights movement. I am not even quite clear as to just what this women's rights movement really is. To me it has seemed a problem of humanity in general. And if you read my books carefully you will understand this. True enough, it is desirable to solve the problem of women's rights, along with all the others; but that has not been the whole purpose. My task has been the *description of humanity*. To be sure, whenever such a description is felt to be reasonably true, the reader will insert his own feelings and sentiments into the work of the poet. These are attributed to the poet; but incorrectly so. Every reader remolds it so beautifully and nicely, each according to his own personality. Not only those who write, but also those who read are poets; they are collaborators; they are often more poetical than the poet himself.

Selection. From Henrik Ibsen, *Speeches and New Letters*, translated by Arne Kildal. Boston: Richard G. Badger, 1910.

August Strindberg 1849–1912

Preface to Miss Julie 1888

Like the arts in general, the theatre has for a long time seemed to me a *Biblia Pauperum*, a picture Bible for those who cannot read, and the playwright merely a lay preacher who hawks the latest ideas in popular form, so popular that the middle classes—the bulk of the audiences—can grasp them without racking their brains too much. That explains why the theatre has always been an elementary school for youngsters and the half-educated, and for women, who still retain a primitive capacity for deceiving themselves and for letting themselves be deceived, that is, for succumbing to illusions and responding hypnotically to the suggestions of the author. Consequently, now that the rudimentary and undeveloped mental processes that operate in the realm of fantasy appear to be evolving to the level of reflection, research, and experimentation, I believe that the theatre, like religion, is about to be replaced as a dying institution for whose enjoyment we lack the necessary qualifications. Support for my view is provided by the theatre crisis through which all of Europe is now passing, and still more by the fact that in those highly cultured lands which have produced the finest minds of our time—England and Germany—the drama is dead, as for the most part are the other fine arts.

Other countries, however, have thought to create a new drama by filling the old forms with new contents. But since there has not been enough time to popularize the new ideas, the public cannot understand them. And in the second place, controversy has so stirred up the public that they can no longer look on with a pure and dispassionate interest, especially when they see their most cherished ideals assailed or hear an applauding or booing majority openly exercise its tyrannical power, as can happen in the theatre. And in the third place, since the new forms for the new ideas have not been created, the new wine has burst the old bottles.

In the play that follows I have not tried to accomplish anything new—that is impossible. I have only tried to modernize the form to satisy what I believe up-to-date people expect and demand of this art. And with that in mind I have seized upon—or let myself be seized by—a theme which may be said to lie outside current party strife, since the question of being on the way up or the way down the social ladder, of being on the top or on the

From *Miss Julie* by August Strindberg, translated by E. M. Sprinchorn. San Francisco: Chandler Publishing Company, 1961. Reprinted by permission of Intext Educational Publishers, Scranton, Pennsylvania. Revised and expanded for this edition by the translator, this is the only English translation of Strindberg's complete text.

bottom, superior or inferior, man or woman, is, has been, and will be of perennial interest. When I took this theme from real life—I heard about it a few years ago and it made a deep impression on me—I thought it would be a suitable subject for a tragedy, since it still strikes us as tragic to see a happily favored individual go down in defeat, and even more so to see an entire family line die out. But perhaps a time will come when we shall be so highly developed and so enlightened that we can look with indifference upon the brutal, cynical, and heartless spectacle that life offers us, a time when we shall have laid aside those inferior and unreliable instruments of thought called feelings, which will become superfluous and even harmful as our mental organs develop. The fact that my heroine wins sympathy is due entirely to the fact that we are still to weak to overcome the fear that the same fate might overtake us. The extremely sensitive viewer will of course not be satisfied with mere expressions of sympathy, and the man who believes in progress will demand that certain positive actions be taken for getting rid of the evil, a kind of program, in other words. But in the first place absolute evil does not exist. The decline of one family is the making of another, which now gets its chance to rise. This alternate rising and falling provides one of life's greatest pleasures, for happiness is, after all, relative. As for the man who has a program for changing the disagreeable circumstance that the eagle eats the dove and that lice eat up the eagle, I should like to ask him why it should be changed? Life is not prearranged with such idiotic mathematical precision that only the larger gets to eat the smaller. Just as frequently the little bee destroys the lion [in Aesop's fable]—or at least drives him wild.

If my tragedy makes most people feel sad, that is their fault. When we get to be as strong as the first French Revolutionists were, we shall be perfectly content and happy to watch the forests being cleared of rotting, superannuated trees that have stood too long in the way of others with just as much right to grow and flourish for a while—as content as we are when we see an incurably ill man finally die.

Recently my tragedy *The Father* was censured for being too unpleasant— as if one wanted amusing tragedies. "The joy of life" is now the slogan of the day. Theatre managers send out orders for nothing but farces, as if the joy of living lay in behaving like a clown and in depicting people as if they were afflicted with St. Vitus's dance or congenital idiocy. I find the joy of living in the fierce and ruthless battles of life, and my pleasure comes from learning something, from being taught something. That is why I have chosen for my play an unusual but instructive case, an exception, in other words— but an important exception of the kind that proves the rule—a choice of subject that I know will offend all lovers of the conventional. The next thing that will bother simple minds is that the motivation for the action is not simple and that the point of view is not single. Usually an event in life— and this is a fairly new discovery—is the result of a whole series of more or less deep-rooted causes. The spectator, however, generally chooses the one that puts the least strain on his mind or reflects most credit on his insight. Consider a case of suicide. "Business failure," says the merchant. "Unhappy love," say the women. "Physical illness," says the sick man. "Lost hopes," says the down-and-out. But it may be that the reason lay in all of these or in none of them, and that the suicide hid his real reason behind a completely different one that would reflect greater glory on his memory.

I have motivated the tragic fate of Miss Julie with an abundance of circumstances: her mother's basic instincts, her father's improper bringing-up of the girl, her own inborn nature, and her fiancé's sway over her weak and degenerate mind. Further and more immediately: the festive atmosphere of Midsummer Eve, her father's absence, her monthly illness, her preoccupation with animals, the erotic excitement of the dance, the long summer twilight, the highly aphrodisiac influence of flowers, and finally chance itself, which drives two people together in an out-of-the-way room, plus the boldness of the aroused man.

As one can see, I have not concerned myself solely with physiological causes, nor confined myself monomaniacally to psychological causes, nor traced everything to an inheritance from her mother, nor put the blame entirely on her monthly indisposition or exclusively on "immorality." Nor have I simply preached a sermon. Lacking a priest, I have let the cook take care of that.

I am proud to say that this complicated way of looking at things is in tune with the times. And if others have anticipated me in this, I am proud that I am not alone in my paradoxes, as all new discoveries are called. And no one can say this time that I am being one-sided.

As far as the drawing of characters is concerned, I have made the people in my play fairly "characterless" for the following reasons. In the course of time the word *character* has acquired many meanings. Originally it probably meant the dominant and fundamental trait in the soul complex and was confused with temperament. Later the middle class used it to mean an automation. An individual who once for all had found his own true nature or adapted himself to a certain role in life, who in fact had ceased to grow, was called a man of character, while the man who was constantly developing, who, like a skillful sailor on the currents of life, did not sail with close-tied sheets but who fell off before the wind in order to luff again, was called a man of no character—derogatorily of course, since he was so difficult to keep track of, to pin down and pigeonhole. This middle-class conception of a fixed character was transferred to the stage, where the middle class has always ruled. A character there came to mean someone who was always one and the same, always drunk, always joking, always moving, and who needed to be characterized only by some physical defect such as a club foot, a wooden leg, or a red nose, or by the repetition of some such phrase as, "That's capital," or

"Barkis is willin'." This uncomplicated way of viewing people is still to be found in the great Molière. Harpagon is nothing but a miser, although Harpagon could have been both a miser and an exceptional financier, a fine father, and a good citizen. Worse still, his "defect" is extremely advantageous to his son-in-law and his daughter who will be his heirs and therefore should not find fault with him, even if they do have to wait a while to jump into bed together. So I do not believe in simple stage characters. And the summary judgments that writers pass on people—he is stupid, this one is brutal, that one is jealous, this one is stingy, and so on—should not pass unchallenged by the naturalists who know how complicated the soul is and who realize that vice has a reverse side very much like virtue.

Since the persons in my play are modern characters, living in a transitional era more hectic and hysterical than the previous one at least, I have depicted them as more unstable, as torn and divided, a mixture of the old and the new. Nor does it seem improbable to me that modern ideas might also have seeped down through newspapers and kitchen talk to the level of the servants. Consequently the valet may belch forth from his inherited slave soul certain modern ideas. And if there are those who find it wrong to allow people in a modern drama to talk Darwin and who recommend the practice of Shakespeare to our attention, may I remind them that the gravedigger in *Hamlet* talks the then fashionable philosophy of Giordano Bruno (Bacon's philosophy), which is even more improbable, seeing that the means of spreading ideas were fewer then than now. And besides, the fact of the matter is that Darwinism has always existed, ever since Moses' history of creation from the lower animals up to man, but it was not until recently that we discovered it and formulized it.

My souls—or characters—are conglomerations from various stages of culture, past and present, walking scrapbooks, shreds of human lives, tatters torn from former fancy dresses that are now old rags—hodgepodges just like the human soul. I have even supplied a little source history into the bargain by letting the weaker steal and repeat words of the stronger, letting them get ideas (suggestions as they are called) from one another, from the environment (the songbird's blood), and from objects (the razor). I have also arranged for *Gedankenübertragung*[1] through an inanimate medium to take place (the count's boots, the servant's bell). And I have even made use of "waking suggestion" (a variation of hypnotic suggestion), which have by now been so popularized that they cannot arouse ridicule or scepticism as they would have done in Mesmer's time.

I say Miss Julie is a modern character not because the man-hating half-woman has not always existed but because she has now been brought out into the open, has taken the stage, and is making noises. Victim of a superstition

[1] Telepathy.

(one that has seized even stronger minds) that woman, that stunted form of human being, standing with man, the lord of creation, the creator of culture, is meant to be the equal of man or could ever possibly be, she involves herself in an absurd struggle with him in which she falls. Absurd because a stunted form, subject to the laws of propagation, will always be born stunted and can never catch up with the one who has the lead. As follows: A (the man) and B (the woman) start from the same point C, A with a speed of let us say 100 and B with a speed of 60. When will Be overtake A? Answer: never. Neither with the help of equal education or equal voting rights—nor by universal disarmament and temperance societies—any more than two parallel lines can never meet. The half-woman is a type that forces itself on others, selling itself for power, medals, recognition, diplomas, as formerly it sold itself for money. It represents degeneration. It is not a strong species for it does not maintain itself, but unfortunately it propagates its misery in the following generation. Degenerate men unconsciously select their mates from among these half-women, so that they breed and spread, producing creatures of indeterminate sex to whom life is a torture, but who fortunately are overcome eventually either by a hostile reality, or by the uncontrolled breaking loose of their repressed instincts, or else by their frustration in not being able to compete with the male sex. It is a tragic type, offering us the spectacle of a desperate fight against nature; a tragic legacy of romanticism that is now being dissipated by naturalism—a movement which seeks only happiness, and for that strong and healthy species are required.

But Miss Julie is also a vestige of the old warrior nobility that is now being superseded by a new nobility of nerve and brain. She is a victim of the disorder produced within a family by a mother's "crime," of the mistakes of a whole generation gone wrong, of circumstances, of her own defective constitution—all of which put together is equivalent to the fate or universal law of the ancients. The naturalists have banished guilt along with God, but the consequences of the act—punishment, imprisonment, or the fear of it—cannot be banished for the simple reason that they remain whether or not the naturalist dismisses the case from his court. Those sitting on the sidelines can easily afford to be lenient; but what of the injured parties? And even if her father were compelled to forgo taking his revenge, Miss Julie would take vengeance on herself, as she does in the play, because of that inherited or acquired sense of honor that has been transmitted to the upper classes from— well, where does it come from? From the age of barbarism, from the first Aryans, from the chivalry of the Middle Ages. And a very fine code it was, but now inimical to the survival of the race. It is the aristocrat's form of hara-kiri, a law of conscience that bids the Japanese to slice his own stomach when someone else dishonors him. The same sort of thing survives, slightly modified, in that exclusive prerogative of the aristocracy, the duel. (Example: the husband challenges his wife's lover to a duel; the lover shoots the husband and runs off with the wife. Result: the husband has saved his *honor* but lost his wife.) Hence the servant Jean lives on; but not Miss Julie, who cannot live without honor. The advantage that the slave has over his master is that he has not committed himself to this defeatist principle. In all of us Aryans there is enough of the nobleman, or of the Don Quixote, to make us sympathize with the man who takes his own life after having dishonored himself by shameful deeds. And we are all of us aristocrats enough to be distressed at the sight of a a great man lying like a dead hulk ready for the scrap pile, even, I suppose, if he were to raise himself up again and redeem himself by honorable deeds.

The servant Jean is the beginning of a new species in which noticeable differentiation has already taken place. He began as the child of a poor worker and is now evolving through self-education into a future gentleman of the upper classes. He is quick to learn, has highly developed senses (smell, taste, sight), and a keen appreciation of beauty. He has already come up in the world, for he is strong enough not to hesitate to make use of other people. He is already a stranger to his old friends, whom he despises as reminders of past stages in his development, and whom he fears and avoids because they know his secrets, guess his intentions, look with envy on his rise and in joyful expectation toward his fall. Hence his character is unformed and divided. He wavers between an admiration of high positions and a hatred of the men who occupy them. He is an aristocrat—he says so himself—familiar with the ins and outs of good society. He is polished on the outside, but coarse underneath. He wears his frock coat with elegance but gives no assurance that he keeps his body clean.

He respects Miss Julie but he is afraid of Christine, for she knows his innermost secrets. Yet he is sufficiently hard-hearted not to let the events of the night upset his plans for the future. Possessing both the coarseness of the slave and the toughmindedness of the born ruler, he can look at blood without fainting, shake off bad luck like water, and take calamity by the horns. Consequently he will escape from the battle unwounded, probably ending up as proprietor of a hotel. And if he himself does not get to be a Rumanian count, his son will doubtless go to college and possibly end up as a government official.

Now his observations about life as the lower classes see it, from below, are well worth listening to—that is, they are whenever he is telling the truth, which is not too often, because he is more likely to say what is advantageous to him than what is true. When Miss Julie supposes that everyone in the lower classes must feel greatly oppressed by the weight of the classes above, Jean naturally agrees with her since he wants to win her sympathy. But he promptly takes it all back when he finds it advisable to separate himself from the mob.

Apart from the fact that Jean is coming up in the world, he is also superior to Miss Julie in that he is a man. In the sexual sphere, he is the aristocrat. He has the strength of the male, more highly developed senses, and the ability to take the initiative. His inferiority is merely the result of his social environment, which is only temporary and which he will probably slough off along with his livery.

His slave nature expresses itself in his awe of the Count (the boots) and in his religious superstitions. But he is awed by the Count mainly because the Count occupies the place he wants most in life; and this awe is still there even after he has won the daughter of the house and seen how hollow that beautiful shell was.

I do not believe that any love in the "higher" sense can be born from the union of two such different souls; so I have let Miss Julie's love be refashioned in her imagination as a love that protects and purifies, and I have let Jean imagine that even his love might have a chance to grow under other social circumstances. For I suppose love is very much like the hyacinth that must strike roots deep in the dark earth *before* it can produce a vigorous blossom. Here it shoots up, bursts into bloom, and turns to seed all at once; and that is why it dies so quickly.

Christine—finally to get to her—is a female slave, spineless and phlegmatic after years spent at the kitchen stove, bovinely unconscious of her own hypocrisy, and with a full quota of moral and religious notions that serve as scapegoats and cloaks for her sins—which a stronger soul does not require since he is able either to carry the burden of his own sins or to rationalize them out of existence. She attends church regularly where she deftly unloads unto Jesus—that straw man—her household thefts and picks up from him another load of innocence. She is only a secondary character, and I have deliberately done no more than sketch her in—just as I treated the country doctor and parish priest in *The Father* where I only wanted to draw ordinary everyday people such as most country doctors and parsons are. That some have found my minor characters one-dimensional is due to the fact that ordinary people while at work are to a certain extent one-dimensional and do lack an independent existence, showing only one side of themselves in the performance of their duties. And as long as the audience does not feel it needs to see them from different angles, my abstract sketches will pass muster.

Now as far as the dialogue is concerned, I have broken somewhat with tradition in refusing to make my characters into interlocutors who ask stupid questions to elicit witty answers. I have avoided the symmetrical and mathematical design of the artfully constructed French dialogue and have let minds work as irregularly as they do in real life, where no subject is quite exhausted before another mind engages at random some cog in the conversation and governs it for a while. My dialogue wanders here and there, gathers material in the first scenes which is later picked up, repeated, reworked, developed, and expanded like the theme in a piece of music.

The action of the play poses no problems. Since it really involves only two people, I have limited myself to these two, introducing only one minor character, the cook, and keeping the unhappy spirit of the father brooding over the action as a whole. I have chosen this course because I have noticed that what interests people most nowadays is the psychological action. Our inveterately curious souls are no longer content to see a thing happen; we want to see how it happens. We want to see the strings, look at the machinery, examine the double-bottom drawer, put on the magic ring to find the hidden seam, look in the deck for the marked cards.

In treating the subject this way I have had in mind the case-history novels of the Goncourt brothers, which appeal to me more than anything else in modern literature.

As far as play construction is concerned, I have made a stab at getting rid of act divisions. I was afraid that the spectator's declining susceptibility to illusion might not carry him through the intermission, when he would have time to think about what he has seen and to escape the suggestive influence of the author-hypnotist. I figure my play lasts about ninety minutes. Since one can listen to a lecture, a sermon, or a political debate for that long or even longer, I have convinced myself that a play should not exhaust an audience in that length of time. As early as 1872 in one of my first attempts at the drama, *The Outlaw*, I tried out this concentrated form, although with little success. I had finished the work in five acts when I noticed the disjointed and disturbing effect it produced. I burned it, and from the ashes there arose a single, completely reworked act of fifty pages that would run for less an hour. This play form is not completely new but seems to be my special property and has a good chance of gaining favor with the public when tastes change. My hope is to educate a public to sit through a full evening's show in one act. But this whole question must first be probed more deeply. In the meantime, in order to establish resting places for the audience and the actors without destroying the illusion, I have made use of three arts that belong to the drama: the monologue, the pantomime, and the ballet, all of which were part of classic tragedy, the monody having become the monologue and the choral dance, the ballet.

The realists have banished the monologue from the stage as implausible. But if I can motivate it, I make it plausible, and I can then use it to my advantage. Now it is certainly plausible for a speaker to pace the floor and read his speech aloud to himself. It is plausible for an actor to practice his part aloud, for a child to talk to her cat, a mother to babble to her baby, an old lady to chatter to her parrot, and a sleeping man to talk in his sleep. And in order to give the actor a chance to work on his own for once and for a moment not be obliged to follow the author's directions, I have not written out the monologues in detail but simply outlined them. Since it makes very little difference what is said while asleep, or to the parrot or the cat, inasmuch as it does not affect the main action, a gifted player who is in the midst of the situation and mood of the play can probably improvise the monologue better than the author, who cannot estimate ahead of time how much may be said and for how long before the illusion is broken.

Some theatres in Italy have, as we know, returned to the art of improvisation and have thereby trained actors who are truly inventive—without, however, violating the intentions of the author. This seems to be a step in the right direction and possibly the beginning of a new, fertile form of art that will be genuinely productive.

In place where the monologue cannot be properly motivated, I have resorted to pantomime. Here I have given the actor even more freedom to be creative and win honor on his own. Nevertheless, not to try the audience beyond its limits, I have relied on music—well motivated by the Midsummer Eve dance—to exercise its hypnotic powers during the pantomime scene. I beg the music director to select his tunes with great care, so that associations foreign to the mood of the play will not be produced by reminders of popular operettas or current dance numbers or by folk music of interest only to ethnologists.

The ballet that I have introduced cannot be replaced by a so-called crowd scene. Such scenes are always badly acted, with a pack of babbling fools taking advantage of the occasion to "gag it up," thereby destroying the illusion. Inasmuch as country people do not improvise their taunts but make use of material already to hand by giving it a double meaning, I have not composed an original lampoon but have made use of a little known round dance that I noted down in the Stockholm district. The words do not fit the situation exactly, which is what I intended, since the slave in his cunning (that is, weakness) never attacks directly. At any rate, let us have no comedians in this serious story and no obscene smirking over an affair that nails the lid on a family coffin.

As far as the scenery is concerned, I have borrowed from impressionistic painting the idea of asymmetrical and open composition, and I believe that I have thereby gained something in the way of greater illusion. Because the audience cannot see the whole room and all the furniture, they will have to surmise what's missing; that is, their imagination will be stimulated to fill in the rest of the picture. I have gained something else by this: I have avoided those tiresome exits through doors. Stage doors are made of canvas and rock at the slightest touch. They cannot even be used to indicate the wrath of an angry father who storms out of the house after a bad dinner, slamming the door behind him "so that the whole house shakes." (In the theatre it sways and billows.) Furthermore, I have confined the action to one set, both to give the characters a chance to become part and parcel of their environment and to cut down on scenic extravagance. If there is only one set, one has a right to expect it to be as realistic as possible. Yet nothing is more difficult than to make a room look like a room, however easy it may be for the scene painter to create waterfalls and erupting volcanos. I suppose we shall have to put up with walls made of canvas, but isn't it about time that we stopped painting shelves and pots and pans on the canvas? There are so many other conventions in the theater which we are told to accept in good faith that we should be spared the strain of believing in painted saucepans.

I have placed the backdrop and the table at an angle to force the actors to play face to face or in half profile when they are seated opposite each other at the table. In a production of *Aïda* I saw a flat placed at such an angle, which led the eye out in an unfamiliar perspective. Nor did it look as if it had been set that way simply to be different or to avoid those monotonous right angles.

Another desirable innovation would be the removal of the footlights. I understand that the purpose of lighting from below is to make the actors look more full in the face. But may I ask why all actors should have full faces? Doesn't this kind of lighting wipe out many of the finer features in the lower part of the face, especially around the jaws? Doesn't it distort the shape of nose and throw false shadows above the eyes? If not, it certainly does something else: it hurts the actor's eyes. The footlights hit the retina at an angle from which it is usually shielded (except in sailors who must look at the sunlight reflected in the water), and the result is the loss of any effective play of the eyes. All one ever sees on stage are goggle-eyed glances sideways at the boxes or upward at the balcony, with only the whites of the eyes being visible in the latter case. And this probably also accounts for that tiresome fluttering of the eyelashes that the female performers are particularly guilty of. If an actor nowadays wants to express something with his eyes, he can only do it looking right at the audience, in which case he makes direct contact with someone outside the proscenium arch—a bad habit known justifiably or not, as "saying hello to friends."[2]

I should think that the use of sufficiently strong side lights (through the use of reflectors or something like them) would provide the actor with a new asset: an increased range of expression made possible by the play of the eyes, the most expressive part of the face.

I have scarcely any illusions about getting actors to play for the audience and not directly at them, although this should be the goal. Nor do I dream of ever seeing an actor play through all of an important scene with his back to the audience. But is it too much to hope that crucial scenes could be played where the author indicated and not in front of the prompter's box as if they were duets demanding applause? I am not calling for a revolution, only for some small changes. I am well aware that transforming the stage into a real room with the fourth wall missing and with some of the furniture placed with

[2] "Counting the house" would be the equivalent in American theatre slang [translator's note].

backs to the auditorium would only upset the audience, at least for the present.

If I bring up the subject of make-up, it is not because I dare hope to be heeded by the ladies, who would rather be beautiful than truthful. But the male actor might do well to consider if it is an advantage to paint his face with character lines that remain there like a mask. Let us imagine an actor who pencils in with soot a few lines between his eyes to indicate great anger, and let us suppose that in that permanently enraged state he finds he has to smile on a certain line. Imagine the horrible grimace! And how can the old character actor wrinkle his brows in anger when his false bald pate is as smooth as a billiard ball?

In a modern psychological drama, in which every tremor of the soul should be reflected more by facial expressions than by gestures and grunts, it would probably be most sensible to experiment with strong side lighting on a small stage, using actors without any make-up or a minimum of it.

And then, if we could get rid of the visible orchestra with its disturbing lights and the faces turned toward the public; if the auditorium floor could be raised so that the spectator's eyes are not level with the actor's knees; if we could get rid of the proscenium boxes and their occupants, giggling diners and drinkers; and if we could have it dark in the auditorium during the performance; and if, above everything else, we could have a small stage and an intimate auditorium—then possibly a new drama might arise and at least one theatre become a refuge for cultured audiences. While we are waiting for such a theatre, we shall have to write for the dramatic stockpile and prepare the repertory that one day shall come.

Here is my attempt. If I have failed, there is still time to try again!

An Effective Play   *c. 1900*

An effective play should contain or make use of:
Hints and intimations
A secret made known to the audience either at the beginning or toward

Translated by Evert Sprinchorn. Copyright © 1974 by Evert Sprinchorn. Printed by permission of the translator.

the end. If the spectator, but not the actors, knows the secret, the spectator enjoys their game of blindman's buff. If the spectator is not in on the secret, his curiosity is aroused and his attention held.

An outburst of emotion, rage, indignation

A reversal, well-prepared

A discovery

A punishment (nemesis), a humiliation

A careful resolution, either with or without a reconciliation

A *quiproquo*[1]

A parallelism

A reversal (*revirement*), an upset, a well-prepared surprise.

Author's Preliminary Note to A Dream Play 1903

Following the example of my previous dream play *To Damascus*, I have in this present dream play sought to imitate the incoherent but ostensibly logical form of our dreams. Anything can happen; everything is possible and probable. Time and space do not exist. Working with some insignificant real events as a background, the imagination spins out its threads of thoughts and weaves them into new patterns—a mixture of memories, experiences, spontaneous ideas, impossibilities, and improbabilities.

The characters split, double, multiply, dissolve, condense, float apart, coalesce. But one mind stands over and above them all, the mind of the dreamer; and for him there are no secrets, no inconsistencies, no scruples, no laws. He does not condemn, does not acquit; he only narrates the story. And since the dream is more often painful than cheerful, a tone of melancholy and of sympathy with all living creatures runs through the pitching and swaying narrative. Sleep, which should free the dreamer, often

[1] A misunderstanding.

plagues and tortures him instead. But when the pain is most excruciating, the moment of waking comes and reconciles the dreamer with reality, which, however agonizing it may be, is a joy and a pleasure at that moment compared to the painful dream.

Nineteenth- and Twentieth-Century England and Ireland

Unlike the neoclassicists, who wrote that theatre should delude the
spectator, through verisimilitude, into belief in what he sees on the stage;
unlike Farquhar and Johnson, who believed the spectator is never deluded,
Coleridge regards as the basis of dramatic illusion the audience's "willing
suspension of disbelief," that is, belief in not what is unreal but "a
negative reality," a temporary willingness not to admit the unreality.
Unlike the neoclassicists, to whom unity meant homogeneity, Coleridge
sees "Multëity in Unitey." In a dramatic or nondramatic poem, he
says, which unlike science has pleasure rather than truth as its immediate
end, the whole provides such pleasure as is compatible with the pleasure
of each part. Those English neoclassicists who admired Shakespeare were
able to reconcile his practice with their theories by considering him
an untutored child of nature who violated rules but succeeded through
sheer natural genius. By contrast, the romantic Coleridge perceives that
Shakespeare follows different rules. To Coleridge, unity is organic, not
imposed, and in Shakespeare "the heterogenous is united, as it is in nature."

Comedy as well as tragedy preoccupied nineteenth-century English
critics. To Hazlitt, both tears and laughter result from the difference
between what is and what should be, but the former focuses on serious, the
latter on trifling matters. Contrast is central to his theory of comedy.
He believes the incongruous to be essential to comedy, which the more
serious it seems, the funnier it may be. Whereas humor describes the
ludicrous in itself, says Hazlitt, wit compares or contrasts it with something
else; whereas humor reveals, wit heightens. Meredith, regarding comedy
as "the fountain of sound sense," distinguishes between satire, irony, comedy,
and humor. According to him, true comedy requires an elite, a cultivated
society with vital intellectual activity and social equality of the sexes. The
test of true comedy is whether it awakens thoughtful laughter and the
test of a country's civilization is whether such comedy flourishes.

The Restoration comedy of manners is a concern of Lamb, to whom it
is "almost . . . a fairyland," where neither morality nor immorality

577

exists. Thus, it should not be judged by moral standards. These plays enable us to escape from real life, with its moral concerns, and then to return, refreshed, to one's "cage" and "shackles." Incompatible with such buoyant comedy, Lamb points out, are the sentimental strains that later entered. Lamb's arguments are "sophistical," claims Macaulay, who (like Collier) asserts that sound morality does exist in Restoration comedy, where it is derided. Such a world, says Macaulay, is far from unreal, it is only too real, and these plays are "a disgrace to our language and our national character."

Whereas the English analyze comic plays, it is the Irish who seem to provide them. As frequently observed, the best English comic playwrights since the Restoration are Irish. Among them are Wilde and Shaw, who are also critics of the drama and of art in general.

To the esthete Wilde, true decadence takes place when, as in the late nineteenth century, life banishes art. The cry of art for art's sake is a defiant social protest against a world that has no place for beauty but instead cherishes profit, in all meanings of the word: utility, morality, financial gain, and so forth. If art is to be exiled, artists like Wilde believe, then let it obey only laws intrinsic to itself and not conform to external standards, whether of morality or even of resemblance to reality.

Shaw felt otherwise. No great art, he says, has ever been produced for its own sake, and " 'for art's sake' alone I would not face the toil of writing a single sentence." But while he proclaims the dramatic viability, social utility, and value of plays dealing with social problems, he recognizes that drama does not have to involve them. Dismissing ordinary dramatists who know nothing of social questions, he observes that the extraordinary ones know about them as about other aspects of human life and society. Still, Shaw recognizes that social problems are too topical and temporal to impel a dramatists to the effort needed to create great poetry. Deriding the well-made play as "Sardoodledom," after one of its practitioners, Victorien Sardou, he hails the Ibsenite drama, which, unlike machine-made plays, revolves around problems of character and conduct, jettisons stereotyped hero and villain, and dialectically dramatizes problems of morality instead of accepting them as premises for a conventional resolution. A major critic of Shakespeare, Shaw condemns "bardolatry" and shocks readers with statements that Shakespeare is a lesser thinker than Ibsen or himself, that he has less to tell audiences of the day, and that he is relevant to them because of his resemblances to Ibsen, not to Webster. Bardolators were too dazed (or angry) to notice Shaw's admission that he himself does not write better plays than Shakespeare, that no one else could write as great a tragedy as *Lear*, that Shakespeare has outlasted and will outlast thousands of abler thinkers, and that he is virtually unexcelled in storytelling gifts, linguistic power, and sense of idiosyncratic character.

Unlike his countryman Shaw, Yeats opposed realistic and didactic drama, and naturalistic acting and production as well. He favored a theatre of passion and poetry, and he advocated acting and stagecraft that had simplicity and beauty. One of the founders of the Irish National Theatre, Yeats worked to create a national drama that would express Irish life and character in the vivid, musical idiom of rural Ireland. Like Yeats, Synge—Ireland's first great playwright in the Irish tradition— opposed didactic drama. Observing that every speech of a good play "should be as fully flavoured as a nut or apple," he asked for both reality and joy in the drama and he provided them.

Like the "English" Shaw, the "English" Murray, Archer, and Esslin were born outside England—in Australia, Scotland, and Hungary, respectively. Greek scholar, translator, and critic, Murray theorizes on the ritual origins of Greek tragedy, which he believes retains ritual features. Archer held a conception of the drama more old-fashioned than Shaw's. An early champion and translator of Ibsen, Archer was nevertheless more tolerant of the well-made play than Shaw was. He wrote what was for many years a standard playwriting manual, *Play-Making*, which disputes Brunetière's *The Law of the Drama* (a long selection from which appears in the next section); Archer offers another law and analyzes such dramatic features as the point of attack and the obligatory scene. Unlike Archer, who charts the structure of conventional drama, Esslin examines a different type of play—without plot, character, or motivation in the usual sense; a nondiscursive, theatrical species based on existential anguish at the absurdity of the human condition—the "theatre of the absurd," a term Esslin himself coined.

Samuel Taylor Coleridge 1772–1834

Greek Drama 1812

The tragic poet idealizes his characters by giving to the spiritual part of our nature a more decided preponderance over the animal cravings and impulses, than is met with in real life: the comic poet idealizes his characters by making the animal the governing power, and the intellectual the mere instrument. But as tragedy is not a collection of virtues and perfections, but takes care only that the vices and imperfections shall spring from the passions, errors, and prejudices which arise out of the soul; so neither is comedy a mere crowd of vices and follies, but whatever qualities it represents, even though they are in a certain sense amiable, it still displays them as having their origin in some dependence on our lower nature, accompanied with a defect in true freedom of spirit and self-subsistence, and subject to that unconnection by contradictions of the inward being, to which all folly is owing.

The ideal of earnest poetry consists in the union and harmonious melting down, and fusion of the sensual into the spiritual—of man as an animal into man as a power of reason and self-government. And this we have represented to us most clearly in the plastic art, or statuary; where the perfection of outward form is a symbol of the perfection of an inward idea; where the body is wholly penetrated by the soul, and spiritualized even to a state of glory, and like a transparent substance, the matter, in its own nature darkness, becomes altogether a vehicle and fixture of light, a mean of developing its beauties, and unfolding its wealth of various colors without disturbing its unity, or causing a division of the parts. The sportive ideal, on the contrary, consists in the perfect harmony and concord of the higher nature with the animal, as with its ruling principle and its acknowledged regent. The understanding and practical reason are represented as the willing slaves of the senses and appetites, and of the passions arising out of them. Hence we may admit the appropriateness to the old comedy, as a work of defined art, of allusions and descriptions, which morality can never justify, and, only with reference to the author himself, and only as being the effect or rather the cause of the circumstances in which he wrote, can consent even to palliate.

Selection. From *The Complete Works of Samuel Taylor Coleridge*, Vol. IV, edited by Professor Shedd. New York: Harper & Brothers, 1854.

On the Principles of Sound Criticism concerning the Fine Arts *1814*

AGREEABLE—We use this word in two senses; in the first for whatever agrees with our nature, for that which is congruous with the primary constitution of our senses. Thus green is naturally agreeable to the eye. In this sense the word expresses, at least involves, a pre-established harmony between the organs and their appointed objects. In the second sense, we convey by the word *agreeable*, that the thing has by force of habit (thence called a second nature) been made to agree with us; or that it has become agreeable to us by its recalling to our minds some one or more things that were dear and pleasing to us; or lastly, on account of some after pleasure or advantage, of which it has been the constant cause or occasion. Thus by force of custom men make the taste of tobacco, which was at first hateful to the palate, agreeable to them; thus too, as our Shakespeare observes,

> Things base and vile, holding no quantity,
> Love can transpose to form and dignity—[1]

the crutch that had supported a revered parent, after the first anguish of regret, becomes agreeable to the affectionate child; and I once knew a very sensible and accomplished Dutch gentleman, who, spite of his own sense of the ludicrous nature of the feeling, was more delighted by the first grand concert of frogs he heard in this country, than he had been by Catalina singing in the compositions of Cimarosa. The last clause needs no illustrations, as it comprises all the objects that are agreeable to us, only because they are the means by which we gratify our smell, touch, palate, and mere bodily feeling.

The BEAUTIFUL, contemplated in its essentials, that is, in kind and not in degree, is that in which the many, still seen as many, becomes one. Take a familiar instance, one of a thousand. The frost on a window-pane has by accident crystallized into a striking resemblance of a tree or a seaweed. With what pleasure we trace the parts, and their relations to each other, and to the whole! Here is the stalk or trunk, and here the branches or sprays—sometimes even the buds or flowers. Nor will our pleasure be less, should the

Selection. From Samuel Taylor Coleridge, *Miscellanies, Aesthetic and Literary*, edited by T. Ashe. London: George Bell & Sons, 1885.

[1] Shakespeare, A *Midsummer Night's Dream*, I, i.

caprice of the crystallization represent some object disagreeable to us, provided only we can see or fancy the component parts each in relation to each, and all forming a whole. A lady would see an admirably painted tiger with pleasure, and at once pronounce it beautiful—nay, an owl, a frog, or a toad, who would have shrieked or shuddered at the sight of the things themselves. So far is the Beautiful from depending wholly on association, that it is frequently produced by the mere removal of associations. Many a sincere convert to the beauty of various insects, as of the dragon-fly, the fangless snake, etc., has Natural History made, by exploding the terror or aversion that had been connected with them.

The most general definition of beauty, therefore, is—that I may fulfill my threat of plaguing my readers with hard words—Multëity in Unity. Now it will be always found, that whatever is the definition of the kind, independent of degree, becomes likewise the definition of the highest degree of that kind. An old coach-wheel lies in the coachmaker's yard, disfigured with tar and dirt (I purposely take the most trivial instances): if I turn away my attention from these, and regard the figure abstractly, "still," I might say to my companion, "there is beauty in that wheel, and you yourself would not only admit, but would feel it, had you never seen a wheel before. See how the rays proceed from the centre to the circumferences, and how many different images are distinctly comprehended at one glance, as forming one whole, and each part in some harmonious relation to each and to all." But imagine the polished golden wheel of the chariot of the Sun, as the poets have described it: then the figure, and the real thing so figured, exactly coincide. There is nothing heterogeneous, nothing to abstract from: by its perfect smoothness and circularity in width, each part is (if I may borrow a metaphor from a sister sense) as perfect a melody, as the whole is a complete harmony. This, we should say, is beautiful throughout. Of all "the many," which I actually see, each and all are really reconciled into unity: while the effulgence from the whole coincides with, and seems to represent, the effluence of delight from my own mind in the intuition of it.

It seems evident then, first, that beauty is harmony, and subsists only in composition, and secondly, that the first species of the Agreeable can alone be a component part of the beautiful, that namely which is naturally consonant with our senses by the pre-established harmony between nature and the human mind; and thirdly, that even of this species, those objects only can be admitted (according to rule the first) which belong to the eye and ear, because they alone are susceptible of distinction of parts.

Biographia Literaria *1815–1816*

The office of philosophical disquisition consists in just distinction; while it is the privilege of the philosopher to preserve himself constantly aware, that distinction is not division. In order to obtain adequate notions of any truth, we must intellectually separate its distinguishable parts; and this is the technical process of philosophy. But having so done, we must then restore them in our conceptions to the unity, in which they actually coexist; and this is the result of philosophy. A poem contains the same elements as a prose composition; the difference therefore must consist in a different combination of them, in consequence of a different object being proposed. According to the difference of the object will be the difference of the combination. It is possible, that the object may be merely to facilitate the recollection of any given facts or observations by artificial arrangement; and the composition will be a poem, merely because it is distinguished from prose by meter, or by rhyme, or by both conjointly. In this, the lowest sense, a man might attribute the name of a poem to the well-known enumeration of the days in the several months:

> Thirty days hath September,
> April, June, and November, etc.

and others of the same class and purpose. And as a particular pleasure is found in anticipating the recurrence of sounds and quantities, all compositions that have this charm superadded, whatever be their contents, *may* be entitled poems.

So much for the superficial form. A difference of object and contents supplies an additional ground of distinction. The immediate purpose may be the communication of truths; either of truth absolute and demonstrable, as in works of science; or of facts experienced and recorded, as in history. Pleasure, and that of the highest and most permanent kind, may result from the attainment of the end; but it is not itself the immediate end. In other works the communication of pleasure may be the immediate purpose; and though truth, either moral or intellectual, ought to be the ultimate end, yet this will distinguish the character of the author, not the class to which the work belongs. . . .

But the communication of pleasure may be the immediate object of a work not metrically composed; and that object may have been in a high degree attained, as in novels and romances. Would then the mere superaddition of meter, with or without rhyme, entitle these to the name of poems? The answer is that nothing can permanently please, which does

Selections from chap. 14. From *The Complete Works of Samuel Taylor Coleridge*, Vol. III, edited by Professor Shedd. New York: Harper & Brothers, 1858.

not contain in itself the reason why it is so, and not otherwise. If meter be superadded, all other parts must be made consonant with it. They must be such, as to justify the perpetual and distinct attention to each part, which an exact correspondent recurrence of accent and sound are calculated to excite. The final definition then, so deduced, may be thus worded. A poem is that species of composition, which is opposed to works of science, by proposing for its *immediate* object pleasure, not truth; and from all other species—having *this* object in common with it—it is discriminated by proposing to itself such delight from the *whole*, as is compatible with a distinct gratification from each component part.

Controversy is not seldom excited in consequence of the disputants attaching each a different meaning to the same word; and in few instances has this been more striking, than in disputes concerning the present subject. If a man chooses to call every composition a poem, which is rhyme, or measure, or both, I must leave his opinion uncontroverted. The distinction is at least competent to characterize the writer's intention. If it were subjoined, that the wole is likewise entertaining or affecting, as a tale, or as a series of interesting reflections, I of course admit this as another fit ingredient of a poem, and an additional merit. But if the definition sought for be that of a *legitimate* poem, I answer, it must be one, the parts of which mutually support and explain each other; all in their proportion harmonizing with, and supporting the purpose and known influences of metrical arrangement. The philosophic critics of all ages coincide with the ultimate judgment of all countries, in equally denying the praises of a just poem, on the one hand, to a series of striking lines or distiches, each of which, absorbing the whole attention of the reader to itself, becomes disjoined from its context, and forms a separate whole, instead of a harmonizing part; and on the other hand, to an unsustained composition, from which the reader collects rapidly the general result unattracted by the component parts. The reader should be carried forward, not merely or chiefly by the mechanical impulse of curiosity, or by a restless desire to arrive at the final solution; but the pleasurable activity of mind excited by the attractions of the journey itself. Like the motion of a serpent, which the Egyptians made the emblem of intellectual power; or like the path of sound through the air—at every step he pauses and half recedes, and from the retrogressive movement collects the force which again carries him onward.

Progress of the Drama *1818*

We call, for we see and feel, the swan and the dove both transcendently beautiful. As absurd as it would be to institute a comparison between their separate claims to beauty from any abstract rule common to both, without reference to the life and being of the animals themselves—or as if, having first seen the dove, we abstracted its outlines, gave them a false generalization, called them the principles or ideal of bird-beauty, and then proceeded to criticise the swan or the eagle—not less absurd is it to pass judgment on the works of a poet on the mere ground that they have been called by the same class-name with the works of other poets in other times and circumstances, or on any ground, indeed, save that of their inappropriateness to their own end and being, their want of significance, as symbols or physiognomy.

O! few have there been among critics, who have followed with the eye of the imagination the imperishable yet ever wandering spirit of poetry through its various metempsychoses, and consequent metamorphoses—or who have rejoiced in the light of clear perception at beholding with each new birth, with each rare avatar, the human race frame to itself a new body, by assimilating materials of nourishment out of its new circumstances, and work for itself new organs of power appropriate to the new sphere of its motion and activity!

I have before spoken of the Romance, or the language formed out of the decayed Roman and the Northern tongues; and comparing it with the Latin, we find it less perfect in simplicity and relation—the privileges of a language formed by the mere attraction of homogeneous parts; but yet more rich, more expressive and various, as one formed by more obscure affinities out of a chaos of apparently heterogeneous atoms. As more than a metaphor, as an analogy of this, I have named the true genuine modern poetry the romantic; and the works of Shakespeare are romantic poetry revealing itself in the drama. If the tragedies of Sophocles are in the strict sense of the word tragedies, and the comedies of Aristophanes comedies, we must emancipate ourselves from a false association arising from misapplied names, and find a new word for the plays of Shakespeare. For they are, in the ancient sense, neither tragedies nor comedies, nor both in one, but a different genus, diverse in kind, and not merely different in degree. They may be called romantic dramas, or dramatic romances.

A deviation from the simple forms and unities of the ancient stage is an essential principle, and, of course, an appropriate excellence, of the romantic

Selections. From *The Complete Works of Samuel Taylor Coleridge*, Vol. IV, edited by Professor Shedd. New York: Harper & Brothers, 1854.

drama. For these unities were to a great extent the natural form of that which in its elements was homogeneous, and the representation of which was addressed preeminently to the outward senses; and though the fable, the language, and the characters appealed to the reason rather than to the mere understanding, inasmuch as they supposed an ideal state rather than referred to an existing reality, yet it was a reason which was obliged to accommodate itself to the senses, and so far became a sort of more elevated understanding. . . .

And here it will be necessary to say a few words on the stage and on stage-illusion.

A theatre, in the widest sense of the word, is the general term for all places of amusement through the ear or eye, in which men assemble in order to be amused by some entertainment presented to all at the same time and in common. Thus, an old Puritan divine says: "Those who attend public worship and sermons only to amuse themselves, make a theatre of the church, and turn God's house into the devil's. *Theatra aedes diabololatricae.*" The most important and dignified species of this genus is, doubtless, the stage (*res theatralis histrionica*), which, in addition to the generic definition above given, may be characterized in its idea, or according to what it does, or ought to, aim at, as a combination of several or of all the fine arts in a harmonious whole, having a distinct end of its own, to which the peculiar end of each of the component arts, taken separately, is made subordinate and subservient—that, namely, of imitating reality— whether external things, actions, or passions—under a semblance of reality. Thus, Claude imitates a landscape at sunset, but only as a picture; while a forest-scene is not presented to the spectators as a picture, but as a forest; and though, in the full sense of the word, we are no more deceived by the one than by the other, yet are feelings very differently affected; and the pleasure derived from the one is not composed of the same elements as that afforded by the other, even on the supposition that the *quantum* of both were equal. In the former, a picture, it is a condition of all genuine delight that we should not be deceived; in the latter, stage-scenery (inasmuch as its principal end is not in or for itself, as is the case in a picture, but to be an assistance and means to an end out of itself), its very purpose is to produce as much illusion as its nature permits. These, and all other stage presentations, are to produce a sort of temporary half-faith, which the spectator encourages in himself and supports by a voluntary contribution on his own part, because he knows that it is at all times in his power to see the thing as it really is. I have often observed that little children are actually deceived by stage-scenery, never by pictures; though even these produce an effect on their impressible minds, which they do not on the minds of adults. The child, if strongly impressed, does not indeed positively think the picture to be the reality; but yet he does not think the contrary. As Sir George Beaumont was showing me a very fine engraving from Rubens, representing a storm at sea without any vessel or boat introduced, my little boy, then about five years old, came dancing and singing into the room, and all at once (if I may so say) *tumbled* in upon the print. He instantly started, stood silent and motionless, with the strongest expression, first of wonder and then of grief in his eyes and countenance, and at length said, "And where is the ship? But that is sunk, and the men are all drowned!" still keeping his eyes fixed on the print. Now what pictures are to little children, stage illusion is to men, provided they retain any part of the child's sensibility; except, that in the latter instance, the suspension of the act of comparison, which permits this sort of negative belief, is somewhat more assisted by the will, than in that of a child respecting a picture.

The true stage-illusion in this and in all other things consists—not in the mind's judging it to be a forest, but, in its remission of the judgment that it is not a forest. And this subject of stage-illusion is so important, and so many practical errors and false criticisms may arise, and indeed have arisen, either from reasoning on it as actual delusion (the strange notion, on which the French critics built up their theory, and on which the French poets justify the construction of their tragedies), or from denying it altogether (which seems the end of Dr. Johnson's reasoning, and which, as extremes meet, would lead to the very same consequences, by excluding whatever would not be judged probable by us in our coolest state of feeling, with all our faculties in even balance), that these few remarks will, I hope, be pardoned, if they should serve either to explain or to illustrate the point. For not only are we never absolutely deluded—or anything like it, but the attempt to cause the highest delusion possible to beings in their senses sitting in a theatre, is a gross fault, incident only to low minds, which, feeling that they can not affect the heart or head permanently, endeavor to call forth the momentary affections. There ought never to be more pain than is compatible with coexisting pleasure, and to be amply repaid by thought.

Table Talk[*] *1822*

Schiller has the material Sublime; to produce an effect, he sets you a whole town on fire, and throws infants with their mothers into the flames, or locks up a father in an old tower. But Shakespeare drops a handkerchief, and the same or greater effects follow.

Lear is the most tremendous effort of Shakespeare as a poet; Hamlet as a philosopher or mediator; and Othello is the union of the two. There is something gigantic and unformed in the former two; but in the latter, everything assumes its due place and proportion, and the whole mature powers of his mind are displayed in admirable equilibrium. . . .

Hamlet's character is the prevalence of the abstracting and generalizing habit over the practical. He does not want courage, skill, will, or opportunity; but every incident sets him thinking; and it is curious, and, at the same time, strictly natural, that Hamlet, who all the play seems reason itself, should be impelled, at last, by mere accident to effect his object. I have a smack of Hamlet myself, if I may say so.

Outline of an Introductory Lecture upon Shakespeare[†] *1836*

Of that species of writing termed tragicomedy, much has been produced and doomed to the shelf. Shakespeare's comic are continually reacting upon his tragic characters. Lear, wandering amidst the tempest, has all his feelings of distress increased by the overflowings of the wild wit of the Fool, as vinegar poured upon wounds exacerbates their pain. Thus even his comic humor tends to the development of tragic passion.

* Selections. From *Specimens of the Table Talk of the Late Samuel Taylor Coleridge*, Vol. I, edited by Henry Nelson Coleridge. London: John Murray, 1835.

† Selection. From *The Complete Works of Samuel Taylor Coleridge*, Vol. IV, edited by Professor Shedd. New York: Harper & Brothers, 1854.

The next characteristic of Shakespeare is his keeping at all times in the high road of life, etc. Another evidence of his exquisite judgment is, that he seizes hold of popular tales; *Lear* and the *Merchant of Venice* were popular tales, but are so excellently managed, that both are the representations of men in all countries and of all times.

His dramas do not arise absolutely out of some one extraordinary circumstance, the scenes may stand independently of any such one connecting incident, as faithful representations of men and manners. In his mode of drawing characters there are no pompous descriptions of a man by himself; his character is to be drawn, as in real life, from the whole course of the play, or out of the mouths of his enemies or friends. This may be exemplified in Polonius, whose character has been often misrepresented. Shakespeare never intended him for a buffoon, etc.

Another excellence of Shakespeare in which no writer equals him, is in the language of nature. So correct is it, that we can see ourselves in every page. The style and manner have also that felicity, that not a sentence can be read, without its being discovered if it is Shakesperian. In observation of living characters—of landlords and postilions—Fielding[1] has great excellence; but in drawing from his own heart, and depicting that species of character, which no observation could teach, he failed in comparison with Richardson,[2] who perpetually places himself, as it were, in a day-dream. Shakespeare excels in both. Witness the accuracy of character in Juliet's Nurse; while for the great characters of Iago, Othello, Hamlet, Richard III, to which he could never have seen any thing similar, he seems invariably to have asked himself, How should I act or speak in such circumstances? His comic characters are also peculiar. A drunken constable was not uncommon; but he makes folly a vehicle for wit, as in Dogberry: everything is a substratum on which his genius can erect the mightiest superstructure.

To distinguish that which is legitimate in Shakespeare from what does not belong to him, we must observe his varied images symbolical of novel truth, thrusting by, and seeming to trip up each other, from an impetuosity of thought, producing a flowing meter and seldom closing with the line.

---

[1] Henry Fielding (1707–1754).
[2] Samuel Richardson (1689–1761).

On the Characteristics
of Shakespeare's Plays 1836

I have said, and I say it again, that great as was the genius of Shakespeare, his judgment was at least equal to it. Of this anyone will be convinced, who attentively considers those points in which the dramas of Greece and England differ, from the dissimiltude of circumstances by which each was modified and influenced. The Greek stage had its origin in the ceremonies of a sacrifice, such as of the goat to Bacchus, whom we most erroneously regard as merely the jolly god of wine—for among the ancients he was venerable, as the symbol of that power which acts without our consciousness in the vital energies of nature, the *vinum mundi*, as Apollo was that of the conscious agency of our intellectual being. The heroes of old under the influence of this Bacchic enthusiasm performed more than human actions; hence tales of the favorite champions soon passed into dialogue. On the Greek stage the chorus was always before the audience; the curtain was never dropped, as we should say; and change of place being therefore, in general, impossible, the absurd notion of condemning it merely as improbable in itself was never entertained by anyone. If we can believe ourselves at Thebes in one act, we may believe ourselves at Athens in the next. If a story lasts twenty-four hours or twenty-four years, it is equally improbable. There seems to be no just boundary but what the feelings prescribe. But on the Greek stage where the same persons were perpetually before the audience, great judgment was necessary in venturing on any such change. The poets never, therefore, attempted to impose on the senses by bringing places to men, but they did bring men to places, as in the well-known instance in the *Eumenides*, where during an evident retirement of the chorus from the orchestra, the scene is changed to Athens, and Orestes is first introduced in the temple of Minerva, and the chorus of Furies come in afterwards in pursuit of him.

In the Greek drama there were no formal divisions into scenes and acts; there were no means, therefore, of allowing for the necessary lapse of time between one part of the dialogue and another, and unity of time in a strict sense was, of course, impossible. To overcome that difficulty of accounting for time, which is effected on the modern stage by dropping a curtain, the judgment and great genius of the ancients supplied music and measured motion, and with the lyric ode filled up the vacuity. In the story of the *Agamemnon* of Aeschylus, the capture of Troy is supposed to be announced by a fire lighted on the Asiatic shore, and the transmission of the signal by

Selection. From *The Literary Remains of Samuel Taylor Coleridge*, Vol. II, edited by Henry Nelson Coleridge. London: William Pickering, 1836.

successive beacons to Mycenae. The signal is first seen at the 21st line, and the herald from Troy itself enters at the 486th, and Agamemnon himself at the 783d line. But the practical absurdity of this was not felt by the audience, who in imagination stretched minutes into hours, while they listened to the lofty narrative odes of the chorus which almost entirely fill up the interspace. Another fact deserves attention here, namely, that regularly on the Greek stage a drama, or acted story, consisted in reality of three dramas, called together a trilogy, and performed consecutively in the course of one day. Now you may conceive a tragedy of Shakespeare's as a trilogy connected in one single representation. Divide *Lear* into three parts, and each would be a play with the ancients; or take the three Aeschylean dramas of Agamemnon, and divide them into, or call them, as many acts, and they together would be one play. The first act would comprise the usurpation of Aegisthus, and the murder of Agamemnon; the second, the revenge of Orestes, and the murder of his mother; and the third, the penance and absolution of Orestes— occupying a period of twenty-two years.

The stage in Shakespeare's time was a naked room with a blanket for a curtain; but he made it a field for monarchs. That law of unity, which has its foundations, not in the factitious necessity of custom, but in nature itself, the unity of feeling, is everywhere and at all times observed by Shakespeare in his plays. Read *Romeo and Juliet*; all is youth and spring— youth with its follies, its virtues, its precipitancies; spring with its odours, its flowers, and its transiency; it is one and the same feeling that commences, goes through, and ends the play. The old men, the Capulets and the Montagues, are not common old men; they have an eagerness, a heartiness, a vehemence, the effect of spring; with Romeo, his change of passion, his sudden marriage, and his rash death, are all the effects of youth; whilst in Juliet love has all that is tender and melancholy in the nightingale, all that is voluptuous in the rose, with whatever is sweet in the freshness of spring; but it ends with a long deep sigh like the last breeze of the Italian evening. This unity of feeling and character pervades every drama of Shakespeare.

It seems to me that his plays are distinguished from those of all other dramatic poets by the following characteristics:

1. Expectation in preference to surprise. It is like the true reading of the passage—"God said, Let there be light, and there was *light*"—not there *was* light. As the feeling with which we startle at a shooting star, compared with that of watching the sunrise at the pre-established moment, such and so low is surprise compared with expectation.
2. Signal adherence to the great law of nature, that all opposites tend to attract and temper each other. Passion in Shakespeare generally displays libertinism, but involves morality; and if there are exceptions to this, they are, independently of their intrinsic value, all of them indic-

ative of individual character, and, like the farewell admonitions of a parent, have an end beyond the parental relation. Thus the Countess's beautiful precepts to Bertram, by elevating her character, raise that of Helena her favorite, and soften down the point in her which Shakespeare does not mean us not to see, but to see and to forgive, and at length to justify. And so it is in Polonius, who is the personified memory of wisdom no longer actually possessed. This admirable character is always misrepresented on the stage. Shakespeare never intended to exhibit him as a buffoon; for although it was natural that Hamlet—a young man of fire and genius, detesting formality, and disliking Polonius on political grounds, as imagining that he had assisted his uncle in his usurpation— should express himself satirically, yet this must not be taken as exactly the poet's conception of him. In Polonius a certain induration of character had arisen from long habits of business; but take his advice to Laertes, and Ophelia's reverence for his memory, and we shall see that he was meant to be represented as a statesman somewhat past his faculties— his recollections of life all full of wisdom, and showing a knowledge of human nature, whilst what immediately takes place before him, and escapes from him, is indicative of weakness.

But as in Homer all the deities are in armour, even Venus; so in Shakespeare all the characters are strong. Hence real folly and dullness are made by him the vehicles of wisdom. There is no difficulty for one being a fool to imitate a fool; but to be, remain, and speak like a wise man and a great wit, and yet so as to give a vivid representation of a veritable fool—*hic labor, hoc opus est.*[1] A drunken constable is not uncommon, nor hard to draw; but see and examine what goes to make up a Dogberry.

3. Keeping at all times in the high road of life. Shakespeare has no innocent adulteries, no interesting incests, no virtuous vice; he never renders that amiable which religion and reason alike teach us to detest, or clothes impurity in the garb of virtue, like Beaumont and Fletcher, the Kotzebues[2] of the day. Shakespeare's fathers are roused by ingratitude, his husbands stung by unfaithfulness; in him, in short, the affections are wounded in those points in which all may, nay, must, feel. Let the morality of Shakespeare be contrasted with that of the writers of his own, or the succeeding, age, or of those of the present day, who boast their superiority in this respect. No one can dispute that the result of such a comparison is altogether in favour of Shakespeare; even the letters of women of high rank in his age were often coarser than his writings. If he occasionally disgusts a keen sense of delicacy, he never injures the mind; he neither excites, nor

---

[1] That is, from this labor derives this work.
[2] August von Kotzebue (1761–1819), German dramatist.

flatters, passion, in order to degrade the subject of it; he does not use the faulty thing for a faulty purpose, nor carries on warfare against virtue, by causing wickedness to appear as no wickedness, through the medium of a morbid sympathy with the unfortunate. In Shakespeare vice never walks as in twilight; nothing is purposely out of its place; he inverts not the order of nature and propriety, does not make every magistrate a drunkard or glutton, nor every poor man meek, humane, and temperate; he has no benevolent butchers, nor any sentimental rat-catchers.

4. Independence of the dramatic interest on the plot. The interest in the plot is always in fact on account of the characters, not vice versa, as in almost all other writers; the plot is a mere canvas and no more. Hence arises the true justification of the same stratagem being used in regard to Benedick and Beatrice, the vanity in each being alike. Take away from the *Much Ado About Nothing* all that which is not indispensable to the plot, either as having little to do with it, or, at best, like Dogberry and his comrades, forced into the service, when any other less ingeniously absurd watchmen and night-constables would have answered the mere necessities of the action; take away Benedick, Beatrice, Dogberry, and the reaction of the former on the character of Hero—and what will remain? In other writers the main agent of the plot is always the prominent character; in Shakespeare it is so, or is not so, as the character is in itself calculated, or not calculated, to form the plot. Don John is the mainspring of the plot of this play; but he is merely shown and then withdrawn.

5. Independence of the interest on the story as the groundwork of the plot. Hence Shakespeare never took the trouble of inventing stories. It was enough for him to select from those that had been already invented or recorded such as had one or other, or both, of two recommendations, namely, suitableness to his particular purpose, and their being parts of popular tradition—names of which we had often heard, and of their fortunes, and as to which all we wanted was, to see the man himself. So it is just the man himself, the Lear, the Shylock, the Richard, that Shakespeare makes us for the first time acquainted with. Omit the first scene in *Lear*, and yet everything will remain; so the first and second scenes in the *Merchant of Venice*. Indeed it is universally true.

6. Interfusion of the lyrical—that which in its very essence is poetical—not only with the dramatic, as in the plays of Metastasio,[3] where at the end of the scene comes the aria as the exit speech of the character—but also in and through the dramatic. Songs in Shakespeare are introduced as songs only, just as songs are in real life, beautifully as some of

---

[3] Pietro Antonio Domenico Buonaventura Metastasio (1698–1782).

them are characteristic of the person who has sung or called for them, as Desdemona's "Willow," and Ophelia's wild snatches, and the sweet carollings in *As You Like It*. But the whole of the *Midsummer's Night's Dream* is one continued specimen of the dramatized lyrical. And observe how exquisitely the dramatic of Hotspur—

> Marry, and I'm glad on't with all my heart;
> I had rather be a kitten and cry—mew, etc.

melts away into the lyric of Mortimer—

> I understand thy looks: that pretty Welsh
> Which thou pourest down from these swelling heavens,
> I am too perfect in, etc.
>
> *Henry IV*, part I, act III, scene 1.

7. The characters of the dramatis personae, like those in real life, are to be inferred by the reader; they are not told to him. And it is well worth remarking that Shakespeare's characters, like those in real life, are very commonly misunderstood, and almost always understood by different persons in different ways. The causes are the same in either case. If you take only what the friends of the character say, you may be deceived, and still more so, if that which his enemies say; nay, even the character himself sees himself through the medium of his character, and not exactly as he is. Take all together, not omitting a shrewd hint from the clown or the fool, and perhaps your impression will be right; and you may know whether you have in fact discovered the poet's own idea, by all the speeches receiving light from it, and attesting its reality by reflecting it.

8. Lastly, in Shakespeare the heterogeneous is united, as it is in nature. You must not suppose a pressure or passion always acting on or in the character; passion in Shakespeare is that by which the individual is distinguished from others, not that which makes a different kind of him. Shakespeare followed the main march of the human affections. He entered into no analysis of the passions or faith of men, but assured himself that such and such passions and faiths were grounded in our common nature, and not in the mere accidents of ignorance or disease. This is an important consideration, and constitutes our Shakespeare the morning star, the guide and the pioneer, of true philosophy.

Notes on
Hamlet 1836

Hamlet was the play, or rather Hamlet himself was the character, in the intuition and exposition of which I first made my turn for philosophical criticism, and especially for insight into the genius of Shakespeare, noticed. This happened first amongst my acquaintances, as Sir George Beaumont will bear witness; and subsequently, long before Schlegel had delivered at Vienna the lectures on Shakespeare, which he afterwards published, I had given on the same subject eighteen lectures substantially the same, proceeding from the very same point of view, and deducing the same conclusions, so far as I either then agreed, or now agree, with him. I gave these lectures at the Royal Institution, before six or seven hundred auditors of rank and eminence, in the spring of the same year, in which Sir Humphry Davy, a fellow-lecturer, made his great revolutionary discoveries in chemistry. Even in detail the coincidence of Schlegel with my lectures was so extraordinary, that all who at a later period heard the same words, taken by me from my notes of the lectures at the Royal Institution, concluded a borrowing on my part from Schlegel. Mr. Hazlitt, whose hatred of me is in such an inverse ratio to my zealous kindness towards him, as to be defended by his warmest admirer, Charles Lamb (who, God bless him! besides his characteristic obstinacy of adherence to old friends, as long at least as they are all down in the world, is linked as by a charm to Hazlitt's conversation) only as "frantic"; Mr. Hazlitt, I say, himself replied to an assertion of my plagiarism from Schlegel in these words: "That is a lie; for I myself heard the very same character of Hamlet from Coleridge before he went to Germany, and when he had neither read nor could read a page of German!" Now Hazlitt was on a visit to me at my cottage at Nether Stowey, Somerset, in the summer of the year 1798, in the September of which year I first was out of sight of the shores of Great Britain. Recorded by me, S. T. Coleridge, 7th January, 1819.

The seeming inconsistencies in the conduct and character of Hamlet have long exercised the conjectural ingenuity of critics; and, as we are always loth to suppose that the cause of defective apprehension is in ourselves, the mystery has been too commonly explained by the very easy process of setting it down as in fact inexplicable, and by resolving the phenomenon into a misgrowth or *lusus*[1] of the capricious and irregular genius of Shakespeare. The

Selection. From *The Literary Remains of Samuel Taylor Coleridge*, Vol. II, edited by Henry Nelson Coleridge. London: William Pickering, 1836.

[1] Game or amusement.

596

shallow and stupid arrogance of these vulgar and indolent decisions I would fain do my best to expose. I believe the character of Hamlet may be traced to Shakespeare's deep and accurate science in mental philosophy. Indeed, that this character must have some connection with the common fundamental laws of our nature may be assumed from the fact, that Hamlet has been the darling of every country in which the literature of England has been fostered. In order to understand him, it is essential that we should reflect on the constitution of our own minds. Man is distinguished from the brute animals in proportion as thought prevails over sense: but in the healthy processes of the mind, a balance is constantly maintained between the impressions from outward objects and the inward operations of the intellect—for if there be an overbalance in the contemplative faculty, man thereby becomes the creature of mere meditation, and loses his natural power of action. Now one of Shakespeare's modes of creating characters is, to conceive any one intellectual or moral faculty in morbid excess, and then to place himself, Shakespeare, thus mutilated or diseased, under given circumstances. In Hamlet he seems to have wished to exemplify the moral necessity of a due balance between our attention to the objects of our senses, and our meditation on the workings of our minds, an equilibrium between the real and the imaginary worlds. In Hamlet this balance is disturbed: his thoughts, and the images of his fancy, are far more vivid than his actual perceptions, and his very perceptions, instantly passing through the medium of his contemplations, acquire, as they pass, a form and a color not naturally their own. Hence we see a great, an almost enormous, intellectual activity, and a proportionate aversion to real action consequent upon it, with all its symptoms and accompanying qualities. This character Shakespeare places in circumstances, under which it is obliged to act on the spur of the moment: Hamlet is brave and careless of death; but he vacillates from sensibility, and procrastinates from thought, and loses the power of action in the energy of resolve. Thus it is that this tragedy presents a direct contrast to that of Macbeth; the one proceeds with the utmost slowness, the other with a crowded and breathless rapidity.

The effect of this overbalance of the imaginative power is beautifully illustrated in the everlasting broodings and superfluous activities of Hamlet's mind, which, unseated from its healthy relation, is constantly occupied with the world within, and abstracted from the world without, giving substance to shadows, and throwing a mist over all commonplace actualities. It is the nature of thought to be indefinite; definiteness belongs to external imagery alone. Hence it is that the sense of sublimity arises, not from the sight of an outward object, but from the beholder's reflection upon it; not from the sensuous impression, but from the imaginative reflex. Few have seen a celebrated waterfall without feeling something akin to disappointment: it is only subsequently that the image comes back full into the mind, and brings with it a train of grand or beautiful associations. Hamlet feels this; his senses are in a state of trance, and he looks upon external things as hieroglyphics. His soliloquy—

O! that this too too solid flesh would melt, etc.

springs from that craving after the indefinite—for that which is not—which most easily besets men of genius; and the self-delusion common to this temper of mind is finely exemplified in the character which Hamlet gives of himself:

—It cannot be
But I am pigeon-livered, and lack gall
To make oppression bitter.

He mistakes the seeing his chains for the breaking them, delays action till action is of no use, and dies the victim of mere circumstance and accident.

Notes on The Tempest 1836

There is a sort of improbability with which we are shocked in dramatic representation, not less than in a narrative of real life. Consequently, there must be rules respecting it; and as rules are nothing but means to an end previously ascertained—inattention to which simple truth has been the occasion of all the pedantry of the French school—we must first determine what the immediate end or object of the drama is. And here, as I have previously remarked, I find two extremes of critical decision—the French, which evidently presupposes that a perfect delusion is to be aimed at, an opinion which needs no fresh confutation; and the exact opposite to it, brought forward by Dr. Johnson, who supposes the auditors throughout in the full reflective knowledge of the contrary.[1] In evincing the impossibility of de-

Selection. From *The Literary Remains of Samuel Taylor Coleridge*, Vol. II, edited by Henry Nelson Coleridge. London: William Pickering, 1836.

[1] See p. 414.

lusion, he makes no sufficient allowance for an intermediate state, which I have before distinguished by the term illusion, and have attempted to illustrate its quality and character by reference to our mental state, when dreaming. In both cases we simply do not judge the imagery to be unreal; there is a negative reality, and no more. Whatever, therefore, tends to prevent the mind from placing itself, or being placed, gradually in that state in which the images have such negative reality for the auditor, destroys this illusion, and is dramatically improbable.

Now the production of this effect—a sense of improbability—will depend on the degree of excitement in which the mind is supposed to be. Many things would be intolerable in the first scene of a play, that would not at all interrupt our enjoyment in the height of the interest, when the narrow cockpit may be made to hold

> The vasty field of France, or we may cram
> Within its wooden O, the very casques,
> That did affright the air at Agincourt.[2]

Again, on the other hand, many obvious improbabilities will be endured, as belonging to the groundwork of the story rather than to the drama itself, in the first scenes, which would disturb or disentrance us from all illusion in the acme of our excitement; as for instance, Lear's division of his kingdom, and the banishment of Cordelia.

But, although the other excellencies of the drama besides this dramatic probability, as unity of interest, with distinctness and subordination of the characters, and appropriateness of style, are all, so far as they tend to increase the inward excitement, means towards accomplishing the chief end, that of producing and supporting this willing illusion, yet they do not on that account cease to be ends themselves; and we must remember that, as such, they carry their own justification with them, as long as they do not contravene or interrupt the total illusion. It is not even always, or of necessity, an objection to them, that they prevent the illusion from rising to as great a height as it might otherwise have attained; it is enough that they are simply compatible with as high a degree of it as is requisite for the purpose. Nay, upon particular occasions, a palpable improbability may be hazarded by a great genius for the express purpose of keeping down the interest of a merely instrumental scene, which would otherwise make too great an impression for the harmony of the entire illusion. Had the panorama been invented in the time of Pope Leo X, Raphael would still, I doubt not, have smiled in contempt at the regret, that the broom-twigs and scrubby bushes at the back of some of his grand pictures were not as probable trees as those in the exhibition.

---

[2] Shakespeare, *Henry V*, Prologue.

The Tempest is a specimen of the purely romantic drama, in which the interest is not historical, or dependent upon fidelity of portraiture, or the natural connexion of events, but is a birth of the imagination, and rests only on the coaptation and union of the elements granted to, or assumed by, the poet. It is a species of drama which owes no allegiance to time or space, and in which, therefore, errors of chronology and geography—no mortal sins in any species—are venial faults, and count for nothing. It addresses itself entirely to the imaginative faculty; and although the illusion may be assisted by the effect on the senses of the complicated scenery and decorations of modern times, yet this sort of assistance is dangerous. For the principal and only genuine excitement ought to come from within, from the moved and sympathetic imagination; whereas, where so much is addressed to the mere external senses of seeing and hearing, the spiritual vision is apt to languish, and the attraction from without will withdraw the mind from the proper and only legitimate interest which is intended to spring from within.

William Hazlitt   *1778–1830*

On Wit and Humour   *1819*

Man is the only animal that laughs and weeps; for he is the only animal that is struck with the difference between what things are and what they ought to be. We weep at what thwarts or exceeds our desires in serious matters: we laugh at what only disappoints our expectations in trifles. We shed tears from sympathy with real and necessary distress, as we burst into laughter from want of sympathy with that which is unreasonable and unnecessary, the absurdity of which provokes our spleen or mirth, rather than any serious reflections on it.

To explain the nature of laughter and tears is to account for the condition of human life, for it is in a manner compounded of these two! It is a tragedy or a comedy—sad or merry, as it happens. The crimes and misfortunes that are inseparable from it shock and wound the mind when they

Selections. From William Hazlitt, *Essays.* London: Walter Scott, 1889.

once seize upon it, and when the pressure can no longer be borne, seek relief in tears; the follies and absurdities that men commit, or the odd accidents that befall them, afford us amusement from the very rejection of these false claims upon our sympathy, and end in laughter. If everything that went wrong, if every vanity or weakness in another, gave us a sensible pang, it would be hard indeed; but as long as the disagreeableness of the consequences of a sudden disaster is kept out of sight by the immediate oddity of the circumstances, and the absurdity or unaccountableness of a foolish action is the most striking thing in it, the ludicrous prevails over the pathetic, and we receive pleasure instead of pain from the farce of life which is played before us, and which discomposes our gravity as often as it fails to move our anger or our pity!

Tears may be considered as the natural and involuntary resource of the mind overcome by some sudden and violent emotion before it has had time to reconcile its feelings to the change of circumstances, while laughter may be defined to be the same sort of convulsive and involuntary movement, occasioned by mere surprise or contrast (in the absence of any more serious emotion), before it has time to reconcile its belief to contradictory appearances. If we hold a mask before our face, and approach a child with this disguise on, it will at first, from the oddity and incongruity of the appearance, be inclined to laugh; if we go nearer to it, steadily, and without saying a word, it will begin to be alarmed, and be half inclined to cry; if we suddenly take off the mask, it will recover from its fears, and burst out a-laughing; but if, instead of presenting the old well-known countenance, we have concealed a satyr's head or some frightful caricature behind the first mask, the suddenness of the change will not in this case be a source of merriment to it, but will convert its surprise into an agony of consternation, and will make it scream out for help, even though it may be convinced that the whole is a trick at bottom.

The alternation of tears and laughter, in this little episode in common life, depends almost entirely on the greater or less degree of interest attached to the different changes of appearance. The mere suddenness of the transition, the mere baulking our expectations, and turning them abruptly into another channel, seems to give additional liveliness and gaiety to the animal spirits; but the instant the change is not only sudden, but threatens serious consequences, or calls up the shape of danger, terror supersedes our disposition to mirth, and laughter gives place to tears. It is usual to play with infants, and make them laugh by clapping your hands suddenly before them; but if you clap your hands too loud, or too near their sight, their countenances immediately change, and they hide them in the nurse's arms. Or suppose the same child, grown up a little older, comes to a place, expecting to meet a person it is particularly fond of, and does not find that person there, its countenance suddenly falls, its lips begin to quiver, its cheek turns pale, its eye glistens, and it vents its little sorrow (grown too big to be concealed) in a flood of tears. Again, if the child meets the same person unexpectedly after long absence, the same effect will be produced by an excess of joy, with different accompaniments; that is, the surprise and the emotion excited will make the blood come into his face, his eyes sparkle, his tongue falter or be mute; but in either case the tears will gush to his relief, and lighten the pressure about his heart. On the other hand, if a child is playing at hide-and-seek, or blindman's buff, with persons it is ever so fond of, and either misses them where it had made sure of finding them, or suddenly runs up against them where it had least expected it, the shock or additional impetus given to the imagination by the disappointment or the discovery, in a matter of this indifference, will only vent itself in a fit of laughter.[1] The transition here is not from one thing of importance to another, or from a state of indifference to a state of strong excitement; but merely from one impression to another that we did not at all expect, and when we had expected just the contrary. The mind having been led to form a certain conclusion, and the result producing an immediate solution of continuity in the chain of our ideas, this alternate excitement and relaxation of the imagination, the object also striking upon the mind more vividly in its loose, unsettled state, and before it has had time to recover and collect itself, causes that alternate excitement and relaxation, or irregular convulsive movement of the muscular and nervous system, which constitutes physical laughter. The *discontinuous* in our sensations produces a correspondent jar and discord in the frame. The steadiness of our faith and of our features begins to give way at the same time. We turn with an incredulous smile from a story that staggers our belief; and we are ready to split our sides with laughing at an extravagance that sets all common sense and serious concern at defiance.

To understand or define the ludicrous, we must first know what the serious is. Now, the serious is the habitual stress which the mind lays upon the expectation of a given order to events, following one another with a certain regularity and weight of interest attached to them. When this stress is increased beyond its usual pitch of intensity, so as to overstrain the feelings by the violent opposition of good to bad, or of objects to our desires, it becomes the pathetic or tragical. The ludicrous, or comic, is the unexpected loosening or relaxing this stress below its usual pitch of intensity, by such an abrupt transposition of the order of our ideas, as taking the mind unawares, throws it off guard, startles it into a lively sense of pleasure, and leaves no time nor inclination for painful reflections.

The essence of the laughable, then, is the incongruous, the disconnecting one idea from another, or the jostling of one feeling against another.

---

[1] A child that has hid himself out of the way in sport is under a great temptation to laugh at the unconsciousness of others as to its situation. A person concealed from assassins is in no danger of betraying his situation by laughing [Hazlitt's note].

The first and most obvious cause of laughter is to be found in the simple succession of events, as in the sudden shifting of a disguise, or some unlooked-for accident, without any absurdity of character or situation. The accidental contradiction between our expectations and the event can hardly be said, however, to amount to the ludicrous: it is merely laughable. The ludicrous is where there is the same contradiction between the object and our expectations, heightened by some deformity or inconvenience, that is, by its being contrary to what is customary or desirable; as the ridiculous, which is the highest degree of the laughable, is that which is contrary not only to custom, but to sense and reason, or is a voluntary departure from what we have a right to expect from those who are conscious of absurdity and propriety in words, looks, and actions.

Of these different kinds of degrees of the laughable, the first is the most shallow and short-lived; for the instant the immediate surprise of a thing's merely happening one way or another is over, there is nothing to throw us back upon our former expectation, and renew our wonder at the event a second time. The second sort, that is, the ludicrous arising out of the improbable or distressing, is more deep and lasting, either because the painful catastrophe excites a greater curiosity, or because the old impression, from its habitual hold on the imagination, still recurs mechanically, so that it is longer before we can seriously make up our minds to the unaccountable deviation from it. The third sort, or the ridiculous arising out of absurdity as well as improbability, that is, where the defect or weakness is of a man's own seeking, is the most refined of all, but not always so pleasant as the last, because the same contempt and disapprobation which sharpens and subtilises our sense of the impropriety, adds a severity to it inconsistent with perfect ease and enjoyment. This last species is properly the province of satire. The principle of contrast is, however, the same in all the stages, in the simply laughable, the ludicrous, the ridiculous; and the effect is only the more complete, the more durably and pointedly this principle operates.

To give some examples in these different kinds. We laugh, when children, at the sudden removing of a pasteboard mask; we laugh, when grown-up, more gravely at the tearing off the mask of deceit. We laugh at absurdity; we laugh at deformity. We laugh at a bottle-nose in a caricature; at a stuffed figure of an alderman in a pantomime; and at the tale of Slaukenbergius. A giant standing by a dwarf makes a contemptible figure enough. Rosinante and Dapple are laughable from contrast, as their masters from the same principle make two for a pair.[2] We laugh at the dress of foreigners, and they at ours. Three chimney-sweepers meeting three Chinese in Lincoln's Inn Fields, they laughed at one another till they were ready to drop down.

---

[2] Rosinante is the name of Don Quixote's horse, Dapple the name of Sancho Panza's ass, in Miguel de Cervantes's *Don Quixote* (completed 1604, published 1605).

Country people laugh at a person because they never saw him before. Anyone dressed in the height of the fashion, or quite out of it, is equally an object of ridicule. One rich source of the ludicrous is distress with which we cannot sympathise from its absurdity or insignificance. Women laugh at their lovers. We laugh at a damned author, in spite of our teeth, and though he may be our friend. "There is something in the misfortunes of our best friends that pleases us." We laugh at people on the top of a stagecoach, or in it, if they seem in great extremity. It is hard to hinder children from laughing at a stammerer, at a Negro, at a drunken man, or even at a mad-man. We laugh at mischief. We laugh at what we do not believe. We say that an argument or an assertion that is very absurd, is quite ludicrous. We laugh to show our satisfaction with ourselves, or our contempt for those about us, or to conceal our envy or our ignorance. We laugh at fools, and at those who pretend to be wise—at extreme simplicity, awkwardness, hypocrisy, and affectation. "They were talking of me," says Scrub, "for they laughed *consumedly*." Lord Foppington's insensibility to ridicule, and airs of ineffable self-conceit, are no less admirable; and Joseph Surface's cant maxims of morality, when once disarmed of their power to do hurt, become sufficiently ludicrous.[3] We laugh at that in others which is a serious matter to ourselves; because our self-love is stronger than our sympathy, sooner takes the alarm, and instantly turns our heedless mirth into gravity, which only enhances the jest to others. Someone is generally sure to be the sufferer by a joke. What is sport to one is death to another. It is only very sensible or very honest people who laugh as freely at their own absurdities as at those of their neighbours. In general the contrary rule holds, and we only laugh at those misfortunes in which we are spectators, not sharers. The injury, the dis-appointment, shame, and vexation that we feel put a stop to our mirth; while the disasters that come home to us, and excite our repugnance and dis-may, are an amusing spectacle to others. The greater resistance we make, and the greater the perplexity into which we are thrown, the more lively and *piquant* is the intellectual display of cross-purposes to the bystanders. Our humiliation is their triumph. We are occupied with the disagreeable-ness of the result instead of its oddity or unexpectedness. Others see only the conflict of motives, and the sudden alternation of events; we feel the pain as well, which more than counterbalances the speculative entertainment we might receive from the contemplation of our abstract situation.

You cannot force people to laugh: you cannot give a reason why they should laugh: they must laugh of themselves, or not at all. As we laugh from a spontaneous impulse, we laugh the more at any restraint upon this impulse. We laugh at a thing merely because we ought not. If we think we

[3] Scrub is a character in *The Beaux' Stratagem* (1707) by George Farquhar; Lord Foppington, in *The Careless Husband* (1704) by Colley Cibber; and Joseph Surface, in *The School for Scandal* (1777) by Richard Brinsley Sheridan.

must not laugh, this perverse impediment makes our temptation to laugh the greater; for by endeavouring to keep the obnoxious image out of sight, it comes upon us more irresistibly and repeatedly; and the inclination to indulge our mirth, the longer it is held back, collects its force, and breaks out the more violently in peals of laughter. In like manner, anything we must not think of makes us laugh, by coming upon us by stealth and unawares, and from the very efforts we make to exclude it. A secret, a loose word, a wanton jest, make people laugh. Aretine laughed himself to death at hearing a lascivious story. Wickedness is often made a substitute for wit; and in most of our good old comedies, the intrigue of the plot and the double meaning of the dialogue go hand-in-hand, and keep up the ball with wonderful spirit between them. The consciousness, however it may arise, that there is something that we ought to look grave at, is almost always a signal for laughing outright: we can hardly keep our countenance at a sermon, a funeral, or a wedding. What an excellent old custom was that of throwing the stocking! What a deal of innocent mirth has been spoiled by the disuse of it! It is not an easy matter to preserve decorum in courts of justice. The smallest circumstance that interferes with the solemnity of the proceedings throws the whole place into an uproar of laughter. People at the point of death often say smart things. Sir Thomas More jested with his executioner. Rabelais and Wycherley both died with a bon mot in their mouths.

Misunderstandings (*mal-entendus*), where one person means one thing, and another is aiming at something else, are another great source of comic humour, on the same principle of ambiguity and contrast. . . . Again, unconsciousness in the person himself of what he is about, or of what others think of him, is also a great heightener of the sense of absurdity. It makes it come the fuller home upon us from his insensibility to it. . . . So wit is often the more forcible and pointed for being dry and serious, for it then seems as if the speaker himself had no intention in it, and we were the first to find it out. Irony, as species of wit, owes its force to the same principle. In such cases it is the contrast between the appearance and the reality, the suspense of belief and the seeming incongruity, that gives point to the ridicule, and makes it enter the deeper when the first impression is overcome. . . .

There is nothing more powerfully humorous than what is called *keeping* in comic character, as we see it very finely exemplified in Sancho Panza and Don Quixote. The proverbial phlegm and the romantic gravity of these two celebrated persons may be regarded as the height of this kind of excellence. The deep feeling of character strengthens the sense of the ludicrous. Keeping in comic character is consistency in absurdity; a determined and laudable attachment to the incongruous and singular. . . .

There is another source of comic humour which has been but little touched on or attended to by the critics—not the infliction of casual pain, but the pursuit of uncertain pleasure and idle gallantry. Half the business and gaiety of comedy turns upon this. Most of the adventures, difficulties, demurs, hair-breadth 'scapes, disguises, deceptions, blunders, disappointments, successes, excuses, all the dexterous manoeuvres, artful innuendoes, assignations, billets-doux, *double entendres*, sly allusions, and elegant flattery, have an eye to this—to the obtaining of those "favours secret, sweet, and precious," in which love and pleasure consist, and which when attained, and the *equivoque* is at an end, the curtain drops, and the play is over. All the attractions of a subject that can only be glanced at indirectly, that is a sort of forbidden ground to the imagination, except under severe restrictions, which are constantly broken through; all the resources it supplies for intrigue and invention; the bashfulness of the clownish lover, his looks of alarm and petrified astonishment; the foppish affectation and easy confidence of the happy man; the dress, the airs, the languor, the scorn, and indifference of the fine lady; the bustle, pertness, loquaciousness, and tricks of the chambermaid; the impudence, lies, and roguery of the valet; the match-making and unmaking; the wisdom of the wise; the sayings of the witty, the folly of the fool; "the soldier's, scholar's, courtier's eye, tongue, sword, the glass of fashion and the mould of form," have all a view to this. . . . It is the life and soul of Wycherley, Congreve, Vanbrugh, and Farquhar's plays. It is the salt of comedy, without which it would be worthless and insipid. It makes Horner decent, and Millimant divine. . . .[4]

Humour is the describing the ludicrous as it is in itself; wit is the exposing it, by comparing or contrasting it with something else. Humour is, as it were, the growth of nature and accident; wit is the product of art and fancy. Humour, as it is shown in books, is an imitation of the natural or acquired absurdities of mankind, or of the ludicrous in accident, situation, and character: wit is the illustrating and heightening the sense of that absurdity by some sudden and unexpected likeness or opposition of one thing to another, which sets off the quality we laugh at or despise in a still more contemptible or striking point of view. Wit, as distinguished from poetry, is the imagination or fancy inverted, and so applied to given objects, as to make the little look less, the mean more light and worthless; or to divert our admiration or wean our affections from that which is lofty and impressive, instead of producing a more intense admiration and exalted passion, as poetry does. . . . Wit hovers round the borders of the light and trifling, whether in matters of pleasure or pain; for as soon as it describes the serious seriously, it ceases to be wit, and passes into a different form. Wit is, in fact, the eloquence of indifference, or an ingenious and striking exposition of those evanescent and glancing impressions of objects which affect us more

---

[4] Characters in Wycherley's *The Country Wife* and Congreve's *The Way of the World*, respectively.

from surprise or contrast to the train of our ordinary and literal preconceptions, than from anything in the objects themselves exciting our necessary sympathy or lasting hatred. The favourite employment of wit is to add littleness to littleness, and heap contempt on insignificance by all the arts of petty and incessant warfare; or if it ever affects to aggrandise, and use the language of hyperbole, it is only to betray into derision by a fatal comparison, as in the mock-heroic; or if it treats of serious passion, it must do it so as to lower the tone of intense and high-wrought sentiment, by the introduction of burlesque and familiar circumstances. . . . Wit or ludicrous invention produces its effect oftenest by comparison, but not always. It frequently effects its purposes by unexpected and subtle distinctions. . . . Almost as happy an instance of the other kind of wit, which consists in sudden retorts, in turns upon an idea, and diverting the train of your adversary's argument abruptly and adroitly into another channel, may be seen in the sarcastic reply of Porson, who hearing someone observe that "certain modern poets would be read and admired when Homer and Virgil were forgotten," made answer—"And not till then! . . ." Wit consists in the truth of the character, and in the happy exposure of the ludicrous contradiction between the pretext and the practice. . . .

. . . Ridicule fastens on the vulnerable points of a cause, and finds out the weak sides of an argument; if those who resort to it sometimes rely too much on its success, those who are chiefly annoyed by it almost always are so with reason, and cannot be too much on their guard against deserving it. Before we can laugh at a thing, its absurdity must at least be open and palpable to common apprehension. Ridicule is necessarily built on certain supposed facts, whether true or false, and on their inconsistency with certain acknowledged maxims, whether right or wrong. It is, therefore, a fair test, if not of philosophical or abstract truth, at least of what is truth according to public opinion and common sense; for it can only expose to instantaneous contempt that which is condemned by public opinion, and is hostile to the common sense of mankind. Or to put it differently, it is the test of the quantity of truth that there is in our favourite prejudices. . . .

It might be made an argument of the intrinsic superiority of poetry or imagination to wit, that the former does not admit of mere verbal combinations. Whenever they do occur, they are uniformly blemishes. It requires something more solid and substantial to raise admiration or passion. The general forms and aggregate masses of our ideas must be brought more into play to give weight and magnitude. Imagination may be said to be the finding out something similar in things generally alike, or with like feelings attached to them; while wit principally aims at finding out something that seems the same, or amounts to a momentary deception where you least expected it—namely, in things totally opposite. The reason why more slight and partial or merely accidental and nominal resemblances serve the purposes of wit, and indeed characterize its essence as a distinct operation and faculty of the mind, is, that the object of ludicrous poetry is naturally to let down and lessen; and it is easier to let down than to raise up; to weaken than to strengthen; to disconnect our sympathy from passion and power, than to attach and rivet it to any object of grandeur or interest; to startle and shock our preconceptions by incongruous and equivocal combinations, than to confirm, enforce, and expand them by powerful and lasting associations of ideas, or striking and true analogies. A slight cause is sufficient to produce a slight effect. To be indifferent or sceptical, requires no effort; to be enthusiastic and in earnest, requires a strong impulse and collective power. Wit and humour (comparatively speaking, or taking the extremes to judge of the gradations by) appeal to our indolence, our vanity, our weakness, and insensibility; serious and impassioned poetry appeals to our strength, our magnanimity, our virtue, and humanity. Anything is sufficient to heap contempt upon an object; even the bare suggestion of a mischievous allusion to what is improper dissolves the whole charm, and puts an end to our admiration of the sublime or beautiful. Reading the finest passage in Milton's *Paradise Lost* in a false tone, will make it seem insipid and absurd. The cavilling at, or invidiously pointing out, a few slips of the pen, will embitter the pleasure, or alter our opinion of a whole work, and make us throw it down in disgust. The critics are aware of this vice and infirmity in our nature, and play upon it with periodical success. The meanest weapons are strong enough for this kind of warfare, and the meanest hands can wield them. Spleen can subsist on any kind of food. The shadow of a doubt, the hint of an inconsistency, a word, a look, a syllable, will destroy our best-formed convictions. What puts this argument in as striking a point of view as anything, is the nature of parody or burlesque, the secret of which lies merely in transposing or applying at a venture to anything, or to the lowest objects, that which is applicable only to certain given things, or to the highest matters. "From the sublime to the ridiculous there is but one step." The slightest want of unity of impression destroys the sublime; the detection of the smallest incongruity is an infallible ground to rest the ludicrous upon. But in serious poetry, which aims at riveting our affections, every blow must tell home. The missing a single time is fatal, and undoes the spell. We see how difficult it is to sustain a continued flight of impressive sentiment: how easy it must be then to travesty or burlesque it, to flounder into nonsense, and be witty by playing the fool. It is a common mistake, however, to suppose that parodies degrade, or imply a stigma on the subject; on the contrary, they in general imply something serious or sacred in the originals. Without this, they would be good for nothing, for the immediate contrast would be wanting, and with this they are sure to tell. The best parodies are, accordingly, the best and most striking things reversed. . . .

Lastly, there is a wit of sense and observation, which consists in the acute illustration of good sense and practical wisdom, by means of some far-fetched conceit or quaint imagery. The matter is sense, but the form is wit. Thus the lines in Pope—

'Tis with our judgments as our watches, none
Go just alike; yet each believes his own

are witty, rather than poetical; because the truth they convey is a mere dry observation on human life, without elevation or enthusiasm, and the illustration of it is of that quaint and familiar kind that is merely curious and fanciful.

Charles Lamb *1775–1834*

On the Artificial Comedy
of the Last Century   *1822*

The artificial Comedy, or Comedy of manners, is quite extinct on our stage. Congreve and Farquhar show their heads once in seven years only, to be exploded and put down instantly. The times cannot bear them. Is it for a few wild speeches, an occasional license of dialogue? I think not altogether. The business of their dramatic characters will not stand the moral test. We screw everything up to that. Idle gallantry in a fiction, a dream, the passing pageant of an evening, startles us in the same way as the alarming indications of profligacy in a son or ward in real life should startle a parent or guardian. We have no such middle emotions as dramatic interests left. We see a stage libertine playing his loose pranks of two hours' duration, and of no after consequence, with the severe eyes which inspect real vices with their bearings upon two worlds. We are spectators to a plot or intrigue (not reducible in life to the point of strict morality), and take it all for truth. We substitute a real for a dramatic person, and judge him accordingly. We try him in our courts, from which there is no appeal to the dramatis personae,

Selection. From Charles Lamb, *The Essays of Elia and the Last Essays of Elia.* New York: Frederick A. Stokes, 1894.

his peers. We have been spoiled with—not sentimental comedy—but a tyrant far more pernicious to our pleasures which has succeeded to it, the exclusive and all-devouring drama of common life; where the moral point is everything; where, instead of the fictitious half-believed personages of the stage (the phantoms of old comedy), we recognize ourselves, our brothers, aunts, kins-folk, allies, patrons, enemies—the same as in life—with an interest in what is going on so hearty and substantial, that we cannot afford our moral judgment, in its deepest and most vital results, to compromise or slumber for a moment. What is *there* transacting, by no modification is made to affect us in any other manner than the same events or characters would do in our relationships of life. We carry our fireside concerns to the theatre with us. We do not go thither like our ancestors, to escape from the pressure of reality, so much as to confirm our experience of it; to make assurance double, and take a bond of fate. We must live our toilsome lives twice over, as it was the mournful privilege of Ulysses to descend twice to the shades. All that neutral ground of character, which stood between vice and virtue; or which in fact was indifferent to neither, where neither properly was called in ques-tion; that happy breathing-place from the burden of a perpetual moral questioning—the sanctuary and quiet Alsatia of hunted casuistry—is broken up and disfranchised, as injurious to the interests of society. The privileges of the place are taken away by law. We dare not dally with images, or names, of wrong. We bark like foolish dogs at shadows. We dread infection from the scenic representation of disorder, and fear a painted pustule. In our anxiety that our morality should not take cold, we wrap it up in a great blanket surtout of precaution against the breeze and sunshine.

I confess for myself that (with no great delinquencies to answer for) I am glad for a season to take an airing beyond the diocese of the strict conscience—not to live always in the precincts of the law-courts, but now and then, for a dream-while or so, to imagine a world with no meddling restrictions—to get into recesses, whither the hunter cannot follow me—

——Secret shades
Of woody Ida's inmost grove,
While yet there was no fear of Jove.[1]

I come back to my cage and my restraint the fresher and more healthy for it. I wear my shackles more contentedly for having respired the breath of an imaginary freedom. I do not know how it is with others, but I feel the better always for the perusal of one of Congreve's—nay, why should I not add even of Wycherley's—comedies. I am the gayer at least for it; and I could never connect those sports of a witty fancy in any shape with any result to be drawn from them to imitation in real life. They are a world of them-

---

[1] Milton, *Il Penseroso* (1631–1632), ll. 28–30.

selves almost as much as fairyland. Take one of their characters, male or
female (with few exceptions they are alike), and place it in a modern play,
and my virtuous indignation shall rise against the profligate wretch as warmly
as the Catos of the pit could desire; because in a modern play I am to
judge of the right and the wrong. The standard of *police* is the measure of
political justice. The atmosphere will blight it; it cannot live here. It has
got into a moral world, where it has no business, from which it must needs
fall headlong, as dizzy, and incapable of making a stand, as a Swedenborgian
bad spirit that has wandered unawares into the sphere of one of his Good
Men, or Angels. But in its own world do we feel the creature is so very
bad?—The Fainalls and the Mirabels, the Dorimants and the Lady Touch-
woods, in their own sphere, do not offend my moral sense; in fact, they do
not appeal to it at all. They seem engaged in their proper element. They
break through no laws or conscientious restraints. They know of none. They
have got out of Christendom into the land—what shall I call it?—of cuckoldry
—the Utopia of gallantry, where pleasure is duty, and the manners perfect
freedom. It is altogether a speculative scene of things, which has no reference
whatever to the world that is. No good person can be justly offended as a
spectator, because no good person suffers on the stage. Judged morally, every
character in these plays—the few exceptions only are *mistakes*—is alike essentially vain and worthless. The great art of Congreve is especially shown in
this, that he has entirely excluded from his scenes—some little generosities
in the part of Angelica perhaps excepted—not only anything like a faultless
character, but any pretensions to goodness or good feelings whatsoever.
Whether he did this designedly, or instinctively, the effect is as happy as
the design (if design) was bold. I used to wonder at the strange power which
his *Way of the World* in particular possesses of interesting you all along
in the pursuits of characters, for whom you absolutely care nothing—for
you neither hate nor love his personages—and I think it is owing to this
very indifference for any, that you endure the whole. He has spread a privation
of moral light, I will call it, rather than by the ugly name of palpable darkness, over his creations; and his shadows flit before you without distinction
or preference. Had he introduced a good character, a single gush of moral
feeling, a revulsion of the judgment to actual life and actual duties, the
impertinent Goshen would have only lighted to the discovery of deformities,
which now are none, because we think them none.

Translated into real life, the characters of his, and his friend Wycherley's
dramas are profligates and strumpets—the business of their brief existence,
the undivided pursuit of lawless gallantry. No other spring of action, or
possible motive of conduct, is recognized; principles which, universally
acted upon, must reduce this frame of things to a chaos. But we do them
wrong in so translating them. No such effects are produced, in *their* world.
When we are among them, we are amongst a chaotic people. We are not

to judge them by our usages. No reverend institutions are insulted by their proceedings—for they have none among them. No peace of families is violated—for no family ties exist among them. No purity of the marriage bed is stained—for none is supposed to have a being. No deep affections are disquieted, no holy wedlock bands are snapped asunder—for affection's depth and wedded faith are not of the growth of that soil. There is neither right nor wrong—gratitude or its opposite—claim or duty—paternity or sonship. Of what consequence is it to Virtue, or how is she at all concerned about it, whether Sir Simon or Dapperwit steal away Miss Martha; or who is the father of Lord Froth's or Sir Paul Pliant's children?

The whole is a passing pageant, where we should sit as unconcerned at the issues, for life or death, as at the battle of the frogs and mice. But, like Don Quixote, we take part against the puppets, and quite as impertinently. We dare not contemplate an Atlantis, a scheme, out of which our coxcombical moral sense is for a little transitory ease excluded. We have not the courage to imagine a state of things for which there is neither reward nor punishment. We cling to the painful necessities of shame and blame. We would indict our very dreams.

Amidst the mortifying circumstances attendant upon growing old, it is something to have seen the *School for Scandal* in its glory. This comedy grew out of Congreve and Wycherley, but gathered some allays of the sentimental comedy which followed theirs. It is impossible that it should be now *acted*, though it continues, at long intervals, to be announced in the bills. Its hero, when Palmer[2] played it at least, was Joseph Surface. When I remember the gay boldness, the graceful solemn plausibility, the measured step, the insinuating voice—to express it in a word—the downright *acted* villainy of the part, so different from the pressure of conscious actual wickedness—the hypocritical assumption of hypocrisy—which made Jack so deservedly a favorite in that character, I must needs conclude the present generation of playgoers more virtuous than myself, or more dense. I freely confess that he divided the palm with me with his better brother; that, in fact, I liked him quite as well. Not but there are passages—like that, for instance, where Joseph is made to refuse a pittance to a poor relation—incongruities which Sheridan was forced upon by the attempt to join the artificial with the comedy, either of which must destroy the other—but over these obstructions Jack's manner floated him so lightly, that a refusal from him no more shocked you, than the easy compliance of Charles gave you in reality any pleasure; you got over the paltry question as quickly as you could, to get back into the regions of pure comedy, where no cold moral reigns. The highly artificial manner of Palmer in this character counteracted every disagreeable impression which you might have received from the contrast,

---

[2] John Palmer (1742–1798) was Joseph Surface in the play's premiere in 1777.

supposing them real, between the two brothers. You did not believe in Joseph with the same faith with which you believed in Charles. The latter was a pleasant reality, the former a no less pleasant poetical foil to it. The comedy, I have said, is incongruous; a mixture of Congreve with sentimental incompatibilities; the gaiety upon the whole is buoyant; but it required the consummate art of Palmer to reconcile the discordant elements.

Thomas Babington Macaulay *1800–1859*

Comic Dramatists of the Restoration *1841*

The plays to which he[1] now acts as introducer are, with few exceptions, such as, in the opinion of many very respectable people, ought not to be reprinted. In this opinion we can by no means concur. We cannot wish that any work or class of works which has exercised a great influence on the human mind, and which illustrates the character of an important epoch in letters, politics, and morals, should disappear from the world. If we err in this matter, we err with the gravest men and bodies of men in the empire, and especially with the Chuch of England and with the great schools of learning which are connected with her. The whole liberal education of our countrymen is conducted on the principle that no book which is valuable, either by reason of the excellence of its style, or by reason of the light which it throws on the history, polity, and manners of nations, should be withheld from the student on account of its impurity. The Athenian comedies,

Selection. From *Miscellaneous Works of Lord Macaulay*, edited by Lady Trevelyan, Vol. III. New York: Harper & Brothers, 1880. The present title is the running title of the article called "Leigh Hunt."

[1] Leigh Hunt, who edited and wrote biographical and critical essays for a volume called *The Dramatic Works of Wycherley, Congreve, Vanbrugh, and Farquhar* (London, 1840). This work occasioned the publication of Macaulay's article, which appeared in the *Edinburgh Review*, January 1841.

in which there are scarcely a hundred lines together without some passage of which Rochester[2] would have been ashamed, have been reprinted at the Pitt Press and the Clarendon Press under the direction of syndics and delegates appointed by the universities, and have been illustrated with notes by reverend, very reverend, and right reverend commentators. Every year the most distinguished young men in the kingdom are examined by bishops and professors of divinity in such works as the *Lysistrata* of Aristophanes and the *Sixth Satire* of Juvenal.[3] There is certainly something a little ludricous in the idea of a conclave of venerable fathers of the Church praising and rewarding a lad on account of his intimate acquaintance with writings compared with which the loosest tale in Prior[4] is modest. But, for our own part, we have no doubt that the great societies which direct the education of the English gentry have herein judged wisely. It is unquestionable that an extensive acquaintance with ancient literature enlarges and enriches the mind. It is unquestionable that a man whose mind has been thus enlarged and enriched is likely to be far more useful to the State and to the Church than one who is unskilled, or little skilled, in classical learning. On the other hand, we find it difficult to believe that in a world so full of temptation as this any gentleman whose life would have been virtuous if he had not read Aristophanes and Juvenal will be made vicious by reading them. A man who, exposed to all the influences of such a state of society as that in which we live, is yet afraid of exposing himself to the influences of a few Greek or Latin verses, acts, we think, much like the felon who begged the sheriffs to let him have an umbrella held over his head from the door of Newgate to the gallows because it was a drizzling morning and he was apt to take cold.

The virtue which the world wants is a healthful virtue, not a valetudinarian virtue; a virtue which can expose itself to the risks inseparable from all spirited exertion, not a virtue which keeps out of the common air for fear of infection, and eschews the common food as too stimulating. It would be, indeed, absurd to attempt to keep men from acquiring those qualifications which fit them to play their part in life with honor to themselves and advantage to their country for the sake of preserving a delicacy which cannot be preserved—a delicacy which a walk from Westminster to the Temple is sufficient to destroy. . . .

. . . We are therefore by no means disposed to condemn this publication,

[2] John Wilmot, Second Earl of Rochester (1647–1680), who wrote several "lewd and profane poems" as well as the "lewd and profane" play, or closet drama, *Sodom* (published posthumously, 1684).

[3] Aristophanes' *Lysistrata* (411 B.C.) and Juvenal's *Sixth Satire* (c. 107–115 A.D.).

[4] Matthew Prior (1664–1721); the reference is to a series of writings, "Public Panegyrics, Amorous Odes, Serious Reflections, and Idle Tales," first published at various times throughout his life.

though we certainly cannot recommend the handsome volume before us as an appropriate Christmas present for young ladies.

We have said that we think the present publication perfectly justifiable. But we can by no means agree with Mr. Leigh Hunt, who seems to hold that there is little or no ground for the charge of immorality so often brought against the literature of the Restoration. We do not blame him for not bringing to the judgment-seat the merciless rigor of Lord Angelo; but we really think that such flagitious and impudent offenders as those who are now at the bar deserved, at least, the gentle rebuke of Escalus. Mr. Leigh Hunt treats the whole matter a little too much in the easy style of Lucio;[5] and perhaps his exceeding lenity disposes us to be somewhat too severe.

And yet it is not easy to be too severe. For, in truth, this part of our literature is a disgrace to our language and our national character. It is clever, indeed, and very entertaining; but it is, in the most emphatic sense of the words, "earthly, sensual, devilish." Its indecency, though perpetually such as is condemned not less by the rules of good taste than by those of morality, is not, in our opinion, so disgraceful a fault as its singularly inhuman spirit. . . . We find ourselves in a world in which the ladies are like very profligate, impudent, and unfeeling men, and in which the men are too bad for any place but Pandemonium. . . .

. . . The crime charged is not mere coarseness of expression. The terms which are delicate in one age become gross in the next. . . . Whether a thing shall be designated by a plain noun substantive or by a circumlocution is mere matter of fashion. Morality is not at all interested in the question. But morality is deeply interested in this—that what is immoral shall not be presented to the imagination of the young and susceptible in constant. connection with what is attractive. For every person who has observed the operation of the law of association in his own mind and in the minds of others knows that whatever is constantly presented to the imagination in connection with what is attractive will itself become attractive. There is undoubtedly a great deal of indelicate writing in Fletcher and Massinger, and more than might be wished even in Ben Jonson and Shakespeare, who are comparatively pure. But it is impossible to trace in their plays any systematic attempt to associate vice with those things which men value most and desire most, and virtue with everything ridiculous and degrading. And such a systematic attempt we find in the whole dramatic literature of the generation which followed the return of Charles the Second. We will take as an instance of what we mean a single subject of the highest importance to the happiness of mankind—conjugal fidelity. We can at present

---

[5] Angelo, Escalus, and Lucio are characters in Shakespeare's *Measure for Measure* (1604).

hardly call to mind a single English play written before the Civil War in which the character of a seducer of married women is represented in a favorable light. We remember many plays in which such persons are baffled, exposed, covered with derision, and insulted by triumphant husbands. Such is the fate of Falstaff,[6] with all his wit and knowledge of the world. Such is the fate of Brisac in Fletcher's *Elder Brother*, and of Ricardo and Ubaldo in Massinger's *Picture*. Sometimes, as in the *Fatal Dowry* and *Love's Cruelty*,[7] the outraged honor of families is repaired by a bloody revenge. If now and then the lover is represented as an accomplished man, and the husband as a person of weak or odious character, this only makes the triumph of female virtue the more signal, as in Jonson's Celia and Mrs. Fitzdottrel, and in Fletcher's Maria.[8] In general, we will venture to say that the dramatists of the age of Elizabeth and James the First either treat the breach of the marriage-vow as a serious crime, or, if they treat it as matter for laughter, turn the laugh against the gallant.

On the contrary, during the forty years which followed the Restoration the whole body of the dramatists invariably represent adultery, we do not say as a peccadillo, we do not say as an error which the violence of passion may excuse, but as the calling of a fine gentleman, as a grace without which his character would be imperfect. It is as essential to his breeding and to his place in society that he should make love to the wives of his neighbors as that he should know French or that he should have a sword at his side. In all this there is no passion, and scarcely anything that can be called preference. The hero intrigues just as he wears a wig; because, if he did not, he would be a queer fellow, a city prig, perhaps a Puritan. All the agreeable qualities are always given to the gallant. All the contempt and aversion are the portion of the unfortunate husband. . . .

Mr. Charles Lamb, indeed, attempted to set up a defence for this way of writing.[9] The dramatists of the latter part of the seventeenth century are not, according to him, to be tried by the standard of morality which exists, and ought to exist, in real life. Their world is a conventional world. Their heroes and heroines belong, not to England, not to Christendom, but to a Utopia of gallantry, to a Fairyland, where the Bible and Burns's *Justice*[10] are unknown, where a prank which on this earth would be rewarded with the pillory is merely matter for a peal of elfish laughter. A real Horner, a real

[6] In Shakespeare's *The Merry Wives of Windsor* (1597).

[7] *The Elder Brother* (1625?), by John Fletcher (with Philip Massinger?); *The Picture* (1629), by Philip Massinger; *The Fatal Dowry* (1616–1619), by Massinger, with Nathan Field; *Love's Cruelty* (1631), by James Shirley.

[8] Celia is a character in Ben Jonson's *Volpone* (1606), Mrs. Fitzdottrel in Jonson's *The Devil Is an Ass* (1616), Maria in Massinger's *The Bashful Lover* (1636).

[9] In *On the Artificial Comedy of the Last Century*. See pp. 609–613.

[10] Robert Burns, D.D. (1789–1869), a theological writer, wrote A *Historical Dissertation on the Law and Practice of Great Britain* (1819).

Careless,[11] would, it is admitted, be exceedingly bad men. But to predicate morality or immorality of the Horner of Wycherley and the Careless of Congreve is as absurd as it would be to arraign a sleeper for his dreams. "They belong to the regions of pure comedy, where no cold moral reigns. When we are among them we are among a chaotic people. We are not to judge them by our usages. No reverend institutions are insulted by their proceedings, for they have none among them. No peace of families is violated, for no family ties exist among them. There is neither right nor wrong, gratitude or its opposite, claim or duty, paternity or sonship."

This is, we believe, a fair summary of Mr. Lamb's doctrine. We are sure that we do not wish to represent him unfairly. For we admire his genius; we love the kind nature which appears in all his writings; and we cherish his memory as much as if we had known him personally. But we must plainly say that his argument, though ingenious, is altogether sophistical. . . .

In the name of art, as well as in the name of virtue, we protest against the principle that the world of pure comedy is one into which no moral enters. If comedy be an imitation, under whatever conventions, of real life, how is it possible that it can have no reference to the great rule which directs life, and to feelings which are called forth by every incident of life? If what Mr. Charles Lamb says were correct, the inference would be that these dramatists did not in the least understand the very first principles of their craft. Pure landscape-painting into which no light or shade enters, pure portrait-painting into which no expression enters, are phrases less at variance with sound criticism than pure comedy into which no moral enters.

But it is not the fact that the world of these dramatists is a world into which no moral enters. Morality constantly enters into that world, a sound morality and an unsound morality; the sound morality to be insulted, derided, associated with everything mean and hateful; the unsound morality to be set off to every advantage, and inculcated by all methods, direct and indirect. It is not the fact that none of the inhabitants of this conventional world feel reverence for sacred institutions and family ties. Fondlewife, Pinchwife, every person, in short, of narrow understanding and disgusting manners, expresses that reverence strongly. The heroes and heroines, too, have a moral code of their own—an exceedingly bad one, but not, as Mr. Charles Lamb seems to think, a code existing only in the imagination of dramatists. It is, on the contrary, a code actually received and obeyed by great numbers of people. We need not go to Utopia or Fairyland to find them. They are near at hand. Every night some of them cheat at the hells in Quadrant, and others pace the Piazza in Covent Garden. Without flying to Nephelococcygia or to the Court of Queen Mab, we can meet with sharpers, bullies,

---

[11] Horner is a character in William Wycherley's *The Country Wife* (1675), Careless in William Congreve's *The Double Dealer* (1693).

hard-hearted impudent debauchees, and women worthy of such paramours. The morality of the *Country Wife* and the *Old Bachelor*[12] is the morality, not, as Mr. Charles Lamb maintains, of an unreal world, but of a world which is a great deal too real. It is the morality, not of a chaotic people, but of low town-rakes, and of those ladies whom the newspapers call "dashing Cyprians." And the question is simply this, whether a man of genius who constantly and systematically endeavors to make this sort of character attractive, by uniting it with beauty, grace, dignity, spirit, a high social position, popularity, literature, wit, taste, knowledge of the world, brilliant success in every undertaking, does or does not make an ill use of his powers. We own that we are unable to understand how this question can be answered in any way but one.

George Meredith   *1828–1909*

An Essay on Comedy   *1877*

There are plain reasons why the Comic poet is not a frequent apparition; and why the great Comic poet remains without a fellow. A society of cultivated men and women is required, wherein ideas are current and the perceptions quick, that he may be supplied with matter and an audience. The semi-barbarism of merely giddy communities, and feverish emotional periods, repel him; and also a state of marked social inequality of the sexes; nor can he whose business is to address the mind be understood where there is not a moderate degree of intellectual activity.

Moreover, to touch and kindle the mind through laughter, demands more than sprightliness, a most subtle delicacy. That must be a natal gift in the Comic poet. The substance he deals with will show him a startling exhibition of the dyer's hand, if he is without it. People are ready to surrender themselves to witty thumps on the back, breast, and sides; all except the head: and it is there that he aims. He must be subtle to penetrate. A corresponding acuteness must exist to welcome him. . . .

Selections. From George Meredith, *An Essay on Comedy and the Uses of the Comic Spirit*. Westminster: Constable, 1897.

[12] (1693) by William Congreve.

Yet should you ask them whether they dislike sound sense, they vow they do not. And question cultivated women whether it pleases them to be shown moving on an intellectual level with men, they will answer that it does; numbers of them claim the situation. Now, Comedy is the fountain of sound sense; not the less perfectly sound on account of the sparkle: and Comedy lifts women to a station offering them free play for their wit, as they usually show it, when they have it, on the side of sound sense. The higher the Comedy, the more prominent the part they enjoy in it. Dorine in the *Tartuffe* is common sense incarnate, though palpably a waiting-maid. Célimène is undisputed mistress of the same attribute in the *Misanthrope*;[1] wiser as a woman than Alceste as man. In Congreve's *Way of the World*,[2] Millament overshadows Mirabel, the sprightliest male figure of English comedy.

But those two ravishing women, so copious and so choice of speech, who fence with men and pass their guard, are heartless! Is it not preferable to be the pretty idiot, the passive beauty, the adorable bundle of caprices, very feminine, very sympathetic, of romantic and sentimental fiction? Our women are taught to think so. The Agnès of the *École des Femmes*[3] should be a lesson for men. The heroines of Comedy are like women of the world, not necessarily heartless from being clear-sighted: they seem so to the sentimentally reared only for the reason that they use their wits, and are not wandering vessels crying for a captain or a pilot. Comedy is an exhibition of their battle with men, and that of men with them: and as the two, however divergent, both look on one object, namely, Life, the gradual similarity of their impressions must bring them to some resemblance. The Comic poet dares to show us men and women coming to this mutual likeness; he is for saying that when they draw together in social life their minds grow liker; just as the philosopher discerns the similarity of boy and girl, until the girl is marched away to the nursery. Philosopher and Comic poet are of a cousinship in the eye they cast on life: and they are equally unpopular with our wilful English of the hazy region and the ideal that is not to be disturbed. . . .

There has been fun in Bagdad. But there never will be civilization where Comedy is not possible; and that comes of some degree of social equality of the sexes. I am not quoting the Arab to exhort and disturb the somnolent East; rather for cultivated women to recognize that the Comic Muse is one of their best friends. They are blind to their interests in swelling the ranks of the sentimentalists. Let them look with their clearest vision abroad and at home. They will see that where they have no social freedom, Comedy is absent: where they are household drudges, the form of Comedy is prim-

---

[1] Both by Molière: 1664 and 1666, respectively.
[2] (1700).
[3] *School for Wives* (1662) by Molière.

itive: where they are tolerably independent, but uncultivated, exciting melodrama takes its place and a sentimental version of them. Yet the Comic will
out, as they would know if they listened to some of the private conversations of
men whose minds are undirected by the Comic Muse: as the sentimental man,
to his astonishment, would know likewise, if he in similar fashion could
receive a lesson. But where women are on the road to an equal footing with
men, in attainments and in liberty—in what they have won for themselves,
and what has been granted them by a fair civilization—there, and only
waiting to be transplanted from life to the stage, or the novel, or the poem,
pure Comedy flourishes, and is, as it would help them to be, the sweetest
of diversions, the wisest of delightful companions. . . .

Taking them generally, the English public are most in sympathy with
this primitive Aristophanic comedy, wherein the comic is capped by the
grotesque, irony tips the wit, and satire is a naked sword. They have the basis
of the Comic in them: an esteem for common sense. They cordially dislike
the reverse of it. . . .

. . . Generally, however, the English elect excel in satire, and they are
noble humourists. The national disposition is for hard-hitting, with a moral
purpose to sanction it; or for a rosy, sometimes a larmoyant, geniality, not
unmanly in its verging upon tenderness, and with a singular attraction for
thick headedness, to decorate it with asses' ears and the most beautiful sylvan
haloes. But the Comic is a different spirit.

You may estimate your capacity for Comic perception by being able to
detect the ridicule of them you love, without loving them less: and more
by being able to see yourself somewhat ridiculous in dear eyes, and accepting
the correction their image of you proposes.

Each one of an affectionate couple may be willing, as we say, to die for the
other, yet unwilling to utter the agreeable word at the right moment; but if
the wits were sufficiently quick for them to perceive that they are in a comic
situation, as affectionate couples must be when they quarrel, they would
not wait for the moon or the almanac, or a Dorine, to bring back the
flood-tide of tender feelings, that they should join hands and lips.

If you detect the ridicule, and your kindliness is chilled by it, you are
slipping into the grasp of Satire.

If instead of falling foul of the ridiculous person with a satiric rod, to
make him writhe and shriek aloud, you prefer to sting him under a semi-
caress, by which he shall in his anguish be rendered dubious whether indeed
anything has hurt him, you are an engine of Irony.

If you laugh all round him, tumble him, roll him about, deal him a
smack, and drop a tear on him, own his likeness to you and yours to your
neighbour, spare him as little as you shun, pity him as much as you expose,
it is a spirit of Humour that is moving you.

The Comic, which is the perceptive, is the governing spirit, awakening and giving aim to to these powers of laughter, but it is not to be confounded with them: it enfolds a thinner form of them, differing from satire, in not sharply driving into the quivering sensibilities, and from humour, in not comforting them and tucking them up, or indicating a broader than the range of this bustling world to them. . . .

The Satirist is a moral agent, often a social scavenger, working on a storage of bile.

The Ironist is one thing or another, according to his caprice. Irony is the humour of satire; it may be savage as in Swift, with a moral object, or sedate, as in Gibbon, with a malicious. The foppish irony fretting to be seen, and the irony which leers, that you shall not mistake its intention, are failures in satiric effort pretending to the treasures of ambiguity.

The Humourist of mean order is a refreshing laugher, giving tone to the feelings and sometimes allowing the feelings to be too much for him. But the humourist of high has an embrace of contrasts beyond the scope of the Comic poet.

Heart and mind laugh out at Don Quixote, and still you brood on him. The juxtaposition of the knight and squire is a Comic conception, the opposition of their natures most humourous. They are as different as the two hemispheres in the time of Columbus, yet they touch and are bound in one by laughter. The knight's great aims and constant mishaps, his chivalrous valiancy exercised on absurd objects, his good sense along the highroad of the craziest of expeditions; the compassion he plucks out of derision, and the admirable figure he preserves while stalking through the frantically grotesque and burlesque assailing him, are in the loftiest moods of humour, fusing the Tragic sentiment with the Comic narrative.

The stroke of the great humourist is worldwide, with lights of Tragedy in his laughter. . . .

The Comic poet is in the narrow field, or enclosed square, of the society he depicts; and he addresses the still narrower enclosure of men's intellects, with reference to the operation of the social world upon their characters. He is not concerned with beginnings or endings or surroundings, but with what you are now weaving. To understand his work and value it, you must have a sober liking of your kind and a sober estimate of our civilized qualities. The aim and business of the Comic poet are misunderstood, his meaning is not seized nor his point of view taken, when he is accused of dishonouring our nature and being hostile to sentiment, tending to spitefulness and making an unfair use of laughter. Those who detect irony in Comedy do so because they choose to see it in life. Poverty, says the satirist, has nothing harder in itself than that it makes men ridiculous. But poverty is never ridiculous to Comic perception until it attempts to make its rags conceal its bareness in a forlorn attempt at decency, or foolishly to rival ostentation. Caleb Balderstone, in his endeavour to keep up the honour of a noble household in a state of beggary, is an exquisitely comic character. In the case of "poor relatives," on the other hand, it is the rich, whom they perplex, that are really comic; and to laugh at the former, not seeing the comedy of the latter, is to betray dullness of vision. Humourist and Satirist frequently hunt together as Ironists in pursuit of the grotesque, to the exclusion of the Comic. That was an affecting moment in the history of the Prince Regent, when the First Gentleman of Europe burst into tears at a sarcastic remark of Beau Brummell's on the cut of his coat. Humour, Satire, Irony, pounce on it altogether as their common prey. The Comic spirit eyes but does not touch it. Put into action, it would be farcical. It is too gross for Comedy.

Incidents of a kind casting ridicule on our unfortunate nature instead of our conventional life, provoke derisive laughter, which thwarts the Comic idea. But derision is foiled by the play of the intellect. Most of doubtful causes in contests are open to Comic interpretation, and any intellectual pleading of a doubtful cause contains germs of an Idea of Comedy.

The laughter of satire is a blow in the back or the face. The laughter of Comedy is impersonal and of unrivalled politeness, nearer a smile; often no more than a smile. It laughs through the mind, for the mind directs it; and it might be called the humour of the mind.

One excellent test of the civilization of a country, as I have said, I take to be the flourishing of the Comic idea and Comedy; and the test of true Comedy is that it shall awaken thoughtful laughter.

If you believe that our civilization is founded in common sense (and it is the first condition of sanity to believe it), you will, when contemplating men, discern a Spirit overhead; not more heavenly than the light flashed upward from glassy surfaces, but luminous and watchful; never shooting beyond them, nor lagging in the rear; so closely attached to them that it may be taken for a slavish reflex, until its features are studied. It has the sage's brows, and the sunny malice of a faun lurks at the corners of the half-closed lips drawn in an idle wariness of half tension. That slim feasting smile, shaped like the longbow, was once a big round satyr's laugh, that flung up the brows like a fortress lifted by gunpowder. The laugh will come again, but it will be of the order of the smile, finely tempered, showing sunlight of the mind, mental richness rather than noisy enormity. Its common aspect is one of unsolicitous observation, as if surveying a full field and having leisure to dart on its chosen morsels, without any fluttering eagerness. Men's future upon earth does not attract it; their honesty and shapeliness in the present does; and whenever they wax out of proportion, overblown, affected, pretentious, bombastical, hypocritical, pedantic, fantastically delicate; whenever it sees them self-deceived or hoodwinked, given to run riot in idolatries, drifting into vanities, congregating in absurdities, planning shortsightedly, plotting dementedly; whenever they are at variance with their professions, and violate the unwritten but perceptible laws binding them in consideration one to another; whenever they offend sound reason, fair justice; are false in humility or mined with conceit, individually, or in the bulk—the Spirit overhead will look humanely malign and cast an oblique light on them, followed by volleys of silvery laughter. That is the Comic Spirit.

Not to distinguish it is to be bull-blind to the spiritual, and to deny the existence of a mind of man where minds of men are in working conjunction.

You must, as I have said, believe that our state of society is founded in common sense, otherwise you will not be struck by the contrasts the Comic Spirit perceives, or have it to look to for your consolation. You will, in fact, be standing in that peculiar oblique beam of light, yourself illuminated to the general eye as the very object of chase and doomed quarry of the things obscure to you. But to feel its presence and to see it is your assurance that many sane and solid minds are with you in what you are experiencing: and this of itself spares you the pain of satirical heat, and the bitter craving to strike heavy blows. You share the sublime of wrath, that would not have hurt the foolish, but merely demonstrate their foolishness. Molière was contented to revenge himself on the critics of the *École des Femmes*, by writing the *Critique de l'École des Femmes*, one of the wisest as well as the playfullest of studies in criticism. A perception of the comic spirit gives high fellowship. You become a citizen of the selecter world, the highest we know of in connection with our old world, which is not supermundane. Look there for your unchallengable upper class! You feel that you are one of this our civilized community, that you cannot escape from it, and would not if you could. Good hope sustains you; weariness does not overwhelm you; in isolation you see no charms for vanity; personal pride is greatly moderated. Nor shall your title of citizenship exclude you from worlds of imagination or of devotion. The Comic spirit is not hostile to the sweetest songfully poetic. Chaucer bubbles with it: Shakespeare overflows: there is a mild moon's ray of it (pale with super-refinement through distance from our flesh and blood planet) in Comus. Pope has it, and it is the daylight side of the night half obscuring Cowper. It is only hostile to the priestly element, when that, by baleful swelling, transcends and overlaps the bounds of its office: and then, in extreme cases, it is too true to itself to speak, and veils the lamp: as, for example, the spectacle of Bossuet over the dead body of Molière: at which the dark angels may, but men do not laugh.

We have had comic pulpits, for a sign that the laughter-moving and the worshipful may be in alliance: I know not how far comic, or how much assisted in seeming so by the unexpectedness and the relief of its appearance: at least they are popular, they are said to win the ear. Laughter is open to perversion, like other good things; the scornful and the brutal sorts are not unknown to us; but the laughter directed by the Comic spirit is a harmless wine, conducing to sobriety in the degree that it enlivens. It enters you like fresh air into a study; as when one of the sudden contrasts of the comic idea floods the brain like reassuring daylight. You are cognizant of the true kind by feeling that you take it in, savour it, and have what flowers live on, natural air for food. That which you give out—the joyful roar—is not the better part; let that go to good fellowship and the benefit of the lungs. Aristophanes promises his auditors that if they will retain the ideas of the comic poet carefully, as they keep dried fruits in boxes, their garments shall smell odoriferous of wisdom throughout the year. The boast will not be thought an empty one by those who have choice friends that have stocked themselves according to his directions. Such treasuries of sparkling laughter are wells in our desert. Sensitiveness to the comic laugh is a step in civilization. To shrink from being an object of it is a step in cultivation. We know the degree of refinement in men by the matter they will laugh at, and the ring of the laugh; but we know likewise that the larger natures are distinguished by the great breadth of their power of laughter, and no one really loving Molière is refined by that love to despise or be dense to Aristophanes, though it may be that the lover of Aristophanes will not have risen to the height of Molière. Embrace them both, and you have the whole scale of laughter in your breast.

Oscar Wilde *1856–1900*

The Decay of Lying *1889*

CYRIL[1] (*coming in through the open window from the terrace*). My dear Vivian, don't coop yourself up all day in the library. It is a perfectly lovely afternoon. The air is exquisite. There is a mist upon the woods like the purple bloom upon a plum. Let us go and lie on the grass, and smoke cigarettes, and enjoy Nature.

Selections. From Oscar Wilde, *Intentions*. London: James R. Osgood McIlvaine, 1894.

[1] Cyril and Vyvyan were the names of Wilde's sons.

VIVIAN Enjoy Nature! I am glad to say that I have entirely lost that faculty. People tell us that Art makes us love Nature more than we loved her before; that it reveals her secrets to us; and that after a careful study of Corot and Constable[2] we see things in her that had escaped our observation. My own experience is that the more we study Art, the less we care for Nature. What Art really reveals to us is Nature's lack of design, her curious crudities, her extraordinary monotony, her absolutely unfinished condition. Nature has good intentions, of course, but, as Aristotle once said, she cannot carry them out. When I look at a landscape I cannot help seeing all its defects. It is fortunate for us, however, that Nature is so imperfect, as otherwise we should have had no art at all. Art is our spirited protest, our gallant attempt to teach Nature her proper place. As for the infinite variety of Nature, that is a pure myth. It is not to be found in Nature herself. It resides in the imagination, or fancy, or cultivated blindness of the man who looks at her.

CYRIL Well, you need not look at the landscape. You can lie on the grass and smoke and talk. ·

VIVIAN But Nature is so uncomfortable. Grass is hard and lumpy and damp, and full of dreadful black insects. Why, even Morris's[3] poorest workman could make you a more comfortable seat than the whole of Nature can. Nature pales before the furniture of "the street which from Oxford has borrowed its name," as the poet you love so much once vilely phrased it. I don't complain. If Nature had been comfortable, mankind would never have invented architecture, and I prefer houses to the open air. . . .

CYRIL . . . However, proceed with your article.

VIVIAN (*reading*). "Art begins with abstract decoration with purely imaginative and pleasurable work dealing with what is unreal and nonexistent. This is the first stage. Then Life becomes fascinated with this new wonder, and asks to be admitted into the charmed circle. Art takes life as part of her rough material, re-creates it, and refashions it in fresh forms, is absolutely indifferent to fact, invents, imagines, dreams, and keeps between herself and reality the impenetrable barrier of beautiful style, of decorative or ideal treatment. The third stage is when life gets the upper hand, and drives Art out into the wilderness. This is the true decadence, and it is from this that we are now suffering.

"Take the case of the English drama. At first in the hands of the monks Dramatic Art was abstract, decorative, and mythological. Then she enlisted Life in her service, and using some of life's external forms, she created an entirely new race of beings, whose sorrows were more terrible

---

[2] Jean Baptiste Camille Corot (1796–1875), French painter; John Constable (1776–1837), English painter.
[3] William Morris (1834–1896), English artist, artisan, poet, and socialist.

than any sorrow man has ever felt, whose joys were keener than lover's joys, who had the rage of the Titans and the calm of the gods, who had monstrous and marvelous sins, monstrous and marvelous virtues. To them she gave a language different from that of actual use, a language full of resonant music and sweet rhythm, made stately by solemn cadence, or made delicate by fanciful rhyme, jeweled with wonderful words, and enriched with lofty diction. She clothed her children in strange raiment and gave them masks, and at her bidding the antique world rose from its marble tomb. A new Caesar stalked through the streets of risen Rome, and with purple sail and flute-led oars another Cleopatra passed up the river to Antioch. Old myth and legend and dream took shape and substance. History was entirely rewritten, and there was hardly one of the dramatists who did not recognize that the object of Art is not simple truth but complex beauty. In this they were perfectly right. Art itself is really a form of exaggeration; and selection, which is the very spirit of art, is nothing more than an intensified mode of overemphasis.

"But Life soon shattered the perfection of the form. Even in Shakespeare we can see the beginning of the end. It shows itself by the gradual breaking up of the blank verse in the later plays, by the predominance given to prose, and by the over-importance assigned to characterization. The passages in Shakespeare—and they are many—where the language is uncouth, vulgar, exaggerated, fantastic, obscene even, are entirely due to Life calling for an echo of her own voice, and rejecting the intervention of beautiful style, through which alone should Life be suffered to find expression. Shakespeare is not by any means a flawless artist. He is too fond of going directly to life, and borrowing life's natural utterance. He forgets that when Art surrenders her imaginative medium she surrenders everything. Goethe says, somewhere—

In der Beschränkung zeigt sich erst der Meister

'It is in working within limits that the master reveals himself,' and the limitation, the very condition of any art is style. However, we need not linger any longer over Shakespeare's realism. *The Tempest* is the most perfect of palinodes. All that we desired to point out was, that the magnificent work of the Elizabethan and Jacobean artists contained within itself the seeds of its own dissolution, and that, if it drew some of its strength from using life as rough material, it drew all its weakness from using life as an artistic method. As the inevitable result of this substitution of an imitative for a creative medium, this surrender of an imaginative form, we have the modern English melodrama. The characters in these plays talk on the stage exactly as they would talk off it; they have neither aspirations nor aspirates; they are taken directly from life and reproduce its vulgarity down to the smallest detail; they present the gait, manner, costume, and accent of real people; they would pass unnoticed in a third-class railway carriage. And yet how wearisome the plays are! The do not succeed in producing even that impression of reality at which they aim, and which is their only reason for existing. As a method, realism is a complete failure. . . .

"Art finds her own perfection within, and not outside of, herself. She is not to be judged by any external standard of resemblance. She is a veil, rather than a mirror. She has flowers that no forests know of, birds that no woodland possesses. She makes and unmakes many worlds, and can draw the moon from heaven with a scarlet thread. Hers are the 'forms more real than living man,' and hers the great archetypes of which things that have existence are but unfinished copies. Nature has, in her eyes, no laws, no uniformity. . . ."

CYRIL   . . . I can quite understand your objection to art being treated as a mirror. You think it would reduce genius to the position of a cracked looking-glass. But you don't mean to say that you seriously believe that Life imitates Art, that Life is in fact the mirror, and Art the reality?

VIVIAN   Certainly I do. Paradox though it may seem—and paradoxes are always dangerous things—it is none the less true that Life imitates Art far more than Art imitates Life. . . .

CYRIL   . . . But in order to avoid making any error I want you to tell me briefly the doctrines of the new aesthetics.

VIVIAN   Briefly, then, they are these. Art never expresses anything but itself. It has an independent life, just as Thought has, and develops purely on its own lines. It is not necessarily realistic in an age of realism, nor spiritual in an age of faith. So far from being the creation of its time, it is usually in direct opposition to it, and the only history that it preserves for us is the history of its own progress. Sometimes it returns upon its footseps, and revives some antique form, as happened in the archaistic movement of late Greek Art, and in the pre-Raphaelite movement of our own day. At other times it entirely anticipates its age, and produces in one century work that it takes another century to understand, to appreciate, and to enjoy. In no case does it reproduce its age. To pass from the art of a time to the time itself is the great mistake that all historians commit.

The second doctrine is this. All bad art comes from returning to Life and Nature, and elevating them into ideals. Life and Nature may sometimes be used as part of Art's rough material, but before they are of any real service to art they must be translated into artistic conventions. The moment Art surrenders its imaginative medium it surrenders everything. As a method Realism is a complete failure, and the two things that every artist should avoid are modernity of form and modernity of subject-matter. To us, who live in the nineteenth century, any century is a suitable subject for art except our own. The only beautiful things are the things that do not concern us. It is, to have the pleasure of quoting myself, exactly because Hecuba is nothing to us that her sorrows are so suitable a motive for a tragedy. Besides, it is only the modern that ever becomes old-fashioned. M. Zola sits down to give us a picture of the Second Empire. Who cares for the Second Empire now? It is out of date. Life goes faster than Realism, but Romanticism is always in front of Life.

The third doctrine is that Life imitates Art far more than Art imitates Life. This results not merely from Life's imitative instinct, but from the fact that the self-conscious aim of Life is to find expression, and that Art offers it certain beautiful forms through which it may realize that energy. It is a theory that has never been put forward before, but it is extremely fruitful, and throws an entirely new light upon the history of Art.

It follows, as a corollary from this, that external Nature also imitates Art. The only effects that she can show us are effects that we have already seen through poetry, or in paintings. This is the secret of Nature's charm, as well as the explanation of Nature's weakness.

The final revelation is that Lying, the telling of beautiful untrue things, is the proper aim of Art.

Preface to
The Picture of Dorian Gray   *1890*

The artist is the creator of beautiful things.

To reveal art and conceal the artist is art's aim.

The critic is he who can translate into another manner or a new material his impression of beautiful things.

From Oscar Wilde, *The Picture of Dorian Gray*. New York: Charterhouse Press, 1904.

The highest as the lowest form of criticism is a mode of autobiography.

Those who find ugly meanings in beautiful things are corrupt without being charming. This is a fault.

Those who find beautiful meanings in beautiful things are the cultivated. For these there is hope.

They are the elect to whom beautiful things mean only Beauty.

There is no such thing as a moral or an immoral book. Books are well written, or badly written. That is all.

The nineteenth-century dislike of Realism is the rage of Caliban[1] seeing his own face in a glass.

The nineteenth-century dislike of Romanticism is the rage of Caliban not seeing his own face in a glass.

The moral life of man forms part of the subject matter of the artist, but the morality of art consists in the perfect use of an imperfect medium.

No artist desires to prove anything. Even things that are true can be proved.

No artist has ethical sympathies. An ethical sympathy in an artist is an unpardonable mannerism of style.

No artist is ever morbid. The artist can express everything.

Thought and language are to the artist instruments of an art.

Vice and virtue are to the artist materials for an art.

From the point of view of form, the type of all the arts is the art of the musician. From the point of view of feeling, the actor's craft is the type.

All art is at once surface and symbol.

Those who go beneath the surface do so at their peril.

Those who read the symbol do so at their peril.

It is the spectator, and not life, that art really mirrors.

Diversity of opinion about a work of art shows that the work is new, complex, and vital.

When critics disagree the artist is in accord with himself.

We can forgive a man for making a useful thing as long as he does not admire it. The only excuse for making a useless thing is that one admires it intensely.

All art is quite useless.

---

[1] The bestial, ugly slave of Prospero in Shakespeare's *The Tempest*.

George Bernard Shaw 1856–1950

Preface to Widowers' Houses* 1893

. . . There must, however, be no mistake as to the ground upon which I challenge criticism for the play, now that I submit it in print to the public. It is a propagandist play—a didactic play—a play with a purpose; but I do not therefore claim any special indulgence for it from people who go to the theatre to be entertained. I offer it as a technically good practicable stage play, one which will, if adequately acted, hold its proper audience and drive its story home to the last word.

But in claiming place for my play among works of art, I must make a melancholy reservation. One or two friendly readers may find it interesting, amusing, even admirable, as far as a mere topical farce can excite admiration; but nobody will find it a beautiful or lovable work. It is saturated with the vulgarity of the life it represents: the people do not speak nobly, live gracefully, or sincerely face their own position: the author is not giving expression in pleasant fancies to the underlying beauty and romance of happy life, but dragging up to the smooth surface of "respectability" a handful of the slime and foulness of its polluted bed, and playing off your laughter at the scandal of the exposure against your shudder at its blackness.

The Problem Play† 1895

Social questions are produced by the conflict of human institutions with human feeling. For instance, we have certain institutions regulating the lives of women. To the women whose feelings are entirely in harmony with these

* Selection. From the Preface to the Independent Theatre Series edition of *Widowers' Houses*, in Bernard Shaw, *Prefaces*. London: Constable, 1934. Printed by permission of The Society of Authors on behalf of the Bernard Shaw Estate.

† Selections. From *Shaw on Theatre*, edited by E. J. West. New York: Hill & Wang, 1958. Printed by permission of The Society of Authors on behalf of the Bernard Shaw Estate.

institutions there is no Woman Question. But during the present century, from the time of Mary Wollstonecraft[1] onwards, women have been developing feelings, and consequently opinions, which clash with these institutions. The institutions assumed that it was natural to a woman to allow her husband to own her property and person, and to represent her in politics as a father represents his infant child. The moment that seemed no longer natural to some women, it became grievously oppressive to them. Immediately there was a Woman Question, which has produced Married Women's Property Acts, Divorce Acts, Woman's Suffrage in local elections, and the curious deadlock to which the Weldon and Jackson cases have led our courts in the matter of conjugal rights. When we have achieved reforms enough to bring our institutions as far into harmony with the feelings of women as they now are with the feelings of men, there will no longer be a Woman Question. No conflict, no question.

Now the material of the dramatist is always some conflict of human feeling with circumstances; so that, since institutions are circumstances, every social question furnishes material for drama. But every drama does not involve a social question, because human feeling may be in conflict with circumstances which are not institutions, which raise no question at all, which are part of human destiny. To illustrate, take Mr Pinero's *Second Mrs. Tanqueray*.[2] The heroine's feelings are in conflict with the human institutions which condemn to ostracism both herself and the man who marries her. So far, the play deals with a social question. But in one very effective scene the conflict is between that flaw in the woman's nature which makes her dependent for affection wholly on the attraction of her beauty, and the stealthy advance of age and decay to take her beauty away from her. Here there is no social question: age, like love, death, accident, and personal character, lies outside all institutions; and this gives it a permanent and universal interest which makes the drama that deals with it independent of period and place. Abnormal greatness of character, abnormal baseness of character, love, and death: with these alone you can, if you are a sufficiently great dramatic poet, make a drama that will keep your language alive long after it has passed out of common use. Whereas a drama with a social question for the motive cannot outlive the solution of that question. It is true that we can in some cases imaginatively reconstruct an obsolete institution and sympathize with the tragedy it has produced: for instance, the very dramatic story of Abraham commanded to sacrifice his son, with the interposition of the angel to make a happy ending; or the condemnation of Antonio to lose a pound of flesh, and his rescue by Portia at the last mo-

---

[1] Mary Wollstonecraft Shelley (1797–1851), wife of the poet Percy Bysshe Shelley, active in promoting rights of women, author of *Vindications of the Rights of Women* (1792), best known for her novel *Frankenstein* (1818).

[2] *The Second Mrs. Tanqueray* (1893) by Sir Arthur Wing Pinero (1855–1934).

ment,[3] have not completely lost their effect nowadays—though it has been much modified—through the obsolescence of sacrificial rites, belief in miracles, and the conception that a debtor's person belongs to his creditors. It is enough that we still have paternal love, death, malice, moneylenders, and the tragedies of criminal law. But when a play depends entirely on a social question—when the struggle in it is between man and a purely legal institution nothing can prolong its life beyond that of the institution. For example, Mr Grundy's *Slaves of the Ring,*[4] in which the tragedy is produced solely by the conflict between the individual and the institution of indissoluble marriage, will not survive a rational law of divorce, and actually fails even now to grip an English audience because the solution has by this time become so very obvious. And that irrepressibly popular play *It's Never Too Late to Mend*[5] will hardly survive our abominable criminal system. Thus we see that the drama which deals with the natural factors in human destiny, though not necessarily better than the drama which deals with the political factors, is likely to last longer.

It has been observed that the greatest dramatists shew a preference for the nonpolitical drama, the greatest dramas of all being almost elementarily natural. But so, though for a different reason, do the minor dramatists. The minor dramatist leads the literary life, and dwells in the world of imagination instead of in the world of politics, business, law, and the platform agitations by which social questions are ventilated. He therefore remains, as a rule, astonishingly ignorant of real life. He may be clever, imaginative, sympathetic, humorous, and observant of such manners as he has any clue to; but he has hardly any wit or knowledge of the world. Compare his work with that of Sheridan,[6] and you feel the deficiency at once. Indeed, you need not go so far as Sheridan: Mr Gilbert's *Trial by Jury*[7] is unique among the works of living English playwrights, solely because it, too, is the work of a wit and a man of the world. Incidentally, it answers the inquiry as to whether social questions make good theatrical material; for though it is pointless, and, in fact, unintelligible except as a satire on a social institution (the breach-of-promise suit), it is highly entertaining, and has made the fortune of the author and his musical collaborator. *The School for Scandal,*[8] the most popular of all modern comedies, is a dramatic sermon, just as *Never Too Late to Mend,* the most popular of modern melodramas, is a dramatic pamphlet: Charles Reade being another example of the distinction which the accomplished man of the world attains

---

[3] Shakespeare's *The Merchant of Venice* (1596–1598).

[4] *Slaves of the Ring* (1894) by Sydney Grundy (1848–1914).

[5] By Charles Reade (1814–1884), based on his own novel of the same name (1853).

[6] Richard Brinsley Sheridan (1751–1816).

[7] *Trial by Jury* (1875) by W. S. Gilbert (1836–1911).

[8] (1777) by Sheridan.

in the theatre as compared to the mere professional dramatist. In fact, it is so apparent that the best and most popular plays are dramatized sermons, pamphlets, satires, or bluebooks, that we find our popular authors, even when they have made a safe position for themselves by their success in purely imaginative drama, bidding for the laurels and the percentages of the sociologist dramatist. Mr Henry Arthur Jones takes a position as the author of *The Middleman* and *The Crusaders*, which *The Silver King*,[9] enormously popular as it was, never could have gained him; and Mr Pinero, the author of *The Second Mrs. Tanqueray* and *The Notorious Mrs. Ebbsmith*,[10] is a much more important person, and a much richer one, than the author of *Sweet Lavender*.[11] Of course, the sociology in some of these dramas is as imaginary as the names and addresses of the characters; but the imitation sociology testifies to the attractiveness of the real article.

We may take it then that the ordinary dramatist only neglects social questions because he knows nothing about them, and that he loses in popularity, standing, and money by his ignorance. With the great dramatic poet it is otherwise. Shakespear and Goethe do not belong to the order which "takes no interest in politics." Such minds devour everything with a keen appetite—fiction, science, gossip, politics, technical processes, sport, everything. Shakespear is full of little lectures of the concrete English kind, from Cassio on temperance to Hamlet on suicide. Goethe, in his German way, is always discussing metaphysical points. To master Wagner's music dramas is to learn a philosophy. It was so with all the great men until the present century. They swallowed all the discussions, all the social questions, all the topics, all the fads, all the enthusiasms, all the fashions of their day in their nonage; but their theme finally was not this social question or that social question, this reform or that reform, but humanity as a whole. To this day your great dramatic poet is never a socialist, nor an individualist, nor a positivist, nor a materialist, nor any other sort of "ist," though he comprehends all the "isms," and is generally quoted and claimed by all the sections as an adherent. Social questions are too sectional, too topical, too temporal to move a man to the mighty effort which is needed to produce great poetry. Prison reform may nerve Charles Reade to produce an effective and businesslike prose melodrama; but it could never produce *Hamlet, Faust,* or *Peer Gynt.*

It must, however, be borne in mind that the huge size of modern populations and the development of the press make every social question more momentous than it was formerly. Only a very small percentage of the population commits murder; but the population is so large that the frequency

9 *The Middleman* (1889), *The Crusaders* (1891), and *The Silver King* (1882) by Henry Arthur Jones (1851–1929).
10 (1895).
11 (1888) by Pinero.

of executions is appalling. Cases which might have come under Goethe's notice in Weimar perhaps once in ten years come daily under the notice of modern newspapers, and are described by them as sensationally as possible. We are therefore witnessing a steady intensification in the hold of social questions on the larger poetic imagination. *Les Misérables*,[12] with its rivulet of story running through a continent of essays on all sorts of questions, from religion to main drainage, is a literary product peculiar to the nineteenth century: it shows how matters which were trifles to Aeschylus become stupendously impressive when they are multiplied by a million in a modern civilized state. Zola's novels are the product of an imagination driven crazy by a colossal police intelligence, by modern hospitals and surgery, by modern war correspondence, and even by the railway system—for in one of his books the hero is Jack the Ripper and his sweetheart a locomotive engine. What would Aristophanes have said to a city with fifteen thousand lunatics in it? Might he not possibly have devoted a comedy to the object of procuring some amelioration in their treatment? At all events, we find Ibsen, after producing, in *Brand, Peer Gynt*, and *Emperor and Galilean*,[13] dramatic poems on the grandest scale, deliberately turning to comparatively prosaic topical plays on the most obviously transitory social questions, finding in their immense magnitude under modern conditions the stimulus which, a hundred years ago, or four thousand, he would only have received from the eternal strife of man with his own spirit. *A Doll's House* will be as flat as ditchwater when *A Midsummer Night's Dream*[14] will still be as fresh as paint; but it will have done more work in the world; and that is enough for the highest genius, which is always intensely utilitarian. . . .

I need not elaborate the matter further. The conclusions to be drawn are:

1. Every social question, arising as it must from a conflict between human feeling and circumstances, affords material for drama.

2. The general preference of dramatists for subjects in which the conflict is between man and his apparently inevitable and eternal rather than his political and temporal circumstances, is due in the vast majority of cases to the dramatist's political ignorance (not to mention that of his audience), and in a few to the comprehensiveness of his philosophy.

3. The hugeness and complexity of modern civilizations and the development of our consciousness of them by means of the press, have the double effect of discrediting comprehensive philosophies by revealing more facts than the ablest man can generalize, and at the same time intensify the urgency of social reforms sufficiently to set even the poetic faculty in action on their behalf.

[12] (1862), novel by Victor Hugo.
[13] Respectively (1865), (1867), (1864–1873).
[14] Respectively: (1879), (1595–1596).

4. The resultant tendency to drive social questions on to the stage, and into fiction and poetry, will eventually be counteracted by improvements in social organization, which will enable all prosaic social questions to be dealt with satisfactorily long before they become grave enough to absorb the energies which claim the devotion of the dramatist, the storyteller, and the poet.

Preface to
Three Plays by Brieux [1] *1909*

Commercially, the classic play was supplanted by a nuisance which was not a failure: to wit, the "well-made play" of Scribe[2] and his school. The manufacture of well-made plays is not an art: it is an industry. It is not at all hard for a literary mechanic to acquire it: the only difficulty is to find a literary mechanic who is not by nature too much of an artist for the job; for nothing spoils a well-made play more infallibly than the least alloy of high art or the least qualm of conscience on the part of the writer. "Art for art's sake" is the formula of the well-made play, meaning in practice "Success for money's sake." Now great art is never produced for its own sake. It is too difficult to be worth the effort. All the great artists enter into a terrible struggle with the public, often involving bitter poverty and personal humiliation, and always involving calumny and persecution, because they believe they are apostles doing what used to be called the Will of God, and is now called by many prosaic names, of which "public work" is the least controversial. And when these artists have travailed and brought forth, and at last forced the public to associate keen pleasure and deep interest with their methods and morals, a crowd of smaller men—art confectioners, we may call them—hasten to make pretty entertainments out of scraps and crumbs from the masterpieces. Offenbach laid hands on Beethoven's Seventh

Selections. From *Three Plays by Brieux*. New York: Brentano's, 1911. Printed by permission of The Society of Authors on behalf of the Bernard Shaw Estate.

[1] Eugène Brieux (1858–1932).
[2] Eugène Scribe (1791–1861).

Symphony and produced *J'aime les militaires,* to the disgust of Schumann, who was nevertheless doing precisely the same thing in a more pretentious way. And these confectioners are by no means mere plagiarists. They bring all sorts of engaging qualities to their work: love of beauty, desire to give pleasure, tenderness, humor, everything except the high republican conscience, the identification of the artist's purpose with the purpose of the universe, which alone makes an artist great.

But the well-made play was not confectionery: it had not even the derived virtue of being borrowed from the great playwrights. Its formula grew up in the days when the spread of elementary schooling produced a huge mass of playgoers sufficiently educated to want plays instead of dog-fights, but not educated enough to enjoy or understand the masterpieces of dramatic art. Besides, education or no education, one cannot live on masterpieces alone, not only because there are not enough of them, but because new plays as well as great plays are needed, and there are not enough Molières and Shakespears in the world to keep the demand for novelty satisfied. Hence it has always been necessary to have some formula by which men of mediocre talent and no conscience can turn out plays for the theatrical market. Such men have written melodramas since the theatre existed. It was in the nineteenth century that the demand for manufactured plays was extended to drawing room plays in which the Forest of Bondy and the Auberge des Adrets, the Red Barn and the Cave at Midnight, had to be replaced by Lord Blank's flat in Whitehall Court and the Great Hall, Chevy Chace. Playgoers, being by that time mostly poor playgoers, wanted to see how the rich live; wanted to see them actually drinking champagne and wearing real fashionable dresses and trousers with a neatly ironed crease down the knee.

How to Write a Popular Play

The formula for the well-made play is so easy that I give it for the benefit of any reader who feels tempted to try his hand at making the fortune that awaits all successful manufacturers in this line. First, you "have an idea" for a dramatic situation. If it strikes you as a splendidly original idea, whilst it is in fact as old as the hills, so much the better. For instance, the situation of an innocent person convicted by circumstances of a crime may always be depended on. If the person is a woman, she must be convicted of adultery. If a young officer, he must be convicted of selling information to the enemy, though it is really a fascinating female spy who has ensnared him and stolen the incriminating document. If the innocent wife, banished from her home, suffers agonies through her separation from her children, and, when one of them is dying (of any disease the dramatist chooses to inflict), disguises herself as a nurse and attends it through its dying convulsion until the doctor, who should be a serio-comic character, and if possible a faithful old admirer of the lady's, simultaneously announces the recovery of the child and the discovery of the wife's innocence, the success of the play may be regarded as assured if the writer has any sort of knack for his work. Comedy is more difficult, because it requires a sense of humor and a good deal of vivacity; but the process is essentially the same: it is the manufacture of a misunderstanding. Having manufactured it, you place its culmination at the end of the last act but one, which is the point at which the manufacture of the play begins. Then you make your first act out of the necessary introduction of the characters to the audience, after elaborate explanations, mostly conducted by servants, solicitors, and other low-life personages (the principals must all be dukes and colonels and millionaires), of how the misunderstanding is going to come about. Your last act consists, of course, of clearing up the misunderstanding, and generally getting the audience out of the theatre as best you can. . . .

. . . No writer of the first order needs the formula any more than a sound man needs a crutch. In his simplest mood, when he is only seeking to amuse, he does not manufacture a plot: he tells a story. He finds no difficulty in setting people on the stage to talk and act in an amusing, exciting or touching way. His characters have adventures and ideas which are interesting in themselves, and need not be fitted into the Chinese puzzle of a plot.

The Interpreter of Life

But the great dramatist has something better to do than to amuse either himself or his audience. He has to interpret life. This sounds a mere pious phrase of literary criticism; but a moment's consideration will discover its meaning and its exactitude. Life as it appears to us in our daily experience is an unintelligible chaos of happenings. You pass Othello in the bazaar in Aleppo, Iago on the jetty in Cyprus, and Desdemona in the nave of St. Mark's in Venice without the slightest clue to their relations to one another. The man you see stepping into a chemist's shop to buy the means of committing murder or suicide, may, for all you know, want nothing but a liver pill or a toothbrush. The statesman who has no other object than to make you vote for his party at the next election, may be starting you on an incline at the foot of which lies war, revolution, or a smallpox epidemic, or five years off your lifetime. The horrible murder of a whole family by the father who finishes by killing himself, or the driving of a young girl on to the streets, may be the result of your discharging an employee in a fit of temper a month before. To attempt to understand life from merely looking on it as it happens in the streets is as hopeless as trying to understand public questions by studying snapshots of public demonstrations. If we possessed a series of cinematographs of all the executions during the Reign of Terror, they might be exhibited a thousand times without enlightening the audiences in the least as to the meaning of the Revolution: Robespierre would perish as "*un monsieur*" and Marie Antoinette as "*une femme.*" Life as it occurs is senseless: a policeman may watch it and work in it for thirty years in the streets and courts of Paris without learning as much of it or from it as a child or a nun may learn from a single play by Brieux. For it is the business of Brieux to pick out the significant incidents from the chaos of daily happenings, and arrange them so that their relation to one another becomes significant, thus changing us from bewildered spectators of a monstrous confusion to men intelligently conscious of the world and its destinies. This is the highest function that man can perform—the greatest work he can set his hand to; and this is why the great dramatists of the world, from Euripides and Aristophanes to Shakespear and Molière, and from them to Ibsen and Brieux, take that majestic and pontifical rank which seems so strangely above all the reasonable pretensions of mere strolling actors and theatrical authors.

The Technical Novelty in Ibsen's Plays   *1913*

It is a striking and melancholy example of the preoccupation of critics with phrases and formulas to which they have given life by taking them into the tissue of their own living minds, and which therefore seem and feel vital and important to them whilst they are to everybody else the deadest and dreariest rubbish (this is the great secret of academic dryasdust), that to this day they remain blind to a new technical factor in the art of popular stage-play making which every considerable playwright has been thrusting under their noses night after night for a whole generation. This technical factor in the play is the discussion. Formerly you had in what was called a well-made play an exposition in the first act, a situation in the second, and unraveling in the third. Now you have exposition, situation, and

From the second edition of *The Quintessence of Ibsenism*. From *Major Critical Essays*. London: Constable, 1948. Printed by permission of The Society of Authors on behalf of the Bernard Shaw Estate.

discussion; and the discussion is the test of the playwright. The critics protest in vain. They declare that discussions are not dramatic, and that art should not be didactic. Neither the playwrights nor the public take the smallest notice of them. The discussion conquered Europe in Ibsen's *Doll's House*; and now the serious playwright recognizes in the discussion not only the main test of his highest powers, but also the real centre of his play's interest. Sometimes he even takes every possible step to assure the public beforehand that his play will be fitted with that newest improvement.

This was inevitable if the drama was ever again to be raised above the childish demand for fables without morals. Children have a settled arbitrary morality: therefore to them moralizing is nothing but an intolerable platitudinizing. The morality of the grown-ups is also very largely a settled morality, either purely conventional and of no ethical significance, like the rule of the road or the rule that when you ask for a yard of ribbon the shopkeeper shall give you thirty-six inches and not interpret the word yard as he pleases, or else too obvious in its ethics to leave any room for discussion: for instance, that if the boots keeps you waiting too long for your shaving water you must not plunge your razor into his throat in your irritation, no matter how great an effort of self-control your forbearance may cost you.

Now when a play is only a story of how a villain tries to separate an honest young pair of betrothed lovers; to gain the hand of the woman by calumny; and to ruin the man by forgery, murder, false witness, and other commonplaces of the *Newgate Calendar*,[1] the introduction of a discussion would clearly be ridiculous. There is nothing for sane people to discuss; and any attempt to Chadbandize[2] on the wickedness of such crimes is at once resented as, in Milton's phrase, "moral babble."[3]

But this sort of drama is soon exhausted by people who go often to the theatre. In twenty visits one can see every possible change rung on all the available plots and incidents out of which plays of this kind can be manufactured. The illusion of reality is soon lost: in fact it may be doubted whether any adult ever entertains it: it is only to very young children that the fairy queen is anything but an actress. But at the age when we cease to mistake the figures on the stage for dramatis personae, and know that they are actors and actresses, the charm of the performer begins to assert itself; and the child who would have been cruelly hurt by being told that the Fairy Queen was only Miss Smith dressed up to look like one, becomes the man who goes to the theatre expressly to see Miss Smith, and is fascinated by her skill or beauty to the point of delighting in plays which would be unendurable to him without her. Thus we get plays "written round" popular performers,

---

[1] *The Newgate Calendar, or Malefactors' Bloody Register*, a series of sensationalized periodicals (eighteenth and nineteenth centuries), which listed notorious crimes.

[2] To be hypocritical; after Chadband, a character in Dickens's *Bleak House*.

[3] In *Comus* (1634), l. 807.

and popular performers who give value to otherwise useless plays by investing them with their own attractiveness. But all these enterprises are,
commercially speaking, desperately precarious. To begin with, the supply of
performers whose attraction is so far independent of the play that their
inclusion in the cast sometimes makes the difference between success and
failure is too small to enable all our theatres, or even many of them, to
depend on their actors rather than on their plays. And to finish with, no
actor can make bricks entirely without straw. From Grimaldi to Sothern,
Jefferson, and Henry Irving[4] (not to mention living actors) we have had
players succeeding once in a lifetime in grafting on to a play which would
have perished without them some figure imagined wholly by themselves; but
none of them has been able to repeat the feat, nor to save many of the plays
in which he has appeared from failure. In the long run nothing can
retain the interest of the playgoer after the theatre has lost its illusion for
his childhood, and its glamor for his adolescence, but a constant supply of interesting plays; and this is specially true in London, where the expense and
trouble of theatregoing have been raised to a point at which it is surprising
that sensible people of middle age go to the theatre at all. As a matter of
fact, they mostly stay at home.

Now an interesting play cannot in the nature of things mean anything
but a play in which problems of conduct and character of personal importance to the audience are raised and suggestively discussed. People have
a thrifty sense of taking away something from such plays: they not only have
had something for their money, but they retain that something as a permanent
possession. Consequently none of the commonplaces of the box office hold
good of such plays. In vain does the experienced acting manager declare
that people want to be amused and not preached at in the theatre; that
they will not stand long speeches; that a play must not contain more than
18,000 words; that it must not begin before nine nor last beyond eleven;
that there must be no politics and no religion in it; that breach of these
golden rules will drive people to the variety theatres; that there must be a
woman of bad character, played by a very attractive actress, in the piece;
and so on and so forth. All these counsels are valid for plays in which
there is nothing to discuss. They may be disregarded by the playwright who
is a moralist and a debater as well as a dramatist. From him, within the
inevitable limits set by the clock and by the physical endurance of the
human frame, people will stand anything as soon as they are matured
enough and cultivated enough to be susceptible to the appeal of his particular form of art. The difficulty at present is that mature and cultivated
people do not go to the theatre, just as they do not read penny novelets;

---

[4] Joseph Grimaldi (1778–1837), E. A. Sothern (1826–1881), Joseph Jefferson (1829–
1905), Henry Irving (1838–1905).

and when an attempt is made to cater for them they do not respond to it in time, partly because they have not the habit of playgoing, and partly because it takes too long for them to find out that the new theatre is not like all the other theatres. But when they do at last find their way there, the attraction is not the firing of blank cartridges at one another by actors, nor the pretence of falling down dead that ends the stage combat, nor the simulation of erotic thrills by a pair of stage lovers, nor any of the other tomfooleries called action, but the exhibition and discussion of the character and conduct of stage figures who are made to appear real by the art of the playwright and the performers.

This, then, is the extension of the old dramatic form effected by Ibsen. Up to a certain point in the last act, *A Doll's House* is a play that might be turned into a very ordinary French drama by the excision of a few lines, and the substitution of a sentimental happy ending for the famous last scene: indeed the very first thing the theatrical wiseacres did with it was to effect exactly this transformation, with the result that the play thus pithed had no success and attracted no notice worth mentioning. But at just that point in the last act, the heroine very unexpectedly (by the wise-acres) stops her emotional acting and says: "We must sit down and discuss all this that has been happening between us." And it was by this new technical feature: this addition of a new movement, as musicians would say, to the dramatic form, that *A Doll's House* conquered Europe and founded a new school of dramatic art.

Since that time the discussion has expanded far beyond the limits of the last ten minutes of an otherwise "well-made" play. The disadvantage of putting the decision at the end was not only that it came when the audience was fatigued, but that it was necessary to see the play over again, so as to follow the earlier acts in the light of the final discussion, before it became fully intelligible. The practical utility of this book is due to the fact that unless the spectator at an Ibsen play has read the pages referring to it beforehand, it is hardly possible for him to get its bearings at a first hearing if he approaches it, as most spectators still do, with conventional idealist prepossessions. Accordingly, we now have plays, including some of my own, which begin with discussion and end with action, and others in which the discussion interpenetrates the action from beginning to end. When Ibsen invaded England discussion had vanished from the stage; and women could not write plays. Within twenty years women were writing better plays than men; and these plays were passionate arguments from beginning to end. The action of such plays consists of a case to be argued. If the case is uninteresting or stale or badly conducted or obviously trumped up, the play is a bad one. If it is important and novel and convincing, or at least disturbing, the play is a good one. But anyhow the play in which there is no argument and no case no longer counts as serious drama. It may still please the child in us as Punch and Judy does, but nobody nowadays pretends to regard the well-made play as anything more than a commercial product which is not in question when modern schools of serious drama are under discussion. Indeed within ten years of the production of A *Doll's House* in London, audiences had become so derisive of the more obvious and hackneyed features of the methods of Sardou[5] that it became dangerous to resort to them; and playwrights who persisted in "constructing" plays in the old French manner lost ground not for lack of ideas, but because their technique was unbearably out of fashion.

In the new plays, the drama arises through a conflict of unsettled ideas rather than through vulgar attachments, rapacities, generosities, resentments, ambitions, misunderstandings, oddities and so forth as to which no moral question is raised. The conflict is not between clear right and wrong: the villain is as conscientious as the hero, if not more so: in fact, the question which makes the play interesting (when it *is* interesting) is which is the villain and which the hero. Or, to put it another way, there are no villains and no heroes. This strikes the critics mainly as departure from dramatic art; but it is really the inevitable return to nature which ends all the merely technical fashions. Now the natural is mainly the everyday; and its climaxes must be, if not everyday, at least everylife, if they are to have any importance for the spectator. Crimes, fights, big legacies, fires, shipwrecks, battles, and thunderbolts are mistakes in a play, even when they can be effectively simulated. No doubt they may acquire dramatic interest by putting a character through the test of an emergency; but the test is likely to be too obviously theatrical, because, as the playwright cannot in the nature of things have much experience of such catastrophes, he is forced to substitute a set of conventions or conjectures for the feelings they really produce.

In short, pure accidents are not dramatic: they are only anecdotic. They may be sensational, impressive, provocative, ruinous, curious, or a dozen other things; but they have no specifically dramatic interest. There is no drama in being knocked down or run over. The catastrophe in *Hamlet* would not be in the least dramatic had Polonius fallen downstairs and broken his neck, Claudius succumbed to delirium tremens, Hamlet forgotten to breathe in the intensity of his philosophic speculation, Ophelia died of Danish measles, Laertes been shot by the palace sentry, and Rosencrantz and Guildenstern drowned in the North Sea. Even as it is, the Queen, who poisons herself by accident, has an air of being polished off to get her out of the way: her death is the one dramatic failure of the piece. Bushels of good paper have been inked in vain by writers who imagined they could produce a tragedy by killing everyone in the last act accidentally. As a

---

[5] Victorien Sardou (1831–1908), who succeeded Eugène Scribe (1791–1861) as France's foremost writer of the well-made play.

matter of fact no accident, however sanguinary, can produce a moment of real drama, though a difference of opinion between husband and wife as to living in town or country might be the beginning of an appalling tragedy or a capital comedy.

It may be said that everything is an accident: that Othello's character is an accident, Iago's character another accident, and the fact that they happened to come together in the Venetian service an even more accidental accident. Also that Torvald Helmer might just as likely have married Mrs Nickelby as Nora. Granting this trifling for what it is worth, the fact remains that marriage is no more an accident than birth or death: that is, it is expected to happen to everybody. And if every man has a good deal of Torvald Helmer in him, and every woman a good deal of Nora,[6] neither their characters nor their meeting and marrying are accidents. *Othello*, though entertaining, pitiful, and resonant with the thrills a master of language can produce by mere artistic sonority is certainly much more accidental than *A Doll's House*; but it is correspondingly less important and interesting to us. It has been kept alive, not by its manufactured misunderstandings and stolen handkerchiefs and the like, nor even by its orchestral verse, but by its exhibition and discussion of human nature, marriage, and jealousy; and it would be a prodigiously better play if it were a serious discussion of the highly interesting problem of how a simple Moorish soldier would get on with a "supersubtle" Venetian lady of fashion if he married her. As it is, the play turns on a mistake; and though a mistake can produce a murder, which is the vulgar substitute for a tragedy, it cannot produce a real tragedy in the modern sense. Reflective people are not more interested in the Chamber of Horrors than in their own homes, nor in murderers, victims, and villains than in themselves; and the moment a man has acquired sufficient reflective power to cease gaping at waxworks, he is on his way to losing interest in Othello, Desdemona, and Iago exactly to the extent to which they become interesting to the police. Cassio's weakness for drink comes much nearer home to most of us than Othello's strangling and throat cutting, or Iago's theatrical confidence trick. The proof is that Shakespear's professional colleagues, who exploited all his sensational devices, and piled up torture on murder and incest on adultery until they had far out-Heroded Herod, are now unmemorable and unplayable. Shakespear survives because he cooly treated the sensational horrors of his borrowed plots as inorganic theatrical accessories, using them simply as pretexts for dramatizing human character as it exists in the normal world. In enjoying and discussing his plays we unconsciously discount the combats and murders: commentators are never so astray (and consequently so ingenious) as when they take Hamlet seriously as a madman, Macbeth as a homicidal High-

[6] Characters in Ibsen's *A Doll's House* (1879).

lander, and impish humorists like Richard and Iago as lurid villains of the Renascence. The plays in which these figures appear could be changed into comedies without altering a hair of their beards. Shakespear, had anyone been intelligent enough to tax him with this, would perhaps have said that most crimes are accidents that happen to people exactly like ourselves, and that Macbeth, under propitious circumstances, would have made an exemplary rector of Stratford, a real criminal being a defective monster, a human accident, useful on the stage only for minor parts such as Don Johns, second murderers, and the like. Anyhow, the fact remains that Shakespear survives by what he has in common with Ibsen, and not by what he has in common with Webster and the rest. Hamlet's surprise at finding that he "lacks gall" to behave in the idealistically conventional manner, and that no extremity of rhetoric about the duty of revenging "a dear father slain" and exterminating the "bloody bawdy villain" who murdered him seems to make any difference in their domestic relations in the palace in Elsinore, still keeps us talking about him and going to the theatre to listen to him, whilst the older Hamlets, who never had any Ibsenist hesitations, and shammed madness, and entangled the courtiers in the arras and burnt them, and stuck hard to the theatrical school of the fat boy in Pickwick ("I wants to make your flesh creep"),[7] are as dead as John Shakespear's mutton.

We have progressed so rapidly on this point under the impulse given to the drama by Ibsen that it seems strange now to contrast him favorably with Shakespear on the ground that he avoided the old catastrophes which left the stage strewn with the dead at the end of an Elizabethan tragedy. For perhaps the most plausible reproach leveled at Ibsen by modern critics of his own school is just that survival of the old school in him which makes the death rate so high in his last acts. Do Oswald Alving, Hedvig Ekdal, Rosmer and Rebecca, Hedda Gabler, Solness, Eyolf, Borkman, Rubeck and Irene[8] die dramatically natural deaths, or are they slaughtered in the classic and Shakespearean manner, partly because the audience expects blood for its money, partly because it is difficult to make people attend seriously to anything except by startling them with some violent calamity? It is so easy to make out a case for either view that I shall not argue the point. The post-Ibsen playwrights apparently think that Ibsen's homicides and suicides were forced. In Tchekov's *Cherry Orchard*,[9] for example, where the sentimental ideals of our amiable, cultured, Schumann playing propertied class are

---

[7] *The Pickwick Papers* (*The Posthumous Papers of the Pickwick Club*) by Charles Dickens.

[8] Characters in (respectively) the following plays of Ibsen: *Ghosts* (1881), *The Wild Duck* (1884), *Rosmersholm* (1886), *Hedda Gabler* (1890), *The Master Builder* (1892), *Little Eyolf* (1894), *John Gabriel Borkman* (1896), *When We Dead Awaken* (1899).

[9] (1904).

reduced to dust and ashes by a hand not less deadly than Ibsen's because it is so much more caressing, nothing more violent happens than that the family cannot afford to keep up its old house. In Granville-Barker's[10] plays, the campaign against our society is carried on with all Ibsen's implacability; but the one suicide (in **W***aste*) is unhistorical; for neither Parnell nor Dilke, who were the actual cases in point of the waste which was the subject of the play, killed himself. I myself have been reproached because the characters in my plays "talk but do nothing," meaning that they do not commit felonies. As a matter of fact we have come to see that it is no true dénouement to cut the Gordian knot as Alexander did with a stroke of the sword. If people's souls are tied up by law and public opinion it is much more tragic to leave them to wither in these bonds than to end their misery and relieve the salutary compunction of the audience by outbreaks of violence. Judge Brack[11] was, on the whole, right when he said that people dont do such things. If they did, the idealists would be brought to their senses very quickly indeed.

But in Ibsen's play the catastrophe, even when it seems forced, and when the ending of the play would be more tragic without it, is never an accident; and the play never exists for its sake. His nearest to an accident is the death of little Eyolf, who falls off a pier and is drowned. But this instance only reminds us that there is one good dramatic use for an accident: it can awaken people. When England wept over the deaths of little Nell and Paul Dombey,[12] the strong soul of Ruskin[13] was moved to scorn: to novelists who were at a loss to make their books sell he offered the formula: When at a loss, kill a child. But Ibsen did not kill little Eyolf to manufacture pathos. The surest way to achieve a thoroughly bad performance of Little Eyolf is to conceive it is a sentimental tale of a drowned darling. Its drama lies in the awakening of Allmers and his wife to the despicable quality and detestable rancors of the life they had been idealizing as blissful and poetic. They are so sunk in their dream that the awakening can be effected only by a violent shock. And that is just the one dramatically useful thing an accident can do. It can shock. Hence the accident that befalls Eyolf.

As to the deaths in Ibsen's last acts, they are a sweeping up of the remains of dramatically finished people. Solness's fall from the tower is as obviously symbolic as Phaeton's fall from the chariot of the sun. Ibsen's dead bodies are those of the exhausted or destroyed: he does not kill Hilda, for instance, as Shakespear killed Juliet. He is ruthless enough with Hedvig and Eyolf because he wants to use their deaths to expose their parents; but if he had written *Hamlet* nobody would have been killed in the last act

[10] Harley Granville-Barker (1877–1946), English actor, director, playwright, and critic.
[11] Ibsen's *Hedda Gabler*.
[12] Dickens's *The Old Curiosity Shop* and *Dombey and Son*.
[13] John Ruskin (1819–1900).

except perhaps Horatio, whose correct nullity might have provoked Fortinbras to let some of the moral sawdust out of him with his sword. For Shakespearean deaths in Ibsen you must go back to *Lady Inger* and the plays of his nonage, with which this book is not concerned.

The drama was born of old from the union of two desires: the desire to have a dance and the desire to hear a story. The dance became a rant: the story became a situation. When Ibsen began to make plays, the art of the dramatist had shrunk into the art of contriving a situation. And it was held that the stranger the situation, the better the play. Ibsen saw that, on the contrary, the more familiar the situation, the more interesting the play. Shakespear had put ourselves on the stage but not our situations. Our uncles seldom murder fathers, and cannot legally marry our mothers; we do not meet witches; our kings are not as a rule stabbed and succeeded by their stabbers; and when we raise money by bills we do not promise to pay pounds of our flesh. Ibsen suplies the want left by Shakespear. He gives us not only ourselves, but ourselves in our own situations. The things that happen to his stage figures are things that happen to us. One consequence is that his plays are much more important to us than Shakespear's. Another is that they are capable both of hurting us cruelly and of filling us with excited hopes of escape from idealistic tyrannies, and with visions of intenser life in the future.

Changes in technique follow inevitably from these changes in the subject matter of the play. When a dramatic poet can give you hopes and visions, such old maxims as that stage-craft is the art of preparation become boyish, and may be left to those unfortunate playwrights who, being unable to make anything really interesting happen on the stage, have to acquire the art of continually persuading the audience that it is going to happen presently. When he can stab people to the heart by shewing them the meanness or cruelty of something they did yesterday and intend to do tomorrow, all the old tricks to catch and hold their attention become the silliest of superfluities. The play called *The Murder of Gonzago*, which Hamlet makes the players act before his uncle, is artlessly constructed; but it produces a greater effect on Claudius than the Oedipus of Sophocles, because it is about himself. The writer who practises the art of Ibsen therefore discards all the old tricks of preparation, catastrophe, dénouement, and so forth without thinking about it, just as a modern rifleman never dreams of providing himself with powder horns, percussion caps, and wads: indeed he does not know the use of them. Ibsen substituted a terrible art of sharpshooting at the audience, trapping them, fencing with them, aiming always at the sorest spot in their consciences. Never mislead an audience, was an old rule. But the new school will trick the spectator into forming a meanly false judgment, and then convict him of it in the next act, often to his grievous mortification. When you despise something you ought to take off your hat to, or admire and imitate something you ought to loathe, you cannot resist the dramatist who knows how to touch these morbid spots in you and make you see that they are morbid. The dramatist knows that as long as he is teaching and saving his audience, he is as sure of their strained attention as a dentist is, or the Angel of the Annunciation. And though he may use all the magic of art to make you forget the pain he causes you or to enhance the joy of the hope and courage he awakens, he is never occupied in the old work of manufacturing interest and expectation with materials that have neither novelty, significance, nor relevance to the experience or prospects of the spectators.

Hence a cry has arisen that the post-Ibsen play is not a play, and that its technique, not being the technique described by Aristotle, is not a technique at all. I will not enlarge on this: the fun poked at my friend Mr A. B. Walkley[14] in the prologue of *Fanny's First Play*[15] need not be repeated here. But I may remind him that the new technique is new only on the modern stage. It has been used by preachers and orators ever since speech was invented. It is the technique of playing upon the human conscience; and it has been practised by the playwright whenever the playwright has been capable of it. Rhetoric, irony, argument, paradox, epigram, parable, the rearrangement of haphazard facts into orderly and intelligent situations: these are both the oldest and the newest arts of the drama; and your plot construction and art of preparation are only the tricks of theatrical talent and the shifts of moral sterility, not the weapons of dramatic genius. In the theatre of Ibsen we are not flattered spectators killing an idle hour with an ingenious and amusing entertainment: we are "guilty creatures sitting at a play"; and the technique of pastime is no more applicable than at a murder trial.

The technical novelties of the Ibsen and post-Ibsen plays are, then: first, the introduction of the discussion and its development until it so overspreads and interpenetrates the action that it finally assimilates it, making play and discussion practically identical; and, second, as a consequence of making the spectators themselves the persons of the drama, and the incidents of their own lives its incidents, the disuse of the old stage tricks by which audiences had to be induced to take an interest in unreal people and improbable circumstances, and the substitution of a forensic technique of recrimination, disillusion, and penetration through ideals to the truth, with a free use of all the rhetorical and lyrical arts of the orator, the preacher, the pleader, and the rhapsodist.

[14] Arthur Bingham Walkley (1855–1926).
[15] (1911) by Shaw.

On Cutting Shakespear *1919*

The moment you admit that the producer's business is to improve Shakespear by cutting out everything that he himself would not have written, and everything that he thinks the audience will either not like or not understand, and everything that does not make prosaic sense, you are launched on a slope on which there is no stopping until you reach the abyss where Irving's Lear lies forgotten. The reason stares us in the face. The producer's disapprovals, and consequently his cuts, are the symptoms of the differences between Shakespear and himself; and his assumption that all these differences are differences of superiority on his part and inferiority on Shakespear's, must end in the cutting down or raising up of Shakespear to his level. Tree[1] thought a third-rate ballet more interesting than the colloquy of Cassio with Iago on the subject of temperance. No doubt many people agreed with him. It was certainly more expensive. Irving, when he was producing *Cymbeline*, cut out of his own part the lines:

> 'Tis her breathing that
> Perfumes the chamber thus. The flame o' the taper
> Bows towards her, and would underpeep her lids
> To see the unclosed lights, now canopied
> Under those windows, white and azure, laced
> With blue of heaven's own tinct.

He was genuinely astonished when he was told that he must not do it, as the lines were the most famous for their beauty of all the purple patches in Shakespear. A glance at the passage will shew how very "sensible" his cut was. Mr Archer wants to cut, "O single-soled jest, solely singular for the singleness," because it is "absolutely meaningless." But think of all the other lines that must go with it on the same ground! The gayer side of Shakespear's poetic ecstasy expressed itself in word-dances of jingling nonsense which are, from the point of view of the grave Scots commentator who demands a meaning and a moral from every text, mere delirium and echolalia. But what would Shakespear be without them? "The spring time, the only merry ring time, when birds do sing hey ding a ding ding" is certainly not good sense nor even accurate ornithological observation! Who ever heard a bird sing "hey ding a ding ding" or anything even remotely resembling it? Out with it, then; and away, too, with such absurdities as Beatrice's obviously untrue statement that a star danced at her birth, which must revolt all the

Selections. From *Shaw on Theatre*, edited by E. J. West. New York: Hill & Wang, 1958. Printed by permission of The Society of Authors on behalf of the Bernard Shaw Estate.

[1] Sir Herbert Beerbohm Tree (1853–1917).

obstetricians and astronomers in the audience. As to Othello's fustian about the Propontick and the Hellespont, is this senseless hullabaloo of sonorous vowels and precipitate consonants to be retained when people have trains to catch? Mr Archer is credulous in imagining that in these orchestral passages the wit has evaporated and the meaning become inscrutable. There never was any meaning or wit in them in his sense any more than there is wit or meaning in the crash of Wagner's cymbals or the gallop of his trombones in the Valkyries' ride. The producer who has a head for syllogisms cuts such passages out. The producer who has an ear for music, like Mr Granville-Barker, breaks his heart in trying to get them adequately executed. . . .

. . . The people who really want Shakespear want all of him, and not merely Mr Archer's or anyone else's favorite bits; and this not in the least because they enjoy every word of it, but because they want to be sure of hearing the words they do enjoy, and because the effect of the judiciously selected passages, not to mention injudiciously selected passages, is not the same as that of the whole play, just as the effect of the currants picked out of a bun is not the same as that of the whole bun, indigestible as it may be to people who do not like buns.

There are plenty of modern instances to go upon. I have seen *Peer Gynt* most judiciously and practically cut by Lugné-Poë,[2] and *The Wild Duck* cut to the bone by Mr Archer. I have seen Wagner at full length at Bayreuth and Munich, and cut most sensibly at Covent Garden. I have actually seen *Il Trovatore*, most swift and concise of operas, cut by Sir Thomas Beecham.[3] My own plays, notoriously too long, have been cut with masterly skill by American managers. Mr Henry Arthur Jones made a capital acting version of *A Doll's House*, entitled *Breaking a Butterfly*. I do not allege that the result has always been disastrous failure, though it has sometimes gone that far. A hash makes a better meal than an empty plate. But I do aver without qualification that the mutilation has always been an offence, and the effect different and worse both in degree and in kind from the effect of a remorselessly faithful performance. Wagner's remark when he heard Rossini's *Barber of Seville* performed for once in its integrity in Turin applies to all the works of the great masters. You get something from such a performance that the selections never give you. And I suggest that this is not wholly a mystery. It occurs only when the work is produced under the direction of a manager who understands its value and can find in every passage the charm or the function which induced the author to write it, and who can dictate or suggest the method of execution that brings out that charm or discharges that function. Without this sense and this skill the

[2] Aurélien-Marie Lugné-Poë (1869–1940).
[3] (1879–1961).

manager will cut, cut, cut, every time he comes to a difficulty; and he will put the interest of the refreshment bars and the saving of electric light and the observance of the conventional hours of beginning the performance before his duty to the author, maintaining all the time that the manager who cuts most is the author's best friend.

In short, there are a thousand more sensible reasons for cutting not only Shakespear's plays, but all plays, all symphonies, all operas, all epics, and all pictures which are too large for the dining-room. And there is absolutely no reason on earth for not cutting them except the design of the author, who was probably too conceited to be a good judge of his own work.

The sane conclusion is therefore that cutting must be dogmatically ruled out, because, as Lao-Tse[4] said, "of the making of reforms there is no end." The simple thing to do with a Shakespear play is to perform it. The alternative is to let it alone. If Shakespear made a mess of it, it is not likely that Smith or Robinson will succeed where he failed.

William Butler Yeats 1865–1939

Windlestraws 1901

Let us learn construction from the masters, and dialogue from ourselves. A relation of mine has just written me a letter, in which he says: "It is natural to an Irishman to write plays, he has an inborn love of dialogue and sound about him, of a dialogue as lively, gallant, and passionate as in the times of great Eliza. In these days an Englishman's dialogue is that of an amateur, that is to say, it is never spontaneous. I mean in *real life*. Compare it with an Irishman's, above all a poor Irishman's, reckless abandonment and naturalness, or compare it with the only fragment that has come down to us of Shakespeare's own conversation." . . .

I have called this little collection of writings *Samhain*, the old name for the beginning of winter, because our plays this year are in October, and because our Theatre is coming to an end in its present shape.

Selections. From *Samhain* (October 1901).

4 (*C.* 600 B.C.)

Notes 1902–1903

The habit of writing for the stage, even when it is not country people who are the speakers, and of considering what good dialogue is, will help to increase our feeling for style. Let us get back in everything to the spoken word, even though we have to speak our lyrics to the Psaltery or the Harp, for, as A. E.[1] says, we have begun to forget that literature is but recorded speech, and even when we write with care we have begun "to write with elaboration what could never be spoken." But when we go back to speech let us see that it is either the idiom of those who have rejected, or of those who have never learned, the base idioms of the newspapers. . . .

. . . Our movement is a return to the people . . . and the drama of society would but magnify a condition of life which the countryman and the artist could but copy to their hurt. The play that is to give them a quite natural pleasure should either tell them of their own life, or of that life of poetry where every man can see his own image, because there alone does human nature escape from arbitrary conditions. Plays about drawing-rooms are written for the middle classes of great cities, for the classes who live in drawing-rooms, but if you would uplift the man of the roads you must write about the roads, or about the people of romance, or about great historical people. We should, of course, play every kind of good play about Ireland that we can get, but romantic and historical plays, and plays about the life of artisans and country people are the best worth getting. In time, I think, we can make the poetical play a living dramatic form again, and the training our actors will get from plays of country life, with its unchanging outline, its abundant speech, its extravagance of thought, will help to establish a school of imaginative acting. The play of society, on the other hand, could but train up realistic actors who would do badly, for the most part, what English actors do well, and would, when at all good, drift away to wealthy English theatres. If, on the other hand, we busy ourselves with poetry and the countryman, two things which have always mixed with one another in life as on the stage, we may recover, in the course of years, a lost art which, being an imitation of nothing English, may bring our actors a secure fame and a sufficient livelihood. . . .

. . . The play which is mere propaganda shows its leanness more obviously than a propagandist poem or essay, for dramatic writing is so full of the stuff of daily life that a little falsehood, put in that the moral may come right in the end, contradicts our experience.

Selections. From *Samhain* (October 1902 and September 1903).

[1] Pen name of George William Russell (1867–1935), Irish poet and painter.

The Reform of the Theatre   1903

I think the theatre must be reformed in its plays, its speaking, its acting, and its scenery. That is to say, I think there is nothing good about it at present.

First We have to write or find plays that will make the theatre a place of intellectual excitement—a place where the mind goes to be liberated as it was liberated by the theatres of Greece and England and France at certain great moments of their history, and as it is liberated in Scandinavia today. If we are to do this we must learn that beauty and truth are always justified of themselves, and that their creation is a greater service to our country than writing that comprises either in the seeming service of a cause. We will, doubtless, come more easily to truth and beauty because we love some cause with all but all our heart; but we must remember when truth and beauty open their mouths to speak, that all other mouths should be as silent as Finn bade the Son of Lugaidh be in the houses of the great. Truth and beauty judge and are above judgment. They justify and have no need of justification.

Such plays will require, both in writers and audiences, a stronger feeling for beautiful and appropriate language than one finds in the ordinary theatre. Sainte-Beuve[1] has said that there is nothing immortal in literature except style, and it is precisely this sense of style, once common among us, that is hardest for us to recover. I do not mean by style words with an air of literature about them, what is ordinarily called eloquent writing. The speeches of Falstaff are as perfect in their style as the soliloquies of Hamlet. One must be able to make a king of faery or an old countryman or a modern lover speak that language which is his and nobody else's, and speak it with so much of emotional subtlety that the hearer may find it hard to know whether it is the thought or the word that has moved him, or whether these could be separated at all.

If one does not know how to construct, if one cannot arrange much complicated life into a single action, one's work will not hold the attention or linger in the memory, but if one is not in love with words it will lack the delicate movement of living speech that is the chief garment of life; and because of this lack the great realists seem to the lovers of beautiful art to be wise in this generation, and for the next generation, perhaps, but not for all generations that are to come.

Selections. From *Samhain* (September 1903).

[1] Charles Augustin Sainte-Beuve (1804–1869), French critic.

Second But if we are to restore words to their sovereignty we must make speech even more important than gesture upon the stage. . . .

Third We must simplify acting, especially in poetical drama, and in prose drama that is remote from real life like my *Hour-Glass*. We must get rid of everything that is restless, everything that draws the attention away from the sound of the voice, or from the few moments of intense expression, whether that expression is through the voice or through the hands; we must from time to time substitute for the movements that the eye sees the nobler movements that the heart sees, the rhythmical movements that seem to flow up into the imagination from some deeper life than that of the individual soul.

Fourth Just as it is necessary to simplify gesture that it may accompany speech without being its rival, it is necessary to simplify both the form and colour of scenery and costume. As a rule the background should be but a single colour, so that the persons in the play, wherever they stand, may harmonize with it and preoccupy our attention. In other words, it should be thought out not as one thinks out a landscape, but as if it were the background of a portrait, and this is especially necessary on a small stage where the moment the stage is filled the painted forms of the background are broken up and lost. Even when one has to represent trees or hills they should be treated in most cases decoratively, they should be little more than an unobtrusive pattern. There must be nothing unnecessary, nothing that will distract the attention from speech and movement. An art is always at its greatest when it is most human. Greek acting was great because it did everything with the voice, and modern acting may be great when it does everything with voice and movement. But an art which smothers these things with bad painting, with innumerable garish colours, with continual restless mimicries of the surface of life, is an art of fading humanity, a decaying art.

First Principles *1904*

What attracts one to drama is that it is, in the most obvious way, what all the arts are upon a last analysis. A farce and a tragedy are alike in this that they are a moment of intense life. An action is taken out of all other actions; it is reduced to its simple form, or at any rate to as simple a form as it can be brought to without our losing the sense of its place in the world. The characters that are involved in it are freed from everything that is not a part of that action; and whether it is, as in the less important kinds of drama, a mere bodily activity, a hair-breadth escape or the like, or as it is in the more important kinds, an activity of the souls of the characters, it is an energy, an eddy of life purified from everything but itself. The dramatist must picture life in action, with an unpreoccupied mind, as the musician pictures her in sound and the sculptor in form.

But if this be true, has art nothing to do with moral judgments? Surely it has, and its judgments are those from which there is no appeal. The character, whose fortune we have been called in to see, or the personality of the writer, must keep our sympathy, and whether it be farce or tragedy, we must laugh and weep with him and call down blessings on his head. This character who delights us may commit murder like Macbeth, or fly the battle for his sweetheart as did Antony, or betray his country like Coriolanus, and yet we will rejoice in every happiness that comes to him and sorrow at his death as if it were our own. It is no use telling us that the murderer and the betrayer do not deserve our sympathy. We thought so yesterday, and we still know what crime is, but everything has been changed of a sudden; we are caught up into another code, we are in the presence of a higher court. Complain of us if you will, but it will be useless, for before the curtain falls a thousand ages, grown conscious in our sympathies, will have cried *Absolvo te.* Blame if you will the codes, the philosophies, the experiences of all past ages that have made us what we are, as the soil under our feet has been made out of unknown vegetations: quarrel with the acorns of Eden if you will, but what has that to do with us? We understand the verdict and not the law; and yet there is some law, some code, some judgment. If the poet's hand had slipped, if Antony had railed at Cleopatra in the tower, if Coriolanus had abated that high pride of his in the presence of death, we might have gone away muttering the Ten Commandments. Yet may be we are wrong to speak of judgment, for we have but contemplated life, and what more is there to say when she that is all virtue, the gift and the giver, the fountain whither all flows again, has given all herself? If the

Selections. From *Samhain* (December 1904).

subject of drama or any other art, were a man himself, an eddy of momentary breath, we might desire the contemplation of perfect characters; but the subject of all art is passion, the flame of life itself, and a passion can only be contemplated when separated by itself, purified of all but itself, and aroused into a perfect intensity by opposition with some other passion, or it may be with the law, that is the expression of the whole whether of Church or Nation or external nature. Had Coriolanus not been a law-breaker neither he nor we had ever discovered, it may be, that noble pride of his, and if we had not seen Cleopatra through the eyes of so many lovers, would we have known that soul of hers to be all flame, and wept at the quenching of it? If we were not certain of law we would not feel the struggle, the drama, but the subject of art is not law, which is a kind of death, but the praise of life, and it has no commandments that are not positive.

But if literature does not draw its substance from history, or anything about us in the world, what is a National literature[?] Our friends have already told us, writers for the Theatre in Abbey Street, that we have no right to the name, some because we do not write in Irish, and others because we do not plead the National cause in our plays, as if we were writers for the newspapers. I have not asked my fellow-workers what they mean by the words National literature, but though I have no great love for definitions, I would define it in some such way as this: It is the work of writers, who are moulded by influences that are moulding their country, and who write out of so deep a life that they are accepted there in the end. It leaves a good deal unsettled—was Rosetti[1] an Englishman, or Swift[2] an Irishman?—but it covers more kinds of National literature than any other I can think of. If one says a National literature must be in the language of the country, there are many difficulies. Should it be written in the language that one's country does speak or the language that it ought to speak? Was Milton an Englishman when he wrote in Latin or Italian, and had we no part in Columbanus[3] when he wrote in Latin the beautiful sermon comparing life to a highway and to a smoke? And then there is Beckford,[4] who is in every history of English litereaure, and yet his one memorable book, a story of Persia, was written in French. . . .

I mean by deep life that men must put into their writing the emotions and experiences that have been most important to themselves. If they say, "I will write of Irish country people and make them charming and picturesque like those dear peasants my great grandmother used to put in the foreground of her water-colour paintings," then they had better be satisfied with the

[1] Dante Gabriel Rossetti (1828–1882).
[2] Jonathan Swift (1667–1745).
[3] St. Columban (543–615), who was indicted in 603 by a synod of French bishops for keeping Easter according to Celtic usage.
[4] William Beckford (1760–1844). The book referred to is a novel, *Vathek* (1782).

word "provincial." If one condescends to one's material, if it is only what a popular novelist would call local colour, it is certain that one's real soul is somewhere else. Mr. Synge, upon the other hand, who is able to express his own finest emotions in those curious ironical plays of his, where, for all that, by the illusion of admirable art, everyone seems to be thinking and feeling as only countrymen could think and feel, is truly a National writer, as Burns was when he wrote finely and as Burns was not when he wrote *Highland Mary* and *The Cotter's Saturday Night*.

A writer is not less National because he shows the influence of other countries and of the great writers of the world.

The Play, the Player, and the Scene *1904*

First Our plays must be literature or written in the spirit of literature. The modern theatre has died away to what it is because the writers have thought of their audiences instead of their subject. An old writer saw his hero, if it was a play of character; or some dominant passion, if it was a play of passion, like *Phèdre* or *Andromache*,[1] moving before him, living with a life he did not endeavour to control. The persons acted upon one another as they were bound by their natures to act, and the play was dramatic, not because he had sought out dramatic situations for their own sake, but because will broke itself upon will and passion upon passion. Then the imagination began to cool, the writer began to be less alive, to seek external aids, remembered situations, tricks of the theatre, that had proved themselves again and again. His persons no longer will have a particular character, but he knows that he can rely upon the incidents, and he feels himself fortunate when there is nothing in his play that has not succeeded a thousand times before the curtain has risen. . . . Falstaff gives one the sensation of reality,

Selections. From *Samhain* (December 1904).

[1] Both plays by Jean Racine.

and when one remembers the abundant vocabulary of a time when all but everything present to the mind was present to the senses, one imagines that his words were but little magnified from the words of such a man in real life. Language was still alive then, alive as it is in Gaelic today, as it is in English-speaking Ireland where the Schoolmaster or the newspaper has not corrupted it. I know that we are at the mere beginning, laboriously learning our craft, trying our hands in little plays for the most part, that we may not venture too boldly in our ignorance; but I never hear the vivid, picturesque, ever-varied language of Mr. Synge's persons without feeling that the great collaborateur has his finger in our business. May it not be that the only realistic play that will live as Shakespeare has lived, as Calderon has lived, as the Greeks have lived, will arise out of the common life, where language is as much alive as if it were new come out of Eden? After all, is not the greatest play not the play that gives the sensation of an external reality but the play in which there is the greatest abundance of life itself, of the reality that is in our minds? Is it possible to make a work of art, which needs every subtlety of expression if it is to reveal what hides itself continually, out of a dying, or at any rate a very ailing language? and all language but that of the poets and of the poor is already bed-ridden. We have, indeed, persiflage, the only speech of educated men that expresses a deliberate enjoyment of words: but persiflage is not a true language. It is impersonal; it is not in the midst but on the edge of life; it covers more character than it discovers: and yet, such as it is, all our comedies are made out of it.

What the ever-moving delicately moulded flesh is to human beauty, vivid musical words are to passion. Somebody has said that every nation begins with poetry and ends with algebra, and passion has always refused to express itself in algebraical terms. . . .

Second   If we are to make a drama of energy, of extravagance, of fantasy, of musical and noble speech, we shall need an appropriate stage management. Up to a generation or two ago, and to our own generation, here and there, lingered a method of acting and of stage-management, which had come down, losing much of its beauty and meaning on the way, from the days of Shakespeare. Long after England, under the influence of Garrick, began the movement towards Naturalism, this school had a great popularity in Ireland, where it was established at the Restoration by an actor who probably remembered the Shakespearean players. . . .

. . . An Irish critic has told us to study the stage management of Antoine,[2] but that is like telling a good Catholic to take his theology from Luther. Antoine, who described poetry as a way of saying nothing, has

[2] André Antoine (1858–1943), French realistic director, founder of the *Théâtre Libre*.

perfected naturalistic acting and carried the spirit of science into the theatre. Were we to study his methods, we might, indeed, have a far more perfect art than our own, a far more mature art, but it is better to fumble our way like children. We may grow up, for we have as good hopes as any other sturdy ragamuffin.

An actor must so understand how to discriminate cadence from cadence, and so cherish the musical lineaments of verse or prose, that he delights the ear with a continually varied music. . . .

If a song is brought into a play it does not matter to what school the musician belongs if every word, if every cadence, is as audible and expressive as if it were spoken. It must be good speech, and one must not listen to the musician if he promise to add meaning to the words with his notes, for one does not add meaning to the word "love" by putting four o's in the middle, or by subordinating it even slightly to a musical note. . . .

Third   We must have a new kind of scenic art. I have been the advocate of the poetry as against the actor, but I am the advocate of the actor as against the scenery. Ever since the last remnant of the old platform disappeared, and the proscenium grew into the frame of a picture, the actors have been turned into a picturesque group in the foreground of a meretricious landscape painting. The background should be of as little importance as the background of a portrait group, and it should, when possible, be of one colour or of one tint, that the persons on the stage, wherever they stand, may harmonise with it or contrast with it and preoccupy our attention. Their outline should be clear and not broken up into the outline of windows and wainscotting, or lost into the edges of colours. In a play which copies the surface of life in its dialogue one may, with this reservation, represent anything that can be represented successfully—a room, for instance—but a landscape painted in the ordinary way will always be meretricious and vulgar. It will always be an attempt to do something which cannot be done successfully except in easel painting, and the moment an actor stands near to your mountain, or your forest, one will perceive that he is standing against a flat surface. Illusion, therefore, is impossible, and should not be attempted. One should be content to suggest a scene upon a canvas, whose vertical flatness one accepts and uses, as the decorator of pottery accepts the roundness of a bowl or a jug. Having chosen the distance from naturalism, which will keep one's composition from competing with the illusion created by the actor, who belongs to a world with depth as well as height and breadth, one must keep this distance without flinching. The distance will vary according to the distance the playwright has chosen, and especially in poetry, which is more remote and idealistic than prose, one will insist on schemes of colour and simplicity of form, for every sign of deliberate order gives remoteness and ideality. But, whatever the distance be, one's treatment will always be more or less decorative. We can only find out the right decoration for the different types of play by experiment, but it will probably range between, on the one hand, woodlands made out of recurring pattern, or painted like old religious pictures upon gold background, and upon the other the comparative realism of a Japanese print. This decoration will not only give us a scenic art that will be a true art because peculiar to the stage, but it will give the imagination liberty, and without returning to the bareness of the Elizabethan stage. The poet cannot evoke a picture to the mind's eye if a second-rate painter has set his imagination of it before the bodily eye; but decoration and suggestion will accompany our moods, and turn our minds to mediation, and yet never become obtrusive or wearisome. The actor and the words put into his mouth are always the one thing that matters, and the scene should never be complete of itself, should never mean anything to the imagination until the actor is in front of it.

If one remembers that the movement of the actor, and the graduation and the colour of the lighting, are the two elements that distinguish the stage picture from an easel painting, one will not find it difficult to create an art of the stage ranking as a true fine art.

John Millington Synge *1871–1909*

Preface to
The Playboy of
the Western World *1907*

In writing *The Playboy of the Western World*, as in my other plays, I have used one or two words only that I have not heard among the country people of Ireland, or spoken in my own nursery before I could read the newspapers. A certain number of the phrases I employ I have heard also from herds and fishermen along the coast from Kerry to Mayo, or from beggar-women and ballad-singers nearer Dublin; and I am glad to acknowledge how much I owe to the folk-imagination of these fine people. Anyone who has lived in real intimacy with the Irish peasantry will know that the wildest sayings and ideas in this play are tame indeed, compared with the fancies one may hear in any little hillside cabin in Geesala, or Carraroe, or Dingle Bay. All art is a collaboration; and there is little doubt that in the happy ages of literature, striking and beautiful phrases were as ready to the story-teller's or the playwright's hand, as the rich cloaks and dresses of his time. It is probable that when the Elizabethan dramatist took his ink-horn and sat down to his work he used many phrases that he had just heard, as he sat at dinner, from his mother or his children. In Ireland, those of us who know the people have the same privilege. When I was writing *The Shadow of the Glen*, some years ago, I got more aid than any learning could have given me from a chink in the floor of the old Wicklow house where I was staying, that let me hear what was being said by the servant girls in the kichen. This matter, I think, is of importance, for in countries where the imagination of the people, and the language they use, is rich and living, it is possible for a writer to be rich and copious in his words, and at the same time to give the reality, which is the root of all poetry, in a comprehensive and natural form. In the modern literature of towns, however, richness is found only in sonnets, or prose poems, or in one or two elaborate books that are far away from the profound and common interests of life. One has, on one side, Mallarmé[1] and Huysmans[2] producing this literature; and on the other, Ibsen and Zola dealing with the reality of life in joyless and pallid words. On the stage one must have reality, and one must have joy; and that is why the intellectual modern drama has failed, and people have grown sick of the false joy of the musical comedy, that has been given them in place of the rich joy found only in what is superb and wild in reality. In a good play every speech should be as fully flavoured as a nut or apple, and such speeches cannot be written by anyone who works among people who have shut their lips on poetry. In Ireland, for a few years more, we have a popular imagination that is fiery and magnificent, and tender; so that those of us who wish to write start with a chance that is not given to writers in places where the springtime of the local life has been forgotten, and the harvest is a memory only, and the straw has been turned into bricks.

---

[1] Stéphane Mallarmé (1842–1898), French poet.
[2] Charles Marie Georges (or Joris Karl) Huysmans (1848–1907), French novelist.

Preface to
The Tinker's Wedding   *1907*

The drama is made serious—in the French sense of the word—not by the degree in which it is taken up with problems that are serious in themselves, but by the degree in which it gives the nourishment, not very easy to define, on which our imaginations live. We should not go to the theatre as we go to a chemist's, or a dramshop, but as we go to dinner, where the food we need is taken with pleasure and excitement. This was nearly always so in Spain and England and France when the drama was at its richest— the infancy and decay of the drama tend to be didactic—but in these days the playhouse is too often stocked with the drugs of many seedy problems, or with the absinthe or vermouth of the last musical comedy.

The drama, like the symphony, does not teach or prove anything. Analysts with their problems, and teachers with their systems, are soon as old-fashioned as the pharmacopoeia of Galen—look at Ibsen and the Germans—but the best plays of Ben Jonson and Molière can no more go out of fashion than the blackberries on the hedges.

Of the things which nourish the imagination humour is one of the most needful, and it is dangerous to limit or destroy it. Baudelaire calls laughter the greatest sign of the Satanic element in man; and where a country loses its humour, as some towns in Ireland are doing, there will be morbidity of mind, as Baudelaire's mind was morbid.

In the greater part of Ireland, however, the whole people, from the tinkers to the clergy, have still a life, and view of life, that are rich and genial and humorous. I do not think that these country people who have so much humour themselves, will mind being laughed at without malice, as the people in every country have been laughed at in their own comedies.

Gilbert Murray *1866–1957*

Excursus on the Ritual Forms Preserved in Greek Tragedy *1912*

The following note presupposes certain general views about the origin and essential nature of Greek Tragedy. It assumes that Tragedy is in origin a Ritual Dance, a *Sacer Ludus*, representing normally the Aition, or supposed historical Cause, of some current ritual practice: e.g., the *Hippolytus* represents the legendary death of that hero, regarded as the Aition of a certain ritual lamentation practised by the maidens of Trozên. Further, it assumes, in accord with the overwhelming weight of ancient tradition, that the Dance in question is originally or centrally that of Dionysus; and it regards Dionysus, in this connection, as the spirit of the Dithyramb or Spring *Drômenon*, an "Eniautos-Daimon," who represents the cyclic death and rebirth of the world, including the rebirth of the tribe by the return of the heroes or dead ancestors. . . .

It is of course clear that Tragedy, as we possess it, contains many non-Dionysiac elements. The ancients themselves have warned us of that. It has been influenced by the epic, by hero cults, and by various ceremonies not connected with Dionysus. Indeed the actual Aition treated in tragedy is seldom confessedly and obviously Dionysiac. It is so sometimes, as sometimes it is the founding of a torch-race or the original reception of suppliants at some altar of sanctuary. But it is much more often the death or *Pathos* of some hero. Indeed I think it can be shown that every extant tragedy contains somewhere towards the end the celebration of a tabu tomb. . . . I wish to suggest, however, that while the content has strayed far from Dionysus, the forms of tragedy retain clear traces of the original drama of the Death and Rebirth of the Year Spirit. . . .

. . . If we examine the kind of myth which seems to underly the various "Eniautos" celebrations we shall find:

1. An *Agon* or Contest, the Year against its enemy, Light against Darkness, Summer against Winter.
2. A *Pathos* of the Year-Daimon, generally a ritual or sacrificial death, in which Adonis or Attis is slain by the tabu animal, the Pharmakos stoned,

Selections. From Jane Ellen Harrison, *Themis*. Cambridge: At the University Press, 1912. Printed by permission of Cambridge University Press.

Osiris, Dionysus, Pentheus, Orpheus, Hippolytus torn to pieces (σπαραγμός).

3. A *Messenger*. For this Pathos seems seldom or never to be actually performed under the eyes of the audience. (The reason of this is not hard to suggest.) It is announced by a messenger. "The news comes" that Pan the Great, Thammuz, Adonis, Osiris is dead, and the dead body is often brought in on a bier. This leads to

4. A *Threnos* or Lamentation. Specially characteristic, however, is a clash of contrary emotions, the death of the old being also the triumph of the new. . . .

5 and 6. An *Anagnorisis*—discovery or recognition—of the slain and mutilated Daimon, followed by his Resurrection or Apotheosis or, in some sense, his Epiphany in glory. This I shall call by the general name *Theophany*. It naturally goes with a *Peripeteia* or extreme change of feeling from grief to joy.

Observe the sequence in which these should normally occur: *Agon, Pathos, Messenger, Threnos, Theophany*, or, we might say, *Anagnorisis* and *Theophany*.

First, however, there is a difficulty to clear away. The Peripeteia which occurs in tragedy, as we have it, is not usually from grief to joy but, on the contrary, from joy to grief, which seems wrong. Our tragedies normally end with a comforting theophany but not with an outburst of joy. No, but it looks as if they once did. We know that they were in early times composed in tetralogies consisting of three tragedies and a Satyr-play.

William Archer   *1856–1924*

Play-Making   *1912*

It may be well, at this point, to consider for a little what we mean when we use the term "dramatic." We shall probably not arrive at any definition which can be applied as an infallible touchstone to distinguish the

Selections. From *Play-Making* by William Archer. Dover Publications, Inc., New York, 1960. Reprinted through the permission of the publisher.

dramatic from the undramatic. Perhaps, indeed, the upshot may rather be to place the student on his guard against troubling too much about the formal definitions of critical theories.

The orthodox opinion of the present time is that which is generally associated with the name of the late Ferdinand Brunetière. "The theatre in general," said that critic, "is nothing but the place for the development of the human will, attacking the obstacles opposed to it by destiny, fortune, or circumstances." And again: "Drama is a representation of the will of man in conflict with the mysterious powers or natural forces which limit and belittle us; it is one of us thrown living upon the stage, there to struggle against fatality, against social law, against one of his fellow-mortals, against himself, if need be, against the ambitions, the interests, the prejudices, the folly, the malevolence of those who surround him."[1]

The difficulty about this definition is that, while it describes the matter of a good many dramas, it does not lay down any true differentia—any characteristic common to all drama, and possessed by no other form of fiction. Many of the greatest plays in the world can with difficulty be brought under the formula, while the majority of romances and other stories come under it with ease. Where, for instance, is the struggle in the *Agamemnon*? There is no more struggle between Clytemnestra and Agamemnon than there is between the spider and the fly who walks into his net. There is not even a struggle in Clytemnestra's mind. Agamemnon's doom is sealed from the outset, and she merely carries out a prearranged plot. There is contest indeed in the succeeding plays of the trilogy; but it will scarcely be argued that the *Agamemnon*, taken alone, is not a great drama. Even the *Oedipus* of Sophocles, though it may at first sight seem a typical instance of a struggle against Destiny, does not really come under the definition. Oedipus, in fact, does not struggle at all. His struggles, in so far as that word can be applied to his misguided efforts to escape from the toils of fate, are all things of the past; in the actual course of the tragedy he simply writhes under one revelation after another of bygone error and unwitting crime. It would be a mere play upon words to recognize as a dramatic "struggle" the writhing of a worm on a hook. And does not this description apply very closely to the part played by another great protagonist—Othello to wit? There is no struggle, no conflict, between him and Iago. It is Iago alone who exerts any will; neither Othello nor Desdemona makes the smallest fight. From the moment when Iago sets his machination to work, they are like people sliding down an ice-slope to an inevitable abyss. Where is the conflict in *As You Like It*? No one, surely, will pretend that any part of the interest or charm of the play arises from the struggle between the

---

[1] *Études Critiques*, Vol. VII, pp. 153 and 207 [Archer's note; see *The Law of the Drama*, pp. 721–726].

banished Duke and the Usurper, or between Orlando and Oliver. There is not even the conflict, if so it can be called, which nominally brings so many hundreds of plays under the Brunetière canon—the conflict between an eager lover and a more or less reluctant maid. Or take, again, Ibsen's *Ghosts*—in what valid sense can it be said that that tragedy shows us will struggling against obstacles? Oswald, doubtless, wishes to live, and his mother desires that he should live; but this mere will for life cannot be the differentia that makes of *Ghosts* a drama. If the reluctant descent of the "downward path to death" constituted drama, then Tolstoy's *Death of Ivan Ilytch* would be one of the greatest dramas ever written—which it certainly is not. Yet again, if we want to see will struggling against obstacles, the classic to turn to is not *Hamlet*, nor *Lear*, but *Robinson Crusoe*; yet no one, except a pantomine librettist, ever saw a drama in Defoe's narrative. In a Platonic dialogue, in *Paradise Lost*, in *John Gilpin*, there is a struggle of will against obstacles; there is none in *Hannele*, which, nevertheless, is a deeply moving drama. Such a struggle is characteristic of all great fiction, from *Clarissa Harlowe* to *The House with the Green Shutters*; whereas in many plays the struggle, if there be any at all, is the merest matter of form (for instance, a quite conventional love story), while the real interest resides in something quite different.

The plain truth seems to be that conflict is *one* of the most dramatic elements in life, and that many dramas—perhaps most—do, as a matter of fact, turn upon strife of one sort or another. But it is clearly an error to make conflict indispensable to drama, and especially to insist—as do some of Brunetière's followers—that the conflict must be between will and will. A stand-up fight between will and will—such a fight as occurs in, say, the *Hippolytus* of Euripides, or Racine's *Andromaque*, or Molière's *Tartuffe*, or Ibsen's *Pretenders*, or Dumas's *Françillon*, or Sudermann's *Heimat*, or Sir Arthur Pinero's *Gay Lord Quex*, or Mr. Shaw's *Candida*, or Mr. Galsworthy's *Strife*—such a stand-up fight, I say, is no doubt one of the intensest forms of drama. But it is comparatively rare, at any rate as the formula of a whole play. In individual scenes a conflict of will is frequent enough; but it is, after all, only one among a multitude of equally telling forms of drama. No one can say that the Balcony Scene in *Romeo and Juliet* is undramatic, or the "Galeoto fú il libro" scene in Mr. Stephen Phillips's *Paolo and Francesca*; yet the point of these scenes is not a clash, but an ecstatic concordance, of wills. Is the death-scene of Cleopatra undramatic? Or the Banquet scene in *Macbeth*? Or the pastoral act in *The Winter's Tale*? Yet in none of these is there any conflict of wills. In the whole range of drama there is scarcely a passage which one would call more specifically dramatic than the Screen Scene in *The School for Scandal*; yet it would be the veriest quibbling to argue that any appreciable part of its effect arises from the clash of will against will. This whole comedy, indeed, suffices to show the emptiness of the theory. With a little strain it is possible to bring it within the letter of the formula; but who can pretend that any considerable part of the attraction or interest of the play is due to that possibility? . . .

What, then, is the essence of drama, if conflict be not it? What is the common quality of themes, scenes, and incidents, which we recognize as specifically dramatic? Perhaps we shall scarcely come nearer to a helpful definition than if we say that the essence of drama is *crisis*. A play is a more or less rapidly developing crisis in destiny or circumstance, and a dramatic scene is a crisis within a crisis, clearly furthering the ultimate event. The drama may be called the art of crises, as fiction is the art of gradual developments. It is the slowness of its processes which differentiates the typical novel from the typical play. If the novelist does not take advantage of the facilities offered by his form for portraying gradual change, whether in the way of growth or of decay, he renounces his own birthright, in order to trespass on the domain of the dramatist. Most great novels embrace considerable segments of many lives; whereas the drama gives us only the culminating points—or shall we say the intersecting culminations?—[of] two or three destinies. Some novelists have excelled precisely in the art with which they have made the gradations of change in character or circumstance so delicate as to be imperceptible from page to page, and measurable, as in real life, only when we look back over a considerable period. The dramatist, on the other hand, deals in rapid and startling changes, the "peripeties," as the Greeks called them, which may be the outcome of long, slow processes, but which actually occur in very brief spaces of time. Nor is this a merely mechanical consequence of the narrow limits of stage presentation. The crisis is as real, though not as inevitable, a part of human experience as the gradual development. Even if the material conditions of the theatre permitted the presentation of a whole *Middlemarch* or *Anna Karénine*—as the conditions of the Chinese theatre actually do—some dramatists, we cannot doubt, would voluntarily renounce that license of prolixity, in order to cultivate an art of concentration and crisis. The Greek drama "subjected to the faithful eyes," as Horace phrases it, the culminating points of the Greek epic; the modern drama places under the lens of theatrical presentment the culminating points of modern experience.

But, manifestly, it is not every crisis that is dramatic. A serious illness, a lawsuit, a bankruptcy, even an ordinary prosaic marriage, may be a crisis in a man's life, without being necessarily, or even probably, material for drama. How, then, do we distinguish a dramatic from a nondramatic crisis? Generally, I think, by the fact that it develops, or can be made naturally to develop, through a series of minor crises, involving more or less emotional excitement, and, if possible, the vivid manifestation of character. . . .

In life there are no such things as beginnings. Even a man's birth is a quite arbitrary point at which to launch his biography; for the determining factors in his career are to be found in persons, events, and conditions that existed before he was ever thought of. For the biographer, however, and for the novelist as a writer of fictitious biography, birth forms a good conventional starting point. He can give a chapter or so to "Ancestry," and then relate the adventures of his hero from the cradle onwards. But the dramatist, as we have seen, deals, not with protracted sequences of events, but with short, sharp crises. The question for him, therefore, is: at what moment of the crisis, or of its antecedents, he had better ring up his curtain? At this point he is like the photographer studying his "finder" in order to determine how much of a given prospect he can "get in."

The answer to the question depends on many things, but chiefly on the nature of the crisis and the nature of the impression which the playwright desires to make upon his audience. If his play be a comedy, and if his object be gently and quietly to interest and entertain, the chances are that he begins by showing us his personages in their normal state, concisely indicates their characters, circumstances, and relations, and then lets the crisis develop from the outset before our eyes. If, on the other hand, his play be of a more stirring description, and he wants to seize the spectator's attention firmly from the start, he will probably go straight at his crisis, plunging, perhaps, into the very middle of it, even at the cost of having afterwards to go back in order to put the audience in possession of the antecedent circumstances. In a third type of play, common of late years, and especially affected by Ibsen, the curtain rises on a surface aspect of profound peace, which is presently found to be but a thin crust over an absolute volcanic condition of affairs, the origin of which has to be traced backwards, it may be for many years. . . .

I do not know whether it was Francisque Sarcey who invented the phrase *scène à faire*;[2] but it certainly owes its currency to that valiant champion of the theatrical theatre, if I may so express it. Note that in this term I intend no disrespect. . . .

An obligatory scene is one which the audience (more or less clearly and consciously) forsees and desires, and the absence of which it may with reason resent. On a rough analysis, it will appear, I think, that there are five ways in which a scene may become, in this sense, obligatory:

1. It may be necessitated by the inherent logic of the theme.
2. It may be demanded by the manifest exigencies of specifically dramatic effect.
3. The author himself may have rendered it obligatory by seeming unmistakably to lead up to it.

[2] Archer translates this as "obligatory scene" (see below).

4. It may be required in order to justify some modification of character or alteration of will, too important to be taken for granted.
5. It may be imposed by history or legend.

These five classes of obligatory scenes may be docketed, respectively, as the Logical, the Dramatic, the Structural, the Psychological, and the Historic. M. Sarcey[3] generally employed the term in one of the first three senses, without clearly distinguishing between them. It is, indeed, not always easy to determine whether the compulsion (assuming it to exist at all) lies in the very essence of the theme or situation, or only in the author's manipulation of it.

Was Sarcey right in assuming such a compulsion to be a constant and dominant factor in the playwright's craft? I think we shall see reason to believe him right in holding that it frequently arises, but wrong if he went the length of maintaining that there can be no good play without a definite *scène à faire*—as eighteenth-century landscape painters are said to have held that no one could be a master of his art till he knew where to place "the brown tree." I remember no passage in which Sarcey explicitly lays down so hard and fast a rule, but several in which he seems to take it for granted.

[3] Francisque Sarcey (1828–1899), in his *Theory of the Theatre* (1876).

Martin Esslin *1918–*

The Theatre
of the Absurd *1961*

The reception of *Waiting for Godot* at San Quentin,[1] and the wide acclaim given to plays by Ionesco, Adamov, Pinter,[2] and others, testify that these plays, which are so often superciliously dismissed as nonsense or mystification, *have* something to say and *can* be understood. Most of the in-

Selection. From Martin Esslin, *The Theatre of the Absurd*. Garden City, New York: Doubleday Anchor Books, 1969. Printed by permission of Doubleday & Co., Inc.

[1] Given by the San Francisco Actor's Workshop in 1957.
[2] Eugene Ionesco (1912–   ), Arthur Adamov (1908–   ), Harold Pinter (1930–   ).

comprehension with which plays of this type are still being received by critics and theatrical reviewers, most of the bewilderment they have caused and to which they still give rise, come from the fact that they are part of a new, and still developing stage convention that has not yet been generally understood and has hardly ever been defined. Inevitably, plays written in this new convention will, when judged by the standards and criteria of another, be regarded as impertinent and outrageous impostures. If a good play must have a cleverly constructed story, these have no story or plot to speak of; if a good play is judged by subtlety of characterization and motivation, these are often without recognizable characters and present the audience with almost mechanical puppets; if a good play has to have a fully explained theme, which is neatly exposed and finally solved, these often have neither a beginning nor an end; if a good play is to hold the mirror up to nature and portray the manners and mannerisms of the age in finely observed sketches, these seem often to be reflections of dreams and nightmares; if a good play relies on witty repartee and pointed dialogue, these often consist of incoherent babblings.

But the plays we are concerned with here pursue ends quite different from those of the conventional play and therefore use quite different methods. They can be judged only by the standards of the Theatre of the Absurd, which it is the purpose of his book to define and clarify.

It must be stressed, however, that the dramatists whose work is here discussed do not form part of any self-proclaimed or self-conscious school or movement. On the contrary, each of the writers in question is an individual who regards himself as a lone outsider, cut off and isolated in his private world. Each has his own personal approach to both subject-matter and form; his own roots, sources, and background. If they also, very clearly and in spite of themselves, have a good deal in common, it is because their work most sensitively mirrors and reflects the preoccupations and anxieties, the emotions and thinking of many of their contemporaries in the Western world.

This is not to say that their works are representative of mass attitudes. It is an oversimplification to assume that any age presents a homogeneous pattern. Ours being, more than most others, an age of transition, it displays a bewildering stratified picture: medieval beliefs still held and overlaid by eighteenth-century rationalism and mid-nineteenth-century Marxism, rocked by sudden volcanic eruptions of prehistoric fanaticisms and primitive tribal cults. Each of these components of the cultural pattern of the age finds its own artistic expression. The Theatre of the Absurd, however, can be seen as the reflection of what seems to be the attitude most genuinely representative of our own time.

The hallmark of this attitude is its sense that the certitudes and unshakable basic assumptions of former ages have been swept away, that they have been tested and found wanting, that they have been discredited as cheap and somewhat childish illusions. The decline of religious faith was masked until the end of the Second World War by the substitute religions of faith in progress, nationalism, and various totalitarian fallacies. All this was shattered by the war. By 1942, Albert Camus[3] was calmly putting the question why, since life had lost all meaning, man should not seek escape in suicide. In one of the great, seminal heart-searchings of our time, *The Myth of Sisyphus*, Camus tried to diagnose the human situation in a world of shattered beliefs:

> A world that can be explained by reasoning, however faulty, is a familiar world. But in a universe that is suddenly deprived of illusions and of light, man feels a stranger. His is an irremediable exile, because he is deprived of memories of a lost homeland as much as he lacks the hope of a promised land to come. This divorce between man and his life, the actor and his setting, truly constitutes the feeling of Absurdity.[4]

"Absurd" originally means "out of harmony," in a musical context. Hence its dictionary definition: "out of harmony with reason or propriety; incongruous, unreasonable, illogical." In common usage, "absurd" may simply mean "ridiculous," but this is not the sense in which Camus uses the word, and in which it is used when we speak of the Theatre of the Absurd. In an essay on Kafka, Ionesco defined his understanding of the term as follows: "Absurd is that which is devoid of purpose. . . . Cut from his religious, metaphysical, and transcendental roots, man is lost; all his actions become senseless, absurd, useless."[5]

This sense of metaphysical anguish at the absurdity of the human condition is, broadly speaking, the theme of the plays of Beckett,[6] Adamov, Ionesco, Genet,[7] and the other writers discussed in this book. But it is not merely the subject matter that defines what is here called the Theatre of the Absurd. A similar sense of the senselessness of life, of the inevitable devaluation of ideals, purity, and purpose, is also the theme of much of the work of dramatists like Giraudoux, Anouilh, Salacrou, Sartre,[8] and Camus himself. Yet these writers differ from the dramatists of the Absurd in an important respect: they present their sense of the irrationality of the human condition in the form of highly lucid and logically constructed reasoning, while the Theatre of the Absurd strives to express its sense of the senseless-

---

[3] (1913–1960).

[4] Albert Camus, *Le Mythe de Sisyphe* (Paris: Gallimard, 1942), p. 18 [Esslin's note].

[5] Eugene Ionesco, "Dans les armes de la ville," *Cahiers de la Compagnie Madeleine Renaud-Jean-Louis Barrault*, Paris, no. 20, October 1957 [Esslin's note].

[6] Samuel Beckett (1906–   ).

[7] Jean Genet (1909–   ).

[8] Jean Giraudoux (1882–1944), Jean Anouilh (1910–   ), Armand Salacrou (1899–   ), Jean-Paul Sartre (1905–   ).

ness of the human condition and the inadequacy of the rational approach by the open abandonment of rational devices and discursive thought. While Sartre or Camus express the new content in the old convention, the Theatre of the Absurd goes a step further in trying to achieve a unity between its basic assumptions and the form in which these are expressed. In some senses, the *theatre* of Sartre and Camus is less adequate as an expression of the *philosophy* of Sartre and Camus—in artistic, as distinct from philosophic, terms—than the Theatre of the Absurd.

If Camus argued that in our disillusioned age the world has ceased to make sense, he did so in the elegantly rationalistic and discursive style of an eighteenth-century moralist, in well-constructed and polished plays. If Sartre argues that existence comes before essence and that human personality can be reduced to pure potentiality and the freedom to choose itself anew at any moment, he presents his ideas in plays based on brilliantly drawn characters who remain wholly consistent and thus reflect the old convention that each human being has a core of immutable, unchanging essence—in fact, an immortal soul. And the beautiful phrasing and argumentative brilliance of both Sartre and Camus in their relentless probing still, by implication, proclaim a tacit conviction that logical discourse can offer valid solutions, that the analysis of language will lead to the uncovering of basic concepts—Platonic ideas.

This is an inner contradiction that the dramatists of the Absurd are trying, by instinct and intuition rather than by conscious effort, to overcome and resolve. The Theatre of the Absurd has renounced arguing *about* the absurdity of the human condition; it merely *presents* it in being—that is, in terms of concrete stage images. This is the difference between the approach of the philosopher and that of the poet; the difference, to take an example from another sphere, between the *idea* of God in the works of Thomas Aquinas or Spinoza and the *intuition* of God in those of St. John of the Cross or Meister Eckhart—the difference between theory and experience.

It is this striving for an integration between the subject-matter and the form in which it is expressed that separates the Theatre of the Absurd from the Existentialist theatre.

It must also be distinguished from another important, and parallel, trend in the contemporary French theatre, which is equally preoccupied with the absurdity and uncertainty of the human condition: the "poetic avant-garde" theatre of dramatists like Michel de Ghelderode,[9] Jacques Audiberti,[10] Georges Neveux,[11] and, in the younger generation, Georges Schehadé,[12]

[9] (1898–1962).
[10] (1899–1965).
[11] (1900–   ).
[12] (1910–   ).

Henri Pichette,[13] and Jean Vauthier,[14] to name only some of its most important exponents. This is an even more difficult dividing line to draw, for the two approaches overlap a good deal. The "poetic avant-garde" relies on fantasy and dream reality as much as the Theatre of the Absurd does; it also disregards such traditional axioms as that of the basic unity and consistency of each character or the need for a plot. Yet basically the "poetic avant-garde" represents a different mood; it is more lyrical, and far less violent and grotesque. Even more important is its different attitude toward language: the "poetic avant-garde" relies to a far greater extent on consciously "poetic" speech; it aspires to plays that are in effect poems, images composed of a rich web of verbal associations.

The Theatre of the Absurd, on the other hand, tends toward a radical devaluation of language, toward a poetry that is to emerge from the concrete and objectified images of the stage itself. The element of language still plays an important part in this conception, but what *happens* on the stage transcends, and often contradicts, the *words* spoken by the characters. In Ionesco's *The Chairs*, for example, the poetic content of a powerfully poetic play does not lie in the banal words that are uttered but in the fact that they are spoken to an ever-growing number of empty chairs.

[13] (1923–   ).
[14] (1910–   ).

Nineteenth- and Twentieth-Century France, Italy, and Spain

Though aged, neoclassicism was far from dead at the start of the nineteenth century. Personifying the classical spirit as an old man and the romantic as a youth, Stendhal (Marie Henri Beyle) calls for an end to the type of play written for periwigged *marquis* and for new plays— expansive and Shakespearean—for "the young people of the year of grace 1823." Four years later, twenty-five-year-old Victor Hugo composed the Preface to *Cromwell*, which is at times as impassioned as (and a good deal livelier than) the lengthy play it introduces. "Let us take the hammer to their theories and systems," cries Hugo, who cites nature as the only lawmaker. Demanding that the restrictions of defunct classicism be abolished, Hugo hails freedom. True poetry, says he, "consists in the harmony of contraries," such as comedy and tragedy, the ugly and the beautiful, the misshapen and the graceful, the grotesque and the sublime. —all of which he would have, in defiance of neoclassical strictures, in the same play. In 1830, the premiere of his *Hernani*, in which he tried to practice what he preached, caused a riot in the theatre. The old guard lost to the new, who paved the way for greater realism.

Between 1823 (the year of Stendhal's essay) and 1900, according to N. C. Arvin's *Eugène Scribe and the French Theatre*, Paris saw 1,163 performances of seven romantic tragedies by Hugo, but during the same period 2,798 of twenty-four "well-made" plays by Scribe and 1,427 of twelve by Dumas *fils*. The well-made play—whose formula Strindberg concisely summarized in *An Effective Play* and Shaw satirically sketched in his Preface to *Three Plays by Brieux*—was (and is) celebrated by middle-class theatregoers. Dumas *fils*, one of its abler practitioners, often regarded (though erroneously) as a dramatist who unflinchingly portrays real-life problems and exposes social evils, reveals how superficial and essentially false to life this genre and his own plays really are. An admirer of the drama of Scribe and Dumas *fils*, Brunetière tries to find the common denominator of all drama. His "law of the drama" applies particularly to the well-made play, from which it may have derived.

Opposed to both the romantic drama and the well-made play, Zola attacks their artificialities and absurdities. Championing naturalistic drama, which "makes the stage a study and a picture of real life," he wants to bring the methods of the natural sciences to the study of human beings and to dramatize the psychological and social aspects of people's lives, their passions and their environment. The naturalists brought to the stage a far greater amount of realism and a sometimes unflinching presentation of class distinctions, milieu, and sex.

Unlike Zola, who advocates the accurate portrayal of both environment and inner forces, Maeterlinck stresses only the latter. To him, "psychological action" is loftier than physical action, which he would banish in favor of "a motionless life" in an experimental drama he calls static. Whereas Maeterlinck's interest is in the tragic, Bergson's is in the comic. Laughter, says Bergson, is a group phenomenon that is characterized in part by an absence of emotional involvement. Analyzing different types of comedy, visual as well as verbal, he perceives the basis of comedy to be "something mechanical inlaid on the living," a formula on which he rings numerous variations. To the Italian playwright Pirandello, contraries form the basis of humor, which he distinguishes from comedy and satire. While the comic writer will laugh at something and the satiric writer be upset by it, the humorist will see both its ridiculous and its serious, grievous side. In his laughter, he feels commiseration.

The neoclassicists were fought by the romanticists, who along with proponents of the well-made play were battled by the naturalists, who themselves were attacked by various types of theatricalists. Although surrealism did not emerge as a movement until 1924, when André Breton published the *First Surrealist Manifesto*, Apollinaire invented the word, which he applied to his play *The Breasts of Tiresias* (written in 1903, he says in his 1917 Preface). To Apollinaire, theatre should depict reality but not copy the surface of life. Cocteau, who also rejects naturalism, calls upon the theatre to create a poetry of its own, a "theatre poetry" as distinguished from "poetry in the theatre" (verbal poetry).

Artaud goes further and would banish the text entirely. Demanding a theatre that will reveal the cruelty of human existence and create experiences that "will shake the organism to its foundations and leave an ineffaceable scar," he condemns poetic drama, psychological drama, escapist drama—all written drama. In their place, he would employ theatrical means—gesture, movement, nonverbal sound, light—to bombard the senses of the spectator, whom he would surround with spectacle and sonorization.

To Absurdist playwright Ionesco, however, theatre includes but is not limited to words. Opposed to realism as a diminution and falsification of reality, to psychological theatre as insufficiently psychological, to ideological and philosophical theatre as oversimplified, he finds the essence of theatre in extreme exaggeration of emotion, dislocation of reality and of language, magnification of effect. Author of "comic dramas" and "tragic farces," Ionesco sees no essential distinction between comedy and tragedy. Comedy, which perceives the absurd, is more hopeless than tragedy, for it offers no escape; and man's helplessness in the face of tragedy and the futility of his efforts may appear comic.

The Spanish philosopher Ortega y Gasset sees a vital difference between modern, avant-garde drama and the art of earlier periods when that art was new. Whereas nineteenth-century art—including both romanticism and naturalism—has essentially mass appeal, modern art—beginning with the antirealistic forms of the late nineteenth-century avant-garde— is essentially unpopular, if not antipopular. Whereas the old guard present at the premiere of Hugo's *Hernani* disliked it because they understood it, today's masses dislike the avant-garde because they do not understand it. Dividing the public into a specially gifted elite who favor it and a large, hostile majority, the new art according to Gasset addresses itself to the former and arouses indignation in the masses, in whom it creates a sense of inferiority. Whereas they like a play when they become interested in its human content, modern avant-garde art is characterized by dehumanization.

Stendhal (Marie Henri Beyle) 1783–1842

Racine and Shakespeare 1823

Nothing resembles less than we do those *marquis* in embroidered coats and big black periwigs costing a thousand *écus* who, about 1670, judged the plays of Racine and Molière.

Those two great men aimed at flattering the taste of the *marquis* and worked for them.

It is my contention that henceforth tragedies should be written for us, the young people of the year of grace 1823, who are argumentative, serious, and a bit envious. Those tragedies should be in prose. In our day, the alexandrine line is often nothing more than a means of concealing stupidity. . . .

The entire dispute between Racine and Shakespeare comes down to whether, while observing the two unities of *time* and *place*, one can write plays that vitally interest nineteenth-century audiences—plays that make them weep and shudder or, in other words, that give them *dramatic* pleasures rather than the *epic* pleasures that make us rush to the fiftieth performance of *Le Paria*[1] or *Régulus*.[2]

I maintain that adherence to the two unities of *time* and *place* is a French habit; a habit with very deep roots; a habit from which we shall free ourselves only with difficulty, because Paris is the salon of Europe and sets the fashion for Europe. But I also maintain that these unities are by no means necessary for producing profound emotion and the genuine dramatic effect.

Why, I will ask the partisans of *Classicism*, do you demand that the action depicted in a tragedy cover not more than twenty-four or thirty-six hours? And that the setting represented on the stage not change—or at any rate, as Voltaire says, that the changes of setting not extend beyond the different rooms of a palace?

THE ACADEMICIAN Because it is not credible that an action represented in two hours should encompass a week or a month; or that in a few

Selections. From Stendhal, *Racine and Shakespeare*, translated by Guy Daniels. New York: The Crowell-Collier Press, 1962. Reprinted with permission of The Macmillan Company from *Racine and Shakespeare*, by Stendhal, translated by Guy Daniels. © The Crowell-Collier Publishing Company, 1962.

[1] (1821) by Jean François Casimir Delavigne (1793–1843).
[2] (1688) by Jacques Pradon (1632–1698).

677

moments the actors should go from Venice to Cyprus, as in Shakespeare's *Othello*, or from Scotland to the English court, as in *Macbeth*.

THE ROMANTIC　Not only is that incredible and impossible; but it is likewise impossible that the action encompass twenty-four or thirty-six hours.

THE ACADEMICIAN　Heaven forbid that we should be so absurd as to claim that the fictitious duration of the action should correspond exactly to the *material* time consumed by the performance. If this were the case, the rules would be actual fetters on genius. In the imitative arts, one must be strict but not rigorous. The spectator can easily imagine that several hours have passed during the interval of the intermissions—all the more so because he is diverted by the symphonies played by the orchestra.

THE ROMANTIC　Be careful of what you say, Monsieur. You are giving me a great advantage. You agree, then, that the spectator can *imagine* that more time is passing than that during which he is seated in the theatre. But tell me: Can he imagine a time passing that is double the real time, triple, quadruple, or a hundred times greater? Where shall we stop?

THE ACADEMICIAN　You are odd, you modern philosophers. You blame poetics because, so you say, it fetters genius. And now you want us to apply the rule of the *unity of time* with all the rigor and exactitude of mathematics, in order for it to be plausible. Is it not enough for you that it obviously contravenes all credibility for the spectator to imagine that a year, a month, or even a week has passed since he got his ticket and entered the theatre?

THE ROMANTIC　And who told you that the spectator cannot imagine that?

THE ACADEMICIAN　It is reason that tells me.

THE ROMANTIC　I beg your pardon. Reason cannot possibly teach you this. How could you know that the spectator can imagine that twenty-four hours have passed, whereas actually he has only been sitting in his box for two hours, unless experience had taught you this? How could you know that those hours that seem so long to a man who is bored, seem to fly when a person is being amused, unless experience had told you. In a word, it is *experience* alone that must settle the issue between you and me.

THE ACADEMICIAN　Yes, no doubt it is experience.

THE ROMANTIC　Well, experience has already spoken against you. In England, for two centuries now, and in Germany during the past fifty years, they have been performing tragedies whose action covers entire months; and the spectators' imagination accommodates itself perfectly to this. . . .

THE ACADEMICIAN　Ah! You will never persuade me that the English and the Germans, even if they are foreigners, really imagine that entire months pass while they are at the theatre.

THE ROMANTIC　Just as you will never persuade me that the French spectators believe that twenty-four hours pass while they are watching a performance of *Iphigénie en Aulide*.[3]

THE ACADEMICIAN (*impatient*)   What a difference!

THE ROMANTIC   Let us not become incensed. And please observe carefully what is going on in your head. Try to draw aside for a moment the veil that habit has thrown over acts which take place so rapidly that you have lost the ability to follow them with your eye and see them *occur*. Let us come to an agreement on the word *illusion*. When one says that the spectator imagines that the time necessary for the events represented on the stage has passed, one does not mean that the spectator's illusion extends to the point of believing that all this time has really elapsed. The fact is that the spectator, caught up and carried along by the story, is not shocked by anything. He gives no thought whatsoever to the time that has passed. Your Parisian spectator sees Agamemnon awaken Arcas at exactly seven o'clock. He witnesses the arrival of Iphigenia; and he sees her led to the altar where the Jesuitic Calchas is waiting for her. If anyone asked him, he would of course reply that these events required several hours. And yet, if during the quarrel between Achilles and Agamemnon he were to take out his watch, it would show the hour of 8:15. What spectator would be surprised by this? Nonetheless, the play that he is applauding has already lasted for several hours.

The truth of the matter is that even your Parisian spectator is accustomed to seeing time move at different rates on the stage and in the other part of the theatre. This is a fact that you cannot deny. It is clear that even in Paris, even at the Théâtre-Français in the Rue de Richelieu, the spectator's imagination lends itself easily to the poet's suppositions. The spectator, quite naturally, pays no attention to the intervals of time required by the poet; just as in sculpture he does not take it into his head to reproach Dupaty or Bosio for the fact that their figures lack movement. This is one of the infirmities of art. The spectator, when he is not a pedant, is concerned only with the acts and developments of passions that are presented to his view. Precisely the same thing happens in the head of the Parisan who applauds *Iphigénie en Aulide* and in that of the Scotsman who admires the story of his former kings, Macbeth and Duncan. The only difference is that the Parisian, being a child of good family, has acquired the habit of mocking others.

THE ACADEMICIAN   In other words, according to you the theatrical illusion is the same for both?

THE ROMANTIC   To have illusions, to be in a state of *illusion*, means to deceive oneself, according to the *Dictionary* of the Academy. An *illusion*,

[3] (1674) by Jean Racine.

M. Guizot says, is the effect of a thing or an idea that deceives us by its misleading appearance. Illusion therefore means the act of a man who believes a thing that does not exist—as in dreams, for example. Theatrical illusion would be the act of a man who believes that the things that take place on the stage really exist.

Last year (August 1822) a soldier who was standing guard in the theatre in Baltimore, upon seeing Othello, in the fifth act of the tragedy of that name, about to kill Desdemona, cried out: "It will never be said that in my presence a damned nigger killed a white woman." At the same moment the soldier shot at the actor who was playing Othello and broke his arm. Not one year passes but what the newspapers report similar incidents.

Now that soldier was entertaining an *illusion*: he believed in the reality of what was happening on the stage. But an ordinary spectator at the moment when his pleasure is most intense—at the moment when he is enthusiastically *applauding* Talma-Manlius[4] saying to his friend, "Do you recognize this writing?"—by virtue of the very fact that he applauds, does not have a *complete illusion*, because he is applauding Talma and not the Roman, Manlius. Manlius does nothing deserving of applause. His act is very simple and entirely in his own interest.

THE ACADEMICIAN   I beg your pardon, my friend, but what you have just said is a commonplace.

THE ROMANTIC   I beg your pardon, my friend, but what you have just said represents the defeat of a man made incapable of close reasoning by an ingrained habit of indulging in elegant phrases.

It is impossible for you not to agree that the illusion one seeks at the theatre is not a complete illusion. *Complete* illusion is the kind experienced by the soldier standing guard in the theatre in Baltimore. It is impossible for you not to agree that the spectators know very well that they are in a theatre and watching a work of art, not a real event.

THE ACADEMICIAN   Who would think of denying that?

THE ROMANTIC   Then you grant that there is *imperfect illusion?* You had better be on your guard.

Do you believe that from time to time—for example, two or three times in one act, and for only a second or two each time—the illusion is complete?

THE ACADEMICIAN   That is by no means clear: In order to give you an answer, I should have to go back to the theatre several times and observe my actions.

---

[4] I.e., François-Joseph Talma, the famous tragic actor, in the leading role of *Manlius Capitolinus*, by Lafosse d'Aubigny, a playwright of the eighteenth century [translator's note].

THE ROMANTIC Ah! That is a charming reply, and one full of good faith. One can easily see that you belong to the Academy and that you no longer need the votes of your colleagues to be admitted. A man who had yet to make his reputation as a learned *littérateur* would take pains to avoid being so clear and reasoning in a manner so precise. You had better be on your guard: if you continue to be of good faith, we shall agree with each other.

It seems to me that these moments of *complete illusion* are more frequent than is generally supposed, especially than is admitted in literary discussions, as a matter of fact. But these moments are of infinitely brief duration—for example, a half-second or a quarter-second. One very quickly forgets Manlius and sees only Talma. Such moments last longer with young women, and that is why they cry so copiously at a tragedy.

But let us try to discover at what moments in a tragedy the spectator can hope to find these delicious instants of *complete illusion*.

Such charming instants do not occur where there is a change of scene; nor at the precise moment when the poet requires the spectator to skip over twelve or fifteen days; nor when the poet is obliged to give a long speech to one of his characters for the sole purpose of informing the spectator of a previous fact about which he must know; nor, again, when there are three or four lines which are admirable and remarkable *as poetry*.

These delicious and very rare instants of *complete illusion* are encountered only in the warmth of a lively scene when there is a rapid exchange of lines among the actors. For example, when Hermione says to Orestes,[5] who has just assassinated Pyrrhus by her order:

Who told you?

One will never encounter these moments of *complete illusion* at the instant when a murder is committed on the stage or when the guards come to arrest a character and take him to prison. We cannot believe any of these things to be real, and they never produce an illusion. These bits are written only to introduce the scenes in which the spectators experience those half-seconds that are so delicious. *Now I maintain that these brief moments of complete illusion are found more often in the tragedies of Shakespeare than in the tragedies of Racine.*

All the pleasure one derives from the tragic spectacle depends upon the frequency of these brief moments of illusion *and upon the state of emotion in which the spectator is left during the intervals between them.*

One of the things most opposed to the birth of these moments of

[5] In *Andromache* (1667) by Racine.

illusion is admiration—however well-founded it may be—for the beautiful poetic lines of a tragedy.

It is much worse if one decides he wants to judge the *poetic lines* of a tragedy. But this is precisely the state of soul of the Parisian spectator when he first goes to see that much lauded tragedy *Le Paria*.

Here we have the question of *romanticism* reduced to its ultimate terms. If you are of bad faith, or if you lack sensitivity, or if you have been petrified by Laharpe, you will deny me my brief moments of perfect illusion.

And I admit that there is nothing I can say in reply to you. Your feelings are not something material that I can extract from your own heart and hold up in front of your eyes to confound you.

I say to you: You should have such and such a feeling at this moment. All men who are generally well organized experience such a feeling at this moment. And you will reply: Please pardon my use of the expression, *but that is not true.*

As for me, I have nothing further to add. I have arrived at the last confines of what logic can grasp in poetry.

THE ACADEMICIAN   Your metaphysics is abominably obscure. Do you hope, with that, to make people hiss Racine?

THE ROMANTIC   First of all, only charlatans claim that they can teach algebra or extract a tooth without some pain. The question we are discussing is one of the most difficult that the human mind can undertake.

As for Racine, I am pleased that you mentioned that great man. His name has been made an insult for us; but his glory is immortal. He will always be one of the greatest geniuses to stir the astonishment and admiration of men. Is Caesar less a great general because gunpowder has been invented since his campaigns against our ancestors, the Gauls? All we claim is that if Caesar were to return to the world, his first concern would be to have cannons in his army. Would anyone say that Catinat or Luxembourg were greater generals than Caesar because they possessed a park of artillery, and because in three days they captured places that would have withstood the Roman legions for a month? It would have been a fine bit of reasoning if someone had said to Francis I at Marignan: "You must not use your artillery. Caesar had no cannons. Do you think you are more clever than Caesar?"

If persons of unquestionable talent like MM. Chénier,[6] Lemercier,[7] and Delavigne had dared to free themselves from rules whose absurdity has been recognized since Racine, they would have given us better plays than *Tibère, Agamemnon,* or *Les Vêpres siciliennes.*[8] Is not *Pinto* a

---

[6] Marie-Joseph Chénier (1764–1811).
[7] Louis Jean Nepomucène Lemercier (1771–1840).
[8] By Chénier (1819), Lemercier (1797), and Delavigne (1819), respectively.

hundred times better than *Clovis, Orovèse, Cyrus,*[9] or any other correct tragedy of M. Lemercier?

Racine did not believe that tragedies could be written any other way. If he lived in our time and dared to follow the new rules, he would do a hundred times better than *Iphigénie.* Instead of arousing only admiration, a rather cold sentiment, he would cause torrents of tears to flow. Is there any man, of even a modicum of education, who does not derive more pleasure from seeing M. Lebrun's *Marie Stuart*[10] at the Théâtre-Français than Racine's *Bajazet?*[11] And yet M. Lebrun's lines of poetry are very weak. The great difference in the degree of pleasure is due to the fact that M. Lebrun has dared to be quasi-romantic.

THE ACADEMICIAN   You have talked a long time. You have perhaps spoken well, but you have not convinced me.

THE ROMANTIC   I was expecting that. But then, too, this rather lengthy intermission is going to end. The curtain is going up. I merely wanted to relieve the boredom by making you a bit angry. You must agree that I have succeeded.

Victor Hugo *1802–1885*

Preface to Cromwell *1827*

Behold then a new religion, a new civilization; upon this twofold foundation a new school of poetry must inevitably spring into life. Hitherto—and we beg pardon for stating a conclusion which the reader must already have drawn for himself from what has been said above—hitherto the purely epic muse of the ancients, following in this respect the old polytheism and the old systems of philosophy, had studied nature in one phase only, pitilessly casting aside almost everything in art which fell short of its type of beauty;

Selections. From Victor Hugo, *Dramas,* Vol. V, translator anonymous. Boston: E. B. Hall & Co., 1896.

[9] By Lemercier (1800), Saint-Sorlin (1657), Lemercier (1802), Philippe Quinault (1658), respectively.
[10] (1820) by Pierre Antoine Lebrun (1785–1873).
[11] (1672).

a type magnificent in the beginning, but which toward the close became false, paltry, and conventional, as always happens with that which is governed by a fixed system. Christianity leads poetry into the paths of truth. Like it, the modern muse will look at things with greater breadth of vision. It will feel that everything in creation is not *beautiful* from the standpoint of mankind, that the ugly exists beside the beautiful, the misshapen beside the graceful, the grotesque beside the sublime, evil with good, darkness with light. It will ask itself if the restricted, relative reasoning of the artist ought to prevail over the infinite, absolute reasoning of the Creator; if it is for man to set God right; if nature will be made more beautiful by mutilation; if anything under heaven will be the better for having its marrow and its source of life taken from it; if art has the right to cut in two, so to speak, man, life, creation; if, in short, harmony is best secured by incompleteness. And thereupon, with its eyes fixed upon occurrences which are at the same time mirth-provoking and awe-inspiring, and under the influence of the spirit of Christian melancholy and critical philosophy to which we adverted a moment since, poetry will take a great step forward, a decisive step, a step which, like an earthquake shock, will change the whole face of the intellectual world. It will strive to do as nature does, to mingle in its creations, but without confounding them, light and darkness, the sublime and the ridiculous, in other words, the body and the soul, the animal and the intellectual; for the point of departure of religion is always identical with the point of departure of poetry.

Thus we see a principle unknown to the ancients, a new type introduced in poetry; and as a new element in the being modifies the whole being, a new form of the art is developed. The new type is the grotesque; the new form is comedy.

And we beg leave to insist upon this point, for we have now pointed out the characteristic feature, the fundamental difference which, in our opinion, separates modern art from ancient art, the present form from the defunct form, or to use more vague but more popular terms, *romantic* literature from *classical* literature.

"At last!" we seem to hear those people say, who for some time *have seen what was coming,* "at last we have you; you are caught red-handed! So then you deem the *ugly* a type to be imitated, the *grotesque* an element of art! But what of the graces? what of the canons of good taste? Do you know that art should set nature right? that we must *ennoble* it? that we must *select?* Did the ancients ever exhibit the ugly or the grotesque? did they ever mingle comedy with tragedy? The example of the ancients, messieurs! And Aristotle. And Boileau. And La Harpe.[1] Upon my word!"

These arguments are sound, no doubt, and are especially remarkable for

---

[1] Jean François de la Harpe (1739–1803).

their novelty. But it is no part of our role to refute them. We are not building up a system—God preserve us from our systems! We are stating a fact. We are a historian, not a critic. Whether the fact gives pleasure or the reverse matters little: it is a fact! Let us resume, therefore, and try to demonstrate that modern genius springs from the fruitful union of the grotesque type and the sublime—modern genius, so complex and varied in its forms, so inexhaustible in its creations, and in that respect diametrically opposed to the uniform simplicity of the genius of the ancients: let us show that that is the point from which we must start to establish the real, radical difference between the two literatures.

It would not be strictly true to say that the grotesque type and the comedy were absolutely unknown to the ancients. Indeed such a thing would be impossible. Nothing grows without a root; the second epoch always exists in germ in the first. In the *Iliad*, Thersites and Vulcan furnish the comedy, one among the mortals, the other among the gods. There is so much that is true to nature, so much originality, in the old Greek tragedy, that a touch of comedy must sometimes creep in. For example, to cite entirely from memory, the scene between Menelaus and the portress at the palace (*Helen*, Act I); the scene of the Phrygian (*Orestes*, Act IV). The Tritons, the Satyrs, the Cyclops are grotesque creatures; Polyphemus is a terrifying example of the same class; Silenus is a grotesque buffoon.

But we can but feel that this part of the art is still in its infancy. The epic, which at this time impresses its form upon everything, weighs heavily upon it and stifles it. The grotesque in the poetry of the ancients is very retiring and always tries to hide his face. We see that he is not upon his own soil, because his nature is disguised. He dissembles to the utmost of his ability. The satyrs, the tritons, and the sirens are hardly deformed. The Parcae and harpies are hideous in their moral attributes rather than in their features; the Furies are beautiful, and are called *Eumenides*, that is to say, *gentle, kindly*. There is a veil of grandeur or of divinity over other grotesques; Polyphemus is a giant; Midas is a king; Silenus is a god.

Thus the comic element is almost imperceptible in the great epic whole of ancient times. Beside the Olympian chariots, of what account is the car of Thespis? Beside the Homeric colossi, Aeschylus, Sophocles, Euripides, what are Aristophanes and Plautus? Homer carries them away with him, as Hercules carried the pygmies, hidden in his lion's skin.

In modern creations, on the other hand, the grotesque plays an enormous part. It is to be found everywhere; on the one hand it creates the deformed and the horrible; on the other hand, the comic, the buffoon.

It surrounds religion with innumerable original superstitions, it surrounds poetry with innumerable picturesque fancies. It sows abundantly, in the air, the water, the earth, the fire, those myriads of intermediate beings which we find instinct with life in the popular traditions of the Middle Ages;

it shows us the ghastly merry-go-round of the witches in the darkness; it gives Satan his horns, his cloven feet, his bat's wings. It is this same grotesque type, which now casts into the Christian hell those hideous forms which the severe genius of Dante and of Milton will evoke, and again peoples it with the absurd figures, among which Callot, the burlesque Michelangelo, will sport. If from the ideal it passes to the real world, it there unfolds an inexhaustible supply of parodies of human foibles. Creations of its fancy are the Scaramouches, Crispins, Harlequins, grinning silhouettes of man, types altogether unknown to the stern-faced ancients, although they had their origin in classical Italy. Lastly, imbuing the same drama with the imagination of the North and the imagination of the South, it exhibits Sganarelle capering about Don Juan, and Mephistopheles crawling about Faust. . . .

. . . We will simply say here that, as a glass through which to examine the sublime, as a means of contrast, the grotesque is, in our judgment, the richest source of inspiration that nature can throw open to art. . . .

It would be no less accurate to say that contact with the deformed has given to the sublime creations of modern artists a purer, grander, aye, a more sublime quality than is to be found in the beautiful creations of antiquity; and so it should be. When art is self-consistent, it guides everything much more surely to its goal. If the Homeric Elysium is very far from suggesting the ethereal charm, the angelic loveliness of the Paradise of Milton, it is because there is beneath the latter a hell far more horrible than the pagan Tartarus. Would Francesca da Rimini and Beatrice seem so enchanting under the hand of a poet who did not confine us in the *Tour de Faim*,[2] and force us to partake of the repulsive banquet of Ugolino? Dante would have less charm, had he less force. Have the fleshly naiads, the brawny tritons, the wanton zephyrs, the diaphanous grace of our sylphs and water-sprites? Is it not because the modern imagination does not fear to picture the ghastly forms of vampires, ogres, ghouls, snake-charmers, and jinns prowling about in cemeteries, that it is able to endow its fairy creations with that incorporeal form, that purity of essence, of which the pagan nymphs fall so far short? The antique Venus is beautiful, and admirable too, beyond doubt; but what is it that imparts to the figures of Jean Goujon their graceful, ethereal, weird delicacy? what is it that gives them that unfamiliar impression of vitality and grandeur, if not the proximity of the rough but powerful sculptures of the Middle Ages?

If the thread of our argument has not been broken off in the reader's mind by these necessary developments of our fundamental idea—developments which might be carried much farther—he realizes doubtless how wonderfully that germ of comedy, the grotesque, when taken up by the modern

---

[2] *The Tower of Starvation* or *The Tower of Hunger*. See Schiller, *The Stage as a Moral Institution*, note 10.

muse, expanded and multiplied, as soon as it was transplanted to a more productive soil than that of paganism and the epic. In the new poetry, while the sublime will represent the soul as it is, purified by Christian morality, the grotesque will play the part of the human animal. The first-named type, freed from all taint of impurity, will be endowed with everything that is beautiful and attractive; it must have the power to create some day a Juliet, a Desdemona, an Ophelia. The second type will take to itself everything that is ridiculous, ugly, inferior mentally or physically. In this partition of humanity and of creation, all the passions, the vices, and crimes will fall to its share; licentiousness, sycophancy, gluttony, avarice, perfidy, and hypocrisy will be its attributes; it will appear, at one time or another, as Iago, Tartuffe, Basile; as Polonius, Harpagon, Bartholo; as Falstaff, Scapin, Figaro. The beautiful has but one type; the ugly has a thousand. The reason is that the beautiful, humanly speaking, is form considered in its simplest aspect, in its most perfect symmetry, in its most absolute harmony with one organization. And so taken as a whole, though complete in its way, it is restricted as we ourselves are. What we call the ugly, on the other hand, is one detail of a great whole, which passes our comprehension, and which is in perfect harmony, not with man, but with all creation. That is why it constantly presents itself in new, but incomplete shapes. . . .

We have now attained the culminating point of modern poetry. Shakespeare is the Drama; and the drama, which combines in one breath the grotesque and the sublime, the terrible and the absurd, tragedy and comedy, is the salient characteristic of the third epoch of poetry, of the literature of today. . . .

On the day when Christianity said to man: Thou art twofold, thou art composed of two beings, the one perishable, the other immortal, the one fleshly, the other ethereal, the one enslaved by appetites and passions, the other borne aloft upon the wings of enthusiasm and reverie; in a word, the one forever bending down toward the earth, its mother, the other constantly darting up toward heaven, its fatherland—on that day the drama was created. Is it, after all, anything more than the contrast we see every day, the never-ceasing conflict between two antagonistic principles which are always present in life, and dispute for the possession of man from the cradle to the tomb?

The poetry born of Christianity, the poetry of our time, is therefore the drama; the characteristic of the drama is the real; the real results from the natural combination of two types, the sublime and the grotesque, which meet in the drama, even as they meet in life and in the creation. For true poetry, complete poetry, consists in the harmony of contraries. It is time, therefore, to proclaim aloud—and in this matter above all others is it true that exceptions prove the rule—everything that exists in nature exists in art. . . .

In the drama, as it may be conceived at least, if not executed, all the parts cohere and everything happens as in real life. The body plays its part as well as the soul; and men and events, set in motion by this twofold agency, pass across the stage, burlesque and terrible by turns, sometimes burlesque and terrible at the same time. . . .

We see how quickly the arbitrary distinction of species vanishes when brought face to face with reason and good taste. It would be no less easy to destroy the pretended rule of the two unities. We say two and not *three* unities, because the unity of action or uniformity, the only true and well-founded one, was long ago left out of the controversy.

Distinguished contemporaries of this and other nations have already attacked, both in practice and theory, this fundamental law of the pseudo-Aristotelian code. Indeed, the combat should not be a long one. At the very first blow it cracked, so worm-eaten was this beam of the old scholastic hovel!

The most extraordinary thing is that the slaves of routine claim to support their rule of the two unities upon probability, whereas the real is the very thing that demolishes it. And indeed what could be more improbable and more absurd than this or that vestibule, peristyle, or antechamber—dreary places where our tragedies obligingly unfold themselves; whither conspirators come, no one knows whence, to declaim against the tyrant, or the tyrant to declaim against the conspirators, each in his turn, as if they had said to themselves, like the clowns they are:

Alternis cantemus; amant alterna Camenae.[3]

Where did one ever see a vestibule of that description? What could be more opposed—we will not say to truth, for the scholastics are very lavish with that—but to probability? The result is that whatever is too characteristic, too private, too closely connected with a particular locality, to take place in the antechamber or the public square, that is to say, the whole of the drama, takes place behind the scenes. We see upon the stage only the elbows of the action, so to speak; its hands are elsewhere. Instead of scenes we have narratives; instead of tableaux, descriptions. Solemn-faced characters stationed, like the old Chorus, between the drama and ourselves, tell us what is taking place in the temple, in the palace, in the public square, so that oftentimes we are tempted to cry out: "Indeed! pray take us thither! That must be very entertaining, a beautiful sight!" To which they would reply, no doubt: "It is possible that it would interest or amuse you, but that isn't the question; we are the guardians of the dignity of the French Melpomene."[4]—God save the mark!

"But," some one will say, "this rule which you cast aside is borrowed

---

[3] Alternately we sing; alternately they love the Muses.
[4] Melpomene is the Muse of Tragedy.

from the Greek stage." Wherein, I pray to know, do the Greek stage and drama resemble our own? Moreover, we have already shown that the vast extent of the ancient stage made it possible to embrace a whole neighborhood, so that the poet could, as the plot required, transport the action from one part of the stage to another, which was equivalent to so many changes of scene. A curious contradiction! the Greek theatre, restricted as it was to the furtherance of a national and religious object, is much freer than our own, which is, however, devoted solely to the entertainment, and, if you please, the instruction of the spectator. The explanation is that the one obeys only those laws which are peculiar to itself, while the other takes to itself attributes which are absolutely foreign to its essence. One is artistic, the other artificial.

We are beginning to realize in our day that exactness in the matter of locality is one of the most essential elements of reality. The speaking or acting characters are not the only ones who leave a faithful impression of the facts upon the mind of the spectator. The place where this or that catastrophe occured is an incorruptible and convincing witness to the catastrophe; and the absence of this species of silent character would render incomplete upon the stage the grandest scenes of history. What poet would dare murder Rizzio elsewhere than in Mary Stuart's chamber? to stab Henri IV elsewhere than in Rue de la Ferronerie, blocked up with drays and carriages? to burn Jeanne d'Arc elsewhere than in the Old Market? to dispatch the Duc de Guise elsewhere than at the Château of Blois where his ambition stirred a popular assembly to frenzy? to behead Charles I and Louis XVI elsewhere than in those ill-omened squares whence Whitehall and the Tuileries can be seen, as if their scaffolds were appurtenances of their palaces?

The unity of time rests on no firmer foundation than the unity of place. Forcibly to confine the action of a play within twenty-four hours is as absurd as to confine it within the narrow limits of a vestibule. Every plot has its proper duration no less than its proper locality. How absurd to dole out the same length of time for every event! to apply the same measure to everything! We should laugh at a cobbler who would fit the same shoe to every foot. What shall we say of the idea of crossing unity of time and unity of place like the bars of a cage, and pedantically forcing to enter the cage thus formed, in the name of Aristotle, all the facts, all the peoples, all the figures which Providence sets before us in such vast messes in real life? It is downright mutilation of men and things! it is forcing history to make wry faces! Let us say rather that they will all die in the operation; and thus the dogmatic mutilators will attain the same results as always; that which was instinct with life in the chronicle is dead in the tragedy. That is why it very often happens that the cage of the unities contains naught but a skeleton.

And then, if twenty-four hours can be comprised in two, it follows logically that forty-eight may be comprised in four. In that case the unity of Shakespeare will not be the unity of Corneille. More's the pity!

But these are the paltry quibbles which genius has had to put up with for two centuries past at the hands of mediocrity, envy, and routine! In this way has the flight of our greatest poets been checked. With the scissors of the unities have their wings been clipped. And what has been given us in exchange for the eagle's feathers stolen from Corneille and Racine? Campestron.[5]

We can imagine what will be said. "A too frequent change of scene tends to confuse and fatigue the spectator, and to produce a dazed condition of his mind; it may happen also that repeated transitions from one place to another, from one time to another, demand explanations which detract from the interest; care must be taken also not to leave gaps in the midst of a plot which prevent the different parts of the drama from adhering closely, and which also tend to confuse the spectator because he does not know what there may be in these empty spaces." But those are precisely the difficulties with which art has to contend. Those are the obstacles peculiar to this or that subject, as to which it would be impossible to pass judgment once for all. It is for genius to overcome, not for would-be poets to evade them.

To demonstrate conclusively the absurdity of the rule of the two unities, it would be enough to evoke another argument, taken from the very bowels of the art. We refer to the existence of the third unity, the unity of action, the only one universally admitted, because it results from the fact that the human eye and the human mind can grasp but one thing at one time. This one is as necessary as the others are useless. This it is which marks the perspective of the drama, and by that very fact it excludes the other two. There can no more be three unities in the drama than three horizons in a picture. We must be careful, however, not to confound the unity of action with simplicity of action. The unity of the whole in no way interferes with the secondary motives upon which the main action rests. It is essential only that these parts, skillfully kept in subordination to the whole, should constantly gravitate toward the main action, and group themselves about it at the different stages of the drama, or rather in connection with its various motives. The unity of the whole is the law of perspective of the stage. . . .

Let us speak out boldly. The time has come to do it, and it would be strange indeed, if at this time liberty, like the light, should extend everywhere, except to the one place where liberty is more logically a native production than anywhere else in the world, the domain of thought. Let us take

---

[5] Jean-Galbert de Campestron (1656–1723), French playwright, member of the Academy, who imitated Racinian tragedy.

the hammer to their theories and systems and treatises. Let us tear down the old stucco-work which conceals the facade of art! There are no rules or models, or rather there are no other rules than the general laws of nature, which extend over the whole domain of art, and the special laws which, in every composition, result from the conditions peculiar to each subject. The former are unchangeable, deep-seated, and abiding; the others variable, external, and can be used but once. The former are the framework of the structure; the latter the scaffolding used in its construction, and rebuilt for each house. The former are the flesh and blood, the latter the clothing of the drama. But these rules are not set down in the treatises. Richelet[6] does not suspect their existence. True genius, which divines rather than learns, deduces, for each work, its general laws from the general order of things, its special laws from the special nature of the subject it treats; not after the fashion of the chemist, who lights the fire under his retort, blows it till it blazes brightly, heats his crucible, analyzes and destroys; but rather like the bee, which flies upon its wings of gold from flower to flower, and steals from each its honey, leaving it as beautiful and fragrant as before.

The poet—upon this point we insist—ought to take counsel of naught but nature, truth, and inspiration, which is, in a certain sense both truth and nature. . . .

Let there be no mistake: if some of our poets have succeeded in attaining greatness, copyists though they be, it is because they have listened often to the voice of nature and to the promptings of their own genius, even while forming themselves after antique models; it is because they have often been themselves to some extent. . . .

We must therefore admit, or be convicted of talking nonsense, that the domain of art and that of nature are entirely distinct. Nature and art are two things, otherwise one or the other of them would not exist. Art, beside its ideal part, has a terrestrial and practical part. Whatever it may do, it is confined between grammar and prosody, between Vaugelas[7] and Richelet. For its most fanciful creations it has forms, means of execution, a complete apparatus to set in motion. For genius there are delicate instruments; for mediocrity rough tools. . . .

Had we the right to say what, in our opinion, should be the style of dramatic poetry, we should declare our liking for free, outspoken, loyal verse, for verse that dares express its meaning without prudery or affectation, that passes naturally from comedy to tragedy, from the sublime to the grotesque; verse that is by turns poetical and practical, always artistic and inspired, profound, dealing in surprises, of wide range, and true: verse that makes bold at fitting times to change the place of the caesura and thereby avoid monotony of Alexandrines; verse that prefers the *enjambement*,

---

[6] César Pierre Richelet (1631–1698), French lexicographer.
[7] Claude Favre Vaugelas (1585–1650), French grammarian.

which lengthens out the line, to the inversion of ideas, which confuses the sense, verse that is faithful to rhyme, that enslaved queen, that supreme beauty of our poetry, that creator of our meter; verse that has a never-failing supply of truth for every turn of thought, and unfathomable secret methods of composition, verse that assumes, like Proteus, a thousand shapes, but changes not its type or characteristics; that avoids *tirade*; sportive in dialogue, ever concealing itself behind the character; verse that is intent before all else upon keeping in its place, and that when it falls to its lot to be *beautiful*, is beautiful only by chance, so to speak, in spite of itself, and unconsciously; verse that is lyric, epic, dramatic, as occasion requires; verse that knows every note in the chromatic scale of poetry, that can descend from high to low, from the loftiest to the most trivial ideas, from the most absurd to the most serious, from the most superficial to the most abstract, without once exceeding the proper limits of a spoken scene; in a word, such verse as the man would write whom a benevolent fairy should endow with the soul of Corneille and the brain of Molière. It seems to us that such verse would be *quite as beautiful as prose*.

Verse of that stamp would have nothing in common with that other variety upon which we were but now holding an autopsy. The distinction between them will be easy to point out, if a certain talented gentleman, to whom the author of this book is personally indebted, will permit us to borrow his trenchant phrase; the other poetry was descriptive, this would be picturesque.

Émile Zola   *1840–1902*

Naturalism on the Stage   *1880*

I

In the first place, is it necessary to explain what I understand by "naturalism"? I have been found fault with on account of this word; some pretend to this day not to understand what I mean by it. It is easy to cut jokes about

From Émile Zola, *The Experimental Novel and Other Essays*, translated by Belle M. Sherman. New York: The Cassell Publishing Co., 1893.

this subject. However, I will explain it again, as one cannot be too clear in criticism.

My great crime, it would seem, has been to have invented and given to the public a new word in order to designate a literary school as old as the world. In the first place, I cannot claim the invention of this word, which has been in use in several foreign literatures; I have at the most only applied it to the actual evolution in our own literature. Further, naturalism, they assure us, dates from the first written works. Who has ever said to the contrary? This simply proves that it comes from the heart of humanity. All the critics, they add, from Aristotle to Boileau, have promulgated this principle, that a work must be based on truth. All this delights me and furnishes me with new arguments. The naturalistic school, by the mouth even of those who deride and attack it, is thus built on an indestructible foundation. It is not one man's caprice, the mad folly of a group of writers; it is born in the eternal depth of things, it started from the necessity which each writer found of taking nature for his basis. Very well, so far we are agreed. Let us start from this point.

Well, they say to me, why all this noise? why do you pose as an innovator and revealer of new doctrines? It is here the misunderstanding commences. I am simply an observer, who states facts. The empiricists alone put forth invented formulas. The savants are content to advance step by step, relying on the experimental method. One thing is certain, I have no new religion in my pocket. I reveal nothing, for the simple reason that I do not believe in revelation; I invent nothing, because I think it more useful to obey the impulses of humanity, the continuous evolutions which carry us along. My role as critic consists in studying from whence we come and our present state. When I venture to foretell where we are going it is purely speculation on my part, a purely logical conclusion. By what has been, and by what is, I think I am able to say what will be. That is my whole endeavor. It is ridiculous to assign me any other role; to place me on a rock, as pope and prophet; to represent me as the head of a school and on familiar terms with God.

But as to this new word, this terrible word of naturalism? I should have pleased my critics better had I used the words of Aristotle. He spoke of the true in art, and that ought to be sufficient for me. Since I accept the eternal basis of things and do not seek to create the world a second time, I no longer have need of a new term. Truly, are they mocking me? Does not the eternal basis of things take upon itself diverse forms, according to the times and the degree of civilization? Is it possible that for six thousand years each race has not interpreted and named, according to its own fashion, the things coming from a common source? Homer is a naturalistic poet—I admit that at once; but our romanticists are not naturalists after his style; between the two literary epochs there is an abyss. This is to judge from an absolute point of view, to efface all history at one stroke; it is to huddle all things together and keep no account of the constant evolution of the human mind. One thing is certain, that any piece of work will always be only a corner of nature as seen through a certain temperament. Only we cannot be content with this truth and go no further. As we approach the history of literature, we must necessarily come upon strange elements, upon manners, events, and intellectual movements which modify, arrest, or precipitate literatures. My personal opinion is that naturalism dates from the first line ever written by man. From that day truth was laid down as the necessary foundation of all art. If we look upon humanity as an army marching through the ages, bent upon the conquest of the true, in spite of every form of wretchedness and infirmity, we must place writers and savants in the van. It is from this point of view that we should write the history of a universal literature, and not from that of an absolute ideal or a common esthetical measure, which is perfectly ridiculous. But it must be understood that I cannot go as far back as that, nor undertake so colossal a work; I cannot examine the marches and countermarches of the writers of all nations, and set down through what darkness and what lights they passed. I must set myself a limit, therefore I go no further back than the last century, where we find that marvelous expansion of intelligence, that wonderful movement from whence came our society of today. And it is just there that I discover a triumphant affirmation of naturalism, it is there that I meet with the word. The long thread is lost in the darkness of the ages; it answers my purpose to take it in hand at the eighteenth century and follow it to our day. Putting aside Aristotle and Boileau, a particular word was necessary to designate an evolution which evidently starts from the first days of the world, but which finally arrives at a decisive development in the midst of circumstances especially favorable to it.

Let us start, then, at the eighteenth century. We have at that period a superb outburst. One fact dominates all, the creation of a method. Until then the savants had worked as the poets did, from individual fantasy, by strokes of genius. A few discovered truths, but they were scattered truths; no tie held them together, and mixed with them were the grossest errors. They wished to create science at one bound the way you write a poem; they joined it on to nature by quack formulas, by metaphysical considerations which would astound us today. All at once a little circumstance revolutionized this sterile field in which nothing grew. One day a savant proposed, before concluding, to experiment. He abandoned supposed truths, he returned to first causes, to the study of bodies, the observation of facts. Like a schoolboy he consented to become humble, to learn to spell nature before reading it fluently. It was a revolution: science detached itself from empiricism, its method consisted in marching from the known to the unknown. They started from an observed fact, they advanced from observation to observation, hesitating to conclude before being in possession of the necessary elements. In one word, instead of setting out with synthesis, they commenced with analysis; they no longer tried to draw the truth from nature by means of divination or revelation; they studied it long and patiently, passing from the simple to the complex, until they were acquainted with its mechanism. The tool was found; such a way of working was to consolidate and extend all the sciences.

Indeed, the benefit was soon apparent. The natural sciences were established, thanks to the minute and thorough exactitude of observation; in anatomy alone an entirely new world was opened up; each day it revealed a little more of the secret of life. Other sciences were created—chemistry and natural philosophy. Today they are still young, but they are growing, and they are bringing truth to light in a manner harassing from its rapidity. I cannot examine each science thus. It is sufficient to name in addition cosmography and geology, two sciences which have dealt so terrible a blow to religious fables. The outburst was general, and it continues.

But everything holds together in civilization. When one side of the human mind is set working other parts are affected, and ere long you have a complete evolution. The sciences, which until then had borrowed their share of imagination from letters, were the first to cut free from fantastic dreams and return to nature; next letters were seen in their turn to follow the sciences, and to adopt also the experimental method. The great philosophical movement of the eighteenth century was a vast inquiry, often hesitating, it is true, but which ended by bringing into question again all human problems and offering new solutions of them. In history, in criticism, the study of facts and surroundings replaces the old scholastic rules. In the purely literary works nature intervenes and reigns with Rousseau and his school; the trees, the waters, the mountains, the great forests, obtain recognition and take once more their place in the mechanism of the world; man is no longer an intellectual abstraction; nature determines and completes him. Diderot remains beyond question the grand figure of the century; he foresees all the truths, he is in advance of his time, waging a continual war against the worm-eaten edifice of conventions and rules. Magnificent outbursts of an epoch, colossal labor from which our society has come forth, new era from which will date the centuries into which humanity is entering, with nature for a basis, method for a tool!

This is the evolution which I have called naturalism, and I contend that you can use no better word. Naturalism, that is, a return to nature; it is this operation which the savants performed on the day when they decided to set out from the study of bodies and phenomena, to build on experiment, and to proceed by analysis. Naturalism in letters is equally the return to nature and to man, direct observation, exact anatomy, the acceptance and depicting of what is. The task was the same for the writer as for the savant. One and the other replaced abstractions by realities, empirical formulas by rigorous analysis. Thus, no more abstract characters in books, no more lying inventions, no more of the absolute; but real characters, the true history of each one, the story of daily life. It was a question of commencing all over again; of knowing man down to the sources of his being before coming to such conclusions as the idealists reached, who invented types of character out of the whole cloth; and writers had only to start the edifice at the foundation, bringing together the greatest number of human data arranged in their logical order. This is naturalism; starting in the first thinking brain, if you wish; but whose greatest evolution, the definite evolution, without doubt took place in the last century.

So great an evolution in the human mind could not take place without bringing on a social overthrow. The French Revolution was this overthrow, this tempest which was to wipe out the old world, to give place to the new. We are the beginning of this new world, we are the direct children of naturalism in all things, in politics as in philosophy, in science as in literature and in art. I extend the bounds of this word naturalism because in reality it includes the entire century, the movement of contemporaneous intelligence, the force which is sweeping us onward, and which is working toward the molding of future centuries. The history of these last one hundred and fifty years proves it, and one of the most typical phenomena is the momentary rebound of the minds which succeeded to Rousseau and Chateaubriand;[1] that singular outburst of romanticism on the very threshold of a scientific age. I will stop here for an instant, for there are some very important observations to make on this subject.

It is rarely the case that a revolution breaks out calmly and sensibly. Brains become deranged, imaginations become frightened, gloomy, and peopled with phantoms. After the rude shocks of the last century, and under the tender and restless influence of Rousseau, we find poets adopting a melancholy and fatal style. They know not where they are going. They throw themselves into bitterness, into contemplation, into the most extraordinary dreams. However, they also have been breathed upon by the spirit of the Revolution. They also are rebels. They bring about a rebellion of color, of passion, of fantasy; they talk of breaking outright with rules, and they renew the language by a burst of lyrical poetry, sparkling and superb. Moreover, truth has touched them, they exact local coloring, they believe in resurrecting the dead ages. This is romanticism. It is a violent reaction against classical literature, it is the first revolutionary use which the writers make of the reconquered literary liberty. They smash windows, they become intoxicated; maddened with their cries they rush into everything extreme from

---

[1] Vicomte François René de Chateaubriand (1768–1848), poet and essayist.

the mere necessity of protesting. The movement is so irresistible that it carries everything with it, not only the flamboyant literature, but painting, sculpture, music, even; they all become romantic; romanticism triumphs and stamps itself everywhere. For one moment, in view of so powerful and so general a manifestation, one could almost believe that this literary and artistic formula had come to remain for a long time. The classical style had lasted at least two centuries; why should not the romantic style, which had taken its place, remain an equal length of time? And people were surprised when, at the end of a quarter of a century, they found romanticism in its last agony, slowly dying a beautiful death. Then truth came forth into the light. The romantic movement was without question but a skirmish. Poets, novelists of great talents, a whole generation full of magnificent enthusiasm had been able to start a wrong scent. But the century did not belong to these overexcited dreamers, to these children of the dawn, blinded by the light of the rising sun. They represented nothing definite; they were but the advance guard, charged with clearing away the debris, and insuring the future conquest by their excesses. The century belongs to the naturalists, to the direct sons of Diderot, whose solid battalions followed, and who will finally found a true state. The ends of the chain came together once more; naturalism triumphed with Balzac.[2] After the violent catastrophes of its infancy, the century at last took the broad path marked out for it. This romantic crisis was bound to be produced, because it corresponded to the social catastrophe of the French Revolution in the same manner that I willingly compare triumphant naturalism to our actual republic, which bids fair to be founded by science and reason.

This is where we stand today. Romanticism, which corresponded to nothing durable, which was simply the restless regret of the old world and the bugle call to battle, gave away before naturalism, which rose up stronger and more powerful, leading the century of which it is in reality the breath. Is it necessary to exhibit it everywhere? It arises from the earth on which we walk; it grows every hour, penetrates and animates all things. It is the strength of our productions, the pivot upon which our society turns. It is found in the sciences, which continued on their tranquil way during the folly of romanticism; it is found in all the manifestations of human intelligence, disengaging itself more and more from the influences of romanticism which once for a moment seemed to have submerged it. It renews the arts, sculpture, and, above all, painting; it extends the field of criticism and history; it makes itself felt in the novel; and it is by means of the novel, by means of Balzac and Stendhal, that it lifts itself above romanticism, thus visibly relinking the chain with the eighteenth century. The novel is its domain, its field of battle and of victory. It seems to have chosen

[2] Honoré de Balzac (1799–1850), novelist and playwright.

the novel in order to demonstrate the power of its method, the glory of the truth, the inexhaustible novelty of human data. Today it takes possession of the stage, it has commenced to transform the theatre, which is the last fortress of conventionality. When it shall triumph there its evolution will be complete; the classical formulas will find themselves definitely and solidly replaced by the naturalistic formula, which should by right be the formula of the new social condition.

It seemed to me necessary to insist upon and to explain at length the meaning of this word naturalism, as a great many pretend not to understand me. But I will drop the question now; I simply wish to study the naturalistic movement on the stage. But I must at the same time speak of the contemporaneous novel, for a point of comparison is indispensable to me. We will see where the novel stands and where the stage stands. The conclusion will thus be easier to reach.

II

I have often talked with foreign writers, and I have found the same astonishment expressed by them all. They are better able than we are to judge of the drift of our literature, for they see us from a distance, and they are outside and away from our daily quarrels. They express great astonishment that there are two distinct literatures with us, cut adrift from each other completely: the novel and the stage. No parallel exists among our neighbors. In France it seems that for half a century literature has been divided in two; the novel has passed to one side, the stage remains on the other; and between is dug a deeper and deeper ditch. Let us examine this situation for a moment; it is very curious and very instructive. Our current criticism—I speak of newspaper critics, whose hard task is to judge from day to day new pieces—our criticism lays down the principle that there is nothing in common between a novel and a dramatic work, neither the frame nor the development; it even goes so far as to say that there are two distinct styles, the theatrical style and the novelist's style, and a subject which could be put in a book could not be placed upon the stage. Why not say at once, as strangers do, that we have two literatures? It is but too true; such criticism has but stated a fact. It only remains to be seen if it does not aid in the detestable task of transforming this fact into a law by saying that this is so, because it cannot be otherwise. Our continual tendency is to draw up rules and codify everything. The worst of it is that, after we have bound ourselves hand and foot with rules and conventions, we have to use superhuman efforts to break the fetters.

In fact, we have two literatures entirely dissimilar in all things. Once a novelist wishes to write for the stage they mistrust him; they shrug their shoulders. Did not Balzac strand himself? It is true that M. Octave

Feuillet[3] has succeeded. I am going to take up this question at the beginning in order to solve it logically. But first let us study the contemporaneous novel.

Victor Hugo wrote poems, even when he descended to prose; Alexandre Dumas *père*[4] was but a prolific story-teller; George Sand[5] gave us the dreams of her imagination in an easy and happy flow of language. I will not go back to those writers who belong to that superb outburst of romanticism, and who have left us no direct descendants. I mean to say that their influence is felt today only by our rebound from it, and in a manner of which I will speak later. The sources of our contemporaneous novel are found in Balzac and in Stendhal. We must look for them and consult them there. Both escaped from the craze of romanticism: Balzac because he could not help himself; and Stendhal from his superiority as a man. While the whole world was proclaiming the triumphs of the lyrics, while Victor Hugo was noisily crowned king of literature, both died almost in obscurity, in the midst of the neglect and disdain of the public. But they left behind them in their works the naturalistic formula of the century; and the future was to show their descendants pressing to their tombs, while the romantic school was dying from bloodlessness, and survived only in one illustrious old man, respect for whom prevented the telling of the truth. This is but a rapid review. There is no need of explaining the new formula which Balzac and Stendhal introduced. They made the inquiry with the novel that the savants made with science. They no longer imagined nor told pretty stories. Their task was to take man and dissect him, to analyze him in his flesh and in his brain. Stendhal remained above all else a psychologist. Balzac studied more particularly the temperaments, reconstructed the surroundings, gathered together human data, and assumed the title of doctor of social sciences. Compare *Père Goriot* or *Cousine Bette*[6] to preceding novels, to those of the seventeenth century as to those of the eighteenth, and you will better understand what the naturalistic evolution accomplished. The name "romance" alone has been kept, which is wrong, for it has lost all significance.

I must now choose among the descendants of Balzac and Stendhal. First, there is M. Gustave Flaubert,[7] and it is he who will complete the actual formula. We shall see in him the reaction from the romantic influence of which I have spoken to you. One of Balzac's most bitter disappointments was that he did not possess Victor Hugo's brilliant form. He

---

[3] Octave Feuillet (1821–1890), novelist and dramatist.

[4] Alexandre Dumas *père* (1802–1870), novelist and dramatist.

[5] George Sand, pen name of Amandine Aurore Lucile Dudevant (née Dupin) (1804–1876), novelist and essayist.

[6] *Father Goriot* (1834–1835) and *Cousin Betty* (1846).

[7] Gustave Flaubert (1821–1880), novelist.

was accused of writing badly, and that made him very unhappy. He sometimes tried to compete with the ringing lyrics, as for instance when he
wrote *La Femme de Trente Ans*, and *Le Lis dans la Vallée*;[8] but in this
he did not succeed; this great writer never wrote better prose than when
he kept his own strong and fluent style. In passing to M. Gustave Flaubert
the naturalistic formula was given into the hands of a perfect artist. It was
solidified, and became hard and shining as marble. M. Gustave Flaubert
had grown up in the midst of romanticism. All his leanings were toward
the movement of 1830. When he published *Madame Bovary*[9] it was as a
defiance to the realism of that time, which prided itself on writing badly.
He intended to prove that you could talk of the little provincial *bourgeoisie*
with the same ampleness and power which Homer has employed in speaking
of the Greek heroes. But happily the work had another result. Whether
M. Gustave Flaubert intended it or not, he had brought to naturalism the
only strength which was lacking to it, that of that perfect and imperishable
style which keeps works alive. From that time the formula was firmly
established. There was nothing for the newcomers to do but to walk in
this broad path of truth aided by art. The novelists went on and continued
M. Balzac's inquiry, advancing more and more in the analysis of man as
affected by the action of his surroundings; only they were at the same time
artists, they had the originality and the science of form, they seemed to
have raised truth from the dead by the intense life of their style.

At the same time as M. Gustave Flaubert, MM. Edmond and Jules
de Goncourt[10] were laboring also for this brillancy of form. They did
not come from the romantic school. They possessed no Latin, no classical
aids; they invented their own language; they jotted down, with an incredible
intensity, their feelings as artists weary of their art. In *Germinie Lacertéaux*[11]
they were the first to study the people of Paris, painting the faubourgs, the
desolate landscapes of the suburbs, daring to tell everything in a refined
language which gave beings and things their proper life. They had a great
influence over the groups of naturalistic novelists. If we found our solidity,
our exact method, in M. Gustave Flaubert, we must add that we were
very much stirred by this new language of the MM. Goncourt: as penetrating as a symphony, giving that nervous shiver of our age to all objects,
going further than the written phrase, and adding to the words of the
dictionary a color, a sound, and a subtle perfume. I do not judge, I but
state my facts. My only end is to establish the source of the contemporaneous novel, and to explain what it is and why it is.

---

[8] *A Woman of Thirty* (1828–1844) and *The Lily of the Valley* (1835).
[9] First in installments in 1856, then as a book in 1857.
[10] Edmond Louis Antoine Huot de Goncourt (1822–1896) and Jules Alfred Huot de
Goncourt (1830–1870), novelists, brothers, collaborators.
[11] (1864).

These, then, are the sources clearly indicated. First, Balzac and Stendhal, a physiologist and a psychologist, weaned from the rhetoric of romanticism, which was nothing but an uprising of word-lovers. Then, between us and these two ancestors, we find M. Gustave Flaubert on one side, and MM. Edmond and Jules de Goncourt on the other, giving us the science of style, fixing the formula in new modes of expression. In these names you have the naturalistic novel. I will not speak of its actual representatives. It will suffice to indicate the distinctive characteristics of this novel.

I have said that the naturalistic novel is simply an inquiry into nature, beings, and things. It no longer interests itself in the ingenuity of a well-invented story, developed according to certain rules. Imagination has no longer place, plot matters little to the novelist, who bothers himself with neither development, mystery, nor dénouement; I mean that he does not intervene to take away from or add to reality; he does not construct a framework out of the whole cloth, according to the needs of a preconceived idea. You start from the point that nature is sufficient, that you must accept it as it is, without modification or pruning; it is grand enough, beautiful enough to supply its own beginning, its middle, and its end. Instead of imagining an adventure, of complicating it, of arranging stage effects, which scene by scene will lead to a final conclusion, you simply take the life study of a person or a group of persons, whose actions you faithfully depict. The work becomes a report, nothing more; it has but the merit of exact observation, of more or less profound penetration and analysis, of the logical connection of facts. Sometimes, even, it is not an entire life, with a commencement and an ending, of which you tell; it is only a scrap of an existence, a few years in the life of a man or a woman, a single page in a human history, which has attracted the novelist in the same way that the special study of a mineral can attract a chemist. The novel is no longer confined to one special sphere; it has invaded and taken possession of all spheres. Like science, it is the master of the world. It touches on all subjects: writes history; treats of physiology and psychology; rises to the highest flights of poetry; studies the most diverse subjects—politics, social economy, religion, and manners. Entire nature is its domain. It adopts the form which pleases it, taking the tone which seems best, feeling no longer bounded by any limit. In this we are far distant from the novel that our fathers were acquainted with. It was a purely imaginative work, whose sole end was to charm and distract its readers. In ancient rhetorics the novel is placed at the bottom, between the fables and light poetry. Serious men disdained novels, abandoned them to women, as a frivolous and comprising recreation. This opinion is still held in the country and certain academical centers. The truth is that the masterpieces of modern fiction say more on the subject of man and nature than do the graver works of philosophy, history, and criticism. In them lies the modern tool.

I pass to another characteristic of the naturalistic novel. It is impersonal; I mean to say by that that the novelist is but a recorder who is forbidden to judge and to conclude. The strict role of a savant is to expose the facts, to go to the end of analysis without venturing into synthesis; the facts are thus: experiment tried in such and such conditions gives such and such results; and he stops there, for if he wishes to go beyond the phenomena he will enter into hypothesis; we shall have probabilities, not science. Well! the novelist should equally keep to known facts, to the scrupulous study of nature, if he does not wish to stray among lying conclusions. He himself disappears, he keeps his emotion well in hand, he simply shows what he has seen. Here is the truth; shiver or laugh before it, draw from it whatever lesson you please, the only task of the author has been to put before you true data. There is, besides, for this moral impersonality of the work a reason in art. The passionate or tender intervention of the writer weakens a novel, because it ruins the clearness of its lines, and introduces a strange element into the facts which destroys their scientific value. One cannot well imagine a chemist becoming incensed with azote, because this body is injurious to life, or sympathizing with oxygen for the contrary reason. In the same way, a novelist who feels the need of becoming indignant with vice, or applauding virtue, not only spoils the data he produces, for his intervention is as trying as it is useless, but the work loses its strength; it is no longer a marble page, hewn from the block of reality; it is matter worked up, kneaded by the emotions of the author, and such emotions are always subject to prejudices and errors. A true work will be eternal, while an impressionable work can at best tickle only the sentiment of a certain age.

Thus the naturalistic novelist never interferes, any more than the savant. This moral impersonality of a work is all-important, for it raises the question of morality in a novel. They reproach us for being immoral, because we put rogues and honest men in our books, and are as impartial to one as to the other. This is the whole quarrel. Rogues are permissible, but they must be punished in the wind-up, or at least we must crush them under our anger and contempt. As to the honest men, they deserve here and there a few words of praise and encouragement. Our impassability, our tranquility in our analysis in the face of the good and bad, is altogether wrong. And they end by saying that we lie when we are most true. What! nothing but rogues, not one attractive character? This is where the theory of attractive characters comes in. There must be attractive characters in order to give a kindly touch to nature. They not only demand that we should have a preference for virtue, but they exact that we should embellish virtue and make it lovable. Thus, in a character, we ought to make a selection, take the good sentiments and pass the wicked by in silence, indeed, we would be more commendable still if we invented a person out of the whole cloth; if we would mold one on the conventional form demanded by propriety and good manners. For this purpose there are ready-made types which writers introduce into a story without any trouble. These are attractive characters, ideal conceptions of men and women, destined to compensate for the sorry impression of true characters taken from nature. As you can see, our only mistake in all this is that we accept only nature, and that we are not willing to correct what is by what should be. Absolute honesty no more exists than perfect healthfulness. There is a tinge of the human beast in all of us, as there is a tinge of illness. These young girls so pure, these young men so loyal, represented to us in certain novels, do not belong to earth; to make them mortal everything must be told. We tell everything, we do not make a choice, neither do we idealize; and this is why they accuse us of taking pleasure in obscenity. To sum up, the question of morality in novels reduces itself to two opinions: the idealists pretend that it is necessary to lie to be moral; the naturalists affirm that there is no morality outside of the truth. Moreover, nothing is so dangerous as a romantic novel; such a work, in painting the world under false colors, confuses the imagination, throws us in the midst of hair-breadth escapes; and I do not speak of the hypocrisies of fashionable society, the abominations which are hidden under a bed of flowers. With us these perils disappear. We teach the bitter science of life, we give the high lesson of reality. Here is what exists; endeavor to repair it. We are but savants, analyzers, anatomists; and our works have the certainty, the solidity, and the practical applications of scientific works. I know of no school more moral or more austere.

Such today is the naturalistic novel. It has triumphed; all the novelists accept it, even those who attempted at first to crush it in the egg. It is the same old story; they deride, and then they praise and finally imitate it. Success is sufficient to turn the source of the current. Besides, now that the impetus has been given, we shall see the movement spreading more and more. A new literary century is beginning for us.

III

I pass now to our contemporaneous stage. We have just seen to what place the novel has risen; we must now endeavor to define the present position of dramatic literature. But before entering upon it I will rapidly recall to the reader's mind the great evolutions of the stage in France.

In the beginning we find unformed pieces, dialogues for two characters, or for three at the most, which were given in the public square. Then halls were built, tragedy and comedy were born, under the influence of the classical renaissance. Great geniuses consecrated this movement—Corneille, Molière, Racine. They were the product of the age in which they lived. The tragedy and comedy of that time, with their unalterable rules, their etiquette of the court, their grand and noble air, their philosophical dissertations and oratorical eloquence are the exact reproduction of contemporaneous society. And this identity, this close affinity of the dramatic formula and the social surroundings, is so strong that for two centuries the formula remains almost the same. It only loses its stiffness, it merely bends in the eighteenth century with Voltaire and Beaumarchais. The ancient society is then profoundly disturbed; the excitement which agitates it even touches the stage. There is a need for greater action, there is a sullen revolt against the rules, a vague return to nature. Even at this period Diderot and Mercier laid down squarely the basis of the naturalistic theatre; unfortunately, neither one nor the other produced a masterpiece, and this is necessary to establish a new formula. Besides, the classical style was so solidly planted in the soil of the ancient monarchy that it was not carried away entirely by the tempest of the Revolution. It persisted for some time longer, weakened, degenerated, gliding into insipidity and imbecility. Then the romantic insurrection, which had been hatching for years, burst forth. The romantic drama killed the expiring tragedy; Victor Hugo gave it its death-blow, and reaped the benefits of a victory for which many others had labored. It is worth noticing that through the necessities of the struggle the romantic drama became the antithesis of the tragedy; it opposed passion to duty, action to words, coloring to psychological analysis, the Middle Ages to antiquity. It was this sparkling contrast which assured its triumph. Tragedy must disappear, its knell had sounded; for it was no longer the product of social surroundings; and the drama brought in its train the liberty that was necessary in order boldly to clear away the debris. But it seems today as though that should have been the liimt of its role. It was but a superb affirmation of the nothingness of rules, of the necessity of life. Notwithstanding all this uproar, it remained the rebellious child of tragedy; in a similar fashion it lied; it costumed facts and characters with an exaggeration which makes us smile nowadays; in a similar fashion it had its rules and its effects—effects much more irritating, as they were falser. In fact, there was but one more rhetoric on the stage. The romantic drama, however, was not to have as long a reign as tragedy. After performing its revolutionary task it died out, suddenly exhausted, leaving the place clear for reconstruction. Thus the history is the same on the stage as in the novel. As a result of this inevitable crisis in romanticism, the traditions of naturalism reappear, the ideas of Diderot and Mercier come more and more to the surface. It is the new social state, born of the Revolution, which fixes little by little a new dramatic formula in spite of many fruitless attempts and of advancing and retreating footsteps. This work was inevitable. It produced itself and it will be produced again by the force of things, and it will never stop until the evolution shall be complete. The naturalistic formula will be to our century what the classical formula has been to past centuries.

Now we have arrived at our own period. Here I find a considerable activity, an extraordinary outlay of talent. It is an immense workroom in which each one works with feverish energy. All is confusion, as yet, there is a great deal of lost labor, very few blows strike out direct and strong; still the spectacle is none the less marvelous. One thing is certain, that each laborer is working toward the definite triumph of naturalism, even those who appear to fight against it. They are, in spite of everything, borne along by the current of the time; they go of necessity where it goes. As none in the theatre has been of large enough caliber to establish the formula at a stroke by the sheer force of his genius, it would almost seem as if they had divided the task, each one giving in turn, and with reference to a definite point, the necessary shove onward. Let us now see who are the best known workers among them.

In the first place, there is M. Victorien Sardou.[12] He is the actual representative of the comedy with a plot. The true heir of M. Scribe,[13] he has renovated the old tricks and pushed scenic art to the point of prestidigitation. This kind of play is a continuous and ever more strongly emphasized reaction against the old-time classical stage. The moment that facts are opposed to words, that action is placed above character, the sure tendency is to a complicated plot, to marionettes led by a thread, to sudden changes, to unexpected dénouements. The reign of Scribe was a notable event in dramatic literature. He exaggerated this new principle of action, making it the principal thing, and he also displayed great ability in producing extraordinary effects, inventing a code of laws and recipes all his own. This was inevitable; reactions are always extreme. What has been for a long time called the fashionable stage had then no other source than an exaggerated principal of action at the expense of the delineation of character and the analysis of emotion. The truth escaped them in their effort to grasp it. They broke one set of rules to invent others, which were falser and more ridiculous. The well-written play—I mean by that the play written on a symmetrical and even pattern—has become a curious and amusing plaything, which diverts the whole of Europe. From this dates the popularity of our repertoire with foreigners. Today it has undergone a slight change; M. Victorien Sardou thinks less of the cabinetwork, but though he has enlarged the frame and laid more stress on legerdemain, he still remains the great representative in the theatre of action, of armorous action, this quality dominating and overpowering everything else. His great quality is movement; he has no life, he has only movement, which carries away the characters, and which often throws an illusive glamour over them; you could almost believe them to be living, breathing beings; but they are in reality only well-staged puppets, coming and going like pieces of perfect mechanism. Ingenuity, dexterity,

---

[12] Victorien Sardou (1831–1908), dramatist.
[13] Eugène Scribe (1791–1861), dramatist.

just a suspicion of actuality, a great knowledge of the stage, a particular talent for episode, the smallest details prodigally and vividly brought forward —such are M. Sardou's principal qualities. But his observation is superficial; the human data which he produces have dragged about everywhere and are only patched up skillfully; the world into which he leads us is a pasteboard world, peopled by puppets. In each one of his works you feel the solid earth giving way beneath your feet; there is always some far-fetched plot, a false emotion carried to the last extremity, which serves as a pivot for the whole play, or else an extraordinary complication of facts, which a magical word is supposed to unravel at the end. Real life is entirely different. Even in accepting the necessary exaggerations of a farce, one looks for and wants more breadth and more simplicity in the means. These plays are never anything more than vaudevilles unnecessarily exaggerated, whose comic strength partakes altogether of caricature. I mean by that that the laughter evoked is not spontaneous, but is called forth by the grimaces of the actors. It is useless to cite examples. Everyone has seen the village which M. Victorien Sardou depicts in *Les Bourgeois de Pont-Arcy*;[14] the character of his observation is here clearly revealed—silhouettes hardly rejuvenated, the stale jokes of the day, which are in everyone's mouth. Compared with Balzac, for instance, of how low an order are these plays. *Rabagas*, for instance, the satire in which is excellent, is spoiled by a very inferior amorous intrigue. *La Famille Benoiton*[15] in which certain caricatures are very amusing, has also its faults—the famous letters, these letters which are to be found throughout M. Sardou's writings, and which are as necessary to him as the jugglery and the presto-change to the conjurer. He has had immense success, a fact easy of explanation, and I am very glad he has. Remark one thing, that, though he very often runs counter to the truth, he has nevertheless been of great service to naturalism. He is one of the workmen of whom I spoke a short time ago, who are of their period, who work according to their strength for a formula which they have not the genius to carry out in its entirety. His personal role is exactness in the stage setting, the most perfect material representation possible of everyday existence. If he falsifies in filling out the frames, at least he has the frames themselves, and that is already something gained. To me his reason for being is that above all things. He has come in his hour, he has given the public a taste for life and tableaux hewn from reality.

I now turn to M. Alexandre Dumas *fils*. Truly, he has done better work still. He is one of the most skillful workmen in the naturalistic workroom. Little remains for him but to find the complete formula, and then let him realize it. To him we owe the physiological studies on the stage; he alone,

---

[14] *The Bourgeois of Pont-Arcy* (1878).
[15] *Rabagas* (1872) and *The Benoiton Family* (1865).

up to the present time, has been brave enough to show us the sex in the young girl, the beast in the man. *La Visite de Noces*, and certain scenes in the *Demi-Monde* and the *Fils Naturel*,[16] possess analysis which is absolutely remarkable and rigorously truthful. Here are human data which are new and excellent; and that is certainly very rare in our modern repertoire. You see I do not make any bones about praising M. Dumas *fils*. But I admire him with reference to a group of ideas which later will cause me to appear very severe upon him. According to my way of thinking, he has had a crisis in his life, he has developed a philosophic vein, he manifests a deplorable desire for legislation, preaching, and conversion. He has made himself God's substitute on this earth, and as a result the strangest freaks of imagination spoil his faculties of observation. He no longer makes use of human observation save to reach superhuman results and astonishing situations, dressed out in full-blown fantasy. Look at *La Femme de Claude*, *L'Étrangère*,[17] and other pieces still. This is not all: cleverness has spoiled M. Dumas. A man of genious is not clever, and a man of genius is necessary to establish the naturalistic formula in a masterly fashion. M. Dumas has imbued all his characters with his wit; the men, the women, even the children in his plays make witty remarks, these famous witticisms which so often give a play success. Nothing can be falser or more fatiguing; it destroys all the truth of the dialogue. Again, M. Dumas, who before everything is a thorough playwriter, never hesitates between reality and a scenic exigency; he sacrifices the reality. His theory is that truth is of little consequence provided he can be logical. A play becomes with him a problem to be solved; he starts out from a given point, he must reach another point without tiring his public; and the victory is gained if you have been agile enough to jump over the break-neck places, and have forced the public to follow you in spite of yourself. The spectators may protest later, cry out against the want of the reality, fight against it; but nevertheless they have belonged to the author during the evening. All M. Dumas's plays are written on this theory. He wins a triumph in spite of paradox, unreality, the most useless and risqué thesis, through the mere strength of his wrists. He who has been touched by the breath of naturalism, who has written such clearly defined scenes, never recoils, however, before a fiction when he needs it for the sake of argument or simply as a matter of construction. It is the most pitiable mixture of imperfect reality and whimsical invention. None of his plays escapes this double current. Do you remember in the *Fils Naturel* the incredible story of Clara Vignot, and in *L'Étrangère* the extraordinary story of La Vierge du Mal?[18] I cite at haphazard. It would seem

[16] *The Wedding Visit* (translated as *A Gay Visit*) (1871), *The Demi-Monde* (1855), *The Illegitimate Son* (1858).
[17] *Claude's Wife* (1873), *The Foreigner* (1876).
[18] The Virgin of Evil.

as though M. Dumas never made use of truth but as a springboard with which to jump into emptiness. He never leads us into a world that we know; the surroundings are always false and painful; the characters lose all their natural accent, and no longer seem to belong to the earth. It is no longer life, with its breadth, its shades, and its good nature; it is a debate, an argument, something cold, dry, and rasping in which there is no air. The philosopher has killed the observer—such is my conclusion, and the dramatic writer has finished the philosopher. It is to be deeply regretted.

Now I come to Émile Augier.[19] He is the real master of our French stage. His was the most constant, the most sincere, and the most regular effort. It must be remembered how fiercely he was attacked by the romanticists; they called him the poet of good sense, they ridiculed certain of his verses, though they did not dare to ridicule verses of a similar character in Molière. The truth was that M. Augier worried the romanticists, for they feared in him a powerful adversary, a writer who took up anew the old French traditions, ignoring the insurrection of 1830. The new formula grew greater with him; exact observation, real life, true pictures of our society in correct and quiet language, were introduced. M. Émile Augier's first works, dramas and comedies in verse, had the great merit of appearing at our classical theatre; they had the same simplicity of plot as the best classical plays, as in *Philiberte*,[20] for example, where the story of an ugly girl who became charming, and whom all the world courted, was sufficient to fill three acts, without the slightest complication; their main point was the elucidating of character, and they possessed also a spirit of genial good nature and the strong, quiet movement that would naturally arise among people who drew apart and then came together again as their emotions impelled them. My conviction is that the naturalistic formula will be but the development of this classical formula, enlarged and adapted to our surroundings. Later M. Émile Augier made his own personality more strongly felt. He could not help employing the naturalistic formula when he began to write in prose, and depicted our contemporaneous society more freely. I mention more particularly *Les Lionnes Pauvres, Le Mariage d'Olympe, Maître Guerin, Le Gendre de M. Poirier*, and those two comedies which created the most talk, *Les Effrontés*, and *Le Fils de Giboyer*.[21] These are very remarkable works, which all, more or less, in some scenes, realize the new theatre, the stage of our time. The bold, unrepentant effrontery, for instance, with which Guerin, the notary, dies, so novel and true in its effect; the excellent picture of the newly enriched bourgeois in the *Gendre de M. Poirer;* both of

---

[19] (1820–1889), dramatist and poet.

[20] (1853).

[21] *The False Steps* (lit., *The Poor Lionesses*), written with Edouard Foussier (1858); *Olympia's Wedding* (1855); *Master Guerin* (1864); *Mr. Poierer's Son-in-Law*, written with Jules Sandeau (1854); *Faces of Brass* (1861); *Giboyer's Son* (1862).

these are admirable studies of human nature; Giboyer, again, is a curious creation, quite true to life, living in the midst of a society depicted with a great deal of excellent sarcasm. M. Augier's strength, and what makes him really superior to M. Dumas *fils* is his more human quality. This human side places him on solid ground; we have no fear that he will take those wild leaps into space; he remains well balanced, not so brilliant, perhaps, but much more sure. What is there to prevent M. Augier from being the genius waited for, the genius destined to make the naturalistic formula a fixture? Why, I ask, does he only remain the wisest and the strongest of the workmen of the present hour? In my opinion it is because he has not known how to disengage himself from conventions from stereotyped ideas, from made-up characters. His stage is constantly belittled by figures *"executés de chic,"*[22] as they say in the studio. Thus it is rarely that you do not find, in his comedies, the pure young girl who is very rich and who does not wish to marry, because she scorns to be married for her money. His young men are equally heroes of honor and loyalty, sobbing when they learn that their fathers made their money unscrupulously. In a word, the interesting character predominates; I mean the ideal type of good and beautiful sentiments always cast in the same mold, that mere symbol, that hieratic personification outside of all true observation. This commandant Guerin, this model of military men, whose uniform aids in the dénouement; Giboyer's son, that archangel of delicacy, born of a man of ill repute, and Giboyer himself, so tender in his baseness; Henri, the son of Charrier in *Les Effrontés*, who goes bond for his father when he has dabbled in an equivocal affair, and who finally induces the latter to reimburse the men whom he has wronged—all these are very beautiful, very touching; only as human data very unlikely. Nature is not so unmixed, neither in the good nor in the evil. You cannot accept these interesting characters except as a contrast and a consolation. This is not all; M. Augier often modifies a character by a stroke of his wand. His reason is easily seen; he wants a dénouement, and he changes a character after an effective scene. For instance, the climax in the *Gendre de M. Poirier*. Really it is very accommodating; you do not make a light man out of a dark one so easily. Considered from the point of genuine observations these brusque changes are to be deplored; a temperament is the same to the end, or at least is only changed by slowly working causes, apparent only to a very minute analysis. M. Augier's best characters, those which will remain longest, because they are the most complete and logical, to my thinking, are Guerin the notary, and Pommeau in *Les Lionnes Pauvres*. The climax in both plays is very good. Reading *Les Lionnes Pauvres* over I bethought me of Mme. Marneffé, married to an honest man. Compare Seraphine to Mme. Marneffé, place M. Émile Augier and Balzac face to

[22] Done without a model, that is, not copied from real life.

face for one instant, and you will understand why, nothwithstanding his good qualities, M. Émile Augier has not firmly established the new formula on the stage. His hand was not bold enough to rid himself of the conventionalities which encumber the stage. His plays are too much of a mixture; not one of them stands out with the decisive originality of genius. He softens his lines too much; still he will remain in our dramatic literature as a pioneer, who possessed great and strong intelligence.

I would like to have spoken of M. Eugène Labiche,[23] whose comic vein is very refreshing; of M. Meilhac and M. Halévy,[24] these sharp observers of Parisian life; of M. Gondinet,[25] who by his witty scenes, depicted without any action, has given the last blow to the downfall of the formula of Scribe.

But it must be sufficient for me to explain myself by means of the three dramatic authors whose work I have just analyzed and who are really the most celebrated. Their talent and their different gifts I greatly admire. Only I must say, once more, I judge them from the point of view of a group of ideas and the place which their works will hold in the literary movement of the century.

IV

Now that all the elements are known I have in my hands all the data which I need for argument and conclusion. On one side, we have seen what the naturalistic novel is at the present time; on the other, we have just ascertained what the first dramatic authors have made of our stage. It remains but to establish a parallel.

No one contests the point that all the different forms of literary expression hold together and advance at the same time. When they have been stirred up, when the ball is once set rolling, there is a general push toward the same goal. The romantic insurrection is a striking example of this unity of movement under a definite influence. I have shown that the force of the current of the age is toward naturalism. Today this force is making itself felt more and more; it is rushing on us, and everything must obey it. The novel and the stage are carried away by it. Only it has happened that the evolution has been much more rapid in the novel; it triumphs there while it is just beginning to put in an appearance on the stage. This was bound to be. The theatre has always been the stronghold of convention for a multiplicity of reasons, which I will explain later. I simply wish, then, to come down to this. The naturalistic formula, however complete and

---

[23] (1815–1888), dramatist.

[24] Henry Meilhac (1831–1897) and Ludovic Halévy (1834–1908), dramatists, collaborators.

[25] Edmond Gondinet (1829–1888), dramatist.

defined in the novel, is very far from being so on the stage, and I conclude from that that it will be completed, that it will assume sooner or later there its scientific rigor, or else the stage will become flat, and more and more inferior.

Some people are very much irritated with me; they cry out: "But what do you ask? what evolution do you want? Is the evolution not an accomplished fact? Have not M. Émile Augier, M. Dumas *fils*, and M. Victorien Sardou pushed the study and the painting of our society to the farthest possible lengths? Let us stop where we are. We have already too much of the realities of this world." In the first place, it is very naïve in these people to wish to stop; nothing is stable in a society, everything is borne along by a continuous movement. Things go in spite of everything where they ought to go. I contend that the evolution, far from being an accomplished fact on the stage, is hardly commenced. Up to the present time we have taken only the first steps. We must wait until certain ideas have wedged their way in, and until the public becomes accustomed to them, and until the force of things abolishes the obstacles one by one. I have tried, in rapidly glancing over MM. Victorien Sardou, Dumas *fils*, and Émile Augier, to tell for what reasons I look upon them as simply laborers who are clearing the paths of débris, and not as creators, not as geniuses who are building a monument. Then after them I am waiting for something else.

This something else which arouses so much indignation and draws forth so many pleasantries is, however, very simple. We have only to read Balzac, M. Gustave Flaubert, and MM. de Goncourt again—in a word, the naturalistic novelists—to discover what it is. I am waiting for them, in the first place to put a man of flesh and bones on the stage, taken from reality, scientifically analyzed, without one lie. I am waiting for them to rid us of fictitious characters, of conventional symbols of virtue and vice, which possess no value as human data. I am waiting for the surroundings to determine the characters, and for characters to act according to the logic of facts, combined with the logic of their own temperament. I am waiting until there is no more jugglery of any kind, no more strokes of a magical wand, changing in one minute persons and things. I am waiting for the time to come when they will tell us no more incredible stories, when they will no longer spoil the effects of just observations by romantic incidents, the result being to destroy even the good parts of a play. I am waiting for them to abandon the cut-and-dried rules, the worked-out formulas, the tears and and cheap laughs. I am waiting until a dramatic work free from declamations, big words, and grand sentiments has the high morality of truth, teaches the terrible lesson that belongs to all sincere inquiry. I am waiting, finally, until the evolution accomplished in the novel takes place on the stage; until they return to the source of science and modern arts, to the study of nature, to the anatomy of man, to the painting of life, in an exact reproduction, more original and powerful than any one has so far dared to place upon the boards.

This is what I am waiting for. They shrug their shoulders and reply to me that I shall wait forever. Their decisive argument is that you must not expect these things on the stage. The stage is not the novel. It has given us what it could give us. That ends it; we must be satisfied.

Now we are at the pith of the quarrel. I am trying to uproot the very conditions of existence on the stage. What I ask is impossible, which amounts to saying that fictions are necessary on the stage; a play must have some romantic corners, it must turn in equilibrium round certain situations, which must unravel themselves at the proper time. They take up the business side; first, any analysis is wearisome; the public demands facts, always facts; then there is the perspective of the stage; an act must be played in three hours, no matter what its length is; then the characters are endowed with a particular value, which necessitates setting up fictions. I will not put forth all the arguments. I arrive at the intervention of the public, which is really considerable; the public wishes this, the public will not have that; it will not tolerate too much truth, it exacts four attractive puppets to one real character taken from life. In a word, the stage is the domain of conventionality; everything is conventional, from the decorations to the footlights which illuminate the actors, even down to the characters, who are led by a string. Truth can only enter by little doses adroitly distributed. They even go so far as to swear that the theatre will cease to exist the day that it ceases to be an amusing lie, destined to console the spectators in the evening for the sad realities of the day.

I know all these reasonings, and I shall try to respond to them presently, when I reach my conclusion. It is evident that each kind of literature has its own conditions of existence. A novel, which one reads alone in his room, with his feet on his andirons, is not a play which is acted before two thousand spectators. The novelist has time and space before him; all sorts of liberties are permitted him; he can use one hundred pages, if it pleases him, to analyze at his leisure a certain character; he can describe his surroundings as much as he pleases; he can cut his story short, can retrace his steps, changing places twenty times—in one word, he is absolute master of his matter. The dramatic author, on the contrary, is inclosed in a rigid frame; he must heed all sorts of necessities. He moves only in the midst of obstacles. Then, above all, there is the question of the isolated reader and the spectators taken en masse; the solitary reader tolerates everything, goes where he is led, even when he is disgusted; while the spectators, taken en masse, are seized with prudishness, with frights, with sensibilities of which the author must take notice under pain of a certain fall. All this is true, and it is precisely for this reason that the stage is the last citadel of conventionality, as I stated further back. If the naturalistic movement had not encountered on the boards a difficult ground, filled with obstacles, it would already have taken root there with the intensity and with the success which have attended the novel. The stage, under its conditions of existence, must be the last, the most laborious, and the most bitterly disputed conquest of the spirit of truth.

I will remark here that the evolution of each century is of necessity incarnated in a particular form of literature. Thus the seventeenth century evidently incarnated itself in the dramatic formula. Our theatre threw forth then an incomparable glitter, to the detriment of lyrical poetry and the novel. The reason was that the stage then exactly responded to the spirit of the period. It abstracted man from nature, studied him with the philosophical tool of the time; it has the swing of a pompous rhetoric, the polite manners of a society which had reached perfect maturity. It is the fruit of the ground; its formula is written from that point where the then civilization flowed with the greatest ease and perfection. Compare our epoch to that, and you will understand the decisive reasons which made Balzac a great novelist instead of a great dramatist. The spirit of the nineteenth century, with its return to nature, with its need of exact inquiry, quitted the stage, where too much conventionality hampered it, in order to stamp itself indelibly on the novel, whose field is limitless. And thus it is that scientifically the novel has become the form, par excellence, of our age, the first path in which naturalism was to triumph. Today it is the novelists who are the literary princes of the period; they possess the language, they hold the method, they walk in the front rank, side by side with science. If the seventeenth century was the century of the stage, the nineteenth will belong to the novel.

Let us admit for one moment that criticism has some show of reason when it asserts that naturalism is impossible on the stage. Here is what they assert. Conventionality is inevitable on the stage; there must always be lying there. We are condemned to a continuance of M. Sardou's juggling; to the theories and witticisms of M. Dumas *fils*; to the sentimental characters of M. Émile Augier. We shall produce nothing finer than the genius of these authors; we must accept them as the glory of our time on the stage. They are what they are because the theatre wishes them to be such. If they have not advanced further to the front, if they have not obeyed more implicitly the grand current of truth which is carrying us onward, it is the theatre which forbids them. That is a wall which shuts the way, even to the strongest. Very well! But then it is the theatre which you condemn; it is to the stage that you have given the mortal blow. You crush it under the novel, you assign it an inferior place, you make it despicable and useless in the eyes of future generations. What do you wish us to do with the stage, we other seekers after truth, anatomists, analysts, searchers of life, compilers of human data, if you prove to us that there we cannot make use of our tools and our methods? Really! The theatre lives only on conventionalities; it must lie; it refuses our experimental literature! Oh, well, then, the century will put the stage to one side, it will abandon it to the hands of the public amusers, while it will perform elsewhere its great and glorious work. You yourselves pronounce the verdict and kill the stage. It is very evident that the naturalistic evolution will extend itself more and more, as it possesses the intelligence of the age. While the novelists are digging always further forward, producing newer and more exact data, the stage will flounder deeper every day in the midst of its romantic fictions, its worn-out plots, and its skillfulness of handicraft. The situation will be the more sad because the public will certainly acquire a taste for reality in reading novels. The movement is making itself forcibly felt even now. There will come a time when the public will shrug its shoulders and demand an innovation. Either the theatre will be naturalistic or it will not be at all; such is the formal conclusion.

And even now, today, is not this becoming the situation? All of the new literary generation turn their backs on the theatre. Question the young men of twenty-five years—I speak of those who possess a real literary temperament; they will show great contempt for the theatre; they will speak of its successful authors with such faint approval that you will become indignant. They look upon the stage as being of an inferior rank. That comes solely from the fact that it does not offer them the soil of which they have need; they find neither enough liberty nor enough truth there. They all veer toward the novel. Should the stage be conquered by a stroke of genius tomorrow you would see what an outpouring would take place. When I wrote elsewhere that the boards were empty I merely meant they had not yet produced a Balzac. You could not, in good faith, compare M. Sardou, Dumas, or Augier to Balzac; all the dramatic authors, put one on top of the other, do not equal him in stature. The boards will remain empty, from this point of view, so long as a master hand has not, by embodying the formula in a work of undying genius, drawn after him tomorrow's generations.

V

I have perfect faith in the future of our stage. I will not admit that the critics are right in saying that naturalism is impossible on the stage, and I am going to explain under what conditions the movement will without question be brought about.

It is not true that the stage must remain stationary; it is not true that its actual conventionalities are the fundamental conditions of its existence.

Everything marches, I repeat; everything marches forward. The authors of today will be overridden; they cannot have the presumption to settle dramatic literature forever. What they have lisped forth others will cry from the house top; but the stage will not be shaken to its foundations on that account; it will enter, on the contrary, on a wider, straighter path. People have always denied the march forward; they have denied to the newcomers the power and the right to accomplish what has not been performed by their elders. The social and literary evolutions have an irresistible force; they traverse with a slight bound the enormous obstacles which were reputed impassable. The theatre may well be what it is today; tomorrow it will be what it should be. And when the event takes place all the world will think it perfectly natural.

At this point I enter into mere probabilities, and I no longer pretend to the same scientific rigor. So long as I have reasoned on facts I have demonstrated the truth of my position. At present I am content to foretell. The evolution will take place, that is certain. But will it pass to the left? will it pass to the right? I do not know. One can reason, and that is all.

In the first place, it is certain that the conditions existing on the stage will always be different. The novel, thanks to its freedom, will remain perhaps the tool, par excellence, of the century, while the stage will but follow it and complete the action. The wonderful power of the stage must not be forgotten, and its immediate effect on the spectators. There is no better instrument for propagating anything. If the novel, then, is read by the fireside, in several instances, with a patience tolerating the longest details, the naturalistic drama should proclaim before all else that it has no connection with this isolated reader, but with a crowd who cry out for clearness and conciseness. I do not see that the naturalistic formula is antagonistic to this conciseness and this clearness. It is simply a question of changing the composition and the body of the work. The novel analyzes at great length and with minuteness of detail which overlooks nothing; the stage can analyze as briefly as it wishes by actions and words. A word, a cry, in Balzac's works is often sufficient to present the entire character. This cry belongs essentially to the stage. As to the acts, they are consistent with analysis in action, which is the most striking form of action one can make. When we have gotten rid of the child's play of a plot, the infantile game of tying up complicated threads in order to have the pleasure of untying them again; when a play shall be nothing more than a real and logical story—we shall then enter into perfect analysis; we shall analyze necessarily the double influence of characters over facts, of facts over characters. This is what has led me to say so often that the naturalistic formula carries us back to the source of our national stage, the classical formula. We find this continuous analysis of character, which I consider so necessary, in Corneille's tragedies and Molière's comedies; plot takes a secondary place, the work is a long dissertation in dialogue on man. Only instead of an abstract man I would make a natural man, put him in his proper surroundings, and analyze all the physical and social causes which make him what he is. In a word, the classical formula is to me a good one, on condition that the scientific method is employed in the study of actual society, in the same way that the chemist studies minerals and their properties.

As to the long descriptions of the novelist, they cannot be put upon the stage; that is evident. The naturalistic novelists describe a great deal, not for the pleasure of describing, as some reproach them with doing, but because it is part of their formula to be circumstantial, and to complete the character by means of his surroundings. Man is no longer an intellectual abstraction for them, as he was looked upon in the seventeenth century; he is a thinking beast, who forms part of nature, and who is subject to the multiplicity of influences of the soil on which he grows and where he lives. This is why a climate, a country, a horizon, a room, are often of decisive importance. The novelist no longer separates his character from the air which he breathes; he does not describe him in order to exercise his rhetorical powers, as the didactic poets did, as Delille[26] does, for example; he simply notes the material conditions in which he finds his characters at each hour, and in which the facts are produced, in order to be absolutely thorough in order that his inquiry may belong to the world's great whole and reproduce the reality in its entirety. But it is not necessary to carry descriptions to the stage; they are found there naturally. Are not the stage settings a continual description, which can be made much more exact and startling ʰhan the descriptions in a novel? It is only painted pasteboard, some say; that may be so, but in a novel it is less than painted pasteboard—it is but blackened paper, notwithstanding which the illusion is produced. After the scenery, so surprisingly true, that we have recently seen in our theatres, no one can deny the possibility of producing on the stage the reality of surroundings. It now remains for dramatic authors to utilize this reality, they furnishing the characters and the facts, the scene painters, under their directions, furnishing the descriptions, as exact as shall be necessary. It but remains for a dramatic author to make use of his surroundings as the novelists do, since the latter know how to introduce them and make them real.

I will add that the theatre, being a material reproduction of life, external surroundings have always been a necessity there. In the seventeenth century, however, as nature was not taken into consideration, as man was looked upon only as a purely intellectual being, the scenery was vague—a peristyle of a temple, any kind of a room, or a public place. Today the naturalistic movement has brought about a more and more perfect exactness in the stage settings. This was produced little by little, almost inevitably. I even find here a proof of the secret work that naturalism has accomplished in the stage since the commencement of the century. I have not time to study any more deeply this question of decorations and accessories; I must

---

[26] Jacques Delille (1738–1813).

content myself by stating that description is not only possible on the stage, but it is, moreover, a necessity which is imposed as an essential condition of existence.

There is no necessity for me to expatiate on the change of place. For a long time the unity of place has not been observed. The dramatic authors do not hesitate to cover an entire existence, to take the spectators to both ends of the world. Here conventionality remains mistress, as it is also in the novel. It is the same as to the question of time. It is necessary to cheat. A play which calls for fifteen days, for example, must be acted in the three hours which we set apart for reading a novel or seeing it played at the theatre. We are not the creative force which governs the world; our power of creation is a second-hand sort; we only analyze, sum up in a nearly always groping fashion, happy and proclaim as geniuses when we can disengage one ray of the truth.

I now come to the language. They pretend to say that there is a special style for the stage. They want it to be a style altogether different from the ordinary style of speaking, more sonorous, more nervous, written in a higher key, cut in facets, no doubt to make the chandelier jets sparkle. In our time, for example, M. Dumas *fils* has the reputation of being a great dramatic author. His *mots*[27] are famous. They go off like skyrockets, falling again in showers to the applause of the spectators. Besides, all his characters speak the same language, the language of witty Paris, cutting in its paradoxes, having a good hit always in view, and sharp and hard. I do not deny the sparkle of this language—not a very solid sparkle, it is true—but I deny its truth. Nothing is so fatiguing as these continual sneering sentences. I would rather see more elasticity, greater naturalness. They are at one and the same time too well and not well enough written. The true style-setters of the epoch are the novelists; to find the infallible, living, original style you must turn to M. Gustave Flaubert and to MM. de Goncourt. When you compare M. Dumas's style to that of these great prose writers you find it is no longer correct—it has no color, no movement. What I want to hear on the stage is the language as it is spoken every day; if we cannot produce on the stage a conversation with its repetitions, its length, and its useless words, at least the movement and the tone of the conversation could be kept; the particular turn of mind of each talker, the reality, in a word, reproduced to the necessary extent. MM. Goncourt have made a curious attempt at this in *Henriette Maréchal*,[28] that play which no one would listen to, and which no one knows anything about. The Grecian actors spoke through a brass tube; under Louis XIV the comedians sang their roles in a chanting tone to give them more pomp; today we are content to say

---

[27] Clever phrases.
[28] (1865).

that there is a particular language belonging to the stage, more sonorous and explosive. You can see by this that we are progressing. One day they will perceive that the best style on the stage is that which best sets forth the spoken conversation, which puts the proper word in the right place, giving it its just value. The naturalistic novelists have already written excellent models of dialogue, reduced to strictly useful words.

There now remains but the question of sentimental characters. I do not disguise the fact that it is of prime importance. The public remain cold and irresponsive when their passion for an ideal character, for some combination of loyalty and honor, is not satisfied. A play which presents to them but living characters taken from real life looks black and austere to them, when it does not exasperate them. It is on this point that the battle of naturalism rages most fiercely. We must learn to be patient. At the present moment a secret change is taking place in the public feeling; people are coming little by little, urged onward by the spirit of the century, to admit the bold reproduction of real life, and are even beginning to acquire a taste for it. When they can no longer stand certain falsehoods we shall very nearly have gained our point. Already the novelists' work is preparing the soil in accustoming them to the idea. An hour will strike when it will be sufficient for a master to reveal himself on the stage to find a public ready to become enthusiastic in favor of the truth. It will be a question of tact and strength. They will see then that the highest and most useful lessons will be taught by depicting what is, and not by oft-dinned generalities, nor by airs of bravado, which are chanted merely to tickle our ears.

The two formulas are before us: the naturalistic formula, which makes the stage a study and a picture of real life; and the conventional formula, which makes it purely an amusement for the mind, an intellectual speculation, an art of adjustment and symmetry regulated after a certain code. In fact, it all depends upon the idea one has of literature, and of dramatic literature in particular. If we admit that literature is but an inquiry about men and things entered into by original minds, we are naturalists; if we pretend that literature is a framework superimposed upon the truth, that a writer must make use of observation merely in order to exhibit his power of invention and arrangement, we are idealists, and proclaim the necessity of conventionality. I have just been very much struck by an example. They have just revived, at the Comédie Française, *Le Fils Naturel* of M. Dumas *fils*. A critic immediately jumps into enthusiasm. Here is what he says: "*Mon Dieu!* but that is well put together! How polished, dove-tailed, and compact! Is not this machinery pretty? And this one, it comes just in time to work itself into this other trick, which sets all the machinery in motion." Then he becomes exhausted, he cannot find words eulogistic enough in which to speak of the pleasure he experiences in this piece of mechanism. Would you not think he was speaking of a plaything, of a puzzle, with which he amused himself by upsetting and then putting all the pieces in order again? As for me, *Le Fils Natural* does not affect me in the least. And why is that? Am I a greater fool than the critic? I do not think so. Only I have no taste for clockwork, and I have a great deal for truth. Yes, truly, it is a pretty piece of mechanism. But I would rather it had been a picture of life. I yearn for life with its shiver, its breath, and its strength; I long for life as it is.

We shall yet have life on the stage as we already have it in the novel. This pretended logic of actual plays, this equality and symmetry obtained by processes of reasoning, which come from ancient metaphysics, will fall before the natural logic of facts and beings such as reality presents to us. Instead of a stage of fabrication we shall have a stage of observation. How will the evolution be brought about? Tomorrow will tell us. I have tried to foresee, but I leave to genius the realization. I have already given my conclusion: Our stage will be naturalistic, or it will cease to exist.

Now that I have tried to gather my ideas together, may I hope that they will no longer put words into my mouth which I have never spoken? Will they still continue to see, in my critical opinions, I know not what ridiculous inflations of vanity or odious retaliations? I am but the most earnest soldier of truth. If I am mistaken, my judgments are there in print; and fifty years from now I shall be judged, in my turn; I may perhaps be accused of injustice, blindness, and useless violence. I accept the verdict of the future.

Alexandre Dumas, Fils   *1824–1895*

How to Write a Play   *1884*

With study, work, patience, memory, energy, a man can gain a reputation as a painter, or a sculptor, or a musician. In those arts there are material and mechanical procedures that he can make his own, thanks to which he can gain talent and particularly ability, and can attain to success.

Selection. Translated by Dudley Miles. From *Papers on Playmaking*, edited by Brander Matthews. New York: Hill and Wang Dramabook, 1957. Reprinted by permission of the Brander Matthews Dramatic Museum of Columbia University.

The public to whom these works are submitted, having none of the technical knowledge involved, from the beginning regard the makers of these works as their superiors: They feel that the artist can always reply to any criticism: "Have you learned painting, sculpture, music? No? Then don't talk so vainly. You cannot judge. You must be of the craft to understand the beauties," and so on. It is thus that the good-natured public is frequently imposed on, in painting, in sculpture, in music, by certain schools and celebrities. It does not dare to protest. But with regard to drama and comedy the situation is altered. The public is an interested party to the proceedings and appears, so to speak, for the prosecution in the case.

The language that we use in our plays is the language used by the spectators every day; the sentiments that we depict are theirs; the persons whom we set to acting are the spectators themselves in instantly recognized passions and familiar situations. No preparatory studies are necessary; no initiation in a studio or school is indispensable; eyes to see, ears to hear—that's all they need. The moment we depart, I will not say from the truth, but from what they think is truth, they stop listening. For in the theatre, as in life, of which the theatre is the reflection, there are two kinds of truth; first, the absolute truth, which always in the end prevails, and secondly, if not the false, at least the superficial truth, which consists of customs, manners, social conventions; the uncompromising truth which revolts, and the pliant truth which yields to human weakness; in short, the truth of Alceste and that of Philinte.[1]

It is only by making every kind of concession to the second that we can succeed in ending with the first. The spectators, like all sovereigns—like kings, nations, and women—do not like to be told the truth, all the truth. Let me add quickly that they have an excuse, which is that they do not know the truth; they have rarely been told it. They therefore wish to be flattered, pitied, consoled, taken away from their preoccupations and their worries, which are nearly all due to ignorance, but which they consider the greatest and most unmerited to be found anywhere, because their own.

This is not all; by a curious optical effect, the spectators always see themselves in the personages who are good, tender, generous, heroic whom we place on the boards; and in the personages who are vicious or ridiculous they never see anyone but their neighbors. How can you expect then that the truth we tell them can do any good?

---

[1] Alceste is the uncompromising title character of Molière's *The Misanthrope*; the moderate Philinte, who compromises, is in the same play.

Ferdinand Brunetière 1849–1906

The Law of the Drama 1894

. . . Whoever grasps a principle grasps all its applications. But the very diversity, multiplicity, perversity, and apparent contradiction of these applications prevent him from seeing the principle. Will any argument, however ingenious, alter the fact that all poetry is either lyric, epic, or dramatic? Certainly not. And if the *Cid*, if *Phèdre*, if *Tartuffe*, if the *Légataire Universel*, if the *Barbier de Seville*, if the *Camaraderie*, if the *Demi-Monde*, if *Célimare le Bien-Aimé*[1] are dramatic, does it not follow that all these works, so different, must nevertheless have not merely a few points of contact or vague resemblance, but an essential characteristic in common? What is this characteristic? That is what I shall try to explain.

Observe, if you please, that I ask only one—no more—and that I leave the dramatist complete freedom in development. That is where I depart from the old school of criticism, that believed in the mysterious power of "Rules" in their inspiring virtues; and consequently we see the old-school critics struggling and striving, exercising all their ingenuity to invent additional Rules; read, for example, the *Cours de Littérature Analytique*[2] by Népomucène Lemercier. But the truth is that there are no Rules in that sense; there never will be. There are only conventions, which are necessarily variable, since their only object is to fulfil the essential aim of the dramatic work, and the means of accomplishing this vary with the piece, the time, and the man. Must we, like Corneille, regularly subordinate character to situation; invent, construct, the situations first, and then, if I may so express it, put the characters inside? We may do so, certainly, since he did it, in the *Cid* and in *Horace*, in *Polyeucte* and in *Rodogune*.[3] Or shall we, like Racine, subordinate situation to character, find the characters first, study them, master them, and then seek the situations which will best bring out their different aspects? We may do so, and that is what he did, as you know, in *Andromaque*, in *Britanicus*, in *Bajazet*,[4] in *Phèdre*. There is an example, then, of a Rule which may be violated, and Racine's dramaturgy is none the less

Selection. From Ferdinand Brunetière, *The Law of the Drama*, translated by Philip M. Hayden. New York: The Dramatic Museum of Columbia University, 1914. Reprinted by permission of The Brander Matthews Dramatic Museum of Columbia University.

[1] Corneille's *The Cid* (1636), Racine's *Phaedra* (1677), Regnard's *The Residuary Legatee* (1708, lit. *Universal Legatee*), Beaumarchais's *Barber of Seville* (1775), Scribe's *Favoritism* (1837), Dumas *fils's The Demi-Monde* (1855), Labiche and Delacour's *Celimare the Beloved* (1863).

[2] *Course in Literary Analysis* (1817).

[3] Corneille's *Horace* (1640), *Polyeucte* (1642), *Rodogune* (1645).

[4] Racine's *Andromache* (1667), *Britannicus* (1669), *Bajazet* (1672).

dramatic for being the opposite of Corneille's dramaturgy. Take another Rule. Shall we oblige the dramatic author to observe the Three Unities? I reply that he will not be hampered by them, if he can choose, like Racine, subjects which properly or necessarily adjust themselves of their own accord, so to speak, to the rule: *Bérénice, Iphigénie, Esther*[5] . . . But if he chooses, like Shakespeare, subjects which are checked by it in their free development, or diverted merely, we will relieve him of the Rule: and *Othello, Macbeth, Hamlet,* will still be a drama. This is another example of a Rule which can be turned in various ways. Or again, shall we mingle tragic and comic, tears and laughter, terror and joy, the sublime and the grotesque, Ariel and Caliban, Bottom and Titania, Triboulet and François I, Don Guritan and Ruy Blas? Shakespeare and Hugo have done it, but Euripides and Sophocles seems to have carefully avoided it; and who will deny that they were both right? We do not feel the need of a comic element to enliven or vary the severe beauty of *Oedipus at Colonos,*[6] but we should certainly be sorry to have King Lear deprived of his Fool. It is unnecessary to continue. Evidently, all these alleged Rules affect or express only the most superficial characteristics of the drama. Not only are they not mysterious, they are not in the least profound. Whether we observe them or not, drama is drama with them or without them. They are only devices which may at any time give place to others. It all depends on the subject, the author, and the public. This is the point to add that there is something which does not depend on them.

To convince ourselves of that fact, let us examine more carefully two or three works whose dramatic value is universally recognized, and let us take them from species as different as the *Cid,* the *Ecole des femmes,*[7] and *Célimare le Bien Aimé.* Chimène *wants* to avenge her father; and the question is how she will succeed. Arnolphe *wants* to marry Agnès, whose stupidity will guarantee her fidelity; and the question is whether he will succeed. Célimare *wants* to get rid of the widowers of his former mistresses; and the question is what means he will employ. But Célimare is hampered in the execution in his *will* by his fear of the vengeance of his friends. Arnolphe is disturbed in the execution of his *will* by the young madcap Horace, who arouses love, and with love a *will,* in Agnès' heart. Chimène is betrayed in the execution of her *will* by the love which she feels for Rodrigue. On the other hand, Chimène's *will* is checked and broken by the insurmountable obstacle which she encounters in a *will* superior to her own. Arnolphe, who is far from being a fool, sees all the plans of his *will* tricked by the conspiracy of youth and love. And Célimare, by the power of his *will,* triumphs over the widowers of his mistresses. Nothing would be

---

[5] *Bérénice* (1670), *Iphigenia* (1674), *Esther* (1689).
[6] (402 B.C.) by Sophocles.
[7] *School for Wives* (1662) by Molière.

easier than to multiply examples. Take the *Tour de Nesles*,[8] and the *Chapeau de Paille d'Italie*.[9] Fadinard *wants* to obtain a Leghorn hat to replace that of Mme. Beauperthuis; and the whole farce consists in the remarkable character of the means which he employs. Suzanne d'Ange *wants* to marry M. de Nanjac; and the whole drama consists only in the means which she formulates. Buridan *wants* to exploit the monstrous secret which exists between him and Marguerite de Bourgogne; and the whole melodrama consists only of the succession of the means which he invents. Buridan's *will* is opposed in its work by Marguerite's pride. Suzanne's *will* is countered by that of Olivier de Jalin. And Fadinard's *will* becomes entangled in the means which he seeks to satisfy it. But chance, more powerful than Fadinard's *will*, brings success at the moment when he least expects it. Oliver's *will* wins out over Suzanne's. And by the exercise of their *will*, Marguerite and Buridan fall into the trap set by their own *will*. Is it not easy now to draw the conclusion? In drama or farce, what we ask of the theatre, is the spectacle of a *will* striving towards a goal, and conscious of the means which it employs.

This essential characteristic of dramatic composition distinguishes it, in the first place, from lyric composition, which I shall not discuss, in order not to complicate the question unnecessarily, and from the composition of the novel, with which, especially in our day, it has so often been confused. "Who is not for us is against us"—you know the phrase. The drama and the novel are not the same thing; or rather, each is exactly the opposite of the other. Read *Gil Blas*[10] again, or go again to see the *Mariage de Figaro*.[11] The setting and the character are the same. Beaumarchais made a trip to Spain, but Lesage's novel was none the less his principal model. I have shown elsewhere that we find in the monologue of Figaro whole sentences from *Gil Blas*. Only, whereas nothing happens to Gil Blas that he has actually *willed*, it is on the contrary Figaro's *will* that conducts the plot of his marriage. Let us pursue this point of comparison.

Gil Blas, like everybody else, wants to live, and if possible to live agreeably. That is not what we call having a will. But Figaro wants a certain definite thing, which is to prevent Count Almaviva from exercising on Suzanne the seigneurial privilege. He finally succeeds—and I grant, since the statement has been made, that it is not exactly through the means which he had chosen, most of which turn against him; but nevertheless he has constantly willed what he willed. He had not ceased to devise means of attaining it, and when these means have failed, he has not ceased to invent new ones. That is what may be called *will*, to set up a goal, and to direct everything

---

[8] *The Tower of Nesle* (1832) by Dumas *père*.

[9] *An Italian Straw Hat* (1851) by Labiche and Marc-Michel.

[10] (1715), a novel by Le Sage.

[11] *The Marriage of Figaro* (1784) by Beaumarchais.

toward it, to strive to bring everything into line with it. Gil Blas really has no goal. Highway robber, doctor's assistant, servant to a canon, to an actress, or to a nobleman, all the positions which he occupies one after another, come to him from fortune or chance. He has no plan, because he has no particular or definite aim. He is subject to circumstances; he does not try to dominate them. He does not *act*; he is *acted upon*. Is not the difference evident? The proper aim of the novel, as of the epic—of which it is only a secondary and derived form, what the naturalists call a subspecies or a variety—the aim of the *Odyssey*, as of *Gil Blas*, of the *Knights of the Round Table*, as of *Madame Bovary*,[12] is to give us a picture of the influence which is exercised upon us by all that is outside of ourselves. The novel is therefore the contrary of the drama; and if I have successfully set forth this opposition, do you not see the consequences which result from it?

It is thus that one can distinguish action from motion or agitation; and that is certainly worthwhile. Is it action to move about? Certainly not, and there is no true action except that of a will conscious of itself, conscious, as I was saying, of the means which it employs for its fulfillment, one which adapts them to its goal, and all other forms of action are only imitations, counterfeits, or parodies. The material or the subject of a novel or of a play may therefore be the same at bottom; but they become drama or novel only by the manner in which they are treated; and the manner is not merely different, it is opposite. One will never be able, therefore, to transfer to the stage any novels except those which are already dramatic; and note well that they are dramatic only to the extent to which their heroes are truly the architects of their destiny. It follows that one could make a novel of the *Mariage de Figaro*, but one will never make a drama or a comedy of *Gil Blas*. One might make a novel of Corneille's *Rodogune*, one will never make a drama of Rousseau's *Héloise*.[13] The general law of the theatre, thus defined, gives us, then, in the first place, a sure means of perceiving what in any subject there is of the novel or the drama. The fact is that people do not know this well enough; and the Naturalist school in France has committed no worse error than confusing the conditions of the two species.

The same law provides, further, the possibility of defining with precision the dramatic species—about as one does the biological species; and for that it is only necessary to consider the particular obstacle against which the will struggles. If these obstacles are recognized to be insurmountable, or reputed to be so, as were, for example, in the eyes of the ancient Greeks, the decrees of Fate; or, in the eyes, of the Christians, the decrees of Providence; as are, for us, the laws of nature, or the passions aroused to frenzy and becoming thus the internal fatality of Phèdre and of Roxane, of Hamlet

[12] (1857), a novel by Flaubert.
[13] *Julia, or the New Héloise* (1761).

or of Othello—it is tragedy. The incidents are generally terrifying, and the conclusion sanguinary, because in the struggle which man undertakes to make against fate, he is vanquished in advance, and must perish. Suppose now that he has a chance of victory, just one, that he still has in himself the power to conquer his passion; or suppose that, the obstacles which he is striving to overcome being the work of his fellow men, as prejudice, for example, or social conventions, a man is for that very reason capable of surmounting them—that is the drama properly speaking, romantic drama or social drama, *Hernani* or *Antony*, the *Fils Naturel* or *Madame Caverlet*.[14] Change once more the nature of the obstacle, equalize, at least in appearance, the conditions of the struggle, bring together two opposing wills, Arnolphe and Agnès, Figaro and Almaviva, Suzanne d'Ange and Olivier de Jalin— that is comedy. *Don Sanche d'Aragon*,[15] heroic comedy—you know this title of one of Corneille's plays. *Bérénice*, for the same reason, is hardly a tragedy. But instead of locating the obstacle in an opposing will, conscious and mistress of its acts, in a social convention or in the fatality of destiny, let us locate it in the irony of fortune, or in the ridiculous aspect of prejudice, or again in the disproportion between the means and the end—that is farce, that is the *Légataire Universel*, the *Chapeau de Paille d'Italie.*

I do not say after that, that the types are always pure. In the history of literature or of art, as in nature, a type is almost never anything but an ideal, and consequently a limit. Where is the man among us, where is the woman, who embodies the perfection of the sex and of the species? There is moreover a natural relationship, we might say a consanguinity between adjoining species. Is a mulatto or a quadroon white or black? They are related to both. Likewise there may be an alliance or mixture of farce and comedy, of drama and tragedy. *Célimare* is almost a comedy; the *Cid* is almost a melodrama: It is neverthless useful to have carefully defined the species; and if the law should only teach authors not to treat a subject of comedy by the devices of farce, that would be something. The general law of the theatre is defined by the action of a will conscious of itself; and the dramatic species are distinguished by the nature of the obstacles encountered by this will.

And the quality of will measures and determines, in its turn, the dramatic value of each work in its species. Intelligence rules in the domain of speculation, but the will governs in the field of action, and consequently in history. It is the will which gives power; and power is hardly ever lost except by a failure or relaxation of the will. But that is also the reason why men think there is nothing grander than the development of the will, whatever the object, and that is the reason for the superiority of tragedy over

[14] Hugo's *Hernani* (1831), Shakespeare's *Antony and Cleopatra* (1607), Dumas *fils's The Illegitimate Son* (1858), Augier's *Madame Caverlet* (1836).
[15] (1649) by Corneille.

the other dramatic forms. One may prefer for one's own taste a farce to a tragedy; one ought even to prefer a good farce to a mediocre tragedy, that goes without saying; and we do it every day. One cannot deny that tragedy is superior to farce: *Athalie*[16] to the *Légataire Universel*, and *Ruy Blas*[17] to the *Trois Epiciers*. Another reason sometimes given is that it implies indifference to death, but that is the same reason, if the supreme effort of the will is to conquer the horror of death. But shall we say that comedy is superior to farce, and why? We will say that, and for the same reason, because the obstacles against which Crispin contends in the *Légataire Universel* do not exist strictly speaking, they are only an invention of Regnard; and so the will is exerting itself to no effect. The goal is only a lure, so the action is only a game. And we will say in conclusion that one drama is superior to another drama according as the quantity of will exerted is greater or less, as the share of chance is less, and that of necessity greater.

Maurice Maeterlinck *1862–1949*

The Tragical in Daily Life *1896*

There is a tragic element in the life of every day that is far more real, far more penetrating, far more akin to the true self that is in us than the tragedy that lies in great adventure. But, readily as we all may feel this, to prove it is by no means easy, inasmuch as this essential tragic element comprises more than that which is merely psychological. It goes beyond the determined struggle of man against man, and desire against desire: it goes beyond the eternal conflict of duty and passion. Its province is rather to reveal to us how truly wonderful is the mere act of living, and to throw light upon the existence of the soul, self-contained in the midst of ever-restless immensities; to hush the discourse of reason and sentiment, so that above the tumult may be heard the solemn, uninterrupted whisperings of

Selections. From Maurice Maeterlinck, *The Treasure of the Humble*. Translated by Alfred Sutro. New York: Dodd, Mead, 1903.

[16] (1691) by Racine.
[17] (1838) by Hugo.

man and his destiny. It is its province to point out to us the uncertain, dolorous footsteps of the being, as he approaches, or wanders from, his truth, his beauty, or his God. And further, to show us, and make us understand, the countless other things therewith connected, of which tragic poets have but vouchsafed us passing glimpses. And here do we come to an essential point, for could not these things, of which we have had only passing glimpses, be placed in front of the others, and shown to us first of all? The mysterious chant of the Infinite, the ominous silence of the soul and of God, the murmur of Eternity on the horizon, the destiny or fatality that we are conscious of within us, though by what tokens none can tell—do not all these underlie *King Lear, Macbeth, Hamlet*? And would it not be possible, by some interchanging of the roles, to bring them nearer to us, and send the actors farther off? Is it beyond the mark to say that the true tragic element, normal, deep-rooted, and universal, that the true tragic element of life only begins at the moment when so-called adventures, sorrows, and dangers have disappeared? Is the arm of happiness not longer than that of sorrow, and do not certain of its attributes draw nearer to the soul? Must we indeed roar like the Atrides, before the Eternal God will reveal Himself in our life? and is He never by our side at times when the air is calm, and the lamp burns on, unflickering? When we think of it, is it not the tranquillity that is terrible, the tranquillity watched by the stars? and is it in tumult or in silence that the spirit of life quickens within us? Is it not when we are told, at the end of the story, "They were happy," that the great disquiet should intrude itself? What is taking place while they are happy? Are there not elements of deeper gravity and stability in happiness, in a single moment of repose, than in the whirlwind of passion? Is it not then that we at last behold the march of time—aye, and of many another onstealing besides, more secret still—is it not then that the hours rush forward? Are not deeper chords set vibrating by all these things than by the dagger-stroke of conventional drama? Is it not at the very moment when a man believes himself secure from bodily death that the strange and silent tragedy of the being and the immensities does indeed raise its curtain on the stage? Is it while I flee before a naked sword that my existence touches its most interesting point? Is life always at its sublimest in a kiss? Are there not other monuments, when one hears purer voices that do not fade away so soon? Does the soul only flower on nights of storm? Hitherto, doubtless, this belief has prevailed. It is only the life of violence, the life of bygone days, that is perceived by nearly all our tragic writers; and truly may one say that anachronism dominates the stage, and that dramatic art dates back as many years as the art of sculpture. Far different is it with the other arts—with painting and music, for instance—for these have learned to select and reproduce those obscurer phases of daily life that are not the less deep-rooted and amazing. They know that all that life has lost, as regards mere superficial ornament, has been more than counterbalanced by the depth, the intimate meaning and the spiritual gravity it has acquired. The true artist no longer chooses Marius triumphing over the Cimbrians, or the assassination of the Duke of Guise, as fit subjects for his art; for he is well aware that the psychology of victory or murder is but elementary and exceptional, and that the solemn voice of men and things, the voice that issues forth so timidly and hesitatingly, cannot be heard amidst the idle uproar of acts of violence. And therefore will he place on his canvas a house lost in the heart of the country, an open door at the end of a passage, a face or hands at rest, and by these simple images will he add to our consciousness of life, which is a possession that it is no longer possible to lose.

But to the tragic author, as to the mediocre painter who still lingers over historical pictures, it is only the violence of the anecdote that appeals, and in his representation thereof does the entire interest of his work consist. And he imagines, forsooth, that we shall delight in witnessing the very same acts that brought joy to the hearts of the barbarians, with whom murder, outrage and treachery were matters of daily occurrence. Whereas it is far away from bloodshed, battle-cry and sword-thrust that the lives of most of us flow on, and men's tears are silent today, and invisible, and almost spiritual.

Indeed, when I go to a theatre, I feel as though I were spending a few hours with my ancestors, who conceived life as something that was primitive, arid, and brutal; but this conception of theirs scarcely even lingers in my memory, and surely it is not one that I can share. I am shown a deceived husband killing his wife, a woman poisoning her lover, a son avenging his father, a father slaughtering his children, children putting their father to death, murdered kings, ravished virgins, imprisoned citizens— in a word, all the sublimity of tradition, but alas, how superficial and material! Blood, surface-tears, and death! What can I learn from creatures who have but one fixed idea, and who have not time to live, for that there is a rival, or a mistress, whom it behooves them to put to death?

I had hoped to be shown some act of life, traced back to its sources and to its mystery by connecting links, that my daily occupations afford me neither power nor occasion to study. I had gone thither hoping that the beauty, the grandeur, and the earnestness of my humble day-by-day existence would, for one instant, be revealed to me, that I would be shown the I know not what presence, power, or God that is ever with me in my room. I was yearning for one of the strange moments of a higher life that flit unperceived through my dreariest hours; whereas, almost invariably, all that I beheld was but a man who would tell me, at wearisome length, why he was jealous, why he poisoned, or why he killed.

I admire Othello, but he does not appear to me to live the august daily life of a Hamlet, who has the time to live, inasmuch as he does not act. Othello is admirably jealous. But is it not perhaps an ancient error to imagine that it is at the moments when this passion, or others of equal violence, possesses us, that we live our truest lives? I have grown to believe that an old man, seated in his armchair, waiting patiently, with his lamp beside him; giving unconscious ear to all the eternal laws that reign about his house, interpreting, without comprehending, the silence of doors and windows and the quivering voice of the light, submitting with bent head to the presence of his soul and his destiny—an old man, who conceives not that all the powers of this world, like so many heedful servants, are mingling and keeping vigil in his room, who suspects not that the very sun itself is supporting in space the little table against which he leans, or that every star in heaven and every fiber of the soul are directly concerned in the movement of an eyelid that closes, or a thought that springs to birth—I have grown to believe that he, motionless as he is, does yet live in reality a deeper, more human and more universal life than the lover who strangles his mistress, the captain who conquers in battle, or "the husband who avenges his honor."

I shall be told, perhaps, that a motionless life would be invisible, that therefore animation must be conferred upon it, and movement, and that such varied movement as would be acceptable is to be found only in the few passions of which use has hitherto been made. I do not know whether it be true that a static theatre is impossible. Indeed, to me it seems to exist already. Most of the tragedies of Aeschylus are tragedies without movement. In both the *Prometheus* and the *Suppliants*, events are lacking; and the entire tragedy of the *Choephorae*—surely the most terrible drama of antiquity—does but cling, nightmare-like, around the tomb of Agamemnon, till murder darts forth, as a lightning flash, from the accumulation of prayers, ever falling back upon themselves. Consider, from this point of view, a few more of the finest tragedies of the ancients: *The Eumenides, Antigone, Electra, Oedipus at Colonos.* "They have admired," said Racine in his preface to *Bérénice*, "they have admired the *Ajax* of Sophocles, wherein there is nothing but Ajax killing himself with regret for the fury into which he fell after the arms of Achilles were denied him. They have admired *Philoctetes*, whose entire subject is but the coming of Ulysses with intent to seize the arrows of Hercules. Even the *Oedipus*, thoughtful of recognitions, contains less subject-matter than the simplest tragedy of our days."

What have we here but life that is almost motionless? In most cases, indeed, you will find that psychological action—infinitely loftier in itself than mere material action, and truly, one might think, well-nigh indispensable —that psychological action even has been suppressed, or at least vastly diminished, in a truly marvelous fashion, with the result that the interest centers solely and entirely in the individual, face to face with the universe. Here we are no longer with the barbarians, nor is man now fretting himself in the midst of elementary passions, as though, forsooth, these were the only things worthy of note: he is at rest, and we have time to observe him. It is no longer a violent, exceptional moment of life that passes before our eyes—it is life itself. Thousands and thousands of laws there are, mightier and more venerable than those of passion; but, in common with all that is endowed with resistless force, these laws are silent, and discreet, and slow-moving; and hence it is only in the twilight that they can be seen and heard, in the meditation that comes to us at the tranquil moments of life. . . .

Indeed, it is not in the actions but in the words that are found the beauty and greatness of tragedies that are truly beautiful and great; and this not solely in the words that accompany and explain the action, for there must perforce be another dialogue besides the one which is superficially necessary. And indeed the only words that count in the play are those that at first seemed useless, for it is therein that the essence lies. Side by side with the necessary dialogue will you almost always find another dialogue that seems superfluous; but examine it carefully, and it will be borne home to you that this is the only one that the soul can listen to profoundly, for here alone is it the soul that is being addressed. You will see, too, that it is the quality and the scope of this unnecessary dialogue that determine the quality and the immeasurable range of the work. Certain it is that, in the ordinary drama, the indispensable dialogue by no means corresponds to reality; and it is just those words that are spoken by the side of the rigid, apparent truth that constitute the mysterious beauty of the most beautiful tragedies, inasmuch as these are words that conform to a deeper truth, and one that lies incomparably nearer to the invisible soul by which the poem is upheld. One may even affirm that a poem draws the nearer to beauty and loftier truth in the measure that it eliminates words that merely explain the action, and substitutes for them others that reveal, not so-called soul-state, but I know not what intangible and unceasing striving of the soul towards its own beauty and truth. And so much the nearer, also, does it draw to the true life. To every man does it happen, in his work-a-day existence, that some situation of deep seriousness has to be unravelled by means of words. Reflect for an instant. At moments such as those—nay, at the most commonplace of times—is it the thing you say or the reply you receive that has the most value? Are not other forces, other words one cannot hear, brought into being, and do not these determine the event? What I say often counts for so little; but my presence, the attitude of my soul, my future and my past, that which will take birth in me and that which is dead, a secret thought, the stars that approve, my destiny, the thousands of mysteries which surround me and float about yourself—all this it is that speaks to you at that tragic moment, all this it is that brings to me your answer. There is all this beneath every one of my words, and each one of yours; it is this, above all, that we see, it is this, above all, that we hear, ourselves notwithstanding. If you have come, you, the "outraged husband," the "deceived lover, the "forsaken wife," intending to kill me, your arm will not be stayed by my most moving entreaty; but it may be that there will come towards you, at that moment, one of these unexpected forces; and my soul, knowing of their vigil near to me, may whisper a secret word whereby, haply, you shall be disarmed. These are the spheres wherein adventures come to issue, this is the dialogue whose echo should be heard. And it is this echo that one does hear—extremely attenuated and variable, it is true—in some of the great works mentioned above. But might we not try to draw nearer to the spheres where it is "in reality" that everything comes to pass?

The Modern Drama   *1904*

. . . The first thing that strikes us in the drama of the day is the decay, one might almost say the creeping paralysis, of external action. Next we note a very pronounced desire to penetrate deeper and deeper into human consciousness, and place moral problems upon a high pedestal; and finally the search, still very timid and halting, for a kind of new beauty, that shall be less abstract than was the old.

It is certain that, on the actual stage, we have far fewer extraordinary and violent adventures. Bloodshed has grown less frequent, passions less turbulent; heroism has become less unbending, courage less material and less ferocious. People still die on the stage, it is true, as in reality they still must die, but death has ceased—or will cease, let us hope, very soon—to be regarded as the indispensable setting, the *ultima ratio*, the inevitable end, of every dramatic poem. In the most formidable crises of our life—which, cruel though it may be, is cruel in silent and hidden ways—we rarely look to death for a solution; and for all that the theatre is slower than the other arts to follow the evolution of human consciousness, it will still be at last compelled, in some measure, to take this into account.

When we consider the ancient and tragical anecdotes that constitute

Translated by Alfred Sutro. Reprinted, with minor omissions, from Maurice Maeterlinck, *The Double Garden*. New York: Dodd, Mead & Co., 1904.

the entire basis of the classical drama; the Italian, Scandinavian, Spanish or mythical stories that provided the plots, not only for all the plays of the Shakespearian period, but also—not altogether to pass over an art that was infinitely less spontaneous—for those of French and German romanticism, we discover at once that these anecdotes are no longer able to offer us the direct interest they presented at a time when they appeared highly natural and possible, at a time, when at any rate, the circumstances, manners, and sentiments they recalled were not yet extinct in the minds of those who witnessed their reproduction.

To us, however, these adventures no longer correspond with a living and actual reality. Should a youth of our time love, and meet obstacles not unlike those which, in another order of ideas and events, beset Romeo's passion, we need no telling that his adventure will be embellished by none of the features that gave poetry and grandeur to the episode of Verona. Gone beyond recall is the entrancing atmosphere of a lordly, passionate life; gone the brawls in picturesque streets, the interludes of bloodshed and splendor, the mysterious poisons, the majestic, complaisant tombs! And where shall we look for that exquisite summer's night, which owes its vastness, its savor, the very appeal that it makes to us, to the shadow of an heroic, inevitable death that already lay heavy upon it? Divest the story of Romeo and Juliet of these beautiful trappings, and we have only the very simple and ordinary desire of a noble-hearted, unfortunate youth for a maiden whose obdurate parents deny him her hand. All the poetry, the splendor, the passionate life of this desire, result from the glamour, the nobility, tragedy, that are proper to the environment wherein it has come to flower; nor is there a kiss, a murmur of love, a cry of anger, grief or despair, but borrows its majesty, grace, its heroism, tenderness—in a word, every image that has helped it to visible form—from the beings and objects around it; for it is not in the kiss itself that the sweetness and beauty are found, but in the circumstance, hour, and place wherein it was given. Again, the same objections would hold if we chose to imagine a man of our time who should be jealous as Othello was jealous, possessed of Macbeth's ambition, unhappy as Lear; or, like Hamlet, restless and wavering, bowed down beneath the weight of a frightful and unrealisable duty.

These conditions no longer exist. The adventure of the modern Romeo— to consider only the external events which it might provoke—would not provide material for a couple of acts. Against this it may be urged that a modern poet, who desires to put on the stage an analogous poem of youthful love, is perfectly justified in borrowing from days gone by a more decorative setting, one that shall be more fertile in heroic and tragical incident. Granted; but what can the result be of such an expedient? Would not the feelings and passions that demand for their fullest, most perfect expression and development the atmosphere of today (for the passions and feelings of a modern poet must, in despite of himself, be entirely and exclusively modern) would not these suddenly find themselves transplanted to a soil where all things prevented their living? . . .

But we need dwell no further on the necessarily artificial poems that arise from the impossible marriage of past and present. Let us rather consider the drama that actually stands for the reality of our time, as Greek drama stood for Greek reality, and the drama of the Renaissance for the reality of the Renaissance. Its scene is a modern house, it passes between men and women of today. The names of the invisible protagonists—the passions and ideas—are the same, more or less, as of old. We see love, hatred, ambition, jealousy, envy, greed; the sense of justice and idea of duty; pity, goodness, devotion, piety, selfishness, vanity, pride, etc. But although the names have remained more or less the same, how great is the difference we find in the aspect and quality, the extent and influence, of these ideal actors! Of all their ancient weapons not one is left them, not one of the marvelous moments of olden days. It is seldom that cries are heard now; bloodshed is rare, and tears not often seen. It is in a small room, round a table, close to the fire, that the joys and sorrows of mankind are decided. We suffer, or make others suffer, we love, we die, there in our corner; and it were the strangest chance should a door or a window suddenly, for an instant, fly open, beneath the pressure of extraordinary despair or rejoicing. Accidental, adventitious beauty exists no longer; there remains only an external poetry, that has not yet become poetic. And what poetry, if we probe to the root of things—what poetry is there that does not borrow nearly all of its charm, nearly all of its ecstasy, from elements that are wholly external? Last of all, there is no longer a God to widen, or master, the action; nor is there an inexorable fate to form a mysterious, solemn, and tragical background for the slightest gesture of man; nor the somber and abundant atmosphere, that was able to ennoble even his most contemptible weaknesses, his least pardonable crimes.

There still abides with us, it is true, a terrible unknown; but it is so diverse and elusive, it becomes so arbitrary, so vague and contradictory, the moment we try to locate it, that we cannot evoke it without great danger; cannot even, without the mightiest difficulty avail ourselves of it, though in all loyalty, to raise to the point of mystery the gestures, actions, and words of the men we pass every day. The endeavor has been made; the formidable, problematic enigma of heredity, the grandiose but improbable enigma of inherent justice, and many others beside, have each in their turn been put forward as a substitute for the vast enigma of the Providence or Fatality of old. And it is curious to note how these youthful enigmas, born but of yesterday, already seem older, more arbitrary, more unlikely, than those whose places they took in an access of pride. . . .

. . . Incapable of outside movement, deprived of external ornament, daring no longer to make serious appeal to a determined divinity or fatality, [the modern drama] has fallen back on itself, and seeks to discover, in the regions of psychology and of moral problems, the equivalent of what once was offered by exterior life. It has penetrated deeper into human consciousness; but has encountered difficulties there no less strange than unexpected.

To penetrate deeply into human consciousness is the privilege, even the duty, of the thinker, the moralist, the historian, novelist, and to a degree, of the lyrical poet; but not of the dramatist. Whatever the temptation, he dare not sink into inactivity, become mere philosopher or observer. Do what one will, discover what marvels one may, the sovereign law of the stage, its essential demand, will always be *action*. With the rise of the curtain, the high intellectual desire within us undergoes transformation; and in place of the thinker, psychologists, mystic or moralist there stands the mere instinctive spectator, the man electrified negatively by the crowd, the man whose one desire it is to see something happen. . . . And there are no words so profound, so noble and admirable, but they will soon weary us if they leave the situation unchanged, if they lead to no action, bring about no decisive conflict, or hasten no definite solution.

But whence is it that action arises in the consciousness of man? In its first stage it springs from the struggle between diverse conflicting passions. But no sooner has it raised itself somewhat—and this is true, if we examine it closely, of the first stage also—than it would seem to be solely due to the conflict between a passion and a moral law, between a duty and a desire. Hence the eagerness with which modern dramatists have plunged into all the problems of contemporary morality; and it may safely be said that at this moment they confine themselves almost exclusively to the discussion of these different problems.

This movement was initiated by the dramas of Alexandre Dumas *fils*, dramas which brought the most elementary of moral conflicts on to the stage; dramas, indeed, whose entire existence was based on problems such as the spectator, who must always be regarded as the ideal moralist, would never put to himself in the course of his whole spiritual existence, so evident is their solution. Should the faithless husband or wife be forgiven? Is it well to avenge infidelity by infidelity? Has the illegitimate child any rights? Is the marriage of inclination—such is the name it bears in those regions—preferable to the marriage for money? Have parents the right to oppose a marriage for love? Is divorce to be deprecated when a child has been born of the union? Is the sin of the adulterous wife greater than that of the adulterous husband? etc., etc.

Indeed, it may be said here that the entire French theatre of today, and a considerable proportion of the foreign theatre, which is only its echo, exist solely on questions of this kind, and on the entirely superfluous answers to which they give rise.

On the other hand, however, the highest point of human consciousness is attained by the dramas of Björnson, of Hauptmann, and, above all, of Ibsen. Here we touch the limit of the resources of modern dramaturgy. For, in truth, the further we penetrate into the consciousness of man, the less struggle do we discover. It is impossible to penetrate far into any consciousness unless that consciousness be very enlightened; for, whether we advance ten steps, or a thousand, in the depths of a soul that is plunged in darkness, we shall find nothing there that can be unexpected, or new; for darkness everywhere will only resemble itself. But a consciousness that is truly enlightened will possess passions and desires infinitely less exacting, infinitely more peaceful and patient, more salutary, abstract, and general, than are those that reside in the ordinary consciousness. Thence, far less struggle—or at least a struggle of far less violence—between these nobler and wiser passions; and this for the very reason that they have become vaster and loftier; for if there be nothing more restless, destructive and savage than a dammed-up stream, there is nothing more tranquil, beneficent and silent than the beautiful river whose banks ever widen.

Again, this enlightened consciousness will yield to infinitely fewer laws, admit infinitely fewer doubtful or harmful duties. There is, one may say, scarcely a falsehood or error, a prejudice, half-truth or convention, that is not capable of assuming, that does not actually assume, when the occasion presents itself, the form of a duty in an uncertain consciousness. It is thus that honor, in the chivalrous, conjugal sense of the word (I refer to the honor of the husband, which is supposed to suffer by the infidelity of the wife), that revenge, a kind of morbid prudishness, pride, vanity, piety to certain gods, and a thousand other illusions, have been, and still remain, the unquenchable source of a multitude of duties that are still regarded as absolutely sacred, absolutely incontrovertible, by a vast number of inferior consciousnesses. And these so-called duties are the pivot of almost all the dramas of the Romantic period, as of most of those of today. But not one of these somber, pitiless duties, that so fatally impel mankind to death and disaster, can readily take root in the consciousness that a healthy, living light has adequately penetrated; in such there will be no room for honor or vengeance, for conventions that clamor for blood. It will hold no prejudices that exact tears, no injustice eager for sorrow. It will have cast from their throne the gods who insist on sacrifice, and the love that craves for death. For when the sun has entered into the consciousness of him who is wise, as we may hope that it will some day enter into that of all men, it will reveal one duty, and one alone, which is that we should do the least possible harm and love others as we love ourselves; and from this duty no drama can spring.

Let us consider what happens in Ibsen's plays. He often leads us far down into human consciousness, but the drama remains possible only because there goes with us a singular flame, a sort of red light, which, somber, capricious—unhallowed, one almost might say—falls only on singular phantoms. And indeed nearly all the duties which form the active principle of Ibsen's tragedies are duties situated no longer within, but without, the healthy, illumined consciousness; and the duties we believe we discover outside this consciousness often come perilously near an unjust pride, or a kind of soured and morbid madness.

Let it not be imagined, however—for indeed this would be wholly to misunderstand me—that these remarks of mine in any way detract from my admiration for the great Scandinavian poet. For, if it be true that Ibsen has contributed few salutary elements to the morality of our time, he is perhaps the only writer for the stage who has caught sight of, and set in motion, a new, though still disagreeable poetry, which he has succeeded in investing with a kind of savage, gloomy beauty and grandeur (surely too savage and gloomy for it to become general or definitive); as he is the only one who owes nothing to the poetry of the violently illumined dramas of antiquity or of the Renaissance.

But, while we wait for the time when human consciousness shall recognize more useful passions and less nefarious duties, for the time when the world's stage shall consequently present more happiness and fewer tragedies, there still remains, in the depths of every heart of loyal intention a great duty of charity and justice that eclipses all others. And it is perhaps from the struggle of this duty against our egoism and ignorance that the veritable drama of our century shall spring. When this goal has been attained—in real life as on the stage—it will be permissible perhaps to speak of a new theatre, a theatre of peace, and of beauty without tears.

Henri Bergson 1859–1941

Laughter 1900

The first point to which we should call attention is that there is no comic outside of what is exclusively *human*. A countryside may be beautiful, graceful, sublime, insignificant, or ugly; it will never be comical. We may laugh at an animal, but only because we have caught in it an attitude of man, or a human expression. We will laugh at a hat; but what we scoff at, then, is not the piece of felt or straw; it is the form that men have given it; it is the human whim from which it has taken shape. How has a fact so important in its simplicity not attracted more of the attention of philosophers? Several have defined man as "an animal who knows how to laugh." They could as well define him as an animal who provokes laughter, because if some animal or an inanimate object succeeds in doing so, it is because of some similarity to man, because of the imprint that man has made on it, or because of the use man makes of it.

Let us point out, now, as a symptom no less worthy of notice, the insensibility which ordinarily accompanies laughter. It is as if the comic can produce its shock only on condition that it brush the surface of a quite calm, quite simple soul. Indifference is its natural milieu. Laughter has no greater enemy than emotion. I do not mean that we might not laugh at a person who inspires pity in us, for example, or even affection: only then for the moment, we must forget this affection, silence this pity. In a society of pure intellectuals, its members would probably not cry more, but they would perhaps still laugh, while invariably sensitive souls, attuned to the harmony of life, whose each event would be drawn out in sentimental resonance, would not laugh, nor understand laughter. Try for a moment to interest yourself in everything that is said and everything that is done; act, in imagination, with those who act; feel with those who feel; in short, give your sympathy its fullest flowering: as though under the stroke of a magic wand, you will see the airiest objects acquire weight, and a harsh coloration sift over everything. Now become detached, look on life as if you were an indifferent spectator: many of the dramas will turn into comedies. We need only shut our ears to the sound of music in a room where people are dancing for the dancers suddenly to appear ridiculous to us. How many human actions would resist a test of this kind? And would we not see many of them move suddenly from solemn to amusing if we separated them from the music of feeling which accompanies them? The comic demands, then, in order to produce its full effect, something like a momentary anesthesia of the heart. It is addressed to pure intellect.

However, this intellect must remain in contact with other intellects. That is the third fact on which we should focus our attention. If we felt isolated, we would have no taste for the comic. It is as though laughter must have an echo. Listen to it closely: it is not an articulated, distinct, finished sound; it is something that wants to be prolonged, reverberating gradually nearer and nearer, something that starts with a clap, only to continue in rolls, like thunder on the mountain. This reverberation, however, should not go on to infinity. It can go around the interior of a circle as large as we like; the circle is none the less closed. Our laughter is always the laughter of a group. Perhaps you have happened, on a train, or in a public dining room, to hear travelers tell stories which must be hilarious to them, since they laugh heartily. If you had been one of their company you would have laughed like them. But since you were not, you had no inclination to laugh. A man who was asked why he did not cry at a sermon where everyone else poured out tears replied: "I am not a member of the parish." What that man thought about tears would be truer of laughter. As ingenuous as one may think it to be, laughter conceals a hidden understanding, I would say almost a complicity with other laughers, real or imaginary. How many times have we not said that the laughter of the audience in the theatre is as broad as the house is full? How many times, on the other hand, have we not remarked that many comic effects cannot be translated from one language to another because they are related to the customs and notions of a specific society? . . .

A man, running in the street, trips and falls. The passers-by laugh. I think they would not laugh at him if they supposed that a whim had suddenly come over him to sit down on the ground. They laugh because he sits down involuntarily. It is not, then, his abrupt change of posture that causes the laughter; it is that there is something involuntary in the change; it is his awkwardness. Perhaps there was a stone on the road. He should have changed his pace or gone around the obstacle. But through lack of suppleness, through inattention, or through the body's obstinacy, *indeed, through inflexibility or momentum,* the muscles have continued to make the same motions when the circumstances called for another one. That is why the man fell and that is at what the passers-by laugh.

Now, here is a person who devotes himself to his little occupations with mathematical regularity. Only the objects which surround him have been meddled with by a practical joker. He dips his pen in the inkwell and when he removes it, it is covered with mud; he thinks he is sitting down on a solid chair and falls full length on the floor; in short, he acts in the wrong way, or functions in a meaningless way, always because of momentum. Habit has dictated the impetus; the movement should have been changed or turned in its course. But no such thing: he continued mechanically in a straight line.

The victim of the practical joke, then, is in a situation analogous to that of the runner who falls. He is comic for the same reason. What is laughable in one case, as in the other, is a certain *mechanical rigidity* exactly where we would hope to find the watchful suppleness and the enduring pliancy of a human being. Between the two cases there is this sole difference, that the first occurred by itself, while the second was brought about artificially. In the first, the passer-by only watched; in the second, the practical joker experimented. . . .

. . . comical facial expression will be one which makes us think of something rigid, stiff, so to speak, in the ordinary mobility of the face. . . .

Attitudes, gestures, and movements of the human body are comic in exactly the same proportion as the body makes us think of a simple machine. . . .

Continuing, now, in this vein, we vaguely perceive the consequences, farther and farther reaching, and of more and more importance, of the law we have just posited. Still more fleeting visions of mechanical effects crowd in on us, visions suggested by man's complex actions and not simply by his gestures. We gather that the usual devices of comedy, the periodic repetition of a word or a scene, the systematic reversals of roles, the geometric progression of a blunder, and many other stage tricks may derive their comic thrust from the same source—the art of the vaudeville writer perhaps being to show us a visibly mechanical articulation of human events, all the while preserving the outward aspect of probability, that is to say, the apparent elasticity of life. . . .

. . . *Something mechanical inlaid on the living*—there is a [sign] at which we must stop, a central image from which the imagination radiates in divergent directions. What are these directions? One perceives three principal ones. We are going to follow one after the other; then we will pick up our road again in a straight line.

First of all, this vision of the mechanical and the living fitted into each other, makes us lean toward the less precise image of some kind of rigidity placed upon the mobility of life, trying unskillfully to follow its lines and counterfeit its elasticity. We see, then, how easy it would be for garments to become ridiculous. We could almost say that all fashion is in some ways comic. . . .

But here, again, we will emphasize the comic by moving it closer to its source. From the idea of travesty, which is derived, we must go back again to the first idea, that of a mechanism superimposed upon life. At once the rigid form of all etiquette suggests to us an image of this sort. As soon as we forget the grave objective of a solemn occasion, or a ceremony, those who take part in it give the effect of moving about like marionettes. Their mobility is ruled by the immobility of a formula. It is purely mechanical movement. But mechanical movement will be perfect, for example, if it is that of a civil servant, functioning like a simple machine, or again, in the unconsciousness of an administrative regulation's being applied with inexorable inevitability and being mistaken for a law of nature. Some years ago a steamer was shipwrecked near Dieppe. With a great deal of difficulty, some passengers were saved in a small craft. A few customs officials, who had bravely gone to their aid, began the conversation by asking them if they had anything to declare. I find something analogous, although the idea is subtler, in the comment of a member of Parliament after questioning a minister on the day after a murder had been committed on a train: "The murderer, after having finished off his victim, must have got off the train on the wrong side, in violation of administrative rules."

A mechanization forced in upon nature, an automatic regulation of society; these, then, are the two kinds of comic effects at which we have arrived. It yet remains for us to put them together and see what will happen. . . .

Something mechanical inlaid on the living—that is again our point of departure. Again, where did the comedy come from? From the living body's becoming stiff like a machine. It seemed to us, then, that the living body ought to have perfect suppleness, its nimbleness always on guard like a principle always at work. But this nimbleness should really belong to the soul rather than to the body. It should be the very flame of life, lighted in us by a higher source and perceived through the body by an impression of transparency. When we see in the living body only grace and suppleness, it is because we do not notice what there is about it that is heavy, resistant, in short, material; we forget its "materialness" so we can think only of its vitality, a vitality that our imagination attributes to the very source of intellectual and moral life. But suppose our attention is called to this material quality of the body. Suppose, instead of partaking of this lightness from the source which animates it, the body is no more, in our eyes, than an ugly and awkward shell, tiresome ballast that keeps on the ground a soul impatient to leave the earth. Then the body will become for the soul what the garment was, just now, for the body itself, inert matter placed upon living energy. And the impression of the comic will be produced as soon as we have a distinct perception of this superimposition. We shall especially have this perception when we are shown the soul *teased* by the needs of the body—on the one hand the moral personality with its intelligently varied energy, on the other the stupidly monotonous body, interfering and interrupting with the stubbornness of a machine. The shabbier and more uniformly repeated these needs of the body are, the more violent the impression will be. But that is only a question of degree and the general law of these phenomena could be stated thus: *Any incident that calls our attention to the physical part of a person when the moral part should be more important is comic.*

Why do we laugh at a speaker who sneezes at the saddest moment of his speech? Where does the comic come from in this sentence from a funeral oration, quoted by a German philosopher: "He was virtuous and quite stout"?

It comes from the fact that our attention is brusquely recalled from the soul to the body. . . .

Let us return, then, for the last time, to our central image: that of the mechanical inlaid on the living. The living being with whom we were concerned here was, above all, a human being, a person. A mechanical device, on the contrary, is a thing. What produced laughter, therefore, if we may regard the image from this point of view, was the momentary transformation of a person into a thing. Let us move, then, from the precise idea of a machine to the less precise one of a thing in general. We will have a new series of comic images which will be obtained by blurring, so to speak, the contours of the first ones, and which will lead us to this new law: *We laugh every time a person gives us the impression that he is a thing.*

We laugh at Sancho Panza thrown into a quilt and hurled into the air like a mere football. . . .

. . . *Any arrangement of acts and events which, when they are in close juxtaposition, gives us the illusion of life and the distinct feeling of a mechanical composition is comic.*

The Jack-in-the-Box   We have all played, long ago, with the fellow who comes up out of his box. He is flattened out, he becomes erect again. He is pushed back lower, he rebounds higher. He is squashed under his lid, and often he makes the whole thing explode. I do not know if this game is old, but the kind of amusement it provides is for all time. It is the conflict between two kinds of stubbornness, one of which—the purely mechanical one—ends up by giving in to the other, who plays with it. The cat playing with the mouse, who lets it go time after time, like a spring, in order to pull it up sharp with a blow from her paw gets amusement of this kind.

Let us now move on to the theater. We should begin with a Punch and Judy show. When the policeman ventures onto the stage he immediately receives, of course, a blow that knocks him down. He stands erect again, a second blow flattens him. Another repetition of the offense, another punishment. With the unvarying rhythm of a spring that coils and releases, the policeman falls down and gets up again while the laughter of the audience grows continuously louder.

Let us imagine, now, a moral spring, an idea that is expressed, quelled, expressed again; a flood of words that gushes forth, is arrested, and starts out again and again. We will have, anew, the vision of one stubborn force against another stubborn force which strives against it. But this vision will have lost its material quality. We will no longer be at the Punch and Judy show; we will be at a real comedy. . . .

. . . *In a comic repetition of words, there are generally two expressions in battle, one repressed opinion that uncoils like a spring, and one idea that amuses itself by repressing the opinion anew.*

When Dorine is telling Orgon about his wife's illness and he continually interrupts her to inquire about the health of Tartuffe, the question that keeps coming back—"And Tartuffe?"—gives us the precise sensation of a spring going off. It is this spring that Dorine amuses herself by pushing back each time she again picks up her recital of Elmire's illness.[1] And when Scapin comes to announce to the old Géronte that his son has been taken prisoner on the famous galley, and that he must ransom him quickly, he toys with the avarice of Géronte exactly as Dorine does with the infatuation of Orgon.[2] The avarice, scarcely repressed, starts up again automatically, and it is this automatism that Molière wanted to emphasize by the mechanical repetition of a question that expresses regret for the money that he is going to have to give: "What the devil was he doing in that galley?" The same observation applies to the scene where Valère shows Harpagon how wrong he would be to marry his daughter to a man she does not love. "But no dowry!" the greed of Harpagon keeps interrupting.[3] And we catch a glimpse, behind this sentence that recurs automatically, of a repeating apparatus made to go by an obsession.

The Puppet   The scenes are innumerable in comedy where a person believes he is speaking and acting freely; where, consequently, this person retains the essential quality of being alive, whereas, from a certain point of view, he appears to be only a toy in the hands of another, who is amusing himself with him. From the puppet that the child manipulates with a piece of string to Géronte and Argante, manipulated by Scapin, the distance is not far. But listen to Scapin himself: "The plot is laid," and again: "It is the gods who have brought them to my net." The spectator, by natural instinct and because he prefers, in imagination at least, to be the duper, rather than the duped, puts himself on the side of the swindlers. He joins up with them, and from now on, like a child who has made a friend lend him his puppet, he himself makes the puppet (whose strings he has taken into his own hands) come and go on the stage. This latter condition, however, is not always indispensable. We can also remain on the outside of what happens if we retain the precise feeling of a mechanical composition. This is what happens when one of the people fluctuates between two opposing sides, each of the sides winning him over in turn—as when Panurge asks every Peter and Paul whether he should get married. Notice that the comic writer takes pains to *personify* the two opposing sides. Lacking spectators, there must at least be actors to hold the strings.

All the profundity of life comes to it from our freedom. The feelings that we have brought to maturity, the emotions that we have hatched, the actions

[1] Molière's *Tartuffe* (1664).
[2] Molière's *Scapin* (1671).
[3] Molière's *The Miser* (1668).

that we have deliberated over, held in check, performed, in short, all that comes from us and is really ours, these are what give life its sometimes dramatic and usually serious aspect. What must happen to transform all that into comedy? It must be imagined that our apparent liberty is covering up a set of puppet strings and that we, here below, are, as the poet[4] said:

. . . humble marionettes
Whose strings are in the hands of necessity.

There is, then, no real, serious, dramatic scene that imagination cannot push into the comic by the evocation of this simple image. There is no game for which there is a wider field.

The Snowball   The further we move in this study of comic methods, the better we understand the role played by childhood recollections. These recollections bear less on any particular game than they do on the mechanical device to which that game is applied. The same general device can be found, moreover, in very different games, like the same musical comedy tune in many musical comedies. What is important here is what the mind retains; what moves, by imperceptible gradations, from the games of the child to those of the man, is the *scheme* of the combination, or, if you like, the abstract formula of which these games are specific illustrations. There is, for example, the rolling snowball which grows bigger as it rolls. We might equally well think of lead soldiers in a file behind each other; if we push the first, it falls on the second, which knocks over the third, and thus the situation grows worse until they are all on the floor. . . .

Inversion   Imagine certain people in a certain situation: you will get a comic scene by turning the situation about and reversing the roles. The double-rescue scene in *The Voyage of Monsieur Perrichon*[5] is of this type. But it is not even necessary that the two symmetrical scenes be placed before us. We need be shown only one, provided that we are surely made to think of the other. Thus it is that we laugh at the accused moralizing to the judges; at the child giving lessons to its parents; in short, at whatever comes under the heading "Upside-down World. . . ."

The truth is that the comic character may, in a sense, be in complete accord with strict morality. He must only come into accord with society. The character of Alceste[6] is that of a completely honest man. But he is unsociable and, because of that, laughable. A malleable vice would be less easy to ridicule than an inflexible virtue. It is the *inflexibility* that is suspect in the eyes of society. Therefore it is the inflexibility that makes us laugh, although the in-

4 Sully-Prudhomme (1839–1907).
5 (1860), by Eugène Labiche and Édouard Martin.
6 In Molière's *The Misanthrope*.

flexibility here betokens honesty. Whoever isolates himself is exposed to ridicule, because the comic is composed, in large measure, of this very isolation. This explains why the comic is so often dependent on the customs, the ideas—to speak plainly, on the prejudices of a society.

However, it must be recognized, to man's credit, that the social ideal and the moral ideal are not essentially different. We can, therefore, admit that, as a general rule, it is the faults of others that make us laugh—even though we must add that these faults make us laugh because of their unsociability rather than their immorality. We must now find out what are the faults which can become comical, and in what cases we judge them too serious to laugh at them.

But we have already answered this question implicitly. The comic, we said, appeals to pure intellect; laughter is incompatible with emotion. Describe to me as unimportant a fault as you wish: if you present it to me in a manner that moves my sympathy, or my fear, or my pity, all is over: I can no longer laugh at it. Pick, on the contrary, a consummate and generally odious vice: you can render it comic, if you first succeed, by appropriate tricks, in rendering it unable to move me. I do not say that the vice will then be comic; I say that, from then on, it may become so. *It must not move me*, that is the sole really necessary condition, although assuredly, it is not enough. . . .

In summary, we have seen that a character may be good or bad, it matters little: if he is unsociable he will become comic. We see now that the gravity of the situation matters little more: grave or gay, it will be able to make us laugh if it is managed so that we are not moved. Unsociability in the character, callousness in the spectator, are together the two essential conditions. There is a third, implied in the two others, that all of our analysis up to now has strained to bring clear.

It is automatism, purely mechanical movement. From the beginning of this work we have made this point and we have never ceased to call attention to it: only what is automatically done is essentially laughable. In a fault, in a virtue, even, the comic is that by which the character betrays himself unknowingly— the involuntary gesture, the unconscious word. All absentmindedness is comic; and the more complete the absentmindedness, the higher the comedy. Systematic absentmindedness, like that of Don Quixote, is the most comical thing in the world: it is the essence of the comic, taken as nearly as possible from its source. Take any other comic character. However conscious he may be of what he says and does, if he is comic it is because there is an aspect of himself which he ignores, a side which escapes him: it is because of that alone that he will make us laugh. Profoundly comic lines are simple lines where a vice is nakedly revealed: how could it show itself thus, if it were capable of seeing itself and judging itself? It is no rare thing for a comic character to disapprove certain conduct in general terms and immediately give an example of it: witness M. Jourdain's philosophy teacher flying into a rage after having preached against anger;[7] Vadius, drawing a poem from his pocket after having railed against readers of poetry;[8] etc. What do these contradictions do if not make us put our fingers on the unconscious of the characters. Inattentiveness to self, and therefore to others; that is what we always find. And if we look closely at these things, we will see that inattentiveness here corresponds to what we have called unsociability. The principal cause of inflexibility is that one fails to look about himself and especially at himself: how can he model his person on that of others if he does not begin to make the acquaintance of others and also of himself? Inflexibility, purely mechanical movement, absentmindedness, unsociability—all these are interwoven, and all these make up the comic character.

Guillaume Apollinaire *1880–1918*

Preface to
The Breasts of Tiresias *1917*

To characterize my drama I have used a neologism which, as I rarely use them, I hope will be excused: I have invented the adjective *surrealist*, which does not at all mean *symbolic*, as Mr. Victor Basch has assumed in his article on the theatre, but defines fairly well a tendency in art which, if it is not the newest thing under the sun, at least has never been formulated as a credo, an artistic and literary faith.

The cheap idealism of the playwrights who followed Victor Hugo sought for verisimilitude in conventional local color, which as "photographic" naturalism produced comedies of manners the originals of which may be found long before Scribe, in the sentimental comedies of Nivelle de la Chaussée.

And in order to attempt, if not a renovation of the theatre, at least an

Selections, translated by Louis Simpson. From *Modern French Theatre*, edited by Michael Benedikt and George E. Wellwarth. New York: E. P. Dutton & Co., 1964. Passages quoted from the Preface to *The Breasts of Tiresias* by permission of Louis Simpson.

[7] In Molière's *The Bourgeois Gentleman.*
[8] In Molière's *The Learned Ladies.*

original effort, I thought it necessary to come back to nature itself, but without copying it photographically.

When man wanted to imitate walking he created the wheel, which does not resemble a leg. In the same way he has created surrealism unconsciously.

However, I cannot possibly decide if this drama is serious or not. Its aim is to interest and entertain. That is the aim of every dramatic work. It also undertakes to emphasize a question of vital importance to those who understand the language in which it is written: the problem of repopulation.

I could have written on this subject, which has never before been treated, a play in the mock-melodramatic style which has been made fashionable by the writers of "problem plays." I preferred a less somber style, for I don't think that the theatre ought to make anyone feel desperate.

I might also have written a play of ideas and flattered the taste of the contemporary public, which likes to think that it thinks. I have preferred to give free rein to the fantasy which is my way of interpreting nature, a fancy which, like life from day to day, is sometimes more and sometimes less melancholy, satiric, and lyrical, but always, and as much as lies within my power, showing a common sense in which there is sometimes enough novelty to shock and anger, but which will be convincing to those who are sincere.

The subject is so moving in my opinion that it permits us to give the word *drama* its most tragic meanings; but it depends on the French whether, because they start making children again, in the future this work is to be called a farce. Nothing else could give me such great patriotic pleasure. I assure you, the reputation which would rightfully be enjoyed by the author of *The Farce of Master Pierre Pathelin*, if his name were known, keeps me awake at night.

It has been said that I have used some of the techniques of vaudeville: I don't really see where. Anyway there is nothing in that criticism that disturbs me, for popular art is an excellent basis and I would congratulate myself for having drawn on it if all my scenes followed the natural sequence of the fable I have imagined, of which the main idea, a man who makes children, is new to the theatre and to literature in general, but can be no more shocking than certain improbable inventions of novelists whose vogue depends on so-called science fiction.

Moreover, there is no symbolism in my play and it is transparent, but you are free to find in it all the symbols you want and to disentangle a thousand meanings, as with the oracles of the sibyl. . . .

Depending on circumstances, tragedy will prevail over comedy or vice versa. But I do not think that from now on you will be able to endure, without impatience, a theatre piece in which these elements are not balanced against each other, for there is such an energy in mankind today and in the writing of the younger generation that the greatest misfortune immediately seems understandable, as though it may be considered not only from the viewpoint of a kindly irony which permits laughter, but also from the perspective of a true optimism which at once consoles us and makes way for hope.

After all, the stage is no more the life it represents than the wheel is a leg. Consequently, it is legitimate, in my opinion, to bring to the theatre new and striking esthetic principles which accentuate the roles of the actors and increase the effect of the production, yet without modifying the pathos or comedy of the situations, which must be self-sufficient.

Finally, may I say that, in abstracting from contemporary literary movements a certain tendency of my own, I am in no way undertaking to form a school, but above all to protest against that "realistic" theatre which is the predominating theatrical art today. This "realism," which is, no doubt, suited to the cinema, is, I believe, as far removed as possible from the art of drama.

Luigi Pirandello *1867–1936*

On Humor *1920*

Comedy and its opposite lie in the same disposition of feeling, and they are inside the process which results from it. In its abnormality, this disposition is bitterly comical, the condition of a man who is always out of tune; of a man who is at the same time violin and bass; of a man for whom no thought can come to mind unless suddenly another one, its opposite and contrary, intervenes; of a man for whom any one reason for saying yes is at once joined by two or three others compelling him to say no, so that yes and no keep him suspended and perplexed for all his life; of a man who cannot let himself go in a feeling without suddenly realizing something inside which disturbs him, disarranges him, makes him angry. . . .

It is a special psychic phenomenon, and it is absolutely arbitrary to attribute to it any determining cause. It may be the result of a bitter experience with life and man—an experience that doesn't allow one the naïve feeling of putting on wings and flying like a lark chirping in the sunshine: it pulls at the tail when one is ready to fly. On the other hand, it leads to the thought that

Selections, translated by Teresa Novel. First published in the *Tulane Drama Review*, Volume X, Number 3 (T 31), Spring 1966. © 1966 by *Tulane Drama Review*. Reprinted by permission. All rights reserved.

man's sadness is often caused by life's sadness, by evils so numerous that not everyone knows how to take them. It leads to the reflection that life, though it has not ordained a clear end for human reason, does not require me to wander in the dark, a reflection that is peculiar and illusive for each man, large or small. It is not important, though, since it is not, nor may it be, the real end which all eagerly try to find and which nobody finds—maybe because it does not exist. The important thing is to give importance to something, vain as it might be. It will be valued as much as something serious, and in the end neither will give satisfaction, because it is true that the ardent thirst for knowledge will always last, the faculty of wishing will never be extinguished—though it cannot be said that man's happiness consists in his progress.

All the soul's fictions and the creations of feeling are subjects for humor; we will see reflection becoming a little devil which disassembles the machine of each image, of each fantasy created by feeling; it will take it apart to see how it is made; it will unwind its spring, and the whole machine will break convulsively. Perhaps humor will do this with the sympathetic indulgence about which those who see only a kind of good humor speak. But it ought not to be trusted. . . .

Every feeling, thought, and idea which arises in the humorist splits itself into contraries. Each yes splits itself into a no, which assumes at the end the same value as the yes. Sometimes the humorist may pretend to take only one side; meanwhile, inside, the other feeling speaks out to him, and appears although he doesn't have the courage to reveal it. It speaks to him and starts by advancing now a faint excuse, an alternative, which cools off the warmth of the first feeling, and then a wise reflection which takes away seriousness and leads to laughter. . . .

Let us start, then, from the construction that illusion offers each of us: the image that everyone has of himself through the work of our illusions. Do we see ourselves in our true reality, as we really are, and not as what we would like to be? Through a spontaneous interior artifice, the result of hidden tendencies or unconscious imitations, don't we believe ourselves to be, in good faith, different from what in substance we are? And we think, work, live according to this factitious but at the same time sincere interpretation of ourselves.

Now, yes, reflection can reveal to the comic and the satirical as well as the humorous writer this concept of illusions. The comic only laughs at it, being pleased to blow away this metaphor of himself created by a spontaneous illusion. The satirical writer will be upset by it. But not the humorist: through the ridiculous side of this perception he will see the serious and grievous side of it. He will analyze the illusion, but not with the intention of laughing at it. Instead of feeling disdain he will, rather, in his laughter, feel commiseration.

The comic and satirical writers know, through reflection, how much nourishment the spider of experience takes from social life to form the web of
morality in any person. And they know how often what is called the moral
sense remains trapped in this web. In the long run, what *are* arrangements of
so-called social convenience? Calculated considerations, in which morality is
almost always sacrificed. The humorist goes deeper, and he laughs without
disdain on finding out how, with naïveté, with the best good faith, through
the spontaneous work of fiction, we are led to interpret as real feeling, as real
moral sense in itself, what is nothing but a feeling of *convenience*, that is, of
mental calculation. He goes even further, and discovers that even the need to
appear worse than what one really is may become conventional, if one is
associated with a social group whose characteristic ideas and feelings are
inferior to what one might desire for oneself. . . .

Simplicity of soul contradicts the historical concept of the human soul.
Its life is a changing equilibrium, a continuous awakening and slumbering of
feelings, tendencies, and ideas. It is an incessant fluctuation between contradictory terms, an oscillation between opposite poles: hope and fear, truth and
falsehood, beauty and ugliness, right and wrong, and so on. If suddenly in
the dark image of the future a brilliant plan of action is drawn, or vaguely a
flower of pleasure shines, soon there also appears, as a result of experience, the
thought of the past, often dark and sad; or the feeling of the agitated present
intervenes to bridle the happy fancy. This conflict of memories, hopes,
prophecies, presentiments, perceptions, and ideals can be represented as a
conflict of souls among themselves; all are fighting for the definite and full
power of personality.

Let's look at an executive, who believes in himself and is a gentleman. The
moral is predominant in him. But one day the instinctive soul, which is like
a wild beast hidden deep in everybody, gives a kick to his moral soul and
the gentleman steals. Now that poor man is the first one who after a while
is shocked, cries, and desperately asks himself. "How, how could I have done
this?"

But—yes, sir—he has stolen. What about another man? A well-to-do man,
indeed a rich man, he has killed. The moral ideal constituted in his personality a soul which was in conflict with his instinctive soul; it constituted an
acquired soul which fought with his hereditary soul, which, left free to itself
for a while, succeeded in committing crime.

Life is a continuous flow which we continually try to stop, to fix in established and determinate forms outside and inside of ourselves because we
are already fixed forms, forms that move among other immovable ones, which
follow the flow of life until the point when they become rigid and their
movement, slowed, stops. The forms in which we try to stop and fix this
continuous flow are the concepts, the ideals, within which we want to keep
coherent all the fictions we create, the condition and the status in which we

try to establish ourselves. But inside ourselves, in what we call our soul, which is the life in us, the flow continues indistinctly, under the wire, past the limits that we set when we formed consciousness and built a personality. During certain stormy moments, inundated by the flow, all our fictitious forms collapse ignominiously. Even what doesn't flow under the wire and beyond the limits—what is revealed distinctly in us carefully channelled by our feelings, in the duties which we have imposed upon ourselves, in the habits that we have formed—in certain moments of flood overflows and topples everything.

There are some restless spirits, almost in a continuous state of confusion, who do not freeze into this or that personality. But even for the quiet ones, those who find rest in one form or other, fusion is always possible. The flow of life is in everybody.

Therefore, it can be, sometimes, a torture for everyone that, in contrast to the soul that moves and changes, our body should be fixed forever in unchanging features. Why are we made exactly so? We sometimes ask the mirror, "Why this face, this body?" We lift a hand; in the unconscious, the act remains suspended. It seems strange that we have done it. *We see ourselves alive.* In that suspended gesture we look like a statue—like that statue of an ancient orator, for example, whom we see in a niche, climbing the stairs of the Quirinal. He has a scroll in one hand and the other hand lifted in a severe gesture. How sad and surprised that ancient orator seems to be that he has remained there, through so many centuries, suspended in that gesture, while so many persons have climbed, are climbing, and will climb those stairs!

During certain moments of interior silence, during which our soul sheds all habitual functions, and our eyes become sharper and more penetrating, we see ourselves in life and we see life as an arid barrenness. Disconcerted, we feel as if taken by a strange impression, as if, in a flash, a different reality from the one we usually perceive were revealed to us, a living reality beyond human vision, beyond the forms of human vision. Very clearly, then, the facts of daily existence, almost suspended in the vacuum of our interior silence, appear to us meaningless and without scope. That different reality appears horrible to us in its stern and mysterious crudeness because all our fictitious relationships, both of feelings and images, have split and disintegrated in it. The interior vacuum expands, surpasses the limits of our body, becomes a vacuum around ourselves, a strange vacuum like a stop of time and life, as our interior silence plunges itself into the abyss of mystery. With a supreme effort we try, then, to recapture the normal sense of things, to tie ourselves again to the usual relationships, to reassemble ideas, to feel alive in the usual way. But we cannot trust this normal consciousness, these rearranged ideas, any more because we know now that they are deceptions which man needs to save himself from death or insanity. It was an instant, but its impressions will last for a long time, with a dizziness in contrast to the stability, quite specious, of things, ambitions, and miserable appearances. Life, which goes on as usual among these appearances, seems as if it isn't real any more. It seems a mechanical phantasmagoria. How can one give importance to it? How can one respect it?

Today we exist, tomorrow we will not. Which face have they given us to represent part of a living person? An ugly nose? How painful to walk around with an ugly nose for the rest of our life! It is good for us that after a while we don't pay any more attention to it. Then we don't know why other people laugh when they look at us. They are so silly! Let us console ourselves by looking at somebody else's lips, one who doesn't even realize it and doesn't have the courage to laugh at us. Masks, masks. They disappear in a breath, giving way to others. A poor lame man, who is he? Running toward death on crutches. Here life steps on somebody's foot, there it blinds somebody's eye—wooden leg, glass eye, and it goes on. Each one fixes his mask up as he can, the exterior mask.

Because inside there is another one, often contradicting the one outside. Nothing is true! True is: the sea, the mountain, a rock, a blade of grass. But man: always wearing a mask, unwillingly, without knowing it, without wanting it, always masked with that thing which he, in good faith, believes to be handsome, good, gracious, generous, unhappy, and so on.

This is funny, if we stop to think of it. Yes, because a dog, after the first ardor of life is gone, eats and sleeps; he lives as he can, as he ought to. He shuts his eyes, with patience, and lets time go by, cold if it is cold, warm if it is warm. If they kick him he takes it because it means that he deserved it. But what about man? Even when he is old he always has that *fever*; he is delirious and doesn't realize it. He cannot help posing, even in front of himself, in any way, and he imagines so many things which he needs to believe are true, which he needs to take seriously. . . .

. . . The discovery of the telescope gave the finishing stroke. This is another infernal machine, comparable to the one which nature wanted to give us. But we invented this one. Instead of being less than nature, with the eye looking from the bottom, out of the smaller lens, and seeing what nature mercifully wanted us to see small, what does our soul do? It jumps to look from the top, so that the telescope becomes a terrible instrument, which destroys earth, man, and all our glory and greatness.

Luckily, we have humorous reflection, from which stems the feeling of incongruity, which in this case says, "But is man really as small as an inverted telescope wants us to see him?" If he can understand and realize his infinite smallness, it means that he also understands and realizes the infinite greatness of the universe. How can we say, then, that man is small? But it is also true that if he feels himself big and a humorist happens to know it, he can have happen to him what happened to Gulliver, the giant in Lilliput who became a toy in the hands of the Giants of Brobdingnag. . . .

From what we have said up to this point about the special activity of reflection in the humorist, the intimate process of humorous art clearly and necessarily develops.

Art, like all ideal or illusory constructions, has the tendency to fix life. It stops it at one moment or in various moments—a statue in a gesture, a landscape in a momentary unchangeable aspect. But what about the perpetual mobility of our successive aspects? What about the continuous fusion in which souls find themselves?

Art in general abstracts and concentrates; that is, it catches and represents only the essential and characteristic ideality of men and things. Now, it appears to the humorist that all this oversimplifies nature, attempting to make life too reasonable, or at least too coherent. It seems to him that art in general does not take into consideration what it ought to, art doesn't consider causes, the real causes which often move this poor human life to strange, absolutely unpredictable actions. For a humorist, causes in real life are never as logical and ordered as in our common works of art, in which all is, in effect, combined and organized to exist within the scope which the writer has in mind. Order? Coherence? What if we have within ourselves four souls fighting among themselves; the instinctive soul, the moral soul, the affective soul, and the social soul? Our consciousness adapts itself according to whichever dominates, and we hold as valid and sincere a false interpretation of our real interior being, which we ignore because it never makes itself manifest as a whole, but now in one way, now in another, according to the circumstances of life.

Yes, an epic or dramatic poet may represent a hero in whom opposite and unacceptable elements are shown fighting; but he will create a character out of these elements and make him coherent in his actions. Well, the humorist will do exactly the reverse: he will take the character apart. While the poet is careful to make him coherent in each action, the humorist is amused by representing him in his incongruities.

A humorist does recognize heroes; even better, he lets others represent them. He, for his own sake, knows what legend is and how it is formed; he knows what history is and how it is formed. They are all compositions more or less ideal; perhaps they are the more ideal if they show a greater pretense of reality. He amuses himself by taking them apart, and one cannot say that this is a pleasant amusement.

He sees the world, if not entirely naked, let's say in only its shirtsleeves. He sees a king in his shirtsleeves, a king who makes a beautiful impression in the majesty of his throne, with his royal staff and crown, his purple robe and ermine. Don't lay people with too much pomp on their deathbeds, in their funeral chambers, because he is capable of profaning even this composition, this scene. He is capable of catching, amid the sadness of the spectators, in that cold and rigid corpse, with his decorations and good suit on, a certain lugubrious grumble of the stomach, an exclamation (since these things are best expressed in Latin), *"Digestio post mortem. . . ."*

And what about the unseen part of life? The abyss which exists in our soul? Don't we often feel a spark inside ourselves, strange thoughts like flashes of folly, illogical thoughts we dare not confide even to ourselves, arising from a soul different from the one we recognize in ourselves? For these, we have in humor research into the most intimate and minute particulars—which might look vulgar or trivial if compared with the ideal syntheses of most art—and work based on contrasts and contradictions in opposition to the coherence sought by the others. We have that disorganized, untied, and capricious element, all the digressions which are seen in a humorous work in opposition to the orderly plan, the *composition*, of most works of art.

They are the result of reflection, which dissects—"If Cleopatra's nose had been longer, who knows what course the world would have had?" This *if*, this little element that can be pinned down, inserted like a wedge in all facts, can produce many different disaggregations; it can cause many disarrangements at the hand of a humorist who, like Sterne for example, sees the whole world regulated by infinite smallnesses.

Let's conclude: humor is the feeling of polarity aroused by that special activity of reflection which doesn't hide itself, which doesn't become, as ordinarily in art, a form of feeling, but its contrary, following the feelings step by step, however, as the shadow follows the body. A common artist pays attention only to the body. A humorist pays attention to the body and its shadow, sometimes more to the shadow than the body. He sees all the tricks of the shadow; it now assumes length or width, as if to mimic the body, which, meanwhile, doesn't pay any attention to it.

Jean Cocteau 1889–1963

Preface to The Eiffel Tower Wedding Party 1922

Every work of the poetic order contains what Gide, in his preface to *Paludes*, so aptly calls "God's share." This "Share," which eludes the poet himself, can surprise him. Such and such a phrase or gesture, which originally meant no more to him than the third dimension means to a painter, has a hidden meaning that each person will interpret in his own way. The true Symbol is never planned: it emerges by itself, so long as the bizarre, the unreal, do not enter into the reckoning.

In a fairyland, the fairies do not appear. They walk invisibly there. To mortal eyes they can appear only on the terra firma of everyday. The unsophisticated mind is more likely than the others to see the fairies, for it will not oppose to the marvelous the resistance of the hardheaded. I might almost say that the Chief Electrician, with his reflections, has often illuminated a piece for me.

I have been reading in Antoine's memoirs of the scandal provoked by the presence on the stage of real quarters of beef and a fountain of real water. But now, thanks to Antoine,[1] we have come to such a pass that the audience is displeased if real objects are *not* used on the stage, and if it is not subjected to a plot precisely as complex, precisely as tedious, as those from which the theatre should serve as a distraction.

The Eiffel Tower Wedding Party, because of its candor, was first of all mistaken for a bit of esoteric writing. The mysterious inspires in the public a sort of fear. Here, I renounce mystery. I illuminate everything, I underline everything. Sunday vacuity, human livestock, ready-made expressions, dissociation of ideas into flesh and bone, the fierce cruelty of childhood, the miraculous poetry of daily life: these are my play, so well understood by the young musicians who composed the score for it.

[1] André Antoine (1858–1943), French actor and director who founded the Théâtre Libre to produce naturalistic plays in a naturalistic manner.

A remark of the Photographer's might do well for my epigraph: "Since these mysteries are beyond me, let's pretend that I arranged them all the time." This is our motto, par excellence. Your prig always finds a last refuge in responsibility. Thus, for example, he will go on fighting a war after the end has been reached.

In *Wedding Party*, God's share is considerable. To the right and left of the scene the human phonographs (like the ancient Chorus, like the *compère* and *commère*[2] of our music-hall stage), describe, without the least "literature," the absurd action which is unfolded, danced, and pantomined between them. I say "absurd" because instead of trying to keep this side of the absurdity of life, to lessen it, to arrange it as we arrange the story of an incident in which we played an uncomplimentary part, I accentuate it, I push it forward, I try to paint *more truly than the truth.*

The poet ought to disengage objects and ideas from their veiling mists; he ought to display them suddenly, so nakedly and so quickly that they are scarcely recognizable. It is then that they strike us with their youth, as though they had never become official dotards. . . .

Every living work of art has its own ballyhoo, and only this is seen by those who stay outside. Now in the case of new work, this first impression so shocks, irritates, angers the spectator that he will not enter. He is repelled from its true nature by its face, by the unfamiliar outward appearance which distracts him as would a clown grimacing at the door. It is this phenomenon which deceives even those critics who are least slaves to convention. They forget that they are at a performance which must be followed just as attentively as a "popular success. . . ."

The action of my piece is pictorial, though the text itself is not. The fact is that I am trying to substitute a "theatre poetry" for the usual "poetry in the theatre." Poetry in the theatre" is a delicate lace, invisible at any considerable distance. "Theatre poetry" should be a coarse lace, a lace of rigging, a ship upon the sea. *Wedding Party* can be as terrifying as a drop of poetry under the microscope. The scenes fit together like the words of a poem.

---

[2] Leading actor and actress in a vaudeville or musical revue.

José Ortega y Gasset 1883–1955

The Dehumanization of Art 1925

. . . All modern art is unpopular, and it is so not accidentally and by chance, but essentially and by fate.

It might be said that every newcomer among styles passes through a stage of quarantine. The battle of *Hernani* comes to mind, and all the other skirmishes connected with the advent of Romanticism. However, the unpopularity of present-day art is of a different kind. A distinction must be made between what is not popular and what is unpopular. A new style takes some time in winning popularity; it is not popular, but it is not unpopular either. The break-through of Romanticism, although a frequently cited example, is, as a sociological phenomenon, exactly the opposite of the present situation of art. Romanticism was very quick in winning "the people" to whom the old classical art had never appealed. The enemy with whom Romanticism had to fight it out was precisely a select minority irretrievably sold to the classical forms of the *"ancien régime"* in poetry. The works of the romanticists were the first, after the invention of printing, to enjoy large editions. Romanticism was the prototype of a popular style. First-born of democracy, it was coddled by the masses.

Modern art, on the other hand, will always have the masses against it. It is essentially unpopular; moreover, it is antipopular. Any of its works automatically produces a curious effect on the general public. It divides the public into two groups: one very small, formed by those who are favorably inclined towards it; another very large—the hostile majority. (Let us ignore that ambiguous fauna—the snobs.) Thus the work of art acts like a social agent which segregates from the shapeless mass of the many two different castes of men.

Which is the differentiating principle that creates these two antagonistic groups? Every work of art arouses differences of opinion. Some like it, some don't; some like it more, some like it less. Such disagreements have no organic character, they are not a matter of principles. A person's chance disposition determines on which side he will fall. But in the case of the new art the split occurs in a deeper layer than that on which differences of personal taste reside. It is not that the majority does not *like* the art of the young and the minority likes it, but that the majority, the masses, do not *understand* it. The old bigwigs who were present at the performance of *Hernani* understood

Selections, translated by Helene Weyl. From José Ortega y Gasset, *The Dehumanization of Art and Other Essays on Art, Culture, and Literature* (rev. ed., copyright © 1968 by Princeton University Press; Princeton Paperback, 1968), pp. 4, 8–10, 11–14, and 54. Reprinted by permission of Princeton University Press.

Victor Hugo's play very well; precisely because they understood it they disliked it. Faithfully adhering to definite esthetic norms, they were disgusted at the new artistic values which this piece of art proposed to them.

"From a sociological point of view" the characteristic feature of the new art is, in my judgment, that it divides the public into the two classes of those who understand it and those who do not. This implies that one group possesses an organ of comprehension denied to the other—that they are two different varieties of the human species. The new art obviously addresses itself not to everybody, as did Romanticism, but to a specially gifted minority. Hence the indignation it arouses in the masses. When a man dislikes a work of art, but understands it, he feels superior to it; and there is no reason for indignation. But when his dislike is due to his failure to understand, he feels vaguely humiliated and this rankling sense of inferiority must be counterbalanced by indignant self-assertion. Through its mere presence, the art of the young compels the average citizen to realize that he is just this—the average citizen, a creature incapable of receiving the sacrament of art, blind and deaf to pure beauty. But such a thing cannot be done after a hundred years of adulation of the masses and apotheosis of the people. Accustomed to ruling supreme, the masses feel that the new art, which is the art of a privileged aristocracy of finer senses, endangers their rights as men. Whenever the new Muses present themselves, the masses bristle.

For a century and a half the masses have claimed to be the whole of society. Stravinski's music or Pirandello's drama have the sociological effect of compelling the people to recognize itself for what it is: a component among others of the social structure, inert matter of the historical process, a secondary factor in the cosmos of spiritual life. On the other hand, the new art also helps the elite to recognize themselves and one another in the drab mass of society and to learn their mission which consists in being few and holding their own against the many.

A time must come in which society, from politics to art reorganizes itself into two orders or ranks: the illustrious and the vulgar. That chaotic, shapeless, and undifferentiated state without discipline and social structure in which Europe has lived these hundred and fifty years cannot go on. Behind all contemporary life lurks the provoking and profound injustice of the assumption that men are actually equal. Each move among men so obviously reveals the opposite that each move results in a painful clash.

If this subject were broached in politics the passions aroused would run too high to make oneself understood. Fortunately the aforementioned unity of spirit within a historical epoch allows us to point out serenely and with perfect clarity in the germinating art of our time the same symptoms and signals of a moral revision that in politics present themselves obscured by low passions. . . .

One point must be clarified before we go on. What is it the majority of people call esthetic pleasure? What happens in their minds when they "like" a work of art; for instance, a theatrical performance? The answer is easy. A man likes a play when he has become interested in the human destinies presented to him, when the love and hatred, the joys and sorrows of the personages so move his heart that he participates in it all as though it were happening in real life. And he calls a work "good" if it succeeds in creating the illusion necessary to make the imaginary personages appear like living persons. In poetry he seeks the passion and pain of the man behind the poet. Paintings attract him if he finds on them figures of men or women whom it would be interesting to meet. A landscape is pronounced "pretty" if the country it represents deserves for its loveliness or its grandeur to be visited on a trip.

It thus appears that to the majority of people esthetic pleasure means a state of mind which is essentially undistinguishable from their ordinary behavior. It differs merely in accidental qualities, being perhaps less utilitarian, more intense, and free from painful consequences. But the object towards which their attention and, consequently, all their other mental activities are directed is the same as in daily life: people and passions. By art they understand a means through which they are brought in contact with interesting human affairs. Artistic forms proper—figments, fantasy—are tolerated only if they do not interfere with the perception of human forms and fates. As soon as purely esthetic elements predominate and the story of John and Mary grows elusive, most people feel out of their depth and are at a loss what to make of the scene, the book, or the painting. As they have never practiced any other attitude but the practical one in which a man's feelings are aroused and he is emotionally involved, a work that does not invite sentimental intervention leaves them without a cue.

Now, this is a point which has to be made perfectly clear. Not only is grieving and rejoicing at such human destinies as a work of art presents or narrates a very different thing from true artistic pleasure, but preoccupation with the human content of the work is in principle incompatible with esthetic enjoyment proper. . . .

During the nineteenth century, artists proceeded in all too impure a fashion. They reduced the strictly esthetic elements to a minimum and let the work consist almost entirely in a fiction of human realities. In this sense all normal art of the last century must be called realistic. Beethoven and Wagner were realistic, and so was Chateaubriand as well as Zola. Seen from the vantage point of our day Romanticism and Naturalism draw closer together and reveal their common realistic root.

Works of this kind are only partially works of art, or artistic objects. Their enjoyment does not depend upon our power to focus on transparencies and images, a power characteristic of the artistic sensibility; all they require is human sensibility and willingness to sympathize with our neighbor's joys and worries. No wonder that nineteenth-century art has been so popular; it is made for the masses inasmuch as it is not art but an extract from life. Let us remember that in epochs with two different types of art, one for minorities and one for the majority, the latter has always been realistic.[1]

I will not now discuss whether pure art is possible. Perhaps it is not; but as the reasons that make me inclined to think so are somewhat long and difficult the subject better be dropped. Besides, it is not of major importance for the matter in hand. Even though pure art may be impossible there doubtless can prevail a tendency toward a purification of art. Such a tendency would effect a progressive elimination of the human, all too human, elements predominant in romantic and naturalistic production. And in this process a point can be reached in which the human content has grown so thin that it is negligible. We then have an art which can be comprehended only by people possessed of the peculiar gift of artistic sensibility—an art for artists and not for the masses, for "quality" and not for hoi polloi.

That is why modern art divides the public into two classes, those who understand it and those who do not understand it—that is to say, those who are artists and those who are not. The new art is an artistic art.

I do not propose to extol the new way in art or to condemn the old. My purpose is to characterize them as the zoologist characterizes two contrasting species. The new art is a world-wide fact. For about twenty years now the most alert young people of two successive generations—in Berlin, Paris, London, New York, Rome, Madrid—have found themselves faced with the undeniable fact that they have no use for traditional art; moreover, that they detest it. With these young people one can do one of two things: shoot them, or try to understand them. As soon as one decides in favor of the latter it appears that they are endowed with a perfectly clear, coherent, and rational sense of art. Far from being a whim, their way of feeling represents the inevitable and fruitful result of all previous artistic achievement. Whimsical, arbitrary, and consequently unprofitable it would be to set oneself against the new style and obstinately remain shut up in old forms that are exhausted and the worse for wear. In art, as in morals, what ought to be done does not depend on our personal judgment; we have to accept the imperative imposed by the time. Obedience to the order of the day is the most hopeful choice open to the individual. Even so he may achieve nothing; but he is much more likely to fail if he insists on composing another Wagnerian opera, another naturalistic novel.

In art repetition is nothing. Each historical style can engender a certain number of different forms within a generic type. But there always comes a

---

[1] For instance in the Middle Ages. In accordance with the division of society in the two strata of noblemen and commoners, there existed an aristocratic art which was "conventional" and "idealistic," and a popular art which was realistic and satirical [Ortega's note].

day when the magnificent mine is worked out. Such, for instance, has been the fate of the romantico-naturalistic novel and theatre. It is a naïve error to believe that the present infecundity of these two genres is due to lack of talent. What happens is that the possible combinations within these literary forms are exhausted. It must be deemed fortunate that this situation coincides with the emergence of a new artistic sensibility capable of detecting other untouched veins.

When we analyze the new style we find that it contains certain closely connected tendencies. It tends (1) to dehumanize art, (2) to avoid living forms, (3) to see to it that the work of art is nothing but a work of art, (4) to consider art as play and nothing else, (5) to be essentially ironical, (6) to beware of sham and hence to aspire to scrupulous realization, (7) to regard art as a thing of no transcending consequence. . . .

But whatever their shortcomings, the young artists have to be granted one point: there is no turning back. All the doubts cast upon the inspiration of those pioneers may be justified, and yet they provide no sufficient reason for condemning them. The objections would have to be supplemented by something positive: a suggestion of another way for art different from dehumanization and yet not coincident with the beaten and worn-out paths.

It is easy to protest that it is always possible to produce art within the bounds of a given tradition. But this comforting phrase is of no use to the artist who, pen or chisel in hand, sits waiting for a concrete inspiration.

Antonin Artaud *1895–1948*

No More Masterpieces *1938*

One of the reasons for the asphyxiating atmosphere in which we live without possible escape or remedy—and in which we all share, even the most revolutionary among us—is our respect for what has been written, formulated, or painted, what has been given form, as if all expression were not at last exhausted, were not at a point where things must break apart if they are to start anew and begin fresh.

We must have done with this idea of masterpieces reserved for a self-styled elite and not understood by the general public; the mind has no such restricted districts as those so often used for clandestine sexual encounters.

Masterpieces of the past are good for the past: they are not good for us. We have the right to say what has been said and even what has not been said in a way that belongs to us, a way that is immediate and direct, corresponding to present modes of feeling, and understandable to everyone.

It is idiotic to reproach the masses for having no sense of the sublime, when the sublime is confused with one or another of its formal manifestations, which are moreover always defunct manifestations. And if for example a contemporary public does not understand *Oedipus Rex*, I shall make bold to say that it is the fault of *Oedipus Rex* and not of the public.

In *Oedipus Rex* there is the theme of incest and the idea that nature mocks at morality and that there are certain unspecified powers at large which we would do well to beware of, call them *destiny* or anything you choose.

There is in addition the presence of a plague epidemic which is a physical incarnation of these powers. But the whole in a manner and language that have lost all touch with the rude and epileptic rhythm of our time. Sophocles speaks grandly perhaps, but in a style that is no longer timely. His language is too refined for this age, it is as if he were speaking beside the point.

However, a public that shudders at train wrecks, that is familiar with earthquakes, plagues, revolutions, wars; that is sensitive to the disordered anguish of love, can be affected by all these grand notions and asks only to become aware of them, but on condition that it is addressed in its own language, and that its knowledge of these things does not come to it through adulterated trappings and speech that belong to extinct eras which will never live again.

Today as yesterday, the public is greedy for mystery: it asks only to become aware of the laws according to which destiny manifests itself, and to divine perhaps the secret of its apparitions.

Let us leave textual criticism to graduate students, formal criticism to esthetes, and recognize that what has been said is not still to be said; that an expression does not have the same value twice, does not live two lives; that all words, once spoken, are dead and function only at the moment when they are uttered, that a form, once it has served, cannot be used again and asks only to be replaced by another, and that the theater is the only place in the world where a gesture, once made, can never be made the same way twice.

If the public does not frequent our literary masterpieces, it is because those masterpieces are literary, that is to say, fixed; and fixed in forms that no longer respond to the needs of the time.

Far from blaming the public, we ought to blame the formal screen we interpose between ourselves and the public, and this new form of idolatry, the idolatry of fixed masterpieces which is one of the aspects of bourgeois conformism.

This conformism makes us confuse sublimity, ideas, and things with the forms they have taken in time and in our minds—in our snobbish, precious, esthetic mentalities which the public does not understand.

How pointless in such matters to accuse the public of bad taste because it relishes insanities, so long as the public is not shown a valid spectacle; and I defy anyone to show me *here* a spectacle valid—valid in the supreme sense of the theatre—since the last great romantic melodramas, i.e., since a hundred years ago.

The public, which takes the false for the true, has the sense of the true and always responds to it when it is manifested. However it is not upon the stage that the true is to be sought nowadays, but in the street; and if the crowd in the street is offered an occasion to show its human dignity, it will always do so.

If people are out of the habit of going to the theatre, if we have all finally come to think of theatre as an inferior art, a means of popular distraction, and to use it as an outlet for our worst instincts, it is because we have learned too well what the theatre has been, namely, falsehood and illusion. It is because we have been accustomed for four hundred years, that is since the Renaissance, to a purely descriptive and narrative theatre—storytelling psychology; it is because every possible ingenuity has been exerted in bringing to life on the stage plausible but detached beings, with the spectacle on one side, the public on the other—and because the public is no longer shown anything but the mirror of itself.

Shakespeare himself is responsible for this aberration and decline, this disinterested idea of the theatre which wishes a theatrical performance to leave the public intact, without setting off one image that will shake the organism to its foundations and leave an ineffaceable scar.

If, in Shakespeare, a man is sometimes preoccupied with what transcends him, it is always in order to determine the ultimate consequences of this preoccupation within him, i.e., psychology.

Psychology, which works relentlessly to reduce the unknown to the known, to the quotidian and the ordinary, is the cause of the theatre's abasement and its fearful loss of energy, which seems to me to have reached its lowest point. And I think both the theatre and we ourselves have had enough of psychology.

I believe furthermore that we can all agree on this matter sufficiently so that there is no need to descend to the repugnant level of the modern and French theatre to condemn the theatre of psychology.

Stories about money, worry over money, social careerism, the pangs of love unspoiled by altruism, sexuality sugar-coated with an eroticism that has lost its mystery have nothing to do with the theatre, even if they do belong to psychology. These torments, seductions, and lusts before which we are nothing but Peeping Toms gratifying our cravings, tend to go bad, and their rot turns to revolution: we must take this into account.

But this is not our most serious concern.

If Shakespeare and his imitators have gradually insinuated the idea of art for art's sake, with art on one side and life on the other, we can rest on this feeble and lazy idea only as long as the life outside endures. But there are too many signs that everything that used to sustain our lives no longer does so, that we are all mad, desperate, and sick. And I call for *us* to react.

This idea of a detached art, of poetry as a charm which exists only to distract our leisure, is a decadent idea and an unmistakable symptom of our power to castrate.

Our literary admiration for Rimbaud, Jarry, Lautréamont, and a few others, which has driven two men to suicide, but turned into café gossip for the rest, belongs to this idea of literary poetry, of detached art, of neutral spiritual activity which creates nothing and produces nothing; and I can bear witness that at the very moment when that kind of personal poetry which involves only the man who creates it and only at the moment he creates it broke out in its most abusive fashion, the theatre was scorned more than ever before by poets who have never had the sense of direct and concerted action, nor of efficacity, nor of danger.

We must get rid of our superstitious valuation of texts and *written* poetry. Written poetry is worth reading once, and then should be destroyed. Let the dead poets make way for others. Then we might even come to see that it is our veneration for what has already been created, however beautiful and valid it may be, that petrifies us, deadens our responses, and prevents us from making contact with that underlying power, call it thought-energy, the life force, the determinism of change, lunar menses, or anything you like. Beneath the poetry of the texts, there is the actual poetry, without form and without text. And just as the efficacity of masks in the magic practices of certain tribes is exhausted—and these masks are no longer good for anything except museums—so the poetic efficacity of a text is exhausted; yet the poetry and the efficacity of the theatre are exhausted least quickly of all, since they permit the *action* of what is gesticulated and pronounced, and which is never made the same way twice.

It is a question of knowing what we want. If we are prepared for war, plague, famine, and slaughter we do not even need to say so, we have only to continue as we are; continue behaving like snobs, rushing en masse· to hear such and such a singer, to see such and such an admirable performance which never transcends the realm of art (and even the Russian ballet at the height of its splendor never transcended the realm of art), to marvel at such and such an exhibition of painting in which exciting shapes explode here and there but at random and without any genuine consciousness of the forces they could rouse.

This empiricism, randomness, individualism, and anarchy must cease.

Enough of personal poems, benefitting those who create them much more than those who read them.

Once and for all, enough of this closed, egoistic, and personal art.

Our spiritual anarchy and intellectual disorder is a function of the anarchy of everything else—or rather, everything else is a function of this anarchy.

I am not one of those who believe that civilization has to change in order for the theatre to change; but I do believe that the theatre, utilized in the highest and most difficult sense possible, has the power to influence the aspect and formation of things: and the encounter upon the stage of two passionate manifestations, two living centers, two nervous magnetisms is something as entire, true, even decisive, as, in life, the encounter of one epidermis with another in a timeless debauchery.

That is why I propose a theater of cruelty. With this mania we all have for depreciating everything, as soon as I have said "cruelty," everybody will at once take it to mean "blood." But *"theatre of cruelty"* means a theatre difficult and cruel for myself first of all. And, on the level of performance, it is not the cruelty we can exercise upon each other by hacking at each other's bodies, carving up our personal anatomies, or, like Assyrian emperors, sending parcels of human ears, noses, or neatly detached nostrils through the mail, but the much more terrible and necessary cruelty which things can exercise against us. We are not free. And the sky can still fall on our heads. And the theatre has been created to teach us that first of all.

Either we will be capable of returning by present-day means to this superior idea of poetry and poetry-through-theatre which underlies the Myths told by the great ancient tragedians, capable once more of entertaining a religious idea of the theatre (without meditation, useless contemplation, and vague dreams), capable of attaining awareness and a possession of certain dominant forces; of certain notions that control all others, and (since ideas, when they are effective, carry their energy with them) capable of recovering within ourselves those energies which ultimately create order and increase the value of life, or else we might as well abandon ourselves now, without protest, and recognize that we are no longer good for anything but disorder, famine, blood, war, and epidemics.

Either we restore all the arts to a central attitude and necessity, finding an analogy between a gesture made in painting or the theatre, and a gesture made by lava in a volcanic explosion, or we must stop painting, babbling, writing, or doing whatever it is we do.

I propose to bring back into the theatre this elementary magical idea, taken up by modern psychoanalysis, which consists in effecting a patient's cure by making him assume the apparent and exterior attitudes of the desired condition.

I propose to renounce our empiricism of imagery, in which the unconscious furnishes images at random, and which the poet arranges at random too, calling them poetic and hence hermetic images, as if the kind of trance that poetry provides did not have its reverberations throughout the whole sensibility, in every nerve, and as if poetry were some vague force whose movements were invariable.

I propose to return through the theatre to an idea of the physical knowledge of images and the means of inducing trances, as in Chinese medicine which knows, over the entire extent of the human anatomy, at what points to puncture in order to regulate the subtlest functions.

Those who have forgotten the communicative power and magical mimesis of a gesture, the theatre can reinstruct, because a gesture carries its energy with it, and there are still human beings in the theatre to manifest the force of the gesture made.

To create art is to deprive a gesture of its reverberation in the organism, whereas this reverberation, if the gesture is made in the conditions and with the force required, incites the organism and, through it, the entire individuality, to take attitudes in harmony with the gesture.

The theatre is the only place in the world, the last general means we still possess of directly affecting the organism and, in periods of neurosis and petty sensuality like the one in which we are immersed, of attacking this sensuality by physical means it cannot withstand.

If music affects snakes, it is not on account of the spiritual notions it offers them, but because snakes are long and coil their length upon the earth, because their bodies touch the earth at almost every point; and because the musical vibrations which are communicated to the earth affect them like a very subtle, very long massage; and I propose to treat the spectators like the snakecharmer's subjects and conduct them *by means of their organisms* to an apprehension of the subtlest notions.

At first by crude means, which will gradually be refined. These immediate crude means will hold their attention at the start.

That is why in the "theatre of cruelty" the spectator is in the center and the spectacle surrounds him.

In this spectacle the sonorization is constant: sounds, noises, cries are chosen first for their vibratory quality, then for what they represent.

Among these gradually refined means light is interposed in its turn. Light which is not created merely to add color or to brighten, and which brings its power, influence, suggestions with it. And the light of a green cavern does not sensually dispose the organism like the light of a windy day.

After sound and light there is action, and the dynamism of action: here the theatre, far from copying life, puts itself whenever possible in communication with pure forces. And whether you accept or deny them, there is nevertheless a way of speaking which gives the name of "forces" to whatever brings to birth images of energy in the unconscious, and gratuitious crime on the surface.

A violent and concentrated action is a kind of lyricism: it summons up supernatural images, a bloodstream of images, a bleeding spurt of images in the poet's head and in the spectator's as well.

Whatever the conflicts that haunt the mind of a given period, I defy any spectator to whom such violent scenes will have transferred their blood, who will have felt in himself the transit of a superior action, who will have seen the extraordinary and essential movements of his thought illuminated in extraordinary deeds—the violence and blood having been placed at the service of the violence of the thought—I defy that spectator to give himself up, once outside the theatre, to ideas of war, riot, and blatant murder.

So expressed, this idea seems dangerous and sophomoric. It will be claimed that example breeds example, that if the attitude of cure induces cure, the attitude of murder will induce murder. Everything depends upon the manner and the purity with which the thing is done. There is a risk. But let it not be forgotten that though a theatrical gesture is violent, it is disinterested; and that the theatre teaches precisely the uselessness of the action which, once done, is not to be done, and the superior use of the state unused by the action and which, *restored*, produces a purification.

I propose then a theatre in which violent physical images crush and hypnotize the sensibility of the spectator seized by the theatre as by a whirlwind of higher forces.

A theatre which, abandoning psychology, recounts the extraordinary, stages natural conflicts, natural and subtle forces, and presents itself first of all as an exceptional power of redirection. A theatre that induces trance, as the dances of Dervishes induce trance, and that addresses itself to the organism by precise instruments, by the same means as those of certain tribal music cures which we admire on records but are incapable of originating among ourselves.

There is a risk involved, but in the present circumstances I believe it is a risk worth running. I do not believe we have managed to revitalize the world we live in, and I do not believe it is worth the trouble of clinging to; but I do propose something to get us out of our marasmus, instead of continuing to complain about it, and about the boredom, inertia, and stupidity of everything.

Eugene Ionesco *1912–*

Experience of the Theatre *1958*

. . . Sometimes it seems to me that I started writing for the theatre because I hated it. . . .

. . . I am not opposed to make-believe. On the contrary, I have always considered imaginative truth to be more profound, more loaded with significance, than everyday reality. Realism, socialist or nor, never looks beyond reality. It narrows it down, diminishes it, falsifies it, and leaves out of account the obsessive truths that are most fundamental to us: love, death, and wonder. It presents man in a perspective that is narrow and alien; truth lies in our dreams, in our imagination: every moment of our lives confirms this statement. Fiction preludes science. Everything we dream about, and by that I mean everything we desire, is true (the myth of Icarus came before aviation, and if Ader or Blériot started flying, it is because all men have dreamt of flight). There is nothing truer than myth: history, in its attempt to "realize" myth, distorts it, stops half way; when history claims to have "succeeded," this is nothing but humbug and mystification. Everything we dream is "realizable." Reality does not have to be: it is simply what it is. It is the dreamer, the thinker or the scientist who is the revolutionary; it is he who tries to change the world.

The fictional element in the novel did not worry me at all and I accepted it in the cinema. I can believe as naturally in the potential reality of fiction as in my own dreams. Film acting did not fill me with the same indefinable malaise, the same embarrassment as acting in the theatre.

Why could I not accept the truth of theatrical reality? Why did it seem false to me? And why did the false seem to want to pass as true and take the place of truth? Was it the fault of the actors? Of the text? Or my own fault? I think I realize now that what worried me in the theatre was the presence of characters in flesh and blood on the stage. Their physical presence destroyed the imaginative illusion. It was as though there were two planes of reality, the concrete, physical, impoverished, empty and limited reality of these ordinary human beings living, moving and speaking on the stage, and the reality of imagination, face to face, overlapping, irreconcilable: two antagonistic worlds failing to come together and unite.

Yes, that was it: every gesture, every attitude, every speech spoken on the stage destroyed for me a world that these same gestures, attitudes and speeches were specifically designed to evoke; destroyed it even before it could be created. It seemed to me an absolute abortion, a fatal mistake, sheer fatuity. . . . The theatre seemed to me essentially impure: the fictional element was mixed with others that were foreign to it; it was imperfectly fictional, yes, raw material that had not yet undergone the transformation or mutation that is indispensable. In short, everything about the theatre exasperated me. When I saw actors, for example, identifying themselves completely with their parts and weeping real tears on the stage, I found it unbearable, positively indecent.

When on the other hand I saw an actor who was too much in control of his part, out of character, dominating it, detached from it, which was what Diderot and Jouvet[1] and Piscator[2] and, after him, Brecht all wanted, I was just as dissatisfied. This too seemed to me an unacceptable mixture of true and false, for I felt a need for the essential transformation or transposition of a reality that only imagination and artistic creation can make more meaningful, more dense, more "true," that the didactic doctrines of realism merely overload, impoverish, and reduce to the level of a second-rate ideology. I did not like stage actors, stars, who for me represented an anarchical principle, breaking up and destroying to their own advantage the organized unity of the stage, attracting all attention to themselves to the detriment of any coherent integration of the elements of drama. But the dehumanization of the actor, as practiced by Piscator or Brecht, a disciple of Piscator, who turned the actor into a simple pawn in the chess game of drama, a lifeless tool, denied passion, participation or personal invention, this time to the advantage of the production, which now, in its turn, attracted all attention to itself—this priority given to organized unity exasperated me just as much and made me feel, quite literally, that something was being smothered: to squash the actor's initiative, to kill the actor, is to kill both life and drama. . . .

I was dissatisfied even by the plays I had managed to read. Not all of them! For I was not blind to the merits of Sophocles, Aeschylus, or Shakespeare, nor a little later to some of the plays of Kleist or Büchner.[3] Why? Because, I thought, all these plays make extraordinary reading on account of their literary qualities, which may well not be specifically theatrical. In any case, after Shakespeare and Kleist, I do not think I have enjoyed reading a play. Strindberg seemed to me clumsy and inadequate. Even Molière bored me. I was not interested in those stories of misers, hypocrites, and cuckolds. I disliked his unmetaphysical mind. Shakespeare raised questions about the whole condition and destiny of man. In the long run Molière's little problems seemed to me of relatively minor importance, sometimes a little sad of

---

[1] Louis Jouvet (1891–1951), French actor and director.
[2] Erwin Piscator (1893–1966), German director.
[3] Heinrich von Kleist (1777–1811) and Georg Büchner (1813–1837), German playwrights.

course, dramatic even, but never tragic; for they could be resolved. The unendurable admits of no solution, and only the unendurable is profoundly tragic, profoundly comic and essentially theatrical.

On the other hand, the greatness of Shakespeare's plays seemed to me diminished in performance. No Shakespearian production ever captivated me as much as my reading of *Hamlet, Othello,* and *Julius Caesar,* etc. As I went so rarely to the theatre, perhaps I have never seen the best productions of Shakespeare's drama? In any case, in performance I had the impression that the unendurable had been made endurable. It was anguish tamed.

So I am really not a passionate theatregoer, still less a man of the theatre. I really hated the theatre. It bored me. And yet . . . when I was a child, I can still remember how my mother could not drag me away from the Punch and Judy show in the Luxembourg Gardens. I would go there day after day and could stay there, spellbound, all day long. But I did not laugh. That Punch and Judy show kept me there open-mouthed, watching those puppets talking, moving, and cudgeling each other. It was the very image of the world that appeared to me, strange and improbable but true as true, in the profoundly simplified form of caricature, as though to stress the grotesque and brutal nature of the truth. And from then until I was fifteen any form of play would thrill me and make me feel that the world is very strange, a feeling so deeply rooted that it has never left me. . . .

Today the theatre is blamed by some for not belonging to its own times. In my view it belongs only too well. This is what makes it so weak and ephemeral. I mean that the theatre *does* belong to its own times, but not quite enough. Every period needs something "out of period" and incommunicable to be introduced into what is "period" and communicable. Everything is a circumscribed moment in history, of course. But all history is contained in each moment of history: any moment in history is valid when it transcends history; in the particular lies the universal.

The themes chosen by many authors merely spring from a certain ideological fashion, which is something *less* than the period it belongs to. Or else these themes are the expression of some particular political attitude, and the plays that illustrate them will die with the ideology that has inspired them, for ideologies go out of fashion. Any Christian tomb, any Greek or Etruscan stele moves us and tells us more about the destiny of man than any number of laboriously committed plays, which are made to serve a discipline, a system of thought and language different from what is properly their own. . . .

Pirandello himself has been left behind the times, for his theatre was built on theories about personality or the multiformity of truth, which now seem clear as daylight since psychoanalysis and psychology plumbed the depths. In testing the validity of Pirandello's theories, modern psychology, inevitably going further than Pirandello in its exploration of the human psyche, certainly confirms Pirandello's findings, but at the same time shows him to be limited and inadequate: for what has been said by Pirandello is now said more thoroughly and scientifically. So the value of his theatre does not rest on his contribution to psychology but on the quality of his drama, which must inevitably lie elsewhere: what interests us in this author is no longer the discovery of the antagonistic elements in human personality, but what he has made of them dramatically. The strictly theatrical interest of his work lies outside science, beyond the limits of his own ideology. All that is left of Pirandello is his dramatic technique, the mechanics of his theatre: which again proves that drama founded on ideology or philosophy, exclusively inspired by them, is built on sand and crumbles away. It is his dramatic idiom, his purely theatrical instinct that keeps Pirandello alive for us today. . . .

. . . Drama of literary subtlety soon wears thin. Half tones are deepened or banished by light that is too brilliant. No shading, no nuance is possible. Problem plays, *pièces à thèse*,[4] are rough approximations. Drama is not the idiom for ideas. When it tries to become a vehicle for ideologies, all it can do is vulgarize them. It dangerously oversimplifies. It makes them too elementary and depreciates them. It is "naïve," but in the bad sense. All ideological drama runs the risk of being parochial. What would, not the *utility*, but the proper *function* of the theatre be, if it was restricted to the task of duplicating philosophy or theology or politics or pedagogy? Psychological drama is not psychological enough. One might as well read a psychological treatise. Ideological drama is not philosophical enough. Instead of going to see a dramatic illustration of this or that political creed I would rather read my usual daily paper or listen to the speeches of my party candidates. . . .

I told myself that the too intelligent playwrights were not intelligent enough: that it was no good thinkers looking to the theatre for the idiom of a philosophical treatise; that when they tried to bring too much subtlety and refinement into the theatre it was not only too much but not enough; that if the theatre was merely a deplorable enlargement of refined subtleties which I found so embarrassing, it merely meant that the enlargement was not sufficient. The overlarge was not large enough, the unsubtle was too subtle.

So if the essence of the theatre lay in magnifying its effects, they had to be magnified still further, underlined and stressed to the maximum. To push drama out of that intermediate zone where it is neither theatre nor literature is to restore it to its own domain, to its natural frontiers. It was not for me to conceal the devices of the theatre, but rather make them still more evident, deliberately obvious, go all out for caricature and the grotesque, way beyond the pale irony of witty drawing-room comedies. No drawing-room comedies, but farce, the extreme exaggeration of parody. Humor, yes, but using the methods of burlesque. Comic effects that are firm, broad, and out-

---

[4] Thesis plays.

rageous. No dramatic comedies either. But back to the unendurable. Everything to raised paroxysm, where the source of tragedy lies. A theatre of violence: violently comic, violently dramatic.

Avoid psychology or rather give it a metaphysical dimension. Drama lies in extreme exaggeration of the feelings, an exaggeration that dislocates flat everyday reality. Dislocation, disarticulation of language too.

Moreover, if the actors embarrassed me by not seeming natural enough, perhaps it was because they too were or tried to be *too* natural: by trying not to be, perhaps they will still appear natural, but in a different way. They must not be afraid of not being natural.

We need to be virtually bludgeoned into detachment from our daily lives, our habits and mental laziness, which conceal from us the strangeness of the world. Without a fresh virginity of mind,-without a new and healthy awareness of existential reality, there can be no theatre and no art either; the real must be in a way dislocated, before it can be reintegrated.

To achieve this effect, a trick can sometimes be used: playing against the text. A serious, solemn, formal production or interpretation can be grafted onto a text that is absurd, wild, and comic. On the other hand, to avoid the ridiculous sentimentality of the tear-jerker, a dramatic text can be treated as buffoonery and the tragic feeling of a play can be underlined by farce. Light makes shadows darker, shadows intensify light. For my part, I have never understood the difference people make between the comic and the tragic. As the "comic" is an intuitive perception of the absurd, it seems to me more hopeless than the "tragic." The "comic" offers no escape. I say "hopeless," but in reality it lies outside the boundaries of hope or despair.

Tragedy may appear to some in one sense comforting, for in trying to express the helplessness of a beaten man, one broken by fate for example, tragedy thus admits the reality of fate and destiny, of sometimes incomprehensible but objective laws that goven the universe. And man's helplessness, the futility of our efforts, can also, in a sense, appear comic.

I have called my comedies "anti-plays" or "comic dramas," and my dramas "pseudo-dramas" or "tragic farces": for it seems to me that comic and tragic are one, and that the tragedy of man is pure derision. The contemporary critical mind takes nothing too seriously or too lightly. In *Victimes du Devoir*[5] I tried to sink comedy in tragedy: in *Les Chaises*[6] tragedy in comedy or, if you like, to confront comedy and tragedy in order to link them in a new dramatic synthesis. But it is not a true synthesis, for these two elements do not coalesce, they coexist: one constantly repels the other, they show each other up, criticize and deny one another and, thanks to their opposition, thus succeed dynamically in maintaining a balance and creating tension. . . .

[5] *Victims of Duty.*
[6] *The Chairs.*

If one believes that "theatre" merely means the drama of the word, it is difficult to grant it can have an autonomous language of its own: it can then only be the servant of other forms of thought expressed in words, of philosophy and morals. Whereas, if one looks on the word as only *one* member of the shock-troops the theatre can marshal, everything is changed. First of all, there is a proper way for the theatre to use words, which is a dialogue, words in action, words in conflict. If they are used by some authors merely for discussion, this is a major error. There are other means of making words more theatrical: by working them up to such a pitch that they reveal the true temper of drama, which lies in frenzy; the whole tone should be as strained as possible, the language should almost break up or explode in its fruitless effort to contain so many meanings.

But the theatre is more than words: drama is a story that is lived and relived with each performance, and we can watch it live. The theatre appeals as much to the eye as to the ear. It is not a series of pictures, like the cinema, but architecture, a moving structure of scenic images.

Nothing is barred in the theatre: characters may be brought to life, but the unseen presence of our inner fears can also be materialized. So the author is not only allowed, but recommended to make actors of his props, to bring objects to life, to animate the scenery and give symbols concrete form.

Just as the words are complemented by gesture, acting, and pantomime, which can take their place when words are no longer adequate, so they can be amplified by the scenic elements of the stage as well. The use of props is yet another question. (Artaud had something to say about that.)

Nineteenth- and Twentieth-Century Germany, Austria, and Switzerland

"I am not a Marxist," said Karl Marx, commenting on the French Marxists of the 1870s. Similarly, both Marx and Engels might disown Socialist Realism, the Soviet doctrine of the arts derived from Marx. In contrast to it, Marx maintains that the highest development of art has neither a necessary nor a direct relationship with a social development or organization. Like Socialist Realism, however, Marx and Engels believe characters should be depicted in their historical context, with their relationships to social classes and conflicting ideologies. Partly for this reason, Engels like Marx prefers the realistic Shakespeare to the idealistic Schiller. Opposed to tendentious literature wherein the author obviously takes sides, serving up the solution on a platter (typical of Socialist Realism), Engels prefers the solution to social problems to inhere in situation and action, and the author's opinions to be concealed.

Marx derived his dialectical materialism from Hegelian dialectics (thesis-antithesis-synthesis); Freytag drew his conception of dramatic action from Hegel's definition of that term. A study of dramatic structure, Freytag's playwriting manual *Technique of the Drama* was long considered one of the more important works of its type. His notions of the dramatic, of play and counterplay, and his famous "Freytag pyramid" were very influential.

Indebted at least in part to Hegel, and to Schopenhauer too, Nietzsche explores the sources and substratum of tragedy. To Nietzsche, the Dionysiac chorus was the origin of Greek tragedy, which combined principles of Dionysos with those of Apollo: the intoxicating and the tranquil, the collective and the individual, the demonic and the intellectual, the lyric and the epic. Responsible for the decline and demise of tragedy, he charges, was Euripides, who sought to eliminate the primitive, Dionysiac element and to rebuild the drama on rationalistic, philosophical

grounds and on more individualized characterization. As tragedy was
born from the spirit of music, Nietzsche believed, so it was being reborn in
Germany through the music of Richard Wagner. According to
Duerrenmatt, Swiss playwright of the atomic age, tragedy was not reborn
at all. Necessary to tragedy, Duerrenmatt holds, are such assumptions
as guilt and a sense of responsibility, which are absent from the grotesquely
comic "Punch-and-Judy show of our century." Nevertheless, he adds,
even though pure tragedy is now impossible, the tragic may emerge from
comedy, as a frightening moment, an abyss suddenly opened.

Wagner, to whom Nietzsche looked for a revival of tragedy, foresaw a
union of separate arts—music, dance, and poetry; architecture and
painting—to form a harmonious "United Artwork of the Future." He
prophesied that on the stage, but not on a printed page, the drama
would flourish as a collective art work, inspired and needed by the popular,
communal spirit of the people.

Whereas Wagner wanted a fusion of the arts, Brecht would have the
different theatrical elements retain their independence in order to
offset and comment on each other, and to provide separate views of the
social context. A Marxist, Brecht wants theatre to reveal a larger
social picture than conventional dramaturgy permits and to communicate
insights into social forces and organization. Rejecting Aristotle's tripartite
division of poetry into epic, lyric, and dramatic, Brecht calls his drama
"epic" and injects lyrical elements as well. To prevent audiences
from becoming mesmerized by the stage action, Brecht wants a drama that
will, by means of alienation, reduce empathy and suspense. The
means of this type of drama also include, paradoxically, a theatrical
presentation of realism. Paradoxically too, the detached audience would
become more engaged than customarily in the depiction of human
beings at odds or in harmony with their society, would consider both clearly,
and then act upon this knowledge. Again paradoxically, alienation
becomes a means of social involvement and action.

Not only were German-speaking social theorists of the nineteenth and
twentieth centuries interested in the drama, so were psychological
theorists, including the Austrian Freud and the Swiss Jung. From the
Sophoclean tragedy Freud drew the name of the Oedipus complex,
and he analyzes both *Oedipus Rex* and *Hamlet,* in which he also finds an
Oedipal situation, as to the title characters, the reason for their impact
on audiences, and what they reveal about the authors. Also exploring comedy,
Freud finds behind jokes defensiveness, hostility, and aggressiveness,
which permit a socially acceptable rebellion against authority and a liberation
from the pressures of those with power, social and sexual. Jung
opposes Freud's "rigid dogmatism." To talk of the poet's relationship with
his parents, says Jung, is not only reductive, it fails to help us understand

his poetry, for a work of art, which is not a disease, does not yield to the medical approach. According to Jung, the source of great art is not the poet's personal unconscious but "primordial images," archetypes, that are part of the collective unconscious, the common heritage of mankind. Archetypes, mythic figures and situations, are behind great art that—activating, elaborating, and shaping these images—"transmutes our personal destiny into the destiny of mankind."

Richard Wagner 1813–1883

The Art-Work of the Future 1849

The path of Science lies from error to knowledge, from fancy to reality, from Religion to Nature. In the beginning of Science, therefore, Man stands toward Life in the same relation as he stood towards the phenomena of Nature when he first commenced to part his life from hers. Science takes over the arbitrary concepts of the human brain, in their totality; while, by her side, Life follows in its totality the instinctive evolution of Necessity. Science thus bears the burden of the sins of Life, and expiates them by her own self-abrogation; she ends in her direct antithesis, in the knowledge of Nature, in the recognition of the unconscious, instinctive, and therefore real, inevitable, and physical. The character of Science is therefore finite: that of Life, unending; just as Error is of time, but Truth eternal. But that alone is true and living which is sentiment, and harkens to the terms of physicality. Error's crowning folly is the arrogance of Science and renouncing and contemning the world of sense; whereas the highest victory of Science is her self-accomplished crushing of this arrogance, in the acknowledgment of the teaching of the senses.

The end of Science is the justifying of the Unconscious, the giving of self-consciousness to Life, the reinstatement of the Senses in their perceptive rights, the sinking of Caprice in the world-Will of Necessity. Science is therefore the vehicle of Knowledge, her procedure mediate, her goal an intermediation; but Life is the great Ultimate, a law unto itself. As Science melts away into the recognition of the ultimate and self-determinate reality, of actual Life itself: so does this avowal win its frankest, most direct expression in Art, or rather in the Work of Art.

True that the artist does not at first proceed directly; he certainly sets about his work in an arbitrary, selective, and mediating mood. But while he plays the go-between and picks and chooses, the product of his energy is not as yet the Work of Art; nay, his procedure is the rather that of Science, who seeks and probes, and therefore errs in her caprice. Only when his choice is made, when this choice was born from pure Necessity—when thus the artist has found himself again in the subject of his choice, as perfected Man finds his true self in Nature—then steps the Art-work into life, then first is it a real thing, a self-conditioned and immediate entity.

The actual Art-work, i.e., *its immediate physical portrayal, in the moment of its liveliest embodiment*, is therefore the only true redemption of

Selections. From *Richard Wagner's Prose Works*, translated by William Ashton Ellis, Vol. I. London: Kegan Paul, Trench, Trübner & Co., Ltd., 1892.

the artist; the uprootal of the final trace of busy, purposed choice; the confident determination of what was hitherto a mere imagining; the enfranchisement of thought in sense; the assuagement of the life-need in Life itself.

The Art-work, thus conceived as an immediate vital act, is therewith the perfect reconcilement of Science with Life, the laurel wreath which the vanquished, redeemed by her defeat, reaches in joyous homage to her acknowledged victor. . . .

The great instinctive errors of the People—which found their earliest utterance in Religion, and then became the starting-points of arbitrary speculation and system-making, in Theology and Philosophy—have reared themselves, in these Sciences and their coadjuatrix and adopted sister, Statecraft, to powers which make no less a claim than to govern and ordain the world and life by virtue of their innate and divine infallibility. Irrevocably, then, would Error reign in destructive triumph throughout eternity: did not the same life-force which blindly bore it, once more effectually annihilate it, by virtue of its innate, natural Necessity; and that so decisively and palpably, that Intellect, with all its arrogant divorce from Life, can see at last no other refuge from actual insanity, than in the unconditional acknowledgement of this only definite and visible force. And this vital force is—The Folk.

Who is then the Folk? . . .

"The Folk," was from of old the inclusive term for *all the units* which made up the total of a *commonality*. In the beginning, it was the family and the tribe; next, the tribes united by like speech into a nation. Practically, by the Roman world-dominion which engulfed the nations, and theoretically, by the Christian religion which admitted of naught but men, i.e., no racial, but only *Christian* men—the idea of "the People" has so far broadened out, or even evaporated, that we may either include in it mankind in general, or, upon the arbitrary political hypothesis, a certain, and generally the propertyless portion of the Commonwealth. But beyond a frivolous, this term has also acquired an ineradicable *moral* meaning; and on account of this it is, that in times of stir and trouble all men are eager to number themselves among the People; each one gives out that he is careful for the People's weal, and no one will permit himself to be excluded from it. Therefore in these latter days also has the question frequently been broached, in the most diverse of senses: Who then is the People? In the sum total of the body politic, can a separate party, a particular fraction of the said body claim this name for itself alone? Rather, are we not all alike "the People," from the beggar to the prince? . . .

The "Folk" is the epitome of all those men *who feel a common and collective Want*. To it belong, then, all of those who recognise their individual want as a collective want, or find it based thereon; ergo, all those who can hope for the stilling of their want in nothing but the stilling of a common want, and therefore spend their whole life's strength upon the stilling of their thus acknowledged common want. For only that want which urges to the uttermost, is genuine Want; but this Want alone is the force of true Need; but a common and collective need is the only true Need; but only he who feels within him a true Need, has a right to its assuagement; but only the assuagement of a genuine Need is Necessity; and it is *the Folk alone that acts according to Necessity's behests,* and therefore irresistibly, victoriously, and right as none besides.

Who now are they who belong *not* to this People, and who are its sworn foes?

All those *who feel no Want;* whose life-spring therefore consists in a need which rises not to the potence of a Want, and thus is artificial, untrue, and egoistic; and not only is not embraced within a common Need, but as the empty need of preserving superfluity—as which alone can one conceive of need without the force of want—is diametrically opposed to the collective Need.

Where there is no Want, there is no true Need; where no true Need, no necessary action. But where there is no *necessary action,* there reigns Caprice; and where Caprice is king, there blossoms every vice, and every criminal assault on Nature. For only by forcing back, by barring and refusing the assuagement of true Need, can the false and artificial need endeavour to assuage itself.

But the satisfaction of an artificial need is *Luxury;* which can only be bred and supported in opposition to, and at the cost of, the necessities of others.

Luxury is as heartless, inhuman, insatiable, and egoistic as the "need" which called it forth, but which, with all its heaping-up and over-reaching, it never more can still. For this need itself is no natural and therefore satisfiable one; by very reason that, being false, it has no true, essential antithesis in which it may be spent, consumed, and satisfied. Actual physical hunger has its natural antithesis, satiety, in which—by feeding—it is spent: but unwanting need, the need that craves for luxury, is in itself already luxury and superfluity. The error of it, therefore, can never go over into truth; it racks, devours, torments and burns, without an instant's stilling; it leaves brain, heart and sense for ever vainly yearning, and swallows up all gladness, mirth, and joy of life. For sake of one sole, and yet unreachable moment of refreshment, it squanders the toil and life-sweat of a thousand needy wanters; it lives upon the unstilled hunger of a thousand thousand poor, though impotent to satiate its own for but the twinkling of an eye; it holds a whole world within the iron chains of despotism, without the power to momentarily break the golden chains of that arch-tyrant which it is unto itself.

And this fiend, this crack-brained need-without-a-need, this need of Need—this *need of Luxury*, which is *Luxury itself* withal—is sovereign of the world. It is the soul of that Industry which deadens men, to turn them to machines; the soul of our State which swears away men's honor, the better then to take them back as lieges of its grace; the soul of our deistic Science, which hurls men down before an immaterial God, the product of the sum of intellectual luxury, for his consumption. It is—alas!—the soul, the stipulation, of our—*Art!*

Who then will bring to pass the rescue from this baleful state?

Want—which shall teach the world to recognize its own *true need*; that need which *by its very nature admits of satisfaction.*

Want will cut short the hell of Luxury; it will teach the tortured, Need-lacking spirits whom this hell embraces in its bounds the simple, homely need of sheer human, physical hunger and thirst; but in fellowship will it point us to the health-giving bread, the clear sweet springs of Nature; in fellowship shall we taste their genuine joys, and grow up in communion to veritable men. In common, too, shall we close the last link in the bond of holy Necessity; and the brother-kiss that seals this bond, will be the *mutual Art-work of the Future*. But in this, also, our great redeemer and well-doer, Necessity's viceregent in the flesh—*the Folk*, will no longer be a severed and peculiar class; for in this Art-work we shall all be *one*—heralds and supporters of Necessity, knowers of the unconscious, willers of the unwilful, betokeners of Nature—*blissful men....*

The three chief artistic faculties of the entire man have once, and of their own spontaneous impulse, evolved to a trinitarian utterance of human Art; and this was in the primal, earliest manifested art-work, the *Lyric*, and its later, more conscious, loftiest completion, the *Drama*.

The arts of *Dance*, of *Tone*, and *Poetry*: thus call themselves the three primeval sisters whom we see at once entwine their measures wherever the the conditions necessary for artistic manifest have arisen. By their nature they are inseparable without disbanding the stately minuet of Art; for in this dance, which is the very cadence of Art itself, they are so wondrous closely interlaced with one another, of fairest love and inclination, so mutually bound up in each other's life, of body and of spirit: that each of the three partners, unlinked from the united chain and bereft thus of her own life and motion, can only carry on an artificially inbreathed and borrowed life—not giving forth her sacred ordinances, as in their trinity, but now receiving despotic rules for mechanical movement....

This is Art the free. The sweet and forceful impulse in that dance of sisters, is the *impulse of Freedom*; the love-kiss of their enlocked embraces, the *transport of a freedom won.*

The solitary unit is unfree, because confined and fettered in un-Love; the *associate is free*, because unfettered and unconfined through Love....

Each separate faculty of man is limited by bounds; but his united, agreed, and reciprocally helping faculties—and thus his faculties in *mutual love* of one another—combine to form the self-completing, unbounded, universal faculty of men. Thus too has every *artistic* faculty of man its natural bounds, since man has not *one only Sense* but separate *Senses*; while every faculty springs from its special sense, and therefore each single faculty must find its bounds in the confines of its correlated sense. But the boundaries of the separate senses are also their joint meeting-points, those points at which they melt in one another and each agrees with each: and exactly so do the faculties that are derived from them touch one another and agree. Their confines, therefore, are removed by this agreement; but only those that love each other can agree, and "to love" means: to acknowledge the other, and at like time to know one's self. Thus Knowledge through Love is Freedom; and the freedom of man's faculties is—*All-faculty*.

Only the Art which answers to this "all-faculty" of man is, therefore, *free*; and not the Art-*variety*, which only issues from a single human faculty. The Arts of Dance, of Tone, of Poetry, are each confined within their several bounds; in contact with these bounds each feels herself unfree, be it not that, across their common boundary, she reaches out her hand to her neighboring art in unrestrained acknowledgment of love. The very grasping of this hand lifts her above the barrier; her full embrace, her full absorption in her sister—i.e., her own complete ascension beyond the set-up barrier—casts down the fence itself. And when every barrier has thus fallen, then are there no more *arts* and no more boundaries, but only *Art*, the universal, undivided.

It is a sorry misconception of Freedom—that of the being who would fain be free in loneliness. The impulse to loose one's self from commonalty, to be free and independent for individual self alone, can only lead to the direct antithesis of the state so arbitrarily striven after: namely to utmost lack of self-dependence. Nothing in Nature is self-dependent excepting that which has the conditionments of its self-standing not merely in itself, but also outside of itself: for the inner are first possible by virtue of the outer. That which would separate itself must, necessarily, first have that from which to separate. He who would fain be nothing but himself, must first know what he is; but this he only learns by distinguishing from what he is not: were he able to lop off entirely that which differs from him, then were he himself no differentiated entity, and thus no longer cognisable by himself. In order to will to be the whole thing which of and in himself he is, the individual must learn to be absolutely not the thing he is not; but the thing that is absolutely what *he* is not, is that thing which lies apart from him; and only in the fullest of communion with that which is apart from him, in the completest absorption into the commonalty of those who differ from him, can he ever be completely *what* he is by nature, what he must be, and as a reasonable being, can but will to be. Thus only in Communism does Egoism find its perfect satisfaction.

That Egoism, however, which has brought such immeasurable woe into the world and so lamentable a mutilation and insincerity into Art, is of another breed to the natural and rational egoism which finds its perfect satisfaction in the community of all. In pious indignation it wards off the name of "Egoism" from it, and dubs itself "Brotherly-" and "Christian-" "Art-" and "Artist-Love"; founds temples to God and Art; builds hospitals, to make ailing old-age young and sound—and schools to make youth old and ailing; establishes 'faculties,' courts of justice, governments, states, and what not else?—merely to prove that it is not Egoism. And this is just the most irredeemable feature of it, and that which makes it utterly pernicious both to itself and to the general commonalty. This is the isolation of the single, in which each severed nullity shall rank as somewhat, but the great commonalty as naught; in which each unit struts as something special and "original," while the whole, forsooth, can then be nothing in particular and for ever a mere imitation. This is the self-dependence of the individual, where every unit lives upon the charges of his fellows, in order to be "free by help of God"; pretends to be what others *are*; and, briefly, follows the inversion of the teaching of Jesus Christ: "To *take* is more blessed than to give."

This is the genuine Egoism, in which each *isolated art-variety* would give itself the airs of universal Art; while, in truth, it only thereby loses its own peculiar attributes. . . .

. . . Thus the Poetic art can absolutely not create the genuine art-work— and this is only such an one as is brought to direct physical manifestment— without those arts to which the physical show belongs directly. Thought, that mere phantom of reality, is formless by itself; and only when it retraces the road on which it rose to birth, can it attain artistic perceptibility. In the Poetic art, the purpose of all Art comes first to consciousness: but the other arts contain within themselves the unconscious Necessity that forms this purpose. The art of Poetry is the creative process by which the Art-work steps into life: but out of Nothing, only the god of the Israelites can make some-thing—the Poet must have that Something; and that something is the whole artistic man, who proclaims in the art of Dance and Tone the physical longing become a longing of the soul, which through its force first generates the poetic purpose and finds in that its absolution, in its attainment its own appeasing.

Wheresoever *the Folk* made poetry—and only by the Folk, or in the footsteps of the Folk, can poetry be really made—there did the Poetic purpose rise to life alone upon the shoulders of the arts of Dance and Tone, as the *head* of the full-fledged human being. The Lyrics of Orpheus would never have been able to turn the savage beasts to silent, placid adoration, if the singer had but given them forsooth some dumb and printed verse to read: their ears must be enthralled by the sonorous notes that came straight from the heart, their carrion-spying eyes be tamed by the proud and graceful movements of the body—*in such a way* that they should recognise instinctively in this whole man no longer a mere object for their maw, no mere objective for their feeding-, but for their hearing- and their seeing-powers—before they could be attuned to duly listen to his moral sentences.

Neither was the true *Folk-epic* by any means a mere recited poem: the songs of Homer, such as we now possess them, have issued from the critical siftings and compilings of a time in which the genuine Epos had long since ceased to live. . . . But before these epic songs became the object of such literary care, they had flourished mid the Folk, eked out by voice and gesture, as a bodily enacted Art-work; as it were, a fixed and crystallised blend of lyric song and dance, with predominant lingering on portrayal of the action and reproduction of the heroic dialogue. These epic-lyrical performances form the unmistakable middle stage between the genuine older Lyric and Tragedy, the normal point of transition from the one to the other.

Tragedy was therefore the entry of the Art-work of the Folk upon the public arena of political life; and we may take its appearance as an excellent touchstone for the difference in procedure between the Art-*creating* of the Folk and the mere literary-historical *Making* of the so-called cultured art-world. At the very time when live-born Epos became the object of the critical dilettantism of the court of Pisistratus, it had already shed its blossoms in the People's life—yet not because the Folk had lost its true afflatus, but since it was already able to surpass the old, and from unstanchable artistic sources to build the less perfect art-work up, until it became the more perfect. For while those pedants and professors in the Prince's castle were laboring at the construction of a *literary Homer,* pampering their own unproductivity with their marvel at their wisdom, by aid of which they yet could not only understand the thing that long had passed from life—*Thespis* had already slid his car to Athens, had set it up beside the palace walls, dressed out his *stage* and, stepping from the chorus of the Folk, had *trodden* its planks; *no longer did he shadow forth* the deeds of heroes, as in the Epos, but *in these heroes' guises enacted them.*

With the Folk, all is reality and deed; it *does,* and then rejoices in the thought of its own doing. . . . Thus it raised the platform of its stage, and decked itself with tragic masks and raiment of some god or hero, in order itself to be a god or hero: and *Tragedy* was born; whose fruits it tasted with the blissful sense of its own creative force, but whose metaphysical basis it handed, all regardless, to the brain-racking speculation of the dramaturgists of our modern court-theatres.

Tragedy flourished for just so long as it was inspired by the spirit of the

Folk, and as this spirit was a veritably popular, i.e., a *communal* one. When the national brotherhood of the Folk was shivered into fragrants, when the common bond of its Religion and primeval Customs was pierced and severed by the sophist needles of the egoistic spirit of Athenian self-dissection —then the Folk's art-work also ceased: then did the professors and the doctors of the literary guilds take heritage of the ruins of the fallen edifice, and delved among its beams and stones; to pry, to ponder, and to rearrange its members. With Aristophanian laughter, the Folk relinquished to these learned insects the refuse of its meal, threw Art upon one side for two millennia, and fashioned of its innermost necessity the history of the world; the while those scholars cobbled up their tiresome history of Literature, by order of the supreme court of Alexander.

The career of Poetry, since the breaking-up of Tragedy, and since her own departure from community with mimetic Dance and Tone, can be easily enough surveyed—despite the monstrous claims which she has raised. The lonely art of Poetry—prophesied no more; she no longer showed, but only *described*; she merely played the go-between, but gave naught from herself; she pieced together what true seers had uttered, but without the living bond of unity; she suggested, without satisfying her own suggestions; she urged to life, without herself attaining life; she gave the catalogue of a picture-gallery, but not the paintings. The wintry stem of Speech, stripped of its summer wreath of sounding leaves, shrank to the withered, toneless signs of Writing: instead of to the Ear, it dumbly now addressed the *Eye*; the poet's strain became a *written dialect*—the poet's breath the *penman's scrawl*. . . .

. . . We need not draw the special subdivision of *literary poesy* within our closer ken. For, with our eyes directed toward the Artwork of the Future, we are seeking out Poetic art where she is struggling to become a living and immediate art, and this is in the *Drama*; not where she renounces every claim to this life-issue, and yet—for all her fill of thought— but takes the terms of her peculiar manufacture from the hopeless artistic unfitness of our modern public life. This Literature-posey supplies the only solace—however sad and impotent!—of the lonely human being of the Present who longs to taste poetic food. Yet the solace that she gives is truly but an access of the *longing after Life*, the longing for the living Artwork; for the urgence of this longing is her very soul—where *this* does not speak out, does not proclaim itself with might and main, there has the last trace of verity departed from this poesy too. The more honestly and tumultuously, however, does it throb within her, so much the more veraciously does she admit her own unsolaceable plight, and confess the only possible assuagement of her longing, to be *her own self-abrogation, her dissolution into Life, into the living Artwork of the Future*.

Let us ponder how this fervent, noble longing of Literary Poesy must one day be responded to; and meanwhile let us leave our modern Dramatic Poetry to the pompous triumphs of her own ridiculous vanity! . . .

In our general survey of the demeanor of each of the three humanistic arts after its severance from their initial communion, we could not but plainly see that exactly where the one variety touched on the province of the next, where the faculty of the second stepped-in to replace the faculty of the first, there did the first one also find its natural bounds. Beyond these bounds, it might stretch over from the second art-variety to the third; and through this third, again, back to itself, back to its own especial individuality—but only in accordance with the natural laws of *Love*, of *self-offering* for the common good impelled by Love. As Man by love sinks his whole nature in that of Woman, in order to pass over through her into a third being, the Child, and yet finds but himself again in all the loving trinity, though in this self a widened, filled, and finished whole: so may each of these individual arts find its own self again in the perfect, thoroughly liberated Artwork—nay, look upon itself as broadened to this Artwork—so soon as, on the path of genuine love and by sinking of itself within the kindred arts, it returns upon itself and finds the guerdon of its love in the perfect work of Art to which it knows itself expanded. Only that art-variety, however, which wills the common art-work, reaches therewith the highest fill of its own particular nature. . . .

Of all these arts not one so sorely needed an espousal with another, as that of *Tone*; for her peculiar character is that of a fluid nature-element poured out betwixt the more defined and individualized substances of the two other arts. Only through the Rhythm of Dance, or as bearer of the Word, could she brace her deliquescent being to definite and characteristic corporeality. But neither of the other arts could bring herself to plunge, in love without reserve, into the element of Tone: each drew from it so many bucketsful as seemed expedient for her own precise and egoistic aims; each took from Tone, but gave not in return; so that poor Tone, who of her life-need stretched out her hands in all directions, was forced at last herself to *take* for very means of maintenance. Thus she engulfed the Word at first, to make of it what suited best her pleasure: but while she disposed of this word as her wilful feeling listed, in Catholic music, she lost its bony framework—so to say—of which, in her desire to become a human being, she stood in need to bear the liquid volume of her blood, and round which she might have crystallised a sinewy flesh. A new and energetic handling of the Word, in order to gain shape therefrom, was shown by *Protestant* church-music; which in the "*Passion-music*," pressed on towards an ecclesiastical drama, wherein the word was no longer a mere shifting vehicle for the expression of feeling, but girt itself to thoughts depicting Action. In this church-drama, Music, while still retaining her predominance and building everything else into her own pedestal, almost compelled Poetry to behave in earnest and like a man towards her. But coward Poetry appeared to dread this challenge; she deemed it as well to cast a few neglected morsels to swell the meal of this mightily waxing monster, Music, and thus to pacify it; only, however, to regain the liberty of staying undisturbed within her own peculiar province, the egoistic sphere of Literature. It is to this selfish, cowardly bearing of Poetry toward Tone that we stand indebted for that unnatural abortion the *Oratorio*, which finally transplanted itself from the church into the concert-hall. The Oratorio would give itself the airs of Drama; but only precisely in so far as it might still preserve to *Music* the unquestioned right of being the chief concern, the only leader of the drama's 'tone.'

Where Poetry fain would reign in solitude, as in the spoken Play, she took Music into her menial service, for her own convenience; as, for instance, for the entertainment of the audience between the acts, or even for the enhancement of the effect of certain dumb transactions, such as the irruption of a cautious burglar, and matters of that sort! Dance did the selfsame thing, when she leapt proudly on to saddle, and graciously condescended to allow Music to hold the stirrup. Exactly so did Tone behave to Poetry in the Oratorio: she merely let her pile the heap of stones, from which she might erect her building as she fancied.

But Music at last capped all this ever-swelling arrogance, by her shameless insolence in the *Opera*. Here she claimed tribute of the art of Poetry down to its utmost farthing: it was no longer to merely make her verses, no longer to merely suggest dramatic characters and sequences, as in the Oratorio, in order to give her a handle for her own distention—but it was to lay down its whole being and all its powers at her feet, to offer up complete dramatic characters and complex situations, in short the entire ingredients of Drama; in order that she might take this gift of homage and make of it whatever her fancy listed.

The *Opera*, as the seeming point of reunion of all the three related arts, has become the meeting-place of these sisters' most self-seeking efforts. Undoubtedly Tone claims for herself the supreme right of legislation therein; nay, it is solely to her struggle—though led by egoism—towards the genuine artwork of the Drama, that we owe the Opera at all. But in degree as Poetry and Dance were bid to be her simple slaves, there rose amid *their* egoistic ranks a growing spirit of rebellion against their domineering sister. The arts of Dance and Poetry had taken a personal lease of Drama *in their own way*: the spectacular Play and the pantomimic Ballet were the two territories between which Opera now deployed her troops, taking from each whatever she deemed indispensable for the self-glorification of Music. Play and Ballet, however, were well aware of her aggressive self-sufficiency: they only lent themselves to their sister against their will, and in any case with the mental reservation that on the first favorable opportunity they each would clear themselves an exclusive field. So Poetry leaves behind her feeling and her pathos, the only fitting wear for Opera, and throws her net of modern Intrigue around her sister Music; who, without being able to get a proper hold of it, must willynilly twist and turn the empty cobweb, which none but the nimble play-sempstress herself can plait into a tissue: and there she chirps and twitters, as in the French confectionary-operas, until at last her peevish breath gives out, and sister Prose steps in to fill the stage. Dance, on the other hand, has only to espy some breach in the breath-taking of the tyrannizing songstress, some chilling of the lava-stream of musical emotion—and in an instant she flings her legs astride the boards; trounces sister Music off the scene, down to the solitary confinement of the orchestra; and spins, and whirls, and runs around, until the public can no longer see the wood for wealth of leaves, i.e., the opera for the crowd of legs.

Thus Opera becomes the mutual compact of the egoism of the three related arts. To rescue her supremacy, Tone contracts with Dance for so many quarters-of-an-hour which shall belong to the latter *alone*: during this period the chalk upon the shoe-soles shall trace the regulations of the stage, and music shall be made according to the system of the *leg-*, and not the *tone-*, vibrations; item, that the singers shall be expressly forbidden to indulge in any sort of graceful bodily motion—this is to be the exclusive property of the dancer, whereas the singer is to be pledged to complete abstention from any fancy for mimetic gestures, a restriction which will have the additional advantage of conserving his voice. With Poetry Tone settles, to the former's highest satisfaction, that she will not employ her in the slightest on the stage; nay, will as far as possible not even articulate her words and verses, and will relegate her instead to the printed text-book, necessarily to be read *after* the performance, in Literature's decorous garb of black and white. Thus, then, is the noble bond concluded, each art again itself; and between the dancing legs and written book, Music once more floats gaily on through all the length and breadth of her desire. *This is modern Freedom in the faithful counterfeit of Art!* . . .

On the stage, prepared by architect and painter, now steps *Artistic Man*, as Natural Man steps on the stage of Nature. What the statuary and the historical painter endeavored to limn on *stone* or *canvas*, they now limn upon *themselves*, their form, their body's limbs, the features of their visage, and raise it to the consciousness of full artistic life. The same sense that led the sculptor in his grasp and rendering of the human figure, now leads the *Mime* in the handling and demeanor of his actual body. The same eye which taught the historical painter, in drawing and in color, in arrangement of his drapery and composition of his groups, to find the beautiful, the graceful and the characteristic, now orders the whole breadth of *actual human show*. Sculptor and painter once freed the Greek Tragedian from his cothurnus and his mask, upon and under which the real man could only move according to a certain religious convention. With justice, did this pair of plastic artists annihilate the last disfigurement of pure artistic man, and thus prefigure in their stone and canvas the tragic Actor of the Future. As they once descried him in his undistorted truth, they now shall let him pass into reality and bring his form, in a measure sketched by them, to bodily portrayal with all its wealth of movement.

Thus the illusion of plastic art will turn to truth in Drama: the plastic artist will reach out hands to the *dancer*, to the *mime*, will lose himself in them, and thus become himself both mime and dancer. So far as lies within his power, he will have to impart the inner man, his feeling and his willing to the eye. The breadth and depth of scenic space belong to him for the plastic message of his stature and his motion, as a single unit or in union with his fellows. But where his power ends, where the fulness of his will and feeling impels him to the uttering of the inner man by means of *Speech*, there will the Word proclaim his plain and conscious purpose: he becomes a *Poet* and, to be poet, a *tone-artist*. But as dancer, tone-artist, and poet, he still is one and the same thing: nothing other than *executant, artistic Man, who, in the fullest measure of his faculties, imparts himself to the highest expression of receptive power.*

It is in him, the immediate executant, that the three sister-arts unite their forces in one collective operation, in which the highest faculty of each comes to its highest unfolding. By working in common, each one of them attains the power to be and do the very thing which, of her own and inmost essence, she longs to do and be. Hereby: that each, where her own power ends, can be absorbed within the other, whose power commences where her's ends—she maintains her own purity and freedom, her independence as *that* which she is. The *mimetic dancer* is stripped of his impotence, so soon as he can sing and speak; the creations of *Tone* win all-explaining meaning through the mime, as well as through the poet's word, and that exactly in degree as Tone itself is able to transcend into the motion of the mime and the word of the poet; while the *Poet* first becomes a Man through his translation to the flesh and blood of the *Performer*: for though he metes to each artistic factor the guiding purpose which binds them all into a common whole, yet this purpose is first changed from "will" to "can" *by the poet's Will descending to the actor's Can.*

Not one rich faculty of the separate arts will remain unused in the United Artwork of the Future; in *it* will each attain its first complete appraisement. Thus, especially, will the manifold developments of Tone, so peculiar to our instrumental music, unfold their utmost wealth within this Artwork; nay, Tone will incite the mimetic art of Dance to entirely new discoveries, and no less swell the breath of Poetry to unimagined fill. For Music, in her solitude, has fashioned for herself an organ which is capable of the highest reaches of expression. This organ is the *Orchestra*. The tone-speech of Beethoven, introduced into Drama by the orchestra, marks an entirely fresh departure for the dramatic artwork. While Architecture and, more especially, scenic Landscape-painting have power to set the executant dramatic Artist in the surroundings of physical Nature, and to dower him from the exhaustless stores of natural phenomena with an ample and significant background, so in the Orchestra, that pulsing body of many-colored harmony, the personating individual Man is given, for his support, a stanchless elemental spring, at once artistic, natural, and human.

The Orchestra is, so to speak, the loam of endless, universal Feeling, from which the individual feeling of the separate actor draws power to shoot aloft to fullest height of growth: it, in a sense, dissolves the hard immobile ground of the actual scene into a fluent, elastic, impressionable ether, whose unmeasured bottom is the great sea of Feeling itself. Thus the Orchestra is like the *Earth* from which Antaeus, soon as ever his foot had grazed it, drew new immortal life-force. By its essence diametrically opposed to the scenic landscape which surrounds the actor, and therefore, as to locality, most rightly placed in the deepened foreground outside the scenic frame, it at like time forms the perfect complement of these surroundings; inasmuch as it broadens out the exhaustless *physical* element of Nature to the equally exhaustless *emotional* element of artistic Man. These elements, thus knit together, enclose the performer as with an atmospheric ring of Art and Nature, in which, like to the heavenly bodies, he moves secure in fullest orbit, and whence, withal, he is free to radiate on every side his feelings and his views of life, broadened to infinity, and showered, as it were, on distances as measureless as those on which the stars of heaven cast their rays of light.

Thus supplementing one another in their changeful dance, the united sister-arts will show themselves and make good their claim; now all together, now in pairs, and again in solitary splendor, according to the momentary need of the only rule- and purpose-giver, the Dramatic Action. Now plastic Mimicry will listen to the passionate plaint of Thought; now resolute Thought will pour itself into the expressive mold of Gesture; now Tone must vent alone the stream of Feeling, the shudder of alarm; and now, in mutual embrace, all three will raise the Will of Drama to immediate and potent Deed. For One thing there is that all the three united arts must will, in order to be free: and that one thing is the Drama: the reaching of the Drama's aim must be their common goal. Are they conscious of this aim, do they put forth all their will to work out that alone: so will they also gain the power to lop off from their several stems the egoistic offshoots of their own peculiar being; that therewith the tree may not spread out in formless mass to every wind of heaven, but proudly lift its wreath of branches, boughs and leaves, into its lofty crown. . . .

But the individual man, in full possession of health of body, heart, and mind, can experience no higher need than that which is common to all his kind; for, to be a *true* Need, it can only be such an one as he can satisfy in Community alone. The most imperious and strongest need of full-fledged artist-man, however, is to impart himself in highest compass of his being to the fullest expression of Community; and this he only reaches with the necessary breadth of general understanding in the *Drama*. In Drama he broadens out his own particular being, by the portrayal of an individual person-ality not his own, to a universally human being. He must completely step outside himself, to grasp the inner nature of an alien personality with that completeness which is needful before he can portray it. This he will only attain when he so exhaustively analyzes this individual in his contact with and penetration and completion by other individualities—and therefore also the nature of these other individualities themselves—when he forms thereof so lively a conception, that he gains a sympathetic feeling of this complementary influence on his own interior being. The perfectly artistic Performer is, therefore, the unit Man expended to the *essence of the Human Species* by the utmost evolution of his own particular nature.

The place in which this wondrous process comes to pass, is the *Theatric stage*; the collective art-work which it brings to light of day, the *Drama*. But to force his own specific nature to the highest blossoming of its con-tents in this *one* and highest art-work, the separate artist, like each several art, must quell each selfish, arbitrary bent toward untimely bushing into outgrowths unfurthersome to the whole; the better then to put forth all his strength for reaching of the highest common purpose, which cannot indeed be realised without the unit, nor, on the other hand, without the unit's recurrent limitation.

This purpose of the Drama, is withal the only true artistic purpose that ever can be fully *realised*; whatsoever lies aloof from that, must necessarily lose itself in the sea of things indefinite, obscure, unfree. This purpose, how-ever, the separate art-branch will never reach *alone*,[1] but only *all together*;

---

[1] The modern *Playwright* will feel little tempted to concede that Drama ought not to belong exclusively to *his* branch of art, the art of *Poesy*; above all will he not be able to constrain himself to share it with the Tone-poet, to wit, as he understands us, allow the Play to be swallowed up by the Opera. Perfectly correct!—so long as Opera subsists, the Play must also stand, and, for the matter of that, the Pantomine too; so long as any dispute hereon is thinkable, the Drama of the Future must itself remain unthinkable. If, however, the Poet's doubt lie deeper, and consist in this, that he cannot conceive how *Song* should be entitled to usurp entirely the place of spoken dialogue: then he must take for rejoinder, that in two several regards he has not as yet a clear idea of the character of the Art-work of the Future. Firstly, he does not reflect that Music has to occupy a very different position in this Art-work to what she takes in modern Opera: that only where her power is the *fittest*, has she to open out her full expanse; while, on the contrary, wherever another power, for instance that of dramatic Speech, is the most *necessary*, she has to subordinate herself to that; still, that Music possesses the peculiar faculty of, without entirely keeping silence, so imperceptibly linking herself to the thought-

and therefore the most *universal* is at like time the only real, free, the only universally *intelligible* Art-work. . . .

Let us . . . first agree as to *whom* we must consider the creator of the Art-work of the Future; so that we may argue back from him to the life-conditions which alone can permit his art-work and himself to take their rise.

Who, then, will be the *Artist of the Future*?

Without a doubt, the Poet.[2]

But *who* will be the Poet?

Indisputably the *Performer*.

Yet *who*, again, will be the Performer?

Necessarily the *Fellowship of all the Artists*.

In order to see the Performer and the Poet take natural rise, we must first imagine to ourselves the artistic Fellowship of the future; and that according to no arbitrary canon, but following the logical course which we are bound to take in drawing from the Art-work itself our conclusions as to those artistic organs which alone can call it into natural life.

The Art-work of the Future is an associate work, and only an associate demand can call it forth. This demand, which we have hitherto merely treated theoretically, as a necessary essential of the being of each separate branch of art, is practically conceivable only in the *fellowship of every artist*; and the union of every artist, according to the exigencies of time and place, and for *one definite aim*, is that which forms this fellowship. This definite aim is the *Drama*, for which they all unite in order by their participation therein to unfold their own peculiar art to the acme of its being; in this unfoldment to permeate each other's essence, and as fruit thereof to generate the living, breathing, moving drama. But the thing that makes this sharing possible to all—nay that renders it necessary, and which without their cooperation can never come to manifestment—is the very kernel of the Drama, the *dramatic Action*.

The dramatic Action, as the first postulate of Drama, is withal that moment in the entire art-work which ensures its widest *understanding*. Directly borrowed from *Life*, past or present, it forms the intelligible bond

---

full element of Speech that she lets the latter seem to walk abroad alone, the while she still supports it. Should the poet acknowledge this, then he has to recognize in the second place, that thoughts and situations to which the lightest and most restrained accompaniment of Music should seem importunate and burdensome, can only be such as are borrowed from the spirit of our modern Play; which, from beginning to end, will find no inch of breathing-space within the Art-work of the Future. The Man who will portray himself in the Drama of the Future has done for ever with all the prosaic hurly-burly of fashionable manners or polite intrigue, which our modern "poets" have to tangle and to disentangle in their plays, with greatest circumstantiality. His nature-bidden action and his speech are: Yea, yea! and Nay, nay!—and all beyond is evil, i.e., modern and superfluous [Wagner's note].

[2] We must beg to be allowed to regard the *Tone*-poet as included in the *Word*-poet—whether personally or by fellowship is here a matter of indifference [Wagner's note].

that links this work therewith; exactly in degrees as it mirrors back the face of Life, and fitly satisfies its claim for understanding. The dramatic Action is thus *the bough from the Tree of Life* which, sprung therefrom by an unconscious instinct, has blossomed and shed its fruit obediently to vital laws, and now, dissevered from the stem, is *planted in the soil of Art*; there, in new, more beautiful, eternal life, to grow into the spreading tree which resembles fully in its inner, necessary force and truth the parent tree of actual Life. But now, become its "objectivation," it upholds to Life the picture of its own existence, and lifts unconscious Life to conscious knowledge of itself.

In the dramatic Action, therefore, the Necessity of the art-work displays itself; without *it*, or some degree of reference thereto, all art-fashioning is arbitrary, unneedful, accidental, unintelligible. The first and truest fount of Art reveals itself in the impulse that urges from *Life* into the work of art; for it is the impulse to bring the unconscious, instinctive principle of Life to understanding and acknowledgment as Necessity. But the impulse toward agreement presupposes *commonality*: the Egoist has need of no one with whom to agree. Therefore, only from a life in common, can proceed the impulse toward intelligible objection of this life by Art-work; the Community of artists alone can give it vent; and only in communion, can they content it. This impulse, however, can only find its full contentment in the faithful representation of an episode taken from Life: whilst only such an episode can be a fitting subject for artistic Treatment as has already come in Life to definite conclusion; as to which, as a series of causes and effects, there can no longer be any doubt; and as to whose possible issue there is no longer room for arbitrary assumption. Only when a thing has been consummated in Life, can we grasp the necessity of its occurrence, the harmony of its separate movements. But an episode is not completed, until the *Man* who brought it about—who stood in the focus of a series of events which, as a feeling, thinking, willing person, he guided by the force of his own innate character—until this man is likewise no longer subject to our arbitrary assumptions as to his possible doings. Now, every man is subject to these so long as he lives: by Death is he first freed from his subjection, for then we know All that he did, and that he was. That action, therefore, must be the best fitted for dramatic art—and the worthiest object of its rendering —which is rounded off together with the life of the chief person that evolved it, and whose denouement is none other than the conclusion of the life of this one man himself.

Only that action is completely truthful—and can thoroughly convince us of its plain necessity—on whose fulfilment a man had set the whole strength of his being, and which was to him so imperative a necessity that he needs must pass over into it with the whole force of his character. But hereof he conclusively persuades us by this alone: that, in the effectuation of his personal force, he literally *went under*, he veritably threw overboard his personal existence, for sake of bringing to the outer world the inner Necessity which ruled his being. He proves to us the verity of his nature, not only in his actions—which might still appear capricious so long as he yet were doing—but by the consummated sacrifice of his personality to this necessary course of action. The last, completest renunciation of his personal egoism, the demonstration of his full ascension into universalism, a man can only show us by his *Death*; and that not by his accidental, but by his *necessary* death, the logical sequel to his actions, the last fulfillment of his being.

The celebration of such a Death is the noblest thing that men can enter on. It reveals to us the nature of this one man, laid bare by death, the whole content of universal human nature. But we fix this revelation in surest hold of memory by the conscious *representation* of that Death itself and, in order to make its purport clear to us, by the representation of those actions which found their necessary conclusion in that death.[3] Not in the repulsive funeral rites which, in our neo-christian mode of life, we solemnise by meaningless hymns and churchyard platitudes; but by the artistic reanimation of the lost one, by life-glad reproduction and portrayal of his actions and his death, in the dramatic Art-work, shall we celebrate that festival which lifts us living to the highest bliss of love for the departed, and turns his nature to our own. . . .

When once the artist has raised his project to a *common* one, by the energy of his own enthusiasm, the artistic undertaking becomes thenceforth *itself an enterprise in common*. But as the dramatic action to be represented has its focus in the Hero of that action, so does the common art-work group itself around the *Representant* of this hero. His fellow-actors, and all his other colleagues, bear to him the same relation in the *art*-work as that which the co-enacting persons—those, that is to say, who formed the foils of the hero's character and the "objects" of his action—and, withal, the general human and natural entourage—bore in *Life* to the Hero; only with this difference, that the hero's impersonator shapes and arranges *consciously* that which came *instinctively* to the actual hero. In his stress for artistic reproduction of the Action, the performer thus becomes a poet; he arranges his own action, and all its living outward issues, in accordance with an artistic standard. But he only attains his special purpose in measure as he raised it to a general aim, as every unit is clamorous to lend himself to the furtherance of this general aim, therefore in exact measure as he himself, above all others, is able to surrender his own specific personal purpose to the general aim; and thus, in a sense, not merely *represents* in the art-work the action

---

[3] We must not forget that, only a few months before writing this essay, Wagner had prepared a sketch for a tragedy on the subject of *Jesus of Nazareth* [translator's note].

of the fêted hero, but *repeats* its moral lesson; insomuch as he proves by this surrender of his personality that he also, in his artistic action, is obeying a dictate of Necessity which consumes the whole individuality of his being.[4]

The *free Artistic Fellowship* is therefore the foundation, and the first condition, of the Art-work itself. From it proceeds the *Performer*, who, in his enthusiasm for this one particular hero whose nature harmonizes with his own, now raises himself to the rank of *Poet*, of artistic *Lawgiver* to the fellowship; from this height, again, to descend to complete absorption in the fellowship. The function of this lawgiver is therefore never more than *periodic*, and is confined to the one particular occasion which has been prompted by his individuality and thereby raised to a common "objective" for the art of all; wherefore his rule can by no means be extended to *all* occasions. The dictatorship of the poet-actor comes to its natural close together with the attainment of his specific purpose: that purpose which he had raised into a common one, and in which his personality was dissolved so soon as ever his message had been shared with the community. Each separate member may lift himself to the exercise of this dictatorship, when he bears a definite message which so far answers to his individuality that in its proclamation he has power to raise it to a common purpose. For in that artistic fellowship which combines for no other aim than the satisfaction of a joint artistic impulse, it is impossible that any other thing should come to definite prescription and resolve, than that which compasses the mutual satisfaction of this impulse: namely, Art herself, and the laws which summon forth her perfect manifestment by the union of the individual with the universal.

---

[4] Whilst we here have only touched upon the *Tragic* element of the Art-work of the Future, in its evolution out of Life, and by artistic fellowship, we may infer its *Comic* element by reversing the conditions which bring the Tragic to a natural birth. The hero of the Comedy will be the obverse of the hero of the Tragedy. Just as the one instinctively directed all his actions to his surroundings and his foils—as a Communist, i.e., as a unit who of his inner, free Necessity, and by his force of character, ascends into the Generality— so the other in his role of Egoist, of foe to the principle of Generality, will strive to withdraw himself therefrom, or else to arbitrarily direct it to his sole self-interest; but he will be withstood by this principle of generality in its most multifarious forms, hard pressed by it, and finally subdued. The Egoist will be *compelled* to ascend into Community; and *this* will therefore be the virtual enacting, many-headed personality which will ever appear to the action-wishing, but never-canning, egoist as a capriciously changing Chance; until it fences him around within its closest circle and, without further breathing space for his self-seeking, he sees at last his only rescue in the unconditional acknowledgment of its necessity. The artistic Fellowship, as the representative of Generality, will therefore have in Comedy an ever directer share in the framing of the poem itself, than in Tragedy [Wagner's note].

Karl Marx *1818–1883*

Introduction to the Critique of Political Economy *1859*

It is well known that certain periods of [the] highest development of art stand in no direct connection with the general development of society, nor with the material basis and the skeleton structure of its organization. Witness the example of the Greeks as compared with the modern nations or even Shakespeare. As regards certain forms of art, as e.g., the epos, it is admitted that they can never be produced in the world-epoch-making form as soon as art as such comes into existence; in other words, that in the domain of art certain important forms of it are possible only at a low stage of its development. If that be true of the mutual relations of different forms of art within the domain of art itself, it is far less surprising that the same is true of the relation of art as a whole to the general development of society. The difficulty lies only in the general formulation of these contradictions. No sooner are they specified than they are explained. Let us take for instance the relation of Greek art and of that of Shakespeare's time to our own. It is a well known fact that Greek mythology was not only the arsenal of Greek art, but also the very ground from which it had sprung. Is the view of nature and of social relations which shaped Greek imagination and Greek [art] possible in the age of automatic machinery, and railways, and locomotives, and electric telegraphs? Where does Vulcan come in as against Roberts & Co.; Jupiter, as against the lightning rod; and Hermes, as against the Credit Mobilier? All mythology masters and dominates and shapes the forces of nature in and through the imagination; hence it disappears as soon as man gains mastery over the forces of nature. What becomes of the Goddess Fame side by side with Printing House Square?[1] Greek art presupposes the existence of Greek mythology, i.e., that nature and even the form of society are wrought up in popular fancy in an unconsciously artistic fashion. That is its material. Not, however, any mythology taken at random, nor any accidental, unconsciously artistic elaboration of nature (including under the latter all objects, hence [also] society). Egyptian mythology could never be the soil or womb which would

Selection. From Karl Marx, *A Contribution to the Critique of Political Economy*, translated by N. I. Stone. Chicago: Charles H. Kerr & Co., 1904.

[1] The site of the *Times* building in London [translator's note].

give birth to Greek art. But in any event [there had to be] *a* mythology. In no event [could Greek art originate] in a society which excludes any mythological explanation of nature, any mythological attitude towards it and which requires from the artist an imagination free from mythology.

Looking at it from another side: is Achilles possible side by side with powder and lead? Or is the *Iliad* at all compatible with the printing press and steam press? Do not singing and reciting and the Muses necessarily go out of existence with the appearance of the printer's bar, and do not, therefore, disappear the prerequisites of epic poetry?

But the difficulty is not in grasping the idea that Greek art and epos are bound up with certain forms of social development. It rather lies in understanding why they still constitute with us a source of aesthetic enjoyment and in certain respects prevail as the standard and model beyond attainment.

A man can not become a child again unless he becomes childish. But does he not enjoy the artless ways of the child and must he not strive to reproduce its truth on a higher plane? Is not the character of every epoch revived perfectly true to nature in child nature? Why should the social childhood of mankind, where it had obtained its most beautiful development, not exert an eternal charm as an age that will never return? There are ill-bred children and precocious children. Many of the ancient nations belong to the latter class. The Greeks were normal children. The charm their art has for us does not conflict with the primitive character of the social order from which it had sprung. It is rather the product of the latter, and is rather due to the fact that the unripe social conditions under which the art arose and under which alone it could appear can never return.

Letter to Ferdinand Lassalle[1] April 19, 1859

I am now coming to *Franz von Sickingen*.[2] In the first instance, I must praise the composition and action, and that is more than can be said of any other modern German drama. In the second instance, leaving aside the purely critical attitude to this work, it greatly excited me on first reading and it will therefore produce this effect in a still higher degree on readers who are governed more completely by their feelings. And this is a second and very important aspect.

Now the other side of the medal: *First*—this is a purely formal matter—now that you have written in verse, you might have polished up your iambs with a bit more artistry. But however much *professional poets* may be shocked by such carelessness I consider it on the whole as an advantage, since our brood of epigonous poets have nothing left but formal gloss. *Second*: The intended collision is not simply tragic but is really the tragic collision that spelled the doom, and properly so, of the revolutionary party of 1848–1849. I can therefore only most heartily welcome the idea of making it the pivotal point of a modern tragedy. But then I ask myself whether the theme you took is suitable for a presentation of this collision. Balthasar[3] may really imagine that if Sickingen had set up the banner of opposition to imperial power and open war against the princes instead of concealing his revolt behind a knightly feud, he would have been victorious. But can we subscribe to this illusion? Sickingen (and with him Hutten,[4] more or less) did not go under because of his cunning. He went under because as a *knight* and a *representative* of a *moribund class* he revolted against that which existed or rather against the new form of what existed. Strip Sickingen of his idiosyncracies and his particular training, natural bents, etc., and what is left is—Götz von Berlichingen.[5] Embodied in adequate form in that last-named *pitiable* fellow is the tragic contrast between knighthood on the

Selection. From Karl Marx and Frederick Engels, *Selected Correspondence*, translated by I. Lasker, edited by S. Ryazanskaya. Moscow: Progress Publishers, 1965.

[1] Ferdinand Lassalle (1825–1864), German socialist leader who was later criticized by Marx and Engels.

[2] A play by Lassalle. Von Sickingen (1481–1523) was a German knight who joined the Reformation movement and led a revolt of knights in 1522–1523.

[3] A character in Lassalle's play, Sler Balthasar was a friend and adviser of von Sickingen; he participated in the Peasant Rebellion in Germany in 1525.

[4] Ulrich von Hutten (1488–1523), a supporter of the Reformation, was with von Sickingen a leader of the knights during their 1522–1523 revolt.

[5] A German knight, Götz von Berlichingen (1480–1562) joined the 1525 Peasant Rebellion but betrayed the peasants. He is the title character of a play by Goethe (1773).

one side and Kaiser and princes on the other; and that is why Goethe rightly made a hero of him. Insofar as Sickingen—and even Hutten himself to a certain extent, although with him, as with all ideologists of a class, such utterances should have been considerably modified—fights against the princes (after all, he takes the field against the Kaiser only because he transformed himself from a kaiser of the knights into a kaiser of the princes), he is in actual fact only a Don Quixote, although one historically justified. Beginning the revolt under color of a knightly feud means nothing else but beginning it in *knightly* fashion. Had he begun it otherwise he would have had to appeal directly and from the very beginning to the cities and peasants, i.e., precisely to the classes whose development was tantamount to the negation of the knighthood.

Therefore, if you did not want to reduce the collision to that presented in *Götz von Berlichingen*—and that was not your plan—then Sickengen and Hutten had to succumb because they imagined they were revolutionaries (the latter cannot be said of Götz) and, just like the *educated* Polish nobility of 1830, on the one hand, made themselves exponents of modern ideas, while on the other they actually represented the interests of a reactionary class.[6] The *noble* representatives of the revolution—behind whose watchwords of unity and liberty there still lurked the dreams of the old empire and of club-law—ought not, in that case, to have absorbed all interest, as they do in your play, but the representatives of the peasants (particularly these) and of the revolutionary elements in the cities should have formed a quite important active background. You could than have had the most modern ideas voiced in their most naïve form and to a much greater extent, whereas now, besides *religious* freedom, civil *unity* actually remains the main idea. You would then have had to *Shakespearize* more of your own accord, while I chalk up against you as your gravest shortcoming your *Schillering*, your transforming of individuals into mere speaking tubes of the spirt of the time. Did you not yourself to a certain extent fall into the diplomatic error, like your Franz von Sickingen, of placing the Lutheran-knightly opposition above the plebian Muncerian opposition? . . .

[6] This refers to the Polish uprising against tsarist rule which began in November 1830. The leadership of the rising was mainly in the hands of the polish nobility. Since the noblemen refused to comply with the demands of the peasants to abolish serfdom, they were unable to gain the support of the peasant masses. This led to the defeat of the rising, which was cruelly put down by the tsarist government [S. Ryazanskaya's note].

Friedrich Engels 1820–1895

Letter to
Ferdinand Lassalle May 18, 1859

. . . Now as far as the historical content[1] is concerned, you have depicted with great clarity and justified reference to subsequent developments the two sides of the movement of that time which were of greatest interest to you: the national movement of the nobility, represented by Sickingen, and the humanistic-theoretical movement with its further development in the theological and ecclesiastical sphere, the Reformation. What I like most here is the scene between Sickingen and the Kaiser and that between the legate and the archbishop of Treves. (Here you succeeded in producing a fine specimen of character drawing—a contrast between the esthetically and classically educated and politically and theoretically foreseeing legate, a man of the world, and the narrowminded German priest-prince—a portrayal which all the same follows directly from the *representative* nature of the two characters.) The pen picture in the Sickingen-Karl scene is also very striking. In Hutten's autobiography, whose *content* you rightly described as essential, you certainly picked a desperate means of working these facts into the drama. Of great importance is also the talk between Balthasar and Franz in Act V, in which the former expounds to his master the *really revolutionary* policy he should have followed. It is here that the really tragic manifests itself; and it seems to me that just because of the significance that attaches to this fact it should have been emphasized somewhat more strongly already in Act III, where there are several convenient places. But I am again lapsing into minor matters.

The position of the cities and the princes of that time is also set forth on several occasions with great clarity and thus the *official* elements, so to speak, of the contemporary movement are fairly well accounted for. But it seems to me that you have not laid due stress upon the nonofficial, the plebeian and peasant, elements and their concomitant representatives in the field of theory. The peasant movement was in its way just as national and just as much opposed to the princes as was that of the nobility, and the colossal dimensions of the struggle in which it succumbed contrast very strongly with the frivolous way in which the nobility, leaving Sickingen

From Karl Marx and Frederick Engels, *Selected Correspondence*, translated by I. Lasker, edited by S. Ryazanskaya. Moscow: Progress Publishers, 1965.

[1] Engels refers to Lassalle's play *Franz von Sickingen*. See Karl Marx's letter to Lassalle (April 19, 1859), notes 1–5.

in the lurch, resigned itself to its historical calling, that of lickspittles. It seems to me, therefore, that also in your conception of the drama which, as you will have seen, is somewhat too abstract, not realistic enough for me, the peasant movement deserved closer attention. While the peasant scene with Fritz Joss[2] is, true enough, characteristic and the individuality of this "agitator" presented very correctly, it does not depict with sufficient force the movement of the peasantry, as opposed to that of the nobility, which already at that time was a swelling torrent. In accordance with *my* view of the drama, which consists in not forgetting the realistic for the idealistic, Shakespeare for Schiller, the inclusion of the sphere of the so superbly variegated plebeian society of that day would have supplied, in addition, quite other material for enlivening the drama, a priceless background for the national movement of the nobility playing in the foreground, and would have set this movement in the proper light. What wonderfully expressive types were produced by this period of the dissolution of feudal bonds as illustrated by the roaming beggar kings, breadless *lansquenets* and adventurers of every description—a Falstaffian background which in an historical drama of *this* kind would have even greater effect than it did in Shakespeare! But apart from this, it seems to me that this relegation of the peasant movement to the rear is precisely the point that erroneously induced you, I believe, to misrepresent also the national movement of the nobility in one respect and at the same time to allow the *really* tragic element in Sickingen's fate to escape you. As I see it, the mass of the nobility directly subject at that time to the emperor had no intention of concluding an alliance with the peasantry. The dependence of their income on the oppressing of the latter did not permit this. An alliance with the cities would have been more feasible. But no such alliance was effected, or was effected only to a very limited extent. But a national revolution of the nobility could have been accomplished only by means of an alliance with the townsmen and the peasants, particularly the latter. Precisely herein lies, in my opinion, the whole tragedy of the thing, that this fundamental condition, the alliance with the peasantry, was impossible, that the policy of the nobility had therefore to be a petty one, that at the very moment when it wanted to take the lead of the national movement, the *mass* of the nation, the peasants, protested against its leadership and it thus necessarily had to collapse. I am unable to judge to what extent your assumption that Sickingen really did have some connection with the peasants has any basis in history. Anyhow, that is wholly immaterial. Moreover, as far as I remember, wherever Hutten in his writings addresses the peasants, he just lightly touches on this ticklish question concerning the nobility and seeks to focus the wrath of the peasants

---

[2] Fritz Joss (?–c. 1517) organized secret peasant societies in Germany in the early sixteenth century.

on the priests. But I do not in the least dispute your right to depict Sickingen and Hutten as having intended to emancipate the peasants. However, this put you at once up against the tragic contradiction that both of them were placed between the nobles, who were decidedly *against* this, and the peasants. Here, I dare say, lay the tragic collison between the historically necessary postulate and the practically impossible execution. By ignoring this aspect you reduce the tragic conflict to smaller dimensions, namely, that Sickingen, instead of at once tackling emperor and empire, tackled only a prince (although here too you tactfully bring in the peasants) and you simply let him perish from the indifference and cowardice of the nobility. Their cowardice would, however, have been motivated quite differently if you had previously brought out more emphatically the rumbling movement of the peasantry and the mood of the nobility, become decidedly more conservative on account of the former "Union Shoes" and "Poor Konrad."[3] However, all this is only *one* way in which the peasant and plebeian movement could have been included in the drama. At least ten other ways of doing this just as well or better are conceivable. . . .

[3] *Bundschuh* (kind of shoe worn by peasants in the Middle Ages), *Armer Konrad* (*Poor Konrad*)—names of secret peasants' confederations, whose activities prepared the ground in Germany for the Peasant War of 1525 [S. Ryazanskaya's note].

Letter to
Minna Kautsky[1]   *November 26, 1885*

. . . it will never do for an author to put his own hero on too high a pedestal and this is the error which to some extent you seem to me to have fallen into here.[2] In Elsa there is still a certain individualization, though verging on idealization, but in Arnold the personality merges still more in the principle.

Selection. From Karl Marx and Frederick Engels, *Selected Correspondence*, translated by I. Lasker, edited by S. Ryazanskaya. Moscow: Progress Publishers, 1965.

[1] Minna Kautsky (1836–1912), German author of novels on social themes, mother of Karl Kautsky (1854–1917), a prominent Marxist.
[2] Engels is discussing Minna Kautsky's novel *Old Ones and the New*.

The novel itself reveals the origins of this shortcoming. You obviously felt a desire to take a public stand in your book, to testify to your convictions before the entire world. This has now been done; that you are through with and need not repeat in this form. I am by no means opposed to tendentious poetry as such. Both Aeschylus, the father of tragedy, and Aristophanes, the father of comedy, were highly tendentious poets, Dante and Cervantes were so no less, and the best thing that can be said about Schiller's *Intrigue and Love*[3] is that it represents the first German political problem drama. The modern Russians and Norwegians, who produce excellent novels, all write with a purpose. I think however that the solution of the problem must become manifest from the situation and the action themselves without being expressly pointed out and that the author is not obliged to serve the reader on a platter the future historical resolution of the social conflicts which he describes. To this must be added that under our conditions novels are mostly addressed to readers from bourgeois circles, i.e., circles which are not directly ours. Thus the socialist problem novel in my opinion fully carries out its mission if by a faithful portrayal of the real relations it dispels the dominant conventional illusions concerning these relations, shakes the optimism of the bourgeois world, and inevitably instils doubt as to the eternal validity of that which exists, without itself offering a direct solution of the problem involved, even without at times ostensibly taking sides.

[3] (1784).

Letter to Margaret Harkness[1] *Beginning of April, 1888*

If I have anything to criticize,[2] it would be that perhaps after all, the tale is not quite realistic enough. Realism, to my mind, implies, besides truth of detail, the truth in reproduction of typical characters under typical circum-

Selection. From Karl Marx and Frederick Engels, *Selected Correspondence*, translated by I. Lasker, edited by S. Ryazanskaya. Moscow: Progress Publishers, 1965.

[1] English novelist, using the pseudonym John Law.
[2] Engels refers to her novel *City Girl*.

stances. Now your characters are typical enough, as far as they go; but the circumstances which surround them and make them act, are not perhaps equally so. In the *City Girl* the working-class figures are a passive mass, unable to help itself and not even showing (making) any attempt at striving to help itself. All attempts to drag it out of its torpid misery come from without, from above. Now if this was a correct description about 1800 or 1810, in the days of Saint-Simon and Robert Owen,[3] it cannot appear so in 1887 to a man who for nearly fifty years has had the honor of sharing in most of the fights of the militant proletariat. The rebellious reaction of the working class against the oppressive medium which surrounds them, their attempts—convulsive, half conscious, or conscious—at recovering their status as human beings, belong to history and must therefore lay claim to a place in the domain of realism.

I am far from finding fault with your not having written a point-blank socialist novel, a *"Tendenzroman,"*[4] as we Germans call it, to glorify the social and political views of the authors. That is not at all what I mean. The more the opinions of the author remain hidden, the better for the work of art. The realism I allude to may crop out even in spite of the author's opinions. Let me refer to an example. Balzac whom I consider a far greater master of realism than all the Zolas *passés, présents et à venir,*[5] in *La Comédie humaine*[6] gives us a most wonderfully realistic history of French "Society," describing, chronicle-fashion, almost year by year from 1816 to 1848 the progressive inroads of the rising bourgeoisie upon the society of nobles, that reconstituted itself after 1815 and that set up again, as far as it could, the standard of *la vieille politesse française.*[7] He describes how the last remnants of this, to him, model society gradually succumbed before the intrusion of the vulgar moneyed upstart, or were corrupted by him; how the grande dame whose conjugal infidelities were but a mode of asserting herself in perfect accordance with the way she had been disposed of in marriage, gave way to the bourgeoisie, who corned her husband for cash or cashmere; and around this central picture he groups a complete history of French Society from which, even in economic details (for instance the rearrangement of real and personal property after the Revolution), I have learned more than from all the professed historians, economists, and statisticians of the period together. Well, Balzac was politically a Legitimist; his great work is a constant elegy on the irretrievable decay of good society; his sympathies are all with the class doomed to extinction. But for all that his satire is never keener, his

[3] Claude Henri Saint-Simon (1760–1825), French Utopian Socialist, and Robert Owen (1771–1858), English Utopian Socialist.
[4] Problem novel.
[5] Past, present, and future.
[6] *The Human Comedy.*
[7] The old French refinement.

irony never bitterer, than when he sets in motion the very men and women with whom he sympathizes most deeply—the nobles. And the only men of whom he always speaks with undisguised admiration are his bitterest political antagonists, the republican heroes of the Cloître Saint Merry,[8] the men, who at that time (1830–1836) were indeed the representatives of the popular masses. That Balzac thus was compelled to go against his own class sympathies and political prejudices, that he *saw* the necessity of the downfall of his favorite nobles, and described them as people deserving no better fate; and that he *saw* the real men of the future where, for the time being, they alone were to be found—that I consider one of the greatest triumphs of Realism, and one of the grandest features in old Balzac.

I must own, in your defence, that nowhere in the civilized world are the working people less actively resistant, more passively submitting to fate, more *hébétés*[9] than in the East End of London. And how do I know whether you have not had very good reasons for contenting yourself, for once, with a picture of the passive side of working-class life, reserving the active side for another work? . . .

Gustav Freytag   *1816–1895*

Technique of the Drama   *1863*

Chapter I
The Dramatic Action

What Is Dramatic?

The dramatic includes those emotions of the soul which steel themselves to will, and to do, and those emotions of the soul which are aroused by a deed or course of action; also the inner processes which man experiences

Selections. From *Freytag's Technique of the Drama*, by Gustav Freytag, translated by Elias J. MacEwan. Chicago: S. C. Griggs, 1896.

[8] Engels refers to the rising started by the Society of the Rights of Man and the Citizen, the Left wing of the Republican Party, which took place in Paris, June 5 and 6, 1832 [S. Ryazanskaya's note].
[9] Dazed, stupefied.

from the first glow of perception to passionate desire and action, as well as the influences which one's own and others' deeds exert upon the soul; also the rushing forth of will power from the depths of man's soul toward the external world, and the influx of fashioning influences from the outer world into man's inmost being; also the coming into being of a deed, and its consequences on the human soul.

An action, in itself, is not dramatic. Passionate feeling, in itself, is not dramatic. Not the presentation of a passion for itself, but of a passion which leads to action is the business of dramatic art; not the presentation of an event for itself, but for its effect on a human soul is the dramatist's mission. The exposition of passionate emotions as such, is in the province of the lyric poet; the depicting of thrilling events is the task of the epic poet.

The two ways in which the dramatic expresses itself are, of course, not fundamentally different. Even while a man is under stress, and laboring to turn his inmost soul toward the external, his surroundings exert a stimulating or repressing influence on his passionate emotions. And, again, while what has been done exerts a reflex upon him, he does not remain merely receptive, but gains new impulses and transformations. Yet, there is a difference in these closely connected processes. The first, the inward struggle of man toward a deed, has always the highest charm. The second stimulates to more external emotion, a more violent cooperation of different forces; almost all that satisfies curiosity belongs to this; and yet, however indispensable it is to the drama, it is principally a satisfying of excited suspense; and the impatience of the hearer, if he has creative power, easily runs in advance, seeking a new vehement agitation in the soul of the hero. . . .

Unity of Action

By *action* is meant, an event or occurrence, arranged according to a controlling idea, and having its meaning made apparent by the characters. It is composed of many elements, and consists in a number of dramatic efficients (*momente*), which become effective one after the other, according to a regular arrangement. The action of the serious drama must possess the following qualities:

It must present complete unity.

This celebrated law has undergone a very different application with the Greeks and Romans, with the Spanish and French, with Shakespeare and the Germans, which has been occasioned partly by those learned in art, partly by the character of the stage. The restriction of its claims through the French classics, and the strife of the Germans with the three unities, of place, of time, and of action, have for us only a literary-historical interest. . . .

From this indispensable introduction, the beginning of the impassioned action must arise, like the first notes of a melody from the introductory chords. This first stir of excitement, this stimulating impulse, is of great importance for the effect of the drama, and will be discussed later. The end of the action must, also, appear as the intelligible and inevitable result of the entire course of the action, the conjunction of forces; and right here, the inherent necessity must be keenly felt; the close must, however, represent the complete termination of the strife and excited conflicts.

Within these limits, the action must move forward with uniform consistency. This internal consistency is produced by representing an event which follows another, as an effect of which that other is the evident cause; let that which occasions be the logical cause of occurrences, and the new scenes and events be conceived as probable, and generally understood results of previous actions; or let that which is to produce an effect be a generally comprehensible peculiarity of a character already made known. . . .

The poet's interest in the characters of his counter-players easily mounts so high that to them is accorded a rich, detailed portrayal, a sympathetic exposition of their striving and their fighting moods, and a peculiar destiny. Thereby arises a double action for the drama; or the action of the piece may be of such a nature as to require for its illumination and completion a subordinate action, which through the exposition of concurrent or opposing relations brings into greater prominence the chief persons, with what they do and what they suffer.

Various defects—especially one-sidedness—in material, may make such a completion desirable. One play is not to run through the whole wide range of affecting and thrilling moods; it is not to play from its sober ground color, through all the possible color-tones; but a variation in mood and modest contrasts in color are as necessary to the drama as it is that in a painting in which there are many figures, the swing of the lesser lines should be in contrast with the ground color, use should be made of dependent, supplementary colors. . . .

If . . . the Greeks classed their plays into those with single action, and those with double action, the modern drama has much less avoided the extension of counter-play into an accessory action. The interweaving of this with the main action has occurred sometimes at the expense of the combined effect. The Germans, especially, who are always inclined, during their labor, to grasp the significance of the accessory persons with great ardor, must guard themselves against too wide an extension of the subordinate action. Even Shakespeare has occasionally, in this way, injured the effect of the drama, most strikingly in *Lear*, in which the whole parallel action of the house of Gloucester, but loosely connected with the main action, and treated with no particular fondness, retards the movement, and needlessly renders the whole more bitter. The poet allowed the episodes in both parts of *Henry IV* to develop into an accessory action, the immortal humor of which outshines the serious effect of the play; and this has made these dramas favorites of the reader. Every admirer of Falstaff will grant, however, that the general effect on the stage has not the corresponding power, in spite of this charm. Let it be noticed, in passing, that in Shakespeare's comedies the double action belongs to the nature of the play; he strives to take from his clowns the episodical, while he interweaves them with the serious action. . . .

It is the business of the action to represent to us the inner consistency of the event, as it corresponds to the demands of the intellect and the heart. Whatever, in the crude material, does not serve this purpose the poet is in duty bound to throw away. And it is desirable that he adhere strictly to this principle, to give only what is indispensable to unity. Yet he may not avoid a deviation from this; for there will be occasional deviations desirable which may strengthen the color of the piece, in a manner conformable to its purpose; which may intensify the meaning of the characters, and enhance the general effect by the introduction of a new color, or a contrast. These embellishing additions of the poet are called episodes. They are of various kinds. At a point where the action suffers a short pause, a characterizing moment may be enlarged into a situation; opportunity may be given a hero to exhibit some significant characteristic of his being in an attractive manner, in connection with some subordinate person; some subordinate role of the piece may, through ampler elaboration, be developed into an attractive figure. By a modest use, which must not take time from what is more important, these may become an embellishment to the drama. . . .

Movement and Rise of the Action

The dramatic action must represent all that is important to the understanding of the play, in the strong excitement of the characters, and in a continuously progressive increase of effects.

The action must, first of all, be capable of the strongest dramatic excitement; and this must be universally intelligible. There are great and important fields of human activity which do not make the growth of a captivating emotion, a passionate desire, or a mighty volition easy; and again, there are violent struggles which force to the outside men's mental processes, while the subject of the struggle is little adapted to the stage, though importance and greatness are not lacking to it. For example, a politic prince, who negotiates with the powerful ones of his land, who wages war and concludes peace with his neighbors, will perhaps do all this without once exhibiting the least excited passion; and if this does come to light as secret desire or resentment toward others, it will be noticeable only by careful observation, and in little ripples. But even when it is allowed to represent his whole being in dramatic suspense, the subject of his volition, a political success or a victory, is capable of being shown only very imperfectly and fragmentarily in its stage setting. And the scenes in which this round of worldly purposes is specially active, state trials, addresses, battles, are for technical reasons not the part most conveniently put on the stage. From this point of view, warning must be given against putting scenes from political history on the boards. Of course the difficulties which this field of the greatest human activity offers are not unsurmountable; but it requires not only maturity of genius but very peculiar and intimate knowledge of the stage to overcome them. . . .

An entirely unfavorable field for dramatic material is the inward struggles which the inventor, the artist, the thinker has to suffer with himself and with his time. Even if he is a reformer by nature, who knows how to impress the stamp of his own spirit on thousands of others; indeed, if his own material misfortunes may lay claim to unusual sympathy, the dramatist will not willingly conclude to bring him forward as the hero of the action. If the mental efforts, the mode of thought of such a hero, are not sufficiently known to the living audience, then the poet will have first to show his warrant for such a character by artful discourse, by a fulness of oral explanation, and by a representation of spiritual import. This may be quite as difficult as it is undramatic. If the poet presupposes in his auditors a living interest in such personages, acquaintance with the incidents of their lives, and makes use of this interest in order to avail himself of an occurrence in the life of such a hero, he falls into another danger. On the stage the good which is known beforehand of a man, and the good that is reported of him, have no value at all, as opposed to what the hero himself does on the stage. Indeed, the great expectations which the hearer brings with him in this case may be prejudicial to the unbiased reception of the action. . . . If the poet is conscientious, he will adopt only those moments from the life of the artist, poet, thinker, in which he shows himself active and suffering quite as significantly toward others as he was in his studio. It is clear that this will be the case only by accident; it is quite as clear that in such a case it will be only an accident, if the hero bears a celebrated name. Therefore, the making use of anecdotes from the life of such great men, the meaning of which does not show itself in the action but in the nonrepresentable activity of their laboratory, is intrinsically right undramatic. The greatness in them is nonrepresentable. . . .

Chapter II
The Construction of the Drama

Play and Counterplay

In an action, through characters, by means of words, tones, gestures, the drama presents those soul-processes which man experiences, from the flashing up of an idea, to passionate desire and to a deed, as well as those inward emotions which are excited by his own deeds and those of others.

The structure of the drama must show these two contrasted elements of the dramatic joined in a unity, efflux and influx of will-power, the accomplishment of a deed and its reaction on the soul, movement and countermovement, strife and counterstrife, rising and sinking, binding and loosing.

In every part of the drama, both tendencies of dramatic life appear, each incessantly challenging the other to its best in play and counterplay; but in general, also, the action of the drama and the grouping of characters is, through these tendencies, in two parts. What the drama presents is always a struggle, which, with strong perturbations of soul, the hero wages against opposing forces. And as the hero must be endowed with a strong life, with a certain one-sidedness, and be in embarrassment, the opposing power must be made visible in a human representative.

It is quite indifferent in favor of which of the contending parties the greater degree of justice lies, whether a character or his adversary is better-mannered, more favored by law, embodies more of the traditions of the time, possesses more of the ethical spirit of the poet; in both groups, good and evil, power and weakness, are variously mingled. But both must be endowed with what is universally, intelligibly human. The chief hero must always stand in strong contrast with his opponents; the advantage which he wins for himself, must be the greater, so much the greater the more perfectly the final outcome of the struggle shows him to be vanquished.

These two chief parts of the drama are firmly united by a point of the action which lies directly in the middle. This middle, the climax of the play, is the most important place of the structure; the action rises to this; the action falls away from this. It is now decisive for the character of the drama which of the two refractions of the dramatic light shall have a place in the first part of the play, which shall fall in the second part as the dominating influence; whether the efflux or influx, the play or the counterplay, maintains the first part. Either is allowed; either arrangement of the structure can cite plays of the highest merit in justification of itself. And these two ways of constructing a drama have become characteristic of individual poets and of the time in which they lived.

By one dramatic arrangement, the chief person, the hero, is so introduced that his nature and his characteristics speak out unembarrassed, even to the moments when, as a consequence of external impulse or internal association of ideas, in him the beginning of a powerful feeling or volition becomes perceptible. The inner commotion, the passionate eagerness, the desire of the hero, increase; new circumstances, stimulating or restraining, intensify his embarrassment and his struggle; the chief character strides victoriously forward to an unrestrained exhibition of his life, in which the full force of his feeling and his will are concentrated in a deed by which the spiritual tension is relaxed. From this point there is a turn in the action; the hero appeared up to this point in a desire, one-sided or full of consequence, working from within outward, changing by its own force the life relations in which he came upon the stage. From the climax on, what he has done reacts upon himself and gains power over him; the external world, which he conquered in the rise of passionate conflict, now stands in the strife above him. This adverse influence becomes continually more powerful and victorious, until at last in the final catastrophe, it compels the hero to succumb to its irresistible force. The end of the piece follows this catastrophe immediately, the situation where the restoration of peace and quiet after strife becomes apparent.

With this arrangement, first the inception and progress of the action are seen, then the effects of the reaction; the character of the first part is determined by the depth of the hero's exacting claims; the second by the counterclaims which the violently disturbed surroundings put forward. This is the construction of *Antigone*, of *Ajax*, of all of Shakespeare's great tragedies except *Othello* and *King Lear*, of *The Maid of Orleans*, less surely of the double tragedy, *Wallenstein*.[1]

The other dramatic arrangement, on the contrary, represents the hero at the beginning in comparative quiet, among conditions of life which suggest the influence of some external forces upon his mind. These forces, adverse influences, work with increased activity so long in the hero's soul, that at the climax, they have brought him into ominous embarrassment, from which, under a stress of passion, desire, activity, he plunges downward to the catastrophe.

This construction makes use of opposing characters, in order to give motive to the strong excitement of the chief character; the relation of the chief figures to the idea of the drama is an entirely different one; they do not give direction in the ascending action, but are themselves directed. Examples of this construction are *King Oedipus*, *Othello*, *Lear*, *Emilia Galotti*, *Clavigo*, *Love and Intrigue*.[2] . . .

It is true, the first kind of dramatic structure conceals a danger, which even by genius, is not always successfully avoided. In this, as a rule, the first part of the play, which raises the hero through regular degrees of commotion to the climax, is assured its success. But the second half, in which greater effects are demanded, depends mostly on the counterplay; and this counterplay must here be grounded in more violent movement and have comparatively greater authorization. This may distract attention rather than attract it more forcibly. It must be added, that after the climax of the action, the hero must seem weaker than the counteracting figures. Moreover, on this account, the interest in him may be lessened. Yet in spite of this difficulty, the poet need be in no doubt to which kind of arrangement to give the preference.

---

[1] The last two works are by Friedrich Schiller.
[2] The last three plays respectively, are by Lessing, Goethe, and Schiller.

His task will be greater in this arrangement; great art is required to make the last act strong. But talent and good fortune must overcome the difficulties. And the most beautiful garlands which dramatic art has to confer, fall upon the successful work. Of course the poet is dependent on his subject and material, which sometimes leaves no choice. Therefore, one of the first questions a poet must ask, when contemplating attractive material, is "does it come forward in the play or in the counterplay?" . . .

Five Parts and Three Crises of the Drama

Through the two halves of the action which come closely together at one point, the drama possesses—if one may symbolize its arrangement by lines— a pyramidal structure. It rises from the *introduction* with the entrance of the exciting forces to the *climax*, and falls from here to the *catastrophe*. Between these three parts lie (the parts of) the *rise* and the *fall*. Each of these five parts may consist of a single scene, or a succession of connected scenes, but the climax is usually composed of one chief scene.

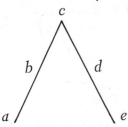

These parts of the drama, (*a*) introduction, (*b*) rise, (*c*) climax, (*d*) return or fall, (*e*) catastrophe, have each what is peculiar in purpose and in construction. Between them stand three important scenic effects, through which the parts are separated as well as bound together. Of these three dramatic moments, or crises, one, which indicates the beginning of the stirring action, stands between the introduction and the rise; the second, the beginning of the counteraction, between the climax and the return; the third, which must rise once more before the catastrophe, between the return and the catastrophe. They are called here the exciting moment or force, the tragic moment or force, and the moment or force of the last suspense. The operation of the first is necessary to every play; the second and third are good but not indispensable accessories. In the following sections, therefore, the eight component parts of the drama will be discussed in their natural order.

The Introduction   It was the custom of the ancients to communicate in a prologue what was presupposed for the action. The prologue of Sophocles and also of Aeschylus is a thoroughly necessary and essential part of the action, having dramatic life and connection, and corresponding exactly to our opening scene; and in the old stage-management signification of the word, it comprised that part of the action which lay before the entrance song of the chorus. In Euripides, it is, by a careless return to the older custom, an epic messenger announcement, which a masked figure delivers to the audience, a figure who never once appears in the play,—like Aphrodite in *Hyppolitus* and the ghost of the slain Polydorus in *Hecuba*. . . . In Shakespeare, as with us, the introduction has come back again into the right place; it is filled with dramatic movement, and has become an organic part of the dramatic structure. Yet, in individual cases, the newer stage has not been able to resist another temptation, to expand the introduction to a situation scene, and set it in advance as a special prelude to the drama. Well-known examples are *The Maid of Orleans* and *Kätchen of Heilbronn*, *Wallenstein's Camp*, and the most beautiful of all prologues, that to *Faust*.[3]

That such a severing of the opening scene is hazardous will be readily granted. . . .

Since it is the business of the introduction of the drama to explain the place and time of the action, the nationality and life relations of the hero, it must at once briefly characterize the environment. Besides, the poet will have opportunity here, as in a short overture, to indicate the peculiar mood of the piece, as well as the time, the greater vehemence or quiet with which the action moves forward. . . . But the greatest master of fine beginnings is Shakespeare. In *Romeo and Juliet*, day, an open street, brawls and the clatter of the swords of the hostile parties; in *Hamlet*, night, the startling call of the watch the mounting of the guard, the appearance of the ghost, restless, gloomy, desperate excitement; in *Macbeth*, storm, thunder, the unearthly witches and dreary heath; and again in *Richard III*, no striking surroundings, a single man upon the stage, the old despotic evil genius, who controls the entire dramatic life of the piece, himself speaking the prologue. So in each of his artistic dramas. . . .

Without forcing all possible cases into the same uniform mold, therefore, the poet may hold firmly to this: the construction of a regular introduction is as follows: a clearly defining keynote, a finished scene, a short transition into the first moment of the excited action.

The Exciting Force   The beginning of the excited action (complication) occurs at a point where, in the soul of the hero, there arises a feeling or volition which becomes the occasion of what follows; or where the counterplay resolves to use its lever to set the hero in motion. Manifestly, this impelling force will come forward more significantly in those plays in which the chief actor governs the first half by his force of will; but in any arrangement, it remains an important motive force for the action. In *Julius Caesar*, this impelling force is the thought of killing Caesar, which, by the conversation with Cassius, gradually becomes fixed in the soul of Brutus. In *Othello*, it comes into play after the stormy night-scene of the exposition, by means of the second conference between Iago and Roderigo, with the agreement to separate the Moor and Desdemona. In *Richard III*, on the contrary, it rises

---

[3] These four plays, respectively, are by Schiller, Kleist, Schiller, and Goethe.

in the very beginning of the piece along with the exposition, and as a matured plan in the soul of the hero. In both cases, its position helps to fix the character of the piece; in *Othello*, where the counterplay leads at the conclusion of a long introduction; in *Richard III*, where the villain alone rules in the first scene. In *Romeo and Juliet*, this occasioning motive comes to the soul of the hero in the interview with Benvolio, as the determination to be present at the masked ball; and immediately before this scene, there runs as parallel scene the conversation between Paris and Capulet, which determines the fate of Juliet; both scenic moments, in such significant juxtaposition, form together the impelling force of this drama, which has two heroes, the two lovers. . . .

From the examples cited, it is evident that this force of the action treads the stage under very diverse forms. It may fill a complete scene; it may be comprised in a few words. It must not always press from without into the soul of the hero or his adversary; it may be, also, a thought, a wish, a resolution, which by a succession of representations may be allured from the soul of the hero himself. But it always forms the transition from the introduction to the ascending action, either entering suddenly, like Mortimer's declaration in *Mary Stuart*, and the rescue of Baumgarten in *William Tell*,[4] or gradually developing through the speeches and mental processes of the characters, like Brutus's resolve to do the murder, where in no place in the dialogue the fearful words are pronounced, but the significance of the scene is emphasized by the suspicion which Caesar, entering meantime, expresses.

Yet it is for the worker to notice, that this force seldom admits of great elaboration. Its place is at the beginning of the piece, where powerful pressure upon the hearer is neither necessary nor advisable. It has the character of a motive which gives direction and preparation, and does not offer a single resting-place. It must not be insignificant; but it must not be so strong that, according to the feeling of the audience, it takes too much from what follows, or that the suspense which it causes, may modify, or perhaps determine, the fate of the hero. Hamlet's suspicion cannot be raised to unconditional certainty by the revelation of the ghost, or the course of the piece must be entirely different. The resolution of Cassius and Brutus must not come out in distinct words, in order that Brutus's following consideration of the matter, and the administration of the oath, may seem a progress. The poet will, probably, sometimes have to moderate the importance attached to this force, which has made it too conspicuous. But he must always bring it into operation as soon as possible; for only from its introduction forward does earnest dramatic work begin.

A convenient arrangement for our stage is to give the exciting force in a temperate scene after the introduction, and closely join to this the first

---

[4] Both plays are by Schiller.

following rising movement, in greater elaboration. *Mary Stuart*, for example, is of this regular structure.

The Rising Movement   The action has been started; the chief persons have shown what they are; the interest has been awakened. Mood, passion, involution have received an impulse in a given direction. . . . The rising movement in *Romeo and Juliet* runs through four stages to the climax. The structure of this ascending group is as follows. First stage: masked ball; three parts, two preparatory scenes (Juliet with her mother, and nurse) (Romeo and his companions); and one chief scene (the ball itself, consisting of one suggestion—conversation of the servants—and four forces—Capulet stirring up matters; Tybalt's rage and setting things to rights; conversation of the lovers; Juliet and the nurse as conclusion). Second stage: The garden scene; short preparatory scene (Benvolio and Mercutio seeking Romeo) and the great chief scene (the lovers determining upon marriage). Third stage: The marriage; four parts; first scene (Laurence and Romeo); second scene (Romeo and companions, and nurse as messenger); third scene (Juliet, and nurse as messenger); fourth scene (Laurence and the lovers, and the marriage). Fourth stage: Tybalt's death; fighting scene.

Then follows the group of scenes forming the climax, beginning with Juliet's words, "Gallop apace you fiery footed steeds," and extending to Romeo's farewell, "It were a grief, so brief to part with thee; farewell." In the four stages of the rise, one must notice the different structure of individual scenes. In the masked ball, little scenes are connected in quick succession to the close; the garden scene is the elaborate great scene of the lovers; in beautiful contrast with this, in the marriage scene-group, the accomplice, Laurence, and the nurse are kept in the foreground, the lovers are concealed. Tybalt's death is the strong break which separates the aggregate rise from the climax; the scenes of this part have a loftier swing, a more passionate movement. The arrangement of the piece is very careful; the progress of both heroes and their motives are specially laid for each in every two adjoining scenes with parallel course. . . .

As to the scenes of this rising movement, it may be said, they have to produce a progressive intensity of interest; they must, therefore, not only evince progress in their import, but they must show an enlargement in form and treatment, and, indeed, with variation and shading in execution; if several steps are necessary, the next to the last, or the last, must preserve the character of a chief scene.

The Climax   The climax of the drama is the place in the piece where the results of the rising movement come out strong and decisively; it is almost always the crowning point of a great, amplified scene, enclosed by the smaller connecting scenes of the rising, and of the falling action. The poet needs to use all the splendor of poetry, all the dramatic skill of his art, in order to make vividly conspicuous this middle point of his artistic creation. It has the highest significance only in those pieces in which the hero, through his own mental processes, impels the ascending action; in those dramas which rise by means of the counterplay, it does not indicate an important place, where this play has attained the mastery of the chief hero, and misleads him in the direction of the fall. Splendid examples are to be found in almost every one of Shakespeare's plays and in the plays of the Germans. The hovel scene in *King Lear,* with the play of the three deranged persons, and the judgment scene with the stool, is perhaps one of the most effective that was ever put on the stage; and the rising action in *Lear,* up to the scene of this irrepressible madness, is of terrible magnificence. The scene is also remarkable because the great poet has here used humor to intensify the horrible effect, and because this is one of the very rare places where the audience, in spite of the awful commotion, perceives with a certain surprise that Shakespeare uses artifices to bring out the effect. Edgar is no fortunate addition to the scene. In another way, the banquet scene in *Macbeth* is instructive. In this tragedy, a previous scene, the night of the murder, had been so powerfully worked out, and so richly endowed with the highest dramatic poetry, that there might easily be despair as to the possibility of any further rise in the action. And yet it is effected; the murderer's struggle with the ghost, and the fearful struggles with his conscience, in the restless scene to which the social festivity and royal splendor give the most effective contrasts, are pictured with a truth, and in a wild kind of poetic frenzy, which make the hearer's heart throb and shudder. In *Othello,*[5] on the other hand, the climax lies in the great scene in which Iago arouses Othello's jealousy. It is slowly prepared, and is the beginning of the convulsing soul-conflict in which the hero perishes. In *Clavigo,*[6] the reconciliation of Clavigo with Marie, and in *Emilia Galotti,*[7] the prostration of Emilia, form the climax, concealed in both cases by the predominating counter-play. Again, in Schiller, it is powerfully developed in all plays.

This outburst of deed from the soul of the hero, or the influx of portentous impressions into the soul; the first great result of a sublime struggle, or the beginning of a mortal inward conflict, must appear inseparably connected with what goes before as well as with what follows; it will be brought into relief through broad treatment or strong effect; but it will, as a rule, be represented in its development from the rising movement and its effect on the environment; therefore, the climax naturally forms the middle point of a group of forces, which, darting in either direction, course upward and downward.

In the case where the climax is connected with the downward movement by a *tragic force,* the structure of the drama presents something peculiar,

[5] (1604) by Shakespeare.
[6] (1774) by Goethe.
[7] (1772) by Lessing.

through the juxtaposition of two important passages which stand in sharp contrast with each other. This tragic force must first receive attention. This beginning of the downward movement is best connected with the climax, and separated from the following forces of the counterplay to which it belongs by a division—our close of an act; and this is best brought about not immediately after the beginning of the tragic force, but by a gradual modulation of its sharp note. It is a matter of indifference whether this connection of the two great contrasted scenes is effected by uniting them into one scene, or by means of a connecting scene. A splendid example of the former is in *Coriolanus*.

In this piece, the action rises from the exciting force (the news that war with the Volscians is inevitable) through the first ascent (fight between Coriolanus and Aufidius) to the climax, the nomination of Coriolanus as consul. The tragic force, the banishment, begins here; what seems about to become the highest elevation of the hero becomes by his untamable pride just the opposite; he is overthrown. This overthrow does not occur suddenly; it is seen to perfect itself gradually on the stage—as Shakespeare loves to have it—and what is overwhelming in the result is first perceived at the close of the scene. The two points, bound together here by the rapid action, form together a powerful group of scenes of violent commotion, the whole of far-reaching and splendid effect. . . .

Somewhat more sharply are the climax and tragic force in *Julius Caesar* separated from each other by a complete connecting scene. The group of murder scenes is followed by the elaborate scene of the conspirators' conversation with Antony—this interpolated passage of beautiful workmanship—and after this the oration scenes of Brutus and Antony; and after this follow little transitions to the parts of the return.

This close connection of the two important parts gives to the drama with tragic force a magnitude and expanse of the middle part, which—if the playful comparison of the lines may be carried out—changes the pyramidal form into one with a double apex.

The most difficult part of the drama is the sequence of scenes in the *downward movement*, or, as it may well be called, the *return*; specially in powerful plays in which the heroes are the directing force, do these dangers enter most. Up to the climax, the interest has been firmly fixed in the direction in which the chief characters are moving. After the deed is consummated, a pause ensues. Suspense must now be excited in what is new. For this, new forces, perhaps new roles, must be introduced, in which the hearer is to acquire interest. On account of this, there is already danger in distraction and in the breaking up of scenic effects. And yet, it must be added, the hostility of the counterparty toward the hero cannot always be easily concentrated in one person nor in one situation; sometimes it is necessary to show how frequently, now and again, it beats upon the soul of the hero; and in this way, in contrast with the unity and firm advance of the first half of the play, the second may be ruptured, in many parts, restless; this is particularly the case with historical subjects, where it is most difficult to compose the counterparty of a few characters only.

And yet the return demands a strong bringing out and intensifying of the scenic effects, on account of the satisfaction already accorded the hearer, and on account of the greater significance of the struggle. Therefore, the first law for the construction of this part is that the number of persons be limited as much as possible, and that the effects be comprised in great scenes. All the art of technique, all the power of invention, are necessary to insure here an advance in interest.

One thing more. This part of the drama specially lays claims upon the character of the poet. Fate wins control over the hero; his battles move toward a momentous close, which affects his whole life. There is no longer time to secure effects by means of little artifices, careful elaboration, beautiful details, neat motives. . . . The second rule is valuable for this part; only great strokes, great effects. Even the episodes which are now ventured must have a certain significance, a certain energy. How numerous the stages must be through which the hero's fall passes cannot be fixed by rule, farther than that the return makes a less number desirable than, in general, the rising movement allows. For the gradual increase of these effects, it will be useful to insert, just before the catastrophe, a finished scene which either shows the contending forces in the strife with the hero, in the most violent activity, or affords a clear insight into the life of the hero. The great scene, Coriolanus and his mother, is an example of the one case; the monologue of Juliet, before taking the sleep potion, and the sleep-walking scene of Lady Macbeth, of the other case.

The Force of the Final Suspense   It is well understood that the catastrophe must not come entirely as a surprise to the audience. The more powerful the climax, the more violent the downfall of the hero, so much the more vividly must the end be felt in advance; the less the dramatic power of the poet in the middle of the piece, the more pains will he take toward the end, and the more will he seek to make use of striking effects. Shakespeare never does this, in his regularly constructed pieces. Easily, quickly, almost carelessly, he projects the catastrophe, without surprising, with new effects; it is for him such a necessary consequence of the whole previous portion of the piece, and the master is so certain to bear forward the audience with him, that he almost hastens over the necessities of the close. This talented man very correctly perceived that it is necessary, in good time, to prepare the mind of the audience for the catastrophe; for this reason, Caesar's ghost appears to Brutus; for this reason, Edmund tells the soldier he must in certain circumstances slay Lear and Cordelia; for this reason, Romeo must, still before Juliet's tomb, slay Paris, in order that the audience, which at this moment, no longer thinks of Tybalt's death, may not, after all, cherish the hope that the piece will close happily; for this reason, must the mortal envy of Aufidius toward Coriolanus be repeatedly expressed before the great scene of the return of the action; and Coriolanus must utter these great words, "Thou hast lost thy son"; for this reason the king must previously discuss with Laertes the murdering of Hamlet by means of a poisoned rapier. Notwithstanding all this, it is sometimes hazardous to hasten to the end without interruption. Just at the time when the weight of an evil destiny has already long burdened the hero, for whom the active sympathy of the audience is hoping relief, although rational consideration makes the inherent necessity of his destruction very evident—in such a case, it is an old, unpretentious poetic device to give the audience for a few moments a prospect of relief. This is done by means of a new, slight suspense; a slight hindrance, a distant possibility of a happy release, is thrown in the way of the already indicated direction of the end. Brutus must explain that he considers it cowardly to kill one's self; the dying Edmund must revoke the command to kill Lear; Friar Laurence may still enter before the moment when Romeo kills himself; Coriolanus may yet be acquitted by the judges; Macbeth is still invulnerable from any man born of woman, even when Birnam Wood is approaching his castle; even Richard III receives the news that Richmond's fleet is shattered and dispersed by the storm. The use of this artifice is old; Sophocles used it to good purpose in *Antigone*; Creon is softened, and revokes the death sentence of Antigone; if it has gone so far with her as he commanded, yet she may be saved. . . .

Yet it requires a fine sensibility to make good use of this force. It must not be insignificant or it will not have the desired effect; it must be made to grow out of the action and out of the character of the persons; it must not come out so prominent that it essentially changes the relative position of the parties. . . .

The Catastrophe   The catastrophe of the drama is the closing action; it is what the ancient stage called the *exodus*. In it the embarrassment of the chief characters is relieved through a great deed. The more profound the strife which has gone forward in the hero's soul, the more noble its purpose has been, so much more logical will the destruction of the succumbing hero be.

And the warning must be given here that the poet should not allow himself to be misled by modern tender-heartedness to spare the life of his hero on the stage. The drama must present an action, including within itself all its parts, excluding all else, perfectly complete; if the struggle of a hero has in fact, taken hold of his entire life, it is not old tradition, but inherent necessity, that the poet shall make the complete ruin of that life impressive. . . .

. . . But the catastrophe contains only the necessary consequences of the action and the characters; whoever has borne both firmly in his soul, can have little doubt about the conclusion of his play. . . .

For the construction of the catastrophe, the following rules are of value: First, avoid every unnecessary word, and leave no word unspoken whereby the idea of the piece can, without effort, be made clear from the nature of the characters. Further, the poet must deny himself broad elaboration of scenes; must keep what he presents dramatically, brief, simple, free from ornament; must give in diction and action, the best and most impressive; must confine the scenes with their indispensable connections within a small body, with quick, pulsating life; must avoid, so long as the action is in progress, new or difficult stage-effects, especially the effects of masses. . . .

. . . It is instructive to set forth distinctly in a scheme, the artistic combination of . . . the constituent parts already discussed. . . . This self-developing organization of the drama, according to a law, will here be briefly analyzed, without regard to the customary division into acts [in *Hamlet*].

Introduction. 1. The key-note; the ghost appears on the platform; the guards and Horatio. 2. The exposition itself; Hamlet in a room of state, before the beginning of the exciting force. 3. Connecting scene with what follows; Horatio and the guards inform Hamlet of the appearance of the ghost. Interpolated exposition scene of the accessory action. The family of Polonius, at the departure of Laertes.

The Exciting Force. 1. Introductory key-note; expectation of the ghost. 2. The ghost appears to Hamlet. 3. Chief part, it reveals the murder to him. 4. Transition to what follows. Hamlet and his confidants.

Through the two ghost scenes, between which the introduction of the chief persons occurs, the scenes of the introduction and of the first excitement are enclosed in a group, the climax of which lies near the end.

Ascending action in four stages. First stage: the counterplayers. Polonius propounds that Hamlet has become deranged through love for Ophelia. Two little scenes: Polonius in his house, and before the king; transition to what follows. Second stage: Hamlet determines to put the king to a test by means of a play. A great scene with episodical performances, Hamlet against Polonius, the courtiers, the actors. Hamlet's soliloquy forms the transition. Third stage: Hamlet's examination by the counterplayers. 1. The king and the intriguers. 2. Hamlet's celebrated monologue. 3. Hamlet warns Ophelia. 4. The king becomes suspicious. These three stages of the rising action are worked out with reference to the effect of the two others; the first becomes an introduction, the broad and agreeable elaboration of the second forms the chief part of the ascent; the third, through the continuation of the monologue, beautifully connected with the second, forms the climax of the group, with sudden descent. Fourth stage, which leads up to the climax: the play, confirmation of Hamlet's suspicion. 1. Introduction. Hamlet, the players and courtiers. 2. The rendering of the play, the king. 3. Transition, Hamlet, Horatio, and the courtiers.

Climax. A scene with a prelude, the king praying. Hamlet hesitating. Closely jointed to this, the

Tragic Force or Incident. Hamlet, during an interview with his mother, stabs Polonius. Two little scenes, as transition to what follows; the king determines to send Hamlet away. These three scene-groups are also bound into a whole, in the midst of which the climax stands. At either side in splendid working-out, are the last stage of the rising action and the tragic force.

The Return. Introductory side-scene. Fortinbras and Hamlet on the way. First stage: Ophelia's madness, and Laertes demanding revenge. Side scene: Hamlet's letter to Horatio. Second stage: A scene; Laertes and the king discuss Hamlet's death. The announcement of the queen that Ophelia is dead forms the conclusion, and the transition to what follows. Third stage: Burial of Ophelia. Introduction scene, with great episodical elaboration. Hamlet and the grave-diggers. The short, restrained chief scene; the apparent reconciliation of Hamlet and Laertes.

Catastrophe. Introductory scene: Hamlet and Horatio, hatred of the king. As transition, the announcement of Osric; the chief scene, the killing. Arrival of Fortinbras.

The three stages of the falling action are constructed less regularly than those of the first half. The little side scenes without action, through which Hamlet's journey and return are announced, as well as the episode with the grave-diggers, interrupt the connection of scenes. The work of the dramatic close is of ancient brevity and vigor.

Friedrich Nietzsche *1844–1900*

The Birth of Tragedy *1871*

Much will have been gained for esthetics once we have succeeded in apprehending directly—rather than merely *ascertaining*—that art owes its continuous evolution to the Apollonian-Dionysiac duality, even as the prop-

Selections. From *The Birth of Tragedy and The Genealogy of Morals* by Friedrich Nietzsche, translated by Francis Golffing. Copyright © 1956 by Doubleday & Co., Inc. Reprinted by permission of the publisher.

agation of the species depends on the duality of the sexes, their constant conflicts and periodic acts of reconciliation. I have borrowed my adjectives from the Greeks, who developed their mystical doctrines of art through plausible *embodiments*, not through purely conceptual means. It is by those two art-sponsoring deities, Apollo and Dionysos, that we are made to recognize the tremendous split, as regards both origins and objectives, between the plastic, Apollonian arts and the nonvisual art of music inspired by Dionysos. The two creative tendencies developed alongside one another, usually in fierce opposition, each by its taunts forcing the other to more energetic production, both perpetuating in a discordant concord that agon which the term *art* but feebly denominates: until at last, by the thaumaturgy of an Hellenic act of will, the pair accepted the yoke of marriage and, in this condition, begot Attic tragedy, which exhibits the salient features of both parents.

To reach a closer understanding of both these tendencies, let us begin by viewing them as the separate art realms of *dream* and *intoxication,* two physiological phenomena standing toward one another in much the same relationship as the Apollonian and Dionysiac. . . .

. . . This deep and happy sense of the necessity of dream experiences was expressed by the Greeks in the image of Apollo. Apollo is at once the god of all plastic powers and the soothsaying god. He who is etymologically the "lucent" one, the god of light, reigns also over the fair illusion of our inner world of fantasy. The perfection of these conditions in contrast to our imperfectly understood waking reality, as well as our profound awareness of nature's healing powers during the interval of sleep and dream, furnishes a symbolic analogue to the soothsaying faculty and quite generally to the arts, which make life possible and worth living. But the image of Apollo must incorporate that thin line which the dream image may not cross, under penalty of becoming pathological, of imposing itself on us as crass reality: a discreet limitation, a freedom from all extravagant urges, the sapient tranquility of the plastic god. His eye must be sunlike, in keeping with his origin. Even at those moments when he is angry and ill-tempered there lies upon him the consecration of fair illusion. In an eccentric way one might say of Apollo what Schopenhauer says, in the first part of *The World as Will and Idea,* of man caught in the veil of Maya: "Even as on an immense, raging sea, assailed by huge wave crests, a man sits in a little rowboat trusting his frail craft, so, amidst the furious torments of this world, the individual sits tranquilly, supported by the *principium individuationis*[1] and relying on it." One might say that the unshakable confidence in that principle has received its most magnificent expression in Apollo, and that Apollo himself may be

---

[1] According to Thomas Aquinas, the principle of individuation.

regarded as the marvelous divine image of the *principium individuationis,* whose looks and gestures radiate the full delight, wisdom, and beauty of "illusion."

In the same context Schopenhauer has described for us the tremendous awe which seizes man when he suddenly begins to doubt the cognitive modes of experience, in other words, when in a given instance the law of causation seems to suspend itself. If we add to this awe the glorious transport which arises in man, even from the very depths of nature, at the shattering of the *principium individuationis,* then we are in a position to apprehend the essence of Dionysiac rapture, whose closest analogy is furnished by physical intoxication. Dionysiac stirrings arise either through the influence of those narcotic potions of which all primitive races speak in their hymns, or through the powerful approach of spring, which penetrates with joy the whole frame of nature. So stirred, the individual forgets himself completely. It is the same Dionysiac power which in medieval Germany drove ever increasing crowds of people singing and dancing from place to place; we recognize in these St. John's and St. Vitus's dancers the bacchic choruses of the Greeks, who had their precursors in Asia Minor and as far back as Babylon and the orgiastic Sacaea. . . .

If this apotheosis of individuation is to be read in normative terms, we may infer that there is one norm only: the individual—or, more precisely, the observance of the limits of the individual: *sophrosyne.* As a moral deity Apollo demands self-control from his people and, in order to observe such self-control, a knowledge of self. And so we find that the esthetic necessity of beauty is accompanied by the imperatives, "Know thyself," and "Nothing too much." Conversely, excess and *hubris* come to be regarded as the hostile spirits of the non-Apollonian sphere, hence as properties of the pre-Apollonian era—the age of Titans—and the extra-Apollonian world, that is to say the world of the barbarians. It was because of his Titanic love of man that Prometheus had to be devoured by vultures; it was because of his extravagant wisdom which succeeded in solving the riddle of the Sphinx that Oedipus had to be cast into a whirlpool of crime: in this fashion does the Delphic god interpret the Greek past.

The effects of the Dionysiac spirit struck the Apollonian Greeks as titanic and barbaric; yet they could not disguise from themselves the fact that they were essentially akin to those deposed Titans and heroes. They felt more than that: their whole existence, with its temperate beauty, rested upon a base of suffering and *knowledge* which had been hidden from them until the reinstatement of Dionysos uncovered it once more. And lo and behold! Apollo found it impossible to live without Dionysos. The elements of titanism and barbarism turned out to be quite as fundamental as the Apollonian element. And now let us imagine how the ecstatic sounds of the Dionysiac rites penetrated ever more enticingly into that artificially restrained and discreet world of illusion, how this clamor expressed the whole outrageous gamut of nature—delight, grief, knowledge—even to the most piercing cry; and then let us imagine how the Apollonian artist with his thin, monotonous harp music must have sounded beside the demoniac chant of the multitude! The muses presiding over the illusory arts paled before an art which enthusiastically told the truth, and the wisdom of Silenus cried "Woe!" against the serene Olympians. The individual, with his limits and moderations, forgot himself in the Dionysiac vortex and became oblivious to the laws of Apollo. Indiscreet extravagance revealed itself as truth, and contradiction, a delight born of pain, spoke out of the bosom of nature. Wherever the Dionysiac voice was heard, the Apollonian norm seemed suspended or destroyed. Yet it is equally true that, in those places where the first assault was withstood, the prestige and majesty of the Delphic god appeared more rigid and threatening than before. . . .

. . . If the earlier phase of Greek history may justly be broken down into four major artistic epochs dramatizing the battle between the two hostile principles, then we must inquire further . . . what was the true end toward which that evolution moved. And our eyes will come to rest on the sublime and much lauded achievement of the dramatic dithyramb and Attic tragedy, as the common goal of both urges; whose mysterious marriage, after long discord, ennobled itself with such a child, at once Antigone and Cassandra. . . .

Thus we have come to interpret Greek tragedy as a Dionysiac chorus which again and again discharges itself in Apollonian images. Those choric portions with which the tragedy is interlaced constitute, as it were, the matrix of the *dialogue,* that is to say, of the entire stage-world of the actual drama. This substratum of tragedy irradiates, in several consecutive discharges, the vision of the drama—a vision on the one hand completely of the nature of Apollonian dream-illusion and therefore epic, but on the other hand, as the objectification of a Dionysiac condition, tending toward the shattering of the individual and his fusion with the original Oneness. Tragedy is an Apollonian embodiment of Dionysiac insights and powers, and for that reason separated by a tremendous gulf from the epic.

On this view the chorus of Greek tragedy, symbol of an entire multitude agitated by Dionysos, can be fully explained. Whereas we who are accustomed to the role of the chorus in modern theatre, especially opera, find it hard to conceive how the chorus of the Greeks should have been older, more central than the dramatic action proper (although we have clear testimony to this effect); and whereas we have never been quite able to reconcile with this position of importance the fact that the chorus was composed of such lowly beings as—originally—goatlike satyrs; and whereas, further, the orchestra in front of the stage has always seemed a riddle to us—we now realize that the stage with its action was originally conceived as pure vision and that the only reality was the chorus, who created that vision out of itself and proclaimed it through the medium of dance, music, and spoken word. Since, in this vision, the chorus beholds its lord and master Dionysos, it remains forever an *attending* chorus; it sees how the god suffers and transforms himself, and it has, for that reason, no need to act. But, notwithstanding its subordination to the god, the chorus remains the highest expression of nature, and, like nature, utters in its enthusiasm oracular words of wisdom. Being compassionate as well as wise, it proclaims a truth that issues from the heart of the world. Thus we see how that fantastic and at first sight embarrassing figure arises, the wise and enthusiastic satyr who is at the same time the "simpleton" as opposed to the god. The satyr is a replica of nature in its strongest tendencies and at the same time a herald of its wisdom and art. He combines in his person the roles of musician, poet, dancer and visionary.

It is in keeping both with this insight and with general tradition that in the earliest tragedy Dionysos was not actually present but merely imagined. Original tragedy is only chorus and not drama at all. Later an attempt was made to demonstrate the god as real and to bring the visionary figure, together with the transfiguring frame, vividly before the eyes of every spectator. This marks the beginning of drama in the strict sense of the word. It then became the task of the dithyrambic chorus so to excite the mood of the listeners that when the tragic hero appeared they would behold not the awkwardly masked man but a figure born of their own rapt vision. If we imagine Admetus brooding on the memory of his recently departed wife, consuming himself in a spiritual contemplation of her form, and how a figure of similar shape and gait is lcd toward him in deep disguise; if we then imagine his tremor of excitement, his impetuous comparisons, his instinctive conviction—then we have an analogue for the excitement of the spectator beholding the god, with whose sufferings he has already identified himself, stride onto the stage. Instinctively he would project the shape of the god that was magically present to his mind onto that masked figure of a man, dissolving the latter's reality into a ghostly unreality. This is the Apollonian dream state, in which the daylight world is veiled and a new world—clearer, more comprehensible, more affecting than the first, and at the same time more shadowy—falls upon the eye in ever-changing shapes. Thus we may recognize a drastic stylistic opposition: language, color, pace, dynamics of speech are polarized into the Dionysiac poetry of the chorus, on the one hand, and the Apollonian dream world of the scene on the other. The result is two completely separate spheres of expression. The Apollonian embodiments in which Dionysos assumes objective shape are very different from the continual interplay of shifting forces in the music of the chorus, from those powers deeply felt by the enthusiast, but which he is incapable of condensing into a clear image. The adept no longer obscurely senses the approach of the god: the god now speaks to him from the proscenium with the clarity and firmness of epic, as an epic hero, almost in the language of Homer. . . .

It is an unimpeachable tradition that in its earliest form Greek tragedy records only the sufferings of Dionysos, and that he was the only actor. But it may be claimed with equal justice that, up to Euripides, Dionysos *remains* the sole dramatic protagonist and that all the famous characters of the Greek stage, Prometheus, Oedipus, etc., are only masks of that original hero. The fact that a god hides behind all these masks accounts for the much-admired "ideal" character of those celebrated figures. Someone, I can't recall who, has claimed that all individuals, as individuals, are comic, and therefore untragic; which seems to suggest that the Greeks did not tolerate individuals at all on the tragic stage. And in fact they must have felt this way. The Platonic distinction between the idea and the eidolon is deeply rooted in the Greek temperament. If we wished to use Plato's terminology we might speak of the tragic characters of the Greek stage somewhat as follows: the one true Dionysos appears in a multiplicity of characters, in the mask of warrior hero, and enmeshed in the web of individual will. The god ascends the stage in the likeness of a striving and suffering individual. That he can *appear* at all with this clarity and precision is due to dream interpreter Apollo, who projects before the chorus its Dionysiac condition in this analogical figure. Yet in truth that hero is the suffering Dionysos of the mysteries. . . .

What were you thinking of, overweening Euripides, when you hoped to press myth, then in its last agony, into your service? It died under your violent hands; but you could easily put in its place an imitation that, like Heracles' monkey, would trick itself out in the master's robes. And even as myth, music too died under your hands; though you plundered greedily all the gardens of music, you could achieve no more than a counterfeit. And because you had deserted Dionysos, you were in turn deserted by Apollo. Though you hunted all the passions up from their couch and conjured them into your circle, though you pointed and burnished a sophistic dialectic for the speeches of your heroes, they have only counterfeit passions and speak counterfeit speeches. . . .

. . . Let us recollect how strangely we were affected by the chorus and by the tragic hero of a kind of tragedy which refused to conform to either our habits or our tradition—until, that is, we discovered that the discrepancy was closely bound up with the very origin and essence of Greek tragedy, as the expression of two interacting artistic impulses, the Apollonian and the Dionysiac. Euripides' basic intention now becomes as clear as day to us: it is to eliminate from tragedy the primitive and pervasive Dionysiac element, and to rebuild the drama on a foundation of non-Dionysiac art, custom and philosophy.

Euripides himself, towards the end of his life, propounded the question of the value and significance of this tendency to his contemporaries in a myth. Has the Dionysiac spirit any right at all to exist? Should it not, rather, be brutally uprooted from the Hellenic soil? Yes, it should, the poet tells us, if only it were possible, but the god Dionysos is too powerful: even the most intelligent opponent, like Pentheus in the *Bacchae*, is unexpectedly enchanted by him, and in his enchantment runs headlong to destruction. The opinion of the two old men in the play—Cadmus and Tiresias—seems to echo the opinion of the aged poet himself: that the cleverest individual cannot by his reasoning overturn an ancient popular tradition like the worship of Dionysos, and that it is the proper part of diplomacy in the face of miraculous powers to make at least a prudent show of sympathy; that it is even possible that the god may still take exception to such tepid interest and—as happened in the case of Cadmus— turn the diplomat into a dragon. We are told this by a poet who all his life had resisted Dionysos heroically, only to end his career with a glorification of his opponent and with suicide—like a man who throws himself from a tower in order to put an end to the unbearable sensation of vertigo. The *Bacchae* acknowledges the failure of Euripides' dramatic intentions when, in fact, these had already succeeded: Dionysos had already been driven from the tragic stage by a daemonic power speaking through Euripides. For in a certain sense Euripides was but a mask, while the divinity which spoke through him was neither Dionysos nor Apollo but a brand-new daemon called Socrates. Thenceforward the real antagonism was to be between the Dionysiac spirit and the Socratic, and tragedy was to perish in the conflict. . . .

. . . The anti-Dionysiac spirit won a mighty victory when it estranged music from itself and made it a slave to appearances. . . .

We see a different aspect of this anti-Dionysiac, antimythic trend in the increased emphasis on character portrayal and psychological subtlety from Sophocles onward. Character must no longer be broadened so as to become a permanent type, but on the contrary must be so finely individualized, by means of shading and nuances and the strict delineation of every trait, that the spectator ceases to be aware of myth at all and comes to focus on the amazing lifelikeness of the characters and the artist's power of imitation. Here, once again, we see the victory of the particular over the general and the pleasure taken in, as it were, anatomical drawing. We breathe the air of a world of theory, in which scientific knowledge is more revered than the artistic reflection of a universal norm. The cult of the characteristic trait develops apace: Sophocles still paints whole characters and lays myth under contribution in order to render them more fully; Euripides concentrates on large single character traits, projected into violent passions; the new Attic comedy gives us masks, each with a single expression: frivolous old men, hoodwinked panders, roguish slaves, in endless repetition. Where is now the mythopoeic spirit? All that remains to music is to excite jaded nerves or call up memory images, as in tone painting.

Sigmund Freud   *1856–1939*

On Oedipus and Hamlet   *1900*

According to my already extensive experience, parents play a leading part in the infantile psychology of all persons who subsequently become psychoneurotics. Falling in love with one parent and hating the other forms part of the permanent stock of the psychic impulses which arise in early childhood, and are of such importance as the material of the subsequent neurosis. But I do not believe that psychoneurotics are to be sharply distinguished in this respect from other persons who remain normal—that is, I do not believe that they are capable of creating something absolutely new and peculiar to themselves. It is far more probable—and this is confirmed by incidental observations of normal children—that in their amorous or hostile attitude toward their parents, psychoneurotics do no more than reveal to us, by magnification, something that occurs less markedly and intensively in the minds of the majority of children. Antiquity has furnished us with legendary matter which corroborates this belief, and the profound and universal validity of the old legends is explicable only by an equally universal validity of the above-mentioned hypothesis of infantile psychology.

I am referring to the legend of King Oedipus and the *Oedipus Rex* of Sophocles. Oedipus, the son of Laius, king of Thebes, and Jocasta, is exposed as a suckling, because an oracle had informed the father that his son, who was still unborn, would be his murderer. He is rescued, and grows up as a king's son at a foreign court, until, being uncertain of his origin, he, too, consults the oracle, and is warned to avoid his native place, for he is destined

This selection is from *The Basic Writings of Sigmund Freud*, trans. and ed. by Dr. A. A. Brill, Copyright 1938 by Random House, Inc. Copyright renewed 1965 by Gioia Bernheim and Edmund R. Brill. Reprinted by permission. [The title of the selection is the present editor's.]

to become the murderer of his father and the husband of his mother. On the road leading away from his supposed home he meets King Laius, and in a sudden quarrel strikes him dead. He comes to Thebes, where he solves the riddle of the Sphinx, who is barring the way to the city, whereupon he is elected king by the grateful Thebans, and is rewarded with the hand of Jocasta. He reigns for many years in peace and honour, and begets two sons and two daughters upon his unknown mother, until at last a plague breaks out—which causes the Thebans to consult the oracle anew. Here Sophocles' tragedy begins. The messengers bring the reply that the plague will stop as soon as the murderer of Laius is driven from the country. But where is he?

> Where shall be found,
> Faint, and hard to be known, the trace of the ancient guilt?

The action of the play consists simply in the disclosure, approached step by step and artistically delayed (and comparable to the work of a psychoanalysis) that Oedipus himself is the murderer of Laius, and that he is the son of the murdered man and Jocasta. Shocked by the abominable crime which he has unwittingly committed, Oedipus blinds himself, and departs from his native city. The prophecy of the oracle has been fulfilled.

The *Oedipus Rex* is a tragedy of fate; its tragic effect depends on the conflict between the all-powerful will of the gods and the vain efforts of human beings threatened with disaster; resignation to the divine will, and the perception of one's own impotence is the lesson which the deeply moved spectator is supposed to learn from the tragedy. Modern authors have therefore sought to achieve a similar tragic effect by expressing the same conflict in stories of their own invention. But the playgoers have looked on unmoved at the unavailing efforts of guiltless men to avert the fulfilment of curse or oracle; the modern tragedies of destiny have failed of their effect.

If the *Oedipus Rex* is capable of moving a modern reader or playgoer no less powerfully than it moved the contemporary Greeks, the only possible explanation is that the effect of the Greek tragedy does not depend upon the conflict between fate and human will, but upon the peculiar nature of the material by which this conflict is revealed. There must be a voice within us which is prepared to acknowledge the compelling power of fate in the *Oedipus*, while we are able to condemn the situations occuring in *Die Ahnfrau*[1] or other tragedies of fate as arbitrary inventions. And there actually is a motive in the story of King Oedipus which explains the verdict of this inner voice. His fate moves us only because it might have been our own, because the oracle laid upon us before our birth the very curse which rested upon him. It may be that we were all destined to direct our first sexual

---

[1] *The Ancestress* (1817) by Franz Grillparzer (1791–1872).

impulses toward our mothers, and our first impulses of hatred and violence toward our fathers; our dreams convince us that we were. King Oedipus, who slew his father Laius and wedded his mother Jocasta, is nothing more or less than a wish-fulfilment—the fulfilment of the wish of our childhood. But we, more fortunate than he, insofar as we have not become psychoneurotics, have since our childhood succeeded in withdrawing our sexual impulses from our mothers, and in forgetting our jealousy of our fathers. We recoil from the person for whom this primitive wish of our childhood has been fulfilled with all the force of the repression which these wishes have undergone in our minds since childhood. As the poet brings the guilt of Oedipus to light by his investigation, he forces us to become aware of our own inner selves, in which the same impulses are still extant, even though they are suppressed. The antithesis with which the chorus departs:

> . . . Behold, this is Oedipus,
> Who unravelled the great riddle, and was first in power,
> Whose fortune all the townsmen praised and envied;
> See in what dread adversity he sank!

—this admonition touches us and our own pride, us who since the years of our childhood have grown so wise and so powerful in our own estimation. Like Oedipus, we live in ignorance of the desires that offend morality, the desires that nature has forced upon us and after their unveiling we may well prefer to avert our gaze from the scenes of our childhood.

In the very text of Sophocles' tragedy there is an unmistakable reference to the fact that the Oedipus legend had its source in dream-material of immemorial antiquity, the content of which was the painful disturbance of the child's relations to its parents caused by the first impulses of sexuality. Jocasta comforts Oedipus—who is not yet enlightened, but is troubled by the recollection of the oracle—by an allusion to a dream which is often dreamed, though it cannot, in her opinion, mean anything:

> For many a man hath seen himself in dreams
> His mothers's mate, but he who gives no heed
> To suchlike matters bears the easier life.

The dream of having sexual intercourse with one's mother was as common then as it is today with many people, who tell it with indignation and astonishment. As may well be imagined, it is the key to the tragedy and the complement to the dream of the death of the father. The Oedipus fable is the reaction of phantasy to these two typical dreams, and just as such a dream, when occurring to an adult, is experienced with feelings of aversion, so the content of the fable must include terror and self-chastisement. The form which it subsequently assumed was the result of an uncomprehending secondary elaboration of the material, which sought to make it serve a theological intention. The attempt to reconcile divine omnipotence with human responsibility must, of course, fail with this material as with any other.

Another of the great poetic tragedies, Shakespeare's *Hamlet,* is rooted in the same soil as *Oedipus Rex.* But the whole difference in the psychic life of the two widely separated periods of civilization, and the progress, during the course of time, of repression in the emotional life of humanity, is manifested in the differing treatment of the same material. In *Oedipus Rex* the basic wish-phantasy of the child is brought to light and realized as it is in dreams; in *Hamlet* it remains repressed, and we learn of its existence—as we discover the relevant facts in a neurosis—only through the inhibitory effects which proceed from it. In the more modern drama, the curious fact that it is possible to remain in complete uncertainty as to the character of the hero has proved to be quite consistent with the overpowering effect of the tragedy. The play is based upon Hamlet's hesitation in accomplishing the task of revenge assigned to him; the text does not give the cause or the motive of this hesitation, nor have the manifold attempts at interpretation succeeded in doing so. According to the still prevailing conception, a conception for which Goethe was first responsible, Hamlet represents the type of man whose active energy is paralysed by excessive intellectual activity: "Sicklied o'er with the pale cast of thought." According to another conception, the poet has endeavoured to portray a morbid, irresolute character, on the verge of neurasthenia. The plot of the drama, however, shows us that Hamlet is by no means intended to appear as a character wholly incapable of action. On two separate occasions we see him assert himself: once in a sudden outburst of rage, when he stabs the eavesdropper behind the arras, and in the other occasion when he deliberately, and even craftily, with the complete unscrupulousness of a prince of the Renaissance, sends the two courtiers to the death which was intended for himself. What is it, then, that inhibits him in accomplishing the task which his father's ghost has laid upon him? Here the explanation offers itself that it is the peculiar nature of this task. Hamlet is able to do anything but take vengeance upon the man who did away with his father and has taken his father's place with his mother—the man who shows him in realization the repressed desires of his own childhood. The loathing which should have driven him to revenge is thus replaced by self-reproach, by conscientious scruples, which tell him that he himself is no better than the murderer whom he is required to punish. I have here translated into consciousness what had to remain unconscious in the mind of the hero; if anyone wishes to call Hamlet an hysterical subject I cannot but admit that this is the deduction to be drawn from my interpretation. The sexual aversion which Hamlet expresses in conversation with Ophelia is perfectly consistent with this deduction—the same sexual aversion which during the next few years was increasingly to take possession of the poet's soul, until it found its supreme utterance in *Timon of Athens.* It can, of course, be only the poet's own psychology with which we are confronted in *Hamlet*; and in a work on Shakespeare by Georg Brandes[2] (1896) I find the statement that the drama was composed immediately after the death of Shakespeare's father (1601)—that is to say, when he was still mourning his loss, and during a revival, as we may fairly assume, of his own childish feelings in respect of his father. It is known, too, that Shakespeare's son, who died in childhood, bore the name of Hamnet (identical with Hamlet). Just as *Hamlet* treats of the relation of the son to his parents, so *Macbeth*, which was written about the same period, is based upon the theme of childlessness. Just as all neurotic symptoms, like dreams themselves, are capable of hyper-interpretation, and even require such hyper-interpretation before they become perfectly intelligible, so every genuine poetical creation must have proceeded from more than one motive, more than one impulse in the mind of the poet, and must admit of more than one interpretation. I have here attempted to interpret only the deepest stratum of impulses in the mind of the creative poet.

[2] Georg Morris Cohen Brandes (1842–1927).

Jokes and Their Relation to the Unconscious *1905*

It is easy to divine the characteristic of jokes on which the difference in their hearers' reaction to them depends. In the one case the joke is an end in itself and serves no particular aim, in the other case it does serve such an aim—it become *tendentious*. Only jokes that have a purpose run the risk of meeting with people who do not want to listen to them.

Non-tendentious jokes were described by Vischer[1] as "abstract" jokes. I prefer to call them "innocent" jokes. . . .

Selections. Reprinted from *Jokes and Their Relation to the Unconscious* by Sigmund Freud. Translated from the German and edited by James Strachey. By permission of W. W. Norton & Company, Inc. Copyright © 1960 by James Strachey.

[1] Friedrich Theodor Vischer (1807–1887), author of *The Humor of Germany* (1879) and *On the Noble and Comical* (1837).

The purposes of jokes can easily be reviewed. Where a joke is not an aim in itself—that is, where it is not an innocent one—there are only two purposes that it may serve, and these two can themselves be subsumed under a single heading. It is either a *hostile* joke (serving the purpose of aggressiveness, satire, or defence) or an *obscene* joke (serving the purpose of exposure). It must be repeated in advance that the technical species of the joke—whether it is a verbal or a conceptual joke—bears no relation to these two purposes.

It is a much lengthier business to show the way in which jokes serve these two purposes. In this investigation I should prefer to deal first not with the hostile jokes but with the exposing jokes. . . .

We know what is meant by "smut": the intentional bringing into prominence of sexual facts and relations by speech. This definition, however, is no more valid than other definitions. In spite of this definition, a lecture on the anatomy of the sexual organs or the physiology of procreation need not have a single point of contact with smut. It is a further relevant fact that smut is directed to a particular person, by whom one is sexually excited and who, on hearing it, is expected to become aware of the speaker's excitement and as a result to become sexually excited in turn. Instead of this excitement the other person may be led to feel shame or embarrassment, which is only a reaction against the excitement and, in a roundabout way, is an admission of it. Smut is thus originally directed towards women and may be equated with attempts at seduction. If a man in a company of men enjoys telling or listening to smut, the original situation, which owing to social inhibitions cannot be realized, is at the same time imagined. A person who laughs at smut that he hears is laughing as though he were the spectator of an act of sexual aggression.

The sexual material which forms the content of smut includes more than what is *peculiar* to each sex; it also includes what is *common* to both sexes and to which the feeling of shame extends—that is to say, what is excremental in the most comprehensive sense. This is, however, the sense covered by sexuality in childhood, an age at which there is, as it were, a cloaca within which what is sexual and what is excremental are barely or not at all distinguished. Throughout the whole range of the psychology of the neuroses, what is sexual includes what is excremental, and is understood in the old, infantile, sense.

Smut is like an exposure of the sexually different person to whom it is directed. By the utterance of the obscene words it compels the person who is assailed to imagine the part of the body or the procedure in question and shows her that the assailant is himself imagining it. It cannot be doubted that the desire to see what is sexual exposed is the original motive of smut. . . .

Generally speaking, a tendentious joke calls for three people: in addition to the one who makes the joke, there must be a second who is taken as the object of the hostile or sexual aggressiveness, and a third in whom the joke's aim of producing pleasure is fulfilled. We shall have later to examine the deeper reasons for this state of things; for the moment let us keep to the fact to which this testifies—namely that it is not the person who makes the joke who laughs at it and who therefore enjoys its pleasurable effect, but the inactive listener. In the case of smut the three people are in the same relation. The course of events may be thus described. When the first person finds his libidinal impulse inhibited by the woman, he develops a hostile trend against that second person and calls on the originally interfering third person as his ally. Through the first person's smutty speech the woman is exposed before the third, who, as listener, has now been bribed by the effortless satisfaction of his own libido. . . .

We are now prepared to realize the part played by jokes in hostile aggressiveness. A joke will allow us to exploit something ridiculous in our enemy which we could not, on account of obstacles in the way, bring forward openly or conspiciously; once again, then, the joke *will evade restrictions and open sources of pleasure that have become inaccessible.* It will further bribe the hearer with its yield of pleasure into taking sides with us without any very close investigation, just as on other occasions we ourselves have often been bribed by an innocent joke into overestimating the substance of a statement expressed jokingly. . . .

. . . Tendentious jokes are especially favoured in order to make aggressiveness or criticism possible against persons in exalted positions who claim to exercise authority. The joke then represents a rebellion against that authority, a liberation from its pressure. The charm of caricatures lies in this same factor: we laugh at them even if they are unsuccessful simply because we count rebellion against authority as a merit. . . .

The comic arises in the first instance as an unintended discovery derived from human social relations. It is found in people—in their movements, forms, actions and traits of character, originally in all probability only in their physical characteristics but later in their mental ones as well or, as the case may be, in the expression of those characteristics. By means of a very common sort of personification, animals become comic too, and inanimate objects. At the same time, the comic is capable of being detached from people, insofar as we recognize the conditions under which a person seems comic. In this way the comic of situation comes about, and this recognition affords the possibility of making a person comic at one's will by putting him in situations in which his actions are subject to these comic conditions. The discovery that one has it in one's power to make someone else comic opens the way to an undreamt-of yield of comic pleasure and is the origin of a highly developed technique. One can make *oneself* comic, too, as easily as other people. The methods that serve to make people comic are: putting them in a comic situation, mimicry, disguise, unmasking, caricature, parody, travesty, and so on. It is obvious that these techniques can be used to serve hostile and aggressive purposes. One can make a person comic in order to make him become contemptible, to deprive him of his claim to dignity and authority. But even if such an intention habitually underlies making people comic, this need not be the meaning of what is comic spontaneously. . . .

. . . The answer to the question of why we laugh at the clown's movements is that they seem to us extravagant and inexpedient. We are laughing at an expenditure that is too large. Let us look now for the determining condition outside the comic that is artificially constructed—where it can be found unintended. A child's movements do not seem to us comic, although he kicks and jumps about. On the other hand, it *is* comic when a child who is learning to write follows the movements of his pen with his tongue stuck out; in these associated motions we see an unnecessary expenditure of movement which we should spare ourselves if we were carrying out the same activity. Similarly, other such associated motions, or merely exaggerated expressive movements, seem to us comic in adults too. Pure examples of this species of the comic are to be seen, for instance, in the movements of someone playing skittles who, after he has released the ball, follows its course as though he could still continue to direct it. Thus, too, all grimaces are comic which exaggerate the normal expression of the emotions, even if they are produced involuntarily as in sufferers from St. Vitus's dance (chorea). And in the same way, the passionate movements of a modern conductor seem comic to any unmusical person who cannot understand their necessity. Indeed, it is from this comic movement that the comic of bodily shapes and facial features branches off; for these are regarded as though they were the outcome of an exaggerated or pointless movement. Staring eyes, a hooked nose hanging down to the mouth, ears sticking out, a hump-back—all such things probably only produce a comic effect insofar as movements are imagined which would be necessary to bring about these features; and here the nose, the ears and other parts of the body are imagined as more movable than they are in reality. There is no doubt that it is comic if someone can "waggle his ears," and it would certainly be still more comic if he could move his nose up and down. A good deal of the comic effect produced on us by animals comes from our perceiving in them movements such as these which we cannot imitate ourselves.

But how is it that we laugh when we have recognized that some other person's movements are exaggerated and inexpedient? By making a comparison, I believe, between the movement I observe in the other person and the one that I should have carried out myself in his place. . . .

Thus a uniform explanation is provided of the fact that a person appears comic to us, if, in comparison with ourselves, he makes too great an expenditure on his bodily functions and too little on his mental ones; and it cannot be denied that in both these cases our laughter expresses a pleasurable sense of the superiority which we feel in relation to him. If the relation in the two cases is reversed—if the other person's physical expenditure is found to be less than ours or his mental expenditure greater—then we no longer laugh, we are filled with astonishment and admiration. . . .

Mankind has not been content to enjoy the comic where they have come upon it in their experience; they have also sought to bring it about intentionally, and we can learn more about the nature of the comic if we study the means which serve to *make* things comic. First and foremost, it is possible to produce the comic in relation to oneself in order to amuse other people—for instance, by making oneself out clumsy or stupid. In that way one produces a comic effect exactly as though one really were these things, by fulfilling the condition of the comparison which leads to the difference in expenditure. But one does not in this way make oneself ridiculous or contemptible, but may in some circumstances even achieve admiration. The feeling of superiority does not arise in the other person if he knows that one has only been pretending; and this affords fresh evidence of the fundamental independence of the comic from the feeling of superiority.

As regards making *other people* comic, the principal means is to put them in situations in which a person becomes comic as a result of human dependence on external events, particularly on social factors, without regard to the personal characteristics of the individual concerned—that is to say, by employing the comic of situation. This putting of someone in a comic situation may be a *real* one (a practical joke)—by sticking out a leg so that someone trips over it as though he were clumsy, by making him seem stupid by exploiting his credulity, or trying to convince him of something nonsensical, and so on—or it may be simulated by speech or play. The aggressiveness, to which making a person comic usually ministers, is much assisted by the fact that the comic pleasure is independent of the reality of the comic situation, so that everyone is in fact exposed, without any defence, to being made comic.

But there are yet other means of making things comic which deserve special consideration and also indicate in part fresh sources of comic pleasure. Among these, for instance, is *mimicry*, which gives quite extraordinary pleasure to the hearer and makes its object comic even if it is still far from the exaggeration of a caricature. It is much easier to find a reason for the comic effect of *caricature* than for that of mere mimicry. Caricature, parody and travesty (as well as their practical counterpart, unmasking) are are directed against people and objects which lay claim to authority and respect, which are in some sense "*sublime.*". . .

Caricature, as is well known, brings about degradation by emphasizing in the general impression given by the exalted object a single trait which is comic in itself but was bound to be overlooked so long as it was only perceivable in the general picture. By isolating this, a comic effect can be attained which extends in our memory over the whole object. This is subject to the condition that the actual presence of the exalted object himself does not keep us in a reverential attitude. If a comic trait of this kind that has been overlooked is lacking in reality, a caricature will unhesitatingly create it by exaggerating one that is not comic in itself; and the fact that the effect of the caricature is not essentially diminished by this falsification of reality is once again an indication of the origin of comic pleasure.

Parody and *travesty* achieve the degradation of something exalted in another way: by destroying the unity that exists between people's characters as we know them and their speeches and actions, by replacing either the exalted figures or their utterances by inferior ones. They are distinguished from caricature in this, but not in the mechanism of their production of comic pleasure.

Carl G. Jung   *1875–1961*

On the Relation
of Analytical Psychology
to Poetry   *1922*

Art by its very nature is not science, and science by its very nature is not art; both these spheres of the mind have something in reserve that is peculiar to them and can be explained only in its own terms. Hence when we speak of the relation of psychology to art, we shall treat only of that aspect of art which can be submitted to psychological scrutiny without violating its nature. Whatever the psychologist has to say about art will be confined to the process of artistic creation and has nothing to do with its innermost essence. He

Selections. From *The Collected Works of C. G. Jung*, edited by G. Adler, M. Fordham, H. Read, trans. by R. F. C. Hull, Bollingen Series XX, vol. 15, *The Spirit in Man, Art, and Literature* (copyright © 1966 by Bollingen Foundation), reprinted by permission of Princeton University Press.

can no more explain this than the intellect can describe or even understand the nature of feeling. . . .

. . . Though the material he works with and its individual treatment can easily be traced back to the poet's personal relations with his parents, this does not enable us to understand his poetry. The same reduction can be made in all sorts of other fields, and not least in the case of pathological disturbances. Neuroses and psychoses are likewise reducible to infantile relations with the parents, and so are a man's good and bad habits, his beliefs, peculiarities, passions, interests, and so forth. It can hardly be supposed that all these very different things must have exactly the same explanation, for otherwise we would be driven to the conclusion that they actually are the same thing. If a work of art is explained in the same way as a neurosis, then either the work of art is a neurosis or a neurosis is a work of art. . . .

The school of medical psychology inaugurated by Freud has undoubtedly encouraged the literary historian to bring certain peculiarities of a work of art into relation with the intimate, personal life of the poet. But this is nothing new in principle, for it has long been know that the scientific treatment of art will reveal the personal threads that the artist, intentionally or unintentionally, has woven into his work. The Freudian approach may, however, make possible a more exhaustive demonstration of the influences that reach back into earliest childhood and play their part in artistic creation. To this extent the psychoanalysis of art differs in no essential form the subtle psychological nuances of a penetrating literary analysis. The difference is at most a question of degree, though we may occasionally be surprised by indiscreet references to things which a rather more delicate touch might have passed over if only for reasons of tact. . . .

. . . Since this kind of anlysis is in no way concerned with the work of art itself, but strives like a mole to bury itself in the dirt as speedily as possible, it always ends up in the common earth that unites all mankind. Hence its explanations have the same tedious monotony as the recitals which one daily hears in the consulting-room. . . .

I have purposely dwelt on the application of medical psychoanalysis to works of art because I want to emphasize that the psychoanalytic method is at the same time an essential part of the Freudian doctrine. Freud himself by his rigid dogmatism has ensured that the method and the doctrine—in themselves two very different things—are regarded by the public as identical. Yet the method may be employed with beneficial results in medical cases without at the same time exalting it into a doctrine. And against this doctrine we are bound to raise vigorous objections. The assumptions it rests on are quite arbitrary. For example, neuroses are by no means exclusively caused by sexual repression, and the same holds true for psychoses. There is no foundation for saying that dreams merely contain repressed wishes whose moral incompatibility requires them to be disguised by a hypothetical dream-censor.

The Freudian technique of interpretation, so far as it remains under the influence of its own one-sided and therefore erroneous hypotheses, displays a quite obvious bias.

In order to do justice to a work of art, analytical psychology must rid itself entirely of medical prejudice, for a work of art is not a disease, and consequently requires a different approach from the medical one. A doctor naturally has to seek out the causes of a disease in order to pull it up by the roots, but just as naturally the psychologist must adopt exactly the opposite attitude towards a work of art. Instead of investigating its typically human determinants, he will inquire first of all into its meaning, and will concern himself with its determinants only insofar as they enable him to understand it more fully. Personal causes have as much or as little to do with a work of art as the soil with the plant that springs from it. We can certainly learn to understand some of the plant's peculiarities by getting to know its habitat, and for the botanist this is an important part of his equipment. But nobody will maintain that everything essential has then been discovered about the plant itself. The personal orientation which the doctor needs when confronted with the question of aetiology in medicine is quite out of place in dealing with a work of art, just because a work of art is not a human being, but is something supra-personal. It is a thing and not a personality; hence it cannot be judged by personal criteria. Indeed, the special significance of a true work of art resides in the fact that it has escaped from the limitations of the personal and has soared beyond the personal concerns of its creator.

I must confess from my own experience that it is not at all easy for a doctor to lay aside his professional bias when considering a work of art and look at it with a mind cleared of the current biological causality. But I have come to learn that although a psychology with a purely biological orientation can explain a good deal about man in general, it cannot be applied to a work of art and still less to man as creator. A purely causalistic psychology is only able to reduce every human individual to a member of the species *Homo sapiens*, since its range is limited to what is transmitted by heredity or derived from other sources. But a work of art is not transmitted or derived—it is a creative reorganization of those very conditions to which a causalistic psychology must always reduce it. The plant is not a mere product of the soil; it is a living, self-contained process which in essence has nothing to do with the character of the soil. In the same way, the meaning and individual quality of a work of art inhere within it and not in its extrinsic determinants. One might almost describe it as a living being that uses man only as a nutrient medium, employing his capacities according to its own laws and shaping itself to the fulfilment of its own creative purpose.

But here I am anticipating somewhat, for I have in mind a particular type of art which I still have to introduce. Not every work of art originates in the way I have just described. There are literary works, prose as well as poetry, that spring wholly from the author's intention to produce a particular result. He submits his material to a definite treatment with a definite aim in view; he adds to it and subtracts from it, emphasizing one effect, toning down another, laying on a touch of colour here, another there, all the time carefully considering the over-all result and paying strict attention to the laws of form and style. He exercises the keenest judgment and chooses his words with complete freedom. His material is entirely subordinated to his artistic purpose; he wants to express this and nothing else. He is wholly at one with the creative process, no matter whether he has deliberately made himself its spearhead, as it were, or whether it has made him its instrument so completely that he has lost all consciousness of this fact. In either case, the artist is so identified with his work that his intentions and his faculties are indistinguishable from the act of creation itself. There is no need, I think, to give examples of this from the history of literature or from the testimony of the artists themselves.

Nor need I cite examples of the other class of works which flow more or less complete and perfect from the author's pen. They come as it were fully arrayed into the world, as Pallas Athene sprang from the head of Zeus. These works positively force themselves upon the author; his hand is seized, his pen writes things that his mind contemplates with amazement. The work brings with it its own form; anything he wants to add is rejected, and what he himself would like to reject is thrust back at him. While his conscious mind stands amazed and empty before this phenomenon, he is overwhelmed by a flood of thoughts and images which he never intended to create and which his own will could never have brought into being. Yet in spite of himself he is forced to admit that it is his own self speaking, his own inner nature revealing itself and uttering things which he would never have entrusted to his tongue. He can only obey the apparently alien impulse within him and follow where it leads, sensing that his work is greater than himself, and wields a power which is not his and which he cannot command. Here the artist is not identical with the process of creation; he is aware that he is subordinate to his work or stands outside it, as though he were a second person; or as though a person other than himself had fallen within the magic circle of an alien will.

So when we discuss the psychology of art, we must bear in mind these two entirely different modes of creation, for much that is of the greatest importance in judging a work of art depends on this distinction. It is one that had been sensed earlier by Schiller, who as we know attempted to classify it in his concept of the *sentimental* and the *naïve*. The psychologist would call "sentimental" art *introverted* and the "naïve" kind *extraverted*. The introverted attitude is characterized by the subject's assertion of his conscious intentions and aims against the demands of the object, whereas the extraverted attitude is characterized by the subject's subordination to the demands which the object makes upon him. In my view, Schiller's plays and most of his poems give one a good idea of the introverted attitude: the material is mastered by the conscious intentions of the poet. The extra-verted attitude is illustrated by the second part of *Faust*: here the material is distinguished by its refractoriness. A still more striking example is Nietzche's *Zarathustra*, where the author himself observed how "one became two."

From what I have said, it will be apparent that a shift of psychological standpoint has taken place as soon as one speaks not of the poet as a person but of the creative process that moves him. When the focus of interest shifts to the latter, the poet comes into the picture only as a reacting subject. This is immediately evident in our second category of works, where the conscious-ness of the poet is not identical with the creative process. But in works of the first category the opposite appears to hold true. Here the poet appears to be the creative process itself, and to create of his own free will without the slightest feeling of compulsion. He may even be fully convinced of his free-dom of action and refuse to admit that his work could be anything else than the expression of his will and ability.

Here we are faced with a question which we cannot answer from the testimony of the poets themselves. It is really a scientific problem that psy-chology alone can solve. As I hinted earlier, it might well be that the poet, while apparently creating out of himself and producing what he consciously intends, is nevertheless so carried away by the creative impulse that he is no longer aware of an "alien" will, just as the other type of poet is no longer aware of his own still speaking to him in the apparently "alien" inspiration, although this is manifestly the voice of his own self. The poet's conviction that he is creating in absolute freedom would then be an illusion: he fancies he is swimming, but in reality an unseen current sweeps him along.

This is not by any means an academic question, but is supported by the evidence of analytical psychology. Researches have shown that there are all sorts of ways in which the conscious mind is not only influenced by the unconscious but actually guided by it. Yet is there any evidence for the sup-position that a poet, despite his self-awareness, may be taken captive by his work? The proof may be of two kinds, direct or indirect. Direct proof would be afforded by a poet who thinks he knows what he is saying but actually says more than he is aware of. Such cases are not uncommon. Indirect proof would be found in cases where behind the apparent free will of the poet there stands a higher imperative that renews its peremptory demands as soon as the poet voluntarily gives up his creative activity, or that produces psychic complications whenever his work has to be broken off against his will.

Analysis of artists consistently shows not only the strength of the creative impulse arising from the unconscious, but also its capricious and wilful char-acter. The biographies of great artists make it abundantly clear that the creative urge is often so imperious that it battens on their humanity and yokes everything to the service of the work, even at the cost of health and ordinary human happiness. The unborn work in the psyche of the artist is a force of nature that achieves its end either with tyrannical might or with the subtle cunning of nature herself, quite regardless of the personal fate of the man who is its vehicle. The creative urge lives and grows in him like a tree in the earth from which it draws its nourishment. We would do well, therefore, to think of the creative process as a living thing implanted in the human psyche. In the language of analytical psychology this living thing is an *autonomous complex*. It is a split-off portion of the psyche, which leads a life of its own outside the hierarchy of consciousness. Depending on its energy charge, it may appear either as a mere disturbance of conscious activities or as a supra-ordinate authority which can harness the ego to its purpose. Accordingly, the poet who identifies with the creative process would be one who acquiesces from the start when the unconscious imperative begins to function. But the other poet, who feels the creative force as something alien, is one who for various reasons cannot acquiesce and is thus caught unawares.

It might be expected that this difference in its origins would be perceptible in a work of art. For in the one case it is a conscious product shaped and designed to have the effect intended. But in the other we are dealing with an event originating in unconscious nature; with something that achieves its aim without the assistance of human consciousness, and often defies it by wilfully insisting on its own form and effect. We would therefore expect that works belonging to the first class would nowhere overstep the limits of comprehension, that their effect would be bounded by the author's intention and would not extend beyond it. But with works of the other class we would have to be prepared for something suprapersonal that transcends our understanding to the same degree that the author's consciousness was in abeyance during the process of creation. We would expect a strangeness of form and content, thoughts that can only be apprehended intuitively, a language pregnant with meanings, and images that are true symbols because they are the best possible expressions for something unknown—bridges thrown out towards an unseen shore.

These criteria are, by and large, corroborated in practice. Whenever we are confronted with a work that was consciously planned and with material that was consciously selected, we find that it agrees with the first class of qualities, and in the other case with the second. The example we gave of Schiller's plays, on the one hand, and *Faust II* on the other, or better still *Zarathustra*, is an illustration of this. But I would not undertake to place the work of an unknown poet in either of these categories without first having examined rather closely his personal relations with his work. It is not enough to know whether the poet belongs to the introverted or to the extraverted type, since it is possible for either type to work with an introverted attitude at one time, and an extraverted attitude at another. This is particularly noticeable in the difference between Schiller's plays and his philosophical writings, between Goethe's perfectly formed poems and the obvious struggle with his material in *Faust II*, and between Nietzsche's well-turned aphorisms and the rushing torrent of *Zarathustra*. The same poet can adopt different attitudes to his work at different times, and on this depends the standard we have to apply.

The question, as we now see, is exceedingly complicated, and the complication grows even worse when we consider the case of the poet who identifies with the creative process. For should it turn out that the apparently conscious and purposeful manner of composition is a subjective illusion of the poet, then his work would possess symbolic qualities that are outside the range of his consciousness. They would only be more difficult to detect, because the reader as well would be unable to get beyond the bounds of the poet's consciousness which are fixed by the spirit of the time. There is no Archimedean point outside his world by which he could lift his time-bound consciousness off its hinges and recognize the symbols hidden in the poet's work. For a symbol is the intimation of a meaning beyond the level of our present powers of comprehension.

I raise this question only because I do not want my typological classification to limit the possible significance of works of art which apparently mean no more than what they say. But we have often found that a poet who has gone out of fashion is suddenly rediscovered. This happens when our conscious development has reached a higher level from which the poet can tell us something new. It was always present in his work but was hidden in a symbol, and only a renewal of the spirit of the time permits us to read its meaning. It needed to be looked at with fresher eyes, for the old ones could see in it only what they were accustomed to see. Experiences of this kind should make us cautious, as they bear out my earlier argument. But works that are openly symbolic do not require this subtle approach; their pregnant language cries out at us that they mean more than they say. We can put our finger on the symbol at once, even though we may not be able to unriddle its meaning to our entire satisfaction. A symbol remains a perpetual challenge to our thoughts and feelings. That probably explains why a symbolic work is so stimulating, why it grips us so intensely, but also why it seldom affords us a purely aesthetic enjoyment. A work that is manifestly not symbolic appeals much more to our aesthetic sensibility because it is complete in itself and fulfills its purpose.

What then, you may ask, can analytical psychology contribute to our fundamental problem, which is the mystery of artistic creation? All that we have said so far has to do only with the psychological phenomenology of art.

Since nobody can penetrate to the heart of nature, you will not expect psychology to do the impossible and offer a valid explanation of the secret of creativity. Like every other science, psychology has only a modest contribution to make towards a deeper understanding of the phenomena of life, and is no nearer than its sister sciences to absolute knowledge.

We have talked so much about the meaning of works of art that one can hardly suppress a doubt as to whether art really "means" anything at all. Perhaps art has no "meaning," at least not as we understand meaning. Perhaps it is like nature, which simply *is* and "means" nothing beyond that. Is "meaning" necessarily more than mere interpretation—an interpretation secreted into something by an intellect hungry for meaning? Art, it has been said, is beauty, and "a thing of beauty is a joy for ever." It needs no meaning, for meaning has nothing to do with art. Within the sphere of art, I must accept the truth of this statement. But when I speak of the relation of psychology to art we are outside its sphere, and it is impossible for us not to speculate. We must interpret, we must find meanings in things, otherwise we would be quite unable to think about them. We have to break down life and events, which are self-contained processes, into meanings, images, concepts, well knowing that in doing so we are getting further away from the living mystery. As long as we ourselves are caught up in the process of creation, we neither see nor understand; indeed we ought not to understand, for nothing is more injurous to immediate experience than cognition. But for the purpose of cognitive understanding we must detach ourselves from the creative process and look at it from the outside; only then does it become an image that expresses what we are bound to call "meaning." What was a mere phenomenon before becomes something that in association with other phenomena has meaning, that has a definite role to play, serves certain ends, and exerts meaningful effects. And when we have seen all this we get the feeling of having understood and explained something. In this way we meet the demands of science.

When, a little earlier, we spoke of a work of art as a tree growing out of the nourishing soil, we might equally well have compared it to a child growing in the womb. But as all comparisons are lame, let us stick to the more precise terminology of science. You will remember that I described the nascent work in the psyche of the artist as an autonomous complex. By this we mean a psychic formation that remains subliminal until its energy-charge is sufficient to carry it over the threshold into consciousness. Its association with consciousness does not mean that it is assimilated, only that it is perceived; but it is not subject to conscious control, and can be neither inhibited nor voluntarily reproduced. Therein lies the autonomy of the complex: it appears and disappears in accordance with its own inherent tendencies, independently of the conscious will. The creative complex shares this peculiarity with every other autonomous complex. In this respect it offers an analogy with pathological processes, since these too are characterized by the presence of autonomous complexes, particularly in the case of mental disturbances. The divine frenzy of the artist comes perilously close to a pathological state, though the two things are not identical. The *tertium comparationis*[1] is the autonomous complex. But the presence of autonomous complexes is not in itself pathological, since normal people, too, fall temporarily or permanently under their domination. . . .

But in what does an autonomous *creative* complex consist? Of this we can know next to nothing so long as the artist's work affords us no insight into its foundations. The work presents us with a finished picture, and this picture is amenable to analysis only to the extent that we can recognize it as a symbol. But if we are unable to discover any symbolic value in it, we have merely established that, so far as we are concerned, it means no more than what it says, or to put it another way, that it *is* no more than what it *seems* to be. I use the word "seems" because our own bias may prevent a deeper appreciation of it. At any rate we can find no incentive and no starting-point for an analysis. But in the case of a symbolic work we should remember the dictum of Gerhard Hauptmann: "Poetry evokes out of words the resonance of the primordial word." The question we should ask, therefore, is: "What primordial image lies behind the imagery of art?"

This question needs a little elucidation. I am assuming that the work of art we propose to analyse, as well as being symbolic, has its source not in the *personal unconscious* of the poet, but in a sphere of unconscious mythology whose primordial images are the common heritage of mankind. I have called this sphere the *collective unconscious,* to distinguish it from the personal unconscious. The latter I regard as the sum total of all those psychic processes and contents which are capable of becoming conscious and often do, but are then suppressed because of their incompatibility and kept subliminal. Art receives tributaries from this sphere too, but muddy ones; and their predominance, far from making a work of art a symbol, merely turns it into a symptom. We can leave this kind of art without injury and without regret to the purgative methods employed by Freud.

In contrast to the personal unconscious, which is a relatively thin layer immediately below the threshold of consciousness, the collective unconscious shows no tendency to become conscious under normal conditions, nor can it be brought back to recollection by any analytical technique, since it was never repressed or forgotten. The collective unconscious is not to be thought of as a self-subsistent entity; it is no more than a potentiality handed down

---

[1] The third thing that can be compared (the first two are divine frenzy and a pathological state).

to us from primordial times in the specific form of mnemonic images or in-herited in the anatomical structure of the brain. There are no inborn ideas, but there are inborn possibilities of ideas that set bounds to even the boldest fantasy and keep our fantasy activity within certain categories: *a priori* ideas, as it were, the existence of which cannot be ascertained except from their effects. They appear only in the shaped material of art as the regulative principles that shape it; that is to say, only by inferences drawn from the finished work can we reconstruct the age-old original of the primordial image.

The primordial image, or archetype, is a figure—be it a daemon, a human being, or a process—that constantly recurs in the course of history and ap-pears wherever creative fantasy is freely expressed. Essentially, therefore, it is a mythological figure. When we examine these images more closely, we find that they give form to countless typical experiences of our ancestors. They are, so to speak, the psychic residua of innumerable experiences of the same type. They present a picture of psychic life in the average, divided up and pro-jected into the manifold figures of the mythological pantheon. But the mythological figures are themselves products of creative fantasy and still have to be translated into conceptual language. Only the beginnings of such a language exist, but once the necessary concepts are created they could give us an abstract, scientific understanding of the unconscious processes that lie at the roots of the primordial images. In each of these images there is a little piece of human psychology and human fate, a remnant of the joys and sorrows that have been repeated countless times in our ancestral history, and on the average follow ever the same course. It is like a deeply graven river-bed in the psyche, in which the waters of life, instead of flowing along as before in a broad but shallow stream, suddenly swell into a mighty river. This happens whenever that particular set of circumstances is encountered which over long periods of time has helped to lay down the primordial image.

The moment when this mythological situation reappears is always char-acterized by a peculiar emotional intensity; it is as though chords in us were struck that had never resounded before, or as though forces whose existence we never suspected were unloosed. What makes the struggle for adaptation so laborious is the fact that we have constantly to be dealing with individual and atypical situations. So it is not surprising that when an archetypal situa-tion occurs we suddenly feel an extraordinary sense of release, as though transported, or caught up by an overwhelming power. At such moments we are no longer individuals, but the race; the voice of all mankind resounds in us. The individual man cannot use his powers to the full unless he is aided by one of those collective representations we call ideals, which releases all the hidden forces of instinct that are inaccessible to his conscious will. The most effective ideals are always fairly obvious variants of an archetype, as is evident from the fact that they lend themselves to allegory. The ideal of the "mother country," for instance, is an obvious allegory of the mother, as is the "fatherland" of the father. Its power to stir us does not derive from the allegory, but from the symbolical value of our native land. The archetype here is the *participation mystique* of primitive man with the soil on which he dwells, and which contains the spirits of his ancestors.

The impact of an archetype, whether it takes the form of immediate experience or is expressed through the spoken word, stirs us because it summons up a voice that is stronger than our own. Whoever speaks in primordial images speaks with a thousand voices; he enthrals and overpowers, while at the same time he lifts the idea he is seeking to express out of the occasional and the transitory into the realm of the ever-enduring. He transmutes our personal destiny into the destiny of mankind, and evokes in us all those beneficent forces that ever and anon have enabled humanity to find a refuge from every peril and to outlive the longest night.

That is the secret of great art, and of its effect upon us. The creative process, so far as we are able to follow it at all, consists in the unconscious activation of an archetypal image, and in elaborating and shaping this image into the finished work. By giving it shape, the artist translates it into the language of the present, and so makes it possible for us to find our way back to the deepest springs of life. Therein lies the social significance of art: it is constantly at work educating the spirit of the age, conjuring up the forms in which the age is most lacking. The unsatisfied yearning of the artist reaches back to the primordial image in the unconscious which is best fitted to compensate the inadequacy and one-sidedness of the present. The artist seizes on this image, and in raising it from deepest unconsciousness he brings it into relation with conscious values, thereby transforming it until it can be accepted by the minds of his contemporaries according to their powers.

Bertolt Brecht 1898–1956

The Modern Theatre
Is the Epic Theatre 1930

The modern theatre is the epic theatre. The following table shows certain changes of emphasis as between the dramatic and the epic theatre.[1]

DRAMATIC THEATRE	EPIC THEATRE
plot	narrative
implicates the spectator in a stage situation	turns the spectator into an observer, but
wears down his capacity for action	arouses his capacity for action
provides him with sensations	forces him to take decisions
experience	picture of the world
the spectator is involved in something	he is made to face something
suggestion	argument
instinctive feelings are preserved	brought to the point of recognition
the spectator is in the thick of it, shares the experience	the spectator stands outside, studies
the human being is taken for granted	the human being is the object of the inquiry
he is unalterable	he is alterable and able to alter
eyes on the finish	eyes on the course
one scene makes another	each scene for itself
growth	montage
linear development	in curves
evolutionary determinism	jumps
man as a fixed point	man as a process
thought determines being	social being determines thought
feeling	reason

When the epic theatre's methods begin to penetrate the opera the first result is a radical *separation of the elements*. The great struggle for supremacy between words, music and production—which always brings up the question "which is the pretext for what?": is the music the pretext for the events on the stage, or are these the pretext for the music? etc.—can simply be by-passed

Selection. From *Brecht on Theatre*, translated by John Willett. Copyright © 1957, 1963, and 1964 by Suhrkamp Verlag, Frankfurt am Main. This translation and notes © 1964 by John Willett. Reprinted by permission of Hill and Wang, Inc.

[1] This table does not show absolute antitheses but mere shifts of accent. In a communication of fact, for instance, we may choose whether to stress the element of emotional suggestion or that of plain rational argument [Brecht's note].

by radically separating the elements. So long as the expression "Gesamtkunst-werk" (or "integrated work of art") means that the integration is a muddle, so long as the arts are supposed to be "fused" together, the various elements will all be equally degraded, and each will act as a mere "feed" to the rest. The process of fusion extends to the spectator, who gets thrown into the melting pot too and becomes a passive (suffering) part of the total work of art. Witchcraft of this sort must of course be fought against. Whatever is intended to produce hypnosis, is likely to induce sordid intoxication, or creates fog, has got to be given up.

Words, music and setting must become more independent of one another.

(a) Music

For the music, the change of emphasis proved to be as follows:

DRAMATIC OPERA	EPIC OPERA
The music dishes up	The music communicates
music which heightens the text	music which sets forth the text
music which proclaims the text	music which takes the text for granted
music which illustrates	which takes up a position
music which paints the psycho-logical situation	which gives the attitude

Music plays the chief part in our thesis.[2]

(b) Text

We had to make something straightforward and instructive of our fun, if it was not to be irrational and nothing more. The form employed was that of the moral tableau. The tableau is performed by the characters in the play. The text had to be neither moralizing nor sentimental, but to put morals and sentimentality on view. Equally important was the spoken word and the written word (of the titles). Reading seems to encourage the audience to adopt the most natural attitude towards the work.

(c) Setting

Showing independent works of art as part of a theatrical performance is a new departure. Neher's[3] projections adopt an attitude towards the events

---

[2] The large number of craftsmen in the average opera orchestra allows of nothing but associative music (one barrage of sound breeding another); and so the orchestra apparatus needs to be cut down to thirty specialists or less. The singer becomes a reporter, whose private feelings must remain a private affair [Brecht's note].

[3] Casper Neher (1897–1962), scene designer.

on the stage; as when the real glutton sits in front of the glutton whom Neher has drawn. In the same way the stage unreels the events that are fixed on the screen. These projections of Neher's are quite as much an independent component of the opera as are Weill's[4] music and the text. They provide its visual aids.

[4] Kurt Weill (1900–1950), composer.

Theatre for Pleasure or Theatre for Instruction *c. 1936*

Many people imagine that the term "epic theatre" is self-contradictory, as the epic and dramatic ways of narrating a story are held, following Aristotle, to be basically distinct. The difference between the two forms was never thought simply to lie in the fact that the one is performed by living beings while the other operates via the written word; epic works such as those of Homer and the medieval singers were at the same time theatrical performances, while dramas like Goethe's *Faust* and Byron's *Manfred* are agreed to have been more effective as books. Thus even by Aristotle's definition the difference between the dramatic and epic forms was attributed to their different methods of construction, whose laws were dealt with by two different branches of esthetics. The method of construction depended on the different way of presenting the work to the public, sometimes via the stage, sometimes through a book; and independently of that there was the "dramatic element" in epic works and the "epic element" in dramatic. The bourgeois novel in the last century developed much that was "dramatic," by which was meant the strong centralization of the story, a momentum that drew the separate parts into a common relationship. A particular passion of utterance, a certain emphasis on the clash of forces are hallmarks of the "dramatic." The epic writer Döblin[1] provided an excellent criterion when he said that with an

Selection. From *Brecht on Theatre*, translated by John Willett. Copyright © 1957, 1963, and 1964 by Suhrkamp Verlag, Frankfurt am Main. This translation and notes © 1964 by John Willett. Reprinted by permission of Hill and Wang, Inc.

[1] Alfred Döblin (1878–1957).

epic work, as opposed to a dramatic, one can as it were take a pair of scissors and cut it into individual pieces, which remain fully capable of life.

This is no place to explain how the opposition of epic and dramatic lost its rigidity after having long been held to be irreconcilable. Let us just point out that the technical advances alone were enough to permit the stage to incorporate an element of narrative in its dramatic productions. The possibility of projections, the greater adaptability of the stage due to mechanization, the film, all completed the theatre's equipment, and did so at a point where the most important transactions between people could no longer be shown simply by personifying the motive forces or subjecting the characters to invisible metaphysical powers.

To make these transactions intelligible the environment in which the people lived had to be brought to bear in a big and "significant" way.

This environment had of course been shown in the existing drama, but only as seen from the central figure's point of view, and not as an independent element. It was defined by the hero's reactions to it. It was seen as a storm can be seen when one sees the ships on a sheet of water unfolding their sails, and the sails filling out. In the epic theatre it was to appear standing on its own.

The stage began to tell a story. The narrator was no longer missing, along with the fourth wall. Not only did the background adopt an attitude to the events on the stage—by big screens recalling other simultaneous events elsewhere, by projecting documents which confirmed or contradicted what the characters said, by concrete and intelligible figures to accompany abstract conversations, by figures and sentences to support mimed transactions whose sense was unclear—but the actors too refrained from going over wholly into their role, remaining detached from the character they were playing and clearly inviting criticism of him.

The spectator was no longer in any way allowed to submit to an experience uncritically (and without practical consequences) by means of simple empathy with the characters in a play. The production took the subject-matter and the incidents shown and put them through a process of alienation: the alienation that is necessary to all understanding. When something seems "the most obvious thing in the world" it means that any attempt to understand the world has been given up.

What is "natural" must have the force of what is startling. This is the only way to expose the laws of cause and effect. People's activity must simultaneously be so and be capable of being different.

It was all a great change.

The dramatic theatre's spectator says: Yes, I have felt like that too—Just like me—It's only natural—It'll never change—The sufferings of this man appal me, because they are inescapable—That's great art; it all seems the most obvious thing in the world—I weep when they weep, I laugh when they laugh.

The epic theatre's spectator says: I'd never have thought it—That's not the way—That's extraordinary, hardly believable—It's got to stop—The sufferings of this man appal me, because they are unnecessary—That's great art: nothing obvious in it—I laugh when they weep, I weep when they laugh.

The Instructive Theatre

The stage began to be instructive.

Oil, inflation, war, social struggles, the family, religion, wheat, the meat market, all became subjects for theatrical representation. Choruses enlightened the spectator about facts unknown to him. Films showed a montage of events from all over the world. Projections added statistical material. And as the "background" came to the front of the stage so people's activity was subjected to criticism. Right and wrong courses of action were shown. People were shown who knew what they were doing, and others who did not. The theatre became an affair for philosophers, but only for such philosophers as wished not just to explain the world but also to change it. So we had philosophy, and we had instruction. And where was the amusement in all that? Were they sending us back to school, teaching us to read and write? Were we supposed to pass exams, work for diplomas?

Generally there is felt to be a very sharp distinction between learning and amusing oneself. The first may be useful, but only the second is pleasant. So we have to defend the epic theatre against the suspicion that it is a highly disagreeable, humourless, indeed strenuous affair.

Well: all that can be said is that the contrast between learning and amusing oneself is not laid down by divine rule; it is not one that has always been and must continue to be.

Undoubtedly there is much that is tedious about the kind of learning familiar to us from school, from our professional training, etc. But it must be remembered under what conditions and to what end that takes place.

It is really a commercial transaction. Knowledge is just a commodity. It is acquired in order to be resold. All those who have grown out of going to school have to do their learning virtually in secret, for anyone who admits that he still has something to learn devalues himself as a man whose knowledge is inadequate. Moreover the usefulness of learning is very much limited by factors outside the learner's control. There is unemployment, for instance, against which no knowledge can protect one. There is the division of labour, which makes generalized knowledge unnecessary and impossible. Learning is often among the concerns of those whom no amount of concern will get any forwarder. There is not much knowledge that leads to power, but plenty of knowledge to which only power can lead.

Learning has a very different function for different social strata. There are strata who cannot imagine any improvement in conditions: they find the conditions good enough for them. Whatever happens to oil they will benefit from it. And: they feel the years beginning to tell. There can't be all that many years more. What is the point of learning a lot now? They have said their final word: a grunt. But there are also strata "waiting their turn" who are discontented with conditions, have a vast interest in the practical side of learning, want at all costs to find out where they stand, and know that they are lost without learning; these are the best and keenest learners. Similar differences apply to countries and peoples. Thus the pleasure of learning depends on all sorts of things; but none the less there is such a thing as pleasurable learning, cheerful and militant learning.

If there were not such amusement to be had from learning the theatre's whole structure would unfit it for teaching.

Theatre remains theatre even when it is instructive theatre, and in so far as it is good theatre it will amuse.

Theatre and Knowledge

But what has knowledge got to do with art? We know that knowledge can be amusing, but not everything that is amusing belongs in the theatre.

I have often been told, when pointing out the invaluable services that modern knowledge and science, if properly applied, can perform for art and specially for the theatre, that art and knowledge are two estimable but wholly distinct fields of human activity. This is a fearful truism, of course, and it is as well to agree quickly that, like most truisms, it is perfectly true. Art and science work in quite different ways: agreed. But, bad as it may sound, I have to admit that I cannot get along as an artist without the use of one or two sciences. This may well arouse serious doubts as to my artistic capacities. People are used to seeing poets as unique and slightly unnatural beings who reveal with a truly godlike assurance things that other people can only recognize after much sweat and toil. It is naturally distasteful to have to admit that one does not belong to this select band. All the same, it must be admitted. It must at the same time be made clear that the scientific occupations just confessed to are not pardonable side interests, pursued on days off after a good week's work. We all know how Goethe was interested in natural history, Schiller in history: as a kind of hobby, it is charitable to assume. I have no wish promptly to accuse these two of having needed these sciences for their poetic activity; I am not trying to shelter behind them; but I must say that I do need the sciences. I have to admit, however, that I look askance at all sorts of people who I know do not operate on the level of scientific understanding: that is to say, who sing as the birds sing, or as people imagine the birds to sing. I don't mean by that I would reject a charming poem about the taste of fried fish or the delights of a boating party just because the writer had not studied gastronomy or navigation. But in my view the great and complicated things that go on in the world cannot be adequately recognized by people who do not use every possible aid to understanding.

Let us suppose that great passions or great events have to be shown which influence the fate of nations. The lust for power is nowadays held to be such a passion. Given that a poet "feels" this lust and wants to have someone strive for power, how is he to show the exceedingly complicated machinery within which the struggle for power nowadays takes place? If his hero is a politician, how do politics work? If he is a business man, how does business work? And yet there are writers who find business and politics nothing like so passionately interesting as the individual's lust for power. How are they to acquire the necessary knowledge? They are scarcely likely to learn enough by going round and keeping their eyes open, though even then it is more than they would get by just rolling their eyes in an exalted frenzy. The foundation of a paper like the *Völkischer Beobachter*[2] or a business like Standard Oil is a pretty complicated affair, and such things cannot be conveyed just like that. One important field for the playwright is psychology. It is taken for granted that a poet, if not an ordinary man, must be able without further instruction to discover the motives that lead a man to commit murder; he must be able to give a picture of a murderer's mental state "from within himself." It is taken for granted that one only has to look inside oneself in such a case; and then there's always one's imagination. . . . There are various reasons why I can no longer surrender to this agreeable hope of getting a result quite so simply. I can no longer find in myself all those motives which the press or scientific reports show to have been observed in people. Like the average judge when pronouncing sentence, I cannot without further ado conjure up an adequate picture of a murderer's mental state. Modern psychology, from psychoanalysis to behaviourism, acquaints me with facts that lead me to judge the case quite differently, especially if I bear in mind the findings of sociology and do not overlook economics and history. You will say: but that's getting complicated. I have to answer that it *is* complicated. Even if you let yourself be convinced, and agree with me that a large slice of literature is exceedingly primitive, you may still ask with profound concern: won't an evening in such a theatre be a most alarming affair? The answer to that is: no.

Whatever knowledge is embodied in a piece of poetic writing has to be wholly transmuted into poetry. Its utilization fulfils the very pleasure that the poetic element provokes. If it does not at the same time fulfill that which is fulfilled by the scientific element, none the less in an age of great discoveries and inventions one must have a certain inclination to penetrate deeper into things—a desire to make the world controllable—if one is to be sure of enjoying its poetry.

---

[2] *The People's Observer*, a Nazi newspaper.

Is the Epic Theatre Some Kind of "Moral Institution"?

According to Friedrich Schiller the theatre is supposed to be a moral institution. In making this demand it hardly occurred to Schiller that by moralizing from the stage he might drive the audience out of the theatre. Audiences had no objection to moralizing in his day. It was only later that Friedrich Nietzsche attacked him by blowing a moral trumpet. To Nietzsche any concern with morality was a depressing affair; to Schiller it seemed thoroughly enjoyable. He knew of nothing that could give greater amusement and satisfaction than the propagation of ideas. The bourgeoisie was setting about forming the ideas of the nation.

Putting one's house in order, patting oneself on the back, submitting one's account, is something highly agreeable. But describing the collapse of one's house, having pains in the back, paying one's account, is indeed a depressing affair, and that was how Friedrich Nietzsche saw things a century later. He was poorly disposed towards morality, and thus towards the previous Friedrich too.

The epic theatre was likewise often objected to as moralizing too much. Yet in the epic theatre moral arguments only took second place. Its aim was less to moralize than to observe. That is to say it observed, and then the thick end of the wedge followed: the story's moral. Of course we cannot pretend that we started our observations out of a pure passion for observing and without any more practical motive, only to be completely staggered by their results. Undoubtedly there were some painful discrepancies in our environment, circumstances that were barely tolerable, and this not merely on account of moral considerations. It is not only moral considerations that make hunger, cold and oppression hard to bear. Similarly the object of our inquiries was not just to arouse moral objections to such circumstances (even though they could easily be felt—though not by all the audience alike; such objections were seldom for instance felt by those who profited by the circumstances in question) but to discover means for their elimination. We were not in fact speaking in the name of morality but in that of the victims. These truly are two distinct matters, for the victims are often told that they ought to be contented with their lot, for moral reasons. Moralists of this sort see man as existing for morality, not morality for man. At least it should be possible to gather from the above to what degree and in what sense the epic theatre is a moral institution.

Friedrich Duerrenmatt 1921–

Problems of the Theatre 1954

Schiller wrote as he did because the world in which he lived could still be mirrored in the world his writing created, a world he could build as a historian. But just barely. For was not Napoleon perhaps the last hero in the old sense? The world today as it appears to us could hardly be encompassed in the form of the historical drama as Schiller wrote it, for the reason alone that we no longer have any tragic heroes, but only vast tragedies staged by world butchers and produced by slaughtering machines. Hitler and Stalin can not be made into Wallensteins.[1] Their power is so enormous that they themselves are no more than incidental, corporeal and easily replaceable expressions of this power; and the misfortune associated with the former and to a considerable extent also with the latter is too vast, too complex, too horrible, too mechanical and usually simply too devoid of all sense. Wallenstein's power can still be envisioned; power as we know it today can only be seen in its smallest part for, like an iceberg, the largest part is submerged in anonymity and abstraction. Schiller's drama presupposes a world that the eye can take in, that takes for granted genuine actions of state, just as Greek tragedy did. For only what the eye can take in can be made visible in art. The state today, however, can not be envisioned for it is anonymous and bureaucratic; and not only in Moscow and Washington, but also in Berne. Actions of state today have become *post hoc* satyric dramas which follow the tragedies executed in secret earlier. True representatives of our world are missing; the tragic heroes are nameless. Any small-time crook, petty government official or policeman better represents our world than a senator or president. Today art can only embrace the victims, if it can reach men at all; it can no longer come close to the mighty. Creon's secretaries close Antigone's case. The state has lost its physical reality, and just as physics can now only cope with the world in mathematical formulas, so the state can only be expressed in statistics. Power today becomes visible, material only when it explodes as in the atom bomb, in this marvelous mushroom which rises and spreads immaculate as the sun and in which mass murder and beauty have become one. The atom bomb can not be reproduced artistically since it is mass-produced. In its face all of man's art that would recreate it must fail,

Selection, translated by Gerhard Nellhaus. First published in *Tulane Drama Review*, Volume III, Number 1 (T 1), October 1958, © 1958 by *Tulane Drama Review*. Reprinted by permission. All rights reserved.

[1] A reference to Schiller's *Wallenstein* trilogy: *Wallenstein's Camp* (1798), *The Piccolomini* (1799), and *Wallenstein's Death* (1799).

since it is itself a creation of man. Two mirrors which reflect one another remain empty.

But the task of art, insofar as art can have a task at all, and hence also the task of drama today, is to create something concrete, something that has form. This can be accomplished best by comedy. Tragedy, the strictest genre in art, presupposes a formed world. Comedy—insofar as it is not just satire of a particular society as in Molière—supposes an unformed world, a world being made and turned upside down, a world about to fold like ours. Tragedy overcomes distance; it can make myths originating in times immemorial seem like the present to the Athenians. But comedy creates distance; the attempt of the Athenians to gain a foothold in Sicily is translated by comedy into the birds undertaking to create their own empire before which the gods and men will have to capitulate. How comedy works can be seen in the most primitive kind of joke, in the dirty story, which, though it is of very dubious value, I bring up only because it is the best illustration of what I mean by creating distance. The subject of the dirty story is the purely sexual, which because it is purely sexual, is formless and without objective distance. To give form the purely sexual is transmuted, as I have already mentioned, into the dirty joke. Therefore this type of joke is a kind of original comedy, a transposition of the sexual onto the plain of the comical. In this way it is possible today in a society dominated by John Doe, to talk in an accepted way about the purely sexual. In the dirty story it becomes clear that the comical exists in forming what is formless, in creating order out of chaos.

The means by which comedy creates distance is the conceit. Tragedy is without conceit. Hence there are few tragedies whose subjects were invented. By this I do not mean to imply that the ancient tragedians lacked inventive ideas of the sort that are written today, but the marvel of their art was that they had no need of these inventions, of conceits. That makes all the difference. Aristophanes, on the other hand, lives by conceits. The stuff of his plays are not myths but inventions, which take place not in the past but the present. They drop into their world like bomb shells which, by throwing up huge craters of dirt, change the present into the comic and thus scatter the dirt for everyone to see. This, of course, does not mean that drama today can only be comical. Tragedy and comedy are but formal concepts, dramatic attitudes, figments of the esthetic imagination which can embrace one and the same thing. Only the conditions under which each is created are different, and these conditions have their basis only in small part in art.

Tragedy presupposes guilt, despair, moderation, lucidity, vision, a sense of responsibility. In the Punch-and-Judy show of our century, in this back-sliding of the white race, there are no more guilty and also, no responsible men. It is always, "We couldn't help it" and "We didn't really want that to happen." And indeed, things happen without anyone in particular being responsible for them. Everything is dragged along and everyone gets caught somewhere in the sweep of events. We are all collectively guilty, collectively bogged down in the sins of our fathers and of our forefathers. We are the offspring of children. That is our misfortune, but not our guilt: guilt can exist only as a personal achievement, as a religious deed. Comedy alone is suitable for us. Our world has led to the grotesque as well as to the atom bomb, and so it is a world like that of Hieronymus Bosch[2] whose apocalyptic paintings are also grotesque. But the grotesque is only a way of expressing in a tangible manner, of making us perceive physically the paradoxical, the form of the unformed, the face of a world without face; and just as in our thinking today we seem to be unable to do without the concept of the paradox, so also in art, and in our world which at times seems still to exist only because the atom bomb exists: out of fear of the bomb.

But the tragic is still possible even if pure tragedy is not. We can achieve the tragic out of comedy. We can bring it forth as a frightening moment, as an abyss that opens suddenly; indeed many of Shakespeare's tragedies are already really comedies out of which the tragic arises.

After all this the conclusion might easily be drawn that comedy is the expression of despair, but this conclusion is not inevitable. To be sure, whoever realizes the senselessness, the hopelessness of this world might well despair, but this despair is not a result of this world. Rather it is an answer given by an individual to this world; another answer would be not to despair, would be an individual's decision to endure this world in which we live like Gulliver among the giants. He also achieves distance, he also steps back a pace or two who takes measure of his opponent, who prepares himself to fight his opponent or to escape him. It is still possible to show man as a courageous being.

In truth this is a principle concern of mine. The blind man, Romulus, Uebelohe, Akki,[3] are all men of courage. The lost world order is restored within them; the universal escapes my grasp. I refuse to find the universal in a doctrine. The universal for me is chaos. The world (hence the stage which represents this world) is for me something monstrous, a riddle of misfortunes which must be accepted but before which one must not capitulate. The world is far bigger than any man, and perforce threatens him constantly. If one could but stand outside the world, it would no longer be threatening. But I have neither the right nor the ability to be an outsider to this world. To find solace in poetry can also be all too cheap; it is more honest to retain one's human point of view. Brecht's thesis, that the world is an accident, which he developed in his *Street Scene* where he shows how this accident

---

[2] (*c.* 1450–1616), Dutch painter. His real name was Van Aeken; Bosch derives from the name of his birthplace, 's-Hertogenbosch (Bois-le-Duc).

[3] Characters in Duerrenmatt's plays, respectively: *The Blind Man* (1948), *Romulus the Great* (1949), *The Marriage of Mr. Mississippi* (1952), *An Angel Comes to Babylon* (1953).

happened, may yield—as it in fact did—some magnificent theatre; but he did it by concealing most of the evidence! Brecht's thinking is inexorable, because inexorably there are many things he will not think about.

And lastly it is through the conceit, through comedy that the anonymous audience becomes possible as an audience, becomes a reality to be counted on, and also, one to be taken into account. The conceit easily transforms the crowd of theatre-goers into a mass which can be attacked, deceived, outsmarted into listening to things it would otherwise not so readily listen to. Comedy is a mousetrap in which the public is easily caught and in which it will get caught over and over again. Tragedy, on the other hand, predicated a true community, a kind of community whose existence in our day is but an embarrassing fiction. Nothing is more ludicrous, for instance, than to sit and watch the mystery plays of the Anthroposophists when one is not a participant.

Nineteenth- and Twentieth-Century United States and Canada

Walt Whitman, who from 1846 to 1848 wrote theatre reviews for *The Brooklyn Eagle*, deplored the state of the American theatre. Denouncing American writing as "copious dribble," he demanded that America rid itself of old-world art and old-world models, Shakespeare included, for he considered these caste-derived, castle-reflecting works to be "poisonous to the idea of the pride and dignity of the common people, the life-blood of democracy." Instead, he messianically called for a native breed of American artist to give expression to the national scope and spirit. Although Eric Bentley, writing a century later, opposes "patrioteering" and "democrateering," his hostility toward money changers in the temple of dramatic art links him with Whitman. Opposed to the commercial theatre not only for what it produces, but also because it discourages potentially great writers from composing plays, Bentley might have been the author of Whitman's observation that the drama, as performed in our theatres, "deserves to be treated with the same gravity, and on a par with the questions of ornamental confectionary at public dinners, or the arrangement of curtains and hangings in a ball-room—nor more, nor less."

Whereas Whitman looked forward optimistically, Krutch looks back regretfully. Analyzing the loss of values and beliefs that characterize *The Modern Temper* (of which his essay on tragedy is a chapter), Krutch discusses science's revelation that our fundamental beliefs are delusions: that absolute right and wrong exist, that love is more than a biological urge, that man has free will, that he can reason rather than rationalize, and that he has inherent dignity and nobility. The notion other ages held about the greatness of man we see as fallacious, but because of that fallacy playwrights were able to create tragedy. Enlightened, we can no longer do so. Our plays deal with smaller people and emotions not because we have become interested in the commonplace but because that is how we have come to regard man's soul and emotions. To Arthur Miller, however, tragedy is still possible, and he sees the common man not as commonplace but as a worthy hero of tragedy.

Miller explores the nature of modern tragedy; two other American playwrights included here treat different aspects of the drama. Building upon Freytag, Brunetière, and Archer, Lawson sees drama as essentially social conflict. Analyzing components of dramatic action—such as the tension between social forces and the individual will, and the nature of conflict and crisis—he demonstrates the relationship between dramatic action and theme as both are resolved in a climax that realizes the theme in terms of an event. A broader field preoccupies Wilder, who examines not the structure of drama but its fundamental conditions that distinguish it from other arts: the collaborative nature of theatre, its addressing itself to a group mind, its basis in pretense, and its action in a perpetual present.

Still broader is the concern of the influential Canadian critic Northrop Frye, who finds conventional generic classifications unsatisfactory because, he believes, such designations as comic and tragic transcend the drama. Employing the archetypal and mythic theories of such writers as Jung and Murray, Frye sets forth central patterns of tragedy and comedy; and he relates the solar cycle of the day, the seasonal cyle of the year, the cycle of human life, mythic subjects and characters, and four archetypal genres that at their peripheries overlap: romance, comedy, satire, and tragedy. Particularly fruitful is his analysis of the mythic structure of comedy.

Walt Whitman 1819–1892

Democratic Vistas 1870

. . . I say that, far deeper than these, what finally and only is to make of our western world a nationality superior to any hither known, and out-topping the past, must be vigorous, yet unsuspected Literatures, perfect personalities and sociologies, original, transcendental, and expressing (what, in highest sense, are not yet express'd at all) democracy and the modern. With these, and out of these, I promulge new races of Teachers, and of perfect Women, indispensable to endow the birth-stock of a New World. For feudalism, caste, the ecclesiastic traditions, though palpably retreating from political institutions, still hold essentially, by their spirit, even in this country, entire possession of the more important fields, indeed the very subsoil, of education, and of social standards and literature.

I say that democracy can never prove itself beyond cavil, until it founds and luxuriantly grows its own forms of art, poems, schools, theology, dis-placing all that exists, or that has been produced anywhere in the past, under opposite influences. It is curious to me that while so many voices, pens, minds, in the press, lecture-rooms, in our Congress, etc., are dis-cussing intellectual topics, pecuniary dangers, legislative problems, the suffrage, tariff and labor questions, and the various business and benevolent needs of America, with propositions, remedies, often worth deep attention, there is one need, a hiatus the profoundest, that no eye seems to perceive, no voice to state. Our fundamental want today in the United States, with closest, amplest reference to present conditions, and to the future, is of a class, and the clear idea of a class, of native authors, literatuses, far different, far higher in grade than any yet known, sacerdotal, modern, fit to cope with our occasions, lands, permeating the whole mass of American mentality, taste, belief, breathing into it a new breath of life, giving it decision, affecting politics far more than the popular superficial suffrage, with results inside and underneath the elections of Presidents or Congresses—radiating, begetting appropriate teachers, schools, manners, and, as its grandest result, accom-plishing (what neither the schools nor the churches and their clergy have hitherto accomplish'd, and without which this nation will no more stand, permanently, soundly, than a house will stand without a substratum) a religious and moral character beneath the political and productive and intellectual bases of the States. For know you not, dear, earnest reader, that the people of our land may all read and write, and may all possess the right

Selections. From Walt Whitman, *Complete Prose Works*. Boston: Small, Maynard & Co., 1898.

to vote—and yet the main things may be entirely lacking?—(and this to suggest them).

View'd, today, from a point of view sufficiently over-arching, the problem of humanity all over the civilized world is social and religious, and is to be finally met and treated by literature. The priest departs, the divine literatus comes. Never was anything more wanted than, today, and here in the States, the poet of the modern is wanted, or the great literatus of the modern. At all times, perhaps, the central point in any nation, and that whence it is itself really sway'd the most, and whence it sways others, is its national literature, especially its archetypal poems. Above all previous lands, a great original literature is surely to become the justification and reliance (in some respects the sole reliance) of American democracy. . . .

I say we had best look our times and lands searchingly in the face, like a physician diagnosing some deep disease. Never was there, perhaps, more hollowness at heart than at present, and here in the United States. Genuine belief seems to have left us. The underlying principles of the States are not honestly believ'd in (for all this hectic glow, and these melodramatic scream-ings) nor is humanity itself believ'd in. What penetrating eye does not every-where see through the mask? The spectacle is appaling. We live in an at-mosphere of hypocrisy throughout. The men believe not in the women, nor the women in the men. A scornful superciliousness rules in literature. The aim of all the *littérateurs* is to find something to make fun of. A lot of churches, sects, etc., the most dismal phantasms I know, usurp the name of religion. Conversation is a mass of badinage. From deceit in the spirit, the mother of all false deeds, the offspring is already incalculable. An acute and candid person, in the revenue department in Washington, who is led by the course of his employment to regularly visit the cities, north, south and west, to investigate frauds, has talk'd much with me about his discoveries. The depravity of the business classes of our country is not less than has been supposed, but infinitely greater. The official services of America, national, state, and municipal, in all their branches and departments, except the judiciary, are saturated in corruption, bribery, falsehood, maladministration; and the judiciary is tainted. The great cities reek with respectable as much as nonrespectable robbery and scoundrelism. In fashionable life, flippancy, tepid amors, weak infidelism, small aims, or no aims at all, only to kill time. In business (this all-devouring modern word, business) the one sole object is, by any means, pecuniary gain. The magician's serpent in the fable ate up all the other serpents; and money-making is our magician's serpent, remaining today sole master of the field. The best class we show, is but a mob of fash-ionably dress'd speculators and vulgarians. True, indeed, behind this fantastic farce, enacted on the visible stage of society, solid things and stupendous labors are to be discover'd, existing crudely and going on in the background, to advance and tell themselves in time. Yet the truths are none the less terrible. I say that our New World democracy, however, great a success in

uplifting the masses out of their sloughs, in materialistic development, products, and in a certain highly deceptive superficial popular intellectuality, is,
so far, an almost complete failure in its social aspects, and in really grand
religious, moral, literary, and esthetic results. In vain do we march with un-
precedented strides to empire so colossal, outvying the antique, beyond
Alexander's, beyond the proudest sway of Rome. In vain have we annex'd
Texas, California, Alaska, and reach north for Canada and south for Cuba.
It is as if we were somehow being endow'd with a vast and more and more
thoroughly-appointed body, and then left with little or no soul. . . .

As to the political section of Democracy, which introduces and breaks
ground for further and vaster sections, few probably are the minds, even in
these republican States, that fully comprehend the aptness of that phrase,
"THE GOVERNMENT OF THE PEOPLE, BY THE PEOPLE, FOR THE PEOPLE," which
we inherit from the lips of Abraham Lincoln; a formula whose verbal shape
is homely wit, but whose scope includes both the totality and all minutiae of
the lesson.

The People! Like our huge earth itself, which, to ordinary scansion, is full
of vulgar contradictions and offence, man, viewed in the lump, displeases, and
is a constant puzzle and affront to the merely educated classes. The rare,
cosmical, artist-mind, lit with the Infinite, alone confronts his manifold and
oceanic qualities—but taste, intelligence and culture (so-called) have been
against the masses, and remain so. There is plenty of glamour about the
most damnable crimes and hoggish meannesses, special and general, of the
feudal and dynastic world over there, with its *personnel* of lords and queens
and courts, so well-dress'd and so handsome. But the People are ungrammati-
cal, untidy, and their sins gaunt and ill-bred.

Literature, strictly consider'd, has never recognized the People, and, whatever may be said, does not today. Speaking generally, the tendencies of
literature, as hitherto pursued, have been to make mostly critical and querulous men. It seems as if, so far, there were some natural repugnance between
a literary and professional life, and the rude rank spirit of the democracies.
There is, in later literature, a treatment of benevolence, a charity business,
rife enough it is true; but I know nothing more rare, even in this country,
than a fit scientific estimate and reverent appreciation of the People—of their
measureless wealth of latent power and capacity, their vast, artistic contrasts
of lights and shades—with, in America, their entire reliability in emergencies,
and a certain breadth of historic grandeur, of peace or war, far surpassing all
the vaunted samples of book-heroes, or any *haut ton* coteries, in all the
records of the world. . . .

Dominion strong is the body's; dominion stronger is the mind's. What has
fill'd, and fills today our intellect, our fancy, furnishing the standards therein,
is yet foreign. The great poems, Shakspere included, are poisonous to the
idea of the pride and dignity of the common people, the life-blood of democracy. The models of our literature, as we get it from other lands, ultra-marine,

have had their birth in courts, and bask'd and grown in castle sunshine; all smells of princes' favors. Of workers of a certain sort, we have, indeed, plenty, contributing after their kind; many elegant, many learn'd, all complacent. But touch'd by the national test, or tried by the standards of democratic personality, they wither to ashes. I say I have not seen a single writer, artist, lecturer, or what-not, that has confronted the voiceless but ever erect and active, pervading, underlying will and typic aspiration of the land, in a spirit kindred to itself. Do you call those genteel little creatures American poets? Do you term that perpetual, pistareen, paste-pot work, American art, American drama, taste, verse? I think I hear, echoed as from some mountain-top afar in the west, the scornful laugh of the Genius of these States. . . .

America has yet morally and artistically originated nothing. She seems singularly unaware that the models of persons, books, manners, etc., appropriate for former conditions and for European lands, are but exiles and exotics here. No current of her life, as shown on the surfaces of what is authoritatively called her society, accepts or runs into social or esthetic democracy; but all the currents set squarely against it. Never, in the Old World, was thoroughly upholster'd exterior appearance and show, mental and other, built entirely on the idea of caste, and on the sufficiency of mere outside acquisition —never were glibness, verbal intellect, more the test, the emulation—more loftily elevated as head and sample—than they are on the surface of our republican States this day. The writers of a time hint the mottoes of its gods. The word of the modern, say these voices, is the word Culture.

We find ourselves abruptly in close quarters with the enemy. This word Culture, or what it has come to represent, involves, by contrast, our whole theme, and has been, indeed, the spur, urging us to engagement. Certain questions arise. As now taught, accepted and carried out, are not the processes of culture rapidly creating a class of supercilious infidels, who believe in nothing? Shall a man lose himself in countless masses of adjustments, and be so shaped with reference to this, that, and the other, that the simply good and healthy and brave parts of him are reduced and clipp'd away, like the bordering of box in a garden? You can cultivate corn and roses and orchards —but who shall cultivate the mountain peaks, the ocean, and the tumbling gorgeousness of the clouds? Lastly—is the readily given reply that culture only seeks to help, systematize, and put in attitude, the elements of fertility and power, a conclusive reply?

I do not so much object to the name, or word, but I should certainly insist, for the purposes of these States, on a radical change of category, in the distribution of precedence. I should demand a program of culture, drawn out, not for a single class alone, or for the parlors or lecture-rooms, but with an eye to practical life, the west, the working-men, the facts of farms and jack-planes and engineers, and of the broad range of the women also of the middle and working strata, and with reference to the perfect equality of women, and of a grand and powerful motherhood. I should demand of this program or theory a scope generous enough to include the widest human area. It must have for its spinal meaning the formation of a typical personality of character, eligible to the uses of the high average of men—and *not* restricted by conditions ineligible to the masses. The best culture will always be that of the manly and courageous instincts, and loving perceptions, and of self-respect—aiming to form, over this continent, an idiocrasy of universalism, which, true child of America, will bring joy to its mother, returning to her in her own spirit, recruiting myriads of offspring, able, natural, perceptive, tolerant, devout believers in her, America, and with some definite instinct why and for what she has arisen, most vast, most formidable of historic births, and is, now and here, with wonderful step, journeying through Time. . . .

Compared with the past, our modern science soars, and our journals serve —but ideal and even ordinary romantic literature, does not, I think, substantially advance. Behold the prolific brood of the contemporary novel, magazine-tale, theatre-play, etc. The same endless thread of tangled and superlative love-story, inherited, apparently from the Amadises and Palmerins of the 13th, 14th, and 15th centuries over there in Europe. The costumes and associations brought down to date, the seasoning hotter and more varied, the dragons and ogres left out—but the *thing*, I should say, has not advanced—is just as sensational, just as strain'd—remains about the same, nor more, nor less. . . .

Of what is called the drama, or dramatic presentation in the United States, as now put forth at the theatres, I should say it deserves to be treated with the same gravity, and on a par with the questions of ornamental confectionery at public dinners, or the arrangement of curtains and hangings in a ball-room —nor more, nor less. Of the other, I will not insult the reader's intelligence (once really entering into the atmosphere of the Vistas) by supposing it necessary to show, in detail, why the copious dribble, either of our little or well-known rhymesters, does not fulfil, in any respect, the needs and august occasions of this land. America demands a poetry that is bold, modern, and all-surrounding and kosmical, as she is herself. It must in no respect ignore science or the modern, but inspire itself with science and the modern. It must bend its vision toward the future, more than the past. Like America, it must extricate itself from even the greatest models of the past, and, while courteous to them, must have entire faith in itself, and the products of its own democratic spirit only. Like her, it must place in the van, and hold up at all hazards, the banner of the divine pride of man in himself (the radical foundation of the new religion). Long enough have the People been listening to poems in which common humanity, deferential, bends low, humiliated, acknowledging superiors. But America listens to no such poems. Erect, inflated, and fully self-esteeming be the chant; and then America will listen with pleased ears. . . .

In the future of these States must arise poets immenser far, and make great poems of death. The poems of life are great, but there must be the poems of the purports of life, not only in itself, but beyond itself. I have eulogized Homer, the sacred bards of Jewry, Aeschylus, Juvenal, Shakspere, etc., and acknowledged their inestimable value. But (with perhaps the exception, in some, not all respects, of the second-mention'd) I say there must, for future and democratic purposes, appear poets (dare I to say so?) of higher class even than any of those—poets not only possess'd of the religious fire and abandon of Isaiah, luxuriant in the epic talent of Homer, or for proud characters as in Shakspere, but consistent with the Hegelian formulas, and consistent with modern science. America needs, and the world needs, a class of bards who will, now and ever, so link and tally the rational physical being of man, with the ensembles of time and space, and with this vast and multiform show, Nature, surrounding him, ever tantalizing him, equally a part, and yet not a part of him, as to essentially harmonize, satisfy, and put at rest. Faith, very old, now scared away by science, must be restored, brought back by the same power that caused her departure—restored with new sway, deeper, wider, higher than ever. Surely, this universal ennui, this coward fear, this shuddering at death, these low, degrading views, are not always to rule the spirit pervading future society, as it has the past, and does the present. What the Roman Lucretius sought most nobly, yet all too blindly, negatively to do for his age and its successors, must be done positively by some great coming literatus, especially poet, who, while remaining fully poet, will absorb whatever science indicates, with spiritualism, and out of them, and out of his own genius, will compose the great poem of death. Then will man indeed confront Nature, and confront time and space, both with science, and *con amore*, and take his right place, prepared for life, master of fortune and misfortune. And then that which was long wanted will be supplied, and the ship that had it not before in all her voyages, will have an anchor.

A Thought on Shakspere   *1888*

The most distinctive poems—the most permanently rooted and with heartiest reason for being—the copious cycle of Arthurian legends, or the almost equally copious Charlemagne cycle, or the poems of the Cid, or

From Walt Whitman, *Complete Prose Works*. Boston: Small, Maynard & Co., 1898.

Scandinavian Eddas, or Nibelungen, or Chaucer, or Spenser, or *bona fide* Ossian, or Inferno—probably had their rise in the great historic perturbations, which they came in to sum up and confirm, indirectly embodying results to date. Then however precious to "culture," the grandest of those poems, it may be said, preserve and typify results offensive to the modern spirit, and long past away. To state it briefly, and taking the strongest examples, in Homer lives the ruthless military prowess of Greece, and of its special god-descended dynastic houses; in Shakspere the dragon-rancors and stormy feudal splendor of medieval caste.

Poetry, largely consider'd, is an evolution, sending out improved and ever-expanded types—in one sense, the past, even the best of it, necessarily giving place, and dying out. For our existing world, the bases on which all the grand old poems were built have become vacuums—and even those of many comparatively modern ones are broken and half-gone. For us today, not their own intrinsic value, vast as that is, backs and maintains those poems—but a mountain-high growth of associations, the layers of successive ages. Everywhere —their own lands included—(is there not something terrible in the tenacity with which the one book out of millions holds its grip?)—the Homeric and Virgilian works, the interminable ballad-romances of the middle ages, the utterances of Dante, Spenser, and others, are upheld by their cumulus-entrenchment in scholarship, and as precious, always welcome, unspeakably valuable reminiscenes.

Even the one who at present reigns unquestion'd—of Shakspere—for all he stands for so much in modern literature, he stands entirely for the mighty esthetic sceptres of the past, not for the spiritual and democratic, the sceptres of the future. The inward and outward characteristics of Shakspere are his vast and rich variety of persons and themes, with his wondrous delineation of each and all—not only limitless funds of verbal and pictorial resource, but great excess, superfetation—mannerism, like a fine, aristocratic perfume, holding a touch of musk (Euphues, his mark)—with boundless sumptuousness and adornment, real velvet and gems, not shoddy nor paste—but a good deal of bombast and fustian—(certainly some terrific mouthing in Shakspere!).

Superb and inimitable as all is, it is mostly an objective and physiological kind of power and beauty the soul finds in Shakspere—a style supremely grand of the sort, but in my opinion stopping short of the grandest sort, at any rate for fulfilling and satisfying modern and scientific and democratic American purposes. Think, not of growths as forests primeval, or Yellowstone geysers, or Colorado ravines, but of costly marble palaces, and palace rooms, and the noblest fixings and furniture, and noble owners and occupants to correspond—think of carefully built gardens from the beautiful but sophisticated gardening art at its best, with walks and bowers and artificial lakes, and appropriate statue-groups and the finest cultivated roses and lilies and japonicas in plenty—and you have the tally of Shakspere. The low characters, mechanics, even the loyal henchmen—all in themselves nothing—serve as capital foils to the aristocracy. The comedies (exquisite as they certainly are) bringing in admirably portray'd common characters, have the unmistakable hue of plays, portraits, made for the divertisement only of the elite of the castle, and from its point of view. The comedies are altogether nonacceptable to America and Democracy.

But to the deepest soul, it seems a shame to pick and choose from the riches Shakspere has left us—to criticize his infinitely royal, multiform quality —to gauge, with optic glasses, the dazzle of his sunlike beams.

The best poetic utterance, after all, can merely hint, or remind, often very indirectly, or at distant removes. Aught of real perfection, or the solution of any deep problem, or any completed statement of the moral, the true, the beautiful, eludes the greatest, deftest poet—flies away like an always uncaught bird.

Joseph Wood Krutch   *1893–1970*

The Tragic Fallacy   *1929*

I

Through the legacy of their art the great ages have transmitted to us a dim image of their glorious vitality. When we turn the pages of a Sophoclean or a Shakespearean tragedy we participate faintly in the experience which created it and we sometimes presumptuously say that we "understand" the spirit of these works. But the truth is that we see them, even at best and in the moments when our souls expand most nearly to their dimensions, through a glass darkly.

It is so much easier to appreciate than to create that an age too feeble to reach the heights achieved by the members of a preceding one can still see those heights towering above its impotence, and so it is that, when we perceive a Sophocles or a Shakespeare soaring in an air which we can never hope to breathe, we say that we can "appreciate" them. But what we mean is that we are just able to wonder, and we can never hope to participate in the glorious vision of human life out of which they were created—not even the the extent of those humbler persons for whom they were written; for while to us the triumphant voices come from far away and tell of a heroic world which no longer exists, to them they spoke of immediate realities and revealed the inner meaning of events amidst which they still lived.

When the life has entirely gone out of a work of art come down to us from the past, when we read it without any emotional comprehension whatsoever and can no longer even imagine why the people for whom it was intended found it absorbing and satisfying, then, of course, it has ceased to be a work of art at all and has dwindled into one of those deceptive "documents" from which we get a false sense of comprehending through the intellect things which cannot be comprehended at all except by means of a kinship of feeling. And though all works from the past age have begun in this way to fade there are some, like the great Greek or Elizabethan tragedies, which are still halfway between the work of art and the document. They no longer can have for us the immediacy which they had for those to whom they originally belonged, but they have not yet eluded us entirely. We no longer live in the world which they represent, but we can half imagine it and we can measure the distance which we have moved away. We write no tragedies today, but we can still talk about the tragic spirit of which we would, perhaps, have no conception were it not for the works in question.

As age which could really "appreciate" Shakespeare or Sophocles would have something comparable to put beside them—something like them, not necessarily in form, or spirit, but at least in magnitude—some vision of life which would be, however different, equally ample and passionate. But when we move to put a modern masterpiece beside them, when we seek to compare them with, let us say, a *Ghosts*[1] or a *Weavers*,[2] we shrink as from the impulse to commit some folly and we feel as though we were about to superimpose Bowling Green upon the Great Prairies in order to ascertain which is the larger. The question, we see, is not primarily one of art but of the two worlds which two minds inhabited. No increased powers of expression, no greater gift for words, could have transformed Ibsen into Shakespeare. The materials out of which the latter created his works—his conception of human dignity, his sense of the importance of human passions, his vision of the amplitude of human life—simply did not and could not exist for Ibsen, as they did not and could not exist for his contemporaries. God and Man and Nature had all somehow dwindled in the course of the intervening centuries, not because the realistic creed of modern art led us to seek out mean people,

---

[1] (1881) by Henrik Ibsen.
[2] (1892) by Gerhart Hauptmann.

but because this meanness of human life was somehow thrust upon us by the operation of that same process which led to the development of realistic theories of art by which our vision could be justified.

Hence, though we still apply, sometimes, the adjective "tragic" to one or another of those modern works of literature which describe human misery and which end more sadly even than they begin, the term is a misnomer since it is obvious that the works in question have nothing in common with the classical examples of the genre and produce in the reader a sense of depression which is the exact opposite of that elation generated when the spirit of a Shakespeare rises joyously superior to the outward calamities which he recounts and celebrates the greatness of the human spirit whose travail he describes. Tragedies, in that only sense of the word which has any distinctive meaning, are no longer written in either the dramatic or any other form, and the fact is not to be accounted for in any merely literary terms. It is not the result of any fashion in literature or of any deliberation to write about human nature or character under different aspects, any more than it is of either any greater sensitiveness of feeling which would make us shrink from the contemplation of the suffering of Medea or Othello or of any greater optimism which would make us more likely to see life in more cheerful terms. It is, on the contrary, the result of one of those enfeeblements of the human spirit not unlike that described in the previous chapter of this essay, and a further illustration of that gradual weakening of man's confidence in his ability to impose upon the phenomenon of life an interpretation acceptable to his desires which is the subject of the whole of the present discussion.

To explain that fact and to make clear how the creation of classical tragedy did consist in the successful effort to impose such a satisfactory interpretation will require, perhaps, the special section which follows, although the truth of the fact that it does impose such an interpretation must be evident to any one who has ever risen from the reading of *Oedipus* or *Lear* with that feeling of exultation which comes when we have been able, by rare good fortune, to enter into its spirit as completely as it is possible for us of a remoter and emotionally enfeebled age to enter it. Meanwhile one anticipatory remark may be ventured. If the plays and the novels of today deal with littler people and less mighty emotions it is not because we have become interested in commonplace souls and their unglamorous adventures but because we have come, willy-nilly, to see the soul of man as commonplace and its emotions as mean.

II

Tragedy, said Aristotle, is the "imitation of noble actions," and though it is some twenty-five hundred years since the dictum was uttered there is only one respect in which we are inclined to modify it. To us "imitation" seems a rather naïve word to apply to that process by which observation is turned into art, and we seek one which would define or at least imply the nature of that interposition of the personality of the artist between the object and the beholder which constitutes his function and by means of which he transmits a modified version, rather than a mere imitation, of the thing which he has contemplated.

In the search for this word the estheticians of romanticism invented the term "expression" to describe the artistic purpose to which apparent imitation was subservient. Psychologists, on the other hand, feeling that the artistic process was primarily one by which reality is modified in such a way as to render it more acceptable to the desires of the artist, employed various terms in the effort to describe that distortion which the wish may produce in vision. And though many of the newer critics reject both romanticism and psychology, even they insist upon the fundamental fact that in art we are concerned, not with mere imitation but with the imposition of some form upon the material which it would not have if it were merely copied as a camera copies.

Tragedy is not, then, as Aristotle said, the *imitation* of noble actions, for, indeed, no one knows what a *noble* action is or whether or not such a thing as nobility exists in nature apart from the mind of man. Certainly the action of Achilles in dragging the dead body of Hector around the walls of Troy and under the eyes of Andromache, who had begged to be allowed to give it decent burial, is not to us a noble action, though it was such to Homer, who made it the subject of a noble passage in a noble poem. Certainly, too, the same action might conceivably be made the subject of a tragedy and the subject of a farce, depending upon the way in which it was treated; so that to say that tragedy is the *imitation* of a *noble* action is to be guilty of assuming, first, that art and photography are the same and, second, that there may be something inherently noble in an acts as distinguished from the motives which prompted it or from the point of view from which it is regarded.

And yet, nevertheless, the idea of nobility is inseparable from the idea of tragedy, which cannot exist without it. If tragedy is not the imitation or even the modified representation of noble actions it is certainly a representation of actions *considered* as noble, and herein lies its essential nature, since no man can conceive it unless he is capable of believing in the greatness and importance of man. Its action is usually, if not always, calamitous, because it is only in calamity that the human spirit has the opportunity to reveal itself triumphant over the outward universe which fails to conquer it; but this calamity in tragedy is only a means to an end and the essential thing which distinguishes real tragedy from those distressing modern works sometimes called by its name is the fact that it is in the former alone that the artist has found himself capable of considering and of making us consider that his people and his actions have that amplitude and importance which make them noble. Tragedy arises then when, as in Periclean Greece or Elizabethan England, a people fully aware of the calamities of life is nevertheless serenely confident of the greatness of man, whose mighty passions and supreme fortitude are revealed when one of these calamities overtakes him.

To those who mistakenly think of it as something gloomy or depressing, who are incapable of recognizing the elation which its celebration of human greatness inspires, and who, therefore, confuse it with things merely miserable or pathetic, it must be a paradox that the happiest, most vigorous, and most confident ages which the world has ever known—the Periclean and the Elizabethan—should be exactly those which created and which most relished the mightiest tragedies; but the paradox is, of course, resolved by the fact that tragedy is essentially an expression, not of despair, but of the triumph over despair and of confidence in the value of human life. If Shakespeare himself ever had that "dark period" which his critics and biographers have imagined for him, it was at least no darkness like that bleak and arid despair which sometimes settles over modern spirits. In the midst of it he created both the elemental grandeur of Othello and the pensive majesty of Hamlet and, holding them up to his contemporaries, he said in the words of his own Miranda, "Oh, rare new world that hath *such* creatures in it."[3]

All works of art which deserve their name have a happy end. This is indeed the thing which constitutes them art and through which they perform their function. Whatever the character of the events, fortunate or unfortunate, which they recount, they so mold or arrange or interpret them that we accept gladly the conclusion which they reach and would not have it otherwise. They may conduct us into the realm of pure fancy where wish and fact are identical and the world is remade exactly after the fashion of the heart's desire or they may yield some greater or less allegiance to fact; but they must always reconcile us in one way or another to the representation which they make and the distinctions between the genres are simply the distinctions between the means by which this reconciliation is effected.

Comedy laughs the minor mishaps of its characters away; drama solves all the difficulties which it allows to arise; and melodrama, separating good from evil by simple lines, distributes its rewards and punishments in accordance with the principles of a naïve justice which satisfies the simple souls of its audience, which are neither philosophical enough to question its primitive ethics nor critical enough to object to the way in which its neat events violate the laws of probability. Tragedy, the greatest and the most difficult of the arts, can adopt none of these methods; and yet it must reach its own happy end in its own way. Though its conclusion must be, by its premise, outwardly calamitous, though it must speak to those who know that the good

---

[3] A misquotation of *The Tempest*, V, i, 183–184: "O brave new world/That has such creatures in't!"

man is cut off and that the fairest things are the first to perish, yet it must leave them, as *Othello* does, content that this is so. We must be and we are glad that Juliet dies and glad that Lear is turned out into the storm.

Milton set out, he said, to justify the ways of God to man,[4] and his phrase, if it be interpreted broadly enough, may be taken as describing the function of all art, which must, in some way or other, make the life which it seems to represent satisfactory to those who see its reflection in the magic mirror, and it must gratify or at least reconcile the desires of the beholder, not necessarily, as the naïver exponents of Freudian psychology maintain, by gratifying individual and often eccentric wishes, but at least by satisfying the universally human desire to find in the world some justice, some meaning, or, at the very least, some recognizable order. Hence it is that every real tragedy, however tremendous it may be, is an affirmation of faith in life, a declaration that even if God is not in his Heaven, then at least Man is in his world.

We accept gladly the outward defeats which it describes for the sake of the inward victories which it reveals. Juliet died, but not before she had shown how great and resplendent a thing love could be; Othello plunged the dagger into his own breast, but not before he had revealed that greatness of soul which makes his death seem unimportant. Had he died in the instant when he struck the blow, had he perished still believing that the world was as completely black as he saw it before the innocence of Desdemona was revealed to him, then, for him at least, the world would have been merely damnable, but Shakespeare kept him alive long enough to allow him to learn his error and hence to die, not in despair, but in the full acceptance of the tragic reconciliation to life. Perhaps it would be pleasanter if men could believe what the child is taught—that the good are happy and that things turn out as they should—but it is far more important to be able to believe, as Shakespeare did, that however much things in the outward world may go awry, man has, nevertheless, splendors of his own and that, in a word, Love and Honor and Glory are not words but realities.

Thus for the great ages tragedy is not an expression of despair but the means by which they saved themselves from it. It is a profession of faith, and a sort of religion; a way of looking at life by virtue of which it is robbed of its pain. The sturdy soul of the tragic author seizes upon suffering and uses it only as a means by which joy may be wrung out of existence, but it is not to be forgotten that he is enabled to do so only because of his belief in the greatness of human nature and because, though he has lost the child's faith in life, he has not lost his far more important faith in human nature. A tragic writer does not have to believe in God, but he must believe in man.

And if, then, the Tragic Spirit is in reality the product of a religious faith in which, sometimes at least, faith in the greatness of God is replaced by faith

[4] *Paradise Lost* (1667), I, 26.

in the greatness of man, it serves, of course, to perform the function of religion, to make life tolerable for those who participate in its beneficent illusion. It purges the souls of those who might otherwise despair and it makes endurable the realization that the events of the outward world do not correspond with the desires of the heart, and thus, in its own particular way, it does what all religions do, for it gives a rationality, a meaning, and a justification to the universe. But it if has the strength it has also the weakness of all faiths, since it may—nay, it must—be ultimately lost as reality, encroaching further and further into the realm of imagination, leaving less and less room in which that imagination can build its refuge.

III

It is, indeed, only at a certain stage in the development of the realistic intelligence of a people that the tragic faith can exist. A naïver people may have, as the ancient men of the north had, a body of legends which are essentially tragic, or it may have only (and need only) its happy and childlike mythology which arrives inevitably at its happy end, where the only ones who suffer "deserve" to do so and in which, therefore, life is represented as directly and easily acceptable. A too sophisticated society on the other hand—one which, like ours, has outgrown not merely the simple optimism of the child but also that vigorous, one might almost say adolescent, faith in the nobility of man which marks a Sophocles or a Shakespeare—has neither fairy tales to assure it that all is always right in the end nor tragedies to make it believe that it rises superior in soul to the outward calamities which befall it.

Distrusting its thought, despising its passions, realizing its impotent unimportance in the universe, it can tell itself no stories except those which make it still more acutely aware of its trivial miseries. When its heroes (sad misnomer for the pitiful creatures who people contemporary fiction) are struck down it is not, like Oedipus, by the gods that they are struck but only, like Oswald Alving, by syphilis, for they know that the gods, even if they existed, would not trouble with them, and they cannot attribute to themselves in art an importance in which they do not believe. Their so-called tragedies do not and cannot end with one of those splendid calamities which in Shakespeare seem to reverberate through the universe, because they cannot believe that the universe trembles when their love is, like Romeo's, cut off or when the place where they (small as they are) have gathered up their trivial treasure is, like Othello's sanctuary, defiled. Instead, mean misery piles on mean misery, petty misfortune follows petty misfortune, and despair becomes intolerable because it is no longer even significant or important.

Ibsen once made one of his characters say that he did not read much because he found reading "irrelevant," and the adjective was brilliantly chosen because it held implications even beyond those of which Ibsen was consciously aware. What is it that made the classics irrelevant to him and to us?

Is it not just exactly those to him impossible premises which make tragedy what it is, those assumptions that the soul of man is great, that the universe (together with whatever gods may be) concerns itself with him and that he is, in a word, noble? Ibsen turned to village politics for exactly the same reason that his contemporaries and his successors have, each in his own way, sought out some aspect of the common man and his common life—because, that is to say, here was at least something small enough for him to be able to believe.

Bearing this fact in mind, let us compare a modern "tragedy" with one of the great works of a happy age, not in order to judge of their relative technical merits but in order to determine to what extent the former deserves its name by achieving a tragic solution capable of purging the soul or of reconciling the emotions to the life which it pictures. And in order to make the comparison as fruitful as possible let us choose *Hamlet* on the one hand and on the other a play like *Ghosts* which was not only written by perhaps the most powerful as well as the most typical of modern writers but which is, in addition, the one of his works which seems most nearly to escape that triviality which cannot be entirely escaped by anyone who feels, as all contemporary minds do, that man is relatively trivial.

In *Hamlet* a prince ("in understanding, how like a god!") has thrust upon him from the unseen world a duty to redress a wrong which concerns not merely him, his mother, and his uncle, but the moral order of the universe. Erasing all trivial fond records from his mind, abandoning at once both his studies and his romance because it has been his good fortune to be called upon to take part in an action of cosmic importance, he plunges (at first) not into action but into thought, weighing the claims which are made upon him and contemplating the grandiose complexities of the universe. And when the time comes at last for him to die he dies, not as a failure, but as a success. Not only has the universe regained the balance which had been upset by what *seemed* the monstrous crime of the guilty pair ("there is nothing either good nor ill but thinking makes it so"), but in the process by which that readjustment is made a mighty mind has been given the opportunity, first to contemplate the magnificent scheme of which it is a part and then to demonstrate the greatness of its spirit by playing a role in the grand style which it called for. We do not need to despair in *such* a world if it has *such* creatures in it.

Turn now to *Ghosts*—look upon this picture and upon that. A young man has inherited syphilis from his father. Struck by a to him mysterious malady he returns to his northern village, learns the hopeless truth about himself, and persuades his mother to poison him. The incidents prove, perhaps, that pastors should not endeavor to keep a husband and wife together unless they know what they are doing. But what a world is this in which a great writer can deduce nothing more than that from his greatest work and how are we to be purged or reconciled when we see it acted? Not only is the failure utter, but it is trivial and meaningless as well.

Yet the journey from Elsinore to Skien is precisely the journey which the human spirit has made, exchanging in the process princes for invalids and gods for disease. We say, as Ibsen would say, that the problems of Oswald Alving are more "relevant" to our life than the problems of Hamlet, that the play in which he appears is more "real" than the other more glamorous one, but it is exactly because we find it so that we are condemned. We can believe in Oswald but we cannot believe in Hamlet, and a light has gone out in the universe. Shakespeare justifies the ways of God to man, but in Ibsen there is no such happy end and with him tragedy, so called, has become merely an expression of our despair at finding that such justification is no longer possible.

Modern critics have sometimes been puzzled to account for the fact that the concern of ancient tragedy is almost exclusively with kings and courts. They have been tempted to accuse even Aristotle of a certain naïveté in assuming (as he seems to assume) that the "nobility" of which he speaks as necessary to a tragedy implies a nobility of rank as well as of soul, and they have sometimes regretted that Shakespeare did not devote himself more than he did to the serious consideration of those common woes of the common man which subsequent writers have exploited with increasing pertinacity. Yet the tendency to lay the scene of a tragedy at the court of a king is not the result of any arbitrary convention but of the fact that the tragic writers believed easily in greatness just as we believe easily in meanness. To Shakespeare, robes and crowns and jewels are the garments most appropriate to man because they are the fitting outward manifestation of his inward majesty, but to us they seem absurd because the man who bears them has, in our estimation, so pitifully shrunk. We do not write about kings because we do not believe that any man is worthy to be one and we do not write about courts because hovels seem to us to be dwellings more appropriate to the creatures who inhabit them. Any modern attempt to dress characters in robes ends only by making us aware of a comic incongruity and any modern attempt to furnish them with a language resplendent like Shakespeare's ends in bombast.

True tragedy capable of performing its function and of purging the soul by reconciling man to his woes can exist only by virtue of a certain pathetic fallacy far more inclusive than that to which the name is commonly given. The romantics, feeble descendants of the tragic writers to whom they are linked by their effort to see life and nature in grandiose terms, loved to imagine that the sea or the sky had a way of according itself with their moods, of storming when they stormed and smiling when they smiled. But the tragic spirit sustains itself by an assumption much more far-reaching and no more justified. Man as it sees him lives in a world which he may not dominate but which is always aware of him. Occupying the exact center of a universe which would have no meaning except for him and being so little below the angels that, if he believes in God, he has no hesitation in imagining Him formed as he is formed and crowned with a crown like that which he or one of his fellows wears, he assumes that each of his acts reverberates through the universe. His passions are important to him because he believes them important throughout all time and all space; the very fact that he can sin (no modern can) means that this universe is watching his acts; and though he may perish, a God leans out from infinity to strike him down. And it is exactly because an Ibsen cannot think of man in any such terms as these that his persons have so shrunk and that his "tragedy" has lost that power which real tragedy always has of making that infinitely ambitious creature called man content to accept his misery if only he can be made to feel great enough and important enough. An Oswald is not a Hamlet chiefly because he has lost that tie with the natural and supernatural world which the latter had. No ghost will leave the other world to warn or encourage him, there is no virtue and no vice which he can possibly have which can be really important, and when he dies neither his death nor ·the manner of it will be, outside the circle of two or three people as unnecessary as himself, any more important than that of a rat behind the arras.

Perhaps we may dub the illusion upon which the tragic spirit is nourished the Tragic, as opposed to the Pathetic, Fallacy, but fallacy though it is, upon its existence depends not merely the writing of tragedy but the existence of that religious feeling of which tragedy is an expression and by means of which a people aware of the dissonances of life manages nevertheless to hear them as harmony. Without it neither man nor his passions can seem great enough or important enough to justify the sufferings which they entail, and literature, expressing the mood of a people, begins to despair where once it had exulted. Like the belief in love and like most of the other mighty illusions by means of which human life has been given a value, the Tragic Fallacy depends ultimately upon the assumption which man so readily makes that something outside his own being, some "spirit not himself"—be it God, Nature, or that still vaguer thing called a Moral Order—joins him in the emphasis which he places upon this or that and confirms him in his feeling that his passions and his opinions are important. When his instinctive faith in that correspondence between the outer and the inner world fades, his grasp upon the faith that sustained him fades also, and Love or Tragedy or what not ceases to be the reality which it was because he is never strong enough in his own insignificant self to stand alone in a universe which snubs him with its indifference.

In both the modern and the ancient worlds tragedy was dead long before writers were aware of the fact. Seneca wrote his frigid melodramas under the impression that he was following in the footsteps of Sophocles, and Dryden probably thought that his *All for Love* was an improvement upon Shakespeare, but in time we awoke to the fact that no amount of rhetorical bombast could conceal the fact that grandeur was not to be counterfeited when the belief in its possibility was dead, and turning from the hero to the common man we inaugurated the era of realism. For us no choice remains except that between mere rhetoric and the frank consideration of our fellow men, who may be the highest of the anthropoids but who are certainly too far below the angels to imagine either that these angels can concern themselves with them or that they can catch any glimpse of even the soles of angelic feet. We can no longer tell tales of the fall of noble men because we do not believe that noble men exist. The best that we can achieve is pathos and the most that we can do is to feel sorry for ourselves. Man has put off his royal robes and it is only in sceptered pomp that tragedy can come sweeping by.

IV

Nietzsche was the last of the great philosophers to attempt a tragic justification of life. His central and famous dogma—"Life is good *because* it is painful"—sums up in a few words the desperate and almost meaningless paradox to which he was driven in his effort to reduce to rational terms the far more imaginative conception which is everywhere present but everywhere unanalyzed in a Sophocles or a Shakespeare and by means of which they rise triumphant over the manifold miseries of life. But the very fact that Nietzsche could not even attempt to state in any except intellectual terms an attitude which is primarily unintellectual and to which, indeed, intellectual analysis is inevitably fatal is proof of the distance which he had been carried (by the rationalizing tendencies of the human mind) from the possibility of the tragic solution which he sought; and the confused, half-insane violence of his work will reveal, by the contrast which it affords with the serenity of the tragic writers whom he admired, how great was his failure.

Fundamentally this failure was, moreover, conditioned by exactly the same thing which has conditioned the failure of all modern attempts to achieve what he attempted—by the fact, that is to say, that tragedy must have a hero if it is not to be merely an accusation against, instead of a justification of, the world in which it occurs. Tragedy is, as Aristotle said, an imitation of noble actions, and Nietzsche, for all his enthusiasm for the Greek tragic writers, was palsied by the universally modern incapacity to conceive man as noble. Out of this dilemma, out of his need to find a hero who could give to life as he saw it the only possible justification, was born the idea of the Superman, but the Superman is, after all, only a hypothetical being, destined to become what man actually was in the eyes of the great tragic writers—a creature (as Hamlet said) "how infinite in capacities, in understanding how like a god." Thus Nietzsche lived half in the past through his literary enthusiasms and half in the future through his grandiose dreams, but for all his professed determination to justify existence he was no more able than the rest of us to find the present acceptable. Life, he said in effect, is not a Tragedy now but perhaps it will be when the Ape-man has been transformed into a hero (the *Ubermensch*), and trying to find that sufficient, he went mad.

He failed, as all moderns must fail when they attempt, like him, to embrace the tragic spirit as a religious faith, because the resurgence of that faith is not an intellectual but a vital phenomenon, something not achieved by taking thought but born, on the contrary, out of an instinctive confidence in life which is nearer to the animal's unquestioning allegiance to the scheme of nature than it is to that critical intelligence characteristic of a fully developed humanism. And like other faiths it is not to be recaptured merely by reaching an intellectual conviction that it would be desirable to do so.

Modern psychology has discovered (or at least strongly emphasized) the fact that under certain conditions desire produces belief, and having discovered also that the more primitive a given mentality the more completely are its opinions determined by its wishes, modern psychology has concluded that the best mind is that which most resists the tendency to believe a thing simply because it would be pleasant or advantageous to do so. But justified as this conclusion may be from the intellectual point of view, it fails to take into account the fact that in a universe as badly adapted as this one to human as distinguished from animal needs, this ability to will a belief may bestow an enormous vital advantage as it did, for instance, in the case at present under discussion where it made possible for Shakespeare the compensations of a tragic faith completely inaccessible to Nietzsche. Pure intelligence, incapable of being influenced by desire and therefore also incapable of choosing one opinion rather than another simply because the one chosen is the more fruitful or beneficent, is doubtless a relatively perfect instrument for the pursuit of truth, but the question (likely, it would seem, to be answered in the negative) is simply whether or not the spirit of man can endure the literal and inhuman truth.

Certain ages and simple people have conceived of the action which passes upon the stage of the universe as of something in the nature of a Divine Comedy, as something, that is to say, which will reach its end with the words "and they lived happily ever after." Others, less naïve and therefore more aware of those maladjustments whose reality, at least so far as outward events are concerned, they could not escape, have imposed upon it another artistic form and called it a Divine Tragedy, accepting its catastrophe as we accept the catastrophe of an *Othello*, because of its grandeur. But a Tragedy, Divine or otherwise, must, it may again be repeated, have a hero, and from the universe as we see it both the Glory of God and the Glory of Man have departed. Our cosmos may be farcical or it may be pathetic but it has not the dignity of tragedy and we cannot accept it as such.

Yet our need for the consolations of tragedy has not passed with the passing of our ability to conceive it. Indeed, the dissonances which it was tragedy's function to resolve grow more insistent instead of diminishing. Our passions, our disappointments, and our sufferings remain important to us though important to nothing else and they thrust themselves upon us with an urgency which makes it impossible for us to dismiss them as the mere trivialities which, so our intellects tell us, they are. And yet, in the absence of tragic faith or the possibility of achieving it, we have no way in which we may succeed in giving them the dignity which would not only render them tolerable but transform them as they were transformed by the great ages into joys. The death of tragedy is, like the death of love, one of those emotional fatalities as the result of which the human as distinguished from the natural world grows more and more a desert.

Poetry, said Santayana in his famous phrase, is "religion which is no longer believed," but it depends, nevertheless, upon its power to revive in us a sort of temporary or provisional credence and the nearer it can come to producing an illusion of belief the greater is its power as poetry. Once the Tragic Spirit was a living faith and out of it tragedies were written. Today these great expressions of a great faith have declined, not merely into poetry, but into a kind of poetry whose premises are so far from any we can really accept that we can only partially and dimly grasp its meaning.

We read but we do not write tragedies. The tragic solution of the problem of existence, the reconciliation to life by means of the tragic spirit is, that is to say, now only a fiction surviving in art. When that art itself has become, as it probably will, completely meaningless, when we have ceased not only to write but to *read* tragic works, then it will be lost and in all real senses forgotten, since the devolution from Religion to Art to Document will be complete.

John Howard Lawson *1894–*

Theory and Technique of Playwriting *1936*

The following definition may serve as a basis for discussion. The essential character of drama is social conflict in which the conscious will is exerted: persons are pitted against other persons, or individuals against groups, or groups against other groups, or individuals or groups against social or natural forces.

The first impression of this definition is that it is still too broad to be of any practical value: a prize fight is a conflict between two persons which has dramatic qualities and a slight but appreciable social meaning. A world war is a conflict between groups and other groups, which has deep social implications.

Either a prize fight or a war might furnish the materials for a dramatic conflict. This is not merely a matter of compression and selection—although both compression and selection are obviously necessary. The dramatic element (which transforms a prize fight or a war from potential material of drama into the actual stuff of drama) seems to lie in the *way* in which the expectations and motives of the persons or groups are projected. This is not a matter solely of the use of the conscious will; it involves the *kind* and *degree* of conscious will exerted. . . .

. . . The crisis, the dramatic explosion, is created by *the gap between the aim and the result*—that is, by a shift of equilibrium between the force of will and the force of social necessity. A crisis is the point at which the balance of forces is so strained that something cracks, thus causing a realignment of forces, a new pattern of relationships.

The will which creates drama is directed toward a specific goal. But the goal which it selects must be sufficiently *realistic* to enable the will to have some effect on reality. We in the audience must be able to understand the goal and the possibility of its fulfillment. The kind of will exerted must spring from a consciousness of reality which corresponds to our own. This is a variable factor, which can be accurately determined by an analysis of the social viewpoint of the audience.

But we are concerned not only with the *consciousness* of will, but with the *strength* of will. The exercise of will must be sufficiently vigorous to sustain and develop the conflict to a point of issue. A conflict which fails to reach a crisis is a conflict of weak wills. In Greek and Elizabethan tragedy, the point of maximum strain is generally reached in the death of the hero: he is crushed by the forces which oppose him, or he takes his own life in recognition of his defeat. . . .

The essential character of drama is social conflict—persons against other persons, or individuals against groups, or groups against other groups, or individuals or groups against social or natural forces—in which the conscious will, exerted for the accomplishment of specific and understandable aims, is sufficiently strong to bring the conflict to a point of crisis. . . .

A debate is not an action, however conscious and willing the participants may be. It is equally obvious that a vast amount of commotion may result in an infinitesimal amount of action. A play may contain a duel in every scene, a pitched battle in every act—and the spectators may be sound asleep, or be kept awake only by the noise.

Let us begin by distinguishing *action* (dramatic movement) from *activity* (by which we mean movement in general). The effectiveness of action does not depend on what people do, but on the *meaning* of what they do. We know that the root of this meaning lies in the conscious will. But how does the meaning express itself in dramatic movement? How are we to judge its objective realization? . . .

. . . The playwright's choice of theme is guided by his conception of the *probable* and *necessary*; the determination to achieve a probable end arouses the conscious will; the "iron framework of fact" sets a necessary limit upon the action of the will. Aristotle spoke simply of "a beginning, a middle and an end." It is obvious that a play which begins by chance and ends because two and one-half hours have passed, is not a play. Its beginning and its end, and the arrangement of the parts in a related design, are dictated by the need of realizing the social conception which constitutes the theme.

The general principle that unity of action is identical with unity of theme is beyond dispute. But this does not solve the problem—because the conception of unity of theme is as abstract as the conception of unity of action. In practice, real unity must be a synthesis of theme and action. . . .

We have observed that the relationship between free will and necessity is a continuously shifting balance of forces: this continuity of movement precludes the idea of absolute beginnings or endings; we cannot conceive of an assertion of free will which is genuinely *free*; this would be an unmotivated decision in an untouched field of experience. When the will is asserted in a certain direction, the decision is based on the sum-total of the necessities which we have previously experienced. This enables us to form a more or less correct picture of future probabilities, which govern our course of action. Then the beginnings of action are not determined merely by the feeling that the will must be asserted; the beginning of the action is rooted in necessity just as firmly as the end—the end constitutes the testing, the acceptance or rejection, of the picture of necessity which motivated the beginning.

This leads us to a genuinely organic conception of unity: the movement of the drama does not move loosely between the opposite poles of free will and necessity: the determination to perform an act includes the picture of *how the act will look and what its effect will be* when performed: there is no dualism of the probable and the necessary; probability is what we imagine necessity to be before it happens.

Therefore every detail of the action is determined by the *end* toward which the action is moving. But this end is no more *absolute* than the beginning: it does not represent necessity in any final form: by necessity we mean the laws that govern reality; reality is fluid and we cannot imagine it in any final form. The climax of the play, being the point of highest tension, gives the fullest expression to the laws of reality as the playwright conceives them.

The climax resolves the conflict by a change of equilibrium which creates a new balance of forces: the necessity which makes this event inevitable is the playwright's necessity: it expresses the social meaning which led him to invent the action.

The climax is the concrete realization of the theme in terms of an event. In practical playwriting, this means that the climax is the point of reference by which the validity of every element of the structure can be determined. . . .

The principle of unity in terms of climax is not a new one; but, as far as I am aware, it has not been clearly analyzed or applied. The nearest approach to a logical statement of the principle may be found in John Dryden's *Essay on Dramatic Poesie*: "As for the third unity, which is that of action, the ancients meant no other by it than what the logicians do by their *finis*, the end, or scope, of any action; that which is first in intention and last in execution."

Many playwrights have pointed to the necessity of testing the action in terms of the ending. "You should not begin your work," said Dumas the Younger, "until you have your concluding scene, movement and speech clear in your mind." Ernest Legouvé[1] gives the same advice: "You ask me how a play is made. By beginning at the end." Percival Wilde is of the same opinion: "Begin at the End and go Back till you come to the Beginning. Then start."[2]

The advice to "begin at the end" is sound as far as it goes. But the author who attempts to apply this advice as a cut-and-dried rule will get very meager results; the mechanical act of writing the climax first cannot be of any value unless one understands the function of the climax and the system of cause and effect which binds it to the play as a whole.

The laws of thought which underlie the creative process require that the playwright begin with a root-idea. He may be unconscious of this; he may think that the creative urge springs from random and purposeless thoughts; but disorganized thought cannot lead to organized activity; however vague his social attitude may be, it is sufficiently conscious and purposive to lead him to the volitional representation of action. Baker[3] says that "a play may start from almost anything; a detached thought that flashes through the mind; a theory of conduct or of art which one firmly believes or wishes only to examine; a bit of dialogue overhead or imagined; a setting, real or imagined, which creates emotion in the observer; a perfectly detached scene, the antecedents and consequences of which are as yet unknown; a figure glimpsed

---

[1] Ernest Legouvé (1807–1903), French playwright.

[2] Percival Wilde (1887–1935), American playwright. Wilde's injunction is a parody of the King's command (*Alice's Adventures in Wonderland*) to begin at the beginning, go on until the middle, continue until the end, and then stop.

[3] George Pierce Baker (1866–1936), teacher of playwriting at Yale University; his students included Eugene O'Neill, Philip Barry, and Sidney Howard.

in a crowd which for some reason arrests the attention of the dramatist, or a figure closely studied; a contrast or similarity between two people or conditions of life; a mere incident—noted in a newspaper or book, heard in idle talk, or observed; or a story, told only in the barest outlines or with the utmost detail."

There is no doubt that a playwright *may* start with any of these odds and ends of fact or fancy. He *may* complete an entire play by spontaneously piecing together bits of experience and information, without ever attaining the slightest understanding of the principles which underlie his activity. But whether he knows it or not, the process is not as spontaneous as it appears. The "bit of dialogue," or figure glimpsed in a crowd," or detailed story, do not appeal to him by chance; the reason lies in a point of view which he has developed as a result of his own experience; his point of view is sufficiently definite to make him feel the need of crystallizing it; he wants to find events which have a bearing on the picture of events which he has formed in his mind. When he finds a "bit of dialogue" or a "figure glimpsed in a crowd" or a story, he is not satisfied that this proves or justifies his point of view—if he were satisfied, he would stop right there, and would not be moved to further activity. What he seeks is the most complete volitional representation of the root-idea. The root-idea is abstract, because it is the sum-total of many experiences. He cannot be satisfied until he has turned it into a living event.

The root-idea is the beginning of the process. The next step is the dis covery of *an action* which expresses the root-idea. This action is the most fundamental action of the play; it is the climax and the limit of the play's development, because it embodies the playwright's idea of social necessity, which defines the play's scope and purpose. In searching for this root-action, the author may collect or invent any number of ideas or incidents or characters; he may suppose that these are of value in themselves; but logically he cannot test their value or put them to work until he has found the fundamental event which serves as climax. The meaning of any incident depends on its relationship to reality; an isolated incident (in a play or in life) assumes a meaning for *us* insofar as it appeals to our sense of what is probable or necessary; but there is no final truth as to probability and necessity; the system of incidents which constitutes a play depends on the *playwright's* sense of what is probable and necessary: until he has defined this, by defining the goal and scope of the action, his efforts can have neither unity nor rational purpose.

While the laws of living movement go forward from cause to effect, the laws of volitional representation go *backward*, from effect to cause. The necessity for this lies in the fact that the representation is volitional; the playwright creates from what he has known and experienced, and therefore must think back over his knowledge and experience to seek out causes which lead to the goal which his conscious will has selected. Thus the concentration on the crisis and the retrospective analysis of causes which we find in much of the world's greatest drama (Greek tragedy and Ibsen's social plays) follow the logic of dramatic thought in its most natural form. The extension of the action in the Elizabethan theatre grows out of a wider and less inhibited social point of view, which permits a freer investigation of causes. The dramatic system of events may attain any degree of extension or complexity, provided the result (the root-action) is clearly defined. . . .

It is customary to speak of tension as a somewhat mystic bond across the footlights, a psychic identification between audience and actors. It is far more enlightening to consider the word in its scientific sense. In electricity it means a difference of potential; in engineering it applies to the amount of stress and strain, which may be carefully calculated.

In play-construction, tension depends on the tensile strength of the elements of the drama, the degree of stress and strain which can be withstood before the final explosion.

The principles of continuity may be summed up as follows: (1) the exposition must be fully dramatized in terms of action; (2) the exposition must present possibilities of extension which are equal to the extension of the stage action; (3) two or more lines of causation may be followed if they find their solution in the root-action; (4) the rising action is divided into an indeterminate number of cycles; (5) each cycle is an action and has the characteristic progression of an action—exposition, rise, clash and climax; (6) the heightening of the tension as each cycle approaches its climax is accomplished by *increasing the emotional load*; this can be done by emphasizing the importance of what is happening, by underlining fear, courage, anger, hysteria, hope; (7) tempo and rhythm are important in maintaining and increasing tension: (8) the linking of scenes is accomplished by abrupt contrast or by overlapping of interest; (9) as the cycles approach the root-action, the tempo is increased, the subsidiary climaxes are more intense and grouped more closely together, and the action between the points is cut down; (10) probability and coincidence do not depend on physical probability, but on the value of the incident in relation to the root-action; (11) the play is not a simple continuity of cause and effect, but the interplay of complex forces; new forces may be introduced without preparation provided their *effect* on the action is manifest; (12) tension depends on the emotional load which the action will bear before the moment of explosion is reached.

Thornton Wilder 1897–

Some Thoughts on Playwriting 1941

Four fundamental conditions of the drama separate it from the other arts. Each of these conditions has its advantages and disadvantages, each requires a particular aptitude from the dramatist, and from each there are a number of instructive consequences to be derived. These conditions are:

1. The theatre is an art which reposes upon the work of many collaborators;
2. It is addressed to the group-mind;
3. It is based upon a pretense and its very nature calls out a multiplication of pretenses;
4. Its action takes place in a perpetual present time.

I. The Theatre Is an Art Which Reposes upon the Work of Many Collaborators

We have been accustomed to think that a work of art is by definition the product of one governing selecting will.

A landscape by Cézanne consists of thousands of brushstrokes each commanded by one mind. *Paradise Lost* and *Pride and Prejudice*, even in cheap frayed copies, bear the immediate and exclusive message of one intelligence.

It is true that in musical performance we meet with intervening executants, but the element of intervention is slight compared to that which takes place in drama. Illustrations:

1. One of the finest productions of *The Merchant of Venice* in our time showed Sir Henry Irving[1] as Shylock, a noble, wronged and indignant being, of such stature that the Merchants of Venice dwindled before him into irresponsible schoolboys. He was confronted in court by a gracious, even queenly, Portia, Miss Ellen Terry.[2] At the Odéon in Paris, however, Gémier[3] played Shylock as a vengeful and hysterical buffoon, confronted in court by a Portia who was a *gamine* from the Paris streets with

From *The Intent of the Artist*, edited by Augusto Centeno. New York: Russell & Russell, 1970. Reprinted by permission of Brandt & Brandt. Copyright © 1941 by Thornton Wilder. Copyright renewed 1969 by Thornton Wilder.

[1] (1838–1905).
[2] (1848–1928).
[3] Fermin Gémier (1866–1934).

a lawyer's quill three feet long over her ear; at the close of the trial scene Shylock was driven screaming about the auditorium, behind the spectator's back and onto the stage again, in a wild Elizabethan revel. Yet for all their divergences both were admirable productions of the play.

2.   If there were ever a play in which fidelity to the author's requirements were essential in the representation of the principal role, it would seem to be Ibsen's *Hedda Gabler,* for the play is primarily an exposition of her character. Ibsen's directions read: "Enter from the left Hedda Gabler. She is a woman of twenty-nine. Her face and figure show great refinement and distinction. Her complexion is pale and opaque. Her steel-gray eyes express an unruffled calm. Her hair is of an attractive medium brown, but is not particularly abundant; and she is dressed in a flowing loose-fitting morning gown." I once saw Eleonora Duse[4] in this role. She was a woman of sixty and made no effort to conceal it. Her complexion was pale and transparent. Her hair was white, and she was dressed in a gown that suggested some medieval empress in mourning. And the performance was very fine.

One may well ask: why write for the theatre at all? Why not work in the novel where such deviations from one's intentions cannot take place?

There are two answers:

1.   The theatre presents certain vitalities of its own so inviting and stimulating that the writer is willing to receive them in compensation for this inevitable variation from an exact image.

2.   The dramatist through working in the theatre gradually learns not merely to take account of the presence of the collaborators, but to derive advantage from them; and he learns, above all, to organize the play in such a way that its strength lies not in appearances beyond his control, but in the succession of events and in the unfolding of an idea, in narration.

The gathered audience sits in a darkened room, one end of which is lighted. The nature of the transaction at which it is gazing is a succession of events illustrating a general idea—the stirring of the idea; the gradual feeding out of information; the shock and countershock of circumstances; the flow of action; the interruption of action; the moments of allusion to earlier events; the preparation of surprise, dread, or delight—all that is the author's and his alone.

For reasons to be discussed later—the expectancy of the group-mind, the problem of time on the stage, the absence of the narrator, the element of pretense—the theatre carries the art of narration to a higher power than the novel or the epic poem. The theatre is unfolding action and in the disposition of events the authors may exercise a governance so complete that

4 (1859–1924).

the distortions effected by the physical appearance of actors, by the fancies of scene-painters and the misunderstandings of directors, fall into relative insignificance. It is just because the theatre is an art of many collaborators, with the constant danger of grave misinterpretation, that the dramatist learns to turn his attention to the laws of narration, its logic and its deep necessity of presenting a unifying idea stronger than its mere collection of happenings. The dramatist must be by instinct a storyteller.

There is something mysterious about the endowment of the storyteller. Some very great writers possessed very litle of it, and some others, lightly esteemed, possessed it in so large a measure that their books survive down the ages, to the confusion of severer critics. Alexandre Dumas had it to an extraordinary degree; while Melville, for all his splendid quality, had it barely sufficiently to raise his work from the realm of nonfiction. It springs, not, as some have said, from an aversion to general ideas, but from an instinctive coupling of idea and illustration; the idea, for a born storyteller, can only be expressed imbedded in its circumstantial illustration. The myth, the parable, the fable are the fountainhead of all fiction and in them is seen most clearly the didactic, moralizing employment of a story. Modern taste shrinks from emphasizing the central idea that hides behind the fiction, but it exists there nevertheless, supplying the unity to fantasizing, and offering a justification to what otherwise we would repudiate as mere arbitrary contrivance, pretentious lying, or individualistic emotional association-spinning. For all their magnificent intellectual endowment, George Meredith and George Eliot were not born storytellers; they chose fiction as the vehicle for their reflections, and the passing of time is revealing their error in that choice. Jane Austen was pure storyteller and her works are outlasting those of apparently more formidable rivals. The theatre is more exacting than the novel in regard to this faculty and its presence constitutes a force which compensates the dramatist for the deviations which are introduced into his work by the presence of his collaborators.

The chief of these collaborators are the actors.

The actor's gift is a combination of three separate faculties or endowments. Their presence to a high degree in any one person is extremely rare, although the ambition to possess them is common. Those who rise to the height of the profession represent a selection and a struggle for survival in one of the most difficult and cruel of the artistic activities. The three endowments that compose the gift are observation, imagination and physical coordination.

1.   An observant and analyzing eye for all modes of behavior about us, for dress and manner, and for the signs of thought and emotion in one's self and in others.

2.   The strength of imagination and memory whereby the actor may, at the indication in the author's text, explore his store of observations and represent the details of appearance and the intensity of the emotions—

joy, fear, surprise, grief, love and hatred, and through imagination extend them to intenser degrees and to differing characterizations.

3.   A physical coordination whereby the force of these inner realizations may be communicated to voice, face and body.

An actor must *know* the appearances and the mental states; he must *apply* his knowledge to the role; and he must physically *express* his knowledge. Moreover, his concentration must be so great that he can effect this representation under conditions of peculiar difficulty—in abrupt transition from the non-imaginative conditions behind the stage, and in the presence of fellow-actors who may be momentarily destroying the reality of the action.

A dramatist prepares the characterization of his personages in such a way that it will take advantage of the actor's gift.

Characterization in a novel is presented by the author's dogmatic assertion that the personage was such, and by an analysis of the personage with generally an account of his or her past. Since in the drama, this is replaced by the actual presence of the personage before us and since there is no occasion for the intervening all-knowing author to instruct us as to his or her inner nature, a far greater share is given in a play to (1) highly characteristic utterances and (2) concrete occasions in which the character defines itself under action and (3) a conscious preparation of the text whereby the actor may build upon the suggestions in the role according to his own abilities.

Characterization in a play is like a blank check which the dramatist accords to the actor for him to fill in—not entirely blank, for a number of indications of individuality are already there, but to a far less definite and absolute degree than in the novel.

The dramatist's principal interest being the movement of the story, he is willing to resign the more detailed aspects of characterization to the actor and is often rewarded beyond his expectation.

The sleep-walking scene from *Macbeth* is a highly compressed selection of words whereby despair and remorse rise to the surface of indirect confession. It is to be assumed that had Shakespeare lived to see what the genius of Sarah Siddons could pour into the scene from that combination of observation, self-knowledge, imagination and representational skill, even he might have exclaimed, "I never knew I wrote so well!"

II.   The Theatre Is an Art
Addressed to a Group-Mind

Painting, sculpture, and the literature of the book are certainly solitary experiences; and it is likely that most people would agree that the audience seated shoulder to shoulder in a concert hall is not an essential element in musical enjoyment.

But a play presupposes a crowd. The reasons for this go deeper than (1) the economic necessity for the support of the play and (2) the fact that the temperament of actors is proverbially dependent on group attention.

It rests on the fact that (1) the pretense, the fiction, on the stage would fall to pieces and absurdity without the support accorded to it by a crowd, and (2) the excitement induced by pretending a fragment of life is such that it partakes of ritual and festival, and requires a throng.

Similarly the fiction that royal personages are of a mysteriously different nature from other people requires audiences, levées, and processions for its maintenance. Since the beginnings of society, satirists have occupied themselves with the descriptions of kings and queens in their intimacy and delighted in showing how the prerogatives of royalty become absurd when the crowd is not present to extend to them the enhancement of an imaginative awe.

The theatre partakes of the nature of festival. Life imitated is life raised to a higher power. In the case of comedy, the vitality of these pretended surprises, deceptions, and *contretemps* becomes so lively that before a spectator, solitary or regarding himself as solitary, the structure of so much event would inevitably expose the artificiality of the attempt and ring hollow and unjustified; and in the case of tragedy, the accumulation of woe and apprehension would soon fall short of conviction. All actors know the disturbing sensation of playing before a handful of spectators at a dress rehearsal or performance where only their interest in pure craftsmanship can barely sustain them. During the last rehearsals the phrase is often heard: "This play is hungry for an audience."

Since the theatre is directed to a group-mind, a number of consequences follow:

1.   A group-mind presupposes, if not a lowering of standards, a broadening of the fields of interest. The other arts may presuppose an audience of connoisseurs trained in leisure and capable of being interested in certain rarefied aspects of life. The dramatist may be prevented from exhibiting, for example, detailed representations of certain moments in history that require specialized knowledge in the audience, or psychological states in the personages which are of insufficient general interest to evoke self-identification in the majority. In the Second Part of Goethe's *Faust* there are long passages dealing with the theory of paper money. The exposition of the nature of misanthropy (so much more drastic than Molière's) in Shakespeare's *Timon of Athens* has never been a success. The dramatist accepts this limitation in subject matter and realizes that the group-mind imposes upon him the necessity of treating material understandable by the larger number.

2.   It is the presence of the group-mind that brings another requirement to the theatre—forward movement.

Maeterlinck said that there was more drama in the spectacle of an old man seated by a table than in the majority of plays offered to the public. He was juggling with the various meanings in the word "drama." In the sense whereby drama means the intensified concentration of life's diversity and signifance he may well have been right; if he meant drama as a theatrical representation before an audience he was wrong. Drama on the stage is inseparable from forward movement, from action.

Many attempts have been made to present Plato's dialogues, Gobineau's fine series of dialogues, *La Renaissance,* and the *Imaginary Conversations* of Landor; but without success. Through some ingredient in the group-mind, and through the sheer weight of anticipation involved in the dressing-up and the assumption of fictional roles, an action is required, and an action that is more than a mere progress in argumentation and debate.

III.   The Theatre Is a World of Pretense

It lives by conventions: a convention is an agreed-upon falsehood, a permitted lie.

Illustrations: Consider at the first performance of the *Medea,* the passage where Medea meditates the murder of her children. An anecdote from antiquity tells us that the audience was so moved by this passage that considerable disturbance took place.

The following conventions were involved:

1.   Medea was played by a man.
2.   He wore a large mask on his face. In the lip of the mask was an accoustical device for projecting the voice. On his feet he wore shoes with soles and heels half a foot high.
3.   His costume was so designed that it conveyed to the audience, by convention: woman of royal birth and oriental origin.
4.   The passage was in metric speech. All poetry is an "agreed-upon falsehood" in regard to speech.
5.   The lines were sung in a kind of recitative. All opera involves this "permited lie" in regard to speech.

Modern taste would say that the passage would convey much greater pathos if a woman "like Medea" had delivered it—with an uncovered face that exhibited all the emotions she was undergoing. For the Greeks, however, there was no pretense that Medea was on the stage. The mask, the costume, the mode of declamation, were a series of signs which the spectator interpreted and reassembled in his own mind. Medea was being re-created within the imagination of each of the spectators.

The history of the theatre shows us that in its greatest ages the stage employed the greatest number of conventions. The stage is fundamental pretense and it thrives on the acceptance of that fact and in the multiplication of additional pretenses. When it tries to assert that the personages in the action "really are," really inhabit such and such rooms, really suffer such and such emotions, it loses rather than gains credibility. The modern world is inclined to laugh condescendingly at the fact that in the plays of Racine and Corneille the gods and heroes of antiquity were dressed like the courtiers under Louis XIV; that in the Elizabethan age scenery was replaced by placards notifying the audience of the location; and that a whip in the hand and a jogging motion of the body indicated that a man was on horseback in the Chinese theatre; these devices did not spring from naïveté, however, but from the vitality of the public imagination in those days and from an instinctive feeling as to where the essential and where the inessential lay in drama.

The convention has two functions:

1. It provokes the collaborative activity of the spectator's imagination; and
2. It raises the action from the specific to the general.

This second aspect is of even greater importance than the first.

If Juliet is represented as a girl "very like Juliet"—it was not merely a deference to contemporary prejudices that assigned this role to a boy in the Elizabethan age—moving about in a "real" house with marble staircases, rugs, lamps and furniture, the impression is irresistibly conveyed that these events happened to this one girl, in one place, at one moment in time. When the play is staged as Shakespeare intended it, the bareness of the stage releases the events from the particular and the experience of Juliet partakes of that of all girls in love, in every time, place and language.

The stage continually strains to tell this generalized truth and it is the element of pretense that reinforces it. Out of the lie, the pretense, of the theatre proceeds a truth more compelling than the novel can attain, for the novel by its own laws is constrained to tell of an action that "once happened"—"once upon a time."

IV.   The Action on the Stage Takes Place in a Perpetual Present Time

Novels are written in the past tense. The characters in them, it is true, are represented as living moment by moment their present time, but the constant running commentary of the novelist ("Tess slowly descended into the valley"; "Anna Karenina laughed") inevitably conveys to the reader the fact that these events are long since past and over.

The novel is a past reported in the present. On the stage it is always now. This confers upon the action an increased vitality which the novelist longs in vain to incorporate into his work.

This condition in the theatre brings with it another important element:

In the theatre we are not aware of the intervening storyteller. The speeches arise from the characters in an apparently pure spontaneity.

A play is what takes place.

A novel is what one person tells us took place.

A play visibly represents pure existing. A novel is what one mind, claiming to omniscience, asserts to have existed.

Many dramatists have regretted this absence of the narrator from the stage, with his point of view, his powers of analyzing the behavior of the characters, his ability to interfere and supply further facts about the past, about simultaneous actions not visible on the stage, and above *all* his function of pointing the moral and emphasizing the significance of the action. In some periods of the theatre he has been present as chorus, or prologue and epilogue or as *raisonneur*.[5] But surely this absence constitutes an additional force to the form, as well as an additional tax upon the writer's skill. It is the task of the dramatist so to coordinate his play, through the selection of episodes and speeches, that though he is himself not visible, his point of view and his governing intention will impose themselves on the spectator's attention, not as dogmatic assertion or motto, but as self-evident truth and inevitable deduction.

Imaginative narration—the invention of souls and destinies—is to a philosopher an all but indefensible activity.

Its justification lies in the fact that the communication of ideas from one mind to another inevitably reaches the point where exposition passes into illustration, into parable, metaphor, allegory and myth.

It is no accident that when Plato arrived at the height of his argument and attempted to convey a theory of knowledge and a theory of the structure of man's nature he passed over into storytelling, into the myths of the Cave and the Charioteer; and that the great religious teachers have constantly had recourse to the parable as a means of imparting their deepest intuitions.

The theatre offers to imaginative narration its highest possibilities. It has many pitfalls and its very vitality betrays it into service as mere diversion and the enhancement of insignificant matter; but it is well to remember that it was the theatre that rose to the highest place during those epochs that aftertime has chosen to call "great ages" and that the Athens of Pericles and the reigns of Elizabeth, Philip II, and Louis XIV were also the ages that gave to the world the greatest dramas it has known.

---

[5] A character who speaks for the author.

Arthur Miller *1915–*

Tragedy and the Common Man *1949*

In this age few tragedies are written. It has often been held that the lack is due to a paucity of heroes among us, or else that modern man has had the blood drawn out of his organs of belief by the skepticism of science, and the heroic attack on life cannot feed on an attitude of reserve and circumspection. For one reason or another, we are often held to be below tragedy—or tragedy above us. The inevitable conclusion is, of course, that the tragic mode is archaic, fit only for the very highly placed, the kings or the kingly, and where this admission is not made in so many words it is most often implied.

I believe that the common man is as apt a subject for tragedy in its highest sense as kings were. On the face of it this ought to be obvious in the light of modern psychiatry, which bases its analysis upon classic formulations, such as the Oedipus and Orestes complexes, for instances, which were enacted by royal beings, but which apply to everyone in similar emotional situations.

More simply, when the question of tragedy in art is not at issue, we never hesitate to attribute to the well-placed and the exalted the very same mental processes as the lowly. And finally, if the exaltation of tragic action were truly a property of the high-bred character alone, it is inconceivable that the mass of mankind should cherish tragedy above all other forms, let alone be capable of understanding it.

As a general rule, to which there may be exceptions unknown to me, I think the tragic feeling is evoked in us when we are in the presence of a character who is ready to lay down his life, if need be, to secure one thing— his sense of personal dignity. From Orestes to Hamlet, Medea to Macbeth, the underlying struggle is that of the individual attempting to gain his "rightful" position in his society.

Sometimes he is one who has been displaced from it, sometimes one who seeks to attain it for the first time, but the fateful wound from which the inevitable events spiral is the wound of indignity, and its dominant force is indignation. Tragedy, then, is the consequence of a man's total compulsion to evaluate himself justly.

In the sense of having been initiated by the hero himself, the tale always reveals what has been called his "tragic flaw," a failing that is not peculiar to grand or elevated characters. Nor is it necessarily a weakness. The flaw, or crack in the character, is really nothing—and need be nothing—but his inherent unwillingness to remain passive in the face of what he conceives to be a challenge to his dignity, has image of his rightful status. Only the passive, only those who accept their lot without active retaliation, are "flawless." Most of us are in that category.

But there are among us today, as there always have been, those who act against the scheme of things that degrades them, and in the process of action everything we have accepted out of fear or insensitivity or ignorance is shaken before us and examined, and from this total onslaught by an individual against the seemingly stable cosmos surrounding us—from this total examination of the "unchangeable" environment—comes the terror and the fear that is classically associated with tragedy.

More important, from this total questioning of what has previously been unquestioned, we learn. And such a process is not beyond the common man. In revolutions around the world, these past thirty years, he has demonstrated again and again this inner dynamic of all tragedy.

Insistence upon the rank of the tragic hero, or the so-called nobility of his character, is really but a clinging to the outward forms of tragedy. If rank or nobility of character was indispensable, then it would follow that the problems of those with rank were the particular problems of tragedy. But surely the right of one monarch to capture the domain from another no longer raises our passions, nor are our concepts of justice what they were to the mind of an Elizabethan king.

The quality in such plays that does shake us, however, derives from the underlying fear of being displaced, the disaster inherent in being torn away from our chosen image of what and who we are in this world. Among us today this fear is as strong, and perhaps stronger, than it ever was. In fact, it is the common man who knows this fear best.

Now, if it is true that tragedy is the consequence of a man's total compulsion to evaluate himself justly, his destruction in the attempt posits a wrong or an evil in his environment. And this is precisely the morality of tragedy and its lesson. The discovery of the moral law, which is what the enlightenment of tragedy consists of, is not the discovery of some abstract or metaphysical quantity.

The tragic right is a condition of life, a condition in which the human personality is able to flower and realize itself. The wrong is the condition which suppresses man, perverts the flowing out of his love and creative instinct. Tragedy enlightens—and it must, in that it points the heroic finger at the enemy of man's freedom. The thrust for freedom is the quality in tragedy which exalts. The revolutionary questioning of the stable environment is what terrifies. In no way is the common man debarred from such thoughts or such actions.

Seen in this light, our lack of tragedy may be partially accounted for by the turn which modern literature has taken toward the purely psychiatric view of life, or the purely sociological. If all our miseries, our indignities, are born and bred within our minds, then all action, let alone the heroic action, is obviously impossible.

And if society alone is responsible for the cramping of our lives, then the protagonist must needs be so pure and faultless as to force us to deny his validity as a character. From neither of these views can tragedy derive, simply because neither represents a balanced concept of life. Above all else, tragedy requires the finest appreciation by the writer of cause and effect.

No tragedy can therefore come about when its author fears to question absolutely everything, when he regards any institution, habit or custom as being either everlasting, immutable or inevitable. In the tragic view the need of man to wholly realize himself is the only fixed star, and whatever it is that hedges his nature and lowers it is ripe for attack and examination. Which is not to say that tragedy must preach revolution.

The Greeks could probe the very heavenly origin of their ways and return to confirm the rightness of laws. And Job could face God in anger, demanding his right and end in submission. But for a moment everything is in suspension, nothing is accepted, and in this stretching and tearing apart of the cosmos, in the very action of so doing, the character gains "size," the tragic stature which is spuriously attached to the royal or the highborn in our minds. The commonest of men may take on that stature to the extent of his willingness to throw all he has into the contest, the battle to secure his rightful place in his world.

There is a misconception of tragedy with which I have been struck in review after review, and in many conversations with writers and readers alike. It is the idea that tragedy is of necessity allied to pessimism. Even the dictionary says nothing more about the word than that it means a story with a sad or unhappy ending. This impression is so firmly fixed that I almost hesitate to claim that in truth tragedy implies more optimism in its author than does comedy, and that its final result ought to be the reinforcement of the onlooker's brightest opinions of the human animal.

For, if it is true to say that in essence the tragic hero is intent upon claiming his whole due as a personality, and if this struggle must be total and without reservation, then it automatically demonstrates the indestructible will of man to achieve his humanity.

The possibility of victory must be there in tragedy. Where pathos rules, where pathos is finally derived, a character has fought a battle he could not possibly have won. The pathetic is achieved when the protagonist is, by virtue of his witlessness, his insensitivity or the very air he gives off, incapable of grappling with a much superior force.

Pathos truly is the mode for the pessimist. But tragedy requires a nicer balance between what is possible and what is impossible. And it is curious, although edifying, that the plays we revere, century after century, are the tragedies. In them, and in them alone, lies the belief—optimistic, if you will, in the perfectibility of man.

It is time, I think, that we who are without kings, took up this bright thread of our history and followed it to the only place it can possibly lead in our time—the heart and spirit of the average man.

Northrop Frye *1912–*

The Archetypes of Literature *1951*

It is clear that criticism cannot be systematic unless there is a quality in literature which enables it to be so, an order of words corresponding to the order of nature in the natural sciences. An archetype should be not only a unifying category of criticism, but itself a part of a total form, and it leads us at once to the question of what sort of total form criticism can see in literature. Our survey of critical techniques has taken us as far as literary history. Total literary history moves from the primitive to the sophisticated, and here we glimpse the possibility of seeing literature as a complication of a relatively restricted and simple group of formulas that can be studied in primitive culture. If so, then the search for archetypes is a kind of literary anthropology, concerned with the way that literature is informed by preliterary categories such as ritual, myth and folk tale. We next realize that the relation between these categories and literature is by no means purely one of descent, as we find them reappearing in the greatest classics—in fact there seems to be a general tendency on the part of great classics to revert to them. This coincides with a feeling that we have all had: that the study of mediocre works of art, however energetic, obstinately remains a random and peripheral form of critical experience, whereas the profound masterpiece seems to draw us to a point at which we can see an enormous number of converging patterns of significance. Here we begin to wonder if we cannot see literature, not only as complicating itself in time, but as spread out in conceptual space from some unseen center.

Selections. From *The Kenyon Review*, XIII (Winter 1951). Copyright by Northrop Frye. Reprinted by permission of the author and *The Kenyon Review*.

This inductive movement towards the archetype is a process of backing up, as it were, from structural analysis, as we back up from a painting if we want to see composition instead of brushwork. In the foreground of the grave-digger scene in *Hamlet*, for instance, is an intricate verbal texture, ranging from the puns of the first clown to the *danse macabre* of the Yorick soliloquy, which we study in the printed text. One step back, and we are in the Wilson Knight and Spurgeon group of critics, listening to the steady rain of images of corruption and decay. Here too, as the sense of the place of this scene in the whole play begins to dawn on us, we are in the network of psychological relationships which were the main interest of Bradley. But after all, we say, we are forgetting the genre: *Hamlet* is a play, and an Elizabethan play. So we take another step back into the Stoll and Shaw group and see the scene conventionally as part of its dramatic context. One step more, and we can begin to glimpse the archetype of the scene, as the hero's *Liebestod*[1] and first unequivocal declaration of his love, his struggle with Laertes and the sealing of his own fate, and the sudden sobering of his mood that marks the transition to the final scene, all take shape around a leap into and return from the grave that has so weirdly yawned open on the stage.

At each stage of understanding this scene we are dependent on a certain kind of scholarly organization. We need first an editor to clean up the text for us, then the rhetorician and philologist, then the literary psychologist. We cannot study the genre without the help of the literary social historian, the literary philosopher and the student of the "history of ideas," and for the archetype we need a literary anthropologist. But now that we have got our central pattern of criticism established, all these interests are seen as converging on literary criticism instead of receding from it into psychology and history and the rest. In particular, the literary anthropologist who chases the source of the Hamlet legend from the pre-Shakespeare play to Saxo, and from Saxo to nature-myths, is not running away from Shakespeare: he is drawing closer to the archetypal form which Shakespeare re-created. . . .

Rhythm, or recurrent movement, is deeply founded on the natural cycle, and everything in nature that we think of as having some analogy with works of art, like the flower or the bird's song, grows out of a profound synchronization between an organism and the rhythms of its environment, especially that of the solar year. With animals some expressions of synchronization, like the mating dances of birds, could almost be called rituals. But in human life a ritual seems to be something of a voluntary effort (hence the magical element in it) to recapture a lost rapport with the natural cycle. A farmer must harvest his crop at a certain time of year, but because this is involuntary, harvesting itself is not precisely a ritual. It is the deliberate expression of a will to synchronize human and natural energies at that time which produces the harvest songs, harvest sacrifices and harvest folk customs that we call

[1] Love-Death.

rituals. In ritual, then, we may find the origin of narrative, a ritual being a temporal sequence of acts in which the conscious meaning or significance is latent: it can be seen by an observer, but is largely concealed from the participators themselves. The pull of ritual is toward pure narrative, which, if there could be such a thing, would be automatic and unconscious repetition. We should notice too the regular tendency of ritual to become encyclopedic. All the important recurrences in nature, the day, the phases of the moon, the seasons and solstices of the year, the crises of existence from birth to death, get rituals attached to them, and most of the higher religions are equipped with a definitive total body of rituals suggestive, if we may put it so, of the entire range of potentially significant actions in human life. . . .

The myth is the central informing power that gives archetypal significance to the ritual and archetypal narrative to the oracle. Hence the myth *is* the archetype, though it might be convenient to say myth only when referring to narrative, and archetype when speaking of significance. In the solar cycle of the day, the seasonal cycle of the year, and the organic cycle of human life, there is a single pattern of significance, out of which myth constructs a central narrative around a figure who is partly the sun, partly vegetative fertility and partly a god or archetypal human being. The crucial importance of this myth has been forced on literary critics by Jung and Frazer[2] in particular, but the several books now available on it are not always systematic in their approach, for which reason I supply the following table of phases:

1

The dawn, spring and birth phase. Myths of the birth of the hero, of revival and resurrection, of creation and (because the four phases are a cycle) of the defeat of the powers of darkness, winter and death. Subordinate characters: the father and the mother. The archetype of romance and of most dithyrambic and rhapsodic poetry.

2

The zenith, summer, and marriage or triumph phase. Myths of apotheosis, of the sacred marriage, and of entering into Paradise. Subordinate characters: the companion and the bride. The archetype of comedy, pastoral and idyll.

3

The sunset, autumn and death phase. Myths of fall, of the dying god, of violent death and sacrifice and of the isolation of the hero. Subordinate characters: the traitor and the siren. The archetype of tragedy and elegy.

[2] Sir James George Frazer (1854–1941), author of *The Golden Bough* (1890–1915).

4

The darkness, winter and dissolution phase. Myths of the triumph of these powers; myths of floods and the return of chaos, of the defeat of the hero, and Götterdämmerung myths. Subordinate characters: the ogre and the witch. The archetype of satire (see, for instance, the conclusion of *The Dunciad*).[3] . . .

. . . It is part of the critic's business to show how all literary genres are derived from the quest-myth, but the derivation is a logical one within the science of criticism: the quest-myth will constitute the first chapter of whatever future handbooks of criticism may be written that will be based on enough organized critical knowledge to call themselves "introductions" or "outlines" and still be able to live up to their titles. . . .

The importance of the god or hero in the myth lies in the fact that such characters, who are conceived in human likeness and yet have more power over nature, gradually build up the vision of an omnipotent personal community beyond an indifferent nature. It is this community which the hero regularly enters in his apotheosis. The world of this apotheosis thus begins to pull away from the rotary cycle of the quest in which all triumph is temporary. Hence if we look at the quest-myth as a pattern of imagery, we see the hero's quest first of all in terms of its fulfillment. This gives us our central pattern of archetypal images, the vision of innocence which sees the world in terms of total human intelligibility. It corresponds to, and is usually found in the form of, the vision of the unfallen world or heaven in religion. We may call it the comic vision of life, in contrast to the tragic vision, which sees the quest only in the form of its ordained cycle.

We conclude with a second table of contents, in which we shall attempt to set forth the central pattern of the comic and tragic visions. One essential principle of archetypal criticism is that the individual and the universal forms of an image are identical, the reasons being too complicated for us just now. We proceed according to the general plan of the game of Twenty Questions, or, if we prefer, of the Great Chain of Being:

1

In the comic vision the *human* world is a community, or a hero who represents the wish-fulfillment of the reader. The archetype of images of symposium, communion, order, friendship and love. In the tragic vision the human world is a tyranny or anarchy, or an individual or isolated man, the leader with his back to his followers, the bullying giant of romance, the deserted or betrayed hero. Marriage or some equivalent consummation belongs to the comic vision; the harlot, witch and other varieties of Jung's

[3] (1728) by Alexander Pope.

"terrible mother" belong to the tragic one. All divine, heroic, angelic or other superhuman communities follow the human pattern.

2

In the comic vision the *animal* world is a community of domesticated animals, usually a flock of sheep, or a lamb, or one of the gentler birds, usually a dove. The archetype of pastoral images. In the tragic vision the animal world is seen in terms of beasts and birds of prey, wolves, vultures, serpents, dragons and the like.

3

In the comic vision the *vegetable* world is a garden, grove or park, or a tree of life, or a rose or lotus. The archetype of Arcadian images, such as that of Marvell's green world or of Shakespeare's forest comedies. In the tragic vision it is a sinister forest like the one in *Comus* or at the opening of the *Inferno*, or a heath or wilderness, or a tree of death.

4

In the comic the *mineral* world is a city, or one building or temple, or one stone, normally a glowing precious stone—in fact the whole comic series, especially the tree, can be conceived as luminous or fiery. The archetype of geometrical images: the "starlit dome" belongs here. In the tragic vision the mineral world is seen in terms of deserts, rocks and ruins, or of sinister geometrical images like the cross.

5

In the comic vision the *unformed* world is a river, traditionally fourfold, which influenced the Renaissance image of the temperate body with its four humors. In the tragic vision this world usually becomes the sea, as the narrative myth of dissolution is so often a flood myth. The combination of the sea and beast images gives us the leviathan and similar water-monsters.

The Mythos of Spring: Comedy 1957

The plot structure of Greek New Comedy, as transmitted by Plautus and Terence, in itself less a form than a formula, has become the basis for most comedy, especially in its more highly conventionalized dramatic form, down to our own day. It will be most convenient to work out the theory of comic construction from drama, using illustrations from fiction only incidentally. What normally happens is that a young man wants a young woman, that his desire is resisted by some opposition, usually paternal, and that near the end of the play some twist in the plot enables the hero to have his will. In this simple pattern there are several complex elements. In the first place, the movement of comedy is usually a movement from one kind of society to another. As the beginning of the play the obstructing characters are in charge of the play's society, and the audience recognizes that they are usurpers. At the end of the play the device in the plot that brings hero and heroine together causes a new society to crystallize around the hero, and the moment when this crystallization occurs is the point of resolution in the action, the comic discovery, *anagnarisis* or *cognitio*.

The appearance of this society is frequently signalized by some kind of party or festive ritual, which either appears at the end of the play or is assumed to take place immediately afterward. Weddings are most common, and sometimes so many of them occur, as in the quadruple wedding at the end of *As You Like It*, that they suggest also the wholesale pairing off that takes place in a dance, which is another common conclusion, and the normal one for the masque. The banquet at the end of *The Taming of the Shrew* has an ancestry that goes back to Greek Middle Comedy; in Plautus the audience is sometimes jocosely invited to an imaginary banquet afterwards; Old Comedy, like the modern Christmas pantomime, was more generous, and occasionally threw bits of food to the audience. As the final society reached by comedy is the one that the audience has recognized all along to be the proper and desirable state of affairs, an act of communion with the audience is in order. Tragic actors expect to be applauded as well as comic ones, but nevertheless the word "plaudite" as the end of a Roman comedy, the invitation to the audience to form part of the comic society, would seem rather out of place at the end of a tragedy. The resolution of comedy comes, so to speak, from the audience's side of the stage; in a tragedy it comes from some mysterious world on the opposite side. In the movie, where darkness permits a more erotically oriented audience, the plot usually moves toward an act which, like death in Greek tragedy, takes place offstage, and is symbolized by a closing embrace.

Selections from Northrop Frye, *Anatomy of Criticism* (copyright © 1957 by Princeton University Press; Princeton Paperback, 1971), pp. 163–168.

The obstacles to the hero's desire, then, form the action of the comedy, and the overcoming of them the comic resolution. The obstacles are usually parental, hence comedy often turns on a clash between a son's and a father's will. Thus the comic dramatist as a rule writes for the younger men in his audience, and the older members of almost any society are apt to feel that comedy has something subversive about it. This is certainly one element in the social persecution of drama, which is not peculiar to Puritans or even Christians, as Terence in pagan Rome met much the same kind of social opposition that Ben Jonson did. There is one scene in Plautus where a son and father are making love to the same courtesan, and the son asks his father pointedly if he really does love mother. One has to see this scene against the background of Roman family life to understand its importance as psychological release. Even in Shakespeare there are startling outbreaks of baiting older men, and in contemporary movies the triumph of youth is so relentless that the moviemakers find some difficulty in getting anyone over the age of seventeen into their audiences.

The opponent to the hero's wishes, when not the father, is generally someone who partakes of the father's closer relation to established society: that is, a rival with less youth and more money. In Plautus and Terence he is usually either the pimp who owns the girl, or a wandering soldier with a supply of ready cash. The fury with which these characters are baited and exploded from the stage shows that they are father-surrogates, and even if they were not, they would still be usurpers, and their claim to possess the girl must be shown up as somehow fraudulent. They are, in short, impostors, and the extent to which they have real power implies some criticism of the society that allows them their power. In Plautus and Terence this criticism seldom goes beyond the immorality of brothels and professional harlots, but in Renaissance dramatists, including Jonson, there is some sharp observation of the rising power of money and the sort of ruling class it is building up.

The tendency of comedy is to include as many people as possible in its final society: the blocking characters are more often reconciled or converted than simply repudiated. Comedy often includes a scapegoat ritual of expulsion which gets rid of some irreconcilable character, but exposure and disgrace make for pathos, or even tragedy. *The Merchant of Venice* seems almost an experiment in coming as close as possible to upsetting the comic balance. If the dramatic role of Shylock is ever so slightly exaggerated, as it generally is when the leading actor of the company takes the part, it is upset, and the play becomes the tragedy of the Jew of Venice with a comic epilogue. *Volpone* ends with a great bustle of sentences to penal servitude and the galleys, and one feels that the deliverance of society hardly needs so much hard labor; but then *Volpone* is exceptional in being a kind of comic imitation of a tragedy, with the point of Volpone's hybris carefully marked.

The principle of conversion becomes clearer with characters whose chief function is the amusing of the audience. The original *miles gloriosus*[1] in Plautus is a son of Jove and Venus who has killed an elephant with his fist and seven thousand men in one day's fighting. In other words, he is trying to put on a good show: the exuberance of his boasting helps to put the play over. The convention says that the braggart must be exposed, ridiculed, swindled, and beaten. But why should a professional dramatist, of all people, want so to harry a character who is putting on a good show—*his* show at that? When we find Falstaff invited to the final feast in *The Merry Wives*, Caliban reprieved, attempts made to mollify Malvolio, and Angelo and Parolles allowed to live down their disgrace, we are seeing a fundamental principle of comedy at work. The tendency of the comic society to include rather than exclude is the reason for the traditional importance of the parasite, who has no business to be at the final festival but is nevertheless there. The word "grace," with all its Renaissance overtones from the graceful courtier of Castiglione to the gracious God of Christianity, is a most important thematic word in Shakespearean comedy.

The action of comedy in moving from one social center to another is not unlike the action of a lawsuit, in which plaintiff and defendant construct different versions of the same situation, one finally being judged as real and the other as illusory. . . .

There are two ways of developing the form of comedy: one is to throw the main emphasis on the blocking characters; the other is to throw it forward on the scenes of discovery and reconciliation. One is the general tendency of comic irony, satire, realism, and studies of manners; the other is the tendency of Shakespearean and other types of romantic comedy. In the comedy of manners the main ethical interest falls as a rule on the blocking characters. The technical hero and heroine are not often very interesting people: the *adulescentes* of Plautus and Terence are all alike, as hard to tell apart in the dark as Demetrius and Lysander, who may be parodies of them. Generally the hero's character has the neutrality that enables him to represent a wish-fulfillment. It is very different with the miserly or ferocious parent, the boastful or foppish rival, or the other characters who stand in the way of the action. In Molière we have a simple but fully tested formula in which the ethical interest is focused on a single blocking character, a heavy father, a miser, a misanthrope, a hypocrite, or a hypochondriac. These are the figures that we remember, and the plays are usually named after them, but we can seldom remember all the Valentins and Angeliques who wriggle out of their clutches. In *The Merry Wives* the technical hero, a man named Fenton, has only a bit part, and this play has picked up a hint or two from Plautus's *Casina*, where the hero and heroine are not even brought on stage at all. Fictional

---

[1] Braggart warrior, a type character of Roman and subsequent comedy, he is also the title character of a play by Plautus.

comedy, especially Dickens, often follows the same practice of grouping its interesting characters around a somewhat dullish pair of technical leads. Even Tom Jones, though far more fully realized, is still deliberately associated, as his commonplace name indicates, with the conventional and typical.

Comedy usually moves toward a happy ending, and the normal response of the audience to a happy ending is "this should be," which sounds like a moral judgment. So it is, except that it is not moral in the restricted sense, but social. Its opposite is not the villainous but the absurd, and comedy finds the virtues of Malvolio as absurd as the vices of Angelo. Molière's misanthrope, being committed to sincerity, which is a virtue, is morally in a strong position, but the audience soon realizes that his friend Philinte, who is ready to lie quite cheerfully in order to enable other people to preserve their self-respect, is the more genuinely sincere of the two. It is of course quite possible to have a moral comedy, but the result is often the kind of melodrama that we have described as comedy without humor, and which achieves its happy ending with a self-righteous tone that most comedy avoids. It is hardly possible to imagine a drama without conflict, and it is hardly possible to imagine a conflict without some kind of enmity. But just as love, including sexual love, is a very different thing from lust, so enmity is a very different thing from hatred. In tragedy, of course, enmity almost always includes hatred; comedy is different, and one feels that the social judgment against the absurd is closer to the comic norm than the moral judgment against the wicked.

Eric Bentley 1916–

What Is Theatre? 1956

Two mistakes are made. First, playwriting is regarded simply as a craft. Now, clearly, playwriting *is* a craft, just as fiction is a craft, *among other things*. It is another question whether it is advisable to isolate the craft from those other things, thus in effect replacing the playwright with the play-doctor, which is rather like replacing fathers and mothers with midwives. The

Selections. From *The Theatre of Commitment* by Eric Bentley. Copyright © 1956, 1967 by Eric Bentley. Reprinted by permission of Atheneum Publishers. All notes, which have been renumbered, are the author's.

notion has spread among writers, play-doctors, critics, producers, actors, public, that plays are "not written, but rewritten"; that is, not written, but pieced together, not composed with one man's passion and intellect but assembled by the ingenuity of all who stop by at the hotel bedroom, preferably during the rehearsal period. In this way, dramaturgy is demoted from the fine to the useful arts; and is unique among the latter by not really being useful.

The second mistake is to write with the audience consciously in mind, instead of in the faith that there will be an audience for good work. Obviously when we say that a play is not a writer's exploration of reality but just a calculated arrangement of effects, there is no need to ask: effects upon whom? The *raison d'être* of these effects is to interest and please the audience. All writers, of course, *hope* to interest and please an audience; the exploratory writer decidedly hopes that his explorations will interest and please an audience. But for the nonexploratory writer, hope is not enough. He is not prepared to leave it, as it were, to chance. He puts his whole mind on audience, audience, audience—by God, he'll *make* them like it—and, perhaps, by foregoing his claim to be an artist, becomes a remarkable craftsman. An artist cannot give *all* his attention to the audience; he needs to keep so much of it for his characters, his story, his subject.[1]

Now I am not prepared to argue with anyone who merely expresses an arbitrary preference for craft and pastime over art and exploration. The argument starts when someone, like Walter Kerr in his book *How Not to Write a Play*, seeks to confer a higher status on the lower phenomenon, raising craft above art, or so defining art that, to all intents and purposes, it *is* craft. Perhaps Mr. Kerr would say he hasn't done this; and it is probably as hard for me to sum up a book of his in terms acceptable to him as it has certainly proved for him to sum up a book of mine in terms acceptable to me. But I think it is true to say that he sees dramaturgy as a matter of adjusting the play to the audience; in no measure or fashion must the audience be asked to adjust itself to the play.[2] They pay their money and they take their choice. V*ox populi, vox dei,* with *populus* defined as nonintellectuals, shopgirls preferred.

What about intellectual shopgirls? That they exist is news that apparently hasn't reached Mr. Kerr, though it is familiar enough to any book publisher; and, of course, they stay away from the plays that Mr. Kerr tries so hard to enjoy on their account. I believe Mr. Kerr's invitation to shopgirls will be turned down because the intellectual ones are busy with paperback books,

---

[1] In his book *The Inmost Leaf*, Alfred Kazin speaks of "that morbid overconsciousness of the audience that afflicts even the most serious writers in this country." The problem is one, not for the theatre alone, but for our culture generally.

[2] Contrast this with the attitude of a great playwright: ". . . no matter how badly my *Carlos* fails as a stage-play, I must insist that our public could see it performed ten times more before it would comprehend and exhaust all the good in it which offsets its defects. . . ."—Friedrich Schiller.

while the nonintellectual ones are quite happy with their TV sets; for, if we want a truly popular alternative to such highbrow pursuits as reading, we have it—in TV. The theatre, as Mr. Kerr presents it, is something neither kind of shopgirl wants.[3] Nor is sociology so up-to-date as he would wish it to be. For example, the notice in the window of the five-and-ten-cent store at the end of my street in Manhattan does not read: SHOPGIRL WANTED. It reads: SALESLADY WANTED. Call it elegance, call it snobbery, the cold fact remains that no candidate who appeals to The Shopgirl Vote, from this time out, is going to get it.

Just as there is a word—patrioteering—for the kind of patriotism that is merely an appeal to the gallery or worse, there ought to be a word for that sort of "democratic" argument which is merely an appeal to mediocrity and the fear of distinction, for in America this is the appeal almost everyone makes when he runs out of real arguments: "democrateering," if I may coin a word and adjust a dictum, is the last refuge of a scoundrel. Mr. Kerr being no scoundrel, I shall dismiss his democrateering as simply unworthy of him, and turn to that part of his argument which calls for an answer. Discussing poetic drama, Mr. Kerr says: "Verse is of no value whatever unless, like every other part of the play, it mirrors the picture people have of themselves. . . . Writing verse is almost like taking the blood pressure of the age." If only Paddy Chayefsky would take up verse, one concludes, he would inevitably become Mr. Kerr's favorite playwright. For, even speaking prose, the actor who played Marty was awarded a golden urn with an inscription stating that he revealed "the meatcutters of America as friendly, humble, sincere, and accredited members of the human race." And this statement is guaranteed to give the picture the meatcutters have of themselves, as the urn was the gift of the Meatcutters Union, Local 587, Santa Monica, California. It seems to me that Mr. Chayefsky is the playwright of the age of conformity, the age of "other-directed" yes-men, the age of democrateering salesmanship; and that Mr. Kerr is in some danger of becoming its critic.

"Every . . . part of the play . . . mirrors the picture people have of themselves." As the metaphor was presumably suggested by a famous passage in *Hamlet,* it may not be unfair to ask what that passage means. Hamlet spoke of the actor as holding up the mirror not to the picture people have of themselves but to nature, that is to people as they really are—a very different matter. In his use of this figure. Shakespeare was following an established tradition according to which the mirror was held up to human affairs to the end that men might be inspired by a good example or warned by a bad one. It was a normative mirror. Though art imitated life, it did not do so just for

---

[3] "By current measurements of audience size, the theatre hardly qualifies as a means of mass communication. But the films assuredly do, and increasingly since the successful marketing of the paper-backs, so does the book."—J. Donald Adams, *The New York Times Book Review,* March 25, 1956.

the record, but in order to improve life; far from saying: "This is how you see yourself, humble, sincere and accredited; keep it that way," it said: "You see what happened to this bad king, go thou and do differently. . . ."

I am told that it is old-fashioned to speak of the "commercial" theatre, for everyone now knows that what Shakespeare and Shaw were after was money. Another false trail! No one denies that, so far from being against money, the artist is most often in the position of having to say to the business man, as Shaw did to Samuel Goldwyn: "You're only interested in art, I'm only interested in money." Human beings like money, and an artist is a human being. But he is also an artist, and while sometimes it may happen that the commercial theatre is mainly favorable to his art, it may sometimes happen that it is not—like the commercial anything else. Today, to choose a contrary example, commercial publishing in this country cannot, in my opinion, be said to be hostile to literature; on the contrary, any novel with merit in it has a strong chance of publication. In theatre, the situation happens to be very different. Not that there are great new plays lying idle in desk drawers; the trouble lies deeper than that. The plays don't get to be written at all, because those who might write them actually write novels. There are many answers to the question: what scares them off the theatre? One typical deterrent is the phenomenon of the Perfect Play.

The commercial play is the Swiss watch of dramaturgy. When properly manufactured, it is perfect, as only a piece of machinery can be perfect. And it is the prospect of such a perfection that current theatre criticism holds out to the young playwright, while enjoying itself noting the imperfections in plays by real writers. In this the newspaper critics live out their manifest destiny as spokesman of the status quo—or rather, like the Devil in *Don Juan in Hell*, not of the status quo as it actually is, but as it aspires to be, not of Broadway as it actually is, but of the Platonic idea of Broadway, not of what people are, but of the picture they have of themselves. The Perfect Play being a good deal easier to put together (though not easy) than a significant imperfect play, one can indeed conceive of a Broadway on which every play is perfect. And since the standard by which perfection is judged is clear and objective (namely, show of hands), all plays in which imperfections are found could be promptly removed from the boards and from the record. I think I have stumbled here on a suggestion that should earn me a medal—or an aisle seat at a perfect play—in whatever mechanized Utopia awaits us in the years to come.

Retreating to my customary persona, I realize that I am left with the unhappy task of championing imperfection. I idealize failure, says Mr. Kerr (to which it seems almost like nose-thumbing to retort: you worship success). Red herring upon red herring! It is not the price to be paid, but the jewel paid for, on which the case rests. But the price does have to be paid; the price of artistic success being, in general, a good deal of failure. To establish oneself as a VIP with a hit written at the age of twenty, and then to manufacture another hit every two years for life—this experience does not resemble that of any artist whose career is known to me. An artist begins as a fumbler, at best a brilliant fumbler, and, even after he has enjoyed some public success, he relapses continually into failures which no one should be so foolish as to idealize, since they represent to him nothing but bitterness and desolation of spirit. The lives of those two notorious career men, Shakespeare and Shaw, are not exceptions. Not even Shaw. The middlebrow critics of the Eighteen Nineties were all against the young highbrow who wrote *Arms and the Man*; he had no success then, and he had very little success with the plays of his last twenty-five years. When today *The Lark* is spoken of as "second only to *Saint Joan*," it is well to remember which show came second as a Broadway run.[4]

(If those who champion pastime tend to be against art, those of us who are for art must make it crystal clear that we are not against pastime. There have grown up particular pastimes, like Perfect Plays, which stand in the way of art, which in a sense are designed to replace art, but, no more than Aristotle when he formulated the distinction, need we in any way disapprove of pastime as such. On the contrary, we acquire in the theatre such respect for certain lighter works and forms that we are ready to speak of the *art* in them, and so to pass beyond the dichotomy I have been using. The works of Labiche and Offenbach are pastimes. Are they therefore not art? The works of Dumas *fils* are not pastimes. Must we therefore rank them higher than Labiche and Offenbach? At this point, the terminology lets us down as, at some point, all critical terminology does. Before continuing to use the art-pastime dichotomy for what it is worth, I want, parenthetically, to concede this, and to insist that what I am trying to measure is the degree, not of earnestness, but of spiritual curiosity.)

I have been maintaining that the "serious" modern playwright is, or should be, engaged, along with other modern writers, in the search for the human essence. If it is possible to state in a word what moral quality the artist engaged in this quest needs above all others, I should say that it is audacity. Conversely, artists who are not searching, not reaching out for anything, but working comfortably within their established resources, and who are completely lacking in daring, who never "cock a snoot," "take a crack" at anything, "stick their necks out"—for them should be reserved the harshest adjective in the critical vocabulary: innocuous. In life there are worse things than innocuousness—forms of rampant evil which render innocuousness

---

[4] Namely, *Saint Joan*, with 218 performances (1923–1924), as against *The Lark's* 229 (1955–1956). Nor is it accurate to say that all runs were short in the Twenties. During the 1923–1924 season there were seventeen plays on Broadway that had run for more than 500 performances, the greatest classics among them being *The Bat* and *Abie's Irish Rose*.

praiseworthy by comparison. But the Devil doesn't write plays. And when Mussolini wrote them he didn't succeed in projecting anything of the force of his iniquity. Like many a better man, he only succeeded in writing innocuously. But that is the worst type of writing there is.

Nineteenth- and Twentieth-Century Russia and Hungary

Recurring themes throughout Russian criticism are a didactic goal, a realistic style, and a mass audience. To Tolstoy, the value of art is its value to humanity. Art should be infectious, he says, and the more people infected, the better the art. Accessible to all the people, not merely one class, art should be Christian, uniting all men with perceptions of their relationship to God or their kinship to each other. Preferring less tendentious drama, as did Engels, Chekhov advocates (and practices) realistic, objective observation of human beings. On the question of drama for the people, he urges that Gogol not be lowered to the unsophisticated level of the masses but that they be raised to an appreciation of Gogol.

According to Lenin, literature and the arts should be infused with the spirit of the class struggle, the overthrow of capitalism, and the dictatorship of the proletariat. His doctrines are the foundations of Socialist Realism, which, in his and Marx's names, and following Tolstoy's emphasis on didacticism, became the official form of Soviet art and criticism: the subjects of art—the ideals the Communists were trying to create or the previous conditions from which socialism would emerge—should be expressed in terms worker-audiences could understand; writing should be realistic, represent revolutionary processes, and contribute to educating audiences in the nature and spirit of socialism. Since the last phrase has first priority, Socialist Realism tends to be conventional realistic drama with a Communist message.

Redefining the function and methods of drama, the Soviets also redefine those of criticism. As explained by Lunacharsky, the U.S.S.R.'s first Commissar of Education, Marxist-Leninist sociological analysis is fundamental to Marxist criticism, which first analyzes the social essence of a work of art (its reflection of the class structure and class interests of a society) and then examines how the form corresponds to it. Lunacharsky spells out the basic evaluative criterion: "everything that aids the development and victory of the proletariat is good; everything that harms

it is evil." Referring approvingly to Tolstoy's dictum that art should
be addressed to the masses, he agrees with Chekhov that to lower all
art to those still uncultured would be a mistake. Applauding writers who
express valuable social ideas in a popular way, he also recognizes the worth
of sophisticated writers who require cultured readers.

Europe's most important Marxist literary critic, the Hungarian
George Lukács, began his work before the Russian Revolution of 1917.
Employing a historical method developed from Marx's analysis of
society, Lukács examines the social dimensions and resonances of modern
European drama, whose heroes he finds more passive and whose
action more internal than those of the old. Bourgeois and historicist,
it is a drama of individualism and of milieu.

Believing that an artist should concern himself less with form than
with content, Soviet Marxist critics consider "formalism" (the
dominance of formal goals over explicit socialist content) an aspect of
bourgeois decadence. To such critics, much of Russia's most exciting
theatre of the 1920s—such as the stage experiments of Eisenstein (before
he became a film director)—is formalistic. To Eisenstein, a theatrical
text is a pretext for stage action. By changes, additions, and subtractions, he
transforms a literary text into a new theatre piece. Anticipating
Artaud and Grotowski, he creates a *Montage of Attractions*: aggressive,
nonliterary, theatrical elements that subject audiences to sensual
or psychological shocks that enable them—unlike those at productions
directed by Artaud and Grotowski—*"to perceive the ideological side of
what is being demonstrated."*

Anton Pavlovich Chekhov *1860–1904*

Letters to A. S. Suvorin[1]

(May 30, 1888)[2]

. . . It seems to me that writers of fiction are not supposed to solve such problems as God, pessimism, etc. The business of a writer of fiction is only to describe who it was that talked or thought about God or pessimism, how they did it, and under what circumstances. An artist is not supposed to be a judge of his characters and of what they say, but only an impartial witness. I heard two Russians carrying on an incoherent conversation about pessimism that didn't resolve anything, and I ought to report this conversation in the same form in which I heard it, and the jury, that is to say the readers, will evaluate it. My business is only to be talented, that is to say, to be able to distinguish the important evidence from the unimportant, to be able to elucidate the characters and speak their language.

(October 27, 1888)[3]

In conversations with my fellow writers I always insist that it is not the artist's business to solve highly specialized problems. It is not right for an artist to take up what he doesn't understand. We have specialists here for specialized problems; their business is to make judgments about the community, about the future of capitalism, about the scourge of drunkenness, about boots, about women's diseases. . . . An artist should make judgments only about what he understands; his range is as limited as that of any other specialist—I repeat this and I always insist on it. Only someone who has never done any writing and who has nothing to do with the workings of the imagination can say that there are no questions in the artist's realm, but only answers. An artist observes, selects, conjectures, composes—these activities in themselves presuppose a problem from the first; if from the first the artist didn't set himself a problem, there wouldn't be anything to conjecture or anything to select. To put it briefly, I will conclude with some psychiatry: if one denies that there is any problem posed or conscious plan in the

[1] (1834–1912), Russian journalist, theatre critic, editor, and publisher.
[2] Selection.
[3] Selections.

creative process, then one must admit that the artist creates unwittingly, without any design, while temporarily insane; therefore, if any author boasted to me that he wrote a story without a previously thought-out plan, but only on the basis of inspiration, I'd call him a madman.

You are right in demanding that the artist have a conscious relation to his work, but you are confusing two ideas: solving a problem and posing a problem correctly. In *Anna Karenina* and *Eugene Onegin*,[4] not one single problem is solved, but those works fully satisfy you simply because all the problems in them are correctly posed. The court is obliged to state the problems correctly, but let the members of the jury solve them, each according to his own views.

(April 1, 1890)[5]

You reproach me for objectivity, calling it indifference to good and evil, an absence of ideals and principles, and so forth. When I describe horse thieves, you want me to say stealing horses is evil. But surely that's been known for a long time now without my having to say it. Let the members of the jury judge them, but my business is only to show what kind of people they are.

[4] By Tolstoy and Pushkin, respectively.
[5] Selection.

Letter to
V. I. Nemirovich-Danchenko[1]

(November 2, 1903)[2]

. . . By the way, both theatre for the people and literature for the people —all that's nonsense, all that's sugar-candy for the people. You mustn't lower Gogol to the level of the people, but raise the people up to the level of Gogol.

[1] (1859–1943), Russian playwright and, with Konstantin Stanislavsky (1863–1938), cofounder of the Moscow Art Theatre (1898).
[2] Selection.

Leo Tolstoy *1828–1910*

What Is Art? *1898*

Chapter XV

Art, in our society, has been so perverted that not only has bad art come to be considered good, but even the very perception of what art really is has been lost. In order to be able to speak about the art of our society, it is, therefore, first of all necessary to distinguish art from counterfeit art.

There is one indubitable indication distinguishing real art from its counterfeit, namely, the infectiousness of art. If a man, without exercising effort and without altering his standpoint, on reading, hearing, or seeing another man's work, experiences a mental condition which unites him with that man and with other people who also partake of that work of art, then the object evoking that condition is a work of art. And however poetical, realistic, effectful, or interesting a work may be, it is not a work of art if it does not evoke that feeling (quite distinct from all other feelings) of joy, and of spiritual union with another (the author) and with others (those who are also infected by it).

It is true that this indication is an *internal* one, and that there are people who have forgotten what the action of real art is, who expect something else from art (in our society the great majority are in this state), and that therefore such people may mistake for this esthetic feeling the feeling of divertisement and a certain excitement which they receive from counterfeits of art. But though it is impossible to undeceive these people, just as it is impossible to convince a man suffering from "Daltonism"[1] that green is not red, yet, for all that, this indication remains perfectly definite to those whose feeling for art is neither perverted nor atrophied, and it clearly distinguishes the feeling produced by art from all other feelings.

The chief peculiarity of this feeling is that the receiver of a true artistic impression is so united to the artist that he feels as if the work were his own and not someone else's—as if what it expresses were just what he had long been wishing to express. A real work of art destroys, in the consciousness of the receiver, the separation between himself and the artist, nor that alone, but also between himself and all whose minds receive this work of art. In this freeing of our personality from its separation and isolation, in this uniting of it with others, lies the chief characteristic and the great attractive force of art.

Selections. From Leo Tolstoy, *What Is Art?*, translated by Aylmer Maude. New York: T. Y. Crowell, 1898.

[1] Color blindness, from the physicist John Dalton (1766–1844).

If a man is infected by the author's condition of soul, if he feels this emotion and this union with others, then the object which has effected this is art; but if there be no such infection, if there be not this union with the author and with others who are moved by the same work—then it is not art. And not only is infection a sure sign of art, but the degree of infectiousness is also the sole measure of excellence in art.

The stronger the infection the better is the art, as art, speaking now apart from its subject-matter, i.e., not considering the quality of the feelings it transmits.

And the degree of the infectiousness of art depends on three conditions:

(1) On the greater or lesser individuality of the feeling transmitted; (2) on the greater or lesser clearness with which the feeling is transmitted; (3) on the sincerity of the artist, i.e., on the greater or lesser force with which the artist himself feels the emotion he transmits.

The more individual the feeling transmitted the more strongly does it act on the receiver; the more individual the state of soul into which he is transferred the more pleasure does the receiver obtain, and therefore the more readily and strongly does he join in it.

The clearness of expression assists infection, because the receiver, who mingles in consciousness with the author, is the better satisfied the more clearly the feeling is transmitted, which, as it seems to him, he has long known and felt, and for which he has only now found expression.

But most of all is the degree of infectiousness of art increased by the degree of sincerity in the artist. As soon as the spectator, hearer, or reader feels that the artist is infected by his own production, and writes, sings, or plays for himself and not merely to act on others, this mental condition of the artist infects the receiver; and, contrariwise, as soon as the spectator, reader, or hearer feels that the author is not writing, singing, or playing for his own satisfaction—does not himself feel what he wishes to express—but is doing it for him, the receiver, a resistance immediately springs up, and the most individual and the newest feelings and the cleverest technique not only fail to produce any infection but actually repel.

I have mentioned three conditions of contagiousness in art, but they may all be summed up into one, the last, sincerity, i.e., that the artist should be impelled by an inner need to express his feeling. That condition includes the first; for if the artist is sincere he will express the feeling as he experienced it. And as each man is different from everyone else, his feeling will be individual for everyone else; and the more individual it is, the more the artist has drawn it from the depths of his nature, the more sympathetic and sincere will it be. And this same sincerity will impel the artist to find a clear expression of the feeling which he wishes to transmit.

Therefore this third condition—sincerity—is the most important of the three. It is always complied with in peasant art, and this explains why such art always acts so powerfully; but it is a condition almost entirely absent from our upper-class art, which is continually produced by artists actuated by personal aims of covetousness or vanity.

Such are the three conditions which divide art from its counterfeits, and which also decide the quality of every work of art apart from its subject-matter.

The absence of any one of these conditions excludes a work from the category of art and relegates it to that of art's counterfeits. If the work does not transmit the artist's peculiarity of feeling, and is therefore not individual, if it is unintelligibly expressed, or if it has not proceeded from the author's inner need for expression—it is not a work of art. If all these conditions are present, even in the smallest degree, then the work, even if a weak one, is yet a work of art.

The presence in various degrees of these three conditions: individuality, clearness, and sincerity, decides the merit of a work of art, as art, apart from subject matter. All works of art take rank of merit according to the degree in which they fulfil the first, the second, and the third of these conditions. In one the individuality of the feeling transmitted may predominate; in another, clearness of expression; in a third, sincerity; while a fourth may have sincerity and individuality but be deficient in clearness; a fifth, individuality and clearness, but less sincerity; and so forth, in all possible degrees and combinations.

Thus is art divided from not art, and thus is the quality of art, as art, decided, independently of its subject matter, i.e., apart from whether the feelings it transmits are good or bad.

But how are we to define good and bad art with reference to its subject matter?

Chapter XVI

How in art are we to decide what is good and what is bad in subject matter?

Art, like speech, is a means of communication, and therefore of progress, i.e., of the movement of humanity forward towards perfection. Speech renders accessible to men of the latest generations all the knowledge discovered by the experience and reflection, both of preceding generations and of the best and foremost men of their own times; art renders accessible to men of the latest generations all the feelings experienced by their predecessors, and those also which are being felt by their best and foremost contemporaries. And as the evolution of knowledge proceeds by truer and more necessary knowledge dislodging and replacing what is mistaken and unnecessary, so the evolution of feeling proceeds through art—feelings less kind and less needful for the well-being of mankind are replaced by others kinder and more needful for that end. That is the purpose of art. And, speaking now of its subject matter, the more art fulfils that purpose the better the art, and the less it fulfils it the worse the art.

And the appraisement of feelings (i.e., the acknowledgment of these or those feelings as being more or less good, more or less necessary for the well-being of mankind) is made by the religious perception of the age.

In every period of history, and in every human society, there exists an understanding of the meaning of life which represents the highest level to which men of that society have attained—an understanding defining the highest good at which that society aims. And this understanding is the religious perception of the given time and society. And this religious perception is always clearly expressed by some advanced men, and more or less vividly perceived by all the members of the society. Such a religious perception and its corresponding expression exists always in every society. If it appears to us that in our society there is no religious perception, this is not because there really is none, but only because we do not want to see it. And we often wish not to see it because it exposes the fact that our life is inconsistent with that religious perception.

Religious perception in a society is like the direction of a flowing river. If the river flows at all, it must have a direction. If a society lives, there must be a religious perception indicating the direction in which, more or less consciously, all its members tend.

And so there always has been, and there is, a religious perception in every society. And it is by the standard of this religious perception that the feelings transmitted by art have always been estimated. Only on the basis of this religious perception of their age have men always chosen from the endlessly varied spheres of art that art which transmitted feeling making religious perception operative in actual life. And such art has always been highly valued and encouraged; while art transmitting feelings already outlived, flowing from the antiquated religious perceptions of a former age, has always been condemned and despised. All the rest of art, transmitting those most diverse feelings by means of which people commune together, was not condemned, and was tolerated, if only it did not transmit feelings contrary to religious perception. Thus, for instance, among the Greeks, art transmitting the feeling of beauty, strength, and courage (Hesiod, Homer, Phidias) was chosen, approved, and encouraged; while art transmitting feelings of rude sensuality, despondency, and effeminacy was condemned and despised. Among the Jews, art transmitting feelings of devotion and submission to the God of the Hebrews and to His will (the epic of Genesis, the prophets, the Psalms) was chosen and encouraged, while art transmitting feelings of idolatry (the golden calf) was condemned and despised. All the rest of art— stories, songs, dances, ornamentation of houses, of utensils, and of clothes— which was not contrary to religious perception, was neither distinguished nor discussed. Thus, in regard to its subject matter, has art been appraised always and everywhere, and thus it should be appraised, for this attitude towards art proceeds from the fundamental characteristics of human nature, and those characteristics do not change.

I know that according to an opinion current in our times, religion is a superstition, which humanity has outgrown, and that it is therefore assumed that no such thing exists as a religious perception common to us by which art, in our time, can be estimated. I know that this is the opinion current in the pseudo-cultured circles of today. People who do not acknowledge Christianity in its true meaning because it undermines all their social privileges, and who, therefore, invent all kinds of philosophic and esthetic theories to hide from themselves the meaninglessness and wrongness of their lives, cannot think otherwise. These people intentionally, or sometimes unintentionally, confusing the conception of a religious cult with the conception of religious perception, think that by denying the cult they get rid of religious perception. But even the very attacks on religion, and the attempts to establish a life-conception contrary to the religious perception of our times, most clearly demonstrate the existence of that religious perception condemning the lives that are not in harmony with it.

If humanity progresses, i.e., mover forward, there must inevitably be a guide to the direction of that movement. And religions have always furnished that guide. All history shows that the progress of humanity is accomplished not otherwise than under the guidance of religion. But if the race cannot progress without the guidance of religion—and progress is always going on, and consequently also in our own times—then there must be a religion of our times. So that, whether it pleases or displeases the so-called cultured people of today, they must admit the existence of religion—not of a religious cult, Catholic, Protestant, or another, but of religious perception—which, even in our times, is the guide always present where there is any progress. And if a religious perception exists among us, then our art should be appraised on the basis of that religious perception; and, as has always and everywhere been the case, art transmitting feelings flowing from the religious perception of our time should be chosen from all the indifferent art, should be acknowledged, highly esteemed, and encouraged; while art running counter to that perception should be condemned and despised, and all the remaining indifferent art should neither be distinguished nor encouraged.

The religious perception of our time, in its widest and most practical application, is the consciousness that our well-being, both material and spiritual, individual and collective, temporal and eternal, lies in the growth of brotherhood among all men—in their loving harmony with one another. This perception is not only expressed by Christ and all the best men of past ages, it is not only repeated in the most varied forms and from most diverse sides by the best men of our own times, but it already serves as a clue to all the complex labor of humanity, consisting as this labor does, on the one hand, in the destruction of physical and moral obstacles to the union of men, and, on the other hand, in establishing the principles common to all men which can and should unite them into one universal brotherhood. And it is on the basis of this perception that we should appraise all the phenomena of our life, and, among the rest, our art also; choosing from all its realms whatever transmits feelings flowing from this religious perception, highly prizing and encouraging such art, rejecting whatever is contrary to this perception, and not attributing to the rest of art an importance not properly pertaining to it.

The chief mistake made by people of the upper classes of the time of the so-called Renaissance—a mistake which we still perpetuate—was not that they ceased to value and to attach importance to religious art (people of that period could not attach importance to it, because, like our own upper classes, they could not believe in what the majority considered to be religion), but their mistake was that they set up in place of religious art which was lacking, an insignificant art which aimed only at giving pleasure, i.e., they began to choose, to value, and to encourage, in place of religious art, something which, in any case, did not deserve such esteem and encouragement.

One of the Fathers of the Church said that the great evil is not that men do not know God, but they have set up, instead of God, that which is not God. So also with art. The great misfortune of the people of the upper classes of our time is not so much that they are without a religious art, as that, instead of a supreme religious art, chosen from all the rest as being specially important and valuable, they have chosen a most insignificant and, usually, harmful art, which aims at pleasing certain people, and which, therefore, if only by its exclusive nature, stands in contradiction to that Christian principle of universal union which forms the religious perception of our time. Instead of religious art, an empty and often vicious art is set up, and this hides from men's notice the need of that true religious art which should be present in life in order to improve it.

It is true that art which satisfies the demands of the religious perception of our time is quite unlike former art, but, notwithstanding this dissimilarity, to a man who does not intentionally hide the truth from himself, it is very clear and definite what does form the religious art of our age. In former times, when the highest religious perception united only some people (who, even if they formed a large society, were yet but one society surrounded by others—Jews, or Athenian or Roman citizens), the feelings transmitted by the art of that time flowed from a desire for the might, greatness, glory, and prosperity of that society, and the heroes of art might be people who contributed to that prosperity by strength, by craft, by fraud, or by cruelty (Ulysses, Jacob, David, Sampson, Hercules, and all the heroes). But the religious perception of our times does not select any one society of men;

on the contrary, it demands the union of all—absolutely of all people without exception—and above every other virtue it sets brotherly love to all men. And, therefore, the feelings transmitted by the art of our time not only cannot coincide with the feelings transmitted by former art, but must run counter to them. . . .

The essence of the Christian perception consists in the recognition by every man of his sonship to God, and of the consequent union of men with God and with one another, as is said in the Gospel (John 17:21).[2] Therefore the subject matter of Christian art is such feeling as can unite men with God and with one another.

The expression *unite men with God and with one another* may seem obscure to people accustomed to the misuse of these words which is so customary, but the words have a perfectly clear meaning nevertheless. They indicate that the Christian union of man (in contradiction to the partial, exclusive union of only some men) is that which unites all without exception.

Art, all art, has this characteristic, that it unites people. Every art causes those to whom the artist's feeling is transmitted to unite in soul with the artist, and also with all who receive the same impression. But non-Christian art, while uniting some people together, makes that very union a cause of separation between these united people and others; so that union of this kind is often a source, not only of division, but even of enmity towards others. Such is all patriotic art, with its anthems, poems, and monuments; such is all Church art, i.e., the art of certain cults, with their images, statues, processions, and other local ceremonies. Such art is belated and non-Christian art, uniting the people of one cult only to separate them yet more sharply from the members of other cults, and even to place them in relations of hostility to each other. Christian art is only such as tends to unite all without exception, either by evoking in them the perception that each man and all men stand in like relation towards God and towards their neighbor, or by evoking in them identical feelings, which may even be the very simplest provided only that they are not repugnant to Christianity and are natural to everyone without exception.

Good Christian art of our time may be unintelligible to people because of imperfections in its forms, or because men are inattentive to it, but it must be such that all men can experience the feelings it transmits. It must be the art, not of some one group of people, nor of one class, nor of one nationality, nor of one religious cult; that is, it must not transmit feelings which are accessible only to a man educated in a certain way, or only to an aristocrat, or a merchant, or only to a Russian, or a native of Japan, or a Roman Catholic, or a Buddhist, etc., but it must transmit feelings accessible

---

[2] "That they may be one; even as thou, Father, art in me, and I in thee, that they also may be in us" [Tolstoy's note].

to everyone. Only art of this kind can be acknowledged in our time to be good art, worthy of being chosen out from all the rest of art and encouraged.

Christian art, i.e., the art of our time, should be catholic in the original meaning of the word, i.e., universal, and therefore it should unite all men. And only two kinds of feeling do unite all men: first, feelings flowing from the perception of our sonship to God and of the brotherhood of man; and next, the simple feelings of common life, accessible to everyone without exception—such as the feeling of merriment, of pity, of cheerfulness, of tranquillity, etc. Only these two kinds of feelings can now supply material for art good in its subject matter.

And the action of these two kinds of art, apparently so dissimilar, is one and the same. The feelings flowing from perception of our sonship to God and of the brotherhood of man—such as a feeling of sureness in truth, devotion to the will of God, self-sacrifice, respect for and love of man —evoked by Christian religious perception; and the simplest feelings— such as a softened or a merry mood caused by a song or an amusing jest intelligible to everyone, or by a touching story, or a drawing, or a little doll: both alike produce one and the same effect—the loving union of man with man. Sometimes people who are together are, if not hostile to one another, at least estranged in mood and feeling, till perchance a story, a performance, a picture, or even a building, but oftenest of all music, unites them all as by an electric flash, and, in place of their former isolation or even enmity, they are all conscious of union and mutual love. Each is glad that another feels what he feels; glad of the communion established, not only between him and all present, but also with all now living who will yet share the same impression; and more than that, he feels the mysterious gladness of a communion which, reaching beyond the grave, unites us with all men of the past who have been moved by the same feelings, and with all men of the future who will yet be touched by them. And this effect is produced both by the religious art which transmits feelings of love to God and one's neighbor, and by universal art transmitting the very simplest feelings common to all men.

The art of our time should be appraised differently from former art chiefly in this, that the art of our time, i.e., Christian art (basing itself on a religious perception which demands the union of man), excludes from the domain of art good in subject matter everything transmitting exclusive feelings, which do not unite but divide men. It relegates such work to the category of art bad in its subject matter, while, on the other hand, it includes in the category of art good in subject matter a section not formerly admitted to deserve to be chosen out and respected, namely, universal art transmitting even the most trifling and simple feelings if only they are accessible to all men without exception, and therefore unite them. Such art cannot, in our time, but be esteemed good, for it attains the end which the religious perception of our time, i.e., Christianity, sets before humanity.

Christian art either evokes in men those felings which, through love of God and of one's neighbor, draw them to greater and even greater union, and make them ready for and capable of such union; or evokes in them those feelings which show them that they are already united in the joys and sorrows of life. And therefore the Christian art of our time can be and is two kinds: (1) art transmitting feelings flowing from a religious perception of man's position in the world in relation to God and to his neighbor—religious art in the limited meaning of the term; and (2) art transmitting the simplest feelings of common life, but such, always, as are accessible to all men in the whole world—the art of common life—the art of a people—universal art. Only these two kinds of art can be considered good art in our time.

The first, religious art, transmitting both positive feelings of love to God and one's neighbor, and negative feelings of indignation and horror at the violation of love, manifests itself chiefly in the form of words, and to some extent also in painting and sculpture: the second kind (universal art) transmitting feelings accessible to all, manifests itself in words, in paintings, in sculpture, in dances, in architecture, and, most of all, in music.

If I were asked to give modern examples of each of these kinds of art, then, as examples of the highest art, flowing from love of God and man (both of the higher, positive, and of the lower, negative kind), in literature I should name *The Robbers* by Schiller; Victor Hugo's *Les Pauvres Gens* and *Les Misérables*; the novels and stories of Dickens—*The Tale of Two Cities, The Christmas Carol, The Chimes*, and others; *Uncle Tom's Cabin*; Dostoevsky's works—especially his *Memoirs from the House of Death*; and *Adam Bede* by George Eliot. . . .

To give examples, from the modern art of our upper classes, of art of the second kind, good universal art or even of the art of a whole people, is yet more difficult, especially in literary art and music. If there are some works which by their inner contents might be assigned to this class (such as *Don Quixote*, Molière's comedies, *David Copperfield* and *The Pickwick Papers* by Dickens, Gogol's and Pushkin's tales, and some things of Maupassant's), these works are for the most part—from the exceptional nature of the feelings they transmit, and the superfluity of special details of time and locality, and, above all, on account of the poverty of their subject matter in comparison with examples of universal ancient art (such, for instance, as the story of Joseph)—comprehensible only to people of their own circle. That Joseph's brethren, being jealous of his father's affection, sell him to the merchants; that Potiphar's wife wishes to tempt the youth; that having attained the highest station, he takes pity on his brothers, including Benjamin the favorite—these and all the rest are feelings accessible alike to a Russian

peasant, a Chinese, an African, a child, or an old man, educated or uneducated; and it is all written with such restraint, is so free from any superfluous detail, that the story may be told to any circle and will be equally
comprehensible and touching to everyone. But not such are the feelings
of Don Quixote or of Molière's heroes (though Molière is perhaps the
most universal, and therefore the most excellent, artist of modern times),
nor of Pickwick and his friends. These feelings are not common to all men
but very exceptional, and therefore, to make them infectious, the authors
have surrounded them with abundant detail of time and place. And this
abundance of detail makes the stories difficult of comprehension to all people
not living within reach of the conditions described by the author.

The author of the novel of Joseph did not need to describe in detail, as
would be done nowadays, the blood-stained coat of Joseph, the dwelling
and dress of Jacob, the pose and attire of Potiphar's wife, and how, adjusting
the bracelet on her left arm, she said, "Come to me," and so on, because
the subject matter of feelings in this novel are so strong that all details,
except the most essential—such as that Joseph went out into another room
to weep—are superfluous, and would only hinder the transmission of feelings.
And therefore this novel is accessible to all men, touches people of all nations
and classes, young and old, and has lasted to our times, and will yet last for
thousands of years to come. But strip the best novels of our times of their
details, and what will remain?

It is therefore impossible in modern literature to indicate works fully
satisfying the demands of universality. Such works as exist are, to a great
extent, spoilt by what is usually called "realism," but would be better termed
"provincialism," in art.

In music the same occurs as in verbal art, and for similar reasons. In
consequence of the poorness of the feeling they contain, the melodies of the
modern composers are amazingly empty and insignificant. And to strengthen
the impression produced by these empty melodies, the new musicians pile
complex modulations on to each trivial melody, not only in their own national
manner, but also in the way characteristic of their own exclusive circle and
particular musical school. Melody—every melody—is free, and may be understood of all men; but as soon as it is bound up with a particular harmony,
it ceases to be accessible except to people trained to such harmony, and it
becomes strange, not only to common men of another nationality, but to
all who do not belong to the circle whose members have accustomed themselves to certain forms of harmonization. . . .

In the arts of painting and sculpture, all pictures and statues in so-called
genre style, depictions of animals, landscapes and caricatures with subjects
comprehensible to everyone and also all kinds of ornaments, are universal
in subject matter. . . . In reality all such objects, if only they transmit a

true feeling experienced by the artist and comprehensible to everyone (however insignificant it may seem to us to be) are works of real, good, Christian art. . . .

So that there are only two kinds of good Christian art: all the rest of art not comprised in these two divisions should be acknowledged to be a bad art, deserving not to be encouraged but to be driven out, denied and despised, as being art not uniting but dividing people. Such, in literary art, are all novels and poems which transmit Church or patriotic feelings, and also exclusive feelings pertaining only to the class of the idle rich; such as aristocratic honor, satiety, spleen, pessimism, and refined and vicious feelings flowing from sex-love—quite incomprehensible to the great majority of mankind.

In painting we must similarly place in the class of bad art all the Church, patriotic, and exclusive pictures; all the pictures representing the amusements and allurements of a rich and idle life; all the so-called symbolic pictures, in which the very meaning of the symbol is comprehensible only to the people of a certain circle; and, above all, pictures with voluptuous subjects—all that odious female nudity which fills all the exhibitions and galleries. And to this class belongs almost all the chamber and opera music of our times—beginning especially from Beethoven (Schumann, Berlioz, Liszt, Wagner)—by its subject matter devoted to the expression of feelings accessible only to people who have developed in themselves an unhealthy, nervous irritation evoked by this exclusive, artificial, and complex music.

"What! the *Ninth Symphony* not a good work of art!" I hear exclaimed by indignant voices.

And I reply: Most certainly it is not. All that I have written I have written with the sole purpose of finding a clear and reasonable criterion by which to judge the merits of works of art. And this criterion, coinciding with the indications of plain and sane sense, indubitably shows me that that symphony by Beethoven is not a good work of art. Of course, to people educated in the adoration of certain productions and of their authors, to people whose taste has been perverted by just being educated in such adoration, the acknowledgement that such a celebrated work is bad is amazing and strange. But how are we to escape the indications of reason and of common sense?

Beethoven's *Ninth Symphony* is considered a great work of art. To verify its claim to be such, I must first ask myself whether this work transmits the highest religious feeling? I reply in the negative, for music in itself cannot transmit those feelings; and therefore I ask myself next, Since this work does not belong to the highest kind of religious art, has it the other characteristic of the good art of our time, the quality of uniting all men in one common feeling: does it rank as Christian universal art? And again I have no option but to reply in the negative; for not only do I not see how the feelings transmitted by this work could unite people not specially trained to submit themselves to its complex hypnotism, but I am unable to imagine to myself a crowd of normal people who could understand anything of this long, confused, and artificial production, except short snatches which are lost in a sea of what is incomprehensible. And therefore, whether I like it or not, I am compelled to conclude that this work belongs to the rank of bad art. . . .

And, just in this same way, in all branches of art, many and many works considered great by the upper classes of our society will have to be judged. By this one sure criterion we shall have to judge the celebrated *Divine Comedy* and *Jerusalem Delivered,* and a great part of Shakespeare's and Goethe's works, and in painting every representation of miracles, including Raphael's "Transfiguration," etc.

Whatever the work may be and however it may have been extolled, we have first to ask whether this work is one of real art or a counterfeit. Having acknowledged, on the basis of the indication of its infectiousness even to a small class of people, that a certain production belongs to the realm of art, it is necessary, on the basis of the indication of its accessibility, to decide the next question, Does this work belong to the category of bad, exclusive art, opposed to religious perception, or to Christian art, uniting people? And having acknowledged an article to belong to real Christian art, we must then, according to whether it transmits the feelings flowing from love to God and man, or merely the simple feelings uniting all men, assign it a place in the ranks of religious art or in those universal art.

Only on the basis of such verification shall we find it possible to select from the whole mass of what, in our society, claims to be art, those works which form real, important, necessary spiritual food, and to separate them from all the harmful and useless art, and from the counterfeits of art which surround us. Only on the basis of such verification shall we be able to rid ourselves of the pernicious results of harmful art, and to avail ourselves of that beneficent action which is the purpose of true and good art, and which is indispensable for the spiritual life of man and of humanity.

V. I. Lenin 1870–1924

Party Organization and Party Literature 1905

The new conditions for Social-Democratic work in Russia which have arisen since the October revolution[1] have brought the question of party literature to the fore. The distinction between the illegal and the legal press, that melancholy heritage of the epoch of feudal, autocratic Russia, is beginning to disappear. It is not yet dead, by a long way. The hypocritical government of our Prime Minister is still running amuck, so much so that *Izvestia Soveta Rabochikh Deputatov*[2] is printed "illegally"; but apart from bringing disgrace on the government, apart from striking further moral blows at it, nothing comes of the stupid attempts to "prohibit" that which the government is powerless to thwart.

So long as there was a distinction between the illegal and the legal press, the question of the party and nonparty press was decided extremely simply and in an extremely false and abnormal way. The entire illegal press was a party press, being published by organizations and run by groups which in one way or another were linked with groups of practical party workers. The entire legal press was nonparty—since parties were banned—but it "gravitated" towards one party or another. Unnatural alliances, strange "bed-fellows" and false cover-devices were inevitable. The forced reserve of those who wished to express party views merged with the immature thinking or mental cowardice of those who had not risen to these views and who were not, in effect, party people.

An accursed period of Aesopian language, literary bondage, slavish speech, and ideological serfdom! The proletariat has put an end to this foul atmosphere which stifled everything living and fresh in Russia. But so far the proletariat has won only half freedom for Russia.

The revolution is not yet completed. While tsarism is *no longer* strong enough to defeat the revolution, the revolution is *not yet* strong enough to defeat tsarism. And we are living in times when everywhere and in everything there operates this unnatural combination of open, forthright, direct and consistent party spirit with an underground, covert, "diplomatic" and dodgy

From V. I. Lenin, *On Literature and Art*. Moscow: Progress Publishers, 1967.

[1] A general political strike in October 1905. This compelled the tsar to issue the Manifesto of October 17, 1905, which granted the people civil rights. The Bolsheviks made use of the new freedom of the press to publish their newspapers legally.

[2] *Bulletin of the Soviet of Workers' Deputies.*

"legality." This unnatural combination makes itself felt even in our news-paper: for all Mr. Guchkov's[3] witticisms about Social-Democratic tyranny forbidding the publication of moderate liberal-bourgeois newspapers, the fact remains that *Proletary*,[4] the Central Organ of the Russian Social-Democratic Labor Party, still remains outside the locked doors of *autocratic*, police-ridden Russia.

Be that as it may, the halfway revolution compels all of us to set to work at once organizing the whole thing on new lines. Today literature, even that published "legally," can be nine-tenths party literature. It must become party literature. In contradistinction to bourgeois customs, to the profit-making, commercialized bourgeois press, to bourgeois literary careerism and individ-ualism, "aristocratic anarchism" and drive for profit, the socialist proletariat must put forward the principle of *party literature*, must develop this principle and put it into practice as fully and completely as possible.

What is this principle of party literature? It is not simply that, for the socialist proletariat, literature cannot be a means of enriching individuals or groups; it cannot, in fact, be an individual undertaking, independent of the common cause of the proletariat. Down with nonpartisan writers! Down with literary supermen! Literature must become *part* of the common cause of the proletariat, "a cog and a screw" of one single great Social-Democratic mechanism set in motion by the entire politically conscious vanguard of the entire working class. Literature must become a component of organized, planned and integrated Social-Democratic Party work.

"All comparisons are lame," says a German proverb. So is my comparison of literature with a cog, of a living movement with a mechanism. And I daresay there will ever be hysterical intellectuals to raise a howl about such a comparison, which degrades, deadens, "bureaucratizes" the free battle of ideas, freedom of criticism, freedom of literary creation, etc., etc. Such out-cries, in point of fact, would be nothing more than an expression of bourgeois-intellectual individualism. There is no question that literature is least of all subject to mechanical adjustment or levelling, to the rule of the majority over the minority. There is no question, either, that in this field greater scope must undoubtedly be allowed for personal initiative, individual inclination, thought and fantasy, form and content. All this is undeniable; but all this simply shows that the literary side of the proletarian party cause cannot be mechanically identified with its other sides. This, however, does not in the least refute the proposition, alien and strange to the bourgeoisie and bour-geois democracy, that literature must by all means and necessarily become an element of Social-Democratic Party work, inseparably bound up with the other elements. Newspapers must become the organs of the various party

[3] Alexander Ivanovich Guchkov (1862–1936), Russian capitalist.
[4] *Proletarian*, an illegal Bolshevik weekly newspaper, published in Geneva from May 14 to November 12, 1905, under Lenin's editorship.

organizations, and their writers must by all means become members of these organizations. Publishing and distributing centers, bookshops and reading-rooms, libraries and similar establishments—must all be under party control. The organized socialist proletariat must keep an eye on all this work, supervise it in its entirety, and, from beginning to end, without any exception, infuse into it the life-stream of the living proletarian cause, thereby cutting the ground from under the old, semi-Oblomov,[5] semishopkeeper Russian principle: the writer does the writing, the reader does the reading.

We are not suggesting, of course, that this transformation of literary work, which has been defiled by the Asiatic censorship and the European bourgeoisie, can be accomplished all at once. Far be it from us to advocate any kind of standardized system, or a solution by means of a few decrees. Cut-and-dried schemes are least of all applicable here. What is needed is that the whole of our Party, and the entire politically conscious Social-Democratic proletariat throughout Russia, should become aware of this new problem, specify it clearly and everywhere set about solving it. Emerging from the captivity of the feudal censorship, we have no desire to become, and shall not become, prisoners of bourgeois-shopkeeper literary relations. We want to establish, and we shall establish, a free press, free not simply from the police, but also from capital, from careerism, and what is more, free from bourgeois-anarchist individualism.

These last words may sound paradoxical, or an affront to the reader. What! some intellectual, an ardent champion of liberty, may shout. What, you want to impose collective control on such a delicate, individual matter as literary work! You want workmen to decide questions of science, philosophy, or esthetics by a majority of votes! You deny the absolute freedom of absolutely individual ideological work!

Calm yourself, gentlemen! First of all, we are discussing party literature and its subordination to party control. Everyone is free to write and say whatever he likes, without any restrictions. But every voluntary association (including the party) is also free to expel members who use the name of the party to advocate antiparty views. Freedom of speech and the press must be complete. But then freedom of association must be complete too. I am bound to accord you, in the name of free speech, the full right to shout, lie and write to your heart's content. But you are bound to grant me, in the name of freedom of association, the right to enter into, or withdraw from, association with people advocating this or that view. The party is a voluntary association, which would inevitably break up, first ideologically and then physically, if it did not cleanse itself of people advocating antiparty views. And to define the borderline between party and antiparty there is the party

---

[5] Chief character of a novel of the same name by I. A. Goncharov. Oblomov, who spends most of his life in his dressing gown, personifies apathy, lethargy, stagnation.

program, the party's resolutions on tactics and its rules and, lastly, the entire experience of international Social-Democracy, the voluntary international associations of the proletariat, which has constantly brought into its parties individual elements and trends not fully consistent, not completely Marxist and not altogether correct and which, on the other hand, has constantly conducted periodical "cleansing" of its ranks. So it will be with us too, supporters of bourgeois "freedom of criticism," *within* the Party. We are now becoming a mass party all at once, changing abruptly to an open organization, and it is inevitable that we shall be joined by many who are inconsistent (from the Marxist standpoint), perhaps we shall be joined even by some Christian elements, and even by some mystics. We have sound stomachs and we are rocklike Marxists. We shall digest those inconsistent elements. Freedom of thought and freedom of criticism within the Party will never make us forget about the freedom of organizing people into those voluntary associations known as parties.

Secondly, we must say to you bourgeois individualists that your talk about absolute freedom is sheer hypocrisy. There can be no real and effective "freedom" in a society based on the power of money, in a society in which the masses of working people live in poverty and the handful of rich live like parasites. Are you free in relation to your bourgeois publisher, Mr. Writer, in relation to your bourgeois public, which demands that you provide it with pornography in novels and paintings, and prostitution as a "supplement" to "sacred" scenic art? This absolute freedom is a bourgeois or an anarchist phrase (since, as a world outlook, anarchism is bourgeois philosophy turned inside out). One cannot live in society and be free from society. The freedom of the bourgeois writer, artist or actress is simply masked (or hypocritically masked) dependence on the money-bag, on corruption, on prostitution.

And we socialists expose this hypocrisy and rip off the false labels, not in order to arrive at a nonclass literature and art (that will be possible only in a socialist extra-class society), but to contrast this hypocritically free literature, which is in reality linked to the bourgeoisie, with a really free one that will be *openly* linked to the proletariat.

It will be a free literature, because the idea of socialism and sympathy with the working people, and not greed or careerism, will bring over new forces to its ranks. It will be a free literature, because it will serve, not some satiated heroine, not the bored "upper ten thousand" suffering from fatty degeneration, but the millions and tens of millions of working people—the flower of the country, its strength and its future. It will be a free literature, enriching the last word in the revolutionary thought of mankind with the experience and living work of the socialist proletariat bringing about permanent interaction between the experience of the past (scientific socialism, the completion of the development of socialism from its primitive, utopian forms) and the experience of the present (the present struggle of the worker comrades).

To work, then, comrades! We are faced with a new and difficult task. But it is a noble and grateful one—to organize a broad, multiform and varied literature inseparably linked with the Social-Democratic working-class movement. All Social-Democratic literature must become Party literature. Every newspaper, journal, publishing house, etc., must immediately set about reorganizing its work, leading up to a situation in which it will, in one form or another, be integrated into one Party organization or another. Only then will "Social-Democratic" literature really become worthy of that name, only then will it be able to fulfil its duty and, even within the framework of bourgeois society, break out of bourgeois slavery and merge with the movement of the really advanced and thoroughly revolutionary class.

On Education and the Arts *October 8, 1920*

It is necessary that a draft resolution (of the Proletcult[1] Congress) should be drawn up with the utmost urgency, and that it should be endorsed by the Central Committee, in time to have it put to the vote *at this very* session of the Proletcult. On behalf of the Central Committee it should be submitted not later than today, for endorsement both by the Collegium of the People's Commissariat of Education and by the Proletcult Congress, because the Congress is closing today.

Draft Resolution

1. All educational work in the Soviet Republic of workers and peasants, in the field of political education in general and in the field of art in particular, should be imbued with the spirit of the class struggle being

From V. I. Lenin, *On Literature and Art.* Moscow: Progress Publishers, 1967.

[1] Proletarian Cultural and Educational Organizations.

waged by the proletariat for the successful achievement of the aims of its dictatorship, i.e., the overthrow of the bourgeoisie, the abolition of classes, and the elimination of all forms of exploitation of man by man.

2.   Hence, the proletariat, both through its vanguard—the Communist Party—and through the many types of proletarian organizations in general, should display the utmost activity and play the leading part in all the work of public education.

3.   All the experience of modern history and, particularly, the more than half-century-old revolutionary struggle of the proletariat of all countries since the appearance of the *Communist Manifesto* has unquestionably demonstrated that the Marxist world outlook is the only true expression of the interests, the viewpoint, and the culture of the revolutionary proletariat.

4.   Marxism has won its historic significance as the ideology of the revolutionary proletariat because, far from rejecting the most valuable achievements of the bourgeois epoch, it has, on the contrary, assimilated and refashioned everything of value in the more than two thousand years of the development of human thought and culture. Only further work on this basis and in this direction, inspired by the practical experience of the proletarian dictatorship as the final stage in the struggle against every form of exploitation, can be recognized as the development of a genuine proletarian culture.

5.   Adhering unswervingly to this stand of principle, the All-Russia Proletcult Congress rejects in the most resolute manner, as theoretically unsound and practically harmful, all attempts to invent one's own particular brand of culture, to remain isolated in self-contained organizations, to draw a line dividing the field of work of the People's Commissariat of Education and the Proletcult, or to set up a Proletcult "autonomy" within establishments under the People's Commissariat of Education and so forth. On the contrary, the Congress enjoins all Proletcult organizations to fully consider themselves in duty bound to act as auxiliary bodies of the network of establishments under the People's Commissariat of Education, and to accomplish their tasks under the general guidance of the Soviet authorities (specifically, of the People's Commissariat of Education) and of the Russian Communist Party, as part of the tasks of the proletarian dictatorship.

George Lukács 1885–1971

The Sociology of Modern Drama 1909

Modern drama is the drama of the bourgeoisie; modern drama is bourgeois drama. By the end of our discussion, we believe, a real and specific content will have filled out this abstract formulation. . . .

The drama has now taken on new social dimensions.[1] This development became necessary, and necessary at this particular time, because of the specific social situation of the bourgeoisie. For bourgeois drama is the first to grow out of conscious class confrontation; the first with the set intention of expressing the patterns of thought and emotion, as well as the relations with other classes, of a class struggling for power and freedom. . . . Although in Elizabethan drama the representatives of several classes appear, the true human beings, the dramatic characters, are derived on the whole from a single class. Infrequently, we find a figure that represents the petty nobility, as in *Arden of Feversham*.[2] The lower classes merely take part in comic episodes, or they are on hand simply so their inferiority will highlight the refinements of the heroes. For this reason, class is not decisive in structuring the character and action of these plays. . . .

A new determinant is joined to the new drama: value judgment. In the new drama not merely passions are in conflict, but ideologies, *Weltanschauungen*,[3] as well. Because men collide who come from differing situations, value judgments must necessarily function as importantly, at least, as purely in-

Selections, translated by Lee Baxandall. Copyright © 1965 by Lee Baxandall. Reprinted by permission of the translator. This translation first appeared in *Tulane Drama Review*, IX (Summer 1965).

[1] Discussed in detail in a portion of the essay here omitted, which dealt chiefly with development of the stage as an institution. Lukács argues that truly bourgeois plays were first written by the Germans Lenz, Grabbe, Goethe, Schiller, and others who were the first dramatists to develop historicist ideas. Emphasis upon reasoned argument, together with environmental determination, is seen to distinguish bourgeois playwrights from their predecessors, who had enjoyed spontaneous communication with their audiences by virtue of shared religious sensibility. According to Lukács, this unity was shattered by a new rationalism, introduced to society by the bourgeoisie's organization of economy and social relations along the most productive lines. The playwright found himself isolated from the broad public; he produced intellectualist compositions for minority audiences, while the public, cut off alike from the rationalist stage and from religious drama, sought theatre offering amusement for its own sake. The Little Theatre movement which emerged after 1885 sought to provide bourgeois drama with a stage, but with poor results [translator's note].

[2] Anon., pub. 1592.

[3] World outlooks.

dividual characteristics. . . . The moral outlooks of Hamlet and Claudius, and even of Richard and Richmond, are at bottom identical. Each man is resolute, and feels contemptible if he acts contrary to this moral view. Claudius knows the murder of his brother to be a sin; he is even incapable of seeking motives that might justify his action, and it is inconceivable that he would attempt a relativist justification (as Hebbel's Herodes will, following the murder of Aristobolus).[4] Also the "skeptical" and "philosophical" Hamlet never for a moment doubts that he is impelled as though by categorical imperative to seek blood revenge. So long as he remains incapable of acting as he knows he must, he feels sinful and blameworthy. Hegel is therefore correct when he says the deeds of Shakespeare's heroes are not "morally justified." For the ethical value judgment of that epoch rested upon such solid metaphysical foundations, showed such little tolerance for any kind of relativity, and gained universality from such mystic, nonanalyzable emotions, that no person violating it—for whatever reasons and motive—could justify his act even subjectively. His deed could be explained by his soul's condition, but no amount of reasoning could provide absolution. . . .

The conflict of generations as a theme is but the most striking and extreme instance of a phenomenon new to drama, but born of general emotion. For the stage has turned into the point of intersection for pairs of worlds distinct in time; the realm of drama is one where "past" and "future," "no longer" and "not yet," come together in a single moment. What we usually call "the present" in drama is the occasion of self-appraisal; from the past is born the future, which struggles free of the old and of all that stands in opposition. The end of each tragedy sees the collapse of an entire world. The new drama brings what in fact is new, and what follows the collapse differs qualitatively from the old; whereas in Shakespeare the difference was merely quantitative. Looked at from an ethical perspective: the bad is replaced by the good, or by something better than the old, and at any rate decidedly different in kind. In *Götz von Berlichingen*[5] Goethe depicts the collapse of a world; a tragedy is possible in this case only because Götz was born at the particular time. A century or perhaps even a generation earlier, and he would have become a hero of legend, perhaps rather like a tragicomic Don Quixote; and a scant generation later as well, this might have been the result. . . .

. . . The heroes of the new drama—in comparison to the old—are more passive than active; they are acted upon more than they act for themselves; they defend rather than attack; their heroism is mostly a heroism of anguish, of despair, not one of bold aggressiveness. Since so much of the inner man has fallen prey to destiny, the last battle is to be enacted within. We can best

---

[4] *Herod and Mariamne* (1848).
[5] (1773).

summarize by saying that the more the vital motivating center is displaced outward (i.e., the greater the determining force of external factors), the more the center of tragic conflict is drawn inward; it bec mes internalized, more exclusively a conflict in the spirit. For up to a certain limit, the inner powers of resistance upon which the spirit can depend become greater and more intense in direct proportion to the greatness and intensity of the outwardly opposing forces. And since the hero now is confronted not only with many more external factors than formerly, but also by actions which have become not his own and turn against him, the struggle in which he engages will be heightened into anguish. He must engage in the struggle: something drives him into it which he cannot resist; it is not his to decide whether he even wishes to resist.

This is the dramatic conflict: man as merely the intersection point of great forces, and his deeds not even his own. Instead something independent of him mixes in, a hostile system which he senses as forever indifferent to him, thus shattering his will. And the why of his acts is likewise never wholly his own, and what he senses as his inner motivating energy also partakes of an aspect of the great complex which directs him toward his fall. The dialectical force comes to reside more exclusively in the idea, in the abstract. Men are but pawns, their will is but their possible moves, and it is what remains forever alien to them (the *abstractum*) which moves them. Man's significance consists only of this, that the game cannot be played without him, that men are the only possible hieroglyphs with which mysterious inscription may be composed. . . .

The new drama is nevertheless the drama of individualism, and that with a force, an intensity and an exclusiveness no other drama ever had. Indeed, one can well conceive an historical perspective on the drama which would see in this the most profound distinction between the old and new drama; such an outlook would place the beginnings of new drama at the point where individualism commences to become dramatic. . . . We said previously that new drama is bourgeois and historicist; we add now that it is a drama of individualism. And in fact these three formulas express a single point of demarcation; they merely view the parting of ways from distinct vantage-points. The first perspective is the question of sociological basis, the foundation on which the other two are based and from which they grow. It states simply that the social and economic forms which the bourgeoisie opposed to remaining vestiges of the feudal order became, from the eighteenth century onward, the prevailing forms. Also, that life proceeds within this framework, and in the tempo and rhythm it dictates, and thus the problems this fact provokes are precisely the problems of life; in a word, that culture today is bourgeois culture. . . . Both historicism and individualism have their roots in the soil of this one culture, and though it may seem from several points of view that they would be sharply conflicting, mutually exclusive opposites, we must nevertheless ask how much this opposition really amounts to an antagonism. . . .

In the course of German Romanticism the historicist sense grew to consciousness together with and parallel to Romantic Individualism, and the two were never felt to exclude one another. We must regard as no accident the way both of these sensibilities rose to consciousness coincidentally and closely associated with the first great event of bourgeois culture, and perhaps its most decisive, the French Revolution, and all that happened around and because of it. . . .

If we examine even the superficial externals of modern life, we are struck by the degree to which it has grown uniform, though it theoretically has engendered a most extreme individualism. Our clothing has grown uniform, as has the communications system; the various forms of employment, from the employee's viewpoint, have grown ever more similar (bureaucracy, mechanized industrial labor); education and the experiences of childhood are more and more alike (the effect and increasing influence of big-city life); and so on. Parallel to this is the ongoing *rationalizing* of our life. Perhaps the essence of the modern division of labor, as seen by the individual, is that ways are sought to make work independent of the worker's capacities, which, always irrational, are but qualitatively determinable; to this end, work is organized according to production outlooks which are objective, super-personal and independent of the employee's character. This is the characteristic tendency of the economics of capitalism. Production is rendered more objective, and freed from the personality of the productive agent. An objective abstraction, capital, becomes the true productive agent in capitalist economy, and it scarcely has an organic relation with the personality of its accidental owner; indeed, personality may often become superfluous, as in corporations.

Also, scientific methodologies gradually cease to be bound up with personality. In medieval science a single individual personally would command an entire sphere of knowledge (e.g., chemistry, astrology), and masters passed on their knowledge or "secret" to the pupils. The same situation was true in the medieval trades and commerce. But the modern specialized methodologies become continually more objective and impersonal. The relation between work and its performers grows more loose; less and less does the work engage the employee's personality, and conversely, the work is related ever less to the workers' personal qualities. Thus work assumes an oddly objective existence, detached from the particularities of individual men, and they must seek means of self-expression outside their work. The relations between men grow more impersonal as well. Possibly the chief characteristic of the feudal order was the way men's dependencies and relations were brought into unity; by contrast, the bourgeois order rationalizes them. The same tendency to depersonalize, with the substitution of quantitative for qualitative categories, is manifested in the overall state organization (electoral system, bureaucracy, military organization, etc.). Together with all this, man too develops a view of life and the world which is inclined toward wholly objective standards, free of any dependency upon human factors.

The style of the new individualism, especially the aspect of importance to us, is defined by this displacement in the relations of liberty and constraint. The transformation can be briefly formulated: previously, life itself was individualistic, now men, or rather their convictions and their outlooks on life, are. Earlier ideology emphasized constraint, because man felt his place within a binding order to be natural and consistent with the world system; and yet, all occasions of concrete living offered him the opportunity to inject his personality into the order of things by means of his deeds. Hence a spontaneous and continuous individualism of this sort was feasible, whereas today it has grown conscious and problematic as a result of the transformation we have sketched. Previously it was—in Schiller's sense—naïve, and today sentimental. The formulation is this, applied to drama: the old drama, by which we mean here primarily that of the Renaissance, was drama of great individuals, today's is that of individualism. In other words, the realization of personality, its per se expression in life, could in no wise become a theme of earlier drama, since personality was not yet problematic. It is, in the drama of today, the chief and most central problem. Though it is true that in most tragedies the action consisted of the clash at some point of someone's maximum attainment with what lay outside him, and the existing order of things refused to let a figure rise to the peak of his possibilities without destroying him, yet this was never associated, consciously at least, with the blunt concept of maximized attainment. The arrangement of the situation was never such that the tragedy had necessarily to result, as it were, from the bare fact of willing, the mere realization of personality. In summary: where the tragedy was previously brought on by the particular *direction* taken by the will, the mere *act* of willing suffices to induce it in the new tragedy. Once again Hebbel offers the most precise definition. He stated that it did not matter for the purposes of drama whether the hero's fall was caused by good or bad actions.

The realization and maintenance of personality has become on the one hand a conscious problem of living; the longing to make the personality prevail grows increasingly pressing and urgent. On the other hand, external circumstances, which rule out this possibility from the first, gain ever greater weight. It is in this way that survival as an individual, the integrity of individuality, becomes the vital center of drama. Indeed the bare fact of Being begins to turn tragic. In view of the augmented force of external circumstance, the least disturbance or incapacity to adjust is enough to induce dissonances which cannot be resolved. Just so, the esthetic of Romanticism regarded tragedy—with a metaphysical rationale and explanation, to be sure—as a consequence of mere being, and the necessary inevitable consequence and natural correlate of individuation. Thus, the contention of these mutually opposed forces is emphasized with increasing sharpness. The sense of being constrained grows, as does its dramatic expression; likewise the longing grows for a man to shatter the bonds which bind men, even though the price he pays is his downfall. . . .

Thus we can say that the drama of individualism (and historicism) is as well the drama of milieu. For only this much-heightened sense of the significance of milieu enables it to function as a dramatic element; only this could render individualism truly problematic, and so engender the drama of individualism. This drama signals the collapse of eighteenth-century doctrinaire individualism. What then was treated as a formal contention between ideologies and life, now becomes a portion of content, an integral part of the historicist drama. Modern life liberates man from many old constraints and it causes him to feel each bond between men (since there are no longer organic) as a bondage. But in turn, man comes to be enclasped by an entire chain of abstract bondages, which are yet more complicated. He feels, whether or not he is conscious of it, that every bond whatsoever is bad and so every bond between men must be resisted as an imposition upon human dignity. In every case, however, the bondage will prove stronger than the resistance. In this perspective Schiller's first play is one typical commencement of the new drama, just as Goethe's play was in another perspective. . . .

In sum, life as the subject of poetry has grown more epic, or to be precise, more novelistic than ever (we refer, of course, to the psychological rather than the primitive form of the novel). The transposition of life into the drama is achieved only by the symptomatic rendering of the life data. For the significance of life's external particulars has declined, if we regard them with the task in mind of rendering man dramatic. Thus, the threat to personality becomes almost of necessity the subject of theoretical discussion. Only if the problem is presented abstractly, dialectically, can we succeed in turning the particular event, which is the basic stuff of drama, into an event touching upon, and expressive of, dramatic man's inner essence. The personage must be consciously aware that in the given case directly involving him, the perpetuation of his personality is at stake. The new drama is on this account the drama of individualism: a drama of demands upon personality made conscious. For this reason men's convictions, their ideologies, are of the highest artistic importance, for they alone can lend a symptomatic significance to the naked data. Only they can bring the vital centers of drama and of character into adjustment. However, this adjustment will always remain problematic; it will never be more than a "solution," an almost miraculous coherence of mutually antagonistic forces, for the ideology threatens in turn to reduce character to a "contrapuntal necessity." . . .

The only ideology which men will not feel to be an ideology is one which prevails absolutely and tolerates no opposition or doubt; only such a one ceases to be abstract and intellectual and is entirely transformed into feeling, so that it is received emotionally just as though no problem of value-judgment were ever involved (e.g., the medieval ideology of Revenge as still found in Shakespeare, or the dictates of Honor among the Spanish). Until the ideologies motivating men became relativized, a man was right or he was wrong. If right, he recognized no relative justification of his opponents whatsoever; nothing might justify them since they were wrong. Were one to suppose that demonic passions drove them to transgress norms which otherwise were absolutely binding, then the nature of the motivating forces was itself enough to forbid sympathy for the others' state of mind, especially with opponents. The final implication of a struggle between persons was such that one could scarcely see in the opponent anyone less than a mortal enemy, and this is precisely because the struggle was irrational. How different are conflicts where the individual is taken for the mere proxy of something external to him, something objective, conflicts where the pairing of particular opponents is virtually accidental, the result of intersected necessities. This is why the man of Shakespeare's time, ripping and tearing his opponent in the wild grip of unbridled passions, could hardly be thought to conceive a sense of community with those whom he destroyed and who destroyed him. . . .

In the main, this explains why intrigue has become superfluous and even disruptive. When every action can be "understood," man's wickedness (though its forms remain unchanged) can no longer be regarded as the ultimate cause of events (as, e.g., Shakespeare's Iago still was). The Count in Lessing's *Emilia Galotti*[6] represents the first stage of this development; and, after the wild excesses of his initial dramas, Schiller comes to this point almost against his will, in the opinion of Philipp.[7] Again it is Hebbel who grasps the situation in its theoretical purity, when he declares that a dramatist's worth is in inverse ratio to the number of scoundrels he requires. . . .

The new life lacks a mythology; what this means is that the thematic material of tragedies must be distanced from life artificially. For the esthetic significance of mythology is twofold. In the first place it projects, in the concrete symbols of concrete fables, man's vital emotions concerning the most profound problems of his life. These fables are not so rigid that they cannot incorporate displacements of the general sensibility, should these occur. Should it happen, however, the retained elements will always outweigh the added elements; the perceptible event will amount to more than the new way of valuing it. The second aspect, and possibly the more important, is that the tragic situation so expressed is held at a constant natural distance

[6] (1772).
[7] *Don Carlos* (1787).

from the public—a constant distance, since the event is projected into vast dark distances of time. A natural distance, since subject and content, and indeed form, have been molded in the public's midst as something their own life partakes of, something passed along from their ancestors and without which life itself could scarcely be imagined. Whatever can be made into myth is by its nature poetic. This means, in the always paradoxical fashion of every poetic work, that it is both distant and near to life, and bears in itself, without conscious stylization, the real and irreal, the naïve and all-signifying, the spontaneous and symbolic, adornment and simple pathos. At its origins, or in the process of turning the past into myth (as for instance, Shakespeare with the War of the Roses), everything that is accidental or superfluous or derives from the individual will, or depends for its effect upon the willfulness of individual taste—everything which, despite its "interestingness," renders the profound trivial—is torn from the subjects of poetry. . . .

The bourgeois drama is by nature problematic, as theory and practice both agree, and countless circumstantial and formal signs indicate. Apart from the general stylistic problems of any new drama, drama becomes problematic at its base as soon as its subject is a bourgeois destiny enacted among bourgeois personages. The thematic material of bourgeois drama is trivial, because it is all too near to us; the natural pathos of its living men is nondramatic and its most subtle values are lost when heightened into drama; the fable is willfully invented and so cannot retain the natural and poetic resonance of an ancient tradition. In consequence, most modern dramas are historical, whether they are set in a definite epoch or the timeless past, and, in view of the foregoing, their historicity gains new meaning. History is meant as a substitute for mythology, creating artificial distances, producing monumentality, clearing away trivia and injecting a new pathos. However, the distance to be gained by projecting back in history is more conscious than formerly, and it is for this reason less spirited and forced to appeal more to the facts, forced, because more timid, to cling more strongly to empirical data. The essence of historical distancing is that it substitutes what happened long ago for what happens today. But always, one event takes the place of another; never does a symbol replace a reality. (Naturally I am not concerned here with trivial "historical truth." A modern fantasy drama is historical; it is less free of the facts than are Shakespeare's historical dramas.) . . .

When a mythology is absent—which explains why this case is perhaps more striking than others—the basis on which everything must be justified is character. When the motivations are wholly based upon character, however, the wholly inward origin of this destiny will drive the character relentlessly to the limits of pathology. The nonpathological Orestes of Aeschylus was driven from without by what drives Goethe's from within; what once was destiny, becomes character for the modern poets. When we find a pathological trait in one or another personage of the ancient poets (Heracles, Ajax, Lear, Ophelia, etc.), then it is the destiny of that personage to so become and his tragedy is that this is what becomes of him; but his tragedy does not originate in his being so. Even where the tragedy is built upon a pathological situation, as in *Phaedra*, it is still projected entirely from without: the gods have inflicted it. Perhaps this seems only a technical problem; it may appear to matter little whether Orestes is pursued by the Furies or his own heated imagination, whether it is the witches' enticing words which bring Macbeth's stormy hunger for power to ripeness, or whether Holophernes seeks his own ruin.[8] In practice, however, we will see that what comes from without, what is sent upon man by the gods, is universal; it is destiny. In the same way, to the same degree, it might happen to anyone, and in the final analysis it becomes a destiny without reference to the composition of the particular character— or at any rate, not solely with reference to it. But when all has become an inner event and can follow only from the character—if, indeed, all is not so infinitely far from the nature of the concerned that they become incapable of dramatic action (as Oswald, Rank)—its intensity must be heightened into an illness if it is to be seen and heard. In pathology and in it alone lies the possibility of rendering undramatic men dramatic. Nothing else is capable of lending them that concentration of action, that intensity of the senses, which will make the act and the situation symbolic and raise the figures above the ordinary, above the everyday. Says Kerr,[9] "in disease we find the permitted poetry of naturalism. . . . The figure is lent infinitely more dimensions and yet can be justified in reality." . . .

[8] Hebbel's *Judith* (1840).
[9] German critic Alfred Kerr (né Kempner, 1867–1948).

Sergei Eisenstein 1898–1948

Montage of Attractions
for the Production of Ostrovsky's
Diary of a Scoundrel[1] 1923

Since this concept is being used for the first time, it requires some explanation.

The spectator himself constitutes the basic material of the theatre; the objective of every utilitarian theatre (agit, poster, health education, etc.) is to guide the spectator in the desired direction (frame of mind). The means of achieving this are all the component parts of the theatrical apparatus (Ostyzhev's[2] "chatter" no more than the color of the prima donna's tights, a stroke on the kettledrum as much as a soliloquy of Romeo's, the cricket on the hearth[3] no less than a salvo under the seats of the spectators) which, in all their heterogeneity, are reduced to a single unit—thereby justifying their presence—by their being attractions.

An attraction (in relation to the theatre) is any aggressive aspect of the theatre; that is, any element of it which subjects the spectator to a sensual or psychological impact, experimentally regulated and mathematically calculated to produce in him certain emotional shocks which, when placed in their proper sequence within the totality, are the only means whereby he is enabled to perceive the ideological side of what is being demonstrated—the ultimate ideological conclusion. (The means of cognition—"through the living play of passions" specifically for the theatre.)

Sensual and psychological, of course, to be understood in the sense of immediate reality, in the way that these are handled, for example, by the Grand Guignol[4] theatre: gouging out eyes or cutting off arms and legs on the stage, or a character on stage participating by telephone in a ghastly event ten miles away, or the plight of a drunkard who senses his approaching death,

Translated by Daniel and Eleanor Gerould. Copyright 1970 by Daniel and Eleanor Gerould. Printed by permission of the translators. A slightly different version of this translation appeared in *Drama and Theatre*, IX (Fall 1970).

[1] A. N. Ostrovsky's play (1868) has also been translated into English as *Enough Simplicity in Every Wise Man* and *The Scoundrel*.

[2] Alexander Ostyzhev (1874–1953), well-known actor of the period, who appeared as Romeo and Othello, and in many other classic roles [notes 2 through 9 to Eisenstein's *Montage . . .* are the translators'].

[3] A reference to the dramatization of Dickens's *The Cricket on the Hearth*, presented at the First Studio of the Moscow Art Theater in 1915.

[4] Parisian theatre famous at the turn of the century for its terrifying horror plays.

and whose cries for help are taken as delirium tremens; and not in terms of the development of psychological problems where the attraction is already the theme of the play itself, a theme which exists and functions even outside of the play's action provided that it is sufficiently topical. (An error into which agit-theatres fall, satisfied with only this kind of attraction in their productions.)

On the formal level, by an attraction I mean an independent and primary element in the construction of a performance—a molecular (that is, component) unit of effectiveness in theatre and of *theatre in general*. It is fully analogous to Grosz's[5] "storehouse of images" or Rodchenko's "elements of photo-illustrations."[6]

"Component"—just as it is difficult to determine where the fascination of the hero's nobility (the psychological aspect) ends and the aspect of his personal charm (that is, his sensual magnetism) begins—the lyric effect of a series of scenes by Chaplin is inseparable from the attraction of the specific mechanics of his movements—so it is difficult to determine when religious pathos gives way to sadistic satisfaction in the scenes of martyrdom in the mystery play theatre, etc. . . .

An attraction has nothing in common with a trick. A trick, or rather, a stunt (it is time to put this term which has been excessively abused back in its proper place) is an accomplishment complete in itself in terms of a certain kind of craftsmanship (chiefly acrobatics). A stunt is only one of the kinds of attractions with its own appropriate method of presentation (or as they say in the circus—its "sale"); since it signifies something absolute and complete *in itself*, in its true meaning it is the direct opposite of an attraction which is based exclusively on an interrelationship—on the reaction of the audience.

A *genuine approach radically changes the possibilities in the principles of building a "construction that has impact" (the performance as a whole), instead of a static "reflection" of a given event necessary for the theme and of the possibility of its resolution solely through effects logically connected with such an event. A new method emerges—free montage of arbitrarily selected independent (also outside of the given composition and the plot links of the characters) effects (attractions), but with a view to establishing a certain final thematic effect—montage of attractions.*

The way of completely freeing the theatre from the weight of the "illusory imitativeness" and "representationality" which up until now has been definitive, inevitable, and solely possible is through a transition to montage of "workable artifices," which allows at the same time interweaving into the montage whole "representational segments" and connected plot lines of ac-

---

[5] George Grosz (1893–1959), German artist.

[6] Alexander Rodchenko, artist, photographer, and stage designer for a number of productions by Meyerhold. One of the creators of photo-montage.

tion, but no longer as something self-contained and all-determining, but as an immediately effective attraction consciously selected for a given purpose; since the sole basis for the effectiveness of a performance does not lie in "the discovery of the playwright's intention," "the correct interpretation of the author," "the true reflection of the period," etc., but only in attractions and a system of attractions. Any director who has become a skilled hand due to a natural flair has intuitively used an attraction in some way or other, but, of course, not in terms of a montage or construction, but "in a harmonious composition" at any rate (hence even its jargon—"effective curtain," "rich exit," "good stunt," etc.) But what is significant is that what was done was only in the framework of logical plot probability ("warranted" by the play), and chiefly, unconsciously in pursuit of something completely different (something that was not in what was calculated "in the beginning"). In terms of working out a system for constructing a performance there remains only to transfer the center of attention to what is proper, what was previously considered secondary and ornamental, but what actually is the basic guide for the production's nonconforming intentions, and, without becoming logically bound by real-life and traditional literary piety, *to establish the given approach as the production method* (the work of the Proletcult workshops[7] from the fall of 1922).

The film and above all the music hall and the circus constitute the school for the montage maker, since, properly speaking, putting on a good show (from the formal point of view) means building a strong music hall-circus program, starting from the basic situation of the play.

As an example, here is an enumeration of a portion of the numbers in the epilogue to *Diary of a Scoundrel.*

1. An expository soliloquy by the hero.
2. A part of a detective film: (explanation of point 1—the theft of the diary).
3. A musical-novelty act: the bride and three rejected suitors (according to the play, only one character) in the role of ushers: a scene of sorrow in the style of the song, "Your fingers smell of incense"[8] and "Let the grave." (As projected, the bride has a xylophone and plays on six rows of bells, the buttons on the officers' uniforms).
4, 5, 6. Three parallel clown acts, two sentences each (motif of payment for organizing the wedding).

[7] The Proletcult, the abbreviation for "Proletarian Cultural and Educational Organizations," was established after the revolution to foster proletarian culture as the basis for the new socialist society. It sought to promote a radically new kind of theatre, revolutionary in content and often avant-garde in form, whose aim was to be agitation and propaganda.

[8] A parody of a popular song by Alexander Vertinskii (1889–1957), who composed and sang his own romances and enjoyed great success throughout Europe in this period.

7. Feature act of the *étoile* (the aunt) and of the three officers (motif of detaining the rejected suitors), punning, (with a transition) through the mention of a horse to a triple-voltage number of an unsaddled horse (because of the impossibility of leading it into the auditorium—traditionally—"three as a horse").

8. Choral-agit song: "The priest had a dog"; to the accompaniment of which, "the priest's bouncing ball"—in the form of a dog (motif of the beginning of the wedding).

9. An interruption of the action (voice of a newsboy for the exit of the hero).

10. The appearance of the villain in a mask, a segment of comic film (a summary of the five acts of the play, in the transformations (of Glumov) the motif of the publication of the diary).

11. A continuation of the action (interrupted) with another group of characters (the wedding ceremony with the three rejected suitors all at the same time).

12. Antireligious song "Allah-Verdi" (punning motif—the necessity of winning over the mullah in view of the great number of suitors and with only one bride), a chorus and a new character used only in this number —a soloist dressed as a mullah.[9]

13. A general dance. Business with a placard "Religion is the opiate of the masses."

14. A farcical scene: putting away the wife and three husbands in a drawer, beating pots on the cover.

15. A scenes-of-domestic-life parody trio—the nuptial song: "And who of us is young."

16. A peak (of the action), the return of the hero.

17. The flight of the hero on a rope up to the cupola (motif of suicide from despair).

18. Break (in the action)—return of the villain, reprieve from suicide.

19. Battle with swords (motif of enmity).

20. Agit-act of the hero and villain on the theme of the NEP.[10]

21. Act on an inclined wire: passage (of the villain) from the ring to the balcony over the heads of the spectators (motif "departure for Russia").

22. Clowns parodying (this) number by the hero and cascade from the wire.

23. Arrival from the balcony along the same wire by a circus clown hanging by his teeth.

[9] The Mullah who performed the wedding ceremony sat cross-legged and rocked to and fro as he sang topical antireligious songs against the Orthodox Church.

[10] New Economic Policy. Instituted by Lenin in 1921 to help the U.S.S.R. recover from World War I and the civil war, and to increase popular support for the Communist Party, especially from the peasantry, the NEP restored a degree of capitalism in agriculture and trade. With Stalin's introduction of the first Five-Year Plan in 1928, the NEP came to an end.

24. The final feature act of two clowns who douse each other with water (traditionally), ending with the announcement "the end."
25. A salvo under the spectators' seats as the final chord.

The connecting moments of the numbers, if there is no direct transition, are used as legato elements and interpreted as the varying arrangement of apparatuses, musical intermission, dance, pantomime, exits by the rug, etc. . . .

Notes to Eisenstein's Discussion of the Epilogue to *Diary of a Scoundrel*[11]

The Epilogue to *Diary of a Scoundrel* consists of twenty-five "attractions" which Eisenstein also enumerates in his essay. Here is the director's rough outline for this epilogue, reconstructed at the request of the editors of the present edition by the still surviving participants in the performance (M.S. Gomorov, A.P. Purkatov, A.I. Levshin, V.P. Sharuev, I.F. Yasykanov, under the general direction of M.M. Shtraukh) in the same sequence of attractions indicated in Eisenstein's essay.

1. On stage (in the ring), Glumov who in a ("expository") soliloquy tells how his diary was stolen from him and how this threatens him with exposure. Glumov decides to marry Mashenka quickly, for which he calls "Menyefa" (a clown) on stage and proposes that he appear as a priest.
2. The lights go out, on the screen the theft of Glumov's diary by a man in a black mask—Golutvin. Parody of an American detective film.
3. Light in the auditorium. Mashenka appears in a motoring outfit, with a bridal veil in a crown, followed by her three rejected suitors—officers (in Ostrovsky's play—Kurchaev), who will be ushers in her wedding with Glumov. The scene of parting ("sorrow") warms up. Mashenka sings a "cruel" romance "Let the grave punish me," the officers perform, as a parody of Vertinskii, "Your fingers smell of incense." (In Eisenstein's original plan this scene was sketched out as a novelty musical number (xylophone), with Mashenka playing on bells sewn like buttons on the officers' uniforms.)
4, 5, 6. After the exit of Mashenka and the three officers, Glumov on stage again. Three clowns, Gorodulin, Joffre, Mamilyukov, come running up to him one after the other out of the auditorium, and each performs his circus number (juggling with small balls, acrobatic leaps, etc.) and demands payment for it. Glumov refuses and goes out. ("A clown act with

---

[11] These constitute the director's rough outline for this Epilogue, reconstituted by participants in the performance: M. S. Gomorov, A. P. Kurbatov, A. I. Levshin, V. P. Sharuev, and I. F. Yasykanov, under the general direction of M. M. Shtraukh, and are in the same sequence of attractions indicated in Eisenstein's essay [translators' note].

paired sentences"—for each exit, two sentences of the text: the comments of the clown and of Glumov.)

7. Mamaeva appears, dressed in provocative splendor ("an *étoile*") with a circus whip in her hand and three officers following her. Mamaeva wants to break Glumov's engagement, console the rejected suitors, and after their remarks about a horse ("My friend the mare neighs") cracks her whip—and the officers scamper off about the ring. Two represent the horse, the third the rider.

8. On stage the priest ("Manyefa"), the "wedding ceremony" begins. All those present for the wedding sing: "The priest had a dog." "Manyefa" performs a circus number ("the bouncing ball"), portraying a dog.

9. The yelling of a newsboy through a megaphone. Glumov, leaving the wedding ceremony, runs off to find out whether his diary has appeared in print.

10. The thief who stole the diary appears—a man in a black mask (Golutvin). The lights go out. On the screen Glumov's diary; in the film it tells about his behavior towards mighty patrons and likewise about his transformations into various temporary shapes (like into an ass with Mamaeva, into a tanker with Joffre, etc. . .).

11. The wedding ceremony is resumed. Glumov's place now that he has run off is taken by the rejected suitors—the three officers ("Kurchaev").

12. In view of the fact that Mashenka is getting married very soon to the three suitors, four uniformed circus attendants carry out on a plank from the auditorium the mullah, who continues the wedding ceremony already in progress, performing a parodistic song on topical themes—"Alla Verdi."

13. When he has finished his song the mullah dances a lezghinka, in which he takes all the parts. The mullah raises up the plank on which he was sitting, on the back is the inscription: "religion is the opiate of the masses." The mullah goes out holding the plank in his hand.

14. Mashenka and the three suitors are put away in drawers (whence they disappear, unnoticed by the spectators). Those taking part in the marriage ceremony beat earthenware pots against the drawers, parodying the old-fashioned wedding ceremony "for putting the young away."

15. Three of those present at the wedding ceremony (Mamilyukov, Mamaev, Gorodulin) perform the wedding song: "And who of us is young, and who not married."

16. Glumov running in with a newspaper in his hand interrupts the wedding song: "Hurrah! There isn't anything in the newspaper!" They all ridicule him and leave him alone.

17. After the publication of his diary and his misfortune with the wedding, Glumov is in a state of despair. He decides to commit suicide, he asks the uniformed circus attendant for a "piece of string." From the ceiling

a rope is lowered down to him. He attaches "angel wings" to his back, and they start to raise him up to the ceiling with a burning candle in his hand. The choir sings "An angel flew across the skies at midnight" to the motif "a beautiful woman's heart." This scene parodies the "Ascension."

18. Golutvin ("the villain") appears on stage. Glumov, once he has seen his enemy, begins to shower him with curses, lowers himself down onto the stage and throws himself down onto the villain.

19. Glumov and Golutvin fight with swords. Glumov wins. Golutkin falls, and Glumov pulls out of Golutvin's pocket a big sticker with "NEP" on it.

20. Golutvin performs a song about the NEP. Glumov joins in the singing. Both dance. Golutvin invites Glumov "to come visit him whenever he wants," to come to Russia.

21. Golutvin, balancing with an umbrella, goes along the inclined wire over the heads of the spectators to the balcony—"he goes off to Russia."

22. Glumov decides to follow his example, climbs up on the wire but falls off (circus "cascade") and with the words: "Oh, slippery, slippery, are these ways, I'd be better off in some back-alley," he follows Golutvin "to Russia," along the less dangerous path through the auditorium.

23. A "red nose" (clown) comes out on stage and weeps, saying over and over again "They went away but they forgot somebody." From the balcony another clown comes down along the wire hanging by his teeth.

24, 25. A squabble arises between the two "red noses"; one of them splashes the other with water and he falls down from surprise. One of them announces: "the end" and bows to the audience. At this moment there is a burst of fireworks under the seats in the auditorium.

Anatoly V. Lunacharsky 1873–1933

Theses on the Problems of Marxist Criticism 1928

I

Our literature is passing through one of the decisive moments in its development. A new life is being built in the country, and literature is learning more and more to reflect this life in its as yet undefined and unstable forms; evidently, too, it can pass to a problem of a still higher order—to the political and, in particular, the moral influence on the very process of construction.

Although our country represents a contrast of individual classes much less than any other, it is still, nonetheless, impossible to consider it entirely classless. Without dwelling on the inevitability of the difference in tendencies between peasant and proletarian literature, it is clear that there are elements in the country which have retained their old attitudes; elements which have either not reconciled themselves with the dictatorship of the proletariat, or which are unable to adapt themselves even to the most basic tendencies of the building of socialism by the proletariat.

The conflict between the old and the new continues. The influence of Europe, of the past, of the remnants of the old ruling class, of the new bourgeoisie which is to a certain extent flourishing under the New Economic Policy[1]—all these are making themselves felt. They are revealed not only in the prevailing moods of individual groups and people, but also in admixtures of every kind. It should be remembered that apart from the direct and deliberately hostile bourgeois currents, there is yet another element which is perhaps more dangerous and which is at any rate harder to defeat—the everyday petty-bourgeois element. This has wormed its way deeply into the everyday attitudes of the proletariat itself, of many Communists even. This explains why the class struggle, in the shape of a struggle for the building of a new way of life which bears the imprint of the socialist aspirations of the proletariat, is not only not abating, but, while retaining its former strength, is acquiring ever more subtle and profound forms. It is these circumstances which make the weapons of art—particularly literature—extremely important at the present time. They cause, however, proletarian and kindred literature to appear, side by side with hostile literary emanations, and by this I mean

From Anatoly Lunacharsky, *On Literature and Art*, translated by Y. Ganushkin. Moscow: Progress Publishers, 1965.

[1] See Eisenstein, *Montage* . . ., note 10, p. 945.

not only the consciously and specifically hostile elements, but also the unconsciously hostile elements—hostile in their passivity, pessimism, individualism, prejudices and distortions, etc.

II

With the significant role that literature has to play under such conditions, Marxist criticism bears a very considerable responsibility. Together with literature it is called upon to partake with intensity and energy in the process of the establishment of the new man and the new way of life.

III

Marxist criticism is distinguished from all other types of literature first of all by the fact that it cannot but be of a sociological nature—in the spirit, of course, of the scientific sociology of Marx and Lenin.

Sometimes a distinction is made between the tasks of a literary critic and those of a literary historian; the distinction is based not so much on an analysis of the past and present, as on, for the literary historian, an objective analysis of the origins of the work, its place in the social fabric and its influence on social life; whereas for the literary critic, it is based on an evaluation of the work from the point of view of its purely formal or social merits and faults.

For the Marxist critic such a distinction loses nearly all its validity. Although criticism in the strict sense of the word must of necessity be a part of a Marxist's critical work, sociological analysis must be an even more essential fundamental element.

IV

How does the Marxist critic carry out this sociological analysis? Marxism looks upon social life as an organic whole in which the separate parts depend one upon the other; and here the decisive role is played by the most natural and material economic relationships, above all, the forms of labor. In a general analysis of an epoch, for example, the Marxist critic must strive to give a complete picture of the entire social development of that epoch. When one single writer or work is being discussed, there is no essential need for an analysis of the basic economic conditions, for here the ever-valid principle, which may be called Plekhanov's[2] principle, comes especially into its own. It states that artistic works depend upon the forms of production in a given

---

[2] Georgi V. Plekhanov (1857–1918), a Russian revolutionist and Marxist critic and theoretician, was a teacher of Lenin and before the revolution collaborated with him in editing a revolutionary magazine, *Iskra* (*The Spark*).

society only to an extremely insignificant extent. They depend on them only through such intermediate links as the class structure of society and the class psychology which has formed as a result of class interests. A work of literature will always reflect, whether consciously or unconsciously, the psychology of the class which the writer represents. Either this or, as often happens, it reflects a mixture of elements in which the influence of various classes on the writer is revealed, and this must be subjected to a close analysis.

V

The ties in every work of literature with the psychology of this or that class or of large groups of a broad social nature are determined chiefly by its content. Literature—the art of the word, the art which is closest to thought—is distinguished from other forms of art by the significance of the content as compared with its form. It is especially evident in literature that it is the artistic content—the flow of thoughts and emotions in the form of images or connected with images—which is the decisive element of the work as a whole. The content strives of itself towards a definite form. It can be said that there is only one optimal form which corresponds to the content. To a greater or lesser extent the writer can find those modes of expression of his thoughts and feelings which reveal them with the greatest clarity and which make the strongest impression on the readers for whom the work is intended.

And so the Marxist critic takes first of all as the object of his analysis the *content* of the work, the *social essence* which it embodies. He determines its connection with these or those social groups and the influence which the force of expression of the work has on social life; only then does he turn to the form, and above all he shows the way in which the form corresponds to the basic aims of the work, that is, to serve the ends of maximum expressiveness and impact.

VI

It is impossible, however, to ignore the specialized task of the analysis of literary *forms*, and the Marxist critic must not turn a blind eye to this. The form of a given work is in fact determined not merely by its content but also by other elements. The psychological thought processes and conversations of a given class, its "style" of living, the general level of the material culture of a given society, the influence of its neighbors, the inertia of the past or the striving for renovation, which can manifest itself in all of life's aspects—all this can affect the form, can act as a subsidiary factor defining it. Often form is linked not just with a single work, but with a whole "school," a whole epoch. It can even be a force which harms or contradicts the content. Sometimes it can become divorced from the content and acquire an isolated, elusive nature. This happens when works of literature are the expression of class tendencies which are devoid of content, which fear real life and which try to hide from this life behind a screen of verbal gymnastics of a highflown, pompous or, on the contrary, facetious and frivolous nature. All such elements must of necessity be a part of a Marxist's analysis. As the reader can see, these formal elements, which arise from a direct formula—in every masterpiece the form is determined wholly by the content, and every literary work aspires to become a masterpiece—are by no means divorced from social life. They, in turn, should be socially interpreted.

VII

We have hitherto confined our attention mainly to the sphere of Marxist criticism as a function of literary scholarship. The Marxist critic appears here as a scientific sociologist, who is specifically applying the methods of Marxist analysis to a special field—literature. The founder of Marxist criticism, Plekhanov, strongly underlined that this is the real role a Marxist is called upon to play. He maintained that the Marxist is distinguished from the "en-lightener," for example, by the fact that the "enlightener" assigns to literature specific aims and specific demands; whereas the "enlightener" judges it from the point of view of specific ideals, the Marxist elucidates the natural causes of the appearance of this or that work.

When Plekhanov rightly opposed the objective and scientific Marxist method of criticism to the old subjectivism, to the capricious approach of the esthete and the gourmet, he did yeoman's service in establishing the true paths for future Marxist criticism to follow.

It must not in any way be thought, however, that it is a characteristic of the proletariat merely to determine and analyze external data. Marxism is not simply a sociological doctrine, but an active program of building. Such building is unthinkable without an objective evaluation of the facts. If a Marxist cannot objectively sense the ties between the phenomena which surround him, then he is finished as a Marxist. But from a genuine, all-round Marxist we demand still more—a definite influence on this environment.

The Marxist critic is not some literary astronomer explaining the inevitable laws of motion of literary bodies, from the large to the very small. He is more than this: he is a fighter and a builder. In this sense the *factor of evaluation* must be regarded as one of the most important and loftiest features of con-temporary Marxist criticism.

VIII

What must be the *criteria* on which the *evaluation* of a work of literature should be based? Let us first of all approach this from the point of view of content. Here, generally, everything is clear. Here the basic criterion is the same as that of proletarian ethics: everything that aids the development and victory of the proletariat is good; everything that harms it is evil.

The Marxist critic must try to find the fundamental social trend in a given work; he must find out where it is heading, whether this process is arbitrary or not. And he must base his evaluation on this fundamental, social and dynamic idea.

Even in the field of the evaluation of the social *content* of a work, however, everything is far from being simple. The Marxist critic needs to be very skilful and extremely sensitive. By this is meant not only specific Marxist training but also specific talent, without which there can be no criticism. In the case of a really great artistic work, there are too many aspects to be weighed, and it is too difficult in this instance to use any kind of thermometer or scales. What is needed here is what is called social sensitivity, otherwise mistakes are inevitable. The Marxist critic must not prize only those works which are devoted to topical problems. Without denying the special importance of burning questions, it is completely impossible to ignore the tremendous significance of issues which at first sight appear too general and remote, but which, in fact, after looking at them more closely, do exert an influence on social life.

Here is the same phenomenon as in science. To demand that science give itself up entirely to practical tasks is a profound error. It is a well-known fact that the most abstract of scientific problems can, when solved, sometimes turn out to be the most fruitful.

And yet, it is just when a writer or a poet turns to the solution of general tasks, striving towards—if he is a proletarian—a proletarian reevaluation of the fundamentals of culture, that a critic can easily become confused. Firstly, in such cases we do not as yet have any true criteria; secondly, hypotheses may be of value here—the most daring hypotheses—for we are concerned not with a final solution to the problems, but with posing the problems and analyzing them. To a certain extent, however, all this refers likewise to literary works of purely topical interest. The artist who illustrates in his works the ideas of our program which have already been fully developed is a bad artist. The artist is valuable when he turns up virgin soil, when he intuitively breaks into a sphere which logic and statistics would find hard to penetrate. To judge whether an artist is right, whether he has correctly combined the truth and the basic aspirations of communism, is by no means easy; here, too, perhaps, the correct judgment can be worked out only in the conflict of opinions between critics and readers. All this does not make the critic's work any less important or necessary.

An extremely important factor in the evaluation of the social content of literary works is the second judgment of a work, which, at first analysis, seemed to belong to a range of phenomena which were alien, sometimes hostile to us. It is indeed very important to know the attitudes of one's foes, to make use of eyewitness accounts coming from a background different from ours. They can often lead us to profound conclusions, and, in any case, can greatly enrich the treasure-store of our knowledge of life's phenomena. The Marxist critic, who has stated that such and such a writer or work is, for example, a purely petty-bourgeois phenomenon, must never dismiss this work or writer with a wave of his hand. A great deal of benefit can be extracted from it. For this reason, a second evaluation from the point of view not of the origin and tendentiousness of a given work, but of its potential use in our constructive effort, is the direct task of a Marxist critic.

I should like to qualify this. Alien and hostile elements in the sphere of literature even if they are of some benefit in the above-mentioned sense can of course be extremely harmful and poisonous and be dangerous manifestations of counterrevolutionary propaganda. It goes without saying that this is the cue for the appearance not of Marxist criticism but of Marxist censorship.

IX

The task of the Marxist critic becomes, perhaps, even more complicated, when he turns from evaluation of content to evaluation of form.

This is an extremely important task, and Plekhanov emphasized its importance. What then, is the general criterion for evaluation here? The form must correspond to the content as closely as possible, giving it maximum expressiveness and assuring the strongest possible impact on the readers for whom the work is intended.

Above all, the most important formal criterion, which Plekhanov also advocated, should be mentioned here; that is that literature is the art of images and every invasion of naked ideas or propaganda is always detrimental to the given work. It is self-evident that this criterion of Plekhanov's is not an absolute. There are excellent works by, for instance, Saltykov-Shchedrin,[3] Uspensky[4] and Furmanov,[5] which clearly sin against this criterion, and this means that hybrid literary works combining belles-lettres with publicist thought can exist in their own right. By and large, these should be cautioned against. Of course, publicistic literature which is brilliant in form is an excellent type of propaganda and literature in the broadest sense of the word, but on the contrary, artistic belles-lettres loaded with purely publicistic elements will leave the reader cold, no matter how brilliant the argument. In this sense, the critic has every right to speak about the inadequacy of the

---

[3] Mikhail Salytkov-Shchedrin (1826–1889), Russian playwright.
[4] Gleb Ivanovich Uspensky (1843 n.s.–1902), Russian novelist and essayist.
[5] Dmitril Andreevich Furmanov (1891–1926), Soviet novelist.

artistic digestion of the content by the author if this content, instead of flowing freely in images of brilliant molten metal in the work, sticks out of this stream in large, cold lumps.

The second particular criterion, which is a natural outgrowth of the whole, as defined above, concerns the originality of the form. In what should this originality consist? Precisely in this: the formal body of a given work should merge into one indivisible whole with its idea, with its content. A genuine work of art should, of course, be new in content. If the content is not new, the work has little value. This is obvious. An artist should express something that has not been expressed before. Reproduction is not art (some painters find this difficult to understand) but only a craft, albeit sometimes very fine. From this point of view, new content in every new work demands new form.

With what can we contrast this genuine originality of form? In the first place there is the stereotyped form which prevents a new idea being really incorporated into the work. A writer can be enthralled by previously used forms, and although his content is new, it is poured into old wineskins. Inadequacies of this kind cannot fail to be noticed. In the second place, the form may simply be weak, i.e., with a new, interesting conception, the artist may not possess the formal resources in the sense of language—a wealth of vocabulary, construction of the phrase, of the entire story, chapter, novel, play, etc.; and in the sense of rhythm and other forms of poetry. All this must be pointed out by the Marxist critic. A genuine Marxist critic—an integral type, so to say, of such a critic—must be a teacher, especially of the young writer or beginner.

Finally, the third major sin against the above-mentioned particular rule for the originality of form, is the "organization" of form, where the emptiness of content is camouflaged by formal inventions and ornamentation. Writers infected by the formalists, those typical representatives of bourgeois decadence, have been known to try to adorn and embellish their honest and weighty content with various trickery, thereby ruining their work.

One must also approach the third criterion of a formal nature—the *universality* of the work—with caution. Tolstoy spoke out strongly for this. We who are extremely interested in the creation of a literature which would be addressed to the masses, and would appeal to them as to the great creators of life, are also interested in this universality. All forms of reticence, of isolation, all forms intended for a small circle of specialized aesthetes, every artistic convention and refinement should be rejected by Marxist criticism. Marxist criticism not only can, but must indicate the inner merits of such works in the past and present, at the same time condemning the frame of mind of the artist who tried with such formal methods to cut himself off from reality.

But as mentioned above, the criterion of universality must be treated with great care. In our press, in our propagandist literature we are going from the very complicated journals and papers, which demand considerable intelligence from the reader, to the most elementary popular level; similarly, we cannot bring all our literature down to the level of the as yet uncultured peasant masses or even of the workers. This would be a very serious mistake.

Glorious is the writer who can express a complex and valuable social idea with such powerful artistic simplicity that he reaches the hearts of millions. Glorious is also the writer who can reach the hearts of these millions with a comparatively simple, elementary content; and the Marxist critic should highly value such a writer. The Marxist critic's special attention and wise assistance are needed here. But of course, one should not deny the value of works which are not sufficiently intelligible for *every* literate person, which are addressed to the upper stratum of the proletariat, to the sophisticated party members, to the reader who has attained a considerable level of culture. Life presents many burning problems to this part of the population which plays an immensely important role in the construction of socialism; and of course these problems should not be left without an artistic answer simply because they have not yet faced the vast masses or because they cannot yet be worked out in universal form. It should, however, be noted that we have gone too far the other way, our writers concentrating their attention on an easier task—writing for a cultured circle of readers at a time when, I repeat, literature for the good of the workers and peasants, provided it is talented and successful literature, must be especially valued.

X

As has already been said, the Marxist critic is also to a significant degree a teacher. It is pointless to criticize unless the criticism results in some kind of progress. And what must this progress be? Firstly, the Marxist critic must be a teacher in his attitude towards the writer. It is quite possible that angry voices will be raised at this, saying that no one gave the critic the right to consider himself superior to the writer, and so on. When the question is properly phrased, such objections become completely invalid. Firstly, once it has been said that the Marxist critic must be the writer's teacher, the conclusion must be drawn from this that he must be an extremely resolute Marxist, an erudite person of irreproachable taste. It will be said that we have no such critics or only a very few. In the first case our opponents will be wrong; in the second they will be closer to the truth. But there is only one conclusion to be drawn from this: it is necessary to learn. There will be no lack of good will and talent in our great country, but there is a lot of hard learning to be done. Secondly, of course, the critic not only teaches the writer without in any way considering himself superior, but he also learns a great deal from the writer. The best critic is the one who can look on the writer with admiration and enthusiasm, and who, at any rate, is well disposed towards him. The Marxist critic can and must be a teacher to the writer in two ways: firstly, he must point out to young writers—and generally to writers capable of making a large number of formal mistakes—the faults in their work. It used to be widely held that we need no Belinskys,[6] for our writers no longer need guidance. This may have been true before the revolution, but it becomes simply laughable after the revolution, when the masses are giving birth to hundreds and thousands of new writers. A firm, guiding criticism, Belinskys of every calibre, including the conscientious workman with a good knowledge of his literary trade—all these are absolutely essential.

The Marxist critic must, on the other hand, be a teacher to the writer in the social sense. Not only is the nonproletarian writer very often merely a child in his social attitudes, committing the crudest of errors as a result of his primitive ideas about the laws of social life and his failure to understand the fundamentals of the epoch, etc., but this also happens only too often with a Marxist, proletarian writer. This is said not as an insult to the writer, but partly almost in his praise. Writers are sensitive beings, immediately receptive to all the influences of reality. In most cases writers possess neither special gifts nor special interest in abstract and scientific thinking; it is for this reason, of course, that they sometimes impatiently refuse any offer of help from the publicist-critic. But this can often be explained by the pedantic way in which such help is offered. Yet it is, in fact, precisely as a result of the cooperation between the important writers and the most gifted literary critics that truly great literature has always arisen and will continue to arise.

XI

The Marxist critic, in trying to teach the writer usefully, must also teach the reader. Yes, the reader must be taught to read. The critic as a commentator, as the person who warns of poison which may taste sweet, as the person who cracks a hard shell to reveal the pearl inside, as the person who dots all the *i*'s, who makes generalizations on the basis of artistic material—this is the guide who is essential now, at a time when so many valuable but as yet inexperienced readers have appeared. This is his relation to our past and to world literature, this is how he must be related to contemporary literature. We once again emphasize, therefore, the exceptional demands which the epoch is making on the Marxist critic. We have no desire to intimidate anyone with our theses. The Marxist critic can begin modestly, he can even start off by making mistakes, but he must remember that he will have to climb a long, steep staircase before he reaches the first landing, and even

---

[6] Vissarion Grigoryevich Belinsky (1811–1848), major Russian critic.

then he must look upon himself only as an apprentice. It is impossible, however, not to count on the gigantic upsurge of general culture and talented literature; it is impossible not to believe that the present—not entirely satis-factory—state of Marxist criticism will very soon improve.

XII

I should like, as a corollary, to touch on two more questions. Firstly, Marxist critics are often accused of what almost amounts to informing. It is indeed quite dangerous now to say about a writer that he entertains "un-conscious" or even "semiconscious," counterrevolutionary ideas. And in those cases when a writer is considered an alien element, a petty-bourgeois element, or a fellow traveler standing way to the Right, or when one of our writers is accused of some deviation or other, then the whole affair seems somewhat dubious. Is it really, people ask, a critic's business to say whether this or that writer is politically suspect, is politically unsound or has political failings? We must hasten to vehemently refute such protests. The critic who uses such a method to settle his personal accounts or deliberately to slander someone, is a villain; and such villainy, sooner or later, always comes to light. It is a heedless and careless critic who, without thinking or weighing the matter, hurls such accusations. But the man who distorts the very essence of Marxist criticism because he is afraid to declare aloud the results of his objective social analysis, must be labeled as careless and politically passive.

Not that the Marxist critic must shout: "Be watchful!" This is not an appeal to state organs; this is objective evaluation of some work or other for our construction. It is for the writer himself to draw conclusions, to correct his line. We are in the sphere of a struggle of ideas. Not a single conscientious and honest Communist can deny the nature of this *struggle* in the question of present-day literature and its evaluation.

XIII

And finally, this question: are sharp and bitter polemics to be allowed?

Generally speaking, sharp polemics are useful in that they keep the reader interested. Polemical articles, especially where both sides are wrong, all other things being equal, have more influence on the public and are better understood. In addition, the martial spirit of the Marxist critic as a revolu-tionary leads him to express his thoughts sharply, but at the same time it should be mentioned that to camouflage the weakness of his arguments with polemical brilliance is one of the critic's great sins. Generally when there are not many arguments but a multitude of various scathing remarks, compari-sons, mocking exclamations, and sly questions, then the impression may be gay but not at all serious. Criticism must be applicable to criticism itself, for Marxist criticism is at the same time scientific and artistic work. Anger is not the best guide in criticism and often means that the critic is wrong.

Admittedly, sometimes biting sarcasm and tirades are torn out of the critic's heart. Always a more or less discerning ear of another critic or reader can from the very beginning distinguish between natural anger and mere malice. In our constructive effort there must be as little malice as possible. It must not be mixed with class hatred. Class hatred strikes with intent, but like a cloud over the earth it is above personal malice. By and large, the Marxist critic, without falling into cheerful indulgence, which would be very wrong on his part, must be a priori benevolent. His supreme joy must be in finding the positive and revealing it to the reader in all its splendor. Assistance must be another of his aims—to channel and to warn—and only rarely should it be necessary to attempt to undo the villain with the piercing arrow of laughter or contempt or with overwhelming criticism, which can easily annihilate any puffed-up nonentity.

Reports and Speeches at the First Soviet Writers' Conference *1934*

Andrei A. Zhdanov *1896–1948*

Soviet Literature– the Richest in Ideas, the Most Advanced Literature

The key to the success of Soviet literature is to be sought for in the success of socialist construction. Its growth is an expression of the success and achievement of our socialist system. Our literature is the youngest of all literatures of all peoples and countries. And at the same time it is the richest in ideas, the most advanced and the most revolutionary literature. Never before has there been a literature which has organized the toilers and oppressed for the struggle to abolish once and for all every kind of exploitation and the yoke of wage slavery. Never before has there been a literature which has based the subject matter of its works on the life of the working class and peasantry and their fight for socialism. Nowhere, in no country in the world, has there been a literature which has defended and upheld the principle of equal rights for the toilers of all nations, the principle of equal rights for women. There is not, there cannot be in bourgeois countries a literature which consistently smashes every kind of obscurantism, every kind of mysticism, priesthood and superstition, as our literature is doing.

Only Soviet literature, which is of one flesh and blood with socialist construction, could become, and has indeed become, such a literature—so rich in ideas, so advanced and revolutionary.

Soviet authors have already created not a few outstanding works, which

Selections. From *Problems of Soviet Literature: Reports and Speeches at the First Soviet Writers' Conference*. New York: International Publishers, n.d. Reprinted by permission of International Publishers Co., Inc. Copyright © 1935.

correctly and truthfully depict the life of our Soviet country. Already there are several names of which we can be justly proud. Under the leadership of the Party, with the thoughtful and daily guidance of the Central Committee and the untiring support and help of Comrade Stalin,[1] a whole army of Soviet writers has rallied around the Soviet power and the Party. And in the light of our Soviet literature's successes, we see standing out in yet sharper relief the full contrast between our system—the system of victorious socialism—and the system of dying, moldering capitalism.

Of what can the bourgeois author write, of what can he dream, what source of inspiration can he find, whence can he borrow this inspiration, if the worker in capitalist countries is uncertain of the morrow, if he does not know whether he will have work the next day, if the peasant does not know whether he will work on his plot of ground tomorrow or whether his life will be ruined by the capitalist crisis, if the brain worker has no work today and does not know whether he will receive any tomorrow?

What can the bourgeois author write about, what source of inspiration can there be for him, when the world is being precipitated once more—if not today, then tomorrow—into the abyss of a new imperialist war?

The present state of bourgeois literature is such that it is no longer able to create great works of art. The decadence and disintegration of bourgeois literature, resulting from the collapse and decay of the capitalist system, represent a characteristic trait, a characteristic peculiarity of the state of bourgeois culture and bourgeois literature at the present time. Gone never to return are the times when bourgeois literature, reflecting the victory of the bourgeois system over feudalism, was able to create works of the period when capitalism was flourishing. Everything now is growing stunted—themes, talents, authors, heroes.

In deathly terror of the proletarian revolution, fascism is wreaking its vengeance on civilization, turning people back to the most hideous and savage periods of human history, burning on the bonfire and barbarously destroying the works of humanity's best minds.

Characteristic of the decadence and decay of bourgeois culture are the orgies of mysticism and superstition, the passion for pornography. The "illustrious persons" of bourgeois literature—of that bourgeois literature which has sold its pen to capital—are now thieves, police sleuths, prostitutes, hooligans.

All this is characteristic of that section of literature which is trying to conceal the decay of the bourgeois system, which is vainly trying to prove that nothing has happened, that all is well in the "state of Denmark," that there is nothing rotten as yet in the system of capitalism. Those repre-

---

[1] Joseph Stalin (1879–1953), then head of the U.S.S.R. and General Secretary of the Soviet Communist Party.

sentatives of bourgeois literature who feel the state of things more acutely are absorbed in pessimism, doubt in the morrow, eulogy of darkness, extolment of pessimism as the theory and practice of art. And only a small section—the most honest and far-sighted writers—are trying to find a way out along other paths, in other directions, to link their destiny with the proletariat and its revolutionary struggle.

The proletariat of capitalist countries is already forging the army of its writers, of its artists—the revolutionary writers whose representatives we are glad to welcome here today at the first Congress of Soviet Writers. The detachment of revolutionary writers in capitalist countries is not large as yet, but it is growing and will continue to grow every day, as the class struggle becomes more intense, as the forces of the world proletarian revolution grow stronger.

We firmly believe that these few dozens of foreign comrades who are here today represent the nucleus, the core of a mighty army of proletarian writers which will be created by the world proletarian revolution in capitalist countries.

That is how matters stand in capitalist countries. Not so with us. Our Soviet writer derives the material for his works of art, his subject-matter, images, artistic language and speech, from the life and experience of the men and women of Dnieprostroy, of Magnitostroy. Our writer draws his material from the heroic epic of the Chelyuskin expedition,[2] from the experience of our collective farms, from the creative action that is seething in all corners of our country.

In our country the main heroes of works of literature are the active builders of a new life—working men and women, men and women collective farmers, Party members, business managers, engineers, members of the Young Communist League, Pioneer. Such are the chief types and the chief heroes of our Soviet literature. Our literature is impregnated with enthusiasm and the spirit of heroic deeds. It is optimistic, but not optimistic in accordance with any "inward," animal instinct. It is optimistic in essence, because it is the literature of the rising class of the proletariat, the only progressive and advanced class. Our Soviet literature is strong by virtue of the fact that it is serving a new cause—the cause of socialist construction.

Comrade Stalin has called our writers engineers of human souls. What does this mean? What duties does the title confer upon you?

In the first place, it means knowing life so as to be able to depict it truthfully in works of art, not to depict it in a dead, scholastic way, not simply as "objective reality," but to depict reality in its revolutionary development.

---

[2] Chelyuskin, named after its discoverer, is in the northernmost part of continental Russia. By 1932 a polar station was established at Cape Chelyuskin.

In addition to this, the truthfulness and historical concreteness of the artistic portrayal should be combined with the ideological remolding and education of the toiling people in the spirit of socialism. This method in belles lettres and literary criticism is what we call the method of socialist realism.

Our Soviet literature is not afraid of the charge of being "tendentious." Yes, Soviet literature is tendentious, for in an epoch of class struggle there is not and cannot be a literature which is not class literature, not tendentious, allegedly nonpolitical.

And I think that every one of our Soviet writers can say to any dull-witted bourgeois, to any philistine, to any bourgeois writer who may talk about our literature being tendentious: "Yes, our Soviet literature is tendentious, and we are proud of this fact, because the aim of our tendency is to liberate the toilers, to free all mankind from the yoke of capitalist slavery."

To be an engineer of human souls means standing with both feet firmly planted on the basis of real life. And this in its turn denotes a rupture with romanticism of the old type, which depicted a nonexistent life and nonexistent heroes, leading the reader away from the antagonisms and oppression of real life into a world of the impossible, into a world of utopian dreams. Our literature, which stands with both feet firmly planted on a materialist basis, cannot be hostile to romanticism, but it must be a romanticism of a new type, revolutionary romanticism. We say that socialist realism is the basic method of Soviet belles lettres and literary criticism, and this presupposes that revolutionary romanticism should enter into literary creation as a component part, for the whole life of our Party, the whole life of the working class and its struggle consist in a combination of the most stern and sober practical work with a supreme spirit of heroic deeds and magnificent future prospects. Our Party has always been strong by virtue of the fact that it has united and continues to unite a thoroughly businesslike and practical spirit with broad vision, with a constant urge forward, with a struggle for the building of communist society. Soviet literature should be able to portray our heroes; should be able to glimpse our tomorrow. This will be no utopian dream, for our tomorrow is already being prepared for today by dint of conscious planned work.

One cannot be an engineer of human souls without knowing the technique of literary work, and it must be noted that the technique of the writer's work possesses a large number of specific peculiarities.

You have many different types of weapons. Soviet literature has every opportunity of employing these types of weapons (genres, styles, forms and methods of literary creation) in their diversity and fullness, selecting all the best that has been created in this sphere by all previous epochs. From this point of view, the mastery of the technique of writing, the critical assimilation of the literary heritage of all epochs, represents a task which you must fulfill without fail, if you wish to become engineers of human souls.

Comrades, the proletariat, just as in other provinces of material and spiritual culture, is the sole heir of all that is best in the treasury of world literature. The bourgeoisie has squandered its literary heritage; it is our duty to gather it up carefully, to study it and, having critically assimilated it, to advance further.

To be engineers of human souls means to fight actively for the culture of language, for quality of production. Our literature does not as yet come up to the requirements of our era. The weaknesses of our literature are a reflection of the fast that people's consciousness lags behind economic life—a defect from which even our writers are not, of course, free. That is why untiring work directed towards self-education and towards improving their ideological equipment in the spirit of socialism represents an indispensable condition without which Soviet writers cannot remold the mentality of their readers and thereby become engineers of human souls. . . .

Karl Radek *1885–1947*

Contemporary World Literature and the Tasks of Proletarian Art

. . . Realism means giving a picture not only of the decay of capitalism and the withering away of its culture, but also of the birth of that class, of that force, which is capable of creating a new society and a new culture. Realism does not mean the embellishment or arbitrary selection of revolutionary phenomena; it means reflecting reality as it is, in all its complexity, in all its contrariety, and not only capitalist reality, but also that other, new reality—the reality of socialism.

An artist who tried to represent the birth of socialism as an idyll, who

Selections. From *Problems of Soviet Literature: Reports and Speeches at the First Soviet Writers' Conference.* New York: International Publishers, n.d. Reprinted by permission of International Publishers Co., Inc. Copyright © 1935.

tried to represent the socialist system, which is being born in hard-fought battles, as a paradise populated by ideal people—such an artist would not be a realist, would not be able to convince anyone by his works. The artist should show how socialism is built out of the bricks of the past, out of the material which the past has left us, out of the material which we ourselves create in the sweat of our brow, in the blood of our toil and struggle, in the hard battles of classes and in the hard toil of man to remold himself.

But there is no such thing as static realism, no such thing as realism which portrays only what is. And if all the great realists of the past, even though unaware of the fact, were dialecticians, portrayed development through the conflict of contradictions, then this dialectic character of our realism is still more strongly stressed by us, when we speak of socialist realism.

Socialist realism means not only knowing reality as it is, but knowing whither it is moving. It is moving towards socialism, it is moving towards the victory of the international proletariat. And a work of art created by a socialist realist is one which shows whither that conflict of contradictions is leading which the artist has seen in life and reflected in his work.

This of itself implies that socialist realism demands a precise knowledge and understanding of this contradictory epoch. The great creations of socialist realism cannot therefore be the result of chance observations of certain sections of reality; they demand that the artist comprehend the tremendous whole. Even when the artist depicts the great in the small, when he wants to show the world in a drop of water, in the destinies of one small man, he cannot accomplish his task without having in his brain an image of the movement of the entire world.

While the literature of dying capitalism invokes the aid of the irrational, of the unconscious and the subconscious, the literature of social realism demands a consciousness of the fate of humanity; it demands tremendous work of the mind, demands an understanding of the position of our planet in the universe and of the position of man on this planet. The literature of socialist realism is a literature of world scales, for its task is to present a picture of the world.

The artists of dying capitalism seek to hide themselves under a cloak of impartiality. They are sceptics; they are convinced that they believe in nothing, although the very essence of their work is a faith that this decaying world will exist forever. The literature of socialist realism does not set out to portray the world in order to satisfy curiosity, in order merely to hold the mirror up to humanity. It sets out to be a participant in the great struggle for the new Renaissance of mankind, or, to speak more exactly, not for the rebirth, but for the birth of mankind.

It is a literature of hatred for putrefying capitalism, which is preparing to let loose a cataclysm, which is steeping mankind in loathsomeness. It is a literature of great love for suffering humanity, for militant humanity, of great love for those whose bones form the piles of the new world edifice.

. . . We must turn the artist away from his "inside," turn his eyes to these great facts of reality which threaten to crash down upon our heads.

Does this mean, however, that the artist should sketch some kind of abstract banks and abstract monopoly capitalism, with Deterding wearing a face like all other capitalists, that he should not be able to clothe these great events in the concrete images of living, typical people, representing classes? If it is a question of being able to present the typical in the individual, we do not need Joyce[1] for that. As teachers, Balzac,[2] Tolstoy are enough for us.

Joyce's specific character, his historical role is not to be sought for in any irrational invention of literary technique. Joyce's form is in keeping with his content, and the content of Joyce is a reflection of that which is most reactionary in the petty bourgeoisie. Joyce can curse at god and curse at imperialist England, but he does not lead artists the right way. Joyce does not choose as the object of his observations the whole world with its mighty contradictions. . . .

This is a profound mistake. If Joyce did not turn his eyes towards the Irish uprising that was preparing, this was not because it took ten years to come, but because all that appealed to Joyce was the medieval, the mystical, the reactionary in the petty bourgeoisie—lust, aberrations; everything capable of impelling the petty bourgeoisie to join the side of revolution was alien to him.

---

[1] James Joyce (1881–1941), Irish writer.
[2] Honoré de Balzac (1799–1850), French novelist.

Nikolai Bukharin 1888–1938

Poetry, Poetics, and the Problems of Poetry in the U.S.S.R.

Let us now revert to the question of socialist realism. Its philosophical basis is dialectical materialism. From this point of view, socialist realism is a distinct method in art the counterpart of dialectical materialism, the translation of the latter into terms of art. (Parenthetically, let us note that it does not by any means follow from this that every good poet must first become a good philosopher; the connection is more complex, but this is a separate question.) What does this mean? What is socialist realism and what are its peculiar features? In what respects does it differ from realism generally?

Socialist realism cannot set out to solve the same problems as dialectical materialism in science—a fact which follows from the very essence of the difference between science and art. From the analysis given in the opening part of this report, it is clear that in describing nature, for instance, socialist realism does not set out to think of it only in terms of electrons, light and heat waves, rays, etc., as against sounds, colors and other directly sensory elements. In depicting society, it cannot set out to employ categories of value, basis and superstructure, and so forth. It employs sensory images first and foremost, and even intellectual elements receive a definite emotional tinge. Without this, there is no art in general or poetry in particular. But realism generally and socialist realism in particular, as a method, is the enemy of everything supernatural, mystic, all other-wordly idealism. This is its principle and definite attribute.

"*Omnis determinatio est negatio*"—"All definition is negation," said old Spinoza. The negative definition of realism is that it is not idealism, not mysticism. But this negative definition is at the same time its positive definition. This means that sensory reality and its motion, and not its fictitious sublimations, that real feelings and passions, real history, and not various versions of the "world spirit," provide the material which it portrays. In conformity with this, the elements of form will also be other than is the case, let us say, in symbolism. The combination of images, the verbal scoring will serve not to conjure up the supernatural but to reproduce

Selections. From *Problems of Soviet Literature: Reports and Speeches at the First Soviet Writers' Conference*. New York: International Publishers, n.d. Reprinted by permission of International Publishers Co., Inc. Copyright © 1935.

reality and the real motions of the feelings with the greatest possible vividness. It does not, however, follow from this that realism, from the point of view of form, precludes the employment of metaphors, including personification. Everything that enhances the sensory effect can and does find a place in the poetic lexicon, because it is perceived as a metaphor. "Terek's stream like a lioness leaping" does not contradict realism just as the reverse metaphor: "He lay like a rock," with its transfer of a dead image to the living, does not contradict realism either.

What distinguishes socialist realism from realism in general? It is distinguished, first of all, by the artistic material it employs. . . . Socialist realism is distinguished from other realism by the fact that it inevitably focuses attention on the portrayal of the building of socialism, the struggle of the proletariat, of the new man, and all the manifold complexities of "connections and settlings" of the great historical process of our day. We must always bear in mind that within poetic unity there coexist intellectual, emotional and volitional elements, forming a single indivisible whole. Certain guiding and evaluating factors—the class token, the aim—form an element which is present in every work, even if only in a very subtle and sublimated form. The point of view of the proletariat's victory is, of course, a constituent trait of all works of socialist realism; it gives them their "social meaning."

Is this distinction, however, the only one? Or are there methodological, and consequently also stylistic, peculiarities of socialist realism, distinguishing it from bourgeois realism?

Of course there are such features.

These features are most intimately connected with the content of the material and with purposefulness of a volitional order, dictated by the class position of the proletariat. In the socialist society which is coming into being, the difference between physical labor and brain work is gradually being effaced. A new type of man is arising in whom intellect and will are not cloven in two: he really knows the world in order to change it. Mere contemplation, mere portrayal of the objective, without elucidation of the motive tendencies, without reference to the practical alteration of the objective world, are here receding into the past. Hence, socialist realism cannot base its views on the naturalism of Zola, who proposed to describe reality *"telle, qu'elle est"* ("such as it is") and nothing more. Neither can it accept his other slogan: *"L'imagination n'a plus d'emploi"* ("imagination is no longer needed"). Socialist realism dares to "dream" and should do so, basing itself on real trends of development.

In connection with this, we must also consider the question of revolutionary romanticism. If socialist realism is distinguished by its active, operative character; if it does not give just a dry photograph of a process; if it projects the entire world of passion and struggle into the future; if it raises the heroic principle to the throne of history—then revolutionary romanticism is a component part of it. Romanticism has usually been contrasted to realism. This was because romanticism in the majority of cases has been connected with idealistic soarings into metaphysical dimensions and "other worlds," with its exalted emotion of the "sublime and beautiful" led beyond the confines of the objective world. This was also because realism expressed a narrow and contemplative so-called objectivism. Narrow, because it did not educe the tendencies leading to the future. Contemplative, because it limited itself to registering what exists, though not, of course, "in its pure form." In our circumstances romanticism is connected above all with heroic themes; its eyes are turned, not on the heaven of metaphysics, but on the earth, in all its senses—on triumph over the enemy and triumph over nature. On the other hand, socialist realism does not merely register what exists, but, catching up the thread of development in the present, it leads it into the future, and leads it actively. Hence an antithesis between romanticism and socialist realism is devoid of all meaning.

The old realism was to a certain extent antilyrical, while the old lyricism was—also to a certain extent—antirealistic. Socialist realism is bound to have its eyes fixed on man. In the final analysis, socialism means the genesis of new human qualities, the enrichment of spiritual content, the development of many-sidedness, the end of squalid misery among people torn asunder into classes, narrow professions, city and country dwellers. . . .

Here we may touch upon yet another question, closely allied to this. Socialist realism is not antilyrical, but it is anti-individualistic. This does not mean that it fails to portray human personality and that it does not develop it. Socialism, as is well known, means the flourishing of personality, the enrichment of its content, the growth of its self-knowledge as a personality. But the growth of individuality is by no means equivalent to the growth of individualism, i.e., of that which disunites people. On the contrary, the feeling of a collective bond between people is one of the principal traits of socialism, and the poetized form of this feeling must inevitably be reflected in the distinguishing stylistic traits of socialist realism. Thus, socialist realism is anti-individualistic.

Twentieth-Century Poland

A playwright and a painter, Witkiewicz was, during the between-wars period, a dramatic theorist as well. Related in technique to surrealism and anticipating in subject matter the theatre of the absurd, his unique, comic, and apocalyptic plays reflect not only metaphysical reality but also social and political developments of his time. Like Artaud, whom he also anticipates, Witkiewicz—or Witkacy, as he called himself—urges a break with the foundations and focus of realistic theatre: psychology and causal action. Instead, seeking to bring theatre into the world of modern art (such as Picasso's), he calls for "Pure Form." Aiming to draw spectators into a sphere of metaphysical feelings where they would apprehend the mysteries of existence, he would synthesize sound, scenery, movement, dialogue, the presence of the actor, changes of lighting, and so forth, and would subordinate them—as independent entities, not as a representation of life—to purely formal goals. To Witkacy, every element in a theatrical production would function as a color or line would in a painting, or a note or chord in a piece of music. In his theatre of Pure Form, reality might be deformed (though not necessarily or consistently), and so might fantasy.

Unlike Witkacy, who during his lifetime exerted no influence outside Poland (and little inside Poland until the mid-fifties), Grotowski during the sixties and seventies has been influencing theatre production throughout Europe and the United States. To this Polish director, the theatre should not be an accessory to dramatic literature (that is, a recitation of a text with accompanying movements). Its appeal should be neither to those in search of frivolous entertainment nor to those anxious for cultural uplift. Grotowski believes that since the theatre cannot be as rich as movies or as lavish as television, it should be "poor," confined to its unique quality, which films and television cannot have: the closeness of living actors and audience. Theatre can exist without costumes, scenery, lighting, music, even without a text. But two features are indispensable to it: actors and an audience. In Grotowski's

"poor theatre," the creative element is the actor, not literature,
which however can stimulate the actor's creativity. Grotowski focuses on
all of the actor's physical and psychic mechanism, he transforms
the text, and, abolishing the physical distance between actors and audience,
he creates a new spatial relationship between them for each production.
Aiming to stimulate the audience into confronting themselves when they
are confronted by the actors, Grotowski—whose words recall Jung's
—would have the theatre "attack . . . the collective complexes of society,
the core of the collective subconscious," and those myths that are
"inherited through one's blood, religion, culture, and climate."

Stanisław Ignacy Witkiewicz *1885–1939*

On a New Type
of Play[1] *1920*

Theatre, like poetry, is a *composite art*, but it is made up of even more elements not intrinsic to it; therefore, it is much more difficult to imagine Pure Form on the stage, essentially independent, in its final result, of the content of human action.

Yet it is not perhaps entirely impossible.

Just as there was an epoch in sculpture and painting when Pure Form was identical with metaphysical content derived from religious concepts, so there was an epoch when performance on stage was identical with myth. Nowadays form alone is the only content of our painting and sculpture, and subject matter, whether concerned with the real world or the fantastic, is only the necessary pretext for the creation of form and has no direct connection with it, except as the "stimulus" for the whole artistic machine, driving it on to creative intensity. Similarly, we maintain that it is possible to write a play in which the performance itself, existing independently in its own right and not as a heightened picture of life, would be able to put the spectator in a position to experience metaphysical feeling, regardless of whether the *fond*[2] of the play is realistic or fantastic, or whether it is a synthesis of both, combining each of their individual parts, provided of course that the play as a *whole* results from a sincere need on the part of the author *to create a theatrical idiom capable of expressing* metaphysical feelings within purely formal dimensions. What is essential is only that the meaning of the play should not necessarily be limited by its realistic or fantastic content, as far as the totality of the work is concerned, but simply that the realistic element should exist for the sake of the purely formal goals—that is, for the sake of a synthesis of all the elements of the theatre: sound, décor, movement on the stage, dialogue, in sum, performance through time, as an uninterrupted whole—so transformed, when viewed realistically, that the performance seems utter nonsense. The idea is to make it possible *to deform either life or the whole of fantasy with complete*

[1] This essay is the last section of *An Introduction to the Theory of Pure Form in the Theatre.*

[2] Foundation, basis.

973

freedom so as to create a whole whose meaning would be defined only by its purely scenic internal construction, and not by the demands of consistent psychology and action according to assumptions from real life. Such assumptions can only be applied as criteria to plays which are heightened reproductions of life. Our contention is not that a play should necessarily be nonsensical, but only that from now on the drama should no longer be tied down to preexisting patterns based solely on life's meaning or on fantastic assumptions. The actor, in his own right, should not exist; he should be the same kind of part within a whole as the color red in a particular painting or the note C-sharp in a particular musical composition. The kind of play under discussion may well be characterized by absolute freedom in the handling of reality, but what is essential is that this freedom, like "nonsensicality" in painting, should be adequately justified and should become valid for the new dimension of thought and feeling into which such a play transports the spectator. At present we are not in a position to give an example of such a play, we are only pointing out that it is possible if only foolish prejudices can be overcome. But let us assume that someone writes such a play: the public will have to get used to it, as well as to that deformed leg in the painting by Picasso. Although we can imagine a painting composed of entirely abstract forms, which will not evoke any associations with the objects of the external world unless such associations are self-induced, yet it is not even possible for us to imagine such a play, because pure performance in time is possible only in the world of sounds, and a theatre without characters who act, no matter how outrageously and improbably, is inconceivable, simply because theatre is a composite art, and does not have its own intrinsic, *homogeneous* elements, like the pure arts: Painting and Music.

The theatre of today impresses us as being something hopelessly bottled up which can only be released by introducing what we have called *fantastic psychology and action.* The psychology of the characters and their actions should only be the pretext for a pure progression of events: therefore, what is essential is that the need for a psychology of the characters and their actions to be consistent and lifelike should not become a bugbear imposing its particular construction on the play. We have had enough wretched logic about characters and enough psychological "truth"—already it seems to be coming out of our ears. Who cares what goes on at 38 Wspólna Street, Apartment 10, or in the castle in the fairy tale, or in past times? In the theatre we want to be in an entirely new world in which the fantastic psychology of characters who are completely implausible in real life, not only in their positive actions but also *in their errors,* and who are perhaps completely unlike people in real life, produces events which by their bizarre interrelationships create a performance in time not limited by any logic except the logic of the form itself of that performance. What is required is that we accept as inevitable a particular movement of a character, a particular phrase having a realistic or only a formal meaning, a particular change of lighting or décor, a particular musical accompaniment, just as we accept as inevitable a particular part of a composition on a canvas or a sequence of chords in a musical work. We must also take into account the fact that such characters' thoughts and feelings are completely unfettered and that they react with complete freedom to any and all events, even though there is no justification for any of this. Still, these elements would have to be suggested on the same level of formal necessity as all the other elements of performance on the stage mentioned above. Of course, the public would have to be won over to this fantastic psychology, as with the square leg in the painting by Picasso. The public has already laughed at the deformed shapes on the canvases of contemporary masters; now they will also have to laugh at the thoughts and actions of characters on the stage, since for the time being these cannot be completely explained. We believe that this problem can be resolved in exactly the same way as it has been in contemporary painting and music: by understanding the essence of art in general and by growing accustomed to it. Just as those who have finally understood Pure Form in painting can no longer even look at other kinds of painting and cannot help understanding correctly paintings which they laughed at before as incomprehensible, so those who become used to the theatre we are proposing will not be able to stand any of the productions of today, whether realistic or heavily symbolic. As far as painting is concerned, we have tested this matter more than once on people who were apparently incapable of understanding Pure Form at the beginning, but who after receiving systematic "injections" over a certain period of time reached a remarkably high level of perfection in making truly expert judgments. There may be a certain amount of perversity in all this, but why should we be afraid of purely artistic perversity? Of course, perverseness in life is often a sad affair, but why should we apply judgments which are reasonable in real life to the realm of art, with which life has essentially so little in common. Artistic perversity (for example, unbalanced masses in a pictorial composition, perversely tense movements or clashing colors in a painting) is only a means, and not an end; therefore, it cannot be immoral, because the goal which it enables us to attain—unity within diversity in Pure Form—cannot be subjected to the criteria of good and evil. It is somewhat different with the theatre, because its elements are beings who act; but we believe that in those new dimensions which we are discussing even the most monstrous situations will be no less moral than what is seen in the theatre today.

Of course, even assuming that a certain segment of the public interested in serious artistic experiences will come to demand plays written in the style described above, such plays would still have to result from a *genuine creative necessity* felt by an author writing for the stage. If such a work were only a kind of *schematic nonsense*, devised in cold blood, artificially, without real need, it would probably arouse nothing but laughter, like those paintings with a bizarre form of subject matter which are created by those who do not suffer from a real "insatiable pursuit of new forms," but who manufacture them for commercial reasons or *pour épater les bourgeois*.[3] Just as the birth of a new form, pure and abstract, without a direct religious basis, took place only through deforming our vision of the external world, so the birth of Pure Form in the theatre is also possible only through deforming human psychology and action.

We can imagine such a play as having complete freedom with respect to absolutely everything from the point of view of real life, and yet being extraordinarily close knit and highly wrought in the way the action is tied together. The task would be to fill several hours on the stage with a performance possessing its own internal, formal logic, independent of anything in "real life." An invented, *not created*, example of such a work can only make our theory appear ridiculous, and, from a certain point of view, even absurd (for some, even infuriating or, to put it bluntly, *idiotic*), but let us try.

Three characters dressed in red come on stage and bow to no one in particular. One of them recites a poem (it should create a feeling of urgent necessity at this very moment). A kindly old man enters leading a cat on a string. So far everything has taken place against a background of a black screen. The screen draws apart, and an Italian landscape becomes visible. Organ music is heard. The old man talks with the other characters, and what they say should be in keeping with what has gone before. A glass falls off the table. All of them fall on their knees and weep. The old man changes from a kindly man into a ferocious "butcher" and murders a little girl who has just crawled in from the left. At this very moment a handsome young man runs in and thanks the old man for murdering the girl, at which point the characters in red sing and dance. Then the young man weeps over the body of the little girl and says very amusing things, whereupon the old man becomes once again kindly and good-natured and laughs to himself in a corner, uttering sublime and limpid phrases. The choice of costumes is completely open: period or fantastic—there may be music during some parts of the performance. In other words, an insane asylum? Or rather a madman's brain on the stage? Perhaps so, but we maintain that, *if the play is seriously written and appropriately produced*, this method can *create works of previously unsuspected beauty*; whether it be drama, tragedy, farce, or the grotesque, all in a uniform style and unlike anything which previously existed.

On leaving the theatre, the spectator ought to have the feeling that

---

[3] In order to shock the bourgeoisie.

he has just awakened from some strange dream, in which even the most ordinary things had a strange, unfathomable charm, characteristic of dream reveries, and unlike anything else in the world. Nowadays the spectator leaves the theatre with a bad taste in his mouth, or he is shaken by the purely biological horror or sublimity of life, or he is furious that he has been fooled by a whole series of tricks. For all its variety, the contemporary theatre almost never gives us the other world, other not in the sense of being fantastic, but truly that other world which brings to us an understanding of purely formal beauty. Occasionally something like this happens in the plays of writers of previous ages, plays which after all have their significance and greatness that we certainly do not want to deny them with any fanatical fury. This element which we are discussing can be found in some of the plays of Shakespeare and Slowacki,[4] for example, but never in its purest form, and, therefore, despite their greatness, these plays do not create the desired effect.

The climax and the conclusion of the kind of play which we are proposing may be created in a complete abstraction from what might be called that debasing feeling of pure curiosity about real life, that tension in the pit of the stomach, with which we watch a drama of real life, and which constitutes precisely the one and only appeal of plays today. Of course we would have to break this bad habit, so that *in a world with which, on the realistic level, we have no contact,* we could experience a metaphysical drama similar to the one which takes place among the notes of a symphony or sonata and only among them, so that the dénouement would not be an event of concern to us as part of real life, but only as something comprehensible *as the inevitable conclusion of the purely formal complications of sound patterns, decorative or psychological, free from the causality found in real life.*

The criticism of absolute freedom made against contemporary artists and their works by people who do not understand art can also be applied here. For example, why three characters, not five? Why dressed in red, not green? Of course, we cannot *prove* the necessity for that number and color, but it should appear inevitable insofar as each element is a necessary part of the work of art once it has been created; while we are watching the play unfold, we ought not to be able to think of any other possible internal interrelationships. And we maintain that, if the work is to be created with complete artistic sincerity, it will have to compel the spectators to accept it as inevitable. It is certainly much more difficult with the theatre than with other arts, because, as a certain expert on the theatre has asserted, the crowd as it watches and listens is an essential part of the performance itself, and moreover the play has to be a box-office success. But we believe that sooner or later the theatre must embark upon the "insatiable pursuit of

---

[4] Juliusz Słowacki (1809–1849), Polish poet and dramatist.

new forms," which it has avoided up until now, and it is to be hoped that
extraordinary works, within the dimensions of Pure Form, still remain to be
created, and that there will not simply be more "renaissance" and "purification" or repetition ad nauseam of the old repertoire which really has
nothing at all to say to anybody.

We must unleash the slumbering Beast and see what it can do. And if
it runs mad, there will always be time enough to shoot it before it is too late.

Jerzy Grotowski *1933–*

The Theatre's
New Testament *1964*

*The very name "Theatre Laboratory" makes one think of scientific research.
Is this an appropriate association?*

The word research should not bring to mind scientific research. Nothing
could be further from what we are doing than science *sensu stricto*,[1] and not
only because of our lack of qualifications, but also because of our lack of
interest in that kind of work.

The word research implies that we approach our profession rather like the
medieval wood carver who sought to re-create in his block of wood a form
which already existed. We do not work in the same way as the artist or the
scientist, but rather as the shoemaker looking for the right spot on the shoe
in which to hammer the nail.

The other sense of the word research might seem a little irrational as it
involves the idea of a penetration into human nature itself. In our age when
all languages are confused as in the Tower of Babel, when all esthetical genres
intermingle, death threatens the theatre as film and television encroach upon

[1] In a narrow sense.

its domain. This makes us examine the nature of theatre, how it differs from the other art forms, and what it is that makes it irreplaceable.

Has your research led you to a definition?

What does the word theatre mean? This is a question we often come up against, and one to which there are many possible answers. To the academic, the theatre is a place where an actor recites a written text, illustrating it with a series of movements in order to make it more easily understood. Thus interpreted the theatre is a useful accessory to dramatic literature. The intellectual theatre is merely a variation of this conception. Its advocates consider it a kind of polemical tribune. Here too, the text is the most important element, and the theatre is there only to plug certain intellectual arguments, thus bringing about their reciprocal confrontation. It is a revival of the medieval art of the oratorical duel.

To the average theatregoer, the theatre is first and foremost a place of entertainment. If he expects to encounter a frivolous Muse, the text does not interest him in the least. What attracts him are the so-called gags, the comic effects and perhaps the puns which lead back to the text. His attention will be directed mainly toward the actor as a center of attraction. A young woman sufficiently briefly clad is in herself an attraction to certain theatregoers who apply cultural criteria to her performance, though such a judgment is actually a compensation for personal frustration.

The theatregoer who cherishes cultural aspirations likes from time to time to attend performances from the more serious repertoire, perhaps even a tragedy provided that it contains some melodramatic element. In this case his expectations will vary widely. On the one hand he must show that he belongs to the best society where "Art" is a guarantee and, on the other, he wants to experience certain emotions which give him a sense of self-satisfaction. Even if he does feel pity for poor Antigone and aversion for the cruel Creon, he does not share the sacrifice and the fate of the heroine, but he nevertheless believes himself to be her equal morally. For him it is a question of being able to feel "noble." The didactic qualities of this kind of emotion are dubious. The audience—all Creons—may well side with Antigone throughout the performance, but this does not prevent each of them from behaving like Creon once out of the theatre. It is worth noticing the success of plays which depict an unhappy childhood. To see the sufferings of an innocent child on the stage makes it even easier for the spectator to sympathize with the unfortunate victim. Thus he is assured of his own high standard of moral values.

Theatre people themselves do not usually have an altogether clear conception of theatre. To the average actor the theatre is first and foremost *himself*, and not what he is able to achieve by means of his artistic technique.

He—his own private organism—*is* the theatre. Such an attitude breeds the impudence and self-satisfaction which enable him to present acts that demand no special knowledge, that are banal and commonplace, such as walking, getting up, sitting down, lighting a cigarette, putting his hands in his pockets, and so on. In the actor's opinion all this is not meant to reveal anything but to be enough in itself for, as I said, he, the actor, Mr. X, *is* the theatre. And if the actor possesses a certain charm which can take in the audience, it strengthens him in his conviction.

To the stage-designer, the theatre is above all a plastic art and this can have positive consequences. Designers are often supporters of the literary theatre. They claim that the décor as well as the actor should serve the drama. This creed reveals no wish to serve literature, but merely a complex towards the producer. They prefer to be on the side of the playwright as he is further removed and consequently less able to restrict them. In practice, the most original stage-designers suggest a confrontation between the text and a plastic vision which surpasses and reveals the playwright's imagination. It is probably no mere coincidence that the Polish designers are often the pioneers in our country's theatre. They exploited the numerous possibilities offered by the revolutionary development of the plastic arts in the twentieth century which, to a lesser degree, inspired playwrights and producers..

Does this not imply a certain danger? The critics who accuse the designers of dominating the stage, put forward more than one valid objective argument, only their premise is erroneous. It is as if they blame a car for traveling faster than a snail. This is what worries them and not whether the designer's vision dominates that of the actor and the producer. The vision of the designer is creative, not stereotyped, and even if it is, it loses its tautological character through an immense magnification process. Nevertheless, the theatre is transformed—whether the designer likes it or not—into a series of living tableaux. It becomes a kind of monumental "camera obscura," a thrilling "laterna magica." But does it not then cease to be theatre?

Finally, what is the theatre to the producer?[2] Producers come to the theatre after failing in other fields. He who once dreamed of becoming a playwright usually ends up as a producer.

The actor who is a failure, the actress who once played the young prima donna and is getting old, these turn to production.

The theatre critic who has long had an impotence complex towards an art which he can do no more than write about takes up producing.

The hypersensitive professor of literature who is weary of academic work considers himself competent to become a producer. He knows what drama is—and what else is theatre to him if not the realization of a text?

---

[2] In the United States, he is called the director.

Because they are guided by such varied psychoanalytic motives, producers' ideas on theatre are about as varied as it is possible to be. Their work is a compensation for various phenomena. A man who has unfilled political tendencies, for instance, often becomes a producer and enjoys the feeling of power such a position gives him. This has more than once led to perverse interpretations, and producers possessing such an extreme need for power have staged plays which polemize against the authorities: hence numerous "rebellious" performances.

Of course a producer wants to be creative. He therefore—more or less consciously—advocates an autonomous theatre, independent of literature which he merely considers as a pretext. But, on the other hand, people capable of such creative work are rare. Many are officially content with a literary and intellectual theatre definition, or to maintain Wagner's theory that the theatre should be a synthesis of all the arts. A very useful formula! It allows one to respect the text, that inviolable basic element, and furthermore it provokes no conflict with the literary and the philological milieu. It must be stated, in parenthesis, that every playwright—even the ones we can only qualify as such out of sheer politeness—feels himself obliged to defend the honor and the rights of Mickiewicz,[3] Shakespeare, etc., because quite simply he considers himself their colleague. In this way Wagner's theory about "the theatre as the total art" establishes *la paix des braves*[4] in the literary field.

This theory justifies the exploitation of the plastic elements of scenography in the performance, and ascribes the results to it. The same goes for the music, whether it be an original work or a montage. To this is added the accidental choice of one or more well-known actors and from these elements, only casually coordinated, emerges a performance which satisfies the ambitions of the producer. He is enthroned on top of all the arts, although in reality he feeds off them all without himself being tied to the creative work which is carried out for him by others—if, indeed, anyone can be called creative in such circumstances.

Thus the number of definitions of theatre is practically unlimited. To escape from this vicious circle one must without doubt eliminate, not add. That is, one must ask oneself what is indispensable to theatre. Let's see.

Can the theatre exist without costumes and sets? Yes, it can.

Can it exist without music to accompany the plot? Yes.

Can it exist without lighting effects? Of course.

And without a text? Yes; the history of the theatre confirms this. In the evolution of the theatrical art the text was one of the last elements to be added. If we place some people on a stage with a scenario they themselves

---

[3] Adam Mickiewicz (1789–1855), Polish poet and playwright.

[4] Literally, the peace of the brave; that is, a reconciliation and calm among the worthy and respectable.

have put together and let them improvise their parts as in the Commedia dell'Arte, the performance will be equally good even if the words are not articulated but simply muttered.

But can the theatre exist without actors? I know of no example of this. One could mention the puppet-show. Even here, however, an actor is to be found behind the scenes, although of another kind.

Can the theatre exist without an audience? At least one spectator is needed to make it a performance. So we are left with the actor and the spectator. We can thus define the theatre as "what takes place between spectator and actor." All the other things are supplementary—perhaps necessary, but nevertheless supplementary. It is no mere coincidence that our own theatre laboratory has developed from a theatre rich in resources—in which the plastic arts, lighting and music, were constantly exploited—into the ascetic theatre we have become in recent years: an ascetic theatre in which the actors and audience are all that is left. All the other visual elements—e.g., plastic, etc.— are constructed by means of the actor's body, the acoustic and musical effects by his voice. This does not mean that we look down upon literature, but that we do not find in it the creative part of the theatre, even though great literary works can, no doubt, have a stimulating effect on this genesis. Since our theatre consists only of actors and audience, we make special demands on both parties. Even though we cannot educate the audience—not systematically, at least—we *can* educate the actor.

How, then, is the actor trained in your theatre, and what is his function in the performance?

The actor is a man who works in public with his body, offering it publicly. If this body restricts itself to demonstrating what it is—something that any average person can do—then it is not an obedient instrument capable of performing a spiritual act. If it is exploited for money and to win the favor of the audience, then the art of acting borders on prostitution. It is a fact that for many centuries the theatre has been associated with prostitution in one sense of the word or another. The words "actress" and "courtesan" were once synonymous. Today they are separated by a somewhat clearer line, not through any change in the actor's world but because society has changed. Today it is the difference between the respectable woman and the courtesan which has become blurred.

What strikes one when looking at the work of an actor as practiced these days is the wretchedness of it: the bargaining over a body which is exploited by its protectors—director, producer—creating in return an atmosphere of intrigue and revolt.

Just as only a greater sinner can become a saint according to the theologians (Let us not forget the Revelation: "So then because thou art lukewarm, and neither cold nor hot, I will spue thee out of my mouth"),[5] in the same way the actor's wretchedness can be transformed into a kind of holiness. The history of the theatre has numerous examples of this.

Don't get me wrong. I speak about "holiness" as an unbeliever. I mean a "secular holiness." If the actor, by setting himself a challenge publicly challenges others, and through excess, profanation and outrageous sacrilege reveals himself by casting off his everyday mask, he makes it possible for the spectator to undertake a similar process of self-penetration. If he does not exhibit his body, but annihilates it, burns it, frees it from every resistance to any psychic impulse, then he does not sell his body but sacrifices it. He repeats the atonement; he is close to holiness. If such acting is not to be something transient and fortuitous, a phenomenon which cannot be foreseen in time or space: if we want a theatre group whose daily bread is this kind of work—then we must follow a special method of research and training.

What is it like, in practice, to work with the "holy" actor?

There is a myth how an actor with a considerable fund of experience can build up what we might call his own "arsenal"—i.e., an accumulation of methods, artifices and tricks. From these he can pick out a certain number of combinations for each part and thus attain the expressiveness necessary for him to grip his audience. This "arsenal" or store may be nothing but a collection of clichés, in which case such a method is inseparable from the conception of the "courtesan actor."

The difference between the "courtesan actor" and the "holy actor" is the same as the difference between the skill of a courtesan and the attitude of giving and receiving which springs from true love: in other words, self-sacrifice. The essential thing in this second case is to be able to eliminate any disturbing elements in order to be able to overstep every conceivable limit. In the first case it is a question of the existence of the body; in the other, rather of its nonexistence. The technique of the "holy actor" is an *inductive technique* (i.e., a technique of elimination), whereas that of the "courtesan actor" is a *deductive technique* (i.e., an accumulation of skills).

The actor who undertakes an act of self-penetration, who reveals himself and sacrifices the innermost part of himself—the most painful, that which is not intended for the eyes of the world—must be able to manifest the least impulse. He must be able to express, through sound and movement, those impulses which waver on the borderline between dream and reality. In short, he must be able to construct his own psychoanalytic language of sounds and gestures in the same way that a great poet creates his own language of words.

If we take into consideration for instance the problem of sound, the

[5] *Revelation* 3:16.

plasticity of the actor's respiratory and vocal apparatus must be infinitely more developed than that of the man in the street. Furthermore, this apparatus must be able to produce sound reflexes so quickly that thought—which would remove all spontaneity—has no time to intervene.

The actor should be able to decipher all the problems of his body, which are accessible to him. He should know how to direct the air to those parts of the body where sound can be created and amplified by a sort of resonator. The average actor knows only the head resonator; that is, he uses his head as a resonator to amplify his voice, making it sound more "noble," more agreeable to the audience. He may even at times, fortuitously, make use of the chest resonator. But the actor who investigates closely the possibilities of his own organism discovers that the number of resonators is practically unlimited. He can exploit not only his head and chest, but also the back of his head (occiput), his nose, his teeth, his larynx, his belly, his spine, as well as a total resonator which actually comprises the whole body and many others, some of which are still unknown to us. He discovers that it is not enough to make use of abdominal respiration on stage. The various phases in his physical actions demand different kinds of respiration if he is to avoid difficulties with his breathing and resistance from his body. He discovers that the diction he learnt at drama school far too often provokes the closing of the larynx. He must acquire the ability to open his larynx consciously, and to check from the outside whether it is open or closed. If he does not solve these problems, his attention will be distracted by the difficulties he is bound to encounter and the process of self-penetration will necessarily fail. If the actor is conscious of his body, he cannot penetrate and reveal himself. The body must be freed from all resistance. It must virtually cease to exist. As for his voice and respiration, it is not enough that the actor learns to make use of several resonators, to open his larynx and to select a certain type or respiration. He must learn to perform all this unconsciously in the culminating phases of his acting and this, in its turn, is something which demands a new series of exercises. When he is working on his role he must learn not to think of adding technical elements (resonators, etc.), but should aim at eliminating the concrete obstacles he comes up against (e.g., resistance in his voice).

This is not merely splitting hairs. It is the difference which decides the degree of success. It means that the actor will never possess a permanently "closed" technique, for at each stage of his self-scrutiny, each challenge, each *excess*, each breaking down of hidden barriers he will encounter new technical problems on a higher level. He must then learn to overcome these too with the help of certain basic exercises.

This goes for everything: movement, the plasticity of the body, gesticulation, the construction of masks by means of the facial musculature and, in fact, for each detail of the actor's body.

But the decisive factor in this process is the actor's technique of psychic penetration. He must learn to use his role as if it were a surgeon's scalpel, to dissect himself. It is not a question of portraying himself under certain given circumstances, or of "living" a part; nor does it entail the distant sort of acting common to epic theatre and based on cold calculation. The important thing is to use the role as a trampoline, and instrument with which to study what is hidden behind our everyday mask—the innermost core of our personality—in order to sacrifice it, expose it.

This is an excess not only for the actor but also for the audience. The spectator understands, consciously or unconsciously, that such an act is an invitation to him to do the same thing, and this often arouses opposition or indignation, because our daily efforts are intended to hide the truth about ourselves not only from the world, but also from ourselves. We try to escape the truth about ourselves, whereas here we are invited to stop and take a closer look. We are afraid of being changed into pillars of salt if we turn around, like Lot's wife.

The performing of this act we are referring to—self-penetration, exposure —demands a mobilization of all the physical and spiritual forces of the actor who is in a state of idle readiness, a passive availability, which makes possible an active acting score.

One must resort to a metaphorical language to say that the decisive factor in this process is humility, a spiritual predisposition: not to *do* something, but to *refrain* from doing something, otherwise the excess becomes impudence instead of sacrifice. This means that the actor must act in a state of trance.

Trance, as I understand it, is the ability to concentrate in a particular theatrical way and can be attained with a minimum of goodwill.

If I were to express all this in one sentence I would say that it is all a question of giving oneself. One must give oneself totally, in one's deepest intimacy, with confidence, as when one gives oneself in love. Here lies the key. Self-penetration, trance, *excess*, the formal discipline itself—all this can be realized, provided one has given oneself fully, humbly and without defence. This act culminates in a climax. It brings relief. None of the exercises in the various fields of the actor's training must be exercises in skill. They should develop a system of allusions which lead to the elusive and indescribable process of self-donation.

All this may sound strange and bring to mind some form of "quackery." If we are to stick to scientific formulas, we can say that it is a particular use of suggestion, aiming at an *ideoplastic* realization. Personally, I must admit that we do not shrink from using these "quack" formulas. Anything that has an unusual or magical ring stimulates the imagination of both actor and producer.

I believe one must develop a special anatomy of the actor; for instance, find the body's various centers of concentration for different ways of acting, seeking the areas of the body which the actor sometimes feels to be his sources of energy. The lumbar region, the abdomen and the area around the solar plexus often function as such a source.

An essential factor in this process is the elaboration of a guiding rein for the form, the artificiality. The actor who accomplishes an act of self-penetration is setting out on a journey which is recorded through various sound and gesture reflexes, formulating a sort of invitation to the spectator. But these signs must be articulated. Expressiveness is always connected with certain contradictions and discrepancies. Undisciplined self-penetration is no liberation, but is perceived as a form of biological chaos.

How do you combine spontaneity and formal discipline?

The elaboration of artificiality is a question of ideograms—sounds and gestures—which evoke associations in the psyche of the audience. It is reminiscent of a sculptor's work on a block of stone: the conscious use of hammer and chisel. It consists, for instance, in the analysis of a hand's reflex during a psychic process and its successive development through shoulder, elbow, wrist and fingers in order to decide how each phase of this process can be expressed through a sign, an ideogram, which either instantly conveys the hidden motivations of the actor or polemizes against them.

This elaboration of artificiality—of the form's guiding rein—is often based on a conscious searching of our organism for forms whose outlines we feel although their reality still escapes us. One assumes that these forms already exist, complete, within our organism. Here we touch on a type of acting which, as an art, is closer to sculpture than to painting. Painting involves the addition of colors, whereas the sculptor takes away what is concealing the form which, as it were, already exists within the block of stone, thus revealing it instead of building it up.

This search for artificiality in its turn requires a series of additional exercises, forming a miniature score for each part of the body. At any rate, the decisive principle remains the following: the more we become absorbed in what is hidden inside us, in the excess, in the exposure, in the self-penetration, the more rigid must be the external discipline; that is to say the form, the artificiality, the ideogram, the sign. Here lies the whole principle of expressiveness.

What do you expect from the spectator in this kind of theatre?

Our postulates are not new. We make the same demands on people as every real work of art makes, whether it be a painting, a sculpture, music, poetry, or literature. We do not cater for the man who goes to the theatre to satisfy a social need for contact with culture: in other words, to have something to talk about to his friends and to be able to say that he has seen this or that play and that it was interesting. We are not there to satisfy his "cultural needs." This is cheating.

Nor do we cater for the man who goes to the theatre to relax after a hard day's work. Everyone has a right to relax after work and there are numerous forms of entertainment for this purpose, ranging from certain types of film to cabaret and music-hall, and many more on the same lines.

We are concerned with the spectator who has genuine spiritual needs and who really wishes, through confrontation with the performance, to analyze himself. We are concerned with the spectator who does not stop at an elementary stage of physic integration, content with his own petty, geometrical, spiritual stability, knowing exactly what is good and what is evil, and never in doubt. For it was not to him that El Greco, Norwid, Thomas Mann, and Dostoevsky spoke, but to him who undergoes an endless process of self-development, whose unrest is not general but directed towards a search for the truth about himself and his mission in life.

Does this infer a theatre for the elite?

Yes, but for an elite which is not determined by the social background or financial situation of the spectator, nor even education. The worker who has never had any secondary education can undergo this creative process of self-search, whereas the university professor may be dead, permanently formed, molded into the terrible rigidity of a corpse. This must be made clear from the very beginning. We are not concerned with just any audience, but a special one.

We cannot know whether the theatre is still necessary today since all social attractions, entertainments, form and color effects have been taken over by film and television. Everybody repeats the same rhetorical question: Is the theatre necessary? But we only ask it in order to be able to reply: Yes, it is, because it is an art which is always young and always necessary. The sale of performances is organized on a grand scale. Yet no one organizes film and television audiences in the same way. If all theatres were closed down one day, a large percentage of the people would know nothing about it until weeks later, but if one were to eliminate cinemas and television, the very next day the whole population would be in an uproar. Many theatre people are conscious of this problem, but hit upon the wrong solution: since the cinema dominates theatre from a technical point of view, why not make the theatre more technical? They invent new stages, they put on performances with lightning-quick changes of scenery, complicated lighting and décor, etc., but can never attain the technical skill of film and television. The theatre must recognize its own limitations. If it cannot be richer than the cinema, then let it be poor. If it cannot be as lavish as

television, let it be ascetic. If it cannot be a technical attraction, let it renounce all outward technique. Thus we are left with a "holy" actor in a
poor theatre.

There is only one element of which film and television cannot rob the
theatre: the closeness of the living organism. Because of this, each challenge from the actor, each of his magical acts (which the audience is incapable of reproducing) becomes something great, something extraordinary,
something close to ecstacy. It is therefore necessary to abolish the distance
between actor and audience by eliminating the stage, removing all frontiers.
Let the most drastic scenes happen face to face with the spectator so that he
is within arm's reach of the actor, can feel his breathing and smell the
perspiration. This implies the necessity for a chamber theatre.

*How can such a theatre express the unrest which one has a right to assume
varies with the individual?*

In order that the spectator may be stimulated into self-analysis when
confronted with the actor, there must be some common ground already
existing in both of them, something they can either dismiss in one gesture
or jointly worship. Therefore the theatre must attack what might be
called the collective complexes of society, the core of the collective subconscious or perhaps superconscious (it does not matter what we call it),
the myths which are not an invention of the mind but are, so to speak,
inherited through one's blood, religion, culture and climate.

I am thinking of things that are so elementary and so intimately associated that it would be difficult for us to submit them to a rational analysis.
For instance, religious myths: the myth of Christ and Mary; biological
myths: birth and death, love symbolism or, in a broader sense, Eros and
Thanatos; national myths which it would be difficult to break down into
formulas, yet whose very presence we feel in our blood when we read Part
III of Mickiewicz's *Forefathers' Eve*, Słowacki's *Kordian*,[6] or the Ave Maria.

Once again, there is no question of a speculative search for certain elements to be assembled into a performance. If we start working on a theatre
performance or a role by violating our innermost selves, searching for the
things which can hurt us most deeply, but which at the same time gives
us a total feeling of purifying truth that finally brings peace, then we
will inevitably end up with *représentations collectives*.[7] One has to be
familiar with this concept so at not to lose the right track once one has found
it. But it cannot be imposed on one in advance.

How does this function in a theatre performance? I do not intend to

[6] (1832) and (1833), respectively.
[7] Collective productions.

give examples here. I think there is sufficient explanation in the description of *Akropolis*,[8] *Dr Faustus*,[9] or other performances. I only wish to draw attention to a special characteristic of these theatre performances which combine fascination and excessive negation, acceptance and rejection, an attack on that which is sacred (*représentations collectives*), profanation and worship.

To spark off this particular process of provocation in the audience, one must break away from the trampoline represented by the text and which is already overloaded with a number of general associations. For this we need either a classical text to which, through a sort of profanation, we simultaneously restore its truth, or a modern text which might well be banal and stereotyped in its content, but nevertheless rooted in the psyche of society.

Is the "holy" actor not a dream? The road to holiness is not open to everyone. Only the chosen few can follow it.

As I said, one must not take the word "holy" in the religious sense. It is rather a metaphor defining a person who, through his art, climbs upon the stake and performs an act of self-sacrifice. Of course, you are right: it is an infinitely difficult task to assemble a troupe of "holy" actors. It is very much easier to find a "holy" spectator—in my sense of the word— for he only comes to the theatre for a brief moment in order to square off an account with himself, and this is something that does not impose the hard routine of daily work.

Is holiness therefore an unreal postulate? I think it is just as well founded as that of movement at the speed of light. By this I mean that without ever attaining it, we can nevertheless move consciously and systematically in that direction, thus achieving practical results.

Acting is a particularly thankless art. It dies with the actor. Nothing survives him but the reviews which do not usually do him justice anyway, whether he is good or bad. So the only source of satisfaction left to him is the audience's reactions. In the poor theatre this does not mean flowers and interminable applause, but a special silence in which there is much fascination but also a lot of indignation, and even repugnance, which the spectator directs not at himself but at the theatre. It is difficult to reach a psychic level which enables one to endure such pressure.

I am sure that every actor belonging to such a theatre often dreams of overwhelming ovations, of hearing his name shouted out, of being covered with flowers or other such symbols of appreciation as is customary in the

---

[8] (1904) by Stanisław Wyspianski (1869–1907), Polish poet, playwright, and painter.
[9] (?1592) by Christopher Marlowe (1564–1593).

commercial theatre. The actor's work is also a thankless one because of the incessant supervision it is subject to. It is not like being creative in an office, seated before a table, but under the eye of the producer who, even in a theatre based on the art of the actor, must make persistent demands on him to a much greater extent than in the normal theatre, urging him on to ever increasing efforts that are painful to him.

This would be unbearable if such a producer did not possess a moral authority, if his postulates were not evident, and if an element of mutual confidence did not exist even beyond the barriers of consciousness. But even in this case, he is nevertheless a tyrant and the actor must direct against him certain unconscious mechanical reactions like a pupil does against his teacher, a patient against his doctor, or a soldier against his superiors.

The poor theatre does not offer the actor the possibility of overnight success. It defies the bourgeois concept of a standard of living. It proposes the substitution of material wealth by moral wealth as the principal aim in life. Yet who does not cherish a secret wish to rise to sudden affluence? This too may cause opposition and negative reactions, even if these are not clearly formulated. Work in such an ensemble can never be stable. It is nothing but a huge challenge and, furthermore, it awakens such strong reactions of aversion that these often threaten the theatre's very existence. Who does not search for stability and security in one form or another? Who does not hope to live at least as well tomorrow as he does today? Even if one consciously accepts such a status, one unconsciously looks around for that unattainable refuge which reconciles fire with water and "holiness" with the life of the "courtesan."

However, the attraction of such a paradoxical situation is sufficiently strong to eliminate all the intrigues, slander, and quarrels over roles which form part of everyday life in other theatres. But people will be people, and periods of depression and suppressed grudges cannot be avoided.

It is nevertheless worth mentioning that the satisfaction which such work gives is great. The actor who, in this special process of discipline and self-sacrifice, self-penetration and molding, is not afraid to go beyond all normally acceptable limits, attains a kind of inner harmony and peace of mind. He literally becomes much sounder in mind and body, and his way of life is more normal than that of an actor in the rich theatre.

This process of analysis is a sort of disintegration of the psychic structure. Is the actor not in danger here of overstepping the mark from the point of view of mental hygiene?

No, provided that he gives himself one hundred percent to his work. It is work that is done half-heartedly, superficially, that is psychically painful and upsets the equilibrium. If we only engage ourselves superficially in this process of analysis and exposure—and this can produce ample esthetical effects—that is, if we retain our daily mask of lies, then we witness a conflict between this mask and ourselves. But if this process is followed through to its extreme limit, we can in full consciousness put back our everyday mask, knowing now what purpose it serves and what it conceals beneath it. This is a confirmation not of the negative in us but of the positive, not of what is poorest but of what is richest. It also leads to a liberation from complexes in much the same way as psychoanalytic therapy.

The same applies to the spectator. The member of an audience who accepts the actor's invitation and to a certain extent follows his example by activiating himself in the same way, leaves the theatre in a state of greater inner harmony. But he who fights to keep his mask of lies intact at all costs, leaves the performance even more confused. I am convinced that on the whole, even in the latter case, the performance represents a form of social psychotherapy, whereas for the actor it is only a therapy if he has given himself wholeheartedly to his task.

There are certain dangers. It is far less risky to be Mr. Smith all one's life than to be Van Gogh.[10] But, fully conscious of our social responsibility, we could wish that there were more Van Goghs than Smiths, even though life is much simpler for the latter. Van Gogh is an example of an incomplete process of integration. His downfall is the expression of a development which was never fulfilled. If we take a look at great personalities like for example Thomas Mann,[11] we do eventually find a certain form of harmony.

It seems to me that the producer has a very great responsibility in this self-analytic process of the actor. How does this interdependence manifest itself, and what might be the consequences of a wrong action on his part?

This is a vitally important point. In the light of what I have just said, this may sound rather strange.

The performance engages a sort of psychic conflict with the spectator. It is a challenge and an excess, but can only have any effect if based on human interest and, more than that, on a feeling of sympathy, a feeling of acceptance. In the same way, the producer can help the actor in this complex and agonizing process only if he is just as emotionally and warmly open to the actor as the actor is in regard to him. I do not believe in the possibility of achieving effects by means of cold calculation. A kind of warmth towards one's fellow men is essential—an understanding of the contradictions in man, and that he is a suffering creature but not one to be scorned.

This element of warm openness is technically tangible. It alone, if

---

[10] Vincent Willem Van Gogh (1853–1890), painter.
[11] Thomas Mann (1875–1955), novelist and essayist.

reciprocal, can enable the actor to undertake the most extreme efforts without any fear of being laughed at or humiliated. The type of work which creates such confidence makes words unnecessary during rehearsals. When at work, the beginnings of a sound or sometimes even a silence are enough to make oneself understood. What is born in the actor is engendered together, but in the end the result is far more a part of him than those results obtained at rehearsals in the "normal" theatre.

I think we are dealing here with an "art" of working which it is impossible to reduce to a formula and cannot simply be learnt. Just as any doctor does not necessarily make a good psychiatrist, not any producer can succeed in this form of theatre. The principle to apply as a piece of advice, and also a warning, is the following: *"Primum non nocere"* (First, do not harm"). To express this in technical language: it is better to suggest by means of sound and gesture than to "act" in front of the actor or supply him with intellectual explanations; better to express oneself by means of a silence or a wink of the eye than by instructions, observing the stages in the psychological breakdown and collapse of the actor in order then to come to his aid. One must be strict, but like a father or older brother. The second principle is one common to all professions: if you make demands on your colleagues, you must make twice as many demands on yourself.

This implies that to work with the "holy" actor, there must be a producer who is twice as "holy": that is, a "super-saint" who, through his knowledge and intuition, breaks the bounds of the history of the theatre, and who is well acquainted with the latest results in sciences such as psychology, anthropology, myth interpretation and the history of religion.

All I have said about the wretchedness of the actor applies to the producer too. To develop the metaphor of the "courtesan actor," the equivalent among producers would be the "producer *souteneur.*" And just as it is impossible to erase completely all traces of the "courtesan" in the "holy" actor, one can never completely eradicate the *"souteneur"*[12] in the "holy" producer.

The producer's job demands a certain tactical *savoir faire*, namely in the art of leading. Generally speaking, this kind of power demoralizes. It entails the necessity of learning how to handle people. It demands a gift for diplomacy, a cold and inhuman talent for dealing with intrigues. These characteristics follow the producer like his shadow even in the poor theatre. What one might call the masochistic component in the actor is the negative variant of what is creative in the director in the form of a sadistic component. Here, as everywhere, the dark is inseparable from the light.

---

12 Pimp.

When I take sides against half-heartedness, mediocrity, and the easy-come-easy-go attitude which takes everything for granted, it is simply because we must create things which are firmly orientated towards either light or darkness. But we must remember that around that which is luminous within us, there exists a shroud of darkness which we can penetrate but not annihilate.

According to what you have been saying, "holiness" in the theatre can be achieved by means of a particular discipline and various physical exercises. In the theatre schools and in traditional as well as experimental theatres, there is no such trend, no consistent attempt to work out or elaborate anything similar. How can we go about preparing the way for and training "holy" actors and producers? To what extent is it possible to create "monastic" theatres as opposed to the day-to-day "parochial" theatre?

I do not think that the crisis in the theatre can be separated from certain other crisis processes in contemporary culture. One of its essential elements—namely, the disappearance of the sacred and of its ritual function in the theatre—is a result of the obvious and probably inevitable decline of religion. What we are talking about is the possibility of creating a secular *sacrum* in the theatre. The question is, can the current pace in the development of civilization make a reality of this postulate on a collective scale? I have no answer to this. One must contribute to its realization, for a secular consciousness in place of the religious one seems to be a psycho-social necessity for society. Such a transition ought to take place but that does not necessarily mean that it will. I believe that it is, in a way, an ethical rule, like saying that man must not act like a wolf towards his fellow men. But as we all know, these rules are not always applied.

In any case, I am sure that this renewal will not come from the dominating theatre. Yet, at the same time, there are and have been a few people in the official theatre who must be considered as secular saints: Stanislavski,[13] for example. He maintained that the successive stages of awakening and renewal in the theatre had found their beginnings amongst amateurs and not in the circles of hardened, demoralized professionals. This was confirmed by Vakhtangov's[14] experience; or to take an example from quite another culture, the Japanese No theatre which, owing to the technical ability it demands, might almost be described as a "super-profession," although its very structure makes it a semiamateur theatre. From where can this renewal come? From people who are dissatisfied with conditions in the normal theatre, and who take it on themselves to create poor theatres

---

[13] Professional name of Konstantin Sergeevich Alekseev (1863–1938), Russian actor, director, and acting teacher.

[14] Eugene Vakhtangov (1883–1922), Russian actor and director.

with few actors, *"chamber ensembles"* which they might transform into institutes for the education of actors; or else from amateurs working on the boundaries of the professional theatre and who, on their own, achieve a technical standard which is far superior to that demanded by the prevailing theatre: in short, a few madmen who have nothing to lose and are not afraid of hard work.

It seems essential to me that an effort be made to organize secondary theatre schools. The actor begins to learn his profession too late, when he is already psychically formed and, worse still, morally molded and immediately begins suffering from *arriviste*[15] tendencies, characteristic of a great number of theatre school pupils.

Age is as important in the education of an actor as it is to a pianist or a dancer—that is, one should not be older than fourteen when beginning. If it were possible, I would suggest starting at an even earlier age with a four-year technical course concentrating on practical exercises. At the same time, the pupil ought to receive an adequate humanistic education, aimed not at imparting an ample knowledge of literature, the history of the theatre and so on, but at awakening his sensibility and introducing him to the most stimulating phenomena in world culture.

The actor's secondary education should then be completed by four year's work as an apprentice actor with a laboratory ensemble during which time he would not only acquire a good deal of acting experience, but would also continue his studies in the fields of literature, painting, philosophy, etc., to a degree necessary in his profession and not in order to be able to shine in snobbish society. On completion of the four years' practical work in a theatre laboratory, the student actor should be awarded some sort of diploma. Thus, after eight years' work of this kind, the actor should be comparatively well equipped for what lies ahead. He would not escape the dangers that threaten every actor, but his capacities would be greater and his character more firmly molded. The ideal solution would be to establish institutes for research which again would be subject to poverty and rigorous authority. The cost of running such an institute would be a half of the amount swallowed up by a state-aided provincial theatre. Its staff should be composed of a small group of experts specializing in problems associated with the theatre: e.g., a psychoanalyst and a social anthropologist. There should be a troupe of actors from a normal theatre laboratory and a group of pedagogues from a secondary theatre school, plus a small publishing house that would print the practical methodical results which would then be exchanged with other similar centers and sent to interested persons doing research in neighboring fields. It is absolutely essential that all research of

---

[15] Aggressive; one who uses any means, even unscrupulous ones, to become successful.

this kind be supervised by one or more theatre critics who, from the outside—rather like the Devil's Advocate—analyze the theatre's weaknesses and any alarming elements in the finished performances, basing their judgments on esthetical principles identical to those of the theatre itself. As you know, Ludwik Flaszen[16] has this task in our theatre.

How can such a theatre reflect our time? I am thinking of the content and analysis of present-day problems.

I shall answer according to our theatre's experience. Even though we often use classical texts, ours is a contemporary theatre in that it confronts our very roots with our current behavior and stereotypes, and in this way shows us our "today" in perspective with "yesterday," and our "yesterday" with "today." Even if this theatre uses an elementary language of signs and sounds—comprehensible beyond the semantic value of the word, even to a person who does not understand the language in which the play is performed —such a theatre must be a national one since it is based on introspection and on the whole of our social superego which has been molded in a particular national climate, thus becoming an integral part of it.

If we really wish to delve deeply into the logic of our mind and behavior and reach their hidden layers, their secret motor, then the whole system of signs built into the performance must appeal to our experience, to the reality which has surprised and shaped us, to this language of gestures, mumblings, sounds and intonations picked up in the street, at work, in cafés—in short, all human behavior which has made an impression on us.

We are talking about profanation. What, in fact, is this but a kind of tactlessness based on the brutal confrontation between our declarations and our daily actions, between the experience of our forefathers which lives within us and our search for a comfortable way of life or our conception of a struggle for survival, between our individual complexes and those of society as a whole?

This implies that every classical performance is like looking at oneself in a mirror, at our ideas and traditions, and not merely the description of what men of past ages thought and felt.

Every performance built on a contemporary theme is an encounter between the superficial traits of the present day and its deep roots and hidden motives. The performance is national because it is a sincere and absolute search into our historical ego; it is realistic because it is an excess of truth; it is social because it is a challenge to the social being, the spectator.

---

[16] Ludwik (or Ludwig) Flaszen, Grotowski's dramaturge.

Selected Bibliography

This bibliography—necessarily selective, since a complete one would require at least a volume the size of this book—may be supplemented or preceded by the books and periodicals cited in the "credits" at the foot of the pages of those critical essays of which selections only have been reprinted here.

ADAMS, HENRY HITCH, and BAXTER HATHAWAY, eds. *Dramatic Essays of the Neoclassic Age.* New York: Benjamin Blom, 1965.

APPIA, ADOLPHE. *Music and the Art of the Theatre*, trans. Robert W. Corrigan and Mary Douglas Dirks. Coral Gables: University of Florida Press (AETA Books of the Theatre Series), 1962.

———. *The Work of Living Art and Man is the Measure of All Things*, trans. H. D. Albright and Barnard Hewitt. Coral Gables: University of Florida Press (AETA Books of the Theatre Series), 1960.

BARZUN, JACQUES. *Classic, Romantic, and Modern.* Garden City: Doubleday, 1961.

BEARDSLEY, MONROE C. *Aesthetics From Classical Greece to the Present: A Short History.* New York: The Macmillan Co., 1966.

BENTLEY, ERIC. *The Life of the Drama.* New York: Atheneum, 1964.

———. *The Playwright as Thinker.* New York: Meridian, 1955.

———. ed. *The Theory of the Modern Stage.* Baltimore: Penguin Books, 1968.

BODKIN, MAUD. *Archetypal Patterns in Poetry.* London: Oxford University Press, 1963.

CLARK, BARRETT H., ed. *European Theories of the Drama*, revised by Henry Popkin. New York: Crown, 1965.

COLE, TOBY, ed. *Playwrights on Playwriting.* New York: Hill and Wang, 1961.

CORRIGAN, ROBERT W., ed. *Comedy: Meaning and Form.* San Francisco: Chandler, 1965.

———. *Theatre in the Twentieth Century.* New York: Grove Press, 1965.

———. *Tragedy: Vision and Form.* San Francisco: Chandler, 1965.

CRAIG, EDWARD GORDON. *On the Art of the Theatre.* New York: Theatre Arts, 1960.

997

DUKORE, BERNARD F., ed. *Documents for Drama and Revolution.* New York: Holt, Rinehart and Winston, 1971.

————, and DANIEL C. GEROULD, eds. *Avant-Garde Drama: Major Plays and Documents.* New York: Bantam, 1969.

GASSNER, JOHN, and RALPH G. ALLEN, eds. *Theatre and Drama in the Making,* 2 vols. Boston: Houghton Mifflin, 1964.

GILBERT, ALLAN H. *Literary Criticism: Plato to Dryden.* Detroit: Wayne State University Press, 1962.

HALL, VERNON, JR. *A Short History of Literary Criticism.* New York: New York University Press, 1963.

HARDISON, O. B., JR., ed. *English Literary Criticism: The Renaissance.* New York: Appleton-Century-Crofts, 1963.

————. *Modern Continental Literary Criticism.* New York: Appleton-Century-Crofts, 1962.

HERRICK, MARVIN T. *Comic Theory in the Sixteenth Century.* Urbana: University of Illinois Press, 1964.

————. *Italian Comedy in the Renaissance.* Urbana: University of Illinois Press, 1960.

————. *Italian Tragedy in the Renaissance.* Urbana: University of Illinois Press, 1965.

————. *Tragicomedy.* Urbana: University of Illinois Press, 1962.

LANGER, SUSANNE K. *Feeling and Form.* New York: Charles Scribner's Sons, 1953.

LAUTER, PAUL, ed. *Theories of Comedy.* Garden City: Doubleday, 1964.

LEVICH, MARVIN, ed. *Aesthetics and the Philosophy of Criticism.* New York: Random House, 1963.

SHAW, BERNARD. *Our Theatres in the Nineties,* 3 vols. London: Constable, 1954.

————. *Shaw on Shakespeare,* ed. Edwin Wilson. New York: Dutton, 1961.

SMITH, JAMES HARRY, and EDD WINFIELD PARKS, eds. *The Great Critics.* New York: Norton, 1951.

SPINGARN, JOEL E. *Literary Criticism in the Renaissance.* New York: Harcourt Brace Jovanovich, 1963.

TAYLOR, EDWARD W., ed. *Literary Criticism of Seventeenth Century England.* New York: Alfred A. Knopf, 1967.

WEITZ, MORRIS, ed. *Problems in Aesthetics.* New York: Macmillan, 1959.

WELLEK, RENÉ. *A History of Modern Criticism,* 4 vols. New Haven: Yale University Press, 1955–1965. Note: the final, fifth volume is forthcoming.

Index of Authors and Titles

999